BUSINESS ESSENTIALS

SECOND CUSTOM EDITION FOR FANSHAWE COLLEGE

Ronald J. Ebert, Ricky W. Griffin and Frederick A. Starke
with contributions by Cyndi Hornby

Taken from:
Business Essentials, Fifth Canadian Edition
by Ronald J. Ebert, Ricky W. Griffin and Frederick A. Starke

Learning Solutions

New York Boston San Francisco
London Toronto Sydney Tokyo Singapore Madrid
Mexico City Munich Paris Cape Town Hong Kong Montreal

Cover Art: Courtesy of the Fanshawe College Marketing and Communications Department

Taken from:

Business Essentials, Fifth Canadian Edition
by Ronald J. Ebert, Ricky W. Griffin and Frederick A. Starke

This special edition published in cooperation with Pearson Learning Solutions.

Pearson Learning Solutions, 501 Boylston Street, Suite 900, Boston, MA 02116
A Pearson Education Company
www.pearsoned.com

Printed in Canada

1 2 3 4 5 6 7 8 9 10 VOZL 15 14 13 12 11 10

000200010270591592

BK

PEARSON

ISBN 10: 0-558-78069-5
ISBN 13: 978-0-558-78069-2

This book is dedicated to E. Allen Slusher III,
a devoted friend, intellectual, colleague, and
humanitarian whose presence has elevated
the lives of so many people.

—R.J.E.

—R.W.G.

To Ann, Eric, and Grant.

—F.A.S.

CONTENTS

PREFACE

Welcome to the fifth Canadian edition of *Business Essentials*! In this edition, we continue to emphasize our long-standing principle of *"Doing the Basics Best."* Cutting-edge firsts, up-to-date issues that shape today's business world, and creative pedagogy help students build a solid foundation of business knowledge. This new, fifth edition continues with the strengths that made the first four editions so successful—comprehensiveness, accuracy, currency, and readability.

What's New to This Edition

The fifth Canadian edition of *Business Essentials* incorporates many of the changes suggested by professors and students who used the fourth edition. This new edition also includes changes suggested by reviewers. The following changes have been made:

- The book opens with a dynamic new "Prologue" that describes the four basic perspectives from which students can approach business—as an *employee*, as an *owner or boss*, as a *customer*, and as an *investor*. In the prologue, we also introduce eight "stories of business" that help students see the excitement, challenge, and satisfaction that are essential parts of business activity.
- More than 95 percent of the opening cases, boxed inserts, and end-of-chapter cases are either new or updated.
- Each chapter opens with a section called "How Will This Benefit You?" In this section, we answer the question by identifying the key elements in the chapter that are most central to students' future careers in business—making it clear why the content in the chapter really matters.
- The chapter on business ethics and social responsibility (Chapter 3, Conducting Business Ethically and Responsibly) now occupies an earlier spot in the text so that students will gain an increased awareness of the importance of this area as they read subsequent chapters in the text.
- Chapter 4 (Entrepreneurship, Small Business, and New Venture Creation) has been significantly revised and much new material has been added that focuses on how new businesses are started.
- Significant new material has been added on decision making in Chapter 6 (Managing the Business Enterprise), leadership and personality in Chapter 9 (Motivating, Satisfying, and Leading Employees), and business strategy and operations management in Chapter 10 (Operations Management and Quality Control).
- Each chapter contains two new boxed inserts. The first of these—entitled "Entrepreneurship and New Ventures"—provides real-life examples of Canadian entrepreneurs who saw an opportunity to provide a new product or service in the marketplace, and the activities they carried out in order to be successful. The second series—entitled "Business Accountability"—focuses student attention on business behaviour that is of significant public concern. Each insert describes an accountability issue that is currently confronting a real Canadian or international company, and the steps that are being taken to make business managers more accountable for their actions. Questions that link the issue to the chapter topics are also included.

- A new team ethics exercise is found at the end of each chapter. These exercises ask students to take on the role of employee, owner, customer, or investor and examine a chapter-related business ethics dilemma through the perspective of that role. By working together as a team, students decide what outcome is ultimately best in each situation, learn how to cooperate with each other, and see an ethical dilemma from various points of view.
- New CBC *Venture* video cases are included at the end of each part.
- A completely rewritten business plan project, tailor-made to match and reinforce book content, appears at the end of each part. This new business plan project is *software-independent* and provides students with an easy-to-understand template that they work from as they create their business plans. Based on reviewer feedback, we've divided the business plan project into logical sections, placing each part of the project at the end of each main part of the book. With five parts in all, students can gradually apply the concepts they've learned in the chapters to their business plans throughout the course.
- A new feature—entitled "Managing Your Personal Finances"—is found in Appendix A at the end of the text. This feature has been overwhelmingly requested by students and instructors, and presents a down-to-earth, hands-on approach that will help students manage their personal finances. The practical information found in this feature includes a worksheet for determining personal net worth, insightful examples demonstrating the time value of money, a method for determining how much money to invest now in order to build a future nest egg of a certain size, suggestions on how to manage credit card debt, guidelines for purchasing a house, and a personalized worksheet for setting financial goals. The information contained in this feature will be immensely useful to students.
- Information technology (IT) has completely changed the business landscape, and we include a completely new appendix on IT that reflects those changes (Appendix B). We discuss the impact IT has had on the business world, the many IT resources businesses have at their disposal, the threats information technology poses for businesses, and the ways in which businesses protect themselves from these threats.

Major Themes

Five major themes are evident throughout this new edition. It is important that students understand these themes, since their careers in business will be significantly affected by them.

The Theme of Change

The dramatic changes that have been occurring during the past decade continue apace. The development of new business processes, new products, and new services all make the study of change in business exciting and necessary. In nearly every aspect of business today there are totally new ways of doing things. These new ways are replacing traditional business practices, usually with surprising speed and often with better competitive results. Given these developments, we as authors felt that our goal had to be to communicate the theme of change by describing how real-world business firms cope with the need for change. Thus, we have tried to capture the flavour and convey the excitement of the "new economy" in all of its rapidly evolving practices.

The Growth of International Business

The globalization of business is one of the dominant challenges of the twenty-first century. To keep students aware of this challenge, we've included many examples and cases that describe the experiences of Canadian companies in the global marketplace. We also describe how global companies have impacted the domestic Canadian market. In addition to these examples throughout the text, we devote an entire chapter to international business (Chapter 5, The Global Context of Business).

The Role of Ethics and Social Responsibility

Business ethics and social responsibility are generating a sharply increased level of discussion and debate as a result of the highly publicized criminal trials of top managers at companies like Enron, WorldCom, and others. We devote an entire chapter to the discussion of ethical and social responsibility issues (Chapter 3, Conducting Business Ethically and Responsibly) because these issues are so important to modern business. Ethical issues are also raised in nearly every chapter of the text, and a team ethics exercise at the end of each chapter further focuses student attention on this important issue.

The Significance of Small Business

Since many students will not work for major corporations, we have provided coverage of both large and small companies throughout the text. In various chapters, the implications of various ideas for small business are discussed. As well, a major part of Chapter 4 (Entrepreneurship, Small Business, and New Venture Creation) contains entirely new material focusing on small business, entrepreneurship, and new business ventures.

The Importance of Information and Communication Technology

In our information-based society, the people and organizations that learn how to obtain and use information will be the ones that succeed. The explosive growth and change in these systems is recognized as we include a new appendix on the management of information (Appendix B).

The Quality Imperative

Quality and productivity became the keys to competitive success for many companies in the global marketplace during the 1990s. These topics continue to dominate the thinking of managers in the twenty-first century, and we devote a substantial part of one chapter to their coverage (Chapter 10, Operations Management and Quality Control).

Major Features of the Text

The text contains the following features to stimulate student interest in, and understanding of, the material that is presented about business.

Part Opener

At the beginning of each of the five major parts of the book is a brief outline introducing the material that will be discussed in that part. These outlines give students a glimpse of the "big picture" as they start reading about a new area of the business world.

Chapter Materials

Each chapter contains several features that are designed to increase student interest in, and understanding of, the material being presented. These features are as follows:

Chapter Learning Objectives. A list of numbered learning objectives is presented at the beginning of each chapter. These objectives—which help students determine what is important in each chapter—are also referenced in the margins opposite the relevant content in the chapter.

Chapter-Opening Case. Each chapter begins with a description of a situation that is faced by a real Canadian or international company. The subject matter of the opening case is relevant to the material presented in the chapter, and therefore helps students bridge the gap between theory and practice.

Boxed Inserts. Each chapter contains two boxed inserts: "Business Accountability" and "Entrepreneurship and New Ventures." As noted above, the Business Accountability boxes raise student consciousness about a business' responsibility to its constituents. Questions for discussion are found at the end of these boxes. The Entrepreneurship and New Ventures boxes tell interesting stories of how Canadian entrepreneurs identified a need for a new product or service and how they set up a company to effectively satisfy that need.

Examples. In addition to the boxed inserts, each chapter contains numerous examples of how businesses operate so that students can gain a better understanding of the dynamics of business practice in both Canada and elsewhere. These examples—which range in length from one sentence to several paragraphs—help students understand concepts that are discussed in the text.

Key Terms. In each chapter, the key terms that students should know are highlighted in the text and defined in the margin.

Figures and Tables. Figures and tables are updated throughout the text.

End-of-Chapter Material

Several important pedagogical features are found at the end of each chapter. These are designed to help students better understand the contents of the chapter.

Summary of Learning Objectives. The material in each chapter is concisely summarized, using the learning objectives as the organizing scheme. This helps students understand the main points that were presented in the chapter.

Questions and Exercises. There are two types of questions here: "Questions for Analysis" (which require students to think beyond simple factual recall and apply the concepts they have read about), and "Application Exercises" (which require students to visit local businesses or to interview managers and gather additional information that will help them understand how business firms operate).

Building Your Business Skills. This feature involves in-depth exercises that allow students to examine in detail some specific aspect of business. The exercise may ask students to work individually or in a group to gather data about an interesting business issue, and then develop a written report or a class presentation based on the information that was gathered. Each exercise begins with a list of goals, a description of the situation, a step-by-step methodology for proceeding, and follow-up questions to help students focus their responses to the challenge.

Exercising Your Ethics: Team Exercise. These new exercises ask students to take on the role of employee, owner, customer, or investor and examine a chapter-related business ethics dilemma through the perspective of that role. By working together as a team, students decide what outcome is ultimately best in each situation, learn how to cooperate with each other, and see an ethical dilemma from various points of view.

Concluding Case. Each chapter concludes with a case study that focuses on a real Canadian or international company. These cases are designed to help students apply the chapter material to a real company that is currently in the news. At the end of each case, several questions guide students in their analysis.

End-of-Part Material

CBC Video Cases. At the end of each of the five major parts of the text, two CBC video cases are presented. The instructor can show the *Venture* episode in class and then either conduct a class discussion using the questions at the end of the written case as a guide, or ask students to complete a written assignment that requires answering the questions at the end of the written case. This approach to teaching adds a positive dynamic to classes because students will be able to relate text material to actual Canadian business situations. The cases are also available through the MyBusinessLab for *Business Essentials,* Fifth Canadian Edition.

Crafting a Business Plan. This new feature helps students gain key insights into what is involved in starting a new business.

Appendices

There are two new appendices found at the end of the text:

Appendix A—Managing Your Personal Finances. This new material gives students extremely practical information about managing their own financial situation.

Appendix B—Information Systems. This material is brand new, and has been written specifically for this appendix.

Supplemental Materials

MyBusinessLab (**www.pearsoned.ca/mybusinesslab**) is an online grading, assessment, and study tool for faculty and students. It engages students and helps them focus on what they need to study. It can help students get a better grade because they are learning in an interactive and focused environment. MyBusinessLab delivers all classroom resources for instructors and students in one place. All resources are organized by learning objective so that lectures and studying can be customized more conveniently than ever before. A complete description of the student and instructor resources available is provided on the MyBusinessLab insert included with this text.

For Instructors

Instructor's Resource Centre. Instructor resources are password protected and available for download via **www.pearsoned.ca**. For your convenience, these resources are also available on the Instructor's Resource CD-ROM (***ISBN 978-0-13-515551-6***) and available online at **www.pearsoned.ca/mybusinesslab** in the instructor area.

MyTest. *MyTest* from Pearson Canada is a powerful online assessment-generation program that helps instructors easily create and print quizzes, tests, and exams, as well as homework or practice handouts. Questions and tests can all be authored online, allowing instructors ultimate flexibility and the ability to efficiently manage assessments at any time, from anywhere.

Pearson TestGen. *Pearson TestGen* is a special computerized test item file that enables instructors to view and edit the existing questions, add questions, generate tests, and print the tests in a variety of formats. Powerful search and sort functions make it easy to locate questions and arrange them in any order desired. TestGen also enables instructors to administer tests on a local area network, have the tests graded electronically, and have the results prepared in electronic or printed reports. The Pearson TestGen is compatible with IBM or Macintosh systems.

Instructor's Resource Manual. The *Instructor's Resource Manual* contains chapter outlines, teaching tips, in-class exercises, and suggestions on how to use the text effectively. It includes material for classroom use, such as careers in business and additional cases. The manual also provides answers to the end-of-chapter questions and cases (including Building Your Business Skills, Exercising Your Ethics, and the CBC Video Cases).

PowerPoint® Presentations. *PowerPoint Presentations* offer an average of about 40 PowerPoint slides per chapter, outlining the key points in the text. The slides include lecture notes that provide page references to the text, summaries, and suggestions for student activities or related questions from the text.

CBC Video Library (VHS: ISBN: 978-0-13-515509-7. DVD: ISBN: 978-0-13-515508-0). The CBC Video Library for *Business Essentials*, Fifth Canadian Edition, includes 10 segments from the CBC program *Venture* that accompany the video cases found at the end of each part in the text. These cases focus on Canadian companies and discuss business issues from a Canadian point of view. The cases can also be viewed online at **www.pearsoned.ca/highered/videocentral**, and answers to the discussion questions are provided in the Instructor's Resource Manual. (Please contact your Pearson Education Canada sales representative for details.)

Additional Videos. Twenty custom videos help students see how real-life businesses and the people who run them apply fundamental business principles on a daily basis. Ask your Pearson Education Canada sales representative for details.

Pearson Custom Publishing (www.prenhall.com/custombusiness). Pearson Custom Publishing can provide you and your students with texts, cases, and articles to enhance your course. Choose material from Darden, Ivey, Harvard Business School Publishing, NACRA, and Thunderbird to create your own custom casebook. Contact your Pearson Education Canada sales representative for details.

Online Learning Solutions. Pearson Education Canada supports instructors interested in using online course management systems. We provide text-related content in Blackboard/WebCT and Course Compass. To find out more about creating an online course using Pearson content in one of these platforms, contact your Pearson Education Canada sales representative.

New! Instructor's ASSET. Pearson Education Canada is proud to introduce Instructor's ASSET, the Academic Support and Service for Educational Technologies. ASSET is the first integrated Canadian service program committed to meeting the customization, training, and support needs for your course. Ask your Pearson Education Canada sales representative for details.

Your Pearson Education Canada Sales Representative. Your Pearson sales rep is always available to ensure you have everything you need to teach a winning course. Armed with experience, training, and product knowledge, your Pearson rep will support your assessment and adoption of any of the products, services, and technology outlined here to ensure our offerings are tailored to suit your individual needs and the needs of your students. Whether it's getting instructions on TestGen software or specific content files for your new online course, your Pearson sales representative is there to help. Ask your Pearson sales representative for details.

For Students

Crafting a Business Plan. A completely rewritten business plan project, tailor-made to match and reinforce book content, appears at the end of each major section of the book. This new business plan project is *software-independent* and provides students with an easy-to-understand template that they work from as they create their business plans.

Acknowledgments

I owe special thanks to Jennifer Therriault, copyeditor; Marisa D'Andrea, Production Editor; Karen Elliott, Acquisitions Editor; Pamela Voves, Developmental Editor; and others at Pearson Education Canada who assisted with the production, marketing, and sales of this edition.

We appreciate the insights and suggestions of the following individuals who provided feedback on the fourth edition or reviewed the manuscript for the new edition:

Laurentiu (Larry) David, Centennial College
Daniel Duyck, Champlain College
Glenn Leonard, University of New Brunswick
Dr. Carolan McLarney, Dalhousie University
Mike Planche, Humber Institute of Technology and Advanced Learning
Lucy Silvestri, Niagara College
Don Wagner, University of Prince Edward Island

Their comments were carefully considered and implemented wherever possible.

Frederick A. Starke, 2008

ABOUT THE AUTHORS

Ronald J. Ebert is Emeritus Professor at the University of Missouri-Columbia where he lectures in the Management Department and serves as advisor to students and student organizations. Dr. Ebert draws upon more than 30 years of teaching experience at such schools as Sinclair College, University of Washington, University of Missouri, Lucian Blaga University of Sibiu (Romania), and Consortium International University (Italy). His consulting alliances include such firms as Mobay Corporation, Kraft Foods, Oscar Mayer, Atlas Powder, and John Deere. He has designed and conducted management development programs for such diverse clients as the American Public Power Association, the United States Savings and Loan League, and the Central Missouri Manufacturing Training Consortium.

His experience as a practitioner has fostered an advocacy for integrating concepts with best business practices in business education. The five business books he has written have been translated into Spanish, Chinese, Malaysian, and Romanian. Dr. Ebert has served as the editor of the *Journal of Operations Management*. He is a past-president and fellow of the Decision Sciences Institute. He has served as consultant and external evaluator for *Quantitative Reasoning for Business Studies*, an introduction-to-business project sponsored by the National Science Foundation.

Ricky W. Griffin is Distinguished Professor of Management and holds the Blocker Chair in Business in the Mays School of Business at Texas A&M University. Dr. Griffin currently serves as executive associate dean. He previously served as head of the Department of Management and as director of the Center for Human Resource Management at Texas A&M. His research interests include workplace aggression and violence, executive skills and decision making, and workplace culture. Dr. Griffin's research has been published in such journals as *Academy of Management Review, Academy of Management Journal, Administrative Science Quarterly,* and *Journal of Management.* He has also served as editor of *Journal of Management*. Dr. Griffin has consulted with such organizations as Texas Instruments, Tenneco, Amoco, Compaq Computer, and Continental Airlines.

Dr. Griffin has served the Academy of Management as chair of the organizational behaviour division. He also has served as president of the southwest division of the Academy of Management and on the board of directors of the Southern Management Association. He is a fellow of both the Academy of Management and the Southern Management Association. He is also the author of several successful textbooks, each of which is a market leader. In addition, they are widely used in dozens of countries and have been translated into numerous foreign languages, including Spanish, Polish, Malaysian, and Russian.

Frederick A. Starke is Emeritus Professor of Organizational Behaviour in the Asper School of Business at the University of Manitoba. He began his career at the University of Manitoba in 1968, and has taught courses in organizational behaviour, organization theory, decision making, and marketing. He has served in several administrative positions, including head of the Department of Business Administration from 1982–1987 and from 1989–1994, and as associate dean from 1996–2005.

Dr. Starke earned his B.A. and M.B.A. from Southern Illinois University, and his Ph.D. in Organizational Behaviour from Ohio State University. He has published research articles in such scholarly journals as the *Administrative Science Quarterly*, the *Journal of Applied Psychology*, the *Academy of Management Journal*, the *Journal of Management Studies*, and the *Review of Religious Research*. He has also written articles for professional journals, such as the *Journal of Systems Management*, *Information Executive*, and the *Canadian Journal of Nursing Administration*.

Dr. Starke also writes textbooks that are used by university and community college students in business programs across Canada. These titles include *Organizational Behaviour*, *Business Essentials*, *Management*, and *Business*. Dr. Starke also presents seminars on the topics of decision making and goal setting to practising managers in both the public and private sectors.

FROM THE AUTHORS

Ron Ebert, Ricky Griffin, and Fred Starke

Businesses today face constant change—change in their competitive landscape, change in their workforce, change in government regulations, change in the economy, change in technology, change in. . . well, you get the idea. As we began to plan this revision, we too recognized the need for change—changing demands from instructors, changing needs and preferences of students, and changing views on what material to cover in this course and how to cover it. These have all affected how we planned and revised the book. This time, though, we took change to a whole new level.

A new team of reviewers gave us great ideas about the content changes we needed to make, and a new editorial team was assembled to guide and shape the creation and development of the book. The business world itself provided us with dozens of new examples, new challenges, new success stories, and new perspectives on what businesses must do to remain competitive. And a new dedication to relevance guided our work from beginning to end. For example, we know that some business students will go to work for big companies. Others will work for small firms. Some will start their own business. Still, others may join a family business. So, we accepted the challenge of striving to make the book as relevant as possible to all students, regardless of their personal and career goals and objectives.

We met this challenge by incorporating many new features in this edition (see the Preface for a list of these new features). We also carefully reviewed the existing book line by line. New material was added and older examples were updated or replaced with newer ones. We worked extra hard to make our writing as clear and as crisp as possible. We think that these changes will help make the material even more alive and personal for you.

We believe that we have taken this book to a new, higher level of excellence. Its content is stronger, its learning framework is better, its design is more reader-friendly, and its support materials are the best on the market. We hope that you enjoy reading and learning from this book as much as we enjoyed creating it. And who knows? Perhaps one day we can tell your story of business success to other students.

PROLOGUE

If you're like many students, you may be starting this term with some questions about why you're here. You may be taking this course at a community college or at a university, and you may be taking it in a traditional classroom setting or online. Whatever the case, you may be wondering just what you're supposed to get from this course and how it will benefit you. In short, you may be wondering, "What's in it for me?"

First, regardless of what it may be called at your school, this is a survey course designed to introduce you to the exciting and challenging world of business, both in Canada and elsewhere. The course is designed to fit the needs of a wide variety of students. You may be taking this course as the first step toward earning a degree in business, or you may be thinking about business and want to know more about it, or you may know you want to study business but are unsure of the area you want to pursue. You may plan to major in another field but want some basic business background and are taking this course as an elective. Or you may be here because, frankly, this course is required or is a prerequisite for another course.

If you don't have a lot of work experience, you may be uncertain as to what the business world is all about. If you have a lot of work experience, you might be a bit skeptical as to what you can actually learn about business from an introductory course. One of our biggest challenges as authors is to write a book that meets the needs of such a diverse student population, especially when we acknowledge the legitimacy of your right to ask "What's in it for me?" We also want to do our best to ensure that you find the course challenging, interesting, and useful. To help lay the foundation for meeting these challenges, let's look at the various "hats" that you may wear, both now and in the future.

WEARING THE HATS

There's an old adage that refers to people wearing different "hats." In general, this is based on the idea that any given person usually has different roles to play in different settings. For example, your roles may include student, child, spouse, employee, friend, and/or parent. You could think of each of these roles as needing a different hat—when you play the role of a student, for example, you wear one hat, but when you leave campus and go to your part-time job, you put on a different hat. From the perspective of studying and interfacing with the world of *business*, there are at least four distinct "hats" that you might wear:

- *The Employee Hat.* One business hat is as an employee working for a business. Most people wear this hat throughout their working career. To wear the hat successfully, you will need to understand your "place" in the organization—your job duties and responsibilities, how to get along with others, how to work with your boss, what your organization is all about, and so on. You'll begin to see how to best wear this hat as you learn more about organizing business enterprises in Chapter 7 and how organizations manage their human resources in Chapter 8, as well as in several other places in this book.
- *The Employer or Boss Hat.* Another business hat that many people wear is as an employer or boss. Whether you start your own business or get

promoted within someone else's business, people will be working for you. You'll still need to know your job duties and responsibilities, but you'll also need to understand how to manage other people—how to motivate and reward them, how to lead them, how to deal with conflict among them, and the legal parameters that may affect how you treat them. Chapters 3, 6, and 9 provide a lot of information about how you can best wear this hat, although the role of employer runs throughout the entire book.

- *The Consumer Hat.* Even if you don't work for a business, you will still wear the hat of a consumer. Whenever you fill your car with PetroCanada gasoline, bid for something on eBay, buy clothes at Urban Outfitters, or download a song from iTunes, you're consuming products or services created by businesses. To wear this hat effectively, you need to understand how to assess the value of what you're buying, your rights as a consumer, and so on. We discuss how you can best wear this hat in Chapters 2, 12, 13, and 14.
- *The Investor Hat.* The final business hat many people wear is that of an investor. You may buy your own business or work for a company that allows you to buy its stock. You may also invest in other companies through the purchase of stocks or shares of a mutual fund. In order for you to invest wisely, you must understand some basics, such as financial markets, business earnings, and the basic costs of investment. Chapters 4, 11, 15, 16, and Appendix A will help you learn how to best wear this hat.

Most people wear more than one of these hats at the same time. Regardless of how many hats you wear or when you may be putting them on, you will interface with many businesses in different ways. Knowing how to best wear all of these hats is what this book is all about.

THE STORIES OF BUSINESS

How do businesses get started? How do they work? Why do some businesses grow, and others struggle or even fail? How do businesses affect us regardless of the hats we may be wearing? These are the questions we'll discuss throughout this book. But first, let's "meet" a few people and see how these questions have affected them.

Google founders Sergey Brin and Larry Page.

Let's Google It

Sergey Brin and Larry Page decided they were tired of internet search engines that yielded an overwhelming mess of random returns so, about 10 years ago, they decided to do something about it—create their own. Today, their creation, Google, has become the world's most popular web search engine, conducting upward of 200 million searches every day. The word "google" has become virtually synonymous with the word search among many computer users.

But Brin and Page are not resting on their laurels as they push to expand Google into more corners of our daily lives. Google now offers Google Talk (instant messaging), Google Maps, Gmail, and Google Desktop, all rapidly growing products. Google also generates more than one-quarter of its revenues from foreign markets and has been translated into 97 languages. And when Google began selling its stock to the public in 2004, it generated over $1.6 billion that it plans to use for even faster expansion. In Chapters 11 and 12 we'll discuss how Google used information technology on its path to success, how companies like it create their lineup of products (their so-called "product mix"), as well as how a company's public stock offerings affect its balance sheet.

Roll Up the Rim

The Tim Hortons coffee and doughnut chain is one of the most famous and well-recognized businesses in Canada. It was founded by NHL player Tim Horton in 1964 in Hamilton, Ontario. In 1967, entrepreneur Ron Joyce became Horton's partner, but when Horton was killed in an automobile accident in 1974, Joyce bought out the Horton family and became the sole owner of the business. Joyce then embarked on a dramatic expansion of the business. By 1991, there were 500 Tim Hortons stores across Canada, and by 2007 the number had increased to 2710. The company has surpassed even McDonald's as Canada's largest food service provider. There are also 336 Tim Hortons outlets in the northeastern United States, but these stores have not fared as well as the Canadian stores.

In Canada, the company is legendary for its community support activities like the Tim Hortons Children Foundation, which sponsors underprivileged children so they can attend summer camps in Canada and the United States. The company also has very high visibility with the Canadian military, and many of its outlets are located near military bases. It has even opened an outlet in Afghanistan to serve Canadian Forces troops that are stationed there. Why has Tim Hortons been such a dramatic success in Canada? Why has it not been as successful in the United States? We'll look at answers to these and other related questions in Chapters 1, 5, and 13.

Hip Hop Hoops

When most people think of athletic footwear, such global brands as Nike and Adidas come to mind. But a small upstart company called And1 is fast making a name for itself as well. Founded by Jay Coen Gilbert, Seth Berger, and Tom Austin, And1 takes a "streetball" approach to basketball. At the core of its business is a growing line of tapes highlighting the skills—and swagger—of playground legends showing incredible moves and turning basketball purists on their heads.

But if the tapes are the catalyst, And1's shoes and shirts are the drivers. Indeed, And1 now trails only Nike in terms of NBA player endorsements. The counterculture firm has 165 employees, generates $180 million in annual revenues, and sells its products in over 125 countries. Among its more recent activities was a smash summer tour showcasing the talents—and footwear—of more than 15 top streetball players. And to help keep itself fresh, And1 hires mostly younger staffers and pays close attention to their advice. And1 is successful because it knows, hires, and promotes to its target market. You'll learn more about these factors in Chapters 4, 8, 13, and 14.

A Boy and His Computer

When Michael Dell was 13, he ran a successful mail-order stamp trading business out of his bedroom, grossing over $2000 a month. When he entered university in 1983, personal computers were just coming onto the market, and Michael saw them as the wave of the future. He realized he could buy computer parts from manufacturers, assemble the computers himself, and then sell them directly to consumers for 40 percent below

Dell Computer founder Michael Dell.

retail. Soon he was grossing $80 000 from his dorm room, so he decided to drop out of school and launch a mail-order computer business.

He named his business Dell Computer, and over the next two decades, Dell became the world's biggest PC maker. It also expanded into other product lines such as printers, MP3 players, and LCD televisions. Michael handed over day-to-day control of the company to Kevin Rollins in 2004, but when Dell's sales slumped in 2006 and Hewlett-Packard became the number one computer company, Michael took over again as CEO of the company. Why and how did a business like Dell prosper, and then run into difficulties? How can you make your own business successful? Chapters 1, 4, 10, and 12 will help you better understand the key reasons for business success and failure.

A Good Cup of Java

Starbucks founder Howard Schultz.

Starbucks has become an important part of the urban landscape in most major cities in Canada. In less than 30 years, the firm has grown to become the largest coffee retailer in the world. It's difficult to provide an accurate count of the number of Starbucks outlets because the firm opens a new store somewhere in the world almost every day. In early 2007, there were 13 168 Starbucks shops in 38 different countries around the world.

The three people who founded Starbucks did not have ambitious retail plans for the firm, but were primarily interested in wholesaling high-quality coffee beans to independent coffeehouses. In 1987, Howard Schultz (a former employee) bought the company from its three original owners and began an aggressive expansion campaign. By combining tight quality control with an uncanny sense of consumer tastes and preferences, Schultz built Starbucks into one of the strongest brand names in the world. The firm has also become a surprisingly important force in the music industry. Managers determined that many premium coffee drinkers also share a passion for music, so the company started selling a small number of hand-picked CDs in its store. As a result, music company executives now line up to try and get their latest offerings on the Starbucks play list. What are the secrets behind Starbucks' success, and how do savvy Starbucks marketers apply their skills to understand Starbucks' customers' preferences? You'll learn about this and more in Chapters 4, 6, 8, and 12.

Going Where Others Fear to Go

Inuktun Services, Ltd. is a Nanaimo, B.C.–based company that designs and produces small, waterproof, remotely operated vehicles (ROVs) that are equipped with lights and a video camera. These ROVs are used to inspect industrial equipment that is located in very small spaces, in dangerous places, and under water—in short, any place where humans can't easily work. The ROVs are used by companies in industries like electrical generation, oil and gas, nuclear, and by the military.

Inuktun was founded in 1989 by Al Robinson and Terry Knight, who chose the name "Inuktun" because in the Inuit language it means "service to mankind." Robinson and Knight originally thought that their ROVs would be of primary interest to boat owners who could guide the robots down into the water to inspect the bottom of their boat and view its condition on a TV monitor. As it turned out, boat owners weren't too interested, but lots of companies were. Now, Inuktun's ROVs travel up and down stairs, around corners, and over obstacles. They can work in water as deep as 300 metres and in pipes as little as 15 centimetres in diameter. Inuktun has been successful, even though its customer base turned out to be somewhat different than the company founders originally planned. In Chapters 12 and 13, we'll look at the issues of customer needs and the new product development process, and how these factors influence business success.

Planting the Seeds

During the heady days of the dot-com boom, new web-based businesses were popping up left and right. Garden.com was founded in 1996 by three friends, Cliff and Lisa Sharples and Jamie O'Neill. In early 2000, their company employed over 200 people, and Garden.com was acclaimed by *Fortune, Forbes,* and *Inc.* as one of the best internet-based retailers in the world. The company also had more cash than it needed and was in the enviable position of being able to turn down investment proposals from venture capitalists.

But by the end of that very same year, the business environment had changed dramatically. Venture capital dried up, operating costs escalated, and investors sought lower risk. These forces combined to drive many of the dot-com companies out of business. Cliff, Lisa, and Jamie were sufficiently realistic to see that their business wasn't going to succeed, and they shut down their operations in a relatively orderly manner. They also managed to pay off all of their obligations and still have a tidy nest egg left over to explore future opportunities. In Chapters 4, 6, and 12 we'll discuss why some businesses succeed and others fail, as well as some of the underlying forces influencing success and failure.

Changing the Urban Landscape

Urban Outfitters sells clothes, accessories, gifts, housewares, and shoes to young metropolitan customers seeking affordable but fashionable lifestyle brands. Urban Outfitters may not have the retailing presence of, say, Old Navy, but the hip retailer nevertheless is a real success story. As of mid-2007, Urban Outfitters had stores in fashion centres in or near large cities in Canada, the United States, the UK, Sweden, Denmark, and Ireland. The firm plans to open 20 or more stores a year.

The company also owns Anthropologie, a similarly focused store that targets consumers in the 30- to 45-year-old range. Its newest venture, called Free People, will offer merchandise similar to that of Urban Outfitters and Anthropologie, but at slightly lower prices. Free People will also offer a wider range of houseware merchandise geared to apartment dwellers. How is one company able to open different kinds of retail stores and operate at different "price points," and do so in several different countries? You'll learn more about these important aspects of business in Chapters 1, 4, 5, and 13.

SO, HOW *WILL* YOU BENEFIT?

We hope that these brief business stories have piqued your interest about what lies ahead in this book. The world today is populated with a breathtaking array of businesses and business opportunities. Big and small businesses, established and new businesses, broad-based and niche businesses, successful and unsuccessful businesses, global and domestic businesses—regardless of where your future plans take you, we hope that you will look back on this course as one of your positive first steps.

Keep in mind that what you get out of this course depends on at least three factors. One factor is this book and the information about business that you will acquire as a result of reading it. Another factor is your instructor. He or she is a dedicated professional who wants to help you grow and develop intellectually and academically.

The third factor is YOU. Learning is an active process that requires you to be a major participant. Simply memorizing the key terms and concepts in this book may help you achieve an acceptable course grade. But true learning requires that you read, study, discuss, question, review, experience, evaluate—and wear the four hats—as you go along. Tests and homework are necessary, but we hope that you will finish this course with new knowledge and increased enthusiasm for the world of business. Your instructor will do his or her part to facilitate your learning. The rest, then, is up to you. We wish you success.

PART ONE

Introducing the Contemporary Business World

In the Opening Cases in Chapters 1 to 5, you will read about five situations that may seem at first glance to have little in common: Canadian megaprojects that focus on the extraction of oil and nickel, the importance of productivity for our standard of living, the unethical behaviour of some business managers, entrepreneurs starting new businesses, and the exporting of Canadian goods and services to other countries. All of these situations, and many more that are described in this text, have a common thread—they all demonstrate the key elements of business as well as the excitement and complexity of business activity. Each case tells a part of the story of our contemporary business world.

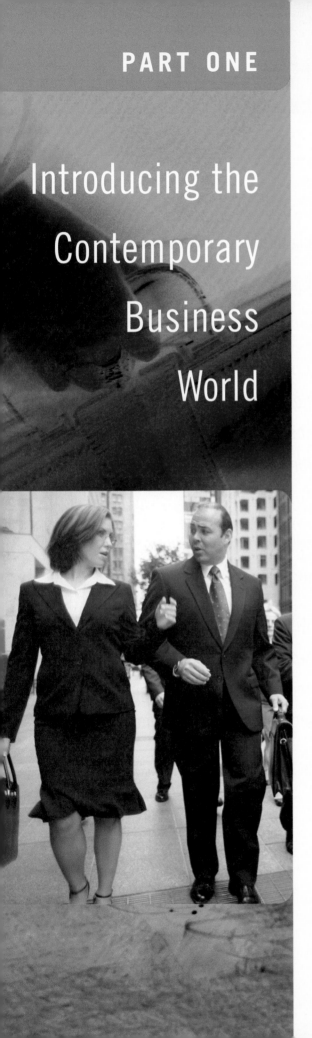

Part One, Introducing the Contemporary Business World, provides a general overview of business today, including its economic roots, the environment in which it operates, the importance of entrepreneurship, the various forms of ownership of business firms, the globalization of business, and the ethical problems and opportunities facing business firms.

- We begin in **Chapter 1, The Canadian Business System**, by examining the role of business in the economy of Canada and other market economies. We also present a brief history of business in Canada.
- Then, in **Chapter 2, The Environment of Business**, we examine the external environments that influence business activity. These include the economic, technological, socio-cultural, legal-political, and general business environments.
- Next, in **Chapter 3, Conducting Business Ethically and Responsibly**, we look at individual ethics and corporate social responsibility, and how these affect the firm's customers, employees, and investors.
- In **Chapter 4, Entrepreneurship, Small Business, and New Venture Creation**, we examine the important concepts of entrepreneurship, small business, and the various forms of business ownership that have evolved to facilitate business activity.
- Finally, in **Chapter 5, The Global Context of Business**, we look at why countries engage in international trade, how companies organize to operate internationally, the development of free trade agreements, and factors that help or hinder international trade.

CHAPTER 1

The Canadian Business System

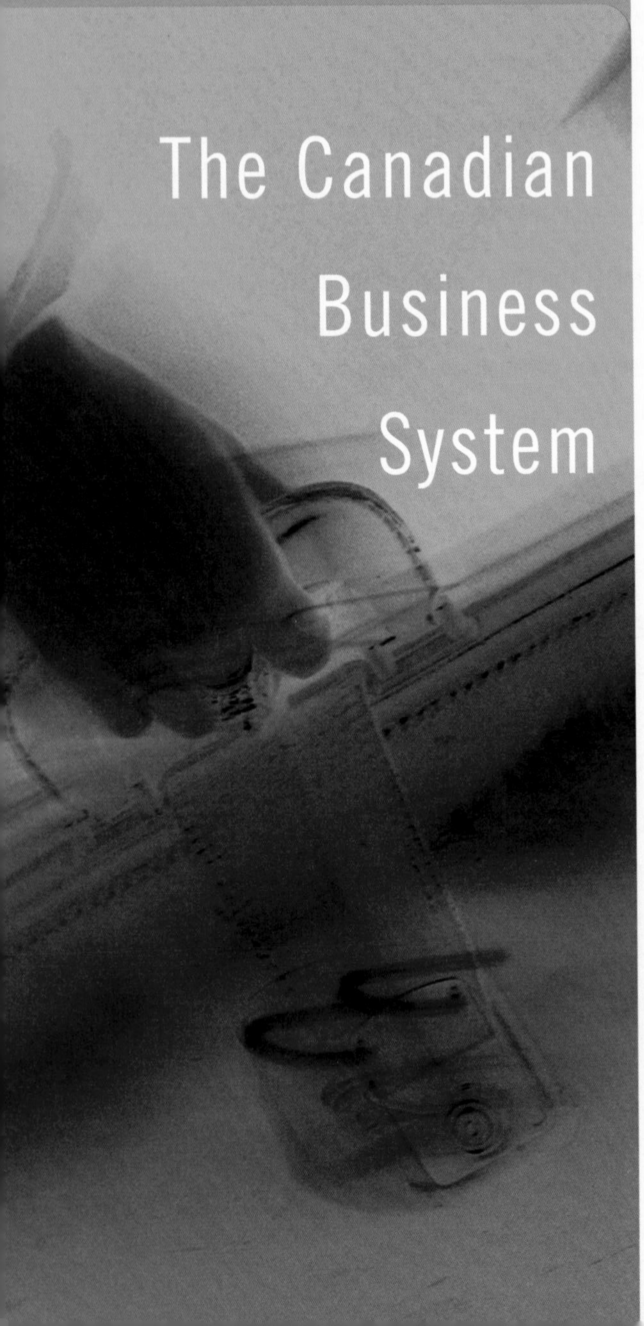

After reading this chapter, you should be able to:

1. Define the nature of Canadian *business* and identify its main goals.
2. Describe different types of global *economic systems* according to the means by which they control the *factors of production* through *input and output markets*.
3. Show how *demand* and *supply* affect resource distribution in Canada.
4. Identify the elements of *private enterprise* and explain the various *degrees of competition* in the Canadian economic system.
5. Trace the *history of business* in Canada.

Canadian Megaprojects

In the world of business, Canada is famous for its rich supply of natural resources such as oil, gas, gold, nickel, and copper. Extracting and selling these resources has long been an important activity for Canadian business firms. Two major projects which are currently underway in Canada's north—the Alberta Tar Sands and Voisey's Bay—illustrate the rewards and risks associated with such business activity. Both of these cases show that the process can be long and complex, particularly for megaprojects.

The Alberta Tar Sands. People have known about the sticky bitumen of northern Alberta for many years. Attempts were made to drill conventional oil wells there nearly 100 years ago but were unsuccessful. In 1967, the Great Canadian Oil Sands Project began the modern era in tar sands development. Ups and downs in oil prices in the 1970s and 1980s led many businesspeople to believe that developing the tar sands was not economically viable. More recently, with the strong surge in oil prices and much talk of developing oil shortages, the rate of development of the tar sands has increased dramatically.

It is estimated that there are 2.5 trillion barrels of oil trapped in the tar sands around Fort McMurray, Alberta. That far exceeds the reserves of Saudi Arabia. Over the last 30 years, various companies have spent about $34 billion dollars to develop this area. Over the next 10 years, another $87 billion is likely to be spent. By then, production will reach about two million barrels of oil each day. This is comparable to the major oil producers in the Middle East. All of this activity is making the rest of the world sit up and take notice of Canada's potential.

Several companies are important players in the development of the tar sands, including Suncor Energy Inc., Canadian Natural Resources Ltd., Petro-Canada, and Syncrude Canada Ltd. The megaprojects currently underway at these companies have generated a huge demand for both people and raw materials. One project at Suncor required 21 million construction hours, 3 million engineering hours, and 150 000 cubic metres of concrete. At its peak, the Syncrude upgrader project employed 6000 workers. By 2010, nearly 30 000 tradespeople will be needed in the area, and this number does not include those who will be needed to work in the mines. Approximately 80 000 people will find work in this area by 2014, and another 240 000 jobs will appear elsewhere as a result of the mining activity in the tar sands.

The plans being made by Canadian Natural Resources Ltd. are typical. The company will spend $25 billion on tar sands development by 2017. This is in addition to the $11 billion it has already spent. The company started operations in 1989, and has already become the number two oil and gas producer in Canada. If events unfold as planned, Canadian Natural Resources Ltd. will be producing approximately one million barrels of oil a day.

Voisey's Bay. After years of delay, the nickel mining project at Voisey's Bay in Labrador is proceeding. The story began in 1993, when two diamond prospectors stumbled upon one of the world's richest nickel finds in the rolling hills of northeast Labrador. In 1996, Inco bought controlling interest in the site for $4.3 billion so it could maintain its dominance in world nickel markets. But in 1997, Inco announced that it would have to delay development of the site because of a time-consuming and expensive environmental review process. To complicate matters, the government of Newfoundland and Labrador was demanding that Inco build a smelter in the province, and the Innu Nation was asking for a 3 percent smelter royalty.

Over the next several years, many further delays were evident as Inco tried to negotiate a deal that was acceptable to the government of Newfoundland and Labrador. After many false starts, an agreement was reached in 2002. The agreement included the provision that the mine become operational in 2006 and that a smelter be built in Argentia in 2011. In 2004 alone, Inco poured nearly $250 million dollars into the project.

The project is not without risk to Inco because it plans to use an unproven technology at Argentia that relies on chemicals instead of heat to produce nickel from concentrate. To explore this new process, Inco has built a test facility in a 1:10 000 scale model. By 2008, Inco must tell the province whether it will use the new technology or the conventional one. Whatever decision is made on the processing technology, once the mine is operational it will produce 110 million pounds of nickel concentrate and 70 million pounds of copper concentrate annually and will add about $300 million to Inco's cash flow. In 2005, the project at Voisey's Bay provided employment for about 1000 people, about one-third of whom are aboriginal, but that will drop to about 400 once regular operations begin. The Argentia smelter will also employ about 400 people.

Industry observers agree that Inco paid too much for Voisey's Bay and that it took far too long to develop the site. But with nickel prices at 16-year highs and customer's demand for the product at high levels as well, Inco is poised to reap considerable rewards from the project. In 2006, Inco was purchased by Brazilian-based Companhia Vale do Rio Doce for $19 billion. ◆

HOW WILL THIS BENEFIT YOU?

The Canadian megaprojects described in the opening case reflect both the opportunities and challenges you'll find in today's business world. All businesses are subject to the influences of economic forces. But these same economic forces also provide astute managers and entrepreneurs with opportunities for profits and growth. By understanding these economic forces and how they interact, you'll be better able to (1) appreciate how managers must contend with the challenges and opportunities resulting from economic forces (from the standpoint of an employee and a manager or business owner), and (2) understand why prices fluctuate (from the perspective of a consumer).

In this chapter, we look at some basic elements of economic systems and describe the economics of market systems. We also introduce and discuss several indicators that are used to gauge the vitality of the Canadian economic system. We conclude the chapter by briefly tracing the history of Canadian business. Let's start with some business basics.

THE IDEA OF BUSINESS AND PROFIT

1 Define the nature of Canadian *business* and identify its main goals.

business
An organization that seeks to earn profits by providing goods and services.

profit
What remains (if anything) after a business's expenses are subtracted from its sales revenues.

What do you think of when you hear the word *business*? Does it conjure up images of huge corporations like Syncrude Canada and Wal-Mart, or smaller companies like your local convenience store? What about one-person operations like the barbershop around the corner? Actually, each of these firms is a **business**—an organization that produces or sells goods or services in an effort to make a profit. **Profit** is what remains after a business's expenses have been subtracted from its revenues. Profits reward the owners of businesses for taking the risks involved in investing their time and money. These amounts can be very large if the business is managed well. Among the most profitable companies in 2005 were Royal Bank of Canada ($3.3 billion), Manulife Financial ($3.2 billion), and Imperial Oil Ltd. ($2.6 billion).[1]

The prospect of earning profits is what encourages people to start and expand businesses. Today, businesses produce most of the goods and services that we consume, and they employ many of the working people in Canada. Profits from these businesses are paid to thousands upon thousands of owners and shareholders, and business taxes help support governments at all levels. In addition, businesses help support charitable causes and provide community leadership.

ECONOMIC SYSTEMS AROUND THE WORLD

A business in Canada is different in many ways from one in China. Both differ from businesses in Japan, France, or Peru. A major determinant of how organizations operate is the kind of economic system that characterizes the country in which they do business. An **economic system** allocates a nation's resources among its citizens. Economic systems differ in terms of who owns and controls these resources, known as the "factors of production" (see Figure 1.1).

2 Describe different types of global *economic systems* according to the means by which they control the *factors of production* through *input and output markets.*

Factors of Production

The key difference between economic systems is the way in which they manage the **factors of production**—the basic resources that a country's businesses use to produce goods and services. Traditionally, economists have focused on four factors of production: *labour, capital, entrepreneurs,* and *natural resources*. Newer perspectives tend to broaden the idea of "natural resources" to include all *physical resources*. In addition, *information resources* are now often included.[2]

economic system
The way in which a nation allocates its resources among its citizens.

factors of production
The resources used to produce goods and services: labour, capital, entrepreneurs, and natural resources.

Labour

The people who work for a company represent the first factor of production, **labour**. Sometimes called *human resources*, labour is the mental and physical capabilities of people. Carrying out the business of such a huge company as Imperial Oil requires a labour force with a wide variety of skills ranging from managers to geologists to truck drivers.

labour
The mental and physical training and talents of people; sometimes called human resources.

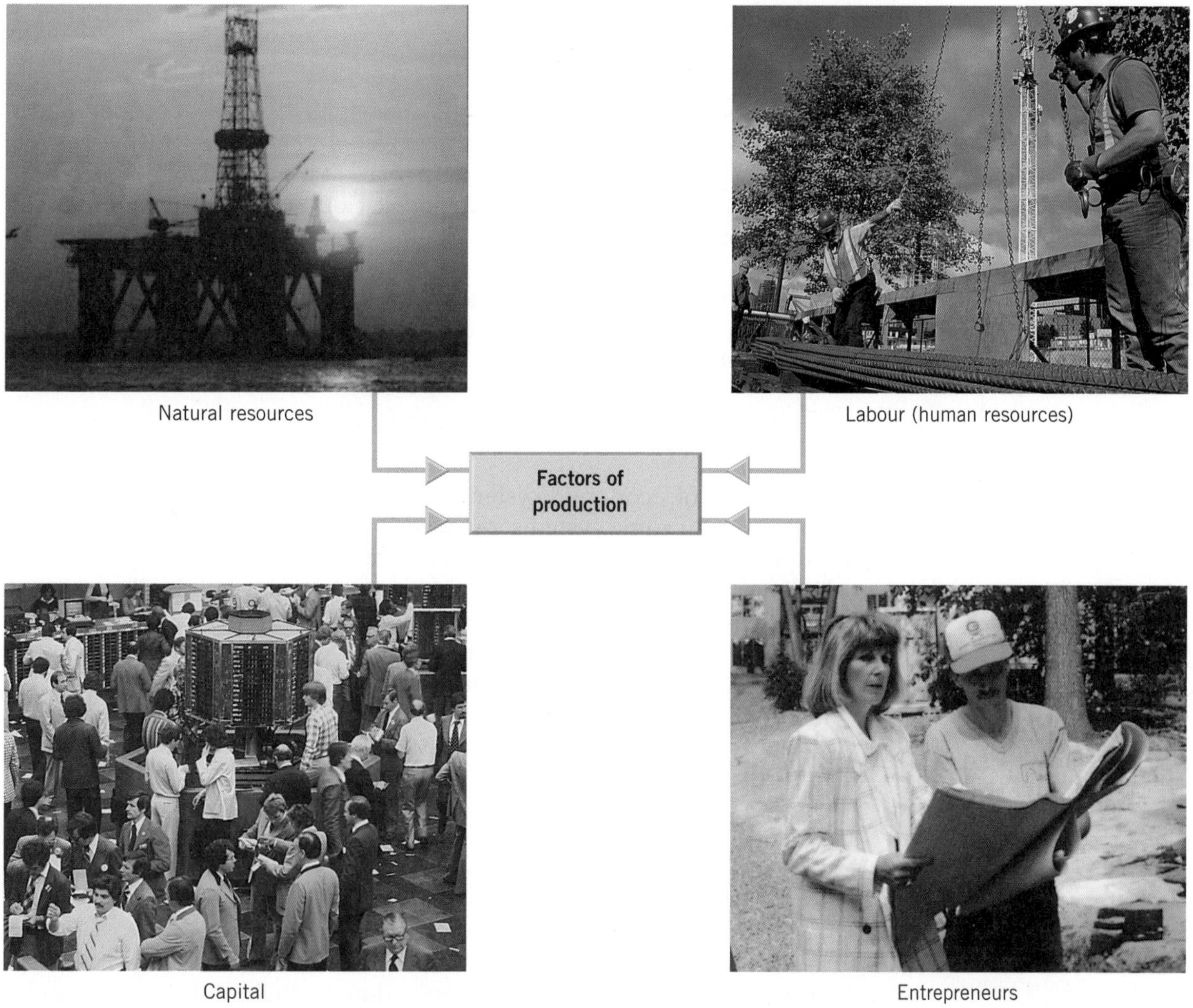

Figure 1.1 Factors of production are the basic resources a business uses to create goods and services. The four basic factors are natural resources, labour, capital, and entrepreneurs.

Capital

capital
The funds needed to operate an enterprise.

Obtaining and using material resources and labour requires **capital**, the funds needed to operate an enterprise. Capital is needed to start a business and to keep the business operating and growing. Imperial Oil's annual drilling costs run into the millions of dollars each year. A major source of capital for most businesses is personal investment by owners, which can be made either by the individual entrepreneurs or partners who start businesses or by investors who buy stock in them. Revenues from the sale of products, of course, are another and important ongoing source of capital.[3] Finally, many firms borrow funds from banks and other lending institutions.

Entrepreneurs

entrepreneur
An individual who organizes and manages labour, capital, and natural resources to produce goods and services to earn a profit, but who also runs the risk of failure.

Entrepreneurs are those people who accept the opportunities and risks involved in creating and operating businesses. They are the people who start new businesses and who make the decisions that allow small businesses to grow into larger ones. Jimmy Pattison is a well-known Canadian entrepreneur.

Natural Resources

natural resources
Items used in the production of goods and services in their natural state, including land, water, mineral deposits, and trees.

Land, water, mineral deposits, and trees are good examples of **natural resources**. For example, Imperial Oil makes use of a wide variety of natural resources. It has vast quantities of crude oil to process each year, but also needs the land where the oil is located, as well as land for its refineries and pipelines.

Information Resources

information resources
Information such as market forecasts, economic data, and specialized knowledge of employees that is useful to a business and that helps it achieve its goals.

While the production of tangible goods once dominated most economic systems, today **information resources** also play a major role. Businesses rely on all sorts of information, including market forecasts, the specialized expertise and knowledge of people, and various forms of economic data about the economy and consumers. Businesses also create new information or repackage existing information for new users and different audiences. AOL, for example, does not produce tangible products. Instead, it provides numerous online services for its millions of subscribers in exchange for a monthly access fee.

Types of Economic Systems

command economy
An economic system in which government controls all or most factors of production and makes all or most production decisions.

market economy
An economic system in which individuals control all or most factors of production and make all or most production decisions.

Different types of economic systems manage the factors of production in different ways. In some systems, ownership is private; in others, the factors of production are owned by the government. Economic systems also differ in the ways decisions are made about production and allocation. A **command economy**, for example, relies on a centralized government to control all or most factors of production and to make all or most production and allocation decisions. In **market economies**, individuals—producers and consumers—control production and allocation decisions through supply and demand. We will describe each of these economic types and then discuss the reality of the *mixed market economy*.

Command Economies

communism
A type of command economy in which the government owns and operates all industries.

The two most basic forms of command economies are communism and socialism. Originally proposed by nineteenth-century German economist Karl Marx, **communism** is a system in which the government owns and operates all sources of production. Marx envisioned a society in which individuals would ultimately contribute according to their abilities and receive economic benefits according to their needs. He also expected government ownership of production factors to be only temporary. Once society had matured, government would "wither away" and the workers would gain direct ownership. But as the Business Accountability box demonstrates, things have not worked out the way Marx predicted and most countries have now abandoned communism in favour of a more market-based economy.

In a less extensive command economic system called **socialism**, the government owns and operates only selected major industries. Smaller businesses such as clothing stores and restaurants may be privately owned. Although workers in socialist countries are usually allowed to choose their occupations or professions, a large proportion generally works for the government. Many government-operated enterprises are inefficient, since management positions are frequently filled based on political considerations rather than ability. Also, extensive public welfare systems result in very high taxes. Because of these factors, socialism is generally declining in popularity.[4]

socialism
A kind of command economy in which the government owns and operates the main industries, while individuals own and operate less crucial industries.

BUSINESS ACCOUNTABILITY

Whatever Happened to Communism?

In 2005, GlobeScan conducted a poll of over 20 000 people in 20 different countries and asked them whether they agreed with the following statement: "the free market economy is the best system." Where do you think the highest support for capitalism was found? Not in the U.S. or Canada or Germany or Italy or Japan, but in *China*, where 74 percent of people polled agreed with the statement. This is a surprising finding, given the Chinese government's strong support of the communist economic ideology. Other countries with high scores were the U.S. (71 percent), India (70 percent), and South Korea (66 percent). Countries with surprisingly low scores were Argentina (42 percent), Brazil (57 percent), and Mexico (61 percent). These low scores are likely the result of rushing free market reforms amid much corruption in Latin American countries.

It is surprising how rapidly free market systems have become popular. Until the 1980s, the former Soviet Union, most Eastern European countries, China, North Korea, Vietnam, Albania, and Cuba all embraced communist economic systems. During the early 1990s, however, one country after another renounced communism as both an economic and a political system. Today, Cuba, North Korea, Vietnam, and the People's Republic of China are among the few nations that claim to have a communist system. But while these countries may claim to be communist, the reality is quite different. They have all been swept up in the worldwide movement toward free market systems (some more than others).

Cuba has been moving toward free markets for more than a decade, but progress is slow. Free-market activities are technically illegal, but they have been increasing since the mid-1990s. Now, special shops that once were reserved for diplomats sell goods to Cubans from all walks of life. These stores are surrounded by paid bicycle-parking lots, car washes, and stalls selling home-grown produce and homemade handicrafts. This "street-corner commerce" reflects a growth in private enterprise as a solution to problems that Cuba's centralized economy has never been able to solve. Raul Castro (Fidel's brother) is now in power, and he seems to be more willing to allow at least limited private enterprise activities.

Even more dramatic and highly publicized changes are taking place in China, which has burst upon the world scene as an awakening economic giant. It seems hard to believe now, but before 1979 people who sold watches on street corners were sentenced to years of hard labour. In 1999, China's constitution was amended to elevate private enterprise to a place alongside the state sector in China's official economic ideology. Since that time, the private sector has become incredibly productive, and China is the world's fastest growing economy. For example, it is estimated that China produces 60 percent of all the toys in the world. It is also a vast and rapidly growing market for many of the products that Canadian firms produce—chemicals, ores, cereals, and wood products. China's reputation for being a low-cost producer of goods is legendary. Over the longer term, it will be difficult for the Chinese government to maintain a communist economic and political ideology while the people of China are eagerly embracing the free market system.

In terms of movement away from the communist ideology, perhaps the most striking changes are those that are occurring in North Korea. Until very recently,

▶▶▶

▶▶▶

North Korea was an extreme example of the communist economic system, and the country was so isolated from world commerce that it was known as the "Hermit Kingdom." Now, large numbers of "sidewalk entrepreneurs" sell items like food and drinks in public places in North Korea, whereas just a few years ago they would have been imprisoned for "profiteering." In the Yanggakdo Hotel, visitors can play slot machines or roulette at the Casino Pyongyang.

As recently as the late 1990s, the official North Korean government position was that merchants were a class of people who should be eradicated because they bought products at low prices and sold them to consumers at high prices (and, it was argued, they used deceit and fraud in the process). Now, the communist party newspaper quotes North Korean dictator Kim Jong Il as saying that he favours profits under socialist economic management. These changes in the government's position have attracted the attention of foreign companies who are becoming more interested in investing in North Korea. In 2005, for example, the London-based Anglo-Sino Capital Partners formed the Chosun Development & Investment Fund and planned to raise $50 million for investment in North Korea. North Korea still has a long way to go toward a free market system, but the movement has started. These changes in so many different countries reflect consumer beliefs that market-based economies are more responsive and accountable to consumer needs.

QUESTIONS FOR DISCUSSION

1. What are the advantages and disadvantages of the free market (capitalist) system? Of the communist system?
2. Why do you think capitalism has displaced communism in so many countries around the world? As part of your answer, consider the differences in government accountability under communism and capitalism.

Market Economies

market
An exchange process between buyers and sellers of a particular good or service.

A **market** is a mechanism for exchange between the buyers and sellers of a particular good or service. To understand how a *market economy* works, consider what happens when a customer goes to a fruit stand to buy apples. Let's say that while one vendor is selling apples for $1 per kilogram, another is charging $1.50. Both vendors are free to charge what they want, and customers are free to buy what they choose. If both vendors' apples are of the same quality, the customer will likely buy the cheaper ones. But if the $1.50 apples are fresher, the customer may buy them instead. In short, both buyers and sellers enjoy freedom of choice.

input market
Firms buy resources that they need in the production of goods and services.

output market
Firms supply goods and services in response to demand on the part of consumers.

Input and Output Markets. A useful and more complete model for understanding how the factors of production work in a pure market economy is shown in Figure 1.2.[5] In the **input market**, firms buy resources from households, which then supply those resources. In the **output market**, firms supply goods and services in response to demand on the part of the households. The activities of these two markets create a circular flow. Ford Motor Co., for example, buys labour directly from households, which may also supply capital from accumulated savings in the form of stock purchases. Consumer buying patterns provide information that helps Ford decide which models to produce and which to discontinue. In turn, Ford uses these inputs in various ways and becomes a supplier to households when it designs and produces various kinds of automobiles, trucks, and sport-utility vehicles and offers them for sale to consumers.

capitalism
An economic system in which markets decide what, when, and for whom to produce.

Individuals are free to work for Ford or an alternative employer and to invest in Ford stock or alternative forms of saving or consumption. Similarly, Ford can create whatever vehicles it chooses and price them at whatever value it chooses. Consumers are free to buy their next car from Ford, Toyota, BMW, or any other manufacturer. The political basis is called **capitalism**, which allows private ownership of the factors of production and encourages entrepreneurship by offering profits as an incentive. This process contrasts markedly with that of a command economy, in which individuals may be told where they can and cannot work, companies may

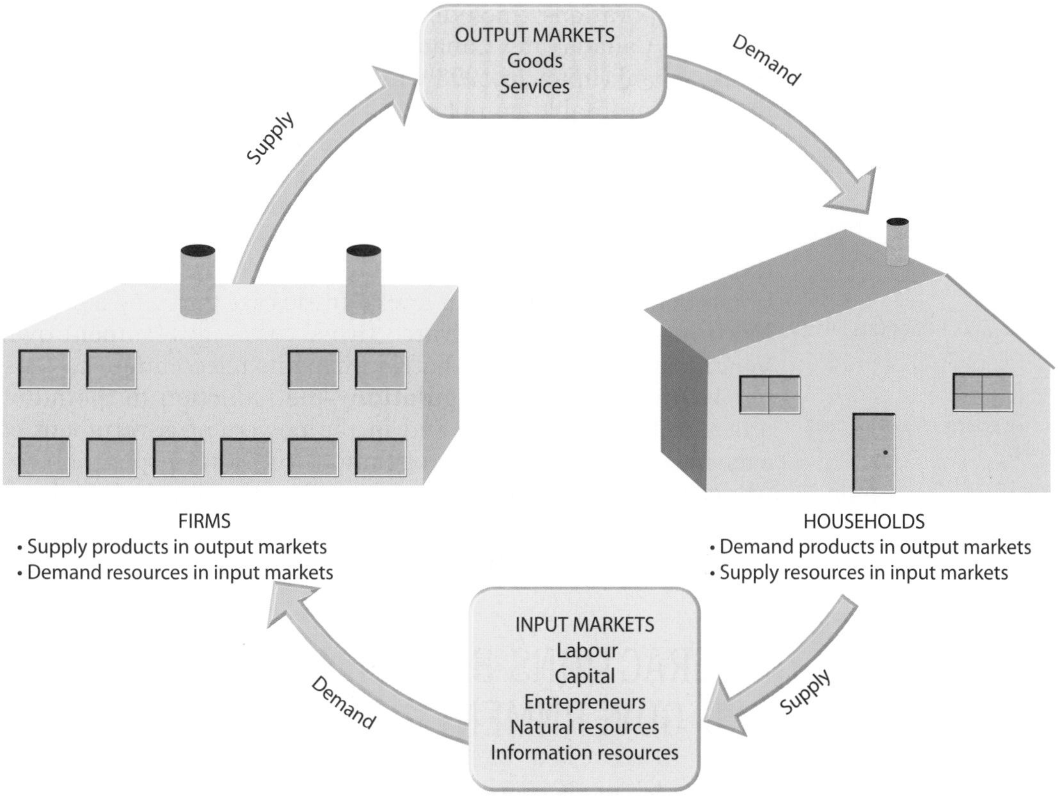

Figure 1.2 Circular flow in a market economy.

be told what they can and cannot manufacture, and consumers may have little or no choice as to what they purchase or how much they pay for items.

Mixed Market Economies

Command and market economies are two extremes, or opposites. In reality, most countries rely on some form of **mixed market economy**—a system featuring characteristics of both command and market economies. But there is a trend toward **privatization**—converting government enterprises into privately owned companies. In Canada, for example, the air traffic control system has been privatized, and the federal government has sold several

mixed market economy
An economic system with elements of both a command economy and a market economy; in practice, typical of most nations' economies.

privatization
The transfer of activities from the government to the private sector.

According to the model of circular flow in a market economy, shoppers at a Wal-Mart de Mexico play the same role in the output market as consumers everywhere. They demand goods supplied by a retail firm. Likewise, you can think of the employees who work for companies from which Wal-Mart buys its products as households that supply the input market with labour, time, and skills.

other corporations, including Canadian National Railway, Air Canada, Teleglobe Canada, and Canadair Ltd. In Russia, Norilsk Nickel was on the brink of bankruptcy in 1998 when it was privatized. By 2001, it was one of the most profitable companies in Russia, and its workers were earning more than double the typical wage in that country.[6] The Netherlands recently began the process of privatizing its TNT Post Group N.V., and India has privatized 18 different industries, including iron, steel, machinery, and telecommunications.[7] After being privatized, companies typically reduce their payroll and boost their efficiency and productivity.[8] While privatization is definitely the trend, a few countries are pursuing a policy of **nationalization**—converting private firms into government-owned firms. Venezuela, for example, is nationalizing its telecommunications industry.

nationalization
The transfer of activities from private firms to the government.

deregulation
A reduction in the number of laws affecting business activity.

Another trend is **deregulation**—the reduction in the number of laws affecting business activity and in the powers of government enforcement agencies. In most cases, deregulation frees the corporation to do what it wants without government intervention, thereby simplifying the task of management. Deregulation is evident in many industries, including airlines, pipelines, banking, trucking, and communications.

INTERACTIONS BETWEEN BUSINESS AND GOVERNMENT

In Canada's economic system, there are many important interactions between business and government. The ways in which government influences business and the ways business influences government are described below.

How Government Influences Business

Government plays several key roles in the Canadian economy and each of these roles influences business activity in some way. The roles government plays are as follows.

Government as a Customer

Government buys thousands of different products and services from business firms, including office supplies, office buildings, computers, battleships, helicopters, highways, water treatment plants, and management and engineering consulting services. Many businesses depend on government purchasing, if not for their survival then at least for a certain level of prosperity. Government expenditures on goods and services amount to billions of dollars each year.

Government as a Competitor

Government also competes with business through Crown corporations, which are accountable to a minister of parliament for their conduct. Crown corporations exist at both the provincial and federal levels, and account for a significant and wide variety of economic activity in Canada.

Government as a Regulator

Canadian Radio-television and Telecommunications Commission (CRTC)
Regulates and supervises all aspects of the Canadian broadcasting system.

Canadian Wheat Board
Regulates the price farmers receive for their wheat.

Despite the move toward deregulation, federal and provincial governments in Canada still regulate many aspects of business activity through many administrative boards, tribunals, or commissions. At the federal level, examples include the **Canadian Radio-television and Telecommunications Commission (CRTC)** (which issues and renews broadcast licences) and the **Canadian Wheat Board** (which regulates the price of wheat). Provincial boards and commissions also regulate business through their decisions.

Reasons for regulating business activity include protecting competition, protecting consumers, achieving social goals, and protecting the environment.

Protecting Competition. Competition is crucial to a market economy, so government regulates business activity to ensure that healthy competition exists among business firms. Without these restrictions, a large company with vast resources could cut its prices and drive smaller firms out of the market. The guidelines for Canada's competition policy are contained in The Competition Act, which prohibits a variety of practices (see Table 1.1). Section 38, for example, prohibits *resale price maintenance*. In 2005, Labatt Brewing Co. pleaded guilty to resale price maintenance and was fined $250 000 after its sales representatives gave money to store operators who agreed not to lower prices on some brands of beer. This activity meant that customers had to pay higher prices for beer. A Labatt competitor, Sleeman Breweries, was fined for resale price maintenance in 2002.[9]

Businesses often complain that the Competition Bureau is too slow in approving (or denying) merger plans. For example, when Labatt Brewing wanted to take over Lakeport Brewing, it was told that the Competition Bureau would need up to six months to determine whether the takeover would lessen competition. After hearing this, Labatt appealed to the Competition Tribunal to speed up the decision. In a surprise decision, the Tribunal agreed with Labatt, and the merger went ahead much sooner than it otherwise would have.[10]

Protecting Consumers. The federal government has initiated many programs that protect consumers. Consumer and Corporate Affairs Canada administers many of these. Important legislation includes the **Hazardous Products Act** (which requires poisonous, flammable, explosive, or corrosive products to be appropriately labelled), the **Tobacco Act** (which prohibits cigarette advertising on billboards and in stores), the **Weights and Measures Act**

Hazardous Products Act
Regulates banned products and products that can be sold but must be labelled hazardous.

Tobacco Act
Prohibits cigarette advertising on billboards and in retail stores, and assigns financial penalties to violators.

Weights and Measures Act
Sets standards of accuracy for weighing and measuring devices.

Table 1.1 The Competition Act

Section 32	Prohibits conspiracies and combinations formed for the purpose of unduly lessening competition in the production, transportation, or storage of goods. Persons convicted may be imprisoned for up to five years or fined up to $1 million or both.
Section 33	Prohibits mergers and monopolies that substantially lessen competition. Individuals who assist in the formation of such a monopoly or merger may be imprisoned for up to two years.
Section 34	Prohibits illegal trade practices. A company may not, for example, cut prices in one region of Canada while selling at a higher price everywhere else if this substantially lessens competition. A company may not sell at "unreasonably low prices" if this substantially lessens competition. (This section does not prohibit credit unions from returning surpluses to their members.)
Section 35	Prohibits giving allowances and rebates to buyers to cover their advertising expenses, unless these allowances are made available proportionally to other purchasers who are in competition with the buyer given the rebate.
Section 36	Prohibits misleading advertising including (1) false statements about the performance of a product, (2) misleading guarantees, (3) pyramid selling, (4) charging the higher price when two prices are marked on an item, and (5) referral selling.
Section 37	Prohibits bait-and-switch selling. No person can advertise a product at a bargain price if there is no supply of the product available to the consumer. (This tactic baits prospects into the store, where salespeople switch them to higher-priced goods.) This section also controls the use of contests to sell goods, and prohibits the sale of goods at a price higher than the advertised one.
Section 38	Prohibits resale price maintenance. No person who produces or supplies a product can attempt to influence upward, or discourage reduction of, the price of the good in question. It is also illegal for the producer to refuse to supply a product to a reseller simply because the producer believes the reseller will cut the price.

(which sets standards of accuracy for weighing and measuring devices), the **Textile Labelling Act** (which regulates the labelling, sale, importation, and advertising of consumer textile articles), and the **Food and Drug Act** (which prohibits the sale of food that contains any poisonous or harmful substances). Consumers are also protected by municipal bylaws such as "no smoking" bylaws.

Textile Labelling Act
Regulates the labelling, sale, importation, and advertising of consumer textile articles.

Food and Drug Act
Prohibits the sale of food unfit for human consumption and regulates food advertising.

Achieving Social Goals. Social goals promote the well-being of our society. Social goals include universal access to health care, safe workplaces, employment insurance, and decent pensions. All of these goals require the interaction of business firms and government. The decisions of foreign governments—as they pursue their own social goals—can affect Canadian businesses. For example, when the U.S. government introduced legislation making it difficult for online gambling companies to operate in the U.S., the stock prices of many companies in that industry, including Canadian firms CryptoLogic Inc. and Chartwell Technology, dropped sharply.[11]

Protecting the Environment. Key government legislation designed to protect the environment includes the **Canada Water Act** (which controls water quality in fresh and marine waters), the **Fisheries Act** (which controls the discharge of any harmful substance into water), and the **Environmental Contaminants Act** (which establishes regulations for airborne substances that are a danger to human health or the environment).

Canada Water Act
Controls water quality in fresh and marine waters of Canada.

Fisheries Act
Regulates the discharge of harmful substances into water.

Environmental Contaminants Act
Establishes regulations for airborne substances that are a danger to human health or to the environment.

Government as a Taxation Agent

Taxes are imposed and collected by federal, provincial, and local governments. **Revenue taxes** (e.g., income taxes) are levied by governments primarily to provide revenue to fund various services and programs. **Progressive revenue taxes** are levied at a higher rate on higher-income taxpayers and at a lower rate on lower-income taxpayers. **Regressive revenue taxes** (e.g., sales tax) are levied at the same rate regardless of a person's income. They cause poorer people to pay a higher percentage of their income than richer people pay. **Restrictive taxes** (e.g., taxes on alcohol, tobacco, and gasoline) are levied partially for the revenue they provide, but also because legislative bodies believe that the products in question should be controlled.

revenue taxes
Taxes whose main purpose is to fund government services and programs.

progressive revenue taxes
Taxes levied at a higher rate on higher-income taxpayers and at a lower rate on lower-income taxpayers.

regressive revenue taxes
Taxes that cause poorer people to pay a higher percentage of income than richer people pay.

restrictive taxes
Taxes levied to control certain activities that legislators believe should be controlled.

Government as a Provider of Incentives and Financial Assistance

Federal, provincial, and municipal governments offer incentive programs that attempt to stimulate economic development. In Quebec, for example, Hyundai Motors received $6.4 million to build a production facility and an additional $682 000 to train workers. Both Toyota and Hyundai have received millions of dollars in incentives from various governments in the form of training incentives, interest-free loans, and the suspension of customs duties.[12]

Governments also offer incentives through the many services they provide to business firms through government organizations. Examples include the (1) Export Development Corporation (which assists Canadian exporters by offering export insurance against non-payment by foreign buyers and long-term loans to foreign buyers of Canadian products), (2) Natural Resources Canada (which provides geological maps of Canada's potential mineral-producing areas), and (3) Statistics Canada (which provides data and analysis on almost every aspect of Canadian society). Additionally, Industry Canada offers many different programs designed to help small businesses. The Canada Business program, for example, provides information on government programs, services, and regulations in order to improve the start-up and survival rates of small and medium-sized businesses. It also encourages businesses to focus on sound business planning and the effective use of market research. The Department of Foreign Affairs and International

Trade (DFAIT) helps Canadian companies doing business internationally by promoting Canada as a good place to invest and to carry on business activities. It also assists in negotiating and administering trade agreements.

There are many other government incentive programs, including municipal tax rebates for companies that locate in certain areas, design assistance programs, and remission of tariffs on certain advanced technology production equipment. Government incentive programs may or may not have the desired effect of stimulating the economy. They may also cause difficulties with our trading partners who claim that Canadian businesses are being unfairly subsidized (see Chapter 5).

Government as a Provider of Essential Services

The federal, provincial, and municipal governments facilitate business activity through the services they supply. The federal government provides highways, the postal service, the minting of money, the armed forces, and statistical data on which to base business decisions. It also tries to maintain stability through fiscal and monetary policy. Provincial and municipal governments provide streets, sewage and sanitation systems, police and fire departments, utilities, hospitals, and education. All of these activities create the kind of stability that encourages business activity.

How Business Influences Government

Businesses also try to influence the government through the use of lobbyists, trade associations, and advertising. A **lobbyist** is a person hired by a company or industry to represent that company's interests with government officials. The Canadian Association of Consulting Engineers, for example, regularly lobbies the federal and provincial governments to make use of the skills possessed by private-sector consulting engineers on projects like city water systems. Business lobbyists may have training in the particular industry, public relations experience, or a legal background. A few have served as legislators or government regulators.

lobbyist
A person hired by a company or an industry to represent its interests with government officials.

The Lobbyists Registration Act came into effect in 1989. Lobbyists must register with the Registrar of Lobbyists so that it is clear which individuals are being paid for their lobbying activity. For many lobbying efforts, there are opposing points of view. For example, the Canadian Cancer Society and the Tobacco Institute present very different points of view on cigarette smoking and cigarette advertising.

Employees and owners of small businesses that cannot afford lobbyists often join **trade associations**. Trade associations may act as an industry lobby to influence legislation. They also conduct training programs relevant to the particular industry, and they arrange trade shows at which members display their products or services to potential customers. Most publish newsletters featuring articles on new products, new companies, changes in ownership, and changes in laws affecting the industry.

trade associations
An organization dedicated to promoting the interests and assisting the members of a particular industry.

Corporations can influence legislation indirectly by influencing voters. A company can, for example, launch an advertising campaign designed to get people to write their MPs, MPPs, or MLAs demanding passage—or rejection—of a particular bill that is before parliament or the provincial legislature.

THE CANADIAN MARKET ECONOMY

Understanding the complex nature of the Canadian economic system is essential to understanding Canadian business. In this section, we will examine the workings of our market economy in more detail. Specifically, we look at markets, demand, supply, private enterprise, and degrees of competition.

Show how *demand* and *supply* affect resource distribution in Canada. 3

Demand and Supply in a Market Economy

market
An exchange process between buyers and sellers of a particular good or service.

In economic terms, a **market** is not a specific place, like a supermarket, but an exchange process between buyers and sellers. Decisions about production in a market economy are the result of millions of exchanges. How much of what product a company offers for sale and who buys it depends on the laws of demand and supply.

The Laws of Supply and Demand

demand
The willingness and ability of buyers to purchase a product or service.

supply
The willingness and ability of producers to offer a good or service for sale.

law of demand
The principle that buyers will purchase (demand) more of a product as price drops.

law of supply
The principle that producers will offer (supply) more of a product as price rises.

Decisions about what to buy and what to sell are determined primarily by the forces of demand and supply. **Demand** is the willingness and ability of buyers to purchase a product or service. **Supply** is the willingness and ability of producers to offer a good or service for sale. The **law of demand** states that buyers will purchase (demand) more of a product as its price drops. Conversely, the **law of supply** states that producers will offer (supply) more for sale as the price rises.

Demand and Supply Schedule

demand and supply schedule
Assessment of the relationships between different levels of demand and supply at different price levels.

To appreciate these laws in action, consider the market for pizza in your town. If everyone in town is willing to pay $25 for a pizza (a relatively high price), the town's only pizzeria will produce a large supply. If, however, everyone is willing to pay only $5 (a relatively low price), the restaurant will make fewer pizzas. Through careful analysis, we can determine how many pizzas will be sold at different prices. These results, called a **demand and supply schedule**, are obtained from marketing research and other systematic studies of the market. Properly applied, they help managers better understand the relationships among different levels of demand and supply at different price levels.

Demand and Supply Curves

demand curve
Graph showing how many units of a product will be demanded (bought) at different prices.

supply curve
Graph showing how many units of a product will be supplied (offered for sale) at different prices.

market price (equilibrium price)
Profit-maximizing price at which the quantity of goods demanded and the quantity of goods supplied are equal.

The demand and supply schedule can be used to construct demand and supply curves for pizza. A **demand curve** shows how many products—in this case, pizzas—will be *demanded* (bought) at different prices. A **supply curve** shows how many pizzas will be *supplied* (baked) at different prices.

Figure 1.3 shows the hypothetical demand and supply curves for pizzas in our illustration. As you can see, demand increases as price decreases, and supply increases as price increases. When the demand and supply curves are plotted on the same graph, the point at which they intersect is the **market price**, or **equilibrium price**—the profit-maximizing price at which the quantity of goods demanded and the quantity of goods supplied are equal. In Figure 1.3, the equilibrium price for pizzas is $10. At this point, the quantity of pizzas demanded and the quantity of pizzas supplied are the same—1000 pizzas per week.

Surpluses and Shortages

surplus
Situation in which quantity supplied exceeds quantity demanded.

shortage
Situation in which quantity demanded exceeds quantity supplied.

What would happen if the owner tried to increase profits by making more pizzas to sell? Or, what if the owner wanted to reduce overhead, cut back on store hours, and reduce the number of pizzas offered for sale? In either case, the result would be an inefficient use of resources. For example, if the restaurant supplies 1200 pizzas and tries to sell them for $10 each, 200 pizzas will not be purchased. The demand schedule clearly shows that only 1000 pizzas will be demanded at this price. The pizza maker will therefore have a **surplus**—a situation in which the quantity supplied exceeds the quantity demanded. The restaurant will thus lose the money that it spent making those extra 200 pizzas.

Conversely, if the pizzeria supplies only 800 pizzas, a **shortage** will result because the quantity demanded will be greater than the quantity supplied. The pizzeria will "lose" the extra money that it could have made by produc-

ENTREPRENEURSHIP AND NEW VENTURES

Putting Canadian Lentils on the International Map

At 33 years of age, Murad Al-Katib has put Canada—and its lentils—on the international map. As president and CEO of Saskcan Pulse Trading of Regina, Al-Katib has, in three years, taken his company from a home-based venture to an award-winning agribusiness that processes and exports pulse (e.g., lentils, chick peas, and peas) to more than 60 countries.

Observing the growth in the export of lentils to Turkey, Al-Katib saw the opportunity for value-added processing. "I didn't want to see the lentil story end up like the mustard story," he said, referring to the province of Saskatchewan supplying the raw material for almost all of the prepared mustards made in France. "I identified potential partners there, including one of the world's largest buyers of red lentils (Arbel) and convinced them that we should do the processing in Saskatchewan. That's how Saskcan was born." The company has attracted millions of dollars in investment, including Arbel's proprietary technology for splitting and oiling the red lentils and their expertise in setting up and operating the processing plant. Indeed, the facility has added about 40 percent to the market value of the crops.

Several factors have contributed to the boom in lentil crops over the past several years: international demand, a desire to produce a commodity that is less volatile in price than wheat, the drive to avoid a price-fixing, central marketing agency such as the Saskatchewan Wheat Board, and the need to rotate traditional crops with ones that restore nitrogen levels to the soil, which lentil plants do.

Product quality is important at Saskcan. "At first, we were a bit of a mystery to clients who wondered if, in Canada, we could produce a red split lentil that lived up to Turkish and Indian quality standards," Al-Katib recalls. "But, the quality of our first shipment of red split lentils was likely among the best in the world. From then on, our business just continued to grow." As Al-Katib explains, "January 2003 was our first load of red split lentils. To go from that to being the second-largest exporter in the world...yeah, we've had to overcome some challenges."

Transportation is one of those challenges, particularly in the face of soaring fuel costs. All the lentils must be containerized and shipped by rail from a land-locked region to international ports. "We are so far from world markets that transit time can take several weeks. Our competitors can deliver faster, so we have to be very competitive with our pricing," explains Al-Katib. The transportation costs alone comprise about 20 percent of the market cost of Canadian lentils, as compared to about 7 percent for rival Turkish lentils. "We've designed an automated system that makes us very efficient at processing, and that has been a big help," he says.

Another challenge is to deal with customers of distinct cultures and languages in 33 different countries. For example, in the Middle East, bright, shiny red lentils are considered the most valuable, while in Europe, a dull finish is more popular. That means some of Saskcan's product is highly polished with oil, while other batches are untouched.

From a relatively minor specialty crop five years ago, Canada's lentil production has grown to more than 900 000 tonnes annually, of which 98 percent is produced in Saskatchewan. "This has become a $1-billion industry in Canada." And Saskcan has grown along with it. The company is the largest processor and exporter of red lentils in the Western Hemisphere, and the second largest exporter of red lentils in the world. For Saskcan's business model to continue working, however, the venture must constantly race to remain the world's lowest cost producer of lentils.

Despite unpredictable growing conditions and the strong Canadian dollar, Al-Katib is optimistic amidst a continuing shift from green to red lentils, crops which command a premium price on international markets, and ongoing investment in the development of new seeds and refined varieties.

ing 200 more pizzas. Even though consumers may pay more for pizzas because of the shortage, the restaurant will still earn lower profits than it would have if it had made 1000 pizzas. In addition, it will risk angering customers who cannot buy pizzas. To optimize profits, therefore, all businesses must constantly seek the right combination of price charged and quantity supplied. This "right combination" is found at the equilibrium point.

Ginseng—a plant known for its healing properties—demonstrates the ideas about shortages and surpluses. In 1982, less than 25 metric tonnes of ginseng were grown in Canada, and growers received about $187 per kilogram for it. There was, essentially, a shortage of ginseng. Many new growers therefore got into the market because they saw a chance to make money supplying ginseng. With more growers, production increased rapidly, and by 1999, 2200 metric tonnes were being produced. By then, growers were getting about $33 per kilogram. By 2001, there was a surplus of ginseng.[13] A practical illustration of the issues of supply and demand is contained in the Exercising Your Ethics feature at the end of the chapter.

Demand and Supply Schedules

Price	Quantity of Pizzas Demanded	Quantity of Pizzas Supplied
$2	2000	100
$4	1700	400
$6	1500	600
$8	1200	800
$10	1000	1000
$12	800	1200
$14	600	1300
$16	400	1600
$18	200	1800
$20	100	2000

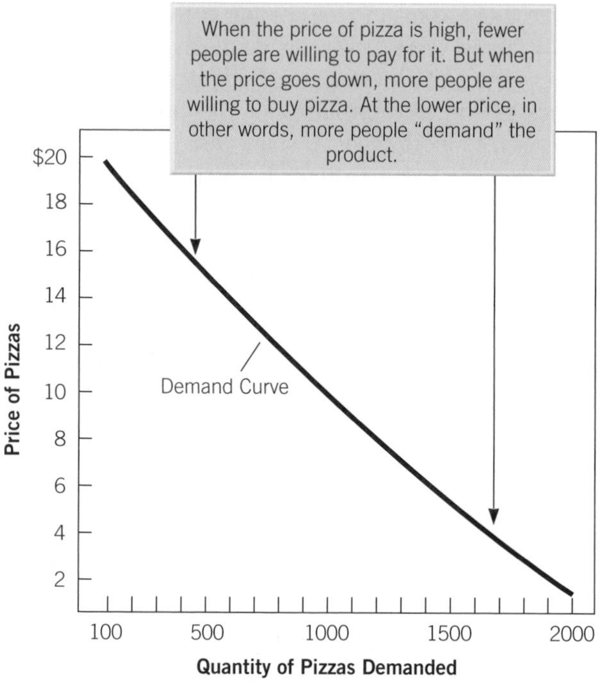

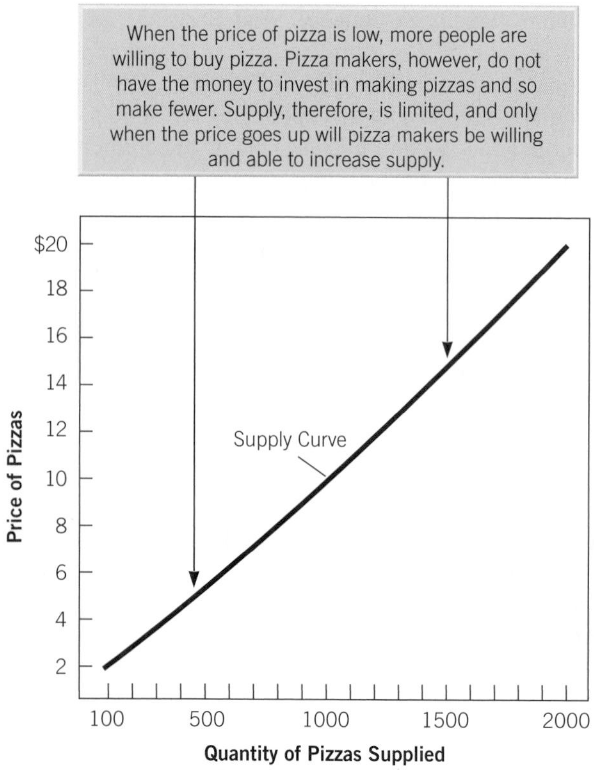

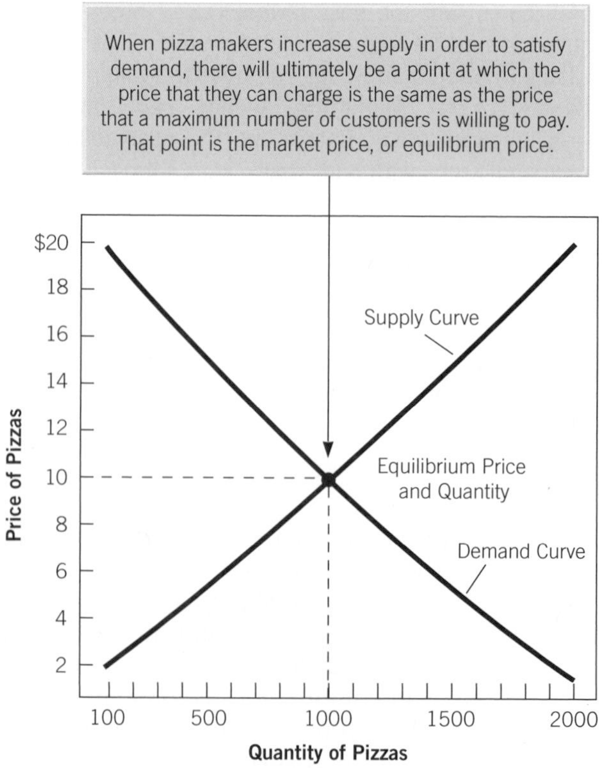

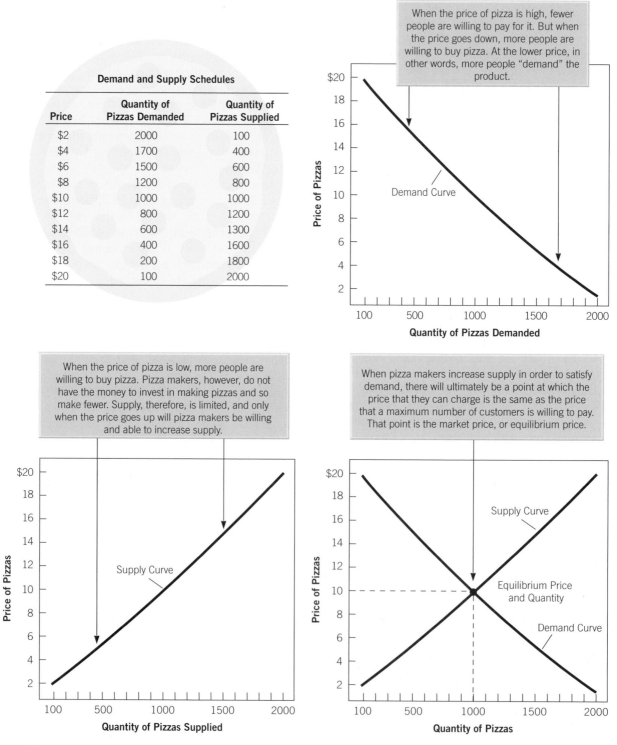

Figure 1.3 Demand and supply.

When demand is high for a commodity like oil, its price goes up, and people try to find substitute commodities that are cheaper. For example, companies have started using corn to make ethanol to add to gasoline, and palm oil is now being used to make diesel fuel (called biodiesel). But as the demand for corn and palm oil increases, the prices of those commodities have risen as well.[14] During 2006, for example, the price of palm oil rose from less than U.S.$400 per metric tonne to more than U.S.$500 per metric tonne.[15]

Price increases aren't the only problem. Criminal behaviour also increases when commodity prices increase. For example, as the price of stainless steel, aluminum, and other commodities has risen during the last few years, thieves have begun stealing items such as beer kegs, railway baggage carts, railroad tracks, light poles, and plastic milk crates made from expensive resins. These items are then sold to scrap yards for cash.[16]

Private Enterprise and Competition

4 Identify the elements of *private enterprise* and explain the various *degrees of competition* in the Canadian economic system.

Market economies rely on a **private enterprise** system—one that allows individuals to pursue their own interests with minimal government restriction. Private enterprise requires the presence of four elements: private property rights, freedom of choice, profits, and competition.

private enterprise
An economic system characterized by private property rights, freedom of choice, profits, and competition.

- *Private property*. Ownership of the resources used to create wealth is in the hands of individuals.[17]
- *Freedom of choice*. You can sell your labour to any employer you choose. You can also choose which products to buy, and producers can usually choose whom to hire and what to produce.
- *Profits*. The lure of profits (and freedom) leads some people to abandon the security of working for someone else and to assume the risks of entrepreneurship. Anticipated profits also influence individuals' choices of which goods or services to produce.
- *Competition*. Profits motivate individuals to start businesses, and competition motivates them to operate those businesses efficiently. **Competition** occurs when two or more businesses vie for the same resources or customers. To gain an advantage over competitors, a business must produce its goods or services efficiently and be able to sell at a reasonable profit. To achieve these goals, it must convince customers that its products are either better or less expensive than those of its competitors. Competition, therefore, forces all businesses to make products better or cheaper.

competition
The vying among businesses in a particular market or industry to best satisfy consumer demands and earn profits.

Degrees of Competition

Economists have identified four basic degrees of competition within a private enterprise system: perfect competition, monopolistic competition, oligopoly, and monopoly.

Perfect Competition. For **perfect competition** to exist, firms must be small in size (but large in number), the products of each firm are almost identical, both buyers and sellers know the price that others are paying and receiving in the marketplace, firms find it easy to enter or leave the market, prices are set by the forces of supply and demand, and no firm is powerful enough individually to influence the price of its product in the marketplace. Agriculture is usually considered to be a good example of pure competition in the Canadian economy. The wheat produced on one farm is essentially the same as wheat produced on another farm. Both producers and buyers are well aware of prevailing market prices. Moreover, it is relatively easy to get started or to quit producing wheat.

perfect competition
A market or industry characterized by a very large number of small firms producing an identical product so that none of the firms has any ability to influence price.

monopolistic competition
A market or industry characterized by a large number of firms supplying products that are similar but distinctive enough from one another to give firms some ability to influence price.

Monopolistic Competition. In **monopolistic competition**, there are fewer sellers than in pure competition, but there are still many buyers. Sellers try to make their products appear to be at least slightly different from those of their competitors by tactics such as using brand names (Tide and Cheer), design or styling (Ralph Lauren and Izod clothes), and advertising (like that done by Coke and Pepsi). Monopolistically competitive businesses may be large or small, because it is relatively easy for a firm to enter or leave the market. For example, many small clothing manufacturers compete successfully with large apparel makers. Product differentiation also gives sellers some control over the price they charge. Thus Ralph Lauren Polo shirts can be priced with little regard for the price of shirts sold at The Bay, even though The Bay's shirts may have very similar styling.

oligopoly
A market or industry characterized by a small number of very large firms that have the power to influence the price of their product and/or resources.

Oligopoly. When an industry has only a handful of very large sellers, an **oligopoly** exists. The entry of new competitors is restricted because a large capital investment is usually necessary to enter the industry. Consequently, oligopolistic industries (such as the automobile, rubber, and steel industries) tend to stay oligopolistic. For example, there are only two companies in the world that make large commercial aircraft: Boeing (a U.S. company) and Airbus (a European consortium). As the trend toward globalization continues, it is likely that more global oligopolies will come into being.[18]

The actions of any one firm in an oligopolistic market can significantly affect the sales of all other firms. When one company reduces prices or offers some type of incentive to increase its sales, the others usually do the same to protect their sales. Likewise, when one company raises its prices, the others generally follow suit. As a result, the prices of comparable products are usually quite similar. Since substantial price competition would reduce every seller's profits, most oligopolistic firms use product differentiation to attract customers. The four major cereal makers (Kellogg, General Mills, General Foods, and Quaker Oats) control almost all of the cereal market, and each charges roughly the same price for its cereal. But each also advertises that its cereals are better tasting or more nutritious than the others. Competition within an oligopolistic market is often fierce.[19]

monopoly
A market or industry with only one producer, who can set the price of its product and/or resources.

Monopoly. When an industry or market has only one producer, a **monopoly** exists. Being the only supplier gives a firm complete control over the price of its product. Its only constraint is how much consumer demand will fall as its price rises. Until 1992, the long-distance telephone business was a monopoly in Canada, and cable TV, which had a local monopoly for years, lost it when telephone companies and satellite broadcasters like Bell ExpressVu and StarChoice were allowed into the cable business.[20]

natural monopoly
A market or industry in which having only one producer is most efficient because it can meet all of consumers' demand for the product.

In Canada, laws such as the Competition Act forbid many monopolies and the prices charged by so-called "natural monopolies" are closely watched by provincial utilities boards. **Natural monopolies** are those where it is generally assumed that one company can most efficiently supply all of the product or service that is needed. For example, your provincial electric company is a "natural" monopoly because it can supply all of the power (product) needed in an area. Duplicate facilities—such as two nuclear power plants, two sets of power lines, and so forth—are seen as wasteful. The assumption that certain activities qualify as natural monopolies is increasingly being challenged. For example, the Royal Mail Group's 350-year monopoly of the British postal service ended in 2006 and rival companies are now allowed to compete with Royal Mail.[21] In India, private couriers like FedEx and United Parcel Service now provide more than half the delivery business in that country after they were allowed to compete with India Post, which had a monopoly on mail delivery for several hundred years.[22]

A BRIEF HISTORY OF BUSINESS IN CANADA

In this section, we will trace the broad outlines of the development of business activity in Canada. Table 1.2 highlights some important dates in Canadian business history.[23]

The Early Years

Trace the *history of business* in Canada. 5

Business activity and profit from commercial fishing were the motivation for the first European involvement in Canada. In the late 1400s, ships financed by English entrepreneurs came to the coast of Newfoundland to fish. By the late 1500s, the Newfoundland coast was being visited by hundreds of fishing vessels each year.

Beginning in the 1500s, French and British adventurers began trading with the native peoples. Items such as cooking utensils and knives were exchanged for beaver and other furs. One trading syndicate made over 1000 percent profit on beaver skins sold to a Paris furrier. Trading was aggressive and, over time, the price of furs rose as more and more Europeans bid for them. Originally the fur trade was restricted to eastern Canada, but by the late 1600s, coureurs de bois were travelling far to the west in search of new sources of furs.

European settlers who arrived in Canada in the sixteenth and seventeenth centuries initially had to farm or starve. Gradually, however, they

Table 1.2 Some Important Dates in Canadian Business History

1490	English fishermen active off the coast of Newfoundland
1534	Account of first trading with native peoples written by Jacques Cartier
1670	Hudson's Bay Company founded
1730–40	Hat-making industry arises in Quebec and is stifled by French home officials
1779	North West Company forms
1785	Molson brewery opens
1805	First Canadian paper mill built at St. Andrew's, Quebec
1809	First steamboat (the *Accommodation*) put into service on the St. Lawrence River by John Molson
1817	Bank of Montreal chartered
1821	Hudson's Bay Company and North West Company merge
1830–50	Era of canal building
1850–60	First era of railroad building
1855	John Redpath opens first Canadian sugar refinery in Montreal
1857–58	First oil well in Canada drilled near Sarnia, Ontario
1861	Toronto Stock Exchange opens
1869	Eaton's opens for business in Toronto
1880–90	First western land boom
1885	Last spike driven to complete the Canadian Pacific Railroad
1896	First large pulp and paper mill in Canada opened at Sault Ste. Marie, Ontario
1897–99	Klondike gold rush
1917–22	Creation of Canadian National Railways
1926	U.S. replaces Great Britain as Canada's largest trading partner
1927	Armand Bombardier sells first "auto-neige" (forerunner of the snowmobile)
1929	Great stock market crash
1929–33	Great Depression
1930	Canadian Airways Limited formed
1932	Canadian Radio Broadcasting Corporation formed (it became the CBC in 1936)
1935	Bank of Canada begins operations
1937	Canadian Breweries Limited is formed
1947–51	Early computer built at the University of Toronto
1947	Leduc Number 1 oil well drilled in Alberta
1949	A.V. Roe (Avro) makes Canada's first commercial jetliner
1965	Auto Pact signed with the U.S.
1969	Canada becomes world's largest potash producer
1989	Free trade agreement with U.S. comes into effect
1993	North American Free Trade Agreement comes into effect
1995–99	Rapid increase in stock prices
2000	Prices of most stocks decline sharply
2003–04	Canadian internet pharmacies begin selling prescription drugs to U.S. citizens
2006	Softwood lumber dispute with U.S. settled

began to produce more than they needed for their own survival. The governments of the countries from which the settlers came (notably England and France) were strong supporters of the mercantilist philosophy. Under *mercantilism*, colonists were expected to export raw materials like beaver pelts and lumber at low prices to the mother country. These raw materials were then used to produce finished goods such as fur coats, which were sold at high prices to settlers in Canada. Attempts to develop industry in Canada were thwarted by England and France, who enjoyed large profits from mercantilism. As a result, Canadian manufacturing was slow to develop.

The Factory System and the Industrial Revolution

British manufacturing took a great leap forward around 1750 with the coming of the **Industrial Revolution**. This revolution was made possible by advances in technology and by the development of the **factory system**. Instead of hundreds of workers turning out items one at a time in their cottages, the factory system brought together in one place all of the materials and workers required to produce items in large quantities, along with newly created machines capable of **mass production**.

Industrial Revolution
A major change in goods production that began in England in the mid-eighteenth century and was characterized by a shift to the factory system, mass production, and specialization of labour.

factory system
A process in which all the machinery, materials, and workers required to produce a good in large quantities are brought together in one place.

mass production
The manufacture of products of uniform quality in large quantities.

specialization
The breaking down of complex operations into simple tasks that are easily learned and performed.

Mass production offered savings in several areas. It avoided unnecessary duplication of equipment. It allowed firms to purchase raw materials at better prices by buying large lots. And most important, it encouraged **specialization** of labour. No longer did production require highly skilled craftspeople who could do all the different tasks required to make an item. A series of semiskilled workers, each trained to perform only one task and supported by specialized machines and tools, greatly increased output.

In spite of British laws against the export of technology and manufacturing to North America, Canadian manufacturing existed almost from the beginning of European settlement. Modest manufacturing operations were evident in sawmills, breweries, grist mills for grinding grain, tanneries, woollen mills, shoemakers' shops, and tailors' shops. These operations were so successful that by 1800, exports of manufactured goods were more important than exports of fur.

With the advent of steam power in the early 1800s, manufacturing activity began to increase rapidly. By 1850, more than 30 factories—employing more than 2000 people—lined the Lachine Canal alone. Exports of timber to England in 1850 were 70 times greater than what they had been in 1800. The demand for reliable transportation was the impetus for canal building in the mid-1800s and then the railroad-building boom in the mid- and late 1800s.

The Entrepreneurial Era

One of the most significant features of the last half of the nineteenth century was the emergence of entrepreneurs willing to take risks in the hope of earning huge profits. Adam Smith in his book *The Wealth of Nations* argued that the government should not interfere in the economy, but should let businesses function without regulation or restriction. This *laissez-faire* attitude was often adopted by the Canadian government. As a result, during the **entrepreneurial era**, some individuals became immensely wealthy through their aggressive business dealings. Some railway, bank, and insurance executives made over $25 000 per year in the late 1800s, and their purchasing power was immense. Entrepreneurs such as Joseph Flavelle, Henry Pellatt, and John MacDonald lived in ostentatious mansions or castles.

entrepreneurial era
The period during the last half of the nineteenth century when businesses operated with very little government regulation and businesses made large profits, often at the expense of consumers.

The size and economic power of some firms meant that other businesses had difficulty competing against them. At the same time, some business executives decided that it was more profitable to collude than to compete. They decided among themselves to fix prices and divide up markets. Hurt by these actions, Canadian consumers called for more regulation of business. In 1889, the first anti-combines legislation was passed in Canada, and legislation regulating business has increased ever since.

The Production Era

The concepts of specialization and mass production that originated in the Industrial Revolution were more fully refined as Canada entered the twentieth century. The Scientific Management Movement focused management's attention on production. Increased efficiency via the "one best way" to accomplish tasks became the major management goal. Henry Ford's introduction of the moving assembly line in the United States in 1913 ushered in the **production era**. During the production era, less attention was paid to selling and marketing than to technical efficiency when producing goods. By using fixed workstations, increasing task specialization, and moving the work to the worker, the assembly line increased productivity and lowered prices, making all kinds of products affordable for the average person. The assembly line also increased the available labour pool because many people could be trained to carry out assembly line tasks. Previously, the labour pool was limited because relatively few people had the high skill levels of craftspeople.

production era
The period during the early twentieth century when businesses focused almost exclusively on improving productivity and manufacturing methods.

During the production era, large businesses began selling stock—making shareholders the owners—and relying on professional managers. The growth of corporations and improved production output resulting from assembly lines came at the expense of worker freedom. The dominance of big firms made it harder for individuals to go into business for themselves. Company towns run by the railroads, mining corporations, and forest products firms gave individuals little freedom of choice over whom to work for and what to buy. To restore some balance within the overall system, both government and labour had to develop and grow. Thus, this period saw the rise of labour unions and collective bargaining. We will look at this development in more detail in Chapter 8. The Great Depression of the 1930s and the Second World War caused the federal government to intervene in the economic system on a previously unimaginable scale. Today, business, government, and labour are frequently referred to by economists and politicians as the three *countervailing powers* in our society. All are big. All are strong. Yet, none totally dominates the others.

The Sales and Marketing Eras

By the 1930s, business's focus on production had resulted in spectacular increases in the amount of goods and services available for sale. As a result, buyers had more choices and producers faced greater competition in selling their wares. Thus began the so-called **sales era**. According to the ideas of that time, a business's profits and success depended on hiring the right salespeople, advertising heavily, and making sure products were readily available. Business firms were essentially production- and sales-oriented, and they produced what they thought customers wanted, or simply what the company was good at producing. This approach is still used by firms that find themselves with surplus goods that they want to sell (e.g., used-car dealerships).

sales era
The period during the 1930s and 1940s when businesses focused on sales forces, advertising, and keeping products readily available.

Following the Second World War, pent-up demand for consumer goods kept the economy rolling. While brief recessions did occur periodically, the 1950s and 1960s were prosperous times. Production increased, technology advanced, and the standard of living rose. During the **marketing era**, business adopted a new philosophy of how to do business—use market research

marketing era
The period during the 1950s and 1960s when businesses began to identify and meet consumer wants in order to make a profit.

to determine what customers want, and then make it for them. Firms like Procter & Gamble and Molson were very effective during the marketing era, and continue to be profitable today. Each offers an array of products within a particular field (e.g., toothpaste or beer), and gives customers a chance to pick what best suits their needs.

The Finance Era

finance era
The period during the 1980s when there were many mergers and much buying and selling of business enterprises.

In the 1980s, emphasis shifted to finance. In the **finance era** there was a sharp increase in mergers and in the buying and selling of business enterprises. Some people now call it the "decade of greed." During the finance era there was a great deal of financial manipulation of corporate assets by so-called corporate raiders. Critics charged that these raiders were simply enriching themselves and weren't creating anything of tangible value by their activity. They also charged that raiders were distracting business managers from their main goals of running the business. The raiders responded that they were making organizations more efficient by streamlining, merging, and reorganizing them.

The Global Era

During the last two decades, we have witnessed the emergence of the global economy and further dramatic technological advances in production, computer technology, information systems, and communication capabilities. Canadians drive cars made in Japan, wear sweaters made in Italy, drink beer brewed in Mexico, and listen to stereos made in Taiwan. But we're not alone in this. In this **global era**, people around the world buy products and services from foreign companies.

global era
The period during the late twentieth and early twenty-first century when a truly global economy emerged.

While some Canadian businesses have been hurt by foreign imports, numerous others have profited by exploring new foreign markets. Global and domestic competition has also forced all businesses to work harder than ever to cut costs, increase efficiency, and improve product and service quality. We will explore a variety of important trends, opportunities, and challenges of the global era throughout this book.

The rapid increase in internet usage facilitates global business activity. Internet usage in North America grew from about 100 users per 1000 people

China opened its economy to foreign investors in the 1980s and joined the World Trade Organization in 2001. Now the Chinese buy as many cars as the Germans and more photographic film than the Japanese. They also buy more cellphones than anyone anywhere, and the opening of the Chinese market has created a windfall for makers of wireless handsets, including Motorola (U.S.), Siemens (Germany), Samsung (South Korea), and Nokia (Finland).

in 1995 to nearly 750 users per 1000 people in 2005. The growth rate in Western Europe has been even faster, and internet usage in the Asia-Pacific region has also become significant. The internet affects both domestic and global business activity in at least three different ways:

- *The internet gives a dramatic boost to trade in all sectors of the economy, especially services.* The internet makes it easier for all trade to grow, and this is particularly true for trade in services on an international scale. The growth of call centres in places like India is an example of this international trade in services.
- *The internet levels the playing field, at least to some extent, between larger and smaller enterprises, regardless of what products or services they sell.* In the past, a substantial investment was typically needed to enter some industries and to enter foreign markets. Now, however, a small business based in central Alberta, southern Italy, eastern Malaysia, or northern Brazil can set up a website and compete quite effectively with much larger businesses located around the world.
- *The internet holds considerable potential as an effective and efficient networking mechanism among businesses.* Business-to-business (B2B) networks can link firms with all of their suppliers, business customers, and strategic partners in ways that make it faster and easier for them to do business together.

Most of these software developers are among the 65 000 engineers that the Indian State of Andhra Pradesh graduates every year—up from 7500 just 10 years ago. Microsoft operates an R&D centre in the capital city of Hyderabad, where Oracle, Computer Associates, and IBM also have facilities. The city is prospering as a hub not only for software programming, but for telephone call centres and pharmaceuticals as well.

Summary of Learning Objectives

1. Define the nature of Canadian *business* and identify its main goals. *Businesses* are organizations that produce or sell goods or services to make a profit. *Profits* are the difference between a business's revenues and expenses. The prospect of earning profits encourages individuals and organizations to open and expand businesses. The benefits of business activities also extend to wages paid to workers and to taxes that support government functions.
2. Describe different types of global *economic systems* according to the means by which they control the *factors of production* through *input and output markets.* An *economic system* is a nation's system for allocating its resources among its citizens. Economic systems differ in terms of who owns or controls the five basic *factors of production*: labour, capital, entrepreneurs, physical resources, and information resources. In *command economies*, the government controls all or most of these factors. In *market economies*, which are based on the principles of *capitalism*, individuals and businesses control the factors of production and exchange them through *input and output markets.* Most countries today have *mixed market economies* that are dominated by one of these systems but include elements of the other. The process of *privatization* is an important means by which many of the world's planned economies are moving toward mixed market systems.
3. Show how *demand* and *supply* affect resource distribution in Canada. The Canadian economy is strongly influenced by markets, demand, and supply. *Demand* is the willingness and ability of buyers to purchase a good or service. *Supply* is the willingness and ability of producers to offer goods or services for sale. Demand and supply work together to set a *market* or *equilibrium price*—the price at which the quantity of goods demanded and the quantity of goods supplied are equal.
4. Identify the elements of *private enterprise* and explain the various *degrees of competition* in the Canadian economic system. The Canadian economy is founded on the principles of *private enterprise: private property rights, freedom of choice, profits,* and *competition.* Degrees of competition vary because not all industries are equally competitive. Under conditions of *pure competition*, numerous small firms compete in a market governed entirely by demand and supply. An *oligopoly* involves a handful of sellers only. A *monopoly* involves only one seller.
5. Trace the *history of business* in Canada. Modern business structures reflect a pattern of development over centuries. Throughout much of the colonial period, sole proprietors supplied raw materials to English manufacturers. The rise of the factory system during the Industrial Revolution brought with it mass production and specialization of

labour. During the entrepreneurial era in the nineteenth century, large corporations—and monopolies—emerged. During the production era of the early twentieth century, companies grew by emphasizing output and production. During the sales and marketing eras of the 1950s and 1960s, business began focusing on sales staff, advertising, and the need to produce what consumers wanted. The 1980s saw the emergence of a global economy. Many Canadian companies have profited from exporting their goods to foreign markets. The most recent development is the use of the internet to boost business. It should level the playing field between large and small companies.

QUESTIONS AND EXERCISES

Questions for Analysis

1. Find an example where a surplus of a product led to decreased prices. Then find an example where a shortage led to increased prices. What eventually happened in each case? Why? Is what happened consistent with what economics predicts?
2. On various occasions, government provides financial incentives to business firms. For example, the Canadian government provided export assistance to Bombardier Inc. with its Technology Transfer Program. Is this consistent with a basically free market system? Explain how this might distort the system.
3. In recent years, many countries have moved from planned economies to market economies. Why do you think this has occurred? Can you envision a situation that would cause a resurgence of planned economies?
4. In your opinion, what industries in Canada should be regulated by the government? Defend your arguments.
5. Familiarize yourself with a product or service that is sold under conditions of pure competition. Explain why it is an example of pure competition and identify the factors that make it so. Then do the same for a product in each of the other three competitive situations described in the chapter (monopolistic competition, oligopoly, and monopoly).
6. Analyze how the factors of production (labour, capital, entrepreneurs, natural resources, and information) work together for a product or service of your choice.
7. Government plays a variety of roles in the Canadian mixed economy (customer, regulator, taxation agent, provider of services, etc.). Consider each of the roles discussed in the text and state your view as to whether government involvement in each role is excessive, insufficient, or about right. What criteria did you use to make your assessments?

Application Exercises

8. Choose a locally owned business. Interview the owner to find out how the business uses the factors of production and have the owner describe the means of acquiring them.
9. Visit a local shopping mall or shopping area. List each store that you see and determine what degree of competition it faces in its immediate environment. For example, if there is only one store that sells shoes in the mall, that store represents a monopoly. Note those businesses with direct competitors (two jewellery stores) and show how they compete with one another.
10. Go to the library or log onto the internet and research 10 different industries. Classify each according to degree of competition.

BUILDING YOUR BUSINESS SKILLS

Analyzing the Price of Doing E-Business

Goal

To encourage students to understand how the competitive environment affects a product's price.

Situation

Assume that you own a local business that provides internet access to individuals and businesses in your community. Yours is one of four such businesses in the local market. Each of the four companies charges the same price: $12 per month for unlimited dial-up service. Your business also provides users with email service; two of your competitors also offer email service. One of these same two competitors, plus the third, also provides the individual user with a free, basic personal Web page. One competitor just dropped its price to $10 per month, and the other two have announced their intentions to follow suit. Your break-even price is

▶▶▶

$7 per customer. You are concerned about getting into a price war that may destroy your business.

Method

Divide into groups of four or five people. Each group is to develop a general strategy for handling competitors' price changes. In your discussion, take the following factors into account:

- how the demand for your product is affected by price changes
- the number of competitors selling the same or a similar product
- the methods—other than price—you can use to attract new customers and/or retain current customers

Analysis

Develop specific pricing strategies based on each of the following situations:

- Within a month after dropping the price to $10, one of your competitors raises its price back to $12.
- Two of your competitors drop their prices further—to $8 per month. As a result, your business falls off by 25 percent.
- One of your competitors that has provided customers with a free Web page has indicated that it will start charging an extra $2 per month for this optional service.
- Two of your competitors have announced that they will charge individual users $8 per month, but will charge businesses a higher price (not yet announced).
- All four providers (including you) are charging $8 per month. One goes out of business, and you know that another is in poor financial health.

Follow-Up Questions

1. Discuss the role that various inducements other than price might play in affecting demand and supply in the market for internet service.
2. Is it always in a company's best interest to feature the lowest prices?
3. Eventually, what form of competition is likely to characterize the market for internet service?

EXERCISING YOUR ETHICS: TEAM EXERCISE

Making the Right Decision

The Situation

Hotel S is a large hotel in a Maritime city. The hotel is a franchise operation run by an international hotel chain. The primary source of revenue for the hotel is convention business. A major tropical storm is working its way up the east coast and is about to hit the city. When that happens, heavy flooding is likely.

The Dilemma

Because Hotel S is a licensed operation, it must maintain numerous quality standards in order to keep its license. This license is important because the international management company handles advertising, reservations, and so on. If it were to lose its license, it is almost certain that the hotel would have to reduce its staff.

For the past few years, members of the Hotel S team have been lobbying the investors who own the hotel to undertake a major renovation. They fear that without such a renovation, the hotel will lose its license when it comes up for renewal in a few months. The owners, however, have balked at investing more of their funds in the hotel itself but have indicated that hotel management can use revenues earned above a specified level for upgrades.

The approaching storm has cut off most major transportation avenues and telephone service is also down. The Hotel S staff are unable to reach the general manager, who has been travelling on business. Because the city is full of conventioneers, hotel rooms are in high demand. Unfortunately, because of the disrepair at the hotel, it only has about 50 percent occupancy. Hotel S staff have been discussing what to do and have identified three options:

1. The hotel can reduce room rates in order to help both local citizens as well as out-of-town visitors. The hotel can also provide meals at reduced rates. A few other hotels are also doing this.
2. The hotel can maintain its present pricing policies. Most of the city's hotels are adopting this course of action.
3. The hotel can raise its rates by approximately 15 percent without attracting too much attention. It can also start charging for certain things it has been providing for free, such as local telephone calls, parking, and morning coffee. The staff members see this option as one way to generate extra profits for the renovation and to protect jobs.

Team Activity

Assemble a group of four students and assign each group member to one of the following roles:

- A member of the hotel staff
- The Hotel S manager
- A customer at the hotel
- A Hotel S investor

Action Steps

1. Before discussing the situation with your group, and from the perspective of your assigned role, which of the three options do you think is the best choice? Write down the reasons for your position.
2. Before discussing the situation with your group, and from the perspective of your assigned role, what are the underlying ethical issues, if any, in this situation? Write down the issues.
3. Gather your group together and reveal, in turn, each member's comments on the best choice of the three options. Next, reveal the ethical issues listed by each member.
4. Appoint someone to record the main points of agreement and disagreement within the group. How do you explain the results? What accounts for any disagreement?
5. From an ethical standpoint, what does your group conclude is the most appropriate action that should have been taken by the hotel in this situation?
6. Develop a group response to the following question: Can your team identify other solutions that might help satisfy both extreme views?

BUSINESS CASE 1

Supply and Demand: Some Practical Lessons

The prices of many different commodities are influenced by the supply of, and demand for, these commodities. Variations in demand and supply have implications for both businesses and for consumers, as the following stories about oil, palladium, and coffee demonstrate.

Oil In 2007, retail gasoline prices in Canada and the United States were very high, exceeding $3.50 per gallon in the U.S. and $1.20 per litre in Canada. Gasoline prices have fluctuated many times in the past. For example, an Arab oil embargo in 1971 led to a major price jump. But the higher prices spurred new exploration, and as new oil fields came online and supplies increased, prices eventually dropped. Subsequent supply disruptions due to political problems in Venezuela, Nigeria, and Iraq have also caused short-term price jumps, after which the price again dropped. But some people who are knowledgeable about oil say that from now on the price of oil is likely to go in only one direction—up. Why? Because the supply of easily recoverable oil is limited, and demand continues to increase because of the surging global economy, particularly in China and India. What's worse, they argue that the global supply of oil will soon peak and then slowly begin to decline.

Sceptics don't buy the doomsday prediction that there is going to be a decline in the supply of oil. They point out that as oil prices rise, the demand for oil will decline because people will be motivated to find alternative sources of fuel. They also argue that the supply of oil will *increase* because more exploration will take place and new oil extraction methods will be found. For example, Chevron used a new, high-tech drilling procedure to find a major oil deposit at 8800 metres below sea level in the Gulf of Mexico. The sceptics point to certain facts as strong support for their argument. They note, for example, that in 1979, experts predicted that global oil reserves would support 1979 consumption rates only until 2007. But even though consumption rates have increased sharply since 1979, experts are now predicting that oil reserves will last until about 2050. Two other interesting statistics are also evident: in 2006, global oil production was at an all-time high (85.2 million barrels per day), and recoverable oil reserves have continued to increase, not decrease.

So, what *is* the future of oil? It seems likely that oil will remain an important commodity for at least another century—but at prices that will likely be as high as or higher than they are today. Firms that can produce alternative sources of energy will also spring up, and those who find viable alternatives to oil will prosper.

Palladium Most people have never heard of palladium, a greyish metal produced primarily in Russia and South Africa. In the 1990s, when automakers adopted tighter pollution emission standards, they switched from platinum to palladium because palladium does a better job of cleaning auto emissions, and because palladium (at $200 per ounce) was much cheaper than platinum (which at that time cost about $1000 per ounce). The automobile manufacturers knew that switching to palladium would cause demand to rise and the price of palladium to increase, but they were not prepared for the price rise that actually occurred when Russian exports of palladium suddenly ceased in 1997. The official explanation was a bureaucratic problem, and when supplies resumed, the price dropped again to about $200 per ounce.

In 1998, the same thing happened, but this time the price of palladium went up to over $400 per ounce. When supplies resumed, the price dropped back to only $300 per ounce. Now the auto manufacturers were becoming very concerned, and they began trying to figure out how to use less palladium and still meet the tighter pollution standards. By 2000, when the price of palladium had risen to over $1000 per ounce, automakers took the unprecedented step of stipulating the maximum amount of palladium that would be allowed in engineers' car designs.

In 2002, Ford Motor Company took a $1 billion write-off on the value of the palladium it had stockpiled for use in its automobile catalytic converters (the price of palladium dropped to $305 in 2001). Ford originally stockpiled this raw material because it thought it would need increasing amounts of palladium, and because it was concerned that palladium was going to be high-priced and hard to get. At the same time, however, Ford's engineers were having success in figuring out ways to reduce the amount of palladium they needed. So, Ford's purchasing agents were buying lots of palladium at high prices (fearing the price would go even higher) while Ford's engineers were figuring out ways to reduce the company's need for the metal.

The price of palladium dropped so sharply because demand dropped (other automakers had also discovered ways to get by with less palladium) and supplies increased (because the extremely high prices of palladium in 1999–2000 had caused more producers to get into the business of supplying the market). By mid-2007, palladium was selling for about $350 per ounce, but some experts were predicting that the price would rise to $500 by the end of 2007. Because it looks a lot like platinum, consumers are now starting to show an interest in palladium engagement rings, which are much cheaper than platinum rings. That will further increase demand and the likelihood of price increases.

Coffee Coffee is another commodity that saw a soaring price in 2005. Between October 2004 and February 2005, for example, the price of high quality Arabica coffee beans (the type used by specialty coffee stores like Starbucks) increased by 79 percent. High demand from consumers, coupled with falling supplies caused the price increase. The increased cost of this popular commodity is quickly passed on to consumers.

Like oil, coffee is a commodity that has experienced many ups and downs over the years. The current high-price situation is a dramatic change from 2001, when coffee prices hit a 30-year low because of an oversupply of coffee beans. The low prices in 2001 were, in turn, caused by the high coffee prices in 1994 and 1995, which motivated farmers to plant a lot of acres of coffee beans in an attempt to cash in on the high prices. Because it takes 3–4 years for a coffee tree to mature, a lot of coffee beans started hitting the market in 1998 and 1999, and that increased the supply and drove prices down. But by 2001 the low prices had discouraged growers from planting more coffee trees, and that caused production to fall, leading to the current drop in supply. This up-and-down cycle is hard to break.

Questions for Discussion

1. What are the basic factors of production in the petroleum industry?
2. Describe the concepts of input and output markets as they apply to the petroleum industry.
3. Explain how the concepts of demand and supply combine to determine market prices for diverse commodities like palladium, oil, and coffee.
4. Does the global energy situation increase or decrease your confidence in a capitalistic system based on private enterprise? Explain your answer.
5. Did automakers respond to increases in the price of palladium in the way predicted by economic theory? Explain.
6. Not everyone agrees that there is an impending oil crisis. Develop arguments that we are not likely to run out of oil any time soon.

MYBUSINESSLAB

To improve your grade, visit the MyBusinessLab website at **www.pearsoned.ca/mybusinesslab**. This online homework and tutorial system allows you to test your understanding and generates a personalized study plan just for you. It provides you with study and practice tools directly related to this chapter's content. MyBusinessLab puts you in control of your own learning!

CHAPTER 2

The Environment of Business

After reading this chapter, you should be able to:

1. Explain the concepts of *organizational boundaries* and *multiple organizational environments*.
2. Explain the importance of the *economic environment* to business and identify the factors used to evaluate the performance of an economic system.
3. Describe the *technological environment* and its role in business.
4. Describe the *political–legal environment* and its role in business.
5. Describe the *socio-cultural environment* and its role in business.
6. Identify emerging challenges and opportunities in the *business environment*.
7. Understand recent trends in the *redrawing of corporate boundaries*.

Productivity and the Standard of Living

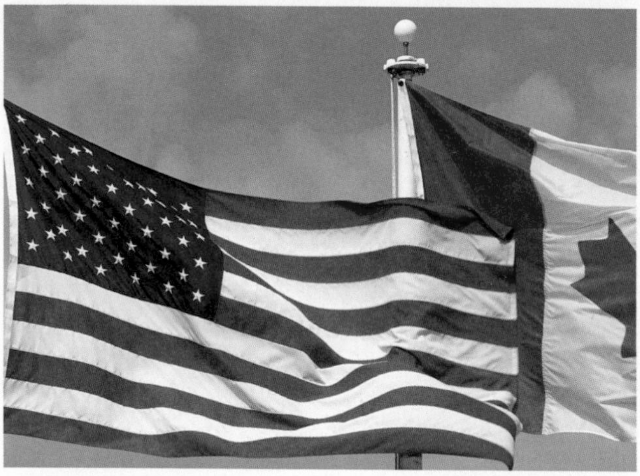

Compared with the United States, Canada's standard of living has been slipping for the last two decades. In 1980, Canada's standard of living was 90 percent of the U.S. level. By 2002, it had slipped to 87 percent, and by 2004 to 84 percent. It is projected to drop to 77 percent by 2010. In 1995, per capita income in Canada lagged behind that in the United States by $8100; by 2005, the gap had widened to $9200. If our standard of living continues to drop, Canadians will experience a decline in the quality of health care, social programs, and overall quality of life. We also risk losing our finest brains, talent, and companies if we fail to hold our own against the United States.

What is causing the standard of living to drop in Canada relative to the United States (and to other countries)? One major factor is Canada's relatively slow *productivity growth rate*. In 2006, the Conference Board of Canada reported that Canada's annual productivity grew just 1 percent per year during the period 2000–05. By contrast, the productivities of the Czech Republic, Hungary, South Korea, and Iceland grew at more than 4 percent each year. Italy, Mexico, and Spain grew at less than 1 percent. The Conference Board of Canada's annual "Performance and Potential Report" rates the world's 24 richest economies on various factors, including productivity. In the 2005 Report, Canada ranked 12th in productivity (down from 3rd place in 2003 and 6th place in 2004). The Conference Board attributed this downward trend to poor productivity growth.

As the number of working-age people decreases over the next several decades, our standard of living will decline further unless the remaining people in the workforce can produce more per person—in other words, productivity must increase. If we are going to compete with the surging economies of India and China in the global market, we must become more productive. If we don't, we will lose export possibilities and the jobs that go with them. That will also contribute to a decline in the Canadian standard of living.

Why is Canadian productivity growing so slowly? Various organizations, including the Ottawa-based Centre for the Study of Living Standards, have identified several different causes:

- Productivity in the information and communications technology sector has dropped off sharply since 2000; prior to that time it was increasing rapidly.
- The prices of commodities like oil and gas have increased dramatically in the last few years, and this has motivated companies to exploit marginal reserves where productivity is low.
- R&D intensity (the ratio of R&D spending to gross GDP) has dropped.
- Exports, as a percent of GDP, dropped from 45.6 percent in 2000 to 38.2 percent in 2004.
- The scale of manufacturing firms in Canada is smaller than in the United States, and small plants are less productive than large ones.
- Worker stress is reducing productivity (in a 2006 AP-Ipsos poll, 75 percent of Canadian workers said they experienced stress on a daily basis, and in a 2005 Ipsos-Reid poll, 66 percent of Canadian CEOs said that employee stress was the biggest drain on productivity).
- The decline of the Canadian dollar between 1995 and 2001 meant that manufacturers had little incentive to increase productivity (because they could sell their goods easily in the United States).
- Canadian business firms conduct less research and development (R&D) than companies in many other countries. For example, Canadian R&D as a percentage of GNP was less than half that of Sweden. In a survey of 24 countries, Canada ranked 11th in R&D spending.

What is the solution to the productivity problem? Clearly, we must boost our productivity growth rate if we are to raise our standard of living. The following actions have been suggested:

- Put more money into post-secondary education
- Develop more partnerships between business and academic institutions
- Invest in upgrading workforce skills, and increase the availability of vocational, technical, and apprenticeship programs for students who don't attend university
- Create greater incentives to rejoin the workforce for those on welfare
- Levy training costs on businesses like some European countries do
- Stop subsidizing uncompetitive industries like shipbuilding
- Cut personal and corporate income tax rates
- Allow more aggressive write-off schedules for capital investments by businesses

What do Canadians think about the issue of productivity and the standard of living? Surveys that have been conducted during the last few years reveal the following answers to several important questions:

- *"How do you think the average personal income for a Canadian worker compares with that for a U.S. worker?"* (half of the respondents said it was lower, one-fifth said it was higher, and one-fifth said it was the same).
- *"How do you think Canada compares with the United States in terms of quality of life?"* (70 percent said it was higher and 18 percent said it was the same).
- *"How do you think Canada compares with the United States in terms of standard of living?"* (37 percent said it is higher in Canada, 34 percent thought it was the same, and 28 percent said it was lower).
- *"How do you think Canada's level of productivity compares with that of the United States?"* (50 percent felt it was worse, 25 percent felt it was the same, and 20 percent felt it was better).

When asked if they agreed or disagreed with the statement "Increasing productivity is essential to improving our standard of living," 82 percent agreed. When asked if they agreed or disagreed with the statement "If we don't improve our productivity, our quality of life will suffer," 70 percent agreed. ◆

HOW WILL THIS BENEFIT YOU?

By understanding the material in this chapter, you'll be better able to assess (1) the impact that events outside a business can have on its owners and managers, (2) how environmental change impacts you as a consumer, and (3) the challenges and opportunities that environmental change provides you as an employee or an investor.

In this chapter, we first introduce the ideas of organizational boundaries and organizational environments. We then describe five key external environments that all businesses must deal with—economic, technological, political–legal, socio-cultural, and business. We conclude with a discussion of how changes in the external environment have motivated businesses to redraw their corporate boundaries through activities like mergers, employee stock ownership plans, and strategic alliances.

ORGANIZATIONAL BOUNDARIES AND ENVIRONMENTS

1 Explain the concepts of *organizational boundaries* and *multiple organizational environments.*

external environment
Everything outside an organization's boundaries that might affect it.

All businesses, regardless of their size, location, or mission, operate within a larger external environment that plays a major role in determining their success or failure. The **external environment** consists of everything outside an organization that might affect it. Managers must understand the key features of the external environment, and then strive to operate and compete within it. No single firm can control the environment, but managers should not simply react to changes in the external environment; rather, they should be proactive and at least try to influence their environment.

We begin our analysis of the environment by briefly discussing the idea of *organizational boundaries,* and then introduce the concept of *multiple organizational environments.*

Organizational Boundaries

organizational boundary
That which separates the organization from its environment.

An **organizational boundary** separates the organization from its environment. Consider the simple case of a small neighbourhood grocery that includes a retail customer area, a storage room, and the owner/manager's office. In many ways, the store's boundary coincides with its physical structure: When you walk through the door, you're crossing the boundary into the business, and when you go back onto the sidewalk, you cross the boundary back into the environment. But this is an oversimplification. During the business day, distributors of soft drinks, snack foods, ice, and bread products may enter the store, inventory the products that they distribute, and refill coolers and shelves just as if they were employees. These distributors are normally considered part of the environment rather than the organization, but during the time they're inside the store, they are essentially part of the business. Customers may even assume that these distributors are store employees and ask them questions as they restock shelves.

For larger firms, the situation is even more complex. McDonald's, for example, has a contract with Coca-Cola, stipulating that it will sell only Coke soft-drink products. McDonald's also has partnerships with Wal-Mart and Disney that allow it to open stores inside those firms' facilities. So when you buy a Coca-Cola soft drink from a McDonald's restaurant located inside a Wal-Mart store or Disney theme park, you are essentially affecting, and being affected by, multiple businesses.

Multiple Organizational Environments

Organizations have multiple environments. Some, like prevailing economic conditions, affect the performance of almost every business. But other dimensions of the environment are much more specific. The neighbourhood grocery, for example, will be influenced not only by an increase in unemployment in its area, but also by the pricing and other marketing activities of its nearest competitors.

Figure 2.1 shows the major elements of the external environment: economic conditions, technology, political–legal considerations, social issues, the global environment, issues of ethical and social responsibility, the business environment itself, and emerging challenges and opportunities. We will cover ethical and global issues in detail in Chapters 3 and 5, respectively, so we discuss them here only as they relate directly to the other areas in this chapter.

THE ECONOMIC ENVIRONMENT

Explain the importance of the *economic environment* to business and identify the factors used to evaluate the performance of an economic system. **2**

economic environment
Conditions of the economic system in which an organization operates.

The **economic environment** refers to the conditions of the economic system in which an organization operates.[1] For example, McDonald's Canadian operations are (as of this writing) functioning in an economic environment characterized by moderate growth, moderate unemployment, and low inflation. Moderate unemployment means that most people can afford to eat out, and low inflation means that McDonald's pays relatively constant prices for its supplies. But it also means that McDonald's can't easily increase the prices it charges because of competitive pressures from Burger King and Wendy's.

Economic Growth

At one time, about half the population of Canada was involved in producing the food that we eat. Today, less than 2.5 percent of the population works in agriculture because agricultural efficiency has improved so much that far fewer people are needed to produce the food we need. We can therefore say that agricultural production has *grown* because the total output of the agricultural sector has increased. We can apply the same idea to a nation's economic system, but the computations are much more complex, as we shall see.

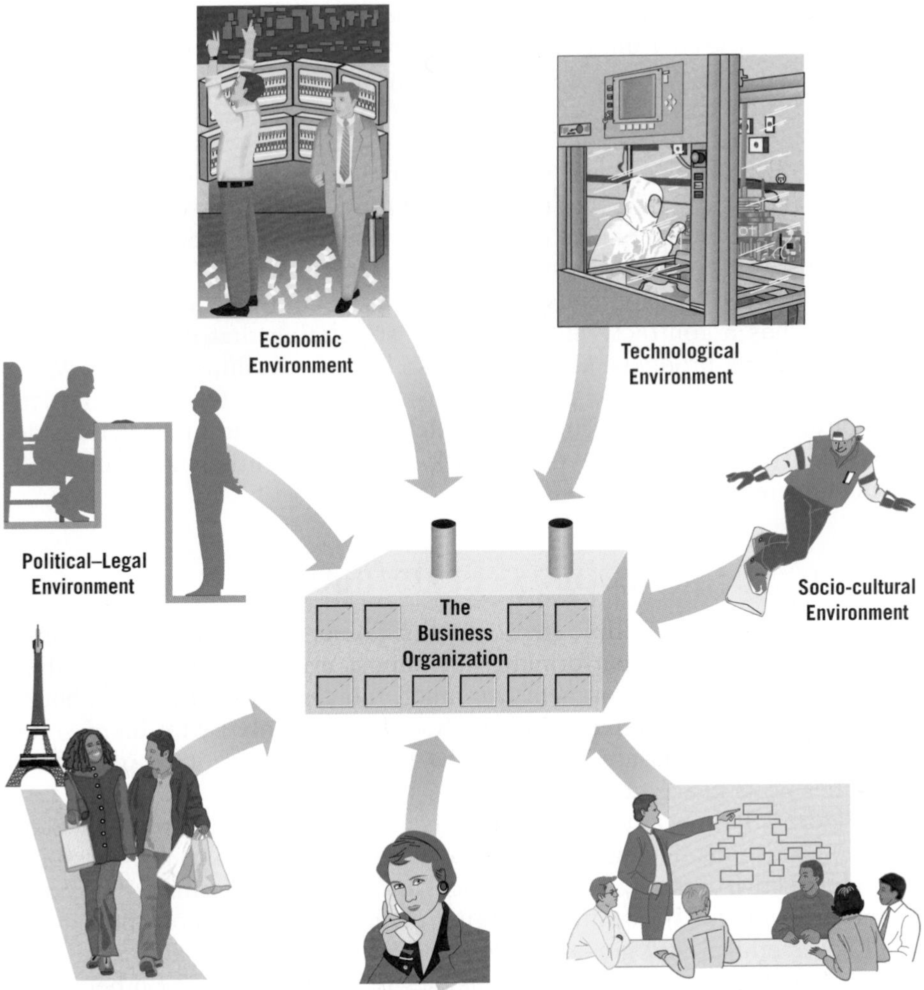

Figure 2.1 Dimensions of the external environment.

Aggregate Output and the Standard of Living

aggregate output
Total quantity of goods and services produced by an economic system during a given period.

standard of living
Total quantity and quality of goods and services that a country's citizens can purchase with the currency used in their economic system.

How do we know whether or not an economic system is growing? The main measure of *growth* is **aggregate output**: the total quantity of goods and services produced by an economic system during a given period.[2] To put it simply, an increase in aggregate output is economic growth.[3] When output grows more quickly than the population, two things usually follow: Output per capita—the quantity of goods and services per person—goes up and the system provides relatively more of the goods and services that people want.[4] And when these two things occur, people living in an economic system benefit from a higher **standard of living**—the total quantity and quality of goods and services that they can purchase with the currency used in their economic system.

The Business Cycle

business cycle
Pattern of short-term ups and downs (expansions and contractions) in an economy.

The growth (and contraction) pattern of short-term ups and downs in an economy is called the **business cycle**. It has four recognizable phases: peak, recession, trough, and recovery (see Figure 2.2). Periods of expansion and contraction can vary from several months to several years. During the latter half of the 1990s, the Canadian economy was continuously expanding, lead-

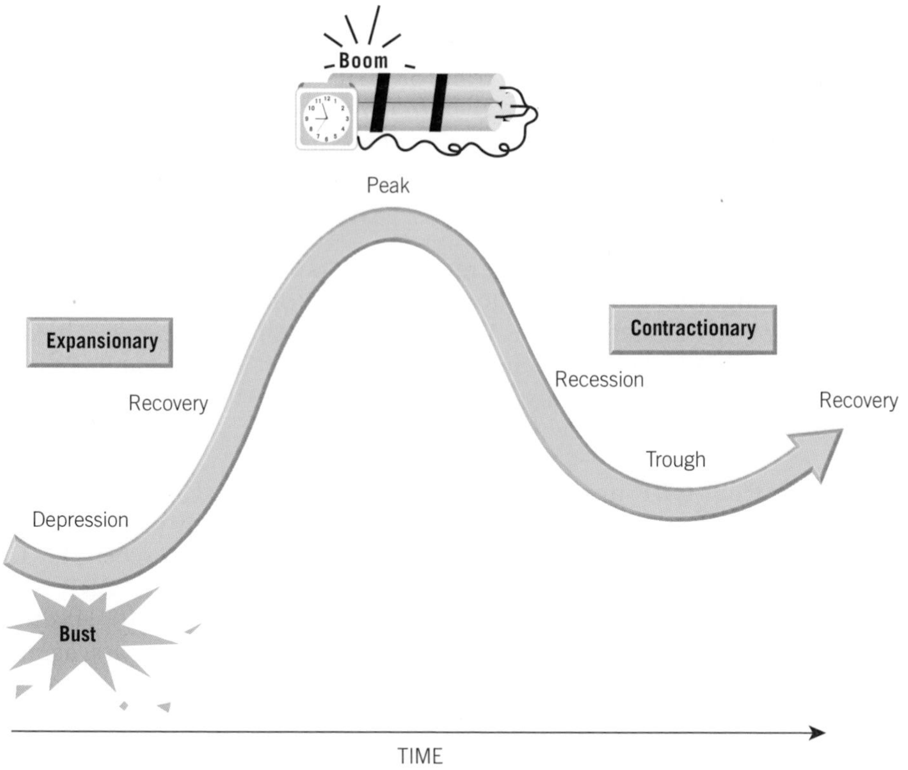

Figure 2.2 The business cycle.

ing some people to believe that the business cycle was a thing of the past. This belief was particularly evident among people who invested in high-tech stocks. They learned a hard lesson when tech stocks crashed in 2000.

Gross Domestic Product and Gross National Product

The term **gross domestic product (GDP)** refers to the total value of all goods and services produced within a given period by a national economy through domestic factors of production. If GDP is going up, the nation is experiencing *economic growth*. Canada's GDP in 2005 was $1.3 trillion.[5]

gross domestic product (GDP) Total value of all goods and services produced within a given period by a national economy through domestic factors of production.

gross national product (GNP) Total value of all goods and services produced by a national economy within a given period regardless of where the factors of production are located.

Economists also use the term **gross national product (GNP)**, which refers to the total value of all goods and services produced by a national economy within a given period regardless of where the factors of production are located. Thus, the profits earned by a Canadian company abroad are included in GNP, but not in GDP. Conversely, profits earned by foreign firms in Canada are included in GDP. Consider the example of a Canadian-owned manufacturing plant in Brazil. The profits earned by the factory are included in Canadian GNP—but not in GDP—because its output is not produced domestically (that is, in Canada). Conversely, those profits are included in Brazil's GDP—but not GNP—because they are produced domestically (that is, in Brazil).

GDP and GNP are useful measures of economic growth because they allow us to track an economy's performance over time. But an organization called Redefining Progress has proposed a more realistic measure to assess economic activity—the Genuine Progress Indicator (GPI). GPI treats activities that harm the environment or our quality of life as costs and gives them negative values. For example, the Exxon Valdez oil spill in 1986 increased GDP because the activities required to clean up the mess were included in measurements of economic growth. But the oil spill was not a good thing. The new GPI measure shows that while GDP has been increasing for many years, GPI has been falling since the 1970s.[6]

Real Growth Rates. GDP and GNP usually differ slightly, but GDP is the preferred method of calculating national income and output. The *real growth rate of GDP*—the growth rate of GDP *adjusted for inflation and changes in the value of the country's currency*—is what counts. Remember that *growth depends on output increasing at a faster rate than population*. If the growth rate of GDP exceeds the rate of population growth, then our standard of living should be improving.

GDP per capita
Gross domestic product per person.

GDP per Capita. **GDP per capita** means GDP per person. We get this figure by dividing total GDP by the total population of a country. As a measure of economic well-being of the average person, GDP per capita is a better measure than GDP. The United States has the highest GDP per capita of any country ($33 123), followed by Ireland ($30 910), Switzerland ($28 684), and Canada ($28 344).[7]

real GDP
GDP calculated to account for changes in currency values and price changes.

nominal GDP
GDP measured in current dollars or with all components valued at current prices.

Real GDP. **Real GDP** means that GDP has been adjusted. To understand why adjustments are necessary, assume that pizza is the only product in an economy. Assume that in 2005, a pizza cost $10, and in 2006 it cost $11. In both years, exactly 1000 pizzas were produced. In 2005, the GDP was $10 000 ($10 × 1000); in 2006, the GDP was $11 000 ($11 × 1000). Has the economy grown? No. Since 1000 pizzas were produced in both years, aggregate output remained the same. If GDP is not adjusted for 2006, it is called **nominal GDP**, that is, GDP measured in current dollars.[8]

Purchasing Power Parity. In our example, *current prices* would be 2006 prices. On the other hand, we calculate real GDP when we account for *changes in currency values and price changes*. When we make this adjust-

ENTREPENEURSHIP AND NEW VENTURES

Want a Macbrioche with that Macespresso?

McDonald's has become an international icon of the fast-food industry. With 30 000 restaurants in over 100 countries, the golden arches have become synonymous with American culture. Yet in recent years, McDonald's seems to have lost its competitive edge both at home and abroad. In the United States, for example, its stores are outdated and its customer service skills seem to be slipping. Moreover, concerns about health (as dramatized in the recent documentary *Supersize Me*) have driven many customers away from Big Macs and French fries. McDonald's no longer leads in technology, with rivals inventing new processing and cooking technologies. The firm's traditional markets—children and young men—are spending less on food while markets McDonald's doesn't target, notably women and older consumers, spend more. Profits have dropped and Starbucks has replaced McDonald's as the food industry's success story.

To grow, McDonald's has had to expand aggressively into foreign markets, especially in Europe and Asia. However, consumers in many of those countries do not always like McDonald's "Americanized" look and products. So the burger maker has had to cater to local tastes. That means serving brioche and espresso in France, salmon sandwiches in Scandinavia, and beer in Germany. McDonald's is also customizing the look of its stores. In France, for example, some stores have ski-chalet décor—hardwood floors, televisions, and armchairs—while others feature 1950s-style booths with their own CD players.

So far, the new menu items and appearance are paying off. U.S. sales continue their downward trend, but French sales increased after the makeover. Ken Clement, a franchisee and former McDonald's vice president, claims the changes are not necessary in the United States. "People are not coming in to swoon over the décor," he says. "They are coming in and getting out of here. They don't give a rip what is inside." However, if the French market continues to improve, the innovations may make it to the United States, where the risk and the return could be great. The change could alienate McDonald's traditional customers or it could revitalize the firm and spark a renaissance for the entire fast-food industry.

ment, we account for both GDP and **purchasing power parity**—the principle that exchange rates are set so that the prices of similar products in different countries are about the same. Purchasing power parity gives us a much better idea of what people can actually buy with the financial resources allocated to them by their respective economic systems. In other words, it gives us a better sense of standards of living across the globe.

purchasing power parity
Principle that exchange rates are set so that the prices of similar products in different countries are about the same.

Productivity

A major factor in the growth of an economic system is **productivity**, which is a measure of economic growth that compares how much a system produces with the resources needed to produce it. Let's say, for instance, that it takes 1 Canadian worker and 1 Canadian dollar to make 10 soccer balls in an 8-hour workday. Let's also say that it takes 1.2 Saudi workers and the equivalent of $1.2 (in riyals, the currency of Saudi Arabia) to make 10 soccer balls in the same 8-hour workday. We can say, then, that the Canadian soccer-ball industry is more *productive* than the Saudi soccer-ball industry. The two factors of production in this extremely simple case are labour and capital.

productivity
Measure of economic growth that compares how much a system produces with the resources needed to produce it.

If more products are being produced with fewer factors of production, what happens to the prices of these products? They go down. As a consumer, therefore, you would need less of your currency to purchase the same quantity of these products. Thus, your standard of living—at least with regard to these products—has improved. If your entire economic system increases its productivity, then your overall standard of living improves. In fact, standard of living improves only through increases in productivity.[9]

The Balance of Trade and the National Debt

There are several factors that can help or hinder the growth of an economic system, but here we focus on just two of them: *balance of trade* and the *national debt*.

Balance of Trade. The **balance of trade** is the economic value of all the products that a country *exports* minus the economic value of its *imported* products. A negative balance of trade is commonly called a *trade deficit*, and a positive balance of trade is called a *trade surplus*. Canada usually has

balance of trade
The total of a country's exports (sales to other countries) minus its imports (purchases from other countries).

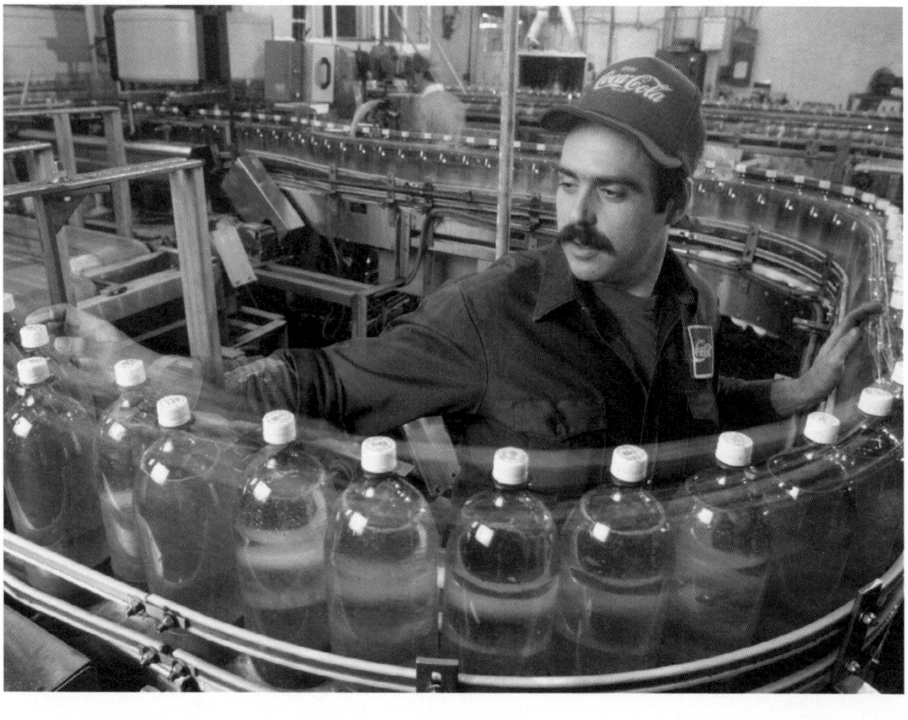

Extremely high productivity levels can be attained using automated equipment such as that in this soft drink bottling operation. Productivity is high because relatively few workers are able to produce large quantities of the product.

a positive balance of trade. It is therefore a *creditor nation* rather than a debtor nation. In 2005, for example, Canada received $66.6 billion more for exports than it spent on imports.[10] By contrast, the United States usually has a negative balance of trade. In 2005, it spent $725 billion more on imports than it received for exports.[11] It is therefore a *debtor nation* rather than a creditor nation. A trade deficit negatively affects economic growth because the money that flows out of a country can't be used to invest in productive enterprises, either at home or overseas.

national debt
The total amount of money that a country owes its creditors.

budget deficits
The result of the government spending more in one year than it takes in during that year.

National Debt. A country's **national debt** is the amount of money that the government owes its creditors. Like a business, the government takes in revenues (primarily in the form of taxes) and has expenses (military spending, social programs, and so forth). For many years, the government of Canada incurred annual **budget deficits**, that is, it spent more money *each year* than it took in. These accumulated annual deficits have created a huge national debt—the amount of money that Canada owes its creditors.

Until the mid-1990s, annual budget deficits and the total national debt were increasing at an alarming rate. From Confederation (1867) to 1981, the total accumulated debt was only $85.7 billion, but in the period 1981–94, *annual deficits* were in the $20 to $40 billion range. Since 1994, however, things have changed dramatically. Annual deficits declined rapidly between 1994 and 1996, and in 1997 the first budget surplus in many years occurred. Canada is the only highly industrialized country in the world that continues to have a budget surplus. In 2005, government revenues were $234.9 billion and expenditures were $219.8 billion, giving a surplus of $15.1 billion.[12]

How does the national debt affect economic growth? When the government of Canada sells bonds to individuals and organizations (both at home and overseas), this affects economic growth because the Canadian government competes with every other potential borrower—individuals, households, businesses, and other organizations—for the available supply of loanable money. The more money the government borrows, the less money is available for the private borrowing and investment that increases productivity.

Economic Stability

stability
Condition in an economic system in which the amount of money available and the quantity of goods and services produced are growing at about the same rate.

A key goal of an economic system is **stability**: a condition in which the amount of money available in an economic system and the quantity of goods and services produced in it are growing at about the same rate. Several factors threaten stability—namely, *inflation, deflation,* and *unemployment*.

Inflation

inflation
Occurrence of widespread price increases throughout an economic system.

Inflation is evident when the amount of money injected into an economic system outstrips the increase in actual output. When inflation occurs, people have more money to spend, but there will still be the same quantity of products available for them to buy. As they compete with one another to buy available products, prices go up. Before long, high prices will erase the increase in the amount of money injected into the economy. Purchasing power, therefore, declines. Figure 2.3 shows how inflation has varied over the last 20 years in Canada.

consumer price index (CPI)
Measure of the prices of typical products purchased by consumers living in urban areas.

Measuring Inflation: the CPI. The **consumer price index (CPI)** measures changes in the cost of a "basket" of goods and services that a typical family buys. What is included in the basket has changed over the years. For example, the first CPI in 1913 included items like coal, spirit vinegar, and fruit, while in 2005 the index included DVD home theatre systems, MP3 portable

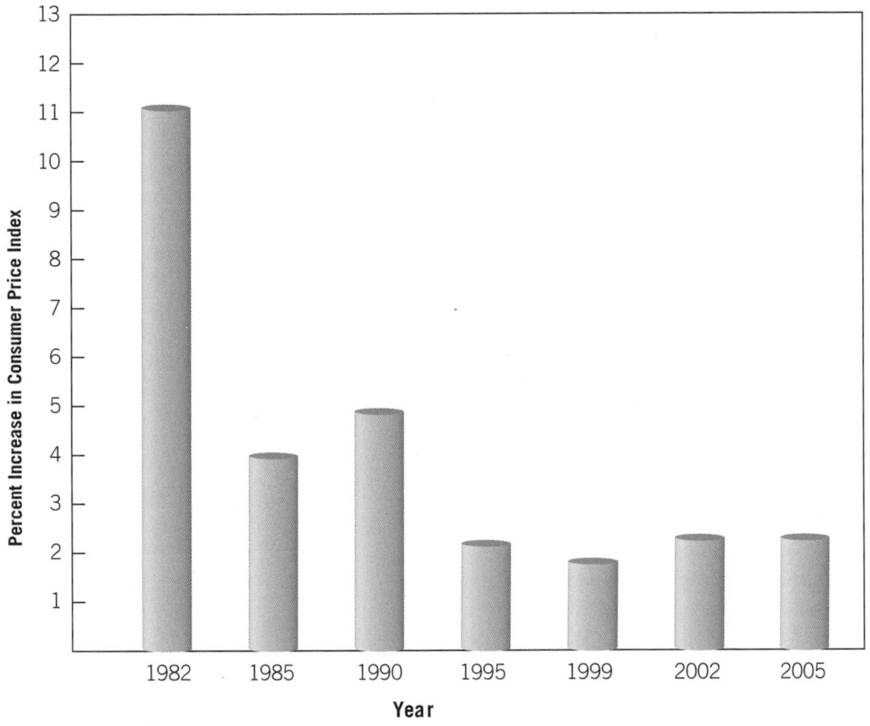

Figure 2.3 During the past decade, the rate of price increases in Canada has been low and quite stable.

players, and plasma televisions.[13] These changes in the CPI reflect changes that have occurred in the pattern of consumer purchases. For example, in 1961, about 53 percent of consumer spending went to necessities like food, housing, and clothing. By 2000, only 40 percent of consumer spending went to necessities.[14]

Deflation

Deflation (falling prices) is evident when the amount of money injected into an economic system lags behind increases in actual output. Prices may fall because industrial productivity is increasing and cost savings are being passed on to consumers (this is good), or because consumers have high levels of debt and are therefore unwilling to buy very much (this is bad).

deflation
A period of generally falling prices.

Unemployment

Unemployment is the level of joblessness among people actively seeking work. There are various types of unemployment: *frictional unemployment* (people are out of work temporarily while looking for a new job); *seasonal unemployment* (people are out of work because of the seasonal nature of their jobs); *cyclical unemployment* (people are out of work because of a downturn in the business cycle); and *structural unemployment* (people are unemployed because they lack the skills needed to perform available jobs). Unemployment rates have varied greatly over the years, as Figure 2.4 shows, with the rates for men generally being higher than the rates for women.

unemployment
The level of joblessness among people actively seeking work in an economic system.

When unemployment is low, there is a shortage of labour available for businesses. As businesses compete with one another for the available supply of labour, they raise the wages they are willing to pay. Then, because higher labour costs eat into profit margins, businesses raise the prices of their products. If prices get too high, consumers will respond by buying

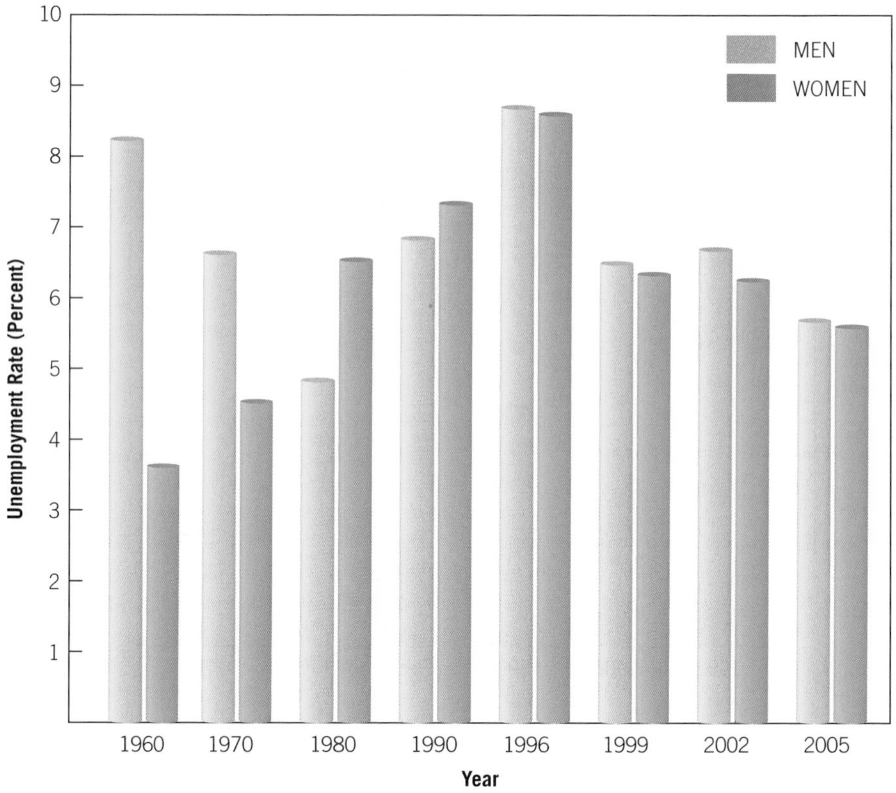

Figure 2.4 Historical unemployment rate. During the period 1970–96, there was a steady upward trend in unemployment rates, but the rate began to decline in the late 1990s.

less. Businesses will then reduce their workforces because they don't need to produce as much. But this causes unemployment to go up and the cycle starts all over again.

Managing the Canadian Economy

fiscal policies
Policies whereby governments collect and spend revenues.

monetary policies
Policies whereby the government controls the size of the nation's money supply.

The federal government manages the Canadian economic system through two sets of policies: fiscal and monetary. **Fiscal policies** involve the collection and spending of government revenues. For example, when the growth rate of the economy is decreasing, tax cuts will normally stimulate renewed economic growth. **Monetary policies** focus on controlling the size of the nation's money supply. Working primarily through the Bank of Canada (see Chapter 15), the government can influence the ability and willingness of banks throughout the country to lend money. The power of the Bank of Canada to make changes in the supply of money is the centrepiece of the Canadian government's monetary policy. The principle is fairly simple:

- Higher interest rates make money more expensive to borrow and thereby reduce spending by both companies that produce goods and services and consumers who buy those goods and services. When the Bank of Canada restricts the money supply, we say that it is practising a *tight monetary policy*.
- Lower interest rates make money less expensive to borrow and thereby increase spending by both companies that produce goods and services and consumers who buy those goods and services. When the Bank of Canada loosens the money supply, we say that it is practising an *easy monetary policy*.

THE TECHNOLOGICAL ENVIRONMENT

As applied to the environment of business, **technology** generally includes all the ways by which firms create value for their constituents. Technology includes human knowledge, work methods, physical equipment, electronics and telecommunications, and various processing systems that are used to perform business activities. Although technology is applied within organizations, the forms and availability of that technology come from the general environment. Boeing, for example, uses computer-assisted manufacturing and design techniques developed by external vendors to simulate the four miles of hydraulic tubing that run through it new 777 aircraft.

3 Describe the *technological environment* and its role in business.

technology All the ways firms create value for their constituents.

Research and Development (R&D)

Technological improvements and innovation in general are important contributors to the economic development of a country. The innovation process includes **research and development (R&D)**, which provides new ideas for products, services, and processes (see Chapter 13 for a discussion of the importance of R&D in the marketing of products). There are two types of R&D. **Basic (or pure) R&D** involves improving knowledge in an area without a primary focus on whether any discoveries that might occur are immediately marketable. For example, chemists in a laboratory might examine how certain chemical compounds behave. The knowledge gained from this activity might or might not result in a marketable product. **Applied R&D**, on the other hand, means focusing specifically on how a technological innovation can be put to use in the making of a product or service that can be sold in the marketplace.

research and development (R&D) Those activities that are necessary to provide new products, services, and processes.

basic (or pure) R&D Improving knowledge in an area without a primary focus on whether any discoveries that might occur are immediately marketable.

applied R&D Focusing specifically on how a technological innovation can be put to use in the making of a product or service that can be sold in the marketplace.

R&D intensity refers to R&D spending as a percentage of the company's sales revenue. Research has shown that companies with a high R&D intensity are better able to gain market share in global markets.[15] If a company has a strategy to be the technological leader in its industry, it will likely have a high R&D intensity. Alternatively, if its strategy is to be a technology follower, it will likely have a much lower R&D intensity.

R&D intensity R&D spending as a percentage of a company's sales revenue.

R&D spending in Canada in 2005 totalled about $13.8 billion.[16] The Canadian private sector accounts for about 54 percent of R&D, the government 9 percent, and universities 35 percent.[17] In the private sector, less than one percent of companies accounted for 56 percent of all R&D performed.[18] A large proportion of GDP is carried out in just a few industries—communications equipment, aerospace products, semiconductor and other electronic components, pharmaceuticals, computer system design, and wholesale trade.[19] Quebec and Ontario accounted for 84 percent of all R&D activities in Canada.[20]

As a proportion of GDP, Canada's level of R&D lags behind that of other countries (see Figure 2.5). When we take into account that the GDP of countries like Japan, the United States, and Germany is much larger in absolute dollars than the GDP of Canada, it means that R&D spending in Canada is a tiny fraction of what is spent in other countries.

Product and Service Technologies

Product and service technologies are employed for creating products—both physical goods and services—for customers. Although many people associate technology with manufacturing, it is also a significant factor in the service sector. Just as an automobile is built as it follows a predetermined pathway along an assembly line, a hamburger at McDonald's is cooked,

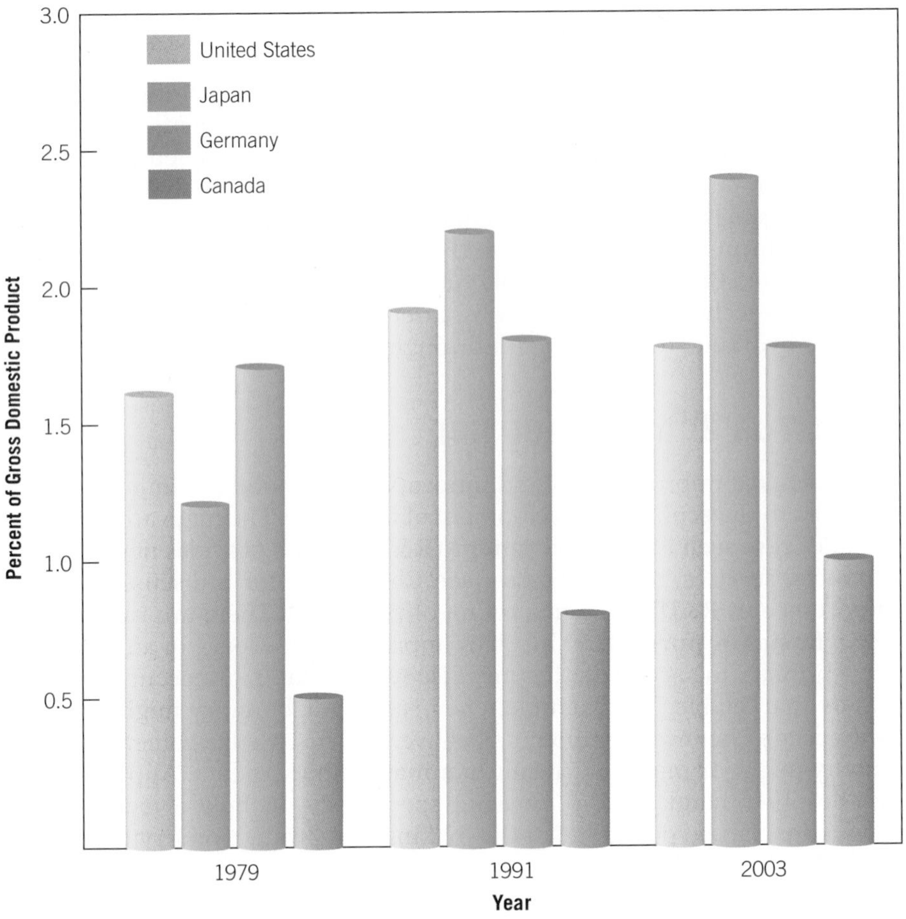

Figure 2.5 R&D expenditures as a proportion of GDP.

assembled, and wrapped as it moves along a predefined path. The rapid advancement of the internet into all areas of business is also a reflection of the technological environment. Indeed, new technologies continue to revolutionize nearly every aspect of business, ranging from the ways that customers and companies interact to where, when, and how employees perform their work.

Companies must constantly be on the lookout for technological breakthroughs that might make their products or services obsolete and thereby threaten their survival. Many of these breakthroughs do not come from direct competitors or even from the industry the company is part of. Microsoft, for example, originally didn't pay much attention to internet technology because it was busy competing with companies like WordPerfect in the word processing and operating software market. When Netscape entered the market with a browser program that threatened to make operating systems unnecessary, Microsoft had to spend a lot of time and money developing its own Internet Explorer browser.[21]

Technology is the basis of competition for some companies, especially when their goal is to be the technology leader in their industry. A company, for example, might focus its efforts on having the most technologically advanced products on the market. Intel exemplifies the challenge and the risks of adopting a strategic dependence on technological leadership. Before co-founding Intel with Bob Noyce in 1968, Gordon Moore made a prediction about microprocessors (the processing components of microcomputers) that eventually became known as Moore's Law: The number of

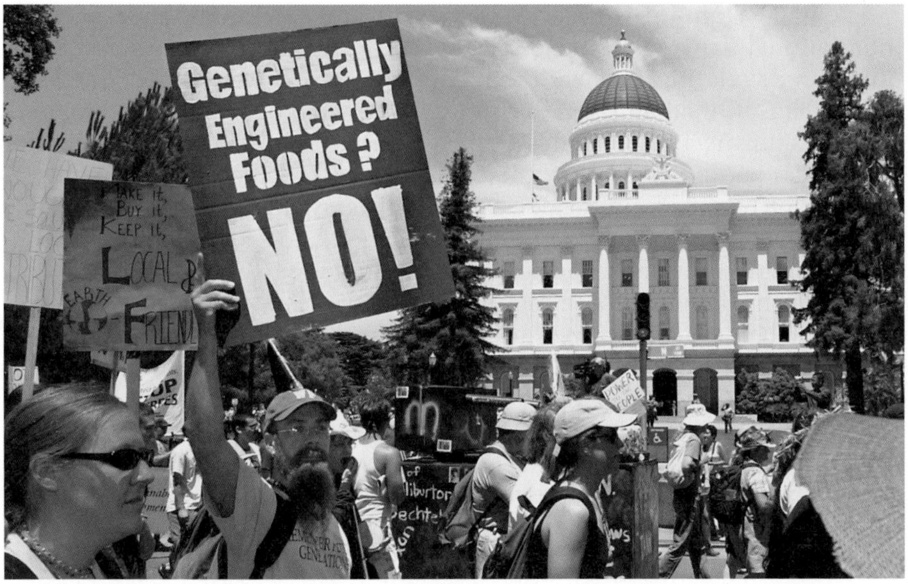

On the surface, low-fat corn and salmon that grow twice as fast would seem to be a good way of improving the food supply. But not everybody is happy about such developments in the modern technological environment. Environmentalists are afraid that genetically modified crops (which they call "Frankenfoods") will sneak into natural populations, outbreed wild species, and threaten biodiversity. Or else they'll cross-pollinate and engineer species that are downright dangerous for human consumption.

transistors in a microprocessor would double every 18 months. In effect, this rate would entail a twofold increase in processing power every 18 months—a seemingly impossible pace. Intel, however, adopted Moore's Law as a performance requirement for each new generation of processor since 1970, up through the Pentium 4.

Because of the rapid pace of new developments, keeping a leadership position based on technology is increasingly difficult. **Technology transfer** refers to the process of getting a new technology out of the lab and into the marketplace where it can generate profits for the company. Efficient technology transfer means an increased likelihood of business success. A related challenge is meeting the constant demand to decrease *cycle time*—the time from beginning to end that it takes a firm to accomplish some recurring activity or function. Since businesses are more competitive if they can decrease cycle times, many companies now focus on decreasing cycle times in areas ranging from developing products to making deliveries and collecting credit payments. Twenty years ago, it took carmakers about five years from the decision to launch a new product until it was available in dealer showrooms. Now most companies can complete the cycle in less than two years.

technology transfer
The process of getting a new technology out of the lab and into the marketplace.

THE POLITICAL–LEGAL ENVIRONMENT

Describe the *political–legal environment* and its role in business. 4

The **political–legal environment** reflects the relationship between business and government, including government regulation of business. The legal system defines what an organization can and can't do. Although Canada is a free market economy, there is still significant regulation of business activity, as we saw in Chapter 1.

Society's general view of business (pro- or anti-) is also important. During periods of anti-business sentiment, companies may find their competitive activities restricted. There may be, for example, fewer opportunities for mergers and acquisitions because of antitrust concerns. When the Royal Bank wanted to merge with the Bank of Montreal, the Canadian government blocked the merger on the grounds that it would reduce competition and harm consumers. During periods of pro-business sentiment, firms find it easier to compete and have fewer concerns about antitrust issues.

political–legal environment
Conditions reflecting the relationship between business and government, usually in the form of government regulation.

Political stability is also an important consideration, especially for international firms. No business wants to set up shop in another country unless trade relationships with that country are relatively well defined and stable. Thus, Canadian firms are more likely to do business with England, Mexico, and the United States than with Haiti and Afghanistan. Similar issues also pertain to assessments of local and provincial governments. A new mayor or provincial leader can affect many organizations, especially small firms that do business in a single location and are susceptible to zoning restrictions, property and school taxes, and the like.

Relations between sovereign governments can also affect business activity. When Canada refused to send troops to support the U.S. invasion of Iraq, relations between the United States and Canada were very cool for a time. A survey revealed that nearly half the Americans polled said they would consider switching away from Canadian goods in favour of goods from other countries because of Canada's lack of support of the war. This would obviously have a negative effect on Canadian exports if U.S. consumers acted on these opinions.[22]

THE SOCIO-CULTURAL ENVIRONMENT

5 Describe the *socio-cultural environment* and its role in business.

The **socio-cultural environment** includes the customs, values, attitudes, and demographic characteristics of the society in which a company operates. The socio-cultural environment influences the customer preferences for goods and services, as well as the standards of business conduct that are seen as acceptable.

socio-cultural environment Conditions including the customs, values, attitudes, and demographic characteristics of the society in which an organization functions.

Customer Preferences and Tastes

Customer preferences and tastes vary both across and within national boundaries. In some countries, consumers are willing and able to pay premium prices for designer clothes with labels such as Armani or Calvin Klein. But the same clothes have virtually no market in other countries. Product usage also varies between nations. In China, bicycles are primarily seen as a mode of transportation, but in Canada, they are marketed primarily for recreational purposes.

Consumer preferences can also vary widely within the same country. Customs and product preferences in Quebec, for example, differ from those in other parts of Canada. In the United States, pre-packaged chili is more popular in the southwest than in the northeast. McDonald's is just one company that is affected by socio-cultural factors. In response to concerns about nutrition and health, McDonald's has added salads to its menus and experimented with other low-fat foods. It was the first fast-food chain to provide customers with information about the ingredients in its products, and it attracted media attention when it announced that it would reduce the fat content in its popular French fries.

Consumer preferences and tastes also change over time. Preferences for colour, style, taste, and so forth change from season to season. In some years, brightly coloured clothes sell best, while in other years, people want more subdued colours. Some of these changes are driven by consumers, and some are driven by companies trying to convince consumers to adopt new styles. These and many other related issues regarding businesses and their customers are explored more fully in Part IV of this book, which deals with the marketing of goods and services.

Socio-cultural factors also influence the way workers in a society feel about their jobs and organizations. In some cultures, work carries meaningful social significance, with certain employers and job titles being highly desired by workers. But in other cultures, because work is simply a means to an end, people are concerned only with pay and job security. McDonald's has occasionally struggled with its operations in the Middle East because many people there are not interested in working in food-service operations.

Ethical Compliance and Responsible Business Behaviour

An especially critical element of the socio-cultural environment is the practice of ethical conduct and social responsibility. We cover these areas in detail in Chapter 3, but they are sufficiently important that we describe one illustrative area of concern briefly at this point: the reporting of a company's financial position. Keeping up with today's increasingly fast-paced business activities is putting a strain on the accounting profession's traditional methods for auditing, financial reporting, and time-honoured standards for professional ethics. The stakeholders of business firms—employees, stockholders, consumers, labour unions, creditors, and the government—are entitled to a fair accounting so they can make enlightened personal and business decisions, but they often get a blurred picture of a firm's competitive health.

The now-famous Enron scandal in the United States involved fast-moving financial transactions among layers of subsidiary firms, some domestic and many offshore, with large-scale borrowing from some of the world's largest financial institutions. The flood of electronic transactions that drove financial flows through a vast network of quickly formed and rapidly dissolved partnerships among energy brokers and buyers was so complex that Enron's accounting reports failed to reflect the firm's disastrous financial and managerial condition. In a blatant display of social irresponsibility, Enron's financial reports concealed many of its partnerships (and debts) with other companies, thus hiding its true operating condition. Arthur Andersen LLP, the accounting firm that audited Enron's finances, did not catch its client's distorted reports. Andersen's unethical and illegal practices—including obstruction of justice for shredding and doctoring documents related to Enron audits—destroyed the public's trust and Arthur Andersen as a company.

The fallout from these activities was not limited to U.S. companies. In 2004, CIBC agreed to pay $480 million to settle allegations that it facilitated accounting fraud at Enron. The CEO of CIBC admitted that the company had "stumbled" in the area of trust and reputation.[23]

THE BUSINESS ENVIRONMENT

Business today is faster paced, more complex, and more demanding than ever before. As businesses aggressively try to differentiate themselves, there has been a trend toward higher quality products, planned obsolescence, and product life cycles measured in weeks or months rather than years. This, in turn, has created customer expectations for instant gratification. Ultimate consumers and business customers want high-quality goods and services—often customized—with lower prices and immediate delivery. Sales offices, service providers, and production facilities are shifting geographically as new markets and resources emerge in other countries. Employees want flexible working hours and opportunities to work at home. Stockholder expectations also add pressure for productivity increases, growth in market share, and larger profits. At the same time, however, a more vocal public demands more honesty, fair competition, and respect for the environment.

A 2007 C-Suite survey found that the three most important issues facing Canadian businesses are (1) the value of the Canadian dollar, (2) a skilled labour shortage, and (3) the environment. These three issues are all important elements of the business environment.[24]

The Industry Environment

Each business firm operates in a specific industry, and each industry has different characteristics. The intensity of the competition in an industry has a big influence on how a company operates. To be effective, managers must understand the competitive situation, and then develop a competitive strategy to exploit opportunities in the industry.

One of the most popular tools to analyze competitive situations in an industry is Michael Porter's five forces model.[25] The model (see Figure 2.6) helps managers analyze five important sources of competitive pressure, and then decide what their competitive strategy should be. We briefly discuss each of the elements of the model in the following paragraphs.

Rivalry Among Existing Competitors

The amount of rivalry among companies varies across industries. Rivalry can be seen in activities like intense price competition, elaborate advertising campaigns, and an increased emphasis on customer service. For many years, the rivalry among Chartered Accountants, Certified General Accountants, and Certified Management Accountants in Canada was low-key, but it has recently become much more intense. These firms are responding by cutting costs, making pricing deals with clients, and trying to find ways to differentiate themselves from their competitors.

Threat of Potential Entrants

When new competitors enter an industry, they may cause big changes. For example, when Microsoft introduced Encarta, it caused the sale of hard-copy encyclopedias by companies like Encyclopaedia Britannica to drop sharply. If it is easy for new competitors to enter a market, competition will

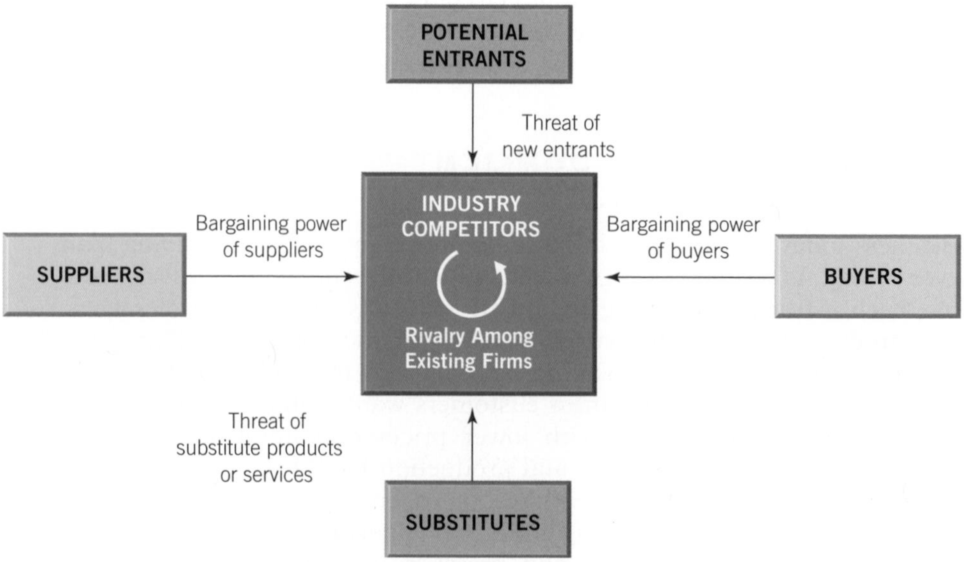

Figure 2.6 Michael Porter's five forces model.

likely be intense and the industry will not be very attractive. Some industries (for example, automobile manufacturing) are very capital-intensive and are therefore difficult to enter, but others (for example, home cleaning or lawn care services) are relatively easy to enter.

Suppliers

The amount of bargaining power suppliers have in relation to buyers helps determine how competitive an industry is. When there are only a few suppliers in an industry, they tend to have great bargaining power. The power of suppliers is influenced by the number of substitute products that are available (i.e., products that perform the same or similar functions). When there are few substitute products, suppliers obviously have more power.

Buyers

When there are only a few buyers and many suppliers, the buyers have a great deal of bargaining power. Retail powerhouse Wal-Mart, for example, is often cited as a buyer that puts tremendous pressure on its suppliers to reduce their prices. Wal-Mart can do this because it buys so much from these suppliers.

Substitutes

If there are many substitute products available, the industry is more competitive. For example, various synthetics fibres can be used as substitutes for cotton.

Managers use Porter's ideas to help them decide the level of competitive intensity in an industry. A good example is the emergence of the internet in the purchase of airline tickets and rental cars. By making it easier for consumers to compare prices, the internet has increased the competitive intensity of these two industries (and many others, for that matter). In effect, the internet has increased the bargaining power of ticket buyers.

Emerging Challenges and Opportunities in the Business Environment

6 Identify emerging challenges and opportunities in the *business environment.*

The most successful firms are dealing with challenges and opportunities in today's business environment by focusing on their **core competencies**—the skills and resources with which they compete best and create the most value for owners. They outsource non-core business processes and pay suppliers and distributors to perform them, thereby increasing their reliance on suppliers. These new business models call for unprecedented coordination—not only among internal activities, but also among customers, suppliers, and strategic partners—and they often involve globally dispersed processes and supply chains.

core competencies
Skills and resources with which an organization competes best and creates the most value for owners.

In this section, we discuss some of the most popular steps that companies have taken to respond to challenges and opportunities in the business environment. These include *outsourcing, viral marketing,* and *business process management*.

Outsourcing

Outsourcing is the strategy of paying suppliers and distributors to perform certain business processes or to provide needed materials or services. For example, the cafeteria in a museum may be important to employees and customers, but the museum's primary focus is on exhibits that will interest the general public, not on food-service operations. That's why museums usually outsource cafeteria operations to food-service management companies whose main line of business is to run cafeterias. The result is more

outsourcing
Strategy of paying suppliers and distributors to perform certain business processes or to provide needed materials or services.

Much concern has been expressed by government officials and labour unions that the outsourcing of jobs will hurt the Canadian economy. Here, women work in one of many call centres in New Delhi, India, that do work for Canadian and U.S. companies.

BUSINESS ACCOUNTABILITY

Outsourcing: Good Or Bad?

Outsourcing is an increasingly popular strategy because it helps firms focus on their core activities and avoid getting sidetracked by secondary activities. The Bank of Montreal (BMO), for example, outsourced its human resource processing services to Exult Inc., which now manages payroll and benefits administration, employee records, HR call centre services, and other functions that used to be performed in-house at BMO. The new arrangement means a 20 percent reduction in HR costs for BMO, and it also frees up BMO managers to concentrate on more "value-added" work. Over 100 people who used to work for BMO now work for Exult.

The Bank of Montreal outsourcing decision involved moving jobs from one company to another within Canada. But a lot of outsourcing involves moving jobs from Canada to a foreign country (often called *offshoring*), and that is why there is so much concern about it. In the short run, it is obvious that Canadian jobs will be lost when outsourcing takes place. But in the longer run, it is possible that outsourcing may be beneficial. How can that be? The reasoning goes something like this: Canadian companies will continue to outsource more manufacturing work in order to take advantage of low-cost foreign suppliers. This will allow the Canadian companies to reduce their costs and be more effective in highly competitive global markets. This, in turn, will raise Canadian productivity and improve the standard of living in Canada.

The chief economist for the Export Development Corporation (EDC) says that the main reason for the large increases in U.S. productivity between 1998 and 2002 was outsourcing, so Canada may get the same benefit if it outsources increasing amounts of work. On the negative side, it will obviously reduce the number of jobs in Canada, at least in the short run. That, in turn, may reduce demand and cause economic growth to decline. But even that may not be as bad as people think. A study conducted by the Peterson Institute for International Economics found that only one in 25 laid-off workers lost their jobs because of outsourcing.

In an increasingly global economy, competitive pressures are intense, and these can cause sweeping change in certain industries. In the automobile business, for example, companies like Ford and GM have to compete with highly efficient Japanese companies like Toyota and Honda. Ford and GM must therefore cut costs wherever possible. But they have rather restrictive labour contracts with their unions that prevent them from easily cutting costs in terms of their own employees, so they have hit upon a new strategy—put pressure on the companies that supply them with auto parts.

The case of Superior Industries International, a California-based company that makes aluminum wheels for Ford and GM, is instructive. Superior got

▶▶▶

▶▶▶

blunt messages from both Ford and General Motors to match the price that Chinese wheel suppliers were charging or they would buy from a company that could match the price. Since 85 percent of Superior's business was with Ford and GM, it had little alternative but to start outsourcing some work to Chinese factories in order to lower their costs. To do this, Superior got involved in a joint venture with a Chinese company near Shanghai to build aluminum wheels. The operation will start small and increase as years go by. This means that there is no guarantee that North American jobs at Superior will continue in the long-run.

Wages in China average about 90 cents per hour compared to $22 per hour in North America. Even after taking into account the large distance between China and North American markets, the cost of Chinese-made radios, cables, brakes, and wheels is still 20 to 40 percent lower than products made in North America. This is causing jobs in the North American auto parts industry to disappear at a rapid rate. What is interesting is that this trend has just started. Since Ford and GM currently buy less than 5 percent of their parts from China, there is room for dramatically increased amounts of outsourcing. The implication for jobs is not positive.

With outsourcing, there are more problems than simply lost jobs. A 2006 study by the Toronto-based Centre for Outsourcing Research and Education found that less than 50 percent of companies that have tried outsourcing are satisfied with it. Members of the "stay-back team"—the individuals who are responsible for managing the new outsourcing relationship—are under pressure to not only cut costs, but also to increase the quality of the services that have been outsourced. In addition, they feel that suppliers too often don't understand what they are supposed to do, that they charge too much, and that they provide poor service. Moreover, when disruptions occur in the supply chain, the costs to both parties can be high. For one thing, replacing failed outsourced operations can be very expensive, especially if the firm wants to go back to performing the outsourced activity itself. In spite of these problems, outsourcing is likely here to stay because of the increasingly global nature of business and because competitive pressures to reduce costs are so intense.

QUESTIONS FOR DISCUSSION

1. Are Canadian companies being accountable to Canadians when they outsource jobs to foreign countries? To what extent do Canadian companies worry about such accountability?
2. "*Canadian companies really don't have any alternative but to outsource. If they don't, they will not be cost-competitive and will lose out in the global market.*" Do you agree or disagree with this statement? Explain.

attention to museum exhibits and better food service for customers. Firms today outsource numerous activities, including payroll, employee training, and research and development. As the Business Accountability box illustrates, concerns about outsourcing have increased as it has become more and more widely used.

Viral Marketing

Combining technology with marketing methods usually results in new ways to attract customers. **Viral marketing**, which uses word of mouth that spreads information like a virus from customer to customer, relies on the vast reach of the internet to replace face-to-face communications. Messages about new cars, sports events, and numerous other goods and services travel on the internet among potential customers who pass the information on to others. Using various formats—games, contests, chat rooms, and bulletin boards—marketers encourage potential customers to try out products and tell other people about them.[26]

viral marketing
Strategy of using the internet and word-of-mouth marketing to spread product information.

The Organic Trade Association (OTA), which promotes organic foods, created a successful viral marketing program when it partnered with Free Range Graphics, and produced a 5-minute online spoof of the latest Star Wars movie. The film—which is called *Store Wars: The Organic Rebellion* and has characters such as Cuke Skywalker and Darth Tater—has been passed around the internet by consumers who favour organic foods.[27]

Viral marketing leads to faster consumer awareness and has a wider reach than traditional media messages, and at a lower cost. The OTA's short film, for example, was seen by 10 million people in its first four months. Viral marketing works because people increasingly rely on the internet for information that they used to get from other media such as newspapers, and because the customer becomes a participant in the process of spreading the word by forwarding information to other internet users.

Business Process Management

process
Any activity that adds value to some input, transforming it into an output for a customer (whether external or internal).

business process management
Approach by which firms move away from department-oriented organization and toward process-oriented team structures that cut across old departmental boundaries.

A **process** is any activity that adds value to some input, transforming it into an output for a customer (whether external or internal).[28] For example, human resource departments perform interviewing and hiring processes; payroll departments perform the employee-payment process; the purchasing department performs the process of ordering materials; accounting performs the financial reporting process; and marketing performs the process of taking orders from customers.

Business process management means moving away from organizing around departments, and moving toward organizing around process-oriented team structures that cut across old departmental boundaries. Often, companies begin by asking, "What must we do well to stay in business and win new orders?" Next, they identify the major processes that must be performed well to achieve these goals. Then they organize resources and skills around those essential processes. By organizing according to processes rather than functional departments, decision making is faster and more customer-oriented, materials and operations are coordinated, and products get to customers more rapidly.[29]

REDRAWING CORPORATE BOUNDARIES

7 Understand recent trends in the *redrawing of corporate boundaries.*

Successful companies are responding to challenges in the external environment by redrawing traditional organizational boundaries, and by joining together with other companies to develop new goods and services. Several trends have become evident in recent years: *acquisitions and mergers, divestitures and spinoffs, employee-owned corporations, strategic alliances,* and *subsidiary/parent corporations*.

Acquisitions and Mergers

acquisition
The purchase of a company by another, larger firm, which absorbs the smaller company into its operations.

merger
The union of two companies to form a single new business.

horizontal merger
A merger of two firms that have previously been direct competitors in the same industry.

vertical merger
A merger of two firms that have previously had a buyer–seller relationship.

conglomerate merger
A merger of two firms in completely unrelated businesses.

friendly takeover
An acquisition in which the management of the acquired company welcomes the firm's buyout by another company.

hostile takeover
An acquisition in which the management of the acquired company fights the firm's buyout by another company.

In an **acquisition**, one firm simply buys another firm. For example, Brazilian-based Companhia Vale do Rio Doce bought Inco, Luxembourg-based Arcelor SA bought Dofasco Inc., and Barrick Gold Corp. bought Placer Dome Inc. The transaction is similar to buying a car that then becomes your property. In contrast, a **merger** is a consolidation of two firms, and the arrangement is more collaborative. In recent years, Canadian National Railways merged with the Illinois Central Railroad, Jean Coutu Group Inc. merged with Eckerd Drugs, Toronto-Dominion Bank merged with Canada Trust, and Molson Inc. merged with Adolph Coors Co. In 2006, there were 1430 mergers and acquisitions in Canada valued at $187 billion.[30]

When the companies are in the same industry, as when Agricore and United Grain Growers merged to form Agricore United, it is called a **horizontal merger**. When one of the companies in the merger is a supplier or customer to the other, it is called a **vertical merger**. When the companies are in unrelated businesses, it is called a **conglomerate merger**. A merger or acquisition can take place in one of several different ways. In a **friendly takeover**, the acquired company welcomes the acquisition, perhaps because it needs cash or sees other benefits in joining the acquiring firm. But in a **hostile takeover**, the acquiring company buys enough of the other company's stock to take control even though the other company is opposed to the takeover.

A **poison pill** is a defence that management adopts to make a firm less attractive to an actual or potential hostile suitor in a takeover attempt. The objective is to make the "pill" so distasteful that a potential acquirer will not want to swallow it. BCE Inc., for example, adopted a poison pill that allowed its shareholders to buy BCE stock at a 50 percent discount if another company announced its intention to acquire 20 percent or more of BCE's shares.[31]

poison pill
A defence that management adopts to make a firm less attractive to an actual or potential hostile suitor in a takeover attempt.

Divestitures and Spinoffs

A **divestiture** occurs when a company decides to sell part of its existing business operations to another corporation. For example, Unilever—the maker of Close-Up toothpaste, Dove soap, Vaseline lotion, and Q-tips—at one time owned several specialty chemical businesses that made ingredients for its consumer products. The company decided that it had to focus more on the consumer products themselves, so it sold the chemical businesses to ICI, a European chemical company.

divestiture
Occurs when a company sells part of its existing business operations to another company.

In other cases, a company might set up one or more corporate units as new, independent businesses because a business unit might be more valuable as a separate company. This is known as a **spinoff**. For example, PepsiCo spun off Pizza Hut, KFC, and Taco Bell into a new, separate corporation called Tricon Global Restaurants (now called Yum! Brands Inc.), and Canadian Pacific spun off Canadian Pacific Railways, CP Ships, PanCanadian Petroleum, and Fording Coal.

spinoff
Strategy of setting up one or more corporate units as new, independent corporations.

Employee-Owned Corporations

Corporations are sometimes owned by the employees who work for them. The current pattern is for this ownership to take the form of **employee stock ownership plans**, or ESOPs. A corporation might decide to set up an ESOP to increase employee motivation or to fight a hostile takeover attempt. The company first secures a loan, which it then uses to buy shares of its stock on the open market. Some of the future profits made by the corporation are used to pay off the loan. The stock, meanwhile, is controlled by a bank or other trustee. Employees gradually gain ownership of the stock, usually on the basis of seniority. But even though they might not have physical possession of the stock for a while, they control its voting rights immediately.

employee stock ownership plans
An arrangement whereby a corporation buys its own stock with loaned funds and holds it in trust for its employees. Employees "earn" the stock based on some condition such as seniority. Employees control the stock's voting rights immediately, even though they may not take physical possession of the stock until specified conditions are met.

A survey of 471 Canadian and U.S. companies conducted by Western Compensation & Benefits Consultants of Vancouver found that three-quarters of the companies that have adopted ESOPs have experienced improvement in both sales and profits. Canadian companies such as Celestica and St. Laurent Paperboard Inc. have found that ESOPs give employees an increased sense of belonging in the company.[32]

Strategic Alliances

A **strategic alliance**, or joint venture, involves two or more enterprises co-operating in the research, development, manufacture, or marketing of a product. For example, GM and Suzuki formed a strategic alliance at the Ingersoll, Ontario, plant where Trackers and Grand Vitaras are made. Northern Empire, Stornoway, and Hunter Exploration Group formed a three-way joint venture to explore for diamonds on Melville Island in the Arctic Ocean. Companies form strategic alliances for two main reasons: (1) to help spread the risk of a project, and (2) to get something of value (like technological expertise) from their strategic partner.

strategic alliance
An enterprise in which two or more persons or companies temporarily join forces to undertake a particular project.

Subsidiary and Parent Corporations

subsidiary corporation
One that is owned by another corporation.

parent corporation
A corporation that owns a subsidiary.

Sometimes corporations own other corporations. A **subsidiary corporation** is one that is owned by another corporation. The corporation that owns the subsidiary is called the **parent corporation**. For example, Unilever is the parent corporation of Lever Brothers, Lipton, and Chesebrough Ponds.

Summary of Learning Objectives

1. Explain the concepts of *organizational boundaries* and *multiple organizational environments.* All businesses operate within a larger *external environment* consisting of everything outside an organization's boundaries that might affect it. An *organizational boundary* is that which separates the organization from its environment. Boundaries were once relatively easy to identify, but are becoming harder to pin down. Organizations have multiple environments. Some environments are relatively general, such as prevailing economic conditions. Others are much more precise, such as the pricing policies of competitors. A full picture of a company's organizational environments would include the following elements: economic conditions, technology, political–legal considerations, social issues, the global environment, issues of ethical and social responsibility, the business environment itself, and numerous other emerging challenges and opportunities.
2. Explain the importance of the *economic environment* to business and identify the factors used to evaluate the performance of an economic system. The *economic environment* is the economic system in which business firms operate. The health of this environment affects business firms. The key goals of the Canadian system are economic growth, economic stability, and full employment. *Gross domestic product (GDP)* is the total value of all goods and services produced within a given period by a national economy through domestic factors of production. The government manages the economy through *fiscal policies* (such as tax increases) and *monetary policies* (controlling the size of the nation's money supply).
3. Describe the *technological environment* and its role in business. *Technology* refers to all the ways by which firms create value for their constituents, including human knowledge, work methods, physical equipment, electronics and telecommunications, and various processing systems. There are two general categories of business-related technologies: *product and service technologies* and *business process technologies.* Product and service technologies create products—both physical goods and services—for customers. Business process technologies are used to improve a firm's performance of internal operations (such as accounting) and to help to create better relationships with external constituents, such as suppliers and customers. *Enterprise resource planning (ERP)* is a large-scale information system for organizing and managing a firm's processes across product lines, departments, and geographic locations.
4. Describe the *political–legal environment* and its role in business. The *political–legal environment* reflects the relationship between business and government, usually in the form of government regulation. The legal system defines in part what an organization can and can't do. Various government agencies regulate important areas such as advertising practices, safety and health considerations, and acceptable standards of business conduct. Pro- or anti-business sentiment in government can further influence business activity. During periods of pro-business sentiment, firms find it easier to compete and have fewer concerns about antitrust issues. During periods of anti-business sentiment, firms may find their competitive activities more restricted.
5. Describe the *socio-cultural environment* and its role in business. *The socio-cultural environment* includes the customs, values, and demographic characteristics of the society in which an organization functions. Socio-cultural processes determine the goods and services as well as the standards of business conduct that a society values and accepts. Appropriate standards of conduct also vary across cultures. The shape of the market, the ethics of political influence, and the attitudes of its workforce are only a few of the many ways in which culture can affect an organization.
6. Identify emerging challenges and opportunities in the *business environment.* Successful companies are responding to challenges in new ways. They are focusing on their core competencies. The innovative ways in which companies respond to emerging challenges and opportunities include *outsourcing, viral marketing,* and *business process management.* Outsourcing is the strategy of

paying suppliers and distributors to perform certain business processes or to provide needed materials or services. Viral marketing relies on the internet to replace face-to-face communications. Many firms are moving away from the department-oriented organization and toward process-oriented team structures that cut across old departmental boundaries—an approach called business process management.

7. Understand recent trends in the *redrawing of corporate boundaries.* An *acquisition* occurs when one firm buys another outright. A *merger* occurs when two firms combine to create a new company. A *divestiture* occurs when a corporation sells a part of its existing business operations or sets it up as a new and independent corporation. When a firm sells part of itself to raise capital, the strategy is known as a *spin-off.* The *employee stock ownership plan* (ESOP) allows employees to own a significant share of the corporation through trusts established on their behalf. In a *strategic alliance,* two or more organizations collaborate on a project for mutual gain.

QUESTIONS AND EXERCISES

Questions for Analysis

1. It has been argued that inflation is both good and bad. How can this be? Explain. Are government efforts to control inflation well-advised? Explain.
2. What are the benefits and risks of outsourcing? What, if anything, should be done about the problem of Canadian companies outsourcing jobs to foreign countries? Defend your answer.
3. Why is it important for managers to understand the environment in which their businesses operate?
4. Explain how current economic indicators such as inflation and unemployment affect you personally. Explain how they affect managers.
5. Using a product or service of your choice, explain how the various environments of business (economic, technological, socio-cultural, global, political–legal, and general business) impact the sales possibilities of the product or service.
6. At first glance, it might seem as though the goals of economic growth and stability are inconsistent with one another. How can this apparent inconsistency be reconciled?
7. What is the current climate in Canada regarding the regulation of business? How might it affect you if you were a manager today?

Application Exercises

8. Select two businesses with which you are familiar. Identify the major elements of their external environments that are most likely to affect them in important and meaningful ways.
9. Assume that you are the owner of an internet pharmacy that sells prescription drugs to U.S. citizens. Analyze the factors in the external environment (economic, technological, political–legal, and socio-cultural) that might facilitate your company's activities. Analyze the factors in the external environment that might threaten your company's activities.
10. Interview two business owners or managers. Ask them to describe for you the following things: (a) what business functions, if any, they outsource; (b) whether or not they are focusing more attention on business process management now than in the past; and (c) how the events of September 11, 2001, have affected their work.

BUILDING YOUR BUSINESS SKILLS

The Letdown from Environmental Upheaval

Goal

To encourage students to understand how local events can affect other businesses in a number of ways.

Situation

The collapse of Enron affected literally hundreds of other businesses. While attention has been directed primarily at the demise of Arthur Andersen, many other businesses suffered as well. For example, Enron's headquarters was located in a large office building on the edge of Houston's downtown business district. Because of both Enron's rapid growth and the prosperity of its employees, numerous other service providers had set up shop nearby—a shoeshine stand, a coffee shop, a bank branch, a dry cleaner, and two restaurants. When Enron collapsed, the demand for services provided by these small businesses dropped sharply.

Larger businesses were also caught up in the ripple effect. Enron, for example, had bought the rights to name the new home of Houston's baseball team, the Astros, Enron Field. The Astros were forced to remove all Enron signage and seek a new sponsor. Continental Airlines dominates the air traffic market out of Houston, and Enron was one of Continental's largest corporate clients. Combined with the events of September 11, 2001, and major staff reductions at Compaq Computer, another big Continental client, the end of business travel by Enron managers cost the airline considerable revenue.

Method

Divide up into groups of four or five students. Each group should begin by doing the following:

Step 1 Identify five kinds of small businesses likely to have been affected by Enron's collapse. You can include some of those identified above, but identify at least two others.

Step 2 Identify five kinds of large businesses likely to have been affected by Enron's collapse. Again, you can use some of those identified above, but identify at least two others.

Step 3 As a group, develop answers to each of the following:

1. For each company that you identify, both small and large, describe the specific effects of the Enron collapse on its business.
2. Describe the most logical organizational response of each company to these effects.
3. What kinds of plans, if any, should each organization develop in the event of similar future events?
4. Identify businesses that might have benefited economically from the collapse of Enron.

Alternative Assignment

Select a different high-profile environmental upheaval, such as the U.S. duties that were placed on Canadian softwood lumber being shipped to the United States, and substitute your choice for Enron. Then proceed with Steps 1–3 above.

Follow-Up Questions

1. What does this exercise demonstrate about the pitfalls of relying too heavily on one business?
2. Could any of these businesses have been better prepared for the Enron collapse?
3. Managers must be on the alert for environmental changes that might negatively affect their business. Is it possible for a manager to spend too much time trying to anticipate future events? Why or why not?

EXERCISING YOUR ETHICS: TEAM EXERCISE

Finding the Balance

The Situation

Managers often find it necessary to find the right balance among the interests of different stakeholders. For instance, paying employees the lowest possible wages can enhance profits, but paying a living wage might better serve the interests of workers. As more businesses outsource production to other countries, these trade-offs become even more complicated.

The Dilemma

The Canadian Delta Company currently uses three different suppliers in Southeast Asia for most of its outsourced production. Due to increased demand for its products, it needs to double the amount of business it currently subcontracts to one of these suppliers. (For purposes of this exercise, assume that the company must award the new supplier contract to a single firm, and that it must be one of these three. You can also assume that the quality provided is about the same for all three companies.)

Subcontractor A provides a plain but clean work environment for its workers. Even though the local weather conditions are hot and humid much of the year, the plant is not air conditioned. Canadian Delta safety experts have verified that the conditions are not dangerous, but are definitely uncomfortable at times. The firm pays its workers the same prevailing wage rate that is paid by its local competitors. While it has never had a legal issue with its workforce, Subcontractor A does push its employees to meet production quotas and it has a very tough policy regarding discipline for tardiness. For instance, an employee who is late gets put on probation; a second infraction within three months results in termination. This subcontractor provides production to Canadian Delta at a level such that it can attach a 25 percent markup.

Subcontractor B also provides a plain work environment. It pays its workers about 5 percent above local wage levels and hence is an attractive employer. Because of its higher pay, this firm is actually quite ruthless with some of its policies, however. For instance, any employee who reports to work more than 15 minutes late without a medical excuse is automatically terminated. This supplier's costs are such that Delta Company can achieve a 20 percent markup.

Subcontractor C runs a much nicer factory than either A or B, and the plant is air conditioned. It also pays its workers about 10 percent above local wage levels. The company also operates an on-site school for the children of its employees, and provides additional training for its workers so they can improve their skills. Due to its higher costs, Canadian Delta's markup on this firm's products is only around 15 percent.

Team Activity

Assemble a group of four students and assign each group member to one of the following roles:

- Canadian Delta executive
- Canadian Delta employee
- Canadian Delta customer
- Canadian Delta investor

Action Steps

1. Before discussing the situation with your group, and from the perspective of your assigned role, which firm do you think should get the additional business? Which firm is your second choice? Write down the reasons for your position.
2. Before discussing the situation with your group, and from the perspective of your assigned role, what are the underlying ethical issues in this situation? Write down the issues.
3. Gather your group together and reveal, in turn, each member's comments on their choices. Next, reveal the ethical issues listed by each member.
4. Appoint someone to record main points of agreement and disagreement within the group. How do you explain the results? What accounts for any disagreement?
5. From an ethical standpoint, what does your group conclude is the most appropriate choice for the company in this situation? Why?

BUSINESS CASE 2

Corporate Reputations: Mixed Evidence

During the last few years, there has been a great deal of negative publicity about business activity. Because of illegal and unethical behaviour, sky-high executive salaries, or simply poor performance, business has lost a lot of respect lately. But there is another side to the story, and it doesn't get enough attention. That story concerns the large number of corporations that perform well and do good things for the constituents in their external environment. And they do it without a lot of fanfare.

Who are these companies? Each year since 1994, KPMG/Ipsos-Reid has published a list of the most respected corporations in Canada. In 2005, 250 leading Canadian CEOs were asked to assess Canadian corporations on eight performance categories such as long-term investment value, innovation and product/service development, financial performance, corporate social responsibility, corporate governance, human resource management, and customer service. The winner for 2005 was the Royal Bank of Canada (RBC) by a wide margin (RBC also came in first in the 2004 survey). The next four companies (in order) were Research in Motion, EnCana Corp., and WestJet Airlines.

Some critics say that banks have an undue advantage in surveys like these because they are so rich that they are able to be very involved in philanthropy. Both CEOs and the general public are likely to be impressed by large charitable donations that banks make, and such activity gives banks a lot of free publicity. On the other hand, Canadian consumers are often not very impressed with banks, arguing that they charge too much for services and do not pay high enough interest on money deposited with them.

Respect and reputation are things that can quickly change. For example, in 1999, Nortel Networks ranked first in the survey, but with its recent troubles it ranked only 40th in the 2005 survey. And Bombardier, which ranked first in 2001, dropped to 28th place in 2005. Negative publicity about a company can obviously cause it to drop in the rankings. Canadian Imperial Bank of Commerce dropped from 10th place in 2004 to 18th place in 2005 after it received negative publicity about its role in the Enron debacle.

Surveys about corporate reputations are also conducted in the United States. The Reputation Quotient study is a joint effort of Harris Interactive Inc., a Rochester, New York-based research firm, and the Reputation Institute of New York. A 2006 survey asked 7886 people to name the two companies they felt had the best reputation and the two companies with the worst reputation. The 60 companies that were mentioned most often were then ranked by 22 480 other respondents on factors such as vision and leadership, emotional appeal, financial performance, social responsibility, and workplace environment. The top three companies were Microsoft, Johnson & Johnson, and 3M. The three worst companies were Comcast, ExxonMobil, and Halliburton. Companies that are ranked poorly often have had significant negative publicity in recent years for various misdeeds. The actions of a relatively small number of companies have influenced how people in the United States view business. In the 2006 survey, 69 percent of respondents rated the reputation of American business as either "not good" or "terrible."

It's not just individual companies that can run into difficulty. During the last few years, the reputations of entire industries have declined. For example, consumer impressions of the pharmaceutical and oil industries are negative because of a widely held belief that these industries are overcharging consumers for the products they sell. The tobacco industry has also had problems because consumers think that information about the negative effects of smoking and nicotine were withheld from the public.

When we consider negative information about business firms, we must remember that only a very small proportion of them are actually engaging in illegal or unethical behaviour. A review of the Canadian and U.S. reputation lists—and the criteria that are used to generate them—provides some reassuring testimony on the vitality and values of many businesses. It also shows the manner in which they conduct their operations, and gives us some insights into how companies must perform to gain the kind of stellar reputation necessary to get on the list.

These criteria all have one underlying theme: They reflect in one way or another the extent to which an organization and its managers effectively meet or exceed the needs and expectations of their external constituents. For example, hiring and developing the brightest and most motivated people from the labour market results in high levels of employee talent. Likewise, respecting the needs of shareholders and other investors affects several criteria, including financial soundness, use of corporate assets, and long-term investment value. Says one expert, "We admire companies that cater to their constituents."

Questions for Discussion

1. What is your opinion of the value of the rankings like those discussed? How might the different ways the Canadian and U.S. surveys are conducted influence the results?
2. Do you think the criteria that are used are appropriate? Can you suggest others?
3. Is the ranking something that investors should rely on in buying stock?
4. If you were a top manager and wanted your firm to move up in the rankings, how would you proceed?

MYBUSINESSLAB

To improve your grade, visit the MyBusinessLab website at **www.pearsoned.ca/mybusinesslab**. This online homework and tutorial system allows you to test your understanding and generates a personalized study plan just for you. It provides you with study and practice tools directly related to this chapter's content. MyBusinessLab puts you in control of your own learning!

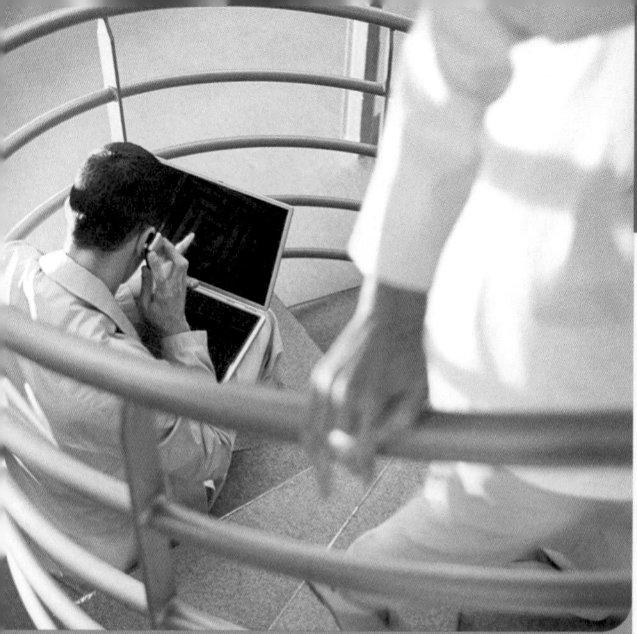

CHAPTER 3

Conducting Business Ethically and Responsibly

After reading this chapter, you should be able to:

1. Explain how individuals develop their personal *codes of ethics* and why ethics are important in the workplace.
2. Distinguish *social responsibility* from *ethics*, identify *organizational stakeholders*, and characterize social consciousness today.
3. Show how the concept of social responsibility applies both to environmental issues and to a firm's relationships with customers, employees, and investors.
4. Identify four general *approaches to social responsibility* and describe the four steps a firm must take to implement a *social responsibility program*.
5. Explain how issues of social responsibility and ethics affect small businesses.

The Price of Bad Behaviour

During the last few years, many business executives have been hit with charges that they made undisclosed loans to shareholders, obstructed justice, engaged in insider trading and tipping, manipulated financial statements, and misled clients and investors. Some of these executives—for example, Garth Drabinsky and Myron Gottlieb (Livent Inc.), Bernie Ebbers (WorldCom), Ken Lay (Enron), Conrad Black (Hollinger International), and Jean Brault (Groupaction Marketing)—received a lot of publicity. Three Canadian banks that were involved in the Enron debacle also received bad press.

Garth Drabinsky and Myron Gottlieb. Livent Inc.—a live theatre company with theatres in Toronto, Vancouver, Chicago, and New York—was started by Drabinsky and Gottlieb. In 1998, questions were raised about Livent's finances by new owners who had bought into the company. Shortly thereafter, Drabinsky and Gottlieb were fired. They were eventually charged with defrauding investors and creditors of about $500 million. Progress in the case has been very slow, and the trial did not start until 2007. Drabinsky and Gottlieb have consistently denied any wrongdoing. In a related development, the Institute of Chartered Accountants of Ontario (ICAO) found three senior Deloitte & Touche LLP auditors guilty of professional misconduct in the Livent case. They could be fined or expelled from the Institute.

Bernie Ebbers. Canadian-born Bernie Ebbers had risen from Alberta milkman and nightclub bouncer to become CEO of WorldCom, one of the largest companies in the U.S. It was alleged that Ebbers conspired with subordinates to "cook the books" when a business downturn occurred. These actions wiped out $100 billion of the company's market value, cost 17 000 people their jobs, and investors lost their life savings. Scott Sullivan, one of Ebbers' subordinates, pled guilty and testified that Ebbers had ordered him to cook the books in order to hit earnings targets. In March 2005, Ebbers was found guilty on nine charges of securities fraud and filing false documents. He was sentenced to 25 years in prison for his role in the collapse of WorldCom Inc.

Ken Lay. The former CEO of Enron was well-known as a "hands-off" manager, and he claimed that he was unaware of the financial manipulations that had been carried out by some of his subordinates, notably Andrew Fastow, the chief financial officer. These manipulations included moving debt "off the balance sheet" to make it look like Enron was in better financial shape than it was. The jury didn't buy Lay's story that he was the victim of his subordinates' misbehaviour, and in 2006 he was convicted of a variety of charges, including conspiracy and securities fraud. His sentencing hearing was scheduled for September 2006, but he died of a heart attack in July 2006.

Conrad Black. In 2005, David Radler, Conrad Black's longtime business partner, pled guilty to his part in a $32 million fraud at Hollinger International where Black was CEO. Radler was given 29 months in jail and a $250 000 fine. He also agreed to cooperate with a criminal investigation of Conrad Black (who became a member of the British House of Lords after renouncing his Canadian citizenship). Radler's guilty plea was not good news for Conrad Black, who was still awaiting trial on charges that he and three associates illegally diverted $84 million out of investors' pockets and into their own. Black denied any wrongdoing and noted that all his actions were approved by the Board of Directors of Hollinger. Prosecutors charged that Black used fraud to obtain board and audit committee approval to make payments to himself, and that he made false statements and omitted facts about the payment to shareholders and regulators. In July 2007, Black was found guilty of three counts of fraud and one count of obstruction of justice.

Jean Brault. In 2002, rumours began circulating that the federal Liberal government had paid millions of dollars to the advertising firm Groupaction Marketing to help raise Canada's profile in Quebec after the 1995 sovereignty referendum. The trouble was no work was ever done. An inquiry resulted in many criminal charges being laid, including six charges of fraud against Jean Brault, who ran Groupaction Marketing. He eventually pled guilty to five of the charges and admitted to paying salaries to Liberal party workers who never did any work. He was sentenced to 30 months in prison.

Canadian banks. The Royal Bank of Canada (RBC), the Toronto-Dominion (TD) bank, and the Canadian Imperial Bank of Commerce (CIBC) were among many defendants in a $25 billion class action suit filed against financial institutions by individuals who lost money when Enron went under in 2001. In 2005, RBC paid $25 million to settle its liability, and the interim CEO at Enron agreed that RBC played only a minor role in Enron's collapse. Also in 2005, CIBC agreed to pay $2.4 *billion* to get out of the Enron Class action lawsuit. That is the biggest payout of any of the financial institutions that were sued (U.S.-based JP Morgan Chase & Co. paid $2.2 billion and Citigroup paid $2 billion). CIBC denied any wrongdoing and said the payment was designed to reduce the uncertainty of future litigation over Enron.

When we consider the examples listed above, we might conclude that the ethical level of business executives has declined in recent years. That's a possibility, but a more likely explanation is that the stock market "bubble" of the late 1990s magnified some already existing human weaknesses, including greed and a tendency to "skate on the edge." Human greed probably hasn't increased in the last few years, but the opportunities to satisfy it have. Another reason is the failure of checks and balances that were supposed to prevent this kind of behaviour. Professionals such as accountants, lawyers, audit committees, government regulators, the press, and securities analysts are supposed to make sure that executives do not do things that are detrimental to shareholders, but critics feel that they often fail to do their job. A third reason is stock options, which may give executives an incentive to behave badly.

The best explanation of unethical executive behaviour is probably a combination of these three reasons. But what does the future hold? Were the excesses of the executives listed above caused by just a "few bad apples," or is the system broken? The view that there are just a "few bad apples" is supported by some statistics. For example, in the U.S. (where much of the high-profile bad behaviour has occurred), the Securities and Exchange Commission (SEC) investigated 570 companies in 2001. That sounds like a lot, but it's only slightly higher than the number investigated in 1994. Another statistic: only about one company in 100 restates its earnings. This suggests that the system needs only a minor fix-up.

The counter view is that there really has been a decline in the general level of ethical behaviour, and that the headline cases are just symptomatic of a very big problem. If we accept this view, it follows that the current legislation is inadequate to deal with the problem, and the only solution is to develop tough new legislation that will control the tendency of executives to behave in an unethical and illegal fashion. ◆

HOW WILL THIS BENEFIT YOU?

There is a growing dilemma in the business world today: the economic imperatives facing managers (real or imagined) versus pressures to function as good citizens. By understanding the material in this chapter, you'll be better able to assess ethical and social responsibility issues that you will face as an employee and as a boss or business owner. It will also help you understand the ethical and social responsibility actions of businesses you deal with as a consumer and as an investor.

In this chapter, we'll look at ethics and social responsibility—what they mean and how they apply to environmental issues and to a firm's relationships with customers, employees, and investors. Along the way, we look at some general approaches to social responsibility, the steps businesses must take to implement social responsibility programs, and how issues of social responsibility and ethics affect small businesses. But first, we begin this chapter by discussing ethics in the workplace—individual, business, and managerial.

ETHICS IN THE WORKPLACE

The situations described in the opening case clearly demonstrate the controversy that often arises when dealing with the issue of ethics in business. **Ethics** are beliefs about what is right and wrong or good and bad. An individual's personal values and morals—and the social context in which they occur—determine whether a particular behaviour is perceived as ethical or unethical. In other words, **ethical behaviour** is behaviour that conforms to individual beliefs and social norms about what is right and good. **Unethical behaviour** is behaviour that individual beliefs and social norms define as wrong and bad. **Business ethics** is a term often used to refer to ethical or unethical behaviours by a manager or employee of an organization.

ethics
Individual standards or moral values regarding what is right and wrong or good and bad.

ethical behaviour
Behaviour that conforms to individual beliefs and social norms about what is right and good.

unethical behaviour
Behaviour that individual beliefs and social norms define as wrong and bad.

business ethics
Ethical or unethical behaviours by a manager or employee of an organization.

Individual Ethics

Explain how individuals develop their personal *codes of ethics* and why ethics are important in the workplace. 1

Because ethics are based on both individual beliefs and social concepts, they vary from person to person, from situation to situation, and from culture to culture. People therefore develop personal codes of ethics reflecting a wide range of attitudes and beliefs. For instance, virtually everyone would agree that if you see someone drop a $20 bill in a store, it would be ethical to return it to the owner. But what if you find $20 and don't know who dropped it? Should you turn it in to the lost-and-found department? Or, since the rightful owner isn't likely to claim it, would it be ethical to just keep it?

Societies generally adopt formal laws that reflect prevailing ethical standards or social norms. For example, because most people regard theft as unethical, we have laws against such behaviour. Unfortunately, applying these laws is sometimes difficult because real-world situations can often be interpreted in different ways, and it isn't always easy to apply statutory standards to real-life behaviour. Consider the case of Samuel Waksal, the former CEO of ImClone, who was convicted of insider trading for tipping off certain investors, including Martha Stewart and members of his own family, about the impending fall of ImClone stock. Stewart was convicted of lying to investigators, but Waksal's daughter, who sold her ImClone stock after getting information from her father, has been treated as an "innocent tippee"—someone who got inside information but didn't think that's what it was at the time.[1]

Unfortunately, the epidemic of business scandals like those described in the opening case show how some managers are willing to take advantage of ethically ambiguous situations. The Business Accountability box describes another situation where there are conflicting views about what is ethical.

Individual Values and Codes

We start to form ethical standards as children in response to our perceptions of the behaviour of parents and other adults. Soon, we enter school where we're influenced by peers, and as we grow into adulthood, experience shapes our lives and contributes to our ethical beliefs and our behaviour. We also develop values and morals that contribute to ethical standards. If you put financial gain at the top of your priority list, you may develop a code of ethics that supports the pursuit of material comfort. If you set family and friends as a priority, you'll no doubt adopt different standards.

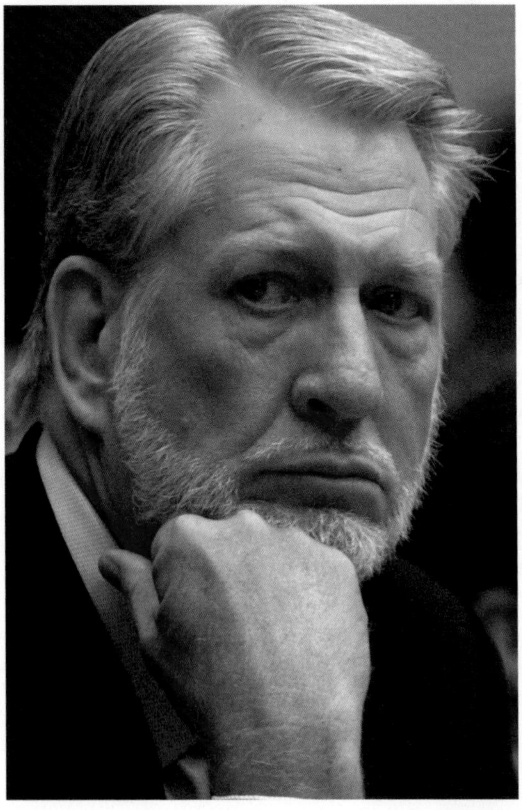

When telecommunications giant WorldCom (now MCI) collapsed amid a record-setting $1 billion bankruptcy in 2003, just about everybody who had anything to do with corporate accounting was arrested. Chief Financial Officer Scott Sullivan pleaded guilty to criminal charges and agreed to testify against his former boss, Canadian-born Bernard Ebbers (pictured here). In 2006, Ebbers was sentenced to 25 years in prison for his role in the collapse.

Because ethics are both personally and culturally defined, differences of opinion can arise as to what is ethical or unethical. For example, many people who would never think of taking a candy bar from a grocery store routinely take home pens and pads of paper from

BUSINESS ACCOUNTABILITY

Crossing the Ethical Line?

In 2005, CIBC World Markets sued 6 former employees after they left the company and started a rival firm, Genuity Capital Markets (a total of 18 people left CIBC for Genuity). While asking for $10 million in damages, CIBC charged that the 6 people (a) planned their new company while they were still on CIBC's payroll, (b) took confidential information with them when they left CIBC, and (c) attempted to steal both top performers and clients from CIBC for the new company. All of this occurred, it is alleged, while the 6 executives were being handsomely paid by CIBC.

The defendants in the lawsuit are David Kassie (formerly CEO of CIBC World Markets), Daniel Daviau (formerly an investment banker at CIBC who specialized in the technology and media sectors), Phil Evershed (former head of mergers and acquisitions at CIBC), Earl Rotman (CIBC World Markets vice-chairman), John Esteireiro (head trader at CIBC), and David Morrison (a top salesman). Evershed, Rotman, and Daviau each received more than $3 million in salary and severance pay from the bank just before they left for Genuity. One of the conditions of their leaving was that they would not try to hire any CIBC employees for 21 months.

In the document it filed with a Toronto court, CIBC provided detailed information from hundreds of pages of e-mails allegedly showing how the 6 former employees had frequently discussed the formation of Genuity while they were still employed at CIBC. It was also alleged that these e-mails listed the names of CIBC employees who were to be recruited for the new company. One other serious allegation has been made by CIBC: that an IT specialist downloaded confidential client information before she left CIBC (the IT specialist claims that she was simply copying disks for her successor, that she didn't give the information to Genuity, and that Genuity is willing to open its computers to support her story).

The founders of Genuity argue that they have done nothing unethical or illegal. One of the key points in their defence is that they didn't break any rules by hiring employees of CIBC to work at Genuity, because these employees had already decided to leave CIBC. Genuity simply provided them with a new place to work.

Some observers think this lawsuit is not so much about Genuity as it is about duty, integrity, honour, and trust. In other words, it's about business ethics. As the leader in the industry, CIBC is not really very concerned about a small new competitor like Genuity being started, but it is concerned about the "slippery" way that it was formed. CIBC also wants to send a message to its remaining employees that CIBC's corporate culture is all about honesty and fair dealing, and that is so important that CIBC will pursue employees (or former employees) who don't act appropriately. CIBC also wants to hold the six former employees to a certain ethical standard because they were paid very well for the work they did.

Others who have analyzed this interesting situation question the quality of the leadership that was evident at CIBC in the year or so before the employee exodus. They ask, for example, what the Board of Directors at CIBC was doing when rumours about the start of Genuity were swirling around Bay Street. They also ask what effect the hiring of Kassie's replacement at CIBC had on employees who did not leave (the defendants claim that once Kassie's replacement was announced, Genuity received many applications from CIBC employees).

It is not clear that this dispute will ever actually be heard in court because both sides have much to lose. CIBC has the financial resources to support an expensive court battle, but if it loses it will not be able to make its point about the importance of ethical behaviour. Genuity, on the other hand, is a new company that needs to establish a reputation of integrity, and a nasty court fight isn't going to do much to help the company achieve that goal.

In the past, lawsuits like this one usually did not result in a full trial, but were settled with a small award (for example, the loser made a contribution to charity). When a full trial does happen, the usual ruling is that individuals have the right to work where they want, but that taking data or enticing a group to leave are not acceptable behaviours. Since CIBC alleged that the latter two things occurred, a full trial would be very interesting. The lawsuit was still unresolved in mid-2007.

QUESTIONS FOR DISCUSSION

1. Do you think it was unethical for CIBC employees to plan the formation of Genuity while they were working for CIBC? Explain your reasoning.
2. Is CIBC right in trying to hold these employees accountable for their actions?

their offices. Other people who view themselves as law abiding citizens have no qualms about using radar detectors to avoid speeding tickets. In each of the situations, people will choose different sides of the issue and argue that their actions are ethical.

Managerial Ethics

Managerial ethics are the standards of behaviour that guide individual managers in their work.[2] Although your ethics can affect your work in any number of ways, it's helpful to classify them in terms of three broad categories.

managerial ethics Standards of behaviour that guide individual managers in their work.

Behaviour Toward Employees

This category covers such matters as hiring and firing, wages and working conditions, and privacy and respect. Ethical and legal guidelines emphasize that hiring and firing decisions should be based solely on ability to perform a job. A manager who discriminates against any ethnic minority in hiring exhibits both unethical and illegal behaviour. But what about the manager who hires a friend or relative when someone else might be more qualified? In Canada, such decisions may not be illegal but may be seen as unethical. In some other countries, however, such a decision may be seen as not only ethical, but as desirable because it helps a friend.

Wages and working conditions, though regulated by law, are also areas for ethical controversy. Consider a manager who pays an employee less than the employee deserves because the manager knows that the employee can't afford to quit or risk his job by complaining. While some people will see this behaviour as unethical, others will see it as simply smart business. Other cases are more clear-cut. For example, Enron managers encouraged employees to invest their retirement funds in company stock and then, when financial problems began to surface, refused to permit them to sell the stock (even though top officials of the company were allowed to sell their stock).

Behaviour Toward the Organization

Ethical issues also arise from employee behaviour toward their employer, especially in such areas as conflict of interest, confidentiality, and honesty. A *conflict of interest* occurs when an activity may benefit the individual to the detriment of his or her employer. Most companies, for example, have policies that forbid company buyers from accepting gifts from suppliers. Businesses in highly competitive industries—software and fashion apparel, for example—have safeguards against designers selling company secrets to competitors. Relatively common problems in the general area of honesty include such behaviour as stealing supplies, padding expense accounts, and using a business phone to make personal long-distance calls. Most employees are honest, but most organizations are nevertheless vigilant.

Behaviour Toward Other Economic Agents

Ethics also comes into play in the relationship between the firm and its customers, competitors, stockholders, suppliers, dealers, and unions. In dealing with such agents, there is room for ethical ambiguity in just about every activity—advertising, financial disclosure, ordering and purchasing, bargaining and negotiation, and other business relationships. For example, when pharmaceutical companies are criticized for the high prices of their drugs, they say that high prices are needed to cover the costs of research and development programs to develop new drugs. To some observers, the solution to such problems is obvious: Find the right balance between reasonable pricing and *price gouging* (responding to increased demand with overly steep price increases). But like so many questions involving ethics, there are significant differences of opinion about what the proper balance is.[3]

Another area of concern is competitive espionage. In 2004, Air Canada sued WestJet for $220 million, claiming that a WestJet executive had electronically snooped on Air Canada's confidential reservation database, which contained important competitive information that would be beneficial to WestJet. WestJet then filed a $30 million counter-suit, claiming that Air Canada was trying to destroy WestJet's reputation. It also claimed that Air Canada had "set up" WestJet by allowing one of WestJet's executives to get into the supposedly confidential Air Canada database. WestJet also charged that Air Canada had hired a firm to steal the garbage of a WestJet executive in the hopes of finding important financial information about WestJet.[4] The resolution of this dispute is described in Video Case I-2 on p. 150.

It is difficult to deal with ethical problems because there is much global variation in business practices. In many countries, bribes are a normal part of doing business. German companies, for example, were formerly allowed to write off bribes as "expenses," but in 2007—after corruption laws had been changed—several executives of Siemens AG were arrested and charged with bribing foreign officials in order to obtain business.[5] In Canada and the U.S., bribes are seen as unethical and illegal. In 2006, the Gemological Institute of America (GIA) fired several employees after they accepted bribes from diamond dealers. In return for the bribes, the GIA employees rated the dealers' diamonds higher than they should have been, and this allowed the dealers to sell them for a much higher price. The GIA also banned two groups of dealers from having their diamonds rated by the GIA.[6]

Assessing Ethical Behaviour

Distinguishing ethical behaviour from unethical behaviour is a complex and often contentious process that leads to major differences of opinion.[7] So, how does one go about deciding whether a particular action or decision is ethical? A three-step model has been suggested as a way of systematically applying ethical judgments to situations that may arise during the course of business activities.

1. Gather the relevant factual information.
2. Determine the most appropriate moral values.
3. Make an ethical judgment based on the rightness or wrongness of the proposed activity or policy.

Let's apply this three-step process to a common dilemma faced by managers—expense accounts. Companies routinely provide managers with accounts to cover work-related expenses when they are travelling on company business and/or entertaining clients for business purposes. Common examples of such expenses include hotel bills, meals, rental cars or taxis, and so forth. Employees are expected to claim only those expenses that are accurate and work-related. For example, if a manager takes a client to dinner while travelling on business and spends $100, submitting a receipt for that dinner to be reimbursed for $100 is clearly accurate and appropriate. Suppose, however, that the manager then has a $100 dinner the next night in that same city with a good friend for purely social purposes and submits that receipt as well. Is that ethical?

We can assess this situation using four different ethical norms:

Utility: Does a particular act optimize what is best for those who are affected by it?
Rights: Does it respect the rights of the individuals involved?

Justice: Is it consistent with what we regard to be fair?
Caring: Is it consistent with people's responsibilities to each other?

Now, let's return to the case of the inflated expense account issue. The *utility* norm would acknowledge that the manager benefits from padding an expense account, but co-workers and owners do not. Likewise, inflating an expense account does not respect the *rights* of others. It is also *unfair* and compromises the manager's responsibilities to others. This particular act, then, appears to be clearly unethical.

But suppose that the manager happens to lose the receipt for the legitimate dinner but does not lose the receipt for the social dinner. Some people will argue that it is acceptable to submit the illegitimate receipt because the manager is only doing so to be reimbursed for what he or she is entitled to. Others, however, will argue that submitting the other receipt is wrong under any circumstances. We won't pretend to arbitrate the case. We simply make the point that changes in the factual information about the case can make ethical issues more or less clear-cut.

Company Practices and Business Ethics

Organizations try to promote ethical behaviour and discourage unethical behaviour in numerous ways. The highly publicized unethical and illegal activities by both managers and employees in recent years have motivated many firms to take additional steps to encourage ethical behaviour in the workplace. Many, for example, establish codes of conduct and develop clear ethical positions on how the firm and its employees will conduct their business.

The single most effective step a company can take is for top management to take decisive action to demonstrate ethical commitment. A classic illustration of this occurred in 1982, when Johnson & Johnson (J&J) discovered that capsules of the company's Tylenol pain reliever had been laced with cyanide. J&J quickly recalled all Tylenol bottles still on retailers' shelves and then went public with candid information throughout the crisis. Both the firm and the brand bounced back much more quickly than most observers had thought possible. More recently, when some Belgian schoolchildren became ill after drinking Coke, the company quickly determined what the problem was, and Coke's CEO made a public apology. The furor died down almost immediately.[8] Two of the most common approaches for formalizing ethical commitment are *adopting written codes* and *instituting ethics programs*.

Adopting Written Codes

Many companies, including Johnson & Johnson, McDonald's, Starbucks, and Dell Computer, have adopted written codes of ethics that formally acknowledge their intent to do business in an ethical manner.

Most codes of ethics are designed to perform one or more of four functions:

1. They increase public confidence in a firm or its industry.
2. They may help stem the tide of government regulation.
3. They improve internal operations by providing consistent standards of both ethical and legal conduct.
4. They help managers respond to problems that arise as a result of unethical or illegal behaviour.

About two-thirds of Canada's largest corporations have codes of ethics (90 percent of large U.S. firms do). More and more regulatory and

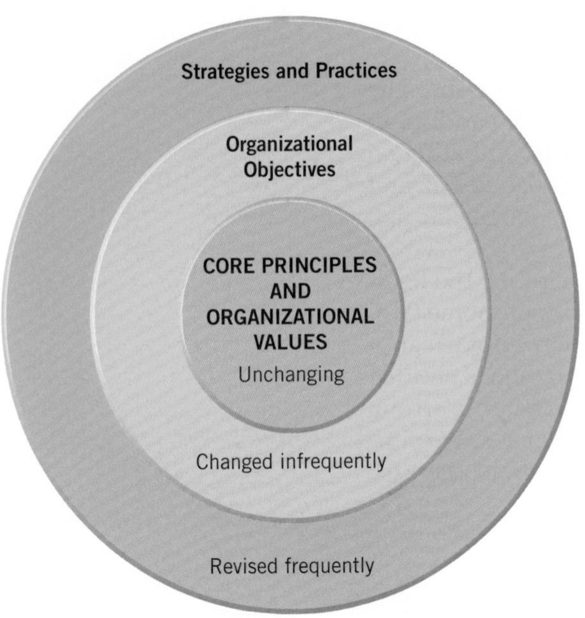

Figure 3.1 Core principles and organization values.

professional associations in Canada are recommending that corporations adopt codes of ethics. The Canada Deposit Insurance Corp., for example, requires that all deposit-taking institutions have a code of conduct that is periodically reviewed and ratified by the board of directors. The Canadian Competition Bureau, the Canadian Institute of Chartered Accountants, and the Ontario Human Rights Commission are all pushing for the adoption of codes of ethics by corporations.[9] Many Canadian and U.S. firms are also adding a position called "Ethics Director" or "Ethics Officer."

Figure 3.1 illustrates the essential role that corporate ethics and values should play in corporate policy. You can use it to see how ethics statements might be structured most effectively. Basically, it suggests that although business strategies and practices can change frequently and business objectives may change occasionally, an organization's core principles and values should remain steadfast. Hewlett-Packard, for example, has had the same written code of ethics, called *The HP Way*, for nearly 50 years, and it has served the firm well. The essential elements of *The HP Way* are as follows:

We have trust and respect for individuals.
We focus on a high level of achievement and contribution.
We conduct our business with uncompromising integrity.
We achieve our common objectives through teamwork.
We encourage flexibility and innovation.

Instituting Ethics Programs

Can business ethics be "taught," either in the workplace or in schools? While business schools have become important players in the debate about ethics education, most analysts agree that companies must take the chief responsibility for educating employees. In fact, more and more firms are doing so. Imperial Oil, for example, conducts workshops for employees that emphasize ethical concerns. The purpose of these workshops is to help employees put Imperial's ethics statement into practice.

But some firms struggle with ethical dilemmas, particularly in international business situations. Nike, for example, manufactures most of its products overseas in order to boost profitability. A scathing report investigating Nike's manufacturing partners in Asia called it just short of slave labour. Nike responded to the report by acknowledging its mistakes and made a commitment to improve working conditions. Nike plants in Asia, for example, no longer force employees to work on Sundays. Wages have been increased, and supervisors are forbidden to use the extreme punishments that were formerly doled out.[10]

SOCIAL RESPONSIBILITY

social responsibility
A business's collective code of ethical behaviour toward the environment, its customers, its employees, and its investors.

organizational stakeholders
Groups, individuals, and organizations that are directly affected by the practices of an organization and that therefore have a stake in its performance.

Social responsibility refers to the way in which a business tries to balance its commitments to the stakeholders in its environment. **Organizational stakeholders** are those groups, individuals, and organizations that are directly affected by the practices of an organization and that therefore have a stake in its performance. Major stakeholders include employees, investors, suppliers, customers, and the local community in which the company operates.

There is a debate about which of these stakeholders should be given the most attention. One view, often called *managerial capitalism*, is held by Nobel laureate Milton Friedman, who says that a company's only social responsibility is to make as much money as possible for its shareholders, as long as it doesn't break any laws in doing so. Friedman also says that a free society is undermined when company managers accept any social responsibility other than making as much money as possible.[11]

Distinguish *social responsibility* from *ethics*, identify *organizational stakeholders*, and characterize social consciousness today. 2

An opposing view is that companies must be responsible to various stakeholders, including *customers, employees, investors, suppliers,* and the *local communities* in which they do business. Some of these stakeholders may be particularly relevant or important to the organization and so it will pay particular attention to their needs and expectations. Whatever the relative emphasis on the various stakeholders, this view says that businesses should not just pursue profit to the exclusion of all else.

Contemporary Social Consciousness

Views about social responsibility have changed dramatically over time, generally in the direction of higher social responsibility expectations of business. The late nineteenth century was characterized by the entrepreneurial spirit and the laissez-faire philosophy. During this era of labour strife and predatory business practices, both individual citizens and the government became concerned about uncontrolled business activity. This concern was translated into laws regulating basic business practices.

During the Great Depression of the 1930s, many people blamed the failure of businesses and banks and the widespread loss of jobs on a general climate of business greed and lack of restraint. Out of the economic turmoil emerged new laws that described an increased expectation that business should protect and enhance the general welfare of society.

During the social unrest of the 1960s and 1970s, business was often characterized as a negative social force. Eventually, increased activism prompted additional government regulation in a variety of areas. Health warnings, for example, were placed on cigarettes, and stricter environmental protection laws were enacted.

Social consciousness and views toward social responsibility continue to evolve in the twenty-first century. Today's attitudes favour a greater social role for business, and greater attention to multiple stakeholders, not simply shareholders. An increased awareness of the global economy and heightened campaigning on the part of environmentalists and other activists have combined to make many businesses more sensitive to various social responsibilities, not simply the pursuit of profit. For example, retailers such as Sears have policies against selling handguns and other weapons, and toy retailer Toys "R" Us refuses to sell toy guns that look too realistic. Electrolux, a Swedish appliance maker, has developed a line of water-efficient washing machines and a solar-powered lawnmower.

Sometimes situations are so complex that it is difficult for companies to determine what is socially responsible. In the 1970s, Nestlé and other makers of infant formula were trying to market their products in developing countries. Problems developed because the formula sometimes was not used properly by mothers, and their babies suffered. Activists organized a boycott of Nestlé, and the United Nations began aggressively promoting breastfeeding. But then the AIDS crisis developed, and it was discovered that some nursing mothers who had AIDS were transmitting the virus to their infants through their milk. Infant formula was then suggested as a possible way to avoid this problem. Suspicion of infant formula makers like Nestlé remains strong, even though the companies are offering to donate infant formula for free.[12]

ENTREPRENEURSHIP AND NEW VENTURES

Mountain Equipment Co-Op

When it comes to corporate social responsibility (CSR), one notable Canadian trailblazer is Mountain Equipment Co-op (MEC). MEC was formed in 1971 by four students from the University of British Columbia whose vision was to "inspire excellence in products and services, passion for wilderness experiences, leadership for a just world, and action for a healthy planet." The company's actions speak louder than words.

MEC's commitment to the environment is demonstrated in many aspects of its business, including the name of its CSR program: Social and Environmental Responsibility. The program's mandate ensures that environmental and social issues are weighed equally.

As a co-operative, MEC does not issue investment shares. Only MEC members—the customers—are permitted to own shares in the company, which are valued at five dollars apiece. Because MEC does not issue investment shares, maximizing shareholder wealth is not its exclusive focus. While MEC members may not see a direct financial return on their shares, in effect, they pass the returns on to the communities and groups that benefit from MEC's altruistic activities.

Some of MEC's revenues each year are allocated to sustainable community development projects, typically through donations for charitable or educational purposes. The MEC Endowment Fund for the Environment—MEC's own registered charity—was created in 1993. Each year, 0.4 percent of the previous year's sales are contributed to MEC's Environment Fund. At first glace, this may not seem like a substantial amount, but that 0.4 percent translates into an average of $750 000 per year in contributions to environmental conservation and wilderness protection projects, research, and education. The endowment fund, which accepts tax deductible donations, is currently valued at $1.2 million and has historically been used to support land acquisition projects.

But to truly practise social and environmental responsibility, MEC recognizes that it must do more than provide money to environmental organizations. Product manufacturers must adhere to a strict set of guidelines established to ensure that the products sold by MEC are manufactured in safe and healthy workplaces where human and civil rights are respected.

The co-op is even more scrupulous about MEC-brand products (58 percent of which are manufactured in Canada), which comprise approximately 60 percent of sales. In addition to its own Supply Team Evaluation Process, MEC uses third-party independent audits to ensure that the suppliers of MEC-brand products avoid the use of child and forced labour, and that workers are treated with respect and dignity and are not subjected to harassment, discrimination, or abuse. Workers must be allowed to join unions and bargain collectively, and they must be paid fairly and directly. Safe and healthy work environments must comply with local health and safety laws and regulations. Suppliers of MEC-brand products are also required to implement and maintain systems to minimize negative impacts of manufacturing and packaging on the environment and to ensure that waste is disposed of in an environmentally responsible manner.

For the past five years, MEC has been greening its buildings by making design, materials, and construction decisions based on environmental considerations. To be considered green by MEC's standards, a building must be built and sustained by resources available within its immediate area. And it should enhance (or at least not detract from) its natural environment. MEC building designers scrutinize every building element and make choices based on a number of criteria, including embodied energy and pollution content, energy efficiency and recycling potential. Some of the more tangible innovations found in MEC's green buildings include the use of geothermal energy heat pumps in Montreal, a demonstration straw-bale wall in Ottawa, and composting toilets in Winnipeg.

When construction on MEC's Winnipeg store was completed in 2002, it became the second retail building in Canada to meet the national C2000 Green Building Standard, second only to MEC's Ottawa location.

AREAS OF SOCIAL RESPONSIBILITY

3 Show how the concept of social responsibility applies both to environmental issues and to a firm's relationships with customers, employees, and investors.

In defining their sense of social responsibility, most firms must determine their social responsibility in four areas: the environment, customers, employees, and investors.

Responsibility Toward the Environment

Controlling **pollution**—the release of harmful substances into the environment—is a significant challenge for contemporary business. Although noise pollution is attracting increased concern, air pollution, water pollution, and land pollution are the subjects of most anti-pollution efforts by business and governments.[13]

pollution
The introduction of harmful substances into the environment.

Air Pollution

Air pollution results when a combination of factors lowers air quality. Large amounts of chemicals such as the carbon monoxide emitted by automobiles contribute to air pollution. So does smoke and other chemicals emitted by manufacturing plants. The rapid industrialization of developing countries has led to increased concerns about air pollution. In China, for example, 100 coal-fired power plants are being built each year, and each plant uses 1.3 million tonnes of coal and gives off 3.4 million tonnes of carbon dioxide. Only 5 percent of the coal-fired power plants in China are equipped with pollution control equipment.[14]

air pollution
Pollution that occurs when a combination of factors lowers air quality.

Figure 3.2 shows world atmospheric carbon dioxide levels for the period between 1750 and 2000, and offers three possible scenarios for future levels under different sets of conditions. The three projections—lowest, middle, highest—were developed by the Intergovernmental Panel on Climate Change, which calculated likely changes in the atmosphere during this century if no efforts were made to reduce so-called *greenhouse emissions*—waste industrial gases that trap heat in the atmosphere. The criteria for estimating changes are population, economic growth, energy supplies, and technologies: The less pressure exerted by these conditions, the less the increase in CO_2 levels. Energy supplies are measured in *exajoules*—roughly the annual energy consumption of a large metropolitan area like New York or London.

Under the lowest, or best-case, scenario, by 2100 the population would only grow to 6.4 billion people, economic growth would be no more than 1.2 to 2.0 percent a year, and energy supplies would require only 8000 exajoules of conventional oil. However, under the highest, or worst-case, scenario, the population would increase to 11.3 billion people, annual economic growth would be between 3.0 and 3.5 percent, and energy supplies would require as much as 18 400 exajoules of conventional oil.

Why would a Western environmental group team up with a domestic logging company to help local villagers log a forest in a remote area of Indonesia? For one thing, the villagers are very poor. For another, the Nature Conservancy believes that it can enforce sustainable practices if the logger, Sumalindo Lestari Jaya, co-operates. The group also thinks that it can trust Sumalindo because it's already been successful in applying pressure to Western retailers like Home Depot and IKEA, who buy wood and paper from the Indonesian supplier.

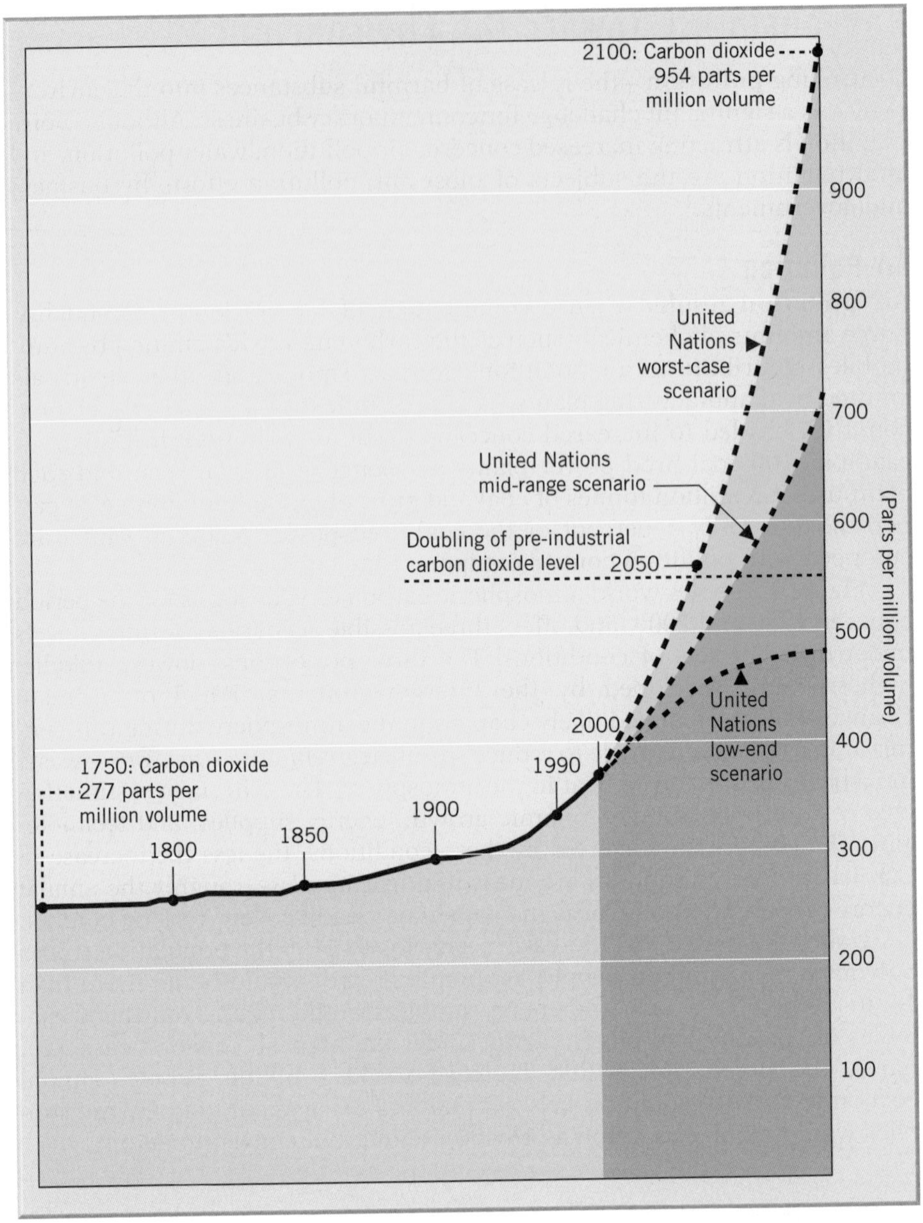

Figure 3.2 CO_2 emissions, past and future.

global warming
An increase in the earth's average temperature.

There is currently a great deal of interest in **global warming**—an increase in the earth's average temperature. Most everyone agrees that global warming is happening, but there is debate about what is causing it. Many scientists are convinced that carbon dioxide emissions are the culprit, but many other scientists argue that climate variation is simply part of the earth's natural cycle and is caused by natural factors. For example, one study of sediments in the fjords of British Columbia showed that climate has varied a great deal over the last 10 000 years, and that climate variation was closely related to sunspot activity, but not to variations in the amount of carbon dioxide.[15] Reid Bryson, the world's most cited climatologist, says that there is no credible proof that global warming is caused by human activity.[16]

There *is* general agreement that global warming will benefit some people and hurt others. In normally icy Greenland, for example, the warming climate has resulted in a longer growing season for grain and vegetables, and farmers are planning to start raising cattle because of the increased forage available in the summertime. In the Peruvian Andes, farmers weren't traditionally able to cultivate crops above the 4300-metre level because of the cold, but they are now planting large potato fields above 4500 metres. But the same process that is warming Greenland and the high Andes is melting the earth's glaciers, and the water released may eventually raise sea levels to the point that many coastal cities around the world would be flooded. Even in Greenland there is a downside to global warming: the traditional lifestyle of Inuit hunters is being disrupted by the thinning ice.[17]

The Kyoto Summit in 1997 was an attempt by various governments to reach an agreement on ways to reduce the threat of pollution. Australia is the world's largest greenhouse gas emitter per capita, contributing 7.3 percent of the world's total. The U.S. (at 6.5 percent) and Canada (at 6.4 percent) are close behind. Alberta is responsible for about 30 percent of Canada's total greenhouse gas emissions, and the oil sands development projects are a big reason.[18] Canada is the only one of the three leading emitters that signed the Protocol, but in 2006, the Conservative government said Canada would not be able to meet the targets for reducing pollution, and that it would continue with the Protocol only if the targets were renegotiated.[19]

Some people have suggested that wind power would be a good way to reduce air pollution. Canada is becoming a world leader in this form of power, and approximately $18 billion will be invested in wind power by 2015.[20] It is possible that 5 percent of Canada's energy needs will be supplied by wind power by 2015. However, experts note that if more than 10 percent of our power needs are supplied by wind power, there will be power interruptions if the wind fails because other forms of power will not be able to immediately cover the shortfall.[21]

Water Pollution

For many years, businesses and municipalities simply dumped their waste into rivers, streams, and lakes with little regard for the effects. Thanks to new legislation and increased awareness on the part of businesses, water quality is improving in many areas. Millar Western Pulp Ltd. built Canada's first zero-discharge pulp mill at Meadow Lake, Saskatchewan. There is no discharge pipe to the river, no dioxin-forming chlorine, and next to no residue. Also, Dow Chemical built a plant at Fort Saskatchewan that will not dump any pollutants into the nearby river.[22]

Land Pollution

Toxic wastes are dangerous chemical and/or radioactive byproducts of various manufacturing processes. In 1998, five million cubic litres of toxic waste escaped from a holding pond at a zinc mine in Spain that was operated by the Canadian mining firm Boliden Ltd. Thousands of hectares of agricultural land were contaminated.[23] Toxic waste spills like this cause destruction of fish, wildlife, and agricultural land.

toxic waste
Pollution resulting from the emission of chemical and/or radioactive byproducts of various manufacturing processes into the air, water, or land.

Changes in forestry practices, limits on certain types of mining, and new forms of solid waste disposal are all attempts to address this issue. A whole new industry—**recycling**—has developed as part of increased consciousness about land pollution. Plant and animal waste can be recycled to produce energy; this is referred to as **biomass**. Waste materials like sawdust, manure, and sludge are increasingly being turned into useful products. Ensyn Corp., for example, converts sawdust into liquid fuel by blasting wood waste with a sand-like substance that is heated. What's left is bio-oil.[24]

recycling
The reconversion of waste materials into useful products.

biomass
Plant and animal waste used to produce energy.

Canadian businesses are now routinely reducing various forms of pollution. However, the road to environmental purity is not easy. Under the Canadian and Ontario Environmental Protection Acts, pollution liability for a business firm can run as high as $2 million per day. To avoid such fines, companies must prove that they showed diligence in avoiding an environmental disaster such as an oil or gasoline spill.[25] The Environmental

Choice program, sponsored by the federal government, licenses products that meet environmental standards set by the Canadian Standards Association. Firms whose products meet these standards can put the logo—three doves intertwined to form a maple leaf—on their products.[26]

An interesting problem that highlights some of the complexities in both waste disposal and recycling involves wooden pallets—those splintery wooden platforms used to store and transport consumer goods. Pallets are popular because they provide an efficient method for stacking and moving large quantities of smaller items. Pallets of merchandise can be easily and efficiently moved from factories to trucks to retail stores. Pallets are very recyclable, but since the cost of new ones is so low, many companies just toss used ones aside and get new ones. Many landfills refuse to take pallets, and others assess surcharges for recycling them. Ironically, some environmentalists argue that abandoned pallets actually serve a useful purpose because, in urban areas, they often become refuges for animals such as raccoons and abandoned pets.[27]

Canadian firms that do business abroad are increasingly being confronted with environmental issues. In many cases, there is opposition to a project by local residents because they fear that some sort of pollution will result. For example, Calgary-based TVI Pacific Inc.'s planned open-pit mine and cyanide processing plant in the Philippines led to violent clashes between the company and the Subanon people. In New Caledonia, indigenous people—who were worried about the environmental impact of a proposed Inco nickel mine—stormed the site and stole millions of dollars of equipment.[28]

Responsibility Toward Customers

There are three key areas that are currently in the news regarding the social responsibility of business toward customers: consumer rights, pricing practices, and ethics in advertising.

Consumer Rights

consumerism
A social movement that seeks to protect and expand the rights of consumers in their dealings with businesses.

Consumerism is a movement dedicated to protecting the rights of consumers in their dealings with businesses. Consumers have the following rights:

1. *The right to safe products*. For example, when you buy a new paint sprayer, it must be safe to use for spraying paint. It must come with instructions on how to use it, and it must have been properly tested by its manufacturer.
2. *The right to be informed about all relevant aspects of a product*. Food products must list their ingredients, clothing must be labelled with information about its proper care, and banks must tell you exactly how much interest you are paying on a loan.
3. *The right to be heard*. Retailers like Kmart offer a money-back guarantee if consumers aren't satisfied, and Procter & Gamble puts a toll-free number on many of its products that consumers can call if they have questions or complaints.
4. *The right to choose what they buy*. Central to this right is free and open competition among companies. In times past, companies divided up a market so that firms did not have to truly compete against each other. Such practices are illegal today and any attempts by businesses to block competition can result in fines or other penalties.
5. *The right to be educated about purchases*. All prescription drugs now come with detailed information regarding dosage, possible side effects, and potential interactions with other medications.

6. *The right to courteous service.* This right is hard to legislate, but as consumers become increasingly knowledgeable, they're more willing to complain about bad service. Consumer hotlines can also be used to voice service-related issues.

Unfair Pricing

Collusion among companies—getting together to "fix" prices—is against the law. Polar Plastic Ltd. of Montreal pled guilty to conspiring to fix prices of disposable cups, glasses, and cutlery in the U.S. market. Although secret meetings and phone conversations took place between executives of competing companies as they tried to fix prices, the conspiracy was not successful.[29]

collusion
An illegal agreement among companies in an industry to "fix" prices for their products.

Pricing fraud is another issue. The U.S. Justice Department is investigating 150 cases of pricing fraud by some of the world's biggest drug companies. The main allegation is that drug companies inflate prices of the drugs they sell to government-paid programs. In 2003 and 2004, several drug companies paid the following penalties: Pfizer ($430 million), Schering-Plough ($345 million), Bayer ($257 million), and GlaxoSmithKline ($88 million). The new charges may mean that up to $1 billion in fines will eventually be levied.[30]

Under some circumstances, firms can also come under attack for *price gouging*—responding to increased demand with steep price increases. For example, when DaimlerChrysler launched its PT Cruiser, demand for the vehicles was so strong that some dealers sold them only to customers willing to pay thousands of dollars over sticker prices. Some Ford dealers adopted a similar practice when the new Thunderbird was launched. As we saw in Chapter 1, this illustrates what can happen when there is a shortage of a product.

Ethics in Advertising

There are several ethical issues in advertising, including truth-in-advertising claims, the advertising of counterfeit brands, the use of stealth advertising, and advertising that is morally objectionable.

Truth-in-advertising. Truth-in-advertising has long been regulated in Canada, but an increased emphasis on truth-in-advertising is now becoming more noticeable on the international scene. In July 2005, for example, Chinese government officials investigated Procter & Gamble's claim that its Pantene shampoo made hair "10 times stronger." A few months earlier, P&G paid a $24 000 fine after one consumer complained that SK-II Skin Cream was not the "miracle water" it claimed to be and that it did not make her skin "look 12 years younger in 28 days."[31]

Advertising of counterfeit brands. Another ethical issue involves the advertising and sale of counterfeit brand names. Canadians tourists who visit New York often go to booths on Canal Street, which is famous for the "bargains" that can be had on supposedly name-brand items like Cartier, Panerai, Vacheron, Mount Blanc, and Vuitton. Many of the items being sold are counterfeit, although it can be very

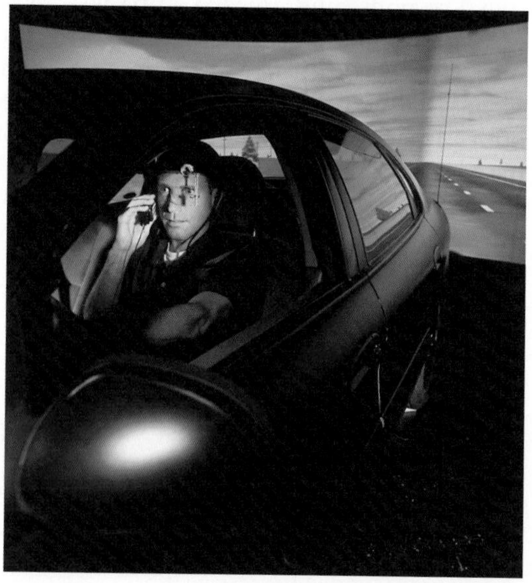

Of all roadway accidents, 25 percent are distraction-related, and the biggest distractions for motorists are handheld gadgets like cellphones and pagers. In fulfilling their responsibility to consumers, some companies are conducting tests that yield important data about roadway accidents. Ford Motor Co., for example, has a Virtual Test Track Experiment simulator that determines how often drivers get distracted. Under normal circumstances, an adult driver will miss about 3 percent of the simulated "events" (like an ice patch or a deer on the road) that Ford contrives for a virtual road trip. If they're on the cellphone, they'll miss about 14 percent. Teenagers miss a scary 54 percent of the events.

hard to tell the difference between these "knockoffs" and the genuine article. A fake Cartier Roadster watch, for example, can be bought on Canal Street for $45 (U.S.), while a real one costs about $3400 (U.S.). Naturally, legitimate manufacturers of these high-end products are trying to stamp out this counterfeit trade in their products.[32]

China is the source of many counterfeit products. For example, knockoffs of Suzuki motorcycles hit the market just a few weeks after the genuine product became available. These were sold to customers as the real thing, but they had not been subjected to the rigorous quality control of real Suzuki motorcycles. Robert Kwauk, a Beijing lawyer, says that the idea of producing knockoffs is tolerated much more in the Chinese culture than it is in Western culture.[33] North Korea has become one of the leading counterfeiters of name brand cigarettes like Marlboros.[34]

stealth (undercover) advertising Companies paying individuals to extol the virtues of their products without disclosing that they are paid to do so.

Stealth (undercover) advertising. A variation of viral marketing that we discussed in Chapter 2, **stealth (or undercover) advertising** involves companies paying individuals to extol the virtues of their products to other individuals. For example, one advertising agency hired models to pose as "tourists." These models asked real tourists to take their picture with a new Sony Ericsson camera cell phone. The models then talked up the advantages of the new product to the unsuspecting real tourists. The ethics of this are questionable when the paid individuals do not reveal that they are being paid by a company, so the recipient of the advertising is not aware that it is advertising. Commercial Alert, a U.S.-based consumer protection group, wants a government investigation of these undercover marketing tactics.[35]

Morally objectionable advertising. A final ethical issue concerns advertising that consumers consider morally objectionable. Benetton, for example, aired a series of commercials featuring inmates on death row. The ads, dubbed "We, on Death Row," prompted such an outcry that Sears dropped the Benetton USA clothing line.[36] Other ads receiving criticism include Victoria's Secret models in skimpy underwear, and campaigns by tobacco and alcohol companies that allegedly target young people.

Responsibility Toward Employees

In Chapter 8, we will describe the human-resource management activities essential to a smoothly functioning business. These same activities—recruiting, hiring, training, promoting, and compensating—are also the basis for social responsibility toward employees. A company that provides its employees with equal opportunities for rewards and advancement without regard to race, sex, or other irrelevant factors is meeting its social responsibilities. Firms that accept this responsibility make sure that the workplace is safe, both physically and emotionally. They would no more tolerate an abusive manager or one who sexually harasses employees than they would a gas leak.

Some progressive companies go well beyond these legal requirements, hiring and training the so-called hard-core unemployed (people with little education and training and a history of unemployment) and those who have disabilities. The Bank of Montreal, for example, sponsors a community college skills upgrading course for individuals with hearing impairments. The Royal Bank provides managers with discrimination awareness training. Rogers Communication provides individuals with mobility restrictions with telephone and customer-service job opportunities.[37]

Business firms also have a responsibility to respect the privacy of their employees. While nearly everyone agrees that companies have the right to exercise some level of control over their employees, there is great controversy about exactly how much is acceptable in areas like drug testing and computer monitoring. When the Canadian National Railway instituted drug testing for train, brake, and yard employees, 12 percent failed. Trucking companies have found that nearly one-third of truckers who had an accident were on drugs.[38]

Whistle-Blowers

Respecting employees as people also means respecting their behaviour as ethically responsible individuals. Employees who discover that their company has been engaging in practices that are illegal, unethical, and/or socially irresponsible should be able to report the problem to higher-level management and be confident that managers will stop the questionable practices. If no one in the organization will take action, the employee might decide to inform a regulatory agency or perhaps the media.

At this point, the person becomes a **whistle-blower**—an employee who discovers and tries to put an end to a company's unethical, illegal, and/or socially irresponsible actions by publicizing them.[39] The Al Pacino–Russell Crowe movie *The Insider* featured the story of a tobacco-industry whistle-blower named Jeffrey Wigand, who was fired when he made his accusations public. Wigand says, "I went from making $300 000 a year, plus stock options, plus, plus, plus—to making $30 000. Yes, there is a price I've paid."[40]

whistle-blower
An individual who calls attention to an unethical, illegal, and/or socially irresponsible practice on the part of a business or other organization.

Melvin Crothers, who worked in the marketing department at WestJet, has also paid a price for his whistle-blowing. In 2003, he discovered that a fellow WestJet employee was accessing a restricted Air Canada website in order to obtain data about Air Canada's "load factor" (the proportion of seats filled) on certain flights. He felt that this was unethical, so he tried to talk to WestJet president Clive Beddoe and tell him what was going on. Beddoe was out of town, so Crothers called a former WestJet president who was heading up an Air Canada discount airline. The conversation led to Air Canada discovering what WestJet was up to, and before long, Air Canada filed a lawsuit against WestJet. Crothers resigned from WestJet four days later.[41] More details about this situation are provided in Video Case I-2 at the end of Part I of the text.

Responsibility Toward Investors

It may sound odd to say that a firm can be irresponsible toward investors, since investors are the owners of the company. But if the managers of a firm abuse its financial resources, the ultimate losers are the owners, since they do not receive the earnings, dividends, or capital appreciation due them. Managers can act irresponsibly in several ways.

Improper Financial Management

Occasionally, organizations are guilty of financial mismanagement. In other cases, executives pay themselves large salaries and spend huge amounts of company money for their own personal comfort. Creditors can do nothing, and even stockholders have few viable options. Trying to force a management changeover is not only difficult, but it can drive down the price of the stock, further penalizing stockholders.

Cheque Kiting

Cheque kiting involves writing a cheque from one account, depositing it in a second account, and then immediately spending money from the second account while the money from the first account is still in transit. A cheque from the second account can also be used to replenish the money in the first account, and the process starts all over again. This practice obviously benefits the person doing the cheque kiting, but is irresponsible because it involves using other peoples' money without paying for it.

cheque kiting
The illegal practice of writing cheques against money that has not yet arrived at the bank on which the cheque has been written, relying on that money arriving before the cheque clears.

Insider Trading

insider trading
The use of confidential information to gain from the purchase or sale of stock.

Insider trading occurs when someone uses confidential information to gain from the purchase or sale of stock. The most famous recent case is that of Martha Stewart, but there are many others as well. Andrew Rankin, an investment banking star with RBC Dominion Securities, was sentenced to six months in jail for "tipping" a friend about several big corporate deals that were pending. The friend used this insider information to make over $4 million by buying and selling the stocks of these companies.[42] In the U.S., 13 Wall Street professionals were arrested in 2007 and charged with insider trading.[43]

Misrepresentation of Finances

Irresponsible and unethical behaviour regarding financial representation is also illegal. All corporations are required to conform to generally accepted accounting principles in maintaining and reporting their financial status. Sometimes, though, managers project profits far in excess of what they truly expect to earn. When the truth comes out, investors are almost always hurt. Occasionally, companies are found guilty of misrepresenting their finances to outsiders, as in the Enron case.

IMPLEMENTING SOCIAL RESPONSIBILITY PROGRAMS

Thus far, we have discussed social responsibility as if consensus existed on how firms should behave in most situations. In fact, differences of opinion exist as to the appropriateness of social responsibility as a business goal. As we have seen, some people oppose any business activity that cuts into profits to investors. Others argue that social responsibility must take precedence over profits.

Even people who share a common attitude toward social responsibility by businesses may have different reasons for their beliefs, and this impacts their beliefs about how social responsibility should be implemented. Some people fear that if businesses become too active in social concerns, they will gain too much control over how those concerns are addressed. They point to the influence many businesses have been able to exert on the government agencies that are supposed to regulate their industries. Other critics of business-sponsored social programs argue that companies lack the expertise needed. They believe that technical experts, not businesses, should decide how best to clean up a polluted river, for example.

Supporters of social responsibility believe that corporations are citizens just like individuals and therefore need to help improve our lives. Others point to the vast resources controlled by businesses and note that since businesses often create many of the problems social programs are designed to alleviate, they should use their resources to help. Still others argue that social responsibility is wise because it pays off for the firm in terms of good public relations.

The late Max Clarkson, formerly a top-level business executive and director of the Centre for Corporate Social Performance and Ethics at the University of Toronto, argued that business firms that have a strong consciousness about ethics and social responsibility outperform firms that don't. After designing and applying a social responsibility rating system for companies, he found that companies that had the highest marks on questions of ethics and social responsibility also had the highest financial performance.[44]

Approaches to Social Responsibility

Given these differences of opinion, it is little wonder that corporations have adopted a variety of approaches to social responsibility. As Figure 3.3 illustrates, the four stances that an organization can take concerning its obligations to society fall along a continuum ranging from the lowest to the highest degree of socially responsible practices.

4 Identify four general *approaches to social responsibility* and describe the four steps a firm must take to implement a *social responsibility program.*

Obstructionist Stance

A few organizations take what might be called an **obstructionist stance** to social responsibility and do as little as possible to solve social or environmental problems. When they cross the ethical or legal line that separates acceptable from unacceptable practices, their typical response is to deny or cover up their actions. Firms that adopt this position have little regard for ethical conduct and will generally go to great lengths to hide wrongdoing.

obstructionist stance A company does as little as possible to solve social or environmental problems.

Defensive Stance

An organization adopting a **defensive stance** will do everything that is required of it legally, but nothing more. Such a firm, for example, would install pollution-control equipment dictated by law, but would not install higher-quality equipment even though it might further limit pollution. Managers who take a defensive stance insist that their job is to generate profits.

Tobacco companies generally take this position in their marketing efforts. In Canada and the United States, they are legally required to include warnings to smokers on their products and to limit advertising to prescribed media. Domestically, they follow these rules to the letter of the law but use more aggressive marketing methods in countries that have no such rules. In many Asian and African countries, for example, cigarettes are heavily promoted, contain higher levels of tar and nicotine than those sold in Canada and the United States, and carry few or no health warning labels.

defensive stance An organization does only what is legally required and nothing more.

Accommodative Stance

A firm that adopts an **accommodative stance** meets its legal and ethical requirements, but will also go further in certain cases. Such firms may agree to participate in social programs, but solicitors must convince them that these programs are worthy of funding. Many organizations respond to requests for donations from community hockey teams, Girl Guides, youth soccer programs, and so forth. The point, however, is that someone has to knock on the door and ask; accommodative organizations do not necessarily or proactively seek avenues for contributing.

accommodative stance A company meets all of its legal and ethical requirements, and in some cases even goes beyond what is required.

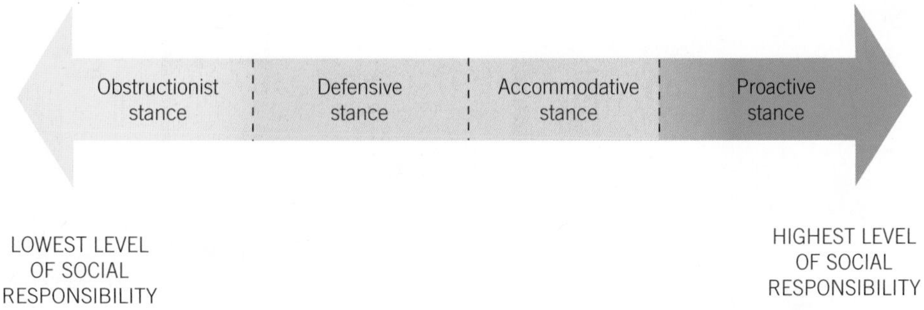

Figure 3.3 Spectrum of approaches to corporate social responsibility.

Proactive Stance

proactive stance
An organization actively seeks opportunities to be socially responsible.

Firms that adopt the **proactive stance** take to heart the arguments in favour of social responsibility. They view themselves as citizens in a society and proactively seek opportunities to contribute. The most common—and direct—way to implement this stance is by setting up a foundation to provide direct financial support for various social programs.

These stances are not sharply distinct; they simply label stages along a continuum of social responsibility. Thus, organizations do not always fit neatly into one category or another. The Ronald McDonald House program has been widely applauded, for example, but McDonald's has also come under fire for allegedly misleading consumers about the nutritional value of its food products. Likewise, while UPS has sincere motives for helping Olympic athletes, the company will also benefit by featuring their photos on its envelopes and otherwise promoting its own benevolence. The Exercising Your Ethics feature at the end of the chapter gives you an opportunity to think more deeply about the pros and cons of the various stances toward social responsibility.

Corporate Charitable Donations. Donating money to different "causes" is one way that business firms try to show that they are socially responsible. A Decima Research survey found that 80 percent of Canadians think that businesses should give some of their profits to social causes.[45] A survey conducted by the Centre for Philanthropy found that Canadian corporations contributed less than 2 percent of all charitable revenue. Canadians think that this number is closer to 20 percent, and that it should be 30 percent.[46]

Corporations that gave substantial amounts of money to charity in 2005 were the RBC Financial Group ($40 million), BMO Financial Group ($29.5 million), and TELUS Corp. ($11 million). Corporations typically give less than half of 1 percent of their pre-tax profits to charity, but many have demonstrated a willingness to give money and products when disasters strike. When seven people died in Walkerton, Ontario, as a result of drinking contaminated water, companies such as Petro-Canada, Shoppers Drug Mart, Sobeys, and Zellers contributed products such as bleach and bottled water. And when thousands of people died in the Asian tsunamis of 2004, companies from around the world rushed aid to the stricken areas. They donated drugs, mobile telephones, machinery, medical equipment, water, and free travel for relief workers.[47] Companies generally receive favourable publicity when they make contributions like these, but they can be accused of being opportunistic if they attempt to publicize their donations.[48]

Ronald McDonald House helps the families of children who are in hospital care. It is supported by McDonald's and is an excellent example of socially responsible behaviour by a business corporation.

Managing Social Responsibility Programs

There are four steps that are required in order for an organization to become truly socially responsible. First, social responsibility must start at the top. Without this support, no program can succeed. Top managers must make the decision that they want to take a stronger stand on social responsibility issues and develop a policy statement outlining their commitment.

Second, a committee of top managers needs to develop a plan detailing the level of support that will be provided. Some companies set aside a percentage of profits for social programs. Levi Strauss, for example, has a policy of giving 2.4 percent of its pre-tax earnings to worthy causes. Managers also need to set specific priorities (for example, should the firm focus on training the hard-core unemployed or supporting the arts?).

Third, one specific executive needs to be given the authority to act as director of the firm's social agenda. This individual must monitor the program and ensure that its implementation is consistent with the policy statement and the strategic plan.

Finally, the organization needs to conduct occasional social audits. A **social audit** is a systematic analysis of how a firm is using funds earmarked for its social-responsibility goals.[49] Canadian businesses also publish sustainability reports which explain how the company is performing on issues such as the environment, employee relations, workplace diversity, and business ethics. A study by Ottawa-based Stratos Inc. found that 70 percent of Canada's largest public companies now report at least some sustainability performance information.[50] Social audits and sustainability reports together constitute **triple bottom line reporting**—measuring the social, environmental, and economic performance of a company.[51]

social audit
A systematic analysis of how a firm is using funds earmarked for social-responsibility goals and how effective these expenditures have been.

triple bottom line reporting
Measuring the social, environmental,and economic performance of a company.

Social Responsibility and the Small Business

Explain how issues of social responsibility and ethics affect small businesses. 5

Small businesses face many of the same ethical and social responsibility issues as large businesses. As the owner of a small garden supply store, how would you respond to a building inspector's suggestion that a cash payment would "expedite" your application for a building permit? As the manager of a nightclub, would you call the police, refuse service, or sell liquor to a customer whose ID card looked forged? Or, as the owner of a small medical laboratory, would you actually call the board of health to make sure that it has licensed the company you want to contract with to dispose of the lab's medical waste? Is a small manufacturing firm justified in overcharging by 5 percent a customer whose purchasing agent is lax? Who will really be harmed if a small firm pads its income statement to help get a much-needed bank loan?

Many small business owners wonder if they can afford a social agenda. Should they sponsor hockey teams, make donations to the United Way, and buy light bulbs from the Lions' Club? Is joining the Chamber of Commerce and supporting the Better Business Bureau too much of a financial drain, or is it just good business? One key to business success is to decide in advance how to respond to these issues because ethics and social responsibility are decisions faced by managers in all organizations, regardless of size.

Summary of Learning Objectives

1. Explain how individuals develop their personal *codes of ethics* and why ethics are important in the workplace. Individual *codes of ethics* are derived from social standards of right and wrong. *Ethical behaviour* is behaviour that conforms to generally accepted social norms concerning beneficial and harmful actions. Because ethics affect the behaviour of individuals on behalf of the companies that employ them, many firms are adopting formal statements of ethics. Unethical behaviour can result in loss of business, fines, and even imprisonment.

2. Distinguish *social responsibility* from *ethics,* identify *organizational stakeholders,* and characterize social consciousness today. *Social responsibility* refers to the way a firm attempts to balance its commitments to organizational stakeholders. One way to understand social responsibility is to view it in terms of *stakeholders*—those groups, individuals, and organizations that are directly affected by the practices of an organization and that therefore have a stake in its performance. Until the second half of the nineteenth century, businesses often paid little attention to stakeholders. Since then, however, both public pressure and government regulation, especially as a result of the Great Depression of the 1930s and the social activism of the 1960s and 1970s, have forced businesses to consider public welfare, at least to some degree. A trend toward increased social consciousness, including a heightened sense of environmental activism, has recently emerged.

3. Show how the concept of social responsibility applies both to environmental issues and to a firm's relationships with customers, employees, and investors. Social responsibility toward the environment requires firms to minimize pollution of air, water, and land. Social responsibility toward customers requires firms to provide products of acceptable quality, to price products fairly, and to respect consumers' rights. Social responsibility toward employees requires firms to respect workers both as resources and as people who are more productive when their needs are met. Social responsibility toward investors requires firms to manage their resources and to represent their financial status honestly.

4. Identify four general *approaches to social responsibility* and describe the four steps a firm must take to implement a *social responsibility program.* An *obstructionist stance* on social responsibility is taken by a firm that does as little as possible to address social or environmental problems and that may deny or attempt to cover up problems that may occur. The *defensive stance* emphasizes compliance with legal minimum requirements. Companies adopting the *accommodative stance* go beyond minimum activities, if asked. The *proactive stance* commits a company to actively seek to contribute to social projects. Implementing a social responsibility program entails four steps: (1) drafting a policy statement with the support of top management, (2) developing a detailed plan, (3) appointing a director to implement the plan, and (4) conducting *social audits* to monitor results.

5. Explain how issues of social responsibility and ethics affect small businesses. Managers and employees of small businesses face many of the same ethical questions as their counterparts at larger firms. Small businesses face the same issues of social responsibility and the same need to decide on an approach to social responsibility. The differences are primarily differences of scale.

QUESTIONS AND EXERCISES

Questions for Analysis

1. Write a one-paragraph description of an ethical dilemma that you (or someone you know) faced recently. What was the actual outcome in the situation? Was it consistent with what you thought should have occurred? Why or why not? Analyze the situation using the ideas presented in the chapter. Make particular reference to the ethical norms of utility, rights, justice, and caring in terms of how they impact the situation. What would each of these suggest about the correct decision? Does this analysis lead you to a different conclusion about the best outcome? Explain.
2. Develop an example of the way in which your personal code of ethics would clash with the practices of some specific company. How might you try to resolve these differences?
3. What kind of wrongdoing would most likely prompt you to be a whistle-blower? What kind of wrongdoing would be least likely? Why?
4. In your opinion, which area of social responsibility is most important? Why? Are there areas other than those noted in the chapter that you consider important?
5. Identify some specific social responsibility issues that might be faced by small-business managers and employees in each of the following areas: environment, customers, employees, and investors.
6. Choose a product or service and explain the social responsibility concerns that are likely to be evident in terms of the environment, customers, employees, and investors.
7. Analyze the forces that are at work from both the company's perspective and the whistle-blower's perspective. Given these forces, what characteristics would a law to protect whistle-blowers have to have to be effective?
8. Pick a product or service that demonstrates the defensive approach to social responsibility. What has been the impact of that stance on the company that is using it? Now pick a product or service for each of the other stances (obstructionist, accommodative, and proactive) and do the same analysis. Why did these companies adopt the particular stance they did?

Application Exercises

9. Develop a list of the major stakeholders of your college or university. As a class, discuss the ways in which you think the school prioritizes these stakeholders. Do you agree or disagree with this prioritization?
10. Using newspapers, magazines, and other business references, identify and describe at least three companies that take a defensive stance to social responsibility, three that take an accommodative stance, and three that take a proactive stance.

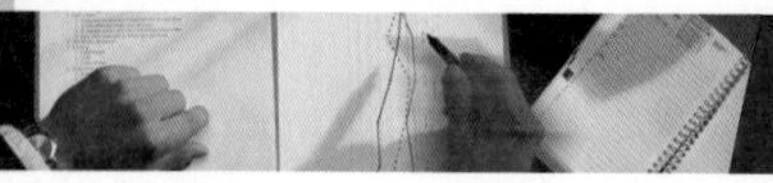

BUILDING YOUR BUSINESS SKILLS

To Lie or Not to Lie: That Is the Question

Goal

To encourage students to apply general concepts of business ethics to specific situations.

Situation

Workplace lying, it seems, has become business as usual. According to one survey, one-quarter of working adults said that they had been asked to do something illegal or unethical on the job. Four in 10 did what they were told. Another survey of more than 2000 secretaries showed that many employees face ethical dilemmas in their day-to-day work.

- Would you lie about your supervisor's whereabouts to someone on the phone?
- Would you lie about who was responsible for a business decision that cost your company thousands of dollars to protect your own or your supervisor's job?
- Would you inflate sales and revenue data on official company accounting statements to increase stock value?
- Would you say that you witnessed a signature when you did not if you were acting in the role of a notary?
- Would you keep silent if you knew that the official minutes of a corporate meeting had been changed?
- Would you destroy or remove information that could hurt your company if it fell into the wrong hands?

Method

Step 1 Working with four other students, discuss ways in which you would respond to the previous ethical dilemmas. When there is a difference of opinion among group members, try to determine the specific factors that influence different responses.

Step 2 Research the commitment to business ethics at Johnson & Johnson (www.jnj.com) and Texas Instruments (www.ti.com/corp/docs/ethics/home.htm) by clicking on their respective websites. As a group, discuss ways in which these statements are likely to affect the specific behaviours mentioned in Step 1.

Step 3 Working with group members, draft a corporate code of ethics that would discourage the specific behaviours mentioned in Step 1. Limit your code to a single typewritten page, but make it sufficiently broad to cover different ethical dilemmas.

Follow-Up Questions

1. What personal, social, and cultural factors do you think contribute to lying in the workplace?
2. Do you agree or disagree with the following statement? "The term *business ethics* is an oxymoron." Support your answer with examples from your own work experience or that of a family member.
3. If you were your company's director of human resources, how would you make your code of ethics a "living document"?
4. If you were faced with any of the ethical dilemmas described in Step 1, how would you handle them? How far would you go to maintain your personal ethical standards?

EXERCISING YOUR ETHICS: TEAM EXERCISE

Assessing the Ethics of Tradeoffs

The Situation

Managers must often make choices among options that are presented by environmental circumstances. This exercise will help you better appreciate the nature and complexity of the kinds of tradeoffs that often result.

The Dilemma

You are the CEO of a medium-sized, unionized manufacturing corporation that is located in a town of about 15 000 people. The nearest major city is about 200 kilometres away. With about 500 workers, your company is one of the five largest employers in town. A regional recession has caused two of the other largest employers to close down (one went out of business and the other relocated to another area). A new foreign competitor has set up shop in the area, but local unemployment has still risen sharply. All in all, the regional economic climate and the new competitor are hurting your business. Your company's sales have dropped 20 percent this year, and you forecast another drop next year before things begin to turn around.

You face two unpleasant choices:

Choice 1: You can tell your employees that you need them to take cuts in pay and benefits. You know that because of the local unemployment rate, you can easily replace anyone who refuses. Unfortunately, you may need your employees to take another cut next year if your forecasts hold true. At the same time, you do have reason to believe that when the economy rebounds (in about two years, according to your forecasts), you can begin restoring pay cuts. Here are the advantages of this choice: You can probably (1) preserve all 500 jobs, (2) maintain your own income, (3) restore pay cuts in the future, and (4) keep the business open indefinitely. And the disadvantages: Pay cuts will (1) pose economic hardships for your employees and (2) create hard feelings and undercut morale.

Choice 2: You can maintain the status quo as far as your employees are concerned, but in that case, you'll be facing two problems: (1) You'll have to cut your own salary. While you can certainly afford to live on less income, doing so would be a blow to your personal finances. (2) If economic conditions get worse and/or last longer than forecast, you may have to close down altogether. The firm has a cash surplus, but because you'll have to dip into these funds to maintain stable wages, they'll soon run out. The advantages of this option: You can (1) avoid economic hardship for your workers and (2) maintain good employee relations. The downside: You will reduce your own standard of living and may eventually cost everyone his or her job.

Team Activity

Assemble a group of four students and assign each group member to one of the following roles:

- CEO of the company
- The vice-president of production
- A stockholder
- An employee who is a member of the union

Action Steps

1. Before discussing the situation with your group, and from the perspective of your assigned role, which of the two options do you think is the best choice? Write down the reasons for your position.
2. Before discussing the situation with your group, and from the perspective of your assigned role, what are the underlying ethical issues in this situation? Write down the issues.
3. Gather the group together and reveal, in turn, each member's comments on the best choice of the two options. Next, reveal the ethical issues listed by each member.
4. Appoint someone to record the main points of agreement and disagreement within the group. How do you explain the results? What accounts for any disagreement?
5. From an ethical standpoint, what does your group conclude is the most appropriate action that should be taken by the company? (You may find the concepts of *utility*, *rights*, *justice*, and *caring* helpful in making your decision.)

BUSINESS CASE 3

High Seas Dumping

Cruising has become a very popular vacation. More than eight million passengers take an ocean voyage each year, cruising many areas of the world's oceans in search of pristine beaches and clear tropical waters. The Caribbean Sea, the Mediterranean Sea, and the coast of Alaska are among the most popular destinations, while the coasts of Europe and Asia are growing in popularity. The tourists and the giant ships that carry them are usually welcome for the revenues that they bring, but these ships also bring something much less desirable—pollution.

A modern cruise ship carries an average of 2000 passengers and 1000 crew members. That many people generate a lot of waste. On a typical day, a ship will produce 6 tonnes of solid garbage, which is incinerated and then dumped (60 litres of highly toxic chemical waste; 114 000 litres of sewage; 27 000 litres of bilge water containing oil; and 850 000 litres of "grey" water from sinks and laundries). Cruise ships also pick up ballast water whenever and wherever it's needed and then discharge it later, releasing animals and pollution from other parts of the world. Multiply this problem by more than 167 ships worldwide, cruising 50 weeks per year, and the scope of the environmental damage is staggering.

Environmental groups see the top pollution-related problem as death of marine life, including extinction. Foreign animals bring parasites and diseases, and, in some cases, replace native species entirely. Bacteria that are harmless to human beings can kill corals that provide food and habitat for many species. Oil and toxic chemicals are deadly to wildlife even in minute quantities. Turtles swallow plastic bags, thinking they are jellyfish, and starve, while seals and birds drown after becoming entangled in the plastic rings that hold beverage cans.

Other problems include the habitat destruction or disease that affects certain industries. For example, cholera, picked up in ships' ballast water off the coast of Peru, caused a devastating loss to fish and shrimp harvesters in the Gulf of Mexico in the 1990s when infected catches had to be destroyed. Heavy metal poisoning of fish is rising, and concern is on the rise that the poisons are moving up the food chain from microscopic animals to fish and, ultimately, to humans. Phosphorus found in detergents causes an overgrowth of algae, which then consume all the available oxygen in the water, making it incapable of supporting any flora or fauna.

Lack of regulation is the biggest obstacle to solving the problem. By international law, countries may regulate oceans for three miles (5 kilometres) off their shores. International treaties provide some additional regulation up to 25 miles (40 kilometres) offshore. Beyond this point, however, ships are allowed free rein. Also, each country's laws and enforcement policies vary considerably, and even when laws are strict, enforcement may be limited. One would think that cruise lines would be cognizant of the importance of clean and safe seas for their own economic well-being. Sadly, however, this is often not the case.

Intentional illegal dumping may be growing in scope. Over the last decade, for instance, as enforcement has tightened, 10 cruise lines have collectively paid U.S.$48.5 million in fines related to illegal dumping. In the largest settlement to date, Royal Caribbean paid U.S.$27 million for making illegal alterations to facilities, falsifying records, lying to the U.S. Coast Guard, and deliberately destroying evidence. The fine may seem high, but it covers 30 different charges and 10 years of violations and seems small compared to the firm's billions in profits over the past few years. Royal Caribbean's fine was less than what the firm would have paid to dispose of the waste properly over a one-year period. In addition, a lawsuit is pending regarding the firing of a whistle-blower, the firm's former vice president for safety and environment. "This [case] is like the Enron of the seas," says attorney William Amlong, who represents the whistle-blower.

Critics are speaking out against the cruise lines' profiteering from an environment that they are destroying, but they note that the companies won't stop as long as the profits continue. Technology exists to make the waste safe, but industry experts estimate that dumping can save a firm millions of dollars annually. From that perspective, Royal Caribbean is making understandable decisions.

Questions for Discussion

1. What are the major legal issues in this case? What are the major ethical issues?
2. Aside from personal greed, what factors might lead a cruise line to illegally dump waste into the ocean?
3. Which approach to social responsibility do cruise lines appear to be taking?
4. Distinguish between ethical issues and social responsibility issues as they apply to this problem.

MYBUSINESSLAB mybusinesslab

To improve your grade, visit the MyBusinessLab website at **www.pearsoned.ca/mybusinesslab**. This online homework and tutorial system allows you to test your understanding and generates a personalized study plan just for you. It provides you with study and practice tools directly related to this chapter's content. MyBusinessLab puts you in control of your own learning!

CHAPTER 4

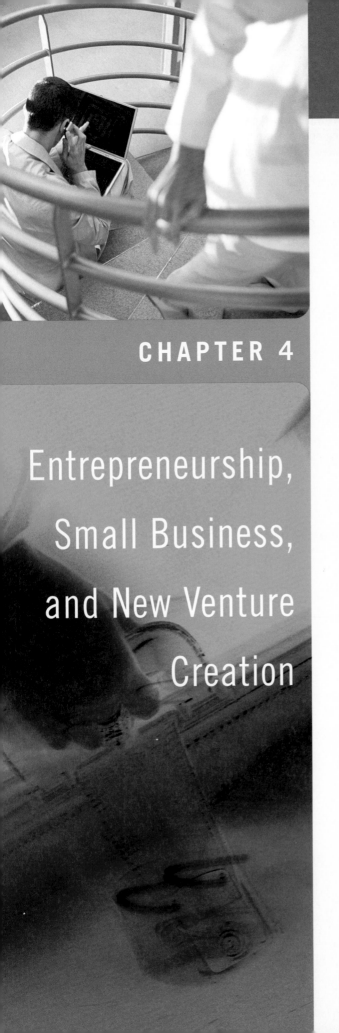

Entrepreneurship, Small Business, and New Venture Creation

After reading this chapter, you should be able to:

1. Explain the meaning and interrelationship of the terms *small business*, *new venture creation*, and *entrepreneurship*.
2. Describe the role of small and new businesses in the Canadian economy.
3. Explain the *entrepreneurial process* and describe its three key elements.
4. Describe three alternative strategies for becoming a business owner—*starting from scratch*, *buying an existing business*, and *buying a franchise*.
5. Describe four forms of *legal organization* for a business and discuss the advantages and disadvantages of each.
6. Identify four key reasons for success in small businesses and four key reasons for failure.

Stepping Up

The year was 1994. Sandra Wilson, a young wife and mother, was downsized out of her airline job. In welcoming the chance to spend more time with her 18-month old son Robert, she was inspired by his tiny feet. Lovingly she handcrafted a pair of brightly coloured, soft-soled leather shoes for young Robert. Indeed, the shoes seemed to improve his balance as the soft soles allowed him to "feel" the floor while he toddled about.

Sandra began to wonder: if these soft-soled shoes worked so well for Robert, perhaps other mothers would find them a good product for their children's developing feet. Sandra saw this as an opportunity to start her own business. Naming the shoes after her son, "Robeez" were born. After hand-stitching 20 pairs of her footwear, she attended the 1994 Vancouver Gift Show trade exhibition. The response? Overwhelming. The orders flooded in and she signed up 15 retailers ready to sell her product.

Sandra threw herself into production. Her home's basement became Robeez Footwear's early headquarters and she quickly immersed herself into learning all there was to know about leather, cutting, sewing, design, sales, and distribution. It was the beginning of an incredible growth story.

To keep up with the booming sales, Sandra hired her first sales representative in March 1995 and by May 1997, Robeez was online. The company moved out of Sandra's basement in May 1999 and into its first commercial space. Since then, the company has relocated and expanded into larger premises to accommodate its rapidly expanding operations. In August 2001, sales topped $1.2 million, and doubled by the following year. Today, sales of this Burnaby, British Columbia business exceed the $25 million mark and continue to grow rapidly.

In June 2006, for the fourth year in a row, Robeez achieved a top-20 spot on the prestigious *Profit* 100 ranking of Canada's fastest-growing companies. Not bad for a business that started out in Wilson's basement with three employees. Wilson says Robeez's relaxed supportive culture is vital to its growth. Robeez weaves fun and training into the routine, which breaks the monotony of many of the sewing jobs. Wilson's belief in her company's culture explains why Robeez's European headquarters were started by a Welsh couple with a passion for Robeez's values. Today, the European office leads plans for cross-Atlantic distribution, with over two dozen full-time employees and regional sales representatives. "People ask, 'What the heck are you doing in Wales?'" says Wilson. "Well, that's where the right people are. We felt it was really important to get the people first, then do the business."

Today, Robeez is recognized as the world's leading manufacturer of soft-soled leather footwear for newborns to four-year-olds. The company has 450 employees and sells more than 90 designs of shoes and booties in over 6500 stores in countries throughout North America, Europe, Australia, and parts of Asia. Recommended by experts and the first choice of parents, the hallmark of the meticulously crafted footwear is the skid-resistant soles that promote the healthy development of little feet by encouraging feet to flex and toes to grip.

HOW WILL THIS BENEFIT YOU?

Robeez Footwear has been successful because its founder, entrepreneur Sandra Wilson, has adhered to sound business practices and made effective decisions. She has maintained a clear focus on what it takes to succeed in business. By understanding the material discussed in this chapter, you'll be better prepared to (1) understand the challenges and opportunities provided in new venture start-ups, (2) assess the risks and benefits of working in a new business, and (3) evaluate the investment potential inherent in a new business.

In this chapter, we begin by looking at the important role that small and new businesses play in the Canadian economy. We then examine entrepreneurship and the process that entrepreneurs use to start a new business from scratch. We also describe two other ways that entrepreneurs can get into business: buying an existing business or buying a franchise. When operating a business, an entrepreneur must also decide which legal form of organization to adopt—sole proprietorship, partnership, corporation, or co-operative—and we discuss the advantages and disadvantages of each form. We conclude the chapter with a discussion of the reasons for success and failure of small businesses.

SMALL BUSINESS, NEW VENTURE CREATION, AND ENTREPRENEURSHIP

Every day, approximately 380 businesses are started in Canada.[1] New firms create the most jobs, are noted for their entrepreneurship, and are typically small.[2] But does this mean that most small businesses are entrepreneurial? Not necessarily.

The terms *small business, new venture,* and *entrepreneurship* are closely linked terms, but each idea is distinct. In the following paragraphs we will explain these terms to help you understand these topics and how they are interrelated.

Small Business

1 Explain the meaning and interrelationship of the terms *small business, new venture creation,* and *entrepreneurship.*

Defining a "small" business can be a bit tricky. Various measures might be used, including the number of people the business employs, the company's sales revenue, the size of the investment required, or the type of ownership structure the business has. Some of the difficulties in defining a small business can be understood by considering the way the Canadian government collects and reports information on small businesses.

Industry Canada is the main federal government agency responsible for small business. In reporting Canadian small business statistics, the government relies on two distinct sources of information, both provided by Statistics Canada: the *Business Register* (which tracks businesses), and the *Labour Force Survey* (which tracks individuals). To be included in the Register, a business must have at least one paid employee, annual sales revenues of $30 000 or more, or be incorporated (we describe incorporation later in the chapter). A goods-producing business in the Register is considered small if it has fewer than 100 employees, while a service-producing business is considered small if it has fewer than 50 employees.

The Labour Force Survey uses information from *individuals* to make estimates of employment and unemployment levels. Individuals are classified as self-employed if they are working owners of a business that is either incorporated or unincorporated, if they work for themselves but do not have a business (some musicians, for example, would fall into this category), or if they work without pay in a family business.[3]

In its publication, *Key Small Business Statistics* (www.strategis.gc.ca/sbstatistics), Industry Canada reports that there are 2.2 million "business

A common type of small business in Canada is the convenience store. It attracts customers from its immediate area through its long hours of operation and the product lines it carries.

establishments" in Canada and about 2.5 million people who are "self-employed."[4] There is no way of identifying how much overlap there is in these two categories, but we do know that an unincorporated business operated by a self-employed person (with no employees) would *not* be counted among the 2.2 million *businesses* in the Register. This is an important point because the majority of businesses in Canada have no employees (just the owner), nor are they incorporated.

These facts need to be kept in mind when considering statistics or research that excludes these firms. When either of these indicators is used to find businesses to study, the number of new firms will be underestimated. A study by the Panel Study of Entrepreneurial Dynamics (PSED), conducted by members of the Entrepreneurship Research Consortium (ERC), tracked a sample of Canadian **nascent entrepreneurs**—people who were trying to start a business—over four years. Only 15 percent of those who reported establishing an operating business had incorporated their firm.[5]

nascent entrepreneurs People who are trying to start a business from scratch.

For our purposes, we define a **small business** as an owner-managed business with less than 100 employees. We do so because it enables us to make better use of existing information, and because you are now aware of how definitions can affect our understanding of small businesses. Industry Canada estimates the percentage of small business's contribution to Canada's GDP over the past decade at 25 percent annually.[6]

small business An independently owned and managed business that does not dominate its market.

The New Venture/Firm

Various criteria can also be used to determine when a new firm comes into existence. Three of the most common are when it was formed, whether it was incorporated, and if it sold goods and/or services.[7] A business is considered to be new if it has become operational within the previous 12 months, if it adopts any of the main organizational forms (proprietorship, partnership, corporation, or cooperative), and if it sells goods or services. Thus, we define a **new venture** as a recently formed commercial organization that provides goods and/or services for sale.

new venture A recently formed commercial organization that provides goods and/or services for sale.

Entrepreneurship

Entrepreneurship is the process of identifying an opportunity in the marketplace and accessing the resources needed to capitalize on that opportunity.[8] **Entrepreneurs** are people who assume the risk of business ownership with a primary goal of making money through selling goods and

entrepreneurship The process of identifying an opportunity in the marketplace and accessing the resources needed to capitalize on it.

entrepreneur A business person who accepts both the risks and the opportunities involved in creating and operating a new business venture.

services to customers. For example, Ken Woods and John Gagliardi are two entrepreneurs who formed the Ontario-based Black Oak Brewing Company with the goal of making the highest quality beer possible. They've already developed several award-winning beers such as Black Oak Nut Brown Ale, Pale Ale, and Premium Lager. A website for Toronto beer lovers called "The Bar Towel" rates these beers very positively.[9]

Each year, the Heritage Foundation publishes an index of economic freedom, which assesses the extent to which entrepreneurs have freedom to pursue new business opportunities. In 2007, the top three countries were Hong Kong, Singapore, and Australia (Canada ranked 10th). North Korea ranked last.[10]

Small businesses often provide an environment to use personal attributes—such as creativity—that have come to be associated with entrepreneurs.[11] Because starting a business involves dealing with a great deal of uncertainty, ambiguity, and unpredictability, every new venture founder needs to exercise some of the personal attributes that entrepreneurs are noted for. But do not assume that only small business owners exhibit entrepreneurial characteristics.[12] Many successful managers in large organizations in both the public and private sectors also exhibit similar characteristics. Entrepreneurship therefore occurs in a wide range of contexts: not just in small or new commercial firms, but also in old firms, in large firms, in firms that grow slowly, in firms that grow rapidly, in nonprofit organizations, and in the public sector.[13]

intrapreneurs
People who create something new within an existing large firm or organization.

People who exhibit entrepreneurial characteristics and create something new within an existing firm or organization are called **intrapreneurs**. One large firm renowned for encouraging intrapreneurship is Proctor & Gamble. It has earned this reputation by having divisions that focus on creating new products for specific markets.[14] The Swiffer product line is one example. Once the basic Swiffer mop was launched successfully, a whole range of products was added such as the Swiffer WetJet and Swiffer Dusters. A key difference between intrapreneurs and entrepreneurs is that intrapreneurs typically don't have to concern themselves with getting the resources needed to bring the new product to market since their employer provides the resources.

Starting a business from scratch involves dealing with a great deal of uncertainty, ambiguity, and unpredictability. For example, who knows how many customers the business will attract or where the needed financial resources will come from? This means that every new venture founder needs to exercise some of the personal attributes that entrepreneurs are noted for. Therefore, when we explore the entrepreneurial process later in the chapter, we will do so within a new venture context. We begin by outlining the role of small and new businesses in the Canadian economy.

THE ROLE OF SMALL AND NEW BUSINESSES IN THE CANADIAN ECONOMY

2 Describe the role of small and new businesses in the Canadian economy.

As we will see in this section, small and new businesses play a key role in the Canadian economy. However, recognition of this role is relatively recent. Prior to the 1980s, large businesses were the focus of attention in terms of economic impact within industrialized nations.

Small Businesses

It may surprise you to learn that close to 98 percent of all businesses in Canada are small, that is, they have less than 100 employees (see Figures 4.1

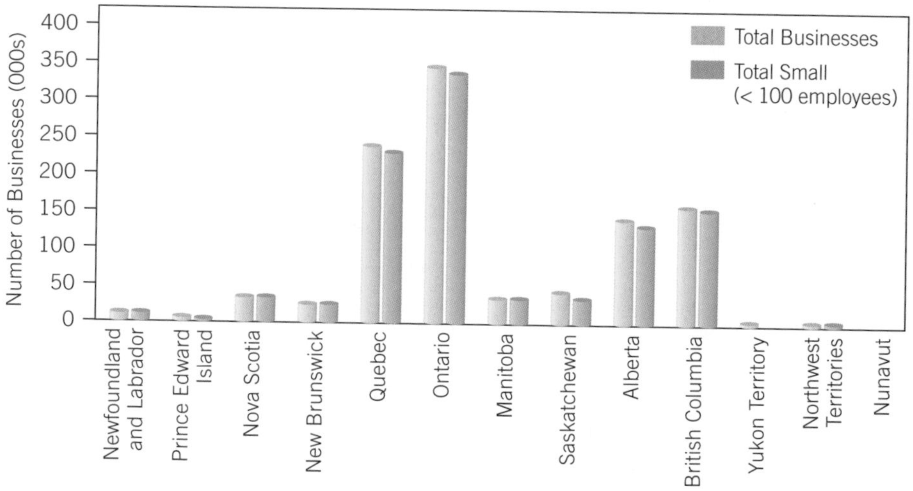

Figure 4.1 Employer businesses by firm size (number of employees) in provinces and territories, June 2005.

and 4.2). While one large business has many more employees than one small business, as a group, small businesses outperform large businesses in terms of employment. New businesses also lead the way when it comes to innovation and new technology.

In terms of distribution, approximately 60 percent of all business establishments in Canada—whether small or large—are located in Ontario and Quebec. Virtually all the rest are found in the western provinces (36 percent) and the Atlantic provinces (6 percent). The Northwest Territories, the Yukon, and Nunavut represent just 0.3 percent of Canada's businesses.

The Canadian allocation of small (fewer than 100 employees), medium (100–499 employees), and large businesses (500+ employees) is very similar to that of the United States. In Canada, 97.6 percent of the 1 048 286 employer businesses (or approximately half of the 2.2 million business establishments) are small, 2.1 percent are medium-sized, and 0.3 percent is large (see Figure 4.2).[15] In the United States, slightly more than 97 percent are small, 2 percent are medium-sized, and 0.3 percent is large. When we further subdivide the Canadian "small" size category, we can see that the majority of small businesses (57 percent) have fewer than five employees (see Figure 4.3).

While the previous figures profile the number of businesses in Canada by size, we now look at how many people work in small- versus medium- and large-sized businesses. According to Statistics Canada, there were

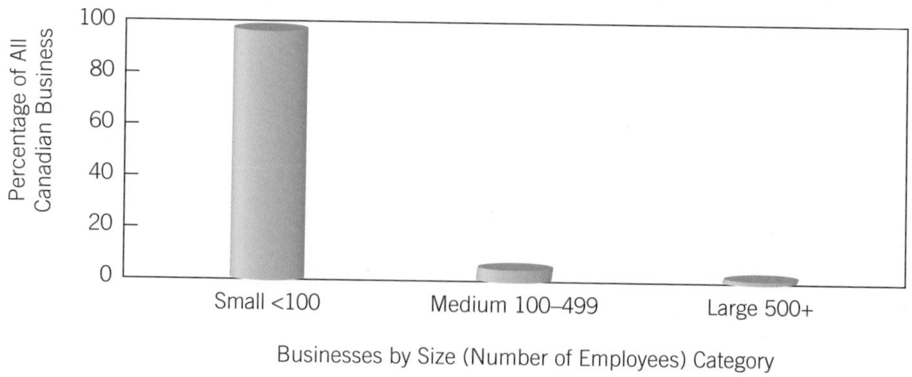

Figure 4.2 Small, medium, and large businesses as a percentage of total businesses.

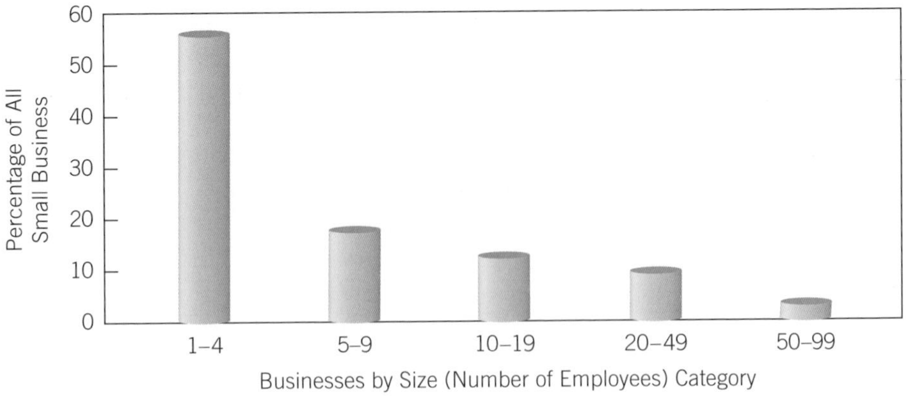

Figure 4.3 Small business size categories as a percentage of all small businesses.

private sector
The part of the economy that is made up of companies and organizations that are not owned or controlled by the government.

10 317 481 **private sector** employees in 2005. The term "private sector" generally refers to the part of the economy that is made up of companies and organizations that are not owned or controlled by the government.

About 49 percent of these employees (5.0 million) worked for small businesses, 16 percent (over 1.6 million) worked for medium-sized enterprises (those with 100 to 499 employees), and 35 percent (3.7 million) for large businesses (see Figure 4.4).[16] These proportions have changed little over the last decade. When the small firm category is further subdivided (fewer than 4 employees, 5 to 19, 20 to 49, and 50 to 99), we see that businesses with between 5 and 19 employees account for the highest percentage of employment (see Figure 4.5).

The distribution of employment by size of firm varies considerably across industries. According to Industry Canada, small businesses account for over two-thirds of employment in four industries: non-institutional health care (90 percent), the construction industry (77 percent), other services (73 percent), and accommodation and food (69 percent).[17] In another five industries at least half of the workforce is employed by small businesses.

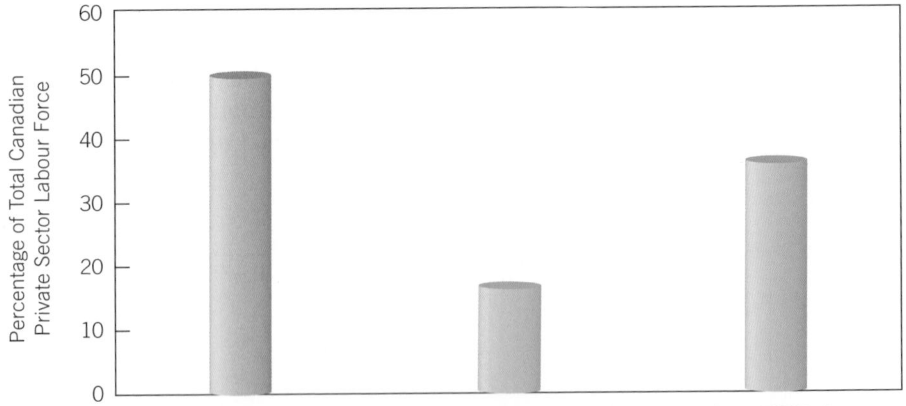

Figure 4.4 Employment in private sector labour force by size of business enterprise.

Note: SEPH data exclude self-employed workers who are not on a payroll and employees in the following industries: agriculture, fishing and trapping, private household services, religious organizations, and military personnel of defence services. The data breaking down employment by size of firm also exclude unclassified industries.

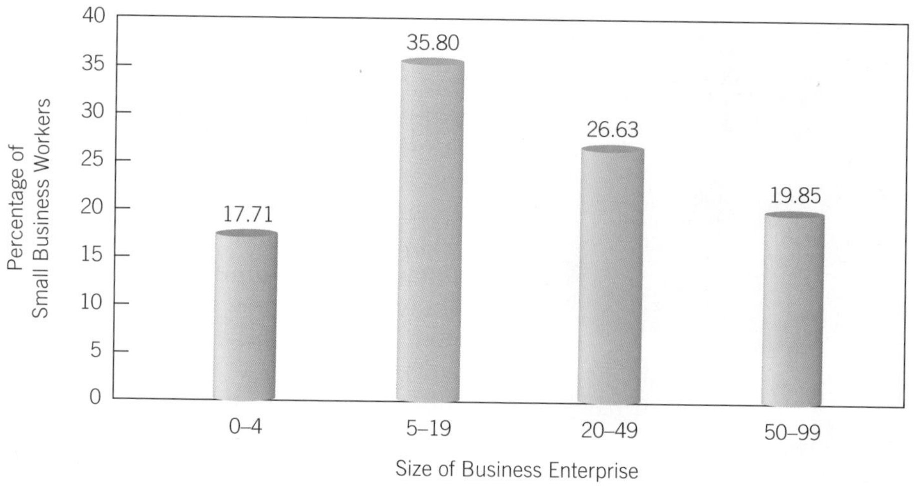

Figure 4.5 Small business employment of private sector labour force by size category.

Note: SEPH data exclude self-employed workers who are not on a payroll and employees in the following industries: agriculture, fishing and trapping, private household services, religious organizations, and military personnel of defence services. The data breaking down employment by size of firm also exclude unclassified industries.

New Ventures

New firms are not only the main source of job creation, they are also responsible for the vast majority of new products and services.[18] According to Statistics Canada, the number of firms in Canada grew 12 percent between 1991 and 2003. Alberta led in growth with 38 percent; British Columbia and Ontario followed with 20 percent and 14 percent, respectively.[19]

Most of the growth in firms occurred in the services-producing sector, with the number of firms in high-knowledge industries such as high-technology and biotechnology nearly doubling (from 32 000 to 62 000 firms). In the goods-producing sector, the number of firms in high-knowledge industries also grew at a much faster pace than in other industries.

Between 1991 and 2003, the number of businesses grew by an average of 9300 each year, with 8800 of these being small- and medium-sized enterprises (SMEs). In terms of who has been responsible for the growth in new firms, it may surprise you to learn that women are playing a far more prominent role than ever before. Kyla Eaglesham, the owner of Madeleines Cherry Pie and Ice Cream Parlour, is typical. After doing a lot of research on the ice cream and dessert industry, she left her job as a flight attendant and opened a dessert café in Toronto's trendy Annex neighbourhood. The store attracts customers who want "a little bit of cottage country in the heart of Toronto."[20]

Research conducted by Industry Canada shows that over the past two decades the number of female entrepreneurs has grown by 208 percent compared with just a 38 percent increase for men.[21] Between 1991 and 2001, self-employment among women increased by 43 percent, as compared to an increase of 21 percent among men. In 2000, majority women-owned SMEs had annual revenues of $72 billion, which is about 8 percent of all revenues from Canada's SMEs; in 2001, majority female-owned businesses employed 974 000 full or contract employees.

According to Statistics Canada, there were 876 000 women entrepreneurs in Canada in 2006.[22] Because many of them run their businesses from home, they are sometimes called "mompreneurs." One such person is Crystal Dallner, who started a marketing business called Outright Communication soon after her first child was born. The Mompreneur

More and more women are starting and successfully operating their own small businesses. They now account for half of all new businesses that are formed.

Networking Group organizes seminars and publishes *Mompreneur*, a free magazine that helps women who want to start a business. Female entrepreneurs are honoured each year at the Canadian Woman Entrepreneur Awards. In 2006, winners included Susan Niczowski (Woodbridge, Ontario-based Summer Fresh Salads), Tracy Gray and Suzanne Mick (Kelowna, B.C.-based Discover Wines Ltd.), and Yvonne Tollens (Okotoks, Alberta-based ComputerAid Professional Services).[23]

Many young entrepreneurs—both men and women—are also involved in creating new ventures in Canada. Consider the following examples:

- Geraldine McManus, who started Ab-Original Wear, buys artwork from Aboriginal artists and then reproduces it on T-shirts, crew-neck shirts, and sweatshirts. The clothing products feature Aboriginal artwork on the front and an inspirational message from a chief or elder on the back. The store also sells crafts made by local Aboriginal artists and miniature log cabins that McManus makes herself from recycled wood.[24]
- The Ben Barry Agency is an Ottawa-based modelling businesses that promotes models who are considered unorthodox—various sizes and ages, different racial backgrounds, and those who have physical disabilities. The models have appeared in government advertising campaigns, and on fashion runways in shopping malls. Barry works with company management to define their clientele and then chooses models who will best reflect the store's typical shoppers.[25]
- Tell Us About Us (TUAU) is a Winnipeg-based company specializing in market research and customer satisfaction programs. Owners Tyler Gompf and Scott Griffith recently signed a seven-figure deal to provide mystery shopper service to Dunkin Donuts, Baskin-Robbins, and Togo's in the United States and Canada. The mystery shoppers will note any problems at a retail site and TUAU will then measure how quickly the problems are fixed.[26]

In considering the government statistics on new ventures we must be mindful that they exclude businesses without employees. Conceivably, a business counted as "new" could have been operating for several years before being statistically counted as a new business. How can this happen? Recall, from our earlier discussion, that an unincorporated business operated by a self-employed person (with no employees) would *not* be included in Statistics Canada's Business Register. If such a business operated for several years prior to hiring employees it would only be classified as a new business when the employees were acquired.

3 Explain the *entrepreneurial process* and describe its three key elements.

THE ENTREPRENEURIAL PROCESS

The entrepreneurial process is like a journey (see Figure 4.6). It is influenced by the social, economic, political, and technological factors in the broader environment, but we will focus our attention on understanding the three key elements in the entrepreneurial process—the entrepreneur, the opportunity, and resources—and how they interact. As these key elements interact, they may be mismatched or well-matched. For example, if an entrepreneur identifies an opportunity for a new health service but does not have the relevant background and skills to deliver the service, the business may never get off the ground. Conversely, if the process elements are well-matched, the new business will likely become operational at some point.

Since the entrepreneur is at the heart of the entrepreneurial process, considerable attention has been paid to identifying the personal characteristics of entrepreneurs. Research shows that these characteristics are wide-ranging. Some are behavioural (for example, taking initiative), others are personality traits (for example, independence), and still others are skills (for example, problem-solving).[27] Some people think that entrepreneurs are rare, but rather than being limited to just a few individuals, entrepreneurial characteristics have been found to be widely distributed in the population.[28] We also know that personal characteristics often have less impact on a person's action than the situation a person is in.[29] What is really important is not who the person *is* but what the person *does*.[30] The two main things that entrepreneurs need to do is to identify an opportunity and access resources.

Identifying Opportunities

Identifying opportunities involves generating ideas for new (or improved) products, processes, or services, screening those ideas so that the one that presents the best opportunity can be developed, and then developing the opportunity.

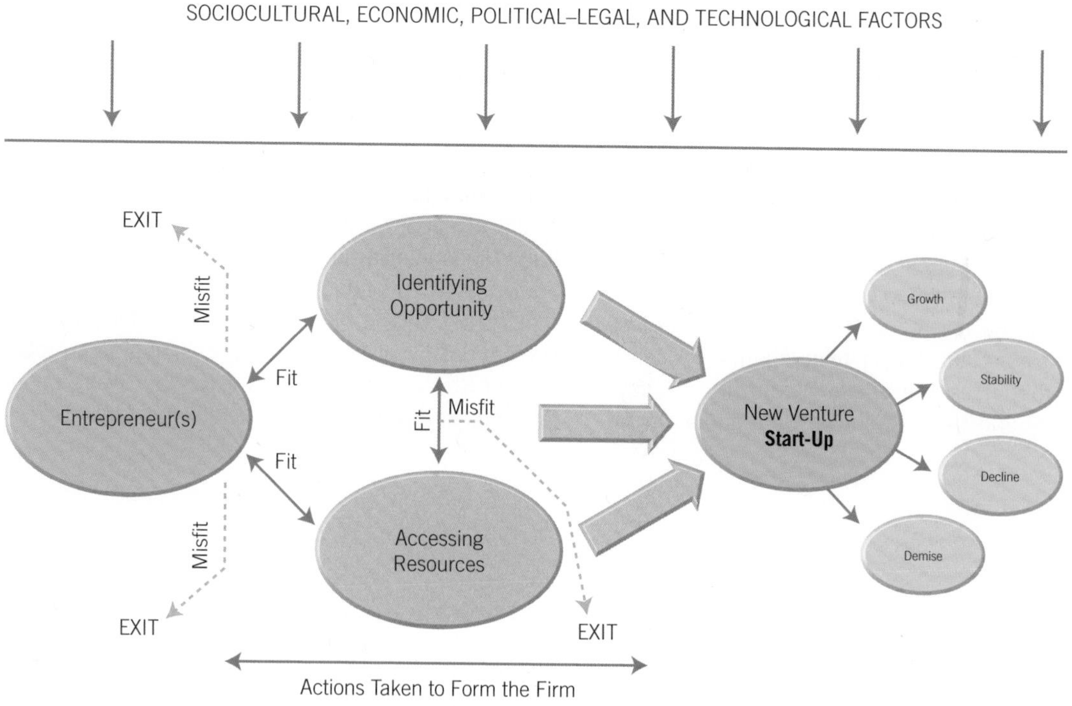

Figure 4.6 The entrepreneurial process in a new venture context.

ENTREPRENEURSHIP AND NEW VENTURES

A Web-Hosting Vision

Vision, they say, is the ability to look at something and see what isn't there. Franc Nemanic's vision was 20/20 back in 1999, when he started eyeing online business opportunities. He noticed that while Canada's big phone companies and cable operators were rushing to offer web access, they weren't doing much to help small businesses build websites to cash in on the internet boom.

Franc's brother John, then the CEO of popular download site Tucows, warned that web hosting is a technically demanding business. But Franc saw that as a plus. If he could sell web-hosting services wholesale rather than retail, he figured complexity would work in his favour, motivating telcos and internet service providers to private-label his services rather than developing their own web-hosting infrastructure.

Nemanic quit his job, wrote a business plan and launched Mississauga, Ont.–based Hostopia.com Inc. Fortunately, he had another asset besides vision: big brother John and his business partners at Tucows, brothers Bill and Colin Campbell, had just sold that firm and were happy to be lead investors in Hostopia's U.S.$2.6-million financing. That first year, Hostopia attracted U.S.$109 202 in revenue. And despite the internet bust—which Nemanic, the firm's 37-year-old president, remembers as "nuclear winter"—sales grew to U.S.$14.3 million, good for five-year sales growth of 13 000 percent and top spot on the 2005 Profit 100.

How did Hostopia survive the meltdown and grow? Nemanic' tactics could fill a textbook on coping with hard times. "You either fight or die," he says. "I never spent a moment not trying to find customers." In September 2000, Nemanic called a staff meeting and explained that Hostopia had to sign up 100 new websites a day by the end of 2001, a fourfold increase that required more and bigger telco clients. "A sense of urgency motivates the whole organization," says Nemanic. "We told them where we were and what we had to accomplish to survive. It made them realize we were all going to sink or swim as a team."

Nemanic kept his team paddling by providing a daily report on Hostopia's progress toward its target. "It was a continuous process of communication." He says even non-sales staff adopted the mission, with administrators and programmers focussing their efforts on helping sales. "As long as you have a customer-centric attitude and you're focussed on helping other people achieve their goals," says Nemanic, "everyone will achieve their goal."

Hopes were rising and so were the numbers when Hostopia signed up Telus Corp. in 2001, a big deal that ensured Hostopia's survival. Better yet, in August 2001, Telus Ventures, the phone giant's venture-capital arm, invested U.S.$5 million in the company. Suddenly, Hostopia was cash-flow positive with a marquee customer.

In the summer of 2002, Nemanic moved to Ft. Lauderdale, Florida, to oversee U.S. sales. Today, he says Hostopia owns 40 percent of the U.S. and Canadian market for private-label, small-biz website hosting. But there's still room for growth, because its biggest rivals are telcos that run these services in-house and they might be persuaded to outsource that business to specialists. Hostopia certainly has an appealing sales pitch: "We cut their operating expenses by 30 to 40 percent," says Nemanic, "and we wipe out their capital expenditures."

Hostopia's three major investors remain active players. Chairman John Nemanic keeps tabs on Hostopia's software development office in Ukraine. Bill Campbell is CEO and CTO, while Colin Campbell is COO. With Franc, they focus on maintaining the company's technological edge, introducing product updates quarterly. Plus, Hostopia is eyeing a public offering in early 2006, Franc says, "provided we build appropriate momentum." That shouldn't be a problem: after growing 60 percent last year, Franc says, Hostopia will probably expand 35 percent more this year, "but we're pushing for a higher number." That's persistence of vision.

Idea Generation

Typically, generating ideas involves abandoning traditional assumptions about how things work and how they ought to be, and seeing what others do not. If the prospective new (or improved) product, process, or service can be profitably produced and is attractive relative to other potential venture ideas, it might present an opportunity.

Where do ideas come from? Most new ventures do not emerge from a deliberate search for viable business ideas. Rather, the majority originate from events relating to work or everyday life.[31] In fact, work experience is the most common source of ideas, accounting for 45 to 85 percent of those generated. This happens because as employees of a company, prospective entrepreneurs are familiar with the product or service, the customers, the suppliers, and the competitors. They are also aware of marketplace needs, can relate those needs to personal capabilities, and can determine whether they are capable of producing products or services that can fill the void.

The next most frequent sources of venture ideas include a personal interest/hobby (16 percent) or a chance happening (11 percent).[32] A chance happening refers to a situation where a venture idea comes about unexpectedly. For example, while on vacation in another country you might try a new snack food that you feel would be in demand if introduced to the Canadian market.

Screening

Entrepreneurs often generate many ideas, and screening them is a key part of the entrepreneurial process. The faster you can weed out the "dead-end" venture ideas, the more time and effort you can devote to the ones that remain. The more of the following characteristics that an idea has, the greater the opportunity it presents.

The Idea Creates or Adds Value for the Customer. A product or service that creates or adds value for the customer is one that solves a significant problem, or meets a significant need in new or different ways. Consider Sally Fox's idea for eliminating the dyeing process in textile operations.[33] By cross-breeding long-fibre white cotton and short-fibre coloured cotton she developed FoxFibre®, an environmentally friendly new cotton fibre that is naturally grown in several colours and is long enough to be spun commercially.

The Idea Provides a Competitive Advantage that Can Be Sustained. A competitive advantage exists when potential customers see the product or service as better than that of competitors. Sustaining a competitive advantage involves maintaining it in the face of competitors' actions or changes in the industry. All other things being equal, the longer markets are in a state of flux, the greater the likelihood of being able to sustain a competitive advantage. The absence of a competitive advantage or developing a competitive advantage that is not sustainable constitute two fatal flaws of many new ventures.[34]

After Sally Fox sold her first crop she was running a $10 million business with well-known companies like Levi's, L.L. Bean, Land's End, and Esprit as customers. But Fox's journey turned out to be bumpy. She had to relocate twice in response to pressure from powerful cotton growers who were afraid that her coloured varieties would contaminate their own crops. Also, once spinning mills began moving to Southeast Asia and South America, Fox's cotton lost the financial advantage it had over traditional cotton. (In their new locations, spinning mills no longer had to treat and dispose of the toxic waste from the cotton-dyeing process—a cost saving of about $4 per kilogram.) Because the overseas mills were unwilling or unable to process the relatively small quantities of cotton her farmers produced, she lost her big customers. Fox now concentrates on smaller mills and smaller customers, and she is rebuilding her business and her network of growers.

The Idea Is Marketable and Financially Viable. While it is important to determine whether there are enough customers who are willing to buy the product or service, it is also important to determine whether sales will lead to profits.[35] Estimating the market demand requires an initial understanding of who the customers are, what their needs are, and how the product or service will satisfy their needs better than competitors' products will. It also requires a thorough understanding of the key competitors who can provide similar products, services, or benefits to the target customer. For example,

10 years ago few people thought that manufacturers of cell phones would be competitors of camera manufacturers in providing real-time photos through digital imaging. Customers define the competition in terms of who can best satisfy their needs.

sales forecast
An estimate of how much of a product or service will be purchased by prospective customers over a specific period.

After learning about the competition and customers, the entrepreneur must prepare a **sales forecast**, which is an estimate of how much of a product or service will be purchased by the prospective customers for a specific period of time—typically one year. Total sales revenue is estimated by multiplying the units expected to be sold by the selling price. The sales forecast forms the foundation for determining the financial viability of the venture and the resources needed to start it.

Determining financial viability involves preparing financial forecasts, which are two- to three-year projections of a venture's future financial position and performance. They typically consist of an estimate of *start-up costs, a cash budget, an income statement*, and a *balance sheet* (see Chapter 11 for more details about these financial documents). These projections serve as the basis for decisions regarding whether to proceed with the venture, and, if so, the amount and type of financing to be used in financing the new business.

The Idea Has Low Exit Costs. The final consideration is the venture's exit costs. Exit costs are low if a venture can be shut down without a significant loss of time, money, or reputation.[36] If a venture is not expected to make a profit for a number of years, its exit costs are high, since the project cannot be reasonably abandoned in the short term. On the other hand, if the venture is expected to make a profit quickly, its exit costs will be lower, making the idea more attractive.

Developing the Opportunity

As the "dead-end" venture ideas are weeded out, a clear notion of the business concept and an entry strategy for pursuing it needs to be developed. As the process proceeds, the business concept often changes from what was originally envisioned. Some new ventures develop entirely new markets, products, and sources of competitive advantage once the needs of the marketplace and the economies of the business are better understood. So, while a vision of what is to be achieved is important, it is equally important to be responsive to new information and to be on the lookout for opportunities that were not originally anticipated. For example, if customers are not placing orders, as was the case with Sally Fox, it is important to find out why and make the appropriate adjustments.

franchise
An arrangement that gives franchisees (buyers) the right to sell the product of the franchiser (the seller).

New ventures use one or more of three main entry strategies: they introduce a totally new product or service; they introduce a product or service that will compete directly with existing competitive offerings but adds a new twist (such as offering the option of customizing the standard product); or they franchise.[37] A **franchise** is an arrangement in which a buyer (franchisee) purchases the right to sell the product or service of the seller (franchiser). We discuss franchising in more detail later in the chapter.

business plan
Document in which the entrepreneur summarizes her or his business strategy for the proposed new venture and how that strategy will be implemented.

When capital requirements are high, such as when a manufacturing operation is being proposed, there is a need for considerable research and planning. Similarly, if product development or operations are fairly complex, research and analysis will be needed to ensure that the costs associated with effectively coordinating tasks will be minimized. In these circumstances, or when the aim is to attract potential investors, then a comprehensive written business plan will be required. A **business plan** is a document that describes the entrepreneur's proposed business venture; explains why it is an opportunity; and outlines its marketing plan, its operational and financial details, and its managers' skills and abilities.[38] The contents of a business plan are shown in Table 4.1.

If market conditions are changing rapidly, the benefits gained from extensive research and planning diminish quickly. By the time the entrepreneur is ready to start, new competitors may have entered the market, prices may have changed, a location may no longer be available, and so on. Similarly, if the product is highly innovative, market research is of less value since the development of entirely new products involves *creating* needs and wants rather than simply responding to existing needs. Consequently, measuring the capacity of the product or service to fill existing customer needs or wants is less critical.

Contrary to what many people might think, planning does not have to be completed before action is taken. For example, if an electrical contracting business is being proposed in an area where there is a shortage of tradespeople, it would be important to seek out qualified employees prior to conducting other analyses that are needed to complete the business plan. Such early action also helps to build relationships that can be drawn on later. Obviously, some ventures do not lend themselves to early action, particularly those which are capital intensive. Since most entrepreneurs have limited resources, it is important to concentrate on the issues that can be dealt with, *and* that will help determine whether to proceed and how to proceed.[39]

Table 4.1 A Business Plan

A well-written business plan is formally structured, easy to read, and avoids confusion. By organizing the information into sections, it makes dealing with the information more manageable. The amount of detail and the order of presentation may vary from one venture to another and according to whom the plan is being prepared for (an investor will require more detail than if the plan is being prepared for internal use by the entrepreneur). An outline for a standard business plan is provided below. While formats vary, with some better suited to the type of venture being proposed than others, most contain the following elements.

I. **Cover Page**: Name of venture and owners, date prepared, contact person, his/her address, telephone and fax numbers, email address, and the name of the organization the plan is being presented to. The easier it is for the reader to contact the entrepreneur, the more likely the contact will occur.

II. **Executive Summary**: A one- to three-page overview of the total business plan. Written after the other sections are completed, it highlights their significant points, and aims to create enough excitement to motivate the reader to continue.

III. **Table of Contents**: This element lists major sections with page numbers for both the body and the appendices of the plan.

IV. **Company Description**: Explains the type of company and tells whether it is a manufacturing, retail, service, or other type of business. It also describes the proposed form of organization: sole proprietorship, partnership, corporation, or co-operative. A typical organization of this section is as follows: name and location; company objectives; nature and primary product or service of the business; current status (start-up, buyout, or expansion) and history if applicable; and legal form of organization.

V. **Product or Service Description**: Describes the product or service and indicates what is unique about it. This section explains the value that is added for customers—why people will buy the product or service; features of the product or service providing a competitive advantage; legal protection (patents, copyrights, trademarks, if relevant); and dangers of technical or style obsolescence.

VI. **Marketing**: This section has two key parts, the market analysis and the marketing plan. The market analysis convinces the reader that the entrepreneur understands the market for the product or service and can deal effectively with the competition to achieve sales projections. The marketing plan explains the strategy for achieving sales projections.

VII. **Operating Plan**: Explains the type of manufacturing or operating system to be used. Describes the facilities, labour, raw materials, and processing requirements.

VIII. **Management**: Identifies the key players—the management team, active investors, and directors—and cites the experience and competence they possess. This section includes a description of the management team, outside investors and directors and their qualifications, outside resource people, and plans for recruiting and training employees.

IX. **Financial Plan**: Specifies financial needs and contemplated sources of financing. Presents projected financial statements, including a cash budget, a balance sheet, and an income statement.

X. **Supporting Details/Appendix**: Provides supplementary materials to the plan such as résumés and other important supporting data.

Accessing Resources

bootstrapping
Doing more with less.

Typically, entrepreneurs acquire the various resources needed to make the venture a reality by **bootstrapping**, which means "doing more with less." Usually the term refers to financing techniques whereby entrepreneurs makes do with as few resources as possible and use other peoples' resources wherever they can. However, bootstrapping can also refer to the acquisition of other types of resources such as people, space, equipment, or materials that are loaned or provided free by customers or suppliers.

Financial Resources

There are two main types of financing—*debt* and *equity* (see Chapter 15 for a discussion of debt and equity financing). Since a business is at its riskiest point during the start-up phase, equity is usually more appropriate and accessible than debt. However, most new venture founders prefer debt because they are reluctant to give up any control to outsiders. To obtain debt financing, the entrepreneur must have an adequate equity investment in the business—typically 20 percent of the business's value—and collateral (or security).

collateral
Assets that a borrower uses to secure a loan or other credit, and that are subject to seizure by the lender if the loan isn't repaid according to the specified repayment terms.

Collateral refers to items (assets) owned by the business (such as a building and equipment) or by the individual (such as a house or car) that the borrower uses to secure a loan or other credit. These items can be seized by the lender if the loan isn't repaid according to the specified terms. To lenders, equity investment demonstrates the commitment of the entrepreneur, as individuals tend to be more committed to a venture if they have a substantial portion of what they own invested in it.

The most common sources of *equity* financing include:

1. **Personal savings**. New venture founders draw heavily on their own finances to start their businesses. Most try to save as much as they can in preparation for start-up.
2. **Love money**. This type of financing includes investments from friends, relatives, and business associates. It is called "love money" because it is often given more on the basis of the family relationship or friendship than on the merit of the business concept.
3. **Private investors**. One popular source of equity capital is informal capital from private investors called *angels*. Usually, these investors are financially well off individuals, many of whom are successful entrepreneurs who wish to recycle their wealth by investing in new businesses. For example, John Phillips agreed to cover the payroll for BPS Corp. when company founder Mark Opausky ran out of operating capital.[40]
4. **Venture capitalists**. Investments by venture capitalists come from professionally managed pools of investor money (venture capital). Since the risk of receiving little or no return on investment is high, only deals that present an attractive, high-growth business opportunity with a return between 35 and 50 percent are considered. Very few new ventures meet this criterion. Venture capital investment in Canada dropped from $5.9 billion in 2001 to $41.7 billion in 2006, so angels are becoming more important in providing start-up money to entrepreneurs.[41]

The most common sources of *debt* financing include:

1. **Financial institutions**. While commercial banks are the main providers of debt financing for established small businesses, it is usually difficult for a new business to borrow from a bank. Banks are risk averse, and loans to new businesses are considered very risky, largely because the business has yet to establish its ability to repay the loan. Typically, if an

entrepreneur is able to get bank financing for a new venture it is because the loan is in the form of a personal loan (as opposed to a business loan). The most common way to obtain a personal loan is to mortgage a house or borrow against the cash value of a life insurance policy.

In addition to commercial banks, other sources of debt financing include trust companies, co-operatives, finance companies, equipment companies, credit unions, and government agencies. Since finance companies lend in high-risk situations, their interest rates tend to be high. The federal and provincial governments have a wide range of financial assistance programs for small businesses. Among the various forms of assistance are low-interest loans, loan guarantees, interest-free loans, and wage subsidies.

2. **Suppliers**. Another source of financing is suppliers who provide goods (such as inventory) or services to the entrepreneur with an agreement to bill them later. This is referred to as *trade credit*. Trade credit can be very helpful in getting started, as it means that inventory, for example, can be acquired without paying cash for it which, in turn, frees up money to pay for other start-up costs. This type of financing is short-term; 30 days is the usual payback period. The amount of trade credit available to a new firm depends on the type of business and the supplier's confidence in the firm. Frequently, though, a new business has trouble getting trade credit since its capacity to repay has yet to be demonstrated.

Besides these conventional sources of financing, the possibilities for bootstrap financing are endless. For example, an entrepreneur might require an advance payment from customers, in full or in part. Equipment can be leased rather than being purchased (which reduces the risk of equipment becoming obsolete). Office furniture can be rented, premises can be shared, and the manufacture of products can be subcontracted, thereby avoiding the expense of procuring material, equipment, and facilities. All of these activities free up cash that can then be used for other purposes.

Other Types of Resources

A business may be owned by one person, but entrepreneurship is not a solo process. There are various stakeholders who provide resources to the venture. These include partners, employees, customers, suppliers, professionals, consultants, government agencies, lenders, shareholders, and venture capitalists. These stakeholders may have management or technical skills that are crucial for the success of the business, or they may have "connections" that help the business get started. Sometimes ownership is shared with one or more of these stakeholders in order to acquire the use of the resources they possess. When ownership is shared, decisions must be made regarding who to share it with, how much each stakeholder will own, at what cost, and under what conditions. The form of legal organization chosen affects whether ownership can be shared and whether resources can be accessed. We discuss this important point later in the chapter.

Deciding whether to share ownership by forming a *venture team* involves consideration of two main issues:

- *the size and scope of the venture*—How many people does the venture require? Is it a one-person operation or does it need contributions from others? Can people be hired to fill the key roles as they are required?
- *personal competencies*—What are the talents, know-how, skills, track-record, contacts, and resources that the entrepreneur brings to the venture? How do these match up with what the venture needs to succeed?

If the entrepreneur does not intend to establish a high-growth venture, going solo may be a realistic option. Some new venture founders bring on additional team members only as the business can afford them. Most successful solo businesses are simple types of ventures, such as small retail stores or services.[42] The odds for survival, growth, profitability, and attracting capital are increased by a team approach.[43]

Assessing the "Fit" Between Elements in the Entrepreneurial Process

Assessing the "fit" between the various elements in the entrepreneurial process is an ongoing task, since the shape of the opportunity, and consequently the resources and people needed to capitalize on it, typically changes as it is developed. It is the entrepreneur that stands to gain the most by attending to these "fits" and any changes they may require, although other stakeholders, such as investors, will be considering them as well.

The Entrepreneur–Opportunity Fit

The first assessment of fit is between the entrepreneur and the opportunity. The entrepreneur needs to decide whether the opportunity, as identified, is something he or she *can do* and *wants to do*. A realistic self-assessment is important. Prospective ventures that are of limited personal interest and require skills and abilities that do not fit well with those of the entrepreneur should be quickly eliminated. For example, it does little good to identify an opportunity for an ecotourism business in a wilderness area if the entrepreneur is a sedentary urban dweller.

Once the entrepreneur has chosen the opportunity he or she wants to pursue, the success of the venture depends heavily upon the individual or individuals involved. No matter how good the product or service concept is, as the opportunity changes shape, it may demand skills a single entrepreneur lacks. This may prompt a decision either to acquire the needed skills by forming a team or by getting further training.

The Opportunity–Resources Fit

Assessing the opportunity–resources fit involves determining whether the resources needed to capitalize on the opportunity can be acquired. As the opportunity changes shape, so too will the resource requirements. When challenges or risks arise, the aim is to determine whether they can be resolved, and if so, to deal with them as quickly as possible. For example, if the venture requires a greater financial investment than originally anticipated, this does not necessarily mean that the venture should be abandoned. Other options such as taking on partners or leasing rather than building a facility may be viable. Of course, some ventures may not be viable regardless of the alternatives considered.

The Entrepreneur–Resources Fit

Once the resource requirements of the venture have been determined, the entrepreneur needs to assess whether he or she has the capacity to meet those requirements. For example, an entrepreneur with a stellar reputation for software development will have an easier time attracting employees for a venture specializing in software than someone with no track record. If that same entrepreneur is well connected with people in the industry, he or she will be more likely to gain commitments from customers, and in turn, investors.

START-UP AND BEYOND

As we have seen, entrepreneurs must make the right start-up decisions, but they must also pay attention to how the business will be run once it is started. In this section, we examine three important topics that are relevant to these issues. First, we describe the three main ways that entrepreneurs start up a small business. Next, we look at the four main organizing options that are available to entrepreneurs. We conclude the chapter with a look at the reasons for success and failure in small business.

Starting up a Small Business

Most entrepreneurs start up a small business in one of three ways: they start from scratch, they buy an existing business, or they buy a franchise. We have already examined the "starting from scratch" alternative in detail in the preceding section, so we turn now to the latter two alternatives.

Buying an Existing Business

Describe three alternative strategies for becoming a business owner—*starting from scratch*, *buying an existing business*, and *buying a franchise*. 4

About one-third of all new businesses that were started in the past decade were bought from someone else. Many experts recommend buying an existing business because it increases the likelihood of success. An existing business has already proven its ability to attract customers. It has also established relationships with lenders, suppliers, and other stakeholders. Moreover, an existing track record gives potential buyers a much clearer picture of what to expect than any estimate of a new business's prospects.

But an entrepreneur who buys someone else's business may not be able to avoid certain problems. For example, there may be uncertainty about the exact financial shape the business is in, the business may have a poor reputation, the location may be poor, or it may be difficult to determine an appropriate purchase price.

Taking Over a Family Business. A special case of buying an existing business involves family businesses. Taking over a family business poses both opportunities and challenges. On the positive side, a family business can provide otherwise unobtainable financial and management resources; it often has a valuable reputation that can result in important community and business relationships; employee loyalty is often high; and an interested, unified family management and shareholders group may emerge. Toronto-based hosiery manufacturer Phantom Industries Inc. is an example of a family-owned business that has been successful through three generations of family members.[44] Another example is Irving Oil Ltd., the giant New Brunswick-based company which now has fifth-generation members running businesses that are part of its empire.[45]

On the other hand, major challenges can be evident in family businesses. There may be disagreements over which family member will control the business, or what price is to be paid if a family member sells his or her interest in the business. Some family members may feel that they have a right to a job, a promotion, or an impressive title simply because they are part of the family.[46] Examples of family businesses that have encountered serious problems are Saskatchewan-based Mitchell's Gourmet Foods (internal family feuding about who would control the company), Cuddy International (disagreements about which of the founder's sons were capable of running the business), and Eatons (inability of third-generation family members to adapt to changing market conditions).[47]

Franchising is very popular in Canada. It offers individuals who want to run their own business an opportunity to establish themselves quickly in a local market.

Buying a Franchise

If you drive around any Canadian town or city, you will notice retail outlets with names like McDonald's, Pizza Pizza, Subway, 7-Eleven, Re/Max, Swiss Chalet, Canadian Tire, Super Lube, Comfort Inn, Blockbuster Video, and Tim Hortons. These diverse businesses all have one thing in common: they are all franchises, operating under licences issued by parent companies to local entrepreneurs who own and manage them. Franchising accounts for 43 percent of retail sales in Canada and generates approximately $30 billion in annual sales revenue.[48]

franchising agreement Stipulates the duties and responsibilities of the franchisee and the franchiser.

A **franchising agreement** outlines the duties and responsibilities of each party. It stipulates the amount and type of payment that franchisees must make to the franchiser. Franchisees usually make an initial payment for the right to operate a local outlet of the franchise. They also make royalty payment to the franchiser ranging form 2 to 30 percent of the franchisee's annual revenues or profits. The franchisee also pays an advertising fee so that the franchiser can advertise in the franchisee's local area. Franchise fees vary widely, from $30 000 for a Fantastic Sam's hair salon, to $1 million for a Burger King franchise, to hundreds of millions for a professional sports franchise.

The Advantages of Franchising. Both franchisers and franchisees benefit from the franchising way of doing business (see Table 4.2).

Is Franchising for You? Do you think you would be happy being a franchisee? The answer depends on a number of factors, including your willingness to work hard, your ability to find a good franchise to buy, and the financial resources you possess. If you are thinking seriously of going into franchising, you should consider several areas of costs that you will incur:

- the franchise sales price
- expenses that will be incurred before the business opens
- training expenses
- operational expenses for the first six months
- personal financial needs for the first six months
- emergency needs

Table 4.2 The Benefits of Franchising

For the Franchiser	For the Franchisee
■ The franchiser can attain rapid growth for the chain by signing up many franchisees in many different locations. ■ Franchisees share in the cost of advertising. ■ The franchiser benefits from the investment money provided by franchisees. ■ Advertising money is spent more efficiently (the franchiser teams up with local franchisees to advertise only in the local area). ■ The franchiser benefits because franchisees are motivated to work hard for themselves; the more revenue the franchisee generates, the more money the franchiser makes. ■ The franchiser is freed from all details of a local operation, which are handled by the franchisee.	■ Franchisees own a small business that has access to big business management skills. ■ The franchisee does not have to build up a business from scratch. ■ Franchisee failure rates are lower than when starting one's own business. ■ A well-advertised brand name comes with the franchise and the franchisee's outlet is recognizable because it looks like all other outlets in the chain. ■ The franchiser may send the franchisee to a training program run by the franchiser (e.g., the Canadian Institute of Hamburgerology run by McDonald's). ■ The franchiser may visit the franchisee and provide expert advice on how to run the business. ■ Economies in buying allow franchisees to get lower prices for the raw materials they must purchase. ■ Financial assistance is provided by the franchiser in the form of loans; the franchiser may also help the franchisee obtain loans from local sources. ■ Franchisees are their own bosses and get to keep most of the profit they make.

Forms of Business Ownership

Whether they intend to run small farms, large factories, or online e-tailers, entrepreneurs must decide which form of legal ownership best suits their goals: *sole proprietorship, partnership, corporation*, or *co-operative*.

Describe four forms of *legal organization* for a business and discuss the advantages and disadvantages of each. 5

The Sole Proprietorship

The **sole proprietorship** is a business owned and operated by one person. Legally, if you set up a business as a sole proprietorship, your business is considered to be an extension of yourself (and not a separate legal entity). Though usually small, a sole proprietorship may be as large as a steel mill or as small as a lemonade stand. While the majority of businesses in Canada are sole proprietorships, proprietorships account for a small proportion of total business revenues.

sole proprietorship
Business owned and usually operated by one person who is responsible for all of its debts.

Advantages of a Sole Proprietorship. Freedom may be the most important benefit of a sole proprietorship. Sole proprietors answer to no one but themselves since they don't share ownership. A sole proprietorship is also easy to form. If you operate the business under your own name, with no additions, you don't even need to register your business name to start operating as a sole proprietor—you can go into business simply by putting a sign on the door. The simplicity of legal setup procedures makes this form appealing to self-starters and independent spirits, as do low the start-up costs.

Another attractive feature is the tax benefits. Most businesses suffer losses in their early stages. Since the business and the proprietor are legally one and the same, these losses can be deducted from income the proprietor earns from personal sources other than the business.

unlimited liability
A person who invests in a business is liable for all debts incurred by the business; personal possessions can be taken to pay debts.

Disadvantages of a Sole Proprietorship. A major drawback is **unlimited liability**, which means that a sole proprietor is personally liable (responsible) for all debts incurred by the business. If the business fails to generate enough cash, bills must be paid out of the owner's pocket. Another disadvantage is lack of continuity: A sole proprietorship legally dissolves when the owner dies. Finally, a sole proprietorship depends on the resources of one person whose managerial and financial limitations may constrain the business. Sole proprietors often find it hard to borrow money to start up or expand. Many bankers fear that they won't be able to recover loans if the owner becomes disabled.

The Partnership

partnership
A business with two or more owners who share in the operation of the firm and in financial responsibility for the firm's debts.

A **partnership** is established when two or more individuals (partners) agree to combine their financial, managerial, and technical abilities for the purpose of operating a business for profit. This form of ownership is often used by professionals such as accountants, lawyers, and engineers. Partnerships are often an extension of a business that began as a sole proprietorship. The original owner may want to expand, or the business may have grown too big for a single person to handle.

general partner
A partner who is actively involved in managing the firm and has unlimited liability.

limited partner
A partner who generally does not participate actively in the business, and whose liability is limited to the amount invested in the partnership.

general partnership
A type of partnership where all partners are jointly liable for the obligations of the business.

limited partnership
A type of partnership with at least one general partner (who has unlimited liability) and one or more limited partners. The limited partners can not participate in the day-to-day management of the business or they risk the loss of their limited liability status.

There are two basic types of partners in a partnership. **General partners** are actively involved in managing the firm and have unlimited liability. **Limited partners** don't participate actively in the business, and their liability is limited to the amount they invested in the partnership. A **general partnership** is the most common type and is similar to the sole proprietorship in that all the (general) partners are jointly liable for the obligations of the business. The other type of partnership—the **limited partnership**—consists of at least one general partner (who has unlimited liability) and one or more limited partners. The limited partners cannot participate in the day-to-day management of the business or they risk the loss of their limited liability status.

Advantages of a Partnership. The most striking advantage of a general partnership is the ability to grow by adding talent and money. Partnerships also have a somewhat easier time borrowing funds than do sole proprietorships. Banks and other lending institutions prefer to make loans to enterprises that are not dependent on a single individual. Partnerships can also invite new partners to join by investing money.

Like a sole proprietorship, a partnership is simple to organize, with few legal requirements. Even so, all partnerships must begin with an agreement of some kind. It may be written, oral, or even unspoken. Wise partners, however, insist on a written agreement to avoid trouble later. This agreement should answer such questions as:

- Who invested what sums of money in the partnership?
- Who will receive what share of the partnership's profits?
- Who does what and who reports to whom?
- How may the partnership be dissolved?
- How will leftover assets be distributed among the partners?
- How would surviving partners be protected from claims by surviving heirs if a partner dies?
- How will disagreements be resolved?

The partnership agreement is strictly a private document. No laws require partners to file an agreement with some government agency. Nor are partnerships regarded as legal entities. In the eyes of the law, a partnership is nothing more than two or more persons working together. The partnership's lack of legal standing means that the partners are taxed as individuals.

Disadvantages of a Partnership. As with sole proprietorships, unlimited liability is the greatest drawback of a general partnership. By law, each partner may be held personally liable for all debts incurred in the name of the partnership. And if any partner incurs a debt, even if the other partners know nothing about it, they are all liable if the offending partner cannot pay up. Another problem with partnerships is lack of continuity. When one partner dies or pulls out, a partnership dissolves legally, even if the other partners agree to stay to continue the business.

A related drawback is the difficulty of transferring ownership. No partner may sell out without the other partners' consent. Thus, the life of a partnership may depend on the ability of retiring partners to find someone compatible with the other partners to buy them out. Finally, a partnership provides little or no guidance in resolving conflicts between the partners. For example, suppose one partner wants to expand the business rapidly and the other wants it to grow slowly. If under the partnership agreement the two are equal, it may be difficult for them to decide what to do.

A practical illustration of the kinds of problems that can arise in partnerships is described in the Exercising Your Ethics assignment found at the end of the chapter.

The Corporation

When you think of corporations you probably think of giant businesses such as Air Canada, Imperial Oil, or Nortel Networks. The very word "corporation" suggests bigness and power. Yet, the tiny corner newsstand has as much right to incorporate as does a giant oil refiner. And the newsstand and oil refiner have the same basic characteristics that all corporations share: legal status as a separate entity, property rights and obligations, and an indefinite lifespan.

A corporation has been defined as "an artificial being, invisible, intangible, and existing only in contemplation of the law." As such, corporations may sue and be sued, buy, hold, and sell property, make and sell products to consumers, and commit crimes and be tried and punished for them. Simply defined, a **corporation** is a business that is a separate legal entity, that is liable for its own debts, and whose owners' liability is limited to their investment.

corporation
A business considered by law to be a legal entity separate from its owners with many of the legal rights and privileges of a person; a form of business organization in which the liability of the owners is limited to their investment in the firm.

Stockholders—investors who buy shares of ownership in the form of stock—are the real owners of a corporation. (The different kinds of stockholders are described in Chapter 15.) Profits may be distributed to stockholders in the form of dividends, although corporations are not required to pay dividends. Instead, they often reinvest any profits in the business. Common stockholders have the last claim to any assets if the company folds. Dividends on **common stock** are paid on a per share basis (if a dividend is declared). Thus, a shareholder with 10 shares receives 10 times the dividend paid a shareholder with one share. *Class A* common shares always have voting rights, but *Class B* common shares usually do not. Shareholder rights advocates argue that Class B common shares prevent democracy from working in companies because controlling shareholders hold most of the Class A stock and sell non-voting Class B stock to the general public. When investors cannot attend a shareholders' meeting, they can grant authority to vote the shares to someone who will attend. This procedure, called voting by *proxy*, is the way almost all individual investors vote.

stockholders
Investors who buy shares of ownership in the form of stock.

common stock
Shares whose owners usually have last claim on the corporation's assets (after creditors and owners of preferred stock) but who have voting rights in the firm.

The **board of directors** is the governing body of a corporation. Its main responsibility is to ensure that the corporation is run in the best interests of the stockholders. The directors choose the president and other officers of the business and delegate the power to run the day-to-day activities of the business to those officers. The directors set policy on paying dividends, on financing major spending, and on executive salaries and benefits. Large

board of directors
A group of individuals elected by a firm's shareholders and charged with overseeing, and taking legal responsibility for, the firm's actions.

corporations tend to have large boards with as many as 20 or 30 directors. Smaller corporations, on the other hand, tend to have no more than five directors. Usually, these are people with personal or professional ties to the corporation, such as family members, lawyers, and accountants. The Business Accountability box describes some recent issues that have arisen regarding boards of directors.

BUSINESS ACCOUNTABILITY

Getting on Boards

Boards of directors today are under pressure to become actively involved in planning and monitoring corporate activity. At WorldCom, Tyco, and other corporations, the boards were either unaware of the misdeeds taking place around them or, in some cases, actually were party to those activities. At Enron, for example, the board of directors several times voted to waive its policies regarding independence and arms-length transactions, allowing executives to continue their fraud unhampered. When the negligence of these boards was publicly exposed, investors cried out for reform.

Investors want boards to take a more active role in decision making and to provide more oversight. Most corporations, eager to distance themselves from scandal, are considering transformation of their boards of directors. The most effective boards are composed of more outsiders than insiders. This allows the directors to have independence from the powerful CEO. To enhance decision-making ability, board members should come from diverse backgrounds and have top-level management experience. Directors should own a substantial amount of the company's stock. Boards should be actively involved in decision making, such as meeting regularly, setting the overall corporate strategy, and having access to confidential information. Boards that do not meet these criteria may be too cozy with corporate executives and thus fail to vigilantly safeguard the interests of shareholders.

Specific questions that should be asked are as follows:

- Are the majority of the board's members independent of the company? (They should not be part of the company's management, they shouldn't work for another company that does business with the company, and they should not come from a parent company that controls the company.)
- Are the majority of the compensation committee's members independent? (The compensation committee determines executive pay.)
- Are the majority of the nominating committee's members independent? (The nominating committee recommends new board members.)
- Does the company have a system for formally evaluating the performance of its board of directors?
- Do the directors and the CEO own stock in the company?
- Do directors have to stand for re-election every year?
- Does the company have a written statement of its corporate governance practices?
- Does the company have only voting common shares and no non-voting shares?

Many high-tech companies are defying these guidelines. For example, the board of Amazon.com has just five members, is chaired by CEO Jeff Bezos, and lacks any real semblance of independence. Pat McGurn, a director at Institutional Shareholder Services, says, "People are coming to view Amazon's problems as the result of poor corporate governance rather than the effect of the economy in general. Unfortunately, the board doesn't seem to see governance as part of the solution."

This problem is not restricted to high-tech companies. In 2003, Gerald Schwartz, CEO of Onex Corporation, named his wife to sit on the board of directors of Onex. Institutional shareholders and corporate governance experts said such a move is contrary to the efforts of most public companies to increase the independence of their directors. One securities lawyer asked how a board member could evaluate a CEO's performance if the CEO is her husband.

Each year the *Report on Business* ranks Canadian corporations in terms of four key areas: board composition, board compensation, shareholder rights, and disclosure. In 2005, the top-ranked companies were SNC-Lavalin Group Inc., Bank of Montreal, Bank of Nova Scotia, and Suncor Energy (in that order). The lowest-ranked companies were Reitmans (Canada) Ltd., Duvernay Oil Corp., and Northern Orion Resources.

Inside directors are employees of the company and have primary responsibility for the corporation. That is, they are also top managers, such as the president and executive vice-president. **Outside directors** are not employees of the corporation in the normal course of its business. Attorneys, accountants, university officials, and executives from other firms are commonly used as outside directors.

inside directors
Members of a corporation's board of directors who are also full-time employees of the corporation.

outside directors
Members of a corporation's board of directors who are not also employees of the corporation on a day-to-day basis.

Types of Corporations. A **public corporation** is one whose shares of stock are widely held and available for sale to the general public. Anyone who has the funds to pay for them can buy shares of companies such as George Weston, Air Canada, or Canadian Pacific. The stock of a **private corporation**, on the other hand, is held by only a few people and is not generally available for sale. The controlling group may be a family, employees, or the management group. Para Paints of Canada and Bata Shoes are private corporations.

public corporation
A business whose stock is widely held and available for sale to the general public.

private corporation
A business whose stock is held by a small group of individuals and is not usually available for sale to the general public.

Most new corporations start out as private corporations, because few investors will buy an unknown stock. As the corporation grows and develops a record of success, it may issue shares to the public as a way of raising additional money. This is called its **initial public offering (IPO)**. In 2005, E.D. Smith, a maker of jams and pie fillings, went public with a $110 million IPO, and Tim Hortons went public in 2006. Internet phenomenon Google Inc. went public in 2004 with an IPO that was expected to net the company nearly $2 billion. IPOs were not very attractive to investors during the stock market decline of 2001–2003, but they have become more popular as the market has recovered. In 2001, for example, there were 1924 IPOs worth $26 billion, but in 2004 there were 2752 IPOs worth over $48 billion.[49]

initial public offering (IPO)
Selling shares of stock in a company for the first time to a general investing public.

A public corporation can also "go private," which is the reverse of going public. In 2004, Cara Operations Ltd.—the parent company of Harvey's, Swiss Chalet, and Second Cup—went private, and in 2007 Magnotta Winery announced that it would go private.[50] **Private equity firms** buy publicly traded companies and then take them private. They often make major changes to the way the company operates in order to increase its value. During 2007, several private equity firms made bids for Bell Canada Enterprises (BCE).[51]

private equity firms
Companies that buy publicly traded companies and then make them private.

In recent years, some corporations have converted to an **income trust** structure which allowed them to avoid paying corporate income tax if they distributed all or most of their earnings to investors. For example, BCE could have avoided an $800 million tax bill for 2008 by becoming an income trust. In a surprise move in 2006, the government announced that it would begin taxing income trusts more like corporations by 2011. This announcement caused a significant decline in the market value of income trusts, and it also means that very few corporations will now convert to an income trust structure.[52]

income trust
A structure allowing companies to avoid paying corporate income tax if they distribute all or most of their earnings to investors.

Formation of the Corporation. The two most widely used methods to form a corporation are federal incorporation under the Canada Business Corporations Act and provincial incorporation under any of the provincial corporations acts. The former is used if the company is going to operate in more than one province; the latter is used if the founders intend to carry on business in only one province. Except for banks and certain insurance and loan companies, any company can be federally incorporated under the Canada Business Corporations Act. To do so, articles of incorporation must be drawn up. These articles include such information as the name of the corporation, the type and number of shares to be issued, the number of directors the corporation will have, and the location of the company's operations. The specific procedures and information required for provincial incorporation vary from province to province.

All corporations must attach the word "Limited" (Ltd./Ltée), "Incorporated" (Inc.), or "Corporation" (Corp.) to the company name to indicate clearly to customers and suppliers that the owners have limited liability for corporate debts. The same sorts of rules apply in other countries. British firms, for example, use PLC for "public limited company" and German companies use AG for "Aktiengesellschaft" (corporation).

limited liability
Investor liability is limited to their personal investments in the corporation; courts cannot touch the personal assets of investors in the event that the corporation goes bankrupt.

Advantages of Incorporation. The biggest advantage of the corporate structure is **limited liability**, which means that the liability of investors is limited to their personal investment in the corporation. In the event of failure, the courts may seize a corporation's assets and sell them to pay debts, but the courts cannot touch the investors' personal possessions. If, for example, you invest $1000 in a corporation that goes bankrupt, you may lose your $1000, but no more. In other words, $1000 is the extent of your liability.

Another advantage of a corporation is continuity. Because it has a legal life independent of its founders and owners, a corporation can, in theory, continue forever. Shares of stock may be sold or passed on to heirs, and most corporations also benefit from the continuity provided by professional management. Finally, corporations have advantages in raising money. By selling **stock**, they expand the number of investors and the amount of available funds. The term "stock" refers to a share of ownership in a corporation. Continuity and legal status tend to make lenders more willing to grant loans to corporations.

stock
A share of ownership in a corporation.

Disadvantages of Incorporation. One of the disadvantages for a new firm in forming a corporation is the cost (approximately $2500). Additionally, corporations also need legal help in meeting government regulations because they are far more heavily regulated than are proprietorships or general partnerships. Some people say that **double taxation** is another problem with the corporate form of ownership. By this they mean that a corporation must pay income taxes on its profits, and then shareholders must also pay personal income taxes on the **dividends** they receive from the corporation. The dividend a corporation pays is the amount of money, normally a portion of the profits, that is distributed to the shareholders. Since dividends paid by the corporation are paid with after-tax dollars, this amounts to double taxation. Others point out that shareholders get a dividend tax credit, which largely offsets the effect of double taxation.

double taxation
A corporation must pay income taxes on its profits, and then shareholders must also pay personal income taxes on the dividends they receive from the corporation.

dividends
The amount of money, normally a portion of the profits, which is distributed to the shareholders.

The Co-operative

co-operative
An organization that is formed to benefit its owners in the form of reduced prices and/or the distribution of surpluses at year-end.

A **co-operative** is an incorporated form of business that is organized, owned, and democratically controlled by the people who use its products and services, and whose earnings are distributed on the basis of use of the co-operative rather than level of investment. As such, it is formed to benefit its owners in the form of reduced prices and/or the distribution of surpluses at year-end. The process works like this: suppose some farmers believe they can get cheaper fertilizer prices if they form their own company and purchase in large volumes. They might then form a co-operative, which can be either federally or provincially chartered. Prices are generally lower to buyers and, at the end of the fiscal year, any surpluses are distributed to members on the basis of how much they purchased. If Farmer Jones bought 5 percent of all co-op sales, he would receive 5 percent of the surplus.

The co-operative's start-up capital usually comes from shares purchased by the co-operative's members. Sometimes all it takes to qualify for membership in a co-operative is the purchase of one share with a fixed (and often nominal) value. Federal co-operatives, however, can raise capital by issuing investment shares to members or non-members. Co-operatives, like investor-owned corporations, have directors and appointed officers.

Types of Co-operatives. There are hundreds of different co-operatives, but they generally function in one of six main areas of business:

- Consumer co-operatives—These organizations sell goods to both members and the general public (e.g., co-op gasoline stations, agricultural implement dealers).
- Financial co-operatives—These organizations operate much like banks, accepting deposits from members, giving loans, and providing chequing services (e.g., credit unions).
- Insurance co-operatives—These organizations provide many types of insurance coverage, such as life, fire, and liability (for example, the Co-operative Hail Insurance Company of Manitoba).
- Marketing co-operatives—These organizations sell the produce of their farm members and purchase inputs for the production process (e.g., seed and fertilizer). Some, like Federated Co-operatives, also purchase and market finished products.
- Service co-operatives—These organizations provide members with services, such as recreation.
- Housing co-operatives—These organizations provide housing for members, who purchase a share in the co-operative, which holds the title to the housing complex.

In terms of numbers, co-operatives are the least important form of ownership. However, they are of significance to society and to their members; they may provide services that are not readily available or that cost more than the members would otherwise be willing to pay. Table 4.3 compares the various forms of business ownership using different characteristics.

Advantages of a Co-operative. Co-operatives have many of the same advantages as investor-owned corporations, such as limited liability of owners and continuity. A key benefit of a co-operative relates to its structure. Each member has only one vote in the affairs of the co-operative, regardless of how many shares he or she owns. This system prevents voting and financial control of the business by a few wealthy individuals.

Whereas investor-owned corporations are typically exposed to double taxation because dividends to shareholders are distributed out of after-tax corporate income, co-operatives are allowed to deduct patronage refunds to members out of before-tax income. Thus, income is only taxed at the

Table 4.3 A Comparison of Four Forms of Business Ownership

Characteristic	Sole Proprietorship	Partnership	Corporation	Co-operative
Protection against liability for bad debts	low	low	high	high
Ease of formation	high	high	medium	medium
Permanence	low	low	high	high
Ease of ownership transfer	low	low	high	high
Ease of raising money	low	medium	high	high
Freedom from regulation	high	high	low	medium
Tax advantages	high	high	low	high

individual member level rather than at both the co-operative and member level. In other words, a co-operative does not pay tax on income that it distributes as patronage dividends.[53]

Disadvantages of a Co-operative. One of the main disadvantages of co-operatives relates to attracting equity investment. Since the benefits from being a member of a co-operative arise through the level of use of the co-operative rather than the level of equity invested, members do not have an incentive to invest in equity capital of the co-operative. Another drawback is that democratic voting arrangements and dividends based purely on patronage turn off some entrepreneurs from forming or joining a co-operative.

SUCCESS AND FAILURE IN SMALL BUSINESS

6 Identify four key reasons for success in small businesses and four key reasons for failure.

Why do some ventures succeed while others fail? This question is difficult to answer since most of what we know is based on businesses that may under- or over-represent firms that succeed or fail. As outlined earlier, when the focus is businesses with employees, as is the case with a great deal of research, businesses run by the self-employed (with no employees) are ignored. Much of what we know about business "failure" is based upon all firms that stopped operating, even though a business can cease operations for a variety of reasons other than failure, such as retirement or a decision by the entrepreneur to move on to something else.[54] Keeping these considerations in mind, we now outline the factors that have typically been associated with success and failure.

Reasons for Success

Beyond the specific findings like the CIBC study, four general factors typically are cited to explain the success of small business owners:

1. *Hard work, drive, and dedication.* Small business owners must be committed to succeeding and be willing to put in the time and effort to make it happen. Long hours and few vacations generally characterize the first few years of new business ownership.
2. *Market demand for the product or service.* Careful analysis of market conditions can help small business people assess the probable reception of their products. If the area around a college has only one pizza parlour, a new pizzeria is more likely to succeed than if there are already 10 in operation.
3. *Managerial competence.* Successful small business people have a solid understanding of how to manage a business. They may acquire competence through training (taking courses), experience, or by using the expertise of others. Few, however, succeed alone or straight out of university or college. Most spend time in successful companies or partner with others to bring expertise to a new business.
4. *Luck.* Luck also plays a role in the success of some firms. For example, after one entrepreneur started an environmental clean-up firm, he struggled to keep his business afloat. Then the government committed a large sum of money for toxic waste clean-up. He was able to get several large contracts, and his business is now thriving.

A 2005 study conducted by CIBC World Markets found that small businesses with above-average revenue growth were run by owners who had more formal education, used professional advisors, adopted the corporate form of ownership, did outsourcing work for other companies, had a high level of internet connectivity, and used the internet to sell outside Canada.[55]

Reasons for Failure

Small businesses fail for many *specific* reasons (see Table 4.4). Entrepreneurs may have no control over some of these factors (for example, weather, fraud, accidents), but they can influence most items on the list. Although no set pattern has been established, four *general* factors contribute to failure:

1. *Managerial incompetence or inexperience.* Some entrepreneurs put their faith in common sense, overestimate their own managerial skills, or believe that hard work alone ensures success. If managers don't know how to make basic business decisions or don't understand basic management principles, they aren't likely to succeed in the long run.
2. *Neglect.* Some entrepreneurs try to launch ventures in their spare time, and others devote only limited time to new businesses. But starting a small business demands an overwhelming time commitment. If an entrepreneur isn't willing to put in the time and effort that a business requires, it isn't likely to survive.
3. *Weak control systems.* Effective control systems keep a business on track and alert managers to potential trouble. If the control systems

Table 4.4 Causes of Small Business Failure

Poor management skills ■ poor delegation and organizational ability ■ lack of depth in management team ■ entrepreneurial incompetence, such as a poor understanding of finances and business markets ■ lack of experience	**Personal reasons** ■ loss of interest in business ■ accident, illness ■ death ■ family problems
Inadequate marketing capabilities ■ difficulty in marketing product ■ market too small, nonexistent, or declines ■ too much competition ■ problems with distribution systems	**Disasters** ■ fire ■ weather ■ strikes ■ fraud by entrepreneur or others
Inadequate financial capabilities ■ weak skills in accounting and finance ■ lack of budgetary control ■ inadequate costing systems ■ incorrect valuation of assets ■ unable to obtain financial backing	**Other** ■ mishandling of large project ■ excessive standard of living ■ lack of time to devote to business ■ difficulties with associates or partners ■ government policies change
Inadequate production capabilities ■ poorly designed production systems ■ old and inefficient production facilities and equipment ■ inadequate control over quality ■ problems with inventory control	

don't signal impending problems, the business may be in serious trouble before you spot more obvious difficulties.

4. *Insufficient capital.* Some entrepreneurs are overly optimistic about how soon they'll start earning profits. In most cases, it takes months or even years. Amazon.com didn't earn a profit for 10 years, but obviously still required capital to pay employees and to cover other expenses. Experts say you need enough capital to operate at least six months without earning a profit; some recommend enough to last a year.[56]

Summary of Learning Objectives

1. Explain the meaning and interrelationship of the terms *small business, new venture creation,* and *entrepreneurship.* A small business has less than 100 employees. A new firm is one that has become operational within the previous 12 months, has adopted any of four main organizational forms—*proprietorship, partnership, corporation, or co-operative*—and sells goods or services. Entrepreneurship is the *process* of identifying an opportunity in the marketplace and accessing the resources needed to capitalize on it. In relation to small and/or new businesses, entrepreneurship is the process by which a small business or a new business is created.

2. Describe the role of small and new businesses in the Canadian economy. While 98 percent of employer businesses in Canada are small (they have less than 100 employees), 49 percent of the total private sector labour force work for small businesses. The distribution of employment by size of firm varies across industries. The small business sector's capacity for entrepreneurship and innovation accounts for much of the job creation this sector contributes to the economy, with start-ups accounting for most of the growth. On average, the number of businesses increased by 9300 each year during the 1991–2003 period, with most of the growth occurring in the services-producing sector. As the number of businesses has increased, so too has the number of women-led firms.

3. Explain the *entrepreneurial process* and describe its three key elements. The entrepreneurial process occurs within a social, political, and economic context and consists of three key elements: the entrepreneur, the opportunity, and resources. The *entrepreneur* is the driving force in identifying an opportunity and accessing the resources to capitalize on it. *Opportunities* don't simply materialize, entrepreneurs create them. Opportunity identification involves: generating ideas, screening them to determine their potential, and developing the ones that remain. Entrepreneurs typically access the various *resources* needed by bootstrapping—doing more with less. These resources are both financial and non-financial. Two types of financing—*debt* and *equity*—can be accessed from a range of sources.

4. Describe three alternative strategies for becoming a business owner—*starting from scratch, buying an existing business,* and *buying a franchise.* It is necessary to work through the entrepreneurial process in order to *start a business from scratch.* Whether start-up efforts will result in a new business often depends upon how well matched the entrepreneur's skills and abilities are with the opportunity and the resources required, as well as how well matched the opportunity and resources are. Of the ventures that are brought to fruition, some will grow, while others will decline, die, or remain stable. Generally, when someone buys an *existing business,* the odds of success are better. An existing business has already proven its ability to attract customers. It has also established relationships with lenders, suppliers, and other stakeholders. Moreover, an existing track record gives potential buyers a much clearer picture of what to expect than any estimate of a new business's prospects. On the other hand, there may be uncertainty about the exact financial shape the business is in, the business may have a poor reputation, the location may be poor, or it may be difficult to determine an appropriate purchase price. A special case of buying an existing business involves family businesses, which pose both opportunities and challenges. In buying a *franchise* the buyer (franchisee) purchases the right to sell the product or service of the seller (franchiser) according to the terms of the franchising agreement. In return the franchiser provides assistance with the business's start-up as well as with ongoing operations once the business opens its doors.

5. Describe four forms of *legal organization* for a business and discuss the advantages and disadvantages of each. The *sole proprietorship* is a business owned and operated by one person. Answering only to themselves, sole proprietors enjoy considerable freedom in running the business. The ease of setting up a sole proprietorship makes it appealing to self-starters, as do the low start-up costs and the tax benefits. A major drawback is unlimited liability. A sole proprietor is personally liable for all debts incurred by the business. Another disadvantage is lack of continuity: A sole proprietorship dissolves when the owner dies. Finally, a sole proprietorship depends on the resources of a single individual.

The *general partnership* is similar to the sole proprietorship in that all partners have unlimited liability for the obligations of the business. The biggest advantage is its ability to grow by adding new talent and money. Because banks prefer to make loans to enterprises that are not dependent on single individuals, it's easier for partnerships to borrow money. They can also invite new partners to join by investing. Although a partnership is easy to form and has few legal requirements, all partnerships should have a partnership agreement. Partners are taxed as individuals, and unlimited liability is a drawback. Each partner may be liable for all partnership debts. Partnerships may lack continuity, and transferring ownership may be hard. No partner may sell out without the consent of the others.

All *corporations* share certain characteristics: they are separate legal entities, they have property rights and obligations, and they have indefinite lifespans. They may sue and be sued; buy, hold, and sell property; make and sell products; commit crimes and be tried and punished for them. The biggest advantage of incorporation is limited liability: Investor liability is limited to one's personal investments in the corporation. If the business fails, the courts may sell a corporation's assets but cannot touch the personal possessions of investors. Another advantage is continuity—a corporation can continue forever. Shares can be sold or passed on to heirs, and most corporations benefit from the continuity of professional management. Finally, corporations have advantages in raising money. By selling stock, they expand the number of investors and the amount of available funds. Legal protections tend to make lenders more willing to grant loans.

Start-up costs and complexity are among the disadvantages of incorporating. Corporations are heavily regulated and must meet complex legal requirements in the provinces in which they're chartered. A potential drawback to incorporation is *double taxation*. A corporation pays income taxes on company profits, and its stockholders pay taxes on income returned by their investments. Thus, corporate profits are taxed twice—at the corporate and at ownership levels (but the dividend tax credit given to owners may offset the effects of double taxation). Of the two types of private-sector corporations—public and privately held—the vast majority are privately held. In forming a corporation, a business will incorporate federally if it is going to operate in more than one province and provincially if it is going to operate in only one province.

A *co-operative* is an organization that is formed to benefit its owners in the form of reduced prices and/or the distribution of surpluses at year-end. It is an incorporated business that is organized, owned, and democratically controlled by the people who use its products and services. The distribution of its earnings (or surpluses) is based upon the use of the co-operative rather than the level of investment. In addition to the two main advantages co-operatives share with corporations—limited liability and continuity—they also have two benefits that corporations don't have. Since all members have one vote, this democratic control ensures a few people cannot dominate the decision-making. Additionally, co-operatives aren't subject to double taxation since surpluses are distributed to members from pre-tax profits. Co-operatives are not without disadvantages. The main drawback is that co-operatives often have difficulty raising equity, since members gain financial benefit according to their use of the co-operative, not according to the amount they have invested. While there are hundreds of different co-operatives, they usually function in one of six areas of business: consumer co-operatives, financial co-operatives, insurance co-operatives, marketing co-operatives, service co-operatives, or housing co-operatives.

6. Identify four key reasons for success in small businesses and four key reasons for failure. Four basic factors explain most small-business success: (1) hard work, drive, and dedication; (2) market demand for the products or services being provided; (3) managerial competence; and (4) luck. Four factors contribute to small-business failure: (1) managerial incompetence or inexperience; (2) neglect; (3) weak control systems; and (4) insufficient capital.

QUESTIONS AND EXERCISES

Questions for Analysis

1. What are some of the problems that are encountered when we try to define the term "small business"?
2. Why are new ventures the main source of job creation and new product/service ideas?
3. Do you think that you would be a successful entrepreneur? Why or why not?
4. Consider a new product or service that has recently become available for purchase by consumers. To what extent did this product or service possess the "screening" characteristics that are described in the chapter (adding value, providing competitive advantage, etc.)?
5. Using the product or service you described in Question 4, analyze the extent to which there is a good "fit" between the various elements in the entrepreneurial process.
6. Why might a private corporation choose to remain private? Why might it choose to "go public"?

Application Exercises

7. Identify three trends—whether in fashion, lifestyle, or something else—and describe at least five ideas for capitalizing on one of them.
8. Find a newspaper or magazine article that describes someone who is an entrepreneur. Use the information provided to explain what makes this person an entrepreneur.
9. Spend some time watching what people do and how they do it, and then (a) identify two ways to make what they do easier, and (b) describe two problems you observed and identify strategies for resolving those problems. Scan the past month's newspapers or magazines to find an article that, in your opinion, describes someone who is an entrepreneur. Using the information provided in the article, explain what makes this person an entrepreneur.
10. Interview the owner-manager of a sole proprietorship or a general partnership. What characteristics of that business form led the owner to choose it? Does he or she ever contemplate changing the form of the business?

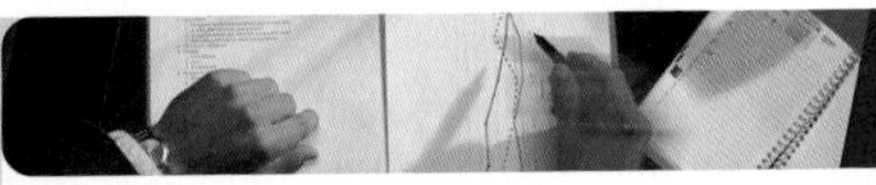

BUILDING YOUR BUSINESS SKILLS

Working the Internet

Goal

To encourage students to define opportunities and problems for small companies doing business on the internet.

Situation

Suppose you and two partners own a gift basket store, specializing in special-occasion baskets for individual and corporate clients. Your business is doing well in your community, but you believe there may be opportunity for growth through a virtual storefront on the internet.

Method

Step 1 Join with two other students and assume the role of business partners. Start by researching internet businesses. Look at books and articles at the library and contact the following websites for help:

- Canada Business Service Centres: www.cbsc.org
- Small Business Administration (United States): www.sba.gov
- IBM Small Business Center: www.businesscenter.ibm.com
- Apple Small Business Home Page: www.apple.com/business/

These sites may lead you to other sites, so keep an open mind.

Step 2 Based on your research, determine the importance of the following small business issues:

- an analysis of changing company finances as a result of expansion to the internet
- an analysis of your new competitive marketplace (the world) and how it affects your current marketing approach, which focuses on your local community
- identification of sources of management advice as the expansion proceeds
- the role of technology consultants in launching and maintaining the website
- customer service policies in your virtual environment

Follow-Up Questions

1. Do you think your business would be successful on the internet? Why or why not?
2. Based on your analysis, how will internet expansion affect your current business practices? What specific changes are you likely to make?
3. Do you think that operating a virtual storefront will be harder or easier than doing business in your local community? Explain your answer.

EXERCISING YOUR ETHICS: TEAM EXERCISE

Public or Private? That Is the Question

The Situation

The Thomas Corporation is a very well-financed, private corporation with a solid and growing product line, little debt, and a stable workforce. However, in the past few months, there has been a growing rift among the board of directors that has created considerable differences of opinion as to the future directions of the firm.

The Dilemma

Some board members believe the firm should "go public" with a stock offering. Since each board member owns a large block of corporate stock, each would make a considerable amount of money if the company went public.

Other board members want to maintain the status quo as a private corporation. The biggest advantage of this approach is that the firm maintains its current ability to remain autonomous in its operations.

The third faction of the board also wants to remain private, but clearly has a different agenda. Those board members have identified a small public corporation that is currently one of the company's key suppliers. Their idea is to buy the supplying company, shift its assets to the parent firm, sell all of its remaining operations, terminate employees, and then outsource the production of the parts it currently buys from the firm. Their logic is that the firm would gain significant assets and lower its costs.

Team Activity

Assemble a group of four students and assign each group member to one of the following roles:

- An employee at the Thomas Corporation
- A customer of the Thomas Corporation
- An investor in the Thomas Corporation
- A board member who has not yet decided which option is best

Action Steps

1. Before discussing the situation with your group, and from the perspective of your assigned role, which option do you think is best? Write down the reasons for your position.
2. Before discussing the situation with your group, and from the perspective of your assigned role, what are the underlying ethical issues, if any, in this situation? Write down the issues.
3. Gather your group together and reveal, in turn, each member's comments on the situation. Next, reveal the ethical issues listed by each member.
4. Appoint someone to record the main points of agreement and disagreement within the group. How do you explain the results? What accounts for any disagreement?
5. From an ethical standpoint, what does your group conclude is the most appropriate action that should be taken by the Thomas Corporation in this situation?
6. Develop a group response to the following question: What do you think most people would do in this situation?

BUSINESS CASE 4

Getting in on the Ground Floor

Larry Gibson, 51, oversees a business empire that employs 80 people full time (plus 110 under contract) and is projected to have sales of $30 million this year. But things didn't start out that way. Gibson got into the flooring business after finding university too slow for his liking. After working as a flooring installer in Halifax, he went west in the late 1970s and worked in Calgary and in the Arctic, honing his commercial estimating skills before returning to Nova Scotia in 1983.

After five years of managing Eaton's flooring business in Halifax, he got word that his division was closing in May, 1988. At the time Eaton's still had contracts and warranties outstanding. "So they came to me and said, 'Will you take these contracts on and go out on your own?'" Using personal savings, he and his wife Patricia bought a dilapidated Halifax building from which to launch a floor-covering business and took over the chain's local flooring accounts, setting up shop under the Install-A-Flor name.

The weekend before opening the doors in July 1988, Patricia started to cry, wondering if they were doing the right thing. Reassurance was not long in coming. Gibson's phone rang at 8:30 opening day, and on the line—unaware that Gibson's phone was resting on a sawhorse, since his office wasn't furnished yet—was Atlantic property developer Armour Construction. Gibson's earlier bid to install flooring in a 185-unit complex had been accepted. The deal was worth $440 000 over 15 months.

He says that first sale taught him that, "if you believe you can do something, then put your mind and heart to it. There's always an element of surprise and the unforeseen, and it can be good or it can be bad. In my case, it was good and lucky." Indeed, Larry Gibson is known for his commitment to hard work, providing the best possible service, and delivering a quality product at a competitive price. He credits the nuns at the convent school in Herring Cove for instilling discipline in him and says the unexpected death of his father when he was 10 helped give him drive.

Mr. Gibson said the first few years of heads-down, all-out work took its toll on his health. "I was gritting my teeth at night and my stomach had a big knot in it, basically, because we started with nothing and always worried about turning that dollar and getting financial institutions and suppliers to believe in me," he recalled. "It was always tight."

Mr. Gibson credits his wife, who handles the business's finances and administration, with helping him through the early days. "I'd go home, we'd sit at the table—most people have salt shakers; we had a calculator. We would do quantity measures on plans and I would bid, bid, bid." That effort resulted in a 633 percent growth over the company's first five years. "When we first started, it was difficult to convince suppliers to sell us their products," recalls Patricia, "because selling to a newcomer is sometimes a bit of a risk. But Larry and I have a policy of 'Never take no for an answer. There's always another way.' We stuck with it and gained people's confidence."

Today, the business includes seven Floors Plus retail stores in Nova Scotia and New Brunswick, as well as specialty and contract divisions that operate internationally and have specialties such as clean room technology—on-site thermal welding and moulding of plastics—that is used in medical operating theatres and food-processing facilities. "Right now we're doing a school in Bermuda," said Mr. Gibson, adding that the business has opened offices in China and Ontario.

Contracting represents 40 percent of the company's business, with retail accounting for another 40 percent and the growing wholesale business, named Dantra (after his two children Daniel and Tracy, who both work in the family firm) representing 20 percent.

"We have a lack of supply here of specialty products," Mr. Gibson said in explaining the company's diversification. "Nobody's going to come in here and say, 'Listen, I want you to do clean rooms.' You've got to search this stuff out and find a market for it. It's not just about money, it's about service, being a leader, and having knowledge about the market."

Market knowledge is market power, and Mr. Gibson has gained that by going all over the world in search of new business opportunities. "We know from travelling the styles that are coming," he said, noting that he is largely in the business of selling fashion. "The (Atlantic) area is a couple of years behind Toronto, New York, and even European or Asian markets. So we know we've got time to react if we react quickly."

Questions for Discussion

1. According to Statistics Canada's Business Register, would Install-a-Flor be considered a small business? Why or why not?
2. Assess the fit between Larry Gibson and the opportunity when Install-a-Flor was started. What personal characteristics contributed most to his success?
3. To what extent did Larry Gibson use bootstrapping in getting his business started? Explain.

4. Assess Larry Gibson's capacity for identifying opportunities according to the characteristics outlined in the opportunity screening section of the chapter.
5. What benefits or drawbacks are evident in this family business?
6. Would you recommend that Install-a-Flor go public?
7. Clearly, Install-a-Flor is no longer a new business. But is it entrepreneurial?

MYBUSINESSLAB PEARSON mybusinesslab

To improve your grade, visit the MyBusinessLab website at **www.pearsoned.ca/mybusinesslab**. This online homework and tutorial system allows you to test your understanding and generates a personalized study plan just for you. It provides you with study and practice tools directly related to this chapter's content. MyBusinessLab puts you in control of your own learning!

CHAPTER 5

The Global Context of Business

After reading this chapter, you should be able to:

1. Describe the rise of international business and identify the *major world marketplaces.*
2. Explain how different forms of *competitive advantage, import–export balances, exchange rates*, and *foreign competition* determine the ways in which countries and businesses respond to the international environment.
3. Discuss the factors involved in deciding to do business internationally and in selecting the *appropriate levels of international involvement* and *international organizational structure.*
4. Describe some of the ways in which *social, cultural, economic, legal*, and *political differences* act as barriers to international trade.
5. Explain how *free trade agreements* assist world trade.

Canadian Exporters: Opportunities and Problems

Approximately 40 percent of all goods and services that are produced in Canada are exported. This means that Canada is one of the most export-focused industrialized countries in the world. Exporting is done by both large and small firms, and by goods-producing and service-producing firms. Consider a few examples:

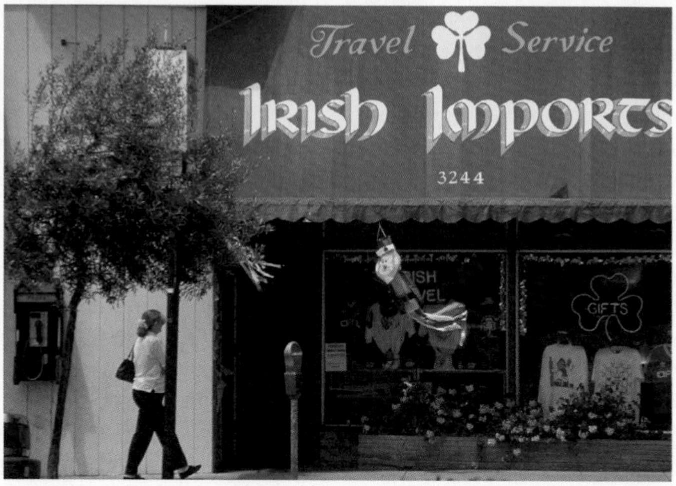

- McCain Foods is a formidable presence in Europe, where it holds a 75 percent share of the market for "oven fries" in Germany. It also dominates the frozen French fry market in France and England.
- Abitibi-Price sells newsprint and other forest products around the world.
- Seagull Pewter & Silversmiths Ltd., Magic Pantry Foods, and LOVAT have all won Canada Export Awards.
- Sabian Cymbals sells 90 percent of its products to 80 different countries.
- Electrovert Ltd. does 95 percent of its business outside Canada.
- Tesma International (which is controlled by Magna International) opened a factory in China in 2004 to produce engine belt tensioners for Volkswagen AG.

The rapid growth in the world economy has created substantial export opportunities for Canadian firms, but Canadian managers must understand foreign cultures if they are to be successful exporters. Recent developments in China and South Africa illustrate both of these aspects of exporting.

China's GDP has been growing by an average of 8 percent annually for the last decade; this is more than double the growth rate achieved in Canada or the United States. China was the world's sixth biggest economy in 2004 and its share of global output is expected to double by 2020. China is now responsible for more than 30 percent of *total* global manufacturing output. It consumes about half of all cement used in the world, more than one-third of all steel, and nearly one-third of all coal.

This dramatic growth in China's GDP means big export opportunities for Canadian companies producing oil, lumber, nickel, coal, zinc, cement, and seafood. Some of these opportunities have already been realized. During the last decade, for example, Canadian exports of fish to China increased by nearly 2000 percent, chemicals and nickel over 1200 percent, and auto parts and wood pulp over 500 percent.

Services are also being successfully exported to China. Manulife Financial Corp., which has made a major commitment to selling insurance in China, entered the Chinese market in 1996 through a joint venture with Sinochem, a state-owned trading company. Manulife trains raw recruits by emphasizing training and team building so that its sales agents can provide good service to customers. The venture now has 8 percent of the Chinese market and Manulife is the second-ranking foreign insurance firm in China.

Canadian managers must be sensitive to foreign cultures when exporting. Jonathan Fischer, the president of Georgetown, Ontario-based Mold-Masters Ltd., discovered this when he went to Shanghai to visit some of his firm's customers. At one meeting he attended, he was dismayed to hear Chinese buyers yelling at his salespeople. When he asked his Chinese managers what was going on, they explained that the buyers were simply demanding lower prices and faster delivery times, and that the shouting was typical of negotiations in China. Fischer learned that the Chinese negotiating style is tough, focuses on price, appears theatrical, and emphasizes hierarchy, but it also requires giving the other side the opportunity to "save face" somewhere in the negotiations. In these negotiations, Western managers have to avoid losing their temper. They must also patiently hold their ground and be prepared to give up something to the other side for the important face saving aspect of negotiations.

The benefits of cultural sensitivity are illustrated by the experience of McCain Foods Ltd., which entered the South African market in 2000. It was initially successful at selling French fries and frozen vegetables to white South Africans, but unsuccessful at selling these products to black South Africans. The company discovered that blacks didn't eat frozen food because they were unfamiliar with it, and because most lived in areas that did not have the electricity needed to run freezers (and they couldn't afford freezers anyway). But there is a growing middle class in South Africa, so McCain began trying to reach this group by providing single-serving packages of frozen vegetables that could be consumed in one meal. This eliminated the need for a freezer.

McCain also adopted a much more unusual strategy. They discovered that funerals were significant events in the South African culture, and that the cost of hosting the traditional funeral lunch was very expensive for the family of the deceased. So the company offered to help grieving families by matching the family's purchases of frozen foods on a one-for-one basis. The families were grateful for the support and were happy to have the McCain name prominently displayed at their funerals. When these individuals go shopping in the future, they will immediately recognize the McCain brand. By 2004, McCain held 70 percent of the market for frozen vegetables and 90 percent of the market for potato products in South Africa.

Cultural sensitivity is only one of the issues that Canadian exporters must deal with. Consider the problems encountered by Kantain Products Ltd. of Kitchener, Ontario. The company makes chemical tank liners and is doing well in Canada because of the environmental movement. Glen Lippert, the President of Kantain, decided that his product was good enough to sell in the United States, but when he tried to buy liability insurance for his anticipated activities in the United States, he discovered the premiums would be at least $50 000 per year. This amount far outweighed the amount of potential profit he thought he could make initially, so he abandoned his plan to sell in the United States.

Many Canadian firms that have actually entered the U.S. market have been given a rough ride. This is particularly true in the retail store business, where companies like Shoppers Drug Mart, Canadian Tire Corp., Future Shop Ltd., Dylex, and Mark's Work Wearhouse all suffered major defeats. In 2004, Jean Coutu Group, based in Longueuil, Quebec, purchased 1549 Eckerd pharmacies in the United States, making Coutu the fourth-largest U.S. chain drug retailer. To date, financial returns have not been as good as the company had hoped. ◆

HOW WILL THIS BENEFIT YOU?

Regardless of whether you see yourself living abroad, working for a big company, or starting your own business, the global economy will affect you in some way. Exchange rates for different currencies and global markets for buying and selling are all of major importance to everyone, regardless of their role or perspective. The material in this chapter will help you to (1) understand how global forces affect you as a customer, (2) understand how globalization affects you as an employee, and (3) assess how global opportunities and challenges can affect you as a business owner and as an investor.

This chapter explores the global context of business. We begin with an exploration of the major world marketplaces. Next, we examine several factors that help determine how countries and businesses respond to international opportunities and challenges. We identify the decisions managers must make if they intend to compete in international markets, and discuss the social, cultural, economic, legal, and political factors that affect international business. We conclude with a description of international trade agreements and how they facilitate international trade.

THE CONTEMPORARY GLOBAL ECONOMY

The total volume of world trade today is immense—around $8 trillion each year. As more and more firms engage in international business, the world economy is fast becoming a single interdependent system—a process called **globalization**. Even so, we often take for granted the diversity of goods and services available today as a result of international trade. Your television set, your shoes, and even the roast lamb on your dinner table may all be **imports**—that is, products made or grown abroad but sold in Canada. At the same time, the success of many Canadian firms depends on **exports**—products made or grown domestically and shipped for sale abroad.

globalization
Process by which the world economy is becoming a single interdependent system.

import
Product made or grown abroad but sold domestically.

export
Product made or grown domestically but shipped and sold abroad.

Trade between nations can be traced back as least as far as 2000 BCE, when North African tribes took dates and clothing to Assyria and Babylonia in the Middle East and traded them for olive oil and spices. So international business is nothing new. But international trade is becoming increasingly central to the fortunes of most nations of the world, as well as to their largest businesses. Whereas in the past many nations followed strict policies to protect domestic businesses, today more and more countries are aggressively encouraging international trade. They are more freely opening their borders to foreign businesses, offering incentives for their own domestic businesses to expand internationally, and making it easier for foreign firms to partner with local firms through various alliances.

Several forces have combined to spark and sustain globalization. For one thing, governments and businesses have simply become more aware of the benefits of globalization to their countries and stockholders. For another, new technologies have made international travel, communication, and commerce easier, faster, and cheaper than ever before. Overseas phone calls and seaborne shipping costs per tonne have both declined sharply over the last several decades. Likewise, transatlantic travel once required several days aboard a ship. Today, conventional transatlantic travel takes less than a day. Finally, there are competitive pressures: Sometimes, a firm simply must enter foreign markets just to keep up with its competitors.

Globalization is not without its critics, who charge that it allows businesses to exploit workers in less developed countries and bypass domestic environmental and tax regulations. They also charge that globalization leads to the loss of cultural heritages and often benefits the rich more than the poor. As a result, many international gatherings of global economic leaders—including the G8 meetings in Germany in 2007—have been marked by protests and demonstrations.

The Major World Marketplaces

Managers involved with international businesses need to understand the global economy, including the major world marketplaces. In this section, we examine some fundamental economic distinctions between countries based on wealth and then look at some of the world's major international marketplaces.

Describe the rise of international business and identify the *major world marketplaces*. 1

Distinctions Based on Wealth

The World Bank, an agency of the United Nations, uses **per-capita income**—average income per person—to make distinctions among countries. Its current classification method consists of four different categories of countries.[1]

per-capita income
The average income per person of a country.

1. *High-income countries.* Those with annual per-capita income greater than U.S.$10 065. These include Canada, the United States, most countries in Europe, Australia, New Zealand, Japan, South Korea, Kuwait, the United Arab Emirates, Israel, Singapore, and Taiwan.

2. *Upper middle-income countries.* Those with annual per-capita income of U.S.$10 065 or less but more than U.S.$3255. This group includes, among others, the Czech Republic, Greece, Hungary, Poland, most of the countries of the former Soviet bloc, Turkey, Mexico, Argentina, and South Africa.

3. *Low middle-income countries.* Those with annual per-capita income of U.S.$3255 or lower but more than U.S.$825. Among the countries in this group are Colombia, Guatemala, Samoa, and Thailand.

4. *Low-income countries* (often called *developing countries*). Those with annual per capita income of U.S.$825 or less. Cambodia, Ethiopia, Haiti, and Vietnam are among the countries in this group. These countries often suffer from low literacy rates, weak infrastructures, and unstable governments; these factors, in turn, make these countries relatively unattractive to international businesses. For example, the East African nation of Somalia, plagued by drought, starvation, and internal strife, plays virtually no role in the world economy.

Geographic Clusters

The world economy revolves around three major marketplaces: North America, Europe, and Asia. In general, these clusters include relatively more of the upper-middle and high-income nations, but relatively few low- and low-middle-income countries. For instance, because Africa consists primarily of low- and low-middle-income countries, it is not generally seen as a major marketplace. The three geographic regions that do warrant this designation are home to most of the world's largest economies, biggest corporations, most influential financial markets, and highest-income consumers.

North America. The United States dominates the North American business region. It is the single largest marketplace and enjoys the most stable economy in the world. Canada also plays a major role in the international economy. Moreover, the United States and Canada are each other's largest trading partner. Many U.S. firms, such as General Motors and Procter & Gamble, have maintained successful Canadian operations for years, and many Canadian firms, such as Nortel Networks and Alcan Aluminum, are also major international competitors.

Mexico has become a major manufacturing centre, especially along the U.S. border, where cheap labour and low transportation costs have encouraged many firms from the United States and other countries to build factories. The auto industry has been especially active, with DaimlerChrysler, General Motors, Volkswagen, Nissan, and Ford all running large assembly plants in the region. Several major suppliers have also built facilities in the area. But Mexico's role as a low-cost manufacturing centre may have peaked. The emergence of China as a low-cost manufacturing centre may lead companies to begin to shift their production from Mexico to China.[2]

Europe. Europe is often regarded as two regions—Western and Eastern. Western Europe, dominated by Germany, the United Kingdom, France, Spain, and Italy, has long been a mature but fragmented marketplace. But the transformation of this region via the European Union (discussed later) into an integrated economic system has further increased its importance. Major international firms, such as Unilever, Renault, Royal Dutch/Shell, Michelin, Siemens, and Nestlé, are all headquartered in Western Europe. E-commerce and technology have also become increasingly important in this region. There has been a surge in internet start-ups in southeastern England, the Netherlands, and the Scandinavian countries; and Ireland is now one of the world's largest exporters of software. Strasbourg, France, is

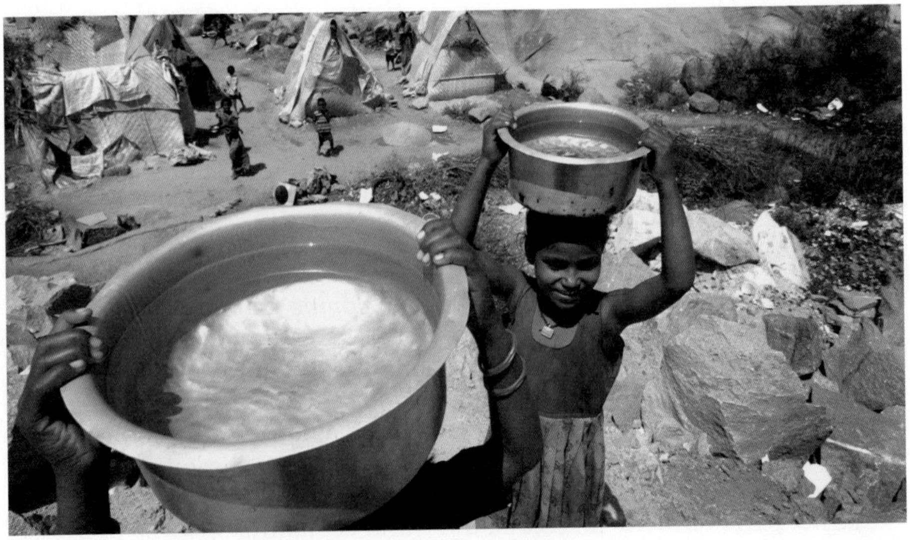

Despite the technology boom that has made its economy one of the fastest-growing in the world, India remains a low-income country. More than 330 million people—nearly 40 percent of the population—live in poverty. Because two-thirds of the population still depends on agriculture, the prosperity generated by the manufacture of auto components and the provision of information-technology services has had little effect on the fortunes of vast numbers of people.

a major centre for biotech start-ups, Barcelona, Spain, has many flourishing software and internet companies, and the Frankfurt region of Germany is dotted with both software and biotech start-ups.

Eastern Europe, once primarily communist, has also gained in importance, both as a marketplace and as a producer. Such multinational corporations as Daewoo, Nestlé, General Motors, and ABB Asea Brown Boveri have all set up operations in Poland. Ford, General Motors, Suzuki, and Volkswagen have all built new factories in Hungary. On the other hand, governmental instability has hampered development in parts of Russia, Bulgaria, Albania, Romania, and other countries.

Pacific Asia. Pacific Asia consists of Japan, China, Thailand, Malaysia, Singapore, Indonesia, South Korea, Taiwan, the Philippines, and Australia (which is technically not in Asia, but is included here because of its proximity to that region.) Some experts still distinguish Hong Kong, though now part of China, as a part of the region, and others include Vietnam. Fuelled by strong entries in the automobile, electronics, and banking industries, the economies of these countries grew rapidly in the 1970s and 1980s. A currency crisis in the late 1990s slowed growth in virtually every country of the region, but that crisis has run its course, and most countries in this region, especially Japan and China, are showing clear signs of revitalization.

Pacific Asia is an important force in the world economy and a major source of competition for North American firms. Led by firms such as Toyota, Toshiba, and Nippon Steel, Japan dominates the region. South Korea (home to such firms as Samsung and Hyundai), Taiwan (owner of Chinese Petroleum and the manufacturing home of many foreign firms), and Hong Kong (a major financial centre) are also successful players in the international economy. China, the world's most densely populated country, has emerged as an important market and now boasts the world's third-largest economy behind that of the United States and only slightly behind that of Japan. During 2006, its economy grew at an annual rate of 11 percent, and it will soon overtake Germany as the world's third-largest producer of automobiles. India, though not part of Pacific Asia, is also rapidly emerging as one of the globe's most important economies. Its economic growth rate in 2006 was over 9 percent.[3]

As in North America and Europe, technology promises to play an increasingly important role in the future of this region. In some parts of Asia, however, the emergence of technology firms has been hampered by poorly developed electronic infrastructures, slower adoption of computers and information technology, and a higher percentage of lower-income consumers. Although the future looks promising, technology companies are facing several obstacles as they work to keep pace with foreign competitors.

Forms of Competitive Advantage

No country can produce all the goods and services that its people need. Thus, countries tend to export those things that they can produce better or less expensively than other countries. The proceeds are then used to import things that they cannot produce effectively. However, this general principle does not fully explain why nations export and import *what* they do. Such decisions hinge partly on the kind of advantages a particular country may enjoy regarding its abilities to create and/or sell various products and resources.[4] Traditionally, economists have focused on *absolute* and *comparative advantage* to explain international trade. But because this approach focuses narrowly on such factors as natural resources and labour costs, the more contemporary view of *national competitive advantage* has emerged.

Explain how different forms of *competitive advantage, import–export balances, exchange rates,* and *foreign competition* determine the ways in which countries and businesses respond to the international environment. **2**

Absolute Advantage

absolute advantage
The ability to produce something more efficiently than any other country.

An **absolute advantage** exists when a country can produce something more cheaply and/or of higher quality than any other country. Saudi oil, Brazilian coffee beans, and Canadian timber approximate absolute advantage, but examples of true absolute advantage are rare. In reality, "absolute" advantages are always relative. For example, most experts say that the vineyards of France produce the finest wines in the world. But the burgeoning wine businesses in California and Ontario attest to the fact that producers there can also produce very good values in wine—wines that are perhaps almost as good as French wines and that also are available in more varieties and at lower prices.

Comparative Advantage

comparative advantage
The ability to produce some products more efficiently than others.

A country has a **comparative advantage** in goods that it can produce more efficiently or better than other goods. For example, if businesses in a given country can make computers more efficiently than they can make automobiles, that nation's firms have a comparative advantage in computer manufacture. Canada has a comparative advantage in farming (because of fertile land and a temperate climate), while South Korea has a comparative advantage in electronics manufacturing (because of efficient operations and cheap labour). As a result, Canadian firms export grain to South Korea and import VCRs and stereos from South Korea. All countries have a comparative advantage in *some* products, but no country has a comparative advantage in *all* products. Developed countries tend to have a comparative advantage in making high-tech products, while developing countries tend to have a comparative advantage in making products that require lots of low-cost labour.

National Competitive Advantage

In recent years, a theory of national competitive advantage has become a more widely accepted model of why nations engage in international trade.[5] **National competitive advantage** derives from four conditions:

national competitive advantage
International competitive advantage stemming from a combination of factor conditions, demand conditions, related and supporting industries, and firm strategies, structures, and rivalries.

1. *Factor conditions* are the factors of production that we identified in Chapter 1.
2. *Demand conditions* reflect a large domestic consumer base that promotes strong demand for innovative products.
3. *Related and supporting industries* include strong local or regional suppliers and/or industrial customers.
4. *Strategies, structures,* and *rivalries* refer to firms and industries that stress cost reduction, product quality, higher productivity, and innovative new products.

When all of these conditions exist in an industry, the companies in that industry are motivated to be very innovative and to excel at what they are doing. This, in turn, increases the likelihood that they will engage in international business. Japan, for instance, has strong domestic demand for automobiles. Its automobile producers have well-developed supplier networks, and Japanese firms have competed intensely with each other for decades. This set of circumstances explains why Japanese automobile companies such as Toyota, Honda, Nissan, and Mazda are generally successful in foreign markets.

international competitiveness
Competitive marketing of domestic products against foreign products.

International competitiveness refers to the ability of a country to generate more wealth than its competitors in world markets. Each year, the World Economic Forum publishes a global competitiveness ranking. The

If local boosters have their way, the success of *The Lord of the Rings*—whose fictional *Middle Earth* is really New Zealand's South Island—will turn the dramatic scenery of New Zealand into an advantage in competing for global business. The national film promotion board appeals to foreign producers by stressing the country's variety of unspoiled landscapes (and largely non-union workforce), and *Rings*-related tourism has already become a thriving business. On the web, Tourism New Zealand invites you to "Experience the Home of Middle Earth," and Air New Zealand bills itself as the "Airline to Middle Earth."

ranking is based on both hard economic data and on a poll of business leaders in many countries. In 2006, the top three countries on the list were Switzerland, Finland, and Sweden. The United States ranked 6th and Canada 16th. Canada's high taxes, regulated industries, and overly conservative capital market institutions were listed as the reasons for Canada's lower rating.[6]

The Balance of Trade

A country's **balance of trade** is the difference in value between its total exports and its total imports. A country that exports more than it imports has a *favourable* balance of trade, or a **surplus**. A country that imports more than it exports has an *unfavourable* balance of trade, or a **deficit**. Canada has enjoyed a favourable balance of merchandise trade for many years. The United States is by far the largest trading partner Canada has, and our overall trade balance is favourable only because Canada exports so much more to the United States than it imports from the United States. We import more from the countries of the European Union and Japan than we export to those countries, and we also import far more than we export from all other countries as well (see Table 5.1).

balance of trade
The economic value of all the products that a country exports minus the economic value of all the products it imports.

surplus
Situation in which a country exports more than it imports, creating a favourable balance of trade.

deficit
Situation in which a country's imports exceed its exports, creating a negative balance of trade.

A study by the World Trade Organization (WTO) found that Canada's economic dependence on the United States is growing, and this trend leaves

Table 5.1 Canadian Exports to and Imports from Selected Countries, 2005

Country	Exports to (in billions of $)	Imports from (in billions of $)
United States	$369.2	$258.4
European Union	28.9	38.3
Japan	10.4	11.1
All others	44.9	78.9

Canada vulnerable. The United States accounts for 80 percent of Canada's merchandise exports and two-thirds of its imports. What's worse, only 50 companies operating in Canada account for nearly half of all merchandise exports, and these companies are often U.S.-owned. Canada has too many of its eggs in one basket.[7]

The Balance of Payments

balance of payments
Flow of all money into or out of a country.

Even if a country has a favourable balance of trade, it can still have an unfavourable balance of payments. A country's **balance of payments** is the difference between money flowing into the country and money flowing out of the country as a result of trade and other transactions. An unfavourable balance means more money is flowing out than in. For Canada to have a favourable balance of payments for a given year, the total of our exports, foreign-tourist spending in this country, foreign investments here, and earnings from overseas investments must be greater than the total of our imports, Canadian-tourist spending overseas, our foreign aid grants, our military spending abroad, the investments made by Canadian firms abroad, and the earnings of foreigners from their investments in Canada. Canada has had an unfavourable balance of payments for about the last 20 years, but it is slowly improving. In 1999, for example, $142 billion more flowed out of Canada than flowed in, but in 2005, that amount was $112 billion.[8]

Exchange Rates

exchange rate
Rate at which the currency of one nation can be exchanged for the currency of another nation.

An **exchange rate** is the rate at which the currency of one nation can be exchanged for that of another.[9] For example, if the exchange rate between Canadian dollars and British pounds is 1 to 2.26, this means that it cost $2.26 in Canadian dollars to "buy" one British pound. Alternatively, it would cost only 0.44 of a British pound to "buy" one Canadian dollar. This exchange rate means that 0.44 of a British pound and one Canadian dollar should have exactly the same purchasing power.

The value of one country's currency relative to that of another country varies with market conditions. For example, when many English citizens want to spend pounds to buy Canadian dollars (or goods), the value of the dollar relative to the pound increases, or becomes "stronger"; *demand* for the Canadian dollar is high. It is also "strong" when there is high demand for goods manufactured in Canada. Thus, the value of the Canadian dollar rises with the demand for Canadian goods. Exchange rates typically fluctuate by very small amounts on a daily basis. More significant variations usually occur over greater spans of time.

Fluctuation in exchange rates can have an important impact on the balance of trade. Suppose, for example, that you wanted to buy some English tea for 10 British pounds per box. At an exchange rate of 2.26 Canadian dollars to the British pound, a box will cost you $22.60 (10 pounds × 2.26 = 22.60). But what if the pound is weaker? At an exchange rate of, say, 1.5 dollars to the pound, the same box of tea would cost you only $15.00 (10 pounds × 1.5 = $15.00).

Changes in the exchange rate, of course, would affect more than just the price of tea. If the Canadian dollar is stronger in relation to the British pound, the prices of all Canadian-made products would rise in England and the prices of all English-made products would fall in Canada. As a result, the English would buy fewer Canadian-made products, and Canadians would spend more on English-made products. The result could conceivably be a Canadian trade deficit with England. This is why the recent increase in the value of the Canadian dollar has Canadian exporters very concerned.

One of the most significant developments in foreign exchange has been the introduction of the **euro**—a common currency among most of the members of the European Union (Denmark, Sweden, and the United Kingdom do not participate). The euro was officially introduced in 2002 and will, for a while, circulate along with currencies of the participating nations. But those currencies will be phased out, and they are to be replaced by the euro as the only accepted currency. The EU anticipates that the euro will become as important as the U.S. dollar and the Japanese yen in international commerce. The euro has risen in value against the U.S. dollar and was worth about U.S.$1.45 in 2007.

euro
A common currency shared among most of the members of the European Union (excluding Denmark, Sweden, and the United Kingdom).

Exchange Rates and Competition

Companies that conduct international operations must watch exchange-rate fluctuations closely because these changes affect overseas demand for their products and can be a major factor in international competition. In general, when the value of a country's domestic currency rises—becomes "stronger"—companies based there find it harder to export products to foreign markets and easier for foreign companies to enter local markets. It also makes it more cost-efficient for domestic companies to move production operations to lower-cost sites in foreign countries. When the value of a country's currency declines—becomes "weaker"—just the opposite patterns occur. Thus, as the value of a country's currency falls, its balance of trade should improve because domestic companies should experience a boost in exports. There should also be a corresponding decrease in the incentives for foreign companies to ship products into the domestic market.

A good case in point is the recent fluctuation of the Canadian dollar relative to the U.S. dollar. In 1990, the Canadian dollar was relatively strong; as a result, Canadian consumers frequently drove south of the border to shop for bargains in the United States. But during the 1990s, the Canadian dollar weakened, and it became cheaper for U.S. consumers to drive to Canada to shop. For example, the same hamburger that cost U.S.$2.39 in Niagara Falls, New York, sold for only U.S.$2.18 just across the border in Ontario.[10] More recently, the value of the Canadian dollar has again risen sharply, and in the fall of 2007 was worth U.S.$1.07. If this trend continues, Canadians will once again be driving to the United States to get bargains just like they used to in 1990.

These same tendencies are evident with other currencies. For example, in 2007 the British pound hit a 14-year high against the U.S. dollar. As a result, U.K. citizens found good price deals in the United States. A Burberry raincoat, which in the U.K. costs 465 British pounds (U.S.$914.14), costs only $695 in New York City.[11]

INTERNATIONAL BUSINESS MANAGEMENT

Wherever a firm is located, its success depends largely on how well it is managed. International business is challenging because the basic management responsibilities—planning, organizing, leading, and controlling—are much more difficult to carry out when a business operates in several markets scattered around the globe. (We discuss these functions of management in detail in Chapter 6.)

3 Discuss the factors involved in deciding to do business internationally and in selecting the *appropriate levels of international involvement* and *international organizational structure.*

Managing means making decisions. In this section, we examine the three most basic decisions that a company's management must make when faced with the prospect of globalization. The first decision is whether to "go international" at all. Often that decision is made because a company feels it has to shift its production to a low-cost foreign country in order to remain competitive. Once that decision has been made, managers must decide on the company's level of international involvement and on the organizational structure that will best meet its global needs.

"Going International"

The world economy is becoming globalized, and more and more firms are conducting international operations. As Figure 5.1 shows, several factors enter into the decision to go international. One overriding factor is the business climate of other nations. Even experienced firms have encountered cultural, legal, and economic roadblocks, as we shall see later in this chapter. In considering international expansion, a company should also consider at least two other questions: Is there a demand for its products abroad? If so, must those products be adapted for international consumption?

Gauging International Demand

Products that are seen as vital in one country may be useless in another. Snowmobiles, for example, are not only popular for transportation and recreation in Canada and the northern United States, but actually revolutionized reindeer herding in Lapland. But there would be no demand at all for this product in Central America. Although this is an extreme example, the point is quite basic to the decision to go international: namely, that foreign demand for a company's product may be greater than, the same as, or weaker than domestic demand. Even when there is demand, advertising may still need to be adjusted. For instance, in Canada bicycles and small motorcycles are mainly used for recreation, but in many parts of Asia they are seen as transportation. Market research and/or the prior market entry of competitors may indicate whether there's an international demand for a firm's products.

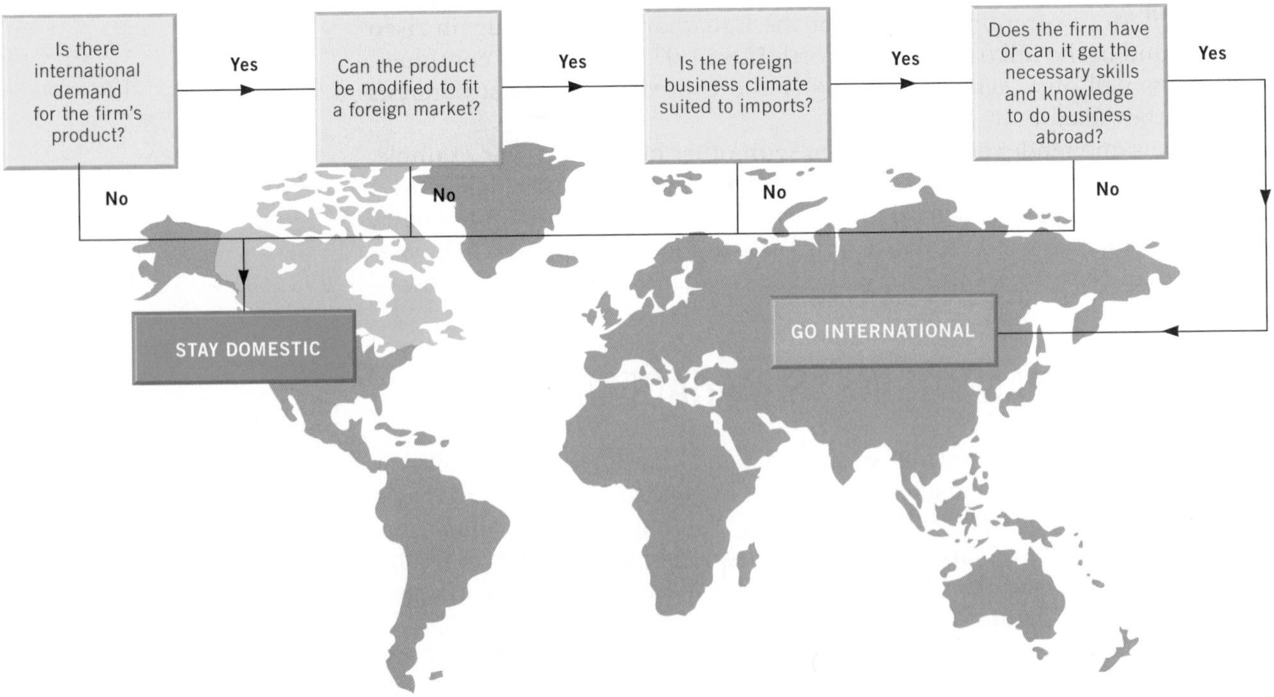

Figure 5.1 The decision to go international.

Some products—like U.S. movies and video games—are popular all over the world. U.S. movies like *Harry Potter* and *Spider-Man* earn significant revenues in the United States, but generate even more revenues overseas. Super Mario Brothers is advertised on billboards in Bangkok, Thailand, and Bart Simpson piñatas are sold at Mexico City bazaars.

Adapting to Customer Needs

If there is international demand for its product, a firm must consider whether and how to adapt that product to meet the special demands and expectations of foreign customers. Movies, for example, have to be dubbed into foreign languages. Likewise, McDonald's restaurants sell wine in France, beer in Germany, and meatless sandwiches in India to accommodate local tastes and preferences. Ford products must have their steering wheels mounted on the right if they are to be sold in England and Japan. When Toyota launches upscale cars at home, it retains the Toyota nameplate; those same cars are sold under the Lexus nameplate in Canada because the firm has concluded that Canadian consumers will not pay a premium price for a "Toyota."

Levels of Involvement in International Business

After a firm decides to go international, it must decide on the level of its international involvement. Several different levels of involvement are possible. At the most basic level, a firm may act as an *exporter* or *importer*, organize as an *international firm*, or operate as a *multinational firm*. Most of the world's largest industrial firms are multinationals.

Exporters and Importers

An **exporter** is a firm that makes products in one country and then distributes and sells them in others. An **importer** buys products in foreign markets and then imports them for resale in its home country. Exporters and importers tend to conduct most of their business in their home nations. Both enterprises entail the lowest level of involvement in international operations and are excellent ways to learn the fine points of global business.

exporter
Firm that distributes and sells products to one or more foreign countries.

importer
Firm that buys products in foreign markets and then imports them for resale in its home country.

Almost 40 percent of all goods and services produced in Canada are exported, and Canada ranks first among the G8 countries in the proportion of its production that is exported.[12] Canada's exports to the world rose from $275 billion in 1996 to $411 billion in 2004.[13] Small firms also export products and services. Lingo Media Inc. is the largest supplier of English-language textbooks in China's primary school system.[14] The Entrepreneurship and New Ventures box on the next page describes another company that became an exporter of an unlikely product.

International Firms

As firms gain experience and success as exporters and importers, they may move to the next level of involvement. An **international firm** conducts a significant portion of its business abroad. International firms also maintain manufacturing facilities overseas. Wal-Mart, for instance, is an international firm. Most of the retailer's stores are still in the United States, but the company is rapidly expanding into Canada and other markets.

international firm
Firm that conducts a significant portion of its business in foreign countries.

Although an international firm may be large and influential in the global economy, it remains basically a domestic firm with international operations: Its central concern is its own domestic market. Despite its obvious presence (and impact) in Canada, Wal-Mart still earns 90 percent of its revenues from U.S. sales.

ENTREPRENEURSHIP AND NEW VENTURES

Rolling in the Worldwide Dough

Is any business more confined to a local market than a bakery? Breads and pastries get stale quickly, and even the largest operations, such as those that make buns for McDonald's, only move products over short distances. But a baker in Paris has refused to accept geographic limitations and is now selling his famous bread in global markets.

When Lionel Poilane took over the family business about 30 years ago, he was determined to return bread making to its roots. As a result of studying the craft of bread making, Poilane built clay ovens based on sixteenth-century plans and technology. Then he trained his bread makers in ancient techniques and soon began selling old-style dark bread known for a thick, chewy, fire-tinged flavour. It quickly became a favourite in Parisian bistros, and demand soared.

To help meet demand, Poilane built two more bakeries in Paris, and today he sells 15 000 loaves of bread a day—about 2.5 percent of all the bread sold in Paris. Poilane has opened a bakery in London, but his efforts to expand to Japan were stymied because local ordinances prohibited wood-burning ovens, and Poilane refused to compromise. During this negotiation process, however, he realized that he didn't really want to build new bakeries all over the world. "I'm not eager to have a business card that says 'Paris, London, New York' on it," he explains.

Instead, he turned to modern technology to expand his old-fashioned business. The key was the big FedEx hub at Roissy-Charles-de-Gaulle Airport near Poilane's largest Paris bakery. After launching a website with minimal marketing support, Poilane started taking international orders. New orders are packaged as the bread cools and then picked up by FedEx. At about four pounds, the basic loaf travels well, and a quick warm-up in the customer's oven gives it the same taste as it had when it came out of Poilane's. Today, a loaf of bread baked in Paris in the morning can easily be reheated for tomorrow night's dinner in more than 20 countries.

Multinational Firms

multinational firm
Firm that designs, produces, and markets products in many nations.

Most **multinational firms** do not ordinarily think of themselves as having domestic and international divisions. Instead, planning and decision making are geared to international markets.[15] The locations of headquarters are almost irrelevant. Royal Dutch/Shell, Nestlé, IBM, and Ford are well-known multinationals.

The economic importance of multinational firms should not be underestimated. Consider, for example, the economic impact of the 500 largest multinational corporations. In 2003, these 500 firms generated $15 trillion in revenues and $382 billion in owner profits. They employed over 51 million people; bought supplies, parts, equipment, and materials from thousands of other firms; and paid billions of dollars in taxes. Moreover, their activities and products have affected the lives of hundreds of millions of consumers, competitors, and investors (sometimes not in a very positive way).[16]

On various occasions, organized protests have been mounted against the activities of multinational corporations. For example, when the Ecuadorian government renewed its commitment to extract oil from the Amazon River basin in 2004, a protest movement began among people in a region called Sarayacu. They battled with both the Ecuadorian government and the Argentine oil company, which was given a 2000 square kilometre concession to explore for oil on Sarayacu land. The protest included lodging a legal complaint against the government, demonstrations, letter writing, sabotage, theft of oil company equipment, and detention of oil company workers. Attempts to resolve problems like these include the development of the Equator Principles, which are a set of guidelines designed to deal with the impact of corporate activity on indigenous people.[17]

International Organizational Structures

Different levels of involvement in international business require different kinds of organizational structure. For example, a structure that would help coordinate an exporter's activities would be inadequate for the activities of a multinational firm. In this section, we briefly consider the spectrum of international organizational strategies, including *independent agents, licensing arrangements, branch offices, strategic alliances,* and *foreign direct investment.*

Independent Agents

An **independent agent** is a foreign individual or organization that agrees to represent an exporter's interests in foreign markets. Independent agents often act as sales representatives: They sell the exporter's products, collect payment, and ensure that customers are satisfied. Independent agents often represent several firms at once and usually do not specialize in a particular product or market. Levi Strauss uses agents to market clothing products in many small countries in Africa, Asia, and South America.

independent agent Foreign individual or organization that agrees to represent an exporter's interests.

Licensing Arrangements

Canadian companies seeking more substantial involvement in international business may opt for **licensing arrangements**. Firms give individuals or companies in a foreign country the exclusive right to manufacture or market their products in that market. In return, the exporter typically receives a fee plus ongoing payments called **royalties**.[18] Royalties are usually calculated as a percentage of the licence holder's sales. For example, Can-Eng Manufacturing, Canada's largest supplier of industrial furnaces, exports its furnaces under licensing arrangements with Japan, Brazil, Germany, Korea, Taiwan, and Mexico.

Franchising is a special form of licensing that is also growing in popularity.[19] McDonald's and Pizza Hut franchise around the world. Similarly, Accor SA, a French hotel chain, franchises its Ibis, Sofitel, and Novotel hotels. Allied-Lyons PLC, a British firm, owns and franchises Baskin-Robbins and Dunkin' Donuts stores in dozens of countries.

licensing arrangement Arrangement in which firms choose foreign individuals or organizations to manufacture or market their products in another country.

royalties Fees that an exporter receives for allowing a company in a foreign country to manufacture or market the exporter's products.

Branch Offices

Instead of developing relationships with foreign companies or independent agents, a firm may simply send some of its own managers to overseas **branch offices**. A company has more direct control over branch managers than over agents or licence holders. Branch offices also give a company a more visible public presence in foreign countries. Potential customers tend to feel more secure when a business has branch offices in their country.

When a business operates branches, plants, or subsidiaries in several countries, it may assign to one plant or subsidiary the responsibility for researching, developing, manufacturing, and marketing one product or line of products. This is known as **world product mandating**. At Nortel Networks, for example, the company's Belleville, Ontario, plant was chosen as the one to produce a new business telephone system designed for the world market. The plant won out in a competition with two other Nortel plants, one in Calgary and one in Santa Clara, California. The Belleville plant also has global mandates for several other product lines.

branch office A location that an exporting firm establishes in a foreign country to sell its products more effectively.

world product mandating The assignment by a multinational of a product responsibility to a particular branch.

Strategic Alliances

The concept of a strategic alliance was introduced in Chapter 2. In international business, it means that a company finds a partner in a foreign country where it would like to conduct business. Each party agrees to invest resources and capital in a new business or else to co-operate in some way for mutual benefit. This new business—the alliance—is then owned by the partners, who divide its profits. For example, Canadian publisher Lingo Media Inc. is involved in a strategic alliance with the state-owned People's Education Press, which is the market leader in providing textbooks to Chinese schools.[20]

The number of strategic alliances among major companies has increased significantly over the last decade and is likely to grow even more. In many countries, including Mexico, India, and China, laws make alliances virtually the only way to do international business within their borders. Mexico, for example, requires all foreign firms investing there to have local partners. Similarly, Disney's new theme park near Hong Kong is a joint venture with local partners. Vancouver-based Westport Innovations, which makes natural gas engines, is now selling its products to China through a strategic alliance with Cummins Inc., a U.S.-based company that is selling buses powered by clean air technology to the city of Beijing.[21]

In addition to easing the way into new markets, alliances give firms greater control over their foreign activities than independent agents and licensing arrangements. (At the same time, of course, all partners in an alliance retain some say in its decisions.) Perhaps most important, alliances allow firms to benefit from the knowledge and expertise of their foreign partners. Microsoft, for example, relies heavily on strategic alliances as it expands into new international markets. This approach has successfully enabled the firm to learn the intricacies of doing business in China and India, two emerging markets that are difficult to crack.

Foreign Direct Investment

foreign direct investment (FDI) Buying or establishing tangible assets in another country.

The term **foreign direct investment (FDI)** means buying or establishing tangible assets in another country.[22] Dell Computer, for example, is building a new assembly plant in Europe, and Volkswagen is building a new factory in Brazil. The establishment of branch offices in foreign countries is also a type of foreign direct investment.

Foreign Investment Review Agency (FIRA) Established in 1973 to screen new foreign direct investment in Canada; supposed to ensure that significant benefits accrued to Canada.

Investment Canada Replaced FIRA in 1985; designed primarily to attract and facilitate foreign investment in Canada.

As we've already seen, many Canadian firms export goods and services to foreign countries, and they also set up manufacturing operations in other countries. But a debate has been going on for many years in Canada about how FDI in Canada by foreign firms affects Canadians. The **Foreign Investment Review Agency (FIRA)**, which was established in 1973, was designed to ensure that FDI benefited Canadians. After FIRA was established, the proportion of various industries controlled by foreign firms declined from a high of 38 percent in the early 1970s to a low of 21 percent in 1985.[23]

In 1985, FIRA's title was changed to **Investment Canada**, and its mandate was changed to focus on attracting foreign investment to Canada. Since the late 1980s, foreign ownership of Canadian industry has again been on the rise, and now stands at 30 percent. But foreign ownership may in fact be higher than it appears since many firms that seem to be Canadian are actually multinational companies. For example, before it was bought by a French company, Seagram had been run from New York City, and Nortel Networks runs all of its business divisions from Dallas, Texas. Table 5.2 lists the 10 largest foreign-owned companies in Canada.[24]

During the past few years, many large Canadian companies like Dofasco, Inco, and Molson have been lost to foreign control, and some people are concerned that this will mean large job losses in Canada. But a Statistics Canada study showed that between 1999 and 2005, foreign companies were responsible for creating all of the new head offices that were created in Canada, and about two-thirds of the new head office jobs.[25] A survey of 150 senior Canadian executives showed that the issue of foreign ownership ranks low on their list of perceived economic challenges.[26]

Table 5.2 The Top 10 Foreign-Controlled Companies in Canada, 2006

Company	Annual Revenues (in billions of $)
1. General Motors of Canada	$34.9
2. Imperial Oil Ltd.	27.7
3. DaimlerChrysler Canada	20.8
4. Shell Canada Ltd.	14.1
5. Ford Motor Co. of Canada Ltd.	13.8
6. Wal-Mart Canada Corp.	13.5
7. Honda Canada Inc.	13.0
8. Ultramar Ltd.	9.5
9. Costco Wholesale Canada	8.1
10. McKesson Canada Corp.	7.1

BARRIERS TO TRADE

Whether a business is selling to just a few foreign markets or is a true multinational, a number of differences between countries will affect its international operations. How a firm responds to and manages social, economic, and political issues will go a long way toward determining its success.

4 Describe some of the ways in which *social, cultural, economic, legal,* and *political differences* act as barriers to international trade.

Social and Cultural Differences

Any firm involved in international business needs to understand something about the society and culture of the countries in which it plans to operate. Unless a firm understands these cultural differences—either itself or by acquiring a partner that does—it will probably not be successful in its international business activities.

Some differences are relatively obvious. Language barriers can cause inappropriate naming of products. In addition, the physical stature of people in different countries can make a difference. For example, the Japanese and French are slimmer and shorter on average than Canadians, an important consideration for firms that intend to sell clothes in these markets. Differences in the average age of the local population can also have ramifications for product development and marketing. Countries with growing populations tend to have a high percentage of young people. Thus, electronics and fashionable clothing would likely do well. Countries with stable or declining populations tend to have more old people. Generic pharmaceuticals might be more successful in such markets.

In addition to such obvious differences, a wide range of subtle value differences can have an important impact on international business. For example, many Europeans shop daily. To Canadians used to weekly trips to the supermarket, the European pattern may seem like a waste of time. But for Europeans, shopping is not just "buying food." It is also meeting friends, exchanging political views, gossiping, and socializing. What implications does this kind of shopping have for firms selling in European markets? First, those who go shopping each day do not need the large refrigerators and freezers common in North America. Second, the large supermarkets one sees in Canada are not an appropriate retail outlet in Europe. Finally, the kinds of food Europeans buy differ from those Canadians buy. While in Canada prepared and frozen foods are important, Europeans often prefer

Tunisian-born French entrepreneur Tawfik Mathlouthi doesn't like U.S. policy in the Middle East, but he does like the American way of doing business. He created Mecca-Cola for Muslims who like Coke but want to protest U.S. foreign policy by boycotting American products. With a core market of Muslims in France, Mecca-Cola is now sold elsewhere in Europe, and Coke (which has taken no legal action regarding the look-alike label) admits that Mecca-Cola and similar products have hurt its international business, mostly in countries like Egypt and Morocco.

to buy fresh ingredients to do their own food preparation "from scratch." These differences are gradually disappearing, however, so firms need to be on the lookout for future opportunities as they emerge.

Even more subtle behavioural differences that can influence business activity exist. For example, crossing your legs in a business meeting in Saudi Arabia is inappropriate, because showing the sole of your foot is viewed as an insult to the other people in the room. In Portugal, it is considered rude to discuss business during dinner, and in Taiwan, tapping your fingers on the table is a sign of appreciation for a meal. Knowledge of local dos and don'ts is important in international business activity.

BUSINESS ACCOUNTABILITY

How to Wake up a Zombie

There is a longstanding tradition in Japan whereby the government often props up failing businesses through low-cost or no-cost loans. The fear has been that if businesses fail, people will lose their jobs and the highly integrated Japanese industrial system will suffer. These businesses, some of which have been bailed out literally dozens of times, are called "Zombie" firms. The major downside of this practice, though, is that it reduces accountability. Managers haven't always had to worry about profits or efficiency, because they knew the government would bail them out. "This kind of intervention can work in the short term. But from a long-term point of view, it has terrible implications: Investors understand that the market is artificial, and accordingly they pull back," states analyst Jean-Marie Eveillard.

In recent years, more Japanese firms are accepting responsibility for their own survival. Cosmetics maker Shiseido held too much inventory and had overly high expenses, leading to a $550 million loss over two years. But rather than call for a government bailout, Shiseido executives focused on making fundamental improvements. Better technology allowed them to control and forecast inventory more effectively. They cut costs throughout the corporation and curtailed their product line. After Shiseido returned to profitability, chief logistics officer Seiji Nishimori boasted, "We're showing other Japanese companies that it's possible to reverse a slide."

Canon, the world's leading maker of copiers and laser printers, has also taken a disciplined approach to performance improvement. CEO Fujio Mitarai replaced every manufacturing line at the firm's 29 Japanese factories with small, self-directed teams of a half dozen workers who do the work previously done by 30 labourers. The teams discovered more efficient inventory management techniques, and Canon was able to close 20 of its 34 parts warehouses. "Manufacturing is where most of the costs lie," Mitarai claims. Canon earnings improved by 53 percent, enabling Mitarai to conclude, "We're much more profitable today because of these changes."

The success of notable high performers such as multinational Toyota has caused Japanese firms to realize the benefit of global cost competitiveness. High-tech companies are abandoning manufacturing and switching attention to research and development to counteract an influx of inexpensive electronics from China, Taiwan, and Korea. For example, NEC has moved out of the unprofitable semiconductor chip-making business and has focused on more lucrative cell phones and software. Sharp, too, has given up on low-margin PC monitors and refocused its operations on innovative products such as liquid crystal displays for PDAs. Sony is working on revolutionary new computer chips while reducing its investment in consumer electronics.

All three companies say they now listen to their consumers more closely. "We were proud of our great technology, and [we] just pumped out products without thinking of our customers' needs," says NEC director Kaoru Tosaka. "Now, we're emphasizing efficiency, profits, and clients."

The zombies need to hear the lessons that these stellar firms have learned. Watch inventory. Cut costs where possible. Use information technology more effectively. Simplify product lines. Experiment with new ways of organizing. Shut down money-losing businesses. Choose areas where the firm can add value. Listen to customer feedback. If the zombies adopt these suggestions, the Japanese—and the rest of the world—would surely benefit.

QUESTIONS FOR DISCUSSION

1. What are the pros and cons of government bailouts of businesses?
2. To what extent is managerial accountability compromised by government bailouts? Explain your reasoning.

Economic Differences

Although cultural differences are often subtle, economic differences can be fairly pronounced. In dealing with economies like those of France and Sweden, for example, firms must be aware of when—and to what extent—the government is involved in a given industry. The French government, for example, is heavily involved in all aspects of airplane design and manufacturing.

Similarly, a foreign firm doing business in a command economy must understand the unfamiliar relationship of government to business, including a host of idiosyncratic practices. General Motors, which entered a $100 million joint venture to build pick-up trucks in China, found itself faced with an economic system that favoured state-owned companies over foreign investors. So, while its Chinese suppliers passed on inflation-based price increases for steel and energy, GM could not in turn pass increases on to Chinese consumers. With subsidized state-owned automakers charging considerably less per truck, GM had no choice but to hold its own prices—and lose money on each sale.

Despite such problems, however, not all companies have had entirely negative experiences. For example, when Motorola opened a factory in China to manufacture paging devices, it planned to export most of the pagers because it forecast limited internal demand. In a pleasant surprise, Motorola was forced to reassess the Chinese market after repeatedly selling out its weekly output of 10 000 units. This experience helped convince Motorola to build a $120 million plant in the northern port city of Tianjin to manufacture pagers, simple integrated circuits, and cellular phones. As part of the largest manufacturing venture in China, it involved Chinese technicians in the production process. Chinese designers and engineers also played key roles in creating an operation that integrates manufacturing, sales, research, and development.

Legal and Political Differences

Closely linked to the structure of the economic systems in different countries are the legal and political issues that confront businesses as they try to expand internationally. These issues include tariffs and quotas, local-content laws, and business-practice laws. An awareness of differences in these areas can be crucial to a business's success.

Quotas, Tariffs, and Subsidies

Even free-market economies often use some form of quota and/or tariff that affects the prices and quantities of foreign-made products in those nations. A **quota** restricts the total number of certain products that can be imported into a country. It indirectly raises the prices of those imports by reducing their supply. The ultimate form of quota is an **embargo**: a government order forbidding exportation and/or importation of a particular product—or even all the products—of a particular country. For example, many countries control bacteria and disease by banning certain plants and agricultural products.

In contrast, a **tariff** is a tax charged on imported products. Tariffs directly affect the prices of products, effectively raising the price of imports to consumers who must pay not only for the products but also for the tariff. Tariffs may take either of two forms. A **revenue tariff** is imposed strictly to raise money for the government. Most tariffs in effect today, however, are **protectionist tariffs** meant to discourage the import of a particular product. In 2004, for example, the Canadian government placed a 34.6 percent

quota
A restriction by one nation on the total number of products of a certain type that can be imported from another nation.

embargo
A government order forbidding exportation and/or importation of a particular product.

tariff
A tax levied on imported products.

revenue tariff
A tariff imposed solely to raise money for the government that imposes it.

protectionist tariffs
A tariff imposed at least in part to discourage imports of a particular product.

tariff on barbecues made in China after complaints were received that Chinese companies were unfairly subsidizing their production.[27]

Governments impose quotas and tariffs for a wide variety of reasons. For example, the U.S. government restricts the number of Japanese automobiles that can be imported into that country. Italy imposes high tariffs on imported electronic goods. Consequently, Sony Walkmans cost almost $150, and CD players are prohibitively expensive. Canada also imposes tariffs on many imported goods.

In 2002, the U.S. Commerce Department imposed a 29 percent tariff on softwood lumber exported from Canada to the United States (84 percent of Canadian lumber is exported to the United States). Ottawa immediately appealed the decision under the provisions of both the North American Free Trade Agreement (NAFTA) and the World Trade Organization (WTO). During 2002 and 2003, both the WTO and NAFTA ruled against the United States on various points in the appeal and said that duties on Canadian lumber must be cut drastically. In spite of these rulings, the United States continued to impose the duties. Since the duties were first imposed, the Canadian lumber industry has paid over $5 billion in duties to the United States.[28] A tentative resolution was reached in July 2006, when the United States agreed to pay back 78 percent of the duties imposed on Canadian lumber, on the condition that Canada agree that its share of the U.S. lumber market would be capped at 34 percent.[29] Several Canadian lumber companies said that they weren't happy with that, but an agreement was eventually reached that went into effect in October 2006.[30]

subsidy
A government payment to help domestic business compete with foreign firms.

A **subsidy** is a government payment to help a domestic business compete with foreign firms. Many European governments subsidize farmers to help them compete with U.S. grain imports, and the U.S. government has for many years paid large subsidies to U.S. cotton farmers. In 2005, U.S. farmers were paid a total of $23 billion by their government.[31]

When the government of a country pays subsidies to one of its domestic industries, it can have a negative effect on producers in other countries. The European Union, for example, pays subsidies to encourage sugar cultivation in unlikely places like Sweden and Finland. This has created a surplus of sugar on the world market, reducing prices and contributing to poverty-level income for sugar producers in some developing countries in the tropics.[32] The WTO has ruled that these subsidies are unreasonable. In another example, in 2005, the WTO ruled that the U.S. government's subsidies to its cotton growers broke trade rules, depressed world cotton prices, and hurt Brazilian

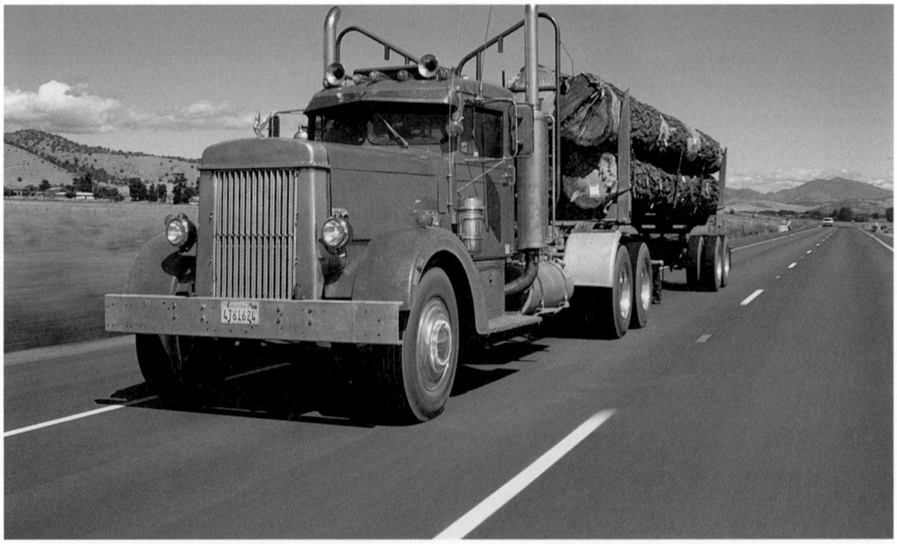

The long-standing softwood lumber dispute between the United States and Canada has hurt Canadian companies in the forestry industry. The dispute was settled in 2006, but much unhappiness is evident, and critics have charged that the Conservative government caved in to American pressure.

cotton producers.[33] These subsidies also hurt small cotton farmers in Africa because they cause highly productive U.S. farmers to produce a lot of cotton which drives down the price African farmers receive.[34] Canada's supply management system, which restricts imports and guarantees markets for producers of chickens, turkeys, eggs, and milk, could also come under fire since the WTO views the system as an unfair subsidy to producers.[35]

Protectionism—the practice of protecting domestic business at the expense of free market competition—has both advocates and critics. Supporters argue that tariffs and quotas protect domestic firms and jobs. In particular, they protect new industries until they are truly able to compete internationally. Some claim that since other nations have such measures, so must we. Still others justify protectionism in the name of national security. They argue that a nation must be able to produce goods needed for its survival in the event of war and that advanced technology should not be sold to potential enemies.

protectionism
Protecting domestic business at the expense of free market competition.

But opponents of protectionism are equally vocal. They note that protectionism reduces competition and drives up prices to consumers. They cite it as a cause of friction between nations. They maintain that, while jobs in some industries would be lost if protectionism ceased, jobs in other industries would expand if all countries abolished tariffs and quotas.

Protectionism sometimes takes on almost comic proportions. Neither Europe nor the United States grows bananas, but both European and U.S. firms buy and sell bananas in foreign markets. Problems arose when the EU put a quota on bananas imported from Latin America—a market dominated by two U.S. firms, Chiquita and Dole—in order to help firms based in current and former European colonies in the Caribbean. The United States retaliated and imposed a 100-percent tariff on certain luxury products imported from Europe, including Louis Vuitton handbags, Scottish cashmere sweaters, and Parma ham.[36]

Local-Content Laws

A country can affect how a foreign firm does business there by enacting local-content laws. **Local-content laws** require that products sold in a particular country be at least partly made in that country. These laws typically mean that firms seeking to do business in a country must either invest directly in that country or have a joint-venture partner from that country. In this way, some of the profits from doing business in a foreign country are shared with the people who live there.

local-content laws
Laws requiring that products sold in a particular country be at least partly made in that country.

Many countries have local-content laws. In a fairly extreme case, Venezuela forbids the import of any product if a like product is made in Venezuela. In 2005, Venezuela's president said he would cancel all mining licences and stop issuing new ones to foreign companies. This move was designed to protect the many small, local miners operating in Venezuela. Oil and gas licenses held by foreign companies had already been cancelled. These actions have made foreign companies much more reluctant to invest in Venezuela.[37]

Local-content laws may even exist within a country; when they do, they act just like trade barriers. In Canada, for example, a low bid on a bridge in British Columbia was rejected because the company that made the bid was from Alberta. The job was given to a B.C. company. A window manufacturer from New Brunswick lost a contract in Nova Scotia despite having made the lowest bid, and the job went to a company in Nova Scotia.

The Agreement on Internal Trade (AIT) requires all 10 Canadian provinces to remove barriers to agricultural trade. But when Quebec—which has a strong dairy lobby—prohibited margarine coloured to look like butter, it was in violation of the agreement.[38] In 2002, Unilever Canada Ltd. challenged the legality of the ban on coloured margarine in court.[39] In another case, Prince

Edward Island ignored a dispute panel ruling that stated P.E.I.'s milk import restrictions also violated the AIT.[40] A third case involves the question of who is allowed to audit the financial statements of public companies. At present, only Chartered Accountants (CAs) are allowed to do this in Quebec. This rule is being challenged by the Certified General Accountants (CGAs), who have auditing rights in most other provinces.[41] If provincial governments do not honour their obligations, the AIT will become meaningless.

Business-Practice Laws

business-practice law Law or regulation governing business practices in given countries.

Many businesses entering new markets encounter problems in complying with stringent regulations and bureaucratic obstacles. Such practices are affected by the **business-practice laws** which host countries use to govern business practices within their jurisdictions. For example, in 2007, the U.S. government crackdown on internet gambling led to the arrest of Canadian entrepreneur John Lefebvre, who was charged with laundering billions of dollars in gambling proceeds through Neteller PLC, an internet payment company he helped create. U.S. authorities have vowed to prosecute online gambling companies even when their executives are outside the United States. Calvin Ayre, the Canadian entrepreneur who runs the gambling site Bodog.com does not enter the United States because he fears he will be arrested.[42]

As part of its entry strategy in Germany, Wal-Mart has had to buy existing retailers rather than open brand-new stores. Why? Because the German government is not currently issuing new licences to sell food products. Wal-Mart also had to stop refunding price differences on items sold for less by other stores because the practice is illegal in Germany. Finally, Wal-Mart must comply with business-hour restrictions: Stores can't open before 7 a.m., must close by 8 p.m. on weeknights and 4 p.m. on Saturday, and must remain closed on Sunday.

Sometimes, what is legal (and even accepted) business practice in one country is illegal in another. The most prominent example is paying bribes to government officials to get business. The Canadian Corruption of Foreign Public Officials Act prohibits bribery of foreign officials, but as more Canadian companies do business abroad, they find themselves competing against companies that are not so reluctant to pay bribes in order to get business. As a result, Canadian companies are losing business to these companies.[43] In an attempt to create fairer competition among multinational companies, ministers from 29 member countries of the Organization for Economic Cooperation and Development (OECD) agreed in 1997 to criminalize bribery of foreign public officials.[44]

Transparency International (TI), an organization devoted to stamping out global corruption, says that Canadian business firms operating abroad are least likely to pay bribes to win business. TI says that bribery is most devastating and common in developing countries because government officials in those countries are poorly paid. TI publishes a "Corruption Perceptions Index" which ranks countries based on the amount of corruption that is perceived to exist, based on ratings by business people, academics, and risk analysts. The 2006 index showed that the least corrupt countries are Finland, Iceland, and New Zealand (ranked 1st, 2nd, and 3rd), while the most corrupt countries are Haiti, Myanmar, and Iraq (ranked 161st, 162nd, and 163rd). Canada ranked 14th and the United States ranked 20th.[45]

Calgary-based Niko Resources experienced first-hand some of the difficulties of doing business in a corrupt country. When it tried to develop two natural gas fields in Bangladesh, the company discovered that it was common for companies to give "gifts" to members of the media so that they would report favourably on company activities. After Niko refused to make any payments (and after two accidents in Niko's gas fields), the media began portraying Niko as an irresponsible company. Then, feuding politicians seized the opportunity to use Niko as a scapegoat during a political campaign. Niko's reputation in Bangladesh has suffered greatly, and the government has demanded $12 million from the company for environmental damage.[46]

Cartels and Dumping. A **cartel** is an association of producers whose purpose is to control the supply and price of a commodity. The most famous cartel is the Organization of Petroleum Exporting Countries (OPEC). It has given oil-producing countries considerable power in the last 25 years. In 1994, the major aluminum-producing countries, including Canada, worked out a deal to curb world aluminum production in an attempt to raise prices.[47] The diamond and shipping cartels have also been successful in keeping the prices they charge artificially high.[48] In 2000, the world's coffee-producing countries formed an OPEC-style cartel to control the price of coffee. They immediately raised coffee prices by 37 percent, which increased the price of a cup of coffee by about 15 cents. Surprisingly, most coffee buyers were sympathetic to the cartel, since coffee prices had been at their lowest level in seven years and coffee farmers in developing countries were struggling.[49]

cartel
Any association of producers whose purpose is to control supply of and prices for a given product.

Many countries forbid **dumping**—selling a product abroad for less than the comparable price charged in the home country. Antidumping legislation typically defines dumping as occurring if products are being sold at prices less than fair value, or if the result unfairly harms domestic industry. In 1992, Canada imposed anti-dumping duties on bicycles made in China, but in 2004 the duties were dropped because Chinese companies provided evidence that they could indeed make bicycles as cheaply as they said they could.[50]

dumping
Selling a product for less abroad than in the producing nation.

OVERCOMING BARRIERS TO TRADE

Despite the barriers described so far, world trade is flourishing. A number of world organizations and treaties exist to promote international business.

Trade Agreements

Explain how *free trade agreements* assist world trade. 5

Various free trade agreements have sparked international trade. Indeed, virtually every nation has formal trade treaties with other nations. Among the most significant agreements are the General Agreement on Tariffs and Trade, the World Trade Organization, the North American Free Trade Agreement, and the European Union.

General Agreement on Tariffs and Trade (GATT)

Governments typically view exports as good (because they create jobs in the country) and imports as bad (because they cause job losses in the country). Because of this, governments may be tempted to erect trade barriers to discourage imports. But if every country does this, international trade is stifled. To overcome this tendency, the **General Agreement on Tariffs and Trade (GATT)**—which was often humorously referred to as the General Agreement to Talk and Talk—was signed after World War II. Its purpose was to reduce or eliminate trade barriers, such as tariffs and quotas. It did so by encouraging nations to protect domestic industries within agreed-upon limits and to engage in multilateral negotiations. While 92 countries signed GATT, not all complied with its rules. The United States was one of the worst offenders.

General Agreement on Tariffs and Trade (GATT)
International trade agreement to encourage the multilateral reduction or elimination or trade barriers.

Fisherman Ratish Karthikeyan can sometimes double the revenue from a day's take by phoning around to compare prices at markets within reach of his boat. India is a thriving export market for cellphones. About half of India's 600 000 rural communities aren't even wired for fixed-line phone service. The number of mobile-phone users in India should jump from 3 million to 30 million in the next few years.

World Trade Organization

World Trade Organization (WTO) Organization through which member nations negotiate trading agreements and resolve disputes about trade policies and practices.

On January 1, 1995, the **World Trade Organization (WTO)** came into existence as the successor to GATT. The 149 member countries are required to open markets to international trade, and the WTO is empowered to pursue three goals:

1. Promote trade by encouraging members to adopt fair trade practices.
2. Reduce trade barriers by promoting multilateral negotiations.
3. Establish fair procedures for resolving disputes among members.

WTO trade liberalization talks in Seattle, Prague, and Montreal have been disrupted by protestors who resent the power of the WTO, and who are concerned about what world trade is doing to both the environment and to the developing countries that are not sharing in its benefits.[51] Protestors include labour unions (who regard imports from developing countries as unfair), environmentalists (who are concerned about business activity harming the environment), social activists (who are concerned about poor working conditions in developing countries), and farmers (who are concerned about the effect of free trade on grain prices). There are also major disagreements between the industrialized countries and developing countries regarding subsidies on agricultural products (see the discussion on subsidies on p. 136). At the Cancun meetings in 2006, developing countries insisted on trade liberalization for agricultural products, but no agreement was reached.

The European Union

European Union (EU) Agreement among major Western European nations to eliminate or make uniform most trade barriers affecting group members.

Originally called the Common Market, the **European Union (EU)** initially included the only the principal Western European nations like Italy, Germany, France, and the United Kingdom. But by 2006, 25 countries belonged to the EU, including eight former communist countries and two Mediterranean islands, which joined in 2004 (see Figure 5.2) Several other countries are also in the process of applying for membership, including Romania, Bulgaria, Turkey, Macedonia, and Croatia. The EU has eliminated most quotas and set uniform tariff levels on products imported and exported within their group. The EU is the largest free marketplace in the world, and produces nearly one-quarter of total global wealth.[52]

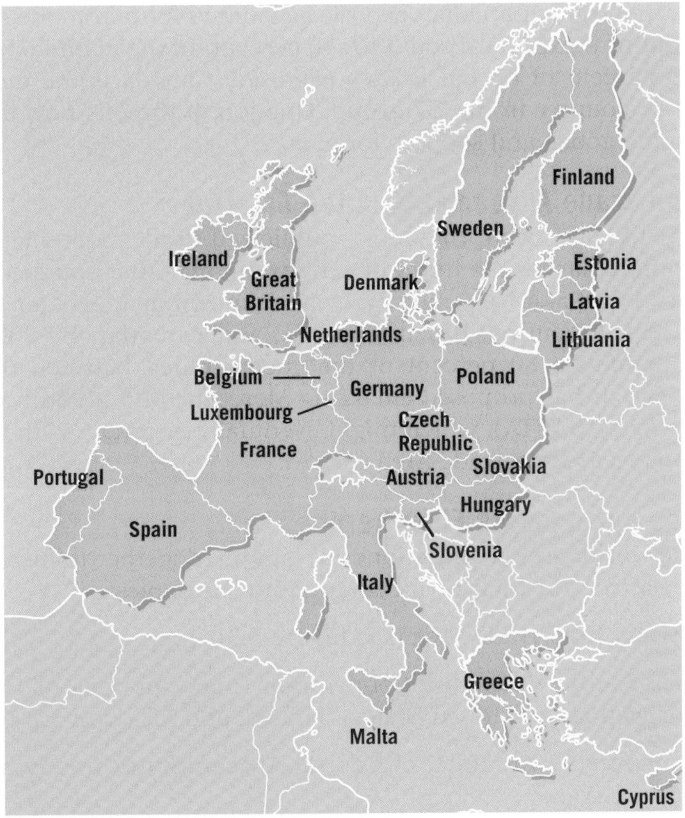

Figure 5.2 The nations of the European Union (EU).

The North American Free Trade Agreement

On January 1, 1994, the **North American Free Trade Agreement (NAFTA)** took effect. The objective of NAFTA is to create a free trade area for Canada, the United States, and Mexico. It eliminates trade barriers, promotes fair competition, and increases investment opportunities. Canada later signed a separate free trade agreement with Chile.

North American Free Trade Agreement (NAFTA) Agreement to gradually eliminate tariffs and other trade barriers among the United States, Canada, and Mexico.

Surveys conducted during the early 1990s showed that the majority of Canadians were opposed to NAFTA. They feared that jobs would be lost to other countries, that Canada's sovereignty would be threatened, and that Canada would be flooded with products manufactured in Mexico, where wages are much lower than they are in Canada. Supporters of NAFTA argued that the agreement would open up U.S. markets for Canadian products and thereby create more employment in Canada, that the agreement would not threaten Canada's sovereignty, and that NAFTA would create more employment possibilities for women.

What has actually happened since NAFTA took effect? In 2004, a group of economists at the Canadian Economics Association concluded that free trade has not been as good for Canada as predicted by its supporters, nor as bad for Canada as predicted by its detractors.[53] Several specific effects are noticeable:

- NAFTA has created a much more active North American market
- direct foreign investment has increased in Canada
- U.S. imports from (and exports to) Mexico have increased
- Canada has become an exporting powerhouse
- trade between the United States and Canada has risen sharply, and Canada enjoys a large trade surplus with the United States

- before free trade, Canadian exports accounted for about one-quarter of GDP, but now exports account for 40 percent. In the manufacturing sector, 60 percent of output is now exported. Canada is the most trade-intensive country in the G7 group. One job in three is now devoted to producing goods and services for export.[54]

Other Free Trade Agreements in the Americas

While NAFTA has been the most publicized trade agreement in the Americas, there has been a flurry of activity among other countries as well. On January 1, 1995, a free trade agreement known as Mercosur went into effect between Argentina, Brazil, Uruguay, and Paraguay. By 2005, tariffs were eliminated on 80 percent of the goods traded between those four countries. Brazil has proposed enlarging Mercosur into a South American Free Trade Area (SAFTA), which might eventually negotiate with NAFTA to form an Americas Free Trade Area (AFTA).

Free Trade Agreements Elsewhere

Around the world, groups of nations are banding together to form regional trade associations for their own benefit. Some examples:

- the ASEAN Free Trade Area (see Figure 5.3)
- the Asia-Pacific Economic Cooperation (many nations of the Pacific Rim, as well as the United States, Canada, and Mexico)
- the Economic Community of Central African States (many nations in equatorial Africa)
- the Gulf Cooperation Council (Bahrain, Kuwait, Oman, Qatar, Saudi Arabia, and United Arab Emirates)

In 2006, a Japanese proposal for the establishment of a new free-trade zone in Asia won support from ASEAN. The zone—which would be established by 2015—would include the ASEAN nations plus China, Japan, South Korea, India, Australia, and New Zealand. It would have a population of 3.1 billion people, and its output would be about one-quarter of the world's GDP.[55]

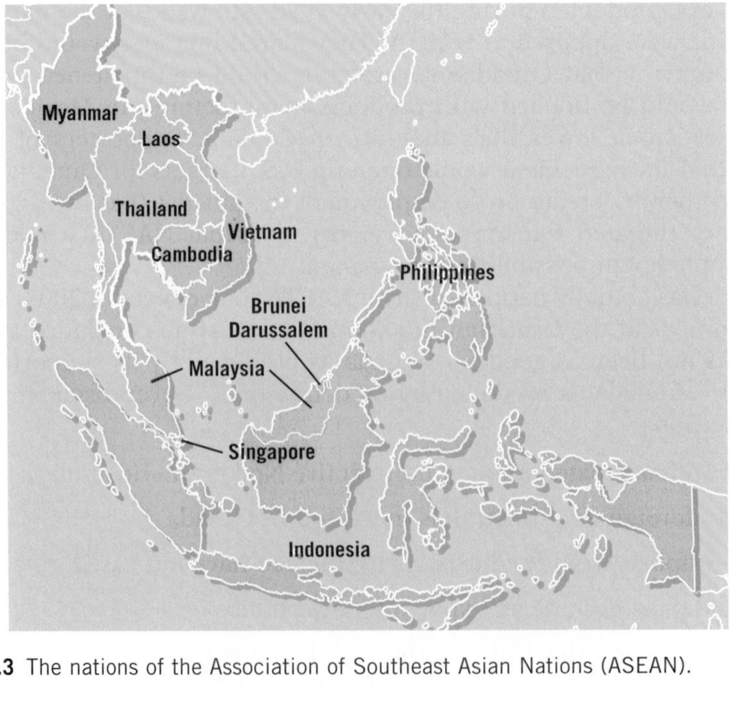

Figure 5.3 The nations of the Association of Southeast Asian Nations (ASEAN).

Summary of Learning Objectives

1. Describe the rise of international business and identify the *major world marketplaces.* More and more business firms are engaged in international business. The term *globalization* refers to the process by which the world economy is fast becoming a single interdependent entity. The global economy is characterized by a rapid growth in the exchange of information and trade in services. The three major marketplaces for international business are *North America* (the United States, Canada, and Mexico), *Western Europe* (which is dominated by Germany, the United Kingdom, France, and Italy), and *Asia–Pacific* (where the dominant country, Japan, is surrounded by such rapidly advancing nations as South Korea, Taiwan, Hong Kong, and China).

2. Explain how different forms of *competitive advantage, import–export balances, exchange rates,* and *foreign competition* determine the ways in which countries and businesses respond to the international environment. With an *absolute advantage*, a country engages in international trade because it can produce a good or service more efficiently than any other nation. But more often countries trade because they enjoy *comparative advantages*, that is, they can produce some items more efficiently than they can produce other items. A country that exports more than it imports has a *favourable balance of trade*, while a country that imports more than it exports has an *unfavourable balance of trade*. If the exchange rate decreases (the value of the Canadian dollar falls), our exports become less expensive for other countries so they will buy more of what we produce. The reverse happens if the value of the Canadian dollar increases. Changes in the exchange rate therefore have a strong impact on our international competitiveness.

3. Discuss the factors involved in deciding to do business internationally and in selecting the *appropriate levels of international involvement* and *international organizational structure.* In deciding whether to do business internationally, a firm must determine whether a market for its product exists abroad, and if so, whether the firm has the skills and knowledge to manage such a business. It must also assess the business climates of other nations to ensure that they are conducive to international operations. A firm must also decide on its level of international involvement. It can choose to be an *exporter* or *importer*, to organize as an *international firm*, or to operate as a *multinational firm*. The choice will influence the organizational structure of its international operations, specifically, its use of *independent agents, licensing arrangements, branch offices, strategic alliances,* and *direct investment.*

4. Describe some of the ways in which *social, cultural, economic, legal,* and *political differences* act as barriers to international trade. *Social* and *cultural differences* that can serve as barriers to trade include language, social values, and traditional buying patterns. Differences in economic systems may force businesses to establish close relationships with foreign governments before they are permitted to do business abroad. *Quotas, tariffs, subsidies,* and *local-content laws* offer protection to local industries. Differences in *business-practice laws* can make standard business practices in one nation illegal in another.

5. Explain how *free trade agreements* assist world trade. Several *trade agreements* have attempted to eliminate restrictions on free trade internationally. The *General Agreement on Tariffs and Trade* (GATT) was instituted to eliminate tariffs and other trade barriers among participating nations, and the WTO promotes trade by encouraging fair trade practices. The *European Union* (EU) has eliminated virtually all trade barriers among the 12 principal Western European nations. The *North American Free Trade Agreement* (NAFTA) eliminates many of the barriers to free trade that exist among the United States, Canada, and Mexico.

QUESTIONS AND EXERCISES

Questions for Analysis

1. Explain how the economic system of a country affects foreign firms interested in doing business there.
2. Make a list of all the major items in your bedroom. Identify the country in which each item was made. Give possible reasons why that nation might have a comparative advantage in producing the product.
3. Assume that you are the manager of a small firm seeking to enter the international arena. What information would you need about the market that you're thinking of entering?
4. Do you think that a firm operating internationally is better advised to adopt a single standard of ethical conduct or to adapt to local conditions? Under what kinds of conditions might each approach be preferable?
5. Explain how it is possible for a country to have a positive balance of trade and a negative balance of payments.
6. Is NAFTA good or bad for Canada? Give supporting reasons for your answer.
7. The EU includes most of the Western European countries, but some (such as Switzerland) have chosen not to join. Why might that be? What are the implications for countries that do not join?
8. What attributes of your province or region (cultural, geographical, economic, etc.) would be of interest to a foreign firm thinking about locating there?

Application Exercises

9. Interview the manager of a local firm that does at least some business internationally. Identify reasons why the company decided to "go international," as well as the level of the firm's international involvement and the organizational structure it uses for its international operations.
10. Select a product familiar to you. Using library references, learn something about the culture of India and identify the problems that might arise in trying to market this product to India's citizens.

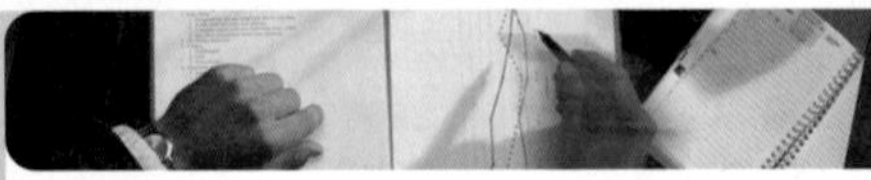

BUILDING YOUR BUSINESS SKILLS

Putting Yourself in Your Place

Goal

To encourage students to apply global business strategies to a small-business situation.

Situation

Some people might say that Yolanda Lang is a bit too confident. Others might say that she needs confidence—and more—to succeed in the business she's chosen. But one thing is certain: Lang is determined to grow INDE, her handbag design company, into a global enterprise. At only 28 years of age, she has time on her side—if she makes the right business moves now.

These days, Lang spends most of her time in Milan, Italy. Backed by $50 000 of her parents' personal savings, she is trying to compete with Gucci, Fendi, and other high-end handbag makers. Her target market is women willing to spend $200 on a purse. Ironically, Lang was forced to set up shop in Italy because of the snobbishness of these customers, who buy high-end bags only if they're European-made. "Strangely enough," she muses, "I need to be in Europe to sell in North America."

To succeed, she must first find ways to keep production costs down—a tough task for a woman in a male-dominated business culture. Her fluent Italian is an advantage, but she's often forced to turn down inappropriate dinner invitations. She also has to figure out how to get her 22-bag collection into stores worldwide. Retailers are showing her bags in Italy and Japan, but she's had little luck in the United States. "I intend to be a global company," says Lang. The question is how to succeed first as a small business.

Method

Step 1 Join together with three or four other students to discuss the steps that Lang has taken so far to break into the U.S. retail market. These steps include:

- Buying a mailing list of 5000 shoppers from high-end department store Neiman Marcus and selling directly to these customers.
- Linking with a manufacturer's representative to sell her line in major U.S. cities while she herself concentrates on Europe.

Step 2 Based on what you learned in this chapter, suggest other strategies that might help Lang grow her business. Working with group members, consider whether the following options would help or hurt Lang's business. Explain why a strategy is likely to work or likely to fail.

- Lang could relocate to the United States and sell abroad through an independent agent.
- Lang could relocate to the United States and set up a branch office in Italy.
- Lang could find a partner in Italy and form a strategic alliance that would allow her to build her business on both continents.

Step 3 Working alone, create a written marketing plan for INDE. What steps would you recommend that Lang take to reach her goal of becoming a global company? Compare your written response with those of other group members.

Follow-Up Questions

1. What are the most promising steps that Lang can take to grow her business? What are the least promising?
2. Lang thinks that her trouble breaking into the U.S. retail market stems from the fact that her company is unknown. How would this circumstance affect the strategies suggested in Steps 1 and 2?
3. When Lang deals with Italian manufacturers, she is a young, attractive woman in a man's world. Often, she must convince men that her purpose is business and nothing else. How should Lang handle personal invitations that get in the way of business? How can she say no while still maintaining business relationships? Why is it often difficult for women to do business in male-dominated cultures?
4. The American consulate has given Lang little business help because her products are made in Italy. Do you think the consulate's treatment of an American business person is fair or unfair? Explain your answer.
5. Do you think Lang's relocation to Italy will pay off? Why or why not?
6. With Lang's goals of creating a global company, can INDE continue to be a one-person operation?

EXERCISING YOUR ETHICS: TEAM EXERCISE

Weighing the Tradeoffs

The Situation

There is a small bank that is headquartered in western Canada. The firm is privately owned and all the managers own stock in the bank. The company's senior managers (and majority owners) have decided to sell the bank to a major international banking company within the next two to three years. First, though, the bank corporation needs to trim its expenses in order to make it more attractive to a potential buyer.

The Dilemma

Because the bank corporation has been a locally owned and operated enterprise, it has maintained a full slate of operations within the local market. For instance, its corporate offices, many banking outlets, and all of its support activities are housed locally. The latter category includes a large call centre—a staff of 30 people who handle most customer calls involving questions about their accounts.

There has been a growing trend in banking, though, to outsource call centres to foreign countries, most notably India. Such markets have an abundance of potential English-speaking employees, excellent technology, and low wages. One senior manager has argued that the bank corporation should outsource its call centre immediately. This would enable the firm to lower its costs, thus making it even more attractive to a potential buyer. When confronted with the prospect of cutting 30 jobs, the manager acknowledges that that will be tough but is certain that any buyer will eventually do the same anyway.

Another vocal senior manager, though, is opposed to this idea. This person argues that because the bank corporation was started locally and has strong ties to the local community, it should maintain its current operations until the bank is sold. Then, this manager argues, if a new owner decides to cut jobs, "it will be on their conscience, not ours."

Team Activity

Assemble a group of four students and assign each group member to one of the following roles:

- Senior manager (majority owner) of the bank
- Call centre employee
- Bank customer
- Bank corporation investor

Action Steps

1. Before discussing the situation with your group, and from the perspective of your assigned role, do you think that the call centre should be outsourced immediately? Write down the reasons for your position.
2. Before discussing the situation with your group, and from the perspective of your assigned role, what are the underlying ethical issues, if any, in this situation? Write down the issues.
3. Gather your group together and reveal, in turn, each member's comments on whether the call centre should be outsourced immediately. Next, reveal the ethical issues listed by each member.
4. Appoint someone to record the main points of agreement and disagreement within the group. How do you explain the results? What accounts for any disagreement?
5. From an ethical standpoint, what does your group conclude is the most appropriate action for the bank to take in this situation?
6. Develop a group response to the following question: Can your team identify other solutions that might help satisfy both senior managers' views?

BUSINESS CASE 5

International Challenges in the Clothing Industry

On January 1, 2005, import quotas in Canada were lifted for members of the World Trade Organization. Prior to that time, the amount of textiles and apparel that could be imported into Canada from countries like China and India was limited in order to protect domestic Canadian industries. The Canadian government unveiled a $600 million aid package to help Canadian companies cope with the expected increase in cheap imports, but many in the industry didn't think this would help much. A mere 7 months after the import quotas were lifted, the Canadian apparel industry had lost about 20 percent of its workforce. Many of these jobs were shifted to low-wage countries as companies tried to reduce their costs to compete with Chinese imports.

The town of Huntingdon, Quebec (population 2600), discovered first-hand what the new trade rules meant even before they were implemented. In December 2004, townspeople learned that Huntingdon Mills was bankrupt and that 215 jobs would be lost, and that Cleyn & Tinker would soon shut down, costing 600 workers their jobs. The closing of the two textile mills meant a 25 percent decline in the town's tax revenue, and increased the unemployment rate (already at 20 percent). Workers don't put all the blame on China. They feel that the Canadian government is accountable because it gave undue import preferences to Caribbean and other poor countries, and that it didn't do enough to keep the Canadian dollar from rising and making Canada's textile exports more expensive.

Two successful apparel companies in Quebec—Peerless Clothing Inc. and Gildan Activewear—are also trying to determine what the dropping of import quotas will mean for them. Peerless operates the largest men's tailored clothing factory in North America, producing 30 000 suits and 40 000 pairs of trousers each week. Annual sales exceed $300 million, and Peerless has captured 20 percent of the U.S. men's suit market. A U.S. retailer who orders a suit on a Monday knows it will show up the next *day* at Peerless' St. Albans, Vermont, shipping centre, ready to be sent anywhere in the United States. Part of Peerless' success is attributed to owner Alvin Segal's invention of the "engineered suit," where a high-quality suit is made using assembly line efficiencies. The company has also benefited from the Canada–U.S. free trade agreement; Segal landed contracts with major U.S. retailers and with labels like Ralph Lauren and Calvin Klein.

Montreal-based Gildan Activewear has become a global T-shirt powerhouse by focusing on being the highest-quality, lowest-cost provider of "blank" 100 percent cotton T-shirts which are sold to wholesalers and then imprinted with logos and designs. Using this strategy, Gildan has achieved annual sales of $600 million and has captured 29 percent of the U.S. imprinted T-shirt market. Its goal is 50 percent of the world market. Unlike Peerless, Gildan aggressively uses offshore manufacturing facilities, mostly in the Caribbean where labour costs are low. In 2006, Gildan announced that it was closing several of its Canadian and U.S. facilities, and transferring even more production work to the Caribbean region in a continuing effort to respond to competitive pressures from low-cost Asian producers.

Both Peerless and Gildan have to keep an eye on future imports from China. The vice-chairman of Peerless says that since the 16 percent tariff on yarn that Peerless imports was dropped, and since Peerless imports most of its textiles from abroad, this will significantly reduce its costs as well and allow it to be price-competitive. Gildan's executive vice-president said his company will be able to meet the threat from China because of Gildan's economies of scale, its state-of-the-art factories, and its already low labour costs.

The government aid package is designed to help both the capital-intensive textile industry and the labour-intensive apparel industry, but the interests of these two industries often do not coincide. The apparel industry pays relatively low wages, buys the lowest-cost fabric it can find, and is able to shift production to wherever it makes the most economic sense. By contrast, the textile industry pays higher wages and invests in new technology to remain competitive in its Canadian base. The irony is that the new regulations will allow Canadian apparel makers to import yarn duty-free. That means that they can use textiles that are not made in Canada, thus hurting Canadian textile mills.

Questions for Discussion

1. Explain how exchange rates and the value of the Canadian dollar have affected the garment industry. Should the Canadian government try to influence the value of the Canadian dollar? Defend your answer.
2. Describe the key arguments made by supporters of protectionism. To what extent are these arguments relevant for the current situation in the garment industry? Describe the key arguments made by those who support free trade. To what extent are these relevant for the current situation in the garment industry?
3. To what extent should the Canadian government intervene and protect industries like the garment industry? Defend your answer.
4. *"There should be no tariffs at all on products moving between any countries. Only then will the world's economic system be operating at full efficiency."* Do you agree or disagree with this statement? Explain.

MYBUSINESSLAB mybusinesslab

To improve your grade, visit the MyBusinessLab website at **www.pearsoned.ca/mybusinesslab**. This online homework and tutorial system allows you to test your understanding and generates a personalized study plan just for you. It provides you with study and practice tools directly related to this chapter's content. MyBusinessLab puts you in control of your own learning!

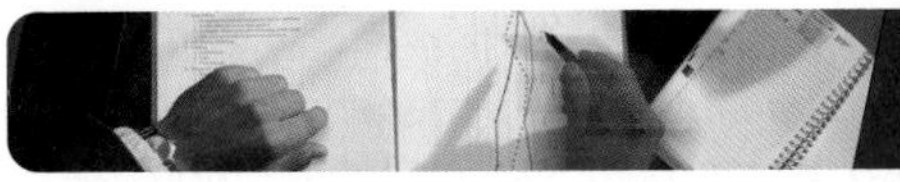

CRAFTING A BUSINESS PLAN

Part 1: The Contemporary Business Environment

Goal of the Exercise

In Chapter 4, we discussed how the starting point for virtually every new business is a *business plan*. Business plans describe the business strategy for any new business and demonstrate how that strategy will be implemented. One benefit of a business plan is that in preparing it, would-be entrepreneurs must develop their idea on paper and firm up their thinking about how to launch their business before investing time and money in it. In this exercise, you'll get started on creating your own business plan.

Exercise Background: Part 1 of the Business Plan

The starting point for any business plan is coming up with a "great idea." This might be a business that you've already considered setting up. If you don't have ideas for a business already, look around. What are some businesses that you come into contact with on a regular basis? Restaurants, childcare services, and specialty stores are a few examples you might consider. You may also wish to create a business that is connected with a talent or interest you have, such as crafts, cooking, or car repair. It's important that you create a company from "scratch" rather than use a company that already exists. You'll learn more if you use your own ideas.

Once you have your business idea, your next step is to create an "identity" for your business. This includes determining a name for your business and an idea of what your business will do. It also includes identifying the type of ownership your business will take, topics we discussed in Chapter 4. The first part of the plan also briefly looks at who your ideal customers are as well as how your business will stand out from the crowd. Part 1 of the plan also looks at how the business will interact with the community and demonstrate social responsibility, topics we discussed in Chapter 3. Finally, almost all business plans today include a perspective on the impact of global business, which we discussed in Chapter 5.

YOUR ASSIGNMENT mybusinesslab

Step 1

To complete this assignment, you first need to download the *Business Plan Student Template* file from the book's MyBusinessLab. This is a Microsoft Word file you can use to complete you business plan. For this assignment, you will fill in "Part 1" of the plan.

Step 2

Once you have the *Business Plan Student Template* file, you can begin to answer the following questions in "Part 1: The Contemporary Business World."

1. What is the name of your business?

   Hint: When you think of the name of your business, make sure that it captures the spirit of the business you're creating.

2. What will your business do?

   Hint: Imagine that you are explaining your idea to a family member or a friend. Keep your description to 30 words or less.

3. What form of business ownership (sole proprietorship, partnership, or corporation) will your business take? Why did you choose this form?

   Hint: For more information on types of business ownership, refer to the discussion in Chapter 4.

4. Briefly describe your ideal customer. What are they like in terms of age, income level, and so on?

   Hint: You don't have to give too much detail in this part of the plan; you'll provide more details about customers and marketing in later parts of the plan.

5. Why will customers choose to buy from your business instead of your competition?

   Hint: In this section, describe what will be unique about your business. For example, is the product special or will you offer the product at a lower price?

6. All businesses have to deal with ethical issues. One way to address these issues is to create a code of ethics. List three core principles your business will follow.

   Hint: To help you consider the ethical issues that your business might face, refer to the discussion in Chapter 3.

7. A business shows social responsibility by respecting all of its stakeholders. What steps will you take to create a socially responsible business?

   Hint: Refer to the discussion of social responsibility in Chapter 3. What steps can you take to be a "good citizen" in the community? Consider also how you may need to be socially responsible toward your customers and, if applicable, investors, employees, and suppliers.

8. Will you sell your product in another country? If so, what countries and why? What challenges will you face?

   Hint: To help you consider issues of global business, refer to Chapter 5. Consider how you will expand internationally (e.g., independent agent, licensing). Do you expect global competition for your product? What advantages will foreign competitors have?

Note: Once you have answered the questions, save your Word document. You'll be answering additional questions in later chapters.

CBC VIDEO CASE I-1

Wormboy

Tom Szaky is a young Canadian who is betting big bucks on his ability to sell worm poop. The son of two doctors, Tom was on track to get a degree from prestigious Princeton University in the United States. But one day he discovered a friend's worm composter, and when he found out that the worms ate garbage, he got an idea for a business. He quit Princeton and started Terra Cycle, a company which makes plant food from worm droppings. Now he is trying to make a fortune off worms.

Terra Cycle's office is in a basement, but the plant food is made in a factory containing 250 000 worms. The worm droppings are mixed with water, pumped into used bottles, and shipped to customers in used boxes. Szaky says he won't harm the environment in his quest to make money. This is eco-capitalism at its finest, because Tom Szaky is turning garbage into gold.

Several of Szaky's friends are working in his company with him. Robin, the vice-president of sales, wants to get Terra Cycle into big box stores like Home Depot and Wal-Mart, but he's also going after smaller chains as well. Robin doesn't have experience with big box stores, and investors want someone experienced to be head of sales. But Szaky finds that it is hard to fire a friend. Another friend, Alex, is a high school buddy who also quit Princeton. He runs Terra Cycle's lawn program. His first big contract was repairing a lawn at Princeton. Alex does a good job of bringing back Princeton's grass, but he hasn't done much to get other sales. So Szaky puts pressure on Alex to get more customers.

In this business, Szaky needs all the help he can get, so he has talked several students into volunteering to work for him. In return for their work, they get business experience and stock options. Szaky bought a run-down mansion and turned it into the staff dorm for the volunteers. He furnished the house with some castoff items that he got from friends at Princeton.

Szaky has several problems he must solve. First, he is spending about $50 000 a month for things like salaries, rent, and food for the worms. So far, he has raised over a million dollars, but he has already spent most of that. Not much money is coming in from sales because Terra Cycle is sold only in a few stores. Second, some of his workers are doing sloppy work. For example, there were errors in a business plan that was given to potential investors, and this did not increase their confidence in the company. Perhaps counting on student volunteers was a mistake.

Third, sales must be increased. Szaky therefore goes on the road to pitch his product—called Plant Jelly—to various companies. One of them is QVC, a home shopping channel that reaches 86 million homes in the United States. He will get 15 minutes of air time to pitch the product. Terra Cycle's chief scientist thinks Szaky is moving too fast because Plant Jelly hasn't really been tested for effectiveness. But Szaky has a gut feeling the product will work, so he goes ahead. (Some time later, Szaky gets test results showing that Plant Jelly does indeed work.)

On his trip, Szaky meets with 7 different retailers, but now some time has passed and he still hasn't heard anything positive from any of them. He is wondering whether eco-capitalism can sell in a big box world. But he believes in his product, so he plans another risky move: he wants to turn a warehouse into a factory that will be able to produce a lot of Plant Jelly if he gets a big box order. It will cost $300 000 to renovate the warehouse, but he doesn't have any money to do the work.

Szaky realizes that he is going to have to start selling reality instead of just potential. In a meeting with venture capitalists, he asks for $4.5 million. He argues that his product has high margins because it is made from garbage. But the venture capitalists are reluctant, partly because of Szaky's age (22).

Finally Szaky gets a call from Wal-Mart and learns that Robin has succeeded in getting a $300 000 order for the spring. Now the company must actually make all that plant food. To do that, the new factory must somehow be financed and set up in very short order. Szaky also has to try to win over another big investor. It's a good thing he works well under pressure. Maybe quitting Princeton wasn't such a bad idea after all.

Questions for Discussion

1. Explain the difference between *entrepreneurship*, *small business*, and *new venture creation* as it applies to Szaky's activities.
2. Use Figure 4.6 on p. 93 to explain Szaky's activities so far.
3. What is *bootstrapping*? How is this idea relevant to Szaky?
4. What kind of financing is Szaky using for his business?
5. What form of business ownership would be most appropriate for Szaky's business?

CBC CBC VIDEO CASE I-2

Corporate Espionage

Spying, intrigue, and shredded documents are activities we normally associate with countries spying on one another. But these activities are also evident in the business world. And make no mistake about it, Canada is just as likely a place for shenanigans as the United States. Norman Inkster, who helps companies fight off corporate spies, says that business firms engage in corporate espionage much more often than we ever hear about. And, he says, "getting a leg up" can be "low down and dirty." Consider the case of Air Canada versus WestJet.

It all started when a WestJet executive got a password that allowed him to access an Air Canada website that was supposed to be confidential and available only to Air Canada employees. The website gave the WestJet executive access to Air Canada's "load factor" on each one of its routes. This was critical information which allowed WestJet to identify Air Canada's strong and weak flights and then to develop a competitive strategy based on that information.

Air Canada learned that someone at WestJet was accessing their website only after they were tipped off. In an attempt to find out just what WestJet knew, Air Canada hired private investigators to steal the WestJet executive's garbage. The garbage contained a lot of shredded paper which was sent to Church Street Technology, a company which has developed a system for reassembling shredded pages. Owner Cody Ford first sorts the strips of shredded paper, then tapes them to a blank sheet of paper and scans them. A specialized computer program then reassembles the original document. Ford says that he can easily reassemble shredded documents.

While this was going on, WestJet was not idle. When the WestJet executive's garbage was stolen, a neighbour noticed and phoned the police. They informed the executive, so he took pictures of the investigators the next time they came for his garbage. The pictures appeared in the *Globe and Mail*.

Once Air Canada had determined what WestJet knew, and once WestJet knew that Air Canada had stolen one of their executive's garbage, the rivalry between the two companies moved from the boardroom to the courtroom, and the companies sued each other over allegations of corporate espionage. Air Canada filed a $220 million lawsuit against WestJet, accusing it of using the website information to schedule competing flights. WestJet counter-sued Air Canada, accusing it of trespassing and stealing private property.

The lawsuit was settled in 2006. WestJet apologized to Air Canada and said that its conduct was both unethical and unacceptable, and that WestJet accepted full responsibility for its misconduct. WestJet agreed to pay $5 million to Air Canada for the expenses Air Canada incurred while investigating the unauthorized accessing of its website. WestJet also agreed to contribute $10 million to children's charities. Clive Beddoe, CEO of WestJet, also apologized to WestJet shareholders and said this shouldn't have happened. WestJet's lawsuit against Air Canada was dismissed.

Questions for Discussion

1. Do you think that WestJet behaved in an unethical fashion? Why or why not? Do you think that Air Canada behaved in an unethical fashion? Why or why not?
2. Analyze this problem using the three-step process described on p. 62. Explain your conclusions at each step in the process. What conclusions do you reach at the end of the process about the behaviour of WestJet and Air Canada?
3. Suppose that you are confronted with a situation where you strongly believe that another person acted in an unethical fashion, but that person totally disagreed with you. How would you go about convincing that person that their behaviour was unethical?
4. *"The WestJet executive who gained access to Air Canada's website did not behave in an unethical fashion. He simply used the information he was given to gather information from Air Canada's website. He then analyzed Air Canada's business activity and developed a strategy for WestJet that took advantage of that knowledge. This is simply an example of a person using information to his advantage."* Do you agree or disagree with this statement? Explain.

PART TWO

The Business of Managing

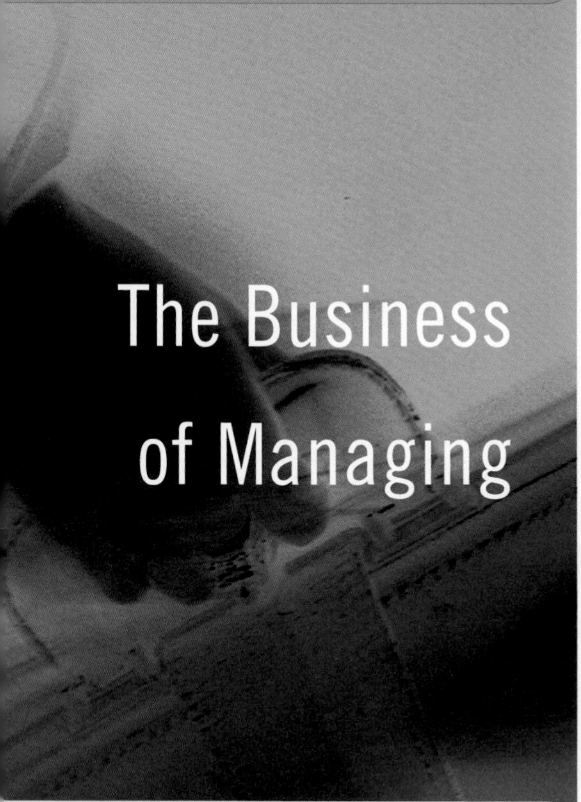

Corporate strategy, organization structure, employee diversity, and motivation are four issues you will read about in the opening cases of Chapters 6–9. These and many other management issues must be dealt with if companies hope to grow and prosper. Managers in all business firms—indeed, in any kind of organization—must carry out the basic management functions of planning, organizing, leading, and controlling. These important functions are the focus of this section of the text.

Part Two, The Business of Managing, provides an overview of business management today. It includes a look at the importance of managers in business firms, how businesses are structured to achieve their goals, the management of the firm's human resources, and the importance of motivating and leading employees.

- We begin in **Chapter 6, Managing the Business Enterprise,** by describing the basic functions of management—planning, organizing, leading, and controlling. We also look at the different types and levels of managers, the skills that managers must possess, the importance of goal setting, and the idea of corporate culture.
- In **Chapter 7, Organizing the Business Enterprise,** we look at the basic organizational structures that companies have adopted, and the different kinds of authority that managers can have. The impact of the informal organization is also examined.
- In **Chapter 8, Managing Human Resources and Labour Relations,** we explore the activities that are necessary to effectively manage employees, including assessing employee needs, training, promoting, and compensating employees. We also look at the union movement in Canada, why and how workers organize, how government legislation has affected workers' rights to organize into unions, and how management and labour interact.
- In **Chapter 9, Motivating, Satisfying, and Leading Employees,** we examine the important issues of motivation and leadership. We look at the reasons why firms should establish good relationships with their employees, how managers' attempts to maintain productivity can affect their relations with employees, and the approaches to leadership that have been evident over time.

CHAPTER 6

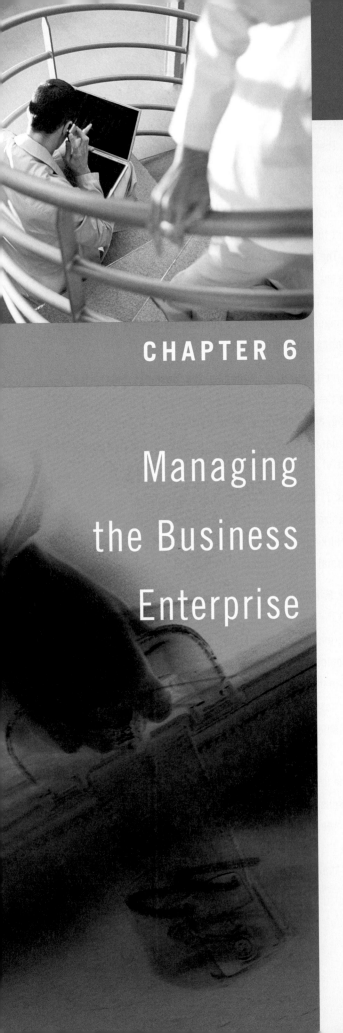

Managing the Business Enterprise

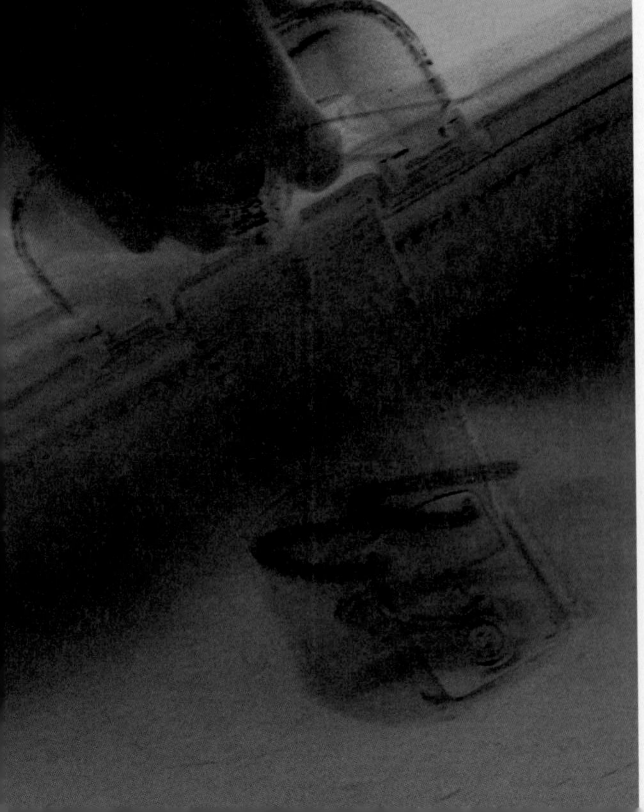

After reading this chapter, you should be able to:

1. Describe the four basic functions that constitute the *management process.*
2. Identify *types of managers* by level and area.
3. Describe the basic *management skills.*
4. Explain the importance of setting *goals* and formulating *strategies* as the starting points of effective management.
5. Discuss *contingency planning* and *crisis management* in today's business world.
6. Explain the idea of *corporate culture* and why it is important.

Looking for Redemption?

Edgar Bronfman, Jr. is the Chairman of Warner Music Group, which includes such record labels as Warner Bros., Atlantic, Electra, and the Christian music producer Word Records. He is the son of Edgar Bronfman, Sr., who was CEO of the Seagram Company. Seagram was started in the 1920s by Sam Bronfman, who sold liquor by mail order. Sam's son, Edgar Bronfman, Sr. became CEO in 1957, and for the next 40 years the company focused on the production of wine and distilled spirits. In the process, it became a household name in Canada.

In the mid-1990s, Edgar Bronfman, Jr. took over leadership of Seagram from his father and made some dramatic strategic moves that turned the company away from its traditional products and moved it toward the high–risk entertainment business. For example, the company bought MCA Inc. (now Universal) and PolyGram NV. These moves caused some people to recall founder Sam Bronfman's observation that third-generation family members often dissipate the family fortune. Edgar Jr. was well aware of this criticism and he was determined not to fulfill his grandfather's prophecy.

Things seemed to go well for a time under Edgar Jr.'s leadership. In 2000, he sold Seagram to the French conglomerate Vivendi SA for $33 billion in Vivendi stock. This looked like a good deal because Seagram was paid the equivalent of $75 for each of its shares, even though Seagram's shares were trading at less than $50 at the time. But things soon turned sour. By the end of 2001, Vivendi was in deep financial trouble, and its stock price had declined from $130 to $50 per share. The Seagram fortune declined along with Vivendi's decline because Bronfman had taken Vivendi stock instead of cash when he sold Seagram. When the merger with Vivendi was originally announced, the Seagram family fortune was worth about U.S.$7 billion, but by 2003, it had declined to less than U.S.$1 billion. People started thinking Sam Bronfman was right after all.

In spite of these setbacks, Edgar Bronfman, Jr. was determined to get back on the winning track. In 2003, he was unsuccessful in his attempt to buy Vivendi's film and TV assets, but in 2004 he and several partners were successful in purchasing Warner Music Group. Bronfman has adopted a corporate strategy based on the assumption that consumers will increasingly bypass traditional music stores and instead buy on-line digital music. He wants Warner Music Group to be a major player in emerging markets such as ringtones and ringbacks (where cellphones are programmed with songs to play for callers). He also thinks that music will be distributed through many more distribution channels than has historically been the case. He predicts that by 2009 about one-quarter of music revenue will come from digital music.

To pursue this strategy, Bronfman has borrowed a lot of money. So far, he is using some of this borrowed money to reward his shareholder partners. The partners have already taken more than $1 billion out of the firm. Standard & Poor's Corp., a bond rating firm, criticized this distribution, saying that it put the company's balance sheet at risk. For the 10 months ending September 30, 2004, Warner Music lost $136 million. Industry observers feel that Bronfman is counting far too much on future revenue, particularly since the music industry's attempts to defeat on-line piracy have not been very successful.

It is too early to tell if Bronfman's strategy is going to work. If it does, he will be seen as a top manager who had the vision and insight to position Warner Music Group so that it could capitalize on a major trend. If the strategy doesn't work, critics will keep saying that old Sam Bronfman was right. ◆

HOW WILL THIS BENEFIT YOU?

After reading this chapter, you will have a clearer understanding of how to effectively carry out various management responsibilities. From the perspective of a consumer or investor, you'll be better able to assess and appreciate the quality of management in various companies.

In this chapter, we begin by introducing the idea of the management process and the functions that are necessary in this process. We then identify the different types of managers that are likely to be found in an organization (by level and by area). Next, we describe the basic management skills, paying particular attention to decision-making skills. We then explore the importance of strategic management and effective goal setting in organizational success. We conclude the chapter by examining the concept of corporate culture.

WHO ARE MANAGERS?

All businesses depend on effective management. Regardless of the type of business they work in, managers like Edgar Bronfman perform many of the same basic functions, are responsible for many of the same tasks, and have many of the same responsibilities. All managers must make plans, organize their work, direct the work of subordinates, and control operations.

Although our focus is on managers in *business* settings, the principles of management apply to all kinds of organizations. Managers work in charities, churches, community organizations, educational institutions, and government agencies. The prime minister of Canada, the president of the University of Toronto, the executive director of the United Way, the dean of your business school, and the chief administrator of your local hospital are all managers. Remember, too, that managers bring to small organizations many of the skills that they bring to large ones. Regardless of the nature and size of an organization, managers are among its most important resources.

THE MANAGEMENT PROCESS

1 Describe the four basic functions that constitute the *management process.*

management
The process of planning, organizing, leading, and controlling a business's financial, physical, human, and information resources in order to achieve its goals.

Management is the process of planning, organizing, leading, and controlling an enterprise's financial, physical, human, and information resources to achieve the organization's goals. The planning, organizing, leading, and controlling aspects of a manager's job are interrelated. This means that a manager is likely to be engaged in all these activities during the course of any given business day. The CEO of Walt Disney Productions is a manager because he regularly carries out these four functions as films are being made. Actors such as Julia Roberts or Tom Cruise may be the stars of the movies, but they are not managers because they don't carry out the four functions of management. The Business Accountability box explains the nature of managerial jobs.

Planning

planning
That portion of a manager's job concerned with determining what the business needs to do and the best way to achieve it.

Planning is the process of determining the firm's goals and developing a strategy for achieving those goals. The planning process involves five steps. In *step 1*, goals are established for the organization. A commercial airline, for example, may set a goal to fill 90 percent of the seats on each flight. In *step 2*, managers identify whether a gap exists between the company's desired and actual position. For example, the airline may analyze load data and find that only 73 percent of the seats on the average flight are filled. In *step 3*, managers develop plans to achieve the desired objectives. For exam-

BUSINESS ACCOUNTABILITY

What Do Managers Actually Do?

Henry Mintzberg of McGill University conducted a detailed study of the work of five chief executive officers and found the following:

1. Managers work at an unrelenting pace.
2. Managerial activities are characterized by brevity, variety, and fragmentation.
3. Managers have a preference for "live" action, and emphasize work activities that are current, specific, and well-defined.
4. Managers are attracted to the verbal media.

Mintzberg believes that a manager's job can be described as 10 roles (in three categories) that must be performed. The manager's formal authority and status give rise to three *interpersonal roles*: (1) *figurehead* (duties of a ceremonial nature, such as attending a subordinate's wedding); (2) *leader* (being responsible for the work of the unit); and (3) *liaison* (making contact outside the vertical chain of command). These interpersonal roles give rise to three *informational roles*: (1) *monitor* (scanning the environment for relevant information); (2) *disseminator* (passing information to subordinates); and (3) *spokesperson* (sending information to people outside the unit).

The interpersonal and informational roles allow the manager to carry out four *decision-making roles*: (1) *entrepreneur* (improving the performance of the unit); (2) *disturbance handler* (responding to high-pressure disturbances, such as a strike at a supplier); (3) *resource allocator* (deciding who will get what in the unit); and (4) *negotiator* (working out agreements on a wide variety of issues, such as the amount of authority an individual will be given).

Managers in a 2005 study conducted by Pace Productivity felt that they should have spent about half their time on activities such as managing staff, providing direction, and coaching, but that they actually were able to spend less than 20 percent of their time on "people management." Managers also thought that they should have spent about 6 percent of their time on administrative tasks, but they actually spent 25 percent of their time on those activities. The amount of time managers thought they should spend on planning was about the same as what they actually spent. Consistent with Mintzberg's original findings, the Pace data also showed that managers' lives are very hectic, and their focus shifts rapidly from activity to activity. For example, 43 different activities lasted an average of just 16 minutes each.

Insight into what managers actually do can also be gained by looking at the *functions* of management (planning, organizing, leading, and controlling). Consider the work of Marina Pyo, who is a Publisher in the School Division at Pearson Education Canada, a publisher of textbooks for elementary and secondary schools, colleges, and universities. Her job is to manage the activities that are necessary to develop resources in math and science for the Canadian elementary school market. Her work is at times intense, fragmented, rewarding, frustrating, and fast-paced. In short, she is a typical manager.

Pyo carries out the *planning* function when she drafts a plan for a new book. She is *organizing* when she develops a new organization chart to facilitate goal achievement. She is *leading* when she meets with a subordinate to discuss that person's career plans. And she is *controlling* when she checks sales prospects for a book before ordering a reprint.

Some of Pyo's activities do not easily fit into this "functions of management" model. For example, it is not clear which function she is performing when she negotiates the size of a reprint run with the manager of the sales division, or when she talks briefly with the president of her division about recent events in her area of responsibility.

QUESTIONS FOR DISCUSSION

1. Just exactly what is it that managers are accountable for?
2. Why do you think managers spend less time on "people management" than they think they should and more time on administrative tasks? How does this affect managerial accountability?

ple, the airline may reduce fares on heavily travelled routes in order to increase the percentage of the seats that are filled. In *step 4*, the plans that have been decided upon are implemented. For example, the fare from Toronto to Montreal may be reduced by 10 percent. In *step 5*, the effectiveness of the plan is assessed. The airline would measure the percentage of seats that were filled after the change was implemented to determine whether the goal was reached.

A more complex example of planning occurred when Yahoo's top managers set a strategic goal of becoming a top firm in the then-emerging market for internet search engines. The company started by assessing the ways in which people actually use the web and concluded that users wanted to be able to satisfy a wide array of needs, preferences, and priorities by going to as few sites as possible to find what they were looking for. One key component of Yahoo's strategy was to foster partnerships and relationships with other companies so that potential web surfers could draw upon several sources through a single site, or portal. Yahoo managers then began fashioning alliances with such diverse partners as Reuters, Standard & Poor's, and the Associated Press, RE/Max, and a wide array of information providers specializing in sports, weather, entertainment, shopping, and travel.

A Hierarchy of Plans

Plans can be made on three general levels, with each level reflecting plans for which managers at that level are responsible. These levels constitute a hierarchy because implementing plans is practical only when there is a logical flow from one level to the next. **Strategic plans** reflect decisions about resource allocations, company priorities, and the steps needed to meet strategic goals. They are usually set by top management. Procter & Gamble's strategy to have its products rank number one or number two in their category is an example of a strategic plan. (We look at strategic planning later in this chapter.) **Tactical plans** are shorter-range plans concerned with implementing specific aspects of the company's strategic plans. They typically involve upper and middle management. Coca-Cola's decision to increase sales in Europe by building European bottling facilities is an example of tactical planning. **Operational plans**, which are developed by middle and lower-level managers, set short-term targets for daily, weekly, or monthly performance. McDonald's, for example, establishes operational plans when it explains precisely how Big Macs are to be cooked, warmed, and served.

strategic plans
Plans that reflect decisions about resource allocations, company priorities, and steps needed to meet strategic goals.

tactical plans
Generally, short-range plans concerned with implementing specific aspects of a company's strategic plans.

operational plans
Plans setting short-term targets for daily, weekly, or monthly performance.

Organizing

Organizing is the process of deciding which jobs must be performed, and how these jobs should be coordinated so that the company's goals are reached. Most businesses prepare organization charts that diagram the various jobs within the company and how those jobs relate to one another. These charts help everyone understand their job and who they report to. In many larger businesses, roles and reporting relationships may be too complex to draw as a simple box-and-line diagram.

organizing
That portion of a manager's job concerned with mobilizing the necessary resources to complete a particular task.

To help you appreciate the importance of the organizing function, consider the example of Hewlett-Packard (HP). The company was once one of the leading-edge, high-tech firms in the world, but it lost its lustre a few years ago. HP had long prided itself on being a corporate confederation of individual businesses, and sometimes these businesses ended up competing with each other. This approach had been beneficial for much of the firm's history. It was easier for each business to make its own decisions quickly and efficiently, and the competition kept each unit on its toes. By the late 1990s, however, problems had become apparent, and no one could quite figure out what was going on. Ann Livermore, then head of the firm's software and services business, realized that the structure that had worked so well in the past was now holding the company back. To regain its competitive edge, HP needed an integrated, organization-wide strategy. Livermore led the charge to create one organization united behind one strategic plan. Eventually, a new team of top managers was handed control of the company, and every major component of the firm's structure was reorganized. The firm is now back on solid footing and has regained its place as one of the world's top technology businesses.[1]

We explore the organizing function in much more detail in Chapter 7.

Leading

When **leading**, managers guide and motivate workers to meet the company's objectives. Clive Beddoe, the CEO of WestJet, has been very successful in motivating employees to go above and beyond normal work practices to ensure the company's (and their own) financial success. By definition, managers have the power to give orders and demand results, but leading goes beyond merely giving orders. Leaders must have the capacity to unite their employees in pursuit of specific goals, and then motivate them to work toward those goals. If managers do this, their employees will respect them, trust them, and believe that by working together, both the firm and its employees will benefit. We discuss leadership more fully in Chapter 9.

leading
That portion of a manager's job concerned with guiding and motivating employees to meet the firm's objectives.

Controlling

Controlling is the process of monitoring a firm's performance to make sure that it is meeting its goals. Managers at WestJet and Air Canada, for example, focus relentlessly on numerous indicators of performance that they can measure and adjust. Everything from on-time arrivals to baggage-handling errors to the number of empty seats on an airplane to surveys of employee and customer satisfaction are regularly and routinely monitored. If on-time arrivals start to slip, managers focus on the problem and get it fixed. No single element of the firm's performance can slip too far before it's noticed and fixed.

controlling
That portion of a manager's job concerned with monitoring the firm's performance and, if necessary, acting to bring it in line with the firm's goals.

Figure 6.1 illustrates the control process, which begins when management establishes standards (often for financial performance). If, for example, a company sets a goal of increasing its sales by 20 percent over the next five years, an appropriate standard to assess progress toward the 20-percent goal might be an increase of about 4 percent a year. Managers then measure actual performance each year against standards. If the two amounts agree, the organization continues along its present course. If they vary significantly, however, one or the other needs adjustment. If sales have increased 3.9 percent by the end of the first year, things are probably fine. But if sales have dropped 1 percent, some revision in plans is needed.

Controlling applies to many activities, including the college or university courses that you are now taking. The instructor first indicates the knowledge areas where you must show competence, and the level of competence you must show. Next, the instructor measures your performance, usually through assignments and exams. The instructor then determines whether your performance meets

Japanese organizations don't usually like radical restructuring, but when Senichi Hoshino took over the hapless Hanshin Tigers, he axed 24 of the team's 70 players and replaced them with free agents. He required everyone on the roster to compete for a position, tracked performance daily, and made individual coaches directly responsible for seeing that players executed certain skills. Soon after that, the Tigers won the pennant—a particularly important achievement, because superstition says that when the Tigers win, Japan will soon enjoy a period of prolonged prosperity.

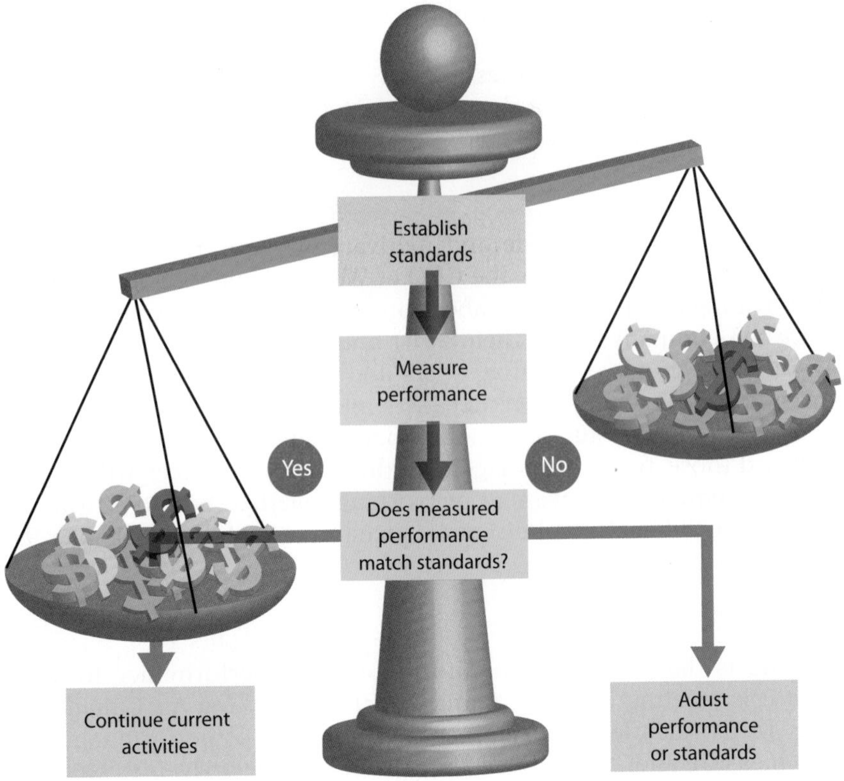

Figure 6.1 The control process.

the standard. If your performance is satisfactory (unsatisfactory), you receive feedback in the form of a passing (or failing) grade in the course.

Control can also show where performance is better than expected, and can serve as a basis for providing rewards or reducing costs. For example, when Chevrolet introduced the Super Sport Roadster (a classic, late-1940s pickup-style vehicle with a two-seat roadster design), the firm hoped it had a major hit on its hands. But poor sales led to Chevrolet's decision to suspend production of the vehicle. On the other hand, after the distributor of the surprise hit movie *The March of the Penguins* saw how popular the movie was becoming, the firm was able to increase advertising and distribution, making the niche movie into a major commercial success.

TYPES OF MANAGERS

2 Identify *types of managers* by level and area.

Although all managers plan, organize, lead, and control, not all managers have the same degree of responsibility for each activity. Moreover, managers differ in the specific application of these activities. Thus we can differentiate between managers based on their *level* of responsibility or their *area* of responsibility.

Levels of Management

The three basic levels of management are top, middle, and first-line management. As Figure 6.2 shows, in most firms there are more middle managers than top managers and more first-line managers than middle managers. Moreover, as the categories imply, the authority of managers and the complexity of their duties increase as we move up the pyramid.

Figure 6.2 Most organizations have three basic levels of management.

Top Managers

The managers who guide the fortunes of most companies are **top managers**. Common titles for top managers include president, vice-president, chief executive officer (CEO), and chief financial officer (CFO). Top managers are responsible to the board of directors and stockholders of the firm for its overall performance and effectiveness. They set general policies, formulate strategies, oversee all significant decisions, and represent the company in its dealings with other businesses and government.[2] In 2006, *Canadian Business* magazine named Denis Turcotte, CEO of Algoma Steel, as the top Canadian CEO for his work in making Algoma the most efficient steel producer in the world.[3]

top managers
Those managers responsible for a firm's overall performance and effectiveness and for developing long-range plans for the company.

middle managers
Those managers responsible for implementing the decisions made by top managers.

first-line managers
Those managers responsible for supervising the work of employees.

Middle Managers

Although below the ranks of the top executives, **middle managers** still occupy positions of considerable autonomy and importance. Titles such as plant manager, operations manager, and division manager are typical of middle-management positions. The producer of a Lion's Gate film like *Monster's Ball* is a middle manager. In general, middle managers are responsible for implementing the strategies, policies, and decisions of the top managers. For example, if top management decides to bring out a new product in 12 months or to cut costs by 5 percent, middle management will have to decide to increase the pace of new product development or to reduce the plant's workforce.

Meg Whitman, the CEO of eBay, understands the importance of human relations in a business whose model is helping sellers find buyers and buyers find sellers. At conventions where 10 000 of eBay's 28 million customers gather to communicate without the medium of cyberspace, Whitman autographs (collectible) eBay trading cards of herself and depends on ordinary users to tell her what works and what doesn't work at the online auction company.

First-Line Managers

Those who hold titles such as *supervisor*, *office manager*, and *group leader* are **first-line managers**. Although they spend most of their time working with and supervising the employees who report to them, first-line managers' activities are not limited to those activities. At a building site, for example, the project manager not only ensures that workers are carrying out construction as specified by the architect, but also interacts extensively with materials suppliers, community officials, and middle and top managers at the home office. The manager of a Canadian Tire store and the flight-services manager for a specific Air Canada flight are first-line managers.

Areas of Management

Within any large company, the top, middle, and first-line managers work in a variety of areas including human resources, operations, information, marketing, and finance.

Human Resource Managers

human resource managers
Those managers responsible for hiring, training, evaluating, and compensating employees.

Every enterprise uses human resources, and **human resource managers** can be found in most companies. They hire employees, train them, evaluate their performance, decide how they should be compensated, and, in some cases, deal with labour unions. Large firms may have several human resource departments, each dealing with specialized activities. Imperial Oil, for example, has separate departments to deal with recruiting and hiring, wage and salary levels, and labour relations. Smaller firms may have a single department, while very small organizations may have a single person responsible for all human resource activities. Chapters 8 and 9 address human resource management issues.

Operations Managers

operations managers
Those managers responsible for controlling production, inventory, and quality of a firm's products.

A firm's operations are the systems by which it creates goods and services. **Operations managers** are responsible for production control, inventory control, and quality control, among other duties. Manufacturing companies like Steelcase, Bristol Aerospace, and Sony need operations managers at many levels. Such firms typically have a vice-president for operations (top), plant managers (middle), and supervisors (first-line). In recent years, sound operations management practices have also become increasingly important to service-producing organizations like hospitals, colleges and universities, and the government. Operations management is the subject of Chapter 10.

Information Managers

information managers
Those managers responsible for the design and implementation of systems to gather, process, and disseminate information.

Dramatic increases in both the amount of information available to managers and the ability to manage it have led to the emergence of **information managers**. These managers are responsible for designing and implementing various systems to gather, process, and disseminate information. Federal Express, for example, has a chief information officer. Middle managers engaged in information management help design information systems for divisions or plants. Computer systems managers within smaller businesses or operations are first-line managers. Information management is discussed in Chapter 11.

Marketing Managers

marketing managers
Those managers responsible for developing, pricing, promoting, and distributing goods and services to buyers.

Marketing includes the development, pricing, promotion, and distribution of products and services. **Marketing managers** are responsible for getting these products and services to buyers. Marketing is especially important for firms dealing in consumer products, such as Procter & Gamble, Coca-Cola, and Sun Ice. These firms often have large numbers of marketing managers at various levels. For example, a large firm will probably have a vice-president for marketing (top manager), regional marketing managers (middle managers), and several district sales managers (first-line managers). For a detailed look at marketing, see Chapters 12–14.

Financial Managers

financial managers
Those managers responsible for planning and overseeing the financial resources of a firm.

Management of a firm's finances is extremely important to its survival. Nearly every company has **financial managers** to plan and oversee its financial resources. Levels of financial management may include a vice-president for finance (top), division controller (middle), and accounting supervisor (first-line). For large financial institutions, effective financial management is the company's reason for being. Chapters 15 and 16 treat financial management in detail.

Other Managers

Some firms have more specialized managers. Chemical companies like CIL have research and development managers, for example, whereas companies like Petro-Canada and Apple have public relations managers. The range of possibilities is almost endless, and the areas of management are limited only by the needs and imagination of the company.

BASIC MANAGEMENT SKILLS

Describe the basic *management skills.* 3

The degree of success that people enjoy in management positions is determined by the skills and abilities they possess. Effective managers must have several skills: *technical, human relations, conceptual, time management*, and *decision-making skills*.

Technical Skills

technical skills
Skills associated with performing specialized tasks within a firm.

Technical skills help people to perform specialized tasks. A secretary's ability to type, an animator's ability to draw a cartoon, and an accountant's ability to audit a company's records are all technical skills. People develop their technical skills through education and experience. The secretary, for example, probably took a keyboarding course and has had many hours of practice both on and off the job. The animator may have had training in an art school and probably learned a great deal from experienced animators on the job. The accountant earned a university degree and a professional certification.

As Figure 6.3 shows, technical skills are especially important for first-line managers. Most first-line managers spend considerable time helping employees solve work-related problems, monitoring their performance, and training them in more efficient work procedures. Such managers need a basic understanding of the jobs they supervise. As a manager moves up the corporate ladder, however, technical skills become less and less important. Top managers,

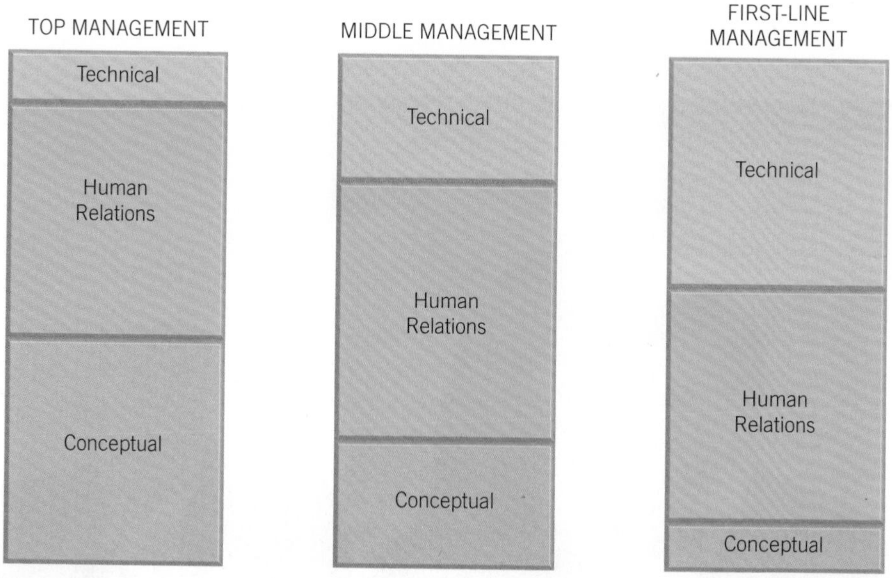

Figure 6.3 Different levels in an organization require different combinations of managerial skills.

for example, often need only a cursory familiarity with the mechanics of basic tasks performed within the company. A top manager at Disney, for example, probably can't draw Mickey Mouse or build a ride for Disney World.

Human Relations Skills

human relations skills
Skills in understanding and getting along with people.

Human relations skills help managers to lead, motivate, communicate with, and get along with their subordinates. Managers with poor human relations skills will likely have conflicts with subordinates, cause valuable employees to quit or transfer, and contribute to poor morale. Figure 6.3 shows that human relations skills are important at all levels of management. This is true because all managers in the hierarchy act as "bridges" between their bosses, their subordinates, and other managers at the same level in the hierarchy. A study by DDI Canada found that the top reason for managerial failure was poor people skills.[4]

Conceptual Skills

conceptual skills
Abilities to think in the abstract, diagnose and analyze different situations, and see beyond the present situation.

Conceptual skills refer to a person's ability to think in the abstract, to diagnose and analyze different situations, and to see beyond the present situation. Conceptual skills help managers recognize new market opportunities and threats. For example, in e-commerce businesses, conceptual skills help mangers foresee how a particular business application will be affected by, or can be translated to, the internet. The need for conceptual skills differs at various management levels. Figure 6.3 shows that top managers depend most on conceptual skills, and first-line managers least, but at least some conceptual skills are needed in almost any management job.

Time Management Skills

time management skills
Skills associated with the productive use of time.

Time management skills refer to the productive use that managers make of their time. In 2006, for example, Research in Motion CEO James Balsillie was paid a total of $54.7 million (including salary, bonuses, and options).[5] Assuming that he worked 50 hours a week and took a two-week vacation, Balsillie earned about $21 880 per hour, or about $365 per minute. Any time that Balsillie wastes represents a large cost to Research in Motion and its stockholders.

National leaders are managers, too, and those at the highest levels, like Russian President Vladimir Putin (centre), set goals for overall economic growth. When Economic Minister German Gref (left) announced an anticipated growth rate of 5.2 percent for the coming year, Putin publicly admonished his entire cabinet for setting their economic sights too low. Applauding his boss's policy (and responding to his management style), Gref quickly revised his estimate to a rosier 6.4 percent, citing the likelihood that oil prices would be higher than he had originally thought.

To manage time effectively, managers must address four leading causes of wasted time:

- *Paperwork.* Some managers spend too much time deciding what to do with letters and reports. Most documents of this sort are routine and can be handled quickly. Managers must learn to recognize those documents that require more attention.
- *The telephone.* Experts estimate that managers are interrupted by the telephone every five minutes. To manage time more effectively, they suggest having a secretary screen all calls and setting aside a certain block of time each day to return the important ones.
- *Meetings.* Many managers spend as much as four hours per day in meetings. To help keep this time productive, the person handling the meeting should specify a clear agenda, start on time, keep everyone focused on the agenda, and end on time.
- *Email.* Managers are relying more heavily on email and other forms of electronic communication. But many email messages are not important, and some are downright trivial. As the number of electronic messages grows, the potential time wasted also increases.

Decision-Making Skills

Decision making means choosing one alternative from among several options. It is a critical management skill because decision making affects all the functions of management.

decision-making skills
Skills in defining problems and selecting the best courses of action.

The Rational Decision-Making Process

Figure 6.4 shows the steps in the rational decision-making process. We explain the key elements of each step below.

Recognizing and Defining the Decision Situation. The first step in rational decision making is recognizing that a decision is necessary. There must be some stimulus or spark to initiate this process. For example, when equipment malfunctions, managers must decide whether to repair it or to replace it. The stimulus for a decision may be either a problem or an opportunity. A manager facing cost overruns on a project is faced with a problem decision, while a manager who is trying to decide how to invest surplus funds is faced with an opportunity decision. Managers also need to understand precisely what the problem or opportunity is. This understanding comes from careful analysis and thoughtful consideration of the situation. Consider the international air travel industry. Because of the growth of international travel related to business, education, and tourism, such global carriers as Singapore Airlines, KLM, JAL, British Airways, and American Airlines need to increase their capacity for international travel. Because most major international airports are already operating at or near capacity, adding a significant number of new flights to existing schedules is not feasible. As a result, the most logical alternative is to increase capacity on existing flights. Thus, Boeing and Airbus, the world's only manufacturers of large commercial aircraft, have recognized an important opportunity and have defined their decision situation as how best to respond to the need for increased global travel capacity.[6]

Identifying Alternatives. Once the need for a decision has been recognized and defined, the second step is to identify alternative courses of effective action. In general, the more important the decision, the more attention is directed to developing alternatives. If the decision involves a multimillion-dollar relocation, a great deal of time and expertise should be devoted to

Step	Detail	Example
1. Recognizing and defining the decision situation	Some stimulus indicates that a decision must be made. The stimulus may be positive or negative.	The plant manager sees that employee turnover has increased by 5 percent.
2. Identifying alternatives	Both obvious and creative alternatives are desired. In general, the more important the decision, the more alternatives should be generated.	The plant manager can increase wages, increase benefits, or change hiring standards.
3. Evaluating alternatives	Each alternative is evaluated to determine its feasibility, its satisfactoriness, and its consequences.	Increasing benefits may not be feasible. Increasing wages and changing hiring standards may satisfy all conditions.
4. Selecting the best alternative	Consider all situational factors and choose the alternative that best fits the manager's situation.	Changing hiring standards will take an extended period of time to cut turnover, so increase wages.
5. Implementing the chosen alternative	The chosen alternative is implemented into the organizational system.	The plant manager may need permission from corporate headquarters. The human resource department establishes a new wage structure.
6. Following up and evaluating the results	At some time in the future, the manager should ascertain the extent to which the alternative chosen in step 4 and implemented in step 5 has worked.	The plant manager notes that six months later, turnover dropped to its previous level.

Figure 6.4 Steps in the rational decision-making process.

identifying alternatives, but if the decision involves choosing a name for the company softball team, much less resources should be devoted to the task (although there may be a lot of arguing about what the name should be!).

Managers must accept that factors such as legal restrictions, moral and ethical norms, and available technology can limit their alternatives. For example, after assessing the question of how to increase international airline capacity, Boeing and Airbus identified three different alternatives: They could independently develop new large planes, they could collaborate in a joint venture to create a single new large plane, or they could modify their largest existing planes to increase their capacity.

Evaluating Alternatives. Once alternatives have been identified, they must be thoroughly evaluated to increase the chance that the alternative finally chosen will be successful. During its analysis of alternatives, Airbus concluded that it would be at a disadvantage if it tried to simply enlarge its existing planes, because the competitive Boeing 747 is already the largest aircraft being made and could readily be expanded. Boeing, meanwhile, was seriously concerned about the risk inherent in building a new and even larger plane, even if it shared the risk with Airbus as a joint venture.

Selecting the Best Alternative. Choosing the best available alternative is the real crux of decision making. Even though many situations do not lend themselves to objective mathematical analysis, managers and leaders can often develop subjective estimates for choosing an alternative. Decision makers should also remember that finding multiple acceptable alternatives may be possible, so selecting just one alternative and rejecting all the others might not be necessary. For example, Airbus proposed a joint venture with Boeing, but Boeing decided that its best course of action was to modify its existing 747 to increase its capacity. Airbus then decided to proceed on its own to develop and manufacture a new jumbo jet called the A380. Meanwhile, Boeing decided that in addition to modifying its 747, it would also develop a new plane (the 787).

Implementing the Chosen Alternative. After an alternative has been selected, managers must implement it. In some situations, implementation is fairly easy, but in others, it is very difficult. In the case of an acquisition, for example, managers must decide how to integrate all the activities of the new business into the firm's existing organizational framework. When Hewlett-Packard first announced its acquisition of Compaq, managers also acknowledged that it would take at least a year to integrate the two firms into a single one.

One of the key things that managers must consider during implementation is employee resistance to change. The reasons for such resistance include insecurity, inconvenience, and fear of the unknown. Managers must also recognize that even when all alternatives have been evaluated as precisely as possible and the consequences of each alternative have been weighed, unanticipated consequences are still likely.

Following Up and Evaluating the Results. The final step in the decision-making process requires managers to evaluate the effectiveness of their decision—that is, they should make sure that the chosen alternative has served its original purpose. If an implemented alternative appears not to be working, they can respond in several ways. One possibility is to adopt an alternative that had previously been discarded. Or they might recognize that the situation was not correctly defined to begin with and start the process all over again. In the Boeing/Airbus case, both companies are getting some feedback about whether or not they made a good decision. Airbus's A380 has experienced delays that are of great concern to the company. Boeing's expanded 747 should be in service sometime in 2007 and its new 787 in 2009. Because of surging fuel prices, the new 787 may prove to be the best decision of all because it is so fuel efficient.

Behavioural Aspects of Decision Making

Many managers make decisions with too little consideration for logic and rationality. Even when managers try to be logical, they sometimes fail. For example, when Starbucks opened its first coffee shops in New York, it relied on scientific marketing research, taste tests, and rational deliberation in making a decision to emphasize drip over espresso coffee. However, that decision proved wrong when it became clear that New Yorkers strongly preferred the same espresso-style coffees that were Starbucks' mainstays in the West. Hence, the firm had to reconfigure its stores hastily to meet customer preferences.

To complicate matters, non-logical and emotional factors often influence managerial decision making. These factors include *organizational politics*, *intuition*, *escalation of commitment*, and *risk propensity*.

Organizational politics. The term **organizational politics** refers to the actions that people take as they try to get what they want. These actions may or may not be beneficial to the organization, but they do influence decision making, particularly if the person taking the action is powerful and can get their way.

organizational politics The actions that people take as they try to get what they want.

Intuition. Managers sometimes decide to do something because it "feels right" or they have a "hunch." **Intuition** is usually based on years of experience and practice in making decisions in similar situations. Such an inner sense may actually help managers make an occasional decision without

intuition An innate belief about something, often without conscious consideration.

going through a rational sequence of steps. For example, the New York Yankees once contacted three major sneaker manufacturers—Nike, Reebok, and Adidas—and informed them that they were looking to make a sponsorship deal. While Nike and Reebok were carefully and rationally assessing the possibilities, managers at Adidas quickly responded to the idea and ended up hammering out a contract while the competitors were still analyzing details.[7] These occasional successes can be very dramatic, but they should not cause managers to rely too heavily on intuition.

escalation of commitment
Condition in which a decision maker becomes so committed to a course of action that she or he stays with it even when there is evidence that the decision was wrong.

Escalation of Commitment. When a manager makes a decision and then remains committed to its implementation in spite of clear evidence that it was a bad decision, **escalation of commitment** has occurred.[8] A good example of this is Expo '86, the world's fair that was held in Vancouver. When the project was first conceived, the deficit was projected at about $56 million. Over the next few years, the projected deficit kept rising until it was over $300 million. In spite of that, the project went forward. Managers can avoid overcommitment by setting specific goals ahead of time that deal with how much time and money they are willing to spend on a given project. These goals make it harder for managers to interpret unfavourable news in a positive light.

risk propensity
Extent to which a decision maker is willing to gamble when making a decision.

Risk Propensity. **Risk propensity** refers to how much a manager is willing to gamble when making decisions. Managers who are very cautious when making decisions are more likely to avoid mistakes, and they are unlikely to make decisions that lead to big losses (or big gains). Other managers are extremely aggressive in making decisions and are willing to take risks.[9] They rely heavily on intuition, reach decisions quickly, and often risk big money on their decisions. These managers are more likely than their conservative counterparts to achieve big successes with their decisions, but they are also more likely to incur greater losses.[10] The organization's culture is a prime ingredient in fostering different levels of risk propensity.

STRATEGIC MANAGEMENT: SETTING GOALS AND FORMULATING STRATEGY

4 Explain the importance of setting *goals* and formulating *strategies* as the starting points of effective management.

strategic management
The process of helping an organization maintain an effective alignment with its environment.

strategic goals
Goals derived directly from a firm's mission statement.

strategy
The broad set of organizational plans for implementing the decisions made for achieving organizational goals.

Managers today are increasingly being called upon to think and act strategically. **Strategic management** is the process of effectively aligning the organization with its external environment. The starting point in effective strategic management is setting **strategic goals**—objectives that a business wants to achieve. Every business needs goals. Remember, however, that deciding what it intends to do is only the first step for an organization. Managers must also make decisions about what actions will and will not achieve company goals. Decisions cannot be made on a problem-by-problem basis or merely to meet needs as they arise. In most companies, a broad program underlies those decisions. That program is called a **strategy**—the broad set of organizational plans for implementing the decisions made for achieving organizational goals.

Setting Business Goals

Goals are performance targets, the means by which organizations and their managers measure success or failure at every level. To properly motivate people to high achievement, goals should be specific, quantitative, challenging, and time-framed. Managers must understand the purposes of goal setting and the kinds of goals that need to be set.

The Purposes of Goal Setting

There are four main purposes in organizational goal setting:

1. *Goal setting provides direction, guidance, and motivation for all managers.* For example, each of the managers at Kanke Seafood Restaurants Ltd. is required to work through a goal-setting exercise each year. Setting and achieving goals is the most effective form of self-motivation.
2. *Goal setting helps firms allocate resources.* Areas that are expected to grow, for example, will get first priority. Thus, 3M allocates more resources to new projects with large sales potential than to projects with low growth potential.
3. *Goal setting helps to define corporate culture.* General Electric's goal, for instance, is to push each of its divisions to number one or number two in its industry. The result is a competitive (and often stressful) environment, and a culture that rewards success and has little tolerance for failure.
4. *Goal setting helps managers assess performance.* If a unit sets a goal of increasing sales by 10 percent in a given year, managers in that unit who attain or exceed the goal can be rewarded. Units failing to reach the goal will also be compensated accordingly.

Kinds of Goals

Goals differ from company to company, depending on the firm's purpose and mission. Every enterprise has a *purpose*—a reason for being. Businesses seek profit, universities work to discover and transmit new knowledge, and government agencies provide services to the public. Most enterprises also have a **mission statement**—a statement of how they will achieve their purpose. DaimlerChrysler's mission statement emphasizes "delighted customers," while Atco Ltd.'s mission is to provide products and services to the energy and resource industries, and to invest in energy-related assets in North America. Mission statements often include some statement about the company's core values and its commitment to ethical behaviour.

mission statement
An organization's statement of how it will achieve its purpose in the environment in which it conducts its business.

Two business firms can have the same purpose—for example, to sell watches at a profit—yet have very different missions. Timex sells low-cost, reliable watches in outlets ranging from department stores to corner drugstores. Rolex, on the other hand, sells high-quality, high-priced fashion watches through selected jewellery stores. Regardless of a company's purpose and mission, it must set long-term, intermediate, and short-term goals.

- **Long-term goals** relate to extended periods of time—typically five years or more into the future. American Express, for example, might set a long-term goal of doubling the number of participating merchants during the next 10 years. Similarly, Kodak might adopt a long-term goal

long-term goals
Goals set for extended periods of time, typically five years or more into the future.

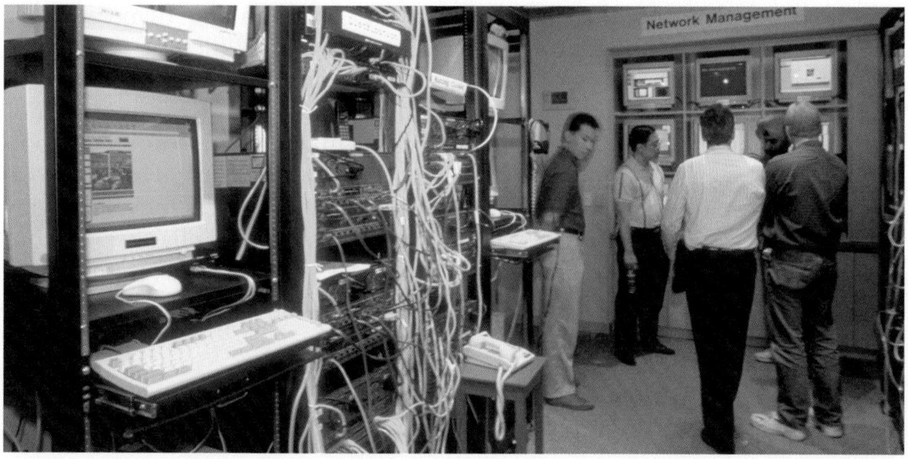

In the wake of a disastrous industry-wide slump in 2001, Cisco Systems, a giant maker of communications equipment, was forced to radically revise its strategic plans. Where engineers once pursued their own pet projects, engineering is now centralized under a group of top managers. Where individual units once chose their own suppliers, a committee now oversees all partnerships. Where the product line once consisted solely of networking apparatus, the company has branched out into a variety of new high-tech markets.

of increasing its share of the digital camera market by 10 percent during the next eight years.

intermediate goals
Goals set for a period of one to five years.

- **Intermediate goals** are set for a period of one to five years into the future. Companies usually have intermediate goals in several areas. For example, the marketing department's goal might be to increase sales by 3 percent in two years. The production department might want to decrease expenses by 6 percent in four years. Human resources might seek to cut turnover by 10 percent in two years. Finance might aim for a 3 percent increase in return on investment in three years.

short-term goals
Goals set for the very near future, typically less than one year.

- Like intermediate goals, **short-term goals**—which are set for perhaps one year—are developed for several different areas. Increasing sales by 2 percent this year, cutting costs by 1 percent next quarter, and reducing turnover by 4 percent over the next six months are all short-term goals.

Formulating Strategy

strategy formulation
Creation of a broad program for defining and meeting an organization's goals.

After a firm has set its goals, it must develop a strategy for achieving them. In contrast to planning, strategy is wider in scope, and is a broad program that describes how a business intends to meet its goals, how it will respond to new challenges, and how it will meet new needs. **Strategy formulation** involves three basic steps: (1) setting strategic goals, (2) analyzing the organization and its environment, and (3) matching the organization and its environment.

Setting Strategic Goals

Strategic goals are long-term goals derived directly from the firm's mission statement. General Electric Co., for example, is pursuing four strategic goals to ensure continued success for the company: an emphasis on quality control, an emphasis on selling services and not just products, concentrating on niche acquisitions, and global expansion.

Analyzing the Organization and Its Environment

SWOT analysis
Identification and analysis of organizational strengths and weaknesses and environmental opportunities and threats as part of strategy formulation.

organizational analysis
The process of analyzing a firm's strengths and weaknesses.

After strategic goals have been set, managers assess both their organization and its environment using a **SWOT analysis**. This involves identifying organizational **S**trengths and **W**eaknesses, and identifying environmental **O**pportunities and **T**hreats. Strengths and weaknesses are factors *internal* to the firm, and are assessed using **organizational analysis**. Strengths might include surplus cash, a dedicated workforce, an ample supply of managerial talent, technical expertise, or weak competitors. For example, Pepsi's strength in beverage distribution through its network of soft drink distributors was successfully extended to distribution of its Aquafina brand of bottled water. Weaknesses might include a cash shortage, aging factories, and a poor public image. Garden.com's total reliance on the emerging internet-based retailing model became its downfall when the dot-com bubble burst.

environmental analysis
The process of scanning the environment for threats and opportunities.

Opportunities and threats are factors *external* to the firm, and are assessed using **environmental analysis**. Opportunities include things like market demand for new products, favourable government legislation, or shortages of raw materials that the company is good at producing. For example, when Pepsi managers recognized a market opportunity for bottled water, they moved quickly to launch their Aquafina brand and to position it for rapid growth. Threats include new products developed by competitors, unfavourable government regulations, and changes in consumer tastes. For example, manufacturers of CDs and CD players now recognize the threat that online music services like iTunes pose.

Matching the Organization and Its Environment

The final step in strategy formulation is matching environmental threats and opportunities with corporate strengths and weaknesses. The matching process is the heart of strategy formulation. More than any other facet of strategy, matching companies with their environments lays the foundation for successfully planning and conducting business. Over the long term, this process may also determine whether a firm typically takes risks or behaves more conservatively. Just because two companies are in the same industry does not mean that they will use the same strategies. The Toronto-Dominion Bank, for example, has been aggressively expanding into the U.S. retail banking industry by acquiring U.S. banks, but the Royal Bank of Canada has been much less aggressive in this area.[11]

ENTREPRENEURSHIP AND NEW VENTURES

Best in Show

When Mark Warren, a Toronto investment banker, returned to Canada from London a few years ago with his four dogs, he was confronted with an underdeveloped market for pet insurance in North America. Pet insurance was sold mainly through veterinary clinics, and coverage was riddled with loopholes and exceptions. Seeing an opportunity to bring increased innovation and customer service to the market, Warren launched Pethealth in 1999.

As people pour emotional equity into their pets (seven in 10 pet owners say their pets have the same rights to health as humans, according to a 2001 Ipsos-Reid study), they're more willing to consider complex medical procedures to extend their lives. With such operations costing in the thousands, pet insurance starts to make sense. "You're effectively replacing the high cost of the unexpected and the unforeseen with a budgetable monthly premium," says Warren.

His strategy has been to avoid the commoditization of Pethealth's insurance services, working hard to out-innovate the competition on all fronts: price, service, sales channels, and technology. Pethealth has led the market by, for example, introducing bigger and faster payouts than its competitors; by partnering with trusted retailers such as U.S. giant Petco to sell its pet insurance; and by befriending the fast-growing channel of animal shelters by providing them with free shelter management software. It also offers free 30-day health insurance on pets adopted from participating pounds—reassuring buyers, eliminating costly liabilities for the shelters, and creating low-cost trial customers, 13 percent of whom renew their policies once the trial ends.

According to Warren, "In 2005, we consolidated our position as Canada's largest provider of pet health insurance and the second largest provider in North America and currently have more than 150 000 policies currently in force. 2005 also marked a watershed year in our journey towards completing our vision of becoming the leading provider of integrated health-related information services to the companion animal industry, bringing unique products and services to veterinarians, shelters, and pet owners."

The transition from a single service pet insurance provider began with the creation in 2003 of 24PetWatch (www.24petwatch.com), a microchip and lost pet recovery network. Pethealth is now the largest provider of RFID technology and related services to veterinary clinics and animal shelters in Canada as well as one of the top providers in the U.S. market. Over 610 000 cats and dogs have been registered in the 24PetWatch registry to date and more than 35 000 new registrations are received each month.

In 2005, Pethealth rolled out additional innovative new services, 24PetMedInfo and 24PetMedAlert (see www.24petwatch.com), that offer pet owners the ability to both track their pets' medical records online and also to allow emergency veterinary personnel to access the information in a lost pet emergency. During 2005, the company also launched its suite of .NET-based software solutions for veterinary clinics and animal welfare organizations throughout North America.

PetPoint™ (www.petpoint.com) is the first web-hosted management software program for animal welfare organizations in North America. In addition to providing a more efficient platform for shelters to manage their day-to-day operations, PetPoint also allows shelters to easily provide Pethealth's ShelterCare insurance and 24PetWatch microchip programs electronically at the point of adoption. To date, 314 animal welfare organizations have licensed PetPoint and more new organizations move to PetPoint each day.

EVE™ (www.eveforclinics.com) is the first web-based claims adjudication software for veterinary clinics. This program, the first of its kind in the pet insurance industry in North America, allows claims to be processed online at the veterinary clinic, thus enhancing the clinic/client relationship. To date, 193 clinics and animal hospitals use EVE.

corporate-level strategy Identifies the various businesses that a company will be in, and how these businesses will relate to each other.

business-level (competitive) strategy Identifies the ways a business will compete in its chosen line of products or services.

functional strategies Identify the basic courses of action that each department in the firm will pursue so that it contributes to the attainment of the business's overall goals.

concentration strategy Involves focusing the company on one product or product line.

market penetration Boosting sales of present products by more aggressive selling in the firm's current markets.

geographic expansion Expanding operations in new geographic areas or countries.

product development Developing improved products for current markets.

horizontal integration Acquiring control of competitors in the same or similar markets with the same or similar products.

vertical integration Owning or controlling the inputs to the firm's processes and/or the channels through which the products or services are distributed.

diversification Expanding into related or unrelated products or market segments.

investment reduction Reducing the company's investment in one or more of its lines of business.

Levels of Strategy

There are three levels of strategy in a business firm (see Figure 6.5). A **corporate-level strategy** identifies the various businesses that a company will be in, and how these businesses will relate to each other. A **business-level (competitive) strategy** identifies the ways a business will compete in its chosen line of products or services. **Functional strategies** identify the basic courses of action that each department in the firm will pursue so that it contributes to the attainment of the business's overall goals. Each of these strategies is discussed below.

Corporate-Level Strategies

There are several different corporate-level strategies that a company might pursue, including concentration, growth, integration, diversification, and investment reduction.

Concentration. A **concentration strategy** involves focusing the company on one product or product line that it knows very well. Organizations that have successfully pursued a concentration strategy include McDonald's and Canadian National Railway.

Growth. Companies have several growth strategies available to them, including **market penetration** (boosting sales of present products by more aggressive selling in the firm's current markets), **geographic expansion** (expanding operations in new geographic areas or countries), and **product development** (developing improved products for current markets). These three strategies focus on *internal* activities that will result in growth.

Integration. There are two basic integration strategies. **Horizontal integration** means acquiring control of competitors in the same or similar markets with the same or similar products. For example, Hudson's Bay Company purchased Kmart and Zellers. **Vertical integration** means owning or controlling the inputs to the firm's processes and/or the channels through which the products or services are distributed. Oil companies like Shell not only drill and produce their own oil, but also sell it through company-controlled outlets across Canada. Horizontal and vertical integration focus on *external* activities that will result in growth.

Figure 6.5 Hierarchy of strategy.

Diversification. **Diversification** helps the firm avoid the problem of having all of its eggs in one basket by spreading risk among several products or markets. *Related diversification* means adding new, but related, products or services to an existing business. For example, Maple Leaf Gardens Ltd., which already owned the Toronto Maple Leafs, also acquired the Toronto Raptors basketball team. *Conglomerate diversification* means diversifying into products or markets that are not related to the firm's present businesses. Conglomerate diversification is not nearly as popular as it was a few years ago.

Investment Reduction. **Investment reduction** means reducing the company's investment in one or more of its lines of business. One investment-reduction strategy is *retrenchment*, which means the reduction of activity or operations. For example,

Federal Industries formerly was a conglomerate with interests in trucking, railways, metals, and other product lines, but it has now retrenched and focuses on a more limited set of products and customers. *Divestment* involves selling or liquidating one or more of a firm's businesses. For example, BCE sold its Yellow Pages and White Pages for $4 billion.

Business-Level (Competitive) Strategies

Whatever corporate-level strategy a firm decides on, it must also have a competitive strategy. A *competitive strategy* is a plan to establish a profitable and sustainable competitive position.[12] Michael Porter identifies three competitive strategies. **Cost leadership** means becoming *the* low-cost leader in an industry. Wal-Mart is the best-known industry cost leader. Montreal-based Gildan Activewear is dedicated to achieving the lowest possible costs in producing its T-shirts. The company has captured 29 percent of the U.S. imprinted T-shirt market with this strategy.[13] A firm using a **differentiation strategy** tries to be unique in its industry along some dimension that is valued by buyers. For example, Caterpillar Tractor emphasizes durability, Volvo stresses safety, Apple Computer stresses user-friendly products, and Mercedes-Benz emphasizes quality. A **focus strategy** means selecting a market segment and serving the customers in that market niche better than competitors. Before it was acquired by Nexfor, Fraser Inc. focused on producing high-quality, durable, lightweight paper that is used in bibles.

cost leadership
Becoming the low-cost leader in an industry.

differentiation strategy
A firm seeks to be unique in its industry along some dimension that is valued by buyers.

focus strategy
Selecting a market segment and serving the customers in that market niche better than competitors.

Functional Strategies

Each business's choice of a competitive strategy (cost leadership, differentiation, or focus) is translated into supporting functional strategies for each of its departments to pursue. A functional strategy is the basic course of action that each department follows so that the business accomplishes its overall goals. To implement its cost-leadership strategy, for example, Wal-Mart's distribution department pursued a functional strategy of satellite-based warehousing that ultimately drove distribution costs down below those of its competitors.

CONTINGENCY PLANNING AND CRISIS MANAGEMENT

Discuss *contingency planning* and *crisis management* in today's business world. 5

Most managers recognize that even the best-laid plans sometimes simply do not work out. For instance, when Walt Disney announced plans to launch a cruise line using Disney characters and themes, managers also began aggressively developing and marketing packages linking three- and four-day cruises with visits to Disney World in Florida. The inaugural sailing was sold out more than a year in advance, and the first year was booked solid six months before the ship was launched. Three months before the first sailing, however, the shipyard constructing Disney's first ship (the *Disney Magic*) notified the company that it was behind schedule and that delivery would be several weeks late. When similar problems befall other cruise lines, they can offer to rebook passengers on alternative itineraries. But because Disney had no other ship, it had no choice but to refund the money it had collected as pre-booking deposits for its first 15 cruises. The 20 000 displaced customers were offered big discounts if they rebooked on a later cruise. Many of them, however, could not rearrange their schedules and requested full refunds. Moreover, quite a few blamed Disney's poor planning for the problem. Fortunately for Disney, the *Disney Magic* was eventually launched and has now become very popular and very profitable.[14]

Commercial airlines have contingency plans to deal with problems like major snowstorms. These contingency plans involve making sure that planes are not stranded at airports that are experiencing snow delays.

Two common methods of dealing with the unknown and unforeseen are *contingency planning* and *crisis management*.

Contingency Planning

contingency planning
Identifying aspects of a business or its environment that might entail changes in strategy.

Contingency planning takes into account the need to find solutions for specific aspects of a problem. By its very nature, a contingency plan is a hedge against changes that might occur. **Contingency planning**, then, is planning for change: It attempts to identify in advance important aspects of a business or its market that might change. It also identifies the ways in which a company will respond to changes.

Suppose, for example, that a company develops a plan to create a new business. It expects sales to increase at an annual rate of 10 percent for the first five years and develops a marketing strategy for maintaining that level. But suppose that sales have increased by only 5 percent by the end of the first year. Does the company abandon the business, invest more in advertising, or wait to see what happens in the second year? Any of these alternatives is possible. However, things will go more smoothly if managers have decided in advance what to do in the event of lower-than-expected sales. Contingency planning can help them do exactly that.

Disney learned from its mistake with its first ship, and when the second ship (the *Disney Wonder*) was launched a year later, managers did several things differently. First, they allowed for an extra two weeks between when the ship was supposed to be ready for sailing and its first scheduled cruise. They also held open a few cabins on *Disney Magic* as a backup for any especially disgruntled customers who might need to be accommodated due to unexpected delays launching *Disney Wonder*.

Crisis Management

crisis management
An organization's methods for dealing with emergencies.

A crisis is an unexpected emergency requiring an immediate organizational response, and **crisis management** refers to an organization's methods for dealing with such emergencies. The terrorist attack on the World Trade Center on September 11, 2001, was an extreme example of the need for crisis management. In the attack, all business firms lost the place where they conducted business, and some firms also lost hundreds of their employees.

When Italian food giant Parmalat Finanziaria SpA couldn't account for $11.7 billion in funds, its Canadian division, headed by CEO Marc Caira, faced a major crisis. Caira responded by auditing the Canadian operation's accounting practices to make sure his division wasn't part of the problem. After he had determined it wasn't, he then took a variety of actions to reassure customers, employees, and investors that everything was fine in the Canadian division. He did this by continuously communicating with the company's key constituents. Caira's actions worked. The year after the Parmalat scandal broke in Italy, the Canadian division recorded its highest sales and profits ever.[15]

To prepare for emergencies better, many organizations maintain crisis plans. These plans—which are designed to help employees cope when disaster strikes—typically outline who will be in charge in different kinds of circumstances, how the organization will respond, and the plans that exist for assembling and deploying crisis-management teams.

MANAGEMENT AND THE CORPORATE CULTURE

Explain the idea of *corporate culture* and why it is important.

6

Just as every individual has a unique personality, every company has a unique identity, called its **corporate culture**: the shared experiences, stories, beliefs, and norms that characterize it. For example, Magna International, a large Canadian producer of auto parts, has a culture that reflects the views of founder Frank Stronach regarding employees, working conditions, daycare centres, unions, the free enterprise system, and profit distribution.[16] Four Seasons Hotels and Resorts has a culture that assesses managers by their deeds, not their words, and where employees take their cues from managers who act as role models.[17]

corporate culture
The shared experiences, stories, beliefs, and norms that characterize a firm.

A 2005 survey of executives at 107 Canadian companies revealed that the companies with the most admired corporate cultures were WestJet Airlines, Tim Hortons, and Royal Bank of Canada. Over 80 percent of the executives surveyed said that corporate culture had an impact on financial performance.[18]

A *strong* corporate culture directs employees' efforts, helps everyone work toward the same goals, and helps newcomers learn accepted behaviours. Some cultures, for example, stress financial success, while others focus more on quality of life. If financial success is the key to a culture, newcomers quickly learn that they are expected to work long, hard hours and that the "winner" is the one who brings in the most revenue. But if quality of life is more fundamental, newcomers learn that it's more acceptable to spend less time at work, and that balancing work and non-work is encouraged. The survey noted above found that only 36 percent of executives felt that the corporate culture of their company was "strong."

Mainframe Entertainment of Vancouver has one of the lowest turnover rates in the animation business. Its culture emphasizes giving young artists and designers opportunities to acquire new skills and develop leadership potential—opportunities not available in the bigger Los Angeles studios.

Communicating the Culture and Managing Change

Managers must carefully consider the kind of culture they want for their organization, then work to nourish that culture by communicating with everyone who works there. Wal-Mart, for example, assigns veteran managers to lead employees in new territories. At Starbucks Coffee, employees are surveyed every 18 months to assess the company's culture and to determine how well it is achieving one of its key values—providing a great work environment where people treat each other with respect and dignity. Royal Bank of Canada also surveys its employees to determine how well it is progressing toward its corporate culture goals.[19]

Communicating the Culture

To use its culture to full advantage, managers must accomplish several tasks, all of which hinge on effective communication. First, managers themselves must have a clear understanding of the culture. Second, they must transmit the culture to others in the organization. Communication is thus one aim in training and orienting newcomers. A clear and meaningful statement of the organization's mission is also a valuable communication tool. Finally, managers can maintain the culture by rewarding and promoting those who understand it and work toward maintaining it.

Managing Change

Organizations must sometimes change their cultures. For example, the RCMP used to have a culture that was influenced by its military tradition. But after it completed a "visioning process," it adopted a new mission statement, a new set of core values, and a commitment to the communities in which it works.[20] Unfortunately, a 2007 report concluded that problems with the culture and management structure of the RCMP were destroying the confidence of rank-and-file members.[21] Another example is CIBC, which, until recently, has had an aggressive, deal-making culture that caused it to go head to head with large Wall Street companies in the U.S. But after several major failures in the U.S., CIBC's culture has become much more conservative. It is now alone among big Canadian banks in not having a foreign growth strategy.[22]

Organizations may experience great difficulty when trying to change their culture. Consider what happened at Nortel Networks, which hired a new president and a new chief technology officer in 2005 in an attempt to resolve some of the company's problems. Both of these individuals had worked at Cisco Systems Inc., and it was thought that they would be a great addition to Nortel. But Cisco has a hard-driving sales culture, while Nortel's culture is much less intense. Within three months, both new managers resigned from Nortel. A "culture clash" caused the new hires to leave the company, and the culture they envisioned will not be implemented at Nortel.[23]

Summary of Learning Objectives

1. Describe the four basic functions that constitute the *management process.* *Management* is the process of planning, organizing, leading, and controlling an organization's financial, physical, human, and information resources to achieve the organization's goals. *Planning* means determining what the company needs to do and how best to get it done. *Organizing* means determining how best to arrange a business's resources and the necessary jobs into an overall structure. *Leading* means guiding and motivating employees to meet the firm's objectives. *Controlling* means monitoring the firm's performance to ensure that it is meeting its goals.
2. Identify *types of managers* by level and area. Managers can be differentiated in two ways: by level and by area. By level, *top managers* set policies, formulate strategies, and approve decisions. *Middle managers* implement policies, strategies, and decisions. *First-line managers* usually work with and supervise employees. By area, managers focus on marketing, finance, operations, human resource, and information. Managers at all levels may be found in every area of a company.
3. Describe the basic *management skills.* Most managers agree that certain basic management skills are necessary for success. *Technical skills* are associated with performing specialized tasks ranging from typing to auditing. *Human relations skills* are associated with understanding and getting along with other people. *Conceptual skills* are the abilities to think in the abstract, to diagnose and analyze different situations, and to see beyond present circumstances. *Decision-making skills* allow managers to define problems and to select the best course of action. *Time management skills* refer to managers' ability to make productive use of the time available to them.

4. Explain the importance of setting *goals* and formulating *strategies* as the starting points of effective management. *Goals*—the performance targets of an organization—can be *long-term, intermediate,* and *short-term.* They provide direction for managers, they help managers decide how to allocate limited resources, they define the corporate culture, and they help managers assess performance. *Strategies*—the methods that a company uses to meet its stated goals—involve three major activities: setting strategic goals, analyzing the organization and its environment, and matching the organization and its environment. These strategies are translated into *strategic, tactical,* and *operational plans.* To deal with crises or major environmental changes, companies develop *contingency plans* and plans for *crisis management.*
5. Discuss *contingency planning* and *crisis management* in today's business world. *Contingency planning* means identifying in advance certain key aspects of a business or its market that might change and thereby affect the operation of the business. This type of planning also identifies the ways the business would respond if the changes actually occurred. *Crisis management* means developing methods and actions for dealing with an emergency that requires an immediate response. To prepare for such emergencies, organizations develop crisis plans.
6. Explain the idea of *corporate culture* and why it is important. *Corporate culture* is the shared experiences, stories, beliefs, and norms that characterize an organization. A strong, well-defined culture can help a business reach its goals and can influence management styles. Culture is determined by several factors, including top management, the organization's history, stories and legends, and behavioural norms. If carefully communicated and flexible enough to accommodate change, corporate culture can be managed for the betterment of the organization.

QUESTIONS AND EXERCISES

Questions for Analysis

1. How are the five basic management *skills* related to the four *functions* of management? Give several specific examples.
2. What is the relationship between Mintzberg's *roles* of management and the more traditional *functions* of management? Use examples to clarify your answer.
3. Select any group of which you are a member (your company, your family, your church, or a club). Explain the relevance of the management functions of planning, organizing, directing, and controlling for that group.
4. Identify managers by level and area at your college or university.
5. Can you identify any organizations where the technical skills of top managers are more important than human relations or conceptual skills? Can you identify organizations where conceptual skills are not important?
6. What differences might you expect to find in the corporate cultures of a 100-year-old manufacturing firm based in Winnipeg and a five-year-old ecommerce firm based in Ottawa?
7. Perform a basic SWOT analysis for the school you are currently attending.
8. Consider the various corporate-level strategies discussed in the text (concentration, growth, integration, diversification, investment reduction). What is the relationship between these various strategies? Are they mutually exclusive? Are they complementary? Defend your answer.

Application Exercises

9. Interview a manager at any level of a local company. Identify that manager's job according to level and area. Show how planning, organizing, directing, and controlling are part of this person's job. Inquire about the manager's education and work experience. Which management skills are most important for this manager's job?
10. Compare and contrast the corporate cultures of two companies that do business in most communities. Be sure to choose two companies in the same industry—for example, a Bay department store and a Wal-Mart discount store.

BUILDING YOUR BUSINESS SKILLS

Speaking With Power

Goal

To encourage students to appreciate effective speaking as a critical human relations skill.

Situation

A manager's ability to understand and get along with supervisors, peers, and subordinates is a critical human relations skill. At the heart of this skill, says Harvard University professor of education Sarah McGinty, is the ability to speak with power and control. McGinty defines "powerful speech" in terms of the following characteristics:

- the ability to speak at length and in complete sentences
- the ability to set a conversational agenda
- the ability to deter interruption
- the ability to argue openly and to express strong opinions about ideas, not people
- the ability to make statements that offer solutions rather than pose questions
- the ability to express humour

Taken together, says McGinty, "all this creates a sense of confidence in listeners."

Method

Step 1 Working alone, compare your own personal speaking style with McGinty's description of powerful speech by taping yourself as you speak during a meeting with classmates or during a phone conversation. (Tape both sides of the conversation only if the person to whom you are speaking gives permission.) Listen for the following problems:

- unfinished sentences
- an absence of solutions
- too many disclaimers ("I'm not sure I have enough information to say this, but... ")
- the habit of seeking support from others instead of making definitive statements of personal conviction (saying, "I recommend consolidating the medical and fitness functions," instead of, "As Emily stated in her report, I recommend consolidating the medical and fitness functions")
- language fillers (saying, "you know," "like," and "um" when you are unsure of your facts or uneasy about expressing your opinion)

Step 2 Join with three or four other classmates to evaluate each other's speaking styles. Finally,

- Have a 10-minute group discussion on the importance of human relations skills in business.
- Listen to other group members, and take notes on the "power" content of what you hear.
- Offer constructive criticism by focusing on what speakers say rather than on personal characteristics (say, "Bob, you sympathized with Paul's position, but I still don't know what you think," instead of, "Bob, you sounded like a weakling").

Follow-Up Questions

1. How do you think the power content of speech affects a manager's ability to communicate? Evaluate some of the ways in which effects may differ among supervisors, peers, and subordinates.
2. How do you evaluate yourself and group members in terms of powerful and powerless speech? List the strengths and weaknesses of the group.
3. Do you agree or disagree with McGinty that business success depends on gaining insight into your own language habits? Explain your answer.
4. In our age of computers and email, why do you think personal presentation continues to be important in management?
5. McGinty believes that power language differs from company to company and that it is linked to the corporate culture. Do you agree, or do you believe that people express themselves in similar ways no matter where they are?

EXERCISING YOUR ETHICS: TEAM EXERCISE

Clean Up Now, or Clean Up Later?

The Situation

The top management team of a medium-sized manufacturing company is on a strategic planning "retreat" where it is formulating ideas and plans for spurring new growth in the company. As one part of this activity, the team, working with the assistance of a consultant, has conducted a SWOT analysis. During this activity, an interesting and complex situation has been identified. Next year, the federal government will be issuing new—and much more stringent—pollution standards for the company's industry. The management team sees this as a potential "threat" in that the company will have to buy new equipment and change some of its manufacturing methods in order to comply with the new standards.

The Dilemma

One member of the team, James Smith, has posed an interesting option—not complying. His logic can be summarized as follows:

1. The firm has already developed its capital budgets for the next two years. Any additional capital expenditures will cause major problems with the company's cash flow and budget allocations.
2. The company has a large uncommitted capital budget entry available in three years; those funds could be used to upgrade pollution control systems at that time.
3. Because the company has a spotless environmental record so far, James Smith argues that if the company does not buy the equipment for three years, the most likely outcomes will be (a) a warning in year 1; (b) a small fine in year 2; and (c) a substantial fine in year 3. However, the total amounts of the fines in years 2 and 3 will be much lower than the cost of redoing the company budgets and complying with the new law next year.

Team Activity

Assemble a group of four students and assign each group member to one of the following roles:

- Management team member
- Lower-level employee at the company
- Company customer
- Company investor

Action Steps

1. Before discussing the situation with your group, and from the perspective of your assigned role, do you think that James Smith's suggestion regarding ignoring pollution standards is a good one? Write down the reasons for your position.
2. Before discussing the situation with your group, and from the perspective of your assigned role, what are the underlying ethical issues in this situation? Write down the issues.
3. Gather your group together and reveal, in turn, each member's comments on James Smith's suggestion. Next, reveal the ethical issues listed by each member.
4. Appoint someone to record the main points of agreement and disagreement within the group. How do you explain the results? What accounts for any disagreement?
5. From an ethical standpoint, what does your group conclude is the most appropriate action that should be taken by the company in this situation?
6. Develop a group response to the following question: "*What are the respective roles of profits, obligations to customers, and obligations to the community for the firm in this situation?*"

BUSINESS CASE 6

Remaking BCE

In the fall of 2007, shareholders of Bell Canada Inc. voted in favour of selling the company to a private equity consortium led by the Ontario Teachers' Pension Plan. The company's CEO, Michael Sabia, also announced that he planned to step down from his position. This was the latest in a series of significant developments at the giant company, most of which focus on the development of a sound corporate strategy. In 2006, Michael Sabia, the CEO of BCE, offered the view that BCE was making good progress on its strategic plan to achieve one of corporate Canada's biggest makeovers, which involved harnessing new revenue streams as old ones declined. Sabia wanted to "blow up" the old culture of the company to make it competitive in the new world where technological boundaries between television, wireless networks, and landline phones are disappearing. There were two parts to Sabia's vision: (1) use internet technology to provide seamless communication across a variety of high-tech devices such as laptops, cellphones, personal digital assistants, televisions, etc., and (2) put together an array of business, information, and entertainment applications to send to all those electronic devices.

The investment community has been skeptical that BCE can achieve its goals, given the rapid pace of change that is occurring in the industry. BCE has long relied on the stable revenue stream from traditional local and long-distance phone service it provides. But recently the profitability of that business has declined, and BCE has been losing large numbers of customers to Vidéotron Ltée, a Quebec cable firm that launched a competing phone product. BCE thinks that the growing demand for new services such as high-speed delivery of wireless data, broadband internet access, and digital television will increase its profitability. But the company's stock value has remained where it was when Sabia became CEO in 2002.

About 60 percent of BCE's revenue comes from providing traditional local and long-distance telephone service, and 40 percent comes from the new, high-growth services. The plan is to increase the proportion of revenue coming from new services. BCE has two other initiatives as part of its strategic plan. First, the company will invest over $1 billion to upgrade its high-definition network so that 85 percent of Quebec homes will have access to high-definition television by 2008. That investment is important since competitors like Canada's cable companies have entered the telephone business with internet-based calling. Second, BCE has embarked on an aggressive cost-cutting program in order to improve profit margins.

Michael Sabia has been focusing on corporate strategy since he became CEO. In 2002, he was faced with a difficult decision, namely what kind of company would BCE be? Would it be a television company, a telecommunications company, a media company, or a New Economy company? A strategic decision was necessary because under former CEO Jean Monty, BCE had been acquiring companies in many different businesses, but several of them were not performing well.

To see why Sabia had a difficult strategic decision to make, consider the makeup of BCE in 2002. It had been pursuing a strategy that was often characterized by industry observers as "commerce, content, and connectivity." The *commerce* part of the equation included BCE Emergis (electronic commerce in the health and financial services industries) and CGI Group Inc. (information technology consulting). The *content* part of the equation was represented by Bell Globemedia, which included CTV (television stations), ROBTv (business reporting), *The Globe and Mail* (a national newspaper), and Sympatico-Lycos (internet portals). The *connectivity* part of the equation included Bell Canada (telephones), Bell ExpressVu (satellite broadcasting), Teleglobe (international voice and data networks), and Bell Canada International (telecom services in emerging markets).

The economic performance of these diverse holdings varied widely. Bell Canada was the most successful and CGI Group was also doing well. But there were problems in each of the other areas. BCE Emergis, for example, has had difficulty reaching revenue projections because new customers simply hadn't materialized. In spite of that, Sabia said that BCE was very committed to making Emergis a success. The same sorts of problems existed with Teleglobe and BCI. Bell Globemedia (BGM) was also losing money, and in 2005 BCE reduced its stake in BGM by selling a 40 percent share to Woodbridge Co. Ltd., a 20 percent share to Torstar Corp., and a 20 percent share to the Ontario Teachers Pension Plan. This reduced BCE's stake in the company to 20 percent. BCE received $1.3 billion as part of the deal.

Questions for Discussion

1. Describe the various corporate-level strategies that a company can pursue. What strategy has BCE been pursuing until recently? What strategy is it pursuing now? To what extent is there a change?
2. What are the main steps in the decision-making process? How do they apply in this case?
3. Describe the skills of management. What skills are particularly important to a person like Michael Sabia? Explain.
4. What is corporate culture? How might the corporate culture have changed at BCE over the last decade? Explain your reasoning.

MYBUSINESSLAB

To improve your grade, visit the MyBusinessLab website at **www.pearsoned.ca/mybusinesslab**. This online homework and tutorial system allows you to test your understanding and generates a personalized study plan just for you. It provides you with study and practice tools directly related to this chapter's content. MyBusinessLab puts you in control of your own learning!

CHAPTER 7

Organizing the Business Enterprise

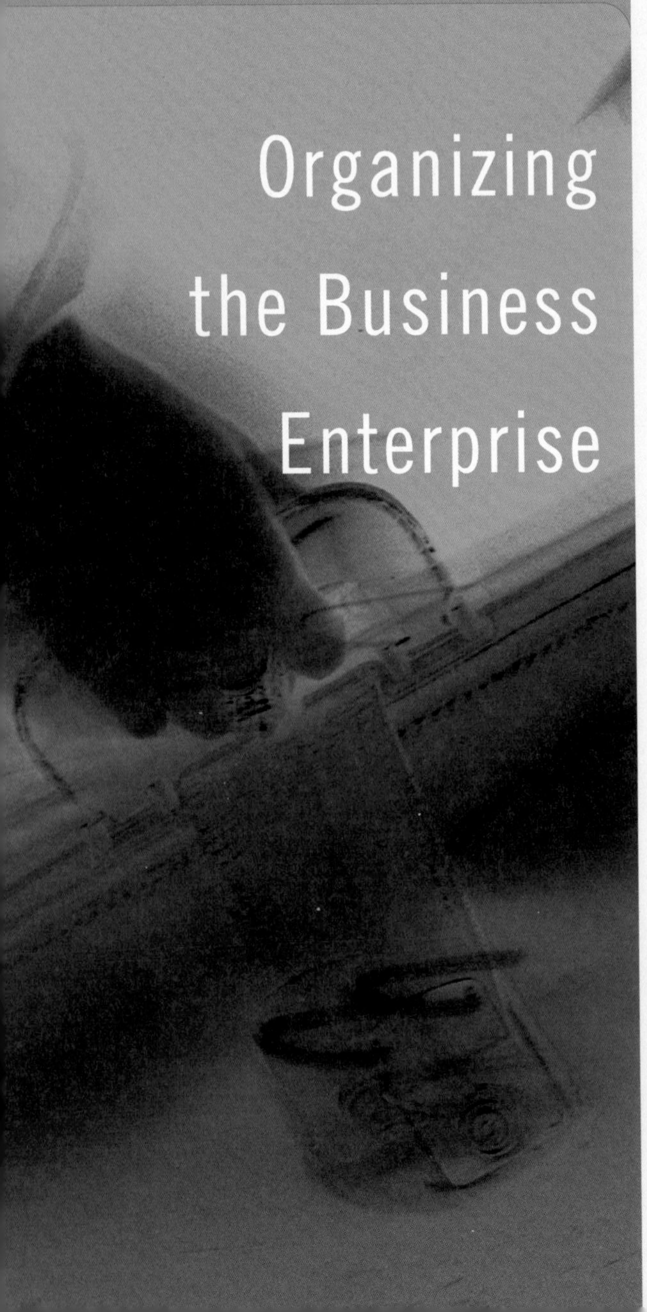

After studying this chapter, you should be able to:

1. Discuss the elements that influence a firm's *organizational structure*.
2. Explain how *specialization* and *departmentalization* are the building blocks of organizational structure.
3. Distinguish between *responsibility* and *authority* and explain the differences in decision making in *centralized* and *decentralized organizations*.
4. Explain the differences between *functional, divisional, project*, and *international organization structures*, and describe the most popular forms of organizational design.
5. Define the *informal organization.*

Frantic Films Is Getting More Organized

Frantic Films is a Winnipeg-based film and TV production company. Founded in 1997, the company has grown rapidly and now has more than 100 employees in four different locations. Shortly after its founding, it was named one of Canada's Hottest 50 Start-Ups by *Profit Magazine*. By 2004, it ranked 23rd on the list of Canada's fastest growing companies, and in 2005 it ranked 5th on the list of Manitoba's fastest growing companies. In addition to being a fast growing company, Frantic has also received numerous awards. A partial list includes the following:

- National Research Council recognition as a Canadian innovation leader
- Lions Gate Innovative Producers award
- Nominated for New Media Visionary Award
- Blizzard Award (for the documentary series "Quest for the Bay")
- Finalist in the Ernst & Young Entrepreneur of the Year award competition (multiple years)

Frantic Films is a private corporation that is owned and managed by three principal shareholders—Jamie Brown (Chief Executive Officer), Chris Bond (President), and Ken Zorniak (Chief Operating Officer). With its rapid growth, the company's organization chart has been revised several times, but its three original divisions—Visual Effects, Live Action, and TV Commercials—continue to be very important (see Figure 7.1).

The *Visual Effects* division produces visual effects for TV and movies. Using visual effects software packages such as Maya, Houdini, Digital Fusion, and 3Dstudio Max, the division has established a reputation as one of the top visual effects providers in North America. The majority of the employees at Frantic are in this division. Its output includes visual effects for films like *Superman Returns, Stay, X-Men 3, The Italian Job, Catwoman, The Core,* and *Swordfish*. The division uses a matrix structure to complete film projects. This means that a project team, made up of specialists in areas like 3D animation, 2D animation, compositing, and hardware/software support, is put together. The teams are typically given specific goals that must be achieved and team members use their technical expertise to decide how they can best achieve the goals. When the project is completed, the team disbands and its members are assigned to other projects.

The *TV Commercial* division produces television commercials for local Winnipeg companies, as well as for national and international clients. It also provides visual effects for commercials produced by other companies. The writers, producers, designers, compositors, animators, and editors have created award-winning spots for local, national, and international companies as divers as the Royal Winnipeg Ballet, the Disney Channel, and Procter & Gamble Canada.

The *Live Action* division produces and owns programs that have been broadcast around the world in over 40 countries. The division first develops the ideas for a program, and then promotes the idea to broadcasters and financiers. If there is a strong interest, a budget is provided and the division produces the program. Frantic has produced documentary programs (e.g., *Pioneer Quest*, one of the highest rated documentary series ever broadcast on a Canadian specialty channel), lifestyle series, (*'Til Debt Do Us Part*), television movies (*Zeyda and the Hitman*), and feature films (*Lucid*). Once a program is

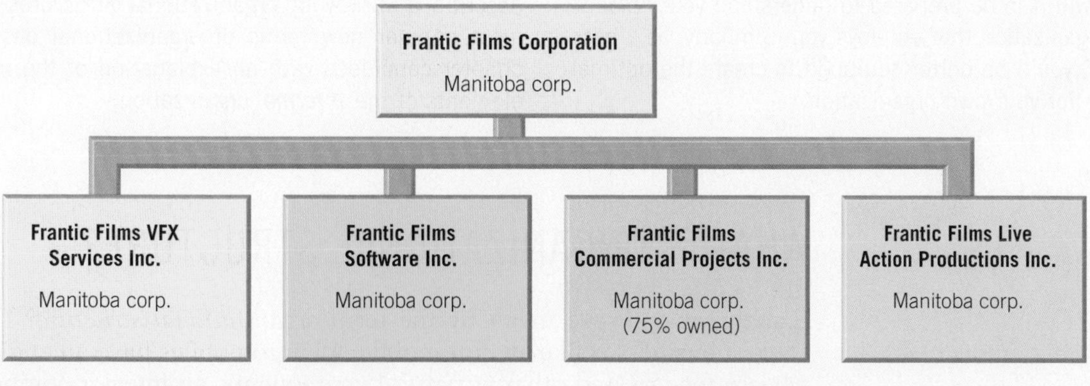

Figure 7.1 Organization chart for Frantic Films.

completed, rights are transferred to the releasing company and the individual, single purpose production companies used for each show are wound up.

Recently, a software division has been created. It comprises seven individuals with specialized expertise, some of whom are computer science grads. When software division employees discovered that off-the-shelf software did not meet their needs, they began creating their own stand-alone software to enhance certain visual effects like virtual water and smoke. This software was used to create the fluid-based character Tar Monster in the movie *Scooby-Doo II*.

Each of the divisions at Frantic Films operates fairly independently, but the company is still small enough that individuals from one division sometimes get involved in decisions in other divisions. For example, since the company does not have a marketing vice-president, marketing decisions are often made jointly by Brown, Bond, and Zorniak for each of the divisions. This means that Frantic Films does not have a "pure" functional or divisional structure.

When the company was first formed, its authority structure was quite centralized because the principal shareholders had both the expertise to make decisions and the motivation to do so. But Brown thinks it is important to increase the involvement of lower-level workers in decisions, so he is trying to delegate more authority to them. Some progress has been made in this area. For example, managers in some of the divisions were recently given the authority to spend up to $5000 without having to get the approval of top management. This change was made because the top managers found that they were spending too much time discussing whether to approve requests for relatively small amounts of money. So, they delegated more authority to division managers by giving them the discretion to spend up to $5000. Brown also encourages employees to make recommendations on various issues to top management. He recognizes that giving employees more discretion can sometimes lead to less-than-optimal decisions, but he also wants to give people more experience in making decisions that affect the company.

Like all rapidly growing companies, Frantic Films has experienced certain "growing pains" with regard to its organizational structure. For example, the California and British Columbia subsidiaries were formed in order to get more visual effects business in those local areas, but until recently, there has not been a dedicated sales force responsible for generating work there. While employees in those offices have been fully employed, they are more costly. The original idea was to have them obtain work that could be sent to the lower cost Winnipeg office, but more work is being done by a growing workforce in the satellite offices. Top management is now in the process of determining the changes that are needed to make the organization's structure more effective.

The other structural problem concerns the division of duties between Brown, Bond, and Zorniak. When the company first formed, all three principals were involved in decision making for all the divisions. But as the company has grown, each individual has gradually become more focused. For example, Brown has primary responsibility for the Live Action division, while Zorniak and Bond have primary responsibility for the Visual Effects division. There have been some discussions among the three principals about having one person be responsible for all three divisions so that work can be better coordinated, but so far they have not been able to agree on a course of action. ◆

HOW WILL THIS BENEFIT YOU?

Companies frequently introduce changes that are designed to improve their organization structures. When this happens, people have to understand their "place" in the organization. By understanding the material in this chapter, you will also be prepared to understand your "place" in the organization that employs you. Similarly, as a boss or owner, you'll be better equipped to create the optimal structure for your own organization.

This chapter examines factors that influence a firm's *formal* organizational structure. We discuss the building blocks of organizational structure—specialization, departmentalization, and decision-making hierarchy. We also describe a variety of organizational structures and the most popular new forms of organizational design. The chapter concludes with an explanation of the important elements of the *informal* organization.

WHAT IS ORGANIZATIONAL STRUCTURE?

Exactly what do we mean by the term *organizational structure*? In many ways, a business is like an automobile. All automobiles have an engine, four wheels, fenders and other structural components, an interior compartment for passengers, and various operating systems including those for fuel, braking, and climate control. Each component has a distinct purpose, but it must also work in harmony with the others. Similarly, all businesses have common structural and operating components, each of which has a specific purpose. Each component must fulfill its own purpose while simultaneously fitting in with the others. And, just like automobiles made by different companies, how these components look and fit together varies from company to company. Thus, **organizational structure** is the specification of the jobs to be done within a business and how those jobs relate to one another.

organizational structure
The specification of the jobs to be done within a business and how those jobs relate to one another.

Every institution—be it a for-profit company like Frantic Films, a not-for-profit organization like the University of Saskatchewan, or a government agency like the Canadian Wheat Board—must develop the most appropriate structure for its own unique situation. What works for Air Canada is not likely to work for the Canada Revenue Agency. Likewise, the structure of the Red Cross will likely not work for the University of Toronto.

Determinants of Organizational Structure

1 Discuss the elements that influence a firm's *organizational structure.*

How is an organization's structure determined? Does it happen by chance or is there some logic that managers use to create structure? Or does it develop by some combination of circumstance and strategy? Ideally, managers carefully assess a variety of important factors as they plan for and then create a structure that will allow their organization to function efficiently.

What are these factors? The organization's *purpose, mission,* and *strategy* are obviously important. A dynamic and rapidly growing enterprise, for example, needs a structure that contributes to flexibility and growth, while a stable organization with only modest growth will function best with a different structure. Size, technology, and changes in environmental circumstances also affect structure. A large manufacturing firm operating in a strongly competitive environment requires a different structure than a local barbershop or video store.

Whatever structure an organization adopts, it is rarely free from tinkering. Indeed, most organizations change their structures almost continually. Ford Motor Co. has, for example, initiated several major structural changes in just the last 15 years. In 1994, the firm announced a major restructuring plan called "Ford 2000," which was intended to integrate all of Ford's vast international operations into a single, unified structure by 2000. By 1998, however, midway through implementation of the plan, top Ford executives announced further modifications, and in 2001 still more changes were announced that were intended to boost the firm's flagging bottom line and stop a decline in product quality.[1, 2] Ford's major problems in 2006 have led to even more changes.

The Chain of Command

Most businesses prepare **organization charts** that illustrate the company's structure and show employees where they fit into the firm's operations. Figure 7.2 shows the organization chart for a hypothetical company. Each box represents a job within the company. The solid lines that connect the boxes define the **chain of command**, or the reporting relationships within the company. Thus, each plant manager reports directly to the vice-president for production who, in turn, reports to the president. When the chain of command is not clear, many different kinds of problems can result. An actual organization chart would, of course, be far more complex and include individuals at many more levels. Large firms cannot easily draw an organization chart with everyone on it.

organization chart
A physical depiction of the company's structure showing employee titles and their relationship to one another.

chain of command
Reporting relationships within a business; the flow of decision-making power in a firm.

THE BUILDING BLOCKS OF ORGANIZATIONAL STRUCTURE

Whether a business is large or small, the starting point in developing its organizational structure is determining who will do what and how people performing certain tasks can most appropriately be grouped together. Job specialization and departmentalization represent the basic building blocks of all businesses.

Specialization

2 Explain how *specialization* and *departmentalization* are the building blocks of organizational structure.

job specialization
The process of identifying the specific jobs that need to be done and designating the people who will perform them.

The process of identifying the specific jobs that need to be done and designating the people who will perform them leads to **job specialization**. In a sense, all organizations have only one major "job"—say, making a profit by manufacturing and selling men's and boys' shirts. But this big job must be broken into smaller components, and each component is then assigned to an individual. Consider the manufacture of men's shirts. Because several steps are required to produce a shirt, each job is broken down into its component parts—that is, into a set of tasks to be completed by a series of individuals or machines. One person, for example, cuts material for the shirt body, another cuts material for the sleeves, and a third cuts material for the collar. Components are then shipped to a sewing room, where a fourth person assembles the shirt. In the final stage, a fifth person sews on the buttons.[3]

Specialization and Growth

In a very small organization, the owner may perform every job. As the firm grows, however, so does the need to specialize jobs so that others can perform them. Consider the case of Mrs. Fields Cookies. When Debbi Fields opened her first store, she did everything herself: bought the equipment,

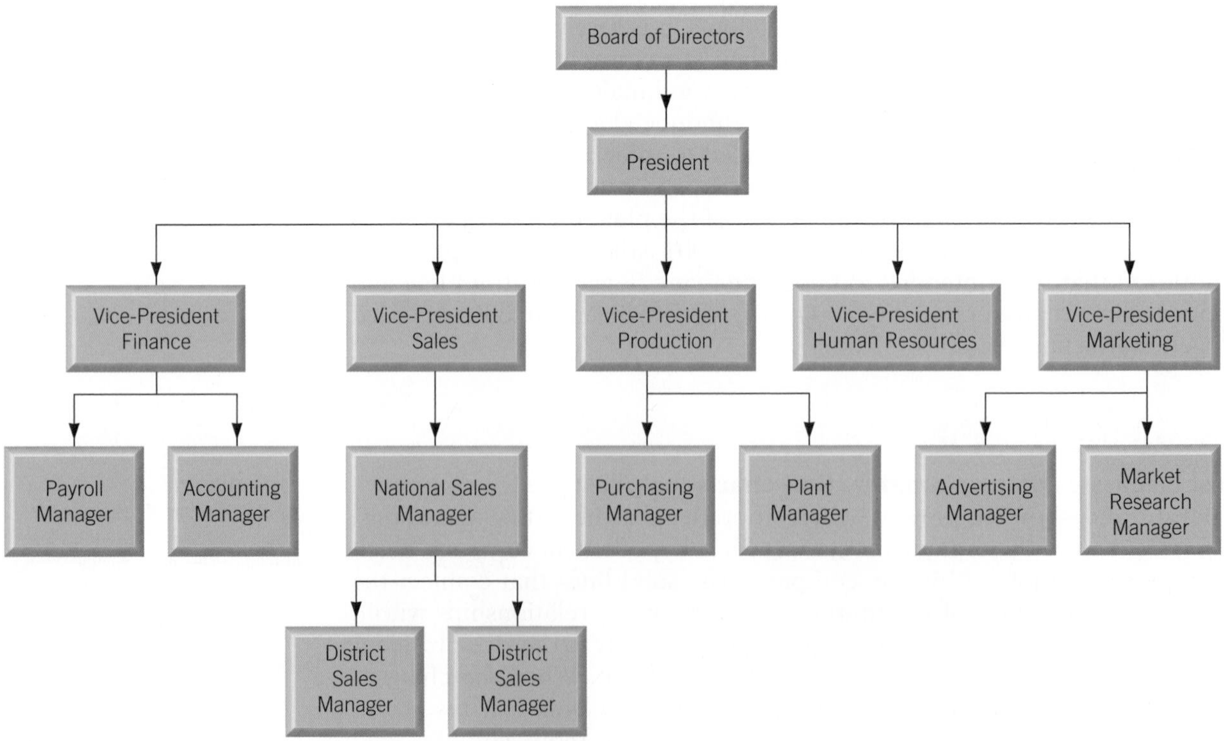

Figure 7.2 An organization chart shows key positions in the organization and interrelationships among them. An actual organization chart would, or course, be far more complex and include individuals at many more levels. Indeed, because of their size, larger firms cannot easily draw a diagram with everyone on it.

Organizational and industry-wide growth don't always result in greater job specialization. Animated feature films like *Toy Story 2* are now created by small teams of people who use point-and-click techniques to perform just abut every job required by a project. The *Toy Story* movies, as well as *Finding Nemo* and *The Incredibles*, were made by Pixar Animation Studios, which works solely with computer-created animation. According to many experts, Pixar may soon take over industry leadership from Disney.

negotiated the lease, baked the cookies, operated the store, and kept the records. As the business grew, however, she found that her job was becoming too much for one person. She first hired a bookkeeper to handle her financial records, then an in-store manager and a cookie baker. Her second store required another set of employees—another manager, another baker, and some salespeople. While Fields focused her attention on other expansion opportunities, she turned promotions over to a professional advertising director. Thus the job that she once did all by herself was increasingly broken down into components and assigned to different individuals.

Job specialization is a natural part of organizational growth. It is neither a new idea nor limited to factory work. It carries with it certain advantages—individual jobs can be performed more efficiently, the jobs are easier to learn, and it is easier to replace people who leave the organization. But if job specialization is carried too far and jobs become too narrowly defined, people get bored, derive less satisfaction from their jobs, and often lose sight of how their contributions fit into the overall organization.

Departmentalization

After jobs are specialized, they must be grouped into logical units. This process is called **departmentalization**. Departmentalized companies benefit from the division of activities because top managers can see more easily how various units are performing. Departmentalization allows the firm to treat a department as a **profit centre**—a separate unit responsible for its own costs and profits. Thus, by assessing profits from sales in a particular area—say, men's clothing—Sears can decide whether to expand or curtail promotions in that area.

departmentalization The process of grouping jobs into logical units.

profit centre A separate company unit responsible for its own costs and profits.

Managers group jobs logically, according to some common thread or purpose. In general, departmentalization may occur along *functional, customer, product, process,* or *geographic* lines (or any combination of these).

Functional Departmentalization

Many service and manufacturing companies develop departments based on a group's functions or activities—**functional departmentalization**. Such firms typically have a production department, a marketing and sales department, a personnel department, and an accounting and finance department. These departments may be further subdivided, just as a university's business school may be subdivided into departments of accounting, finance, marketing, and management.

functional departmentalization Departmentalization according to functions or activities.

Customer Departmentalization

customer departmentalization Departmentalization according to the types of customers likely to buy a given product.

Stores like HMV are divided into departments—a classical music department, an R&B department, a pop department, and so on. Each department targets a specific customer category (people who want different genres of music). **Customer departmentalization** makes shopping easier by providing identifiable store segments. Thus, a customer shopping for Shania Twain's latest CD can bypass World Music and head straight for Country. Stores can also group products in locations designated for deliveries, special sales, and other service-oriented purposes. In general, the store is more efficient and customers get better service—in part because salespeople tend to specialize and gain expertise in their departments.[4]

Product Departmentalization

product departmentalization Departmentalization according to the products being created or sold.

Product departmentalization means dividing an organization according to the specific product or service being created. A bank, for example, may handle consumer loans in one department and commercial loans in another. 3M Corp., which makes both consumer and industrial products, operates different divisions for Post-it brand tape flags, Scotch-Brite scrub sponges, and the Sarns 9000 perfusion system for open-heart surgery.

Process Departmentalization

process departmentalization Departmentalization according to the production process used to create a good or service.

Process departmentalization means dividing the company according to the production process used. Vlasic, a pickle maker, has separate departments that transform cucumbers into fresh-packed pickles, relishes, or pickles cured in brine.

Geographic Departmentalization

geographic departmentalization Departmentalization according to the area of the country or world supplied.

Some firms may be divided according to the area of the country—or even the world—they serve. This is known as **geographic departmentalization**. The Personal Services division of Montreal Trust, for example, is organized around four regions—Atlantic, Quebec, Central, and BC/Western.

The Business Accountability box describes some difficulties that companies can encounter when they try to choose between product and geographic departmentalization.

Many department stores are departmentalized by product. Concentrating different products in different areas of the store makes shopping easier for customers.

BUSINESS ACCOUNTABILITY

Product Versus Geographic Departmentalization: What's the Right Choice?

Geographic departmentalization ensures quick, responsive reaction to the needs of the company's customers in certain geographic areas. On the other hand, it may also lead to duplicate production and other facilities, and compartmentalization of knowledge in those same geographic areas. So, it's not easy to decide whether to organize geographically or around products.

Organizing geographically grew in popularity as globalization occurred and firms expanded across national borders. Years ago, when relatively limited communications made it difficult to take the pulse of consumer needs or monitor operations abroad, it made sense to let local managers in foreign countries run their regional or country businesses as more or less autonomous companies. However, two trends are making this structure less popular today. First, information technology is reducing the impediments to cross-border communication. Second, global competition is so intense that firms can't afford to miss an opportunity to quickly transfer product improvements from one region to another.

Many firms are therefore switching from geographic to product departmentalization. For example, food company Heinz abandoned geographic departmentalization and is now organized by products. Managers in the United States work with those in Europe, Asia, and other regions to apply the best ideas from one region to all the others.

The Canadian Imperial Bank of Commerce (CIBC) also reorganized in order to break down the walls between the conservative and traditional retail/commercial banking side, and the more volatile investment banking side. The company is now organized around product lines.

Exide Corp., the world's largest producer of automotive and industrial batteries, has also shifted from geographic to product departmentalization. Previously, Exide's structure consisted of about 10 "country organizations." The head of each country organization had considerable latitude to make decisions that were best for that person's country. It also meant that each country manager focused on products that were marketable in that country. Under the new product system, global business units have been formed to oversee the company's various product lines such as car and industrial batteries. But the change has not been without problems. For example, when Exide made an acquisition, some top executives got upset when their unit was made subordinate to the newly acquired unit. It wasn't long before Exide was tinkering with its organization chart again.

Either approach—products or geography—can cause problems if taken to an extreme. If a company organizes by products, it can standardize manufacturing, introduce new products around the world faster, and eliminate overlapping activities. But if too much emphasis is placed on product and not enough on geography, a company is likely to find that local decision making is slowed, pricing flexibility is reduced, and products are not tailored to meet the needs of a specific country's customers.

Ford Motor Co. experienced exactly these problems when it decided to move toward the product model. The reorganization saved the company $5 billion in its first few years of operation, but Ford's market share declined during the same period. This is what we would expect to happen when too much emphasis is placed on product departmentalization. Ford responded to this drop in market share by giving executives in various regions more authority to decide what types of vehicles were best for their local market. In other words, it moved back toward the geographic model.

Procter & Gamble also encountered problems after it replaced country organizations with global business units in an attempt to globalize P & G brands like Tide, Pampers, and Crest. The reorganization caused great upheaval within the company as thousands of employees shifted into new jobs. As many as half of all company executives took on new roles. The CEO who ordered the change left the company just 17 months into his job.

QUESTIONS FOR DISCUSSION

1. In your own words, explain the dilemma that managers face when they are trying to decide between product departmentalization and geographic departmentalization.
2. How does the notion of managerial accountability enter into the "product vs. geographic departmentalization" decision?

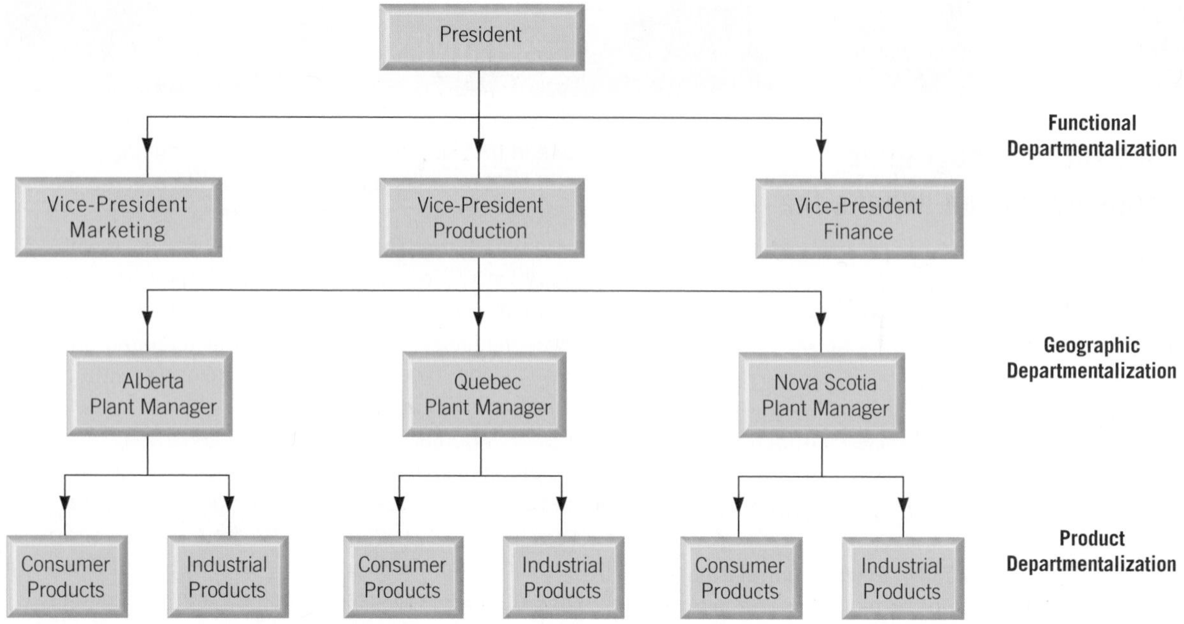

Figure 7.3 Most organizations use multiple bases of departmentalization. This organization, for example, is using functional, geographic, and product departmentalization.

Because different forms of departmentalization offer different advantages, larger companies tend to adopt different types of departmentalization at various levels of the corporation. For example, the company illustrated in Figure 7.3 uses functional departmentalization at the top level, geographic departmentalization in its production department, and product departmentalization in its marketing unit.

ESTABLISHING THE DECISION-MAKING HIERARCHY

A major question that must be asked about any organization is this: *Who makes which decisions?* This leads to a consideration of the decision-making hierarchy, which generally results from a three-step process:

1. *Assigning tasks:* determining who can make decisions and specifying how they should be made.
2. *Performing tasks:* implementing decisions that have been made.
3. *Distributing authority:* determining whether the organization is to be centralized or decentralized.

To see this process in action, consider what happened at McDonald's, where executives systematically changed the firm's decision-making hierarchy. McDonald's has always been highly centralized, but executives restructured both the company's decision-making processes and its operations. For instance, they reduced staff at the corporate headquarters in Illinois, and established five regional offices throughout the United States. Now, many decisions are made at the regional level. They also clamped a lid on U.S. growth and increased international expansion. In addition, they purchased stakes in three new restaurant chains with an eye on expansion: Donatos Pizza, Chipotle Mexican Grill, and Aroma, a British coffee chain. Four new managers have been installed, one to head up international operations and the others to oversee the three new restaurant partner groups. All four of these executives report directly to the CEO.[5]

Assigning Tasks

The question of who is supposed to do what and who is entitled to do what in an organization is complex. In any company with more than one person, individuals must work out agreements about responsibilities and authority. **Responsibility** is the duty to perform an assigned task, while **authority** is the power to make the decisions necessary to complete the task. The amount of authority and responsibility a person has must be consistent. Imagine a mid-level buyer for The Bay who encounters an unexpected opportunity to make a large purchase at an extremely good price but does not have the authority to make such a purchase without confirmation from above. The company's policies on delegation and authority are inconsistent, since the buyer is *responsible* for purchasing clothes that will be sold in the upcoming season but lacks the *authority* to make the needed purchases.

3 Distinguish between *responsibility* and *authority* and explain the differences in decision making in *centralized* and *decentralized organizations.*

responsibility The duty to perform an assigned task.

authority The power to make the decisions necessary to complete a task.

Performing Tasks

When appropriate levels of responsibility and authority are not clearly spelled out, difficulties arise between managers and subordinates around the issues of delegation and accountability. **Delegation** begins when a manager assigns a task to a subordinate. **Accountability** then falls to the subordinate, who must complete the task. If the subordinate does not perform the assigned task properly and promptly, he or she may be reprimanded, punished, or possibly even dismissed.

delegation Assignment of a task, a responsibility, or authority by a manager to a subordinate.

accountability Liability of subordinates for accomplishing tasks assigned by managers.

If managers do not delegate the authority necessary to do the job, subordinates face a major dilemma: They cannot do what the boss demands, but the boss still holds them accountable. In contrast, effective managers surround themselves with a team of strong subordinates and then delegate sufficient authority to those subordinates to get the job done. There are four things to keep in mind when delegating:

- decide on the nature of the work to be done
- match the job with the skills of subordinates
- make sure the person chosen understands the objectives he or she is supposed to achieve
- make sure subordinates have the time and training necessary to do the task

Distributing Authority

In a **centralized organization**, top management retains the right to make most decisions that need to be made. Most lower-level decisions must be approved by upper management before they can be implemented.[6] McDonald's, for example, practises centralization as a way to maintain standardization. All restaurants must follow precise steps in buying products and making and packaging burgers and other menu items. Most advertising is handled at the corporate level, and any local advertising must be approved by a regional manager. Restaurants even have to follow prescribed schedules for facilities' maintenance and upgrades like floor polishing and parking lot cleaning.[7]

centralized organization Top managers retain most decision-making rights for themselves.

In a **decentralized organization**, more decision-making authority is delegated to managers at lower levels in the hierarchy. The purpose of decentralization is to make a company more responsive to its environment. Jack Welch, former CEO of General Electric, said "If you don't let managers make their own decisions, you're never going to be anything more than a one-person business."

decentralized organization Lower- and middle-level managers are allowed to make significant decisions.

There are both advantages and disadvantages of decentralization, and they can clearly be seen in the long history of General Motors. In the 1920s, GM's legendary president, Alfred Sloan, introduced a decentralized structure that gave each car division considerable autonomy to produce cars that would attract whatever market segment the division was pursuing. This decentralized structure continued as the company expanded from the United States into Canada and other markets. It worked so well that GM became the largest automobile manufacturer in the world. Even though the company was large, in many parts of the world it operated more like a small regional company because its executives were given a great deal of autonomy over issues like car design. This helped GM offer cars that appealed to people in local markets.

But all this autonomy resulted in widely differing car designs that were very expensive to produce. As costs soared, and as competition from cost-conscious Japanese car makers became ferocious, GM's sales and overall profitability plummeted. Something had to be done. So GM *re*centralized and head office took away much of the autonomy that managers in various international divisions had. Now, GM requires its world-wide units to work

ENTREPRENEURSHIP AND NEW VENTURES

The Techie Trio

When the three young owners of Triotech Amusement Inc.—Frederic Lachance, 35, David Lachance, 27, and Ernest Yale, 34—took their video game prototype to a trade show in Atlanta in 1999, it was their "make it or break it" chance. On the last day of the show, they made a sale, and from that first success have gone on to build a business that now has sales of close to $8 million annually.

Brothers David and Frederic Lachance were operating an internet café in Joliette, Quebec, in 1998 when they started providing "cabins" where people could play games over a network. This led to the idea of creating and selling closed cabins for game playing. With the help of software developer Ernest Yale they came up with their first product, Cyberpod. The three invested everything they had in the machine, rented a truck, and drove it to the Atlanta tradeshow where it was sold to an American distributor. "That's how Triotech got started," says Frederic. "We sold about 100 units through that distributor." In 2001, with their second product ready for launching, they hired their own sales representatives. They now have some 30 employees in Quebec and sales offices in California and Texas.

The products Triotech Amusement develops and manufactures include video games, arcade machines and multi-seat 3D theatres. The business is known for its technologically advanced motion system and the sleek design of its products. Trademark products include Mad Wave Motion Theater, a two-seat coin-operated ride simulator; Wasteland Racer 2071, a driving simulator; and the XD Theater, a multi-seat motion-simulated thrill ride with 3D films. Known internationally, Triotech sells its products to amusement parks, entertainment centres and arcade operators in the United States, England, Mexico, Russia, India, Australia, and Saudi Arabia. "Nothing beats watching people playing one of our games or enjoying one of our thrill rides," says Ernest. "Seeing their reactions makes it all worthwhile."

Frederic, David, and Ernest combine their complementary skills to run Triotech. Ernest, a video game developer since he was 12, heads the R&D unit in Montréal where he and his team develop software for new products. Frederic, President of the company, designs the actual machines that house the games and theatres and is responsible for sales and marketing strategy in Lavaltrie, Quebec. David uses his technical skills in overseeing the day-to-day operations of manufacturing the units and designing the technology behind the hardware. Triotech has assembled a team of passionate people who care as much about the company as they do. "If there is anything that we're proud of it's our team," says Frederic.

As the company has grown, the three partners have faced the challenges of managing a larger organization and learning to delegate tasks. Frederic says the secret to handling growth is seeking out information, learning from others, and building a solid network of contacts. "There is no equivalent for our company in Canada," says Frederic, "and we operate in a sector that is virtually unknown in Quebec. But we've shown great growth potential; we're young and we've only touched the tip of what the possibilities are."

"Since the beginning, we have dreamed of success," says Frederic. "But it's surprising how fast the business has grown. Dreams don't always come true, but for us this one has."

much more closely together to design cars that can be sold (with modest variations) worldwide in order to reduce GM's cost per car.

The new, more centralized structure means that engineers in various regions have less authority than they used to have when they are designing cars and determining the parts that will be used in those cars. A "Global Council" in Detroit now makes key decisions about how much will be spent on new car development. And the Council can say "no" to proposed new car designs. For example, when GM engineers at its Daewoo joint venture with South Korea wanted to develop a sport utility vehicle especially suited for the South Korean market, the request was denied.[8]

Span of Control

The distribution of authority in an organization affects how many people work for any individual manager—the **span of control**. The span of control may be *wide* (many subordinates reporting to a boss) or *narrow* (few subordinates reporting to a boss). Factors influencing the span of control include employees' abilities, the supervisor's managerial skills, the nature of the tasks being performed, and the extent to which tasks are interrelated. For example, when many employees perform the same simple task or a group of interrelated assembly line tasks, a wide span of control is possible. Because all the jobs are routine, one supervisor may well control an entire assembly line having 40 or more workers. Since tasks are interrelated—if one work station stops, they all stop—having one supervisor ensures that all stations receive equal attention. In contrast, when jobs are not routine, or when they are unrelated, a narrower span of control is preferable.

span of control
The number of people managed by one manager.

Downsizing refers to the planned reduction in the scope of an organization's activity. It usually means cutting large numbers of managers and workers, and reducing the number and variety of products the company produces. Downsizing may mean that entire layers of management are eliminated. When this happens, the remaining managers often end up with larger spans of control. Because spans of control are wider, corporate structures are flatter after downsizing.

downsizing
The planned reduction in the scope of an organization's activity.

Three Forms of Authority

As individuals are delegated responsibility and authority, a complex web of interactions develops. These interactions may take one of three forms of authority: *line, staff,* or *committee and team*. In reality, like departmentalization, all three forms may be found in a given company, especially if it is a large one.

Line Authority

Line authority is authority that flows up and down the chain of command (refer back to Figure 7.2). Most companies rely heavily on **line departments**—departments directly linked to the production and sale of specific products. For example, Clark Equipment Corp. has a division that produces forklifts and small earth movers (see Figure 7.4). In this division, line departments include purchasing, materials handling, fabrication, painting, and assembly (all of which are directly linked to production) along with sales and distribution (both of which are directly linked to sales).

line authority
An organizational structure in which authority flows in a direct chain of command from the top of the company to the bottom.

line department
A department directly linked to the production and sale of a specific product.

Each line department is essential in achieving the goals the company has set. Line employees are the "doers" and producers in a company. If any line department fails to complete its task, the company cannot sell and deliver finished goods. Thus, the authority delegated to line departments is important. A bad decision by the manager in one department can hold up production for an entire plant. For example, say that the painting department manager at Clark Equipment changes a paint application on a batch of forklifts, which

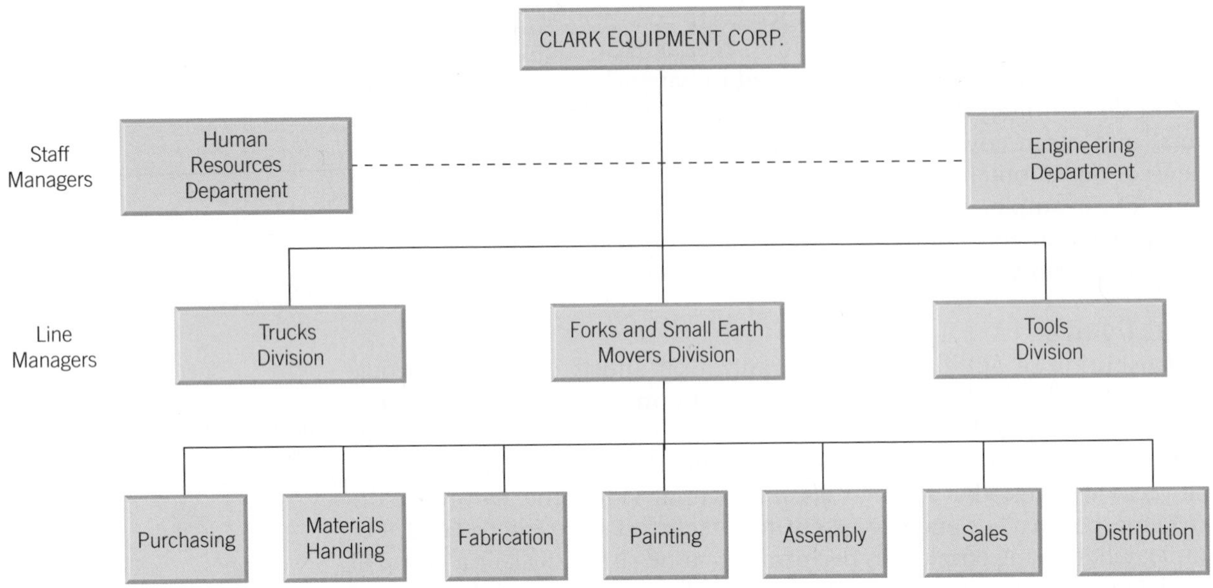

Figure 7.4 Line and staff organization: Clark Equipment Corp.

then show signs of peeling paint. The batch will have to be repainted (and perhaps partially reassembled) before the machines can be shipped.

Staff Authority

staff authority Authority that is based on expertise and that usually involves advising line managers.

Staff authority is sometimes given to employees with expertise in areas like law, accounting, and human resources. Staff members help line departments in making decisions but do not have the authority to make final decisions. Suppose, for example, that the fabrication department at Clark Equipment has an employee with a drinking problem. The manager of the department could consult a human resource staff expert for advice on handling the situation. The staff expert might suggest that the worker stay on the job but enter a counselling program. But if the line manager decides that the job is too dangerous to be handled by a person whose judgment is often impaired by alcohol, the line manager's decision will most likely prevail.

Typically, the separation between line authority and staff authority is clearly delineated. As Figure 7.4 shows, this separation is usually shown in organization charts by solid lines (line authority) and dotted lines (staff authority). It may help to understand this separation by remembering that while staff members generally provide services to management, line managers are directly involved in producing the firm's products or services.

Committee and Team Authority

committee and team authority Authority granted to committees or work teams involved in a firm's daily operations.

More and more organizations have started to use **committee and team authority**—authority granted to committees or work teams that play central roles in the firm's daily operations. A committee, for example, may consist of top managers from several major areas. If the work of the committee is especially important, and if the committee will be working together for an extended time, the organization may even grant it special authority as a decision-making body that goes beyond the individual authority possessed by each of its members.

At the operating level, many firms today are also using work teams—groups of operating employees empowered to plan and organize their own work and to perform that work with a minimum of supervision. As with permanent committees, the organization will usually find it beneficial to grant special authority to work teams so that they may function more effectively.[9]

BASIC ORGANIZATIONAL STRUCTURES

A glance at the organization charts of many organizations reveals what appears to be an infinite variety of structures. However, closer examination shows that most of them fit into one of three basic categories: functional, divisional, or project. As business has become more globalized, more and more firms are adopting an international organizational structure. These structures are described below.

4 Explain the differences between *functional, divisional, project,* and *international organization structures,* and describe the most popular forms of organizational design.

The Functional Structure

In the **functional structure**, the various units in the organization are formed based on the functions that must be carried out to reach organizational goals. The functional structure makes use of departmentalization by function. An example of a functional structure was shown in Figure 7.2. The advantages and disadvantages of the functional structure are summarized in Table 7.1.

functional structure
Various units are included in a group based on functions that need to be performed for the organization to reach its goals.

The Divisional Structure

The **divisional structure** divides the organization into several divisions, each of which operates as a semi-autonomous unit and profit centre. Divisions in organizations can be based on products, customers, or geography. Bell Canada, for example, created three divisions based on which *customers* were being served: consumers, small- and medium-sized businesses, and large corporations. This structure replaced the former divisional structure that was geographically based.[10] Whatever basis is used, divisional performance can be assessed easily each year because the division operates as a separate company.

divisional structure
Divides the organization into divisions, each of which operates as a semi-autonomous unit.

H.J. Heinz, one of the world's largest food-processing companies, makes thousands of different products and markets them around the world. The firm is organized into seven basic *product* divisions: food service (selling small packaged products such as mustard and relish to restaurants), infant foods, condiments (Heinz ketchup, steak sauce, and tomato sauce), StarKist tuna, pet foods, frozen foods, and miscellaneous products (which includes new lines being test-marketed and soups, beans, and pasta products). Because of its divisional structure, Heinz can evaluate the performance of each division independently.[11]

Divisionalized companies are free to buy, sell, create, and disband divisions without disrupting the rest of their operations. Divisions can maintain healthy competition among themselves by sponsoring separate advertising campaigns, fostering different corporate identities, and so forth. They can also share certain corporate-level resources (such as market research data). Of course, if too much control is delegated to divisional managers, corporate managers may lose touch with daily operations. Competition between divisions has also been known to become disruptive, and efforts of one division may be duplicated by those of another.

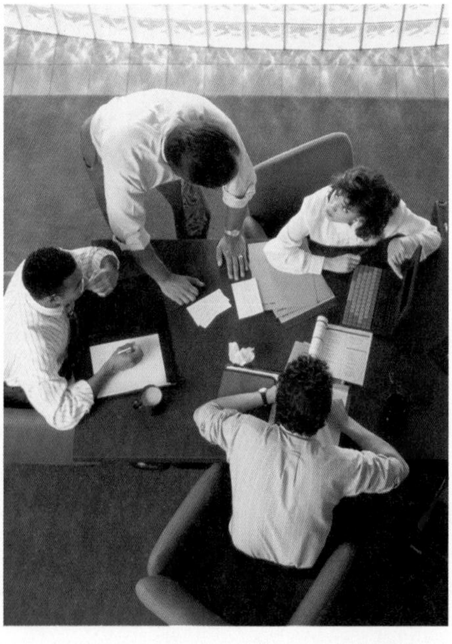

Business firms are increasingly using work teams and allowing groups of employees to plan and organize their own work with a minimum of supervision. This contributes to employee empowerment.

Table 7.1 Advantages and Disadvantages of a Functional Structure

Advantages	Disadvantages
1. It focusses attention on the key activities that must be performed.	1. Conflicts may arise among the functional areas.
2. Expertise develops within each function.	2. No single function is responsible for overall organizational performance.
3. Employees have clearly defined career paths.	3. Employees in each functional area have a narrow view of the organization.
4. The structure is simple and easy to understand.	4. Decision making is slowed because functional areas must get approval from top management for a variety of decisions.
5. It eliminates duplication of activities.	5. Coordinating highly specialized functions may be difficult.

The advantages and disadvantages of the divisional structure are summarized in Table 7.2.

Project Organization

A typical organization is characterized by unchanging vertical authority relationships. It has such a setup because the organization produces a product or service in a repetitive and predictable way. Procter & Gamble, for example, produces millions of tubes of Crest toothpaste each year using standardized production methods. The company has done this for years and intends to do so indefinitely. But some organizations find themselves faced with new product opportunities, or with projects that have a definite starting and end point. These organizations often use a project structure to deal with the uncertainty encountered in new situations. **Project organization** involves forming a team of specialists from different functional areas of the organization to work on a specific project.[12] A project structure may be temporary or permanent; if it is temporary, the project team disbands once the project is completed and team members return to their regular functional area or are assigned to a new project.

project organization
An organization that uses teams of specialists to complete specific projects.

Project organization is used extensively by Canadian firms, for example, in the construction of hydroelectric generating stations like those developed by Hydro-Québec on the La Grande River, and by Manitoba Hydro on the Nelson River. Once the generating station is complete, it becomes part of the traditional structure of the utility. Project organization is also used at Genstar Shipyards Ltd. in Vancouver. Each ship that is built is treated as a project and supervised by a project manager; the project manager for a given ship is responsible for ensuring that the ship is completed on time and within budget.[13] Project organization has also proven useful for co-ordinating the many elements needed to extract oil from the tar sands.

matrix organization
A project structure in which the project manager and the regular line managers share authority until the project is concluded.

A **matrix organization** is a variation of project structure in which the project manager and the regular line managers share authority. When a

Table 7.2 Advantages and Disadvantages of a Divisional Structure

Advantages	Disadvantages
1. It accommodates change and expansion.	1. Activities may be duplicated across divisions.
2. It increases accountability.	2. A lack of communication among divisions may occur.
3. It develops expertise in the various divisions.	3. Adding diverse divisions may blur the focus of the organization.
4. It encourages training for top management.	4. Company politics may affect the allocation of resources.

project is concluded, the matrix is disbanded. Ford, for example, uses a matrix organization to design new car models. A design team composed of people from engineering, marketing, operations, and finance is created to design the new car. After the team's work is completed, team members move back to their permanent functional jobs.

In some companies, the matrix organization is a semi-permanent fixture. Figure 7.5 shows how Martha Stewart Living Omnimedia Inc. has created a permanent matrix organization for its burgeoning lifestyle business. The company is organized broadly into media and merchandising groups, each of which has specific product and product groups. Layered on top of this structure are teams of lifestyle experts organized into groups such as cooking, crafts, weddings, and so forth. Although each group targets specific customer needs, they all work across all product groups. A wedding expert, for example, might contribute to an article on wedding planning for a Martha Stewart magazine, contribute a story idea for a Martha Stewart cable television program, and supply content for a Martha Stewart website. This same individual might also help select fabrics suitable for wedding gowns that are to be retailed.[14]

International Organization

Several **international organizational structures** have emerged as competition on a global scale becomes more intense and companies experiment with the ways in which they might respond. For example, when Wal-Mart opened its first store outside the United States in 1992, it set up a special projects team to handle the logistics. As more stores were opened abroad in the mid-1990s, the firm created a small international department to handle overseas expansion. By 1999, however, international sales and expansion

international organizational structure
An organizational structure that is designed to help a company succeed in international markets. International departments, international divisions, or an integrated global organization are all variations of the international organizational structure.

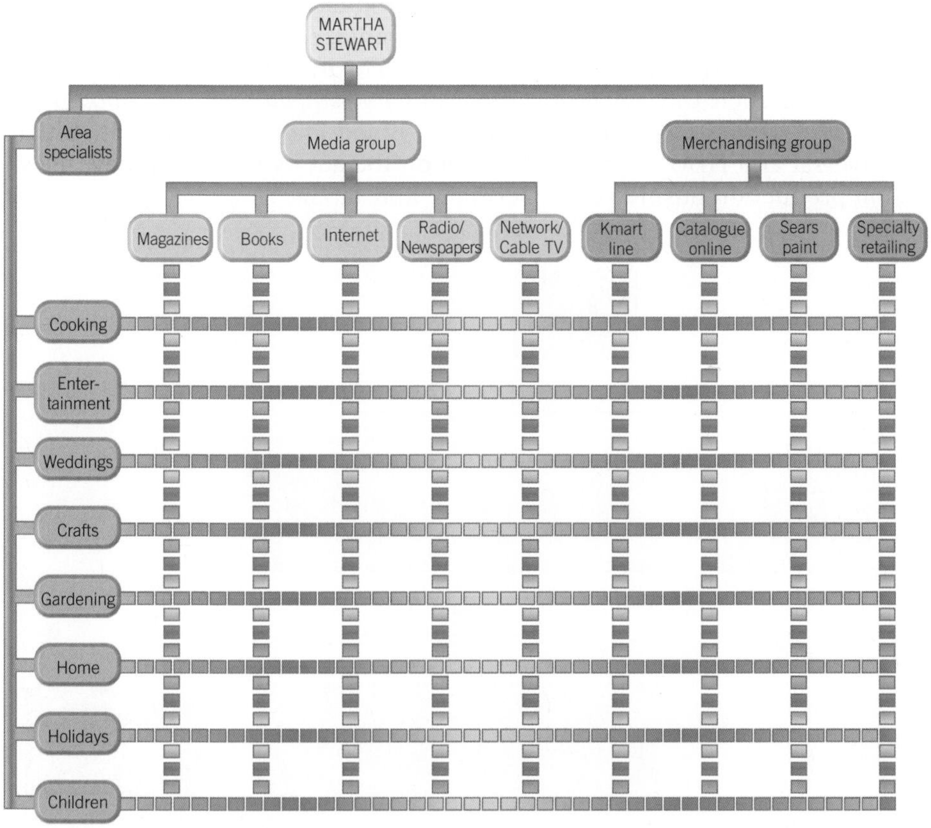

Figure 7.5 Matrix organization of Martha Stewart.

All the signs at this 8000-square-metre store in Numazu identify it as a Seiyu outlet run by Japan's fifth-largest supermarket chain. However, Wal-Mart owns 38 percent of Seiyu, and this giant store is part of Wal-Mart's effort to enter the world's second-largest retail market.

had become such a major part of Wal-Mart's operations that the firm created a separate international division headed up by a senior vice-president. By 2002, international operations had become so important to Wal-Mart that the international division was further divided into geographic areas where the firm does business, such as Mexico and Europe. Wal-Mart's structure is of the general type shown in Figure 7.6.

Other companies have adopted other international structures. The French food giant Danone Group, for instance, has three major product groups: dairy products (Danone yogurt), bottled water (Evian), and cookies (Pim's). Danone's structure does not differentiate internationally, but rather integrates global operations within each product group.[15] In contrast, U.S. entertainment companies are finding it advantageous to create a more local identity when they enter foreign markets. For instance, Columbia TriStar, known for such U.S. television programs as *Seinfeld* and *Mad About You*, launched *Chinese Restaurant*, a sitcom filmed and shown only in China. Universal and HBO are also getting in on the act by setting up new television production businesses in Germany and Japan.[16]

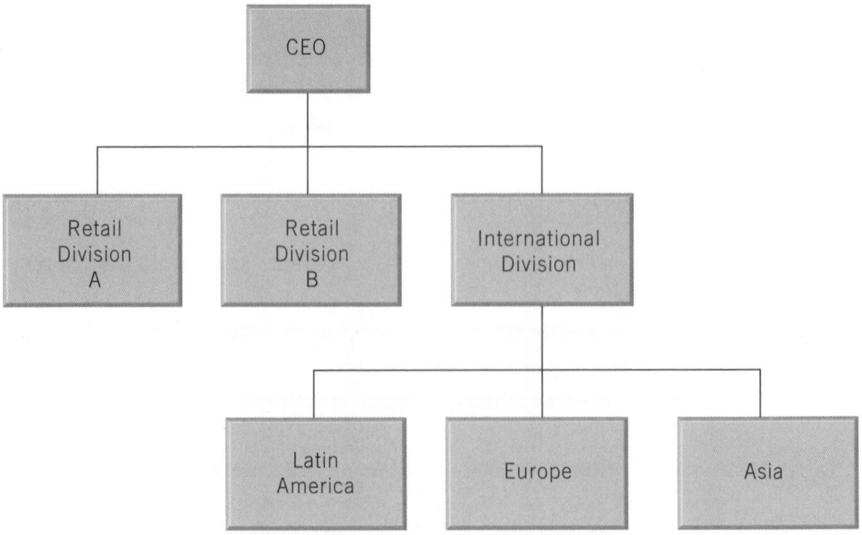

Figure 7.6 International division structure.

Some companies adopt a truly global structure in which they acquire resources (including capital), produce goods and services, engage in research and development, and sell products in whatever local market is appropriate, without any consideration of national boundaries. Until a few years ago, for example, General Electric kept its international business operations as separate divisions. Now, however, the company functions as one integrated global organization. GE businesses around the world connect and interact with each other constantly, and managers freely move back and forth among them.[17]

ORGANIZATIONAL DESIGN FOR THE TWENTY-FIRST CENTURY

As the world grows increasingly complex and fast paced, organizations continue to seek new forms of organization that permit them to compete effectively. Among the most popular of these new forms are the *boundaryless organization*, the *team organization*, the *virtual organization*, and the *learning organization*.

Boundaryless Organization

The *boundaryless organization* is one in which traditional boundaries and structures are minimized or eliminated altogether. For example, General Electric's fluid organizational structure, in which people, ideas, and information flow freely between businesses and business groups, approximates this concept. Similarly, as firms partner with their suppliers in more efficient ways, external boundaries disappear. Some of Wal-Mart's key suppliers are tied directly into the retailer's information system. As a result, when Wal-Mart distribution centres start running low on, say, Wrangler blue jeans, the manufacturer receives the information as soon as the retailer does. Wrangler proceeds to manufacture new inventory and restock the distribution centre without Wal-Mart having to place a new order.

Team Organization

Team organization relies almost exclusively on project-type teams, with little or no underlying functional hierarchy. People "float" from project to project as dictated by their skills and the demands of those projects. At Cypress Semiconductor, units or groups that become large are simply split into smaller units. Not surprisingly, the organization is composed entirely of small units. This strategy allows each unit to change direction, explore new ideas, and try new methods without having to deal with a rigid bureaucratic superstructure. Although few large organizations have actually reached this level of adaptability, Apple Computer and Xerox are among those moving toward it.

Virtual Organization

Closely related to the team organization is the virtual organization. A *virtual organization* has little or no formal structure. Typically, it has only a handful of permanent employees, a very small staff, and a modest administrative facility. As the needs of the organization change, its managers bring in temporary workers, lease facilities, and outsource basic support services to meet the demands of each unique situation. As the situation changes, the temporary workforce changes in parallel, with some people leaving the organization and others entering it. Facilities and subcontracted services also change. In other words, the virtual organization exists only in response to its own needs.

Global Research Consortium (GRC) is a virtual organization. GRC offers research and consulting services to firms doing business in Asia. As clients request various services, GRC's staff of three permanent employees subcontracts the work to an appropriate set of several dozen independent consultants and/or researchers with whom it has relationships. At any given time, therefore, GRC may have several projects underway and 20 or 30 people working in various capacities. As the projects change, so does the composition of the organization. Figure 7.7 illustrates a hypothetical virtual organization.

Learning Organization

A *learning organization* facilitates the lifelong learning and personal development of all of its employees while continually transforming itself to respond to changing demands and needs. While managers might approach the concept of a learning organization from a variety of perspectives, the most frequent goals are improved quality, continuous improvement, and performance measurement. The idea is that the most consistent and logical strategy for achieving continuous improvement is to upgrade employee talent, skill, and knowledge constantly. For example, if each employee in an organization learns one new thing each day and can translate that knowledge into work-related practice, continuous improvement will logically follow. Organizations that embrace this approach believe that only through constant employee learning can continuous improvement really occur.

In recent years, many different organizations have implemented this approach on various levels. Shell Oil Co., for example, purchased an execu-

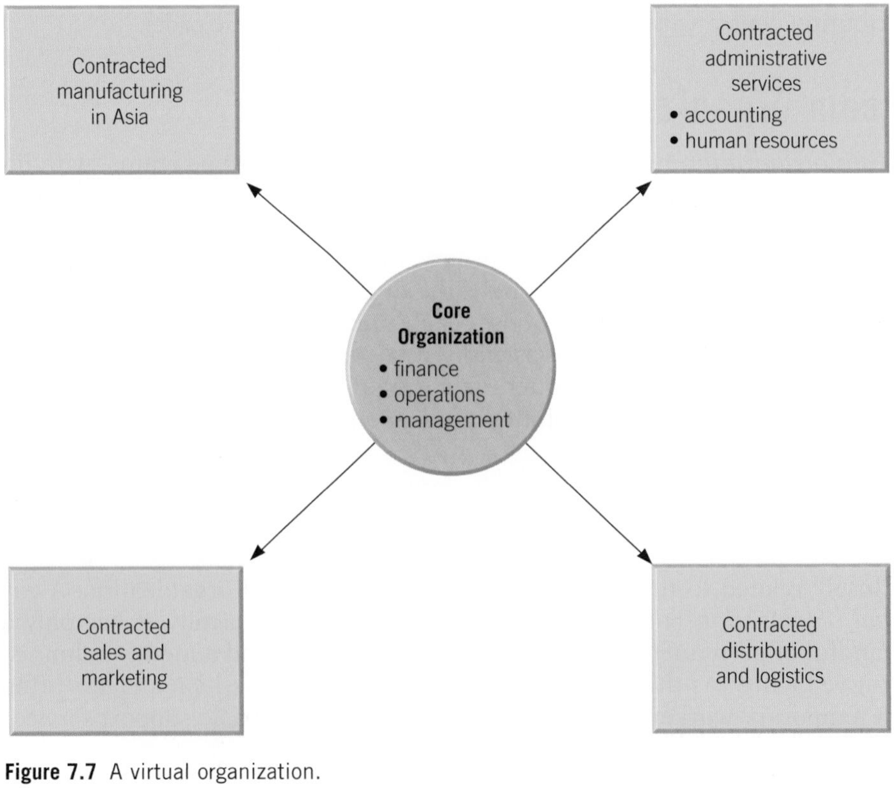

Figure 7.7 A virtual organization.

tive conference centre called the Shell Learning Center. The facility boasts state-of-the-art classrooms and instructional technology, lodging facilities, a restaurant, and recreational amenities such as a golf course, a swimming pool, and tennis courts. Line managers at the firm rotate through the centre and serve as teaching faculty. All Shell employees routinely attend training programs, seminars, and related activities, gathering the latest information they need to contribute more effectively to the firm.

THE INFORMAL ORGANIZATION

Describe the *informal organization.* 5

Our discussion so far has focused on an organization's *formal* structure—its "official" arrangement of jobs and job relationships. In reality, however, all organizations also have another dimension—an *informal* organization within which people do their jobs in different ways and interact with each other in ways that do not follow formal lines of communication. The Exercising Your Ethics box at the end of the chapter presents an interesting situation that illustrates the informal organization.

Formal Versus Informal Organizational Systems

The formal organization of a business is the part that can be seen and represented in chart form. The structure of a company, however, is not limited to the organization chart and the formal assignment of authority. Frequently, the **informal organization**—the everyday social interactions among employees that transcend formal jobs and job interrelationships—effectively alters a company's formal structure. Indeed, this level of organization is sometimes just as powerful, if not more powerful, than the formal structure.

informal organization
A network of personal interactions and relationships among employees unrelated to the firm's formal authority structure.

The informal organization can have a very positive effect on an organization by facilitating work behaviour that helps the company achieve its goals. It can, however, also have a negative side. It can, for example, reinforce office politics that put the interests of individuals ahead of those of the firm. Likewise, it can cause harm by distorting and communicating information without management input or review. For example, if the informal organization is highlighting false information about impending layoffs, valuable employees may act quickly (and unnecessarily) to seek other employment. Among the more important elements of the informal organization are *informal groups* and the *organizational grapevine*.

Informal Groups

Informal groups are simply groups of people who decide to interact among themselves. They may be people who work together in a formal sense or who simply get together for lunch, during breaks, or after work. They may talk about business, the boss, or non-work related topics such as families, movies, or sports. For example, at the New York Metropolitan Opera, musicians and singers play poker during the intermissions. Most pots are in the $30 to $40 range. Luciano Pavarotti, the famed tenor, once played (he lost big).[18]

The Organizational Grapevine

The **grapevine** is the informal communication network that runs through the entire organization.[19] Grapevines—which are found in all organizations—do not always follow the same patterns as formal channels of authority and communication. The internet is a worldwide grapevine. Formerly, when people gathered around the water cooler or on the golf course to exchange gossip and pass on information, they had names and faces. But with the internet, you may not know who you are talking to, or how reliable the person is who is providing the information.[20]

grapevine
An informal communications network that carries gossip and other information throughout an organization.

The grapevine is a powerful communications network in most organizations. These workers may be talking about any number of things—an upcoming deadline on an important project, tonight's football game, the stock market, rumours about an impending takeover, gossip about forthcoming promotions, or the weather.

Because the grapevine typically passes information orally, messages often become distorted in the process. Attempts to eliminate the grapevine are fruitless, but managers do have at least some control over it. By maintaining open channels of communication and responding vigorously to inaccurate information, they can minimize the damage the grapevine can do. In fact, the grapevine can actually be an asset. By getting to know the key people in the grapevine, the manager can partially control the information received and use the grapevine to determine employee reactions to new ideas (e.g., a change in human resource policies or benefit packages).

Wise managers will tune in to the grapevine's message because it is often a corporate early warning system. Ignoring this valuable source of information can cause managers to be the last to know that they are about to get a new boss, or that they have a potentially fatal image problem. The grapevine is not infallible, however. In addition to miscommunication and attempts by some people to manipulate it for their own ends, it may carry rumours with absolutely no basis in fact. Such rumours are most common when there is a complete lack of information. Apparently, human nature abhors a vacuum and wants to fill it with something, even if they are just rumours. Baseless rumours can be very hard to kill, however.

Summary of Learning Objectives

1. Discuss the elements that influence a firm's *organizational structure.* Every business needs structure to operate. *Organizational structure* varies according to a firm's mission, purpose, and strategy. Size, technology, and changes in environmental circumstances also influence structure. In general, while all organizations have the same basic elements, each develops the structure that contributes to the most efficient operations.
2. Explain how *specialization* and *departmentalization* are the building blocks of organizational structure. The building blocks of organizational structure are *job specialization* and *departmentalization.* As a firm grows, it usually has a greater need for people to perform specialized tasks (specialization). It also has a greater need to group types of work into logical units (departmentalization). Common forms of departmentalization are *customer, product, process, geographic,* and *functional.* Large businesses often use more than one form of departmentalization.
3. Distinguish between *responsibility* and *authority* and explain the differences in decision making in *centralized* and *decentralized organizations. Responsibility* is the duty to perform a task; *authority* is the power to make the decisions necessary to complete tasks. *Delegation* begins when a manager assigns a task to a subordinate; *account-*

ability means that the subordinate must complete the task. *Span of control* refers to the number of people who work for any individual manager. The more people supervised by a manager, the wider his or her span of control. Wide spans are usually desirable when employees perform simple or unrelated tasks. When jobs are diversified or prone to change, a narrower span is generally preferable.

In a *centralized organization*, only a few individuals in top management have real decision-making authority. In a *decentralized organization*, much authority is delegated to lower-level management. Where both *line* and *line-and-staff systems* are involved, *line departments* generally have authority to make decisions while *staff departments* have a responsibility to advise. A relatively new concept, *committee and team authority*, empowers committees or work teams involved in a firm's daily operations.

4. Explain the differences between *functional, divisional, project,* and *international organization structures,* and describe the most popular forms of organizational design. In a *functional organization*, authority is usually distributed among such basic functions as marketing and finance. In a *divisional organization*, the various divisions of a larger company, which may be related or unrelated, operate in a relatively autonomous fashion. In *project organization*, in which individuals report to more than one manager, a company creates teams to address specific problems or to conduct specific projects. A company that has divisions in many countries may require an additional level of *international organization* to coordinate those operations. Four of the most popular new forms of organizational design are (a) boundaryless organizations (traditional boundaries and structures are minimized or eliminated), (b) team organizations (rely on project-type teams, with little or no functional hierarchy), (c) virtual organizations (have little formal structure and only a handful of permanent employees, a small staff, and a modest administrative facility), and (d) learning organizations (work to facilitate employees' lifelong learning and personal development while transforming the organization to meet changing demands and needs).

5. Define the *informal organization.* The informal organization consists of the everyday social interactions among employees that transcend formal jobs and job interrelationships. It may have a positive or negative effect on the organization. The informal organization exists in every formal organization, and attempts by managers to suppress it will not be effective.

QUESTIONS AND EXERCISES

Questions for Analysis

1. Explain the significance of size as it relates to organizational structure. Describe the changes that are likely to occur as an organization grows.

2. Why do some managers have difficulties in delegating authority? Why does this problem tend to plague smaller businesses?

3. Draw up an organization chart for your college or university.

4. Describe a hypothetical organizational structure for a small printing firm. Describe changes that might be necessary as the business grows.

5. Compare and contrast the matrix and divisional approaches to organizational structure. How would you feel personally about working in a matrix organization in which you were assigned simultaneously to multiple units or groups?

6. If a company has a formal organization structure, why is the informal organization so important?

7. Consider the organization where you currently work (or one where you previously worked). Which of the three basic structural types was it most consistent with (functional, divisional, project)? What was the basis of departmentalization in the company? Why was that particular basis of departmentalization used?

8. What kinds of problems might develop in a matrix organization? Why would these problems develop?

Application Exercises

9. Interview the manager of a local service business—a fast-food restaurant. What types of tasks does this manager typically delegate? Is the appropriate authority also delegated in each case?

10. We introduced the idea of entrepreneurship in Chapter 4. *Intrapreneurship*—which means creating and maintaining innovation and flexibility in a formal organizational structure—is also important. Using books, magazines, or personal interviews, identify a person who has succeeded as an intrapreneur. In what ways did the structure of the intrapreneur's company help this individual succeed? In what ways did the structure pose problems?

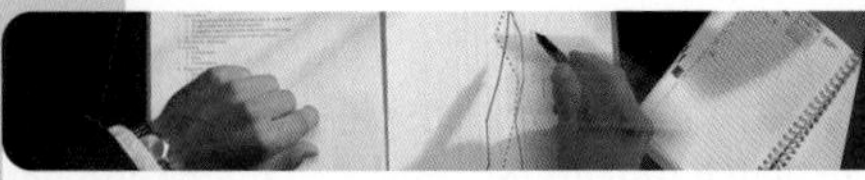

BUILDING YOUR BUSINESS SKILLS

Getting With the Program

Goal

To encourage students to understand the relationship between organizational structure and a company's ability to attract and keep valued employees.

Situation

You are the founder of a small but growing high-technology company that develops new computer software. With your current workload and new contracts in the pipeline, your business is thriving except for one problem: You cannot find computer programmers for product development. Worse yet, current staff members are being lured away by other high-tech firms. After suffering a particularly discouraging personnel raid in which competitors captured three of your most valued employees, you schedule a meeting with your director of human resources to plan organizational changes designed to encourage worker loyalty. You already pay top dollar, but the continuing exodus tells you that programmers are looking for something more.

Method

Working with three or four classmates, identify some ways in which specific organizational changes might improve the working environment and encourage employee loyalty. As you analyze the following factors, ask yourself the obvious question: If I were a programmer, what organizational changes would encourage me to stay?

- *Level of job specialization.* With many programmers describing their jobs as tedious because of the focus on detail in a narrow work area, what changes, if any, would you make in job specialization? Right now, for instance, few of your programmers have any say in product design.
- *Decision-making hierarchy.* What decision-making authority would encourage people to stay? Is expanding employee authority likely to work better in a centralized or decentralized organization?
- *Team authority.* Can team empowerment make a difference? Taking the point of view of the worker, describe the ideal team.
- *Intrapreneuring.* What can your company do to encourage and reward innovation?

Follow-Up Questions

1. With the average computer programmer earning nearly $70 000, and with all competitive firms paying top dollar, why might organizational issues be critical in determining employee loyalty?
2. If you were a programmer, what organizational factors would make a difference to you? Why?
3. As the company founder, how willing would you be to make major organizational changes in light of the shortage of qualified programmers?

EXERCISING YOUR ETHICS: TEAM EXERCISE

To Poach or not to Poach...

The Situation

The Hails Corporation, a manufacturing plant, has recently moved toward an all-team-based organization structure. That is, all workers are divided into teams. Each team has the autonomy to divide up the work assigned to it among its individual members. In addition, each team handles its own scheduling for members to take vacations and other time off. The teams also handle the interviews and hiring of new team members when the need arises. Team A has just lost one of its members who moved to another city to be closer to his ailing parents.

The Dilemma

Since moving to the team structure, every time a team has needed new members, it has advertised in the local newspaper and hired someone from outside the company. However, Team A is considering a different approach to fill its opening. Specifically, a key member of another team (Team B) has made it known that she would like to join Team A. She likes the team members, sees the team's work as being enjoyable, and is somewhat bored with her team's current assignment.

The concern is that if Team A chooses this individual to join the team, several problems may occur. For one thing, her current team will clearly be angry with the members of Team A. Further, "poaching" new team members from other teams inside the plant is likely to become a common occurrence. On the other hand, though, it seems reasonable that she should have the same opportunity to join Team A as an outsider would. Team A needs to decide how to proceed.

Team Activity

Assemble a group of four students and assign each group member to one of the following roles:

- Member of Team A
- Member of Team B
- Manager of both teams
- Investor in Hails Corporation

Action Steps

1. Before discussing the situation with your group, and from the perspective of your assigned role, do you think that the member of Team B should be allowed to join Team A? Write down the reasons for your position.
2. Before discussing the situation with your group, and from the perspective of your assigned role, what are the underlying ethical issues, if any, in this situation? Write down the issues.
3. Gather your group together and reveal, in turn, each member's comments on the situation. Next, reveal the ethical issues listed by each member.
4. Appoint someone to record the main points of agreement and disagreement within the group. How do you explain the results? What accounts for any disagreement?
5. From an ethical standpoint, what does your group conclude is the most appropriate action that should be taken by Hails in this situation? Should Team B's member be allowed to join Team A?
6. Develop a group response to the following questions: Assuming Team A asks the Team B member to join its team, how might it go about minimizing repercussions? Assuming Team A does not ask the Team B member to join its team, how might it go about minimizing repercussions?

BUSINESS CASE 7

Cooking Up a New Structure

A few years ago, Sara Lee CEO John H. Bryan realized that he had a problem. During the 25 years of his tenure, the firm had grown beyond its foundation in food products to encompass dozens of lines of business—everything from cake mixes to insecticide to lingerie. The new businesses were acquisitions, and the original managers controlled each one as if it were a separate company. Calculating the cost of all this duplication, Bryan reached the conclusion that the company could not afford high costs at a time when price competition was heating up.

In an effort to fix things, starting in 1997, Bryan sold or eliminated about one-quarter of the firm's 200 products. He cut redundant factories and the workforce, reduced the number of products, and standardized companywide processes. He called his extensive restructuring program "deverticalization," and his goal was to remove Sara Lee from manufacturing while strengthening its focus and effectiveness as a marketer. In the meantime, however, he continued to acquire rival firms in order to sustain the company's growth. Despite Bryan's efforts, Sara Lee continued to suffer from high costs and remained unfocused and inefficient. One industry analyst said, about Bryan's strategy, "Sometimes, the more chairs you move around, the more dust you see behind the chairs."

In 2000, C. Steven McMillan took over from Bryan at Sara Lee, and in the immortal words of Yogi Berra, "It was *déjà vu* all over again." McMillan quickly realized that Bryan's moves had had little impact on the firm's performance and that he would need to start making some big changes. Borrowing a page from rival Kraft Foods, he began by merging the sales forces that specialized in various brands to create smaller, customer-focused teams. In meats alone, for instance, Sara Lee had 10 different brands, including Ball Park, Hillshire Farms, Bryan, and Jimmy Dean. "So if you're a Safeway," explained McMillan, "you've got to deal with 10 different organizations and multiple invoices." Teams reduced duplication and were more convenient for buyers—a win-win situation. National retailers like Wal-Mart responded by increasing their orders for Sara Lee products.

McMillan also centralized decision making at the firm by shutting down 50 weaker regional brands and reorganizing the firm into three broad product categories: Food and Beverage, Intimates and Underwear, and Household Products. He abolished several layers of corporate hierarchy, including many of the middle managers whom the firm had inherited from its acquisitions. He created category managers to oversee related lines of business, and the flattened organizational structure led to improved accountability and more centralized control over Sara Lee's far-flung operations.

McMillan also borrowed some tactics from his predecessor, divesting 15 businesses, including Coach Leather Goods, and laying off 10 percent of his workers. In another move that was widely questioned by industry observers, he paid $2.8 billion for breadmaker Earthgrains. The move increased Sara Lee's market share in baked goods, but many observers felt that McMillan paid too much for a small potential return.

McMillan still had a few tricks up his sleeves. One bold move was developing a chain of retail stores named Inner Self. Each store features a spa-like atmosphere in which to sell Sara Lee's Hanes, Playtex, Bali, and Wonderbra products. Susan Nedved, head of development for Inner Self, thinks that the company-owned stores provide a more realistic and comforting environment for making underwear purchases than do some specialty outlets. "There seems to be an open void for another specialty concept that complements Victoria's Secret," says Nedved. "There was a need for shopping alternatives that really cater to the aging population."

McMillan remains confident that his strategy—more centralization, coordination, and focus—will do the trick at Sara Lee. "I do believe the things we're doing will enhance the growth rate of our company," he says. But many observers are less optimistic. As for Inner Self and underwear, one analyst points out that "even if you fix that business, it's still apparel, and it's not really viewed as a high-value-added business."

Even if McMillan's strategy does manage to cut costs and increase market share, skeptics point out that there is no logic behind the idea of housing baked goods, meats, coffee, underwear, shoe polish, and household cleaners under one corporate roof. Unless McMillan can find some as yet–undiscovered synergy among such disparate units, Sara Lee is probably headed for a breakup into several smaller, more focused, more profitable companies.

Questions for Discussion

1. Describe the basic structural components at Sara Lee.
2. What role does specialization play at Sara Lee?
3. What kinds of authority are reflected in this case?
4. What kind of organizational structure does Sara Lee seem to have?
5. What role has the informal organization played in Sara Lee's various acquisitions and divestitures?

MYBUSINESSLAB mybusinesslab

To improve your grade, visit the MyBusinessLab website at **www.pearsoned.ca/mybusinesslab**. This online homework and tutorial system allows you to test your understanding and generates a personalized study plan just for you. It provides you with study and practice tools directly related to this chapter's content. MyBusinessLab puts you in control of your own learning!

CHAPTER 8

Managing Human Resources and Labour Relations

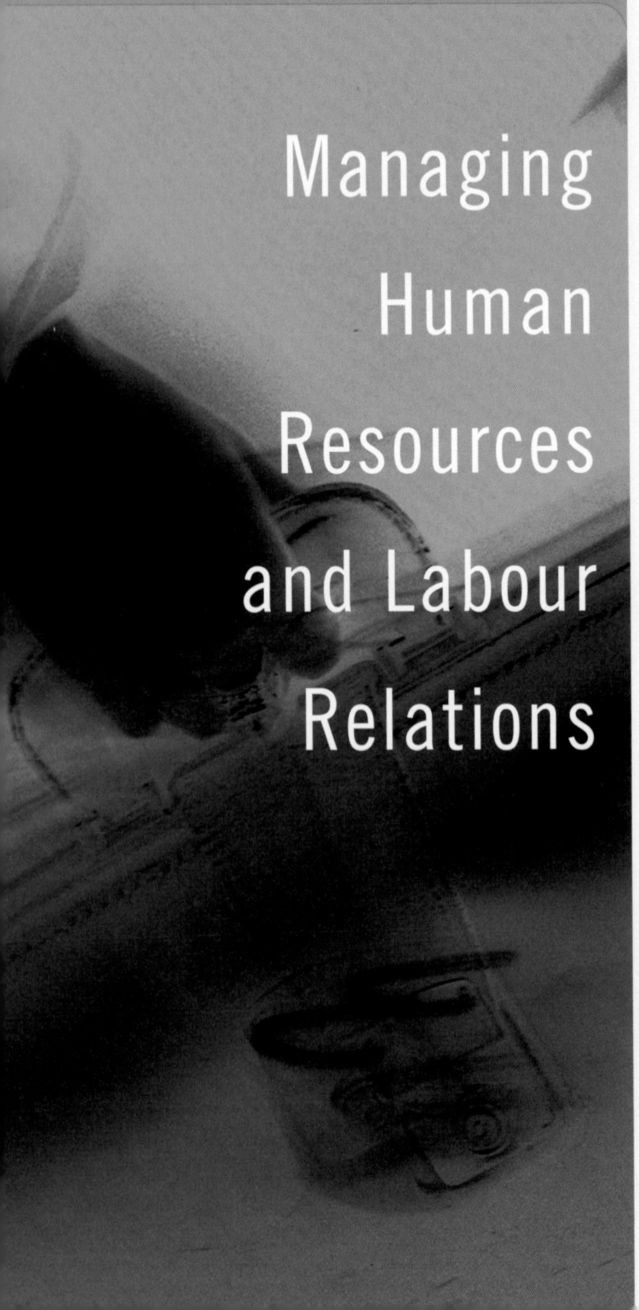

After reading this chapter, you will be able to:

1. Define *human resource management*, discuss its strategic significance, and explain how managers plan for human resources.
2. Identify the issues involved in *staffing* a company, including *internal* and *external recruiting* and *selection*.
3. Discuss different ways in which organizations go about developing the capabilities of employees and managers.
4. Discuss the importance of *wages and salaries, incentives*, and *benefit programs* in attracting and keeping skilled workers.
5. Describe some of the key legal issues involved in hiring, compensating, and managing workers in today's workplace.
6. Discuss *workforce diversity*, the management of *knowledge workers*, and the use of *contingent and temporary workers* as important changes in the contemporary workplace.
7. Trace the evolution of, and discuss trends in, *unionism* in Canada.
8. Describe the *major laws governing unionism*.
9. Identify the steps in the *collective bargaining process*.

Celebrating Workforce Diversity

The following facts about visible minorities show just how important the issue of workforce diversity has become:

- 73 percent of the people who immigrated to Canada during the 1990s were visible minorities
- 18 percent of Canada's population was born outside Canada
- 20 percent of Saskatchewan's population will be Aboriginal by 2015
- In 2001, approximately 4 million Canadians were visible minorities; by 2017, that number could increase to as many as 8.5 million
- The largest visible minority group in Canada in 2001 was Chinese, but the South Asian population is expected to grow more quickly during the next decade
- Visible minorities currently make up 40 percent of the population of Vancouver
- By 2017, visible minorities will form more than 50 percent of the populations of Toronto and Vancouver
- By 2017, 22 percent of the total Canadian population will be visible minorities

Changes of this magnitude simply cannot be ignored, either by Canadian politicians or by Canadian business firms. Procter & Gamble Canada is one of the many Canadian businesses that are taking steps to deal with the challenges and opportunities that come with a rapidly changing population demographic.

Thirty years ago, P & G was like a lot of other Canadian companies—most of its employees were white males. But that's changing rapidly. In 2005, for example, the 800 people who are employed at P & G's Toronto headquarters organized a major social gathering to celebrate the diverse nature of the P & G workforce (employees come from 40 different countries and speak at least 30 different languages). But the event wasn't just for fun. Like other companies, P & G has learned that employees are more productive when their differences are respected in the work environment. And that translates into increased corporate success. Since the top management ranks of P & G are still predominantly white male, the company has set a strategic goal to diversify its workforce.

P & G thinks that a diverse workforce also helps the company market its well-known brands—Pampers, Crest, Tide, Mr. Clean, etc.—to a diverse group of consumers. And the Statistics Canada report clearly shows that Canadian consumers are becoming more diverse at a dizzying pace. As consumer demographics change, it is important to get more diverse people involved in making marketing decisions. The president of P & G Canada, Tim Penner, says that a diverse workforce enriches everyone in the company because they are exposed to other cultures; also, the diversity gives employees a better understanding of P & G's customers.

There are multiple "affinity groups" at P & G, such as the Women's Leadership Council, the French Canadian Network, the Asian Professional Network, the Christian Network, and the Jewish Network. The goal of these networks is to help employees feel comfortable about participating in corporate life, and to act as resource groups for employees who want insights about how to target certain specific markets.

Western Union is another company that is focusing on diversity, and it may be further along than most companies given the nature of its business—moving money overseas to the families of new Canadians who are working here and want to help their families back in their home country. The potential customers of Western Union are not easily reached by traditional marketing methods, so the company hires people who speak the language of their target market and who know what it feels like to be an immigrant in Canada. When recruiting new employees, Western Union does not demand "Canadian experience" as many other companies do. Rather, they want employees with international experience because of the nature of the company's business. After Western Union hires these people, they seek out local business operators to act as Western Union agents for their own ethnic community.

Marketing Manager Marco Amoranto is typical of the kind of employees that are hired at Western Union. He was born in the Philippines and originally worked for Colgate-Palmolive. He wanted to work in Canada but had trouble landing a job because he didn't have Canadian experience. At Western Union, he is responsible for marketing to Asian and Europeans. He recently returned from a "road show" where the company sponsored concerts featuring several top Philippine entertainers, including Freestyle, Basil Valdez, and Jaya.

The Western Union approach has yielded some interesting benefits. In one area of Toronto, for example, customers who wanted to transfer money back to the Philippines got a free loaf of Pan de Sel bread from a local Filipino baker. Thus, the results were positive for Western Union, its customers, and the baker. Western Union also brings in entertainers from its customers' home countries and then gives customers free tickets to the concerts.

In the current rapidly changing demographic environment, companies are discovering that they cannot ignore workforce (and customer) diversity. One company that has had some bad press recently in this area is Wal-Mart, which has been confronted with a class-action sex discrimination lawsuit, as well as a lot of negative publicity about alleged low wages and lack of health care available to its employees. In response to these concerns, the company has hired a director of diversity.

Lee Scott, the CEO of Wal-Mart, says that Wal-Mart is a "pretty good company," but with 1.5 million employees, there are bound to be some racists and sexists among them. The company has also built in incentives to motivate top managers to reach certain diversity goals. If the goals are not met, Scott could forfeit up to $600 000 of his salary. Scott says that in the past, if an employee made a racist or sexist remark, the person might just be transferred. But in today's more enlightened environment, that kind of behaviour can no longer be tolerated and the person will be terminated. With Wal-Mart opening more stores in areas where a larger proportion of customers are Hispanic and black, there will be less tolerance of unacceptable behaviour among employees.

HOW WILL THIS BENEFIT YOU?

Effectively managing human resources is critical to the success of organizations. A firm that handles this activity well has a much better chance for success than does a firm that simply goes through the motions. After reading the material in this chapter, you'll be better able to understand—from the perspective of a manager—the importance of properly managing human resources in a department or business you own or supervise. You'll also understand—from the perspective of an employee—why your employer has adopted certain approaches to dealing with issues like hiring, training, compensation, and benefits.

We start this chapter by explaining how managers plan for their organization's human resource needs. We then discuss ways in which organizations select, develop, appraise, and compensate employees. We also look at some key legal issues involved in managing workers, and we pay special attention to managing workforce diversity. Finally, we explain why workers organize into labour unions, and how the collective bargaining process works. Let's get started with some basic concepts of human resource management.

THE FOUNDATIONS OF HUMAN RESOURCE MANAGEMENT

1 Define *human resource management*, discuss its strategic significance, and explain how managers plan for human resources.

human resource management (HRM)
Set of organizational activities directed at attracting, developing, and maintaining an effective workforce.

Human resource management (HRM) is the set of organizational activities directed at attracting, developing, and maintaining an effective workforce. Human resource management takes place within a complex and ever-changing environmental context and is increasingly being recognized for its strategic importance.[1]

The Strategic Importance of HRM

Human resources are critical for effective organizational functioning. HRM (or *personnel*, as it is sometimes called) was once relegated to second-class status in many organizations, but its importance has grown dramatically in the last two decades. This new importance stems from increased legal complexities, the recognition that human resources are a valuable means for improving productivity, and the awareness today of the costs associated with poor human resource management.

Managers now realize that the effectiveness of their HR function has a substantial impact on a firm's bottom-line performance. Poor human resource planning can result in spurts of hiring followed by layoffs—a process that is costly in terms of unemployment compensation payments, training expenses, and morale. Haphazard compensation systems do not attract, keep, and motivate good employees, and outmoded recruitment practices can expose the firm to expensive and embarrassing legal action. Consequently, the chief human resource executive of most large businesses is a vice-president directly accountable to the CEO, and many firms are developing strategic HR plans that are integrated with other strategic planning activities.

Human Resource Planning

The starting point in attracting qualified human resources is planning. HR planning involves *job analysis*, *forecasting* the demand for and supply of labour, and *matching* supply and demand.

Job Analysis

Job analysis is a systematic analysis of jobs within an organization. A job analysis is made up of two parts:

- The **job description** lists the duties of a job, its working conditions, and the tools, materials, and equipment used to perform it.
- The **job specification** lists the skills, abilities, and other credentials needed to do the job.

Job analysis information is used in many HR activities. For instance, knowing about job content and job requirements is necessary to develop appropriate selection methods and job-relevant performance appraisal systems and to set equitable compensation rates.

job analysis
A detailed study of the specific duties in a particular job and the human qualities required for that job.

job description
The objectives, responsibilities, and key tasks of a job; the conditions under which it will be done; its relationship to other positions; and the skills needed to perform it.

job specification
The specific skills, education, and experience needed to perform a job.

Forecasting HR Demand and Supply

After managers fully understand the jobs to be performed within an organization, they can start planning for the organization's future HR needs. The manager starts by assessing trends in past HR usage, future organizational plans, and general economic trends. A good sales forecast is often the foundation, especially for smaller organizations. Historical ratios can then be used to predict demand for types of employees, such as operating employees and sales representatives. Large organizations, of course, use much more complicated models to predict HR needs.

Forecasting the supply of labour involves two tasks:

- Forecasting *internal supply*—the number and type of employees who will be in the firm at some future date
- Forecasting *external supply*—the number and type of people who will be available for hiring from the labour market at large

The simplest approach merely adjusts present staffing levels for anticipated turnover and promotions. Large organizations often use extremely sophisticated models to keep track of the present and future distributions of professionals and managers.

Replacement Charts. At higher levels of the organization, managers plan for specific people and positions. The technique most commonly used is the **replacement chart**, which lists each important managerial position, who occupies it, how long he or she will probably stay in it before moving on, and who (by name) is now qualified or soon will be qualified to move into it.

replacement chart
An HR technique that lists each important managerial position, who occupies it, how long he or she will probably stay in it before moving on, and who (by name) is now qualified or soon will be qualified to move into it.

employee information systems (skills inventories) Computerized systems that contain information on each employee's education, skills, work experience, and career aspirations.

Skills Inventories. To facilitate planning and to identify people for transfer or promotion, some organizations also have **employee information systems**, or **skills inventories**. These systems are usually computerized and contain information on each employee's education, skills, work experience, and career aspirations. Such a system can quickly locate every employee in the company who is qualified to fill a position requiring, say, a degree in chemical engineering, three years of experience in an oil refinery, and fluency in French.

Forecasting the external supply of labour is more difficult. To get an idea of the future availability of labour, planners must rely on information from outside sources, including population and demographic statistics and figures supplied by colleges and universities on the number of students in major fields. These statistics show that Canada is likely to face a severe labour shortage within the next 10 years. The problem is already evident in the hot economy of Alberta, but labour shortages are likely to appear in almost all provinces over the next few years as thousands of "baby boomers" approach retirement age.[2] The worst shortages are in the construction, retail, and transportation industries.[3]

Matching HR Supply and Demand

After comparing future demand and internal supply, managers can make plans to manage predicted shortfalls or overstaffing. If a shortfall is predicted, new employees can be hired, present employees can be retrained and transferred into understaffed areas, individuals approaching retirement can be convinced to stay on, or labour-saving or productivity-enhancing systems can be installed.

If the organization needs to hire, the external labour-supply forecast helps managers plan how to recruit according to whether the type of person needed is readily available or scarce in the labour market. The use of temporary workers also helps managers in staffing by giving them extra flexibility. If overstaffing is expected to be a problem, the main options are transferring the extra employees, not replacing individuals who quit, encouraging early retirement, and laying people off.

STAFFING THE ORGANIZATION

Once managers have decided what positions they need to fill, they must find and hire individuals who meet the job requirements. A study by the Canadian Federation of Independent Business found that the top three characteristics employers are looking for when they hire people are a good work ethic, reliability, and willingness to stay on the job.[4] In this section, we will describe both the process of acquiring staff from outside the company (*external staffing*) and the process of promoting staff from within (*internal staffing*). Both external and internal staffing start with effective recruiting.

2 Identify the issues involved in *staffing* a company, including *internal* and *external recruiting* and *selection.*

Recruiting Human Resources

recruiting The phase in the staffing of a company in which the firm seeks to develop a pool of interested, qualified applicants for a position.

internal recruiting Considering present employees as candidates for job openings.

Recruiting is the process of attracting qualified persons to apply for the jobs that are open. Some recruits are found internally; others come from outside the organization. **Internal recruiting** means considering present employees as candidates for openings. Promotion from within can help build morale and keep high-quality employees from leaving. In unionized firms, the procedures for notifying employees of internal job-change opportunities are usually spelled out in the union contract. For higher-level positions, a skills inventory system may be used to identify internal candidates, or managers may be asked to recommend individuals who should be considered.

External recruiting means attracting people outside the organization to apply for jobs. External recruiting methods include advertising, campus interviews, employment agencies or executive search firms, union hiring halls, referrals by present employees, and hiring "walk-ins" (people who show up without being solicited). Private employment agencies can be a good source of clerical and technical employees, and executive search firms specialize in locating top-management talent. Newspaper ads are often used because they reach a wide audience and thus allow minorities "equal opportunity" to learn about and apply for job openings.

external recruiting Attracting people outside the organization to apply for jobs.

The old-fashioned job fair has survived in spite of internet career postings and the proliferation of employment agencies and headhunters. At a job fair, candidates browse through the positions available and employers can see a sample of the skills candidates have. Sears Canada held a three-day job fair at the Marriott Hotel in Toronto's Eaton Centre because it was looking for hundreds of new employees.[5] Some companies carry on external recruiting in non-traditional ways. For example, Nortel Networks recruited at a rock concert outside Boston, near one of its manufacturing facilities. Recruiters handed out lip balm, ran a raffle, and chatted about Nortel to people who were arriving to hear Counting Crows and Live.[6]

One increasingly popular method of external recruiting involves offering college and university students **internships**—short-term paid positions where students focus on a specific project. At IBM Canada's "Extreme Blue" internship program, for example, students are responsible for turning an idea into a marketable product.[7] If the placement works out well, the company often hires the student full-time upon graduation.

Selecting Human Resources

Once the recruiting process has attracted a pool of applicants, the next step is to select someone to hire. The intent of the selection process is to gather information from applicants that will predict their job success and then to hire the candidates likely to be most successful. The process of determining the predictive value of information is called **validation**.

validation The process of determining the predictive value of information.

To reduce the element of uncertainty, managers use a variety of selection techniques, the most common of which are shown in Figure 8.1. Each organization develops its own mix of selection techniques and may use them in almost any order.

At job fairs, students and recruiters can talk face to face about jobs that are available. Here, recruiters talk to students about the opportunities at the company.

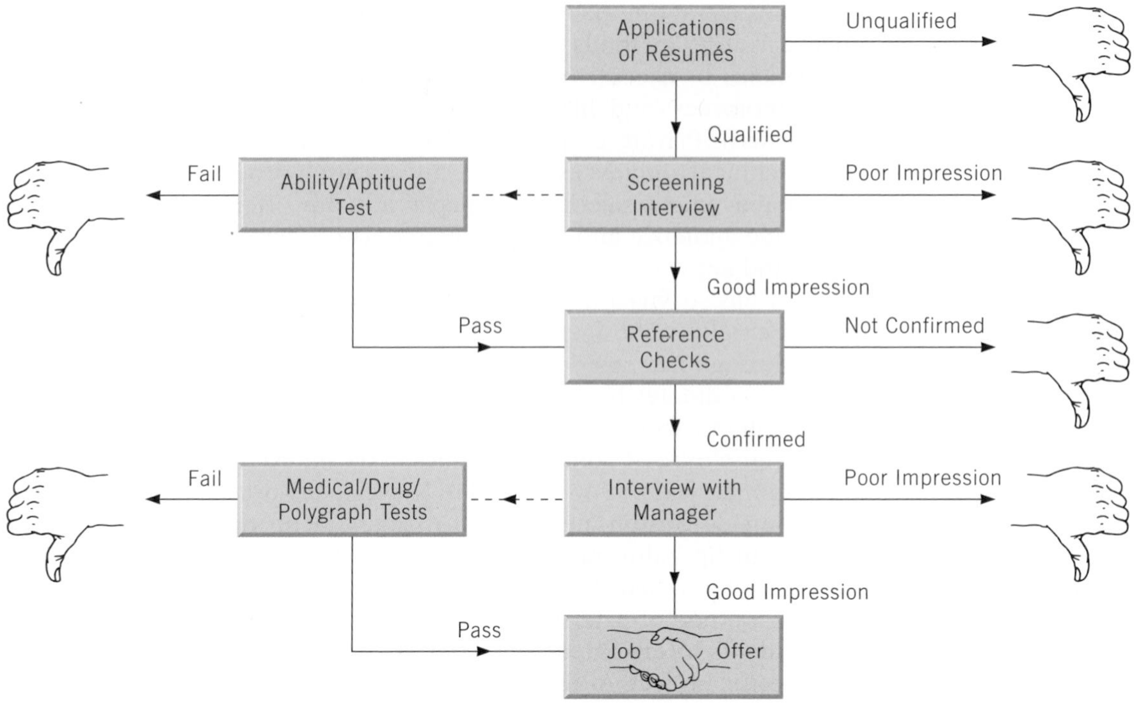

Figure 8.1 General steps in the selection process.

Application Forms

The first step in selection is asking the candidate to fill out an application form. An application form is an efficient method of gathering information about the applicant's previous work history, educational background, and other job-related demographic data. It should not contain questions about areas unrelated to the job, such as gender, religion, or national origin. Application-form data are generally used informally to decide whether a candidate merits further evaluation, and interviewers use application forms to familiarize themselves with candidates before interviewing them.

Tests

Employers sometimes ask candidates to take tests during the selection process. Tests of ability, skill, aptitude, or knowledge relevant to a particular job are usually the best predictors of job success, although tests of general intelligence or personality are occasionally useful as well. At Astral Media Inc. of Montreal, for example, job candidates are required to take a series of tests that measure verbal and numerical skills, as well as psychological traits.[8] Some companies administer tests to determine how well applicants score on the "big five" personality dimensions discussed in Chapter 9. These scores are used to help make hiring decisions. In addition to being validated, tests should be administered and scored consistently. All candidates should be given the same directions, allowed the same amount of time, and offered the same testing environment, including temperature, lighting, and distractions.

assessment centre
A series of exercises in which management candidates perform realistic management tasks while being observed by appraisers.

An **assessment centre** is a series of exercises in which candidates perform realistic management tasks under the watchful eye of expert appraisers. During this time, potential managers take selection tests, engage in management simulations, make individual presentations, and conduct group discussions. Assessors check to see how each participant reacts to stress or to

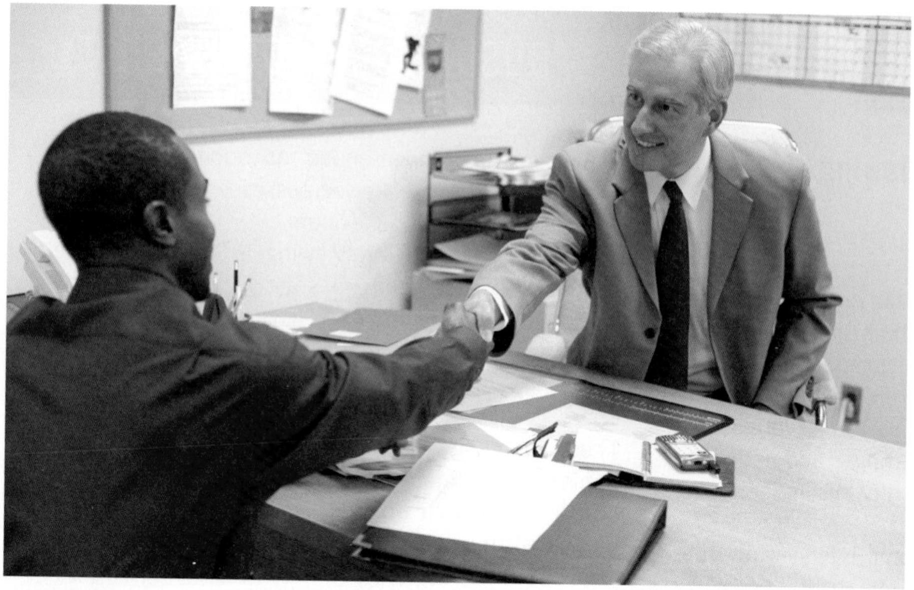

An in-depth interview with a prospective employee is often part of the recruiting process, particularly for managerial jobs.

criticism by colleagues. A relatively new type of test is **video assessment**, which involves showing potential hires videos of realistic work situations and asking them to choose a course of action to deal with the situation.

video assessment
Involves showing potential hires videos of realistic work situations and asking them to choose a course of action to deal with the situation.

Interviews

The interview is a popular selection device, but it is sometimes a poor predictor of job success because biases inherent in the way people perceive and judge others on first meeting affect subsequent evaluations. Many companies are placing more emphasis on testing and less emphasis on interviewing because job candidates are becoming very clever at giving all the "right" answers during interviews.[9] Interview validity can be improved by training interviewers to be aware of potential biases, and by writing out questions in advance and asking all interviewees the same set of questions. Interviewers can also increase interview validity by asking "curveball" questions—that is, questions that job applicants would never expect to be asked—to see how well they think on their feet. Questions such as "How would you move Mount Fuji?" or "How would you sell me a glass of water?" are curveball questions.[10] The Business Accountability box describes further actions that interviewers can take to make interviews useful.

Other Techniques

Organizations also use other selection techniques that vary with the circumstances. A manufacturer afraid of injuries to workers on the job might require new employees to have a physical examination. This gives the company some information about whether the applicants are physically fit to do the work and what (if any) pre-existing injuries they might have. Polygraph (lie detector) tests are largely illegal now, and drug tests are also coming under fire. For example, the Toronto-Dominion Bank wanted to give drug tests to all new employees because it wanted to have the public's trust. However, a federal court ruled that the bank's policy was discriminatory and that it wasn't related closely enough to job performance.[11] Reference checks with previous employers are also used, but may be of limited value because individuals are likely to only provide the names of references who will give them positive recommendations.

BUSINESS ACCOUNTABILITY

Behaviour-Based Interviewing

Behaviour-based interviewing assesses how you reacted to difficult and/or important job situations in the past, and assumes that these are a good indicator of how you will react to similar job situations in the future. The approach can be used to test for technical skills (e.g., accounting, welding, computer programming), management skills (e.g., organizing, motivating others, communicating), and individual characteristics (e.g., dependability, discipline, ability to work on a team).

Instead of asking a traditional interviewing question like "Do you often take the initiative?," behaviour-based interviewing asks questions like "Tell me about a situation where you became aware of a problem. What did you do?" Asking questions like this focuses the interview much more on your *behaviour* than on what you *say* you would do if the problem arose in the future. Other typical questions that interviewers ask in behaviour-based interviewing are as follows:

- Think of a time when you were asked to analyze information and then make a specific recommendation. What kind of reasoning and thought processes did you use?
- Think of a time when you had to deal with a customer that you thought was being unreasonable. How did you deal with that person?
- Think of a time when you had to cope with a major change in your job. What did you do?
- Think of a time when you had to work with a person that was not "pulling their weight." What, if anything, did you do?

Behaviour-based interviewing requires the person who is interviewing candidates to first identify the characteristics, skills, and behaviours that are important in the job that needs to be filled. The interviewer then constructs open-ended questions which will determine if the interviewee possesses those characteristics, skills, and behaviours.

Behaviour-based interviewing is becoming more common because companies are facing increasingly competitive environments. These competitive environments have meant downsizing, which places increasing demands on the workers who remain. There is also more emphasis on working in teams. These changing work situations have motivated companies to be much more focused in their hiring because they want workers who are more skilled and motivated than were available previously.

The increasing use of behaviour-based interviewing means that you are likely to be exposed to it at some point in your job search. What should you do to prepare for a behaviour-based interview? The main thing is to think about the job you are interviewing for and the skills that will be required to do it. Try to tell an interesting story (from a previous paid or volunteer position) that succinctly describes a situation you faced, the actions you took, and the outcome that resulted from your actions. If the outcome was good, the interviewer will likely be favourably impressed with your logical thinking and actions. Even if the outcome wasn't so good, you can indicate what you learned from the experience and how that experience will benefit your new employer.

QUESTIONS FOR DISCUSSION

1. Do you think that behaviour-based interviewing will give employers better insights about potential employees than traditional interviewing does?
2. "*We should only hire people who have been through a behaviour-based interview because such people will feel more accountable for their job performance and will do a better job for the company.*" Do you agree or disagree with this statement? Explain your reasoning.

DEVELOPING HUMAN RESOURCES

3 Discuss different ways in which organizations go about developing the capabilities of employees and managers.

After a company has hired new employees, it must acquaint them with the firm and their new jobs. Managers also take steps to train employees and to further develop necessary job skills. In addition, every firm has some system for performance appraisal and feedback.

Training and Development

On-the-job training occurs while employees are in the actual work situation. Much on-the-job training is informal, as when one employee shows another how to operate the photocopy machine. Training may also be formal, as when a trainer shows employees how to operate a new software program. In **job rotation**, employees learn a wide array of tasks and acquire more abilities as they are moved from one job to another.

on-the-job training
Those development programs in which employees gain new skills while performing them at work.

job rotation
A technique in which an employee is rotated or transferred from one job to another.

Off-the-job training is performed at a location away from the work site. For example, during their stay at Coffee College—a two-week cram course run by Second Cup Ltd.—managers learn how to hire workers, keep the books, detect employee theft, and boost Christmas sales.[12] Another off-the-job training program is **vestibule training**, which involves having employees perform work under conditions closely *simulating* the actual work environment. For example, engineers at Montreal-based CAE Inc. built a simulator for the world's largest passenger jet, the Airbus A380. Airline pilots use the simulator to learn how to fly the new jet without ever leaving the ground.[13]

off-the-job training
Those development programs in which employees learn new skills at a location away from the normal work site.

vestibule training
A work simulation in which the job is performed under conditions closely simulating the actual work environment.

Management development programs try to enhance conceptual, analytical, and problem-solving skills. Most large companies run formal in-house management development programs or send managers to programs on university campuses. Some management development takes place informally, often through processes such as networking and mentoring. **Networking** refers to informal interactions among managers for the purpose of discussing mutual problems, solutions, and opportunities. Networking takes place in a variety of settings, both inside and outside the office. **Mentoring** means having a more experienced manager sponsor and teach a less experienced manager.

management development programs
Development programs in which managers' conceptual, analytical, and problem-solving skills are enhanced.

networking
Informal interactions among managers, both inside and outside the office, for the purpose of discussing mutual problems, solutions, and opportunities.

mentoring
Having a more experienced manager sponsor and teach a less experienced manager.

Evaluating Employee Performance

Performance appraisals are designed to show how well workers are doing their jobs. Typically, the appraisal process involves a written assessment issued on a regular basis. As a rule, however, the written evaluation is only one part of a multi-step process. The appraisal process begins when a manager defines performance standards for an employee. The manager then observes the employee's performance. If the standards are clear, the manager should have little difficulty comparing expectations with performance. The process is completed when the manager and employee meet to discuss the appraisal.

performance appraisals
A formal program for evaluating how well an employee is performing the job; helps managers to determine how effective they are in recruiting and selecting employees.

Organizations rely on a variety of different information sources when conducting performance appraisals. Some organizations systematically gather information from peers, subordinates, customers, and bosses. This comprehensive approach is called **360-degree feedback**. At McMaster University, for example, President Peter George had his performance evaluated by staff, union leaders, and board members.[14]

360-degree feedback
Gathering information from a manager's subordinates, peers, and superiors when assessing the manager's performance.

Performance appraisal in many organizations tends to focus on negatives. As a result, managers may have a tendency to avoid giving feedback because they know that an employee who receives negative feedback may be angry, hurt, discouraged, or argumentative. But clearly, if employees are not told about their shortcomings, they will have no concrete reason to try to improve and receive no guidance as to *how* to improve.

Methods for Appraising Performance

simple ranking method
A method of performance appraisal that requires a manager to rank-order from top to bottom or from best to worst each member of a particular work group or department.

forced distribution method
A method of performance appraisal that involves grouping employees into predefined frequencies of performance ratings.

graphic rating scale
A statement or question about some aspect of an individual's job performance for which the rater must select the response that fits best.

critical incident method
A technique of performance appraisal in which raters recall examples of especially good or poor performance by an employee and then describe what the employee did (or did not do) that led to success or failure.

The **simple ranking method** requires a manager to rank-order from top to bottom or from best to worst each member of a particular workgroup or department. The individual ranked first is the top performer, the individual ranked second is the second-best performer, and so forth. Another ranking method, the **forced distribution method**, involves grouping employees into predefined frequencies of performance ratings. Those frequencies are determined in advance and are imposed on the rater. A decision might be made, for instance, that 10 percent of the employees in a workgroup will be categorized as "outstanding," 20 percent as "very good," 40 percent as "average," 20 percent as "below average," and the remaining 10 percent as "poor." The forced distribution method is familiar to many students because it is the principle used by professors who grade on a so-called "bell curve" or "normal curve."

One of the most popular and widely used methods is the **graphic rating scale**, which consists simply of a statement or question about some aspect of an individual's job performance. Figure 8.2 shows a sample graphic rating scale.

The **critical incident method** focuses attention on an example of especially good or poor performance on the part of the employee. Raters then describe what the employee did (or did not do) that led to success or failure. This technique not only provides information for feedback but defines performance in fairly clear behavioural terms.

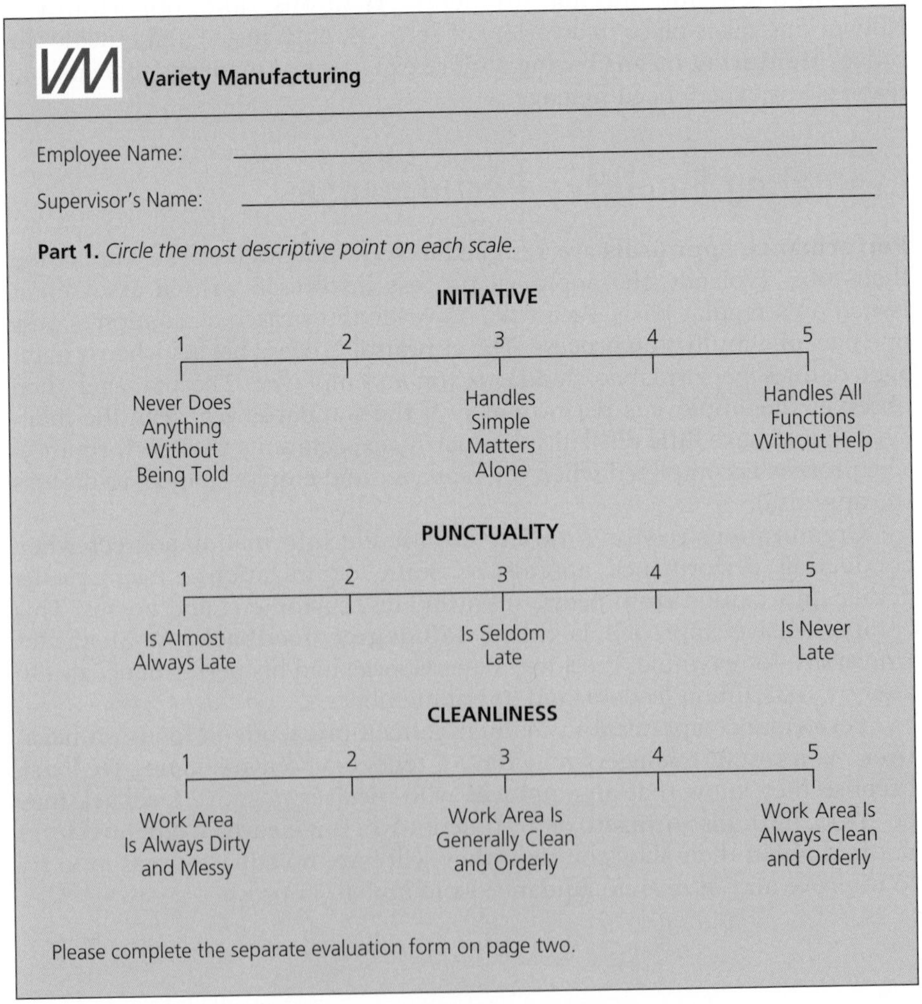
Variety Manufacturing

Employee Name: ____________________

Supervisor's Name: ____________________

Part 1. *Circle the most descriptive point on each scale.*

INITIATIVE

1 — Never Does Anything Without Being Told
2
3 — Handles Simple Matters Alone
4
5 — Handles All Functions Without Help

PUNCTUALITY

1 — Is Almost Always Late
2
3 — Is Seldom Late
4
5 — Is Never Late

CLEANLINESS

1 — Work Area Is Always Dirty and Messy
2
3 — Work Area Is Generally Clean and Orderly
4
5 — Work Area Is Always Clean and Orderly

Please complete the separate evaluation form on page two.

Figure 8.2 Performance rating scale.

COMPENSATION AND BENEFITS

Compensation refers to the rewards that organizations provide to individuals in return for their willingness to perform various jobs and tasks within the organization. Compensation includes a number of different elements, including base salary, incentives, bonuses, benefits, and other rewards. The compensation received by CEOs can be extremely large, especially when bonuses are included. The most highly paid managers in the 2005 *Globe and Mail* Survey of Compensation were Hank Swartout of Precision Drilling Trust (who earned $74.8 million), Hunter Harrison of Canadian National Railway ($56.2 million), Frank Stronach of Magna International ($40.3 million), and Mike Zafirovski of Nortel Networks ($37.4 million).[15] Critics have frequently questioned the wisdom of giving executives such large amounts of money, but most attempts to rein in executive salaries have failed. A study done by a University of Southern California professor showed that the average CEO's pay in 1976 was about 36 times as much as that of the average worker, but by 2005, it was 369 times as much.[16]

4 Discuss the importance of *wages and salaries, incentives,* and *benefit programs* in attracting and keeping skilled workers.

compensation What a firm offers its employees in return for their labour.

Determining Basic Compensation

Wages generally refer to hourly compensation paid to operating employees. Most of the jobs that are paid on an hourly wage basis are lower-level and/or operating-level jobs. Rather than expressing compensation on an hourly basis, the organization may instead describe compensation on an annual or monthly basis. Many college and university graduates, for example, compare job offers on the basis of annual **salary**, such as $40 000 versus $38 000 a year.

wages Dollars paid based on the number of hours worked.

salary Dollars paid at regular intervals in return for doing a job, regardless of the amount of time or output involved.

Companies often use **pay surveys** to determine pay levels. These surveys show the compensation that is being paid to employees by other employers in a particular geographic area, an industry, or an occupational group. For example, the Canadian Federation of Business School Deans publishes an annual summary of salaries for professors teaching in business schools in Canadian universities. The internet allows job seekers and current employees to more easily get a sense of what their true market value is. If they can document the claim that their value is higher than what their current employer now pays or is offering, they are in a position to demand a higher salary.

pay surveys A survey of compensation paid to employees by other employers in a particular geographic area, an industry, or an occupational group.

Another means of determining basic compensation is **job evaluation**, a method for determining the relative value or worth of a job to the organization so that individuals who perform it can be compensated appropriately. In other words, it is mostly concerned with establishing internal pay equity. There should be a logical rank-ordering of compensation levels from the most valuable to the least valuable jobs throughout the organization.

job evaluation A method for determining the relative value or worth of a job to the organization so that individuals who perform it can be appropriately compensated.

Incentive Programs

Employees feel better about themselves and their company when they believe that they are being fairly compensated. However, as we discussed in Chapter 9, studies have shown that beyond a certain point, more money will not produce better performance. As well, money motivates employees only if it is tied directly to performance. The most common method of establishing this link is the use of **incentive programs**—special pay programs designed to motivate high performance. Some programs are available to individuals, whereas others are distributed on a companywide basis.

incentive programs Special compensation programs designed to motivate high performance.

Individual incentive plans have been a big part of professional sports for many years. Some players receive multi-million dollar annual compensation for outstanding individual performance.

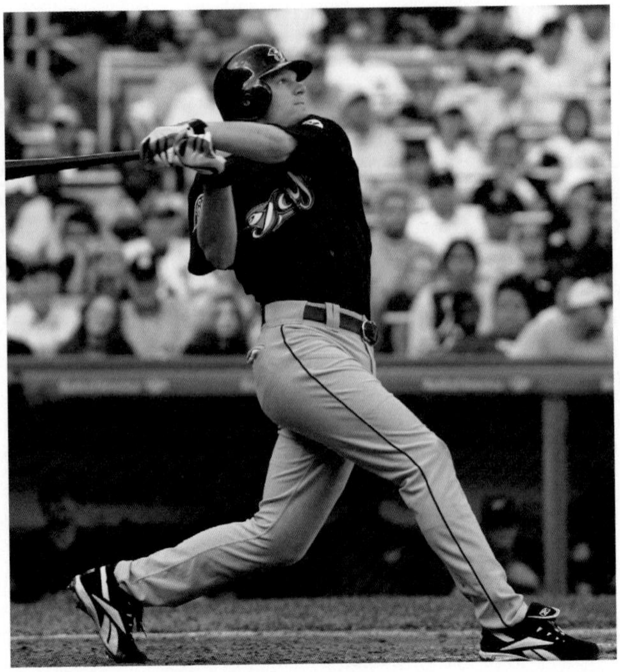

Individual Incentives

piece-rate incentive plan A compensation system in which an organization pays an employee a certain amount of money for every unit produced.

bonus Individual performance incentive in the form of a special payment made over and above the employee's salary.

pay for performance (variable pay) Individual incentive that rewards a manager for especially productive output.

Under a **piece-rate incentive plan**, employees receive a certain amount of money for every unit they produce. An assembly-line worker, for example, might be paid $1 for every 12 units of a product successfully completed. Sales employees are often paid a **bonus**—a special payment above their salaries—when they sell a certain number or certain dollar amount of goods for the year. Bonuses are also given in non-sales jobs. For example, many baseball players have contract clauses that pay them bonuses for hitting over .300, making the All-Star team, or being named Most Valuable Player.

With **pay for performance** (or **variable pay**) schemes, managers are rewarded for especially productive output—for producing earnings that significantly exceed the cost of bonuses. Such incentives go to middle managers on the basis of companywide performance, business unit performance, personal record, or all three factors. Eligible managers must often forgo merit or entitlement raises (increases for staying on and reporting to work every day), but many firms say that variable pay is a better motivator because the range between generous and mediocre merit raises is usually quite small anyway.

Companywide Incentives

profit-sharing plans An incentive program in which employees receive a bonus depending on the firm's profits.

gainsharing plans An incentive program in which employees receive a bonus if the firm's costs are reduced because of greater worker efficiency and/or productivity.

pay-for-knowledge plans Incentive plan to encourage employees to learn new skills or become proficient at different jobs.

Some incentive programs apply to all the employees in a firm. Under **profit-sharing plans**, for example, profits earned above a certain level are distributed to employees. In one recent year, Ipsco Steel's profit-sharing plan distributed over $9 million to employees.[17] Conversely, **gainsharing plans** distribute bonuses to employees when a company's costs are reduced through greater work efficiency. Palliser Furniture Ltd., for example, introduced a gainsharing plan that rewards employees for increasing production. Any profit resulting from production above a certain level is split 50–50 between the company and the employees.[18] **Pay-for-knowledge plans** encourage workers to learn new skills and to become proficient at different jobs. These workers receive additional pay for each new skill or job that they master.

Benefits

Benefits are rewards, incentives, and other things of value that an organization gives to employees in addition to wages, salaries, and other forms of direct financial compensation. Because these benefits have tangible value, they represent a meaningful form of compensation even though they are not generally expressed in financial terms.

benefits
What a firm offers its workers other than wages and salaries in return for their labour.

Mandated Protection Plans

Protection plans assist employees when their income is threatened or reduced by illness, disability, unemployment, or retirement. **Employment insurance** provides a basic subsistence payment to employees who are unemployed but are actively seeking employment. Both employers and employees pay premiums to an employment insurance fund. As of 2007, employee premiums were $1.80 per hundred dollars of earnings, and employer premiums were $2.52.[19]

protection plans
A plan that protects employees when their income is threatened or reduced by illness, disability, death, unemployment, or retirement.

employment insurance
A protection plan that provides a basic subsistence payment to employees who are between jobs.

The **Canada Pension Plan** provides income to retired individuals to help them supplement their personal savings, private pensions, part-time work, and so forth. It is funded through employee and employer taxes that are withheld from payroll. In 2006, the Canada Pension Plan had a surplus of almost $100 billion.[20]

Canada Pension Plan
A plan that provides income to retired individuals through employee and employer taxes that are withheld from payroll.

Workers' compensation is mandated insurance that covers individuals who suffer a job-related illness or accident. Employers bear the cost of workers' compensation insurance. The premium is related to each employer's past experience with job-related accidents and illnesses. For example, a steel company might pay $20 per $100 of wages, while an accounting firm might pay only $0.10 per $100 of wages.

workers' compensation
Mandated insurance that covers individuals who suffer a job-related illness or accident.

Optional Protection Plans

Health insurance is the most important type of coverage, and has expanded in recent years to include vision care, mental health services, dental care, and prescription drugs. Employee prescription drug plan costs are doubling about every five years, and companies are increasingly concerned about their ability to offer this kind of coverage.[21] Pension liabilities are also a problem.

Paid Time Off

Paid vacations are usually for periods of one, two, or more weeks during which an employee can take time off from work and continue to be paid. Most organizations vary the amount of paid vacation with an individual's seniority, but some companies are reducing the time required to qualify for paid vacations. At Carlson Wagonlit Travel Canada, employees get four weeks of paid vacation after working at the company for just five years. Formerly, 10 years of service was required.[22]

Another common paid time off plan is *sick leave*, which is provided when an individual is sick or otherwise physically unable to perform his or her job. Sometimes an organization will allow an employee to take off a small number of days simply for "personal business." The Catholic Children's Aid Society, for example, provides its child protection workers with time off when they need it because the workers face high stress situations.[23]

Other Types of Benefits

In addition to protection plans and paid time off, many organizations offer a number of other benefit programs. **Wellness programs**, for example, concentrate on preventing illness in employees rather than simply paying

wellness programs
A program that concentrates on preventing illness in employees rather than simply paying their expenses when they become sick.

their expenses when they become sick. Childcare benefits are also popular. Any organization that wants to be considered "family-friendly" must have some type of childcare benefit, and being a "family-friendly" company is increasingly becoming a competitive advantage. The childcare centre run by Husky Injection Molding Systems in Bolton, Ontario, provides on-site haircuts, music lessons, and a pyjama party on Valentine's Day so parents can spend time together.[24] Eldercare is also going to become increasingly important as the population ages and workers care for their elderly parents.

cafeteria-style benefit plans
A flexible approach to providing benefits in which employees are allocated a certain sum to cover benefits and can "spend" this allocation on the specific benefits they prefer.

Cafeteria-style benefit plans allow employees to choose the benefits they really want. The organization typically establishes a budget, indicating how much it is willing to spend, per employee, on benefits. Employees are then presented with a list of possible benefits and the cost of each. They are free to put the benefits together in any combination they wish.

THE LEGAL CONTEXT OF HRM

5 Describe some of the key legal issues involved in hiring, compensating, and managing workers in today's workplace.

HRM is heavily influenced by federal and provincial law, so managers must be aware of the most important and far-reaching areas of HR regulation. These include *equal employment opportunity, comparable worth, sexual harassment, employee health and safety,* and *retirement*.

Equal Employment Opportunity

equal employment opportunity regulations
Regulations to protect people from unfair or inappropriate discrimination in the workplace.

The basic goal of all **equal employment opportunity regulations** is to protect people from unfair or inappropriate discrimination in the workplace. Note that differentiating between employees—for example, giving one person a raise and denying the raise to another person—is not illegal. As long as the basis for this distinction is purely job-related (made, for instance, on the basis of performance or qualifications) and is applied objectively and consistently, the action is legal and appropriate. Problems arise when distinctions among people are not job-related. In such cases, the resulting discrimination is illegal.

Anti-Discrimination Laws

Canadian Human Rights Act
Ensures that any individual who wishes to obtain a job has an equal opportunity to apply for it.

The key federal anti-discrimination legislation is the **Canadian Human Rights Act** of 1977 (each province has also enacted human rights legislation). The goal of the Act is to ensure that any individual who wishes to obtain a job has an equal opportunity to compete for it. The Act applies to all federal agencies, federal Crown corporations, any employee of the federal government, and business firms that do business interprovincially. The Act prohibits a wide variety of practices in recruiting, selecting, promoting, and dismissing personnel. It specifically prohibits discrimination on the basis of age, race and colour, national and ethnic origin, physical handicap, religion, gender, marital status, or prison record (if pardoned). Some exceptions to these blanket prohibitions are permitted. Discrimination cannot be charged if a blind person is refused a position as a train engineer, bus driver, or crane operator. Likewise, a firm cannot be charged with discrimination if it does not hire a deaf person as a telephone operator or as an audio engineer.

bona fide occupational requirement
When an employer may choose one applicant over another based on overriding characteristics of the job.

Difficulties in determining whether discrimination has occurred are sometimes dealt with by using the concept of **bona fide occupational requirement**. That is, an employer may choose one person over another based on overriding characteristics of the job in question. If a fitness centre wants to hire only women to supervise its women's locker room and sauna, it can do so without being discriminatory because it established a bona fide occupational requirement.

Enforcement of the federal Act is carried out by the Canadian Human Rights Commission. The commission can either respond to complaints from individuals who believe they have been discriminated against, or launch an investigation on its own if it has reason to believe that discrimination has occurred. During an investigation, data are gathered about the alleged discriminatory behaviour and, if the claim of discrimination is substantiated, the offending organization or individual may be ordered to compensate the victim.

The **Employment Equity Act of 1986** addresses the issue of discrimination in employment by designating four groups as employment-disadvantaged—women, visible minorities, Aboriginal people, and people with disabilities. These four groups contain six of every 10 individuals in the Canadian workforce, and it is estimated that their underemployment costs the Canadian economy around $50 billion each year.[25] Companies covered by the Employment Equity Act are required to publish statistics on their employment of people in the four designated groups.

Employment Equity Act of 1986 Federal legislation that designates four groups as employment disadvantaged—women, visible minorities, Aboriginal people, and people with disabilities.

In 2007, the Bank of Nova Scotia received an award from Catalyst recognizing the bank's success in promoting women to higher management levels. Women now occupy 31 percent of senior management positions, up from 19 percent in 2003. The bank also has set targets for other traditionally disadvantaged groups.[26]

Comparable Worth

In spite of recent advances, the average woman still earns only about three-quarters of what the average man earns; the average *single* woman, however, earns 99 percent of what the average single man earns. The average woman also spends a lower proportion of her potential years of work actually working. For example, for men aged 55–64, the proportion of potential years of work spent actually working is 92.3 percent; for women of that age, the figure is 64.2 percent.[27]

Comparable worth is a legal concept that aims at paying equal wages for jobs that are of comparable value to the employer. This might mean comparing dissimilar jobs, such as those of nurses and mechanics or secretaries and electricians. Proponents of comparable worth say that all the jobs in a company must be evaluated and then rated in terms of basic dimensions such as the level of skill they require. All jobs could then be compared based on a common index. People in different jobs that rate the same on this index would be paid the same. Critics of comparable worth object on the grounds that it ignores the supply and demand aspects of labour. They say, for example, that legislation forcing a company to pay people more than the open market price for their labour (which may happen in jobs where there is a surplus of workers) is another example of unreasonable government interference in business activities.

comparable worth A legal idea that aims to pay equal wages for work of equal value.

In a long-standing comparable worth dispute, the Supreme Court of Canada ruled in 2006 that flight attendants at Air Canada—who have been trying for years to achieve pay equity with male-dominated groups of employees—could compare their pay with the pay of ground crews and pilots because all these employees work for the same company. In spite of this ruling, the president of the Air Canada Canadian Union of Public Employees was concerned that it might take many years before the flight attendants actually saw a wage increase.[28]

In 2005, the Canadian Human Rights Tribunal ruled that a wage gap between male and female clerical workers at Canada Post was the result of systemic sex discrimination. It ordered the company to pay a total of $150 million in back pay to 6000 female clerical workers.[29] In an earlier case, the Tribunal required the federal government to pay a total of more than $3 billion to thousands of civil servants because it had discriminated against workers in female-dominated job classifications. About 85 percent of these workers were women.

Sexual Harassment

sexual harassment
Requests for sexual favours, unwelcome sexual advances, or verbal or physical conduct of a sexual nature that creates an intimidating or hostile environment for a given employee.

quid pro quo harassment
Form of sexual harassment in which sexual favours are requested in return for job-related benefits.

hostile work environment
Form of sexual harassment deriving from off-colour jokes, lewd comments, and so forth.

Within the job context, **sexual harassment** refers to requests for sexual favours, unwelcome sexual advances, or verbal or physical conduct of a sexual nature that creates an intimidating or hostile environment for a given employee. The Canadian Human Rights Act takes precedence over any policies that a company might have developed on its own to deal with sexual harassment problems.

Quid pro quo harassment is the most blatant form of sexual harassment. It occurs when the harasser offers to exchange something of value for sexual favours. A male supervisor, for example, might tell or suggest to a female subordinate that he will recommend her for promotion or give her a raise in exchange for sexual favours. The creation of a **hostile work environment** is a subtler form of sexual harassment. A group of male employees who continually make off-colour jokes and decorate the work environment with questionable photographs may create a hostile work environment for a female colleague. Regardless of the pattern, the same bottom-line rules apply: Sexual harassment is illegal, and the organization is responsible for controlling it. If a manager is found guilty of sexual harassment, the company is liable because the manager is an agent of the company.

Prominent managers who verbally express certain sentiments can find themselves in trouble. When Neil French, a legendary advertising executive and the creative director of WPP Group PLC, gave a speech in Toronto in 2005, he was asked why there were so few women who were creative advertising directors. He replied that women focus too much on their family duties and this usually prevents them from succeeding in management. His comments caused quite a stir, and French soon resigned from his position. It is interesting to note that the Toronto office of Ogilvy & Mather (a subsidiary of WPP) is headed by two creative directors, both of whom are women.[30]

Employee Health and Safety

Employee health and safety programs help to reduce absenteeism and turnover, raise productivity, and boost morale by making jobs safer and more healthful. In Canada, each province has developed its own workplace health and safety regulations. The Ontario Occupational Health and Safety Act illustrates current legislation in Canada. It requires all employers to ensure that equipment and safety devices are used properly. Employers must also show workers the proper way to operate machinery. At the job site, supervisors are charged with the responsibility of ensuring that workers use equipment properly. The Act also requires workers to behave appropriately on the job. Employees have the right to refuse to work on a job if they believe it is unsafe; a legal procedure exists for resolving any disputes in this area. In most provinces, the Ministry of Labour appoints inspectors to enforce health and safety regulations. If the inspector finds a sufficient hazard, he or she has the authority to clear the workplace. Inspectors can usually arrive at a firm unannounced to conduct an inspection.

repetitive strain injuries (RSIs)
Injuries that occur when workers perform the same functions over and over again.

Some industrial work—logging, construction, fishing, and mining—can put workers at risk of injury in obvious ways. But other types of work—such as typing or lifting—can also cause painful injuries. **Repetitive strain injuries (RSIs)** occur when workers perform the same functions over and over again. These injuries disable more than 200 000 Canadians each year and account for nearly half of all work-related lost-time claims.

Retirement

Until the 1990s, Canadian courts generally upheld 65 as the mandatory retirement age, but most Canadian provinces have now abolished mandatory retirement. In spite of this, workers are actually retiring earlier than they used to. In the late 1970s, the average retirement age in Canada was 65, but by 2003 it had dropped to 62.3 years.[31] A Statistics Canada study showed that "boomer" couples are unlikely to retire at the same time, with the woman often staying in the workforce longer than her husband.[32]

Some managers fear that the abolition of mandatory retirement will allow less productive employees to remain at work after age 65, but research shows that the employees who stay on the job past 65 are usually the most productive ones. But there are two other interesting facts that should not be ignored: workers over age 65 are nearly four times as likely to die from work-related causes as are younger workers, and older workers have double the health-care costs that workers in their forties do.[33]

NEW CHALLENGES IN THE CHANGING WORKPLACE

As we have seen throughout this chapter, HR managers face various challenges in their efforts to keep their organizations staffed with effective workers. To complicate matters, new challenges arise as the economic and social environments of business change. Several of the most important HRM issues facing business today are: *managing workforce diversity, managing knowledge workers,* and *managing contingent and temporary workers.*

6 Discuss *workforce diversity,* the management of *knowledge workers,* and the use of *contingent and temporary workers* as important changes in the contemporary workplace.

Managing Workforce Diversity

As we saw in the opening case, one extremely important set of human resource challenges centres on **workforce diversity**—the range of workers' attitudes, values, beliefs, and behaviours that differ by gender, race, age, ethnicity, physical ability, and other characteristics. In the past, organizations tended to work toward homogenizing their workforces, getting everyone to think and behave in similar ways. Partly as a result of affirmative action efforts, however, many organizations are now creating more diverse workforces by embracing more women, ethnic minorities, and foreign-born employees than ever before.

workforce diversity The range of workers' attitudes, values, beliefs, and behaviours that differ by gender, race, age, ethnicity, physical ability, and other relevant characteristics.

Organizations are increasingly recognizing that diversity can be a competitive advantage. By hiring the best people available from every group rather than hiring from just one or a few groups, a firm can develop a higher-quality workforce. Similarly, a diverse workforce can bring a wider array of information to bear on problems and can provide insights on marketing products to a wider range of consumers.

Managing Knowledge Workers

Traditionally, employees added value to organizations because of what they did or because of their experience. In the "information age," however, many employees add value because of what they *know*.[34]

The Nature of Knowledge Work

These employees are usually called **knowledge workers**, and the skill with which they are managed is a major factor in determining which firms will be successful in the future. Knowledge workers, including computer scientists, engineers, and physical scientists, provide special challenges for the HR manager. They tend to work for high-tech firms and are usually experts in some

knowledge workers Workers who are experts in specific fields like computer technology and engineering, and who add value because of what they know, rather than how long they have worked or the job they do.

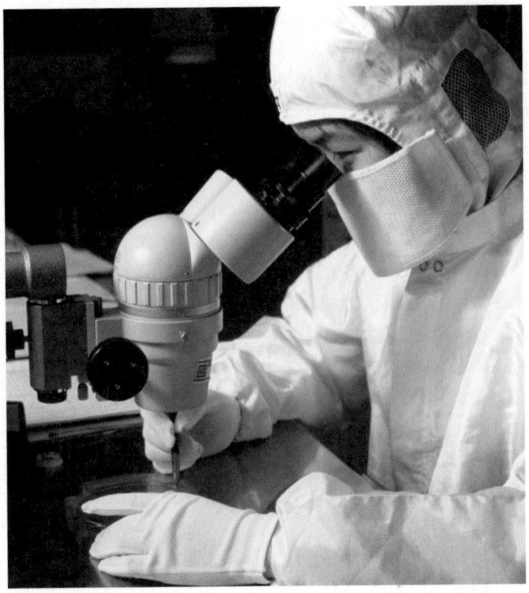

This worker has the extensive training and highly specialized skills that are needed in this high-tech manufacturing process. Management of such knowledge workers is increasingly important for business success.

abstract knowledge base. They often prefer to work independently and tend to identify more strongly with their profession than with the organization that pays them—even to the extent of defining performance in terms recognized by other members of their profession.

As the importance of information-driven jobs grows, the need for knowledge workers continues to grow as well. But these employees require extensive and highly specialized training, and not every organization is willing to make the human capital investments necessary to take advantage of these employees. Even after knowledge workers are on the job, training updates are critical to prevent their skills from becoming obsolete. The failure to update such skills not only results in the loss of competitive advantage, it also increases the likelihood that knowledge workers will move to another firm that is more committed to updating their knowledge.

Knowledge Worker Management and Labour Markets

Organizations that need knowledge workers must introduce regular market adjustments (upward) to pay them enough to keep them. This is especially critical in areas in which demand is growing, as even entry-level salaries for these employees are skyrocketing. Once an employee accepts a job with a firm, the employer faces yet another dilemma. Once hired, workers are subject to the company's internal labour market, which is not likely to be growing as quickly as the external market for knowledge workers as a whole. Consequently, the longer knowledge workers remain with a firm, the further behind the market their pay lags.

The growing demand for knowledge workers has inspired some fairly extreme measures for attracting them in the first place.[35] High starting salaries and sign-on bonuses are common. British Petroleum Exploration was recently paying starting petroleum engineers with undersea platform-drilling knowledge—not experience, just knowledge—salaries in the six figures, plus sign-on bonuses of over U.S.$50 000 and immediate profit sharing. Even with these incentives, HR managers complain that they cannot retain specialists because young engineers soon leave to accept sign-on bonuses from competitors.

Managing Contingent Workers

A contingent worker is one who works for an organization on something other than a permanent or full-time basis. Categories of contingent workers include independent contractors (freelancers), on-call workers, temporary employees (usually hired through outside agencies), leased employees, and part-time workers.

Given the widespread use of contingent workers, HR managers must understand how to use such employees most effectively. One key is careful planning. Even though one of the presumed benefits of using contingent workers is flexibility, it is still important to integrate such workers in a coordinated fashion. Rather than having to call workers in sporadically and with no prior notice, organizations should try to bring in specified numbers of workers for well-defined periods of time.

A second key is understanding contingent workers and acknowledging both their advantages and their disadvantages. The organization must recognize what it can and cannot achieve by using contingent workers. Expecting too much from contingent workers, for example, is a mistake that managers should avoid.

Third, managers must carefully assess the real cost of using contingent workers. Many firms adopt this course of action to save labour costs. The organization should be able to document its labour-cost savings precisely. How much would it be paying people in wages and benefits if they were on permanent staff? How does this cost compare with the amount spent on contingent workers? Even if there are apparent financial advantages in using contingent workers, this might be misleading because contingent workers may be less effective performers than permanent and full-time employees. Organizations must learn to adjust the direct differences in labour costs to account for differences in productivity and performance.

Finally, managers must fully understand their own strategies and decide in advance how they intend to manage temporary workers, specifically focusing on how to integrate them into the organization. For example, an organization with a large contingent workforce must make some major and minor decisions about the treatment of contingent workers relative to the treatment of full-time, permanent workers. Should contingent workers be invited to the company holiday party? Should they have the same access to such employee benefits as counselling services and childcare? Managers need to develop a strategy for integrating contingent workers according to some sound logic and then follow that strategy consistently over time.[36]

DEALING WITH ORGANIZED LABOUR

7 Trace the evolution of, and discuss trends in, *unionism* in Canada.

A **labour union** is a group of individuals working together to achieve shared job-related goals, such as higher pay, shorter working hours, greater benefits, or better working conditions.[37] Labour unions grew in popularity in Canada in the nineteenth and early twentieth centuries. At that time, work hours were long, pay was minimal, and working conditions were

labour union
A group of individuals who work together to achieve shared job-related goals.

This young woman is one of 1500 temporary workers at Sola Optical. Sola keeps at least 100 temps working at all times, because it gives human resource managers both scheduling flexibility and the opportunity to try potential permanent employees.

often unsafe. Workers had no job security and received few benefits. Many companies employed large numbers of children and paid them poverty-level wages. If people complained, they were fired.

Unions forced management to listen to the complaints of all workers rather than to just those few who were brave enough to speak out. Thus the power of unions comes from collective action. **Collective bargaining** is the process by which union leaders and company management negotiate terms and conditions of employment for those workers represented by unions. We discuss the role of collective bargaining in more detail below.

collective bargaining
The process through which union leaders and management personnel negotiate common terms and conditions of employment for those workers represented by the union.

Unionism Today

Although 4.3 million workers in Canada belonged to unions in 2005, union membership *as a proportion of the total workforce* has stagnated during the past few decades, and less than one-third of workers now belong to unions.[38] The highest rates of unionization are found in Newfoundland (37.7 percent) and Quebec (37.5 percent). The lowest rates are found in Alberta (23.0 percent) and New Brunswick (26.4 percent). Nearly half of all union members are women, and they are concentrated in the public sector, which is heavily unionized (72.7 percent). The private sector is not heavily unionized (18.1 percent).[39] In some occupations—for example, teaching and nursing—over 80 percent of workers are unionized. In other occupations—for example, management and food and beverage workers—less than 10 percent of the workers belong to unions.[40] The union movement is more successful in Canada than it is in the United States, where only 13 percent of the workforce is unionized.

Many years ago, unions routinely won certification votes. But in recent years, they have had less success. One reason is that today's workforce is increasingly composed of women and ethnic minorities. Because these groups have much weaker traditions of union affiliation than white males, their members are less likely to join unions when they enter the private-sector workforce. The workforce is also increasingly employed in the service sector, which traditionally has been less heavily unionized.

Another reason is that companies have become far more aggressive in opposing unions. Federal and provincial labour legislation restricts what management of a company can do to keep out a union, but companies are free to pursue certain strategies to minimize unionization, such as creating a more employee-friendly work environment. For example, Japanese manufacturers who have set up shop in North America have avoided unionization efforts by the United Auto Workers (UAW) by providing job security, higher wages, and a work environment in which employees are allowed to participate and be actively involved in plant management.

An employee from Wal-Mart in Chicoutimi stands outside the store after it became the first Wal-Mart in Canada to become unionized. The Quebec Labour Relations Board gave the United Food and Commercial Workers Union the nod to represent the 180 workers.

Trends in Union–Management Relations

The problems that have been experienced by unions have caused some significant changes in union–management relations. Not so long ago, most union–management bargaining was very adversarial, with unions making demands for dramatic improvements in wages, benefits, and job security for members. But with organizational downsizing and a decade of low inflation in Canada, many unions today find themselves able to achieve only modest improvements in wages and benefits for their members. A common goal of union strategy is therefore to preserve what has already been won. For example, unions are well aware that companies have an incentive to relocate jobs to lower-wage foreign countries, so unions have to work hard to keep jobs in Canada and thus maintain job security for members.

This means that unions must co-operate with employers if both companies and unions are to survive and prosper. The goal is to create effective partnerships in which managers and workers share the same goals: profitability, growth, and effectiveness, with equitable rewards for everyone. Even in those sectors of the economy where unions remain quite strong—most notably in the automobile and steel industries—unions have changed their tactics. In the automobile industry, for example, Buzz Hargrove, the president of the Canadian Auto Workers, has been urging members of the union bargaining team to come up with new ideas for improving quality and productivity so that Canadian factories will be more attractive for new investment.[41] The Entrepreneurship and New Ventures box describes an interesting development in labour–management co-operation.

ENTREPRENEURSHIP AND NEW VENTURES

Benchmarking Labour Relations Through Sustainable Development

Arcelor is a leading player in the global steel industry. With a turnover of 30 billion euros in 2004, the company holds leading positions in its main markets: automotive, construction, household appliances, and packaging, as well as general industry. The company—the number one steel producer in Europe and Latin America—has ambitions to further expand internationally to capture the growth potential of developing economies and offer technologically advanced steel solutions to its global customers. Arcelor employs 95 000 associates in over 60 countries, including Canada. The company places its commitment to sustainable development at the heart of its strategy and has ambitions to be a benchmark for economic performance, labour relations, and social responsibility.

Arcelor has signed a worldwide agreement on principles of corporate social responsibility with the International Metalworkers' Federation (IMF) and the European Metalworkers' Federation (EMF). The global steelmaker is the first company in the steel industry to sign such an agreement. Arcelor CEO, Guy Dollé, said: "This agreement is an expression and a confirmation of our principles of responsibility and of our commitment to the respect and fair treatment of each and every member of our staff. As a global company we apply the same high ethical and social standards wherever we operate. We are convinced that this commitment will help us to grow internationally in a sustainable way."

Rob Johnston of the IMF welcomed the international agreement with Arcelor and the value the company places on its workforce. "This agreement not only gives recognition to the vital importance of Arcelor's workforce, but also sets out in clear terms how the company will respect its workers worldwide. We look forward to working with Arcelor to implement this agreement, the first of its kind in the steel sector." Peter Scherrer of the EMF said: "As a major global steel producer, Arcelor is setting high standards in corporate social responsibility and we hope that this will set a trend and that we will see other companies in the steel sector follow this example."

Fundamental social rights covered by the agreement include freedom of choice of employment, non-discrimination, banning of child labour, freedom of association, and the right to collective bargaining. In addition, the agreement covers a number of labour-related matters given a high priority by Arcelor such as health and safety, the environment, social dialogue, communication, and the anticipative management of industrial and economic change. A joint committee will monitor the implementation and application of the agreement.

The Future of Unions

Despite declining membership and loss of power, labour unions remain a significant factor in Canadian business. The labour organizations in the Canadian Labour Congress and independent major unions such as the International Brotherhood of Teamsters and the Canadian Union of Public Employees can disrupt the economy by refusing to work. The votes of their members are still sought by politicians at all levels. In addition, the concessions they have won for their members—better pay, shorter working hours, and safer working conditions—now cover many non-unionized workers as well.

The big question is this: Will unions be able to cope with the many challenges that are currently facing them, or will their power continue to dwindle? The challenges facing unions are many, including the decline of the so-called "smokestack industries" (where union power has traditionally been very strong), employment growth in service industries (where union power has traditionally not been strong), the globalization of business (which has raised the very real possibility of many jobs being moved to areas of the world with lower labour costs), and technological change (which often reduces the number of workers that are needed).

THE LEGAL ENVIRONMENT FOR UNIONS IN CANADA

8 Describe the *major laws governing unionism.*

Political and legal barriers to collective bargaining existed until well into the twentieth century. Courts held that some unions were conspirators in restraint of trade. Employers viewed their employees' efforts to unionize as attempts to deprive the employers of their private property. The employment contract, employers contended, was between the individual worker and the employer—not between the employer and employees as a group. The balance of bargaining power was very much in favour of the employer.

The employer–employee relationship became much less direct as firms grew in size. Managers were themselves employees, and hired managers dealt with other employees. Communication among owners, managers, and workers became more formalized. Big business had more power than workers. Because of mounting public concern, laws were passed to place the worker on a more even footing with the employer.

In 1900, government concern about labour disputes resulted in the passage of the Conciliation Act. The Act was designed to help settle labour disputes through voluntary conciliation and was a first step in creating an environment more favourable to labour. A more comprehensive law came into effect in 1907. The **Industrial Disputes Investigation Act** provided for compulsory investigation of labour disputes by a government-appointed board before a strike was allowed. However, this Act was later found to violate a fundamental provision of the British North America (BNA) Act.

Industrial Disputes Investigation Act
Provided for compulsory investigation of labour disputes by a government-appointed board before a strike was allowed.

Privy Council Order 1003
Recognized the right of employees to bargain collectively.

In 1943, **Privy Council Order 1003** was issued. This order recognized the right of employees to bargain collectively, prohibited unfair labour practices on the part of management, established a labour board to certify bargaining authority, and prohibited strikes and lockouts except in the course of negotiating collective agreements.

Constitution Act
Divided authority over labour regulations between the federal and provincial governments.

The **Constitution Act** (originally the BNA Act), passed in 1867, has also affected labour legislation. This Act allocated certain activities to the federal government (e.g., labour legislation for companies operating interprovincially) and others to individual provinces (labour relations regulations in general). Thus, labour legislation emanates from both the federal and provincial governments but is basically a provincial matter. That is why certain groups of similar employees might be allowed to go on strike in one province but not in another.

Federal Legislation—The Canada Labour Code

Canada Labour Code Legislation that applies to the labour practices of firms operating under the legislative authority of parliament.

The **Canada Labour Code** is a comprehensive piece of legislation that applies to the labour practices of firms operating under the legislative authority of parliament. In 2005, a sweeping review of the Canada Labour Code was announced by the federal Minister of Labour. One of the issues that the review will focus on is whether managers and supervisors should also be protected by labour code restrictions on the number hours they work each week, and whether they should receive overtime pay. The issue came to the forefront after the Manitoba Labour Board ruled that Sharon Michalowski, a manager at Nygard International, was entitled to overtime pay, even though she was a manager and had signed a contract stipulating that she would work whatever hours were required to earn her annual salary of $42 000.[42]

The Canada Labour Code has four main sections.

Fair Employment Practices

This section prohibits an employer from either refusing employment on the basis of a person's race or religion or using an employment agency that discriminates against people on the basis of their race or religion. These prohibitions apply to trade unions as well, but not to non-profit, charitable, and philanthropic organizations. Any individual who believes a violation has occurred may make a complaint in writing to Labour Canada. The allegation will then be investigated and, if necessary, an Industrial Inquiry Commission will be appointed to make a recommendation in the case. Since 1982, fair employment practices have been covered by the Canadian Human Rights Act; they are also covered by the Canadian Charter of Rights and Freedoms.

Standard Hours, Wages, Vacations, and Holidays

This section deals with a wide variety of mechanical issues such as standard hours of work (8-hour day and 40-hour week), maximum hours of work per week (48), overtime pay (at least one and a half times the regular pay), minimum wages, equal wages for men and women doing the same jobs, vacations, general holidays, and parental leave. The specific provisions are changed frequently to take into account changes in the economic and social structure of Canada, but their basic goal is to ensure consistent treatment of employees in these areas.

Safety of Employees

This section requires that every person running a federal work project do so in a way that will not endanger the health or safety of any employee. It also requires that safety procedures and techniques be implemented to reduce the risk of employment injury. This section requires employees to exercise care to ensure their own safety; however, even if it can be shown that the employee did not exercise proper care, compensation must still be paid. This section also makes provisions for a safety officer whose overall duty is to assure that the provisions of the code are being fulfilled. The safety officer has the right to enter any federal project "at any reasonable time."

Canada Industrial Relations Regulations

The final major section of the Canada Labour Code deals with all matters related to collective bargaining.

Provincial Labour Legislation

Each province has enacted legislation to deal with the personnel practices covered in the Canada Labour Code. These laws vary across provinces and are frequently revised; however, their basic approach and substance is the same as in the Canada Labour Code. Certain provinces may exceed the minimum code requirements on some issues (e.g., the minimum wage).

COLLECTIVE BARGAINING

9 Identify the steps in the *collective bargaining process.*

People often associate collective bargaining with the specific act of signing of a contract between a union and a company or industry. In fact, collective bargaining is an ongoing process involving both the drafting and administration of the terms of a labour contract.

Reaching Agreement on the Contract's Terms

The collective bargaining process begins when the union is recognized as the exclusive negotiator for its members. The bargaining cycle begins when union leaders meet with management representatives to begin working on a new contract. By law, both parties must negotiate "in good faith." When each side has presented its demands, sessions focus on identifying the *bargaining zone*. For example, although an employer may initially offer no pay raise, it may expect that it may eventually have to grant a raise of up to 6 percent. Likewise, the union may initially demand a 10 percent pay raise while expecting to accept a raise as low as 4 percent. The bargaining zone, then, is a raise between 4 and 6 percent. Obviously, compromise is needed on both sides if agreement is to be reached. The new tentative agreement is then submitted for a ratification vote by union membership.

Contract Issues

Most of the issues in the labour contract arise from demands that unions make on behalf of their members. Issues that are typically most important to union negotiators include *compensation, benefits,* and *job security.* Certain *management rights* issues are also negotiated in most bargaining agreements.

Compensation

The most common issue is compensation. Unions want their employees to earn higher wages immediately, so they try to convince management to raise wages for all or some employees. Of equal concern to unions is future compensation which is to be paid during subsequent years of the contract. One common tool for securing wage increases is a **cost-of-living adjustment (COLA)**. Most COLA clauses tie future raises to the *Consumer Price Index (CPI)*, a government statistic that reflects changes in consumer purchasing power.

cost-of-living adjustment (COLA) A contract clause specifying that wages will increase automatically with the rate of inflation.

A **wage reopener clause** is now included in some labour contracts as well. Such a clause allows wage rates to be renegotiated at preset times during the life of the contract. For example, a union might be uncomfortable with a long-term contract based solely on COLA wage increases.

wage reopener clause A contract clause that allows wage rates to be renegotiated at preset times during the life of the contract.

Benefits

Benefits that are commonly addressed during negotiations include insurance, retirement benefits, paid holidays, working conditions, and the cost of supplementary health care (prescription drugs, eye care, dental care, etc.). The health care issue is becomingly increasingly contentious during negotiations because the cost of health care is rapidly increasing. General Motors, for example, spends more on health care benefits for its 1.1 million workers than it does on steel. And insurance premiums for drug plans are doubling every five years.[43]

Job Security

In some cases, a contract may dictate that if the workforce is reduced, seniority will be used to determine which employees keep their jobs. Unions are also increasingly setting their sights on preserving jobs for workers in Canada in the face of business efforts to outsource production in some sectors to countries where labour costs are cheaper.

Other Union Issues

Other possible issues might include such specific details as working hours, overtime policies, rest periods, differential pay plans for shift employees, the use of temporary workers, grievance procedures, and allowable union activities (dues collection, union bulletin boards, and so forth). In addition, some contracts are beginning to include formal mechanisms for greater worker input into management decisions.

Management Rights

Management wants as much control as possible over hiring policies, work assignments, and so forth. Unions, meanwhile, often try to limit management rights by specifying hiring, assignment, and other policies. At one DaimlerChrysler plant, for example, the contract stipulates that three workers are needed to change fuses in robots: a machinist to open the robot, an electrician to change the fuse, and a supervisor to oversee the process. Such contracts often bar workers in one job category from performing work that falls within the domain of another. Unions try to secure jobs by defining as many different categories as possible (the DaimlerChrysler plant has over 100). Of course, management resists this practice, which limits flexibility and makes it difficult to reassign workers.

When Bargaining Fails

An impasse occurs if management and labour fail to agree on a new contract. Although it is generally agreed that both parties suffer when an impasse is reached and action is taken, each side can employ several tactics to support its cause until the impasse is resolved.

Union Tactics

A **strike** occurs when employees temporarily walk off the job and refuse to work. On February 10, 2007, nearly 2800 workers at Canadian National Railway went on strike. The strike caused major disruptions in the movement of raw materials and finished goods in Canada, and Ford closed its auto assembly plant at St. Thomas, Ontario, because it couldn't get enough supplies by rail to keep running. On February 24, employees returned to work after reaching a tentative one-year agreement with management.[44] During a strike, unions may picket or launch a boycott. **Picketing** involves having workers march at the entrance to the company with signs explaining their reasons for striking.

strike
A tactic of labour unions in which members temporarily walk off the job and refuse to work to win concessions from management.

picketing
A tactic of labour unions in which members march at the entrance to the company with signs explaining their reasons for striking.

During the period 1996–2005, OECD countries averaged 42 working days lost as a result of strikes. The UK averaged just 23 days lost, France 53, Italy 99, and Canada 208.[45] During the 1981–2003 period, Spain had the highest number of days lost to strikes per thousand employees (418), followed by Italy (315), and then Canada (310). Germany lost only 17 days. The most strike-prone sectors in Canada were mining and energy, and transport/communication.[46] After a strike is over, employees may exhibit low morale, anger, increased absenteeism, and decreased productivity. In these situations, care must be taken to improve communications between management and workers.

Sometimes a union is not permitted to strike. In 2001, the province of Nova Scotia passed a law that forbids strikes by health-care workers in that province.[47] Hospital workers cannot strike in Alberta, PEI, or Ontario either. Strikes may also be illegal if the union does not go through certain necessary steps before striking. The Ontario primary and secondary school teachers' strike in 1997 against the province of Ontario and the nurses' strikes in Quebec and Saskatchewan in 1999 were illegal for this reason.

Management Tactics

lockout
A tactic of management in which the firm physically denies employees access to the workplace to pressure workers to agree to the company's latest contract offer.

strikebreaker
An individual hired by a firm to replace a worker on strike; a tactic of management in disputes with labour unions.

employers' associations
A group of companies that get together to plan strategies and exchange information about how to manage their relations with unions.

decertification
The process by which employees terminate their union's right to represent them.

Management can also respond forcefully to an impasse. A **lockout** occurs when employers physically deny employees access to the workplace. Management might lock workers out, for example, if they fear that workers will damage expensive equipment. In 2005, the CBC locked its employees out for eight weeks when union and management could not agree on the terms of a new collective agreement. As an alternative to a lockout, firms can hire temporary or permanent replacements (**strikebreakers**) for the absent employees.

Companies can also lessen the impact of unions by contracting out—to non-union contractors—a lot of assembly work they used to do themselves. This results in fewer union workers within the company. Companies can also join **employers' associations**—groups of companies that get together to plan strategies and exchange information about how to manage their relations with unions.

The threat of **decertification**—the process by which employees legally terminate their union's right to represent them—is also a deterrent to unions. In 2005, the Manitoba Labour Board decertified Local 832 of the United Food and Commercial Workers for workers at the Hampton Inn & Suites in Winnipeg. The workers said they weren't getting value for the dues they were paying to the union.[48]

In extreme cases, management may simply close down a plant if an agreement cannot be reached with the union. When production workers at a Versatile tractor plant went on strike, no settlement was in sight after many months. The union offered to go back to work, but then management locked the workers out. Eventually, the union agreed to a deal that paid the workers for the entire period they were on strike, but the plant was closed and all the workers lost their jobs.[49]

Mediation and Arbitration

mediation
A method of settling a contract dispute in which a neutral third party is asked to hear arguments from both the union and management and offer a suggested resolution.

voluntary arbitration
A method of settling a contract dispute in which the union and management ask a neutral third party to hear their arguments and issue a binding resolution.

compulsory arbitration
A method of settling a contract dispute in which the union and management are forced to explain their positions to a neutral third party who issues a binding resolution.

Rather than using their weapons on one another, labour and management can agree to call in a third party to help resolve a dispute. In **mediation**, the neutral third party (a mediator) advises the parties about how to reach a settlement. In **voluntary arbitration**, the neutral third party (an arbitrator) dictates a settlement between two sides who have agreed to submit to outside judgment. In some cases, arbitration is legally required to settle bargaining disputes. This **compulsory arbitration** is used to settle disputes between government and public employees such as firefighters and police officers.

Summary of Learning Objectives

1. Define *human resource management*, discuss its strategic significance, and explain how managers plan for human resources. Human resource management, or HRM, is the set of organizational activities directed at attracting, developing, and maintaining an effective workforce. HRM plays a key strategic role in organizational performance. Planning for human resource needs entails several steps. Conducting a *job analysis* enables managers to create detailed, accurate job descriptions and specifications. After analysis is complete, managers must forecast demand and supply for both the numbers and types of workers they will need. Then they consider steps to match supply with demand.

2. Identify the issues involved in *staffing* a company, including *internal* and *external recruiting* and *selection.* Recruiting is the process of attracting qualified persons to apply for jobs that an organization has open. *Internal recruiting* involves considering present employees for new jobs. This approach helps build morale and rewards an organization's best employees. *External recruiting* means attracting people from outside the organization to apply for openings. When organizations are actually selecting people for jobs, they generally use such selection techniques as *application forms, tests, interviews,* and other techniques. Regardless of what selection techniques are used, they must be valid predictors of an individual's expected performance in the job.

3. Discuss different ways in which organizations go about developing the capabilities of employees and managers. If a company is to get the most out of its workers, it must develop both those workers and their skills. Nearly all employees undergo some initial *orientation* process that introduces them to the company and to their new jobs. Many employees are given the opportunity to acquire new skills through various *work-based* and/or *instructional-based programs.*

4. Discuss the importance of *wages and salaries, incentives,* and *benefit programs* in attracting and keeping skilled workers. *Wages and salaries, incentives,* and *benefit packages* may all be parts of a company's *compensation program.* By paying its workers as well as or better than competitors, a business can attract and keep qualified personnel. Incentive programs can also motivate people to work more productively. *Indirect compensation* also plays a major role in effective and well-designed compensation systems.

5. Describe some of the key legal issues involved in hiring, compensating, and managing workers in today's workplace. In hiring, compensating, and managing workers, managers must obey a variety of federal and provincial laws. *Equal employment opportunity* and *equal pay* laws forbid discrimination other than action based on legitimate job requirements. The concept of *comparable worth* states that equal wages should be paid for jobs that are of comparable value to the employer. Firms are also required to provide employees with safe working environments, as set down by the guidelines of provincial occupational health and safety acts. *Sexual harassment* is another key contemporary legal issue in business.

6. Discuss *workforce diversity*, the management of *knowledge workers*, and the use of *contingent and temporary workers* as important changes in the contemporary workplace. *Workforce diversity* refers to the range of workers' attitudes, values, beliefs, and behaviours that differ by gender, race, ethnicity, age, and physical ability. Today, many businesses are working to create workforces that reflect the growing diversity of the population as it enters the labour pool. Although many firms see the diverse workforce as a competitive advantage, not all are equally successful in or eager about implementing diversity programs.

   Many firms today also face challenges in managing *knowledge workers.* The recent boom in high-tech companies has led to rapidly increasing salaries and high turnover among the workers who are best prepared to work in those companies. *Contingent workers* are temporary and part-time employees hired to supplement an organization's permanent workforce. Their numbers have grown significantly since the early 1980s and are expected to rise further. The practice of hiring contingent workers is gaining in popularity because it gives managers more flexibility and because temps are usually not covered by employers' benefit programs.

7. Trace the evolution of, and discuss trends in, *unionism* in Canada. The first unions were formed in the early nineteenth century in the maritime provinces. Many labour organizations sprang up and then faded away during the nineteenth century. In the twentieth century, unions began to develop in earnest. In 1943, *Privy Council Order 1003* gave unions the right to bargain collectively with employers.

Since the mid-1970s, labour unions in Canada have experienced increasing difficulties in attracting new members. While millions of workers still belong to labour unions, union membership as a percentage of the total workforce has begun to decline. Increasingly, unions recognize that they do not have as much power as they once held and that it is in their own best interests, as well as the best interests of the workers they represent, to work with management instead of against it. Bargaining perspectives have also altered in recent years.

8. Describe the *major laws governing unionism.* *Privy Council Order 1003* gave unions the right to bargain collectively in Canada. The *Constitution Act of 1867* allows the federal government to pass labour legislation (e.g., the *Canada Labour Code*) for companies that operate interprovincially, and allows the provincial governments to pass legislation (e.g., the Ontario *Labour Relations Act*) for companies that operate in only one province.

9. Identify the steps in the *collective bargaining process.* Once certified, the union engages in collective bargaining with the organization. The initial step in collective bargaining is reaching agreement on a *labour contract.* Contract demands usually involve wages, job security, or management rights.

Both labour and management have several tactics that can be used against the other if negotiations break down. Unions may attempt a *strike* or a *boycott* of the firm or may engage in a *slowdown.* Companies may hire replacement workers (*strikebreakers*) or *lock out* all workers. In extreme cases, mediation or arbitration may be used to settle disputes. Once a contract has been agreed on, union and management representatives continue to interact to settle worker grievances and interpret the contract.

QUESTIONS AND EXERCISES

Questions for Analysis

1. Why is a good employee–job match important? Who benefits more, the organization or the employee? Why?

2. What benefits do you consider most and least important in attracting workers? In keeping workers? In motivating workers to perform their jobs well? How much will benefit considerations affect your choice of an employer after graduation?

3. Select a job currently held by you or a close friend. Draw up a job description and job specification for this position.

4. Why is the formal training of workers so important to most employers? Why don't employers simply let people learn about their jobs as they perform them?

5. Suppose you are a manager in a non-unionized company. You have just heard a rumour that some of your workers are discussing forming a union. What would you do? Be specific.

6. What training do you think you are most likely to need when you finish school and start your career?

7. Workers at some automobile manufacturers (e.g., Ford, GM, and DaimlerChrysler) are represented by a union, but workers at some other automobile manufacturers are not (e.g., Toyota, Nissan, and Honda). Why is this so?

Application Exercises

8. Interview a human resource manager at a local company. Select a position for which the firm is currently recruiting applicants and identify the steps in the selection process.

9. Interview the managers of two local companies, one unionized and one non-unionized. Compare the wage and salary levels, benefits, and working conditions of workers at the two firms.

10. Obtain a copy of an employment application. Examine it carefully and determine how useful it might be in making a hiring decision.

BUILDING YOUR BUSINESS SKILLS

Getting Online for a Job

Goal

To introduce students to career-search resources available on the internet.

Situation

If companies are on one side of the external staffing process, people looking for work are on the other. Companies need qualified candidates to fill job openings, and candidates need jobs that are right for them. The challenge, of course, is to make successful matches. Increasingly, this matchmaking is being conducted on the internet, where companies are posting jobs and job seekers are posting résumés in response. The number of job postings has grown dramatically in recent years. On a typical Sunday, you might find as many as 50 000 postings on Monster.com, a leading job site. With so many companies looking for qualified candidates online, it makes good business sense to learn how to use the system.

Method

Using internet career resources means locating job databases and preparing and posting a résumé. (You will therefore need access to the internet to complete this exercise.)

Step 1 Team up with three classmates to investigate and analyze specific job databases. In each case, write a short report describing the database (which you and other group members may use during an actual job search). Summarize the site and its features, as well as its advantages, disadvantages, and costs. Start with the following sites and add others you may find on your own:

- Monster, **www.monster.com**
- Careerbuilder.com, **www.careerbuilder.com**
- College Grad Job Hunter, **www.collegegrad.com**

Step 2 Investigate the job opportunities listed on the home pages of various companies. Consider trying the following companies:

- Air Canada, **www.aircanada.ca**
- Dofasco, **www.dofasco.ca**
- Royal Bank, **www.royalbank.com**
- IBM Canada, **www.ibm.com/ca/en/**
- Wal-Mart, **www.walmartstores.com**
- McDonald's, **www.mcdonalds.com**
- Bombardier, **www.bombardier.com**

Write a summary of the specific career-related information you find on each site.

Step 3 Working with group members, research strategies for composing effective cyber-résumés. The following websites provide some helpful information on formats and personal and job-related information that should be included in your résumé. They also offer hints on the art of creating a scannable résumé:

- Spherion, **www.spherion.com/corporate/careercenter/ home.jsp**
- JobSource, **www.jobsource.com**
- CareerMagazine, **www.careermag.com**

Two books by Joyce Lain Kennedy, *Electronic Job Search Revolution* and *Electronic Résumé Revolution*, also contain valuable information.

Step 4 Working as a group, create an effective electronic résumé for a fictitious college or university graduate looking for a first job. Pay attention to format, language, style, and the effective communication of background and goals.

Step 5 Working as a group, learn how to post your résumé online. (Do not submit the résumé you created for this exercise; it is, after all, fictitious.) The databases provided will guide you in this process.

Follow-Up Questions

1. Why is it necessary to learn how to conduct an electronic job search? Do you think it will be more or less necessary in the years ahead?
2. Why do you think more computer-related jobs than non-technical jobs are posted online? Do you think this situation will change?
3. Why is it a waste of time to stylize your résumé with different fonts, point sizes, and centred headings?
4. What is the advantage of emailing your résumé directly to a company rather than applying for the same job through an online databank?

EXERCISING YOUR ETHICS: TEAM EXERCISE

Handling the Layoffs

The Situation

The CEO of a moderate-sized company is developing a plan for laying off some members of the company workforce. He wants each manager to rank his or her employees according to the order in which they should be laid off, from first to last.

The Dilemma

One manager has just asked for help. He is new to his position and has little experience to draw from. The members of the manager's team are as follows:

- Tony Jones: white male, 10 years with the company, average performer, reportedly drinks a lot after work
- Amanda Wiggens: white female, very ambitious, 3 years with company, above-average performer, puts in extra time at work; is known to be abrasive when dealing with others
- George Sinclair: Aboriginal, 20 years with the company, average performer, was previously laid off but called back when business picked up
- Dorothy Henderson: white female, 25 years with company, below-average performer, has filed five sexual harassment complaints in last 10 years
- Wanda Jackson: black female, 8 years with company, outstanding performer, is rumoured to be looking for another job
- Jerry Loudder: white male, single parent, 5 years with company, average performer
- Martha Strawser: white female, 6 years with company, excellent performer but spotty attendance, is putting husband through university

Team Activity

Assemble a group of four students. Your group has agreed to provide the manager with a suggested rank ordering of the manager's employees.

Action Steps

1. Working together, prepare this list, ranking the manager's employees according to the order in which they should be laid off, from first to last. Identify any disagreements that occurred along the way, and indicate how they were resolved.
2. As a group, discuss the underlying ethical issues in this situation and write them down.
3. As a group, brainstorm any legal issues involved in this situation and write them down.
4. Do the ethical and legal implications of your choices always align?
5. Do the ethical and performance implications of your choices always align?

BUSINESS CASE 8

Galt Contracting

Galt Contracting is a small B.C.-based company that plants trees for lumber companies like Canfor, Gorman Brothers, and Riverside. In the spring of each year, Donald Galt, the owner–manager of Galt Contracting, bids on tree-planting contracts that will be available during the upcoming summer. He visits the block of land that is up for bid and looks it over with a lumber company representative. He then develops a bid and submits it to the lumber company. If he is awarded the job, Galt's profit is determined by the amount of the lumber company contract minus the amount he pays his workers.

The Business of Tree Planting

Once Galt knows that he has gotten a contract, he hires tree planters to do the actual tree planting. Galt usually hires university students who are looking for good-paying summer jobs. The work is hard, but tree planters can make very good money because they are paid on a piece-rate system, that is, they are paid a certain amount of money for each tree that they plant. The amount usually varies between 16 and 32 cents per tree, depending on the terrain and the kind of tree that is being planted. The more difficult the terrain is, the higher the piece rate that planters receive.

A tree planter may plant as few as 1000 trees or as many as 2500 each day, depending on the terrain and the planter's skill. On an average day, a reasonably experienced planter can put 1300 seedlings in the ground. Planters don't not have a set lunch break, but eat on the run. They usually leave their lunch boxes at the main cache, and eat about halfway through the day on one of their return trips to the cache to pick up more seedlings.

Each planter is assigned a "piece" to plant for the day, usually an area equal in size to a football field, but not necessarily symmetrical. The limits of each planter's area are marked with flags by the planters as they begin planting in the morning. Planters leave the main cache and begin planting trees in a straight line. As they plant, they "flag a line" which indicates the boundaries of their piece. This involves staking out strips of brightly coloured tape close to the line of trees. This line helps each planter determine where their piece begins and ends. Planting is then done in a back-and-forth pattern within each piece as planters work back toward the main cache as their bag gradually empties. They monitor the number trees left in their planting bags so they can end up near the main cache when they run out of trees.

Trees must be planted in different concentrations on different pieces, and a certain jargon has arisen to describe this activity. For example, if spacing is "2.9," this means that trees must be planted 2.9 metres apart; if spacing is "3.1," this means that trees must be planted 3.1 metres apart. Planters prefer "2.9" days over "3.1" days because they don't have to cover as much ground and can therefore plant more trees and make more money.

Quality Control

A checker—who works for the lumber company—inspects the work of the planters to ensure that they are planting properly. Checkers use a cord to inscribe a circle on randomly chosen part of a piece. On "2.9" days, the checker will ensure that 7 trees are contained in the circle within the cord. The checker also determines whether the trees are planted properly. Trees must not have any air pockets around the roots, there must be no "j-rooted" (crooked) roots, and trees must be planted on the south (sunny) side of any obstacles on the piece. Trees must also be planted close to obstacles so that they are not trampled by the cattle that sometimes graze in the area. If a planter consistently plants too many or too few trees on a piece, the checker can demand that the piece be replanted. This happens infrequently, but when it does, the planter's pay is sharply reduced.

Galt sometimes checks workers himself, especially if he has reason to believe that they are doing a sloppy job. The biggest problem he has encountered is workers who plant large numbers of trees, but do so very poorly. Planters know that if Galt is following them around for any significant period of time, he is suspicious about the quality of their planting. Planters are very hard on each other in terms of quality. They become very upset if one of their group tries to make more money by planting large numbers of trees by cutting corners. Planters put pressure on each other to do a good job because the reputation of the whole group suffers if one or two planters do poor quality work. As well, planters resent those among them who make more money simply by planting large numbers of trees in a poor quality way. A planter who is known to do a sloppy job or who is forced to replant an area might, for example, be nicknamed "j-root."

Planters don't know when the checker will come by. If a planter "gets in good" with a checker, the checker may go easy when checking the planter's work. The checkers are themselves checked by other lumber company employees to ensure that they are doing reasonable quality control work. In turn, the lumber company is

▶▶▶

checked by the provincial government to see that trees are planted properly.

The Problem

Galt has been paying planters on a piece-rate basis for many years, but recently he has become very concerned about it because too many trees are improperly planted and die soon after planting. Galt thinks this is happening because planters are focusing on quantity at the expense of quality (they are so motivated by the money they can earn if they plant a lot of trees that they are doing sloppy work). At the end of last year's planting season, Galt was told in no uncertain terms by one lumber company that if he did not improve the quality of his tree planting, he would not get any more jobs.

The problem is significant enough that Galt has been thinking about dropping the piece-rate system and moving toward a "flat rate" system which would give planters a fixed amount of pay for each day's work. Galt thinks that this would cause planters to take more time and care when planting each tree since they would not have to worry about how much money they were going to make for the day. In the past, Galt has occasionally paid workers on a flat rate, particularly when the terrain was uneven. But this system is not problem-free either. For example, Galt gets the impression that when he pays on a flat-rate basis that planters don't work as hard, and they take more breaks. Galt also knows that planters *like* the piece rate system because they can make good money. The piece-rate system generates friendly competition among planters to see who can be the most productive. Those who plant the most trees have higher status among their peers, and they also earn more money. Overall, Galt thinks that this friendly competition increases the number of trees that are planted.

When the piece rate system is used, there is not much socializing among workers on the site, except when they are bagging up at the main cache at various times throughout the day. Socializing is generally seen as counterproductive because workers who stand around and talk aren't planting trees, and this reduces their pay.

As Galt considered all these facts, the wondered what he should do regarding the payment system he uses for planters.

Questions for Discussion

1. What are the advantages and disadvantages of paying tree planters on a piece-rate system? On a flat-rate system?
2. Review the motivation theories in Chapter 9. What does each of those theories say (or imply) about Galt's idea of dropping the piece-rate system and paying planters a flat rate for each day of work?
3. Devise a payment system for tree planters that minimizes negative consequences. Describe the impact of your proposal on each of the following factors:
   - the motivation levels of the planters
   - the activities of the quality control checkers
   - the level of quality needed in tree planting
   - the needs of the lumber companies
   - Donald Galt's need to run a profitable company
4. What should Donald Galt do?

MYBUSINESSLAB PEARSON mybusinesslab

To improve your grade, visit the MyBusinessLab website at **www.pearsoned.ca/mybusinesslab**. This online homework and tutorial system allows you to test your understanding and generates a personalized study plan just for you. It provides you with study and practice tools directly related to this chapter's content. MyBusinessLab puts you in control of your own learning!

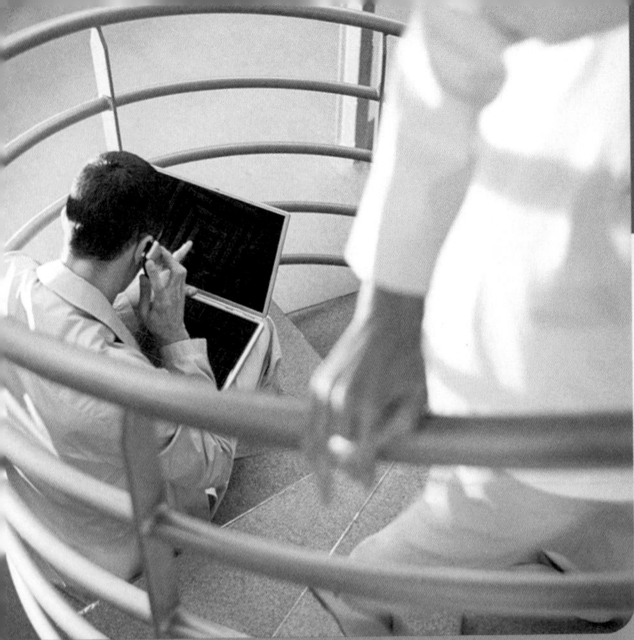

CHAPTER 9

Motivating, Satisfying, and Leading Employees

After reading this chapter, you should be able to:

1. Identify and discuss the basic *forms of behaviour* that employees exhibit in organizations.
2. Describe the nature and importance of *individual differences* among employees.
3. Explain the meaning and importance of *psychological contracts* and the *person–job fit* in the workplace.
4. Identify and summarize the most important *models of employee motivation*.
5. Describe the *strategies* used by organizations to improve job satisfaction and employee motivation.
6. Define *leadership* and distinguish it from *management*.
7. Summarize the *approaches to leadership* that developed in the twentieth century.
8. Describe the most recent ideas about effective leadership.

Keeping Employees Satisfied and Motivated

Managers would like to have employees who are satisfied and motivated to work hard. These attitudes typically cause positive employee behaviour like persisting even in the face of difficulties, being interested in continuous learning and improvement, and being on the lookout for ways to improve quality and productivity. Behaviours like these, in turn, lead to positive outcomes like higher customer satisfaction, greater profits, higher quality, and lower employee turnover.

Because employee motivation and satisfaction are so important, many employee satisfaction surveys are conducted each year. Some companies organize their own in-house surveys, while others hire independent research firms to do the work. These surveys, which ask employees to give their views about a wide range of issues, provide managers with some interesting insights into how Canadian workers feel about their jobs.

One independent research firm, Sirota Survey Intelligence, measured employee satisfaction at 237 different companies during the period 1994–2003. They found that only 14 percent of these companies had workforces that could be classified as "enthusiastic." One interesting conclusion was that the level of enthusiasm of the workforce made a difference in the company's stock prices. When the stock prices of 28 companies with enthusiastic workforces were compared to the average for publicly traded companies, it was found that they outperformed the average prices by more than two-and-a-half times. (Companies with *un*enthusiastic workforces lagged far behind the average stock prices). Companies with enthusiastic workforces also had fewer customer complaints, lower employee turnover, and higher quality in their products.

Various other surveys have also been conducted on issues that relate closely to employee enthusiasm and motivation. A Watson Wyatt Canada survey of more than 3000 Canadian employees revealed the following:

- 46 percent would consider changing jobs if a comparable job became available.
- Only 40 percent of employees believe they have real opportunities for advancement with their current employer.
- Only 27 percent of employees see any connection between their job performance and their pay.

Yet another survey, this one conducted by the Gallup Organization, studied the attitudes of 7200 workers in Canada, the United States, and Great Britain. On most measures of job satisfaction, Canadian workplaces rank behind those of the United States. For example, only 47 percent of Canadian workers were completely satisfied with their boss, while 60 percent of American workers were. Only 29 percent of Canadian workers were completely satisfied with their opportunities for promotion, while 40 percent of Americans were. And 37 percent of Canadian workers were completely satisfied with the recognition they received, while 48 percent of Americans were. Canadian workers were also less satisfied than U.S. workers on several other issues, including the flexibility of their work hours, workplace safety, relationships with co-workers, and the amount of vacation time they received (even though they usually received more than Americans).

The Gallup survey also asked workers about their religious beliefs and found that 90 percent of Americans said they believe in God, but only 71 percent of Canadians do. Industrial psychologist Guy Beaudin thinks this statistic might explain why Canadian workers are less satisfied than American workers. He speculates that since faith is more important in the lives of Americans, they do not rely as much on their work for fulfillment as Canadians do. Canadians may have higher expectations about work as they attempt to give their life a sense of meaning, and this may explain why Canadian workers are less satisfied than American workers. Of course, other factors may explain the difference. For example, Canadian workers are less satisfied with their bosses than American workers are, and this may negatively influence the overall job satisfaction of Canadian workers.

Most employees start work with considerable enthusiasm, but they often lose it. Why? Much of the blame is laid at the feet of managers whose attitudes and behaviours depress employee enthusiasm. These include failing to express appreciation to employees for jobs well done, assuming that employees are lazy and irresponsible, treating employees as disposable objects, failing to build trust with workers, and quickly laying people off when the business gets in trouble. Managerial assumptions about employee satisfaction with pay can be particularly problematic. For example, many managers assume that workers will never be satisfied with their pay. But research by Sirota Survey Intelligence showed that only 23 percent of workers rate their pay as "poor" or "very poor," and 40 percent rate it as "good" or "very good."

One of the simplest ways for managers to motivate workers is to praise them. Yet this occurs far less often than it should. A 2005 *Globe and Mail* web poll showed that 27 percent of the 2331 respondents had *never* received a compliment from their boss. Another 10 percent had not received a compliment in the last year, and 18 percent had not received a compliment in the last month. This result is disturbing, since another survey showed that 89 percent of employees rate recognition of their work as "very important" or "extremely important."

Bad management practices are not the only factor in reducing employee motivation to do their job well. Stress and mental disability (particularly depression) also play a large part. WarrenShepell, a company that provides employee assistance programs, found that 51 percent of the 41 000 people who sought assistance under one of its plans cited high stress as a cause. A Watson Wyatt Staying at Work survey of 100 large Canadian companies found that 56 of them identified rapidly increasing employee mental health disability claims as their top concern (these claims usually include stress as a component).

A report by the Business and Economic Roundtable on Mental Health (BERMH) concluded that employee stress is costing Canadian industry about $60 billion each year, and more than half of that is in lost productivity. The top sources of stress for employees were identified as too much (or too little) work to do, lack of two-way communication up and down the hierarchy, being unappreciated, inconsistent performance review processes, career uncertainty, unclear company policies, and office politics. In 2005, BERMH announced two initiatives to identify the causes of stress and depression among workers. One study will survey more than 100 000 Canadian employees to determine the benefits of early treatment of depression. Another will be a 10-year study of mental health in the workplace.

HOW WILL THIS BENEFIT YOU?

The connections that employees have with their jobs can go a long way toward determining how happy they are with their work. Some people love their jobs, while others hate them. Most people, however, fall somewhere in between. Some of these feelings are caused by the type of leadership employees are experiencing. By understanding the information in this chapter, you'll be better able to understand (1) your own feelings toward your work from the perspective of an employee, (2) the feelings of others toward their work from the perspective of a boss or owner, (3) how you can more effectively function as a leader, and (4) how your manager or boss strives to motivate you through his or her own leadership.

Some employees work hard and have a positive attitude toward their work, while others do just enough to get by and constantly grumble about how awful things are. Successful managers understand what accounts for such differences. To start developing your understanding, we begin by describing the different forms of behaviour that employees can exhibit at work and how employee attitudes and personality influence their work. Then we look at some important ideas about employee motivation, some strategies and techniques used by organizations to improve employee motivation, and how leadership facilitates employee motivation and performance.

1 Identify and discuss the basic *forms of behaviour* that employees exhibit in organizations.

FORMS OF EMPLOYEE BEHAVIOUR

employee behaviour
The pattern of actions by the members of an organization that directly or indirectly influences the organization's effectiveness.

performance behaviours
The total set of work-related behaviours that the organization expects employees to display.

organizational citizenship
Positive behaviours that do not directly contribute to the bottom line.

Employee behaviour is the pattern of actions by the members of an organization that directly or indirectly influences the organization's effectiveness. **Performance behaviours** are the behaviours directly targeted at performing a job. For example, an assembly-line worker who sits by a moving conveyor and attaches parts to a product as it passes by has relatively simple performance behaviours. By contrast, a research-and-development scientist who works in a lab trying to find new scientific breakthroughs that have commercial potential has much more complex performance behaviours.

Other behaviours—called **organizational citizenship**—provide positive benefits to the organization but in more indirect ways. An employee who does satisfactory work in terms of quantity and quality, but refuses to work overtime, won't help newcomers learn the ropes, and is generally unwilling to make any contribution beyond the strict performance requirements of the job is not a good organizational citizen. By contrast, an employee with a satisfactory level of performance who works late when the boss asks and takes time to help newcomers learn their way around is a good organizational citizen.

Counterproductive behaviours are those that detract from organizational performance. **Absenteeism** occurs when an employee does not show up for work. When an employee is absent, legitimately or not, that person's work does not get done and a substitute must be hired to do it, or others in the organization must pick up the slack. **Turnover** occurs when people quit their jobs. It results from a number of factors, including aspects of the job, the organization, the individual, a poor person–job fit, the labour market, and family influences. An organization usually incurs costs in replacing workers who have quit (e.g., lost productivity while seeking a replacement, training someone new).

counterproductive behaviours Behaviours that detract from organizational performance.

absenteeism When an employee does not show up for work.

turnover Annual percentage of an organization's workforce that leaves and must be replaced.

In 2005, the average turnover rate in Canada was 8 percent, up from 6.6 percent in 2004. The turnover rate varied across industries, with retail trade having the highest rate (20.4 percent), followed by services (16.9 percent). The lowest turnover rates were in natural resources (4.1 percent) and communications/telecommunications (4.3 percent). A Conference Board of Canada survey of 347 companies found that 67 percent of them had trouble retaining employees; only 43 percent reported such difficulties in 2004.[1]

Other forms of counterproductive behaviour may be even more costly for an organization. *Theft and sabotage*, for example, result in direct financial costs for an organization. *Sexual and racial harassment* also cost an organization, both indirectly (by lowering morale, producing fear, and driving off valuable employees) and directly (through financial liability if the organization responds inappropriately). *Workplace aggression and violence* are also counterproductive.

INDIVIDUAL DIFFERENCES AMONG EMPLOYEES

Individual differences are physical, psychological, and emotional attributes that vary from one person to another. The individual differences that characterize a specific person make that person unique. *Personality* and *attitudes* are two main categories of individual differences.

2 Describe the nature and importance of *individual differences* among employees.

individual differences Personal attributes that vary from one person to another.

Personality

Personality is the relatively stable set of psychological attributes that distinguish one person from another. In recent years, researchers have identified five fundamental traits that are especially relevant to organizations. These *"big five" personality traits* (shown in Figure 9.1) can be summarized as follows:

personality The relatively stable set of psychological attributes that distinguish one person from another.

- *Agreeableness* is a person's ability to get along with others. A person with a *high* level of agreeableness is gentle, co-operative, forgiving, understanding, and good-natured in their dealings with others. A person with a *low* level of agreeableness is often irritable, short-tempered, uncooperative, and generally antagonistic toward other people. Highly agreeable people are better at developing good working relationships with co-workers, whereas less agreeable people are not likely to have particularly good working relationships.
- *Conscientiousness* refers to the number of things a person tries to accomplish. *Highly conscientious* people tend to focus on relatively few tasks at one time; as a result, they are likely to be organized, systematic, careful, thorough, responsible, and self-disciplined. *Less conscientious* people tend to pursue a wider array of tasks; as a result, they are often

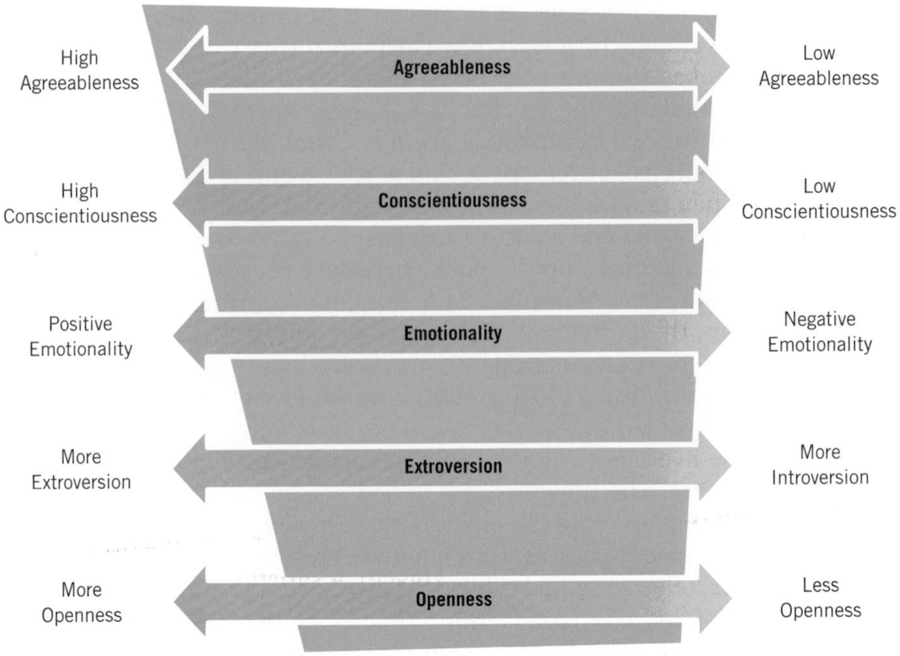

Figure 9.1 The "big five" personality traits.

more disorganized and irresponsible, as well as less thorough and self-disciplined. Highly conscientious people tend to be relatively higher performers in a variety of different jobs.

- *Emotionality* refers to the degree to which people tend to be positive or negative in their outlook and behaviours toward others. People with *positive* emotionality are relatively poised, calm, resilient, and secure; people with negative emotionality are more excitable, insecure, reactive, and subject to mood swings. People with positive emotionality are better able to handle job stress, pressure, and tension. Their stability might also cause them to be seen as more reliable than their less-stable counterparts.
- *Extroversion* refers to a person's comfort level with relationships. *Extroverts* are sociable, talkative, assertive, and open to establishing new relationships, while *introverts* are much less sociable, talkative, and assertive, and more reluctant to begin new relationships. Extroverts tend to be higher overall job performers than introverts and are more likely to be attracted to jobs based on personal relationships, such as sales and marketing positions.
- *Openness* reflects how open or rigid a person is in terms of his or her beliefs. People with *high* levels of openness are curious and willing to listen to new ideas and to change their own ideas, beliefs, and attitudes in response to new information. People with *low* levels of openness tend to be less receptive to new ideas and less willing to change their minds. People with more openness are often better performers due to their flexibility and the likelihood that they will be better accepted by others in the organization.

emotional intelligence (emotional quotient [EQ])
The extent to which people are self-aware, can manage their emotions, can motivate themselves, express empathy for others, and possess social skills.

Emotional Intelligence

Emotional intelligence, while not part of the "big five," also plays a large role in employee personality. **Emotional intelligence**, or **emotional quotient (EQ)**, refers to the extent to which people are self-aware, can manage their emotions, can motivate themselves, can express empathy for others, and possess social skills.[2] Research suggests that people with high EQs may perform better than others, especially in jobs that require a high degree of interpersonal interaction and that involve influencing or directing the work of others. Moreover, EQ appears to be something that isn't biologically based but which can be developed.[3]

Attitudes

People's attitudes also affect their behaviour in organizations. **Attitudes** reflect our beliefs and feelings about specific ideas, situations, or other people. People in organizations have attitudes about many different things: their salary, their promotion possibilities, their boss, their employee benefits, and so on. Especially important attitudes are *job satisfaction* and *organizational commitment*.

attitudes
A person's beliefs and feelings about specific ideas, situations, or people.

- **Job satisfaction** is the degree of enjoyment that people derive from performing their jobs (a related concept—*morale*—refers to the overall attitude people have toward their workplace). A satisfied employee tends to be absent less often, to be a good organizational citizen, and to stay with the organization. Dissatisfied employees may be absent more often, may experience stress that disrupts co-workers, and may be continually looking for another job. Contrary to what a lot of managers believe, high levels of job satisfaction do not automatically lead to higher levels of productivity.
- **Organizational commitment**, sometimes called *job commitment*, reflects an individual's identification with the organization and its mission. Highly committed employees see themselves as a true member of the firm, overlook minor sources of dissatisfaction, and see themselves remaining a member of the organization. Less committed employees are more likely to see themselves as outsiders, to express more dissatisfaction about the work situation, and to not see themselves as a long-term member of the organization.

job satisfaction
Degree of enjoyment that people derive from performing their jobs.

organizational commitment
An individual's identification with the organization and its mission.

MATCHING PEOPLE AND JOBS

Given the array of individual differences that exist across people and the many different forms of employee behaviour that can occur in organizations, it is important to have a good match between people and the jobs they are performing. Two key methods for facilitating this match are *psychological contracts* and the *person–job fit*.

3 Explain the meaning and importance of *psychological contracts* and the *person–job fit* in the workplace.

Psychological Contracts

A **psychological contract** is the set of expectations held by an employee concerning what he or she will contribute to an organization (referred to as *contributions*) and what the organization will provide the employee in return (referred to as *inducements*). If either party perceives an inequity in the contract, that party may seek a change. The employee, for example, might ask for a pay raise, promotion, or a bigger office, or might put forth less effort or look for a better job elsewhere. The organization can also initiate change by training workers to improve their skills, transferring them to new jobs, or terminating them. Unlike a business contract, a psychological contract is not written on paper, nor are all of its terms explicitly negotiated. Figure 9.2 illustrates the essential features of a psychological contract.

psychological contract
The set of expectations held by an employee concerning what he or she will contribute to an organization (contributions) and what the organization will provide the employee (inducements) in return.

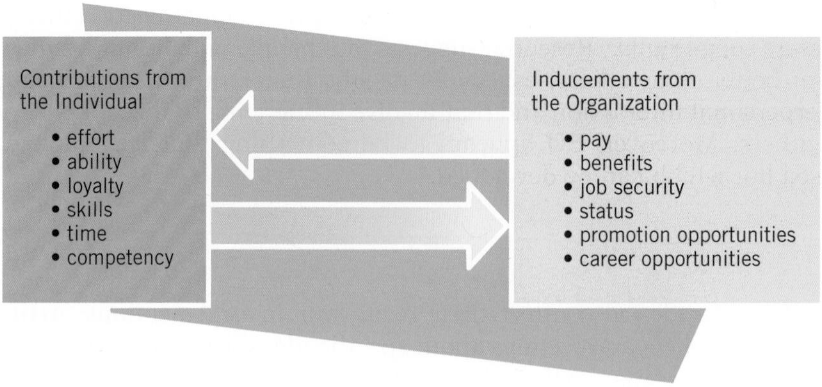

Figure 9.2 The psychological contract.

The downsizing and cutbacks that have occurred in Canadian businesses in recent years have complicated the process of managing psychological contracts. Many organizations, for example, used to offer at least reasonable assurances of job permanence as a fundamental inducement to employees. Now, however, because job permanence is less likely, alternative inducements—such as improved benefits packages or more flexible working hours—may be needed instead.

The Person–Job Fit

person–job fit
The extent to which a person's contributions and the organization's inducements match one another.

The **person–job fit** refers to the extent to which a person's contributions and the organization's inducements match one another. Each employee has a specific set of needs that he or she wants fulfilled, and a set of job-related behaviours and abilities to contribute. If the organization can take perfect advantage of those behaviours and abilities and exactly fulfill those needs, it will have achieved a perfect person–job fit. A good person–job fit, in turn, can result in higher performance and more positive attitudes. A poor person–job fit can have just the opposite effects.

MOTIVATION IN THE WORKPLACE

motivation
The set of forces that causes people to behave in certain ways.

Motivation is the set of forces that causes people to behave in certain ways. For example, while one worker may be motivated to work hard to produce as much as possible, another may be motivated to do just enough to get by. Effective managers recognize that today's workers have a complex set of needs and must be motivated in increasingly complicated ways.

One survey asked workers to identify the things they most wanted at work. Among the things noted were flexible working hours (67 percent), casual dress (56 percent), unlimited internet access (51 percent), opportunities to telecommute (43 percent), nap time (28 percent), massages (25 percent), daycare (24 percent), espresso machines (23 percent), and the opportunity to bring pets to work (11 percent).[4] In another study focusing on fathers, many men also said they wanted more flexible working hours to spend more time with their families.[5] Canadian businesses are starting to respond to these employee preferences. For example, a Conference Board of Canada survey of 312 companies showed the following:[6]

- flexible working hours are offered by 75 percent
- leave for family-related reasons is provided by 74 percent
- childcare assistance or programs are offered by 54 percent

- telecommuting is offered by 49 percent
- eldercare is offered by 48 percent
- unpaid sabbaticals are provided by 43 percent

Over the years, many theories have been proposed to address the issue of motivation. In this section, we will focus on three major approaches to motivation in the workplace that reflect a chronology of thinking in the area: *classical theory* and *scientific management, early behavioural theory,* and *contemporary motivational theories*.

Classical Theory

According to the so-called **classical theory of motivation**, workers are motivated solely by money. In his book, *The Principles of Scientific Management* (1911), industrial engineer Frederick Taylor proposed a way for both companies and workers to benefit from this widely accepted view of life in the workplace.[7] If workers are motivated by money, Taylor reasoned, then paying them more would prompt them to produce more. Meanwhile, the firm that analyzed jobs and found better ways to perform them would be able to produce goods more cheaply, make higher profits, and thus pay—and motivate—workers better than its competitors.

classical theory of motivation A theory of motivation that presumes that workers are motivated almost solely by money.

Taylor's approach is known as **scientific management**. His ideas captured the imagination of many managers in the early twentieth century. Soon, plants across Canada and the United States were hiring experts to perform **time-and-motion studies**. Industrial-engineering techniques were applied to each facet of a job to determine how to perform it most efficiently. These studies were the first "scientific" attempts to break jobs down into easily repeated components and to devise more efficient tools and machines for performing them.[8]

scientific management Analyzing jobs and finding better, more efficient ways to perform them.

time-and-motion studies The use of industrial-engineering techniques to study every aspect of a specific job to determine how to perform it most efficiently.

Early Behavioural Theory

In 1925, a group of Harvard researchers began a study at the Hawthorne Works of the Western Electric Company. Their intent was to examine the relationship between changes in the physical environment and worker output, with an eye to increasing productivity. The results of the experiment at first confused, then amazed, the scientists. Increasing lighting levels improved productivity, but so did lowering lighting levels. And against all expectations, raising the pay of workers failed to increase their productivity. Gradually they pieced together the puzzle: The explanation for the lighting phenomenon lay in workers' response to attention. In essence, they determined that almost any action on the part of management that made workers believe they were receiving special attention caused worker productivity to rise. This result, known as the **Hawthorne effect**, convinced many managers that paying attention to employees is indeed good for business.

Hawthorne effect The tendency for workers' productivity to increase when they feel they are receiving special attention from management.

Following the Hawthorne studies, managers and researchers alike focused more attention on the importance of good human relations in motivating employee performance. Stressing the factors that cause, focus, and sustain workers' behaviour, most motivation theorists became concerned with the ways in which management thinks about and treats employees. The major motivation theories include the *human resources model*, the *hierarchy of needs model*, and *two-factor theory*.

4 Identify and summarize the most important *models of employee motivation.*

The Human-Resources Model: Theories X and Y

In an important study, behavioural scientist Douglas McGregor concluded that managers had radically different beliefs about how best to use the human resources at a firm's disposal. He classified these beliefs into sets of

The Hawthorne studies were an important step in developing an appreciation for the human factor at work. These women worked under different lighting conditions as researchers monitored their productivity. The researchers were amazed to find that productivity increased regardless of whether lighting levels increased or decreased.

Theory X
A management approach based on the belief that people must be forced to be productive because they are naturally lazy, irresponsible, and unco-operative.

Theory Y
A management approach based on the belief that people want to be productive because they are naturally energetic, responsible, and co-operative.

assumptions that he labelled "Theory X" and "Theory Y."[9] The two theories convey very different assumptions about people at work. Managers who subscribe to **Theory X** tend to believe that people are naturally lazy and unco-operative and must therefore be either punished or rewarded to be made productive. Managers who incline to **Theory Y** tend to believe that people are naturally energetic, growth-oriented, self-motivated, and interested in being productive.

McGregor generally favoured Theory Y beliefs. Thus, he argued that Theory Y managers are more likely to have satisfied, motivated employees. Of course, Theory X and Y distinctions are somewhat simplistic and offer little concrete basis for action. Their value lies primarily in their ability to highlight and analyze the behaviour of managers in light of their attitudes toward employees.

Maslow's Hierarchy of Needs Model

hierarchy of human needs model
Theory of motivation describing five levels of human needs and arguing that basic needs must be fulfilled before people work to satisfy higher-level needs.

Psychologist Abraham Maslow's **hierarchy of human needs model** proposed that people have a number of different needs that they attempt to satisfy in their work. He classified these needs into five basic types and suggested that they are arranged in the hierarchy of importance shown in Figure 9.3. According to Maslow, needs are hierarchical because lower-level needs must be met before a person will try to satisfy those on a higher level.[10]

- *Physiological needs* are necessary for survival; they include food, water, shelter, and sleep. Businesses address these needs by providing both comfortable working environments and salaries sufficient to buy food and shelter.
- *Security needs* include the needs for stability and protection from the unknown. Many employers thus offer pension plans and job security.
- *Social needs* include the needs for friendship and companionship. Making friends at work can help to satisfy social needs, as can the feeling that you "belong" in a company.
- *Esteem needs* include the need for status and recognition as well as the need for self-respect. Respected job titles and large offices are among the things that businesses can provide to address these needs.

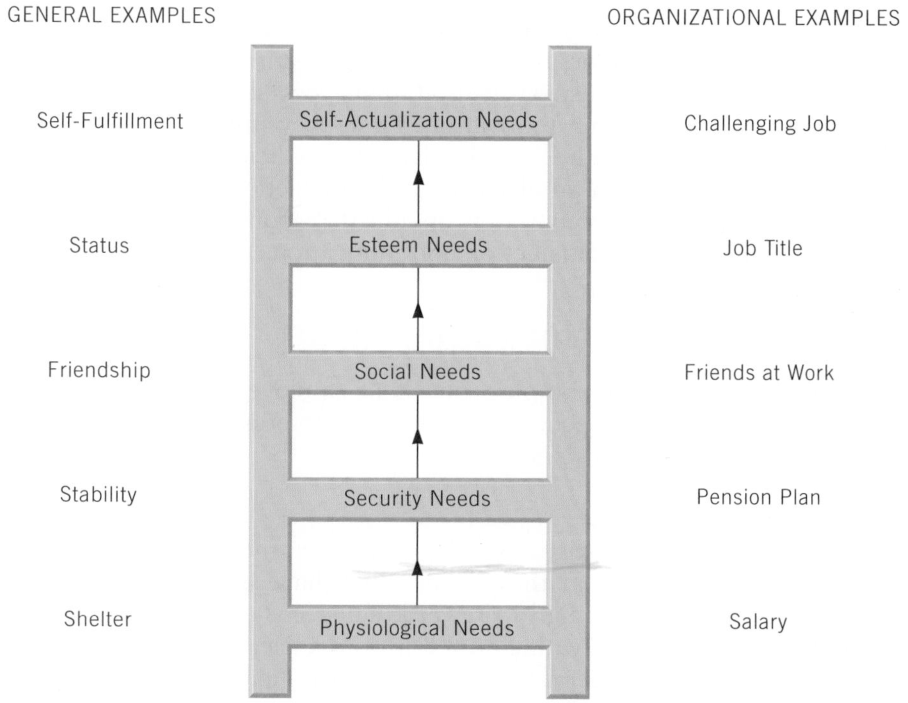

Figure 9.3 Maslow's hierarchy of human needs provides a useful categorization of the different needs people have.

- Finally, *self-actualization needs* are needs for self-fulfillment. They include the needs to grow and develop one's capabilities and to achieve new and meaningful goals. Challenging job assignments can help satisfy these needs.

According to Maslow, once one set of needs has been satisfied, it ceases to motivate behaviour. For example, if you feel secure in your job, a new pension plan will probably be less important to you than the chance to make new friends and join an informal network among your co-workers. If, however, a lower-level need suddenly becomes unfulfilled, most people immediately refocus on that lower level. Suppose, for example, that you are seeking to meet your esteem needs by working as a divisional manager at a major company. If you learn that your division—and consequently your job—may be eliminated, you might very well find the promise of job security at a new firm as motivating as a promotion once would have been in your old company.

Two-Factor (Motivator–Hygiene) Theory

After studying a group of accountants and engineers, psychologist Frederick Herzberg concluded that job satisfaction and dissatisfaction depend on two factors: *hygiene factors*, such as working conditions, and *motivating factors*, such as recognition for a job well done.[11] According to **two-factor theory**, hygiene factors affect motivation and satisfaction only if they are *absent* or *fail* to meet expectations. For example, workers will be dissatisfied if they believe that they have poor working conditions. If working conditions are improved, however, they will not necessarily become *satisfied*; they will simply be *not dissatisfied*. On the other hand, if workers receive no recognition for successful work, they may be neither dissatisfied nor satisfied. If recognition is provided, they will likely become more satisfied.

two-factor theory
A theory of human relations developed by Frederick Herzberg that identifies factors that must be present for employees to be satisfied with their jobs and factors that, if increased, lead employees to work harder.

Motivation factors lie along a continuum from *satisfaction* to *no satisfaction*. Hygiene factors, on the other hand, are likely to produce feelings that lie on a continuum from *dissatisfaction* to *no dissatisfaction*. While motivation factors are directly related to the work that employees actually perform, hygiene factors refer to the environment in which they perform it.

This theory thus suggests that managers should follow a two-step approach to enhancing motivation. First, they must ensure that hygiene factors—working conditions, clearly stated policies—are acceptable. This practice will result in an absence of dissatisfaction. Then they must offer motivating factors—recognition or added responsibility, for example—as means of improving satisfaction and motivation.

Contemporary Motivation Theory

Recently, other more complex models of employee behaviour and motivation have been developed. Two of the more interesting and useful ones are *expectancy theory* and *equity theory*.

Expectancy Theory

expectancy theory
The theory that people are motivated to work toward rewards that they want and that they believe they have a reasonable chance of obtaining.

Expectancy theory suggests that people are motivated to work toward rewards they want and they believe they have a reasonable chance—or expectancy—of obtaining.[12] A reward that seems out of reach, for example, is not likely to be motivating even if it is intrinsically positive. Consider the case of an assistant department manager who learns that a division manager has retired and that the firm is looking for a replacement. Even though she wants the job, she does not apply for it because she doubts that she would be selected. She also learns that the firm is looking for a production manager on a later shift. She thinks that she could get this job but does not apply because she does not want to change shifts. Finally, she learns of an opening one level higher—full department manager—in her own division. She may well apply for this job because she both wants it and thinks that she has a good chance of getting it.

Expectancy theory helps to explain why some people do not work as hard as they can when their salaries are based purely on seniority: Because they are paid the same whether they work very hard or just hard enough to get by, there is no financial incentive for them to work harder. Similarly, if hard work will result in one or more *undesirable* outcomes—say, a transfer to another location or a promotion to a job that requires more travel—employees may not be motivated to work hard.

Equity Theory

equity theory
The theory that people compare (1) what they contribute to their job with what they get in return, and (2) their input/output ratio with that of other employees.

Equity theory focuses on social comparisons—people evaluating their treatment by the organization relative to the treatment of others. This approach says that people begin by analyzing what they contribute to their jobs (time, effort, education, experience, and so forth) relative to what they get in return (salary, benefits, recognition, security). The result is a ratio of contribution to return. Then they compare their own ratios to those of other employees. Depending on their assessments, they experience feelings of equity or inequity.[13]

For example, suppose a new college graduate gets a starting job at a large manufacturing firm. His starting salary is $38 000 per year, he gets a compact company car, and he shares an office with another new employee. If he later learns that another new employee has received the same salary, car, and office arrangement, he will feel equitably treated. If the other newcomer, however, has received $40 000, a full-size company car, and a private office, he may feel inequity.

When people feel that they are being inequitably treated, they may do various things to restore fairness. For example, they may ask for raises, reduce their effort, work shorter hours, or just complain to their bosses.

They may also rationalize their situation ("management succumbed to pressure to promote a woman"), find different people with whom to compare themselves, or leave their jobs altogether.

STRATEGIES FOR ENHANCING MOTIVATION

Understanding what motivates workers and provides job satisfaction is only part of the manager's job. The other part is to apply that knowledge. Experts have suggested—and many companies have instituted—a wide range of programs designed to make jobs more interesting and rewarding and the work environment more pleasant. In this section, we will consider six of the most common types of programs: *reinforcement/behaviour modification theory, goal setting, participative management and empowerment, team management, job enrichment and redesign,* and *modified work schedules.*

Describe the *strategies* used by organizations to improve job satisfaction and employee motivation. 5

Reinforcement/Behaviour Modification Theory

Some companies try to control, and even alter or modify, workers' behaviour through systematic rewards and punishments for specific behaviours. In other words, they first try to define the specific behaviours they want their employees to exhibit (working hard, being courteous to customers, stressing quality) and the specific behaviours they want to eliminate (wasting time, being rude to customers, ignoring quality). Then they try to shape employee behaviour by linking reinforcement with desired behaviours and punishment with undesired behaviours.

Positive reinforcement is used, for example, when a company pays *piecework* rewards—when workers are paid for each piece or product completed. In reinforcement strategies, rewards refer to all of the positive things people receive for working (pay, praise, promotions, job security, and so forth). When rewards are tied directly to performance, they serve as *positive reinforcement*. For example, paying large cash bonuses to salespeople who exceed quotas prompts them to work even harder during the next selling period. Farm equipment manufacturer John Deere uses a reward system based on positive reinforcement, and gives pay increases when workers complete college or university courses and demonstrate mastery of new job skills. Workers at Maple Leaf Sports & Entertainment receive "good job" cards when they do outstanding work. These cards can be redeemed for prizes.[14] Incentive reward systems that are based on positive reinforcement are also used by companies like BC TEL and Drexis Inc.

positive reinforcement
Reward that follows desired behaviours.

Punishment is designed to change behaviour by presenting people with unpleasant consequences if they fail to change in desirable ways. Employees who are repeatedly late for work, for example, may be suspended or have their pay docked. When the National Hockey League or Major League Baseball fines or suspends players found guilty of substance abuse, the organization is seeking to change players' behaviour.

punishment
Unpleasant consequences of an undesirable behaviour.

Goal Setting

Performance goals are commonly used to direct and motivate behaviour. Effective goals have two basic characteristics. First, they are moderately difficult: While a goal that is too easy does little to enhance effort and motivation, a goal that is too difficult also fails to motivate people. Second, they are specific. A goal of "do your best," for instance, does not motivate people nearly as much as a goal like "increase profits by 10 percent." The specificity and clarity of this goal serves to focus attention and energy on exactly what needs to be done.[15]

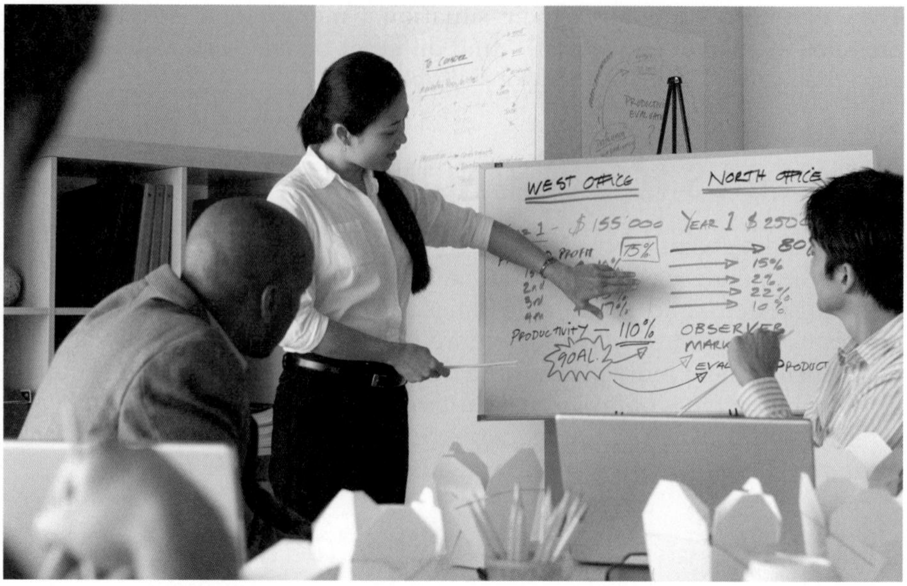

Research has shown that goals that are specific, measurable, and moderately difficult to achieve result in high performance for employees.

management by objectives (MBO) A system of collaborative goal setting that extends from the top of an organization to its bottom.

The most frequent method for setting performance goals is called **management by objectives (MBO)**, which is a system of collaborative goal setting that extends from the top of an organization to the bottom. MBO involves managers and subordinates in setting goals and evaluating progress. After the program is started, the organization specifies its overall goals and plans. Managers then collaborate with each of their subordinates to set individual goals that will best contribute to the organization's goals. Managers meet periodically to review progress toward individual goals, and then, usually on an annual basis, goal achievement is evaluated and used as a basis for starting the cycle over again.

Investors Group Financial Services uses MBO to motivate its sales force in selling financial services. The MBO process begins when the vice-president of sales develops general goals for the entire sales force. This sets the stage for Planning Week, which is held annually in 73 regional centres across Canada. Sales reps review their financial accomplishments and think through their personal and financial goals for the coming year. During Planning Week, sales reps meet with their division managers and reach a consensus about the specific goals the sales reps will pursue during the next year. Each division manager then forwards the proposed objectives for his or her division to the appropriate regional manager. This process continues all the way up to the vice-president of sales, who gives final approval to the overall sales objectives of the company for the coming year.[16]

Participative Management and Empowerment

participative management and empowerment Method of increasing job satisfaction by giving employees a voice in the management of their jobs and the company.

Participative management and empowerment involves giving employees a voice in how they do their jobs and how the company is managed. Such participation should make employees feel more committed to the goals of the organization because they help shape them. Participative management has become more popular in recent years in Canada, as management and labour have become increasingly co-operative. At CP Express and Transport, for example, truck drivers were allowed to decide how to spend \$8 million on new equipment.[17] At Toronto's Delta Chelsea Hotel, employees noticed that in the summer months there were fewer business guests and more vacationers' children in the hotel. As a result of employee suggestions, the hotel installed a waterslide, appointed a "kids' concierge," and set

Participative management gets employees involved in analyzing problems and suggesting solutions. This increases employee satisfaction with, and commitment to, decisions that are made.

up a game room for teens to better serve this market segment.[18] More employers are using **wikis**—websites that allow employees to add content whenever they want on issues that are of use to the business—as a way to enhance employee productivity. Toronto-based technology strategist Don Tapscott says that wikis are part of the move to "mass collaboration" that is going on in business.[19]

wikis
Websites that allow employees to add content whenever they want on issues that are of use to the business.

One popular technique to encourage participative management is the **quality circle**, a group of employees who meet regularly to consider solutions for problems in their work area. The Great-West Life Assurance Company, for example, has reported success with its quality circle program.

quality circle
A technique for maximizing quality of production. Employees are grouped into small teams that define, analyze, and solve quality and other process-related problems within their area.

Participation and empowerment can be used in large firms or small firms, and with managers and operating employees. For example, managers at General Electric who once needed higher-level approval for any expenditure over $5000 now have the autonomy to make their own expense decisions up to as much as $50 000. At WestJet, front-line staff have the right to issue travel credits to customers they feel have not been treated properly. WestJet thinks that the goodwill generated by the practice will increase repeat business.[20]

As the Business Accountability box shows, managers must accept the fact that participation is not desired by all employees. Some will be frustrated by responsibilities they are not equipped to handle. Participative programs may actually result in dissatisfied employees if workers see the invitation to participate as more symbolic than substantive. A good approach is to invite participation only to the extent that employees want to have input, and only if participation will have real value for an organization.

Team Management

One benefit that companies get from using teams is increased motivation and enhanced job satisfaction among those employees working in teams. Although teams are often less effective in traditional and rigidly structured bureaucratic organizations, they often help smaller, more flexible organizations make decisions more quickly and effectively, enhance companywide communication, and encourage organizational members to feel more like a part of an organization. In turn, these attitudes usually lead to higher levels of both employee motivation and job satisfaction.[21]

BUSINESS ACCOUNTABILITY

Encouraging Employees to Share Ideas

The empowerment movement involves tapping into workers' knowledge about the job, encouraging them to be self-motivated and to make suggestions for improvements, and giving them more authority and responsibility so that they feel they are a real part of the company's success. The South Bend, Indiana, manufacturing plant of the Eaton Corporation, illustrates empowerment in practice. The traditional factory hierarchy is avoided, and everyone wears the same blue uniforms. There are no time clocks, and workers report their hours on an honour basis. Production statistics for each work team are posted where everyone can see them. Each work team is responsible for keeping its own members productive and motivated. Empowerment has meant more authority and more responsibility for workers.

Many workers respond favourably to empowerment opportunities, but others do not. Empowerment can be a tricky process, particularly in an era when layoffs are common and employees may not trust management. The empowerment process typically requires workers to share their job knowledge with other workers or with management, but some workers fear that such sharing will allow others to take credit for their hard-earned knowledge, or that sharing their knowledge will weaken their position in the company. So, managers who assume that all workers want to be empowered may be in for a rude shock. The following examples demonstrate this difficulty:

- One employee who cut metal shafts for industrial pumps at Blackmer/Dover Resources Inc. in Grand Rapids, Michigan, had a reputation for being both fast and accurate in his work. He refused to share his knowledge with management (or his fellow workers) because he feared that management would use the knowledge to speed up the workflow and that he would then have to work faster. He is not alone. Many workers have developed extra-fast ways of doing their work, but are reluctant to share those ideas with management. Since managers are always under pressure to improve productivity, the refusal of these workers to share information is frustrating.
- One long-time employee at a small Canadian manufacturing plant taught a younger replacement worker how to run a complicated machine. Shortly thereafter, the older worker became ill and was off work for several weeks. When he returned, he found that the younger worker had essentially taken over his job. The older worker had this to say: "To pass on your experience or your knowledge to others, or to pass on to your fellow workers your secrets, how you assemble it faster, better, or more efficiently for the company, be careful; tomorrow you might have lost your job."

Robin Miller, the executive director of the Winnipeg-based Centre for Education and Work, says that there is a lot of "informal learning" that goes on in companies, but it is not generally recognized or rewarded in Canadian workplaces. If informal learning is not rewarded, we should not be surprised if employees do not share with management the efficient short-cuts they have discovered that allow them to work faster.

The main reason workers conceal knowledge seems to be related to job security. Workers fear that if they share their knowledge, management will use that knowledge to increase output. The increased output will mean that management can get by with fewer workers, so some people will lose their jobs.

In some companies, workers don't share their knowledge because they have become convinced that management doesn't think they have anything to contribute. At the Blackmer/Dover plant, for example, a new plant manager was trying to resolve some production problems that had developed under his predecessor. He asked for worker participation so that he could understand what was wrong in the plant and how things might be improved. Workers were surprised they were being asked for their ideas, because previous management had not solicited worker input. But in this case the workers agreed to help, and the story eventually had a happy ending.

QUESTIONS FOR DISCUSSION

1. What sorts of things can managers do to show that they are being accountable to workers who share their job insights with managers?
2. What sorts of things can employees do to show that they are being accountable to the business for the wages they are receiving for doing their job?

As with participative management, managers must remember that teams are not for everyone. Levi Strauss, for example, encountered major problems when it tried to use teams. Individual workers previously performed repetitive, highly specialized tasks, such as sewing zippers into jeans, and were paid according to the number of jobs they completed each day. In an attempt to boost productivity, company management reorganized everyone into teams of 10 to 35 workers and assigned tasks to the entire group. Each team member's pay was determined by the team's level of productivity. But faster workers became resentful of slower workers because they reduced the group's total output. Slower workers, meanwhile, resented the pressure put on them by faster-working co-workers. As a result, motivation, satisfaction, and morale all dropped, and Levi Strauss eventually abandoned the teamwork plan altogether.

Job Enrichment and Redesign

While MBO programs and participative management can work in a variety of settings, job enrichment and job redesign programs can increase satisfaction only if a job lacks motivating factors to begin with.[22]

Job Enrichment Programs

Job enrichment means adding one or more motivating factors to a job. At one company, a group of eight typists worked in isolated cubicles. Their job involved taking calls from any of dozens of field sales representatives and typing up service orders. They had no client contact; if they had a question about the order, for example, they had to call the sales representative. They also received little performance feedback. Interviews with these workers suggested that they were bored with their jobs and did not feel valued. As part of a job enrichment program, each typist was paired with a small group of designated sales representatives and became a part of their team. Typists were also given permission to call clients directly if they had questions about the order. Finally, a new feedback system was installed to give the typists more information about their performance. As a result, their performance improved and absenteeism decreased markedly.[23]

job enrichment
A method of increasing employees' job satisfaction by extending or adding motivating factors such as responsibility or growth.

Job Redesign Programs

Job redesign recognizes that different people want different things from their jobs. By restructuring work to achieve a more satisfactory person–job fit, job redesign can motivate individuals who have a high need for growth or achievement.[24] Three typical ways of implementing job redesign are to combine tasks, to form natural workgroups, and to establish client relationships.

job redesign
A method of increasing employees' job satisfaction by improving the person–job fit through combining tasks, creating natural work groups, and/or establishing client relationships.

Combining Tasks. This involves enlarging jobs and increasing their variety to make employees feel that their work is more meaningful. In turn, workers are more motivated. For example, the job done by a computer programmer who maintains computer systems might be redesigned to include some system design and development work. The programmer is then able to use additional skills and is involved in the overall system package.

Forming Natural Workgroups. People who do different jobs on the same project are good candidates for natural workgroups. On the one hand, these groups help employees get an overview of their jobs and see their importance in the total structure. On the other hand, these groups help management, and the firm in general, because the people working on a project are usually the most knowledgeable about it and are thus able to solve problems related to it. To see how natural workgroups affect motivation, consider a group where each employee does a small part of the job of assembling radios. One person sees his job as attaching red wires while another sees hers as attaching control knobs. The jobs could be redesigned to allow the group to decide who does what and in what order. The workers can exchange jobs and plan their work schedules. Now they all see themselves as part of a team that assembles radios.

Establishing Client Relationships. A third way of redesigning a job is to establish client relationships—to let employees interact with customers. This approach increases the variety of a job. It also gives workers greater feelings of control over their jobs and more feedback about their performance. Lotus Software uses this approach as a means of granting necessary independence to creative employees. Instead of responding to instructions from marketing managers on how to develop new products, software writers are encouraged to work directly with customers. Similarly, software writers at Microsoft watch test users work with programs and discuss problems with them directly rather than receive feedback from third-party researchers.

Modified Work Schedules

As another way of increasing job satisfaction, many companies are trying out different approaches to working hours and the workweek. Several types of modified work schedules have been tried, including *flextime, compressed workweeks, telecommuting,* and *workshare programs*.

Flextime

flextime
A method of increasing employees' job satisfaction by allowing them some choice in the hours they work.

Some modifications involve adjusting a standard daily work schedule. **Flextime** allows people to pick their working hours. Figure 9.4 illustrates how a flextime system might be arranged and how different people might use it. The office is open from 6 a.m. until 7 p.m. Core time is 9 a.m. until

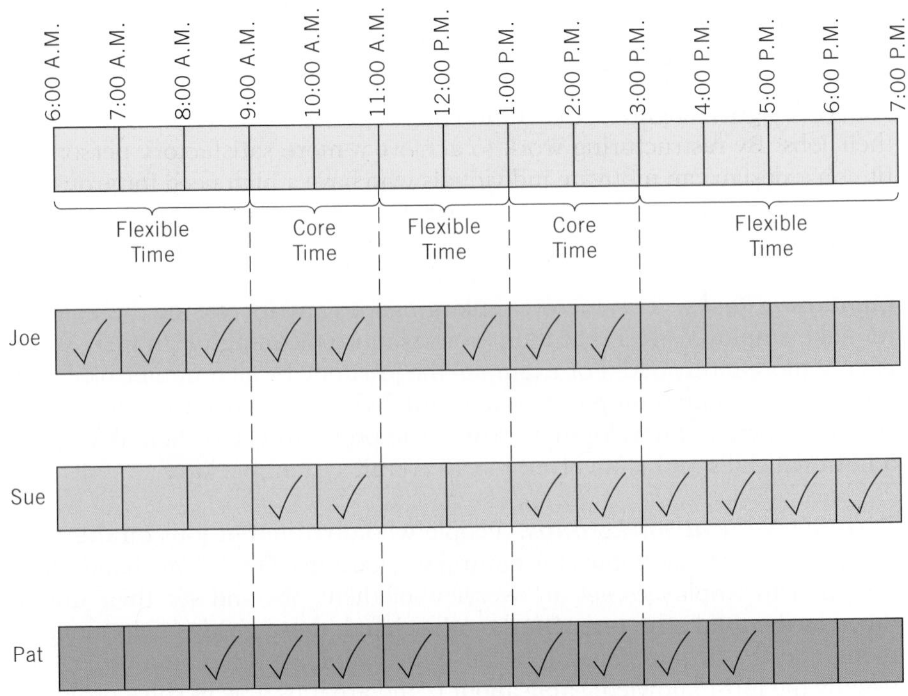

Figure 9.4 Flextime schedules include core time, when everyone must be at work, and flexible time, during which employees can set their own working hours.

11 a.m. and 1 p.m. until 3 p.m. Joe, an early riser, comes in at 6 a.m., takes an hour lunch between 11 a.m. and noon, and finishes his day by 3 p.m. Sue, on the other hand, prefers a later day. She comes in at 9 a.m., takes a long lunch from 11 a.m. to 1 p.m., and then works until 7 p.m. Pat works a more traditional day from 8 a.m. until 5 p.m. At Kraft Canada, employees can choose to arrive at work any time from 7 a.m. to 10 a.m.[25]

A survey conducted by Mercer Human Resources Consulting showed that almost 60 percent of Canadian employers now offer flextime as an option for their workers.[26] Flextime programs give employees more flexibility in their professional and personal lives. Such programs allow workers to plan around the work schedules of spouses and the school schedules of young children, for example. The increased feeling of freedom and control over their work life also reduces individuals' levels of stress.

Compressed Workweeks

In **compressed workweeks**, employees work fewer days per week, but more hours on the days they do work. The most popular compressed workweek is 4 days, 10 hours per day, but some companies have also experimented with 3 days, 12 hours per day. Tellers at the Bank of Montreal in Oakville Place work long days (up to 14 hours), but enjoy a short workweek. Some tellers work 7 a.m. to 9 p.m. Thursday and Friday, and 7:30 a.m. to 5:30 p.m. Saturdays. Others work Monday to Wednesday for 14 hours each day. Employees like the system because it allows them to do personal errands during the day on the weekdays they do not have to be at work.[27]

compressed workweeks
Employees work fewer days per week, but more hours on the days they do work.

Telecommuting

A third variation in work design is **telecommuting**, which allows people to do some or all of their work away from their office. The availability of networked computers, fax machines, cellular telephones, and overnight delivery services makes it possible for many independent professionals to work at home or while travelling. The Mercer Human Resource survey found that 47 percent of professionals telecommute.[28] Statistics Canada estimates that a total of 1.3 million Canadians were telecommuting in 2001.[29] As an extreme example, David Longstaff, a software developer, "commutes" from Waterloo, Ontario, to Leeds, England, each day to provide support for computer programs he has written for the company.[30]

telecommuting
Allowing employees to do all or some of their work away from the office.

The advent of computers and fax machines has made telecommuting an increasingly popular job strategy. Many people in Canada telecommute.

While employees like telecommuting because it saves them time and money, the federal government is concerned that holes may be developing in the health and safety net because employers may not extend workplace health and safety coverage to telecommuters who work at home. That is not the only problem with telecommuting. Workers often report feeling isolated and lonely. To avoid this problem, BC TEL and Bentall Development Inc. jointly developed a satellite telecommuting office in Langley, B.C. It allows workers who used to commute to Burnaby or Vancouver to reduce their travel time considerably and still be able to interact with other workers.[31]

But telecommuting may not be for everyone. Would-be telecommuters must ask themselves several important questions: Can I meet deadlines even when I'm not being closely supervised? What will it be like to be away from the social context of the office five days a week? Can I renegotiate family rules, so my spouse doesn't come home expecting to see dinner on the table just because I've been home all day?

Another obstacle to establishing a telecommuting program is convincing management that it will be beneficial for everyone involved. Telecommuters may have to fight the perception—from both bosses and co-workers—that if they are not being supervised, they are not working. Managers are often very suspicious about telecommuting, asking "How can I tell if someone is working when I can't see them?"

Workshare Programs

worksharing (job sharing) A method of increasing employee job satisfaction by allowing two people to share one job.

A fourth type of modified work schedule, **worksharing** (also called **job sharing**), benefits both employee and employer. This approach allows two people to share one full-time job. For example, Kim Sarjeant and Loraine Champion, who are staff lawyers for NOVA Chemicals in Calgary, share a position advising the human resources department. Sarjeant works Monday through Wednesday, and Champion works Wednesday through Friday.[32] A Statistics Canada survey showed that 8 percent of all part-time workers in Canada share a job with someone. People who share jobs are more likely to be women, to be university educated, and to have professional occupations like teaching and nursing. In addition, job sharers earned more than regular part-time workers.[33]

LEADERSHIP AND MOTIVATION

6 Define *leadership* and distinguish it from *management*.

leadership The process of motivating others to work to meet specific objectives.

Leadership refers to the processes and behaviours used by managers to motivate, inspire, and influence the behaviours of others to meet specific objectives. Each year a "most respected corporate leader" study is sponsored by KPMG and conducted by Ipsos-Reid. In 2005, 250 Canadian CEOs were asked to list the corporate leaders they most respected (other than themselves). Gwyn Morgan, the CEO of EnCana Corp. of Calgary topped the list. Other CEOs that ranked highly were Dominic d'Alessandro (CEO of Manulife Financial Corp.), Gordon Nixon (CEO of Royal Bank of Canada), and Clive Beddoe (CEO of WestJet Airlines).[34]

People often assume that "leadership" and "management" mean the same thing, but they are really different concepts. A person can be a manager, a leader, both, or neither.[35] To illustrate the differences between leadership and management, consider a hospital setting. The chief of staff (chief physician) of a large hospital is clearly a manager by virtue of the position itself. But this individual may or may not be respected or trusted by others, and may have to rely solely on the authority vested in the position to get people to do things. Thus, being a manager does not ensure that a person is also a leader.

On the other hand, an emergency-room nurse with no formal authority may be quite effective at taking charge of a chaotic situation and directing others in how to deal with specific patient problems. Others in the emergency room may respond because they trust the nurse's judgment and have confidence in the nurse's decision-making skills. In this case, the emergency-room nurse is a leader but not a manager.

And finally, the head of pediatrics, supervising a staff of 20 other doctors, nurses, and attendants, may also enjoy the staff's complete respect, confidence, and trust. They readily take her advice and follow directives without question, and often go far beyond what is necessary to help carry out the unit's mission. Thus, the head of pediatrics is both a manager and a leader.

The key distinctions between leadership and management are summarized in Table 9.1.

Organizations need both management and leadership if they are to be effective. For example, leadership is necessary to create and direct change and to help the organization get through tough times.[36] Management is necessary to achieve coordination and systematic results and to handle administrative activities during times of stability and predictability. Management—in conjunction with leadership—can help achieve planned orderly change. Leadership—in conjunction with management—can keep the organization properly aligned with its environment. In addition, managers and leaders also play a major role in establishing the moral climate of the organization and in determining the role of ethics in its culture.[37]

Approaches to Leadership

Summarize the *approaches to leadership* that developed in the twentieth century. 7

Political, religious, and business leaders have profoundly influenced the course of human events throughout history, but careful scientific study of leadership began only about a century ago. In the following paragraphs, we briefly summarize the development of this research.

The Trait Approach

In the first two decades of the twentieth century, researchers believed that leaders had unique traits that distinguished them from their peers. The

Table 9.1 Kotter's Distinctions Between Management and Leadership

Activity	Management	Leadership
Creating an Agenda	Planning and budgeting. Establishing detailed steps and timetables for achieving needed results; allocating the resources necessary to make those needed results happen.	Establishing direction. Developing a vision of the future, often the distant future, and strategies for producing the changes needed to achieve that vision.
Developing a Human Network for Achieving the Agenda	Organizing and Staffing. Establishing some structure for accomplishing plan requirements, staffing that structure with individuals, delegating responsibility and authority for carrying out the plan, providing policies and procedures to help guide people, and creating methods or systems to monitor implementation.	Aligning people. Communicating the direction by words and deeds to all those whose co-operation may be needed to influence the creation of teams and coalitions that understand the vision and strategies and accept their validity.
Executing Plans	Controlling and problem solving. Monitoring results vs. plan in some detail, identifying deviations, and then planning and organizing to solve these problems.	Motivating and Inspiring. Energizing people to overcome major political, bureaucratic, and resource barriers to change by satisfying very basic, but often unfulfilled, human needs.
Outcomes	Produces a degree of predictability and order and has the potential to consistently produce major results expected by various shareholders (e.g., for customers, always being on time; for stockholders, being on budget).	Produces change, often to a dramatic degree, and has the potential to produce extremely useful change (e.g., new products that customers want, new approaches to labour relations that help make a firm more competitive)

trait approach
A leadership approach focused on identifying the essential traits that distinguished leaders.

trait approach therefore focused on identifying the traits that would differentiate leaders from non-leaders. Many traits were proposed as important, including intelligence, dominance, self-confidence, energy, activity (versus passivity), height, and knowledge about the job. As time passed, the list became so long that it lost any practical value. The trait approach was all but abandoned by the middle of the twentieth century, but in recent years it has resurfaced once again. Some researchers now argue that certain traits (for example, intelligence, drive, motivation, honesty, integrity, and self-confidence) provide the *potential* for effective leadership, but only if the person is really motivated to be a leader. The implication is that people without these traits are not likely to be successful leaders even if they try.

The *emotional intelligence* idea that was mentioned earlier in this chapter suggests that successful leaders possess five basic traits: *self-awareness* (the ability to understand your mood), *self-regulation* (the ability to control disruptive impulses), *motivation* (a passion for work), *empathy* (the ability to understand the emotional makeup of others), and *social skill* (proficiency in managing relationships). Managers who do not have these traits, it is argued, will not be successful regardless of how intelligent or highly trained they are.[38]

The Behavioural Approach

behavioural approach
A leadership approach focused on determining what behaviours are employed by leaders.

In the 1940s and 1950s, researchers shifted away from the trait approach and began to look at actual leader behaviours. The goal of the **behavioural approach** was to determine how the behaviours of effective leaders differed from the behaviours of less effective leaders. This research led to the identification of two basic forms of leader behaviour. While different researchers applied different names, the basic leader behaviours identified during this period were:

task-focused leader behaviour
Leader behaviour focusing on how tasks should be performed in order to meet certain goals and to achieve certain performance standards.

employee-focused leader behaviour
Leader behaviour focusing on satisfaction, motivation, and well-being of employees.

- **Task-focused leader behaviour**: Task-focused leader behaviour occurs when a leader focuses on how tasks should be performed in order to meet certain goals and to achieve certain performance standards.
- **Employee-focused leader behaviour**: Employee-focused leader behaviour occurs when a leader focuses on the satisfaction, motivation, and well-being of his or her employees.

A given leader usually tends toward one or the other of these behaviours. But sometimes one leader can change from an emphasis on one type to an emphasis on another type. Consider the case of Andrall (Andy) Pearson, the former chairman and new director of Yum! Brands Inc. (formerly Tricon Global Restaurants), the parent company of Pizza Hut, Taco Bell, and KFC. He has evolved from feared dictator to beloved guru. During his 14-year stint as President and COO of PepsiCo, he was known for being abrasive, numbers-oriented, and hard to please. *Fortune* named him one of the top-10 toughest bosses in 1980, in part because he often drove employees to tears or to quitting if they failed to meet his expectations. In fact, he helped people out the door—his policy was to fire the lowest-performing 10 to 20 percent of all his employees each year.

But over the years Pearson has softened and transformed. When he says, "If I could only unleash the power of everybody in the organization, instead of just a few people... we'd be a much better company," he seems to truly care about employees. And his thinking about leadership has matured: "Great leaders find a balance between getting results and how they get them. A lot of people make the mistake of thinking that getting results is all there is to a job.... Your real job is to get results *and* to do it in a way that makes your organization a great place to work."[39]

The Situational Approach

As time passed, researchers began to realize that there are other leader behaviours that need to be considered besides just the task-focused and employee-focused behaviours, and that there are circumstances in which different combinations of leader behaviour might be more effective than other combinations. For instance, suppose a new manager takes over a work site where workers are satisfied, but they are not very motivated to work hard. The leader should most likely focus on task-focused behaviours in order to improve productivity. But now suppose the situation is different—productivity is high but workers are stressed out about their jobs and therefore have low levels of job satisfaction. In this instance, the manager should most likely concentrate on employee-focused behaviours so as to help improve job satisfaction. This line of thinking led to the development of the *situational approach to leadership*.

The **situational approach**, which emerged during the 1960s, assumed that appropriate leader behaviour varied from one situation to another. This approach was first proposed as a continuum of leadership behaviour (see Figure 9.5). At one extreme, the leader makes decisions alone; at the other extreme, the leader has employees make decisions with only minimal guidance from the leader. Each point on the continuum is influenced by *characteristics of the leader* (including the manager's value system, confidence in subordinates, personal inclinations, and feelings of security), *characteristics of the subordinates* (including the subordinates' need for independence, readiness to assume responsibility, tolerance for ambiguity, interest in the problem, understanding of goals, knowledge, experience, and expectations), and the *characteristics of the situation* (include the type of organization, group effectiveness, the problem itself, and time pressures).

situational approach
Leadership approach that assumes that appropriate leader behaviour varies from one situation to another.

The leadership continuum focused attention on leader behaviours as a continuum instead of being two simple alternatives, and pointed out that various elements of any given situation affect the success of any given leadership style. Although this framework proposed the importance of certain situational factors, it was only speculative. Later models have developed more detailed predictions of how different forms of leader behaviour influence subordinate satisfaction and productivity.

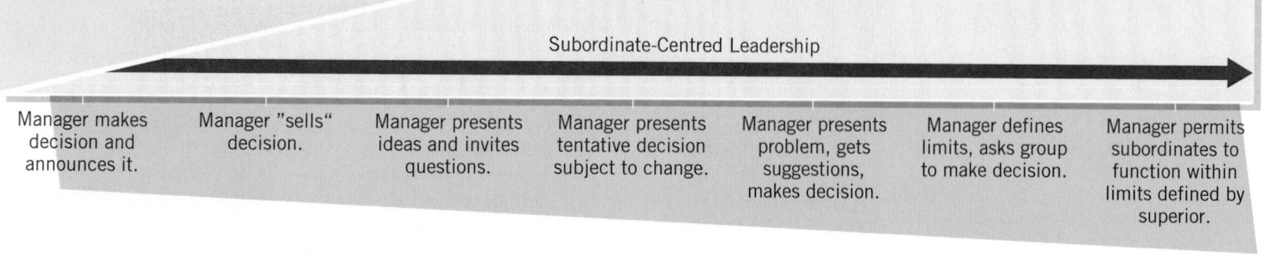

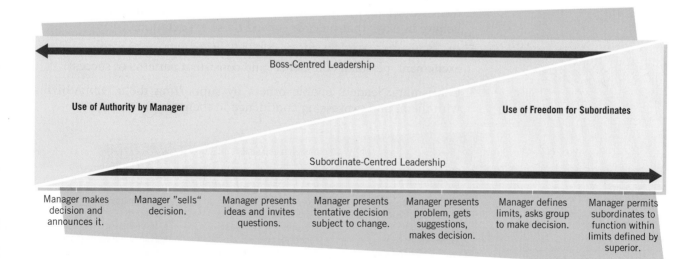

Figure 9.5 The leadership continuum.

Recent Trends in Leadership

8 Describe the most recent ideas about effective leadership.

During the late twentieth and early twenty-first centuries, many new ideas about leadership have been developed. We conclude this chapter with a brief discussion of several of these ideas.

Transformational Leadership

transformational leadership The set of abilities that allows a leader to recognize the need for change, to create a vision to guide that change, and to execute the change effectively.

transactional leadership Comparable to management, it involves routine, regimented activities.

Transformational leadership focuses on the importance of leading for change (as opposed to leading during a period of stability). Thus, **transformational leadership** is the set of abilities that allows a leader to recognize the need for change, to create a vision to guide that change, and to execute the change effectively. By contrast, **transactional leadership** involves routine, regimented activities.

Many leaders may find it difficult to exercise both types of leadership. For example, when Michael Eisner took over the Walt Disney organization in the early 1990s, the company was stagnant and was heading into decline. Relying on transformational skills, Eisner turned things around in dramatic fashion. Among many other things, he quickly expanded the company's theme parks, built new hotels, improved Disney's movie business, created a successful Disney cruise line, launched several other major initiatives, and changed the company into a global media powerhouse. But when the firm began to plateau and needed some time to let the changes all settle in, Eisner was unsuccessful at changing his own approach from transformational leadership to transactional leadership and was pressured into retiring.

Charismatic Leadership

charismatic leadership Type of influence based on the leader's personal charisma.

Charismatic leadership is a type of influence based on the leader's personal charisma. All else being equal, someone with charisma is more likely to be able to influence others than someone without charisma. For example, a highly charismatic supervisor will be more successful in influencing a subordinate's behaviour than a supervisor who lacks charisma.

Charismatic leaders typically have a lot of self-confidence and a strong need to influence others. They also tend to communicate high expectations about follower performance and to express confidence in their followers. Figure 9.6 portrays the three key elements of charismatic leadership that most experts acknowledge today:

1. Charismatic leaders are able to envision likely future trends and patterns, to set high expectations for themselves and for others, and to behave in ways that meet or exceed those expectations.
2. Charismatic leaders are able to energize others by demonstrating personal excitement, personal confidence, and consistent patterns of success.
3. Charismatic leaders enable others by supporting them, empathizing with them, and expressing confidence in them.[40]

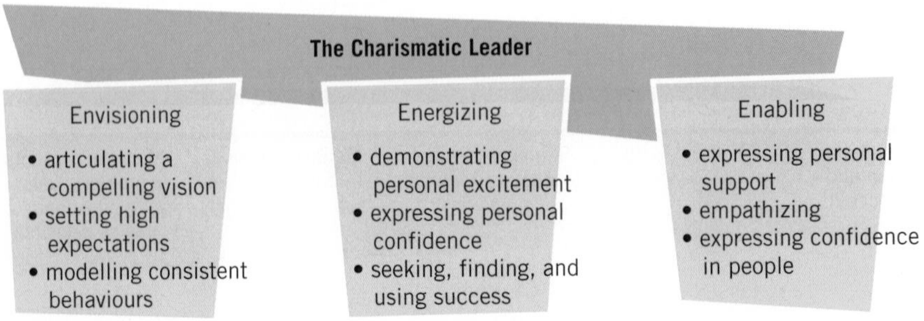

Figure 9.6 Charismatic leadership.

Charismatic leadership ideas are popular among managers today and are the subject of numerous books and articles.[41] Unfortunately, few studies have specifically attempted to test the meaning and impact of charismatic leadership. There are also concerns that some charismatic leaders will inspire such blind faith in their followers that the followers may engage in inappropriate, unethical, or even illegal behaviours simply because the leader instructed them to do so. This tendency likely played a role in the collapse of both Enron and Arthur Andersen, as people followed orders from their charismatic bosses to hide information, shred documents, and mislead investigators.

Leaders as Coaches

Many organizations are now attempting to become less hierarchical—that is, to eliminate the old-fashioned command-and-control mentality often inherent in bureaucratic organizations—and to motivate and empower individuals to work independently. This changes the role of leaders. Whereas leaders were once expected to control situations, direct work, supervise people, closely monitor performance, make decisions, and structure activities, many leaders today are being asked to become a *coach* instead of an *overseer*.[42]

Consider the parallel with an athletic team. The coach selects the players for the team and decides on the general direction to take (such as emphasizing offence versus defence). The coach also helps develop player talent and teaches team members how to execute specific plays. But at game time, it's up to the players to execute plays and get the job done. While the coach may get some of the credit for the victory, he or she didn't actually score any of the points.

For business leaders, a coaching perspective calls for the leader to help select team members and other new employees, to provide some general direction, to help train and develop the team and the skills of its members, and to help the team get the information and other resources it needs. The leader may also have to help resolve conflict among team members and mediate other disputes that arise. And coaches from different teams need to link the activities and functions of their respective teams. But beyond these activities, the leader is expected to keep a low profile and let the group get its work done, with little or no direct oversight from the leader.

Gender and Leadership

Another factor that is altering the face of leadership is the growing number of women advancing to the highest levels in organizations. Given that most leadership theories and research studies have focused on male leaders, developing a better understanding of how women lead is clearly an important next step. For example, do women and men lead differently? Some early observers, for instance, predicted that (consistent with prevailing stereotypes) female leaders would be relatively warm, supportive, and nurturing as compared to their male counterparts. But in reality, research suggests that female leaders are not necessarily more nurturing or supportive than male leaders. Likewise, male leaders are not systematically more harsh, controlling, or task focused than female leaders. Women do seem to have a tendency to be more democratic when making decisions, whereas men have a tendency to be somewhat more autocratic.[43]

Cross-Cultural Leadership

Culture is a broad concept that encompasses both international differences and diversity-based differences within one culture. For instance, when a Japanese firm sends an executive to head up the firm's operation in

Canada, that person will need to be sensitive to the cultural differences that exist between the two countries and consider changing his or her leadership style accordingly. Japan is generally characterized by *collectivism* (group before individual), whereas Canada is based more on *individualism* (individual before group). The Japanese executive, then, will find it necessary to recognize the importance of individual contributions and rewards and the differences in individual and group roles that exist in Japanese and Canadian businesses.

Cross-cultural factors also play a growing role in organizations as their workforces become more diverse. Most leadership research, for instance, has analyzed white male leaders because those individuals dominated leadership positions in North America. But as Asians, Blacks, Aboriginals, and Hispanics achieve leadership positions, it will be necessary to reassess how applicable current models of leadership are when applied to the increasingly diverse pool of leaders.

Canadian Versus American Management Styles. Many Canadian-born managers have achieved significant success in companies that operate outside of Canada. When Bob Kelly was passed over in the race to replace the retiring CEO of the Toronto-Dominion Bank in 2000, he moved to the United States and became the Chief Financial Officer of First Union Corp. In 2006, he was appointed CEO of the Bank of New York Mellon Corp., the 11th largest financial services firm in the United States.[44] Other Canadians who have achieved high positions include Henry McKinnell (CEO of Pfizer, the world's largest pharmaceutical company), Steven McArthur (President of online travel company Expedia), Patricia Arnold, Vice-President of Credit Suisse First Boston), Clara Furse (CEO of the London Stock Exchange), Simon Cooper (CEO of Ritz-Carlton Hotel), and Dominic Barton (Chairman of McKinsey & Company's Asia Region), to name just a few.[45]

The management style of Canadian managers might look a lot like that of Americans, but there are several notable differences. Most fundamentally, Canadian managers are more subtle and subdued than American managers. Canadian managers also seem more committed to their companies, less willing to mindlessly follow the latest management fad, and more open to different cultures because of the multicultural nature of Canada. All of these characteristics are advantageous for Canadian companies that will increasingly be competing in global markets.[46]

Strategic Leadership

strategic leadership
Leader's ability to understand the complexities of both the organization and its environment and to lead change in the organization so as to enhance its competitiveness.

Strategic leadership—which explicitly relates leadership to the role of top management—is a leader's ability to understand the complexities of both the organization and its environment in order to lead change in the organization which will enhance its competitiveness. Steve Jobs, CEO of Apple Computer, is an effective strategic leader. A few years ago, Jobs recognized the potential growth of MP3 players and the fact that those devices used technology that is similar to that found in computers. He therefore directed the development of the Apple iPod, which has become an enormously successful and profitable product.

Ethical Leadership

ethical leadership
Leader behaviours that reflect high ethical standards.

In the wake of recent corporate scandals at firms like Enron and WorldCom, faith in business leaders has been shaken. High standards of ethical conduct are therefore being held up as a prerequisite for effective leadership. More specifically, business leaders are being called on to maintain high ethical standards for their own conduct, to unfailingly exhibit ethical behaviour, and to hold others in their organizations to the same standards—in short, to practise **ethical leadership**.

ENTREPRENEURSHIP AND NEW VENTURES

An Apple a Day

Steve Jobs, a cofounder of Apple Computer, was the visionary behind the first mass-market personal computer, while his cofounder, Steve Wozniak, was the technical wizard. The quirky, creative, and unique culture of Apple was greatly influenced by Jobs, the nonconformist CEO. Apple's unprecedented success helped paved the way for the PC boom of the 1980s. However, under pressure of competition from mainstream computer makers, such as IBM and Compaq, Apple's performance declined.

As the computer maker lost its strategic direction, Jobs was seen by some investors as having failed, and he reluctantly left Apple in 1985. One biography of Jobs sums up the turnover, saying, "While Jobs was a persuasive and charismatic evangelist for Apple, critics also claimed he was an erratic and tempestuous manager." In 1986, Jobs purchased Pixar from George Lucas and became CEO. The computer animation studio produced its first film, *Toy Story*, in 1995. And after a decade of mediocre results at Apple, Jobs was then coaxed into again taking the helm in 1997.

As Apple CEO, Jobs developed a reputation for brilliance, originality, and charm. At the same time, he could be arrogant and hypercritical. He expected others to meet his very high standards and was insulting when disappointed. One industry observer portrayed Jobs as intimidating and power hungry, while others said he commanded "a cult-like following from employees and consumers."

Yet, despite occasional criticism, Jobs is clearly a leader who can deliver success in businesses that are evolving, highly technical, and demanding. Writer Steven Berglas says, "Jobs, the enfant terrible widely reputed to be one of the most aggressive egotists in Silicon Valley, has an unrivaled track record when it comes to pulling development teams through startups." Referring to the bitter battles waged in the PC industry during the period of rapid growth, Berglas believes that Jobs is an empire builder who "held up IBM as the enemy he needed to destroy."

But would Jobs' charisma, confidence, and vision allow him to be a successful leader during times of prosperity and success? Berglas and some other industry observers predicted that Jobs would not be able to switch his leadership behaviour to effectively manage the company during good times. However, as Apple's shares reached an all-time high of $80 and the company had the highest revenues and profits in its history in January 2006, Jobs has proved them wrong.

Indeed, he seems more unbeatable than ever. In a recent interview, Jobs discussed how his passion and focus enable the company to succeed in any type of situation or environment. "Lots of companies have tons of great engineers and smart people," said Jobs. "But ultimately, there needs to be some gravitational force that pulls it all together.... That's what was missing at Apple for a while. There were bits and pieces of interesting things floating around, but not that gravitational pull."

Today, Jobs is riding high. Pixar has released a series of wildly successful movies, such as *Monsters, Inc.*, *Finding Nemo*, and *The Incredibles*. Each film has grossed more than the previous one. *The Incredibles* had sales of $143 million in its opening weekend; the DVD sold five million copies on the first day of release, setting a daily record of $100 million. In early 2006, Disney bought Pixar, making Jobs the largest shareholder of that company.

As for Apple, it's also riding high. For instance, it has released several versions of the hugely popular iPod, supported by the company's online music store, iTunes. The recent iMac and Mac mini have also been bestsellers. And Apple has started making computers using Intel technology, making them much more compatible with PCs. Jobs' confidence is justified by the company's tremendous success and his confidence is growing. "Apple is doing the best work in its history," he says, "and there's a lot more coming." Jobs' uncanny blend of leadership and entrepreneurship has contributed in myriad ways to the successes of both Apple and Pixar, and will likely give Disney a boost as well.

The behaviours of top leaders are being scrutinized more than ever, and those responsible for hiring new leaders for a business are looking more closely at the backgrounds of those being considered. And the emerging pressures for stronger corporate governance models are likely to further increase commitment to select only those individuals with high ethical standards for leadership positions in business and to hold them more accountable than in the past for both their actions and the consequences of those actions.

Virtual Leadership

virtual leadership
Leadership in settings where leaders and followers interact electronically rather than in face-to-face settings.

Finally, **virtual leadership** is also emerging as an important issue for organizations. In earlier times, leaders and their employees worked together in the same physical location and engaged in personal (i.e., face-to-face) interactions on a regular basis. But in today's world, both leaders and their employees may work in locations that are far from one another. Such arrangements might include people telecommuting from a home office one or two days a week to people actually living and working far from company headquarters and seeing one another in person only very infrequently.

How do managers carry out leadership activities when they do not have regular personal contact with their followers? And how do they help mentor and develop others? Communication between leaders and their subordinates will still occur, but it may be largely by telephone and email. In the future, leaders may simply have to work harder at creating and maintaining relationships with their employees that go beyond words on a computer screen. While nonverbal communication, such as smiles and handshakes, may not be possible online, managers can make a point of adding a few personal words in an email (whenever appropriate) to convey appreciation, reinforcement, or constructive feedback. Building on this, managers should then also take advantage of every opportunity whenever they are in face-to-face situations to go further than they might have done under different circumstances to develop a strong relationship.

Beyond these simple prescriptions, there is not much theory or research to guide managers functioning in a virtual world. Hence, as electronic communication continues to pervade the workplace, researchers and managers alike need to work together to first help frame the appropriate issues and questions regarding virtual leadership and then to help address those issues and answer those questions.

Summary of Learning Objectives

1. Identify and discuss the basic *forms of behaviour* that employees exhibit in organizations. *Employee behaviour* is the pattern of actions by the members of an organization that directly or indirectly influences the organization's effectiveness. *Performance behaviours* are the total set of work-related behaviours that the organization expects employees to display. *Organizational citizenship* refers to the behaviour of individuals who make a positive overall contribution to the organization. *Counterproductive behaviours* detract from, rather than contribute to, organizational performance.
2. Describe the nature and importance of *individual differences* among employees. *Individual differences* are personal attributes that vary from one person to another. *Personality* is the relatively stable set of psychological attributes that distinguish one person from another. The "*big five" personality traits* are *agreeableness*, *conscientiousness*, *emotionality*, *extroversion*, and *openness*. *Emotional intelligence*, or *emotional quotient (EQ)*, refers to the extent to which people are self-aware, can manage their emotions, can motivate themselves, express empathy for others, and possess social skills. *Attitudes* reflect our beliefs and feelings about specific ideas, situations, or other people. Especially important attitudes are *job satisfaction* and *organizational commitment*.
3. Explain the meaning and importance of *psychological contracts* and the *person–job fit* in the workplace. A *psychological contract* is the overall set of expectations held by employees and the organization regarding what employees will contribute to the organization and what the organization will provide in return. A good *person–job fit* is achieved when the employee's contributions match the inducements the organization offers. Having a good match between people and their jobs can help enhance performance, job satisfaction, and motivation.
4. Identify and summarize the most important *models of employee motivation*. *Motivation* is the set of forces that cause people to behave in certain ways. Early approaches to motivation were based first on the assumption that

people work only for money and then on the assumption that social needs are the primary way to motivate people. The *hierarchy of human needs* model holds that people at work try to satisfy one or more of five different needs. The *two-factor theory* argues that satisfaction and dissatisfaction depend on *hygiene factors*, such as working conditions, and *motivation factors*, such as recognition for a job well done. *Expectancy theory* suggests that people are motivated to work toward rewards that they have a reasonable expectation of obtaining. *Equity theory* focuses on social comparisons—people evaluating their treatment by the organization relative to the treatment of others.

5. Describe the *strategies* used by organizations to improve job satisfaction and employee motivation. There are several major strategies and techniques often used to make jobs more interesting and rewarding. *Positive reinforcement* is used when a company or manager provides a reward when employees exhibit desired behaviours. *Punishment* is designed to change behaviour by presenting employees with unpleasant consequences if they exhibit undesired behaviours. *Management by objectives (MBO)* is a system of collaborative goal setting that extends from the top of an organization to the bottom. In *participative management and empowerment*, employees are given a voice in how they do their jobs and in how the company is managed. Using *teams* can also enhance motivation. *Job enrichment* adds motivating factors to job activities. *Job redesign* is a method of increasing job satisfaction by designing a more satisfactory fit between workers and their jobs. Some companies also use *modified work schedules*—different approaches to working hours. Common options include *work sharing (job sharing), flextime programs*, and *telecommuting*.

6. Define *leadership* and distinguish it from *management*. *Leadership* refers to the processes and behaviours used by someone to motivate, inspire, and influence the behaviours of others. While leadership and management are often related, they are not the same thing. Leadership involves such things as developing a vision, communicating that vision, and directing change. Management, meanwhile, focuses more on outlining procedures, monitoring results, and working toward outcomes.

7. Summarize the *approaches to leadership* that developed in the twentieth century. The *trait approach to leadership* focused on identifying the traits of successful leaders. The earliest researchers believed that important leadership traits included intelligence, dominance, self-confidence, energy, activity (versus passivity), and knowledge about the job. More recent researchers have started to focus on traits such as emotional intelligence, drive, honesty, integrity, self-confidence, and charisma. The *behavioural approach* identified two basic and common leader behaviours: *task-focused* and *employee-focused* behaviours. The *situational approach to leadership* proposes that there is no single best approach to leadership. Instead, situational factors influence the approach to leadership that is most effective. This approach was proposed as a continuum of leadership behaviour, ranging from having the leader make decisions alone to having employees make decisions with minimal guidance from the leader. Each point on the continuum is influenced by *characteristics of the leader, his or her subordinates*, and the *situation*.

8. Describe the most recent ideas about effective leadership. *Transformational leadership* (as distinguished from *transactional leadership*) focuses on the set of abilities that allow a leader to recognize the need for change, to create a vision to guide that change, and to execute the change effectively. *Charismatic leadership* is influence based on the leader's personal charisma. The basic concept of charisma suggests that charismatic leaders are likely to have self-confidence, confidence in their beliefs and ideals, and a need to influence people. They also tend to communicate high expectations about follower performance and to express confidence in their followers.

Many organizations expect their leaders to play the role of *coach*—to select team members, provide direction, train and develop, but otherwise allow the group to function autonomously. Another factor that is altering the face of leadership is the number of women advancing to higher levels. While there appear to be few differences between men and women leaders, the growing number of women leaders suggests a need for more study. Another changing perspective on leadership relates to cross-cultural issues. In this context, *culture* encompasses international differences and diversity-based differences within one culture. *Strategic leadership* is the leader's ability to lead change in the organization so as to enhance its competitiveness. Business leaders are also being called on to practise *ethical leadership*—that is, to maintain high ethical standards for their own conduct, and to hold others in their organizations to the same standards. As more leaders and employees work in different settings, a better understanding of *virtual leadership* is also becoming more important.

QUESTIONS AND EXERCISES

Questions for Analysis

1. Describe the psychological contract you currently have or have had in the past with an employer. If you have never worked, describe the psychological contract that you have with the instructor in this class.
2. How is the job enrichment/job redesign approach to motivation different from the modified work schedules (flextime, compressed workweek) approach to motivation? Are there similarities between the two approaches? Explain.
3. How can participative management programs enhance employee satisfaction and motivation? Why do some employees not want to get involved in participative management?
4. Research suggests that right after graduation from college or university, students have high levels of job satisfaction on their first job. Levels then drop dramatically as they reach their late twenties, only to increase gradually once they get older. What might account for this pattern?
5. Describe the type of circumstance in which it would be appropriate to apply each of the theories of motivation discussed in this chapter. Which would be easiest to use? Which would be hardest? Why?
6. The impact of virtual leadership is likely to grow in the future. As a potential follower in a virtual leadership situation, what issues would be of most concern to you? What do you think would be the issues of most concern for your boss in such a situation?
7. List three Canadian managers who you think would also qualify as great leaders. Explain why you think they are great leaders.

Application Exercises

8. Assume that you are going to start your own business. What actions should you take to ensure that your employees will be satisfied and motivated? When listing the actions you would take, be specific. As well, explain how each of your proposed actions is consistent with one or more motivation theories.
9. The situational approach to leadership assumes that leaders can change their style as the situation demands. Do you think this is a reasonable assumption? Support your conclusion by finding information about a real manager in a business publication like the *Globe and Mail* or the *Financial Post*.
10. Interview the manager of a local manufacturing company. Identify as many different strategies for enhancing job satisfaction at that company as you can.

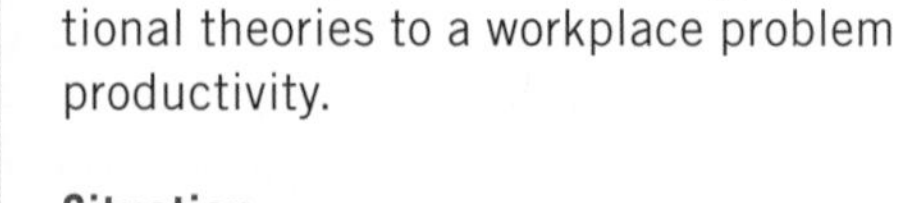

BUILDING YOUR BUSINESS SKILLS

Too Much of a Good Thing

Goal

To encourage students to apply different motivational theories to a workplace problem involving poor productivity.

Situation

Consider a small company that makes its employees feel as if they were members of a large family. Unfortunately, this company is going broke because too few members are working hard enough to make money for it. They are happy, comfortable, complacent—and lazy. With sales dropping, the company brings in management consultants to analyze the situation and make recommendations. The outsiders quickly identify a motivational problem affecting the sales force: Sales reps are paid a handsome salary and receive automatic year-end bonuses regardless of performance. They are also treated to bagels every Friday and regular group birthday lunches that cost as much as $200 each. Employees feel satisfied, but have little incentive to work very hard. Eager to return to profitability, the company's owners wait to hear your recommendations.

Method

Step 1 In groups of four, step into the role of management consultants. Start by analyzing your client's workforce motivation problems from the following perspectives (the questions focus on key motivational issues):

- *Job satisfaction and morale.* As part of a long-standing family-owned business, employees are happy and loyal, in part because they are treated so well. Can high morale have a downside? How can it breed stagnation, and what can managers do to prevent stagnation from taking hold?

- *Theory X versus Theory Y.* Although the behaviour of these workers seems to make a case for Theory X, why is it difficult to draw this conclusion about a company that focuses more on satisfaction than on sales and profits?
- *Two-factor theory.* Analyze the various ways in which improving such motivational factors as recognition, added responsibility, advancement, and growth might reduce the importance of hygiene factors, including pay and security.
- *Expectancy theory.* Analyze the effect on productivity of redesigning the company's sales force compensation structure; namely, by paying lower base salaries while offering greater earnings potential through a sales-based incentive system. How would linking performance with increased pay that is achievable through hard work motivate employees? How would the threat of job loss motivate greater effort?

Step 2 Write a short report based on your analysis, and make recommendations to the company's owners. The goal of your report is to change the working environment in ways that will motivate greater effort and generate greater productivity.

Follow-Up Questions

1. What is your group's most important recommendation? Why do you think it is likely to succeed?
2. Changing the corporate culture to make it less paternalistic may reduce employees' sense of belonging to a family. If you were an employee, would you consider a greater focus on profits to be an improvement or a problem? How would it affect your motivation and productivity?
3. What steps would you take to improve the attitude and productivity of long-time employees who resist change?

EXERCISING YOUR ETHICS: TEAM EXERCISE

Taking One for the Team

The Situation

You are a skilled technician who has worked for a major electronics firm for the past 10 years. You love your job—it is interesting, stimulating, and enjoyable, and you are well paid for what you do. The plant where you work is one of five manufacturing centres your firm operates in a major metropolitan area. The firm is currently developing a new prototype for one of its next-generation products. To ensure that all perspectives are reflected, the company has identified a set of technicians from each plant who will work together as a team for the next two months.

The Dilemma

You have just met with your new teammates and are quite confused about what you might do next. As it turns out, the technicians from two of the manufacturing centres have heard rumours that your company is planning to close at least three of the centres and move production to a lower-cost factory in another country. These individuals are very upset. Moreover, they have made it clear that they (1) do not intend to put forth much extra effort on this project and (2) they are all looking for new jobs. You and the other technicians, though, have heard none of these rumours. Moreover, these individuals seem as excited as you about their jobs.

Team Activity

First, working alone, write a brief summary of how you would handle this situation. For instance, would you seek more information or just go about your work? Would you start looking for another job, would you try to form a sub-group just with those technicians who share your views, or would you try to work with everyone?

Second, form a small group with some of your classmates. Share with each other the various ideas you each identified. Then, formulate a group description of what you think most people in your situation would do. Then, share your description with the rest of the class.

BUSINESS CASE 9

Bringing the Bounty Back to P&G

As the 1990s drew to a close, consumer products powerhouse Procter & Gamble (P&G) found itself in an unfamiliar rut. Fuelled by such megabrands as Tide, Crest, Charmin, Downy, Pampers, Folgers, Bounty, and Pringles, the 1980s had been a decade of phenomenal growth, but in the 1990s—for the first time ever—P&G failed to meet its goal of doubling sales growth each decade. Part of the problem was clear—turnover at the top. P&G had gone through three different CEOs during the 1990s, each with his own unique personality and individual view of how the firm should be run.

The last of the three, Durk Jager, was appointed in 1998. Jager was an avid reorganizer who moved no fewer than 110 000 workers into new jobs. His strategy also called for focusing attention on new products rather than best-sellers. Unfortunately, the innovations that he championed, such as Olay cosmetics, often bombed. He also liked the idea of putting American brand names on P&G's global products, but shoppers in Germany and Hong Kong didn't recognize such brands as "Pantene" and "Dawn," and overseas sales plummeted. Jager tried to acquire drugmakers Warner-Lambert and American Home Products but dropped the idea under pressure from investors who thought the prices too high.

Under Jager's leadership, P&G missed earnings targets and lost $70 billion in market value. To make matters worse, his aggressive personality didn't endear Jager to P&G employees. Insiders reported that morale was falling daily, and many senior managers felt as if they no longer knew what they were supposed to be doing. "I was lost," said one vice president. "It was like no one knew how to get anything done anymore." Jager was fired in mid-2000, after only 17 months on the job.

The announcement of his replacement, 25-year P&G veteran Alan Lafley, was met with yawns and a $4 per share drop in share price. According to conventional wisdom, Durk Jager had saddled the company with so many problems that only a dynamic, strong-willed successor stood a chance of turning things around. And by most accounts, that wasn't Alan Lafley, whose low-key style and bespectacled appearance caused one industry analyst to comment that "If there were 15 people sitting around the conference table, it wouldn't be obvious that he was the CEO." *Fortune* magazine dubbed him "the un-CEO."

But to the surprise of many—and the shock of some—the quiet and unassuming Lafley has succeeded in turning around the stumbling manufacturer when other, more flamboyant leaders might well have failed. In some ways, he's even made it seem easy, demonstrating the virtues of back-to-basics strategy and honest, straightforward leadership. Lafley has also succeeded in restoring a sense of pride in the company and its products and has lifted employee morale in dramatic style.

From day one as CEO, Alan Lafley knew that P&G could do a better job of selling its proven winners. One of his first acts was to allocate more resources to the managers of the company's top 10 brands. "The trick," he recalls, "was to find the few things that were really going to sell, and sell as many of them as you could.... The essence of our strategy," he adds, "is incredibly simple, but I believe the simplicity is its power.... It's Sesame Street–simple, but it works." For example, hair-care managers reinvented the way they marketed Pantene, the company's top-selling hair-care brand. Rather than position products by hair type (for oily hair or fine hair), new campaigns focused on the looks that customers wanted—say, more curls or more volume. Sales went up by 8 percent.

Instead of insisting that new products be developed internally, Lafley also started acquiring small, idea-driven firms. He announced that 50 percent of the company's product innovations should come through such acquisitions. If the strategy proves successful, Lafley explains, "We would double the productivity of our current investment in R&D." Lafley also demands more marketability in new products, reminding researchers, "Innovation is in the consumer's eyes.... It isn't a great innovation until [the customer] loves it and purchases it."

Lafley is shaking up P&G's staid culture in other ways, too. "I have made a lot of symbolic, very physical changes," he says, "so people understand we are in the business of change." At the company's headquarters, product managers have moved out of executive suites to work more closely with employees. Wood paneling and oil paintings are coming down so that top managers can work as teams in modern, open spaces. The penthouse floor is now a learning centre, where top executives conduct lessons and share knowledge with the workforce. "I really believe knowledge is power," says Lafley, "and translating knowledge into action in the marketplace is one of the things that distinguishes leadership."

Not surprisingly, communication between managers, workers, board members, and even competitors has opened up. "You can tell him bad news or things you'd be afraid to tell other bosses," says one vice president of Lafley. The CEO rewards managers for financial results, but is harsh on poor performers—half of the top team is new.

With a series of small changes, Alan Lafley has had a powerful impact on P&G's performance. Since he took over, earnings regularly beat expectations, and stock price has risen 70 percent. Profits are up 49 percent over last year. As for Lafley himself, he continues to emphasize the basics. "Nearly 2 billion times a day," he reminds his employees, "P&G products are put to the test when consumers use [them].... When we get this right... then we begin to earn the trust on which great brands are built."

Questions for Discussion

1. Discuss the role of psychological contracts at Procter & Gamble.
2. How important are job satisfaction and morale to a large firm such as P&G?
3. Show how various theories of motivation apply to P&G.
4. What does this case illustrate about the nature of leadership?
5. Compare and contrast the leadership approaches used by Durk Jager and Alan Lafley.

MYBUSINESSLAB

To improve your grade, visit the MyBusinessLab website at **www.pearsoned.ca/mybusinesslab**. This online homework and tutorial system allows you to test your understanding and generates a personalized study plan just for you. It provides you with study and practice tools directly related to this chapter's content. MyBusinessLab puts you in control of your own learning!

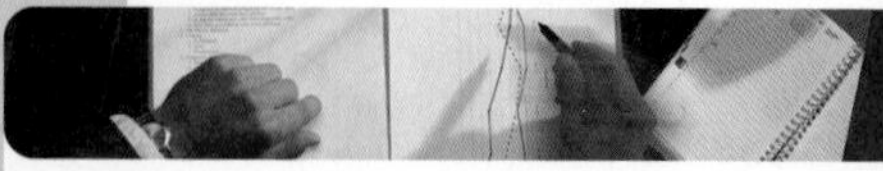

CRAFTING A BUSINESS PLAN

Part 2(a): The Business of Managing

Goal of the Exercise

In Part 1 of the business plan project, you formulated a basic identity for your business. Part 2(a) of the business plan project asks you to think about the goals of your business, some internal and external factors affecting the business, and the organizational structure of the business.

Exercise Background: Part 2(a) of the Business Plan

As you learned in Chapter 6, every business sets goals. In this part of the plan, you'll define some of the goals for your business. Part 2(a) of the business plan also asks you to perform a basic SWOT analysis for your business. As you'll recall from Chapter 6, a SWOT analysis looks at the business's *strengths*, *weaknesses*, *opportunities*, and *threats*. The strengths and weaknesses are internal factors—things that the business can control. The opportunities and threats are generally external factors that affect the business:

Sociocultural forces—Will changes in population or culture help your business or hurt it?
Economic forces—Will changes in the economy help your business or hurt it?
Technological forces—Will changes in technology help your business or hurt it?
Competitive forces—Does your business face much competition or very little?
Political–legal forces—Will changes in laws help your business or hurt it?

Each of these forces will affect different businesses in different ways, and some of these may not apply to your business at all.

Part 2(a) of the business plan also asks you to determine how the business is to be run. One thing you'll need to do is create an organizational chart to get you thinking about the different tasks needed for a successful business.

YOUR ASSIGNMENT mybusinesslab

Step 1

Open the saved *Business Plan* file you began working on in Part 1. You will continue to work from the same file you started working on in Part 1.

Step 2

For the purposes of this assignment, you will answer the questions in "Part 2(a): The Business of Managing."

1. Provide a brief mission statement for your business.

   Hint: Refer to the discussion of mission statements in Chapter 6. Be sure to include the name of your business, how you will stand out from your competition, and why a customer will buy from you.

2. Consider the goals for your business. What are three of your business goals for the first year? What are two intermediate to long-term goals?

   Hint: Refer to the discussion of goal setting in Chapter 6. Be as specific and realistic as possible with the goals you set. For example, if you plan on selling a service, how many customers do you want by the end of the first year, and how much do you want each customer to spend?

3. Perform a basic SWOT analysis for your business, listing its main strengths, weaknesses, opportunities, and threats.

   Hint: We explained previously what factors you should consider in your basic SWOT analysis. Look around at your world, talk to classmates, or talk to your instructor for other ideas in performing your SWOT analysis.

4. Who will manage the business?

   Hint: Refer to the discussion of managers in Chapter 6. Think about how many levels of management as well as what kinds of managers your business needs.

▶▶▶

▶▶▶

5. Show how the "team" fits together by creating a simple organization chart for your business. Your chart should indicate who will work for each manager as well as each person's job title.

Hint: As you create your organizational chart, consider the different tasks involved in the business. Whom will each person report to? Refer to the discussion of organizational structure in Chapter 7 for information to get you started.

CRAFTING A BUSINESS PLAN

Part 2(b): The Business of Managing

Goal of the Exercise

At this point, your business has an identity and you've described the factors that will affect your business and how you will operate it. Part 2(b) of the business plan project asks you to think about your employees, the jobs they will be performing, and the ways in which you can lead and motivate them.

Exercise Background: Part 2(b) of the Business Plan

To complete this part of the plan, you need to refer back to the organizational chart that you created in Part 2(a). In this part of the business plan exercise, you'll take the different job titles you created in the organizational chart and give thought to the *skills* that employees will need to bring to the job *before* they begin. You'll also consider the *training* you'll need to provide *after* they are hired, as well as how you'll compensate your employees. Part 2(b) of the business plan also asks you to consider how you'll lead your employees and keep them happy and motivated.

YOUR ASSIGNMENT

PEARSON mybusinesslab

Step 1

Open the *Business Plan* file you have been working on.

Step 2

For the purposes of this assignment, you will answer the questions in "Part 2(b): The Business of Managing."

1. What do you see as the "corporate culture" of your business? What types of employee behaviours, such as organizational citizenship, will you expect?

   Hint: Will your business demand a casual environment or a more professional environment? Refer to the discussion on employee behaviour in Chapter 9 for information on organizational citizenship and other employee behaviours.

2. What is your philosophy on leadership? How will you manage your employees day-to-day?

   Hint: Refer to the discussion on leadership in Chapter 9 to help you formulate your thoughts.

3. Looking back at your organizational chart in Part 2(a), briefly create a job description for each team member.

   Hint: As you learned in Chapter 8, a job description lists the duties and responsibilities of a job, its working conditions, and the tools, materials, equipment, and information used to perform it. Imagine your business on a typical day. Who is working and what is each person's responsibilities?

4. Next, create a job specification for each job, listing the skills and other credentials and qualifications needed to perform the job effectively.

   Hint: As you write your job specifications, consider what you would write if you were making an ad for the position. What would the new employee need to bring to the job in order to qualify for the position?

5. What sort of training, if any, will your employees need once they are hired? How will you provide this training?

   Hint: Refer to the discussion of training in Chapter 8. Will you offer your employees on-the-job training? Off-the-job training? Vestibule training?

6. A major factor in retaining skilled workers is a company's compensation system—the total package of rewards that it offers employees in return for their labour. Part of this compensation system includes wages/salaries. What wages or salaries will you offer for each job? Why did you decide on that pay rate?

   Hint: Refer to Chapter 8 for more information on forms of compensation.

7. As you learned in Chapter 8, incentive programs are special programs designed to motivate high performance. What incentives will you use to motivate your workforce?

   Hint: Be creative and look beyond a simple answer, such as giving pay increases. Ask yourself, who are my employees and what is important to them? Refer to Chapter 8 for more information on the types of incentives you may want to consider.

Note: Once you have answered the questions, save your Word document. You'll be answering additional questions in later chapters.

CBC VIDEO CASE II-1

God in the Workplace

Bruce Smith used to play in the CFL. Now he is a "chaplain on call" who counsels managers in the heart of Toronto's financial district (for free). He is decidedly Christian in his views, and presents Jesus as an alternative for people who are having problems. His approach is to present this as an option. He thinks there is as much of a hunger for religion in Canada as there is in the United States, since he talks to people everyday in the marketplace who want to talk about Christian values. But, says Smith, Canadians are not as open about religion as Americans are. Smith feels that Canadian companies need certain basic values and convictions to function well. Smith is one of only a few people doing corporate chaplaincy in Canada and he wants to find more chaplains so he can expand his service.

In Canada, Jesus hasn't made it into business plans like He has in the United States, but some Canadian companies are making money by satisfying the demand for religiously themed movies. Cloud 10 is a movie making company started by Peter and Paul Lalonde from North Bay, Ontario. They have married entertainment with the Christian end of the world by making Christian films about the apocalypse (using B-actors from Hollywood). These films have been seen by millions of moviegoers, and have made Cloud 10 the most profitable independent film studio in North America.

Christian-themed entertainment is not limited to movies. Toronto-based Harlequin, which is well-known for its racy novels, now has a Steeple Hill Division that churns out Christian romance novels. Its target market is the 30 million women in the United States who want romance novels that contain no swearing, drinking, or sex. The division has achieved double digit growth in its line of Christian books; the biggest hit is the Whitney Chronicles. Editors at Harlequin say the Christian market is easy to target. More generally, Christian entrepreneurs are finding that these are boom times, and that barriers between business, religion, and the workplace are disappearing.

In the United States, religion has always been a big part of life and now it's becoming a big part of business. More Americans than ever call themselves Christians, and more and more of them are taking their faith into the workplace. This means that there is a growing demand for products related to Jesus, and in activities that connect Christianity with commerce. Consider the case of Liz Golden, the owner of a struggling embroidery business. It's not every day that you pray with your banker, but that's what Liz did when she talked to Chuck Ripka about getting a loan from the Riverview Community Bank in Otsego, Minnesota. Riverview is the first Christian bank in the United States, and Ripka says it is doing very well. He says that God promised him that if he would do the things God called him to do, God would take care of the bottom line. Once a week during lunch Chuck networks with other Christian businesspeople. They consider Jesus their business partner, and they pray for courage to spread their brand of faith to customers, co-workers, and employees. Ripka realizes that his bank's openly Christian focus probably turns some people off, but he points out that neither the employees nor the customers have to be Christians. But the staff who are Christians pray for the business on a daily basis.

In Dallas, Texas, corporate chaplain Gil Strickland wants to convince others that chaplains in the workplace will boost the bottom line. He served as a U.S. Army chaplain for 37 years, taking care of the emotional needs of soldiers. He says you have to reach out and love and encourage people in the Army, and he thought it would be a good idea to do that in corporate America as well. His company, Marketplace Chaplains, hires out Christian chaplains to business firms. He has 1600 people on the payroll. Marketplace Chaplains brings in $7 million a year in revenue, but Strickland says the business is not about the money; the real satisfaction comes from helping people.

It is left up to employees if they want to avail themselves of the services provided by the chaplain. The chaplains offer more than just a pat on the back. For example, when a long-distance driver is on the road, someone will check that his wife is O.K. Or, if one of his children gets sick, a chaplain from the company will visit at the hospital. At one electrical wire company where Marketplace Chaplains operates, turnover has been reduced by 40 percent since the arrival of the chaplain.

Questions for Discussion

1. What is motivation? What are the factors that motivate people at work? Can a Christian emphasis in the workplace motivate those who are interested?
2. How is job satisfaction different from morale? What is the likely effect on job satisfaction of introducing religion and/or spirituality in the workplace for those who are interested?
3. What are the advantages and disadvantages of bringing religion and spirituality into the workplace?

CBC VIDEO CASE II-2

The Big Switcheroo

Vancouver City Savings Credit Union (Van City for short) is Canada's biggest credit union. With 41 branches, 2000 employees, and $9 billion in assets, it is hard to miss the Van City signs around Vancouver.

Dave Mowat is the CEO of the company and he is a powerful man. Lisa Paille, who is a front-line worker in a suburban Van City branch, doesn't have any of Mowat's responsibilities, and she isn't so powerful. A company-wide contest picks Lisa Paille as the person who will switch jobs with Mowat. Here is the story of what happened when these two people switched jobs. Who will get the bigger reality check?

On her first day as CEO, Paille finds that her day is booked solid. Her first duty is conducting the head office manager's meeting. As Lisa conducts the meeting, she really feels that she has been put on the spot. She isn't doing well, and she keeps nervously looking at her notes as she speaks. Afterwards, her vice-presidents line up to meet with her, but by the time the finance vice-president shows up, she is running 30 minutes behind schedule. She is already looking weary and it's not even 1 p.m. Lisa doesn't have time to contact her family during the day, and when she arrives home, it is past her kids' bedtime.

Mowat isn't having an easy time of it on his first day, either. His first job is as a teller. He discovers that he is breaking dress rules by not wearing a tie (this violates the dress code which states that business attire is required). He is also experiencing front-line stress at the branch. The people who are waiting in line are impatient, and Mowat gets flustered trying to deal with them. He doesn't work fast enough. He doesn't get to go home until his money balances. He comes close (just 10 cents out). His day ends early, and he gets to eat dinner with his family while it is still daylight. That doesn't often happen when he stays late at work to attend to CEO duties.

On day 2, it's more of the same for Paille. It is difficult keeping the top executives in line, running meetings, and doing everything on time, but she is doing a little better today, and she actually finishes one meeting ahead of schedule. But later she gets behind schedule again. Lunch is sent in to save time, but Paille doesn't feel comfortable eating in front of the other managers. As she deals with her work backlog, she is learning that there is never an early end to a CEO's day. She heads to a company hockey game to boost morale, and talks on the phone during the game trying to reduce her work backlog.

On his second day, Mowat is answering the phones at the call centre. He has to act quickly and move on to other calls. But he spends about twice as long on each call as he is supposed to spend. He also discovers the stress of having his supervisor monitor his calls. Later in the day, he hustles business at Save-On Foods, a partner of Van City. His job is to sign up new customers.

On day 3, Lisa arrives at 8:45 a.m. and her day is again filled with appearances, ending with another speech to a group of managers. She also gladhands at the Vancouver Board of Trade (the Van City CEO is a member of the board). She is beginning to understand the importance of networking. She also speaks at an employee's anniversary party and presents him with a gift.

On his third day, Mowat starts at 6 a.m. in the Van City mail room. He delivers mail to all the offices, including the CEO's (where he observes that Paille is not yet in her office). He also does some information technology work by changing backup tapes. He finds that the process is complicated, and comments on how important the person doing that work is. Mowat does maintenance duties in the afternoon.

At the end of the three days, Lisa leaves the executive suite and returns to the front lines. Mowat puts down his tools and resumes his CEO duties. They both report on what they learned from their job switch. Paille says she enjoyed the experience, but she is glad it is over because she had to wear a lot of different hats. She has a new appreciation for how hectic and complex the work of a top manager is. Mowat feels that he did pretty well during the switch, but his productivity was judged as too low. He says he is impressed at how well the company's systems work.

Questions for Discussion

1. Briefly describe the four functions of management. Give several examples from the case of how the four functions of management are evident at Van City. Using the four functions of management as a basis, show how the jobs of Lisa Paille and Dave Mowat are different.
2. How are technical skills, human relations skills, and conceptual skills different? Explain the relative importance of each of these skills for a CEO like Dave Mowat and for a front-line worker like Lisa Paille. Give examples from the case to demonstrate the use of these skills.
3. Briefly summarize what Henry Mintzberg discovered about the work of CEOs. Was Lisa Paille's experience as the CEO consistent with what Mintzberg found? Give examples of how Lisa Paille performed some of the roles that Mintzberg identified.
4. What kind of insights do you think Mowat and Paille gained as a result of their switching jobs? To what extent will these insights make each of them more effective in their jobs? Defend your answer.

PART THREE

Managing Operations and Information

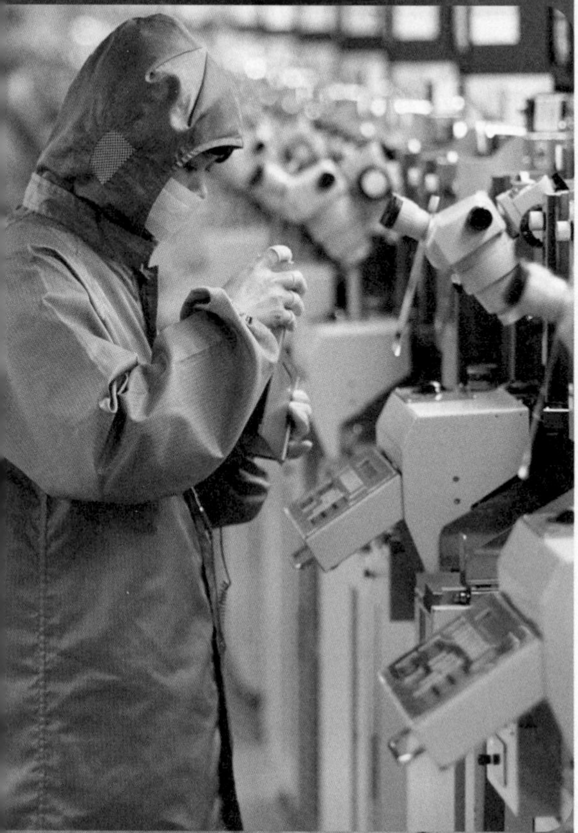

Producing high-quality goods and services in an efficient way is at the heart of all business operations. The opening case for Chapter 10 describes how the increasingly global nature of manufacturing has created productivity challenges for Canadian manufacturers. The opening case for Chapter 11 describes the concerns that have arisen about the under-funding of pension plans and possible changes that may be necessary in accounting rules so that the information provided to stakeholders is more realistic in terms of pension reporting.

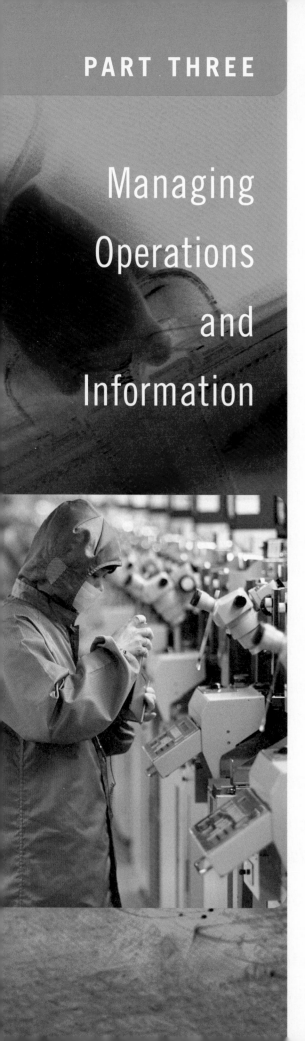

Part Three, Managing Operations and Information, provides an overview of three aspects of business that are important to a firm's survival: the efficient production of goods and services, increasing levels of productivity and quality, and understanding principles of accounting.

- In **Chapter 10, Operations Management and Quality Control**, we examine how business firms manage the production of both physical goods and intangible services, and how they plan, organize, and control the production process. Included in this chapter is a discussion of the importance of both productivity and quality, and the various approaches that companies have taken to improve the productivity and quality of their output.

- In **Chapter 11, Understanding Accounting**, we examine the role of accountants in gathering, assembling, and presenting financial information about a company. We also look at the tools accountants use and the statements they prepare to report a firm's financial standing.

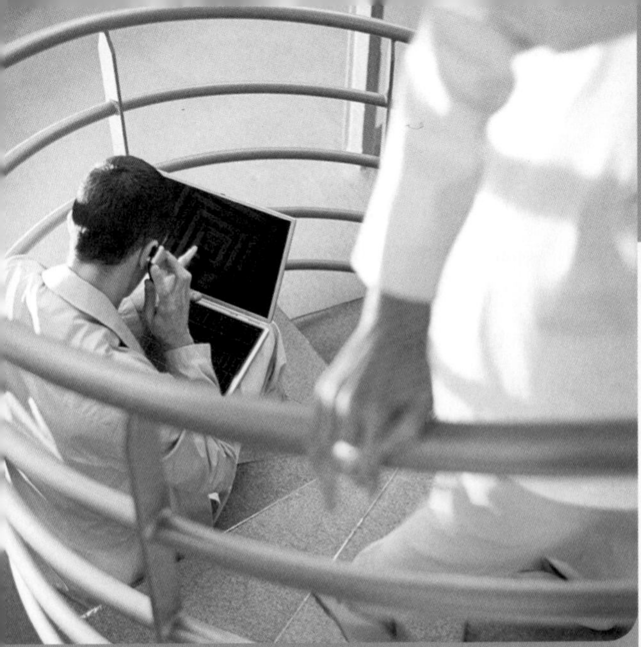

CHAPTER 10

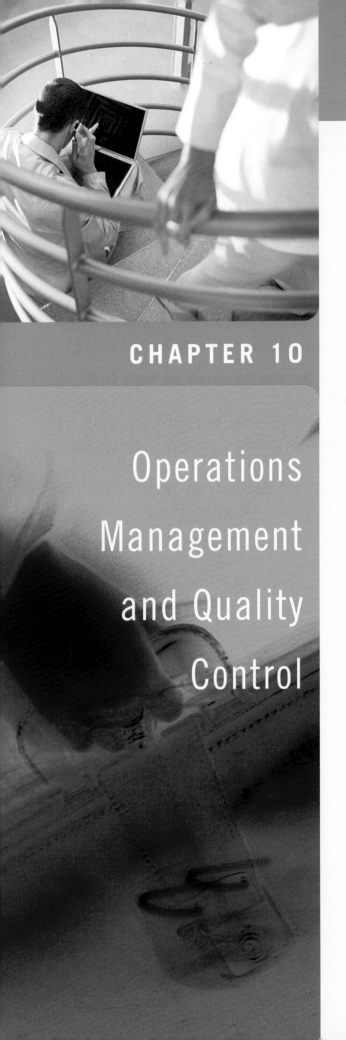

Operations Management and Quality Control

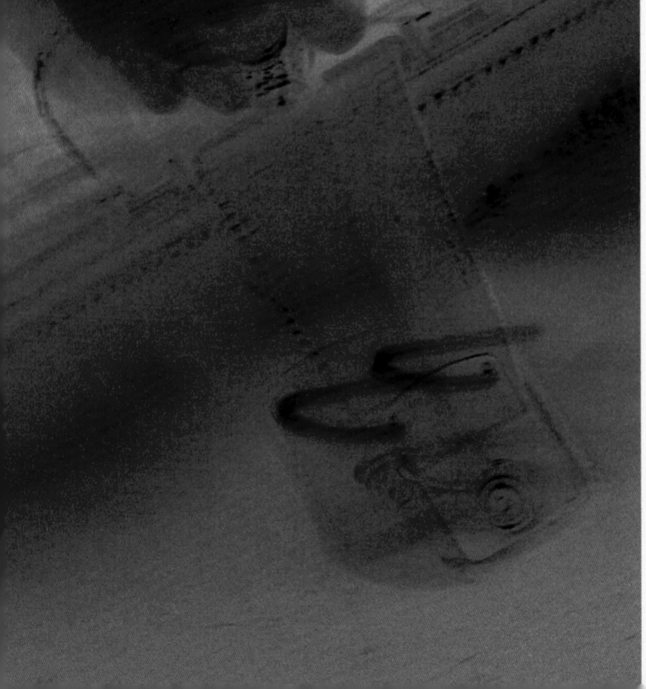

After reading this chapter, you will be able to:

1. Explain the meaning of the term *production* (or *operations*) and describe the four kinds of *utility* it provides.
2. Identify the characteristics that distinguish *service operations* from *goods production* and explain the main differences in the *service focus*.
3. Describe and explain the three classifications of *operations processes*.
4. Describe the factors involved in *operations planning*.
5. Explain the activities involved in *operations control*, including *materials management* and the use of *operation control tools*.
6. Describe the connection between *productivity* and *quality*.
7. Identify the activities involved in *total quality management* and describe nine tools that companies can use to achieve it.

Meeting the Productivity Challenge

During the past few years, considerable publicity has been given to the economic revolution that is taking place in China. With wage rates that are far below those in Canada, China has become a formidable competitor because it is such a low-cost producer of goods. The most obvious way to cope with this competitive threat is to reduce the number of hours of labour that are required to make a product, and thereby reduce the product's cost. In other words, Canadian companies must increase labour productivity.

Growth rates in labour productivity (GDP per hour worked) vary across countries, and Canada has not fared well in recent years. In 2004, for example, Canadian labour productivity did not increase at all, while many other countries increased their labour productivity by 1.5–2.5 percent.

The productivity news is not all bad. In some industries—primary metals, wood products, construction, transport equipment, paper, and chemicals—Canadian productivity actually exceeds that of the U.S. Algoma Steel, for example, is the most efficient steel producer in the *world*. It earned $131 for each tonne of steel it sold in 2004, and that was more than twice the amount achieved by the number two company, U.S. Steel. In many other industries, however—including computers and electronics, fabricated metal products, textiles, furniture, retail trade, financial services, and electrical equipment—Canadian productivity lags far behind the United States'.

Consider the case of the automobile industry. In 2005, Harbour Consulting ranked GM Canada's Oshawa Plant Number 1 at the top of its list of the most productive plants in North America. The plant, which makes Chevrolet Impalas and Monte Carlos, takes 15.85 hours to produce one car. The second most productive plant is a Nissan plant in Tennessee that takes 15 minutes longer. Oshawa Plant Number 2 was in fourth place at 17.47 hours. This sounds pretty good for Canada, but car manufacturing is a world-wide phenomenon, and car makers in Japan are even more efficient than in North America. Nissan led the way, and made $1603 on the average vehicle, followed by Toyota ($1488), and Honda ($1250). Chrysler made only $186 per vehicle and Ford $620. In spite of its good productivity showing, GM *lost* $2311 on each vehicle it sold because of declining demand from consumers and high pension and health care costs.

But how can labour productivity be increased? As we saw in the Opening Case in Chapter 2, a variety of approaches have been suggested, including changes in tax policies that would encourage manufacturers to invest in more productive equipment. Consider the issue of capital cost allowance (CCA). In the United States, manufacturers are allowed to write off equipment much faster than in Canada. This means that U.S. companies pay less tax than Canadian companies. Standen's Ltd., a Canadian company, is a clear example of the disincentive that tax policy can create. The company, which produces truck springs, was considering buying an automotive springs plant in Wallaceburg, Ontario, but eventually decided it wouldn't make the purchase because the after-tax cost of the investment was too high. If Canadian tax laws allowed greater deductions for investment in machinery, the purchase would have been feasible.

But these suggestions are not without controversy. The Canadian Labour Congress, for example, accepts the importance of productivity and the need to increase it, but says there are good and bad ways to do that. A "bad" way, in their view, is to cut jobs, while a "good" way is to invest in innovation and employee training. The Information Technology Association of Canada says that U.S. companies in the information and communications technology sector spend more than twice as much per worker as Canadian companies do.

There is also debate about the role that managers play in this problem. Some people argue that Canadian managers are not expending enough energy or do not have enough imagination, and that is why Canadian productivity is lagging. But Jack Mintz, the head of the C.D. Howe Institute, says that Canadian managers are very good and are simply responding to their environment—in this case, the tax environment. Specifically, he notes that Canadian managers invest outside Canada because of lower tax rates on capital investment in other countries. He says that a comparison of 36 industrialized countries shows that Canada has the second-highest marginal tax rate on capital investment.

Of particular importance to Canadian businesses is the productivity comparison with their U.S. counterparts. While productivity comparisons with the much larger U.S. economy may seem unfair, Canada's immense trade with the United States makes such comparisons important. Output per hour in Canadian manufacturing was about 14 percent below the United States for the period 1977–1994. Since 1994, the situation has actually worsened—output per hour in Canada was 29 percent lower than the United States in 2000 and 32 percent lower in 2001. Put another way, labour productivity growth was 3.8 *percentage points* higher in the United States than in Canada during the period 1994–2000.

To catch up to the United States, Canada will have to exceed the rate of productivity growth in the United States each year by about one percentage point for the next 15 years. One percentage point might not sound like much, but it would require Canadian industry to achieve an annual productivity growth rate of over 3 percent. That rate of productivity growth has been achieved only twice in Canada in the last 25 years.

When making productivity comparisons, we must be careful that we consider certain factors that may give one country an inherent advantage over another. For example, Canadian oil and gas producers are less productive than their U.S. counterparts. This is so partly because Canadian companies are spending large amounts of money developing expensive offshore and non-conventional oil sands deposits, while U.S. oil and gas producers continue to extract energy from wells that use technology developed long ago. Another example: Canadian retailers are less productive than U.S. retailers, partly because Wal-Mart has forced its U.S. competitors to cut costs in order to survive. This cost cutting does raise productivity and benefits *consumers*, but *employees* often suffer. One study showed that Wal-Mart workers earned 31 percent less than the average wage paid by large retailers and that less than half of Wal-Mart's workers had health insurance.

A delicate balancing act is required to achieve higher productivity while not reducing worker well-being. Companies need to foster a competitive climate (which drives productivity growth) and at the same time promote social, environmental, and employee welfare.

HOW WILL THIS BENEFIT YOU?

You will benefit in two ways by reading and understanding methods that managers use for managing production operations and improving quality: (1) as an employee, you'll have a clearer picture of who your customers are, what they want, and how your job depends on the goods and services your company provides, and (2) you'll better understand how all companies—even successful ones—remain competitive by continually analyzing their production methods so they can efficiently produce high quality products and services that consumers will want.

In this chapter, we'll look at how businesses create value through production operations, and the many facets of operations planning, scheduling, and controlling. We'll also talk about productivity (how businesses can increase the efficiency of their operations) and quality (how businesses can improve and manage product quality, and why it's important that they do so).

WHAT DOES "PRODUCTION" MEAN TODAY?

1 Explain the meaning of the term *production* (or *operations*) and describe the four kinds of *utility* it provides.

service operations Production activities that yield tangible and intangible service products.

goods production Production activities that yield tangible products.

Everywhere you go today, you encounter business activities that provide goods and services to their customers. You wake up in the morning, for example, to the sound of your favourite radio station. You stop at the corner store for a newspaper on your way to the bus stop, where you catch the bus to work or school. Your instructors, the bus driver, the clerk at the 7-Eleven store, and the morning radio announcer are all examples of people who work in **service operations**. They provide you with tangible and intangible service products, such as entertainment, transportation, education, and food preparation. Firms that make tangible products—radios, newspapers, buses, textbooks—are engaged in **goods production**.

Although the term *production* has historically referred to companies engaged in goods production, the concept as we now use it also means services. Many of the things that we need or want, from health care to fast food, are produced by service operations. As a rule, service-sector managers focus less on equipment and technology than on the human element in operations. Why? Because success or failure may depend on provider–customer contact. Employees who deal directly with customers affect customer feelings about the service, and as we will see, a key difference between production and service operations is the customer's involvement in the latter.

While companies are typically classified as either goods producers or service providers, the distinction is often blurred. All businesses are service operations to some extent. When you think of General Electric, for example, you most likely think of appliances and jet engines. However, GE is not just a goods producer. According to its annual report, GE's "growth engines"—its most vibrant business activities—are service operations, including media and entertainment (NBC-Universal), consumer and commercial finance, investment, transportation services, health care information, and real estate, which account for over 80 percent of the company's revenues.[1]

CREATING VALUE THROUGH PRODUCTION

To understand the production processes of a firm, you need to understand the importance of products—both goods and services. Products provide businesses with both economic results (profits, wages, goods purchased from other companies) and non-economic results (new technology, innovations, pollution), and they provide consumers with what economists call **utility**—want satisfaction.

Four basic kinds of utility would not be possible without production. By making a product available at a time when consumers want it, production creates **time utility**, as when a company turns out ornaments in time for Christmas. By making a product available in a place convenient for consumers, production creates **place utility**, as when a local department store creates a "Trim-A-Tree" section. By making a product that consumers can take pleasure in owning, production creates **ownership (possession) utility**, as when you take a box of ornaments home and decorate your tree. But above all, production makes products available in the first place. By turning raw materials into finished goods, production creates **form utility**, as when an ornament maker combines glass, plastic, and other materials to create tree decorations.

Operations (or **production**) **management** is the systematic direction and control of the processes that transform resources into finished goods and services. As Figure 10.1 shows, **production managers** must bring raw materials, equipment, and labour together under a production plan that effectively uses all the resources available in the production facility. As

utility
The power of a product to satisfy a human want; something of value.

time utility
That quality of a product satisfying a human want because of the time at which it is made available.

place utility
That quality of a product satisfying a human want because of where it is made available.

ownership (possession) utility
That quality of a product satisfying a human want during its consumption or use.

form utility
That quality of a product satisfying a human want because of its form; requires raw materials to be transformed into a finished product.

operations (or production) management
A set of methods and technologies used in the production of a good or a service.

production managers
Managers responsible for ensuring that operations processes create value and provide benefits.

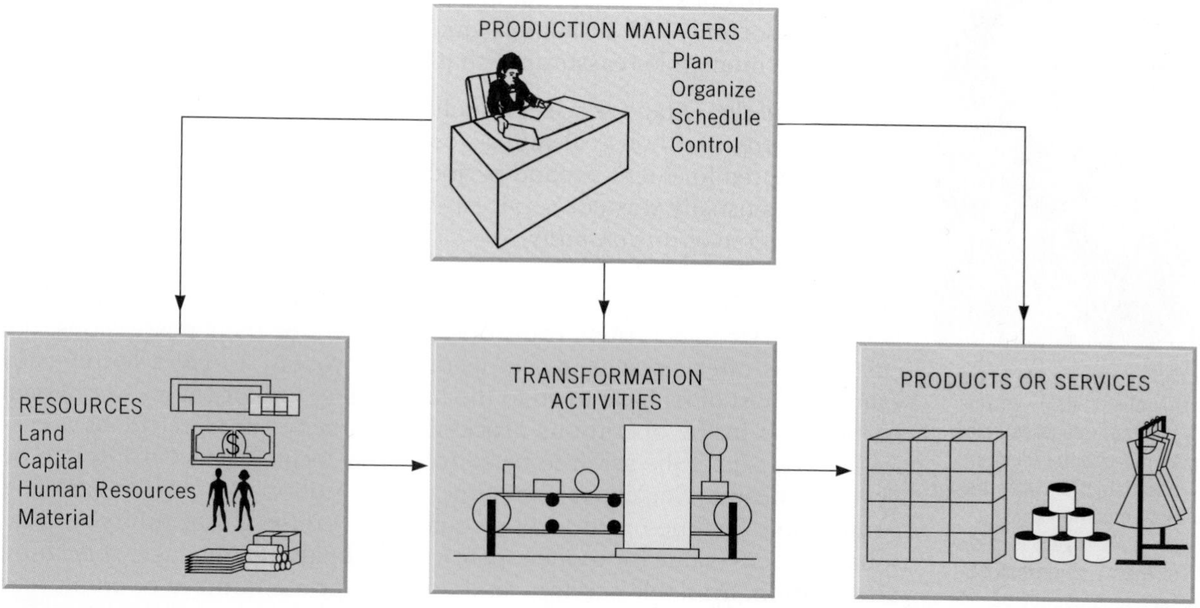

Figure 10.1 The transformation system.

demand for a good increases, they must schedule and control work to produce the amount required. Meanwhile, they must control costs, quality levels, inventory, and plant and equipment.

Differences Between Service and Manufacturing Operations

2 Identify the characteristics that distinguish *service operations* from *goods production* and explain the main differences in the *service focus.*

Both service and manufacturing operations transform raw materials into finished products. In service operations, however, the raw materials, or inputs, are not things like glass or steel. Rather, they are people who have either unsatisfied needs or possessions needing care or alteration. In service operations, finished products or outputs are people with needs met and possessions serviced.

Thus, there is at least one obvious difference between service and manufacturing operations. Whereas goods are *produced*, services are *performed*. Four aspects of service operations can make such operations more complicated than simple goods production. These include (1) interacting with consumers, (2) the intangible and unstorable nature of some services, (3) the customer's presence in the process, and (4) service quality considerations.

Interacting with Consumers

Manufacturing operations emphasize outcomes in terms of physical goods—for example, a new jacket. But the products of most *service* operations are really combinations of goods and services—both making a pizza *and* delivering (serving) it. Service workers need different skills. For example, gas company employees may need interpersonal skills to calm frightened customers who have reported gas leaks. Thus, the job includes more than just repairing pipes. In contrast, factory workers who install gas pipes in manufactured homes without any customer contact don't need such skills.

The hair styling service being provided to this customer illustrates the three key features of services operations: intangibility (customer pleasure or satisfaction with the service), customization (the service each person gets is customized for them), and unstorability (the services cannot be produced ahead of time).

Services Can Be Intangible and Unstorable

Two prominent characteristics—*intangibility* and *unstorability*—set services apart from physical goods.

- *Intangibility*. Often, services can't be touched, tasted, smelled, or seen, but they're still there. An important satisfier for customers, therefore, is the *intangible* value they receive in the form of pleasure, gratification, or a feeling of safety. For example, when you hire an attorney, you purchase not only the intangible quality of legal expertise but also the equally intangible reassurance that help is at hand.
- *Unstorability*. Many services—such as trash collection, transportation, child care, and house cleaning—can't be produced ahead of time and then stored for high-demand periods. If a service isn't used when available, it's usually wasted. Services, then, are typically characterized by a high degree of *unstorability*.

The Customer's Presence in the Operations Process

Because service operations transform customers or their possessions, the customer is often present in the operations process. To get a haircut, for example, most of us have to go to the barbershop or hair salon. As physical participants in the operations process, consumers can affect it. As a customer, you expect the salon to be conveniently located (place utility), to be open for business at convenient times (time utility), to provide safe and comfortable facilities, and to offer quality grooming (form utility) at reasonable prices (value for money spent). Accordingly, the manager sets hours of operation, available services, and an appropriate number of employees to meet customer requirements. But what happens if a customer, scheduled to receive a haircut, also asks for additional services, such as highlights or a shave when they arrive? In this case, the service provider must balance customer satisfaction with a tight schedule. High customer contact has the potential to significantly affect the process.

The growth of ecommerce has introduced a "virtual presence" of the customer, as opposed to a physical presence. Consumers interact electronically, in real time, with sellers, collecting information about product features, delivery availability, and after-sales service. Many companies have invited "the virtual customer" into their service systems by building customer-communications relationships. For example, the online travel agency Expedia.ca responds to your personalized profile with a welcome email letter, presents you with a tailor-made web page the next time you sign on, offers chat rooms in which you can compare notes with other customers, and notifies you of upcoming special travel opportunities.

Intangibles Count for Service Quality

Consumers use different measures to judge services and goods because services include intangibles, not just physical objects. Most service managers know that quality of work and quality of service are not necessarily the same thing. Your car, for example, may have been flawlessly repaired (quality of work), but you'll probably be unhappy with the service if you're forced to pick it up a day later than promised (quality of service).

Operations Processes

Describe and explain the three classifications of *operations processes*. **3**

An **operations process** is a set of methods and technologies used in the production of a good or a service. We classify various types of production according to differences in their operations processes. In other words, we can describe goods according to the kind of *transformation technology* they require, or according to whether their operations process combines resources or breaks them into component parts. We can describe services according to the *extent of customer contact* required.

operations process
A set of methods and technologies used in the production of a good or a service.

Goods-Producing Processes

All goods-producing processes can be classified in two different ways: by the *type of transformation technology* that transforms raw materials into finished goods, and by the *analytic or synthetic nature of the transformation process*.

Types of Transformation Technology. Manufacturers use the following types of transformation processes to turn raw materials into finished goods:

- In *chemical processes*, raw materials are chemically altered. Such techniques are common in the aluminum, steel, fertilizer, petroleum, and paint industries.
- *Fabrication processes* mechanically alter the basic shape or form of a product. Fabrication occurs in the metal forming, woodworking, and textile industries.
- *Assembly processes* put together various components. These techniques are common in the electronics, appliance, and automotive industries.
- In *transport processes*, goods acquire place utility by being moved from one location to another. For example, bicycles are routinely moved by trucks from manufacturing plants to consumers through warehouses and discount stores.
- *Clerical processes* transform information. Combining data on employee absences and machine breakdowns into a productivity report is a clerical process. So is compiling inventory reports at a retail outlet.

ENTREPRENEURSHIP AND NEW VENTURES

The Silencers

In just eight years, Scott MacDonald, 30, and his father have seen their business grow from a two-person operation into a 29-person team of experts that attracts clients locally and from the United States. Noise Solutions Inc., an innovative company in the emerging sector of noise control, aims to facilitate a peaceful coexistence between industries and residents.

Founded in 1997, Noise Solutions helps large-scale industries suppress noise pollution created by their activities. The Calgary-based enterprise thrives by providing turn-key solutions, mainly for companies in the energy and mining sectors. Noise Solutions' clients include notable organizations like United Space Alliance/NASA and Canadian Natural Resources. Responding to the needs of residents living near industrial sites and to help industries comply with Alberta Energy and Utilities Board guidelines, the company assesses industrial noise sources, then selects and installs appropriate sound-reducing mufflers and silencers.

"I'm particularly proud of the team that we've put together," says Scott. "They have the ability to meet any sort of challenge head-on, whether it be of a technical nature, an accounting challenge, or solving a problem in the field."

"A huge part of our growth is attributable to the fact that we go beyond what our clients' needs are and improve the end result for them," explains Scott. "In fact, in the first five years, word of mouth from satisfied customers was responsible for our entire growth. They see and understand that we tend to go the extra mile for them."

Scott, a believer in continuous education, has created a work environment that focuses on learning. To attract customers from farther afield, he taught himself website design and built the Noise Solutions website, which helped spark interest from industrial users in the United States. "We continuously try to keep ourselves up to date with new products, programs, and developmental concepts and we work to educate the industry," says Scott. "We try to look far enough into the future to anticipate challenges and ensure that nothing can stop us or get in our way."

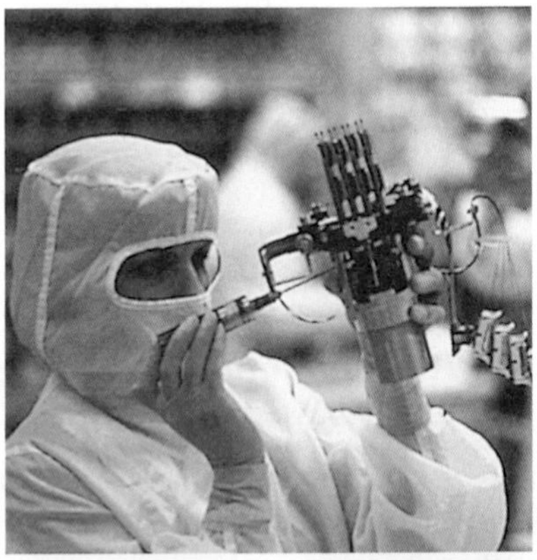

As these photos show, various industries use different transformation techniques: (from left, top) chemical, fabrication, and assembly; (bottom) transport and clerical.

Analytic Versus Synthetic Processes. A second way of classifying production processes is by the way in which resources are converted into finished goods. An **analytic process** breaks down the basic resources into components. For example, Alcan manufactures aluminum by extracting it from an ore called bauxite. The reverse approach, a **synthetic process**, combines a number of raw materials to produce a finished product such as fertilizer or paint.

analytic process
Any production process in which resources are broken down.

synthetic process
Any production process in which resources are combined.

Service-Producing Processes

One way of classifying services is to ask whether a given service can be provided without the customer being part of the production system. In answering this question, services are classified according to the extent of *customer contact*.

High-Contact Processes. Think for a moment about the service provided by your local public transit system. When you purchase transportation, you must board a bus or train, so public transit is a **high-contact system**. For this reason, transit managers must worry about the cleanliness of the trains and buses and the appearance of the stations. This is usually not the case in low-contact systems. Large industrial concerns that ship coal in freight trains, for example, are generally not concerned with the atmosphere inside those trains.

high-contact system
A system in which the service cannot be provided without the customer being physically in the system (e.g., transit systems).

Low-Contact Processes. Consider the cheque-processing operations at your bank. Workers sort the cheques that have been cashed that day and dispatch them to the banks on which they were drawn. This operation is a **low-contact system** because customers are not in contact with the bank while the service is performed. They receive the service—their funds are transferred to cover their cheques—without ever setting foot in the cheque-processing centre. Gas and electric utilities, auto repair shops, and lawn care services are also low-contact systems.

low-contact system
A system in which the service can be provided without the customer being physically in the system (e.g., lawn care services).

Business Strategy as the Driver of Operations

There is no one standard way for doing production. Rather, it is a flexible activity that can be moulded into many shapes to give quite different production, or operations, capabilities for different purposes. How, then, do companies go about selecting the kind of production that is best for their company? Its design is best driven from above by the firm's larger business strategy.

In this section we present examples of four firms—two in goods production and two in services—that have contrasting business strategies and, as we shall see, have chosen different operations capabilities. All four firms are successful, but they've taken quite different operations paths to get there. As shown in Table 10.1, each company has identified a business strategy that it can use for attracting customers in its industry. For Toyota, *quality* was chosen as the strategy for competing in selling autos. Save-A-Lot grocery stores, in contrast to others in the grocery industry, offer customers *lower prices*. The *flexibility* strategy at 3M emphasizes new product development in an ever-changing line of products for home and office. FedEx captures the overnight delivery market by emphasizing delivery *dependability*.

Business Strategy Determines Operations Capabilities

Successful firms design their operations to support the company's business strategy.[2] In other words, production operations are adjusted to support the firms' target markets. Since our four firms use different business strategies, we should expect to see differences in their operations. The top-priority **operations capability (production capability)**—the activity or process that production must do especially well, with high proficiency—is listed for

operations capability (production capability)
The activity or process that production must do especially well and with high proficiency.

Table 10.1 Business Strategies That Win Customers for Four Companies

Company	Strategy for Attracting Customers	What the Company Does to Implement Its Strategy
Toyota	Quality	Cars perform reliably, have an appealing fit-and-finish, and consistently meet or exceed customer expectations at a competitive price
Save-A-Lot	Low Price	Foods and everyday items offered at savings up to 40 percent less than conventional food chains
3M	Flexibility	Innovation, with more than 55 000 products in a constantly changing line of convenience items for home and office
FedEx	Dependability	Every delivery is fast and on time, as promised

each firm in Table 10.2, along with key operations characteristics for implementing that capability. Each company's operations capability matches up with its business strategy so that the firm's activities—from top to bottom—are focused in a particular direction.

As you can see in Table 10.2, Toyota's top priority focuses on quality, so its operations—inputs, transformation activities, and outputs—are devoted first and foremost to quality. Its car designs emphasize appearance, reliable performance, and desirable features at a reasonable price. All production processes, equipment, and training are designed to build better cars. The entire culture supports a quality emphasis among employees, suppliers, and dealerships. Had Toyota instead chosen to compete as the low-price car in the industry, as some successful car companies do, then a cost-minimization focus would have been appropriate, giving Toyota's operations an altogether different form. Toyota's operations support its chosen business strategy and do it successfully.

Table 10.2 Operations Capabilities and Characteristics for Four Companies

Operations Capability	Key Operations Characteristics
Quality (Toyota)	• High-quality standards for materials suppliers • Just-in-time materials flow for lean manufacturing • Specialized, automated equipment for consistent product build-up • Operations personnel are experts on continuous improvement of product, work methods, and materials
Low Cost (Save-A-Lot)	• Avoids excessive overhead and costly inventory (no floral departments, sushi bars, or banks that drive up costs) • Limited assortment of products, staples, in one size only for low-cost restocking, lower inventories, and less paperwork • Many locations; small stores—less than half the size of conventional grocery stores—for low construction and maintenance costs • Reduces labour and shelving costs by receiving and selling merchandise out of custom shipping cartons
Flexibility (3M)	• Maintains some excess (expensive) production capacity available for fast startup on new products • Adaptable equipment/facilities for production changeovers from old to new products • Hires operations personnel who thrive on change • Many medium- to small-sized facilities in diverse locations, which enhances creativity
Dependability (FedEx)	• Customer automation: uses electronic and online tools with customers to shorten shipping time • Wireless information system for package scanning by courier, updating of package movement, and package tracking by customer • Maintains a company air force, global weather forecasting centre, and ground transportation for pickup and delivery, with backup vehicles for emergencies • Each of 30 automated regional distribution hubs processes up to 45 000 packages per hour for next-day deliveries

Expanding into Additional Capabilities

Over time, excellent firms learn how to achieve more than just one competence. Our four example firms eventually became excellent in several capabilities. FedEx, for example, in addition to dependability, is noted for world-class service quality and cost containment, too. But in its earlier years, its primary and distinguishing capability—that which set it apart from the competition—was dependability, the foundation upon which future success was built.

OPERATIONS PLANNING

Describe the factors involved in *operations planning.* 4

Managers from many departments contribute to the firm's decisions about operations management. As Figure 10.2 shows, however, no matter how many decision makers are involved, the process can be described as a series of logical steps. The success of any firm depends on the final result of this logical sequence of decisions.

The business plan and forecasts developed by top managers guide operations planning. The business plan outlines goals and objectives, including the specific goods and services that the firm will offer. Managers also develop long-range production plans through **forecasts** of future demand for both new and existing products. Covering a two-to-five-year period, the production plan specifies the number of plants or service facilities and the amount of labour, equipment, transportation, and storage that will be needed to meet demand. It also specifies how resources will be obtained. There are five main categories of operations planning: *capacity, location, layout, quality,* and *methods planning*.

forecasts
Estimates of future demand for both new and existing products.

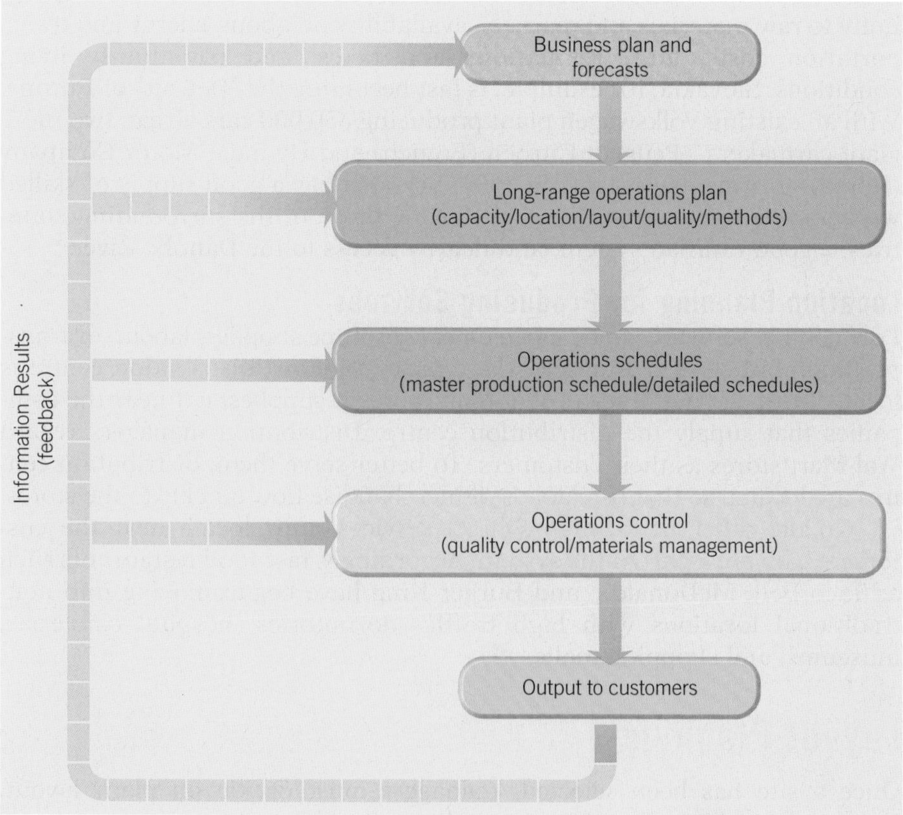

Figure 10.2 Operations planning and control.

Capacity Planning

capacity The amount of a good that a firm can produce under normal working conditions.

The amount of a product that a company can produce under normal working conditions is its **capacity**. A firm's capacity depends on how many people it employs and the number and size of its facilities.

Capacity Planning for Producing Goods

Capacity planning means ensuring that a firm's capacity just *slightly* exceeds the normal demand for its product. If capacity is too small to meet demand, the company must turn away customers, and it will forego profit opportunities. If capacity is too large, the firm wastes money by having a plant that is too large and has too many employees.

Capacity Planning for Producing Services

In low-contact systems, capacity should be set at the level of *average demand*. Orders that arrive faster than expected can be set aside in a "to be done" file and processed later during a slower period. In high-contact systems, managers must plan capacity to meet *peak demand*. A supermarket, for instance, has far more cash registers than it needs on an average day. But on a Saturday morning or during the three days before Christmas, all registers will be running at full speed.

Location Planning

Because the location of a factory, an office, or a store affects its production costs and flexibility, sound location planning is crucial. Depending on the site of its facility, a company may be capable of producing a low-cost product or may find itself at an extreme cost disadvantage relative to its competitors.

Location Planning for Producing Goods

In goods-producing operations, location decisions are influenced by proximity to raw materials and markets, availability of labour, energy and transportation costs, local regulations and taxes, and community living conditions. Slovakia, for example, is fast becoming the "Detroit" of Europe. With an existing Volkswagen plant producing 850 000 cars a year, two more giant carmakers—Peugeot Citroën (French) and Hyundai Motor Company (Korea)—opened new plants in 2006. Slovakia has a good supply of skilled workers, a good work ethic, wages below those of the surrounding countries, a good railroad system, and nearby access to the Danube River.[3]

Location Planning for Producing Services

Low-contact services can be located near resource supplies, labour, or transportation outlets. For example, the typical Wal-Mart distribution centre is located near the hundreds of Wal-Mart stores it supplies, not near the companies that supply the distribution centre. Distribution managers regard Wal-Mart stores as their customers. To better serve them, distribution centres are located so that truckloads of merchandise flow quickly to the stores.

On the other hand, high-contact services must locate near the customers who are a part of the system. Accordingly, fast-food restaurants such as Taco Bell, McDonald's, and Burger King have begun moving into nontraditional locations with high traffic—dormitories, hospital cafeterias, museums, and shopping malls.

Layout Planning

Once a site has been selected, managers must decide on plant layout. Layout of machinery, equipment, and supplies determines whether a company can respond quickly and efficiently to customer requests for more and different products or find itself unable to match competitors' production speed or convenience of service.

Layout Planning for Producing Goods

In facilities that produce goods, layout must be planned for three different types of space:

- *Productive facilities:* workstations and equipment for transforming raw materials
- *Non-productive facilities:* storage and maintenance areas
- *Support facilities:* offices, restrooms, parking lots, cafeterias, and so forth

When producing goods, alternatives for layout planning include *process, cellular,* and *product layouts*.

Process Layouts. In a **process layout**, which is well suited to *job shops* specializing in custom work, equipment and people are grouped according to function. In a woodworking shop, for example, machines cut the wood in an area devoted to sawing, sanding occurs in a dedicated area, and jobs that need painting are taken to a dust-free area where all the painting equipment is located. The various tasks are each performed in specialized locations.

process layout A way of organizing production activities such that equipment and people are grouped together according to their function.

The job shop produces many one-of-a-kind products, and each product requires different kinds of work (see Figure 10.3a). Whereas Product X needs only three production steps prior to packaging, Product Y needs four. Machine shops, custom bakeries, and dry cleaning shops often feature process layouts.

Cellular Layouts. The **cellular layout** is used when a group of similar products follows a fixed flow path. A clothing manufacturer, for example, may establish a cell, or designated area, dedicated to making a family of pockets—for example, pockets for shirts, coats, blouses, trousers, and slacks. Within the cell, various types of equipment (for cutting, trimming, and sewing) are arranged close together in the appropriate sequence. Figure 10.3b shows two production cells, one each for Products X and Y, while all smaller-volume products are produced elsewhere in the plant.

cellular layout Used to produce goods when families of products can follow similar flow paths.

Product Layouts. In a **product layout**, equipment and people are set up to produce one type of product in a fixed sequence of steps that are arranged according to its production requirements (see Figure 10.3c). Product layouts are efficient for producing large volumes of product quickly and often use **assembly lines**. Automobile, food processing, and television assembly plants use product layouts. In an attempt to improve productivity even more, many companies are now emphasizing **lean manufacturing**, which involves getting rid of traditional assembly lines altogether. Suppliers pre-assemble many specific parts into modules, and then production workers combine the various modules to make the finished product. This requires fewer production workers, less factory space, and less investment in equipment. Louis Vuitton, a maker of luxury handbags, has adopted lean manufacturing in order to quickly respond to changes in customer preferences.[4]

product layout A way of organizing production activities such that equipment and people are set up to produce only one type of good.

assembly line A type of product layout in which a partially finished product moves through a plant on a conveyor belt or other equipment.

lean manufacturing A system designed for smooth production flows that avoid inefficiencies, eliminate unnecessary inventories, and continuously improve production processes.

Other Developments in Layout Flexibility. With a **flexible manufacturing system (FMS)**, a single factory can produce a wide variety of products. Automobile manufacturers, for example, now build several different models of cars using the same basic "platform" (the underbody of the car). Nissan, Toyota, and Honda make the majority of their cars using FMS, and North American car makers are now rapidly adopting the strategy.[5] The Oakville, Ontario, Ford plant is the first flexible assembly plant in Canada.[6]

flexible manufacturing system (FMS) A production system that allows a single factory to produce small batches of different goods on the same production line.

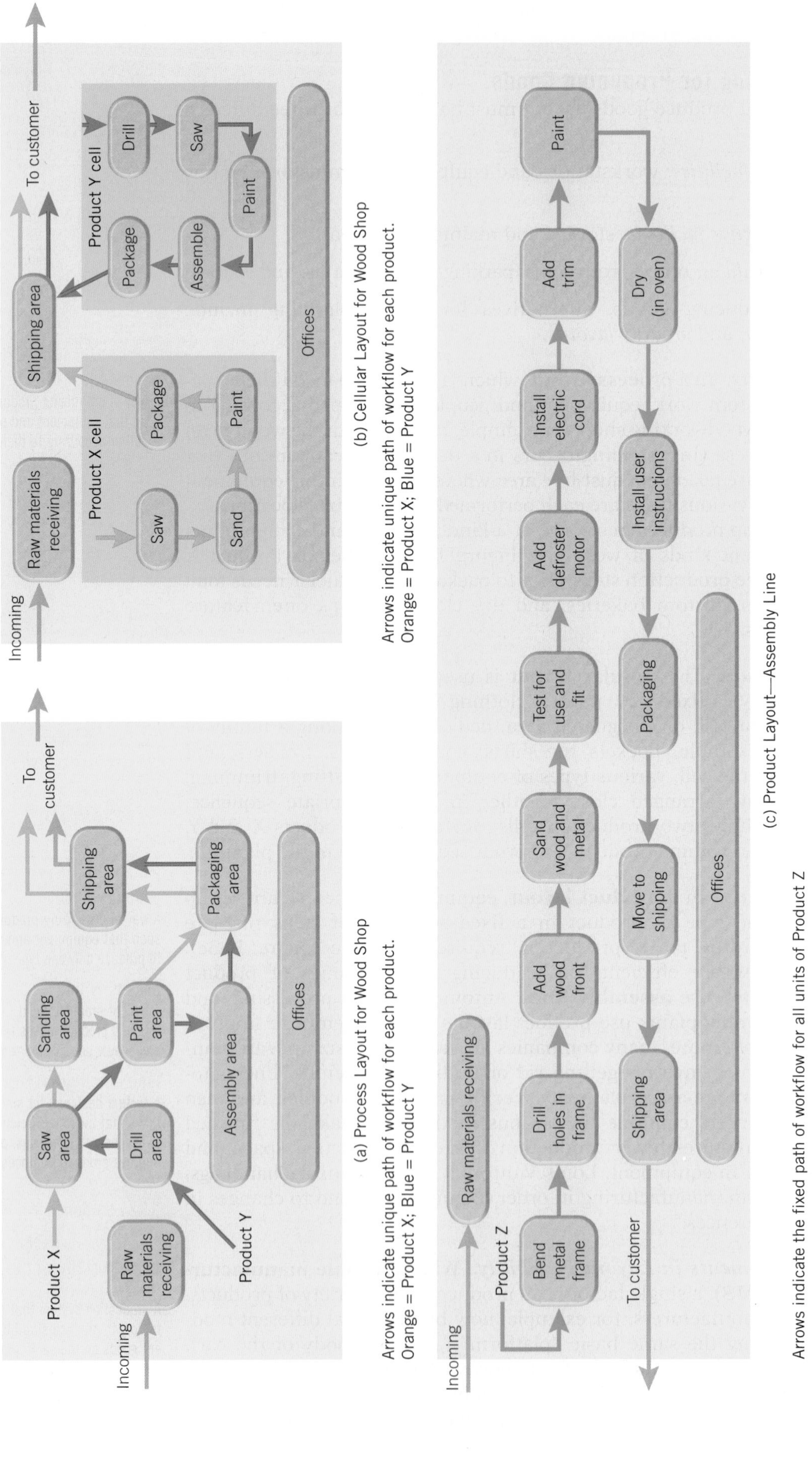

Figure 10.3 Layouts for producing goods.

Some companies have experimented with so-called **soft manufacturing**—reducing huge FMS operations to smaller, more manageable groups of machines. Automation is less likely to fail when relegated to jobs it does best, while human workers perform the assembly-line jobs that require dexterity and decision making. Both are supported by networks of computers programmed to assist in all sorts of tasks.

soft manufacturing
Emphasizes computer software and computer networks instead of production machines.

The very latest development is the **moveable factory**. Because FMS is so expensive, some developing countries with lots of labour but little capital are buying up equipment that is still relatively modern from industrialized countries and then using it to produce new and untested products in their own country. For example, the Chinese want to buy the Campo Largo factory in Brazil that was built by BMW in 1998. They plan to dismantle the machinery and equipment and ship it to Chongqing, China where it will be used to produce an all-Chinese car.[7]

moveable factory
Purchasing relatively modern production equipment and transporting it to another location to create a new manufacturing plant, typically in a developing country.

Layout Planning for Services

In a low-contact system like the mail-processing facility at UPS or Federal Express, the system looks very much like a product layout in a factory. Machines and people are arranged in the order in which they are used in the mass processing of mail. In contrast, FedEx Kinko's Office and Print Centers use process layouts for diverse custom jobs. Specific functions such as photocopying, computing, binding, photography, and laminating are each performed in specialized areas of the store.

High-contact service systems are arranged to meet customer needs and expectations. For example, a cafeteria focuses both layout and services on the groups that constitute its primary market—families and elderly people. As shown in Figure 10.4, families enter to find an array of highchairs and rolling baby beds that make it convenient to wheel children through the line. Meanwhile, servers are willing to carry trays for elderly people and for those pushing strollers.

Quality Planning

In planning production systems and facilities, managers must keep in mind the firm's quality goals.[8] Thus, any complete production plan includes systems for ensuring that goods are produced to meet the firm's quality standards. The issues of productivity and quality are discussed in more detail later in this chapter.

Methods Planning

In designing both production and service systems, managers must clearly identify all production steps and the specific methods for performing them.

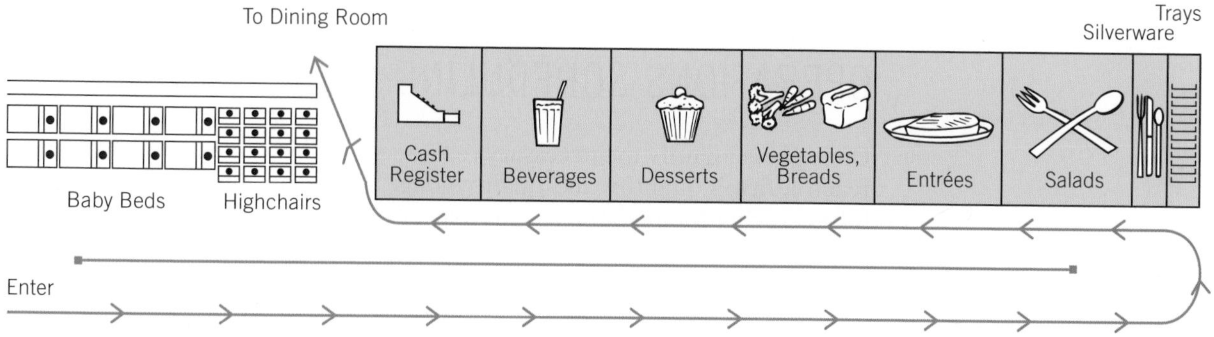

Figure 10.4 Layout of a typical Piccadilly cafeteria.

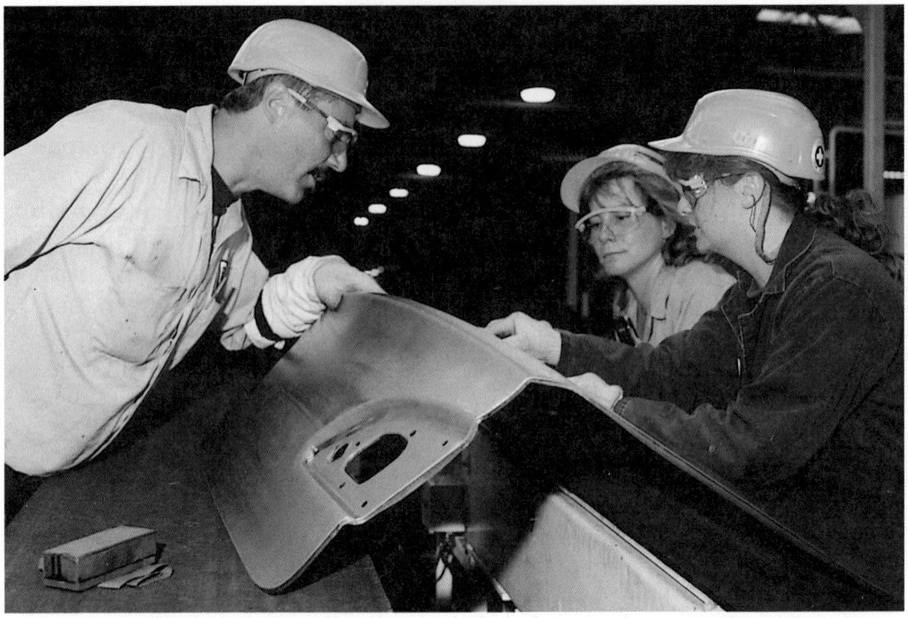

Employees at the Toyota manufacturing plant in Cambridge, Ontario, discuss a production problem. At this plant, employees are responsible not only for making automobiles, but also for monitoring quality control and for maintaining a clean work area.

They can then work to reduce waste, inefficiency, and poor performance by examining procedures on a step-by-step basis, an approach sometimes called *methods improvement*.

Methods Improvements in Goods

Improvement of production for goods begins when a manager documents the current method using a diagram called the *process flow chart*. The chart identifies the sequence of production activities, movements of materials, and work performed at each stage as the product flows through production. The flow can then be analyzed to identify wasteful activities, sources of delay in production flows, and other inefficiencies.

Methods Improvements in Services

Similar procedures are useful in designing and evaluating low-contact service systems. At a bank, for example, the cash-management unit collects accounts receivable for corporate clients; the sooner cheques are collected and deposited, the sooner the client begins collecting interest.

In high-contact services, the demands of systems analysis are somewhat different. Here, for example, the steps to be analyzed include such operations as exchanging information or money, delivering and receiving materials, and even making physical contact. The next time you are at your dentist's office, for instance, notice the way in which dental hygienists "scrub up" and wear disposable gloves.

OPERATIONS SCHEDULING

Once plans identify the necessary resources and how to use those resources to reach a firm's quantity and quality goals, managers must develop timetables for acquiring the resources. This aspect of operations is called *scheduling*.

Scheduling Goods Operations

master production schedule
Schedule showing which products will be produced, when production will take place, and what resources will be used.

A **master production schedule** shows which products will be produced, when production will occur, and what resources will be used during the scheduled time period. Consider the case of Logan Aluminum Inc., which produces coils of aluminum that its main customers, Atlantic Richfield and Alcan Aluminum, use to produce aluminum cans. Logan's master schedule extends out to 60 weeks and shows how many coils will be made during each week. For various types of coils, the master schedule specifies how many of each will be produced.

This information is not complete, however. For example, manufacturing personnel must also know on which days each type of coil will be run. Machine start-up and stop times must be assigned, and employees must be given scheduled work assignments. Short-term *detailed schedules* answer questions like these on daily or weekly bases. These schedules use incoming orders and weekly sales forecasts to determine what size and variety of coils to make within a specified time period. A classic dilemma in production scheduling is described in the Exercising Your Ethics exercise at the end of this chapter.

Scheduling Service Operations

In a low-contact service, *work scheduling* may be based either on the desired completion date or on the time of order arrival. For example, several cars may be scheduled for repairs at a local garage. Thus, if your car is not scheduled for work until 3:30 p.m., it may sit idle for several hours even if it was the first to be dropped off. In such businesses, reservation and appointment systems can help to smooth demand.

In high-contact services, the customer is part of the system and must be accommodated. Thus, precise scheduling of services may not be possible in high-contact systems. For example, if a hospital emergency room is overloaded, patients cannot be asked to make an appointment and come back later.

OPERATIONS CONTROL

Explain the activities involved in *operations control,* including *materials management* and the use of *operation control tools.* 5

Operations control requires production managers to monitor production performance by comparing results with detailed plans and schedules. If schedules or quality standards are not met, these managers must take corrective action. **Follow-up**—checking to ensure that production decisions are being implemented—is an essential and ongoing facet of operations control. Operations control features *materials management* and *production process control.* Both activities ensure that schedules are met and that production goals are fulfilled, both in quantity and in quality.

operations control
Managers monitor production performance by comparing results with plans and schedules.

follow-up
Checking to ensure that production decisions are being implemented.

Materials Management

Materials management involves planning, organizing, and controlling the flow of materials. Even before production starts, materials management focuses on product design by emphasizing materials **standardization**—the use, where possible, of standard and uniform components rather than new or different components. Standardization simplifies paperwork, reduces storage requirements, eliminates unnecessary materials flows, and saves money by reducing the number of different parts that are needed. The five major areas of materials management are *transportation, warehousing, inventory control, supplier selection,* and *purchasing.*

- **Transportation** includes the means of transporting resources to the company and finished goods to buyers.
- **Warehousing** is the storage of both incoming materials for production and finished goods for physical distribution to customers.

materials management
Planning, organizing, and controlling the flow of materials from purchase through distribution of finished goods.

standardization
Using standard and uniform components in the production process.

transportation
The means of transporting resources to the company and finished goods to buyers.

warehousing
The storage of both incoming materials for production and finished goods for physical distribution to customers.

inventory control
In materials management, receiving, storing, handling, and counting of all raw materials, partly finished goods, and finished goods.

supplier selection
Finding and determining suppliers to buy from.

purchasing
The acquisition of all the raw materials and services that a company needs to produce its products.

- **Inventory control** includes the receiving, storing, handling, and counting of all raw materials, partly finished goods, and finished goods. It ensures that enough materials inventories are available to meet production schedules.
- **Supplier selection** means finding and choosing suppliers of services and materials to buy from. It includes evaluating potential suppliers, negotiating terms of service, and maintaining positive buyer–seller relationships.
- **Purchasing** is the acquisition of all the raw materials and services that a company needs to produce its products; most large firms have purchasing departments to buy proper materials in the amounts needed.

Tools for Operations Process Control

Tools for assisting managers in controlling operations include *worker training, just-in-time production systems, material requirements planning,* and *quality control.*

Worker Training

When providing services, employees are both the producers of the product and the salespeople. Thus, human relations skills are vital for anyone who has contact with the public. Managers realize how easily service employees with a poor attitude can reduce sales. Conversely, the right attitude is a powerful sales tool. Disney World has a team of sweepers constantly at work picking up bits of trash as soon as they fall to the ground. When visitors have questions about directions or time, they often ask one of the sweepers. Because their responses affect visitors' overall impressions of Disney World, sweepers are trained to respond in appropriate ways. Their work is evaluated and rewarded based on strict performance appraisal standards.[9]

Just-in-Time Production Systems

just-in-time (JIT) production systems
A method of inventory control in which materials are acquired and put into production just as they are needed.

To minimize manufacturing inventory costs, many companies use **just-in-time (JIT) production systems**. JIT brings together all the needed materials and parts at the precise moment they are required for each production stage, not before. JIT reduces inventory of goods in process to practically nothing, and saves money by replacing stop-and-go production with smooth movement. Once smooth movements become the norm, disruptions become more visible and thus are resolved more quickly. At Mount Sinai Hospital in Toronto, individual suppliers no longer go to the hospital to deliver the items. Rather, all suppliers deliver their products to Livingston Healthcare Services Inc., which stores these items and fills Mount Sinai's order once each day. Mount Sinai no longer keeps any inventory.[10]

In Chapter 2, we saw how events in the external environment can influence what goes on inside a business firm. In the case of JIT, increased security at Canada–United States border crossings has created increased uncertainty about delivery times, and this has forced some exporters to drop JIT and return to their former practice of stockpiling goods in inventory.[11]

material requirements planning (MRP)
A method of inventory control in which a computerized bill of materials is used to estimate production needs so that resources are acquired and put into production only as needed.

bill of materials
Production control tool that specifies the necessary ingredients of a product, the order in which they should be combined, and how many of each are needed to make one batch.

Material Requirements Planning

Material requirements planning (MRP) uses a **bill of materials** that is basically a "recipe" for the finished product. It specifies the necessary ingredients (raw materials and components), the order in which they should be combined, and the quantity of each ingredient needed to make one "batch" of the product (say, 2000 finished telephones). The recipe is fed into a computer that controls inventory and schedules each stage of production. The result is fewer early arrivals, less-frequent stock shortages, and lower storage costs.

Manufacturing resource planning (also called **MRP II**), is an advanced version of MRP that ties together all parts of the organization into the company's production activities. For example, MRP inventory and production schedules are translated into cost requirements for the financial management department and personnel requirements for the human resources department. Information on capacity availability for new-customer orders goes to the marketing department.

manufacturing resource planning (MRP II)
An advanced version of MRP that ties together all parts of the organization into the company's production activities.

Quality Control

Quality control refers to the management of the production process so as to manufacture goods or supply services that meet specific quality standards. McDonald's, for example, is a pioneer in quality control in the restaurant industry. The company oversees everything from the farming of potatoes for French fries to the packing of meat for Big Macs. Quality-assurance staffers even check standards for ketchup sweetness and French fry length. We discuss quality control in more detail in the following section, where we focus on the connection between productivity and quality.

quality control
The management of the production process so as to manufacture goods or supply services that meet specific quality standards.

THE PRODUCTIVITY–QUALITY CONNECTION

Explain the connection between *productivity* and *quality*. 6

Productivity measures how much is produced relative to the resources used to produce it. Productivity considers both the amounts and the quality of what is produced. By using resources more efficiently, the quantity of output will be greater. But unless the resulting goods and services are of satisfactory quality, consumers will not want them. **Quality**, then, means fitness for use—offering features that consumers want.

quality
A product's fitness for use in terms of offering the features that consumers want.

Responding to the Productivity Challenge

As we noted in the opening case, productivity is an international issue with major domestic effects. A nation's productivity determines how large a piece of the global economic resource pie it gets. A country with more resources has more wealth to divide among its citizens. A country whose productivity fails to increase as rapidly as that of other countries will see its people's standard of living fall relative to the rest of the world.

Measuring Productivity

How do we know how productive a country is? Most countries use **labour productivity** to measure their level of productivity:

labour productivity
Partial productivity ratio calculated by dividing gross domestic product by total number of workers.

$$\text{Labour productivity of a country} = \frac{\text{Gross domestic product}}{\text{Total number of workers}}$$

The focus on labour, rather than on other resources (such as capital or energy), is preferred because most countries keep accurate records on employment and hours worked.

Productivity Among Global Competitors

A study by the Organization for Economic Cooperation and Development (OECD) reports productivity levels in 23 countries. Figure 10.5 compares productivity among several OECD countries. As you can see, economic output per hour worked in Belgium is about 28 percent higher than the average for OECD members. At 31 percent below average, output in New Zealand is lowest among the nations listed.

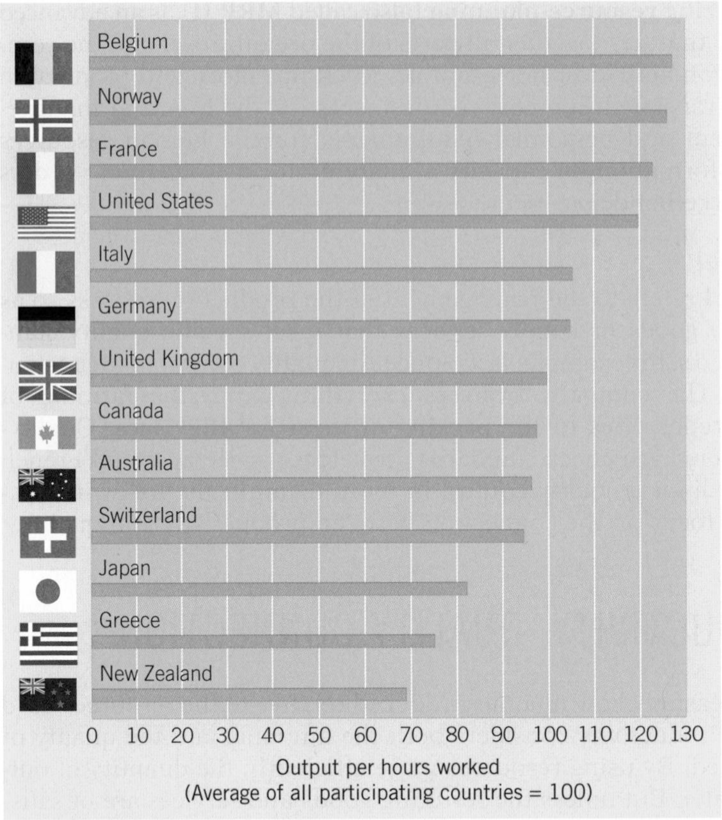

Figure 10.5 International productivity comparisons.

Michael Porter, a Harvard University expert on international competitiveness, says that Canada's competitiveness is a concern because we have been living off our rich diet of natural resources. In Porter's view, Canada will have to start emphasizing innovation and develop a more sophisticated mix of products if it hopes to be successful in international markets. Porter criticizes Canadian business, government, and labour for failing to abandon outdated ways of thinking regarding productivity and innovation.[12]

Domestic Productivity

Nations must pay attention to their domestic productivity regardless of their global standing. A country that improves its ability to make something out of its existing resources can increase the wealth of all its inhabitants. Conversely, a decline in productivity shrinks a nation's total wealth. Additional wealth from higher productivity can be shared among workers (as higher wages), investors (as higher profits), and customers (as stable prices). When productivity drops, however, wages can be increased only by reducing profits (penalizing investors) or by increasing prices (penalizing customers).

Manufacturing Versus Service Productivity

Manufacturing productivity is higher than service productivity. For many years, it was widely believed that the service sector suffered from "Baumol's Disease," named after economist William Baumol. He argued that since the service sector focused more on hands-on activity that machines couldn't replace, it would be more difficult to increase productivity in services. Baumol noted, for example, that it would always require four musicians to play a Mozart quartet. But the Opera Company of Brooklyn is challenging that notion. It now puts on the opera *The Marriage of Figaro* with only 12 musicians and a technician who oversees a computer program that plays all the other parts. The orchestra's productivity has increased sharply because it does not have to pay for the usual complement of musicians.[13]

Industry Productivity

Industries differ in terms of their productivity. Agriculture is more productive in Canada than in many other nations because we use more sophisticated technology. Technological advances have also given the computer industry a productivity edge. In the forestry industry, Canfor Corp. is using Genus—a computerized database containing geographic information and other essential data about Canfor's vast lumber and pulp operations in British Columbia and Alberta—as a strategic planning tool to determine how the company should adjust its logging plans to reflect market demand.[14] Forestry firms in other countries are also increasing their productivity. In Brazil, for example, genetic engineering has resulted in the development of eucalyptus trees that are ready for harvest just seven years after they are planted (in Canada, the wait is often 50 years). A eucalyptus plantation in 1980 produced about 30 cubic metres of wood per hectare each year, but by 2002 that number had increased to 45 cubic metres of wood.[15]

Company Productivity

High productivity gives a company a competitive edge because its costs are lower. As a result, it can offer its product at a lower price (and gain more customers), or it can make a greater profit on each item sold. The productivity of individual companies is therefore important to investors, workers, and managers.

MEETING THE QUALITY CHALLENGE

Business has not always recognized the importance of quality. In the decades following the Second World War, American business consultant

On the left, workers assemble a truck the old way, manually lowering and bolting frames onto axles. On the right, the process is highly automated (and safer), with robotic grippers to flip and align the bulky frames.

W. Edwards Deming tried to persuade U.S. firms that they needed to improve quality at least as much as quantity. Like many a prophet, he was not honoured in his homeland. But his arguments won the Japanese over. Through years of meticulous hard work, Japan's manufacturers have changed "Made in Japan" from a synonym for cheap, shoddy merchandise into a hallmark of reliability. Eventually, North American businesses came to understand that Deming was right. A current example of an attempt to convey quality to consumers is described in the Business Accountability box.

BUSINESS ACCOUNTABILITY

Rating the Quality of Diamonds

How do you rate the quality of diamonds? Historically, diamond quality has been assessed by reference to four Cs: *cut, colour, clarity,* and *carat.* But perhaps a fifth C is emerging, and that is "country of origin." Better yet, the fifth C may also stand for "Canada."

Until just a few years ago, Canada was not even a player in the international diamond business. But in 1991, a promising diamond field was located in the Northwest Territories and the race was on to exploit the possibilities. Skeptics said that even if diamonds were found in commercial quantities in Canada, the diamonds would have to be sold to DeBeers, the company that controlled the world diamond trade. But once diamond wholesalers were shown the first Canadian diamonds, they realized that the quality was as high as that from the best diamond mines in the world, and they eagerly bought them. The myth of DeBeers' control soon evaporated.

The first Canadian diamond mine was opened in the Northwest Territories in 1998 and by 2003 it was already producing 6 percent of the total world's supply of rough diamonds. A second mine opened in 2003, and another in 2006. Canada produces 12 percent of the world's diamonds. There are also promising developments in diamond mining in Nunavut and in Saskatchewan (where core samples drilled by Shore Gold show that high quality diamonds exist there).

In recent years, there has been much publicity (and a Hollywood movie) about so-called "blood diamonds," that is, diamonds that are mined by armed workers in war-torn African countries like Sierra Leone. These diamonds are then exported, and the money used to support further military campaigns. The developing Canadian diamond industry has no such image problems. Diamonds in Canada are mined under very ethical and environmentally strict conditions. And there's one added advantage: the quality of Canadian diamonds is very high. Canadian rough diamonds from the Northwest Territories average U.S.$170 per carat in value, far above the U.S.$100 level at which diamonds are considered precious. The new samples from Saskatchewan are valued at about U.S.$135 per carat.

But is country of origin important enough to influence consumers when they purchase a diamond? In the minds of many consumers, the quality of certain products *is* associated with the product's country of origin. Think, for example, of Swiss watches, Italian leather, and French wines. Oren Sofer, CEO of diamond wholesaler Beny Sofer & Sons LLC, says that if you can brand water, you certainly should be able to brand diamonds. He wants consumers to eventually recognize "Canadian diamonds" as an important brand name.

This is not an impossible goal. The move is already underway to establish a high quality reputation for Canadian diamonds. Sirius Diamond Inc., a Vancouver diamond wholesaler, engraves a tiny polar bear on the Canadian diamonds it sells, and Birks & Sons Inc. engraves a maple leaf on its diamonds. The government of the Northwest Territories provides a certificate for each diamond that has come from its mines. This ensures that diamonds from other countries cannot be passed off as Canadian stones. For example, the Clay Pot, a diamond retailer in New York, guarantees conflict-free diamonds from Canada.

QUESTIONS FOR DISCUSSION

1. How can business firms be made accountable for the conditions under which they produce diamonds? Be specific and practical in your suggestions.
2. Read the arguments of critics who say that the "blood diamonds" issue is phoney, and that there really aren't any "blood diamonds" at all. Compare these arguments with those who say there is a real problem with "blood diamonds." Who do you think has the better arguments? Explain your reasoning.

Quality advocates such as Joseph Juran and Kaoru Ishikawa introduced methods and tools for implementing quality. Ishikawa, for example, developed so-called "fishbone diagrams," also known as "cause-and-effect diagrams" or "Ishikawa diagrams, that help employees figure out the causes of quality problems in their work areas. The diagram in Figure 10.6, for instance, was designed to help an airport manager find out why his facility had so many delayed departures. Focusing on five major categories of possible causes, he then noted several potential causes of the problem in each. (It turns out that there weren't enough tow trucks to handle baggage transfers.)[16]

Managing for Quality

Explain the concept of *total quality management* and describe nine tools that companies can use to achieve it. 7

Total quality management (TQM) includes all of the activities necessary for getting high-quality goods and services into the marketplace. TQM emphasizes that no defects are tolerable, and that employees are responsible for maintaining quality standards. At Toyota's Cambridge, Ontario, plant, for example, workers can push a button or pull a rope to stop the production line when something is not up to standard.[17]

total quality management (TQM) A concept that emphasizes that no defects are tolerable and that all employees are responsible for maintaining quality standards.

A customer focus is the starting point for TQM. It includes using methods for determining what customers want, and then making sure that all the company's activities and people are focused on fulfilling those needs. Total participation is critical; if all employees are not working toward improved quality, the firm is wasting potential contributions from its human resources, and is missing a chance to become a stronger competitor in the marketplace. TQM in today's competitive markets demands unending and continuous improvement of products, after-sales services, and all of the company's internal processes, such as accounting, delivery, billing, and information flow.

Consider the example of Standard Aero in Winnipeg, which is in the business of aircraft overhaul. When the company instituted TQM, the process began with the formation of a "change council" consisting of the CEO and five senior managers. Next, a nine-person task force was formed

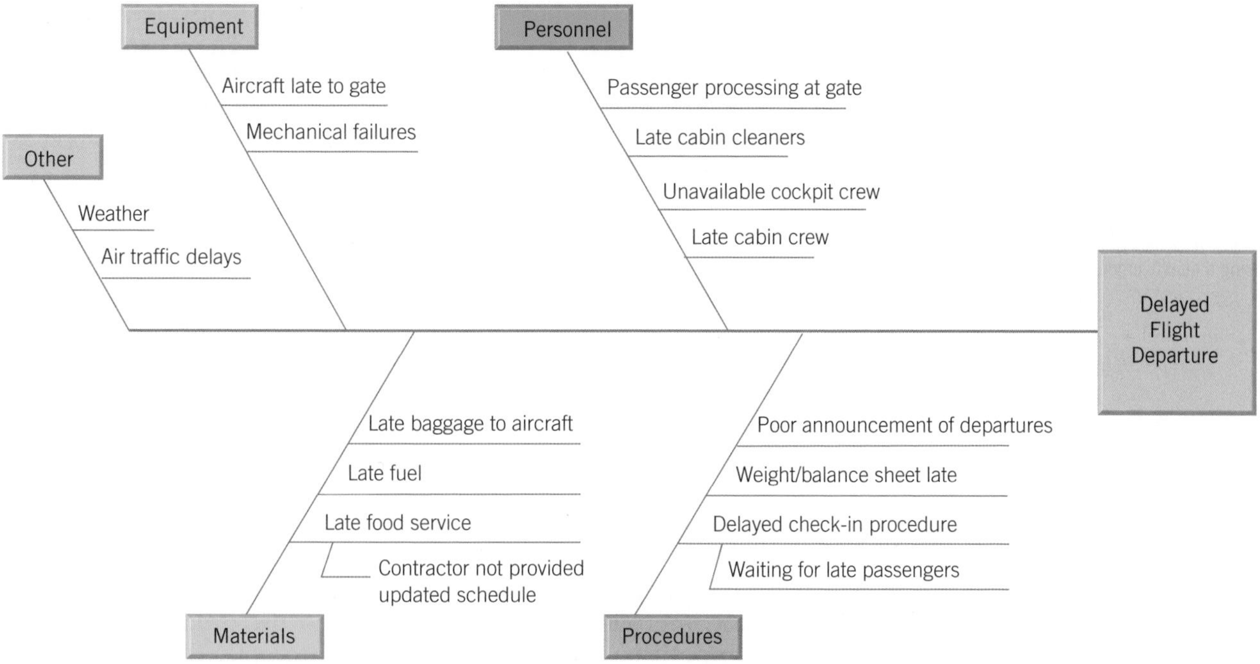

Figure 10.6 "Fishbone" or cause-and-effect diagram.

that consisted of employees who had done the full range of jobs on one of Standard's major overhaul contracts. Its first job was to find out what the customer wanted. It did this by designing a questionnaire and visiting customer plants around the world to gather information. The task force also worked within Standard Aero to determine exactly how the company did its aircraft overhaul work. After weeks of analysis, the task force was able to reduce the time required for overhaul work significantly. For example, the number of times a certain gearbox was handled as it moved through the repair process was reduced by 84 percent.[18]

Planning for Quality

Planning for quality should begin before products are designed or redesigned. Managers need to set goals for both quality levels and quality reliability in the beginning. **Performance quality** refers to the features of a product and how well it performs. For example, Maytag gets a price premium because its washers and dryers offer a high level of performance quality. Customers perceive Maytags as having more advanced features and being more durable than other brands.

performance quality
The overall degree of quality; how well the features of a product meet consumers' needs and how well the product performs.

Performance quality may or may not be related to quality reliability in a product. **Quality reliability** refers to the consistency or repeatability of performance. Toyota's small cars have high quality reliability, and the firm has a reputation for producing very few "lemons."

quality reliability
The consistency of quality from unit to unit of a product.

Organizing for Quality

The old idea of a separate "quality control" department is no longer enough. Everyone from the chair of the board to the part-time clerk—purchasers, engineers, janitors, marketers, machinists, and other personnel—must work to assure quality. At Germany's Messerschmitt-Bölkow-Blohm aerospace company, for example, all employees are responsible for inspecting their own work. The overall goal is to reduce eventual problems to a minimum by making the product correctly from the beginning.

Leading for Quality

Too often, firms fail to take the initiative to make quality happen. Leading for quality means that managers must inspire and motivate employees throughout the company to achieve quality goals. They need to help employees see how they affect quality and how quality affects their jobs and their company. If managers succeed, employees will ultimately accept **quality ownership**—the idea that quality belongs to each person who creates or destroys it while performing a job.

quality ownership
The concept that quality belongs to each employee who creates or destroys it in producing a good or service; the idea that all workers must take responsibility for producing a quality product.

Controlling for Quality

By monitoring its products and services, a company can detect mistakes and make corrections. To do so, however, managers must first establish specific quality standards and measurements. In a bank, for example, supervisors periodically evaluate transactions against a checklist. Specific aspects of each teller's work—appearance, courtesy, efficiency, and so on—are recorded. The results, reviewed with employees, either confirm proper performance or indicate changes that are needed to bring performance up to standards.

Tools for Quality Assurance

In managing for quality, companies rely on assistance from proven tools. Often, ideas for improving both the product and the production process come from **competitive product analysis**. For example, Toshiba will take apart a Xerox photocopier and test each component to see how it compares with Toshiba's competing product. They then can decide which Toshiba

competitive product analysis
Process by which a company analyzes a competitor's products to identify desirable improvements.

product features are satisfactory, which product features need to be upgraded, and whether Toshiba's production processes need improvement.

There are many specific tools that can be used to achieve the desired level of quality: *value-added analysis, statistical process control, quality/cost studies, quality improvement teams, benchmarking, getting closer to the customer, ISO 9000:2000 and ISO 14000, re-engineering,* and *adding value through supply chains*.

Value-Added Analysis

Value-added analysis means evaluating all work activities, material flows, and paperwork to determine the value that they add for customers. Value-added analysis often reveals wasteful or unnecessary activities that can be eliminated without harming customer service. For example, when Hewlett-Packard reduced its customer contracts from 20 pages to as few as 2, computer sales rose by more than 18 percent.

value-added analysis
The evaluation of all work activities, material flows, and paperwork to determine the value they add for customers.

Statistical Process Control

Companies can improve uniformity in their outputs by understanding the sources of variation. **Statistical process control (SPC)** methods—especially process variation studies and control charts—allow managers to analyze variations in production data.

statistical process control (SPC)
Statistical analysis techniques that allow managers to analyze variations in production data and to detect when adjustments are needed to create products with high quality reliability.

Process Variation. While some amount of **process variation** is acceptable, too much can result in poor quality and excessive operating costs. Consider the box-filling operation for Honey Nuggets cereal. Each automated machine fills two 400-gram boxes per second. Even under proper conditions, slight variations in cereal weight from box to box are normal. Equipment and tools wear out, the cereal may be overly moist, machinists make occasional adjustments. But how much variation is occurring? How much is acceptable?

process variation
Any change in employees, materials, work methods, or equipment that affects output quality.

Information about variation in a process can be obtained from a *process capability study*. Boxes are taken from the filling machines and weighed. The results are plotted, as in Figure 10.7, and compared with the upper and lower *specification limits* (quality limits) for weight. These limits define good and bad quality for box filling. Boxes with more than 410 grams are a wasteful "giveaway." Underfilling has a cost because it is unlawful.

In Figure 10.7, we see that none of Machine A's output violates the quality limits, and it is fully capable of meeting the company's quality standards. But Machines B and C have problems and cannot reliably meet Honey Nuggets' quality standards. The company must take special—and costly—actions to sort the good from the bad boxes before releasing the cereal for shipment.

Control Charts. Knowing that a process is capable of meeting quality standards is not enough. Managers must still monitor the process to prevent its going astray during production. To detect the beginning of bad conditions, managers can check production periodically and plot the results on a **control chart**. For example, several times a day, a machine operator at Honey Nuggets might weigh several boxes of cereal together to ascertain the average weight.

control chart
A statistical process control method in which results of test sampling of a product are plotted on a diagram that reveals when the process is beginning to depart from normal operating conditions.

Quality/Cost Studies for Quality Improvement

Statistical process controls help keep operations up to existing capabilities. But in today's competitive environment, firms must consistently *raise* quality capabilities. Managers thus face the challenge of identifying the improvements that offer the greatest promise. **Quality/cost studies** are helpful to managers, because they not only identify a firm's current costs but also reveal areas with the largest cost-saving potential.[19]

quality/cost studies
A method of improving product quality by assessing a firm's current quality-related costs and identifying areas with the greatest cost-saving potential.

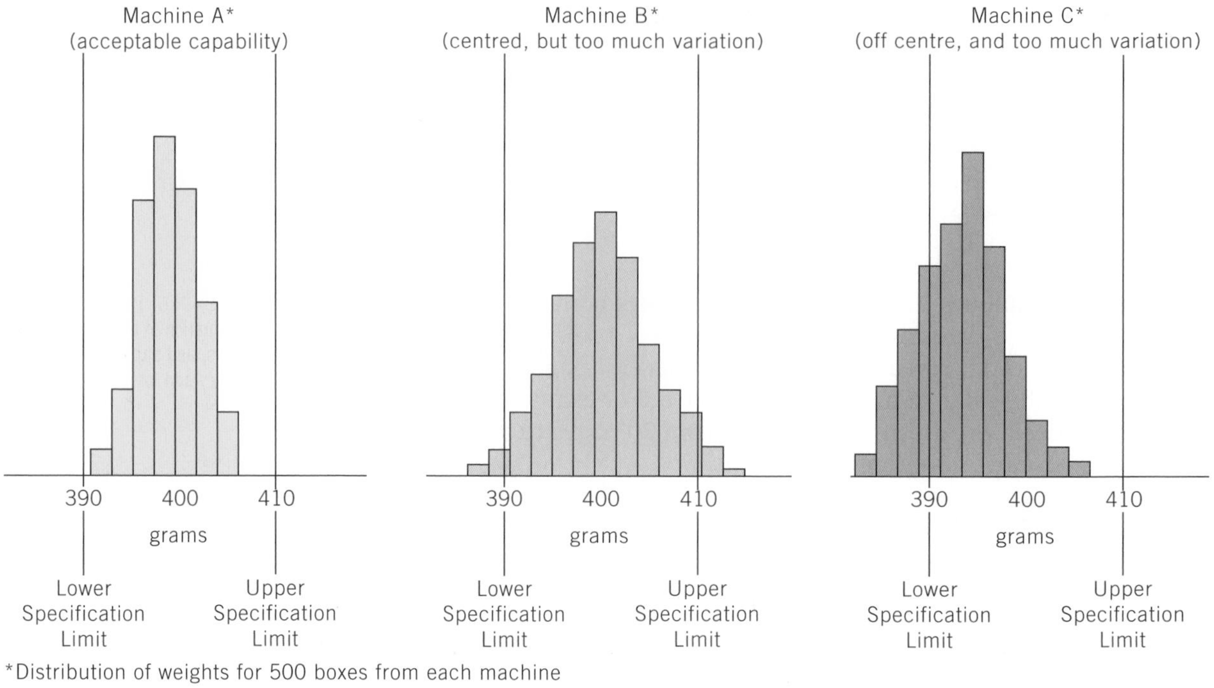

Figure 10.7 Process variation in box filling for Honey Nuggets cereal.

internal failures
Expenses incurred during production and before bad product leaves the plant.

external failures
Allowing defective products to leave the factory and get into consumers' hands.

For example, Honey Nuggets must determine its costs for **internal failures**. These are expenses—including the costs of overfilling boxes and the costs of sorting out bad boxes—incurred during production and before bad product leaves the plant. Despite quality control procedures, however, some bad boxes may get out of the factory, reach the customer, and generate complaints from grocers and cereal eaters. These are **external failures** that occur outside the factory. The costs of correcting them—refunds to customers, transportation costs to return bad boxes to the factory, possible lawsuits, factory recalls—should also be tabulated in the quality/cost study.

Quality Improvement Teams

Quality improvement (QI) teams are groups of employees from various work areas who meet regularly to define, analyze, and solve common production problems. Their goal is to improve both their own work methods and the products they make.[20] Many QI teams organize their own work,

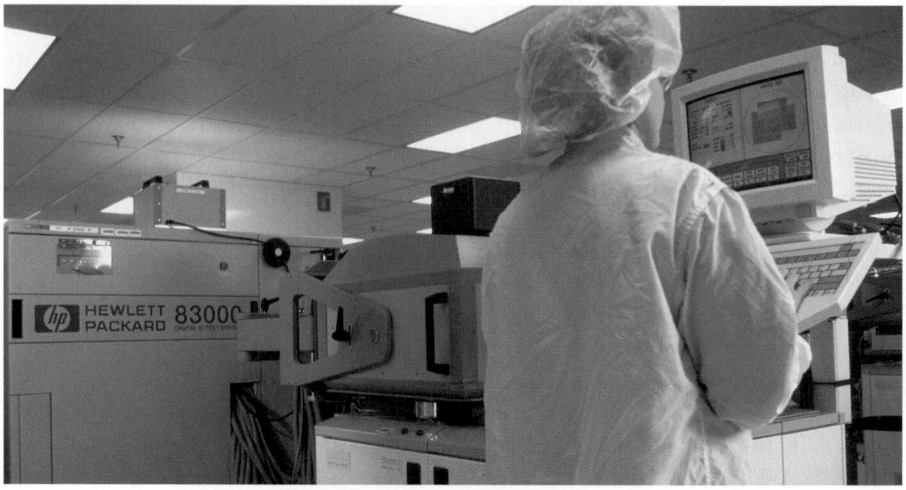

At Hewlett-Packard, testing machines use tiny probes to ensure that the electronic characteristics of every semiconductor are correct. Such systems are designed to check primarily for so-called "class defects"—problems that can affect a whole range of products on the assembly line. One bad wafer at the end of the line can represent a waste of $10 000 in costs, and its commercial value is zero.

select leaders, and address problems in the workplace. Motorola, for example, sponsors company-wide team competitions to emphasize the value of the team approach, to recognize outstanding team performance, and to reaffirm the team's role in the company's continuous-improvement culture. Teams get higher marks for dealing with projects closely tied to Motorola's key initiatives.[21]

Benchmarking

With **benchmarking**, a company compares its current performance against its own past performance (internal benchmarking), or against the performance of its competitors (external benchmarking). As an example of the former, the percentage of customer phone calls last month requiring more than two minutes of response time may be compared to the required response time the month before that. As an example of the latter, Toronto Hospital gathered performance data on 26 indicators from various Canadian hospitals so it could determine how well it was performing compared to other organizations in the health-care industry.[22]

benchmarking Comparing the quality of the firm's output with the quality of the output of the industry's leaders.

Getting Closer to the Customer

Says one advocate of quality improvement, "Customers are an economic asset. They're not on the balance sheet, but they should be." Struggling companies have often lost sight of customers as the driving force behind all business activity. Such companies may design products that customers do not want, or ignore customer reactions to existing products, or fail to keep up with changing tastes. Meanwhile, successful businesses take steps to know what their customers want in the products they consume.

Caterpillar Financial Services won a recent Malcolm Baldrige National Quality Award—the prestigious award for excellence in quality—for high ratings by its customers (dealers and buyers of Caterpillar equipment). Buying and financing equipment from Cat Financial became easier as Cat moved its services increasingly online. Customers now have 24/7 access to information on how much they owe on equipment, and they can make payments around the clock. In the past, the 60 000 customers had to phone a Cat representative, who was often unavailable, resulting in delays and wasted time. The improved online system is testimony to Cat Financial's dedication in knowing what customers want and then providing it.[23]

At Greyhound Lines of Canada, the marketing and operations vice-president wanted to drive home the point to managers that clean restrooms are important to customers. He warned regional managers that he would visit bus depots on one hour's notice to see if the restrooms were clean enough to eat dinner in. Within weeks, photos of regional managers having dinner in spotless restrooms began pouring in to the vice-president's office.[24]

ISO 9000:2000 and ISO 14000

DuPont Co. had a problem: A moulding press used to make plastic connectors for computers had a 30-percent defect rate. Efforts to solve the problem went nowhere until, as part of a plant-wide quality program, press operators were asked to submit detailed written reports describing how they did their jobs. After comparing notes, operators realized that they were incorrectly measuring the temperature of the moulding press; as a result, temperature adjustments were often wrong. With the mystery solved, the defect rate dropped to 8 percent.

The quality program that led to this solution is called *ISO 9000*—a certification program attesting to the fact that a factory, a laboratory, or an office has met the rigorous quality management requirements set by the International Organization for Standardization. ISO 9000 (pronounced *ICE-o nine thousand*) originated in Europe as an attempt to standardize materials received from suppliers in such high-tech industries as electronics, chemicals, and aviation. Today, more than 140 countries have adopted ISO 9000 as a national standard, and more than 400 000 certificates have been issued in 160 countries.[25]

The latest version, *ISO 9000:2000*, indicates that it was revised in 2000. Revised standards allow firms to show that they follow documented procedures for testing products, training workers, keeping records, and fixing defects. To become certified, companies must document the procedures followed by workers during every stage of production. The purpose is to ensure that a manufacturer's product is exactly the same today as it was yesterday and as it will be tomorrow. Ideally, standardized processes would ensure that goods are produced at the same level of quality even if all employees were replaced by a new set of workers.

ISO 14000
Certification program attesting to the fact that a factory, laboratory, or office has improved environmental performance.

The **ISO 14000** program certifies improvements in *environmental* performance. Extending the ISO approach into the arena of environmental protection and hazardous waste management, ISO 14000 requires a firm to develop an *environmental management system (EMS)*, which is a plan documenting how the company has acted to improve its performance in using resources (such as raw materials) and in managing pollution. A company must not only identify hazardous wastes that it expects to create, but it must also stipulate plans for treatment and disposal. ISO 14000 covers practices in environmental labelling—the use of such terms as *energy efficient* and *recyclable*—and assesses the total environmental impact of the firm's products, not just from manufacturing, but also from use and disposal.

Business Process Re-Engineering

business process re-engineering
Redesigning of business processes to improve performance, quality, and productivity.

Business process re-engineering focuses on improving business processes by rethinking each of its steps, starting from scratch. *Re-engineering* is the fundamental rethinking and radical redesign of business processes to achieve dramatic improvements as measured by cost, quality, service, and speed.[26] The example given above of Caterpillar's changeover to an online system for customers is an example. Cat re-engineered the whole payments and financing process by improving equipment, retraining employees, and connecting customers to Cat's databases. As the example illustrates, redesign is guided by a desire to improve operations and thereby provide higher-value services for the customer.

Adding Value Through Supply Chains

Managers sometimes forget that a company belongs to a network of firms that must coordinate their activities. As each firm performs its transformation processes, it relies on others in the network. A **supply chain (or value chain)** for any product is the flow of information, materials, and services that starts with raw-materials suppliers and continues adding value through other stages in the network of firms until the product reaches the end customer.[27]

supply chain (value chain)
Flow of information, materials, and services that starts with raw materials suppliers and continues through other stages in the operations process until the product reaches the end customer.

Figure 10.8 shows the supply chain activities involved in supplying baked goods to consumers. Each stage adds value for the final customer. The chain begins with raw materials (grain harvested from the farm). It also includes additional storage and transportation activities, factory operations for baking and wrapping, and distribution to retailers. Each stage depends on the others for success in getting fresh-baked goods to consumers.

supply chain management (SCM)
Principle of looking at the chain as a whole to improve the overall flow through the system.

Supply chain management (SCM) tries to improve the overall flow through a system composed of companies working together. Because customers ultimately get better value, SCM gains competitive advantage for each supply-chain member.[28] A traditionally managed bakery, for example,

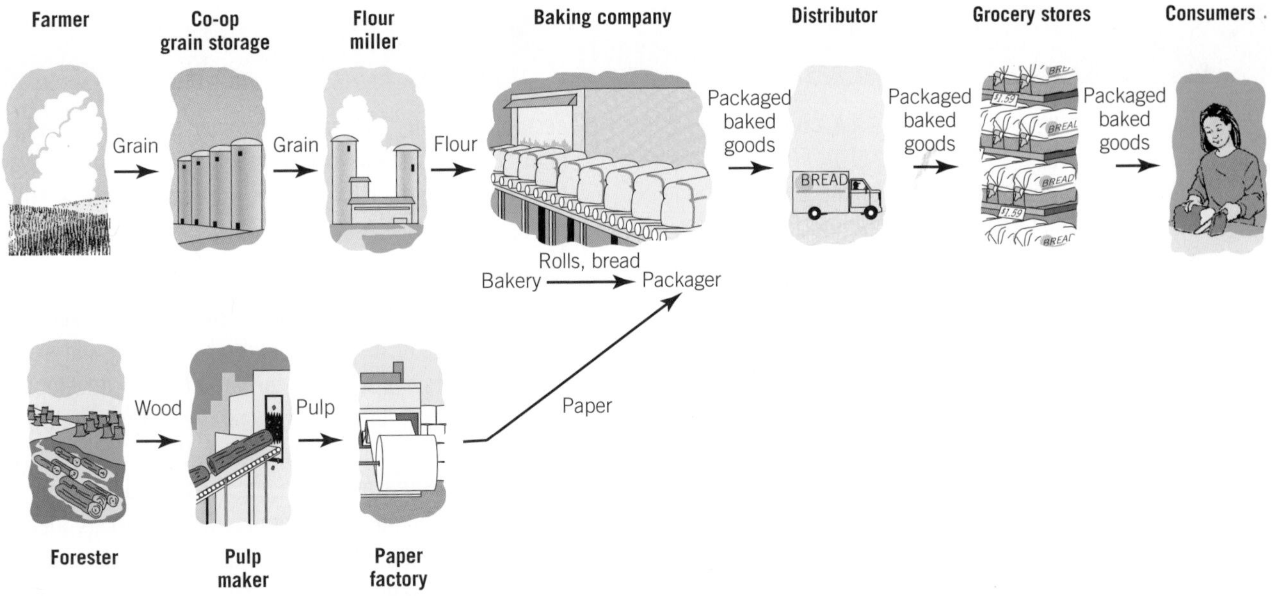

Figure 10.8 Supply chain for baked goods.

would focus simply on getting production inputs from flour millers and paper suppliers and supplying baked goods to distributors. Unfortunately, this approach limits the chain's performance and doesn't allow for possible improvements when activities are more carefully coordinated. Supply chain management can improve performance and, as a result, provide higher quality at lower prices.

An innovative supply chain strategy was at the heart of Michael Dell's vision when he established Dell Inc. The process starts when customer orders are automatically translated into updated production schedules in the factory. These schedules are used not only by operations managers at Dell but also by parts suppliers such as Sony, which adjust their own production and shipping activities to better meet Dell's production needs. In turn, parts suppliers' updated schedules are transmitted to their materials suppliers, and so on up the chain. As Dell's requirements change, suppliers up and down the chain synchronize their schedules to produce only the right materials and parts. As a result, Dell's prices are low and turnaround time for shipping PCs to customers is reduced to a matter of hours instead of days.

Fashion house Louis Vuitton, which produces upscale products like its "Reade" totebag, used to focus mainly on product image and product design. When an item became a hot seller, retailers often ran out of product because the company's production system and supply chain was not responsive to increased consumer demand. Vuitton has revamped its systems in order to ensure that retailers always have a supply of in-demand Vuitton products on their shelves. Other luxury-goods manufacturers like Armani, Gucci, and Versace are doing the same thing.[29]

Summary of Learning Objectives

1. Explain the meaning of the term *production* (or *operations*) and describe the four kinds of *utility* it provides. *Production* (or *operations*) refers to the processes and activities for transforming resources into finished services and goods for customers. Resources include knowledge, physical materials, equipment, and labour that are systematically combined in a production facility to create four kinds of *utility* for customers: *time utility* (which makes products available when customers want them), *place utility* (which makes products available where they are convenient for customers), possession or *ownership utility* (by which customers benefit from possessing and using the product), and *form utility* (which results from the creation of the product).

2. Identify the characteristics that distinguish *service operations* from *goods production* and explain the main differences in the *service focus*. Although the creation of both goods and services involves resources, transformations, and finished products, service operations differ from goods manufacturing in several important ways. In service production, the raw materials are not, say, glass or steel, but rather people who choose among sellers because they have unsatisfied needs or possessions that require care or alteration. Therefore, whereas services are typically performed, goods are physically produced. In addition, services are largely *intangible*, more likely than physical goods to be *customized* to meet the purchaser's needs, and more *unstorable* than most products. Service businesses therefore focus explicitly on these characteristics of their products. Because services are intangible, for instance, providers work to ensure that customers receive value in the form of pleasure, satisfaction, or a feeling of safety. Often, they also focus on both the transformation process and the final product (say, making the loan interview a pleasant experience as well as providing the loan itself). Finally, service providers typically focus on the *customer-service link*, often acknowledging the customer as part of the operations process.

3. Describe and explain the three classifications of *operations processes*. Operations managers in manufacturing use one of two classifications to describe operations processes. Criteria include the *type of technology* used (chemical, fabrication, assembly, transport, or clerical) to transform raw materials into finished goods and whether products are submitted to *analytic* or *synthetic processes* (that is, whether the process breaks down resources into components or combines raw materials into finished products). Service operations are classified according to the *extent of customer contact*, as either high-contact systems (the customer is part of the system) or low-contact (customers are not in contact while the service is provided).

4. Describe the factors involved in *operations planning*. *Operations planning* involves the analysis of six key factors. *Forecasts* of future demand for both new and existing products provide information for developing production plans. In *capacity planning*, the firm analyzes how much of a product it must be able to produce. In high-contact services, managers must plan capacity to meet peak demand. Capacity planning for goods means ensuring that manufacturing capacity slightly exceeds the normal demand for its product. *Location planning* for goods and for low-contact services involves analyzing proposed facility sites in terms of proximity to raw materials and markets, availability of labour, and energy and transportation costs. Location planning for high-contact services, in contrast, involves locating the service near customers, who are part of the system. *Layout planning* involves designing a facility so that customer needs are supplied for high-contact services and so as to enhance production efficiency. Layout alternatives include product, process, and cellular configurations. In *quality planning*, systems are developed to ensure that products meet a firm's quality standards. Finally, in *methods planning*, specific production steps and methods for performing them are identified. *Service flow analysis* and *process flow charts* are helpful for identifying all operations activities and eliminating wasteful steps from production.

5. Explain the activities involved in *operations control*, including *materials management* and the use of *operation control tools*. *Operations control* requires production managers to monitor production performance, by comparing results with detailed plans and schedules, and then to take corrective action as needed. *Materials management* is the planning, organizing, and controlling of the flow of materials. It focuses on the control of *transportation* (transporting resources to the manufacturer and products to customers), *warehousing* (storing both incoming raw materials and finished goods), *purchasing* (acquiring the raw materials and services that a manufacturer needs), *supplier selection*, and *inventory control*. To control operations processes, managers use various methods. For example, *worker training* programs can assist in quality control, the management of the operations process so as to ensure that services and goods meet specific quality standards. *Just-in-time (JIT) production systems* bring

together all materials and parts needed at each production stage at the precise moment they are required. JIT reduces manufacturing inventory costs and reveals production problems that need improvement. *Material requirements planning (MRP)* is another method for ensuring that the right amounts of materials are delivered to the right place at the right time for manufacturing. It uses computer-controlled schedules for moving inventories through each stage of production.

6. Describe the connection between *productivity* and *quality*. *Productivity* is a measure of economic performance; it compares how much is produced with the resources used to produce it. *Quality* is a product's fitness for use. However, an emphasis solely on productivity or solely on quality is not enough. Profitable competition in today's business world demands high levels of both productivity and quality.

7. Identify the activities involved in *total quality management* and describe nine tools that companies can use to achieve it. *Total quality management (TQM)* is the planning, organizing, leading, and controlling of all the activities needed to get high-quality goods and services into the marketplace. Managers must set goals for and implement the processes needed to achieve high quality and reliability levels. *Value-added analysis* evaluates all work activities, materials flows, and paperwork to determine what value they add for customers. *Statistical process control methods*, such as *process variation studies* and *control charts*, can help keep quality consistently high. *Quality/cost studies*, which identify potential savings, can help firms improve quality. *Quality improvement teams* also can improve operations by more fully involving employees in decision making. *Benchmarking*—studying the firm's own performance and the best practices of other companies to gather information for improving a company's own goods and services—has become an increasingly common TQM tool. *Getting closer to the customer* provides a better understanding of what customers want so that firms can satisfy them more effectively. *ISO 9000:2000* is a certification program attesting to the fact that a factory, a laboratory, or an office has met the rigorous quality management requirements set by the International Organization for Standardization. *Re-engineering* is the process of rethinking and redesigning business processes to achieve improvements in productivity. *Supply chain management* focuses on the activities that are needed to coordinate movement of products from the raw materials stage to the point of consumer ownership.

QUESTIONS AND EXERCISES

Questions for Analysis

1. What are the resources needed and the finished "products" that are produced in the following services: real estate firm, childcare facility, bank, city water and electric department, and hotel?
2. Find good examples of a synthetic production process and an analytic process. Then classify each according to whether it is chemical, fabrication, assembly, transport, or clerical. Explain your analysis.
3. Pick three products (not services) that you regularly use. Then do some research to determine which of the basic production processes are used to produce these products (chemical, fabrication, assembly, transport, or clerical processes). To what extent are multiple processes used in the production of the product?
4. Pick three services (not products) that you regularly use. Explain what customization, unstorability, and intangibility mean for each of the services. How do these factors influence the way the service is delivered to customers?
5. Develop a service flow analysis for some service that you use frequently, such as buying lunch at a cafeteria, having your hair cut, or riding a bus. Identify areas of potential quality or productivity failures in the process.
6. High productivity in the service sector has historically been difficult to achieve. Why was this so? What might be changing in this area that will cause service productivity to increase during the next decade?
7. Pick a consumer product that you use regularly and trace the supply chain for the product.
8. What are the similarities and differences in location planning for goods versus location planning for services?

Application Exercises

9. Using a local firm as an example, show how you would conduct a quality/cost study. Identify the cost categories and give some examples of the costs in each category. Which categories do you expect to have the highest and lowest costs? Why?

10. Interview the owner of a local service business, such as a laundry or dry-cleaning shop. Identify the major decisions that were necessary in planning its service operations. Prepare a report suggesting areas for improvement.

BUILDING YOUR BUSINESS SKILLS

Making Your Benchmark in the World

Goal

To encourage students to understand ways in which benchmarking can improve quality and productivity.

Situation

As the director of maintenance for a regional airline, you are disturbed to learn that the cost of maintaining your 20-plane fleet is skyrocketing. A major factor is repair time; when maintenance or repairs are required, work often proceeds slowly. As a result, additional aircraft are required to meet the schedule. To address the problem, you decide to use a powerful total quality management tool called benchmarking. You will approach your problem by studying ways in which other companies have successfully managed similar problems. Your goal is to apply the best practices to your own maintenance and repair operation.

Method

Step 1 Working with three or four other students, choose your benchmarking target from among the following choices:

- the maintenance and repair operations of a competing airline
- the pit crew operations of a race car team
- the maintenance and repair operations of a national trucking company

Write a memo explaining the reasons for your choice.

Step 2 Write a list of benchmarking questions that will help you learn the best practices of your targeted company. Your goal is to ask questions that will help you improve your own operation. These questions will be asked during on-site visits.

Step 3 As part of a benchmarking project, you will be dealing with your counterparts in other companies. You have a responsibility to prepare for these encounters, and you must remember that what you learn during the exchange process is privileged information. Given these requirements, describe the steps you would take before your first on-site visit and outline your benchmarking code of ethics.

Follow-Up Questions

1. Why is benchmarking an important method for improving quality?
2. Why did you make your benchmarking choice? Explain why the company you selected holds more promise than other companies in helping you to solve your internal maintenance problems.
3. What kind of information would help you to improve the efficiency of your operations? Are you interested in management information, technical information, or both?
4. In an age of heightened competition, why do you think companies are willing to benchmark with each other?

EXERCISING YOUR ETHICS: TEAM EXERCISE

Calculating the Cost of Conscience

The Situation

Product quality and cost affect every firm's reputation and profitability, as well as the satisfaction of customers. This exercise will expose you to some ethical considerations that pertain to certain cost and service decisions that must be made by operations managers.

The Dilemma

As director of quality for a major appliance manufacturer, Ruth was reporting to the executive committee on the results of a program for correcting problems with a newly redesigned compressor that the company had recently begun putting in its refrigerators. Following several customer complaints, the quality lab had determined that some of the new compressor units ran more loudly than expected. One corrective option was simply waiting until customers complained and responding to each complaint if and when it occurred. Ruth, however, decided that this approach was inconsistent with the company's policy of being the high-quality leader in the industry. Insisting on a proactive, "pro-quality" approach, Ruth initiated a program for contacting all customers who had purchased refrigerators containing the new compressor.

Unfortunately, her "quality-and-customers-first" policy was expensive. Service representatives across Canada had to phone every customer, make appointments for home visits, and replace original compressors with a newer model. Because replacement time was only 30 minutes, customers were hardly inconvenienced, and food stayed refrigerated without interruption. Customer response to the replacement program was overwhelmingly favourable.

Near the end of Ruth's report, an executive vice-president was overheard to comment, "Ruth's program has cost this company $400 million in service expenses." Two weeks later, Ruth was fired.

Team Activity

Assemble a group of four students and assign each group member to one of the following roles:

- Ruth
- Ruth's boss
- a customer
- a company investor

Action Steps

1. Before discussing the situation with your group, and from the perspective of your assigned role, do you think that Ruth's firing is consistent with the company's desire for industry leadership in quality? Write down the reasons for your position.
2. Before discussing the situation with your group, and from the perspective of your assigned role, what are the underlying ethical issues, if any, in this situation? Write down the issues.
3. Gather your group together and reveal, in turn, each member's comments on Ruth's firing. Next, reveal the ethical issues listed by each member.
4. Appoint someone to record the main points of agreement and disagreement within the group. How do you explain the results? What accounts for any disagreement?
5. From an ethical standpoint, what does your group conclude is the most appropriate action that should have been taken by the company in this situation?
6. Develop a group response to the following question: What are the respective roles of profits, obligations to customers, and employee considerations for the firm in this situation?

BUSINESS CASE 10

Supply Chain Management at Loblaws

Loblaw Companies Limited is one of Canada's biggest sellers of groceries, and its Real Canadian Superstores—which sell both groceries and general merchandise—are a prominent feature on the Canadian retail scene. Loblaw also operates stores under the Provigo, Fortinos, and No Frills names. Because price-conscious consumers are always looking for the best prices, in 2005 Loblaw embarked on an ambitious plan to improve its supply chain system in order to compete with Wal-Mart (which had seven Supercentres with a full range of food and non-food merchandise by early 2007). But Loblaw's aggressive strategy has run into problems, and it has now decided to close some of its stores, lay off 1000 head office staff, and cut back on the number of non-food items it carries in an attempt to regain its former market position.

In 2005, Loblaw came to the conclusion that it was taking too long for its products to get from its warehouses to its retail grocery stores. To fight off Wal-Mart, and to better serve customers, Loblaw embarked on a $62 million restructuring project, which involved improving its supply chain network, reorganizing grocery merchandising, procurement, and operations groups, updating its information technology systems, consolidating work formerly done in regional offices into its new Ontario head office building, reducing the number of warehouses from 32 to 26, consolidating operations in state-of-the-art facilities, and cutting 1400 jobs.

But problems developed as system implementation began, and Loblaw president John Lederer admitted to financial analysts that the company had moved too fast in trying to implement too many changes. For example, too many distribution facilities were closed before the newer, high-tech ones were ready to cope with increased volume. One supplier shipped merchandise to the Calgary warehouse, but the shipment was refused. Many weeks passed before the shipment was finally accepted and the supplier was paid. These distribution problems forced Loblaw to pull back on marketing its general merchandise offerings. Since it is well known in the retail business that customers get very unhappy when advertised items are not on the shelf, it made little sense to spend money on marketing if the company couldn't guarantee product availability.

Loblaw also incurred some other not-so-obvious costs because of distribution problems. For example, it had to mark down many toys because they were received too late for the Christmas season. Loblaw discovered that it isn't only groceries that are perishable. Another problem: since customers don't know all the products that the superstores carry, there are often noticeably fewer people in the non-grocery sections. In 2005, Loblaw store productivity declined 2.4 percent.

The company also experienced problems as it tried to move 2000 administrative employees to the company's new headquarters in Brampton, Ontario. When about 75 general merchandise product buyers decided to quit the company rather than move, this turnover made it difficult to maintain continuity with suppliers. These missteps not only cost the company millions, they set back its plans for implementation by at least a year. If Loblaw cannot effectively sell both groceries and general merchandise, they will be at a disadvantage compared to Wal-Mart.

Loblaw must compete with Wal-Mart's legendary supply chain management system. To do so, it must develop its own system for keeping in-demand products on its shelves. Such a system will also allow Loblaw to lower its prices and compete with Wal-Mart. Loblaw has hired a supply chain expert from Wal-Mart to spearhead the resolution of its distribution problems. Loblaw is wise to not underestimate the Wal-Mart threat. In the United States, Wal-Mart went from a zero share in groceries to that country's largest grocer in less than a decade. If Wal-Mart has that kind of success in Canada, it will obviously have a detrimental effect on Canadian retailers like Loblaw and Sobey's. Loblaw predicted that it would not return to profitability until at least 2009.

Not all of Loblaw's problems are logistical. In an attempt to compete with Wal-Mart—which is well-known for its anti-union stance—Loblaw's is trying to reduce labour costs by getting the union to agree to wage cuts. Its employees are represented by the United Food and Commercial Workers union, and the union is likely to put up significant resistance to wage cuts.

Questions for Discussion

1. What is a supply chain? Why is efficiency in its supply chain so crucial to Loblaw?
2. What is supply chain management? How is it relevant for Loblaw?
3. What is the relationship between supply chain management, productivity, and quality?

MYBUSINESSLAB

To improve your grade, visit the MyBusinessLab website at **www.pearsoned.ca/mybusinesslab**. This online homework and tutorial system allows you to test your understanding and generates a personalized study plan just for you. It provides you with study and practice tools directly related to this chapter's content. MyBusinessLab puts you in control of your own learning!

CHAPTER 11

Understanding Accounting

After reading this chapter, you should be able to:

1. Explain the role of *accountants* and distinguish among the three types of professional accountants in Canada.
2. Describe how the *accounting equation* is used.
3. Describe three basic *financial statements* and show how they reflect the activity and financial condition of a business.
4. Explain the key standards and principles for reporting financial statements.
5. Explain how computing *financial ratios* can help in analyzing the financial strengths of a business.

Accounting for Pensions

Traditional pension plans have historically been defined benefit plans, that is, the company promises to pay a certain defined amount of money to employees when they retire. But a CGA-Canada report showed that the total deficit of the country's largest pension plans at the end of 2004 was $26 billion. If the indexation of pension benefits is taken into account, the number soars to $190 billion. In terms of proportions, 59 percent of traditional pension plans were experiencing pension shortfalls; this number jumps to 96 percent if the indexation of benefits is taken into account. But the news is not all bad. With the strong showing of the stock market during 2004–2006, the situation has improved considerably. Now, about half of the pension plans in Canada have a surplus, and half have a deficit.

There are also problems in funding retiree *benefits* (not pensions). A study of 71 of Canada's largest companies showed that their liabilities for retiree *benefits* amounted to $16 billion. In one recent year at Suncor Energy Inc., for example, the company's benefits liability was $98 million (almost as much as its pension liability of $99 million). With baby boomers living longer, and with large numbers of them heading into retirement, the situation for both retiree pensions and retiree benefits is likely to get worse before it gets better.

The problems in pension plans have been caused by a variety of factors, but two factors stand out. First, there were lower than anticipated returns on investments held by the pension plans. In the 1990s, returns on pension plan investments averaged 11 percent. This rate of return was higher than the 7.5 percent that had been predicted. But during the period 2001–2003, the average rate of return for pension plan investments was just 3.1 percent. This was far below the 7 percent that had been assumed. This situation was made even worse because companies began to invest more heavily in equities as a result of their positive experience in the stock market boom of the 1990s. In 1990, 64 percent of pension assets were invested in fixed-income securities and only 36 percent in the more risky equities. By 2004, however, 56 percent of pension assets were invested in equities and only 37 percent in fixed-income securities.

Second, because pension plan investments had achieved such high returns in the 1990s, many companies took pension plan contribution "holidays" and did not contribute anything to the plans they were sponsoring. When the lower investment returns of the twenty-first century started showing up, pension surpluses quickly became pension deficits. In retrospect, companies should not have taken contribution holidays.

The crisis in defined benefit pension plans has caused employers to examine alternative ways to deal with pensions. The simplest solution is to drop defined *benefit* pension plans and instead offer employees defined *contribution* pension plans. When the latter is used, the company's liability is known, but the value of the pension plan when a person retires is unknown (its value is determined solely by the rate of return that the investments in the plan have achieved). Defined contribution plans obviously reduce the uncertainty for the company, but create more uncertainty for retirees.

Companies are increasingly shifting to defined contribution pension plans. In the United States, for example, there were 112 000 defined benefit plans in 1985, but now there are only about 29 000. The move away from defined benefit plans is also occurring in Canada, although at a slower rate. But that is likely to change, since Canadian legislation requires companies to bear the full financial burden of pension deficits. The current crisis in defined benefit plans means that over the next five years, $15 billion extra dollars will have to be put into those plans to make up for past investment losses. Companies therefore have an incentive to move away from defined benefit plans and toward defined contribution plans, because with the latter they at least know what their contribution requirements are.

Canadian accounting rules may also need to be reexamined. Under current rules, companies can delay recognizing changes in the value of their pension plans. Using a practice called "smoothing," companies can spread the reporting of changes over several years. When stock markets were booming, no one scrutinized pension plans much because their value was going up. But when stock markets started dropping in 2000, large liabilities began building up (but companies kept that information off their balance sheets). National Bank Financial studied 79 Canadian companies—representing 80 percent of the capitalization of the S&P/TSX—and found that their off-balance sheet pension deficits totalled $21 billion.

Canadian and international accounting regulators are working on changes to accounting rules that will bring more realism to pension reporting. The most obvious change involves ending the practice of smoothing and reporting pension fund returns as they actually take place. This means that income from the pension fund would be reported as investment income and the costs of running the pension fund would be reported as expenses. Regulators recognize that a change like this will increase the volatility in the earnings that corporations report, but they point out that investors will be able to more clearly see what is happening (good or bad) in a company's pension fund.

HOW WILL THIS BENEFIT YOU?

By understanding the material presented in this chapter, you'll benefit in three ways: (1) if you're an *entrepreneur* thinking about starting your own business, you'll discover your obligations for reporting your firm's financial status, (2) as an *employee*, you'll learn how to evaluate your company's financial condition and its prospects for the future, and (3) as an interested *citizen*, you'll learn about accounting ethics and the regulatory requirements for maintaining the public's trust in the Canadian business system.

In this chapter, we focus on the development and use of accounting information. We begin by looking at the role of accountants in providing information. We examine how the accounting equation is used in accounting, and describe the three basic financial statements. We conclude the chapter with an explanation of the key standards and principles for reporting financial information.

WHAT IS ACCOUNTING?

accounting
A comprehensive system for collecting, analyzing, and communicating financial information.

Accounting is a comprehensive information system for collecting, analyzing, and communicating financial information. It measures business performance and translates the findings into information for management decisions. Accountants prepare performance reports for owners, the public, and regulatory agencies. To perform these functions, accountants keep records of such transactions as taxes paid, income received, and expenses incurred, and they analyze the effects of these transactions on particular business activities. By sorting, analyzing, and recording thousands of transactions, accountants can determine how well a business is being managed and how financially strong it is. **Bookkeeping** is just one phase of accounting—the recording of accounting transactions.

bookkeeping
Recording accounting transactions.

accounting information system (AIS)
An organized procedure for identifying, measuring, recording, and retaining financial information so that it can be used in accounting statements and management reports.

Because businesses engage in many thousands of transactions, ensuring that financial information is consistent and dependable is mandatory. This is the job of the **accounting information system (AIS)**: an organized procedure for identifying, measuring, recording, and retaining financial information so that it can be used in accounting statements and management reports. The system includes all of the people, reports, computers, procedures, and resources for compiling financial transactions.[1]

Users of accounting information are numerous:

- *Business managers* use accounting information to set goals, develop plans, set budgets, and evaluate future prospects
- *Employees and unions* use accounting information to get paid and to plan for and receive such benefits as health care, insurance, vacation time, and retirement pay

- *Investors and creditors* use accounting information to estimate returns to stockholders, determine a company's growth prospects, and determine whether it is a good credit risk before investing or lending
- *Tax authorities* use accounting information to plan for tax inflows, determine the tax liabilities of individuals and businesses, and ensure that correct amounts are paid on time
- *Government regulatory agencies* rely on accounting information to fulfill their duties. Provincial securities regulators, for example, require firms to file financial disclosures so that potential investors have valid information about a company's financial status.

WHO ARE ACCOUNTANTS AND WHAT DO THEY DO?

1 Explain the role of *accountants* and distinguish among the three types of professional accountants in Canada.

At the head of the accounting system is the **controller**, who manages all of the firm's accounting activities. As chief accounting officer, the controller ensures that the accounting system provides the reports and statements needed for planning, controlling, and decision-making activities. This broad range of activities requires different types of expertise among accounting specialists. In this section, we will begin by distinguishing between the two main fields of accounting: *financial* and *managerial*. Then we will discuss the different functions and activities of the three professional accounting groups in Canada.

controller The individual who manages all the firm's accounting activities.

Financial and Managerial Accounting

In any company, two fields of accounting—financial and managerial—can be distinguished by the different users they serve. As we have just seen, it is both convenient and accurate to classify users of accounting information as users outside the company and users inside the company. This same distinction allows us to categorize accounting systems as either *financial* or *managerial*.

Financial Accounting

A firm's **financial accounting system** is concerned with external users of information: consumer groups, unions, stockholders, and government agencies. It prepares and publishes income statements and balance sheets at regular intervals, as well as other financial reports that are published for stockholders and the general public. All of these documents focus on the activities of the company *as a whole*, rather than on individual departments or divisions.

financial accounting system The process whereby interested groups are kept informed about the financial condition of a firm.

Managerial Accounting

In contrast, **managerial (or management) accounting** serves internal users. Managers at all levels need information to make decisions for their departments, to monitor current projects, and to plan for future activities. Other employees also need accounting information. Engineers, for instance, want to know the costs for materials and production so that they can make product operation improvements. To set performance goals, salespeople need data on past sales by geographic region. Purchasing agents use information on material costs to negotiate terms with suppliers.

managerial (or management) accounting Internal procedures that alert managers to problems and aid them in planning and decision making.

Professional Accountants

Three professional accounting organizations have developed in Canada to certify accounting expertise.

BUSINESS ACCOUNTABILITY

Who's Accountable for Offshore Oversight?

Planning on an accounting career for job security? If so, you might want to take a second look at what's happening with business process outsourcing (BPO), which is the use of third parties to perform services that a company would otherwise do internally. As we saw in Chapter 2, outsourcing is an increasingly popular option for businesses. Universities and hospitals outsource cafeteria operations to food service firms, retailers outsource human resources activities to HR firms, and manufacturing companies outsource shipping and delivery activities to companies like UPS and FedEx. Offshoring is also popular for professional services that have low customer contact and require little customization, such as radiology analysis (e.g., x-rays, CT scans, MRIs), computer software development, and engineering (e.g., product design, testing, and analysis). Worldwide, the outsourcing of finance and accounting services exceeds $40 billion.

The basic philosophy of outsourcing is that businesses do best when they focus on their core activities rather than getting sidetracked into non-core activities. John Gillespie, a partner at Accenture, says that outsourcing of accounting services makes sense because there are a lot of people involved in accounting activities, and there is much routine work that doesn't need to be done by highly paid executives. Accounting's basic number-crunching activities—payroll, accounts receivable, accounts payable, cash accounting, and inventory valuation—are easily outsourced because once the overseas outsourcing provider learns Canadian or U.S. accounting rules, they apply equally to all customers. Data for these activities are transmitted for offshore processing, and results are then transmitted back to the outsourcer. More information about the outsourcing of accounting services is provided in the "African Accountants" Video Case on p. 335.)

In addition to cost savings, clients also expect more accurate and faster reporting from outsourcing. On the downside, however, outsourcing increases the risk to data security. Placing private information in faraway hands, especially in the absence of clear-cut legislation on data privacy and security (as in India), increases the chance of violating the client's trust in accounting integrity. In determining what practices to employ for protecting clients, some advocates suggest that, at the very least, accountants seek clients' permission for using offshore outsourcing. While the accounting profession searches for answers to these outsourcing-related issues, one principle remains clear: The use of third parties in no way diminishes the accountants' accountability for privacy, confidentiality, and security to their clients.

India, with its abundance of well-educated and highly skilled employees, has become the back office of the world. Accounting skills are plentiful, and salaries average just one-fifth of those in Western countries. With over one-third of its university graduates speaking more than two languages fluently, and many speaking as many as six, India is well-positioned as an international outsourcing provider. Its Chartered Accountant designation for ensuring professionalism is similar in rigour and esteem to the CPA certification in the United States. The accounting firm Deloitte Touche Tohmatsu forecasts that by 2008 India's financial and accounting services will be boosted by some one million new back-office jobs and technology-related positions, moved there by the world's top 100 financial companies.

While India holds the premier position today in offshore work, other countries—Australia, Ireland, Malaysia, the Philippines, and South Africa—are gearing up with low-cost, high-technology expertise in the battle of accounting outsourcing destinations. Among the brightest contenders, if it can overcome a non-English-speaking tradition, is China, with its population of one billion, rapid economic growth, low-cost labour, and heavy investment in technical education. Its stated goal is to become the world's top outsourcing destination for accounting.

QUESTIONS FOR DISCUSSION

1. What factors do you think are most important to consider in deciding which parts of a firm's accounting system, if any, are appropriate for outsourcing?
2. Suppose the accounting firm that prepares your income tax return outsources the work to a third-party tax-service provider overseas. Do you think the accounting firm should get your permission before outsourcing the work? Explain why or why not.
3. What ethical issues, if any, are involved in a decision about outsourcing a firm's accounting activities? Explain.

Chartered Accountants

The Canadian Institute of Chartered Accountants (CICA) grants the **chartered accountant (CA)** designation. To achieve this designation, a person must earn a university degree, then complete an educational program and pass a national exam. About half of all CAs work in CA firms that offer accounting services to the public; the other half work in government or industry. CA firms typically provide audit, tax, and management services. CAs focus on external financial reporting, that is, certifying for various interested parties (stockholders, lenders, the Canada Revenue Agency, etc.) that the financial records of a company accurately reflect the true financial condition of the firm. In 2006, there were about 70 000 CAs in Canada.[2]

chartered accountant (CA)
An individual who has met certain experience and education requirements and has passed a licensing examination; acts as an outside accountant for other firms.

Certified General Accountants

The Certified General Accountants Association of Canada grants the **certified general accountant (CGA)** designation. To become a CGA, a person must complete an education program and pass a national exam. To be eligible, a person must have an accounting job with a company. Formerly, CGAs were not allowed to audit the financial statements of publicly held companies, but this is rapidly changing, and now CGAs can audit corporate financial statements in most provinces. Most CGAs work in private companies, but there are a few CGA firms. Some CGAs also work in CA firms. CGAs also focus on external financial reporting, and emphasize the use of the computer as a management accounting tool. In 2006, there were about 41 000 CGAs in Canada.[3]

certified general accountant (CGA)
An individual who has completed an education program and passed a national exam; works in private industry or a CGA firm.

Certified Management Accountants

The Society of Management Accountants of Canada grants the **certified management accountant (CMA)** designation. To achieve the designation, a person must have a university degree, pass a two-part national entrance examination, and complete a strategic leadership program while gaining practical experience in a management accounting environment. CMAs work in organizations of all sizes, and focus on applying best management practices in all of the operations of a business. CMAs bring a strong market focus to strategic management and resource deployment, synthesizing and analyzing financial and non-financial information to help organizations maintain a competitive advantage. CMAs emphasize the role of accountants in the planning and overall strategy of the firm in which they work. In 2006, there were about 37 000 CMAs in Canada.[4]

certified management accountant (CMA)
An individual who has completed a university degree, passed a national examination, and completed a strategic leadership program; works in industry and focuses on internal management accounting.

Accounting Services

CAs and CGAs usually perform several accounting services for their clients. The most common of these are auditing, tax services, and management services.

Auditing

In an **audit**, the accountant examines a company's AIS to determine whether the company's financial reports fairly present its financial operations. Companies normally must provide audited financial reports when applying for loans or when selling stock. The audit will determine if the firm has controls to prevent errors or fraud from going undetected. Auditors also examine receipts such as shipping documents, cancelled cheques, payroll records, and cash receipts records. In some cases, an auditor may physically check inventories, equipment, or other assets, even if it means descending 200 metres underground in a lead mine.

audit
An accountant's examination of a company's financial records to determine if it used proper procedures to prepare its financial reports.

A financial report is an integral component of the financial accounting system.

Detecting fraud is not the primary purpose of audits, but in recent years there has been much publicity about the alleged failure of auditors to detect fraud. Therefore, when audits are being conducted, **forensic accountants** may be used to track down hidden funds in business firms. Because white-collar crime is on the increase, the number of forensic accountants has increased in recent years. Forensic accountants were used to examine Swiss bank accounts for assets deposited by victims of Nazi persecution during the Second World War.[5]

forensic accountant
An accountant who tracks down hidden funds in business firms, usually as part of a criminal investigation.

One of the auditor's responsibilities is to ensure that the client's accounting system adheres to generally accepted accounting principles. **Generally accepted accounting principles (GAAP)** are a body of theory and procedure developed and monitored by the CICA. At the end of an audit, the auditor will certify whether the client's financial reports comply with GAAP. By 2011, Canadian companies will adopt the International Financial Reporting Standards.[6] This will make it easier for investors in other countries to understand the financial statements of Canadian companies, thus making for improved access to global capital markets.

generally accepted accounting principles (GAAP)
Standard rules and methods used by accountants in preparing financial reports.

Tax Services

Tax services include helping clients not only with preparing their tax returns but also in their tax planning. Tax laws are complex. A CA's advice can help a business structure (or restructure) its operations and investments and save millions of dollars in taxes. To serve their clients best, of course, accountants must stay abreast of changes in tax laws—no simple matter.

Management Consulting Services

Management consulting services range from personal financial planning to planning corporate mergers. Other services include plant layout and design, marketing studies, production scheduling, computer feasibility studies, and design and implementation of accounting systems. Some CA firms even assist in executive recruitment. Small wonder that the staff of CA firms include engineers, architects, mathematicians, and even psychologists.

management consulting services
Specialized accounting services to help managers resolve a variety of problems in finance, production scheduling, and other areas.

Private Accountants

To assure the fairness of their reports, CAs and CGAs must be independent of the firms they audit. They are employees of accounting firms and provide services for many clients. But businesses also hire their own

private accountants as salaried employees to deal with the company's day-to-day accounting needs.

private accountant
An accountant hired as a salaried employee to deal with a company's day-to-day accounting needs.

Private accountants perform a variety of accounting jobs. An internal auditor at Petro-Canada, for example, might fly to the Hibernia site to confirm the accuracy of oil-flow meters on the offshore drilling platform. But a supervisor responsible for $200 million in monthly accounts payable to vendors and employees may travel no farther than the executive suite. The nature of the accounting job thus depends on the specific business and the activities needed to make that business a success. Large businesses employ specialized accountants in such areas as budgets, financial planning, internal auditing, payroll, and taxation. Each accounting area has its own challenges and excitement. In small businesses, a single individual may handle all accounting tasks.

THE ACCOUNTING EQUATION

2 Describe how the *accounting equation* is used.

All accountants, whether public or private, rely on record keeping. Underlying all record-keeping procedures is the most basic tool of accounting: the **accounting equation**. At various points in the year, accountants use the following equation to balance the data pertaining to financial transactions:

Assets = Liabilities + Owners' equity

accounting equation
Assets = Liabilities + Owners' Equity; the formula used by accountants to balance data for the firm's financial transactions at various points in the year.

After each transaction (e.g., payments to suppliers, sales to customers, wages to employees, etc.) the accounting equation must be in balance. To understand the importance of this equation, we must first understand the terms *assets, liabilities,* and *owners' equity*.[7]

Assets and Liabilities

An **asset** is any economic resource that is expected to benefit a firm or an individual who owns it. Assets include land, buildings, equipment, inventory, and payments due the company (accounts receivable). A **liability** is a debt that the firm owes to an outside party.

asset
Anything of economic value owned by a firm or individual.

liability
Any debt owed by a firm or individual to others.

Owners' Equity

You may have heard of the equity that a homeowner has in a house—that is, the amount of money that could be made by selling the house and paying off the mortgage. Similarly, **owners' equity** is the amount of money that owners

owners' equity
Any positive difference between a firm's assets and its liabilities; what would remain for a firm's owners if the company were liquidated, all its assets were sold, and all its debts were paid.

The inventory at this car dealership is part of the company's assets. The cars constitute an economic resource because the firm will benefit financially as it sells them. When they are sold, at the end of the company's accounting period, the dealership will convert the cost of the cars to expenses and show it as the cost of goods sold.

would receive if they sold all of a company's assets and paid all of its liabilities. We can rewrite the accounting equation to highlight this definition:

$$\text{Assets} - \text{Liabilities} = \text{Owners' equity}$$

If a company's assets exceed its liabilities, owners' equity is *positive*; if the company goes out of business, the owners will receive some cash (a gain) after selling assets and paying off liabilities. If liabilities outweigh assets, owners' equity is *negative*; assets are insufficient to pay off all debts. If the company goes out of business, the owners will get no cash and some creditors won't be paid. Owners' equity is meaningful for both investors and lenders. Before lending money to owners, for example, lenders want to know the amount of owners' equity in a business. Owners' equity consists of two sources of capital:

1. The amount that the owners originally invested
2. Profits earned by and reinvested in the company

When a company operates profitably, its assets increase faster than its liabilities. Owners' equity, therefore, will increase if profits are retained in the business instead of paid out as dividends to stockholders. Owners' equity also increases if owners invest more of their own money to increase assets. However, owners' equity can shrink if the company operates at a loss or if owners withdraw assets.

FINANCIAL STATEMENTS

3 Describe three basic *financial statements* and show how they reflect the activity and financial condition of a business.

If your business purchases inventory with cash, you do two things: (1) decrease your cash and (2) increase your inventory. Similarly, if you purchase supplies on credit, you: (1) increase your supplies and (2) increase your accounts payable. If you invest more money in your business, you: (1) increase your cash and (2) increase your owners' equity. In other words, *every transaction affects two accounts*. Accountants thus use a **double-entry accounting system** to record the *dual effects* of financial transactions.

double-entry accounting system
A bookkeeping system, developed in the fifteenth century and still in use, that requires every transaction to be entered in two ways—how it affects assets and how it affects liabilities and owners' equity—so that the accounting equation is always in balance.

As we noted earlier, the primary purpose of accounting is to summarize the results of a business's transactions and to issue reports that can help managers and others make informed decisions. Some of the most important reports, called **financial statements**, fall into three broad categories: *balance sheets, income statements,* and *statements of cash flows*.[8]

financial statements
Any of several types of broad reports regarding a company's financial status; most often used in reference to balance sheets, income statements, and/or statements of cash flows.

Balance Sheets

Balance sheets supply detailed information about the accounting equation factors: assets, liabilities, and owners' equity. Figure 11.1 shows the balance sheet for Perfect Posters.

balance sheet
A type of financial statement that summarizes a firm's financial position on a particular date in terms of its assets, liabilities, and owners' equity.

Assets

As we have seen, an asset is any economic resource that a company owns and from which it can expect to derive some future benefit. From an accounting standpoint, most companies have three types of assets: *current, fixed,* and *intangible*.

Current Assets. **Current assets** include cash, money in the bank, and assets that can be converted into cash within a year. They are normally listed in order of **liquidity**: the ease with which they can be converted into cash. Business debts, for example, can usually be satisfied only through payments of cash. A company that needs but cannot generate cash—in other words, a company that is not liquid—may thus be forced to sell assets at sacrifice prices or even go out of business.

current assets
Cash and other assets that can be converted into cash within a year.

liquidity
The ease and speed with which an asset can be converted to cash; cash is said to be perfectly liquid.

Perfect Posters, Inc.
555 Riverview, Toronto, Ontario

Perfect Posters, Inc.
Balance Sheet
As of December 31, 2006

Assets			
Current Assets:			
Cash		$7 050	
Marketable securities. . . .		2 300	
Accounts receivable.	$26 210		
Less: Allowance for doubtful accounts.	(650)	25 560	
Merchandise inventory.		21 250	
Prepaid expenses		1 050	
Total current assets			**$57 210**
Fixed Assets:			
Land		18 000	
Building	65 000		
Less: Accumulated depreciation	(22 500)	42 500	
Equipment	72 195		
Less: Accumulated depreciation	(24 815)	47 380	
Total fixed assets. . .			**107 880**
Intangible Assets:			
Patents	7 100		
Trademarks	900		
Total intangible assets			**8 000**
Total assets			**$173 090**

Liabilities and Owners' Equity			
Current liabilities:			
Accounts payable.	$16 315		
Wages payable.	3 700		
Taxes payable.	1 920		
Total current liabilities			**$21 935**
Long-term liabilities:			
Notes payable, 8% due 2009	10 000		
Bonds payable, 9% due 2011	30 000		
Total long-term liabilities			**40 000**
Total liabilities			**$61 935**
Owners' Equity			
Common stock, $5 par		40 000	
Additional paid-in capital		15 000	
Retained earnings		56 155	
Total owners' equity			**111 155**
Total liabilities and owners' equity . . .			**$173 090**

Figure 11.1 Perfect Posters' balance sheet shows clearly that the firm's total assets equal its total liabilities and owners' equity.

By definition, cash is completely liquid. *Marketable securities* purchased as short-term investments are slightly less liquid but can be sold quickly if necessary. Marketable securities include stocks or bonds of other companies, government securities, and money market certificates. There are three other important non-liquid assets held by many companies: *accounts receivable, merchandise inventory,* and *prepaid expenses*.

Accounts receivable are amounts due from customers who have purchased goods on credit. Most businesses expect to receive payment within 30 days of a sale. In our hypothetical example, the entry labelled *Less: Allowance for doubtful accounts* in Figure 11.1 indicates $650 in receivables that Perfect Posters does not expect to collect. Total accounts receivable assets are decreased accordingly.

accounts receivable
Amounts due to the firm from customers who have purchased goods or services on credit; a form of current asset.

Following accounts receivable on the Perfect Posters balance sheet is **merchandise inventory**—the cost of merchandise that has been acquired for sale to customers and is still on hand. Accounting for the value of inventories on the balance sheet is difficult because inventories are flowing in and out throughout the year. Therefore, assumptions must be made about which ones were sold and which ones remain in storage.

merchandise inventory
The cost of merchandise that has been acquired for sale to customers but is still on hand.

Prepaid expenses include supplies on hand and rent paid for the period to come. They are assets because they have been paid for and are available to the company. In all, Perfect Posters' current assets as of December 31, 2006, totalled $57 210.

prepaid expenses
Includes supplies on hand and rent paid for the period to come.

Fixed Assets. **Fixed assets** (for example, land, buildings, and equipment) have long-term use or value. As buildings and equipment wear out or

fixed assets
Assets that have long-term use or value to the firm such as land, buildings, and machinery.

become obsolete, their value decreases. To reflect decreasing value, accountants use depreciation to spread the cost of an asset over the years of its useful life. There are various methods used to calculate depreciation, but in its simplest sense, **depreciation** means determining an asset's useful life in years, dividing its worth by that many years, and subtracting the resulting amount each year. Each year, therefore, the asset's remaining value decreases on the books. In Figure 11.1, Perfect Posters shows fixed assets of $107 880 after depreciation.

depreciation
Distributing the cost of a major asset over the years in which it produces revenues; calculated by each year subtracting the asset's original value divided by the number of years in its productive life.

Intangible Assets. Although their worth is hard to set, intangible assets have monetary value. **Intangible assets** usually include the cost of obtaining rights or privileges such as patents, trademarks, copyrights, and franchise fees. **Goodwill** is the amount paid for an existing business beyond the value of its other assets. Perfect Posters has no goodwill assets; however, it does own trademarks and patents for specialized storage equipment. These are intangible assets worth $8000. Larger companies, of course, have intangible assets that are worth much more.

intangible assets
Non-physical assets, such as patents, trademarks, copyrights, and franchise fees, that have economic value but whose precise value is difficult to calculate.

goodwill
The amount paid for an existing business beyond the value of its other assets.

Liabilities

Just as assets are separated into different categories, so are liabilities. **Current liabilities** are debts that must be paid within one year. These include **accounts payable**: unpaid bills to suppliers for materials as well as wages and taxes that must be paid in the coming year. Perfect Posters has current liabilities of $21 935.

Long-term liabilities are debts that are not due for at least one year. These normally represent borrowed funds on which the company must pay interest. Perfect Posters' long-term liabilities are $40 000.

current liabilities
Any debts owed by the firm that must be paid within one year.

accounts payable
Amounts due from the firm to its suppliers for goods and/or services purchased on credit; a form of current liability.

long-term liabilities
Any debts owed by the firm that are not due for at least one year.

Owners' Equity

The final section of the balance sheet in Figure 11.1 shows owners' equity broken down into *common stock, paid-in capital,* and *retained earnings*. When Perfect Posters was formed, the declared legal value of its common stock was $5 per share. By law, this $40 000 ($5 multiplied by 8000 shares) cannot be distributed as dividends. **Paid-in capital** is additional money invested in the firm by its owners. Perfect Posters has $15 000 in paid-in capital.

Retained earnings are net profits minus dividend payments to stockholders. Retained earnings accumulate when profits, which could have been distributed to stockholders, are kept instead for use by the company. At the close of 2006, Perfect Posters had retained earnings of $56 155.

paid-in capital
Any additional money invested in the firm by the owners.

retained earnings
A company's net profits less any dividend payments to shareholders.

Income Statements

4 Explain the key standards and principles for reporting financial statements.

The **income statement** is sometimes called a **profit-and-loss statement**, because its description of revenues and expenses results in a figure showing the firm's annual profit or loss. In other words,

Revenues – Expenses = Profit (or loss)

Popularly known as "the bottom line," profit or loss is probably the most important figure in any business enterprise. Figure 11.2 shows the 2006 income statement for Perfect Posters, whose bottom line that year was $12 585. The income statement is divided into three major categories: *revenues, cost of goods sold,* and *operating expenses*.

income statement (profit-and-loss statement)
A type of financial statement that describes a firm's revenues and expenses and indicates whether the firm has earned a profit or suffered a loss during a given period.

Revenues

When a law firm receives $250 for preparing a will or when a supermarket collects $65 from a customer buying groceries, both are receiving **revenues**—the funds that flow into a business from the sale of goods or services. In 2006, Perfect Posters reported revenues of $256 425 from the sale of art prints and other posters.

revenues
Any monies received by a firm as a result of selling a good or service or from other sources such as interest, rent, and licensing fees.

Perfect Posters, Inc.
555 Riverview, Toronto, Ontario

Perfect Posters, Inc.
Income Statement
Year ended December 31, 2006

Revenues (gross sales)			**$256 425**
Costs of goods sold:			
Merchandise inventory, January 1, 2006	$22 380		
Merchandise purchases during year	103 635		
Goods available for sale		$126 015	
Less: Merchandise inventory, December 31, 2006		21 250	
Cost of goods sold			**104 765**
Gross profit			**151 660**
Operating expenses:			
Selling and repackaging expenses:			
Salaries and wages	49 750		
Advertising	6 380		
Depreciation—warehouse and repackaging equipment	3 350		
Total selling and repackaging expenses		59 480	
Administrative expenses:			
Salaries and wages	55 100		
Supplies	4 150		
Utilities	3 800		
Depreciation—office equipment	3 420		
Interest expense	2 900		
Miscellaneous expenses	1 835		
Total administration expenses		71 205	
Total operating expenses			**130 685**
Operating income (income before taxes)			20 975
Income taxes			8 390
Net income			**$12 585**

Figure 11.2 Perfect Posters' income statement. The final entry on the income statement, the bottom line, reports the firm's profit or loss.

Revenue Recognition and Matching. **Revenue recognition** is the formal recording and reporting of revenues in the financial statements. Although any firm earns revenues continuously as it makes sales, earnings are not reported until the earnings cycle is completed. This cycle is complete under two conditions:

revenue recognition
The formal recording and reporting of revenues in the financial statements.

1. The sale is complete and the product has been delivered
2. The sale price to the customer has been collected or is collectible (accounts receivable)

The completion of the earning cycle, then, determines the timing for revenue recognition in the firm's financial statements. Revenues are recorded for the accounting period in which sales are completed and collectible (or collected). This practice assures the reader that the statement gives a fair comparison of what was gained for the resources that were given up.

Cost of Goods Sold

In Perfect Posters' income statement, the **cost of goods sold** category shows the costs of obtaining materials to make the products sold during the year. Perfect Posters began 2006 with posters valued at $22 380. Over the year, it spent $103 635 to purchase posters. During 2006, then, the company had $126 015 worth of merchandise available to sell. By the end of the year, it had sold all but $21 250 of those posters, which remained as merchandise inventory. The cost of obtaining the goods sold by the firm was thus $104 765.

cost of goods sold
Any expenses directly involved in producing or selling a good or service during a given time period.

gross profit (gross margin)
A firm's revenues (gross sales) less its cost of goods sold.

Gross Profit (or Gross Margin). To calculate **gross profit** (or **gross margin**), subtract the cost of goods sold from revenues. Perfect Posters' gross profit in 2006 was $151 660 ($256 425 minus $104 765). Expressed as a percentage of sales, gross profit is 59.1 percent ($151 660 divided by $256 425).

Gross profit percentages vary widely across industries. In retailing, Home Depot reports 30 percent. In manufacturing, Harley-Davidson reports 34 percent; and in pharmaceuticals, American Home Products reports 75 percent. For companies with low gross margins, product costs are a big expense. If a company has a high gross margin, it probably has low cost-of-goods-sold but high selling and administrative expenses.

Operating Expenses

operating expenses
Costs incurred by a firm other than those included in cost of goods sold.

In addition to costs directly related to acquiring goods, every company has general expenses ranging from erasers to the president's salary. Like cost of goods sold, **operating expenses** are resources that must flow out of a company for it to earn revenues. As you can see in Figure 11.2, Perfect Posters had operating expenses of $130 685 in 2006. This figure consists of $59 480 in selling and repackaging expenses and $71 205 in administrative expenses.

Selling expenses result from activities related to selling the firm's goods or services. These may include salaries for the sales force, delivery costs, and advertising expenses. General and administrative expenses, such as management salaries, insurance expenses, and maintenance costs, are expenses related to the general management of the company.

operating income
Compares the gross profit from business operations against operating expenses.

net income (net profit or net earnings)
A firm's gross profit less its operating expenses and income taxes.

Operating Income and Net Income. Sometimes managers must determine **operating income**, which compares the gross profit from business operations against operating expenses. This calculation for Perfect Posters ($151 660 minus $130 685) reveals an operating income, or *income before taxes*, of $20 975. Subtracting income taxes from operating income ($20 975 minus $8390) reveals **net income** (also called **net profit** or **net earnings**). In 2006, Perfect Posters' net income was $12 585.

Statements of Cash Flows

statement of cash flows
A financial statement that describes a firm's generation and use of cash during a given period.

In order to survive, a business must earn a *profit* (that is, its sales revenues must exceed its expenses), but it must also make sure it has *cash* available when it needs it (for example, to pay employees). Cash flow management requires the development of a **statement of cash flows**, which describes a company's yearly cash receipts and cash payments. It shows the effects on cash of three important business activities:

- *Cash flows from operations.* This part of the statement is concerned with the firm's main operating activities: the cash transactions involved in buying and selling goods and services. It reveals how much of the year's profits result from the firm's main line of business (for example, Jaguar's sales of automobiles) rather than from secondary activities (for example, licencing fees that a clothing firm paid to Jaguar for using the Jaguar logo on shirts).
- *Cash flows from investing.* This section reports net cash used in or provided by investing. It includes cash receipts and payments from buying and selling stocks, bonds, property, equipment, and other productive assets.
- *Cash flows from financing.* The final section reports net cash from all financing activities. It includes cash inflows from borrowing or issuing stock as well as outflows for payment of dividends and repayment of borrowed money.

The overall change in cash from these three sources provides information to lenders and investors. When creditors and stockholders know how firms obtained and used their funds during the course of a year, it is easier for them to interpret the year-to-year changes in the firm's balance sheet and income statement. The importance of cash flow is noted in the Entrepreneurship and New Ventures box.

The Budget: An Internal Financial Statement

In addition to financial statements, managers need other types of accounting information to aid in internal planning, controlling, and decision making. Probably the most crucial internal financial statement is the budget. A **budget** is a detailed statement of estimated receipts and expenditures for a

budget
A detailed financial plan for estimated receipts and expenditures for a period of time in the future, usually one year.

ENTREPRENEURSHIP AND NEW VENTURES

How Can You Account for a Good Beer?

An article in the Canadian trade journal *World of Beer* lamented that Denison's "has closed, and with it has gone our sole opportunity to enjoy Canada's finest Bavarian-style wheat beer and some of the best lagers in the land." The failure of Denison's Brewing Co., a favourite among brewpub aficionados in Toronto, issued a stark warning to all local brewers: Even a great-tasting beer will go sour if you can't produce and sell it profitably.

The lesson of Denison's rise and fall has been studied seriously at Black Oak Brewing Co., where founders Ken Woods and John Gagliardi may be the perfect pair to survive in Canada's highly competitive beer market. Although each brings different skills to the joint venture, they share a vision: to make—and sell—the highest-quality beer possible. Gagliardi, certified as a brewmaster by the world-renowned Siebel Institute in 1993, is the quality-control expert whose responsibilities include ensuring the consistency and character of every batch of Black Oak. He admits that as a businessman, he is "first and foremost" a beer lover, and he continues to refresh the company's brand mix by releasing seasonal brews, such as Oktoberfest and Christmas Nutcracker—a practice that permits him to conduct brewing experiments without too much risk. "We're bent on making the highest-quality beer possible," says Gagliardi. "It's got to have the right taste and the perfect clarity and quality. We won't settle for anything less than the best, because we know our customers are going to be expecting a high-quality beer."

Woods, meanwhile, is a Certified Management Accountant (CMA) and a member of the Society of Management Accountants of Canada, but he shares his partner's enthusiastic interest in beer and brewing. For 10 years, he devoted his evenings to developing both his bartending skills and his business contacts, while both would-be entrepreneurs refined their concepts of beers and brewery operations. Since opening Black Oak in 1999, they've managed to develop award-winning beers such as Black Oak Nut Brown Ale, Pale Ale, and Premium Lager, which *The Bar Towel,* a website for Toronto beer lovers, calls "fine, flavourful brews."

Just as importantly, they've also managed to cultivate successful business operations. Woods' accounting background enables him to set up and monitor management and financial procedures, such as the cost controls that made it possible for the company to buy a vintage 1940s labelling machine. "It doesn't matter that it's old," explains Woods. "It's a great piece of equipment and we got it at the right price." Woods and Gagliardi also take care to buy high-quality raw materials at the right price. That's why toasted wheat comes from the nearby town of Fergus while malt is imported from western Canada.

Accounting expertise is especially important because the company's cash flows are affected by the terms of payment negotiated with suppliers and by its procedures for collecting sales revenues. Working in finance and purchasing departments while earning his CMA credentials, Woods learned a lot about payables and receivables. He also produced staff expense reports and tax documents and set up standards for keeping operating costs under control. Finally, his management-accountant training has been especially useful in dealing with the numerous guidelines and rafts of government forms that characterize Ontario's highly regulated beer industry. Being a CMA, says Woods "is really helpful because it firms up everything you need to know in the marketplace."

period of time in the future. Although that period is usually one year, some companies also prepare budgets for three- or five-year periods, especially when considering major capital expenditures.

Budgets are also useful for keeping track of weekly or monthly performance. Procter & Gamble, for example, evaluates all of its business units monthly by comparing actual financial results with monthly budgeted amounts. Discrepancies in "actual versus budget" totals signal potential problems and initiate action to get financial performance back on track.

ANALYZING FINANCIAL STATEMENTS

5 Explain how computing *financial ratios* can help in analyzing the financial strengths of a business.

solvency ratios
Ratios that estimate the financial risk that is evident in a company.

profitability ratios
Measures of a firm's overall financial performance in terms of its likely profits; used by investors to assess their probable returns.

activity ratios
Measures of how efficiently a firm uses its resources; used by investors to assess their probable returns.

Financial statements present a great deal of information, but what does it all mean? How, for example, can statements help investors decide what stock to buy or help managers decide whether to extend credit? Statements provide data, which in turn can be applied to various ratios (comparative numbers). These ratios can then be used to analyze the financial health of one or more companies. They can also be used to check a firm's progress by comparing current and past statements. Ratios are normally grouped into three major classifications:

- **Solvency ratios**, both short-term and long-term, estimate risk
- **Profitability ratios** measure potential earnings
- **Activity ratios** reflect management's use of assets

Depending on the decisions to be made, a user may apply none, some, or all of the ratios in a particular classification.

Solvency Ratios

What are the chances that a borrower will be able to repay a loan and the interest due? This question is first and foremost in the minds of bank lending officers, managers of pension funds and other investors, suppliers, and the borrowing company's own financial managers. Solvency ratios provide measures of the firm's ability to meet its debt obligations.

Short-Term Solvency

short-term solvency ratio
Financial ratio for measuring a company's ability to pay immediate debts.

current ratio
Financial ratio for measuring a company's ability to pay current debts out of current assets.

Short-term solvency ratios measure a company's liquidity and its ability to pay immediate debts. The most commonly used ratio is the **current ratio**, which reflects a firm's ability to generate cash to meet obligations through the normal, orderly process of selling inventories and collecting revenues from customers. It is calculated by dividing current assets by current liabilities. The higher a firm's current ratio, the lower the risk to investors. For many years, the guideline was a current ratio of 2:1 or higher—which meant that current assets were at least double current liabilities. More recently, many firms that are financially strong operate with current ratios of less than 2:1.

How does Perfect Posters measure up? Look again at the balance sheet in Figure 11.2. Judging from its current assets and current liabilities at the end of 2006, we see that the company looks like a good credit risk:

$$\frac{\text{Current assets}}{\text{Current liabilities}} = \frac{\$57\ 210}{\$21\ 935} = 2.61$$

Long-Term Solvency

Stakeholders are also concerned about long-term solvency. Has a company been overextended by borrowing so much that it will be unable to repay debts in future years? A firm that can't meet its long-term debt obligations is in danger of collapse or takeover—a risk that makes creditors and investors quite cautious. To evaluate a company's risk of running into this problem, creditors turn to the balance sheet to see the extent to which a firm is financed through borrowed money. Long-term solvency is calculated by dividing **debt**—total liabilities—by owners' equity. The lower a firm's debt, the lower the risk to investors and creditors. Companies with **debt-to-equity ratios** above 1.0 may be relying too much on debt. In the case of Perfect Posters, we can see from the balance sheet in Figure 11.2 that the debt-to-equity ratio calculates as follows:

debt
A company's total liabilities.

debt-to-equity ratios
A form of debt ratio calculated as total liabilities divided by owners' equity.

$$\frac{\text{Debt}}{\text{Owners' equity}} = \frac{\$61\ 935}{\$111\ 155} = \$0.56$$

Sometimes, high debt can be not only acceptable but also desirable. Borrowing funds gives a firm **leverage**—the ability to make otherwise unaffordable investments. In *leveraged buyouts*, firms have sometimes taken on huge debt in order to get the money to buy out other companies. If owning the purchased company generates profits above the cost of borrowing the purchase price, leveraging makes sense. Unfortunately, many buyouts have caused problems because profits fell short of expected levels or because rising interest rates increased payments on the buyer's debt.

leverage
Using borrowed funds to make purchases, thus increasing the user's purchasing power, potential rate of return, and risk of loss.

Profitability Ratios

Although it is important to know that a company is solvent in both the long term and the short term, safety or risk alone is not an adequate basis for investment decisions. Investors also want some measure of the returns they can expect. Return on equity, return on sales, and earning per share are three commonly used profitability ratios (sometimes these are called *shareholder return ratios* or *performance ratios*).

Return on Equity

Owners are interested in the net income earned by a business for each dollar invested. **Return on equity** measures this performance by dividing net income (see Figure 11.2) by total owners' equity (see Figure 11.1). For Perfect Posters, the return on equity ratio in 2006 is as follows:

return on equity
A form of profitability ratio calculated as net income divided by total owners' equity.

$$\frac{\text{Net income}}{\text{Total owners' equity}} = \frac{\$12\ 585}{\$111\ 155} = 11.3\%$$

Is this figure good or bad? There is no set answer. If Perfect Posters' ratio for 2006 is higher than in previous years, owners and investors should be encouraged, but if 11.3 percent is lower than the ratios of other companies in the same industry, they will likely be concerned.

Return on Sales

Companies want to generate as much profit as they can from each dollar of sales revenue they receive. The **return on sales** ratio is calculated by dividing net income by sales revenue (see Figure 11.2). For Perfect Posters, the return on sales ratio for 2006 is as follows:

return on sales
Ratio calculated by dividing net income by sales revenue.

$$\frac{\text{Net income}}{\text{Sales revenue}} = \frac{\$12\ 585}{\$256\ 425} = 4.9\%$$

Is this figure good or bad? Once again, there is no set answer. If Perfect Posters' ratio for 2006 is higher than in previous years, owners and investors should be encouraged, but if 4.9 percent is lower than the ratios of other companies in the same industry, they will likely be concerned.

The inventory turnover ratio measures the average number of times that a store sells and restocks its inventory in one year. The higher the ratio, the more products that get sold and the more revenue that comes in. Supermarkets must have a higher turnover ratio than, say, auto supply or toy stores. In almost all retail stores, products with the highest ratios get the shelf spaces that generate the most customer traffic and sales.

Earnings per Share

earnings per share
A form of profitability ratio calculated as net income divided by the number of common shares outstanding.

The **earnings per share** ratio—which is calculated by dividing net income by the number of shares of common stock outstanding—is used by investors to decide whether to buy or sell a company's stock. As the ratio gets higher, the stock value increases, because investors know that the firm can better afford to pay dividends. The stock will likely lose market value if the latest financial statements report a decline in earnings per share. For Perfect Posters, we can use the net income total from the income statement in Figure 11.2 to calculate earning per share as follows:

$$\frac{\text{Net income}}{\text{Number of common shares outstanding}} = \frac{\$12\,585}{8000} = \$1.57 \text{ per share}$$

Activity Ratios

The efficiency with which a firm uses resources is linked to profitability. As a potential investor, then, you want to know which company gets more mileage from its resources. Activity ratios measure this efficiency. For example, suppose that two firms use the same amount of resources or assets. If Firm A generates greater profits or sales, it is more efficient and thus has a better activity ratio.

inventory turnover ratio
An activity ratio that measures the average number of times inventory is sold and restocked during the year.

One of the most important activity ratios is the **inventory turnover ratio**, which calculates the average number of times that inventory is sold and restocked during the year—that is, how quickly inventory is produced and sold.[9] A company needs to know its *average inventory* (which can be calculated by adding end-of-year inventory to beginning-of-year inventory and dividing by 2). The company can then calculate the inventory turnover ratio, which is expressed as the cost of goods sold divided by average inventory:

$$\frac{\text{Cost of goods sold}}{\text{Average inventory}} = \frac{\text{Cost of goods sold}}{(\text{Beginning inventory} + \text{Ending inventory}) \div 2}$$

To calculate Perfect Posters' inventory turnover ratio for 2006, we take the merchandise inventory figures for the income statement in Figure 11.2. The ratio can be expressed as follows:

$$\frac{\$104\,765}{(\$22\,380 + \$21\,250) \div 2} = 4.8$$

In other words, new merchandise replaces old merchandise every 76 days (365 days divided by 4.8). The 4.8 ratio is below the industry average of 7.0 for comparable wholesaling operations, indicating that the business is somewhat inefficient.

Summary of Learning Objectives

1. Explain the role of *accountants* and distinguish among the three types of professional accountants in Canada. By collecting, analyzing, and communicating financial information, accountants provide business managers and investors with an accurate picture of a firm's financial health. *Chartered Accountants* (CAs) and *Certified General Accountants* (CGAs) provide accounting expertise for client organizations who must report their financial condition to external stakeholders. *Certified Management Accountants* (CMAs) provide accounting expertise for the firms that employ them.
2. Describe how the *accounting equation* is used. Accountants use the following equation to balance the data pertaining to financial transactions:

   Assets – Liabilities = Owners' equity

   After each financial transaction (e.g., payments to suppliers, sales to customers, wages to employees), the accounting equation must be in balance. If it isn't, then an accounting error has occurred. The equation also provides an indication of the firm's financial health. If assets exceed liabilities, owners' equity is positive; if the firm goes out of business, owners will receive some cash (a gain) after selling assets and paying off liabilities. If liabilities outweigh assets, owners' equity is negative; assets aren't enough to pay off debts. If the company goes under, owners will get no cash and some creditors won't be paid, thus losing their remaining investments in the company.
3. Describe three basic *financial statements* and show how they reflect the activity and financial condition of a business. The *balance sheet* summarizes a company's assets, liabilities, and owners' equity at a given point in time. The *income statement* details revenues and expenses for a given period of time and identifies any profit or loss. The *statement of cash flows* reports cash receipts and payment from operating, investing, and financial activities.
4. Explain the key standards and principles for reporting financial statements. Accountants follow standard reporting practices and principles when they prepare financial statements. Otherwise, users wouldn't be able to compare information from different companies, and they might misunderstand—or be led to misconstrue—a company's true financial status. *Revenue recognition* is the formal recording and reporting of revenues in financial statements. All firms earn revenues continuously as they make sales, but earnings are not reported until the earnings cycle is completed. This cycle is complete under two conditions: (a) The sale is complete and the product delivered; (b) The sale price has been collected or is collectible. This practice assures interested parties that the statement gives a fair comparison of what was gained for the resources that were given up.
5. Explain how computing *financial ratios* can help in analyzing the financial strengths of a business. Drawing upon data from financial statements, ratios can help creditors, investors, and managers assess a firm's finances. The *current, liquidity,* and *debt-to-owners' equity ratios* all measure solvency, a firm's ability to pay its debt in both the short and long runs. *Return on sales, return on equity,* and *earnings per share* are all ratios that measure profitability. The *inventory turnover ratio* shows how efficiently a firm is using its funds.

QUESTIONS AND EXERCISES

Questions for Analysis

1. Balance sheets and income statements are supposed to be objective assessments of the financial condition of a company. But the accounting scandals of the last few years show that certain pressures may be put on accountants as they audit a company's financial statements. Describe these pressures. To what extent do these pressures make the audit more subjective?
2. If you were planning to invest in a company, which of the three types of financial statements would you want most to see? Why?
3. A business hires a professional accountant like a CA or CGA to assess the financial condition of the company. Why would the business also employ a private accountant?
4. Explain how the double entry system reduces the chances of mistakes or fraud in accounting.
5. Explain how financial ratios allow managers to monitor their own efficiency and effectiveness.

6. Suppose that Inflatables Inc., makers of air mattresses for swimming, has the following transactions in one week:
   - Sale of three deluxe mattresses to Al Wett (paid cash—$75) on 7/16
   - Received cheque from Ima Flote in payment for mattresses bought on credit ($90) on 7/13
   - Received new shipment of 200 mattresses from Airheads Inc. (total cost $2000) on 7/17

   Construct a journal for Inflatables Inc.

7. Dasar Co. reports the following data in its September 30, 2007 financial statements:
   - Gross sales $225 000
   - Current assets 40 000
   - Long-term assets 100 000
   - Current liabilities 16 000
   - Long-term liabilities 44 000
   - Owners' equity 80 000
   - Net income 7 200
   - Number of outstanding shares 5 000

   Compute the following ratios: *current ratio, debt-to-equity, return on owners' equity,* and *earnings per share.*

Application Exercises

8. Interview an accountant at a local manufacturing firm. Determine what kinds of budgets the firm uses, and the process by which budgets are developed. Also determine how budgeting helps managers plan their business activities. Give specific examples.
9. Interview the manager of a local retail or wholesale business about taking inventory. What is the firm's primary purpose in taking inventory? How often is it done?
10. Interview the manager of a local business and ask about the role of ethics in the company's accounting practices. Is ethics in accounting an important issue to the manager? What steps are taken to ensure ethical practices internally?

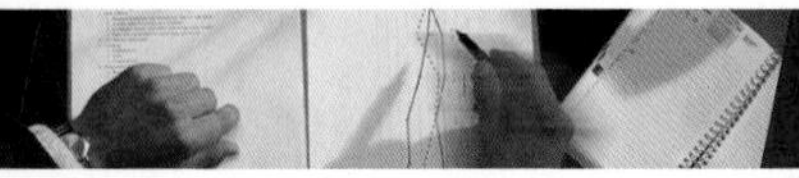

BUILDING YOUR BUSINESS SKILLS

Putting the Buzz in Billing

Goal

To encourage you to think about the advantages and disadvantages of using an electronic system for handling accounts receivable and accounts payable.

Method

Step 1 As the CFO of a utility company, you are analyzing the feasibility of switching from a paper to an electronic system. You decide to discuss the ramifications of the choice with three associates (choose three classmates to take on these roles). Your discussion requires that you research electronic payment systems now being developed. Specifically, using online and library research, you must find out as much as you can about the electronic bill-paying systems being developed by companies like Visa International, Intuit, IBM, and the Checkfree Corporation.

Step 2 After you have researched this information, brainstorm the advantages and disadvantages of switching to an electronic system.

Follow-Up Questions

1. What cost savings are inherent in the electronic system for both your company and its customers? In your answer, consider such costs as handling, postage, and paper.
2. What consequences would your decision to adopt an electronic system have on others with whom you do business, including manufacturers of cheque-sorting equipment, Canada Post, and banks?
3. Switching to an electronic system would mean a large capital expense for new computers and software. How could analyzing the company's income statement help you justify this expense?
4. How are consumers likely to respond to paying bills electronically? Are you likely to get a different response from individuals than you get from business customers?

EXERCISING YOUR ETHICS: TEAM EXERCISE

Confidentially Yours

The Situation

Accountants are often entrusted with private, sensitive information that should be used confidentially. In this exercise, you're encouraged to think about ethical considerations that might arise when an accountant's career choices come up against a professional obligation to maintain confidentiality.

The Dilemma

Assume that you're the head accountant in Turbatron, a large electronics firm that makes components for other manufacturing firms. Your responsibilities include preparing Turbatron's financial statements that are then audited for financial reporting to shareholders. In addition, you regularly prepare confidential budgets for internal use by managers responsible for planning departmental activities, including future investments in new assets. You've also worked with auditors and CA consultants that assess financial problems and suggest solutions.

Now let's suppose that you're approached by another company, Electrolast, one of the electronics industry's most successful firms, and offered a higher-level position. If you accept, your new job will include developing Electrolast's financial plans and serving on the strategic planning committee. Thus, you'd be involved not only in developing strategy but also in evaluating the competition, perhaps even using your knowledge of Turbatron's competitive strengths and weaknesses.

Your contractual commitments with Turbatron do not bar you from employment with other electronics firms.

Team Activity

Assemble a group of four to five students and assign each group member to one of the following roles:

- Head accountant (leaving Turbatron)
- General manager of Turbatron
- Shareholder of Turbatron
- Customer of Turbatron
- General manager of Electrolast (if your team has five members)

Action Steps

1. Before discussing the situation with your group, and from the perspective of your assigned role, are any ethical issues confronting the head accountant in this situation? If so, write them down.
2. Return to your group and reveal ethical issues identified by each member. Were the issues the same among all roles or did differences in roles result in different issues?
3. Among the ethical issues that were identified, decide as a group which one is most important for the head accountant. Which is most important for Turbatron?
4. What does your group finally recommend be done to resolve the most important ethical issue(s)?
5. What steps do you think Turbatron might take in advance of such a situation to avoid any difficulties it now faces?

BUSINESS CASE 11

Continuing Concerns in the Accounting Profession

The corporate accounting and insider trading scandals of a few years ago have caused users of financial data to be increasingly concerned that the balance sheets and income statements of corporations may not be exactly what they seem. Those concerns prompted a Canadian Senate Banking Committee to analyze ways to restore investor confidence in financial data. The Committee made several recommendations, including forcing CEOs to vouch for the truthfulness of their financial statements, passing new legislation governing the conflicts of interest faced by investment analysts, and requiring companies to have only independent directors on their audit committees.

Most of the really dramatic cases of corporate fraud have occurred in the United States, but Canada has the dubious distinction of having one of its own in the limelight. Canadian-born Bernard Ebbers had risen from Alberta milkman and nightclub bouncer to become CEO of WorldCom, one of the largest companies in the United States. It was alleged that Ebbers conspired with subordinates to "cook the books" when a business downturn occurred. These actions wiped out $100 billion of the company's market value, cost 17 000 people their jobs, and investors lost their life savings. Scott Sullivan, one of Ebbers' subordinates, pled guilty and testified that Ebbers had ordered him to cook the books in order to hit earnings targets. In 2005, Ebbers was found guilty on nine charges of securities fraud and filing false documents. He was sentenced to 25 years in prison for his role in the collapse of WorldCom Inc.

In addition to outright accounting fraud, concerns have been expressed about the difficulty investors have in understanding what accounting statements really mean. In recent years, two issues in this area have received attention: overstating sales revenue and understating pension liabilities. The problem of overstating sales revenue is discussed below (see the chapter-opening vignette on pp. 313–314 for a discussion of the pension liability issue).

Overstating Sales Revenue

Many companies are tempted to use "creative accounting" to inflate sales revenue, and this yields a distorted picture of how much product or service a company is actually selling. This is done so that the company will not disappoint the expectations of the stock market and then see their stock price drop. There are different ways that sales revenue can be overstated. For example, some software makers sell a lot of product at the end of a quarter and then count all those sales as revenue without taking into account the future costs the firm will incur to support the software or to provide the free upgrades they promised. Or, a company that acts as a sales agent for an airline might include the ticket price, plus the commission it earns, as revenue. When the airline firm is paid, the cost goes on the expense line. This approach vastly overstates revenue (but not profit). The company should have included only its sales commissions as revenue.

High-tech firms in particular are seen as too liberal in recording revenues on their financial statements. Because of this, the Ontario Securities Commission (OSC) is shifting its emphasis from examining prospectuses to analyzing the way companies report income. It has set up a continuous disclosure team to review the financial reports of corporations in a systematic manner. To get a better understanding of the revenue problem, the OSC is also asking companies how they account for revenue from things like service contracts, and whether they benchmark their accounting practices against those used by other firms in their industry.

Other Concerns

A variety of other concerns have also been raised during recent years, including the following:

- there is sometimes a "chummy" relationship between auditors and their clients; this makes it more difficult for auditors to be completely objective
- there is considerable "elasticity" in the application of generally accepted accounting principles; thus, companies have a lot of leeway in their accounting practices
- if a person from an accounting firm takes a management position with a firm that is a client, future audits may be too "cozy" and fail to be objective
- self-regulation by the accounting industry doesn't work
- there has been much fruitless debate in accounting firms about how to deal with stock options that are given to executives (if these are shown as expenses, they depress corporation earnings and lower the stock price)
- the accounting profession has moved away from establishing broad accounting principles and instead spent much of its time drafting detailed rules; even if these detailed rules are followed, the financial statements that are produced can present a distorted picture of a company's financial condition

What should be done to resolve these problems? A few of the more commonly heard solutions are as follows:

- auditors should clarify their language so that readers of financial statements will have a better idea of how a company is doing before they invest in it

- auditors should give more consideration to the users of financial statements, perhaps emphasizing different data for different user groups
- auditors should be charged with detecting fraud and reporting when they find it
- firms should be required to change their auditors on a regular basis (for example, once every five years) to prevent "chummy" relationships from developing
- auditors should not be allowed to take jobs with former clients until after a specified time period has passed (say, 3–5 years)
- a truly independent monitoring group should be formed that would assess the extent to which companies are meeting standards in their financial reporting
- stock options should be shown as expenses
- when earnings forecasts are made, there must be a clear statement of how the forecasted numbers were arrived at
- companies should be required to show how much they paid for auditing services, and how much they paid for management consulting from the same auditor
- auditors should be required to rank a company's accounting practices in terms of how "aggressive" they are, rather than just saying the books are okay or not okay

Questions for Discussion

1. Who are the various users of accounting information? How will each of these users be influenced if sales revenues are overstated and pension liabilities are understated?
2. What are the three basic financial statements that accountants generate for business firms? What does each one show? How will overstating sales revenue and understating pension liabilities affect each of these statements?
3. Read the section in the chapter on revenue recognition and matching. How is that material helpful in dealing with the "overstating of sales revenue" problem noted in the case?
4. Consider the following statement: "*Since sales revenues and pension returns are measured in dollars, and since dollars are easy to quantify, it should be very clear what sales revenues and investment income a firm had in a given period. It is therefore unnecessary to have policies about how sales revenues and pension returns should be reported.*" Do you agree or disagree? Explain.

MYBUSINESSLAB

To improve your grade, visit the MyBusinessLab website at **www.pearsoned.ca/mybusinesslab**. This online homework and tutorial system allows you to test your understanding and generates a personalized study plan just for you. It provides you with study and practice tools directly related to this chapter's content. MyBusinessLab puts you in control of your own learning!

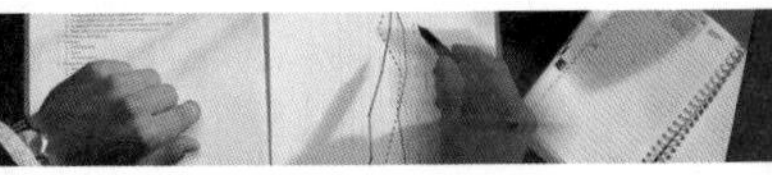

CRAFTING A BUSINESS PLAN

Part 3: Managing Operations and Information

Goal of the Exercise

This part of the business plan project asks you to think about your business in terms of operations, accounting concepts, and information technology (IT) needs and costs. (See Appendix B for material on IT.)

Exercise Background: Part 3 of the Business Plan

An increasingly important part of a business plan is a consideration of how IT—computers, the internet, software, and so on—influences businesses. This part of the business plan asks you to assess how you will use technology to improve your business. Will you, for example, use a database to keep track of your customers? How will you protect your business from hackers and other IT security risks?

This part of the business plan also asks you to consider the costs of doing business, such as salaries, rent, and utilities. You'll also be asked to complete the following financial statements:

- *Balance Sheet.* The balance sheet is a foundation for financial reporting. This report identifies the valued items of the business (its *assets*) as well as the debts that it owes (its *liabilities*). This information gives the owner and potential investors a "snapshot" into the health of the business.

- *Income Statement (or Profit-and-Loss Statement).* This is the focus of the financial plan. This document will show you what it takes to be profitable and successful as a business owner for your first year. You'll also be asked to consider various factors relating to operating your business.

YOUR ASSIGNMENT mybusinesslab

Step 1

Open the saved *Business Plan* file you have been working on.

Step 2

For the purposes of this assignment, you will answer the following questions in "Part 3: Managing Operations and Information":

1. What kinds of IT resources will your business require?

   Hint: Think about the employees in your business and what they will need in order to do their jobs. What computer hardware and software will they need? Will your business need a network and an internet connection? What type of network? Refer to Appendix B for a discussion on IT resources you may want to consider.

2. How will you use IT to keep track of your customers and potential customers?

   Hint: Many businesses—even small businesses—use databases to keep track of their customers. Will your business require a database? What about other information systems? Refer to Appendix B for more information on these topics.

3. What are the *costs* of doing business? Equipment, supplies, salaries, rent, utilities, and insurance are just some of these expenses. Estimate what it will cost to do business for one year.

   Hint: The Business Plan Student Template provides a table for you to insert the costs associated with doing business. Note that these are just estimates—just try your best to include accurate costs for the expenses you think will be a part of doing business.

4. How much will you charge for your product? How many products do you believe that you can sell in one year (or how many customers do you think your business can attract)? Multiply the price that you will charge by the number of products that you hope to sell or the amount you hope each customer will spend. This will give you an estimate of your *revenues* for one year.

   Hint: You will use the amounts you calculate in the costs and revenues questions in this part of the plan in the accounting statements, so be as realistic as you can.

5. Create a balance sheet and an income statement (profit-and-loss statement) for your business.

   Hint: You will have two options for creating these reports. The first option is to use the Microsoft Word versions that are found within the Business Plan Student Template itself. The second option is to use the specific Microsoft Excel templates created for each statement, which are found on the book's MyBusiness Lab. These Excel files are handy to use because they already have the worksheet calculations preset—all you have to do is "plug in" the numbers and the calculations will be performed automatically for you. If you make adjustments to the different values in the Excel worksheets, you'll automatically see how changes to expenses, for example, can improve the "bottom line."

6. Create a floor plan of the business. What does it look like when you walk through the door?

   Hint: When sketching your floor plan, consider where equipment, supplies, and furniture will be located.

7. Explain what types of raw materials and supplies you will need to run your business. How will you produce your good or service? What equipment do you need? What hours will you operate?

   Hint: Refer to the discussion of operations in Chapter 10 for information to get you started.

8. What steps will you take to ensure that the quality of the product or service stays at a high level? Who will be responsible for maintaining quality standards?

   Hint: Refer to the discussion of quality improvement and TQM in Chapter 10 for information to get you started.

Note: Once you have answered the questions, save your Word document. You'll be answering additional questions in later chapters.

CBC VIDEO CASE III-1

Handmaster

Dr. Terry Zachary is a chiropractor turned entrepreneur who has developed a product that is designed to strengthen all the muscles in the human hand. The product looks pretty simple (a polyurethane sponge ball and a plastic cord), but as Terry was looking into how to produce it, he discovered that if he had it manufactured in China he could cut the production cost by 50 percent compared to what it would cost to produce in Canada.

So, Zachary decided to make a trip to China to look at potential manufacturers. He wants to have different companies produce the ball and the cord to reduce the chance that his product will be counterfeited and copied. His plan was to visit eight potential manufacturers in five different Chinese cities to determine who might be best to work with. His first visit is to a company called Changzhou Yuming. Zachary meets with the managers and shows them a sample of the cord that he might want them to produce. He tells them that the quality must be high. Zachary tours their production facilities and is impressed by what he sees. The Yuming managers are very aggressive in assuring him that they can do the work he wants. They clearly want him as a customer, but Zachary finds that communicating through an interpreter is difficult and frustrating.

His next meeting is with managers from Erison, the company that Zachary thinks might be able to make the foam ball for his product. He tells the Erison managers that he wants three different densities for the ball (firm, medium, soft), and that the density must be just right. Later, Zachary takes a bus to the Lelpro factory in Wuxi; that company makes various items including basketballs. Eventually, Zachary decides that Lelpro will make the foam ball for his product. He then heads home.

Six weeks later, Zachary is back in China to see how things are progressing. This is make-or-break time for him. His company has orders for the Handmaster, but he has had problems getting the Chinese manufacturing companies up to speed. At Yuming, the company that is making the cord, Zachary sees the machine that will make it. A test run is underway, and the Yuming production managers say they are getting close to what Zachary wants. Communication is still difficult, and Zachary feels that it is hard to pin down exact dates for when the product will be ready. He is also frustrated because there seems to be a difference between what is being promised and what is actually being delivered. Still, progress is being made, and Zachary feels that his manufacturer is actually getting close to what he wants.

Zachary then goes to check on the production of the foam ball at Lelpro. He checks the all-important density and finds it is good. He thinks that Lelpro is a pretty good company to deal with, but he is taking a chance that they can actually deliver the product in 20 days as required. He didn't put a penalty clause in the contract if they don't deliver on time, but thinks perhaps he should have.

Back at Yuming, there are still problems. Zachary wants to see a final product, but is having trouble conveying that to the Yuming managers. They say they are getting close. Zachary forcefully tells the interpreter to find out the exact time a crucial mould is supposed to arrive at the factory. He also continually asks the interpreter what the Chinese managers are saying. All of this is frustrating, but Zachary can do nothing but wait. Finally, just in time, he gets the final version of the cord for the product. All of the manufacturing jobs that Zachary's product will create will stay in China, but product packaging will be done in Canada.

In the end, Zachary is impressed with the way that the Yuming managers worked through the problems that developed. He says a cordial good-bye to the people at Yuming and returns to Canada.

Questions for Discussion

1. What are the different kinds of utility? What kind of utility is being generated by these Chinese manufacturers?
2. What five types of transformation technology are available? Which one is being used by the manufacturers in this situation?
3. What is the difference between analytic and synthetic processes? Which process is being used here?
4. What kind of layout is likely used in the manufacture of the Handmaster product?
5. Which of the total quality management techniques might be useful in the production of the Handmaster product?

Source: "Handmaster: Made in China," *Venture*, March 14, 2004.

CBC VIDEO CASE III-2

African Accountants

In Canada's business jungle, all tracks lead to Bay Street, where lions of modern industry reign. Accountants keep Bay Street's books, but the heat is on to keep better books. Accountants don't like people who bring in shoeboxes full of receipts and then ask the accountant to organize them. Instead, accountants want the material organized before they try to do any calculations. But all this organizing costs money, and small- and mid-sized businesses don't usually have the money to pay for it.

For George Wall, of Wall & Associates, finding enough casual workers to do data organization and entry was a big challenge. He had to pay them up to $20 an hour, and that service was way too pricey for many of his clients. But what if Wall could find workers who would do this work for one-tenth the hourly wage he had to pay people in Toronto? He found the solution by adopting global outsourcing. It works like this: when that shoebox arrives, each piece of paper is first fed into a high-speed scanner, then stored on a server, and then sent to the internet. While Bay Street sleeps, the material is sent to Kampala, Uganda, where the data are keyed in by African accountants who are paid only about $1 a day.

In a freshly painted office in Kampala, a dozen computers have just been taken out of their boxes, and a dozen workers have just been hired. Their boss is 20-something Abu Luaga, a Ugandan with a commerce degree who has the contract to do accounting work for Wall & Associates. He teaches the new hires what to do. His start-up funds came from his family, and he got involved with Wall & Associates through his connections with a Canadian business consultant.

There is much competition from other developing countries to get this kind of business. But his workers are keen, and they're already trained as bookkeepers. They're eager to see what the developed world has to offer, but many have never had a computer before and need training so that they can recognize various financial documents and learn Canadian accounting jargon. They're also being trained to think the way Canadian businesses do. As well, Luaga reminds them about deadlines and privacy. Because these workers are dealing with sensitive information, no cellphones are allowed in the office and the copying or saving of files or images is prohibited.

What are the implications of all this information flowing from the first world to the third world and back again? It may be just the kind of miracle Uganda needs. The telecommunications industry has been a bright spot in the Ugandan economy, but Ugandans still make only about $1 a day. The country still relies on money earned by exporting coffee, and the government is dependent on foreign donors for part of its budget. Officials admit that the technical skills of workers aren't as good as those of people in some Asian countries, but this system allows educated Ugandans to work in their home country.

Luaga's workers say the work has already changed their career prospects. But not all Canadian clients have jumped at the chance to zip their documents to Africa. George Wall is convinced they will eventually be comfortable with the idea, and Luaga is banking on it. He's leasing bigger and better office space because he thinks that a new office and clients in Canada will impress other potential clients in Africa.

Questions for Discussion

1. What is the difference between financial and managerial accounting? Is the work that the African accountants are doing financial or managerial accounting? Explain.
2. Why might Canadian clients be reluctant to have Wall & Associates send their data to Africa for organizing? What can George Wall do to respond to their concerns?
3. Suppose that you read a newspaper editorial condemning the practice of sending documents to Africa on the grounds that this was yet another example of exporting Canadian jobs overseas to low-wage countries. How would you respond?

Source: "African Accountants," *Venture*, February 16, 2003.

PART FOUR

Managing Marketing

What is the first thing you think of when you hear the names Coffee Crisp, Post-it, Crest, and Eno? If you grew up in Canada, you probably didn't hesitate at all before picturing candy, little slips of paper with one sticky edge, toothpaste, and something to calm your stomach. Your rapid association of company names and the goods or services they provide is a tribute to the effectiveness of the marketing managers of the firms that produce these goods. These and many other names have become household words because companies have developed the right products to meet customers' needs, have priced those products appropriately, have made prospective customers aware of the products' existence and qualities, and have made the products readily available.

Part Four, Managing Marketing, provides an overview of the many elements of marketing, including developing, pricing, promoting, and distributing various types of goods and services.

- We begin in **Chapter 12, Understanding Marketing Processes and Consumer Behaviour**, by examining the ways in which companies distinguish their products, determine customer needs, and otherwise address consumer buying preferences.
- Then, in **Chapter 13, Developing and Promoting Goods and Services**, we explore the development of different types of products, the effect of brand names and packaging, how promotion strategies help a firm meet its objectives, and the advantages and disadvantages of several promotional tools.
- Finally, in **Chapter 14, Pricing and Distributing Goods and Services**, we look at the strategies firms use to price their products. We also consider the various outlets business firms use to distribute their products, and we discuss the problems of storing goods and transporting them to distributors.

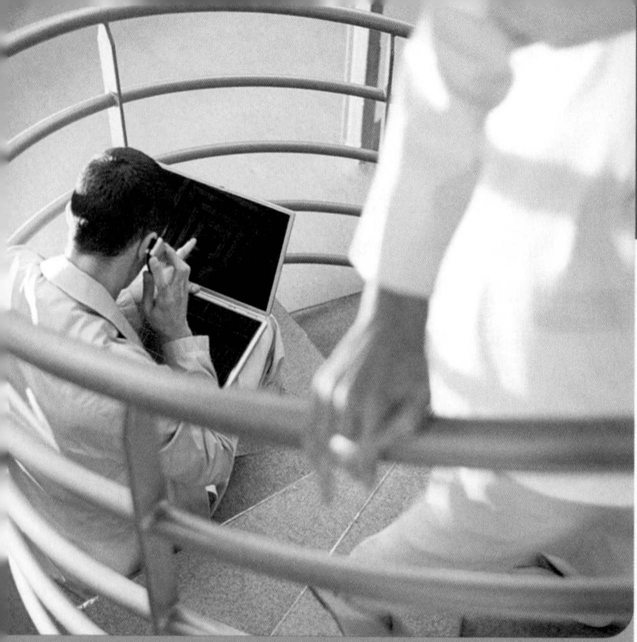

CHAPTER 12

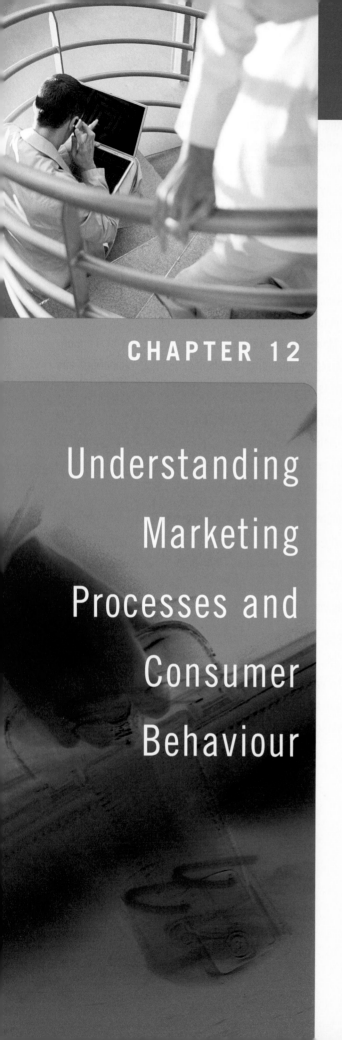

Understanding Marketing Processes and Consumer Behaviour

After reading this chapter, you should be able to:

1. Explain the concept of *marketing*.
2. Explain the purpose of a *marketing plan* and identify the four components of the *marketing mix*.
3. Explain *market segmentation* and show how it is used in target marketing.
4. Explain the purpose and value of *marketing research*.
5. Describe the key factors that influence the *consumer buying process*.
6. Describe the *international* and *small business marketing mixes*.

Marketers Pay Attention to the Older Folks

For many years, marketers directed their attention to consumers in the 18–35 age bracket because it was assumed that if they could get younger consumers to like their products, these consumers would continue to be loyal to them as they grew older. But this assumption has been called into question by marketing research data which shows that customers are quite willing to switch brands if given the incentive to do so. Companies are also realizing that older consumers simply have a lot more money to spend than younger consumers do. For example, the net worth of people aged 65–69 is about 15 times the net worth of people aged 34 and younger.

Another factor is demographics: by 2010, about one-third of the Canadian population will be over 50 years of age. Between 2003 and 2016, the number of Canadians aged 55–64 will increase by 51 percent, and the number over 65 will increase by 41 percent. The number of Canadians aged 18–24 will increase by only 5 percent during that same period.

Is it possible for a company to attract older customers while still making younger ones think their products are cool? Sony thinks so. Its advertisement showing a grandmother taking underwater pictures of sharks scored well with younger viewers who liked the adventure aspect of the advertisement. Sony calls customers in the 50–64 age bracket "zoomers" to reflect the fact that they have more active lifestyles than their parents did. Here are several other examples of marketing to older people:

- Ford Motor Co. is introducing the Ford Five Hundred, a sedan (which older drivers like) that has some of the features of an SUV (it also has a roomy trunk for golf bags)
- Procter & Gamble has identified about 30 different products, including Puffs and Downy fabric softener) that can be marketed to people over 50; it has targeted older women with two new products (Rejuvenating Effects toothpaste and Olay Anti-Aging Cream, and has also developed Actonel, an osteoporosis drug, which is likely to do well in Japan, Italy, and France because of the aging populations there
- Motorola introduced a new phone that should be of interest to older consumers because its zoom function allows the user to increase the font size so that it's more readable; the phone also has speakers that can be connected to a hearing aid
- Vodafone introduced a new phone that shows a clear message that the batteries need recharging rather than some tiny icon that is hard for older folks to see
- In Japan, Meiji Dairies Corp. started making a yogurt brand for people over 40
- Walt Disney World developed a program aimed at people over 50 called "Magical Gatherings" that allows customers to use a website to plan trips with golf buddies or old schoolmates
- Anheuser-Busch attracted older drinkers away from wine and other less-filling beverages by introducing a low-carb Michelob beer called "Michelob Ultra"; it was introduced in three Florida retirement communities
- Francine Tremblay launched *Le Bel Age*, a French-language magazine for "mature" Canadians; she also produced *Good Times*, an English-language magazine aimed at the same age group

Of course, companies are not giving all their attention to older people. Rather, they are using demographics (studying characteristics of the population such as age, income, and ethnic background) to determine how to best market to their customers. The age distribution of a country's population is important and it has a big impact on the marketing strategies of companies that are trying to sell everything from diapers to arthritis medicine. For example, the strategy of focusing on the youth market still looks pretty good in places like Brazil, Mexico, and Vietnam (because a large proportion of the population in these countries is young), but not so good in countries like Japan, Germany, and France (where a large proportion of the population is old).

In North America, the importance of demographics in marketing can be seen in a variety of situations. Consider the following:

- Ford Motor of Canada gives graduates a $750 rebate on their first-time purchase of a car
- In 2003, the *Toronto Star* started a youth-oriented newspaper aimed at kids 9 to 14; this offering complements the existing *Starship* feature, which is aimed at kids 6 to 12 and the boom! feature (aimed at teenagers)
- The soundtrack of Hannah Montana, the fictional 14-year-old Disney Channel character, sold over 1.6 million copies in the first two months after its release (that was more than Jay-Z's new album); the Hannah Montana album targets tweens—children between the ages of 8 and 12
- Major League Baseball Enterprises tracks demographic trends to set marketing goals for its $6 billion-a-year business; 20 years ago, the typical fan was a child, but today's average fan is about 37 years old

HOW WILL THIS BENEFIT YOU?

Marketing is a business activity that focuses on providing value to customers so they will want to purchase goods and services that companies offer for sale. If you understand the marketing methods and ideas that are presented in this chapter, you will benefit in two ways: (1) you'll be better prepared to enhance your career by using effective marketing ideas, both as an employee and as a manager, and (2) you'll be a more informed consumer with greater awareness of how businesses use marketing to influence your purchases.

We start this chapter by looking at how marketing provides value, satisfaction, and utility to customers in order to motivate them to purchase goods and services. We then look at the marketing plan and the components of the marketing mix, and discuss market segmentation and how it is used in target marketing. Next, we look at the idea of market research, and how this activity helps companies develop and sell goods and services. The chapter concludes with a discussion of the key factors that influence the buying processes of consumers and organizational buyers.

WHAT IS MARKETING?

1 Explain the concept of *marketing*.

marketing
Planning and executing the development, pricing, promotion, and distribution of ideas, goods, and services to create exchanges that satisfy both buyers' and sellers' objectives.

marketing concept
The idea that the whole firm is directed toward serving present and potential customers at a profit.

What do you think of when you think of marketing? If you are like most people, you probably think of advertising for something like detergent or soft drinks. But marketing includes much more than advertising. **Marketing** is "the process of planning and executing the conception, pricing, promotion, and distribution of ideas, goods, and services to create exchanges that satisfy individual and organizational objectives."[1] The **marketing concept** means that the whole firm is coordinated to achieve one goal—to serve its present and potential customers and to do so at a profit. This concept means that a firm must get to know what customers really want and closely follow the changes in tastes that occur. The various departments of the firm—marketing, production, finance, and human resources—must operate as a system, well coordinated and unified in the pursuit of a common goal: customer satisfaction.

Providing Value and Satisfaction

value
Relative comparison of a product's benefits versus its costs.

Consumers buy products that offer the best value when it comes to meeting their needs and wants. **Value** compares a product's benefits with its costs. *Benefits* include not only the features of the product or service, but also the emotional satisfaction associated with owning, experiencing, or possessing it. *Costs* include the price, the expenditure of the buyer's time, and the emotional costs of making a purchase decision. The satisfied buyer perceives the benefits derived from the purchase to be greater than its costs. Thus, the simple but important ratio for value:

$$\text{Value} = \frac{\text{Benefits}}{\text{Costs}}$$

To understand how marketing creates value for customers, we need to know the kind of benefits that buyers get from a firm's goods or services. As we saw in Chapter 10, products provide consumers with time, place, ownership, and form utility. These utilities yield products that satisfy human wants or needs.

Goods, Services, and Ideas

Marketing of tangible goods is obvious in our everyday life. You walk into a department store and a woman with a clipboard asks if you'd like to try a new cologne. A pharmaceutical company proclaims the virtues of its new cold medicine. Your local auto dealer offers you a special deal on a car. These **consumer goods** are products that you, the consumer, buy for personal use. Firms that sell their products to the end user are engaged in *consumer marketing*.

consumer goods
Products purchased by individuals for their personal use.

Marketing is also important for **industrial goods**—items that are used by companies for production purposes or further assembly. Conveyors, lift trucks, and earth movers are all industrial goods, as are components and raw materials such as integrated circuits, coal, steel, and plastic. Firms that sell their products to other manufacturers are engaged in *industrial marketing*.

industrial goods
Products purchased by companies to use directly or indirectly to produce other products.

Marketing is also relevant for **services**—intangible products such as time, expertise, or some activity that you can purchase. *Service marketing* has become a major area of growth in Canada. Insurance companies, airlines, investment counsellors, health clinics, and exterminators are a few examples of companies that engage in service marketing.

services
Intangible products, such as time, expertise, or an activity that can be purchased.

Finally, marketing is also used to promote *ideas*. Television ads, for example, remind us that teaching is an honourable profession, that drinking and driving is irresponsible behaviour, and that smoking is detrimental to your health.

Relationship Marketing

Marketing often focuses on single transactions for products, services, or ideas, but **relationship marketing** emphasizes longer-term relationships with customers and suppliers. Stronger relationships, including stronger economic and social ties, can result in greater long-term satisfaction and retention of customers.[2] Harley-Davidson, for example, offers social incentives through the Harley Owners Group (HOG), the largest motorcycle club in

relationship marketing
A type of marketing that emphasizes lasting relationships with customers and suppliers.

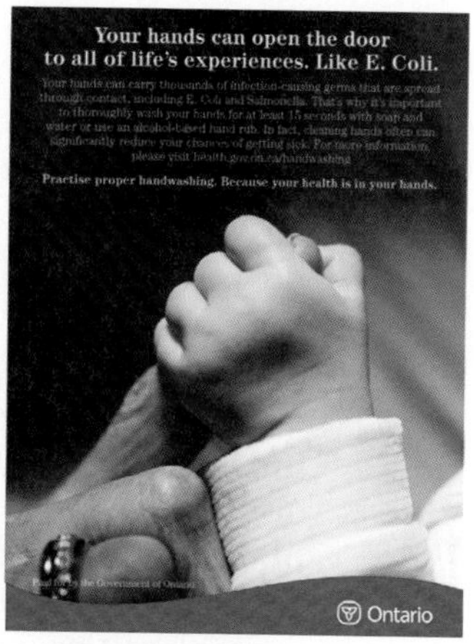

Each of these advertisements provides information about a specific product, service, or idea. The soy milk, for example, is a tangible consumer product. The advertisement for the fitness club promotes a service that can be enjoyed. The public service ad promotes the idea of healthy behaviour.

BUSINESS ACCOUNTABILITY

When Smoke Gets in Your Eyes

In Canada, government restriction on the advertising of cigarettes has a long history. Television advertising of cigarettes has been prohibited since 1971, and various other restrictions (including some rather dramatic label requirements) have come into force since then. Recent legislation discourages tobacco companies from sponsoring sports and cultural events so that they can get their brands prominently displayed to consumers. At a charity dinner in Toronto in 2004, for example, the Rothmans Benson & Hedges table simply said "anonymous" in spite of the fact that the company had paid thousands of dollars to sponsor the table. Tobacco companies are still allowed to advertise in magazines and newspapers, but the rules are so restrictive they generally don't try anymore. Yves-Thomas Dorval, a spokesman for Imperial Tobacco Canada Ltd., says that since "promotion" is essentially prohibited by law, tobacco companies are focusing on the three other "P's" of marketing (price, place, and product).

Clashes between stop-smoking groups and tobacco companies are common, particularly when tobacco companies appear to be ignoring the spirit of the restrictions that have been placed on them. For example, as part of the TD Canada Downtown Jazz Festival, Imperial Tobacco set up an outdoor smoking lounge in Toronto's Nathan Phillips Square. The lounge was criticized by the Ontario Free-Tobacco Network, which called on the mayor of Toronto to stop Imperial from using "scantily clad girls" to promote cigarettes on city property.

All of these situations are interesting, but an important question remains: Who is accountable for the negative effects of tobacco use? Government agencies in both Canada and the United States (Health Canada and the American Public Health Association, respectively) seem to take the position that it is the companies who sell cigarettes that bear most of the responsibility. Not surprisingly, cigarette companies argue that because tobacco use is an individual behaviour choice for which potential health risks are well known, accountability falls to the consumer instead of the producer of the product.

Coalitions of health advocacy groups—including the World Health Organization and other grassroots public health organizations—are insisting that corporate accountability be formally acknowledged. In the United States, the $39 billion in settlement revenues that was given to states during a recent five-year period is cited as tangible recognition of the industry's accountability, but only for after-effects. Not far enough, insist the health advocates, arguing that the more than 400 000 tobacco-related deaths each year in North America are preventable: Companies should also be accountable for effective preventive measures that are absent now and are likely to remain so until more regulation is imposed on them. Tobacco firms, in response, point to several recent court rulings in the United States that denied more than $50 billion in claims brought by HMOs and insurance companies for reimbursement of tobacco-related health expenses. They point to these cases as supportive of the industry's argument that it is not accountable.

the world, with nearly 300 000 members and approximately 900 dealer-sponsored chapters worldwide. HOG, explain Harley marketers, "is dedicated to building customers for life. HOG fosters long-term commitments to the sport of motorcycling by providing opportunities for our customers to bond with other riders and develop long-term friendships."[3]

2 Explain the purpose of a *marketing plan* and identify the four components of the *marketing mix*.

marketing managers
Managers responsible for planning and implementing all the marketing-mix activities that result in the transfer of goods or services to customers.

marketing plan
A detailed strategy for gearing the marketing mix to meet consumer needs and wants.

Strategy: The Marketing Mix

Although many individuals contribute to the marketing of a product, a company's **marketing managers** are typically responsible for planning and implementing all the marketing activities that result in the transfer of goods or services to its customers. These activities culminate in the **marketing plan**: a detailed and focused strategy for gearing marketing activities to meet consumer needs and wants. Marketing begins, therefore, when a company identifies a consumer need and develops a product to meet it.

In planning and implementing their strategies, marketing managers rely on four principal elements of marketing. These four elements—called the *four Ps of marketing*—are *p*roduct (including developing goods, services,

While the issue of accountability simmers, marketing finds itself on both sides of the controversy. Advertising expenditures by Canadian and U.S. tobacco companies have soared to more than $11 billion each year. Health advocates cite "predatory marketing practices" as the industry advertises in youth magazines and develops advertising campaigns targeted at Hispanic, Asian, and other population groups that as yet may not be fully aware of health risks from smoking. Young adults with low incomes and lower education levels are representative of the target-market demographics of smoking. Consider the following statistics:

- The rate of smoking among people who did not complete high school is three times the rate for those with an undergraduate university degree.
- Smoking among pregnant women is 15 times greater for those who did not graduate from high school than it is for those with a university education.
- About one-third of people living below the poverty line are smokers, compared with only one-quarter of those above the poverty line.
- Low-wage workers smoke more than those with high wages.

Health advocates say that tobacco companies have increasingly paid retailers to display tobacco advertising, have used "buy one, get one free" promotions, and have set up promotional racks and giveaways that make cigarettes easier to buy among these targeted smokers.

Marketing by health advocacy groups has embraced "idea-and-information" messages to promote the stop-smoking idea and to appeal for more corporate accountability. The American Legacy Foundation's award-winning TV "truth" campaign, debunks the idea that smoking is glamorous, and features information about the social costs and health consequences of tobacco. A report by the U.S. National Cancer Institute publicized the idea that "light" cigarettes don't reduce health risks and often simply lead to brand switching rather than quitting. Community-based and grassroots efforts include counter-marketing campaigns to educate higher risk groups—targeted by the tobacco industry—about tobacco's harmful effects. Media ads and promotional materials targeted at legislators and regulators are appealing for more regulation and explicit acknowledgement of industry's accountability for reducing the ill effects from tobacco. Meanwhile, both sides know that each day brings with it hundreds of new smokers, quitters, and tobacco-related deaths.

QUESTIONS FOR DISCUSSION

1. Who is more accountable for the health risks associated with smoking: the tobacco companies or the people who decide to smoke cigarettes? Explain your reasoning.
2. Should tobacco companies be held more accountable for the health problems of low-income, low-education smokers than for the health problems of high-income, high-education smokers?
3. "*There is overwhelming evidence that cigarettes cause a variety of serious health problems. The Canadian government, in its role of protecting consumers, should therefore ban the sale of cigarettes.*" Do you agree or disagree with this statement? Explain your reasoning.

and ideas), *p*ricing, *p*romotion, and *p*lace (distribution).[4] The sellers' four Ps are a mirror image of the buyers' four Cs: customer solution (product), customer cost (price), customer convenience (place), and customer communication (promotion).[5] Together, these elements are known as the **marketing mix**, depicted in Figure 12.1.

marketing mix The combination of product, pricing, promotion, and distribution strategies used in marketing a product.

The importance of these four elements varies, depending on the product that is being sold. Price might play a large role in selling fresh meat but a very small role in selling newspapers. Distribution might be crucial in marketing gasoline but not so important for lumber. Promotion is vital in toy marketing, but of little consequence in marketing nails. The product is important in every case, but probably less so for toothpaste than for cars.

Product

Marketing begins with a **product**—a good, a service, or an idea designed to fill a consumer need or want. Meeting consumer needs is a constant challenge, and often means changing existing products to keep pace with changing markets and competitors. Marketers try to promote particular features of products to distinguish them from their competitors in the marketplace.

product A good, service, or idea that satisfies buyers' needs and demands.

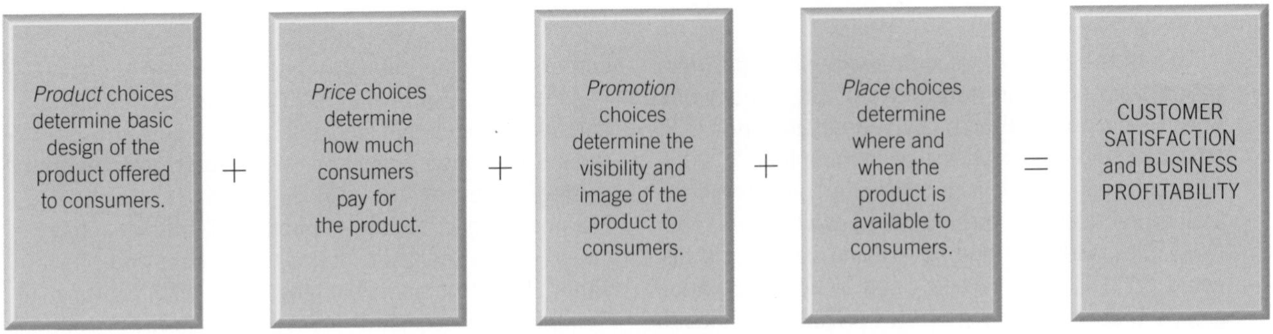

Figure 12.1 Choosing the marketing mix for a business.

product differentiation
The creation of a product or product image that differs enough from existing products to attract consumers.

Product differentiation is the creation of a feature or image that makes a product differ enough from competitive products to attract consumers. For example, Volvo automobiles provide newer, better safety features to set them apart from competitors. Customers of E*Trade™, the online investment service, gain value from after-hours trading not offered by conventional investment-service firms. One company has developed a system that allows its customers at retail home centres and lumber yards to custom-design decks and shelving. As a result, the company has differentiated a commodity—two-by-fours—by turning them into premium products. *Mass customization*, which was explained in Chapter 10, allows marketers to provide products that satisfy very specific needs of consumers. We discuss products and product development in more detail in Chapter 13.

Price

price
That part of the marketing mix concerned with choosing the appropriate price for a product to meet the firm's profit objectives and buyers' purchasing objectives.

Price refers not only to the actual amount of money that consumers pay for a product or service, but also to the total value of the other things that consumers are willing to give up in return for being able to have the benefits of the product or service. For example, if a person wants to own a Chrysler 300C, that person may have to take money out of a savings account in order to pay for the car. The value of the interest that would have been earned on the savings account is part of the value that the customer gives up in order to own the car.

Determining the best price at which to sell a product is a balancing act. On one hand, prices must support the organization's operating, administrative, research, and marketing costs. On the other hand, prices cannot be so high that consumers turn to competing products. Both low- or high-price strategies may be effective, depending on the situation. Low prices will generally lead to a larger volume of sales. High prices will usually limit the size of the market, but will increase a firm's profits per unit. In some cases, however, high prices may actually attract customers by implying that the product is especially good or rare. We will discuss pricing in more detail in Chapter 14.

Place (Distribution)

distribution
That part of the marketing mix concerned with getting products from the producer to the buyer, including physical transportation and choice of sales outlets.

In the marketing mix, *place* refers to **distribution**. Placing a product in the proper outlet—say, a retail store—requires decisions about warehousing, inventory control, and transportation that are needed to get the product from the producer to the consumer. Firms must also make decisions about the *channels* through which they distribute products. Many manufacturers, for instance, sell goods to other companies which, in turn, distribute them to retailers. Others sell directly to major retailers such as Sears, Wal-Mart, or Safeway. Still others sell directly to final consumers. We explain distribution decisions further in Chapter 14.

By providing both distribution and advertising for Grand & Toy, this truck plays a dual role in the company's marketing.

Promotion

The most visible component of the marketing mix is **promotion**, which refers to those activities that are designed to sell products and services to consumers. Promotional tools include advertising, personal selling, sales promotions, publicity, and public relations. Chapter 13 explores the promotion of products in more depth.

promotion That part of the marketing mix concerned with selecting the appropriate technique for selling a product to a consumer.

TARGET MARKETING AND MARKET SEGMENTATION

Explain *market segmentation* and show how it is used in target marketing. 3

Marketing managers realize that they cannot be "all things to all people" because people have different tastes, different interests, different goals, and different lifestyles. The marketing concept's recognition of consumers' various needs and wants leads marketing managers to think in terms of **target markets**—groups of people with similar wants and needs. Target marketing clearly requires **market segmentation**—dividing a market into categories of customer types or "segments." For example, Mr. Big-and-Tall sells to men who are taller and heavier than average. Special-interest magazines are oriented toward people with certain interests like fishing, home decorating, or gardening.

target market Any group of people who have similar wants and needs and may be expected to show interest in the same product(s).

market segmentation Dividing a market into categories according to traits customers have in common.

Once they have identified market segments, companies may adopt a variety of product strategies. Some firms decide to provide a range of products to the market in an attempt to market their products to more than one segment. For example, General Motors of Canada offers compact cars, vans, trucks, SUVs, luxury cars, and sports cars with various features and prices. Its strategy is to provide an automobile for nearly every segment of the market. In contrast, some businesses restrict production to one market segment. Rolls-Royce, for example, understands that only a relatively small number of people are willing to pay $310 000 for an exclusive touring limousine. Rolls-Royce, therefore, makes no attempt to cover the entire range of possible products; instead, it markets only to a very small segment of the total automobile buyers market.

Table 12.1 shows how a marketer of home-electronic equipment might segment the radio market. Note that segmentation is a strategy for analyzing consumers, not products. The analysis identifies consumer-users—joggers, commuters, travellers. Only *indirectly*, then, does it focus on the uses of the product itself.

Table 12.1 Possible Segmentation of the Radio Market

Segmentation	Product/Target Market
Age	Inexpensive, unbreakable, portable models for young children Inexpensive equipment—possibly portable—for teens Moderate-to-expensive equipment for adults
Consumer attitude	Sophisticated components for audio buffs All-in-one units in furniture cabinets for those concerned with room appearance
Product use	Miniature models for joggers and commuters "Boom box" portables for taking outdoors Car stereo systems for travelling Components and all-in-one units for home use
Location	Battery-powered models for use where electricity is unavailable AC current for North American users DC current for other users

Identifying Market Segments

The members of a market segment must share some common traits or behaviours that will affect their purchasing decisions. In identifying market segments, researchers look at geographic, demographic, psychographic, and product-use variables.

Geographic Variables

geographic variables Geographical units that may be considered in a segmentation strategy.

Geographic variables are the geographical units, from countries to neighbourhoods, which may be important in a segmentation strategy. For example, the heavy rainfall in British Columbia prompts its inhabitants to purchase more umbrellas than do people living in Arizona's desert. Urban dwellers have less demand for pickup trucks than do their rural counterparts. Sailboats sell better along both coasts than they do in the Prairie Provinces.

These patterns affect marketing decisions about what products to offer, at what price to sell them, how to promote them, and how to distribute them. For example, consider marketing down parkas in rural Saskatchewan. Demand will be high, price competition may be limited, local newspaper advertising may be very effective, and the best location may be one easily reached from several small towns.

Demographic Variables

demographic variables Characteristics of populations that may be considered in developing a segmentation strategy.

Demographic variables describe populations by identifying characteristics such as age, income, gender, ethnic background, marital status, race, religion, and social class. Note that these are objective criteria that cannot be altered. Marketers must work with or around them. We saw in the opening case how important one demographic variable—the age distribution of a country's population—is to marketing managers.

Depending on the marketer's purpose, a segment can be a single classification (for example, *aged 20–34*) or a combination of categories (for example, *aged 20–34, married with children, earning $25 000–$34 999*). Foreign competitors, for example, are gaining market share in auto sales by appealing to young buyers (*under 30*) with limited incomes (*under $30 000*). While companies such as Hyundai, Kia, and Daewoo are winning entry-level customers with high quality and generous warranties, Volkswagen targets under-35 buyers with its entertainment-styled VW Jetta.[6]

Canada's great ethnic diversity requires companies to pay close attention to ethnicity as a segmentation variable. Visible minorities in Canada control $76 billion in annual buying power, and to be effective in **multicultural marketing**, companies must understand the underlying values that ethnic minority customers hold. For example, Rogers Communication Inc.'s television advertising campaign for its Bollywood Oye! video-on-demand service is designed to promote its business to South Asian communities in Canada. Rogers currently has 32 multicultural channels and wants to be a leader in customizing services to suit specific ethnic groups.[7]

multicultural marketing Marketing activities directed at various identifiable ethnic groups in Canada.

Psychographic Variables

Members of a market can also be segmented according to **psychographic variables** such as lifestyles, opinions, interests, and attitudes. One company that is using psychographic variables to revive its brand is Burberry, whose plaid-lined gabardine raincoats have been a symbol of British tradition since 1856. After a recent downturn in sales, Burberry is repositioning itself as a global luxury brand, like Gucci and Louis Vuitton. The strategy calls for luring top-of-the-line, fashion-conscious customers. Burberry pictures today's luxury-product shopper as a world traveller who identifies with prestige fashion brands and monitors social and fashion trends in magazines like *Harper's Bazaar*.[8]

psychographic variables Psychological traits that a group has in common, including motives, attitudes, activities, interests, and opinions.

Unlike demographics and geographics, psychographics can sometimes be changed by marketing efforts. For example, many companies in Poland have succeeded in overcoming consumer resistance to credit by promoting the safety and desirability of using credit rather than depending solely on cash. One outcome of such changed attitudes is a booming economy and the emergence of a growing middle class. The increasing number of Polish households that own televisions, appliances, automobiles, and houses is fuelling the status of Poland's middle class as the most stable in the former Soviet bloc.[9]

Product-Use Variables

This fourth way of segmenting looks at why people purchase the product in question, how they use the product, and their brand loyalty to the product.[10] For example, a woman buying an *athletic* shoe will probably not care much about its appearance, but she will care a great deal about arch support, traction offered by the sole, and sturdiness. In contrast, a woman buying a *casual* shoe will want it to look good but be comfortable. A woman buying a *dress* shoe may require a specific colour or style and accept some discomfort and a relatively fragile shoe.

Whatever basis is used for segmenting a market, care must be taken to *position* the product correctly. **Product positioning** is based on the important attributes that consumers use to assess the product. For example, a low-priced car like a Ford Focus tends to be positioned on the basis of *economy*, while a Porsche is positioned in terms of *high performance*. The product positioning chart in Figure 12.2 shows that Tim Hortons emphasizes a standardized product and provides fast service to people in a hurry, while Starbucks provides more customized products in more leisurely surroundings.

product positioning The establishment of an easily identifiable image of a product in the minds of consumers.

Market Segmentation: A Caution

Segmentation must be done carefully. A group of people may share an age category, income level, or some other segmentation variable, but their spending habits may be quite different. Look at your friends in school. You may all be approximately the same age, but you have different needs and wants. Some of you may wear cashmere sweaters while others wear sweatshirts. The same holds true for income. University professors and truck

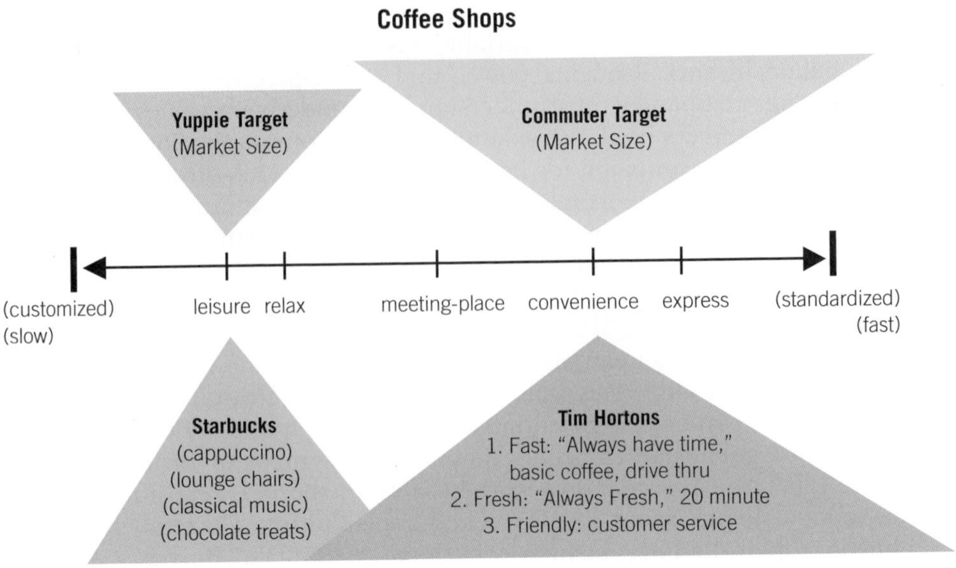

Figure 12.2 Product positioning.

drivers frequently earn about the same level of income; however, their spending patterns, tastes, and wants are generally quite different.

In Canada, the two dominant cultures—English and French—have historically shown significant differences in consumer attitudes and behaviour. Researchers have found, for example, that compared with English Canadians, French Canadians are more involved with home and family, attend ballet more often, travel less, eat more chocolate, and are less interested in convenience food. But this does not necessarily mean that companies must have different product offerings in Quebec. When Headspace Marketing Inc. asked 1000 Quebecers to rate how well 12 different retail brands had adapted to the needs and expectations of Quebecers, they found that the top three brands were Tim Hortons, Canadian Tire, and Bureau en gros (in that order). Interestingly, Tim Hortons ranked much higher than Starbucks (which ranked number 12) in spite of the fact that Tim Hortons did very little to adapt its product line to the Quebec market and Starbucks did a lot. What Tim Hortons *did* do well was get involved with community charities and activities that brought it closer to local residents. The company also used two Quebec actors in their ad campaigns. This apparently made the Tim Hortons brand "resonate" better with Quebecers. The situation is similar for second-ranked Canadian Tire. The chain sells pretty much the same product line in Quebec as in the rest of Canada, but it also got involved in local charities and used Quebec singer Jici Lauzon as a spokesperson.[11]

MARKET RESEARCH

4 Explain the purpose and value of *marketing research.*

market research
The systematic study of what buyers need and how best to meet those needs.

Market research, which is the study of what buyers need and how best to meet those needs, can address any element in the marketing mix. Business firms spend millions of dollars each year as they try to figure out their customers' habits and preferences. Market research can greatly improve the accuracy and effectiveness of market segmentation.[12] Failure to do market research can lead to significant problems. For example, in 2004 the CEO of Coca-Cola admitted that the company had missed the change in consumer tastes away from carbonated drinks and toward healthier, non-carbonated drinks. PepsiCo Inc., on the other hand, capitalized on these trends with its Propel Fitness Water and Gatorade.[13]

The Research Process

Market research can occur at almost any point in a product's existence, but it is most frequently used when a new or altered product is being considered. There are five steps in performing market research:[14]

1. *Study the current situation.* What is the need and what is being done to meet it at this point?
2. *Select a research method.* In choosing a method, marketers must bear in mind the effectiveness and costs of different methods.
3. *Collect data.* **Secondary data** are information already available as a result of previous research by the firm or other organizations. For example, Statistics Canada publishes a great deal of data that are useful for business firms. Using secondary data can save time, effort, and money. But in some cases secondary data are unavailable or inadequate, so **primary data**—new research by the firm or its agents—must be obtained. Hostess Frito-Lay, the maker of Doritos, spent a year studying how to best reach its target market—teenagers. The researchers hung around shopping malls, schools, and fast-food outlets to watch them.[15]
4. *Analyze the data.* As we learned in Chapter 11, data are not useful until they have been organized into information.
5. *Prepare a report.* This report normally includes a summary of the study's methodology and findings, various alternative solutions (where appropriate), and recommendations for an appropriate course of action.

secondary data
Information already available to market researchers as a result of previous research by the firm or other agencies.

primary data
Information developed through new research by the firm or its agents.

Research Methods

The four basic types of methods used by market researchers are *observation, survey, focus groups,* and *experimentation.*

Observation

Probably the oldest form of market research is simple **observation** of what is happening. It is also a popular research method because it is relatively low in cost, often drawing on data that must be collected for some other reason, such as reordering. In earlier times, when a store owner noticed that customers were buying red children's wagons, not green ones, the owner reordered more red wagons, the manufacturer's records showed high sales of red wagons, and the marketing department concluded that customers wanted red wagons. But observation is now much more sophisticated. For example, Procter & Gamble sent video crews into about 80 households in the U.K., Germany, and China to capture people's daily routines and how they used products. P&G can use this information to develop new products to satisfy needs that consumers didn't even know they had.[16]

observation
A market research technique involving viewing or otherwise monitoring consumer buying patterns.

Using video equipment to observe consumer behaviour is called *video mining*. It is being adopted by many retailers in North America who use hidden cameras to determine the percentage of shoppers that buy and the percentage that only browse. They do this by comparing the number of people taped with the number of transactions the store records. Some consumer organizations are raising privacy concerns about this practice, since shoppers are unaware that they are being taped.[17]

Survey

Sometimes, observation of current events is not enough and marketers need to conduct a **survey** to find out what consumers want. When United Parcel Service (UPS) surveyed customers to find out how it could improve

survey
A market research technique based on questioning a representative sample of consumers about purchasing attitudes and practices.

service, it found that customers wanted more interaction with drivers because they could offer practical advice on shipping. UPS thus added extra drivers, freeing up some time for drivers to get out of their trucks and spend time with customers.[18]

The heart of any survey is a questionnaire that contains carefully constructed questions designed to give the company honest answers about specific issues that are being researched. Surveys can be expensive to carry out and may vary widely in their accuracy. Because no firm can afford to survey everyone, marketers must be careful to get a representative group of respondents.

In the past, surveys have been mailed to individuals for their completion, but online surveys are now gaining in popularity because the company gets immediate results, and because the process is a less intrusive way of gathering data. At Hudson's Bay Co., customers can use online surveys to tell the company how happy or unhappy they are about the service they received at any of The Bay's department stores. The company can then make any changes that are needed to keep customers happy. The Bay used to hire mystery shoppers to find out how well it was serving the public, but that program was ended when the online survey system was adopted.[19]

Focus Groups

focus group
A market research technique involving a small group of people brought together and allowed to discuss selected issues in depth.

Many firms also use **focus groups**, where 6 to 15 people are brought together to talk about a product or service. A moderator leads the group's discussion, and employees from the sponsoring company may observe the proceedings from behind a one-way mirror. The comments of people in the focus group are taped, and then researchers go through the data looking for common themes. The people in the focus group are not usually told which company is sponsoring the research.

When Procter & Gamble was developing a new air freshener, it asked people in focus groups to describe their "desired scent experience." They discovered that people get used to a scent after about half an hour and no longer notice it. P&G used this information to develop a "scent player" called Febreze Scentstories that gives off five different scents every 30 minutes.[20]

Consumers don't necessarily tell the truth when participating in focus groups or when filling out surveys. They may say one thing and think something else. This has led marketers to look at other ways of gathering information. Sensory Logic Inc., for example, studies facial expressions and eye movements to determine what consumers really think of a product.[21]

As they watch a sitcom with six commercial breaks, these women are participating in a marketing research experiment. The researchers think that their results will be more accurate than questionnaire and focus-group responses because they're getting them straight from the subjects' brains. A spike in a subject's left prefrontal cortex means that she probably likes a product or an ad. A spike in the right prefrontal cortex is bad news for the advertiser. Using machines designed to detect brain tumours, researchers can even tell which part of an ad makes a dent in the subject's long-term memory.

Experimentation

Experimentation compares the responses of the same or similar individuals under different circumstances. For example, a firm that is trying to decide whether to include walnuts in a new candy bar probably would not learn much by asking people what they thought of the idea. But if it made some bars with nuts and some without and then asked people to try both, the responses could be very helpful.[22]

experimentation
A market research technique in which the reactions of similar people are compared under different circumstances.

UNDERSTANDING CONSUMER BEHAVIOUR

Market research in its many forms can be of great help to marketing managers in understanding how the common traits of a market segment affect consumers' purchasing decisions. Why do people buy a certain product? What desire are they fulfilling with the product? Is there a psychological or sociological explanation for why consumers purchase one product and not another? These questions and many others are addressed in the area of marketing known as **consumer behaviour**, which focuses on the decision process customers use when deciding what products to buy.

consumer behaviour
The study of the process by which customers come to purchase and consume a product or service.

Influences on Consumer Behaviour

To understand consumer behaviour, marketers draw heavily on the fields of psychology and sociology. Four influences are most active, and marketers use these to explain consumer choices and predict future purchasing behaviour:

- *Psychological influences* include an individual's motivations, perceptions, ability to learn, and attitudes.
- *Personal influences* include lifestyle, personality, economic status, and life-cycle stage.
- *Social influences* include family, opinion leaders (people whose opinions are sought by others), and reference groups such as friends, coworkers, and professional associates.
- *Cultural influences* include culture (the "way of living" that distinguishes one large group from another), subculture (smaller groups, such as ethnic groups, with shared values), and social class (the cultural ranking of groups according to criteria such as background, occupation, and income).

Although these factors can have an impact on a consumer's choices, their effect on actual purchases varies. Some consumers, for example, regularly purchase certain products because they are satisfied with their performance. Such people are less subject to influence and stick with brand names they have experience with. On the other hand, the clothes you wear and the food you eat often reflect social and psychological influences on your consuming behaviour.

The Consumer Buying Process

Describe the key factors that influence the *consumer buying process*. 5

Researchers who have studied consumer behaviour have constructed models that help marketing managers understand how consumers come to purchase products. Figure 12.3 presents one such model. At the foundation of this and similar models is an awareness of the psychosocial influences that lead to consumption. Ultimately, marketing managers use this information to develop marketing plans.

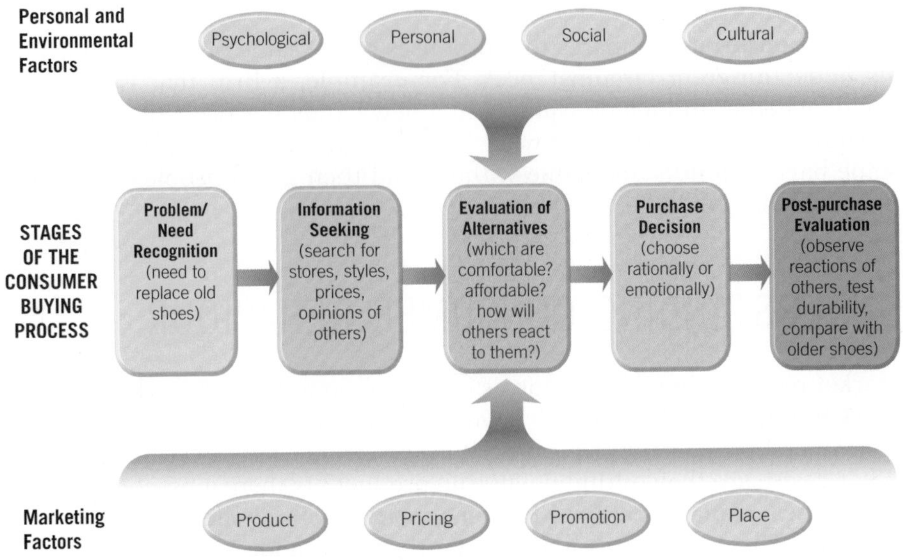

Figure 12.3 Consumer buying process.

Problem/Need Recognition

The buying process begins when a consumer becomes aware of a problem or need. For example, after strenuous exercise, you may recognize that you are thirsty and need refreshment. After the birth of twins, you may find your one-bedroom apartment too small for comfort. After standing in the rain to buy movie tickets, you may decide to buy an umbrella. Need recognition also occurs when you have a chance to change your purchasing habits. For example, the income from your first job after graduation will let you purchase items that were too expensive when you were a student. You may also discover a need for professional clothing, apartment furnishings, and cars. Visa and The Bay recognize this shift and therefore market their credit cards to graduates.

Information Seeking

Having recognized a need, consumers seek information. This search is not always extensive. If you are thirsty, you may ask where the pop machine is, but that may be the extent of your information search. Other times, you simply rely on your memory for information. Before making major purchases, however, most people seek additional information. For example, if you move to a new city, you will want to find out who is the best local dentist, physician, hair stylist, butcher, or pizza maker. To get this information, you may check with personal sources such as acquaintances, co-workers, and relatives. Before buying an exercise bike, you may go to the library and read the latest *Consumer Reports*—a public source of consumer ratings—on such equipment. You may also ask market sources such as the salesclerk or rely on direct experience. For example, you might test-ride the bike to learn more before you buy. The internet has become an important source of information, with one-third of consumers relying on it to gather information.[23]

Evaluation of Alternatives

If you are in the market for a set of golf clubs, you probably have some idea of who produces clubs and how they differ. You may have accumulated some of this knowledge during the information-seeking stage and combined it with what you knew before. Based on product attributes such as colour, taste, price, prestige, quality, and service record, you will decide which product best meets your needs.

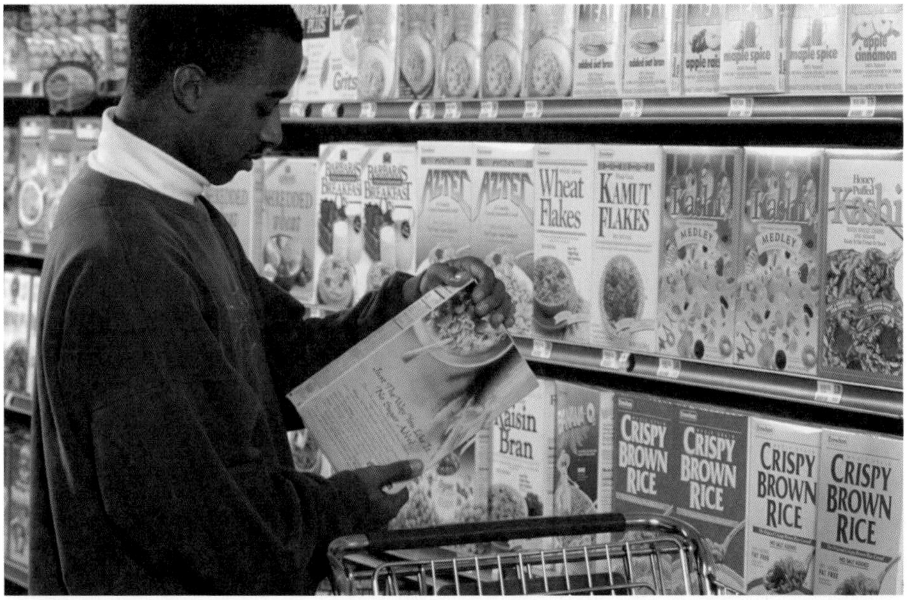

What information is this shopper looking for to decide on his purchase? Marketers would like to know how and why consumers buy the products they buy. A better understanding of the customer buying process allows sellers to tailor their products to meet customer needs.

Purchase Decision

Ultimately, you make a purchase decision. "Buy" decisions are based on rational and emotional motives. **Rational motives** involve a logical evaluation of product attributes like cost, quality, and usefulness. **Emotional motives** like fear, sociability, imitation of others, and aesthetics can lead to less-than-ideal purchase decisions. Many spur-of-the-moment decisions are emotionally driven. You might buy mouthwash to avoid ostracism. You might buy the same brand of jeans as your friends so that you "fit in." And you might buy a chocolate milkshake simply because you like the taste.

rational motives
Those reasons for purchasing a product that involve a logical evaluation of product attributes such as cost, quality, and usefulness.

emotional motives
Those reasons for purchasing a product that involve non-objective factors.

Post-Purchase Evaluation

Marketing does not stop with the sale of a product or service, but includes the process of consumption. What happens *after* the sale is very important. A marketer wants consumers to be happy after the consumption of the product so that they will buy the product again. In fact, since consumers do not want to go through a complex decision process for every purchase, they often choose a product they have used and liked.

Not all consumers are satisfied with their purchases, of course. Dissatisfied consumers may complain, file a lawsuit, or publicly criticize the product and the company. They are unlikely to purchase the product again, and they are much more likely to speak about their negative experience with a product than are satisfied customers. People can complain about products or services at www.complaints.com. Dissatisfied customers can have a very negative impact on a company's marketing effort. **Word of mouth marketing** (also known as "**buzz marketing**") is therefore a very powerful marketing tool. It can, however, be the most devastating, since businesses cannot control it.[24] The Exercising Your Ethics feature at the end of the chapter describes a situation where the customer's buying process did not fit with the marketing methods being used by the company. The result was an unhappy customer.

word of mouth marketing ("buzz marketing")
Opinions about the value of products passed among consumers in informal discussions.

THE INTERNATIONAL MARKETING MIX

Describe the *international* and *small business marketing mixes.* **6**

Marketing products internationally means mounting a strategy to support global business operations. Obviously, this is no easy task. Foreign customers, for example, differ from domestic buyers in language, customs, business practices, and consumer behaviour. When they decide to go global, marketers must therefore reconsider each element of the marketing mix.

International Products

Some products can be sold in many different countries with virtually no changes. Budweiser, Coca-Cola, and Marlboros are exactly the same in Toronto, Tokyo, and Timbuktu. In other cases, firms can create products with built-in flexibility—for instance, electric shavers that adapt to either 110- or 220-volt outlets. At other times only a redesigned—or completely different—product will meet the needs of foreign buyers. To sell the Macintosh in Japan, for example, Apple Computer had to develop a Japanese-language operating system.

ENTREPRENEURSHIP AND NEW VENTURES

When in Rome

When Art Aylesworth first tried to sell solar-powered LED lights for bus stops in Britain's capital, he was stymied. Oh, they might speak English in London, but the strategy he used to sell lights to the North American marine industry didn't translate to both a new country and sector.

Five years later, Aylesworth's Carmanah Technologies Corp. targets nine industries in 115 countries. Exports, which yield 92 percent of sales, powered five-year revenue growth of 1246 percent, with Carmanah now ranked number one in the world in sales of solar-powered LED lights. Its new winning strategy? Customizing sales and marketing to each industry and country. That may sound daunting, but, like it or not, the rules of play are set by prospective clients. "You have to be a chameleon in the way you present your products and do business," says Aylesworth, Carmanah's CEO. "Figure out how they do things and join in."

Shape-shifting is hard and complicated work, but Aylesworth says it's worth it: "Had we stuck with the [original] strategy, the business would have grown about fivefold in five years. By adapting the way we have, it has grown about 35 times as big." Rather than offer a single website, Carmanah has 11 tailored to various industries and subsectors (e.g., railwaylights.com and solarairportlights.com), with more in the works. Customers want to know you understand their world, says Aylesworth, and a customized site yields opportunities more easily and affordably than a sales rep. Carmanah has also added new sales channels to suit client preferences. It used to sell only through distributors, but now also uses its own salespeople, contracted sales agents and strategic partnerships.

Geographically, it tailors its technology to each market as regulations or local practices require. But, Aylesworth says, Carmanah's main export challenge has been learning foreign cultures and business processes, which takes time and no small amount of trial and error. Deals in Europe and Asia, for example, require far more patience and relationship-building than in Canada. Indeed, Carmanah's five-year, $16-million deal with London's transit authority was four years in the making.

Carmanah crafts a strategy for each prospect by first asking a series of questions: which products they want and use, how and why they use them, how they buy or replace technology (including regulatory and approval procedures), who they partner with and which sales channels they prefer. It's crucial to find the right "lead investigator" to gather such market feedback. The first senior manager Carmanah sent to the Middle East failed to earn the trust of locals, even after many trips and meetings. Aylesworth now stresses the importance of hiring a business-development manager who's hard to deter, astute, and "tough-natured but nice when they need to be."

Shape-shifting isn't cheap, either. Carmanah invested $5 million over five years to develop new products and markets. Still, the approach doesn't require vast resources: Carmanah had just 12 staff when it adopted this strategy. What you do need, advises Aylesworth, is enough money to invest for the long haul. You should also hone your communication skills and hire people with relevant geographical or industry expertise to shorten the learning curve. Above all, weigh carefully your decision to enter a market so you don't misjudge your resources, opportunity, or desire. "If you ever walk away," warns Aylesworth, "you won't get back in easily."

International Pricing

When pricing for international markets, marketers must handle all the considerations of domestic pricing while also considering the higher costs of transporting and selling products abroad. Some products cost more overseas than in Canada because of the added costs of delivery. Due to the higher costs of buildings, rent, equipment, and imported meat, a McDonald's Big Mac that sells for $2.99 in Canada has a price tag of over $10 in Japan. In contrast, products like jet airplanes are priced the same worldwide because delivery costs are incidental; the huge development and production costs are the major considerations regardless of customer location.

International Promotion

Some standard Canadian promotional techniques like advertising do not always succeed in other countries. In fact, many Europeans believe that a product must be inherently shoddy if a company does *any* advertising. International marketers must also be aware that cultural differences can cause negative reactions to products that are advertised improperly. For example, since many Europeans are offended by television commercials that show weapons or violence, Dutch commercials for toys do not feature the guns and combat scenes that are commonplace on Saturday morning television in North America. Meanwhile, cigarette commercials that are banned from Canadian and U.S. television are thriving in many Asian and European markets.

Symbolism, too, is a sometimes surprising consideration. In France, for instance, yellow flowers suggest infidelity. In Mexico, they are signs of death—an association made in Brazil by the colour purple. Clearly, product promotions must be carefully matched to the customs and cultural values of each country.

International Distribution

In some industries, delays in starting new distribution networks can be costly. Therefore, companies with existing distribution systems often enjoy

Feathercraft is a small British Columbia manufacturer that has been successful selling kayaks in the Japanese market.

an advantage over new businesses. Several companies have gained advantages in time-based competition by buying existing businesses. Procter & Gamble, for example, saved three years of start-up time by buying Revlon's Max Factor and Betrix cosmetics, both of which are well established in foreign markets. P&G can thus immediately use these companies' distribution and marketing networks for selling its own brands in the United Kingdom, Germany, and Japan.

Other companies contract with foreign firms or individuals to distribute and sell their products abroad. Foreign agents may perform personal selling and advertising, provide information about local markets, or serve as exporters' representatives. But having to manage interactions with foreign personnel complicates a marketing manager's responsibilities. In addition, packaging practices in Canada must sometimes be adapted to withstand the rigours of transport to foreign ports and storage under conditions that differ radically from domestic conditions.

SMALL BUSINESS AND THE MARKETING MIX

Many of today's largest firms were yesterday's small businesses. McDonald's began with one restaurant, a concept, and one individual (Ray Kroc) who had a lot of foresight. Behind the success of many small firms lies a skilful application of the marketing concept and careful consideration of each element in the marketing mix.

Small-Business Products

Some new products—and firms—are doomed from the start simply because few consumers want or need what they have to offer. Too often, enthusiastic entrepreneurs introduce products that they and their friends like, but they fail to estimate realistic market potential. Other small businesses offer new products before they have clear pictures of their target markets and how to reach them. They try to be everything to everyone, and they end up serving no one well. In contrast, sound product planning has paid off for many small firms. "Keep it simple" is a familiar key to success—that is, fulfill a specific need and do it efficiently.

Small-Business Pricing

Haphazard pricing that is often little more than guesswork can sink even a firm with a good product. Most often, small business pricing errors result from a failure to predict operating expenses accurately. Owners of failing businesses have often been heard to utter statements like "I didn't realize how much it costs to run the business!" and "If I price the product high enough to cover my expenses, no one will buy it!" But when small businesses set prices by carefully assessing costs, many earn very satisfactory profits—sometimes enough to expand or diversify.

Small-Business Promotion

Successful small businesses plan for promotional expenses as part of start-up costs. Some hold costs down by taking advantage of less expensive promotional methods. Local newspapers, for example, are sources of publicity when they publish articles about new or unique businesses. Other small businesses have succeeded by identifying themselves and their products with associated groups, organizations, and events. Thus a custom-crafts gallery might join with a local art league and local artists to organize public showings of their combined products.

Small-Business Distribution

Problems in arranging distribution can also make or break small businesses. Perhaps the most critical aspect of distribution is facility location, especially for new service businesses. The ability of many small businesses—retailers, veterinary clinics, gourmet coffee shops—to attract and retain customers depends partly on the choice of location.

In distribution, as in other aspects of the marketing mix, however, smaller companies may have advantages over larger competitors. They may be quicker, for example, in applying service technologies. Everex Systems Inc. sells personal computers to wholesalers and dealers through a system the company calls "Zero Response Time." Phone orders are reviewed every two hours so that the factory can adjust assembly to match demand.

Summary of Learning Objectives

1. Explain the concept of *marketing.* Marketing is "the process of planning and executing the conception, pricing, promotion, and distribution of ideas, goods, and services to create exchanges that satisfy individual and organizational goals." Products provide consumers with utility—the ability of a product to satisfy a human want or need. Marketing can be used to promote consumer and industrial goods and services, as well as ideas.

2. Explain the purpose of a *marketing plan* and identify the four components of the *marketing mix.* Marketing managers plan and implement all the marketing activities that result in the transfer of products to customers. These activities culminate in the marketing plan—a detailed strategy for focusing the effort to meet consumer needs and wants. Marketing managers rely on the "Four Ps" of marketing, or the marketing mix. (1) *Product:* Marketing begins with a product, a good, a service, or an idea designed to fill a consumer need or want. Product differentiation is the creation of a feature or image that makes a product differ from competitors. (2) *Pricing:* Pricing is the strategy of selecting the most appropriate price at which to sell a product. (3) *Place (Distribution):* All distribution activities are concerned with getting a product from the producer to the consumer. (4) *Promotion:* Promotion refers to the techniques used to communicate information about products to customers.

3. Explain *market segmentation* and show how it is used in target marketing. Marketers think in terms of target markets—groups of people who have similar wants and needs and who can be expected to show interest in the same products. Target marketing requires market segmentation—dividing a market into customer types or "segments." Four of the most important influences are: (1) *geographic variables* (the geographical units that may be considered in developing a segmentation strategy); (2) *demographic variables* (describe populations by identifying such traits as age, income, gender, ethnic background, marital status, race, religion, and social class); (3) *psychographic variables* (such as lifestyles, interests, and attitudes); and (4) *behavioural variables* (the ways in which consumers use a product, the benefits they expect from it, their reasons for purchasing it, and their loyalty to it).

4. Explain the purpose and value of *marketing research.* Market research is the study of what buyers need and of the best ways to meet those needs. This process involves a study of the current situation, the selection of a research method, the collection of data, the analysis of data, and the preparation of a report that may include recommendations for action. The four most common research methods are observation, surveys, focus groups, and experimentation.

5. Describe the key factors that influence the *consumer buying process.* Consumer behaviour is the study of the process by which customers decide to purchase products. The result is a focus on four major influences on consumer behaviour: (1) *psychological influences* include motivations, perceptions, ability to learn, and attitudes; (2) *personal influences* include lifestyle, personality, and economic status; (3) *social influences* include family,

opinion leaders, and such reference groups as friends, co-workers, and professional associates; and (4) *cultural influences* include culture, subculture, and social class. By identifying which influences are most active in certain circumstances, marketers try to explain consumer choices and predict future purchasing behaviour.

6. Describe the *international* and *small business marketing mixes.* When they decide to go global, marketers must reconsider each element of the marketing mix: (1) *product* (whereas some products can be sold abroad with virtually no changes, sometimes only a redesigned product will meet the needs of foreign buyers); (2) *price* (when pricing for international markets, marketers must consider the higher costs of transporting and selling products abroad); (3) *distribution* (in some industries, companies have gained advantages by buying businesses already established in foreign markets); (4) *promotion* (occasionally, a good ad campaign can be transported to another country virtually intact, but often Canadian promotional tactics do not succeed in other countries).

Behind the success of many small firms lies an understanding of each element in the marketing mix. (1) *small-business products:* Understanding of what customers need and want has paid off for many small firms; (2) *small-business pricing:* Haphazard pricing can sink even a firm with a good product. Small-business pricing errors usually result from failure to project operating expenses accurately; (3) *small-business distribution:* Perhaps the most critical aspect of distribution is facility location, since the ability of many small businesses to attract and retain customers depends partly on the choice of location; (4) *small-business promotion:* Successful small businesses plan for promotional expenses as part of start-up costs.

QUESTIONS AND EXERCISES

Questions for Analysis

1. Why and how is market segmentation used in target marketing?

2. Select an everyday product (books, CDs, skateboards, dog food, or shoes, for example). Show how different versions of your product are aimed toward different market segments. Explain how the marketing mix differs for each segment.

3. Select another product and describe the consumer buying process that likely occurs before it is purchased.

4. Select another everyday product and describe the consumer buying process that typically goes into its purchase.

5. Consider a service product, such as transportation, entertainment, or health care. What are some ways that more customer value might be added to this product? Why would your improvements add value for the buyer?

6. How does the branding and packaging of convenience, shopping, and specialty goods differ? Why? Give examples of actual products to defend your answer.

7. If you were starting a small business, what are the key *marketing* pitfalls you would try to avoid?

8. Select a product or service that you regularly use. Explain the relative importance of each of the four elements in the marketing mix (product, price, promotion, and place). Then select another product and determine the extent to which the relative emphasis changes. If it changed, why did it change?

Application Exercises

9. Interview the marketing manager of a local business. Identify the degree to which this person's job is focused on each element in the marketing mix.

10. Select a product made by a foreign company and sold in Canada. What is the product's target market? What is the basis on which the target market is segmented? Do you think that this basis is appropriate? How might another approach, if any, be beneficial? Why?

BUILDING YOUR BUSINESS SKILLS

Dealing in Segments and Variables

Goal

To encourage students to analyze the ways in which various market segmentation variables affect business success.

Situation

You and four partners are thinking of purchasing a heating and air conditioning (H/AC) dealership that specializes in residential applications priced between $2000 and $40 000. You are now in the process of deciding where that dealership should be. You are considering four locations: Miami, Florida; Toronto, Ontario; Vancouver, British Columbia; and Dallas, Texas.

Method

Step 1 Working with four classmates (your partnership group), do library research to learn how H/AC makers market their residential products. Check for articles in *The Globe and Mail, Canadian Business, The Wall Street Journal*, and other business publications.

Step 2 Continue your research. This time, focus on the specific marketing variables that define each prospective location. Check Statistics Canada data at your library and on the internet and contact local chambers of commerce (by phone and via the internet) to learn about the following factors for each location:

- geography
- demography (especially age, income, gender, family status, and social class)
- psychographic variables (lifestyles, interests, and attitudes)

Step 3 Meet with group members to analyze which location holds the greatest promise as a dealership site. Base your decision on your analysis of market segment variables and their effects on H/AC sales.

Follow-Up Questions

1. Which location did you choose? Describe the market segmentation factors that influenced your decision.
2. Identify the two most important variables you believe will have the greatest impact on the dealership's success. Why are these factors so important?
3. Which factors were least important in your decision? Why?
4. When equipment manufacturers advertise residential H/AC products, they often show them in different climate situations (in winter, summer, or high-humidity conditions). Which market segments are these ads targeting? Describe these segments in terms of demographic and psychographic characteristics.

EXERCISING YOUR ETHICS: TEAM EXERCISE

A Big Push for Publicity

The Situation

Marsden Corp. is known as a "good citizen" and prides itself on publicity it receives from sponsoring civic programs and other community projects. The company's executive vice president, Jane Martin, has just been named chairperson of annual fundraising for the Coalition for Community Services (CCS), which is a group of community services organizations that depend on voluntary donations. In the highly visible chairperson's role, Martin has organized the support of officials at other firms to ensure that the fundraising target is met or surpassed.

The Dilemma

Martin began a meeting of 30 department managers to appeal for 100 percent employee participation in CCS giving in the fundraising drive. As follow-up the week before the drive officially started, she met with each manager, saying: "I expect you to give your fair share and for you to ensure that all your employees do likewise. I don't care what it takes, just do it. Make it clear that employees will at least donate cash. Even better, get them to sign up for weekly payroll deductions to the CCS fund because it nets more money than one-time cash donations."

An hour after meeting with Martin, Nathan Smith was both surprised and confused. As a newly appointed department manager, he was unsure how to go about soliciting donations from his 25 employees. Remembering Martin's comment, "I don't care what it takes, just do it," Nathan wondered what to do if someone did not give. Personally, too, he was feeling uneasy. How much should he give? With his family's pressing financial needs, he would rather not give money to CCS. He began to wonder if his donation to CCS would affect his career at Marsden.

▶▶▶

Team Activity

Assemble a group of four to five students and assign each group member to one of the following roles:

- Nathan Smith (employee)
- Jane Martin (employer)
- Director of CCS (customer)
- Marsden stockholder (investor)
- Marsden CEO (use this role only if your group has five members)

Action Steps

1. Before discussing the situation with your group, and from the perspective of your assigned role, do you think there are any *ethical issues* with Marsden's fundraising program? If so, write them down.
2. Before discussing the situation with your group, and from the perspective of your assigned role, are any *problems* likely to arise from Marsden's fundraising program? If so, write them down.
3. Together with your group, share the ethical issues you identified. Then share the potential problems you listed. Did the different roles you were assigned result in different ethical issues and problems?
4. For the various ethical issues that were identified, decide as a group which one is the most important for Marsden to resolve. Likewise, for potential problems that were identified, which is the most important one for Marsden?
5. From an ethical standpoint, what does your group recommend be done to resolve the most important ethical issue? How should the most important problem be resolved? Identify the advantages and drawbacks of your recommendations.

BUSINESS CASE 12

Television Viewership: How Do You Measure It?

Business firms spend a lot of money each year on marketing research trying to figure out customers' habits and preferences. Advertisers, for example, want to know what television programs consumers are watching so they can effectively direct their advertisements. If it can be demonstrated that some TV shows are more popular than others, advertisers are willing to pay more to have their ads appear on those programs.

Not surprisingly, when there is a need for information like this, one or more companies will agree to provide it (for a price, of course). Nielsen Media Research is the most well-known company providing such information. It gets its revenues by selling its viewer data to advertising agencies and television companies. Nielsen has reported on the TV viewing habits of Canadians and Americans for many years. Until recently, the system involved having selected viewers write down the channel number they were watching and who was watching TV each quarter hour of the day. But this system was cumbersome, and consumers often made errors when they were filling out the forms. The system gradually began to break down as technology changed. For example, when remote controls became popular, so did channel surfing, but channel surfing is virtually impossible to reflect in a diary. The introduction of digital video recorders (DVR) and the delivery of shows via cellphone, computer, and iPod is quickly making Nielsen's old system obsolete. One consultant says it is ridiculous to expect people to accurately write down what they view in this new, high-tech environment.

Nielsen initially responded to criticisms by attaching electronic meters to household TVs. The meter determined what channel was being watched and who was watching, but viewers still had to punch in a pre-assigned number on their remote control whenever they started to watch. These meters likely improved the accuracy of in-home viewing data, but they did not address the growing problem of measuring viewing habits of people when they were not at home but who were still watching TV. For example, measuring the viewing habits of students who live away from home at university is not easy. "The O.C."—a drama about teen life in Orange County, California—is very popular with students attending U.S. universities, but almost none of these viewers are counted in Nielsen ratings because Nielsen's system doesn't capture the viewing habits of university students. Not only that, it continues to count these students as if they are living at home and watching no TV at all. Nielsen also doesn't monitor viewing in offices, bars, hotels, prisons, and many other out-of-home venues.

Dissatisfaction with Nielsen is also evident at cable companies, who argue that Nielsen's system doesn't accurately capture the large number of people who watch cable TV. Differences can be substantial with different measuring systems. For example, in a side-by-side analysis in New York City, an episode of *The Simpsons* on the Fox Network showed a 27 percent decline when the new electronic meters were used, but new shows on Comedy Central cable saw gains of 225 percent using the same electronic measurement.

In Montreal and Quebec City, consumers are being paid a few dollars a month to carry a pager-sized device that records each advertisement they see or hear and every store or restaurant they go into. BBM Canada is using something called the Personal Portable Meter (PPM) to determine television ratings. These devices, which listen for cues that broadcasters have embedded in their broadcasts, enable BBM to assess television viewing *outside* peoples' homes. They reduce the errors that were evident in the old hard-wired systems where people had to press buttons to indicate who was watching what. The new system will eventually allow advertisers to correlate the advertisements people hear with the products they buy. They can therefore determine how effective their advertisements are. Early tests of the PPM show recorded audiences about 15 percent higher than traditional methods. Nielsen is studying the PPM technology, but says it needs much more work. It likes the idea that the PPM measures out-of-home viewership and that it measures audio very well.

Nielsen is still getting a lot of criticism and not much sympathy. Nielsen's system was developed long ago when families gathered around the sole TV in the house to watch a program. But times have changed. While Dad is watching a sporting event in the den, junior is watching MTV in the basement, and Mom is channel surfing in the bedroom. In 2006, Nielsen announced that it would introduce technology that would allow it to capture DVR viewing on a daily basis. It will also begin measuring video-on-demand and testing ways of measuring viewing on the internet and on hand-held devices such as iPods and cellphones. If these new measuring systems show significantly differing viewing patterns than historical data, it will likely result in advertisers shifting their money around accordingly. It could also result in increased advertising rates for some programs and decreased rates for others.

But even if these improvements are made, some critics will not be happy. The vice-president at one advertising space-buying company, for example, says that the only thing that is important to measure is "live" viewing. That's because people who are watching a DVR program are probably not even watching the ads. Not surprisingly, TV companies disagree with that assessment. They argue that ad rates should be determined by the total viewership an ad gets.

Questions for Discussion

1. What are the various methods that are available to market researchers as they gather data about customers? Which method does Nielsen use?
2. The viewership data that Nielsen's develops is important in determining how much advertisers pay to place their ads on TV. What are the advantages and disadvantages of the system? Are there alternative systems that might work better? Explain.
3. The argument has been made that counting DVR viewing isn't useful because people either don't watch program advertisements when using a DVR, or that advertisements simply don't have the same urgency if they are watched. Do you agree or disagree with this argument? Give reasons. Whatever your position, how does uncertainty over issues like this influence the value of marketing research data? What could be done to improve the data?
4. Suppose that you are buying advertising space on TV. Would you be more likely to accept Nielsen data for, say, sports programs than you would for dramas? Explain. What kind of biases might you have and why?

CHAPTER 13

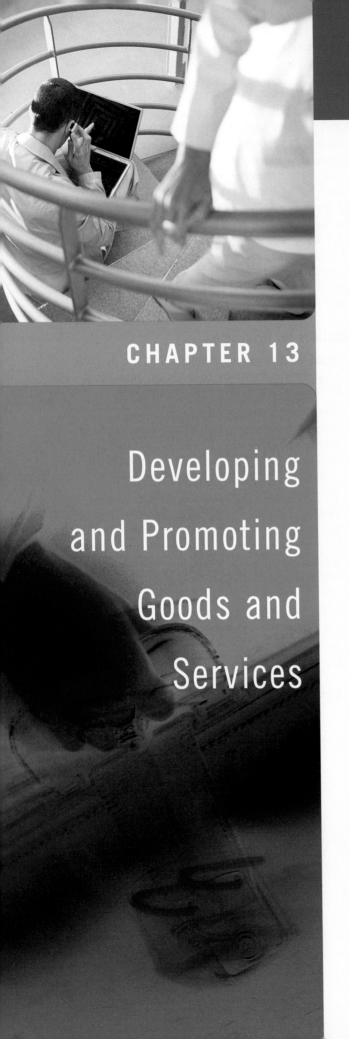

Developing and Promoting Goods and Services

After reading this chapter, you should be able to:

1. Identify a *product*, distinguish between *consumer* and *industrial products*, and explain the *product* mix.
2. Describe the *new product development process* and trace the stages of the *product life cycle*.
3. Explain the importance of *branding, packaging*, and *labelling*.
4. Identify the important objectives of *promotion* and discuss the considerations in selecting a *promotional mix*.
5. Describe the key *advertising media*.
6. Outline the tasks involved in *personal selling*.
7. Describe the various types of *sales promotions* and distinguish between *publicity* and *public relations*.

The Fuel Cell: Still a Long, Rough Road Ahead

At the 2004 annual meeting of Vancouver-based Ballard Power Systems Inc., shareholders listened to CEO Dennis Campbell explain what progress was being made on a radical new product—the hydrogen fuel cell, which combines hydrogen (one of the earth's most common elements) with oxygen to produce electricity. The only exhaust is warm water. The electricity generated by the fuel cell can be used to power anything that runs on electricity, including cars. The fuel cell greatly interests car makers because they have been trying for years to develop a new engine to replace the internal combustion engine that has powered automobiles for over a century.

All of this sounds very promising, but Ballard shareholders were not happy with what they heard because their company has been developing the fuel cell for over a decade and progress has been very slow. Back in the mid-1990s, Ballard had generated great excitement when it first announced that it was going to develop a fuel cell that would solve the world's energy problems and save the environment at the same time. Initially, enthusiasm for the hydrogen fuel cell was high. DaimlerChrysler invested \$450 million in Ballard, and Ford Motor Co. put in another \$600 million to pursue the development of fuel cells. A DaimlerChrysler executive even said a few years ago that the company expected to sell 100 000 cars powered by fuel cells by 2004. Ballard sold prototypes to several automobile companies for testing, the Chicago Transit Authority put three fuel cell-powered buses into service, and the provincial government of British Columbia purchased three buses.

But significant problems have arisen for Ballard as it has tried to make the fuel cell commercially viable. Sales revenues haven't kept up with development costs, and the revolution, which was always just around the corner, has stayed tantalizingly in the future. In 2003, Ballard estimated that it wouldn't become profitable until 2007. Reality has hit the company hard. From a high of \$210 per share in 2000, Ballard stock now sells for less than \$10. What's worse, skepticism about the commercial viability of the fuel cell is steadily increasing. It is clear that fuel-cell powered cars are not going to be on sale anytime soon, and some skeptics wonder if they ever will be.

Why has the fuel cell not lived up to its earlier promise? Consider the following list of daunting problems facing the development of fuel cells:

- hydrogen must first be extracted from substances that contain it (e.g., natural gas), but stripping the hydrogen from natural gas creates carbon dioxide, which is precisely what the standard internal combustion car engines emit
- safety is an issue (when the word "hydrogen" is mentioned, many people immediately think of the spectacular explosion and fire that destroyed the hydrogen-powered Hindenburg dirigible in 1937)
- if insufficient numbers of hydrogen-dispensing gas stations are built, consumer demand will never be high enough to encourage mass production of cars that are powered by fuel cells; it is going to be a long time before there will be enough such stations
- the hydrogen fuel cell is likely to be very expensive because the most environmentally sound way to make hydrogen—extracting it from water using electricity made from solar or wind power—is costly and requires large areas of land covered in solar panels that produce the required electricity
- other costs associated with the product are also high; for example, it currently costs about \$4500 per kilowatt to produce the fuel "stacks" in the hydrogen fuel cell, but experts estimate that this cost needs to be reduced to about \$45 per kilowatt in order to be commercially viable
- hybrid cars like the Toyota Prius and the Honda Civic have been very successful and are providing strong competition for the hydrogen fuel cell; in 2006, Toyota sold over 1 million hybrid cars
- improvements are being made in the internal combustion engine, and this reduces the incentive to develop the hydrogen fuel cell
- there are now at least 50 different companies in competition with Ballard to build a successful fuel cell

If there are so many problems, why has so much time and money been invested in the development of hydrogen fuel cells? The answer is both environmental (less air pollution) and political (less reliance on foreign oil). This new product may be commercially viable in 20 or 30 years, but there are still many developmental problems to be overcome. General Motors and Ford, which formerly invested large amounts of money in fuel cell research, now seem to be more interested in developing hybrid cars.

But maybe the hydrogen fuel cell will eventually become common in automobiles. Keep in mind what critics said when internal combustion-powered automobiles were introduced a hundred years ago: "They'll never become popular because there would have to be gas stations all over the place." Well, that's exactly what happened.

HOW WILL THIS BENEFIT YOU?

By understanding the material in this chapter, you can benefit in three ways: (1) as an employee and as a manager, you'll be better able to use the concepts of developing and promoting products in your career; (2) as a consumer, you'll have a clearer picture of how the complex process of new product development and promotion leads to more consumer choice; and (3) as an investor, you'll be better prepared to evaluate a company's marketing program and its competitive potential before buying the company's stock.

In Chapter 12, we introduced the four basic elements in the marketing mix. In this chapter, we focus on two of these components—products and how they are promoted. We begin by looking at the different classifications of products, the new product development process, the product life cycle idea, and the branding of products. We then move to a discussion of the various aspects of promotion: advertising, personal selling, sales promotion, and publicity.

WHAT IS A PRODUCT?

1 Identify a *product*, distinguish between *consumer* and *industrial products*, and explain the *product mix*.

In developing the marketing mix for any products—whether goods, services, or ideas—marketers must consider what consumers really buy when they purchase products. Only then can they plan their strategies effectively. We begin where product strategy begins—with an understanding of product *features* and *benefits*. Next, we will describe the major *classifications of products*, both consumer and industrial. Finally, we will discuss the most important component in the offerings of any business—its *product mix*.

Features and Benefits

Products are much more than just *visible* features and benefits. In buying a product, consumers are also buying an image and a reputation. The marketers of Swatch Chrono watch, for example, are well aware that brand name, packaging, labelling, and after-the-purchase service are also indispensable parts of their product. Advertisements remind consumers that they don't just get "real" features like shock and water resistance, quartz precision, and Swiss manufacture; they also get Swatch's commitment that its products will be young and trendy, active and sporty, and stylistically cool and clean.

value package
Product marketed as a bundle of value-adding attributes, including reasonable cost.

Today's consumer regards a product as a bundle of attributes which, taken together, marketers call the **value package**. Increasingly, buyers expect to receive products with greater *value*—with more benefits at reasonable costs. For example, the possible attributes in a personal computer value package are things like easy access to understandable pre-purchase information, choices of colour, attractive software packages, fast ordering via the internet, assurance of speedy delivery, and internet chat room capability. Although the computer includes physical *features*—like processing devices and other hardware—most items in the value package are services or intangibles that, collectively, add value by providing *benefits* that increase the customer's satisfaction.

Classifying Goods and Services

Product buyers fall into two groups: buyers of *consumer* products and buyers of *industrial* products. Because the consumer and industrial buying processes are different, marketing products to consumers is different from marketing them to other companies.

Classifying Consumer Products

Consumer products are commonly divided into three categories that reflect buyers' behaviour: *convenience*, *shopping*, and *specialty* goods.

- **Convenience goods** (such as milk and newspapers) and **convenience services** (such as those offered by fast-food restaurants) are consumed rapidly and regularly. They are relatively inexpensive and are purchased frequently and with little expenditure of time and effort.
- **Shopping goods** (such as stereos and tires) and **shopping services** (such as insurance) are more expensive and are purchased less frequently than convenience goods and services. Consumers often compare brands, sometimes in different stores. They also may evaluate alternatives in terms of style, performance, colour, price, and other criteria.
- **Specialty goods** (such as wedding gowns) and **specialty services** (such as catering for wedding receptions) are important and expensive purchases. Consumers usually decide on precisely what they want and will accept no substitutes. They will often go from store to store, sometimes spending a great deal of time and money to get exactly the product they want.

convenience goods and services
Relatively inexpensive consumer goods or services that are bought and used rapidly and regularly, causing consumers to spend little time looking for them or comparing their prices.

shopping goods and services
Moderately expensive consumer goods or services that are purchased infrequently, causing consumers to spend some time comparing their prices.

specialty goods and services
Very expensive consumer goods or services that are purchased rarely, causing consumers to spend a great deal of time locating the exact item desired.

Classifying Industrial Products

Industrial products can be divided into two categories: *expense items* and *capital items*.

- **Expense items** are any materials and services that are consumed within a year. The most obvious expense items are industrial goods used directly in the production process, for example, bulkloads of tea processed into tea bags. In addition, *support materials* help to keep a business running without directly entering the production process. Oil, for instance, keeps the tea-bagging machines running but is not used in the tea bags. Similarly, *supplies*—pencils, brooms, gloves, paint—are consumed quickly and regularly by every business. Finally, *services* such as window cleaning, equipment installation, and temporary office help are essential to daily operations. Because these items are used frequently, purchases are often automatic or require little decision making.
- **Capital items** are "permanent"—that is, expensive and long-lasting—goods and services. All these items have expected lives of more than a year—typically up to several years. Expensive buildings (offices, factories), fixed equipment (water towers, baking ovens), and accessory equipment (computers, airplanes) are capital goods. Capital services are those for which long-term commitments are made. These may include purchases for employee food services, building and equipment maintenance, or legal services.

expense items
Relatively inexpensive industrial goods that are consumed rapidly and regularly.

capital items
Expensive, long-lasting industrial goods that are used in producing other goods or services and have a long life.

The Product Mix

The group of products a company has available for sale, be it consumer or industrial, is known as the firm's **product mix**. Black & Decker, for example, makes toasters, vacuum cleaners, electric drills, and a variety of other appliances and tools. Nike has introduced a whole line of sports-related products like baseball gloves and bats, hockey sticks, basketballs, and in-line skates.

product mix
The group of products a company has available for sale.

product line
A group of similar products intended for a similar group of buyers who will use them in a similar fashion.

A **product line** is a group of products that are closely related because they function in a similar manner or are sold to the same customer group who will use them in similar ways. ServiceMaster, for example, was among the first successful home services that offered mothproofing and carpet cleaning. Subsequently, the company expanded into other closely related services for homeowners—lawn care (TruGreen, ChemLawn), pest control (Terminix), and cleaning (Merry Maids).

Companies may extend their horizons and identify opportunities outside existing product lines. The result is *multiple* (or *diversified*) *product lines*. After years of serving residential customers, ServiceMaster has added business and industry services (landscaping and janitorial), education services (management of schools and institutions, including physical facilities and financial and personnel resources), and health-care services (management of support services—plant operations, asset management, laundry/linen supply—for long-term care facilities). Multiple product lines allow a company to grow rapidly and can help to offset the consequences of slow sales in any one product line.

DEVELOPING NEW PRODUCTS

2 Describe the *new product development process* and trace the stages of the *product life cycle.*

All products and services—including once-popular TV shows like *Seinfeld, Everyone Loves Raymond, Friends,* and *Frasier*—eventually reach the end of their life cycles and expire. Firms must therefore develop and introduce streams of new products. Levi's jeans, for example, were once one of Canada's most popular brands, but the company failed to keep pace with changing tastes and lost market share. But the company got back on track when it introduced the new Signature brand of casual clothing. The brand has become very popular, and Levi's has opened Signature stores in several countries.

Sometimes companies develop a new product to meet what they think is a demand in one industry, only to find that the product is really more viable in another industry. For example, Inuktun Services Ltd. developed a small, submersible, remotely operated vehicle (ROV) equipped with lights and a video camera that was designed for use by boat owners. The boat owners weren't interested, but the nuclear industry was. Now, Inuktun's ROVs travel up and down stairs, around corners, over obstacles, in water up to 300 metres deep, and through ducts and pipes as little as 15 centimetres in diameter.[1]

The Time Frame of New Product Development

Companies often face multi-year time horizons and high risks when developing new products. In 1989, discussions about the possibility of manufacturing a new long-range executive jet began at Bombardier Inc. of Montreal. Over the next few years, the company spent millions of dollars developing the product, which finally became available in 1998. But there is a lot of uncertainty in new product development. In 2005, Bombardier announced that it would build a new line of passenger jets, but in 2006 it announced that it was shelving the project.[2]

As we saw in the Opening Case, the hydrogen fuel cell has taken much longer to develop than expected. High-definition television (HDTV)—which gives much-improved picture quality—is another example of a new product that has been slower to develop than expected. The technology of HDTV clearly works, but this promising new product suffers from a classic "chicken-and-egg" problem. *Broadcasters* haven't offered a lot of high-definition programs because to do so requires special transmitters and cameras. *Manufacturers* of HDTVs have been holding back because they don't know whether broadcasters are going to produce high-definition programs for consumers to watch. *Consumers* have been slow to buy HDTV sets because they are expensive, so they have waited to see how many programs would be broadcast in HDTV format. There were about 3 million HDTVs in Canadian homes at the end of 2006, but experts predict that about 40 percent of Canadian homes will have an HD set by 2011.[3] The Entrepreneurship & New Ventures box provides another example of new product development.

Product Mortality Rates

It takes about 50 new product ideas to generate one product that finally reaches the market. Even then, only a few of these survivors become *successful* products. Many seemingly great *ideas* have failed as *products*. Indeed, creating a successful new product has become increasingly difficult—even for the most experienced marketers. Why? The number of new products hitting the market each year has increased dramatically, and thousands of new

ENTREPRENEURSHIP AND NEW VENTURES

The Patriotic Entrepreneur

Serious discussions about biotechnology seldom touch on Malaysia. That situation, however, may soon change as Malaysia takes its first steps toward what officials hope will be world-class status in the biotech sector. The Malaysian vision calls for developing not one dominant product but rather families or streams of biologically based products to compete on world markets.

Unfortunately, Malaysians are starting from scratch. Malaysia, critics scoff, doesn't have the science community necessary to compete with Europe and the United States to attract the needed investment. In fact, experts question whether Malaysia can even compete with regional neighbours such as Singapore, which has similar ambitions and more money to lure talent from abroad. Malaysia's response to seemingly insurmountable odds is simple: Bring in Kim Tan, regarded by many as the world's top biochemistry entrepreneur.

Tan has already built three major biotech companies, with facilities in Canada, China, Britain, and the United States, while amassing a personal fortune estimated at $500 million. He has decided to collaborate with the Malaysian government to set up the country's first biotech venture fund—dubbed Springhill Biotech Ventures. As founding father of the country's biotech industry, Tan will manage Malaysia's planned life-sciences activities from its new biotech hub—called Biovalley—near the capital of Kuala Lumpur. The plan calls for Springhill to invest in new technologies from abroad that are almost ready to hit the market and that hold promise for future Biovalley research. The fund will also form joint ventures with companies that agree to locate facilities and conduct research in Malaysia.

Just how valuable is Tan's participation? Born in Malaysia and educated in Britain in the 1970s, Tan is an ideal role model for biotech entrepreneurs. "We really need more people like him to jump-start this industry," says Gurinder Shahi, a Singapore-based biotech consultant. "He's a good example of people that were part of the brain drain that now are returning and combining science and business skills that pay off." Tan's patents have already led to new drugs for treatment of cancer and chronic illnesses, and his research in genetic engineering has developed hormones for treating diabetes and arthritis.

In addition to his contributions of money and scientific knowledge to Biovalley, Tan also brings biotech-management and business skills. In 1986, he sold his first company, a diagnostics firm, using the proceeds to form KS Biomedics to commercialize his ideas for growing cancer-fighting antibodies in sheep. More recently, he formed TranXenoGen for genetic engineering in chickens to produce eggs containing therapeutic proteins for use in drugs. Yet another company—Genemedix—mass-produces low-cost generic drugs for reducing the fatal side effects of chemotherapy.

Tan has no illusions about the monumental task ahead: Biovalley starts with an inexperienced scientific base, few patents, and little venture capital. So, after all his success, why is Tan risking yet another start-up project? "Nationalism," he says. "I could make far more money and it's easier over there [in Britain]. The main reason: I'm a Malaysian. One has a responsibility to [his] country." Significantly, the country did not recruit Tan for the job; rather, it was Tan who took the initiative. "I took it to them. I've been waiting to see what the government was going to do [about building the sector]. They are committed. So I decided, right, let's do something."

household, grocery, and drugstore items are introduced annually. But at any given time, the average supermarket carries a total of only 20 000 to 25 000 different items. Because of lack of space and customer demand, about 9 out of 10 new products will fail. Those with the best chances are innovative and deliver unique benefits.

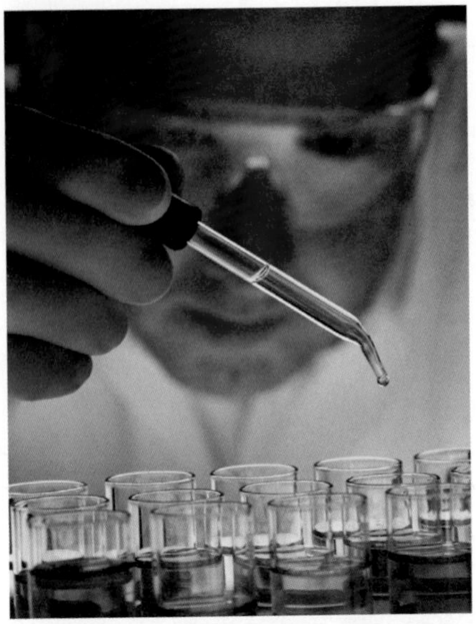

Pharmaceutical companies spend large amounts of money on research and development, yet bring relatively few products to market.

Speed to Market

The more rapidly a product moves from the laboratory to the marketplace, the more likely it is to survive. By introducing new products ahead of competitors, companies quickly establish market leaders that become entrenched in the market before being challenged by late-arriving competitors. **Speed to market**—that is, a firm's success in responding to customer demand or market changes is very important. One study estimated that a product that is only three months late to the market (that is, three months behind the leader) loses 12 percent of its lifetime profit potential. A product that is six months late loses 33 percent.[4]

speed to market
Strategy of introducing new products to respond quickly to customer and/or market changes.

The Seven-Step Development Process

To increase their chances of developing a successful new product, many firms adopt some variation on a basic seven-step process.

1. *Product ideas*. Product development begins with a search for ideas for new products. Product ideas can come from consumers, the sales force, research and development people, or engineering personnel.
2. *Screening*. In this stage, the goal is to eliminate all product ideas that do not mesh with the firm's abilities, expertise, or objectives. Representatives from marketing, engineering, and production must have input at this stage.
3. *Concept testing*. Once ideas have been culled, companies use market research to solicit consumers' input. In this way, firms can identify benefits that the product must provide as well as an appropriate price level for the product.
4. *Business analysis*. This stage involves developing estimates of costs versus benefits for the proposed product. The aim is not to determine precisely how much money the product will make, but to see whether the product can meet minimum profitability goals.
5. *Prototype development*. At this stage, product ideas begin to take shape. Using input from the concept-testing phase, engineering and/or research and development produce a preliminary version of the product. Prototypes can be extremely expensive, often requiring extensive hand crafting, tooling, and development of components.
6. *Product testing and test marketing*. Using what it learned from the prototype, the company goes into limited production of the item. This stage is very costly, since promotional campaigns and distribution channels must be established for test markets. But test marketing gives a company its first information on how consumers will respond to a product under real market conditions.
7. *Commercialization*. If test-marketing results are positive, the company will begin full-scale production and marketing of the product. Gradual commercialization, with the firm providing the product to more and more areas over time, prevents undue strain on the firm's initial production capabilities.

THE PRODUCT LIFE CYCLE

The **product life cycle (PLC)** is the idea that successfully commercialized products have a limited profit-producing life for a company. This life may be a matter of months, years, or decades, depending on the ability of the product to attract customers over time. Products such as Kellogg's Corn Flakes, Coca-Cola, Ivory soap, Argo corn starch, and Caramilk candy bars have had extremely long productive lives.

product life cycle (PLC)
The concept that the profit-producing life of any product goes through a cycle of introduction, growth, maturity (levelling off), and decline.

Stages in the Product Life Cycle (PLC)

The product life cycle is a natural process in which products are born, grow in stature, mature, and finally decline and die.[5] The life cycle is typically divided into four states through which products pass as they "age" in the market. In Figure 13.1a, the four phases of the PLC are applied to several products with which you are familiar.

1. *Introduction.* The introduction stage begins when the product reaches the marketplace. During this stage, marketers focus on making potential consumers aware of the product and its benefits. Because of extensive promotional and development costs, profits are nonexistent.
2. *Growth.* If the new product attracts and satisfies enough consumers, sales begin to climb rapidly. During this stage, the product begins to show a profit. Other firms in the industry move rapidly to introduce their own versions.

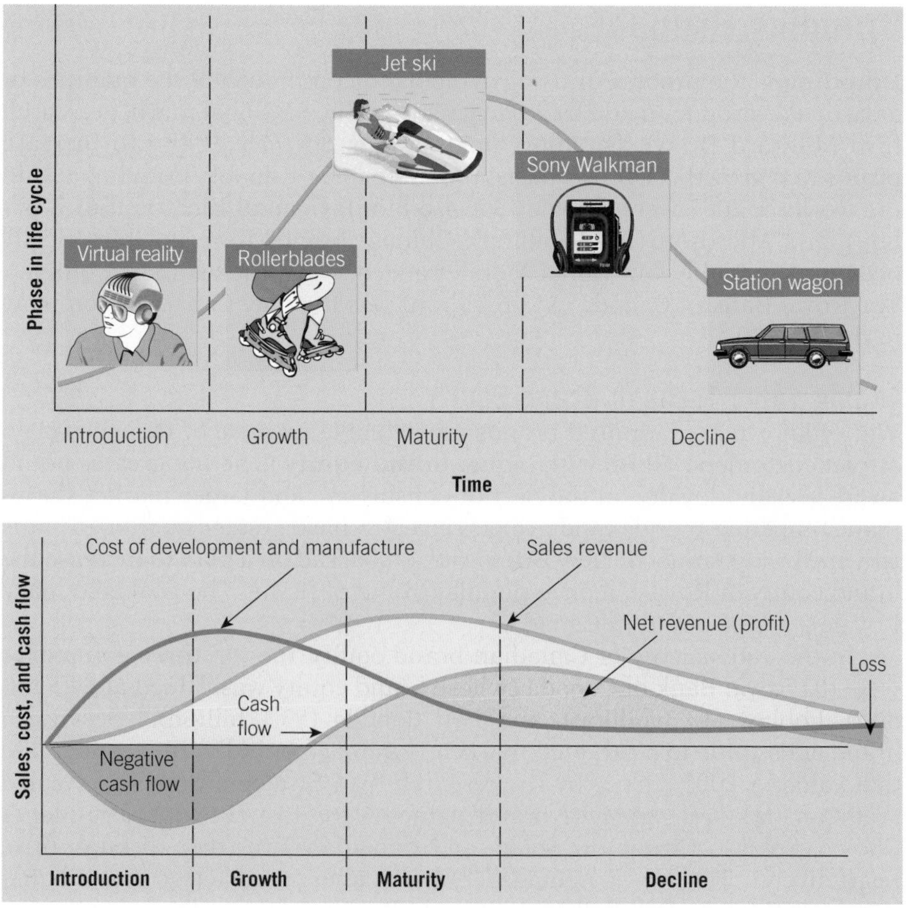

(a)

(b)

Figure 13.1 The product life cycle: stages, sales, cost, and profit.

3. *Maturity.* Sales growth begins to slow. Although the product earns its highest profit level early in this stage, increased competition eventually leads to price cutting and lower profits. Toward the end of this stage, sales start to fall.
4. *Decline.* During this final stage, sales and profits continue to fall. New products in the introduction stage take sales away. Companies remove or reduce promotional support (ads and salespeople) but may let the product linger to provide some profits.

Figure 13.1b plots the relationship of the PLC to a product's typical sales, costs, and profits. Although the early stages of the PLC often show no profit, successful products usually continue to generate profits until the decline stage. For most products, profitable life spans are short—thus, the importance placed by so many firms on the constant replenishment of product lines. At some point, the company must decide to cease production of a product in the decline stage. For example, in 2003 sales of digital cameras surpassed film cameras for the first time, and Kodak announced stoppage of film camera production, after decades as the market leader.

IDENTIFYING PRODUCTS

3 Explain the importance of *branding*, *packaging*, and *labelling*.

As noted earlier in the chapter, developing the features of a product is only part of a marketer's job. Identifying that product in consumers' minds through the use of brand names, packaging, and labelling is also important.

Branding Products

branding
Process of using symbols to communicate the qualities of a product made by a particular producer.

Branding is the process of using symbols to communicate the qualities of a particular product made by a particular producer. Global market research firm Millward Brown Optimor ranks brands on their ability to increase profits and growth.[6] On this basis, the three most valuable brand names in the world in 2007 were Google ($66.4 billion), General Electric ($61.8 billion), and Microsoft ($54.9 billion), Chinese brands have not historically been ranked highly, but China Mobile ranked 5th on the list ($39.1 billion). The Royal Bank of Canada ($13.6 billion) was the only Canadian company in the top 100.[7]

Adding Value Through Brand Equity

brand equity
Degree of consumers' loyalty to and awareness of a brand and its resultant market share.

Widely known and admired brands are valuable because of their power to attract customers. Those with higher **brand equity** generate greater brand awareness and loyalty on the part of consumers, and larger market shares than competing brands (and are perceived to have greater quality). That is why the Irving family of New Brunswick embarked on a plan to increase the brand equity of Royale, a once-popular brand of tissue. The goal is to make Royale a major brand in Canada.[8]

In the 2005 survey of Canadian brand equity, the top three companies were the Royal Bank of Canada (whose brand equity was valued at $4.5 billion), Loblaw ($3.3 billion), and Bell Canada ($3.1 billion).[9] Because a brand adds value to a product, marketers manage brand names to increase that value. A 2005 survey by the research firm Strategic Counsel revealed that Canada's *best managed* brand names were Tim Hortons, President's Choice, Loblaw, Cirque du Soleil, and Canadian Tire (first through fifth, respectively). The worst managed brand names were Jetsgo (now bankrupt), Air Canada, Bell/Bell Mobility, and Rogers Wireless.[10]

Firms that sell products internationally face an issue of growing importance in branding strategy. They must consider how product names will translate in various languages. In Spanish, for example, the name of Chevrolet's now-defunct Nova simply became *no va*—"it does not go." Sales were particularly poor in South America. Similarly, Rolls-Royce was once going to name a new touring car "Silver Mist." Rolls changed the name to "Silver Shadow" when it discovered that *mist* is German for "manure."[11]

Types of Brand Names

National brands are those that are produced and distributed by the manufacturer across the entire country (e.g., Scotch Tape, Crest Toothpaste). When a company with a well-known brand sells another company the right to place that brand on its products, these are called **licensed brands**. For example, the Canadian company Nelvana has licensed Sears to set up Franklin the Turtle boutiques at more than 850 stores).[12] Harley-Davidson's famous logo—emblazoned on boots, eyewear, gloves, purses, lighters, and watches—brings the motorcycle maker more than $210 million annually. Along with brands such as Coors and Ferrari, licensing for character-based brands—Punisher, Spider-Man, and Pokeman—are equally lucrative.

national brands
Products distributed by and carrying a name associated with the manufacturer.

licensed brands
Selling the right to use a brand name, a celebrity's name, or some other well-known identification mark to another company to use on a product.

Private brands are those developed by retailers who then have certain manufacturers place their brand name on the product when it is being produced. For example, Loblaw Cos. Ltd. has created a line of upscale products under the private brand "President's Choice." Clever advertising, fancy labels, and exotic product names differentiate the line and draw consumer attention to items such as peanut butter and cookies. Shoppers Drug Mart produces a line of products under the "Life" label. It hopes to make the Life label as prestigious as the President's Choice label.[13] E.D. Smith, a maker of jams and pie fillings, makes private label items for retailers like Wal-Mart and Pizza Pizza Ltd.[14]

private brands
Products promoted by and carrying a name associated with the retailer or wholesaler, not the manufacturer.

Brand Loyalty

Companies want **brand loyalty** from customers, that is, they want customers who, when they need a particular item, will consistently buy the company's products. Brand loyalty can have a major impact on a company's profits. In the beer industry, for example, each market share point is worth about $25 million in profit. This is why companies like Labatt and Molson have such fierce competitive battles for market share.[15]

brand loyalty
Customers' recognition of, preference for, and insistence on buying a product with a certain brand name.

SpongeBob macaroni and cheese is Kraft Foods' top-selling licensed pasta product, and SpongeBob Band-Aids now outsell Scooby Doo bandages. There are SpongeBob dolls and bowling balls, and the brand also appears on toothpaste and underwear. SpongeBob belongs to Nickelodeon Enterprises, a children's TV programmer that's been the highest-rated basic cable network since 1995. Product licensing is worth about $2.5 billion to Nickelodeon each year.

Brand loyalty exists at three levels: *brand awareness* (customers recognize the brand name), *brand preference* (consumers have a favourable attitude toward the product), and *brand insistence* (consumers demand the product and are willing to go out of their way to get it). Brand insistence implies a lot of consumer trust in a brand, but a survey sponsored by *Reader's Digest Canada* found that Canadians have less trust in brands than they did 20 years ago. However, some well-known brands like Becel Margarine, Robin Hood flour, Wal-Mart, and Black & Decker are still viewed postively.[16]

Ebusiness Branding

The expensive and fierce struggle for brand recognition is very evident in the branding battles among dot-com firms. Collectively, the top internet brands—Google, America Online, Yahoo!, and Amazon.com—spend billions a year. Even with hundreds of millions of visitors each month, Yahoo! still faces formidable competitors in AOL Time Warner and Microsoft. The mounting costs of brand identity mean that many would-be ebusinesses will fail.[17]

It takes a long time to establish national or global brand recognition.[18] After years of work, Cisco Systems Inc., the network-equipment manufacturer, finally reached new heights in branding for business-to-business, or B2B, ecommerce. The company's "Cisco Internet Generation" promotional campaign stressed reliability and innovation, and in analyzing the campaign, Cisco found that its brand awareness had increased by 80 percent (boosting it past rivals Lucent Technologies and Nortel Networks). The campaign also lifted Cisco's reputation as an internet expert above that of Microsoft, IBM, and Lucent.[19]

Trademarks, Patents, and Copyrights

Because brand development is very expensive, a company does not want another company using its name and confusing consumers into buying a substitute product. Many companies apply to the Canadian government and receive a **trademark**, the exclusive legal right to use a brand name. Trademarks are granted for 15 years and may be renewed for further periods of 15 years, but only if the company continues to protect its brand name.

trademark
The exclusive legal right to use a brand name.

Just what can be trademarked is not always clear. If the company allows the name to lapse into common usage, the courts may take away protection. Common usage occurs when the company fails to use the ® symbol for its brand. It also occurs if the company fails to correct those who do not acknowledge the brand as a trademark. Windsurfer, a popular brand of sailboards, lost its trademark, and the name can now be used by any sailboard company. The same thing has happened to other names that were formerly brand names—trampoline, yo-yo, thermos, snowmobile, kleenex, and aspirin. But companies like Xerox, Coca-Cola, Jell-O, and Scotch tape have successfully defended their brand names.

A **patent** protects an invention or idea for a period of 20 years. The cost is $1000 to $1500; it takes nine months to three years to secure a patent from the Canadian Patent Office.[20] Patents can be very valuable. In 2006, Waterloo, Ontario-based Research in Motion (RIM), maker of the immensely popular Blackberry device, agreed to pay $612.5 million to NTP Inc., a U.S. firm that claimed RIM was infringing on some patents that NTP held.[21]

patent
Protects an invention or idea for a period of 20 years.

Copyrights give exclusive ownership rights to the creators of books, articles, designs, illustrations, photos, films, and music. Computer programs and even semiconductor chips are also protected. Copyrights extend to creators for their entire lives and to their estates for 50 years thereafter. Copyrights apply to the tangible expressions of an idea, not to the idea itself. For example, the idea of cloning dinosaurs from fossil DNA cannot be

copyright
Exclusive ownership rights granted to creators for the tangible expression of an idea.

copyrighted, but Michael Crichton, the author of *Jurassic Park*, could copyright his novel because it is the tangible result of the basic idea.

Packaging Products

With a few exceptions, including fresh fruits and vegetables, structural steel, and some other industrial products, almost all products need some form of **packaging** so they can be transported to the market. Packaging serves as an in-store advertisement that makes the product attractive, clearly displays the brand, identifies product features and benefits, and reduces the risk of damage, breakage, or spoilage. It is the marketer's last chance to say "buy it" to the consumer. Packaging costs can be as high as 15 percent of the total cost to make a product, and features like zip-lock tops can add 20 percent to the price that is charged.

packaging
The physical container in which a product is sold, including the label.

Companies are paying close attention to consumer concerns about packaging. Beyond concerns about product tampering, packaging must be tight enough to withstand shipping, but not so tight that it frustrates consumers when they try to open the package. Nestlé—which spends more than $6 billion annually on packaging—spent nine months coming up with a new easier-opening lid and an easier-to-grip container for its new Country Creamery Ice Cream.[22]

Labelling Products

Labels *identify*, *promote*, and *describe* the product. The federal government regulates the information on package labels. The **Consumer Packaging and Labelling Act** has two main purposes: to provide a comprehensive set of rules for packaging and labelling of consumer products, and to ensure that the manufacturer provides full and factual information on labels. All prepackaged products must state in French and English the quantity enclosed in metric units, as well as the name and description of the product.

labels
That part of a product's packaging that identifies the product's name and contents and sometimes its benefits.

Consumer Packaging and Labelling Act
A federal law that provides comprehensive rules for packaging and labelling of consumer products.

Sellers are very sensitive to what is on the label of the products they sell. For example, the Maple Leaf is on all beer that Labatt Brewing Co. Ltd. sells in Canada—except in Quebec. There, the label has a stylized sheaf of wheat instead of the Maple Leaf. Interestingly, the Maple Leaf is much more prominent on Labatt's beer sold in the United States.[23] Many companies have different labels for their products in Quebec, partly because "Canadian" symbols may not resonate well with Quebec sovereigntists.

PROMOTING PRODUCTS AND SERVICES

4 Identify the important objectives of *promotion* and discuss the considerations in selecting a *promotional mix*.

The ultimate objective of promotion is to increase sales. However, marketers also use promotion to increase consumer awareness of their products, to make consumers more knowledgeable about the features of their products, to persuade consumers to like their products, and to persuade consumers to actually purchase their products. Today's value-conscious customers gain benefits when the specific elements in the promotional mix are varied so as to communicate value-added benefits in its products. Burger King, for example, shifted its promotional mix by cutting back on advertising and using those funds instead for customer discounts. Receiving the same food at a lower price is "value added" for Burger King's customers. Many companies, such as Hallmark Cards, experience seasonal sales patterns. By increasing their promotional activities in slow periods, these firms can achieve a more stable sales volume throughout the year. As a result, they can keep their production and distribution systems running evenly.

In rare cases, a company may purposely do very little promotion of its products. For example, Langlitz Leathers makes leather jackets that cost as much as $800. They are worn by rebels like Hell's Angels, rockers like Bruce Springsteen, and actors like Sylvester Stallone. Even though the company does virtually no advertising, customers who want a Langlitz have to wait several months to get one after they place their order.[24]

Promotional Strategies

push strategy
A promotional strategy in which a company aggressively pushes its product through wholesalers and retailers, which persuade customers to buy it.

pull strategy
A promotional strategy in which a company appeals directly to customers, who demand the product from retailers, which demand the product from wholesalers.

Once a firm's promotional objectives are clear, it must develop a promotional strategy to achieve these objectives. Promotional strategies may be of the push or pull variety. A company with a **push strategy** will "push" its product to wholesalers and retailers, who then persuade customers to buy it. In contrast, a company with a **pull strategy** appeals directly to customers, who demand the product from retailers, who in turn demand the product from wholesalers, who in turn demand the product from the manufacturer. Advertising "pulls" while personal selling "pushes."

Makers of industrial products often use a push strategy, while makers of consumer products often use a pull strategy. Many large firms use a combination of the two strategies. For example, General Foods uses advertising to create consumer demand (pull) for its cereals. It also pushes wholesalers and retailers to stock these products.

The Promotional Mix

promotional mix
That portion of marketing concerned with choosing the best combination of advertising, personal selling, sales promotions, and publicity to sell a product.

As we noted in Chapter 12, there are four basic types of promotional tools: *advertising, personal selling, sales promotions,* and *publicity and public relations*. The best combination of these tools—the best **promotional mix**—depends on many factors. The company's product, the costs of different tools versus the promotions budget, and characteristics in the target audience all play a role. Figure 13.2 shows different combinations of products, promotional tools, and target consumers.

ADVERTISING PROMOTIONS

What candy bar is "one of life's sweet mysteries"? What soap is "99 and 44/100 pure"? What product is "only available in Canada—Pity"? What is the store where "the lowest price is the law"? If you are like most Canadians, you can answer these questions because of advertising. (The answers are Caramilk, Ivory soap, Red Rose Tea, and Zellers, respectively.)

Consumers remember brand names more easily if the company has a catchy advertising slogan. Buckley's Mixture, a well-known product in Canada, is trying to crack the U.S. market. In one advertisement on U.S. television, the announcer intones "Buckley's Mixture, the famous Canadian cough remedy, is now available here. It tastes awful, and it works."[25]

5 Describe the key *advertising media.*

As important and high profile as advertising is, it has limits. Both Eaton's and Canadian Airlines were enthusiastic advertisers, but that didn't keep them in business. Advertising can convince customers to try a company's product or service, but it is the customer's experience with the product or service that determines whether they will make repeat purchases.

Advertising Media

advertising medium
The specific communication device—television, radio, newspapers, direct mail, magazines, billboards—used to carry a firm's advertising message to potential customers.

In developing advertising strategies, marketers must consider what is the best **advertising medium** for their message. IBM, for example, uses televi-

Goods Promotion: House (real estate)
Tool: Personal selling
Consumer: House buyer

Service Promotion:
Weight-loss program
Tool: Sales promotion (coupon)
Consumer: Overweight person

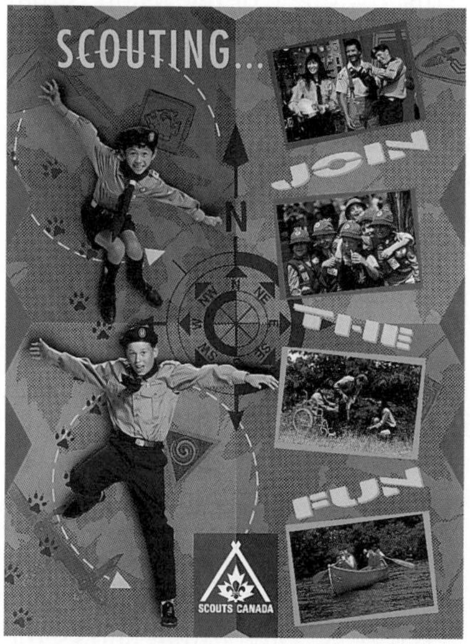

Organizational Promotion: Scouts Canada
Tool: Publicity
Consumer: Young men and women

Event Promotion: Rock concert
Tool: Advertising
Consumer: Cheering fan

Person or Idea Promotion:
Candidate for prime minister
Tool: Publicity/advertising/personal sales
Consumer: Voter

Figure 13.2 Each promotional tool should be properly matched with the product being promoted and the target customer.

sion ads to keep its name fresh in consumers' minds. But it also uses newspaper and magazine ads to educate consumers on products' abilities and trade publications to introduce new software.

An advertiser selects media with a number of factors in mind. The marketer must first ask: Which medium will reach the people I want to reach? If a firm is selling hog breeding equipment, it might choose a business magazine read mostly by hog farmers. If it is selling silverware, it might choose a magazine for brides. If it is selling toothpaste, the choice might be a general audience television program or a general audience magazine such as *Reader's Digest* (or *Sélection du Reader's Digest* for exposure to a similar audience of francophones). Each advertising medium has its own advantages and disadvantages.

Newspapers

Newspapers are a widely used advertising medium, and advertisers spent $2.2 billion in Canada in 2005 in this medium.[26] Newspapers offer excellent coverage, since each local market has at least one daily newspaper, and many people read the paper every day. This medium offers flexible, rapid coverage, since ads can change from day to day. Newspapers also offer believable coverage, since ads are presented side by side with news. However, newspapers do not generally allow advertisers to target their audience well. In recent years, the volume of classified ads placed in newspapers has declined as advertisers have shifted their emphasis to the internet. The *Toronto Star* has tried to counter this trend by giving a free internet posting to anyone who buys a classified ad in the newspaper.[27]

Television

Television allows advertisers to combine sight, sound, and motion, thus appealing to almost all the viewer's senses. Information on viewer demographics for a particular program allows advertisers to promote to their target audiences. National advertising is done on television because it reaches more people than any other medium. One disadvantage of television is that too many commercials cause viewers to confuse products. Most people, for example, can't recall whether a tire commercial was sponsored by Firestone, Goodyear, or B.F. Goodrich. In addition, VCR or digital video recording viewers often fast-forward past the ads of TV shows that they have recorded. Moreover, because "commercial spots" last only a short time (usually 30 seconds), the impact of the commercial is lost if the viewer is not paying attention. The brevity of TV ads also makes television a poor medium in which to educate viewers about complex products. Finally, television is the most expensive medium in which to advertise.

Worldwide, advertisers spent U.S.$146.8 billion on television advertising in 2005.[28] Spending on television advertising in Canada totalled $2.5 billion in 2005.[29] A 30-second commercial during the 2005 NFL Super Bowl cost U.S.$2.4 million.[30] Ads during prime-time evening hours cost less but are still expensive, at upwards of U.S.$190 000 for a 30-second commercial.

Direct Mail

direct mail
Printed advertisements, such as flyers, mailed directly to consumers' homes or places of business.

Direct mail involves flyers or other types of printed advertisements mailed directly to consumers' homes or places of business. Direct mail allows the company to select its audience and personalize its message. Although many people discard "junk mail," targeted recipients with stronger-than-average interest are more likely to buy. Although direct mail involves the largest advance costs of any advertising technique, it does appear to have the highest cost-effectiveness. Particularly effective have been "fax attacks," in which advertisers send their "mail" messages electronically via fax machines and get higher response rates than they would if they used Canada Post.

Radio

Large numbers of people listen to the radio each day, and radio ads are inexpensive. In addition, since most radio is programmed locally, this medium gives advertisers a high degree of customer selectivity. For example, radio stations are already segmented into listening categories such as rock and roll, country and western, jazz, talk shows, news, and religious programming. Like television, radio ads are over quickly. And radio permits only an audio presentation. As well, people tend to use the radio as "background" while they are doing other things, so they may pay little attention to advertisements. Spending on radio advertisements totalled $1 billion in Canada in 2005.[31]

Magazines

The many different magazines on the market provide a high level of consumer selectivity. The person who reads *Popular Photography* is more likely to be interested in the latest specialized lenses from Canon than is a *Gourmet* magazine subscriber. Magazine advertising allows for excellent reproduction of photographs and artwork that not only grab buyers' attention but may also convince them of the product's value. And magazines allow advertisers plenty of space for detailed product information. Magazines have a long life and tend to be passed from person to person, thus doubling and tripling the number of exposures. Spending on magazine advertisements totalled $739 million in Canada in 2005.[32]

Outdoor Advertising

Outdoor advertising—billboards, signs, and advertisements on buses, taxis, and subways—is one of the oldest forms of advertising. Worldwide, spending on outdoor advertising in 2005 totalled $23.2 billion, while in Canada the total was $264 million.[33] Outdoor advertising has gone high-tech, and many billboards now feature animation and constantly changing images. Billboard messages are relatively inexpensive, face little competition for customers' attention, and are subject to high repeat exposure. On the downside, outdoor ads can present only limited information, and sellers have little control over who sees their advertisements. Because roadside billboards are prohibited on some major Ontario arteries, Moving Impressions Inc. has introduced "rolling billboards"—advertisements attached to the sides of large freight trucks. The truck companies get a piece of the action.[34]

Word of Mouth

Consumers form very strong opinions about products as a result of conversations with friends and acquaintances. Marketers have known about the power of **word of mouth** for many years. When consumers start talking about a new product or idea, the information can build momentum and spread like wildfire. If word of mouth (also called *buzz marketing*) says that a product is good, higher product sales are likely. Nike, for example, spent very little money advertising its Presto line of stretchy sneakers, but kids and teens spread the word to each other about the shoes and the fashion statement they could make by having them.[35]

word of mouth
Opinions about the value of products passed among consumers in informal discussions.

The Internet

Ecommerce refers to buying and selling processes that make use of electronic technology, while **internet marketing** refers to the promotional efforts of companies to sell their products and services to consumers over the internet.[36] Worldwide, internet advertising expenditures were $18.1 billion in 2005.[37] The internet is the most recent advertising medium to arise, and thousands of well-known and lesser-known firms have placed ads there.

ecommerce
The use of the Internet and other electronic means for retailing and business-to-business transactions

internet marketing
The promotional efforts of companies to sell their products and services to consumers over the internet.

Speed and creativity have given billboards like these a new prominence in the world of advertising media. Instead of relying on highly skilled human artists, outdoor ad sellers can now commission digital creations that not only turn heads but also cost less than most other media. Whereas it used to take a month to launch a billboard-based campaign, it now takes just days.

In 2006, online advertising in Canada exceeded $1 billion for the first time.[38] Craigslist.org offers free local classified advertising on 204 websites around the world. Eleven cities in Canada had Craigslist sites in 2006.[39]

Internet advertising offers advantages for both buyers and sellers. For buyers, advantages include *convenience* (websites can be accessed 24 hours a day, and there is no need to fight traffic at shopping malls), *privacy* (no face-to-face high-pressure sales tactics are possible), *selection* (the products and services that are available are almost unlimited), *useful information* (about competing products and services), and *control* (consumers can "build" custom products for themselves).

For sellers, advantages include *reach* (access to consumers around the world), *direct distribution* (eliminating intermediaries), *reduced expenses* (which would normally be incurred when owning "bricks-and-mortar" outlets), *relationship building* (with customers on interactive websites), *flexibility* (sellers can quickly change prices or the terms of sale based on market developments), and *feedback* (sellers can measure the success of messages by counting how many people see each ad and track the number of click-throughs to their own website).[40]

Internet marketing also has some weaknesses, including *profitability problems* (many internet marketers are unprofitable and the failure rate is high), *information overload* (consumers may not know what to do with all the information available to them), and *limited markets* (consumers who use the web are typically more highly educated).

In addition to these weaknesses, internet marketers must also cope with consumer concerns about two security-related issues. First, an Angus Reid/*Globe and Mail* poll of 1500 Canadians found that their main concern about internet marketing was security. People who had made at least one purchase on the internet were *more* likely to list security as their top concern than were those who had never purchased anything on the internet. In particular, people were concerned that their credit card number might end up in the wrong hands, and that their privacy would be invaded if they purchased on the internet.[41]

Second, consumers object to "spyware" software, which monitors websites they visit and observes their shopping habits. This software is often implanted on their personal computers as they wander the web. It then generates "pop-up" advertisements that are targeted to that particular consumer. Because people are often unaware that such spyware is on their computer, the technique has generated a lot of anger among consumers. Consumers can, however, get free anti-spyware software that removes spyware from their computer. Spyware is also a concern for companies that sell from their own websites because the pop-ups are designed to divert web surfers from the products offered by the website.[42] If it is going to reach its full potential, internet marketing is going to have to improve its image.

Virtual Advertising

An even newer method of advertising, called *virtual advertising*, uses digital implants of brands or products onto live or taped programming, giving the illusion that the product is part of the show. With this technique, an advertiser's product can appear as part of the television show—when viewers are paying more attention—instead of during commercial breaks. In a televised basketball game, for example, the digital image of a brand—for example, the round face of a Rolex watch or an Acura hubcap—can be electronically enlarged and superimposed on centre court without physically changing the playing floor. For videotaped movies, digital images can be inserted easily. A K-Mart shopping bag can be digitally added to the table in a kitchen scene, or a Philips Flat TV can be superimposed on the wall for display during a dramatic scene in the den.[43]

Other Advertising Media

A combination of many additional media—including catalogues, sidewalk handouts, *Yellow Pages,* skywriting, telephone calls, special events, and door-to-door communications—make up the remaining advertisements to which Canadians are exposed. The combination of media that a company chooses to advertise its products is called its **media mix**. Although different industries use different mixes, most depend on multiple media to advertise their products and services. The newest medium for advertising is cellphones. There are two billion cellphones in use around the world, and advertisers are looking for ways to effectively advertise on these phones.[44]

media mix
The combination of media through which a company chooses to advertise its products.

BUSINESS ACCOUNTABILITY

Who's Accountable for Results?

New frontiers in ad accountability are changing relationships among advertisers, ad agencies, and media outlets. Many companies, instead of conducting their own advertising programs, outsource to advertising agencies for media planning and strategy. Consider just one example, Masterfoods, a division of Mars Inc., and its ad account of U.S.$325 million with Starcom MediaVest Group, which is responsible for media buying and planning for Masterfoods brands such as Snickers, Uncle Ben's, and Whiskas. Extend this to thousands of companies, and the stakes become enormous in this mega-billion-dollar industry. But are clients getting results from ad agencies? That question reflects a new movement toward closer scrutiny of ad agencies by marketers who, themselves, are accountable for demonstrating bottom-line results in return for their firms' huge ad expenditures.

Under growing accountability for media effectiveness, clients are gearing up to ask agencies more probing questions about ad programs and media buys: How are the media plans developed, who buys the current mix of media, and how well have they performed? Up to now, marketing managers at client firms have had little grounding in the technical details of media, so they're not at ease with practices that seem routine to advertising agency managers. "Generally, marketing executives don't come in with that kind of training and oftentimes they're intimidated by some of the terms and the more technical areas of media. For many of them it is a black box," explains Allan Linderman, president of the Linderman Media Group. To overcome this deficiency, two kinds of help are on the way: (1) Schools to teach media are being conducted by the Association of National Advertisers along with the Center for Marketing Excellence, and (2) third-party intermediaries—ad agency auditors—are helping clients assess value received from ad campaigns and agencies.

Faced with growing accountability to perform, ad agencies are, in turn, gearing up to impose more accountability from media outlets. Local and national TV may no longer rely solely on Nielsen ratings as evidence for ad effectiveness; more convincing proof of performance would show how much they contribute to advertiser's sales. Newspaper, magazines, radio, and other media will be asked for more convincing evidence of effectiveness. While reliable proof-of-performance measures don't currently exist, research is underway to develop them. Media research is testing new models to measure the effects of media on consumer attention, persuasion and consumer thinking, and responsiveness in buying behaviour. Reliable measurements will allow agencies' media planners to compare bottom-line results from alternative media expenditures—newspaper, radio, magazines, local TV, national TV—and to pinpoint the best combination of media buys for the agency's client. They will also be evidence of success or failure in accountability-for-performance by media, agencies, and clients alike.

QUESTIONS FOR DISCUSSION

1. Suppose that you were an account executive in an advertising agency and you were asked by an important client to prove that the advertisements your agency developed were actually causing the sales revenues of the client to increase. How would you respond to this request?
2. "*Companies spend millions of dollars on advertisements in the hope that they will cause an increase in sales of the companies' products. But companies don't really know how effective their advertisements are, so they are not being accountable to their shareholders for these expenditures. Companies are probably wasting large amounts of shareholders' money by advertising.*" Do you agree or disagree with this argument? Explain your reasoning.

PERSONAL SELLING PROMOTIONS

6 Outline the tasks involved in *personal selling.*

personal selling
Promotional tool in which a salesperson communicates one-on-one with potential customers.

Virtually everyone has done some selling. Perhaps you had a lemonade stand or sold candy for the drama club. Or you may have gone on a job interview, selling your abilities and services as an employee to the interviewer's company. In personal selling, a salesperson communicates one to one with a potential customer to identify the customer's need and match that need with the seller's product.

Personal selling—the oldest form of selling—provides the personal link between seller and buyer. It adds to a firm's credibility because it gives buyers a contact person who will answer their questions. Because it involves personal interaction, personal selling requires a level of trust between the buyer and the seller. When a buyer feels cheated by the seller, that trust has been broken and a negative attitude toward salespeople in general can develop.

Personal selling is the most expensive form of promotion per contact because presentations are generally made to one or two individuals at a time. Personal selling expenses include salespeople's compensation and their overhead, usually travel, food, and lodging. The average cost of an industrial sales call has been estimated at nearly $300.[45] The Exercising Your Ethics exercise at the end of the chapter describes an interesting personal selling dilemma.

Costs have prompted many companies to turn to *telemarketing:* using telephone solicitations to conduct the personal selling process. Telemarketing is useful in handling any stage of this process and in arranging appointments for salespeople. For example, it cuts the cost of personal sales visits to industrial customers, each of whom requires about four visits to complete a sale. Telemarketing has saved some sellers $1000 or more in sales visits per customer. Such savings are stimulating the growth of telemarketing, which places billions of phone calls each year and is responsible for billions of dollars of sales in North America. It averages more than a $7 return for every dollar invested.[46]

SALES PROMOTIONS

7 Describe the various types of *sales promotions* and distinguish between *publicity* and *public relations.*

sales promotions
Short-term promotional activities designed to stimulate consumer buying or co-operation from distributors and other members of the trade.

Sales promotions are short-term promotional activities designed to stimulate consumer buying or co-operation from distributors, sales agents, or other members of the trade. They are important because they increase the likelihood that buyers will try products. They also enhance product recognition and can increase purchase size and amount. For example, soap is often bound into packages of four with the promotion, "Buy three and get one free."

To be successful, sales promotions must be convenient and accessible when the decision to purchase occurs. If Harley-Davidson has a one-week motorcycle promotion and you have no local dealer, the promotion is neither convenient nor accessible to you, and you will not buy. But if The Bay offers a 20 percent-off coupon that you can save for use later, the promotion is convenient and accessible.

Types of Sales Promotions

The best known sales promotions are coupons, point-of-purchase displays, purchasing incentives (such as free samples, trading stamps, and premiums), trade shows, and contests and sweepstakes.

- Certificates entitling the bearer to stated savings off a product's regular price are **coupons**. Coupons may be used to encourage customers to try new products, to attract customers away from competitors, or to induce current customers to buy more of a product. They appear in newspapers and magazines and are often sent through direct mail.

coupon
A method of sales promotion featuring a certificate that entitles the bearer to stated savings off a product's regular price.

- To grab customers' attention as they walk through a store, some companies use **point-of-purchase (POP) displays**. Displays located at the end of the aisles or near the checkout in supermarkets are POP displays. POP displays often coincide with a sale on the item(s) being displayed. They make it easier for customers to find a product and easier for manufacturers to eliminate competitors from consideration. The cost of shelf and display space, however, is becoming more and more expensive.

point-of-purchase (POP) display
A method of sales promotion in which a product display is so located in a retail store as to encourage consumers to buy the product.

- Free samples and premiums are *purchasing incentives*. Free samples allow customers to try a product for a few days without any risk. They may be given out at local retail outlets or sent by manufacturers to consumers via direct mail. **Premiums** are free or reduced-price items, such as pens, pencils, calendars, and coffee mugs, given to consumers in return for buying a specified product. For example, during one promotion Molson Canadian included a free T-shirt with certain packages of its beer.[47] Premiums may not work as well as originally hoped, since customers may switch to a competitor's brand simply to get the premiums that company is offering.

premium
A method of sales promotion in which some item is offered free or at a bargain price to customers in return for buying a specified product.

- Periodically, industries sponsor **trade shows** for their members and customers. Trade shows allow companies to rent booths to display and demonstrate their products to customers who have a special interest in the products or who are ready to buy. Trade shows are relatively inexpensive and are very effective, since the buyer comes to the seller already interested in a given type of product. International trade shows are becoming more important.

trade show
A method of sales promotion in which members of a particular industry gather for displays and product demonstrations designed to sell products to customers.

- Customers, distributors, and sales representatives may all be persuaded to increase sales of a product through the use of *contests*. Distributors and sales agents, for example, may win a trip to Hawaii for selling the most pillows in the month of February.

Best Buy, a 1900-store chain once known for consumer electronics and appliances, has added software and entertainment to its inventory and is now a major retailer of CDs and DVDs. To promote its entertainment products, Best Buy uses promotional tie-ins, such as deals to become the exclusive retailer of U2's latest DVD. In return, Best Buy spent $10 million to put U2 in newspaper circulars and on the sides of buses. Meanwhile, CEO Richard Schultze (right) pursues his strategy of putting electronics and entertainment under one roof.

PUBLICITY AND PUBLIC RELATIONS

publicity
Information about a company that is made available to consumers by the news media; not controlled by the company, but it does not cost the company any money.

Much to the delight of marketing managers with tight budgets, **publicity** is free. Moreover, because it is presented in a news format, consumers see publicity as objective and believable. However, marketers may have little control over bad publicity, and that can have a very negative effect on the company. In August 2003, for example, the New Delhi-based Center for Science and Environment published a report claiming that pesticide residues in Coke and Pepsi were 30 times the acceptable limits in Europe. The two companies jointly called a press conference to deny the allegations. In spite of that, sales of Coke and Pepsi dropped 30–40 percent in the weeks following publication of the report.[48]

public relations
Public-service announcements by the company designed to enhance the company's image.

In contrast to publicity, **public relations** is company-influenced publicity. It attempts to create goodwill between the company and its customers through public-service announcements that enhance the company's image. For example, a bank may announce that senior citizens' groups can have free use of a meeting room for their social activities. Corporate sponsorships of athletic events also help promote a company's image. Roots has been successful in getting high-profile individuals to wear its products. In spite of doping and bribery scandals at the Olympic Games, big-name sponsors such as McDonald's, Coca-Cola, and UPS have continued to sponsor Olympic athletes.

Most large firms have a department to manage their relations with the public and to present a desired company image. As well, company executives may make appearances as guest speakers representing their companies at professional meetings and civic events. They also may serve as leaders in civic activities like the United Way campaign and university fund-raising.

INTERNATIONAL PROMOTIONAL STRATEGIES

As we saw in Chapter 5, recent decades have witnessed a profound shift from "home-country" marketing to "multi-country" and now to "global" marketing. Nowhere is this rapidly growing global orientation more evident than in marketing promotions, especially advertising.

Emergence of the Global Perspective

global perspective
Company's approach to directing its marketing toward worldwide rather than local or regional markets.

Every company that markets products in several countries faces a basic choice: use a *decentralized approach*, maintaining separate marketing management for each country, or adopt a *global perspective*, directing a coordinated marketing program at one worldwide audience. Thus, the **global perspective** is a philosophy that directs marketing toward a worldwide rather than toward local or regional markets.

The Movement Toward Global Advertising

A truly global perspective means designing products for multinational appeal—that is, genuinely global products.[49] A few brands, such as Coca-Cola, McDonald's, Mercedes Benz, Rolex, and Xerox, enjoy global recognition and have become truly global brands. Not surprisingly, globalization is affecting the promotional activities of such firms. In effect, they have already posed the question, "Is it possible to develop global advertising?" McDonald's thinks it is possible, and has embarked on a global promotion campaign with the "I'm Lovin' It" slogan, which was developed by the

German advertising agency Heye and Partners. In December 2003, Cossette Communication Group of Toronto was awarded the contract to handle McDonald's first-ever global product promotion for French fries.[50]

One universal advertising program would be more efficient and cost-effective than developing different programs for each of many countries, but global advertising is not feasible for many companies. Four factors make global advertising a challenging proposition:

- *Product variations.* Even if a product has universal appeal, some variations, or slightly different products, are usually preferred in different cultures. In the magazine business, Hearst Corp. has expanded to 33 editions of *Cosmopolitan* magazine, including one for Central America; English and Spanish editions for the United States; and local editions for Italy, Turkey, Russia, Hong Kong, and Japan. *Reader's Digest* has 48 editions in 19 languages.
- *Language differences.* Compared with those in other languages, ads in English require less print space and airtime because English is a more efficient and precise language than most others. Moreover, translations are often inexact and confusing: When Coke first went to China, the direct translation of "Coca-Cola" came out "Bite the wax tadpole." Advertising agencies have set up worldwide agency networks that can coordinate a campaign's central theme while allowing regional variations.
- *Cultural receptiveness.* There is a lot of difference across nations regarding the mass advertising of sensitive products (such as birth control or personal hygiene products), not to mention those for which advertising may be legally restricted (alcohol, cigarettes). A Canadian in Paris may be surprised to see nudity in billboard ads and even more surprised to find that France is the only country in the European Union (EU) that bans advertising or selling wine on the internet. In the EU and through much of Asia, comparative advertising is considered distasteful or even illegal.
- *Image differences.* Any company's image can vary from nation to nation, regardless of any advertising appeals for universal recognition. American Express, IBM, and Nestlé have better images in the United States than in the United Kingdom, where Heinz, Coca-Cola, and Ford have better images.

Universal Messages and Regional Advertising Skills

Although universal advertising themes are cost-effective and promote brand awareness, major companies have found that without a local or national identity, universal ads don't cause consumers to buy. Coca-Cola's "think global, act local" strategy and Nestlé's approach to small-scale local advertising call for ads tailored to different areas. Such ads are designed to toy with variations on a universal theme while appealing to local emotions, ideas, and values.

Summary of Learning Objectives

1. Identify a *product*, distinguish between *consumer* and *industrial products*, and explain the *product mix*. A *product* is a good, service, or idea that is marketed to fill consumer needs and wants. Customers buy products because of the *value* that they offer. *Consumer products* are divided into three categories that reflect buyer behaviour: (i) *Convenience goods* are inexpensive and purchased often, with little expenditure of time and effort. (ii) *Shopping goods* are more expensive; consumers often compare brands and evaluate alternatives. (iii) *Specialty goods* are important and expensive purchases; consumers usually decide on precisely what they want and accept no substitutes. *Industrial products* can be divided into two categories: (i) *Expense items* (goods and services consumed within a year by firms producing other goods or services); and (ii) *Capital items* (expensive and long-lasting goods and services). The group of products that a company makes available for sale, whether consumer, industrial, or both, is its *product mix*.

2. Describe the *new product development process* and trace the stages of the *product life cycle*. Many firms adopt some version of a basic seven-step process: (1) *Product ideas:* Searching for ideas for new products. (2) *Screening*: Eliminating all product ideas that do not mesh with the firm's abilities or objectives. (3) *Concept testing:* Using market research to get consumers' input about product benefits and prices. (4) *Business analysis:* Comparing manufacturing costs and benefits to see whether a product meets minimum profitability goals. (5) *Prototype development:* Producing a preliminary version of a product. (6) *Product testing and test marketing:* Going into limited production, testing the product to see if it meets performance requirements, and, if so, selling it on a limited basis. (7) *Commercialization:* Beginning full-scale production and marketing.

   The *product life cycle (PLC)* is a series of four stages or phases characterizing a product's profit-producing life: (1) *Introduction:* Marketers focus on making potential consumers aware of the product and its benefits. (2) *Growth:* Sales begin to climb and the product begins to show a profit. (3) *Maturity:* Although the product earns its highest profit level, increased competition eventually leads to price cutting and lower profits; sales start to fall. (4) *Decline:* Sales and profits are further lost to new products in the introduction stage.

3. Explain the importance of *branding*, *packaging*, and *labelling*. *Branding* is a process of using symbols to communicate the qualities of a particular product made by a particular producer. With a few exceptions, a product needs some form of *packaging*—a physical container in which it is sold, advertised, or protected. A package makes the product attractive, displays the brand name, and identifies features and benefits. It also reduces the risk of damage, breakage, or spoilage, and it lessens the likelihood of theft. Every product has a *label* on its package that identifies its name, manufacturer, and contents; like packaging, labelling can help market a product.

4. Identify the important objectives of *promotion* and discuss the considerations in selecting a *promotional mix*. Besides the ultimate objective of increasing sales, marketers may use promotion to accomplish any of the following four goals: (1) *Communicating information:* Information tells customers that a product exists or educates them about its features. (2) *Positioning products: Positioning* is the process of establishing an easily identifiable product image in the minds of consumers. (3) *Adding value:* Not only is promotion the main means of establishing a product's perceived value, but customers gain when the promotional mix includes value-added benefits (say, consumer discounts). (4) *Controlling sales volume:* Firms can compensate for seasonal sales patterns and achieve more stable sales volume throughout the year.

5. Describe the key *advertising media*. Marketers use several different *advertising media*—specific communication devices for carrying a seller's message to potential customers. The most common media—television, newspapers, direct mail, radio, magazines, outdoor advertising, internet advertising, and virtual advertising—differ in their cost and their ability to segment target markets. The combination of media through which a company advertises is its *media mix*.

6. Outline the tasks involved in *personal selling*. In *personal selling*, a salesperson communicates one to one with potential customers to identify their needs and align them with a seller's products. It adds to a firm's credibility because it allows buyers to interact with and ask questions of the seller. Unfortunately, expenses are high, and high costs have turned many companies to *telemarketing*—the use of telephone solicitations to conduct the personal selling process.

7. Describe the various types of *sales promotions* and distinguish between *publicity* and *public relations*. *Sales promotions* are short-term promotional activities designed to stimulate consumer buying or co-operation from members of the trade. They increase the likelihood that buyers will try products; they also enhance product recognition and can increase purchase size and amount. The following are the best-known forms of promotions: (1) Certificates entitling bearers to savings off regular prices are *coupons*. (2) To grab customers' attention as they move through stores, companies use *point-of-purchase (POP) displays*. (3) Free samples and premiums are *purchasing incentives* that allow customers to try products without risk. (4) *Premiums* are gifts to consumers in return for buying certain products. (5) Industries sponsor *trade shows*, at which companies rent booths to display and demonstrate products to customers with a special interest in them. (6) Customers, distributors, and sales reps may all be persuaded to increase sales by means of *contests*.

Publicity is a promotional tool in which information about a company or product is created and transmitted by general mass media. It is free, and because it is presented in a news format, consumers often see it as objective and credible. However, marketers often have little control over it, and it can be as easily detrimental as beneficial. *Public relations* is company-influenced publicity that seeks to build good relations with the public and to deal with unfavourable events.

QUESTIONS AND EXERCISES

Questions for Analysis

1. What impact do the different levels of brand loyalty (recognition, preference, insistence) have on the consumer buying process that was described in Chapter 12?

2. Why would a business use a "push" strategy rather than a "pull" strategy?

3. Which promotional tools have proven most useful in mounting global advertising campaigns? Why?

4. Is publicity more or less available to small firms than to larger firms? Why?

5. How would you expect the branding, packaging, and labelling of convenience, shopping, and specialty goods to differ? Why? Give examples to illustrate your answers.

6. Choose two advertising campaigns that have recently been conducted by businesses based in your area. Choose one that you think is effective and one that you think is ineffective. What differences in the campaigns made one better than the other?

7. Find examples of publicity about some business, either a local firm or a national firm. Did the publicity have, or is it likely to have, positive or negative consequences for the business? Why?

Application Exercises

8. Interview the manager of a manufacturing firm that produces at least three or four different products. Identify each of the company's products in terms of their stage in the product life cycle. Are all the products in the same stage of the product life cycle, or does the company have products in each stage?

9. Select a product that is sold nationally. Identify as many media used in its promotion as you can. Which medium is used most often? On the whole, do you think the campaign is effective? Why or why not?

10. Check out your college or university's website and assess its effectiveness as a tool for promoting your school. What improvements can you suggest?

BUILDING YOUR BUSINESS SKILLS

Greeting Start-Up Decisions

Goal

To encourage students to analyze the potential usefulness of two promotional methods—personal selling and direct mail—for a start-up greeting card company.

Situation

You are the marketing adviser for a local start-up company that makes and sells specialty greeting cards in a city of 400 000. Last year's sales totalled 14 000 cards, including personalized holiday cards, birthday cards, and special-events cards for individuals. Although revenues increased last year, you see a way of further boosting sales by expanding into card shops, grocery stores, and gift shops. You see two alternatives for entering these outlets:

1. Use direct mail to reach more individual customers for specialty cards.
2. Use personal selling to gain display space in retail stores.

Your challenge is to convince the owner of the start-up company which alternative is the more financially sound decision.

Method

Step 1 Get together with four or five classmates to research the two kinds of product segments: *personalized cards* and *retail store cards*. Find out which of the two kinds of marketing promotions will be more effective for each of the two segments. What will be the reaction to each method by customers, retailers, and card company owners?

Step 2 Draft a proposal to the company owner. Leaving budget and production details to other staffers, list as many reasons as possible for adopting direct mail. Then list as many reasons as possible for adopting personal selling. Defend each reason. Consider the following reasons in your argument:

- *Competitive environment:* Analyze the impact of other card suppliers that offer personalized cards and cards for sale in retail stores.
- *Expectations of target markets:* Who buys personalized cards, and who buys ready-made cards from retail stores?
- *Overall cost of the promotional effort:* Which method—direct mail or personal selling—will be more costly?
- *Marketing effectiveness:* Which promotional method will result in greater consumer response?

Follow-Up Questions

1. Why do you think some buyers want personalized cards? Why do some consumers want ready-made cards from retail stores?
2. Today's computer operating systems provide easy access to software for designing and making cards on home PCs. How does the availability of this product affect your recommendation?
3. What was your most convincing argument for using direct mail? For using personal selling?
4. Can a start-up company compete in retail stores against industry giants such as Hallmark?

EXERCISING YOUR ETHICS: TEAM EXERCISE

Cleaning Up in Sales

The Situation

Selling a product—whether a good or a service—requires the salesperson to believe in it, to be confident of his or her sales skills, and to keep commitments made to clients. Because so many people and resources are involved in delivering a product, numerous uncertainties and problems can give rise to ethical issues. This exercise encourages you to examine some of the ethical issues that can surface in the selling process for industrial products.

The Dilemma

Cleaning Technologies Corporation (CTC) is a U.S.-based company that manufactures equipment for industrial cleaners. The Canadian division of CTC has just hired Denise Skilsel and six other new graduates, and these seven individuals have just completed the sales training program for a new line of high-tech machinery that CTC has developed. As a new salesperson, Skilsel is eager to meet potential clients, all of whom are professional buyers for companies—such as laundries and dry cleaners, carpet cleaners, and military cleaners—that use CTC products or those of competitors. Skilsel is especially enthusiastic about several facts that she learned during training: CTC's equipment is the most technically advanced in the industry, carries a 10-year performance guarantee, and is safe—both functionally and environmentally.

The first month was difficult but successful. In visits to seven firms, Skilsel successfully closed three sales, earning large commissions (pay is based on sales results) as well as praise from the sales manager. Moreover, after listening to her presentations, two more potential buyers had given verbal commitments and were about to sign for much bigger orders than any Skilsel had closed to date. As she was catching her flight to close those sales, Skilsel received two calls—one from a client and one from a competitor. The client, just getting started with CTC equipment, was having some trouble: Employees stationed nearby were getting sick when the equipment was running. The competitor told Skilsel that the U.S. Environmental Protection Agency (EPA) had received complaints from some of CTC's U.S. customers that the new technology was environmentally unsafe because of noxious emissions.

Team Activity

Assemble a group of four students and assign each group member to one of the following roles:

- Denise Skilsel: CTC salesperson (employee)
- CTC sales manager (employer)
- CTC customer
- CTC investor

Action Steps

1. Before discussing the situation with your group, and from the perspective of your assigned role, what do you recommend Skilsel should say to the two client firms she is scheduled to visit? Write down your recommendation.
2. Gather your group together and reveal, in turn, each member's recommendation.
3. Appoint someone to record the main points of agreement and disagreement within the group. How do you explain the results? What accounts for any disagreement?
4. Identify any ethical issues involved in group members' recommendations. Which issues, if any, are more critical than others?
5. From an ethical standpoint, what does your group finally recommend Skilsel should say to the two client firms she is scheduled to visit? Explain your result.
6. Identify the advantages and drawbacks resulting from your recommendations.

BUSINESS CASE 13

Advertising: Not What It Used to Be

A long time ago (in the 1960s and 1970s), advertising was simple. Sellers of products paid for radio, TV, and newspaper advertisements to get the attention of prospective customers. Consumers basically put up with advertisements because they knew that advertisers were providing the content in return for their advertisements being shown. But consumers have never liked most advertisements, and when they are given an opportunity to avoid them, they'll take it. And that opportunity has increasingly been provided as consumers are given the tools to help them avoid advertisements.

In TV, the problem (from the advertisers perspective) is caused by VCRs and digital video recorders like TiVo. While primarily designed to allow consumers to tape TV shows when they had other commitments, consumers quickly discovered that they could fast forward through those annoying advertisements. This obviously defeated the purpose for which TV advertisements were produced. It is estimated that by 2010, almost half of all television programming will be watched this way, and that consumers will fast forward through 80 percent of the advertisements they might have otherwise seen.

In radio, the development of satellite radio poses another threat to advertisers. Earth-based radio stations beam their signal to orbiting satellites, which in turn beam the signal to a satellite radio company such as Sirius Satellite or XM Satellite (in 2007, the two companies announced plans to merge). These companies then make the signal available to consumers who pay a monthly fee for the service. In 2005, the CRTC approved licenses for Canadian companies to start providing ad-free satellite radio service. In addition to allowing listeners to avoid advertisements, satellite radio may threaten the competitive position of existing AM radio stations because the satellite radio companies are required to have only 10 percent Canadian content, while existing AM radio stations are required to have 35 percent Canadian content. Consumer interest in satellite radio has to date been much higher in the United States than in Canada; there were about 8 million subscribers in the United States at the end of 2005, and the number was rapidly growing.

Advertisers are not sitting idly by as these trends unfold. Instead, they are using several new tactics to reach consumers. These include *stealth advertising, product placement*, *cellphone advertising*, and *interactive television advertising*.

Stealth advertising. As the name implies, stealth advertising is designed to advertise a company's product without consumers knowing that they are the target of an actual advertisement. (For a description of stealth advertising, see p. 72 in Chapter 3).

Product placement. In the area of television advertising, one of the newer tactics is something called "product placement," which involves using brand name products as part of the actual storyline of TV shows. For example, Home Depot has been able to embed its brand name into shows like *Trading Spaces*, *Survivor*, and *The Apprentice*. On one episode of *The Apprentice*, teams had to run a workshop inside a Home Depot store. The winning team developed a workshop to build a storage chest, and after that episode, Home Depot stores ran their own workshops on how to build the chests. Many other companies are using product placement, including Bell Canada (on CBC's *Making the Cut*), Coke (on *American Idol*), and Buick (on *Desperate Housewives*).

Product placement is not limited to TV advertising; it can also be found in movies, novels, video games, pop songs, music videos, and Broadway plays. It is also rapidly increasing in importance. A PQ Media survey showed that from 2003 to 2004, product placement increased by 46 percent. The increased importance of product placement has influenced how companies spend their promotion dollars. In 2005, Procter & Gamble cut the amount of money it spent on traditional TV advertising and shifted some of that money into product placement. P&G's global marketing officer, Jim Stengel, says that companies must "embrace the consumer's point of view about TV and create advertising consumers choose to watch."

Product placement must be done carefully because it is a complex type of advertising. Pat Wilkinson, director of Marketing for Home Depot Canada, says that for every dollar the company spends on branded entertainment, it must spend an additional \$3–\$5 to make it deliver further results. And Michael Beckerman, the chief marketing officer for the Bank of Montreal, says that product placements must be "natural." He says that if a person is watching, say, *Desperate Housewives* and the characters started talking about BMO mutual funds, viewers would likely see it as a blatant advertisement, and it would not likely be effective.

The Canadian Radio-Television and Telecommunications Commission (CRTC) is looking into product placement advertising because Canadian broadcasters cannot have more than 12 minutes of advertising per hour of programming. If there are more than 12 minutes of advertising, the show is classified as an infomercial, and is no longer considered Canadian content (and is not eligible for government funding incentives). For example, when Global TV's *Rona Dream Home* contained too much time featuring the sponsor, it was ruled non-Canadian content.

Cellphone advertising. Capitalizing on new technology and the popularity of cellphones, Maiden Group PLC and Filter UK Ltd. have developed a system where transmitters detect cellphones that are equipped with Bluetooth, a short-range wireless technology, and then the transmitters beam out text messages to these cellphones. For example, passengers in the first-class lounge who were waiting to board Virgin Atlantic Airways flights at London's Heathrow airport were asked if they would like to watch a video-clip about a new SUV on their phone. The transmitters are also installed in billboards in train stations in the United Kingdom. In one test, the transmitters discovered 87 000 Bluetooth-equipped phones at the railway station; of those, 13 000 people agreed to view the advertisement when asked. Cellphone advertising is important to advertisers because people are spending less time watching TV or reading newspapers.

Interactive television advertising. Another possibility for advertisers is something called interactive television advertising. It allows viewers of advertisements to opt for more information about products if they are interested. Consider this example: Sony Corp. produced a TV advertisement for the action movie "XXX: State of the Union" that included an icon which appeared on TV screens. The icon invited viewers to press a button on their remote to learn more about the movie. If they pushed the button, they got access to a 30-minute program which included 10 minutes of the actual movie as well as interviews with the stars. A unit of DaimlerChrysler has also developed an interactive ad that lets viewers go to a special screen where they can customize a car. And Mercedes ran an interactive ad in 2005 that generated 15 000 requests for more information. This far exceeded the advertiser's expectations.

The idea of giving consumers an opportunity to interact with advertisers is also evident on the internet. Procter & Gamble developed an online contest for its Crest Whitening Expressions brand where internet users voted for their favourite potential new flavour. Crest promised to make a product based on the winning flavour. Over 785 000 votes were recorded over a three-month period. To promote its Malibu Maxx vehicle, General Motors of Canada ran an online search for the Canadian couple with the greatest height difference. Contestants logged on to *LongandShort.gmcanada.com* and completed a survey.

Questions for Discussion

1. Consumers are taking advantage of ways to avoid seeing advertisements, but companies are also developing new techniques in order to increase the visibility of their products. What do you think will be the eventual outcome in this "contest"? Give examples to demonstrate your reasoning.
2. Will the emphasis on each of the four Ps of marketing (product, price, promotion, and place) change in importance as consumers get more opportunities to avoid viewing advertisements? Why or why not?
3. To what extent will the changes that are occurring in advertising affect the new product development process in companies?
4. Does the value of brand names increase or decrease when consumers are able to take advantage of ways to avoid seeing advertisements?

MYBUSINESSLAB

To improve your grade, visit the MyBusinessLab website at **www.pearsoned.ca/mybusinesslab**. This online homework and tutorial system allows you to test your understanding and generates a personalized study plan just for you. It provides you with study and practice tools directly related to this chapter's content. MyBusinessLab puts you in control of your own learning!

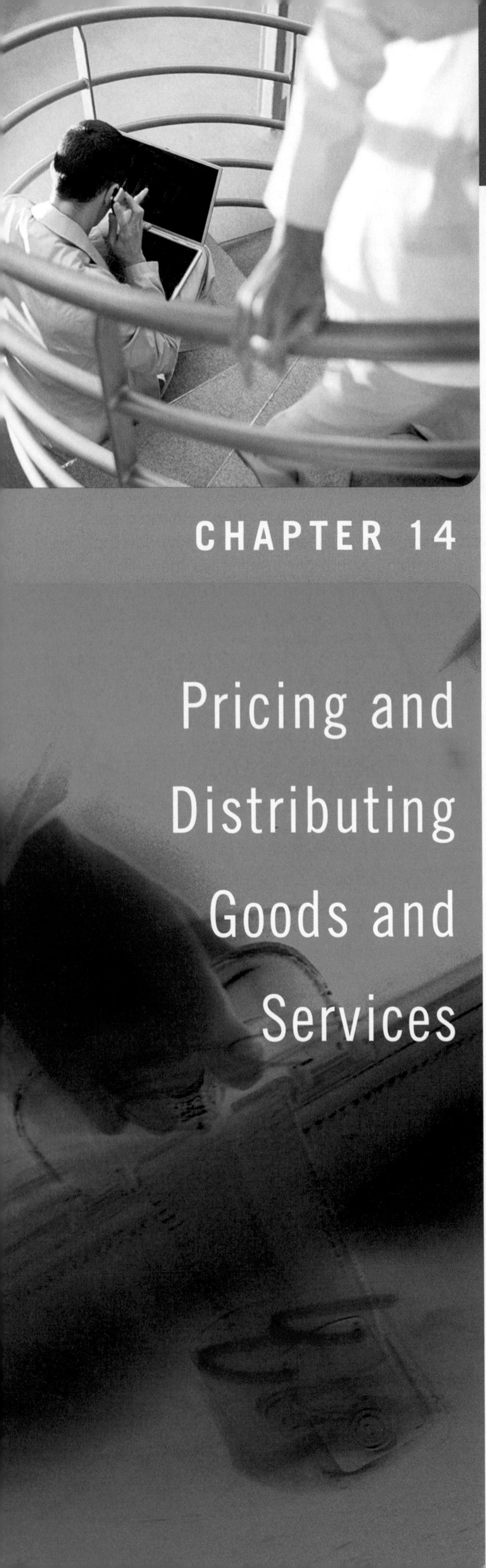

CHAPTER 14

Pricing and Distributing Goods and Services

After reading this chapter, you should be able to:

1. Identify the various *pricing objectives* that govern pricing decisions and describe the price-setting tools used in making these decisions.
2. Discuss *pricing strategies* and *tactics* for existing and new products.
3. Explain the *distribution mix*, the different *channels of distribution*, and different *distribution strategies*.
4. Explain the differences among *retailers, wholesalers*, and *agents/brokers*.
5. Identify the different types of *retail stores* and the activities of *e-intermediaries*.
6. Define *physical distribution* and describe the major activities in *warehousing* operations.
7. Compare the five basic forms of *transportation* and explain how distribution can be used as a marketing strategy.

The Importance of Price

There has always been a tension between sellers of goods and the customers who buy them. The seller naturally wants to get the highest price possible, and the buyer, just as naturally, wants to get the lowest price possible. In the last few years, the tension between buyers and sellers over price has reached a new intensity in several different areas, including retailing, online auctions, beer, automobiles, and cigarettes.

The retailing industry. The most obvious example of consumer pressure for low prices is the success of Wal-Mart. But there are many other examples of how consumers have become obsessed with paying the least amount possible for goods and services. Consider the recent success of so-called dollar stores—retailers that offer ultra-cheap prices on a limited selection of goods. These include stores like The Silver Dollar, Dollarama, and Buck or Two. Sales revenues for this type of retail outlet have doubled in the last five years, and the number of stores has tripled. While dollar stores originally targeted low-income shoppers, they now are appealing to buyers at all income levels, and they are gaining the attention of companies that once ignored them. Procter & Gamble, for example, created a special version of Dawn dish soap that sells for $1, and Kraft Foods sells boxes of macaroni and cheese in dollar stores. All of this activity is driven by consumers who demand low prices. As one customer said, "Why should I pay $4 for a greeting card when I can get one at a dollar store for $1?"

The online auction industry. In 2005, eBay announced that it was increasing the fees it charges those who sell their goods online. For goods advertised at $25 or less, eBay formerly charged 5.25 percent of the closing price. That rate has now increased to 8 percent of the closing price. When eBay announced this increase, thousands of users threatened to stop using eBay's service. Trisha Dixon is typical. She had been selling scrapbooks, children's clothes, and health products on eBay for six years in order to make a little extra money. But when eBay announced its price increases, Dixon estimated that her monthly eBay bill would increase from $750 to $1500. Like Dixon, many eBay sellers operate small businesses from their homes, and they say they cannot afford to pay higher monthly fees and still make their business work. But eBay is popular with many different kinds of sellers, and its dollar volume of goods sold continues to rapidly increase, so these complaints may not have much effect on eBay's business. Small business owners who are unhappy with the price increases may have no alternative but to go to some less well-known online auction service such as *iOffer.com* or *Wagglepop.com* to sell their goods.

The beer industry. Price wars have long been common in the Canadian beer market, but in recent years competition from wineries, liquor manufacturers, discount beers, and imported beers has made it difficult to raise prices. In 2004, when Sleeman Breweries Ltd., Canada's third-largest brewer, tried to increase the price of its beer to $42 a case, it quickly found that consumers wouldn't accept the increase because they had cheaper alternatives. Shortly thereafter, it dropped the price to $36 per case. Sleeman and the two largest brewers—Molson and Labatt—have found the discount brewers hard to ignore. For example, Hamilton-based Lakeport Brewing Corp. began selling its Honey Lager brew for $1 a bottle in 2003. Since then, its share of the Ontario at-home market has risen from 1.8 percent to nearly 10 percent. Waterloo-based Brick Brewing Co. more than doubled its volume by pricing significantly lower than either Molson Canadian or Labatt Blue. The title of an article that appeared in the *Globe and Mail* nicely summed up the price dilemma facing beer makers. It read: "In Hamilton, they like beer cold... and cheap." Discount beer is taking market share away from long-time industry leaders like Labatt and Molson.

The automobile industry. While the absolute price that a company charges for its products is important, it's not the only issue causing tension between buyers and sellers. The pricing *system* can also raise the ire of consumers. It used to be the case when you purchased a new car that you got involved in much haggling with the salesperson over the price you would pay. Some consumers liked the give-and-take, but most of them didn't. So, in 2000, Toyota introduced what seemed like a consumer-friendly idea: a "no-haggle" policy (one-price) policy. But in 2004 Toyota announced that it was terminating the program. It is not exactly clear why Toyota decided to drop the idea. It may have been that their dealers had become less aggressive in the marketplace, or because lawsuits challenging the legality of the program were filed against the company in Quebec and B.C., or because the Competition Bureau had looked into allegations that the pricing system amounted to price fixing. One study by CarCost Canada found that buyers who purchased a Toyota Sequoia under the one-price system in B.C. paid an average of $63 171, while buyers in Ontario (where the one-price policy was not in effect) paid only $57 881. Evidence like this does not make consumers happy.

The cigarette industry. For many years, the North American cigarette market has been an oligopoly that is dominated by a few very large tobacco companies like Imperial Tobacco, R.J. Reynolds, Philip Morris, Brown & Williamson, and Lorillard Tobacco. The pricing strategy that has historically been used by these companies is to increase prices to maintain (or increase) profits. This strategy worked for decades because customers were very loyal to their favourite brand. But the cigarette business has become much more difficult for the major cigarette companies in the last few years for three reasons. First, cigarettes are highly taxed by the government, class action lawsuits have resulted in some billion-dollar judgments against the major companies, they must put explicit warnings on their products indicating that cigarettes are dangerous, and the number of smokers is dropping. Second, some new cigarette manufacturing companies have started up and are pricing their cigarettes as much as 50 percent lower than the majors. The majors are responding with incentives like 2-for-1 deals, but that has reduced their profits by 50 percent or more. Third, contraband cigarettes are an increasing problem. These are cigarettes containing no health warnings and for which no tax has been paid. A bag containing 200 contraband cigarettes can be purchased for as little as $10. All these developments mean that the major cigarette companies have less control over the market than they used to, and they are going to have much more difficulty simply raising prices in the future.

Companies are well aware that raising prices can cause customers to be unhappy, so they may try to raise prices without *appearing* to have done so. Consider these examples:

- Kimberly-Clark Corp. cut the price of its diapers, but cut the quantity in the package even more (this was, in effect, a 5 percent price increase).
- General Motors started charging extra for antilock brakes instead of including them at no charge as it used to do (this also constituted a price increase).
- Goodyear Tire & Rubber Co. tire distributors had routinely been given big discounts on the tires they purchased. But the company discovered that the discounts were so deep that the distributors were ordering large quantities of tires and selling them outside their normal business area. This reduced the sales of smaller distributors in other areas that Goodyear also sold tires to, and had the overall effect of reducing the price of Goodyear tires in the marketplace. In 2003, Goodyear reduced the discounts it had been giving to its biggest distributors, and found that revenue per tire went up.

HOW WILL THIS BENEFIT YOU?

By understanding the material presented in this chapter, you will benefit in three ways: (1) as a consumer, you will have a better understanding of how a product's development, promotion, and distribution affect its selling price; (2) as an investor, you'll be better prepared to evaluate a company's marketing program and its competitive potential before buying the company's stock; and (3) as an employee and/or manager, you'll be able to use your knowledge about product pricing and distribution to further your career.

In this chapter, we continue with our analysis of the four basic elements in the marketing mix by looking at *price* and *place* (channels of distribution). Price is an important element of the marketing mix because it influences both consumer demand for a product and a company's profitability. As the opening case shows, this element of the marketing mix has become intensely competitive during the last few years. But price is not the only important element. We also analyze the distribution function of marketing, because consumers also want products and services to be available in the right places and at the right time.

PRICING OBJECTIVES AND TOOLS

1 Identify the various *pricing objectives* that govern pricing decisions and describe the price-setting tools used in making these decisions.

In **pricing**, managers decide what the company will receive in exchange for its products. In this section, we first discuss the objectives that influence a firm's pricing decisions. Then we describe the major tools that companies use to meet those objectives.

pricing
Deciding what the company will receive in exchange for its product.

Pricing to Meet Business Objectives

The pricing structure used on eBay is simple: Let buyers make offers until a price is finally settled. While eBay sellers hope for a high price, they sometimes are willing to give up some profit in return for a quick sale. Unfortunately, the eBay pricing model of one-on-one price setting isn't feasible for all companies with lots of customers and products. **Pricing objectives** are the goals that sellers hope to achieve in pricing products for sale. Some companies set prices to maximize profits while others try to secure a high market share. Pricing decisions are also influenced by the need to compete in the marketplace, by social and ethical concerns, and even by corporate image.

pricing objectives Goals that sellers hope to attain in pricing products for sale.

Profit-Maximizing Objectives

Pricing to maximize profits is tricky. If prices are set too low, the company will sell all of its output, but it may miss the opportunity to make additional profit on each unit. If prices are set too high, the company will make a large profit on each item but may not sell all its output. To avoid these problems, companies try to set prices to sell the number of units that will generate the highest possible total profits.

The strategy of charging prices based on market conditions is increasingly evident in both the public and private sectors. For example, in professional baseball, the New York Mets charge fans twice as much for tickets when home run king Barry Bonds plays with the visiting San Francisco Giants. The Ottawa Senators increase prices 20 percent for games against the Toronto Maple Leafs and the champion Detroit Red Wings.[1] An experimental dynamic-pricing system of toll road fees has been introduced in Stockholm, Sweden, in an attempt to reduce traffic congestion. In the busiest time of the day, road users must pay fees that are double those charged during lighter traffic times. During the trial period, declines were evident in the number of vehicles using the roads, the number of personal injuries, and the amount of emissions from motor vehicles.[2] In the United Kingdom, one auto insurer has introduced a system where car insurance premiums vary depending on how much, where, and when a person drives. For example, a 40-year-old driver who is driving on a divided highway at 2 p.m. might pay only one pence per mile to drive, but a teenager driving at 1 a.m. would pay dramatically more (about one *pound* per mile).[3]

In calculating profits, managers weigh receipts against costs for materials and labour used to create the product. But they also consider the capital resources (plant and equipment) that the company must tie up to generate that level of profit. The costs of marketing (such as maintaining a large sales staff) can also be substantial. Concern over the efficient use of these resources has led many firms to set prices so as to achieve a targeted level of return on sales or capital investment.[4]

Market-Share Objectives

Some companies initially set low prices for new products. They are willing to accept minimal profits—even losses—to get buyers to try their products. These companies are using price to establish **market share**—a company's percentage of the total market sales for a specific product. Even with established products, market share objectives may outweigh profits in setting price. For a product like Philadelphia Brand Cream Cheese, dominating a market means that consumers are more likely to buy it because they are familiar with a well-known, highly visible brand name.

market share A company's percentage of the total market sales for a specific product.

Price-Setting Tools

Whatever a company's objectives, managers must measure the potential impact before deciding on final prices. Two basic tools are often used for this purpose: *cost-oriented pricing* and *break-even analysis*. As a rule, these tools are combined to identify prices that will allow the company to reach its objectives.

Cost-Oriented Pricing

Cost-oriented pricing considers the firm's desire to make a profit and takes into account the need to cover production costs. A music store manager, for instance, would begin to price CDs by calculating the cost of making them available to shoppers. Included in this figure would be store rent, employee wages, utilities, product displays, insurance, and, of course, the cost of buying CDs from the manufacturer.

Let's assume that the cost from the manufacturer is \$8 per CD. If the store sells CDs for this price, it will not make any profit. Nor will it make a profit if it sells CDs for \$8.50 each, nor even for \$10 or \$11. The manager must account for product and other costs and set a figure for profit. Together, these figures constitute markup. In this case, a reasonable markup of \$7 over costs would result in a \$15 selling price. Markup is usually stated as a percentage of selling price. Markup percentage is thus calculated as follows:

$$\text{Markup percentage} = \frac{\text{Markup}}{\text{Sales price}}$$

In the case of our CD retailer, the markup percentage is 46.7:

$$\text{Markup percentage} = \frac{\$7}{\$15} = 46.7\%$$

In other words, out of every dollar taken in, 46.7 cents will be gross profit for the store. From this profit, the store must still pay rent, utilities, insurance, and all other costs. Markup can also be expressed as a percentage of cost: The \$7 markup is 87.5 percent of the \$8 cost of a CD (\$7 divided by \$8).

In some industries, cost-oriented pricing doesn't seem to work. When you go to a first-run movie theatre, for example, you pay the same price for each film you see. But it may cost as little as \$2 million or as much as \$200 million to make a film. Shouldn't the admission price be based on how much the film cost to make? After all, you pay a lot more for a Lincoln Continental than you do for a Ford because the Lincoln costs more to make. Shouldn't the same pricing system apply to Hollywood? Apparently not. Market-based pricing is at work here (i.e., consumers are simply not willing to pay more than a certain amount to see a movie).

Some homeowners have the opportunity to take out fixed-price fuel oil contracts to lock in the heating oil prices they'll pay during the winter. In some years, it's a good bet. If a homeowner locks in at \$1.15 per gallon and prices go up to \$1.80 per gallon, the homeowner obviously benefits. But if prices decline to \$0.85 per gallon, the homeowner loses. "It's like buying insurance," says one analyst. "When you buy a fixed-price deal, you're saying you want the peace of mind."

Break-Even Analysis: Cost–Volume–Profit Relationships

Using cost-oriented pricing, a firm will cover its **variable costs**—costs that change with the number of goods or services produced or sold. It will also make some money toward paying its **fixed costs**—costs that are unaffected by the number of goods or services produced or sold. But how many units must the company sell before all of its fixed costs are covered and it begins to make a profit? To determine this figure, it needs a **break-even analysis**.

variable costs
Those costs that change with the number of goods or services produced or sold.

fixed costs
Those costs unaffected by the number of goods or services produced or sold.

break-even analysis
An assessment of how many units must be sold at a given price before the company begins to make a profit.

To continue our music store example, suppose again that the variable cost for each CD (in this case, the cost of buying the CD from the producer) is \$8. This means that the store's annual variable costs depend on how many CDs are sold—the number of CDs sold multiplied by \$8 cost per CD. Assume that fixed costs for keeping the store open for one year are \$100 000. These costs are unaffected by the number of CDs sold; costs for lighting, rent, insurance, and salaries are steady however many CDs the store sells. How many CDs must be sold to cover both fixed and variable costs and to start to generate some profit? The answer is the **break-even point**, which is 14 286 CDs. We arrive at this number through the following equation:

break-even point
The number of units that must be sold at a given price before the company covers all of its variable and fixed costs.

$$\text{Break-even point (in units)} = \frac{\text{Total fixed costs}}{\text{Price} - \text{Variable cost}}$$

$$= \frac{\$100\ 000}{\$15 - \$8} = 14\ 286 \text{ CDs}$$

Figure 14.1 shows the break-even point graphically. If the store sells fewer than 14 286 CDs, it loses money for the year. If sales exceed 14 286 CDs, profits grow by \$7 for each CD sold. If the store sells exactly 14 286 CDs, it will cover all of its costs but will earn zero profit. Zero profitability at the break-even point can also be seen by using the following profit equation:

$$\text{Profit} = \text{Total revenue} - (\text{Total fixed costs} + \text{Total variable costs})$$

$$\$0 = (14\ 286 \text{ CDs} \times \$15) - (\$100\ 000 \text{ fixed costs} + [14\ 286 \text{ CDs} \times \$8 \text{ variable costs}])$$

$$\$0 = (214\ 290) - (\$100\ 000 + 114\ 288)$$
(rounded to the nearest whole CD)

The music store owner would certainly like to hit the break-even quantity as early as possible so that profits will start rolling in. Why not charge

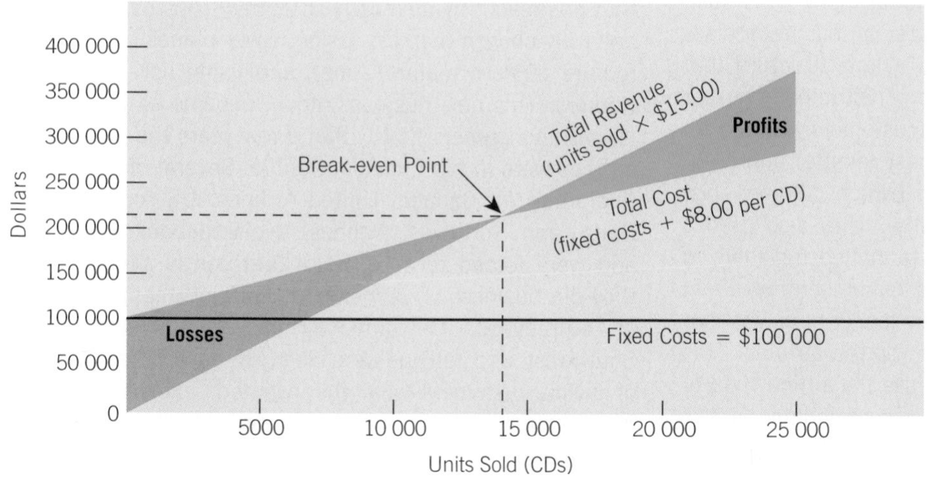

Figure 14.1 Break-even analysis.

$20 per CD and reach the break-even point earlier? The answer lies in the downward-sloping demand curve we discussed in Chapter 1. At a price of $20 per CD, sales at the store would drop. In setting a price, the manager must consider how much CD buyers will pay and what the store's local competitors charge.

PRICING STRATEGIES AND TACTICS

2 Discuss *pricing strategies* and *tactics* for existing and new products.

In this section, we discuss *pricing strategy*—that is, pricing as a planning activity that affects the marketing mix. We then describe some basic *pricing tactics*—ways in which managers implement a firm's pricing strategies.

Pricing Strategies

How important is pricing as an element in the marketing mix? Because pricing has a direct impact on revenues, it is extremely important. Moreover, it is a very flexible tool. It is certainly easier to change prices than to change products or distribution channels. In this section, we focus on the ways in which pricing strategies can result in widely differing prices for very similar products.

Pricing Existing Products

A firm has three options available in pricing its existing products. It can set prices for its product: (1) above prevailing market prices charged for similar products; (2) below market; or (3) at or near the market price. Companies pricing above the market play on customers' beliefs that higher

BUSINESS ACCOUNTABILITY

Pricing in the Airline Industry: The Sky Is no Longer the Limit

For the last 40 years, major airlines like Air Canada and United Airlines dominated the industry. Their business model involved providing many frills such as in-flight meals, movies, special business class seats with more legroom, and a fare structure that featured relatively low-priced "restricted" tickets (that included a penalty if customers wanted to change their schedule at the last minute) and high-priced "unrestricted" tickets (which allowed last minute changes with no penalty). They also used a "hub-and-spoke" system that funnelled travellers in from various regional areas to major centres. From there they transferred to other, longer-haul destinations that were more lucrative for the airlines. This was an expensive system, because the airlines had to lease many airport gates to accommodate all the transferring passengers.

In the 1990s, several airlines (including Southwest Airlines in the United States and WestJet in Canada) introduced a far different business model which involved abandoning the hub-and-spoke system, selling all tickets at bargain prices (many of them on the internet), offering good customer service (but no meals), flying mostly short-haul trips between carefully chosen markets, using newer planes (which require far less maintenance), and using non-union workers. This new business model became so popular with consumers that within a few years the major airlines were in big financial trouble. Several of them (including Air Canada, United Airlines, US Airways, Delta, and Northwest Airlines) declared bankruptcy and were forced to do a major overhaul of the way they did business. This included laying off thousands of employees. Discount airlines like WestJet, Southwest, and JetBlue were clearly doing a better job of giving customers what they wanted, namely low-priced air travel. The discount airlines essentially "Wal-Marted" the airline business.

Just a few years ago, the pricing system used by the major airlines meant that a business traveller flying from Toronto to Vancouver might pay five to 10 times what a leisure traveller in the next seat was paying. This is very much less likely now because of the impact of the discount airlines. A study by Sabre Holdings Corp. revealed that in 2001, 15 percent of the passengers on a New York to Los Angeles flight paid over $2000 for a round-trip ticket; in 2004, only 3 percent paid that much. In 2001, only 28 percent of passengers paid between $200 and $400; in 2004, 55 percent paid that amount.

It is now widely recognized that the so-called "major" airlines have a major problem: their costs exceed their revenues, and they can't cut costs or raise fares enough to make a profit. In terms of *cost-cutting*, the airlines' unionized workers naturally resist wage and benefit cuts. One study showed that major airlines spend U.S.$4.53 on labour costs per seat for each mile flown, while the discount airlines, with their non-unionized workforces, spend only $2.42. In terms of *raising fares*, competition is so fierce that this is generally not possible. Airline tickets have increased in price only 4 percent over the last decade, while prices of other products and services have increased by 27 percent.

In the 1980s, airlines developed so-called "yield-management systems" that were designed to get the most revenue out of each flight. The system was built on many complex assumptions about which travellers would be willing to pay which amounts for seats. But with the advent of discount airlines, the assumptions underlying the yield management systems are no longer accurate. Pricing assumptions are now much simpler: everyone (both business and leisure travellers) wants low-priced seats. That fact, coupled with the oversupply of airline seats and the ability of customers to do price comparisons on the internet before buying a ticket, has driven down the prices that airlines can charge.

The move to low fares for all flyers is now putting pressure on all airlines, including the discounters. Initially, Southwest Airlines was the most successful of the discount airlines. Its emphasis on reliability and customer service, combined with a dedication to cost control and a corporate culture that attracts only the best employees, allowed Southwest to remain virtually unchallenged. Then along came Blue—JetBlue. Since its founding in 1999, it has become one of the most profitable start-up carriers in the United States, and it has done so in large part by applying many of the ideas introduced by Southwest.

CEO David Neeleman's creativity as a manager and marketer is a major factor in JetBlue's success. He originally worked at Southwest, but after he was fired, he decided to form a rival airline that would beat his former employer at its own game. He copied elements of Southwest's discount strategy, such as point-to-point scheduling, reliance on a single type of aircraft, and use of non-union employees. Then he added some extras of his own: reserved seats, upscale snacks, leather chairs, and seat-back televisions with 24 channels of DirecTV. Relying on his extensive industry experience (including a stint at WestJet), Neeleman focused most of his energy on a few key factors that he felt would make or break his company. By hiring younger workers and giving them stock options in lieu of high wages, JetBlue kept labour expenses down to 25 percent of revenues (compared to Southwest's 33 percent and Delta's 44 percent). JetBlue fills planes to capacity, gets more flying hours out of each aircraft, and saves on maintenance costs because its fleet is brand new. Even the luxurious leather seats are cost-effective because they're easier to clean. Neeleman regards on-time arrival as a critical element in customer service and his pager (which he wears to bed) beeps whenever a JetBlue flight touches down more than one minute late.

Neeleman's dedication to monitoring JetBlue's performance is matched by his passion for feedback. He jumps on a plane once a week or so, and not just to ride: He loads baggage and serves drinks. Along the way, he smiles politely when passengers tell him how well he's doing, but he prefers to hear their complaints. No concern is too small or too large, whether a desire for better biscotti or a request for more flights to a certain destination. Neeleman gives employees the authority to make immediate customer-service decisions. "Employees at other airlines," he explains, "get so caught up in procedure—rules, rules, rules—that they often forget there is a paying customer there." JetBlue passengers get discount coupons and free accommodations if their flight is diverted, compensation that rival airlines don't always provide.

QUESTIONS FOR DISCUSSION

1. In what ways are companies—in this case airline companies—accountable to customers? Do the discount airlines have a different view of accountability than the major airlines do?
2. "*The discount airlines are satisfying customers who want low prices, but they are not satisfying customers who want a wider range of services (for example, meals) when they fly. Airlines are failing to be accountable to consumers if they do not provide these services (which used to be available to customers).*" Do you agree or disagree with this statement? Explain your reasoning.

price means higher quality. Companies such as Godiva chocolates and Rolls-Royce have also succeeded with this pricing philosophy. In contrast, both Budget and Discount car rental companies promote themselves as low-priced alternatives to Hertz and Avis.

Pricing New Products

Companies introducing new products into the market have to consider two contrasting pricing policy options: coming in with either a very high price or a very low one. **Price skimming**—setting an initially high price to cover costs and generate a profit—may generate a large profit on each item sold. The revenue is often needed to cover development and introduction costs. High-definition television (HDTV) is an example. In contrast, **penetration pricing**—setting an initially low price to establish a new product in the market—seeks to create consumer interest and stimulate trial purchases.

price skimming
The decision to price a new product as high as possible to earn the maximum profit on each unit sold.

penetration pricing
The decision to price a new product very low to sell the most units possible and to build customer loyalty.

Fixed Versus Dynamic Pricing for Ebusiness

The electronic marketplace has introduced a highly variable pricing system as an alternative to the more conventional—and more stable—pricing structures for both consumer and business-to-business products. Dynamic pricing is feasible because the flow of information on the internet notifies millions of buyers around the world of instantaneous changes in product availability.[5] To attract sales that might be lost under traditional fixed-price structures, sellers can alter prices privately on a one-to-one, customer-to-customer basis.[6] Roy Cooper, for example, scours the markets of Quito, Ecuador, for tapestries, baskets, and religious relics. He pays $10 to $15 for selected items and then posts them on eBay, where they usually sell at substantial markups.

At present, *fixed pricing* remains the most widely available option for cybershoppers. Amazon.com, for example, has maintained this practice as the pricing strategy for its 16 million retail items. That situation is beginning to change, however, as dynamic-price challengers—such as eBay and Priceline.com grow in popularity.

Pricing Tactics

Regardless of its pricing strategy, a company may adopt one or more *pricing tactics*. Companies selling multiple items in a product category often use **price lining**—offering all items in certain categories at a limited num-

price lining
The practice of offering all items in certain categories at a limited number of predetermined price points.

If the manufacturer says a product should retail for $349, why does every retailer sell it for, say, $229? Such discrepancies between a manufacturer's suggested retail price and the actual retail price are the norm in the electronics industry, and consumers have come to expect discounted prices. "You can't have a discount until there's a price to discount it from," explains an editor at *Consumer Reports*, but the practice raises an interesting question: If no one charges suggested retail prices, is anyone really getting a discount?

ber of prices. With price lining, a department store, for example, predetermines three or four *price points* at which a particular product will be sold. If price points for men's suits are $175, $250, and $400, all men's suits will be priced at one of these three prices.

Psychological pricing takes advantage of the fact that customers are not completely rational when making buying decisions.[7] One type of psychological pricing, **odd-even pricing**, is based on the theory that customers prefer prices that are not stated in even dollar amounts. Thus, customers regard prices of $1000, $100, $50, and $10 as significantly higher than $999.95, $99.95, $49.95, and $9.95, respectively. Finally, sellers must often resort to price reductions—**discounts**—to stimulate sales. Cash, seasonal, trade, and quantity discounts are the most common forms.

psychological pricing
The practice of setting prices to take advantage of the illogical reactions of consumers to certain types of prices.

odd-even pricing
A form of psychological pricing in which prices are not stated in even dollar amounts.

discount
Any price reduction offered by the seller to persuade customers to purchase a product.

THE DISTRIBUTION MIX

Explain the *distribution mix*, the different *channels of distribution*, and different *distribution strategies*. 3

The success of any product is affected by its **distribution mix**: the combination of distribution channels by which a firm gets products to end-users. In addition to consumers, industrial users are important because every company is a customer that buys other companies' products. In this section, we describe the role of intermediaries, identify the basic distribution strategies, and explain channel conflict and leadership.

distribution mix
The combination of distribution channels a firm selects to get a product to end-users.

Intermediaries and Distribution Channels

Intermediaries are the individuals and firms who help to distribute a producer's goods. **Wholesalers** sell products to other businesses, which resell them to final consumers. **Retailers** sell products directly to consumers. While some firms rely on independent intermediaries, others employ their own distribution networks and sales forces.

intermediaries
Any individuals or firms other than the producer that participate in a product's distribution.

wholesalers
Intermediaries who sell products to other businesses, which in turn resell them to the end-users.

retailers
Intermediaries who sell products to end-users.

Distribution of Goods and Services

A **distribution channel** is the path that a product follows from producer to end-user. Figure 14.2 shows how four popular distribution channels can be identified according to the kinds of channel members involved in getting products to buyers. All channels begin with a producer and end either with a consumer or an industrial (business) user.

distribution channel
The path a product follows from the producer to the end-user.

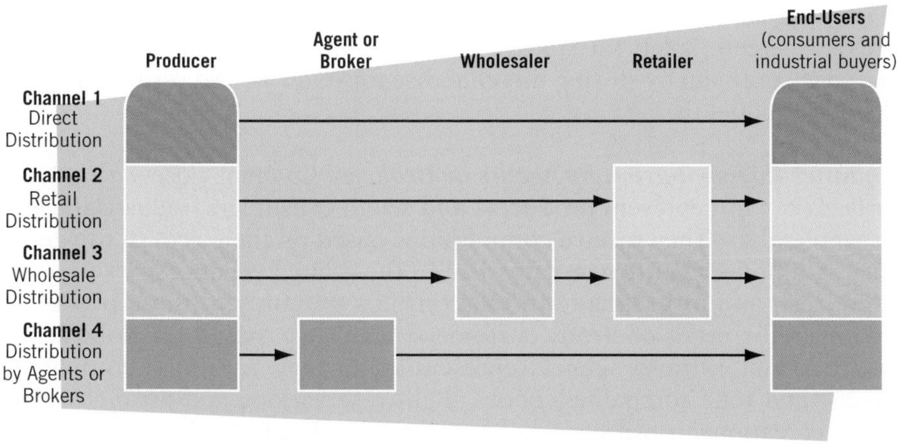

Figure 14.2 Channels of distribution.

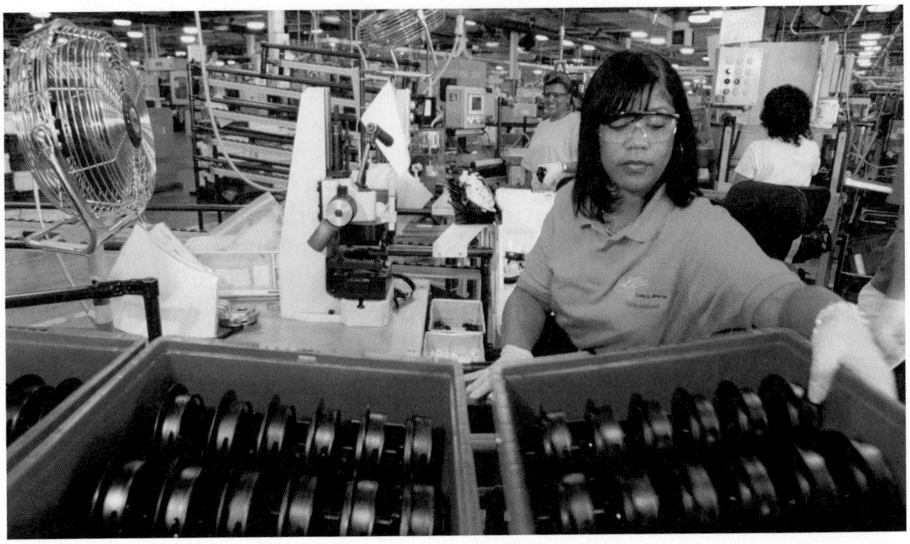

At the plant of the world's largest auto parts supplier, Delphi Automotive Systems, Jessica V. Prince assembles fuel pumps according to a process that she helped engineers and consultants design. The auto parts are shipped from the plant to an auto manufacturer, illustrating a direct (product to customer) channel distribution.

direct channel
A distribution channel in which the product travels from the producer to the consumer without passing through any intermediary.

Channel 1: Direct Distribution. In a **direct channel**, the product travels from the producer to the consumer or to the industrial buyer without intermediaries. Using their own sales forces, companies such as Avon, Dell, Geico, and Tupperware use this channel. Direct distribution is prominent on the internet for thousands of products ranging from books and automobiles to insurance and vacation packages sold directly by producers to users. Most business goods, especially those bought in large quantities, are sold directly by the manufacturer to the industrial buyer.

Channel 2: Retail Distribution. Producers often distribute consumer products through retailers. Goodyear and Levi's have their own retail outlets. Large outlets, such as Wal-Mart, buy merchandise directly from producers and sell to consumers. Many industrial buyers also rely on Channel 2 as they shop at office supply retailers such as Staples, Office Depot, and Office Max.

Channel 3: Wholesale Distribution. Channel 2 was once the most widely used method of nondirect distribution. But it requires a large amount of floor space, both for storing merchandise and for displaying it in stores. Faced with the rising cost of store space, many retailers found that they could not afford both retail and storage space. Thus, wholesalers entered the distribution network to take over more of the storage function. The combination convenience store/gas station is an example of Channel 3. With approximately 90 percent of the space used to display merchandise, only 10 percent is left for storage and office facilities. Wholesalers relieve the space problem by storing merchandise for retailers and restocking store displays frequently.

sales agent
An independent business person who represents a business and receives a commission in return, but never takes legal possession of the product.

broker
Independent intermediary who matches numerous sellers and buyers as needed, often without knowing in advance who they will be.

Channel 4: Distribution by Agents or Brokers. Channel 4 uses *sales agents* or *brokers* who represent producers and sell to consumers, industrial users, or wholesalers. They receive commissions based on the prices of the goods they sell. **Sales agents** generally deal in the related product lines of a few producers, and form long-term relationships to represent those producers and meet the needs of steady customers. Vancouver-based Uniglobe Travel International, a travel agency representing airlines, car-rental companies, hotels, and tour companies, books flight reservations and arranges complete recreational travel services for consumers. The firm also services companies whose employees need lodging and transportation for business travel. In contrast to agents, **brokers** match numerous sellers and buyers as needed, often without knowing in advance who they will be. Both the real estate industry and stock exchanges rely on brokers to match buyers and sellers of property.

The Pros and Cons of Non-Direct Distribution

Each link in the distribution chain makes a profit by charging a markup or commission. Thus, nondirect distribution means higher prices: The more members in the channel, the higher the final price. Intermediaries, however, can provide *added value* by saving consumers both time and money. Moreover, the value accumulates with each link in the supply chain. Intermediaries provide time-saving information and make the right quantities of products available where and when consumers need them. Consider Figure 14.3, which illustrates the problem of making chili without the benefit of a common intermediary—the supermarket. As a consumer, you would obviously spend a lot more time, money, and energy if you tried to gather all the ingredients from one producer at a time.

Eliminating intermediaries does not magically eliminate the tasks they perform and the costs they incur in performing those tasks. In this do-it-yourself era, more and more people are trying to save money by opting to sell their homes without using the services of a real estate agent. Since the agent's fee is normally between 5 and 6 percent of the purchase price of the house, the savings can be substantial. But the seller then has to do all the work that brokers would normally do to earn their fee.

Although intermediaries like real estate agents provide an essential service, this does not mean that they necessarily provide a *low-cost* service. E-brokers have emerged who charge a flat rate for selling a home, and that rate is far below what traditional real estate brokers charge. It is not surprising that this development has been viewed with some alarm by traditional real estate agents. What's worse, in 2007 the Canadian Competition Bureau launched an inquiry into changes the Canadian Real Estate Association (CREA) made to its operating procedures. E-brokers claimed these changes were designed to maintain high fees for traditional real estate brokers by cutting e-brokers out of the CREAs Multiple Listing Service.[8]

Intermediaries are even appearing in places where most people might think they aren't needed. A Canadian company called Imagine This Sold Ltd. began operating in 2004. For a percentage of the selling price, it provides expertise to people who are trying to sell items on eBay. This company exists because trading has become so competitive on eBay that more expertise is needed to succeed than a lot of people thought.[9]

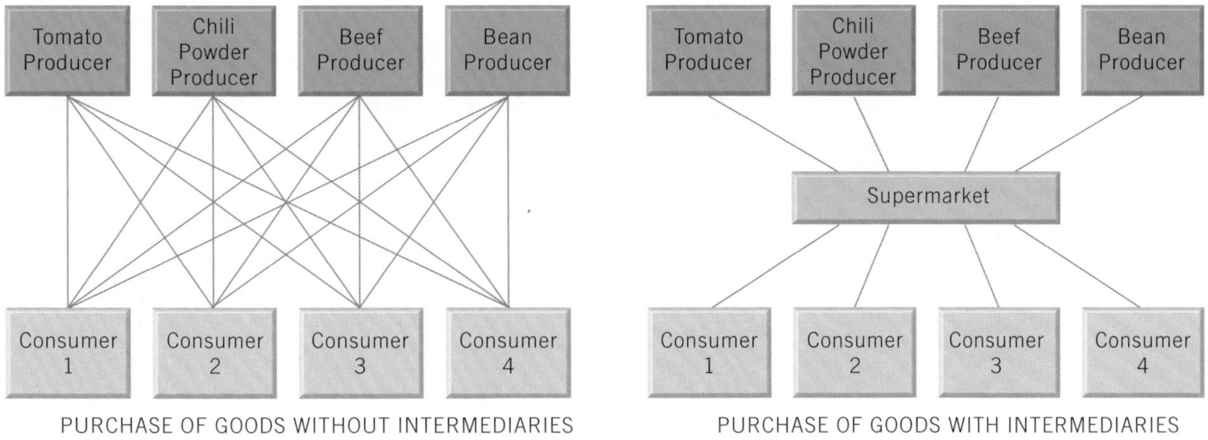

Figure 14.3 Advantages of intermediaries.

Distribution Strategies

intensive distribution
A distribution strategy in which a product is distributed in nearly every possible outlet, using many channels and channel members.

exclusive distribution
A distribution strategy in which a product's distribution is limited to only one wholesaler or retailer in a given geographic area.

selective distribution
A distribution strategy that falls between intensive and exclusive distribution, calling for the use of a limited number of outlets for a product.

The choice of distribution strategy determines the amount of market exposure the product gets and the cost of that exposure. **Intensive distribution** occurs when a product is distributed through as many channels and channel members as possible. For example, as Figure 14.4 shows, Caramilk bars flood the market through all suitable outlets. Intensive distribution is normally used for low-cost consumer goods such as candy and magazines. In contrast, **exclusive distribution** occurs when a manufacturer grants the exclusive right to distribute or sell a product to one wholesaler or retailer in a given geographic area. For example, Jaguar automobiles are sold by only a single dealer servicing a large metropolitan area. **Selective distribution** falls between intensive and exclusive distribution. A company that uses this strategy selects only wholesalers and retailers who will give special attention to the product in terms of sales efforts, display position, etc. This method is usually embraced by companies like Black & Decker, whose product lines do not require intense market exposure to increase sales.

Channel Conflict and Channel Leadership

channel conflict
Conflict arising when the members of a distribution channel disagree over the roles they should play or the rewards they should receive.

channel captain
The channel member that is the most powerful in determining the roles and rewards of organizations involved in a given channel of distribution.

Channel conflict occurs when members of the distribution channel disagree over the roles they should play or the rewards they should receive. John Deere, for example, would no doubt object if its dealers began distributing Russian and Japanese tractors. Channel conflict may also arise if one member has more power than the others or is viewed as receiving preferential treatment. Such conflicts defeat the purpose of the system by disrupting the flow of goods to their destinations. Usually, one channel member—the **channel captain**—is the most powerful in determining the roles and rewards of other members. The channel captain might be a manufacturer, or it might be a large retailer like Wal-Mart that generates large sales volumes.

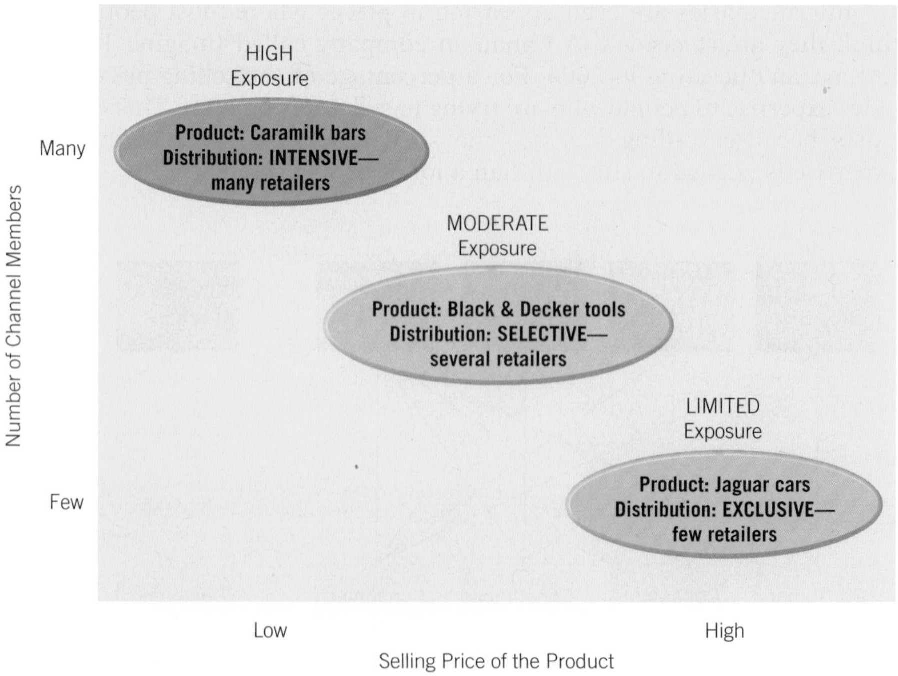

Figure 14.4 Amounts of market exposure from the three kinds of distribution.

To overcome the problems posed by channel conflict, the **vertical marketing system (VMS)** has emerged. In a VMS, separate businesses join to form a unified distribution channel, with one member coordinating the activities of the whole channel. In a *corporate VMS*, all stages in the channel are under single ownership. The Limited, for example, owns both the production facilities that manufacture its apparel and the retail stores that sell it. In a *contractual VMS*, channel members sign contracts agreeing to specific duties and rewards. The Independent Grocers' Alliance (IGA), for example, consists of independent retail grocers joined with a wholesaler who contractually leads—but does not own—the VMS. Most franchises are contractual VMSs.

vertical marketing system (VMS) A system in which there is a high degree of coordination among all the units in the distribution channel so that a product moves efficiently from manufacturer to consumer.

WHOLESALING

4 Explain the differences among *retailers*, *wholesalers*, and *agents/brokers*.

Now that you know something about distribution channels, we can consider more closely the role of intermediaries. Wholesalers, for example, provide a variety of services to buyers of products for resale or business use. In addition to storing and providing an assortment of products, some wholesalers offer delivery, credit, and product information.

Most wholesalers are independent operations that sell various consumer or business goods produced by a variety of manufacturers. They buy products from manufacturers and sell them to other businesses. They own the goods that they resell and usually provide storage and delivery. They provide additional value-adding services for customers, including credit, marketing advice, and merchandising services, such as marking prices and setting up displays.

Unlike wholesalers, agents and brokers do not own their merchandise. Rather, they serve as sales and merchandising arms for producers or sellers who do not have their own sales forces. The value of agents and brokers lies in their knowledge of markets and their merchandising expertise. They show sale items to potential buyers and, for retail stores, they provide such services as shelf and display merchandising and advertising layout. They remove open, torn, or dirty packages, arrange products neatly, and generally keep goods attractively displayed. Many supermarket products are handled through brokers.

RETAILING

5 Identify the different types of *retail stores* and the activities of *e-intermediaries*.

You probably have had little contact with wholesalers, but like most Canadians, you buy nearly all the goods and services you consume from retailers. Most retailers are small operations, often consisting of just the owners and part-time help. But there are some very large retailers, and these account for billions dollars of sales each year. Wal-Mart is the largest retailer in Canada.

Types of Retail Outlets

Canadian retail operations vary widely by type as well as size. We can classify them in various ways: by their pricing strategies, location, range of services, or range of product lines. Choosing the right types of retail outlets is a crucial aspect of every seller's distribution strategy. In this section, we describe retail stores by using three classifications: *product line retailers*, *bargain retailers*, and *convenience stores*.

Product Line Retailers

department stores
Large retail stores that offer a wide variety of high-quality items divided into specialized departments.

supermarkets
Large retail stores that offer a variety of food and food-related items divided into specialized departments.

specialty stores
Small retail stores that carry one line of related products.

Retailers featuring broad product lines include **department stores** like The Bay, which are organized into specialized departments: shoes, furniture, women's petite sizes, and so on. Stores are usually large, handle a wide range of goods, and offer a variety of services, such as credit plans and delivery. Similarly, **supermarkets** like Loblaw and Safeway are divided into departments of related products: food products, household products, and so forth. They stress low prices, self-service, and wide selection. In contrast, **specialty stores** are small stores that carry one line of related products. They serve specific market segments with full product lines in narrow product fields and often feature knowledgeable sales personnel. Sunglass Hut International stores, for example, have a deep selection of competitively priced sunglasses.

Bargain Retailers

bargain retailers
Retail outlets that emphasize low prices as a means of attracting consumers.

discount houses
Bargain retail stores that offer major items such as televisions and large appliances at discount prices.

Bargain retailers carry wide ranges of products and come in many forms. The first **discount houses** sold large numbers of items (such as TVs and other appliances) at substantial price reductions to cash-only customers. As name-brand items became more common, they offered better product assortments while still transacting cash-only sales in low-rent facilities. As they became more firmly entrenched, they began moving to better locations, improving their decor, and selling better-quality merchandise at higher prices. They also began offering a few department store services, such as credit plans and noncash sales.

catalogue showroom
A bargain retail store in which customers place orders for items described in a catalogue and pick up those items from an on-premises warehouse.

factory outlets
Bargain retail stores that are owned by the manufacturers whose products they sell.

wholesale clubs
Huge, membership-only, combined retail-wholesale operations that sell brand-name merchandise.

Catalogue showrooms mail catalogues to attract customers into showrooms to view display samples, place orders, and wait briefly while clerks retrieve orders from attached warehouses. **Factory outlets** are manufacturer-owned stores that avoid wholesalers and retailers by selling merchandise directly from factory to consumer. **Wholesale clubs** such as Costco offer large discounts on a wide range of brand-name merchandise to customers who pay annual membership fees.

Convenience Stores

convenience stores
Retail stores that offer high accessibility, extended hours, and fast service on selected items.

Neighbourhood food retailers, such as 7-Eleven and Circle K stores, are **convenience store** chains, which offer ease of purchase: They stress easily accessible locations, extended store hours, and speedy service. They differ from most bargain retailers in that they do not feature low prices. Like bargain retailers, they control prices by keeping in-store service to a minimum.

Nonstore Retailing

Not all goods and services are sold in stores. In fact, some of the nation's largest retailers sell all or most of their products without bricks-and-mortar stores. For example, certain types of consumer goods—soft drinks, candy, and cigarettes—lend themselves to distribution in vending machines. However, vending machine sales still represent only a small proportion of all retail sales. Another kind of nonstore retailing is described in the Entrepreneurship & New Ventures box.

direct-response retailing
A type of retailing in which firms make direct contact with customers both to inform them about products and to receive sales orders.

direct selling
Form of non-store retailing typified by door-to-door sales.

Nonstore retailing also includes **direct-response retailing**, in which firms contact customers directly to inform them about products and to receive sales orders. The oldest form of retailing, **direct selling**, is still used by companies like Avon and Tupperware that sell door-to-door or through home-selling parties. The Fuller Brush Company was started in 1906 by Arthur Fuller, a self-described "country bumpkin" from Nova Scotia. The company used to be well known in door-to-door selling, but sweeping changes in North American society—women leaving the home to work,

ENTREPRENEURSHIP AND NEW VENTURES

There Must Be a Better Way to Distribute Confusion, Demand, and Dysfunction

Bolivian Marcelo Claure started his distribution career selling cellphones out of the trunk of his car when he was just 23. Today his Brightstar Corp. is a dominant distributor in Latin America, with 700 employees working at 21 facilities in 16 countries and annual revenues topping $1.2 billion. This constant-talking empire builder thinks big and plays for high stakes, meets rival distributors head on, and is always looking for new opportunities and an innovative advantage for future business growth.

As an entrepreneur, Claure sees opportunities where others perceive only obstacles. After deciding to go into global distribution, for example, he and three friends chose Latin America as the ideal starting place because, as Claure says, it has three perfect characteristics for would-be entrepreneurs—*confusion, demand,* and *dysfunction. Confusion* stems from the region's many countries with various currencies, trade restrictions, dissimilar government regulations, import tariffs, and volatile economic conditions. This mix of problems poses a headache for foreign manufacturers who would willingly pay a middleman to handle the confusion. *Demand* is on the rise with the region's rapidly growing population and their fondness for phones. *Dysfunction* stems from the limited availability of telephone landlines—only 17 percent of the Latin American people have access—so affordable satellite service can capture the untapped phone market. They eagerly set up for business where other companies wouldn't.

Brightstar's operations started by distributing lacklustre Ericsson cellphones that for years held only a tiny share of market in the region. Phone companies complained about the phone's ugly appearance and high price, which Brightstar couldn't control. All Brightstar controlled was shipping, so newcomer Claure took a different tack, saying, "What if we make Ericsson the easiest brand to do business with?" He promised irresistible shipping, with direct delivery to phone carriers—Brightstar handled all the complications of importing the phones and getting them through customs—no minimum order, longer than 30 days to pay, and immediate delivery. Ericsson's market share doubled within a year. "After a while," says Claure, "the carriers got dependent on us. They knew that if they needed a phone tomorrow, they could get one from Brightstar."

Claure is quick to notice what competitors are doing wrong and then he capitalizes on it. An example is Brightstar's first encounter with Motorola, using a manoeuvre that didn't endear them to the giant cellphone manufacturer. After discovering that Motorola was selling phones cheaper to Bell Canada than in the United States, Marcelo talked Bell Canada into buying extra phones that were, in turn, sold to Brightstar, who resold them at bargain prices to U.S. retailers. While undercutting Motorola's U.S. prices, Brightstar made millions of sales for weeks and, says Claure, "We managed to make Motorola miserable." After further thought, however, Motorola came to Claure's way of thinking: By using Brightstar's strength in distributing, Motorola is freed up for what it does best—making phones. Having learned that lesson, Motorola signed Brightstar as its main Latin America distributor after Ericsson's contract with Brightstar expired in 2000. By 2003, Motorola's market share had jumped from 16 percent to 33 percent, tying it for leadership with Nokia, whose share fell from 60 percent during the same period. When asked how it all happens, the answer is simple: "The secret was," Claure says, "that I changed the rules of distribution."

mass retailing, and the globalization of business—caused the company to fall on hard times. Two of its most famous salesmen were the Reverend Billy Graham and disc jockey Dick Clark.

Mail order (or catalogue marketing) is a popular form of direct-response retailing. So is **telemarketing**—the use of the telephone to sell directly. It is growing rapidly in Canada and Great Britain, but suffered a downturn in the United States with recent state and national do-not-call registries. **E-intermediaries** are internet-based channel members who perform one or both of the following functions: (1) they collect information about sellers and present it to consumers, or (2) they help deliver internet products to buyers. We will examine three types of e-intermediaries: *syndicated sellers, shopping agents,* and *e-retailers.*

mail order (catalogue marketing) A form of nonstore retailing in which customers place orders for merchandise shown in catalogues and receive their orders via mail.

telemarketing Use of the telephone to sell directly to consumers.

e-intermediaries Internet-based distribution-channel members that collect information about sellers and present it in convenient form to consumers and/or help deliver internet products to consumers.

Syndicated Sellers

syndicated selling
Occurs when a website offers other websites a commission for referring customers.

Syndicated selling occurs when one website offers another a commission for referring customers. With nearly 20 million users each month, Expedia.com is the world's leading online travel service. Expedia's webpage shows a list of car rental companies, such as Dollar Rent A Car. When Expedia customers click on the Dollar banner for a car rental, they are transferred from the Expedia site to the Dollar site. Dollar pays Expedia a fee for each booking that comes through this channel. Although the new intermediary increases the cost of Dollar's supply chain, it adds value for customers. Travellers avoid unnecessary cyberspace searches and are efficiently guided to a car-rental agency.[10]

Shopping Agents

shopping agent (e-agent)
A type of intermediary that helps internet consumers by gathering and sorting information they need to make purchases.

Shopping agents (e-agents) help internet consumers by gathering and sorting information. Although they don't take possession of products, they know which websites and stores to visit, give accurate comparison prices, identify product features, and help consumers complete transactions by presenting information in a usable format—all in a matter of seconds. PriceScan.com is among the better known cyber-shopping agents, but there are many others as well. Since e-agents have become so plentiful, unsure shoppers are turning to rating sites, such as eSmarts.com, that evaluate and compare e-agents.

Ecommerce intermediaries called *business-to-business (B2B) brokers* have also emerged for business customers. The pricing process between B2B buyers and sellers of commodities can be outsourced, for example, to an internet company like FreeMarkets Inc. (which recently merged with Ariba). As a pricing broker, FreeMarkets links any large-volume buyer with potential suppliers that bid to become the supplier for the industrial customer. Client companies (the commodity buyers), such as Quaker Oats or Emerson Electric, pay FreeMarkets a fixed annual subscription fee and receive networking into FreeMarkets's auction headquarters, where real-time bids come in from suppliers at remote locations. The website (www.freemarkets.com) provides up-to-date information until the bidding ends with the low-price supplier. In conducting the pricing transactions electronically, FreeMarkets doesn't take possession of any products. Rather, it brings together timely information and links businesses to one another.[11]

Electronic Retailing

electronic retailing
Nonstore retailing in which information about the seller's products and services is connected to consumers' computers, allowing consumers to receive the information and purchase the products in the home.

Electronic retailing (also called *etailing*) allows consumers to shop from home using the internet. Sears Canada, one of the most popular etailers in Canada, offers more than 10 000 items for sale on its website.[12] Etailing is made possible by communications networks that let sellers post product information on consumers' PCs. Etailing sales are expected to increase sharply during the next few years as more people shop online with their personal computers. Electronic retailing is evident in *electronic catalogues*, *internet-based stores*, *electronic storefronts and cybermalls*, and *interactive and video marketing*.

e-catalogues
Nonstore retailing that uses the internet to display products and services for both retail shoppers and business customers.

Electronic catalogues. **E-catalogues** use the internet to display products for both retail and business customers. Using electronic displays (instead of traditional mail catalogues), firms give millions of users instant access to pages of product information. The seller avoids mail-distribution and printing costs, and once an online catalogue is in place, there is little cost in maintaining and accessing it. Recognizing these advantages, about 85 percent of all catalogues are now on the internet, with sales via websites accounting for 10 percent of all catalogue sales. The top 10 consumer e-catalogues include JCPenney (number 1), Fingerhut (number 3), L.L. Bean (number 7), and Victoria's Secret (number 8). Top B2B e-catalogues include Dell Computer (number 1) and Office Depot (number 5).[13]

Internet-Based Stores. Use of the internet to interact with customers—to inform, sell to, and distribute to them—is growing rapidly. For example, Ice.com, a Montreal-based company, sells mid- and low-priced jewellery over the internet. Almost all of the company's customers are in the United States. The company is profitable because margins on jewellery are higher than they are for books or electronics. Jewellery fits well in the ecommerce environment because it is high in value but small in size. This makes it easy to ship products to customers. Most of the items that Ice.com sells cost between $50 and $750. More than two-thirds of the Ice.com shoppers are female.[14]

In 2006, Canadian consumers spent $8.3 billion while shopping online, and sales are expected to increase to $16 billion by 2009. But as large as these numbers are, they still represent only a small proportion of the $762 billion dollars that consumers spent on goods and services in 2005.[15] Ecommerce is still in its infancy and there is a lot of room for growth. Using the internet to do *comparison shopping* is also increasing rapidly. Internet sites like Ask Jeeves Inc., Google Inc., and Yahoo! Inc. allow consumers to compare prices and products before making a purchase.

Electronic Storefronts and Cybermalls. Today, a seller's website is an **electronic storefront** (or *virtual storefront*) from which consumers collect information about products and buying opportunities, place orders, and pay for purchases. Producers of large product lines, such as Dell Computer, dedicate storefronts to their own product lines. Other sites, such as CDNOW, which offers CDs and audio and videotapes, are category sellers whose storefronts feature products from many manufacturers.

electronic storefront
A seller's website in which consumers collect information about products and buying opportunities, place sales orders, and pay for their purchases.

Search engines like Yahoo! serve as **cybermalls**: collections of virtual storefronts representing diverse products. After entering a cybermall, shoppers can navigate by choosing from a list of stores (L.L. Bean or Lands' End), product listings (computers or MP3 players), or departments (apparel or bath/beauty). When your virtual shopping cart is full, you check out and pay your bill. The value-added properties of cybermalls are obvious: speed, convenience, 24-hour access, and efficient searching.

cybermalls
Collections of virtual storefronts representing diverse products.

Interactive and Video Marketing. Today, both retail and B2B customers interact with multimedia sites using voice, graphics, animation, film clips, and access to live human advice. One good example of **interactive marketing** is LivePerson.com, a leading provider of real-time sales and customer service for over 3000 websites. When customers log on to the sites of

interactive marketing
Selling products and services by allowing customers to interact with multimedia websites using voice, graphics, animation, film clips, and access to live human advice.

Veteran QVC host Bob Bowersox is getting ready to offer bedding made by a company called Northern Lights, which distributes regularly through the TV home shopping channel. Northern Lights, which sells sheets, pillows, and other bedding products, markets through such electronic retailing outlets as eBay and Shopping.com as well as QVC.

Toyota, Earthlink, Hewlett Packard, Verizon, Microsoft—all of which are LivePerson clients—they can enter a live chat room where a service operator initiates a secure one-on-one text chat. Questions and answers go back and forth to help customers get answers to specific questions before deciding on a product. Another form of interaction is the so-called banner ad that changes as the user's mouse moves about the page, revealing new drop-down, check, and search boxes.

video marketing
Selling to consumers by showing products on television that consumers can buy by telephone or mail.

Video marketing, a long-established form of interactive marketing, lets viewers shop at home from TV screens by phoning in or emailing orders. Most cable systems offer video marketing through home-shopping channels that display and demonstrate products and allow viewers to phone in or email orders. One U.S. network, QVC, also operates in the United Kingdom, Germany, Mexico, and South America.

PHYSICAL DISTRIBUTION

6 Define *physical distribution* and describe the major activities in *warehousing* operations.

physical distribution
Those activities needed to move a product from the manufacturer to the end consumer.

Physical distribution refers to the activities needed to move products efficiently from manufacturer to consumer. The goals of physical distribution are to keep customers satisfied, to make goods available when and where consumers want them, and to keep costs low. Thus, physical distribution includes *warehousing* and *transporting operations*, as well as distribution for e-customers.

Warehousing Operations

warehousing
That part of the distribution process concerned with storing goods.

private warehouse
A warehouse owned and used by just one company.

public warehouse
An independently owned and operated warehouse that stores the goods of many firms.

Storing or **warehousing** products is a major function of distribution management. There are two basic types of warehouses: *private* and *public*. Within these categories, we can further divide warehouses according to their use as *storage warehouses* or as *distribution centres*. **Private warehouses** are owned by and provide storage for just one company, be it a manufacturer, a wholesaler, or a retailer. Most are used by large firms that deal in mass quantities and need storage regularly. **Public warehouses** are independently owned and operated. Companies that use these warehouses pay for the actual space used. Public warehouses are popular with firms that need such storage only during peak business periods. They are also used by manufacturers who want to maintain stock in numerous locations to get their products to many markets quickly.

Transportation Operations

7 Compare the five basic forms of *transportation* and explain how distribution can be used as a marketing strategy.

Because the highest cost faced by many companies is that of physically moving a product, cost is a major consideration in choosing transportation methods. But firms must also consider other factors: the nature of the product, the distance it must travel, the speed with which it must be received, and customer wants and needs.

Transportation Modes

The major transportation modes are trucks, railroads, planes, water carriers, and pipelines. Differences in cost are most directly related to delivery speed.

Trucks. The advantages of trucks include flexibility, fast service, and dependability. Nearly all sections of Canada, except the far north, can be reached by truck. Trucks are a particularly good choice for short-distance distribution and more expensive products. Large furniture and appliance retailers in major cities, for example, use trucks to shuttle merchandise between their stores and to make deliveries to customers. Trucks can, however, be delayed by bad weather. They also are limited in the volume they can carry in a single load.

Planes. Air is the fastest available transportation mode. In Canada's far north, it may be the only available transportation. Other advantages include greatly reduced costs in packing, handling, unpacking, and final preparations necessary for sale to the consumer. Also, inventory carrying costs can be reduced by eliminating the need to store certain commodities. Fresh fish, for example, can be flown to restaurants each day, avoiding the risk of spoilage that comes with packaging and storing a supply of fish. However, air freight is the most expensive form of transportation. In recent years, a whole new industry has evolved to meet the customer's need to receive important business papers and supplies "overnight."

Railroads. Railroads have been the backbone of our transportation system since the late 1800s. Until the 1960s, when trucking firms lowered their rates and attracted many customers, railroads were fairly profitable. They are now used primarily to transport heavy, bulky items such as cars, steel, and coal.

Water carriers. Of all the transportation modes, water transportation is the least expensive, but slowest, way to ship. Boats and barges are mainly used for extremely heavy, bulky materials and products (like sand, gravel, oil, and steel) for which transit times are unimportant. The St. Lawrence Seaway is a vital link in Canada's water transportation system, and water transportation is particularly important in Canada's far north, where barges deliver commodities like fuel oil to various isolated hamlets along the western edge of Hudson's Bay during the summer months. Northern Transportation Company Ltd. moves freight on the Athabasca River because of demand created by the oilsands projects in Northern Alberta.[16]

Pipelines. Like water transportation, pipelines are slow in terms of overall delivery time. They are also completely inflexible, but they do provide a constant flow of the product and are unaffected by weather conditions. Traditionally, this delivery system has transported liquids and gases. Lack of adaptability to other products and limited routes make pipelines a relatively unimportant transportation method for most industries.

A container train crosses the Salmon River Bridge in New Brunswick.

intermodal transportation
The combined use of different modes of transportation.

Intermodal Transportation. **Intermodal transportation**—the combined use of different modes of transportation—has come into widespread use. For example, shipping by a combination of truck and rail ("piggy-back"), water and rail ("fishy-back"), or air and rail ("birdy-back") has improved flexibility and reduced costs.

Physical Distribution and E-Customer Satisfaction

order fulfillment
All activities involved in completing a sales transaction, beginning with making the sale and ending with on-time delivery to the customer.

New ecommerce companies often focus on sales, only to discover that delays in after-sale distribution cause customer dissatisfaction. Any delay in physical distribution is a breakdown in fulfillment. **Order fulfillment** begins when the sale is made: It involves getting the product to each customer in good condition and on time. But the volume of a firm's transactions can be huge, and fulfillment performance—in terms of timing, content, and terms of payment—has been a source of irritation to many ebusiness customers.

To improve on-time deliveries, many businesses maintain distribution centres and ship from their own warehouses. Other etailers, however, outsource order filling to distribution specialists, such as the giant UPS e-logistics and the much smaller CaseStack, to gain reliable performance. Both CaseStack and UPS process orders, ship goods, provide information about product availability and order status, and handle returns. To perform these tasks, the client's computer system must be networked with that of the distribution specialist.

Physical Distribution as a Marketing Strategy

Distribution is an increasingly important way of competing for sales. Instead of just offering advantages in product features and quality, price, and promotion, many firms have turned to distribution as a cornerstone of business strategy. This approach means assessing and improving the entire stream of activities—wholesaling, warehousing, and transportation—involved in getting products to customers.

Consider, for example, the distribution system of National Semiconductor, one of the world's largest computer-chip makers. Finished microchips are produced in plants around the world and shipped to customers, such as IBM, Toshiba, and Compaq, which also run factories around the globe. Chips originally sat waiting at one location after another—on factory floors, at customs, in distributors' facilities, and in customers' warehouses. Typically, they travelled 20 000 different routes on as many as 12 airlines and spent time in 10 warehouses before reaching customers. National has streamlined the system by shutting down six warehouses and now airfreights chips worldwide from a single centre in Singapore. Every activity—storage, sorting, and shipping—is run by FedEx. By outsourcing the activities, National's distribution costs have fallen, delivery times have been reduced by half, and sales have increased.

Summary of Learning Objectives

1. Identify the various *pricing objectives* that govern pricing decisions and describe the price-setting tools used in making these decisions. (1) *Pricing to maximize profits:* If prices are too low, the company will probably sell many product units but miss the chance to make additional profits on each one. If prices are set too high, it will make a large profit on each unit but will sell fewer units. (2) *Market share objectives:* Many companies are willing to accept minimal profits, even losses, to get buyers to try products. Sometimes, neither profit maximizing nor market share is the best objective. During difficult economic times, loss containment and survival may be the main objectives. Price-setting tools include (1) *Cost-oriented pricing,* which considers both the firm's desire to make a profit and need to cover production costs. Managers price products by calculating the cost of making them available to shoppers (including rent, wages, and manufacturer's cost); and (2) *Break-even analysis,* which assesses total costs versus revenues for various sales volumes. It shows, at any particular sales price, the financial result—the amount of loss or profit—for each possible sales volume.
2. Discuss *pricing strategies* and *tactics* for existing and new products. There are three options for *pricing existing products:* (1) *pricing above the market,* (2) *pricing below the market,* and (3) *pricing at or near market prices.* Companies *pricing new products* must often choose between two pricing policy options: (1) *price skimming*—setting an initially high price to cover costs and generate a profit, or (2) *penetration pricing*—setting an initially low price to establish a new product in the market. *Pricing tactics* include *price lining* (offering all items in certain categories at a limited number of prices), *psychological pricing* (appealing to buyers' perceptions of relative prices), and *discounting* (reducing prices to stimulate sales).
3. Explain the *distribution mix,* the different *channels of distribution,* and different *distribution strategies.* In selecting a *distribution mix,* a firm may use all or any of eight distribution channels. The first four are aimed at getting products to consumers, the fifth is for consumers or business customers, and the last three are aimed at getting products to business customers. Channel 1 involves direct sales to consumers. Channel 2 includes a *retailer.* Channel 3 involves both a retailer and a *wholesaler,* and Channel 4 includes an *agent* or *broker* who enters the system before the wholesaler and retailer. Channel 5 includes only an agent between the producer and the customer. Channel 6, which is used extensively for ecommerce, involves a direct sale to an industrial user. Channel 7, which is used infrequently, entails selling to business users through wholesalers. Channel 8 includes retail superstores that get products from producers or wholesalers (or both) for reselling to business customers. *Distribution strategies* include *intensive, exclusive,* and *selective distribution,* which differ in the number of products and channel members involved and in the amount of service performed in the channel.
4. Explain the differences among *retailers, wholesalers,* and *agents/brokers. Wholesalers* sell products to other businesses, which resell them to final consumers. *Retailers* sell products directly to consumers. *Agents and brokers* are independent individuals who represent many companies and serve as sales and merchandising arms of producers that don't have sales forces.
5. Identify the different types of *retail stores* and the activities of *e-intermediaries.* Retail operations fall under two classifications: (1) *product line retailers* include department stores, supermarkets, and specialty stores; and (2) *bargain retailers* include discount houses, catalogue showrooms, factory outlets, warehouse clubs, and convenience stores. Important forms of *nonstore retailing* include direct-response retailing, mail order, telemarketing, direct selling, electronic retailing, e-catalogues, electronic storefronts, and cybermalls. *E-intermediaries* are internet-based channel members who perform one or both of two functions: (1) they collect information about sellers and present it to consumers; (2) they help deliver internet products. There are three types of e-intermediaries: (1) *syndicated selling* occurs when a website offers other websites a commission for referring customers. (2) *shopping agents* (or *e-agents*) help internet consumers by gathering and sorting information (such as comparison prices and product features) for making purchases. (3) *business-to-business brokers* are ecommerce intermediaries for business customers. They may provide up-to-date market information and price and product data.
6. Define *physical distribution* and describe the major activities in *warehousing* operations. *Physical distribution* refers to the activities needed to move products from manufacturer to consumer. These activities make goods available when and where consumers want them, keep costs low, and provide customer services. They include *warehousing,* or the storage of goods. *Private warehouses*

are owned and used by a single manufacturer, wholesaler, or retailer. *Public warehouses* are independently owned and operated and permit companies to rent only the space they need. Facilities can be further divided according to their uses: *Storage warehouses* provide storage for extended periods. *Distribution centres* store products whose market demand is constant and high. Retail chains, wholesalers, and manufacturers use them to break down large quantities of merchandise into the smaller quantities that stores or customers demand.

7. Compare the five basic forms of *transportation* and explain how distribution can be used as a marketing strategy. There are five different modes of transportation, and differences in cost are most directly related to delivery speed. (1) *Trucks:* The advantages of trucks include flexibility, fast service, and dependability. (2) *Railroads:* Railroads are now used primarily to transport heavy, bulky items such as cars and steel. Railroad services now include faster delivery and piggyback service, in which truck trailers are placed on railcars. (3) *Planes:* Air is the fastest available mode of transportation and also boasts lower costs in handling and packing and unpacking. However, air freight is the most expensive form of transportation. (4) *Water carriers:* Water is the least expensive and the slowest. (5) *Pipelines:* Used to transport liquids and gases, pipelines are slow and inflexible but do provide a constant flow of products and are unaffected by weather. Many firms regard distribution as a cornerstone of business strategy. This approach means assessing and streamlining the entire range of activities involved in getting products to customers. One approach to streamlining is the use of *hubs:* central distribution outlets that control all or most of a firm's distribution activities.

QUESTIONS AND EXERCISES

Questions for Analysis

1. How do cost-oriented pricing and break-even analysis help managers measure the potential impact of prices?
2. From the manufacturer's point of view, what are the advantages and disadvantages of using intermediaries to distribute products? From the end-user's point of view?
3. In what ways do the four channels of distribution used only for consumer products differ from the channels used only for industrial products?
4. Explain how the activities of e-agents (internet shopping agents) or brokers differ from those of traditional agents/brokers.
5. A small publisher selling to book distributors has fixed operating costs of $600 000 each year and variable costs of $3 per book. How many books must the firm sell to break even if the selling price is $6? If the company expects to sell 50 000 books next year and decides on a 40 percent markup, what will the selling price be?
6. Novelties Ltd. produces miniature Canadian flag decals. The fixed costs for their latest project are $5000. The variable costs are $0.70/flag, and the company should be able to sell them for $2 apiece. How many flags must Novelties Ltd. sell to break even? How many flags must the company sell to make a profit of $2000? If the maximum number of flags the company can sell is 5000, should it get involved in this project?
7. Consider the various kinds of nonstore retailing. Give examples of two products that typify the kinds of products sold to at-home shoppers through each form of nonstore retailing. Are different products best suited to each form of nonstore retailing? Explain.
8. A retailer buys a product from a manufacturer for $25 and sells it for $45. What is the markup percentage? Explain what the term "markup percentage" means.

Application Exercises

9. Select a product with which you are familiar and analyze various possible pricing objectives for it. What information would you want to have if you were to adopt a profit-maximizing objective? A market share objective?
10. Interview the manager of a local manufacturing firm. Identify the firm's distribution strategy and the channels of distribution that it uses. Where applicable, describe the types of wholesalers or retail stores used to distribute the firm's products.

BUILDING YOUR BUSINESS SKILLS

Are You Sold on the Net?

Goal

To encourage students to consider the value of online retailing as an element in a company's distribution system.

Situation

As the distribution manager of a privately owned clothing manufacturer specializing in camping gear and outdoor clothing, you are convinced that your product line is perfect for online distribution. However, the owner of the company is reluctant to expand distribution from a successful network of retail stores and a catalogue operation. Your challenge is to convince the boss that retailing via the internet can boost sales.

Method

Step 1 Join together with four or five classmates to research the advantages and disadvantages of an online distribution system for your company. Among the factors to consider are the following:

- The likelihood that target consumers are internet shoppers. Camping gear is generally purchased by young, affluent consumers who are comfortable with the web.
- The industry trend to online distribution. Are similar companies doing it? Have they been successful?
- The opportunity to expand inventory without increasing the cost of retail space or catalogue production and mailing charges.
- The opportunity to have a store that never closes.
- The lack of trust many people have about doing business on the web. Many consumers are reluctant to provide credit card data over the web.
- The difficulty that electronic shoppers have in finding a website when they do not know the store's name.
- The frustration and waiting time involved in web searches.
- The certainty that the site will not reach consumers who do not use computers or who are uncomfortable with the web.

Step 2 Based on your findings, write a persuasive memo to the company's owner stating your position about expanding to an online distribution system. Include information that will counter expected objections.

Follow-Up Questions

1. What place does online distribution have in the distribution network of this company?
2. In your view, is online distribution the wave of the future? Is it likely to increase in importance as a distribution system for apparel companies? Why or why not?

EXERCISING YOUR ETHICS: TEAM EXERCISE

The Chain of Responsibility

The Situation

Because several stages are involved when distribution chains move products from supply sources to end consumers, the process offers ample opportunity for ethical issues to arise. This exercise encourages you to examine some of the ethical issues that can emerge during transactions among suppliers and customers.

The Dilemma

A customer bought an expensive wedding gift at a local store and asked that it be shipped to the bride in another province. Several weeks after the wedding, the customer contacted the bride, who had not confirmed the arrival of the gift. It hadn't arrived. Charging that the merchandise had not been delivered, the customer requested a refund from the retailer. The store manager uncovered the following facts:

- All shipments from the store are handled by a well-known national delivery firm.
- The delivery firm verified that the package had been delivered to the designated address two days after the sale.
- Normally, the delivery firm does not obtain recipient signatures; deliveries are made to the address of record, regardless of the name on the package.

The gift giver argued that even though the package had been delivered to the right address, it had not been delivered to the named recipient. It turns out that, unbeknownst to the gift giver, the bride had moved. It stood to reason, then, that the gift was in the

▶▶▶

hands of the new occupant at the bride's former address. The manager informed the gift giver that the store had fulfilled its obligation. The cause of the problem, she explained, was the incorrect address given by the customer. She refused to refund the customer's money and suggested that the customer might want to recover the gift by contacting the stranger who received it at the bride's old address.

Team Activity

Assemble a group of four students and assign each group member to one of the following roles:

- Customer (the person who had originally purchased the gift)
- Employee (of the store where the gift was purchased)
- Bride (the person who was supposed to receive the gift)
- Customer Service Manager (of the delivery company)

Action Steps

1. Before discussing the situation with your group, and from the perspective of your assigned role, do you think there are any ethical issues in this situation? If so, write them down.
2. Before discussing the situation with your group, and from the perspective of your assigned role, decide how this dispute should be resolved.
3. Together with your group, share the ethical issues that were identified. What responsibilities does each party—the customer, the store, and the delivery company—have in this situation?
4. What does your group recommend be done to resolve this dispute? What are the advantages and disadvantages of your recommendations?

BUSINESS CASE 14

Changes in Distribution Channels: Downloading Music from the Internet

An important new channel of distribution developed during the last decade: the internet. To the delight of consumers, and the dismay of music and movie industry people, this new channel of distribution allowed consumers to download—for free—a wide variety of music and movies. All of this was made possible by something called file-sharing. As often happens, new technology made this revolution possible. How it will all end is anybody's guess, but here is the story as it has unfolded so far.

For many years, music was distributed through record stores. Consumers visited the stores, looked over their merchandise, and then decided what to buy. Then came internet stores, many of them offering discount prices. You could go to a site like www.cdhitlist.com, which offered thousands of titles among CDs, cassettes, and VHS/DVD movies, search the lists, place orders electronically or over the phone, and then receive your music or movie by mail.

Then came an online music service called Napster. You first went to the website to obtain Napster software, which you could download (for free) onto your computer. The software found albums that you had stored (in MP3 format) on your hard disk and published that information on Napster's website, along with similar lists from millions of other users. Then you could start trading with anyone else who was live on the internet at the same time. It is easy to see why Napster was so popular: it was accessible 24 hours per day, you didn't have to leave your home to shop, and it was free.

Not surprisingly, recording industry executives were not impressed with this new channel of distribution. They argued that file-sharing denied music artists the royalties they were due. If consumers didn't pay for an album, how could the costs of production be recovered? And if the market price of an album was essentially zero, record stores could not hope to stay in business. The threat from Napster was seen as so great that a recording industry trade organization, the Recording Industry Association of America (RIAA), decided to prosecute. Napster proclaimed its innocence, arguing that it did nothing more than supply software. It neither took possession of albums nor did it buy or sell them. The trading of albums occurred solely among individuals on the open market. The courts didn't buy this argument, and Napster was shut down for copyright infringement. To the recording industry's dismay, the victory was short-lived, as other file-sharing services like Morpheus, KaZaA, and Grokster popped up.

As part of their overall strategy to combat illegal downloading, the recording industry launched two online music services—MusicNet and Pressplay. If you use MusicNet, you pay $9.95 a month and get 100 downloads (but you can't copy them and the deal expires at the end of the month). If you use Pressplay, you get 100 downloads for $24.95 per month (and the right to burn 20 tracks to a CD). Other similar services are offered by iTunes (the industry leader), Microsoft, Yahoo!, Ruckus, Cdigix, and a rejuvenated Napster. To date, consumer demand for these services is much weaker than the demand for free downloading. A study by NPD Group Inc. revealed that in 2004, 243 million songs were downloaded through services such as Grokster, while only 26 million songs were purchased from online stores.

The recording industry also filed lawsuits against Grokster and StreamCast Networks (the makers of Morpheus). The defendants initially succeeded in getting a ruling from a U.S. appeals court that what they were doing was not illegal, but in 2005, the U.S. Supreme Court ruled that the entertainment industry could sue companies like Grokster and Morpheus. A few months later, Grokster agreed to shut down and pay $50 million to settle piracy complaints by the music industry. Grokster then announced plans to launch a legal service called 3G, which will require customers to pay a fee to get access to songs that can be downloaded.

Will this court ruling stop the illegal downloading of music and movies that has become so popular in recent years? Not likely. Unlike pioneer Napster (which had a central server that could be shut down), Grokster and Morpheus software is in the hands of millions of consumers who can still engage in illegal downloading. And more file-sharing software is becoming available all the time. Another problem for the entertainment industry is overseas programmers who offer new software to consumers. They are beyond the reach of the law in North America. A survey by Forrester Research found that 80 percent of consumers who were surveyed said they were not going to stop free downloading.

Companies should never underestimate how clever consumers can be when they are highly motivated to get something (like music) for free. Consider what has happened with Apple's iTunes software. There is an option on the software called "share my music," which allows users to make their library of songs available to any other computer running iTunes. The software allows people to *listen* to other peoples' collection of music, but not to *copy* it. Or so Apple thought when it developed the software. Now, some clever programmers have figured out a way to get around the restriction and they are using iTunes software to facilitate illegal downloading.

Some record industry executives are beginning to recognize that people who download music are big music fans, and that harassing them is not a good idea. Maybe it's better to capitalize on their activity. In 2006, an 8-minute video clip of a Jay-Z concert appeared on several music sharing sites. But Jay-Z was not upset because he had agreed to allow distribution of the video clip, which contains advertisements for Coca-Cola. Advertisers are now capitalizing on downloading instead of trying to stamp it out.

Questions for Discussion

1. Consider the traditional channels of distribution for music albums. Which channel elements are most affected by the presence of services like Grokster, KaZaA, and Morpheus? Explain how those elements are affected.
2. Why is the music industry so concerned about internet distribution? Are there any opportunities for the recording industry in internet distribution?
3. Develop arguments opposing the legality of services offered by Grokster and Morpheus. Then take the reverse position and develop an argument in favour of these services.
4. What types of ethical or social responsibility issues does file-sharing raise?
5. What other products, besides music albums, are the most likely candidates for distribution on the internet, now and in the future?

MYBUSINESSLAB

To improve your grade, visit the MyBusinessLab website at **www.pearsoned.ca/mybusinesslab**. This online homework and tutorial system allows you to test your understanding and generates a personalized study plan just for you. It provides you with study and practice tools directly related to this chapter's content. MyBusinessLab puts you in control of your own learning!

CRAFTING A BUSINESS PLAN

Part 4: Managing Marketing

Goal of the Exercise

So far, your business has an identity, you've described the factors that will affect your business, and you've examined your employees, the jobs they'll be performing, and the ways in which you can motivate them. Part 4 of the business plan project asks you to think about marketing's Four *Ps—product, price, place (distribution)*, and *promotion*—and how they apply to your business. You'll also examine how you might target your marketing toward a certain group of consumers.

Exercise Background: Part 4 of the Business Plan

In Part 1, you briefly described what your business will do. The first step in Part 4 of the plan is to more fully describe the product (good or service) you are planning to sell. Once you have a clear picture of the product, you'll need to describe how this product will "stand out" in the marketplace—that is, how will it differentiate itself from other products?

In Part 1, you also briefly described who your customers would be. The first step in Part 4 of the plan is to describe your ideal buyer, or target market, in more detail, listing their income level, educational level, lifestyle, age, and so forth. This part of the business plan project also asks you to discuss the price of your products, as well as where the buyer can find your product.

Finally, you'll examine how your business will get the attention and interest of the buyer through its *promotional mix*—advertising, personal selling, sales promotions, and publicity and public relations.

This part of the business plan encourages you to be creative. Have fun! Provide as many details as you possibly can, as this reflects an understanding of your product and your buyer. Marketing is all about finding a need and filling it. Does your product fill a need in the marketplace?

YOUR ASSIGNMENT mybusinesslab

Step 1

Open the saved *Business Plan* file you have been working on.

Step 2

For the purposes of this assignment, you will answer the following questions in "Part 4: Managing Marketing."

1. Describe your target market in terms of age, education level, income, and other demographic variables.

   Hint: Refer to Chapter 12 for more information on the aspects of target marketing and market segmentation that you may want to consider. Be as detailed as possible about who you think your customers will be.

2. Describe the features and benefits of your product or service.

   Hint: As you learned in Chapter 13, a product is a bundle of attributes—features and benefits. What features does your product have—what does it look like and what does it do? How will the product benefit the buyer?

3. How will you make your product stand out in the crowd?

   Hint: There are many ways to stand out in the crowd, such as a unique product, outstanding service, or a great location. What makes your great idea special? Does it fill an unmet need in the marketplace? How will you differentiate your product to make sure that it succeeds?

4. What pricing strategy will you choose for your product, and what are the reasons for this strategy?

   Hint: Refer to Chapter 14 for more information on pricing strategies and tactics. Since your business is new, so is the product. Therefore, you probably want to choose between price skimming and penetration pricing. Which will you choose, and why?

5. Where will customers find your product or service? (That is, what issues of the distribution mix should you consider?)

   Hint: If your business does not sell its product directly to consumers, what types of retail stores will sell your product? If your product will be sold to another business, which channel of distribution will you use? Refer to Chapter 14 for more information on aspects of distribution you may want to consider.

6. How will you advertise to your target market? Why have you chosen these forms of advertisement?

   Hint: Marketers use several different advertising media—specific communication devices for carrying a seller's message to potential customers—each having its advantages and drawbacks. Refer to Chapter 13 for a discussion of the types of advertising media you may wish to consider here.

7. What other methods of promotion will you use, and why?

   Hint: There's more to promotion than simple advertising. Other methods include personal selling, sales promotions, and publicity and public relations. Refer to the discussion of promotion in Chapter 14 for ideas on how to promote your product that go beyond just advertising.

Note: Once you have answered the questions, save your Word document. You'll be answering additional questions in later chapters.

CBC VIDEO CASE IV-1

Buying into Sexy

Girls in the 8- to 12-year-old age group (often called "tweens") are increasingly the target of advertisements that use sex to sell products. Companies are bombarding kids with sexy images to try to get them to buy their products. They are also using an "age compression" strategy—which involves pushing adult products on younger and younger kids. Chains like Miss Teen and LaSenza sell these products to tween girls, and Tween Brands, Inc., a U.S.-based specialty retailer, is expanding into Canada to challenge LaSenza. Advertisers say there is a demand for these products, but critics argue that advertisers have created the demand.

Kids may not get all the innuendo in the advertisements, but they have reached the conclusion that sexy is cool. Tweens see hundreds of sexual images each day, and this seems to be causing them to move out of childhood more quickly than children in earlier generations did. In short, tweens don't want to be kids, even though that's what they are.

Parents are put in a very tough spot when they are confronted with a daughter who wants to go to school wearing a suggestive outfit. Consider 12-year-old Amanda, who says she wants to look sexy. Where did she get these ideas? The answer is that young girls are bombarded with sexy images every day from pop stars, from magazines like *Tween*, from the internet, and from television. Entire chains are devoted to tween shoppers, and they sell racy clothing, makeup, and lingerie. This is a multi-billion-dollar industry.

When tween girls are asked *why* they buy sexy clothes, they give several reasons. They say, for example, that they like the attention they get when they wear such clothes. It's also a reaction against their parents, who don't like them wearing such clothes. Peer pressure is also important; if girls don't wear sexy clothes, they fear they won't be popular and will become isolated from their friends.

Parents are very concerned about the trend to sexy clothes among tween girls. Amanda's mother, for example, prefers that Amanda wear a baggy t-shirt and jeans, but she also wants her daughter to be popular, and wearing "cool" clothes is seen to facilitate popularity. Amanda's dad is uncomfortable with the clothes she wears. The parents of another girl, Alexia, are also concerned. Alexia's mother was raised in a strict Italian home where sexy clothing was forbidden. But, she says she wants her daughter to "fit in," so she usually doesn't say no to Alexia's clothes. Her father says he feels powerless because Alexia sees so many sexy images and then she imitates what she sees. Alexia is very unhappy when her parents don't agree with her choice of clothes.

Where do girls learn about sexy fashions? One place is dolls, where Bratz has replaced Barbie. Bratz books give tips on being a flirt and how to attract boys. One critic says the magazine is "Cosmopolitan for 6-year-olds." Young girls are encouraged to be very conscious about their looks, but child psychologists say this is not age appropriate. Parents are often too busy to have an effect. Couple that with the increasing money that kids have and their access to the media promoting sex, and you have a potent mixture.

Pop stars like Ashley Simpson also convey mixed messages to tween girls. Her posters, for example, show both teddy bears and high heels. Tweens are also big consumers of music videos that have much sexual content. MuchMusic says it doesn't show sexual images during prime time viewing hours, but one analysis of MuchMusic videos shown in the late afternoon and early evening clearly showed a great deal of explicit sexual content. The target audience of MuchMusic (18- to 24-year-olds) is obviously not tweens, but that doesn't stop tweens from watching MuchMusic.

What do boys think of all this? When a Candie's shoe advertisement was shown to boys, they said the model was "hot." Boys seem to be consuming a "bimbo" image of women. Even skateboarding games have sexy images. The storyline of one Tony Hawk skateboarding game, for example, involves a strip club and scantily clad women. Hawk says that the game contains these images because teenage boys like girls.

Critics of sexualized content worry that it teaches boys to devalue women and to lose respect for them. The images that are being sent to tween girls are apparently received quite differently by the girls than they are by the boys.

Questions for Discussion

1. There are several different variables that marketers use to segment markets. Which variable(s) is (are) being used in marketing that is directed at tween girls?
2. What is a brand? How do brand names fit into the issues described in the case?
3. Do advertisers merely respond to what consumers want, or do advertisers actually create wants in consumers for certain products? Defend your answer.
4. Consider the following statement: "*Advertisers are using their expertise to convince tween girls to buy products that sexualize their image and are inappropriate for their age group. By doing this, advertisers are robbing tween girls of the innocence of childhood, and at the same time are demeaning the value of women in the eyes of men.*" Do you agree or disagree? Defend your answer.

Sources: "Buying Into Sexy," *CBC Marketplace*, January 5, 2004; Marina Strauss, "U.S. Retailer Eyes 'Tween' Market," *The Globe and Mail*, January 30, 2007, pp. B1–B2.

CBC VIDEO CASE IV-2

Avery's Brandman

Venture found a business on the brink of bankruptcy and a marketing expert who thought he could revive the brand. The business was a B.C. vineyard and winery run by David and Liz Avery. Their vineyard produced a very fine wine, but for some reason sales were very poor. Six years of work and eight acres of heartache had put the Averys $1 million in debt. They decided they needed a new image, a new name, and a new label for their wine, so they called on Joseph Beauregard (Bernie) to help them out.

Bernie is an expert on names and branding. He dreams up new names and new looks for products and services: things as diverse as chocolates, beer, and garbage trucks. But he wants to make wine brands his specialty. He has already successfully re-branded two wines, and he needs a third success to seal his reputation. It's a good thing that Bernie loves a challenge, because the Avery wine challenge is big one. After he chooses a new name for the Avery's wine (Lotusland), he is in for a couple of surprises: his client's are less-than-enthusiastic about the new name, and he has to schmooze famous people and tell them about the Avery label.

Because his wine has been selling poorly, David Avery is not on good terms with his bank, and he badly needs to make some changes. But the cooperation between Bernie and the Averys leaves a lot to be desired. There is a crisis getting labels designed, approved, and printed because the Averys at various times refuse to communicate with Bernie. In frustration, Bernie sends them an email indicating that their refusal to communicate is preventing him from doing an effective job of re-branding their wine. David responds that he is preoccupied with winemaking, and that he can't deal with several different projects at once. He says he can only wear the winemaker's hat at certain times of the year. Finally, these coordination problems are solved and the bottles get labelled.

Bernie aggressively touts the new Lotusland brand to a multitude of retail outlets. His reputation is on the line. In the end, he is able to get 30 different restaurants signed on to sell Lotusland wine. David and Liz are happy.

Eighteen months later, Bernie's branding business is booming, and he is branding wines all over British Columbia. He has come up with provocative names like *Dirty Laundry*, and bottles with wild looks like *Star Galaxy*. And that's not all. His success has been noticed in other countries. Brand man Bernie has been hired by a winery from the state of Washington, and someone in New Zealand is also interested in his work. Bernie is busy pursuing his dream of transforming the world of wine.

As for the Averys, their new Lotusland wine is doing very well, and their world has been changed forever thanks to Bernie. David says their business is "awesome," and the bank is finally happy because the increased sales mean increased cash flow to pay the winery's bills. The company should be out of debt soon. David is so positive about these developments that he wants to start another organic vineyard in partnership with a land developer. David won't own the land the vineyard will be on, but the vineyard and the winery will be the centrepiece of a subdivision of luxurious homes.

But Bernie is doubtful about working again with David because of the frustrations he experienced the first time around. For his part, David says he would love to work with Bernie again and would like to have his expertise on this new project, but David thinks that maybe he (David) is too hard to work with.

Questions for Discussion

1. What is branding? How does branding add value to a product like Lotusland Wine?
2. Describe the different kinds of brands that Canadian consumers see. In which brand category does Lotusland Wine fit?
3. What are the different levels of brand loyalty? What level of brand loyalty does Lotusland Wine likely have at the moment?
4. What are the key differences between advertising and personal selling? What kind of promotion did Bernie do for the Averys? What kind of promotion is called for in the future?

Source: "Avery Wine's Brandman," *Venture*, March 27, 2005.

PART FIVE

Managing Financial Issues

Management of the financial transactions of a business firm is absolutely critical to the firm's survival. Whether it involves raising money to start a new firm, accurately assessing the riskiness of the firm's investments, or monitoring the firm's activities in securities markets, financial management is a key business activity. The opening cases of the two chapters in this section illustrate the importance of securities markets in the Canadian economy (and how their manipulation can harm investors), and the importance of sound risk management practices in the survival of business firms (and how failure to properly manage risk can harm both employees and investors).

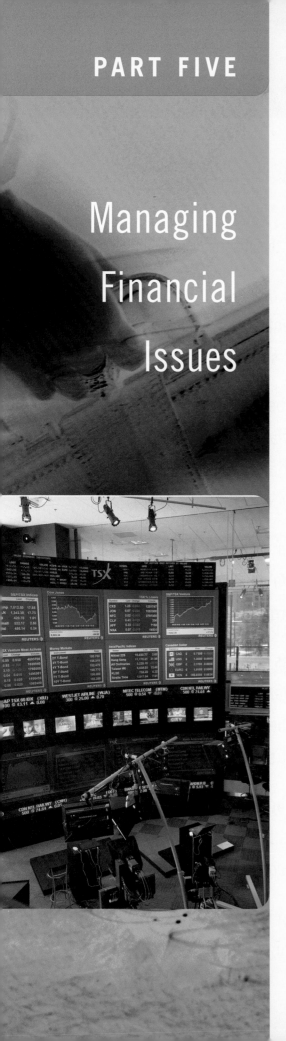

Part Five, Managing Financial Issues, provides an overview of the importance of money and banking in the modern business environment, how firms raise and manage money, how they define and manage risk, and how they use Canadian securities markets to meet their financial needs.

- In **Chapter 15, Money, Banking, and Securities Markets,** we explore the nature of money, its creation through the banking system, and the role of the Bank of Canada in the nation's financial system. We also look at the securities markets in which Canadian firms raise long-term funds, how these markets operate, and how they are regulated.
- In **Chapter 16, Financial Decisions and Risk Management,** we look at the reasons businesses need funds and how financial managers raise both long- and short-term funds. We also examine the kinds of risks businesses encounter and the ways in which they deal with these risks.

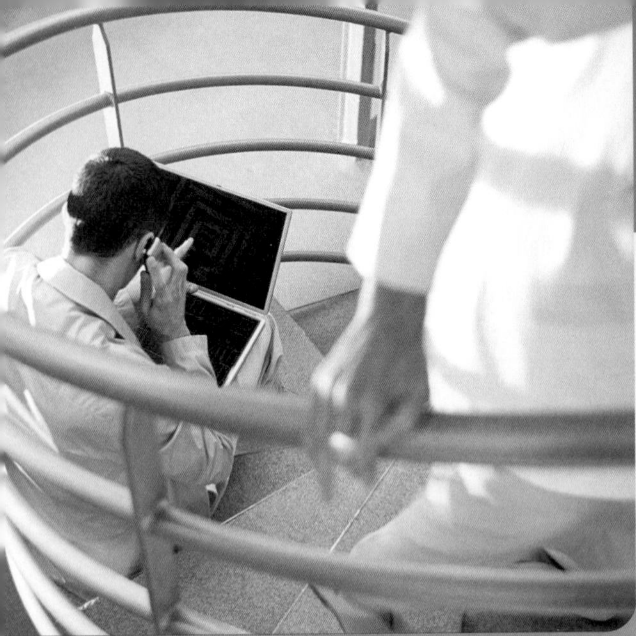

CHAPTER 15

Money, Banking, and Securities Markets

After reading the chapter, you should be able to:

1. Define *money* and identify the different forms it takes in Canada's money supply.
2. Describe the different kinds of *financial institutions* that make up the Canadian financial system and explain the services they offer.
3. Explain the functions of the *Bank of Canada* and describe the tools it uses to control the money supply.
4. Discuss the value of *common stock* and *preferred stock* to stockholders and describe the secondary market for each type of security.
5. Describe the investment opportunities offered by *bonds*, *mutual funds*, and *commodities*.
6. Explain the process by which securities are bought and sold.

Who Could Have Imagined This?

On May 2, 2006 David Watt, an economist at BMO Nesbitt Burns, predicted that the Canadian dollar would reach 95 cents U.S. by the spring of 2007. The chief economist at the National Bank of Canada went even further and predicted that the Canadian dollar would be on par with the U.S. dollar by the fall of 2007. These were dramatic predictions, given that the Canadian dollar was worth only 62 cents as recently as 2003. Yet the Canadian dollar did, in fact, achieve parity with the U.S. dollar in the fall of 2007. Why did this happen?

First, a bit of history. Back in the 1960s, the Canadian dollar was worth slightly more than the U.S. dollar, but by 1976, the two currencies were equal in value. After that, the Canadian dollar began a long slide downward as prices of commodities like oil weakened and as government deficits rose. By 2003, the Canadian dollar was valued at just 62 cents U.S., and it looked the dollar might drop even further.

But then several factors conspired to drive the Canadian dollar sharply upward. For one thing, the U.S. dollar started declining in value, partly because of the huge budget deficits that the United States was incurring as a result of its military activities in Iraq and Afghanistan. In this same period, Canada had budget surpluses. Another factor was interest rates. Economists concluded that the U.S. Federal Reserve was not going to increase U.S. interest rates further, but that the Bank of Canada was not yet finished increasing Canadian interest rates. This would make Canada a more attractive place to invest money, and this would put upward pressure on the loonie. Yet another factor was the high demand for oil, partly caused by the rapid growth of the economies of China and India. This increased demand developed at the same time that Canada's massive tar sands oil development was finally starting to produce significant amounts of oil. As the tar sands output increases in the future, Canada will become a truly significant player on the world oil scene, and this will put further upward pressure on the Canadian dollar.

Canadians have lived for many years with a dollar that was worth less than the U.S. dollar, so many Canadians feel good about the newfound strength of the Canadian dollar. But there are both winners and losers when the Canadian dollar rises in value.

Winners. The following groups are better off when the Canadian dollar increases in value:

- *Canadian consumers* (giant retailers like Wal-Mart can cut prices because they also benefit when the value of the Canadian dollar increases)
- *Canadian professional sports teams* (they pay their players in U.S. funds, so when the Canadian dollar goes up, it costs them less money; an NHL team with a U.S.$30 million payroll, for example, would have had to pay $46.78 million in 2002 when the Canadian dollar was worth just 62 cents, but in 2006, the team would have had to pay only $33.02 million because the Canadian dollar was worth 90 cents)
- *Canadians travelling to the United States* (the Canadian dollar is worth more, so it costs less to travel in the United States)
- *Canadian firms with U.S. dollar debt* (their debt declines as the value of the Canadian dollar increases)

The increase in the value of the Canadian dollar is having a direct, positive effect on Canadian consumers by putting downward pressure on the price of products that consumers buy. For example, the price of California strawberries dropped from $8 a kilogram early in 2006 to just over $4 a kilogram by mid-2006. Price reductions were also evident for many other products.

Losers. The following groups are worse off when the Canadian dollar increases in value:

- *The domestic Canadian tourism industry* (a high Canadian dollar discourages foreign visitors and encourages Canadians to travel abroad)
- *Canadian farmers who export grain* (for every one cent rise in the Canadian dollar, there is a $2 dollar per tonne loss in revenue)
- *Canadian manufacturers who export to the United States* (Canadian products cost more in the United States when the Canadian dollar rises)
- *Canadian railroads* (they take in much of their revenue in U.S. dollars, so when the Canadian dollar increases in value, they get less money than they did when the Canadian dollar was low)

- *Canadian film production* (the cost of Canadian film production rises for U.S. companies, so they are less likely to come to Canada)
- *Canadians who invest in U.S. stocks* (if the increase in the value of the Canadian dollar exceeds the increase in the value of U.S. stocks, Canadian investors' mutual funds will be worth less than when the Canadian dollar was low)
- *Canadians who keep U.S. dollar savings accounts* (the value of the U.S. dollar has declined relative to the Canadian dollar)

The rise in the value of the Canadian dollar has caused great consternation in Canada's manufacturing sector. As the dollar approached 90 cents U.S. in the spring of 2006, more and more doomsday predictions were being made. For example, Rob McBain, co-chair of the Canadian Manufacturers and Exporters, said that even a 90-cent dollar was having a devastating effect on Canada's manufacturing sector. He said that manufacturers need the Canadian dollar to be in the high 70s or low 80s. When the dollar is higher than that, Canadian goods are not as competitive in export markets, *and* Canadian retailers are more likely to buy foreign-made products. He fears that Canadian manufacturers will have no alternative but to go out of business or move their operations out of Canada. If that happens, thousands of jobs will be lost.

Many manufacturers want the federal government to help them cope with the rapid rise of the loonie. The most commonly heard suggestion is to allow companies to increase the pace at which they write off capital investments that are designed to increase productivity. This equipment is needed to allow them to compete more effectively.

HOW WILL THIS BENEFIT YOU?

By understanding the material in this chapter, you will benefit in two ways: (1) as a consumer, you'll learn what money is, where it comes from, how the supply of money grows, and the kinds of services that are available to you from the financial services industry; (2) as an investor, you'll be better prepared to evaluate investment opportunities that will improve your personal financial situation.

In the first half of this chapter, we note the different forms that money takes and the different kinds of financial institutions that make up the Canadian financial system. We also examine how financial institutions create money and the means by which these institutions are regulated. We also discuss the role of the Bank of Canada, ways in which the money and banking system is changing, and key concepts and activities in international banking and finance. In the second half of the chapter, we describe the role of securities markets and securities as a stimulus for business. We discuss common stock, preferred stock, and the various types of bonds, the markets where they are bought and sold, and the regulation of securities markets.

WHAT IS MONEY?

1 Define *money* and identify the different forms it takes in Canada's money supply.

When someone asks you how much money you have, what do you say? Do you count the bills and coins in your pockets? Do you mention the funds in your chequing and savings accounts? What about stocks, or bonds, or your car? Taken together, the value of everything you own is your personal *wealth*. Not all of it, however, is *money*.

The Characteristics of Money

money Any object generally accepted by people as payment for goods and services.

Under the Celts some 2500 years ago, ancient Ireland had a simple agrarian economy. Instead of using coins, the cow was the unit of exchange. Over the centuries, items as diverse as stone wheels, salt, wool, livestock, shells, and spices have been used as money. As early as 1100 BCE, the Chinese were using metal money that represented the objects they were exchanging (for example, bronze spades and knives). Coins probably came into use sometime around 600 BCE and paper money around 1200 CE. Modern money usually takes the form of stamped metal or printed paper—Canadian dollars, U.S. dollars, British pounds, Japanese yen—that is issued by governments. Just about any object can serve as **money** if it is portable, divisible, durable, and stable. To understand why these qualities are important, imagine using as money something valuable that lacks them—a 35-kilogram salmon, for example.

- *Portability.* If you wanted to use the salmon to buy goods and services, you would have to lug a 35-kilogram fish from shop to shop. Modern currency, by contrast, is lightweight and easy to handle.
- *Divisibility.* Suppose you wanted to buy a hat, a book, and some milk from three different stores—all using the salmon as money. How would you divide the fish? First, out comes a cleaver at each store. Then, you would have to determine whether a kilogram of its head is worth as much as a kilogram from its middle. Modern currency is easily divisible into smaller parts with fixed values for each unit. In Canada, for example, a dollar can be exchanged for 4 quarters, 10 dimes, 20 nickels, 100 pennies, or any combination of these coins.
- *Durability.* Fish seriously fail the durability test. Each day, whether or not you "spend" it, the salmon will be losing value (and gaining scents). Modern currency, on the other hand, does not spoil, it does not die, and, if it wears out, it can be replaced with new coins and paper money.
- *Stability.* If salmon were in short supply, you might be able to make quite a deal for yourself. But in the middle of a salmon run, the market would be flooded with fish. Since sellers would have many opportunities to exchange their wares for salmon, they would soon have enough fish and refuse to trade for salmon. While the value of the paper money we use today has fluctuated over the years, it is considerably more stable than salmon.

The Functions of Money

Imagine a successful fisherman who needs a new sail for his boat. In a *barter economy*—one in which goods are exchanged directly for one another—he would have to find someone who not only needs fish but who is willing to exchange a sail for it. If no sailmaker wants fish, the fisherman must find someone else—say, a shoemaker—who wants fish and will trade for it. Then the fisherman must hope that the sailmaker will trade for his new shoes. Contrast this with a money economy, where the fisherman would sell his catch, receive money, and exchange the money for such

This 100-kilogram gold coin—produced by the Royal Canadian Mint—is the largest gold coin ever produced. It is 99.999 percent pure gold and sells for $3 million.

goods as a new sail. The barter economy is quite inefficient, but it is still used in various places around the world. It is active in Russia, where major problems have arisen as the country tries to move toward a market-based system and away from the command economy that existed under communism. As recently as the late 1990s, barter accounted for more than half of the business transactions in Russia.[1]

Money serves three functions:

- *Medium of exchange.* Like the fisherman "trading" money for a new sail, we use money as a way of buying and selling things. Without money, we would be bogged down in a system of barter.
- *Store of value.* Pity the fisherman who catches a fish on Monday and wants to buy a few bars of candy on, say, the following Saturday. By then, the fish would have spoiled and be of no value. In the form of currency, however, money can be used for future purchases and so "stores" value.
- *Unit of account.* Finally, money lets us measure the relative values of goods and services. It acts as a unit of account because all products can be valued and accounted for in terms of money. For example, the concepts of "$1000-worth of clothes" or "$500 in labour costs" have universal meaning because everyone deals with money every day.

The Spendable Money Supply: M-1

For money to serve as a medium of exchange, a store of value, or a unit of account, buyers and sellers must agree on its value. The value of money, in turn, depends in part on its supply, that is, how much money is in circulation. When the money supply is high, the value of money drops. When the money supply is low, the value of money increases.

It is not easy to measure the supply of money, nor is there complete agreement on exactly how it should be measured. The "narrow" definition of the money supply is called **M-1**, which includes only the most liquid forms of money: currency and demand deposits (chequing accounts) in banks. As of February 2006, M-1 totalled $190.8 billion.[2]

M-1
Only the most liquid forms of money (currency and demand deposits).

currency
Paper money and coins issued by the government.

Currency is paper money and coins issued by the Canadian government. It is widely used to pay small bills. Canadian currency—which clearly states "This note is legal tender"—is money the law requires a creditor to accept in payment of a debt. Counterfeiting of paper currency, which has been a problem for many years, is now a worldwide problem, partly because new technologies like scanners and colour copiers allow counterfeiters to make real-looking bills rather easily. In 2004, 553 000 counterfeit Canadian bills (worth $13 million) were discovered. Most of these were $20 bills.[3] In 2005, there were about 326 phoney Canadian bills in circulation for every million genuine bills.[4] In an attempt to reduce counterfeiting, the Bank of Canada has issued new $20 and $5 bills with more sophisticated security features.[5] Further information about counterfeiting is provided in Video Case V-1 on p. 482.

A **cheque** is an order instructing the bank to pay a given sum to a specified person or firm. Cheques enable buyers to make large purchases without having to carry large amounts of cash. Money in chequing accounts, known as **demand deposits**, is counted in M-1 because such funds may be withdrawn at any time without notice.

cheque
An order instructing the bank to pay a given sum to a specified person or firm.

demand deposits
Money in chequing accounts; counted as M-1 because such funds may be withdrawn at any time without notice.

M-1 Plus the Convertible Money Supply: M-2

M-2 includes everything in M-1 plus items that cannot be spent directly but that are easily converted to spendable forms: *time deposits, money market*

M-2
Everything in M-1 plus savings deposits, time deposits, and money market mutual funds.

The hub of operations at Amazon.com is this 840 000 square-foot warehouse, where workers can ship as many as 11 000 boxes an hour. The key to the efficiency of the facility is technology—all orders are processed electronically. The most important technology of all may be the credit card. If you had nothing but cash, you'd find it hard to shop on the internet, and internet retailers who depend on credit card transactions (like Amazon, Dell, and eBay) couldn't exist in a cash-only world.

mutual funds, and *savings deposits*. M-2 accounts for nearly all the nation's money supply. As this overall supply of money increases, more is available for consumer purchases and business investment. When this supply decreases, less is available for consumer purchases and business investment. As of February 2006, M-2 totalled $670.4 billion.[6]

Unlike demand deposits, **time deposits** require prior notice of withdrawal and cannot be transferred by cheque. The supply of money in time deposits—such as *certificates of deposit (CDs)* and *savings certificates*—grew rapidly in the 1970s and 1980s as interest rates rose to levels never before seen in Canada.

time deposit
A deposit that requires prior notice to make a withdrawal; cannot be transferred to others by cheque.

Money market mutual funds are operated by investment companies that pool the assets of many investors and then buy short-term, low-risk financial securities. Ownership of and profits (or losses) from the sale of these securities are shared among the fund's investors. These funds attracted many investors in the 1980s and 1990s because of high payoffs.

money market mutual funds
Funds operated by investment companies that bring together pools of assets from many investors to buy short-term, low-risk financial securities.

Credit Cards: Plastic Money?

Although not included in M-1 or M-2, credit—especially credit cards—has become a major factor in the purchase of consumer goods in Canada. The use of MasterCard, Visa, American Express, Discover, and credit cards issued by individual businesses has become so widespread that many people refer to credit cards as "plastic money." In 2005, Canadians spent $190 billion using credit cards.[7] Credit cards are actually a *money substitute*; they serve as a temporary medium of exchange but are not as a store of value. More detail about credit cards is provided in Appendix B.

THE CANADIAN FINANCIAL SYSTEM

Describe the different kinds of *financial institutions* that make up the Canadian financial system and explain the services they offer. 2

Many forms of money, especially demand deposits and time deposits, depend on the existence of financial institutions to provide a broad spectrum of services to both individuals and businesses. In this section, we describe the major types of financial institutions, explain how they work, and describe some of the special services they offer. We also explain their role as creators of money and discuss the regulation of the Canadian banking system.

Financial Institutions

The main function of financial institutions is to facilitate the flow of money from users with surpluses to those with deficits. They do this by attracting funds into chequing and savings accounts. These funds are then loaned to individuals and businesses, and perhaps invested in government securities.

There are many different financial intermediaries in Canada. For many years, they were divided rather clearly into four distinct legal areas. Often called the "four financial pillars," they were: (1) chartered banks; (2) alternate banks, such as trust companies and credit unions; (3) life insurance companies and other specialized lending and saving intermediaries, and (4) investment dealers. We will discuss the role of these four financial divisions in a moment, but it is important to remember that so many changes have taken place in the financial services industry that the differences across the four divisions are now very blurred.

The crumbling of the four financial pillars began in 1980 when several changes were made to the Bank Act. Additional changes were made in 1987 and 1992. Canadian banks, for example, are now permitted to own securities dealers and to sell commercial paper and to own insurance companies (although they are not allowed to sell insurance in their own bank branches). Banks have also established subsidiaries to sell mutual funds. Trust companies have declined in importance during the last few years, and many trust companies have been bought by banks or insurance companies. The largest trust company—Canada Trust—merged with the Toronto-Dominion Bank and is now called TD Canada Trust. Insurance companies are facing increased challenges since banks can now sell insurance. The mutual fund business is now much larger than it used to be. These (and other) significant changes must be kept in mind as we now turn to a discussion of the four financial pillars of the Canadian economy.

FINANCIAL PILLAR #1—CHARTERED BANKS

chartered bank
A privately owned, profit-seeking firm that serves individuals, non-business organizations, and businesses as a financial intermediary.

A **chartered bank** is a privately owned, profit-seeking financial intermediary that serves individuals, businesses, and non-business organizations. Chartered banks are the largest and most important financial institution in Canada. In March 2006, Canadian chartered banks had assets totalling $1.3 trillion.[8] Chartered banks offer chequing and savings accounts, make loans, and provide many other services to their customers. They are the main source of short-term loans for business firms.

Unlike the United States, where there are hundreds of banks, each with a few branches, in Canada there are only a few banks, each with hundreds of branches. The largest bank in Canada (based on annual revenues) is the Royal Bank. The five largest Canadian banks account for about 90 percent of total bank assets. *Schedule I* banks are those which are Canadian-owned and have no more than 10 percent of voting shares controlled by a single interest. *Schedule II* banks are those which may be domestically owned but do not meet the 10 percent limit, or may be foreign-controlled. Several foreign banks have set up Schedule II subsidiaries in Canada.

Services Offered by Banks

Because the banking business today is highly competitive, banks no longer just accept deposits and make loans. They also offer financial advice and an array of electronic money transfer options.

Financial Advice

Banks help their customers manage their money. Depending on the customer's situation, the bank may recommend different investment opportunities. The recommended mix might include guaranteed investment certificates, mutual funds, stocks, or bonds. Banks also help customers establish savings plans for *retirement*. Banks also offer **trust services**—the management of funds left "in the bank's trust." In return for a fee, the trust department performs such tasks as making your monthly bill payments and managing your investment portfolio.

trust services
The management of funds left in the bank's trust.

Electronic Funds Transfer

Electronic funds transfer (EFT) combines computer and communication technology to transfer funds or information into, from, within, and among financial institutions. Examples include the following:

electronic funds transfer (EFT)
A combination of computer and communications technology that transfers funds or information into, from, within, and among financial institutions.

automated banking machines (ABMs)
Electronic machine that allows bank customers to conduct account-related activities 24 hours a day, 7 days a week.

Automated Banking Machines (ABMs). **ABMs**, or 24-hour tellers (called automated teller machines—ATMs in the United States), are electronic terminals that let you bank at almost any time of day or night. You insert a special card and enter your own secret identification number to withdraw cash, make deposits, or transfer funds between accounts. Banks typically charge about $1.50 per transaction, but at the Dragonfly Nightclub in the Niagara Fallsview Casino Resort, the ABM surcharge is $2.99. In terms of consumer access, Canada ranks first in the world in ABMs. Only one-third of ABMs are owned by banks; the other two-thirds—so-called "white label" machines—are owned by private companies.[9]

Pay-by-Phone. These systems let you telephone your financial institution and instruct it, by pushing the proper buttons on your phone, to pay certain bills or to transfer funds between accounts.

ENTREPRENEURSHIP AND NEW VENTURES

Check It Out!

In the fall of 2005, Calgary-based CHEQ-IT Ltd. announced that six new clients had joined the fold. Arcan Resources Ltd., Dual Energy Ltd., Focus Energy Trust, Grizzly Resources Ltd., Thunder Energy Trust, and Yoho Resources have all implemented the CHEQ-IT system to process their vendor payments in recent months.

CHEQ-IT Ltd. has come a long way since its founding in 1992 when its focus was on being a supplier of cheque printing software and hardware. At that time its niche was in the oil and gas sector. Now, CHEQ-IT's client base includes companies in financial services, transportation, consulting, and other business sectors. Companies as diverse as Greyhound and Price Waterhouse/Coopers depend on CHEQ-IT products.

Currently considered a leading edge provider of electronic funds transfer capability, CHEQ-IT Ltd. develops, sells and supports payment processing for Electronic Funds Transfer (EFT), Electronic Data Interchange (EDI), cheque printing software systems and related supplies. The Systems, currently in use by companies across Canada, work with a variety of corporate accounting systems, and provide a robust, secure, and efficient means to process payments at a low cost. The CHEQ-IT system, with security encryption, is one of the most secure and efficient methods of making payments and preventing fraudulent acts. In addition to the immediate income from the system sales, the ongoing maintenance and transaction fees from these installations contribute to the increasing recurring revenue base of CHEQ-IT.

The rationale cited for selecting the CHEQ-IT solution by the company's recently acquired clients was that after examining the alternatives, the CHEQ-IT system was the most advantageous to implement with their existing accounting applications. Additionally, most of these clients received a recommendation from their accounting system provider Q-Byte systems, with whom CHEQ-IT has a close and ongoing relationship.

Follow-up comments from these new clients indicated that the implementation of the CHEQ-IT system was virtually seamless, facilitating payment processing shortly after installation.

Direct Deposits and Withdrawals. This system allows you to authorize in advance specific, regular deposits and withdrawals. You can arrange to have paycheques and social assistance cheques automatically deposited and recurring expenses, such as insurance premiums and utility bills, automatically paid.

debit card
A type of plastic money that immediately on use reduces the balance in the user's bank account and transfers it to the store's account.

Point-of-Sale Transfers. These let you pay for retail purchases with your **debit card**, a type of plastic money that immediately reduces the balance in the user's bank account when it is used. For example, if you use a debit card at a grocery store, the clerk simply runs the card through the machine and asks you to punch in a personal identification number on a keypad next to the cash register. The price of the groceries is then deducted electronically from your chequing account, and money moves from your chequing account to the grocery store's account. In 2005, there were 4 billion debit card transactions in Canada, and 35 million debit cards in peoples' wallets (that's more than the population of Canada).[10]

smart cards
A credit card-sized computer that can be programmed with "electronic money."

Smart Cards. **Smart cards**—also known as "electronic purses" or "stored-value cards"—can be programmed with "electronic money" at ATM machines or, with special telephone hookups, even at home. After using your card to purchase an item, you can then check an electronic display to see how much money is left on your card. Phone callers and shoppers in Europe and Asia are the most avid users. In North America, smart cards are most popular in gas pump payments, followed by prepaid phone service, ATMs, self-operated checkouts, and automated banking services.[11] Analysts predict that in the near future smart cards will function as much more than electronic purses. For example, travel industry experts predict that people will soon book travel plans at home on personal computers and then transfer their reservations onto their smart cards. The cards will then serve as airline tickets and boarding passes.

ecash
Money that moves among consumers and businesses via digital electronic transmissions.

Ecash. Electronic money, known as **ecash**, is money that moves along multiple channels of consumers and businesses via digital electronic transmissions. Ecash moves outside the established network of banks, cheques, and paper currency. How does ecash work? Traditional currency is used to buy electronic funds, which are downloaded over phone lines into a PC or a portable "electronic wallet" that can store and transmit ecash. Ecash is purchased from any company that sells it, including banks. When shopping online—say, to purchase jewellery—a shopper sends digital money to the merchant instead of using traditional cash, cheques, or credit cards. Businesses can purchase supplies and services electronically from any merchant that accepts ecash. The money flows from the buyer to the seller's ecash funds, which are instantaneously updated and stored on a microchip.

Although ecash transactions are cheaper than handling cheques and the paper records involved with conventional money, there are some potential problems. Hackers, for example, may break into ecash systems and drain them instantaneously. Moreover, if the issuer's computer system crashes, it is conceivable that money "banked" in memory may be lost forever. Finally, regulation and control of ecash systems remains largely nonexistent; there is virtually none of the protection that covers government-controlled money systems.

Figure 15.1 summarizes the services that chartered banks offer. Banks are chartered by the federal government and are closely regulated when they provide these services.

- Long- and short-term loans
- Automated teller machines
- Safeguard property entrusted to it
- Debit and credit cards
- Savings accounts
- Guaranteed investment certificates

- Chequing accounts
- Buy and sell securities for customer accounts
- Exchange Canadian dollars for foreign currencies
- Exchange foreign currencies for Canadian dollars
- Advise customers on financial matters

Figure 15.1 Examples of services by many chartered banks and trust companies.

Bank Loans

Banks are the major source of short-term loans for business. Although banks make long-term loans to some firms, they prefer to specialize in providing short-term funds to finance inventories and accounts receivable. A *secured* loan is backed by collateral such as accounts receivable or a life insurance policy. If the borrower cannot repay the loan, the bank sells the collateral. An *unsecured* loan is backed only by the borrower's promise to repay it. Only the most creditworthy borrowers can get unsecured loans.

Borrowers pay interest on their loans. Large firms with excellent credit records pay the **prime rate of interest**, which is the lowest rate charged to borrowers. This rate changes from time to time owing to changes in the demand for and supply of loanable funds as well as to policies of the Bank of Canada. The so-called "Big Six" Canadian banks (Royal Bank, CIBC, Bank of Montreal, Bank of Nova Scotia, TD Canada Trust, and National Bank of Canada) typically act in concert with respect to the prime rate.

prime rate of interest
The lowest rate charged to borrowers.

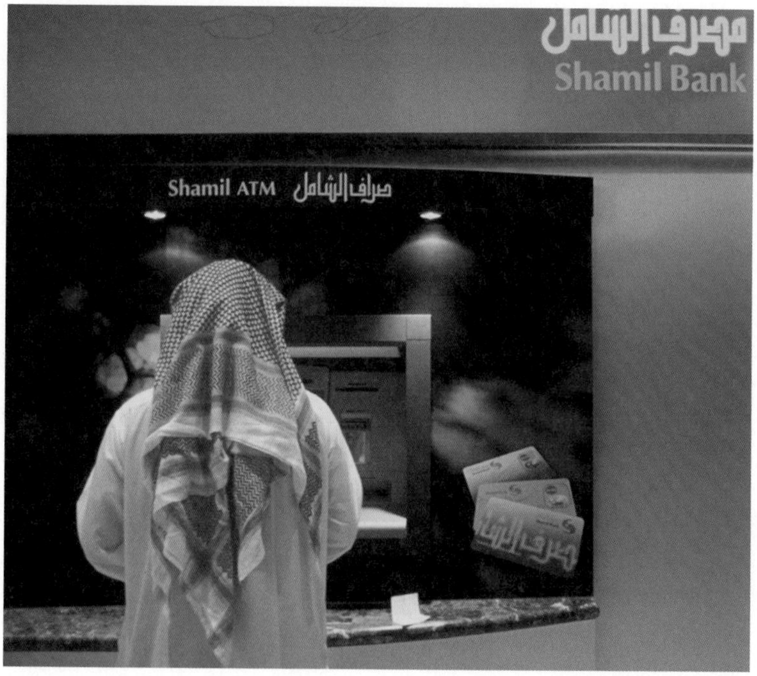

Devout Muslims can't pay or receive interest, a fact that complicates banking operations. Because money has to work to earn a return, institutions like the Shamil Bank in Bahrain invest deposits directly in such ventures as real estate and then pay back profit shares rather than interest. Buying a car is possible through a complex arrangement in which the bank takes temporary ownership and then sells the car to the individual at a profit. Mortgage arrangements are similar but even more complicated.

Banks as Creators of Money

In the course of their activities, financial institutions provide a special service to the economy—they create money. They don't mint bills and coins, but by taking in deposits and making loans, they *expand the money supply*. We will first look at how this expansion process works, assuming that banks have a **reserve requirement**, that is, that they must keep a portion of their chequable deposits in vault cash or as deposits with the Bank of Canada. (This reserve requirement was dropped in 1991 and the implications of this change are described later.)

reserve requirement
The requirement (until 1991) that banks keep a portion of their chequable deposits in vault cash or as deposits with the Bank of Canada.

Suppose you saved $100, took it to a bank, and opened a chequing account. Let's assume for the moment that there is a reserve requirement, and that it is 10 percent. Your bank must therefore keep $10 of your $100 deposit in reserve, so it has only $90 to lend to other borrowers. Now suppose a person named Jennifer Leclerc borrows $90 from your bank. She now has $90 added to her chequing account. Assume that she writes a cheque for $90 payable to Canadian Tire. Canadian Tire's bank ends up with a $90 deposit, and that bank is also required to keep $9 in reserve. It therefore has $81 to lend out to someone else. This process of deposit expansion can continue as shown (in abbreviated form) in Figure 15.2, and your original deposit of $100 could result in an increase of $1000 in new deposits for all banks in the system.

But, what happens if there is no reserve requirement? At the extreme, it means that banks could (theoretically) create infinite amounts of money because they don't have to keep any in reserve. But banks will not do this because it is risky. So, in practice, the dropping of the reserve requirement simply means that banks will be able to create more money than they did when there was a reserve requirement.

Other Changes in Banking

Substantial changes in addition to those already described are taking place in banking, including changes in consumer preferences, deregulation, and international banking.

Changes in Customer Preferences

Banks have shifted away from their historical role as intermediaries between depositors and borrowers, and are diversifying to provide a wider array of financial products to their clients. Training bankers to be effective

Deposit	Money Held in Reserve by Bank	Money to Lend	Total Supply
$100.00	$10.00	$90.00	**$190.00**
90.00	9.00	81.00	**271.00**
81.00	8.10	72.90	**343.90**
72.90	7.29	65.61	**409.51**
65.61	6.56	59.05	**468.56**

Figure 15.2 How the chartered banking system creates money.

in this environment is necessary. For example, over 100 executives at TD Canada Trust attended a Harvard University course that taught them to think like investment bankers. The Bank of Montreal conducted a similar course for over 400 executives.

Household consumers are increasingly turning to non-traditional, electronic banks like ING Direct and President's Choice Financial that have very few tellers or branches. As well, retailers like Sears and Canadian Tire are opening their own branches.[12] Traditional banks are responding by selling a growing array of corporate and government securities through their branches. All of this activity is transforming the profit base of banks. In the past, they made most of their money from the spread between interest rates paid to depositors and the rates charged on loans. Investment banking, on the other hand, is fee-based. Banks are now making a larger proportion of their profits from fees, and this is further blurring the traditional boundary between banks and securities firms.

Deregulation

In the last few years, large companies have reduced their use of bank loans. To compensate for this loss, banks are setting up money market operations. Before deregulation, only securities firms were allowed to sell commercial paper (see Chapter 16), but banks expect to dominate in this area before too long. Banks have been allowed to sell commercial paper since 1987, when deregulation opened up this possibility. The Bank of Montreal and TD Canada Trust have been the most active in this new market.

International Banking

U.S. and other foreign banks are now allowed to do business in Canada, and Canada's banks are responding to this competitive threat with a variety of tactics, including attempts to merge with one another so they can afford the millions of dollars in technology investment that will be needed to remain competitive. In 1998, for example, the Canadian Imperial Bank of Commerce and the Toronto-Dominion Bank tried to merge, as did the Royal Bank and Bank of Montreal. But both of these mergers were blocked by the federal government because it feared the mergers would reduce competition and harm consumers. But, as we saw earlier, the government did allow Canada Trust and Toronto-Dominion Bank to merge. Banks are also trying other things to be more competitive, like co-operating to spread their fixed costs. Syncor Services, for example, is a joint venture between three banks that provides cheque-clearing services across Canada.[13]

The Bank of Canada

3 Explain the functions of the *Bank of Canada* and describe the tools it uses to control the money supply.

The **Bank of Canada**, formed in 1935, is Canada's central bank. It has a crucial role to play in managing the Canadian economy and in regulating certain aspects of chartered bank operations. The Bank of Canada is managed by a board of governors composed of a governor, a deputy governor, and 12 directors appointed from different regions of Canada.

The rate at which chartered banks can borrow from the Bank of Canada is called the **bank rate**, or **rediscount rate**. It serves as the basis for establishing the chartered banks' prime interest rates. In practice, chartered banks seldom have to borrow from the Bank of Canada. However, the bank rate is an important instrument of monetary policy as a determinant of interest rates.

Bank of Canada Canada's central bank; formed in 1935.

bank rate (rediscount rate) The rate at which chartered banks can borrow from the Bank of Canada.

The Money Supply and the Bank of Canada

The Bank of Canada plays an important role in managing the money supply in Canada (see Figure 15.3). If the Bank of Canada wants to *increase* the

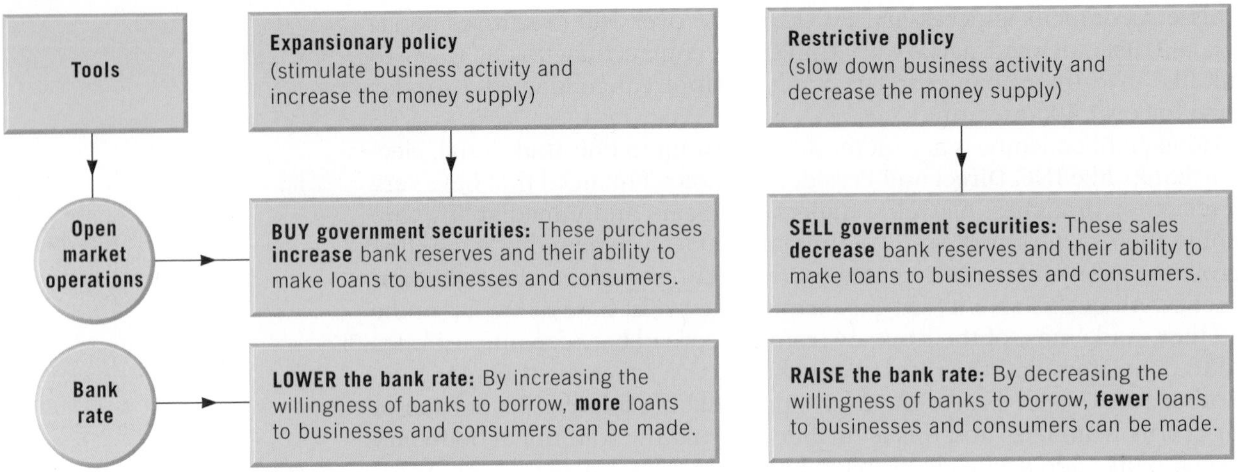

Figure 15.3 Bank of Canada monetary policy actions.

money supply, it can buy government securities. The people who sell these bonds then deposit the proceeds in their banks. These deposits increase banks' reserves and their willingness to make loans. The Bank of Canada can also lower the bank rate; this action will cause increased demand for loans from businesses and households because these customers borrow more money when interest rates drop.

If the Bank of Canada wants to *decrease* the money supply, it can sell government securities. People spend money to buy bonds, and these withdrawals bring down banks' reserves and reduce their willingness to make loans. The Bank of Canada can also raise the bank rate; this action will cause decreased demand for loans from businesses and households because these customers borrow less money when interest rates rise. The Business Accountability box provides additional information on the Bank of Canada.

FINANCIAL PILLAR #2—ALTERNATE BANKS

Trust Companies

trust company
Safeguards funds and estates entrusted to it; may also serve as trustee, transfer agent, and registrar for corporations.

A **trust company** safeguards property—funds and estates—entrusted to it. It may also serve as trustee, transfer agent, and registrar for corporations and provide other services. For example, a corporation selling bonds to investors appoints a trustee, usually a trust company, to protect the bondholders' interests. A trust company can also serve as a transfer agent and registrar for corporations. A *transfer agent* records changes in ownership of a corporation's shares of stock, and a *registrar* certifies to the investing public that stock issues are correctly stated and comply with the corporate charter. Other services include preparing and issuing dividend cheques to stockholders and serving as trustee for employee profit-sharing funds. Trust companies also accept deposits and pay interest on them.

Credit Unions/Caisses Populaires

credit unions
Co-operative savings and lending association formed by a group with common interests.

Credit unions and *caisses populaires* are co-operative savings and lending associations formed by a group with common interests. They are important because they lend money to businesses and to consumers (who use the money to buy durable goods such as cars and furniture from businesses). Members (owners) can add to their savings accounts by authorizing deductions from their paycheques or by making direct deposits. They can borrow

BUSINESS ACCOUNTABILITY

Fixing the System on a National Scale

Bankers and economists recently did a follow-up evaluation of the Bank of Canada's fixed-date system, launched in December 2000, for announcing its key policy interest rate—the overnight rate that individual banks pay to borrow from one another. The overnight rate is among the bank's strongest tools for influencing short-term interest rates that, in turn, affect mortgage rates, prime rates charged by chartered banks, and other asset prices in Canada's financial markets. Under the old system, the bank's monetary policy decisions could be made on any business day, without warning, and were governed largely by tactical considerations. That's quite different from today's announcements on eight pre-specified or "fixed" dates each year.

The changeover to fixed dates was launched with four objectives in mind, including one that involves the bank's accountability. First, policymakers wanted to reduce uncertainty in Canada's financial markets by eliminating investors' guesswork about when rate changes would be announced. Knowing that the bank would make changes only on specific dates would allow financial institutions to plan ahead without fear of unexpected rate changes. A second objective was to overcome an unfavourable public perception that Canada was taking its cues for monetary policies from those of the U.S. Federal Reserve. The new system would provide greater focus on Canada's economic context rather than its relationship to U.S. conditions. The third objective was to increase the public's awareness of the forward-looking nature of monetary policy, requiring 18 to 24 months to have its full impact on the economy instead of thinking only of its short-term results. The final objective concerns the bank's accountability to the public. In addition to making monetary policy understandable by explaining clearly to Canadians the how's and why's of its decisions, the bank has an obligation to let citizens know how well it's doing its job and report its progress in meeting the objectives.

Follow-up evaluations on the first objective indicate a reduction of economic uncertainties resulting from reduced volatility of interest rates under the fixed-date system. For the second objective—greater focus on Canada's economic context—media coverage has shifted more to Canadian economic issues as separate from U.S. conditions. Writing in the *Globe and Mail* on monetary policy two years into the fixed-date system, for example, Bruce Little commented, "Our economy has followed a different path than that of the United States.... [W]hat happens in the U.S. affects Canada, but Canada's economy is not a clone of the U.S. economy." Shifting of the public's perspective from short to medium term still poses a significant challenge because the public tends to be impatient about looking beyond a week or month for monetary policy to take affect.

Regarding accountability, the fixed-date system has helped in several ways. Among the bank, investors, and financial institutions, regularity of communications has brought a convergence of expectations on the overall direction of monetary policy. It has improved the predictability of Bank of Canada decisions by eliminating surprises in terms of timing and enables financial institutions to better anticipate the general direction of interest rates. Finally, fixed-announcement dates have given Canadians a regular opportunity to hear the bank's recent views about the economy and its current thinking about monetary policy. The net effect is a more stable economic environment, an obligation for which the bank is accountable to the Canadian public.

QUESTIONS FOR DISCUSSION

1. The changes that have been made at the Bank of Canada seem very positive. Can you think of any negative aspects of announcing interest rate changes only on set dates?
2. "*Because the U.S. has a much larger economy than Canada does, it is not really realistic to think that Canada can chart a different economic course than the U.S. can. We really have no alternative but to move pretty much in lock-step with the U.S.*" Do you agree or disagree with this statement? Explain your reasoning.

short-term, long-term, or mortgage funds from the credit union. Credit unions invest substantial amounts of money in corporate and government securities and sell certificates of deposits to the general public.

FINANCIAL PILLAR #3—SPECIALIZED LENDING AND SAVINGS INTERMEDIARIES

Life Insurance Companies

life insurance company
A mutual or stock company that shares risk with its policyholders for payment of premiums.

A **life insurance company** shares risk with its policyholders in return for payment of a premium by policyholders. It lends some of the money it collects from premiums to borrowers. Life insurance companies are substantial investors in real estate mortgages and in corporate and government bonds. Next to chartered banks, they are the largest financial intermediaries in Canada. We discuss insurance in Chapter 16.

Factoring Companies

factoring company (or factor)
Buys accounts receivable from a firm for less than their face value, and then collects the face value of the receivables.

An important source of short-term funds for many firms is factoring companies. A **factoring company (or factor)** buys accounts receivable (amounts due from credit customers) from a firm. It pays less than the face value of the accounts but collects the face value of the accounts. The difference, minus the cost of doing business, is the factor's profit. A firm that sells its accounts receivable to a factor shifts the risk of credit loss to the factor. If an account turns out to be uncollectible, the factor suffers the loss.

Financial Corporations

sales finance company
Specializes in financing instalment purchases made by individuals or firms.

A **sales finance company** specializes in financing instalment purchases made by individuals and firms. When you buy durable goods from a retailer on an instalment plan with a sales finance company, the loan is made directly to you. The item itself serves as security for the loan. Sales finance companies enable many firms to sell on credit, even though the firms could not afford to finance credit sales on their own. General Motors Acceptance Corporation (GMAC) is a sales finance company that finances instalment contracts resulting from sales made by General Motors. Industrial Acceptance Corporation is a large Canadian sales finance company.

consumer finance company
Makes personal loans to consumers.

A **consumer finance company** makes personal loans to consumers. Often, the borrower pledges no security (collateral) for the loan. For larger loans, collateral may be required, such as a car or furniture. These companies do not make loans to businesses but they do provide the financing that allows consumers to buy goods and services from businesses. Household Finance Corporation is an example of a consumer finance company.

Venture Capital Firms

venture capital firm
Provides funds for new or expanding firms thought to have significant potential.

A **venture capital firm** provides funds for new or expanding firms that seem to have significant potential. Venture capital firms typically buy shares in companies they are interested in. They may demand an ownership stake of 50 percent or more before they will buy into the company. Because financing new, untested businesses is risky, venture capital firms also want to earn a higher-than-normal return on their investment. They may therefore insist that they be given at least one seat on the board of directors so they can observe first-hand how their investment is faring. A venture capital firm would ideally want a situation where a company they invest in becomes very successful and experiences substantial increases in its stock value.

Venture capital firms obtain their funds from initial capital subscriptions, from loans from other financial intermediaries, and from retained earnings. The amount of venture capital that is raised varies according to economic conditions. For example, during May 2005, Canadian companies raised $434 million through venture capital firms. That was up sharply from earlier months and indicated continuing improvement in the Canadian economy.[14] In recent years, U.S.-based venture capital firms have become a significant presence in the Canadian market, and are pushing aside smaller Canadian venture capital firms.

Pension Funds

A **pension fund** accumulates money that will be paid out to plan subscribers at some time in the future. The money collected is invested in corporate stocks and bonds, government bonds, or mortgages until it is to be paid out.

pension fund
Accumulates money that will be paid out to plan subscribers in the future.

FINANCIAL PILLAR #4—INVESTMENT DEALERS

Investment dealers (called stockbrokers or underwriters) are the primary distributors of new stock and bond issues (the underwriting function). They also facilitate secondary trading of stocks and bonds, both on stock exchanges and on over-the-counter stock and bond markets (the brokerage function). These functions are described in more detail later in this chapter.

In 2004, Canadian corporations raised $44.2 billion in equity funds and $56.3 billion in debt funds. CIBC World Markets Inc. was the largest equity (stock) underwriter, selling $10.7 billion.[15] RBC Dominion Securities was the largest debt seller, with $11.4 billion in bond sales.[16]

OTHER SOURCES OF FUNDS

Government Financial Institutions and Granting Agencies

In Canada, a number of government suppliers of funds are important to business. In general, they supply funds to new and/or growing companies. However, established firms can also use some of them.

The *Business Development Bank of Canada (BDC)* makes term loans, primarily to smaller firms judged to have growth potential but unable to secure funds at reasonable terms from traditional sources. It provides proportionally more equity financing and more management counselling services. A variety of provincial industrial development corporations also provide funds to developing business firms in the hope that they will provide jobs in the province. A number of federal and provincial programs are specifically designed to provide loans to agricultural operators. Most of these, with the exception of farm improvement loans that guarantee bank loans to farmers, are long-term loans for land purchase.

The federal government's *Export Development Corporation* finances and insures export sales for Canadian companies. The *Canada Mortgage and Housing Corporation (CMHC)* is involved in providing and guaranteeing mortgages. The CMHC is particularly important to the construction industry.

In addition to these activities, governments are involved in providing grants to business operations. For example, the federal government, through the *Department of Regional Industrial Expansion (DRIE)*, gives grants for certain types of business expansion in designated areas of the country. Other federal government grants are available for activities such as new product development.

International Sources of Funds

The Canadian capital market is just one part of the international capital market. Canadian provinces borrow extensively in foreign markets such as those in London and in New York. Canadian corporations likewise find it attractive to borrow in foreign markets. Foreign sources of funds have been important in the economic development of Canada. Although many groups and individuals have expressed concern about foreign ownership of Canadian businesses, projections of Canada's future capital requirements indicate that we will continue to need foreign sources of funds. Canadian financial institutions will continue to play a large role in making these funds available.

INTERNATIONAL BANKING AND FINANCE

Banks and other financial institutions play an important role in the international movement of money and in the value that is placed on the currency of various countries. Each nation tries to influence its currency exchange rates for economic advantage in international trade. The subsequent country-to-country transactions result in an *international payments* process that moves money between buyers and sellers on different continents.

Exchange Rates and International Trade

The value of a given currency (say, the Canadian dollar) reflects the overall supply and demand for Canadian dollars both at home and abroad. This value changes with economic conditions. Worldwide, therefore, firms will watch those trends, and decisions about doing business in Canada will be affected by more or less favourable exchange rates. At one point in 2007, for example, the Canadian dollar was valued at U.S.$0.99. This was up sharply from its 2002 value of $0.63, but lower than its value in the 1960s, when the U.S. and Canadian dollars were about equal.

The Law of One Price

When a country's currency is overvalued, its exchange rate is higher than warranted by its economic conditions, and its high costs make it less competitive. In contrast, an undervalued currency means low costs and low prices. When a currency becomes overvalued, a nation's economic authorities may *devalue* the nation's currency. This causes a decrease in the country's exchange value, making it less expensive for other countries to buy the country's products. If a nation's currency is undervalued, the government can *revalue* the currency, which will make it more expensive for other countries to buy its products.

But how do we know whether a currency is overvalued or undervalued? One method involves a simple concept called the **law of one price**: the principle that identical products should sell for the same price in all countries. In other words, if the different prices of a Rolex watch in different countries were converted into a common currency, the common-denominator price should be the same everywhere.

law of one price
The principle that identical products should sell for the same price in all countries.

A simple example that illustrates over- and undervalued currencies is the Big Mac Currencies, an index published annually in the British magazine *The Economist*. The identical product here is always McDonald's Big Mac, which is made locally in many countries. Table 15.1 lists selected countries and Big Mac prices in terms of U.S. dollars. As you can see, the Icelandic kronur is the most overvalued, while the Chinese yuan is the most undervalued. In theory, this means that you could buy Big Macs in China (using yuan) and resell them in Iceland (for kronur) at a handsome profit. In China, therefore, the demand for burgers would increase, driving the price up toward the higher prices in the other countries. In other words, the law of one price would set in.

The International Payments Process

Transactions among buyers and sellers in different countries are simplified through the services provided by their banks. For example, payments from buyers flow through a local bank that converts them from the local currency into the foreign currency of the seller. Likewise, the local bank receives and converts incoming money from the banks of foreign buyers. This *international payments process* is shown in Figure 15.4.[17]

Step 1. A Canadian olive importer withdraws $1000 from its chequing account to buy olives from a Greek exporter. The local Canadian bank *converts* those dollars into euros at the current exchange rate (0.626032 euros per dollar).

Step 2. The Canadian bank sends the cheque for 626.03 euros (EUR 626.03—0.626032 multiplied by 1000) to the exporter in Greece.

Steps 3 and 4. The exporter sends olives to its Canadian customer and deposits the cheque in its local Greek bank. While the exporter now has euros that can be spent in Greece, the importer has olives to sell in Canada. At the same time, a separate transaction is being made between a Canadian machine exporter and a Greek olive oil producer. This time,

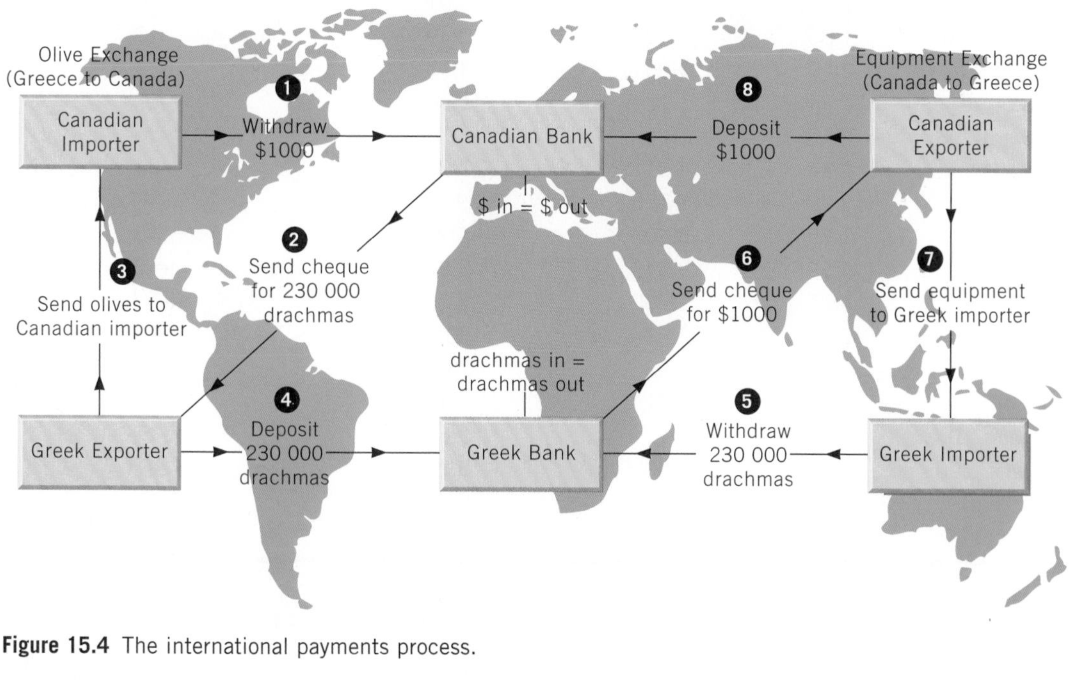

Figure 15.4 The international payments process.

Table 15.1 Big Mac Currency Index

Country	Big Mac Prices In Local Currency	Big Mac Prices In Dollars	Implied PPP* of the Dollar	Actual Dollar Exchange Rate Jan 31st	Under (–)/Over (+) Valuation Against the Dollar, %
United States†	$3.22	3.22			
Argentina	Peso 8.25	2.65	2.56	3.11	–18
Australia	A$3.45	2.67	1.07	1.29	–17
Brazil	Real 6.4	3.01	1.99	2.13	–6
Britain	£1.99	3.90	1.62‡	1.96‡	+21
Canada	C$3.63	3.08	1.13	1.18	–4
Chile	Peso 1,670	3.07	519	544	–5
China	Yuan 11.0	1.41	3.42	7.77	–56
Colombia	Peso 6,900	3.06	2,143	2,254	–5
Costa Rica	Colones 1,130	2.18	351	519	–32
Czech Republic	Koruna 52.1	2.41	16.2	21.6	–25
Denmark	DKr27.75	4.84	8.62	5.74	+50
Egypt	Pound 9.09	1.60	2.82	5.70	–50
Estonia	Kroon 30	2.49	9.32	12.0	–23
Euro area§	€ 2.94	3.82	1.10**	1.30**	+19
Hong Kong	HK$12.0	1.54	3.73	7.81	–52
Hungary	Forint 590	3.00	183	197	–7
Iceland	Kronur509	7.44	158	68.4	+131
Indonesia	Rupiah 15,900	1.75	4,938	9,100	–46
Japan	¥280	2.31	87.0	121	–28
Latvia	Lats 1.35	2.52	0.42	0.54	–22
Lithuania	Litas 6.50	2.45	2.02	2.66	–24
Malaysia	Ringgit 5.50	1.57	1.71	3.50	–51
Mexico	Peso 29.0	2.66	9.01	10.9	–17
New Zealand	NZ$4.60	3.16	1.43	1.45	–2
Norway	Kroner 41.5	6.63	12.9	6.26	+106
Pakistan	Rupee 140	2.31	43.5	60.7	–28
Paraguay	Guarani 10,000	1.90	3,106	5,250	–41
Peru	New Sol 9.50	2.97	2.95	3.20	–8
Philippines	Peso 85.0	1.74	26.4	48.9	–46
Poland	Zloty 6.90	2.29	2.14	3.01	–29
Russia	Rouble 49.0	1.85	15.2	26.5	–43
Saudi Arabia	Riyal 9.00	2.40	2.80	3.75	–25
Singapore	S$3.60	2.34	1.12	1.54	–27
Slovakia	Crown 57.98	2.13	18.0	27.2	–34
South Africa	Rand 15.5	2.14	4.81	7.25	–34
South Korea	Won 2,900	3.08	901	942	–4
Sri Lanka	Rupee 190	1.75	59.0	109	–46
Sweden	SKr32.0	4.59	9.94	6.97	+43
Switzerland	SFr6.30	5.05	1.96	1.25	+57
Taiwan	NT$75.0	2.28	23.3	32.9	–29
Thailand	Baht 62.0	1.78	19.3	34.7	–45
Turkey	Lire 4.55	3.22	1.41	1.41	nil
UAE	Dirhams 10.0	2.72	3.11	3.67	–15
Ukraine	Hryvnia 9.00	1.71	2.80	5.27	–47
Uruguay	Peso 55.0	2.17	17.1	25.3	–33
Venezuela	Bolivar 6,800	1.58	2,112	4,307	–51

Sources: McDonald's; *The Economist*

*Purchasing-power parity: local price divided by price in United States. †Average of New York, Atlanta, Chicago, and San Francisco; ‡Dollars per pound; §Weighted average of prices in euro area; **Dollars per euro.

the importer/exporter roles are reversed between the two countries: The Greek firm needs to *import* a $1000 olive oil press from Canada.

Steps 5 and 6. EUR 626.03 withdrawn from a local Greek bank account is converted into $1000 Canadian and sent via cheque to the Canadian exporter.

Steps 7 and 8. The olive oil press is sent to the Greek importer, and the importer's cheque is deposited in the Canadian exporter's local bank account.

The International Bank Structure

There is no worldwide banking system that is comparable, in terms of policy-making and regulatory power, to the system of any single industrialized nation. Rather, worldwide banking stability relies on a loose structure of agreements among individual countries or groups of countries.

The World Bank and the IMF

Two United Nations agencies, the World Bank and the International Monetary Fund, help to finance international trade. Unlike true banks, the **World Bank** (technically the International Bank for Reconstruction and Development) actually provides only a very limited scope of services. For instance, it funds national improvements by making loans to build roads, schools, power plants, and hospitals. The resulting improvements eventually enable borrowing countries to increase productive capacity and international trade.

World Bank
A United Nations agency that provides a limited scope of financial services, such as funding national improvements in undeveloped countries.

The **International Monetary Fund (IMF)** is a group of some 150 nations that have combined their resources for the following purposes:

International Monetary Fund (IMF)
U.N. agency consisting of about 150 nations that have combined resources to promote stable exchange rates, provide temporary short-term loans, and serve other purposes.

- promote the stability of exchange rates
- provide temporary, short-term loans to member countries
- encourage members to co-operate on international monetary issues
- encourage development of a system for international payments

SECURITIES MARKETS

So far in this chapter we have talked about the importance of money, the various organizations in the Canadian financial system, and international finance. We now turn to our attention to securities markets, where the role of money is very obvious. Stocks and bonds are both known as **securities** because they represent a secured (asset-based) claim on the part of investors. Collectively, the market in which stocks and bonds are sold is called the *securities market*.

securities
Stocks, bonds, and mutual funds representing secured, or asset-based, claims by investors against issuers.

Primary and Secondary Markets for Securities

Primary securities markets handle the buying and selling of new stocks and bonds by firms or governments. When new securities are sold to one buyer or a small group of buyers, these *private placements* allow the businesses that use them to keep their plans confidential. Most new stocks and some bonds are sold to the public market. To bring a new security to market, the issuing corporation must obtain approval from a provincial securities commission. It also needs the services of an investment banker.

primary securities market
Market in which new stocks and bonds are bought and sold

investment bankers
Financial specialists in issuing new securities.

Investment bankers serve as financial specialists in issuing new securities. Such well-known firms as RBC Dominion Securities and TD Securities *advise* companies on the timing and financial terms for a new issue, *underwrite* (buy) the new securities, and *create* the distribution network that moves the new securities through groups of other banks and brokers into the hands of individual investors.

secondary securities market
The sale and purchase of previously issued stocks and bonds.

New securities represent only a small portion of securities traded. The market for existing stocks and bonds—the **secondary securities market**—is handled by organizations like the Toronto Stock Exchange. We will consider the activities of these markets later in this chapter.

STOCKS

4 Discuss the value of *common stock* and *preferred stock* to stockholders and describe the secondary market for each type of security.

Each year, millions of investors buy and sell the stocks of thousands of Canadian and international companies. This widespread ownership has become possible because of the availability of different types of stocks and because markets have been established for conveniently buying and selling them. In this section, we will focus on *common* and *preferred stock* as securities and the *stock exchanges* where they are bought and sold.

Common Stock

Individuals and companies buy a firm's common stock, hoping that the stock will increase in value (a capital gain) and/or will provide dividend income. Stock values are expressed in three different ways: par value, market value, and book value.

Par Value

par value
The arbitrary value of a stock set by the issuing company's board of directors and stated on stock certificates; used by accountants but of little significance to investors.

The face value of a share of stock, its **par value**, is set by the issuing company's board of directors. Each company must preserve money in the amount of its stock's par value in its retained earnings, and cannot distribute it as dividends.

Market Value

market value
The current price of one share of a stock in the secondary securities market; the real value of a stock.

A stock's real value is its **market value**—the current price of a share in the stock market. The price of a stock can be influenced by both objective factors (e.g., company profits) and by subjective factors, including *rumours* (unverified information such as a claim that a company has made a big gold strike), *investor relations* (publicizing the positive aspects of a company's financial condition to financial analysts and financial institutions), and *stockbroker recommendations* (a recommendation to buy a stock may increase demand for the stock and cause its price to increase, while a recommendation to sell can decrease demand and cause the price to fall). None of these actions are illegal.

market capitalization
The dollar value (market value) of stocks listed on a stock exchange.

The **market capitalization** of a company's stock is computed by multiplying the number of a company's outstanding shares times the market value of each share. Because stock prices change every day, so does market capitalization. The Royal Bank topped the list in 2006 with a market capitalization of approximately $61 billion. In the late 1990s, some dot-com companies had very high market capitalizations, but when the stock market declined, the market value of those companies dropped drastically. The market capitalization of Nortel Networks, for example, was $221.9 billion in 2000 (the highest of any Canadian company), but the company wasn't even in the top 10 by 2003.

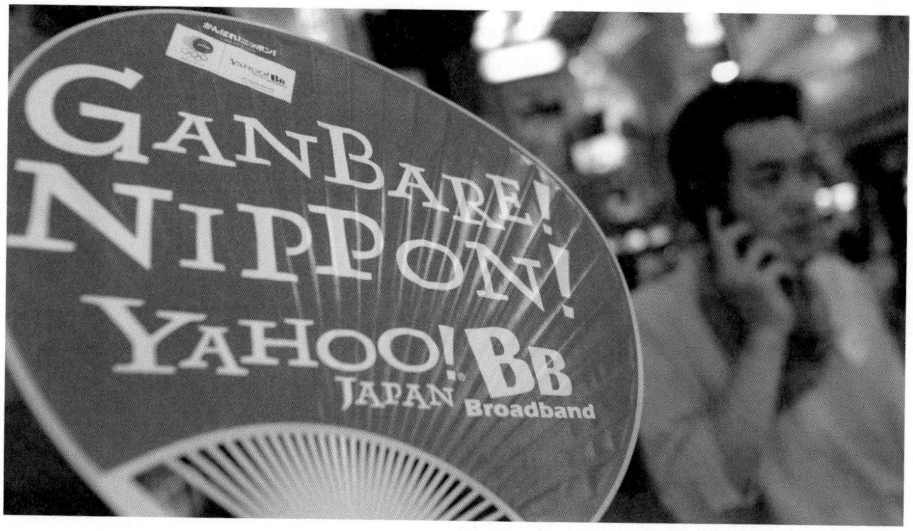

Yahoo! Japan is just one of dozens of net-related companies in the portfolio of Japan's Softbank Corp., which is riding the crest of an 83 percent surge in profits from online retail transactions. Softbank has sunk its profits in Yahoo! BB, a high-speed consumer broadband service that's already attracted 4.3 million users at $20–$30 per month. To strengthen its hold on broadband service in Japan, Softbank also delved into the "old economy," buying up the country's third largest fixed line provider, Japan Telecom.

Book Value

Recall from Chapter 11 our definition of *stockholders' equity*—the sum of a company's common stock par value, retained earnings, and additional paid-in capital. The **book value** of common stock represents stockholders' equity divided by the number of shares. Book value is used as a comparison indicator because, for successful companies, the market value is usually greater than its book value. Thus, when market price falls to near book value, some investors buy the stock on the principle that it is under-priced and will increase in the future.

book value
Value of a common stock expressed as total stockholders' equity divided by the number of shares of stock.

Preferred Stock

Preferred stock is usually issued with a stated par value, such as $100. Dividends paid on preferred stock are usually expressed as a percentage of the par value. For example, if a preferred stock with a $100 par value pays a 6 percent dividend, stockholders would receive an annual dividend of $6 on each share. Some preferred stock is *callable,* that is, the issuing firm can require the preferred stockholders to surrender their shares in exchange for a cash payment. The amount of this cash payment, known as the *call price,* is specified in the agreement between the preferred stockholders and the firm.

Stock Exchanges

A **stock exchange** is an organization of individuals formed to provide an institutional setting in which stock can be bought and sold. The exchange enforces certain rules to govern its members' trading activities. Most exchanges are non-profit corporations established to serve their members. To become a member, an individual must purchase one of a limited number of memberships—called "seats"—on the exchange. Only members (or their representatives) are allowed to trade on the exchange. In this sense, because all orders to buy or sell must flow through members, they have a legal monopoly. Memberships can be bought and sold like other assets.

stock exchange
A voluntary organization of individuals formed to provide an institutional setting where members can buy and sell stock for themselves and their clients in accordance with the exchange's rules.

A **stockbroker** receives buy and sell orders from those who are not members of the exchange and executes the orders. In return, the broker earns a commission from the order placer. Like many products, brokerage assistance can be purchased at either discount or at full-service prices. Buying 200 shares of a $20 stock costs an investor $9.99 to $12.99 at

stockbroker
An individual licensed to buy and sell securities for customers in the secondary market; may also provide other financial services.

E*Trade, and up to $100 at a full-service brokerage firm. Price differences are obvious even among the discount brokers, but the highest discount price is well below the price of the full-service broker.[18]

Discount brokerage services cost less because sales personnel receive fees or salaries, not commissions. Unlike many full-service brokers, discount brokers do not offer investment advice or person-to-person sales consultations. They do, however, offer automated online services, such as stock research, industry analysis, and screening for specific types of stocks.

Online trading is increasing in popularity because of convenient access to the internet, fast no-nonsense transactions, and the opportunity for self-directed investors to manage their own investments while paying low fees for trading. In 2005, the volume of online trading reached 25 percent of all shares traded, and competition among brokers has driven prices downward.[19]

Canadian Stock Exchanges

The *Toronto Stock Exchange (TSE)* is the largest stock exchange in Canada. It is made up of about 100 individual members who hold seats. The securities of most major corporations are listed here. A company must pay a fee before it can list its security on the exchange. Formerly, there were also stock exchanges in Calgary, Vancouver, and Montreal, but in 1999 an agreement was reached that (1) created the new *Canadian Venture Exchange (CDNX)* from the Vancouver and Alberta stock markets, (2) shifted all derivative trading to the Montreal stock exchange, and (3) consolidated all senior equity trading at the TSE.[20] The CDNX now focuses on junior companies.

Foreign Stock Exchanges

Many foreign countries also have active stock exchanges, and several foreign stock exchanges—most notably those in the United States and United Kingdom—trade far more shares each day than the TSE does.

The New York and American Stock Exchanges. For many people, "the stock market" means the *New York Stock Exchange (NYSE)*. Founded in 1792 and located at the corner of Wall and Broad Streets in New York City, the largest of all U.S. exchanges is the model for exchanges worldwide. An average of 1.4 billion shares valued at $44 billion change hands each day. About 59 percent of all shares traded on U.S. exchanges are traded here. Only firms meeting certain minimum requirements—earning power, total

The Toronto Stock Exchange is one of several in Canada where shares of stock in Canadian companies are bought and sold.

value of outstanding stock, and number of shareholders—are eligible for listing on the NYSE.[21] The American Stock Exchange is the second-largest U.S. stock exchange. It accounts for 2 percent of shares traded.

Other Foreign Stock Exchanges. In 1980, the U.S. stock market accounted for more than half the value of the *world* market in traded stocks. Market activities, however, have shifted as the value of shares listed on foreign exchanges continues to grow rapidly. The annual dollar value of trades on exchanges in London, Tokyo, and other cities is now in the trillions. In fact, the London exchange exceeds even the NYSE in number of stocks listed. Exchanges are also flourishing in cities from Shanghai to Warsaw, but risk levels in some of these markets are very high. In China, for example, stock prices doubled during 2006, but in 2007 the market lost 9 percent of its value in *one day*. The Chinese stock market has been likened to that of a casino, and it is plagued with corruption, lax government regulation, and financially troubled companies.[22]

The Over-the-Counter Market

The **over-the-counter (OTC) market** is so called because its original traders were somewhat like retailers: they kept supplies of shares on hand and, as opportunities arose, sold them over the counter to interested buyers. Even today, the OTC market has no trading floor. Rather, it consists of many people in different locations who hold an inventory of securities that are not listed on any of the major exchanges. The OTC consists of independent dealers who own the securities that they buy and sell at their own risk.

over-the-counter (OTC) market
Organization of securities dealers formed to trade stock outside the formal institutional setting of the organized stock exchanges.

NASDAQ

The **National Association of Securities Dealers Automated Quotation (NASDAQ)** is the world's first electronic stock market.[23] The NASDAQ telecommunications system operates the NASDAQ Stock Market by broadcasting trading information on an intranet to over 350 000 terminals worldwide. NASDAQ orders are paired and executed on a computer network. The stocks of nearly 3300 companies are traded by NASDAQ, and it accounts for about 38 percent of shares traded. Newer firms are often listed here when their stocks first become available in the secondary market. Current listings include Starbucks and such well-known technology stocks as Intel, Dell Computer, Oracle Technology, and Microsoft.

National Association of Securities Dealers Automated Quotation (NASDAQ)
A stock market implemented by NASD that operates by broadcasting trading information on an intranet to more than 350 000 terminals worldwide.

BONDS

A **bond** is an IOU—a written promise that the borrower will pay the lender, at some stated future date, a sum of money (the principal) and a stated rate of interest. Bondholders have a claim on a corporation's assets and earnings that comes before the claims of common and preferred stockholders. Bonds differ from one another in terms of maturity date and level of risk. To help bond investors make assessments, several services rate the quality of bonds from different issuers. Table 15.2 shows ratings by Moody's and Standard & Poor's (which recently acquired the former Canadian Bond Rating Service). The rating measures the bond's *default risk*—the chance that one or more promised payments will be deferred or missed altogether.

bond
A written promise that the borrower will pay the lender, at a stated future date, the principal plus a stated rate of interest.

All corporations issue common stock, but not all issue bonds. Stockholders provide equity (ownership) capital, while bondholders are lenders (although they are also considered "investors" as far as the securities market is concerned). Stock certificates represent ownership, while bond certificates represent indebtedness.

Table 15.2 Bond Ratings

	High Grade	Medium Grade (Investment Grade)	Speculative	Poor Grade
Moody's	Aaa Aa	A Baa	Ba B	Caa to C
Standard & Poor's	AAA AA	A BBB	BB B	CCC to D

Government Bonds

Government bonds—for example, New Canada Savings Bonds—are among the safest investments available. However, securities with longer maturities are somewhat riskier than short-term issues because their longer lives expose them to more political, social, and economic changes. All federal bonds are, however, backed by the Canadian government. Government securities are sold in large blocks to institutional investors who buy them to ensure desired levels of safety in portfolios.

Provincial and local governments also issue bonds (called municipal bonds) to finance school and transportation systems and a variety of other projects. Banks invest in bonds nearing maturity because they are relatively safe, liquid investments. Pension funds, insurance companies, and private citizens also make longer-term investments in municipals.

Corporate Bonds

Corporate bonds are a major source of long-term financing for Canadian corporations. They have traditionally been issued with maturities ranging from 20 to 30 years. In the 1980s, 10-year maturities came into wider use. As with government bonds, longer-term corporate bonds are somewhat riskier than shorter-term bonds. Unlike stocks, nearly all secondary trading in bonds occurs in the over-the-counter market rather than on any organized exchange. Like stocks, market values and prices of bonds change from day to day. The direction of bond prices moves opposite to interest rate changes—as interest rates move up, bond prices tend to go down. The prices of riskier bonds fluctuate more than those of higher-grade bonds and often exceed the interest rate of the economy.

Corporate bonds may be categorized in one of two ways: (1) according to methods of interest payment and (2) according to whether they are *secured* or *unsecured*.

Interest Payment: Registered and Bearer Bonds

registered bonds
The names of holders are registered with the company.

bearer (or coupon) bonds
Require bondholders to clip coupons from certificates and send them to the issuer to receive interest payments.

Registered bonds register the names of holders with the company, which simply mails out cheques. Certificates are of value only to registered holders. **Bearer (or coupon) bonds** require bondholders to clip coupons from certificates and send them to the issuer in order to receive payment. Coupons can be redeemed by anyone, regardless of ownership.

Bond Security

secured bonds
Bonds issued by borrowers who pledge assets as collateral in the event of non-payment.

Borrowers can reduce the risk of their bonds by pledging assets to bondholders in the event of default. **Secured bonds** can be backed by first mortgages, other mortgages, or other specific assets. If the corporation does not pay interest when it is due, the firm's assets can be sold and the proceeds used to pay the bondholders. Unsecured bonds are called **debentures**. No specific property is pledged as security for these bonds. Holders of unsecured bonds generally have claims against property not otherwise pledged in the company's other bonds. Accordingly, debentures have inferior claims on the corporation's assets. Financially strong corporations often use debentures.

The Retirement of Bonds

Maturity dates on bonds of all kinds may be very long. But at some point, all bonds must be paid off. In terms of maturity dates, there are three types of bonds: *callable, serial,* and *convertible*.

Callable Bonds

The issuer of a **callable bond** has the right at almost any time to call the bonds in and pay them off at a price stipulated in the bond indenture (contract). Usually the issuer cannot call the bond for a certain period of time after issue, but some are callable at any time. Issuers are most likely to call in existing bonds when the prevailing interest rate is lower than the rate being paid on the bond. But the price the issuer must pay to call in the bond, the *call price*, usually gives a premium to the bondholder. For example, a bond might have a $100 face value and be callable by the firm for $108.67 any time during the first year after being issued. The call price and the premium decrease annually as the bond nears maturity.

Bonds are often retired by the use of a **sinking-fund provision** in the bond indenture. This method requires the issuing company to put a certain amount of money into a special bank account each year. At the end of a number of years, the money in this account (including interest) is sufficient to redeem the bonds. Failure to meet the sinking-fund provision places the bond issue in default. Bonds with sinking funds are generally regarded as safer investments than bonds without them.

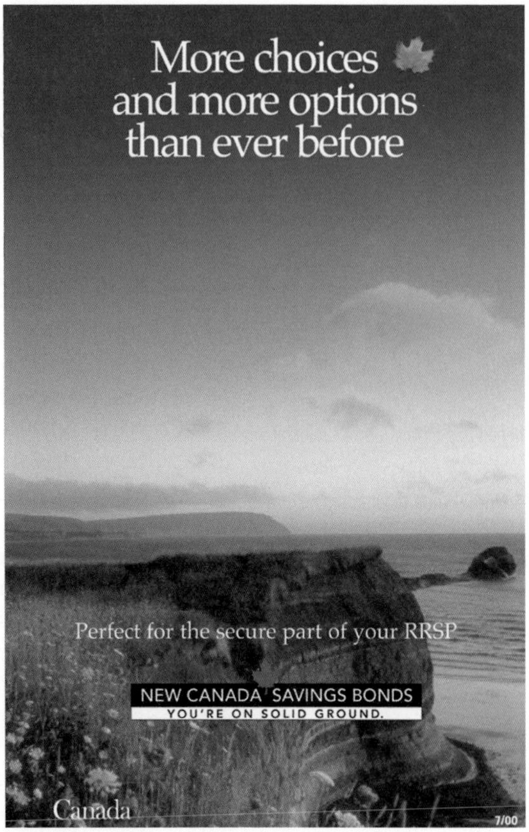

Private corporations are not the only organizations that issue bonds. The Government of Canada issues Canada Savings Bonds to finance its debt.

debentures
Unsecured bonds.

callable bond
A bond that may be paid off by the issuer before the maturity date.

sinking-fund provision
A clause in the bond indenture (contract) that requires the issuing company to put enough money into a special bank account each year to cover the retirement of the bond issue on schedule.

serial bond
A bond issue in which redemption dates are staggered so that a firm pays off portions of the issue at different predetermined dates.

convertible bond
Any bond that offers bondholders the option of accepting common stock instead of cash in repayment.

Serial and Convertible Bonds

As an alternative to sinking funds, some corporations issue serial or convertible bonds. In a **serial bond** issue, the firm retires portions of the bond issue at different predetermined dates. For example, in a $100 million serial bond issue maturing in 20 years, the company may retire $5 million of the issue each year.

Convertible bonds can be paid off in (converted to) common stock of the issuing company, at the option of the bondholder. Since this option gives bondholders a chance for capital gains, the company can offer lower interest rates when issuing the bonds. Suppose that in 1999, Canadian Arctic Explorations sold a $100 million issue of 4.5 percent convertible bonds. The bonds were issued in $1000 denominations; they mature in 2009. At any time before maturity, each debenture of $1000 is convertible into 19.125 shares of the company's common stock. Assume that between October 1999 and March 2007, the stock price ranged from a low of $28 to a high of $67. In that time, then, 19.125 common shares had a market value ranging from $535 to $1281. In other words, the bondholder could have exchanged the $1000 bond in return for stock to be kept or sold at a possible profit (or loss).

OTHER INVESTMENTS

5 Describe the investment opportunities offered by *bonds, mutual funds,* and *commodities.*

Although stocks and bonds are very important, they are not the only marketable securities for businesses. Financial managers are also concerned with investment opportunities in *mutual funds, commodities,* and *stock options*.

Mutual Funds

mutual fund
Any company that pools the resources of many investors and uses those funds to purchase various types of financial securities, depending on the fund's financial goals.

no-load fund
A mutual fund in which investors are not charged a sales commission when they buy into or sell out of the fund.

load fund
A mutual fund in which investors are charged a sales commission when they buy into or sell out of the fund.

Companies called **mutual funds** pool investments from individuals and other firms to purchase a portfolio of stocks, bonds, and short-term securities. For example, if you invest $1000 in a mutual fund that has a portfolio worth $100 000, you own 1 percent of the portfolio. Mutual funds usually have portfolios worth many millions of dollars. Investors in **no-load funds** are not charged a sales commission when they buy into or sell out of the mutual fund. **Load funds** carry a charge of between 2 and 8 percent of the invested funds. Mutual funds give small investors access to professional financial management. Their managers have up-to-date information about market conditions and the best large-scale investment opportunities.

Mutual funds vary by the investment goals they stress. Some stress safety. The portfolios of these mutual funds include treasury bills and other safe issues that offer immediate income (liquidity). Other funds seek higher current income and are willing to sacrifice some safety. Long-term municipal bond mutual funds, corporate bond mutual funds, and income mutual funds (which invest in common stocks with good dividend-paying records) all fall into this category. Still other mutual funds stress growth. Examples include balanced mutual funds, which hold a mixture of bonds, preferred stocks, and common stocks. Aggressive growth mutual funds seek maximum capital appreciation. To get it, these funds sacrifice current income and safety. They invest in stocks of new companies, troubled companies, and other high-risk securities.

Ethical Funds

ethical funds
Mutual funds that stress socially responsible investing.

Mutual funds that stress socially responsible investing are called **ethical funds**. They avoid investing in companies like cigarette manufacturers or companies that make weapons, and instead focus on investing in companies that produce safe and useful products and show concern for their employees, for the environment, and for human rights. Clean Environment Equity, Ethical Growth, and Summa Investors are all ethical funds. In spite of the many corporate scandals in recent years, ethical funds have not attracted as much interest in Canada as they have in the United States and Europe. They have also not performed as well as other mutual funds.[24]

Hedge Funds

hedge funds
Private pools of money that try to give investors a positive return regardless of stock market performance.

Hedge funds are private pools of money that try to give investors a positive return regardless of stock market performance. Hedge funds often engage in risky practices like *short-selling* (essentially betting that a company's stock price will go down) and *leveraging* (borrowing money against principal). Historically, interest in hedge funds has been limited to wealthy people (called "accredited investors") who are assumed to be very knowledgeable about financial matters and are able to weigh the risks of investing. But recently, hedge funds have begun marketing their products to the average investor with something called "principal-protected notes." These guarantee that investors will get their original investment back at a certain time, but they do not guarantee that any additional returns will be forthcoming.

The number of hedge funds has increased rapidly in recent years—from less than 2000 in 1993 to over 6000 in 2005—and the majority of money invested in hedge funds is now in the form of principal-protected notes.[25] Hedge funds are not as closely regulated as mutual funds, and are not required to report management fees. But these management fees can be higher than those charged by mutual funds, so there is increasing concern that investors will be short-changed. As a result, there are now calls for increased regulation of hedge funds.[26]

Traders deal in futures contracts—agreements to buy or sell commodities for certain prices at a future time. This day (May 18, 2004) was an interesting one. The assassination of an Iraqi leader rekindled concerns about supplies of crude oil, so the price went up to (at that time) a record of $41.55 per barrel. Since that time, other uncertainties on the world scene have caused the price of oil to rise above $90 per barrel.

Commodities

Futures contracts—agreements to purchase a specified amount of a commodity at a given price on a set date in the future—are available for commodities ranging from coffee beans and live hogs to propane and platinum, as well as for stocks. Since selling prices reflect traders' beliefs about the future, prices of such contracts are very volatile, and futures trading is very risky.

Consider an example. On November 1, 2003, the price of gold on the open market was $387 per ounce. Futures contracts for June 2004 gold were selling for $385 per ounce. This price reflected investors' judgment that gold prices would be slightly lower the following June. Now suppose that you purchased a 100-ounce gold futures contract in November for $38 500 ($385 × 100). If in January 2004 the June gold futures sold for $418 (which they really did), you could sell your contract for $41 800. Your profit after the two months would be $3300. Of course, if the futures contract had been selling for less than $385, you would have lost money.

futures contracts Agreement to purchase specified amounts of a commodity (or stock) at a given price on a set future date.

margin The percentage of the total sales price that a buyer must put up to place an order for stock or a futures contract.

Margins

Usually, buyers of futures contracts need not put up the full purchase amount. Rather, the buyer posts a smaller amount—the **margin**—that may be as little as $3000 for contracts up to $100 000. Let us look again at our gold futures example. As we saw, if you had posted a $3000 margin for your July gold contract, you would have earned a $3300 profit on that investment of $3000 in only two months.

However, you also took a big risk involving two big *ifs*: If you had held onto your contract until June *and* if gold had dropped, say to $340, you would have lost $4500 ($38 500 – $34 000). If you had posted a $3000 margin to buy the contract, you would have lost that entire margin and would owe an additional $1500. As it turns out, June gold prices increased to $394, so your investment of $38 500 would have gained $900 in June. In fact, however, between 75 and 90 percent of all small-time investors lose money in the futures market.

Stock Options

A **stock option** is the right to buy or sell a stock. A **call option** gives its owner the right to buy a particular stock at a certain price, with that right lasting until a particular date. A **put option** gives its owner the right to sell a particular stock at a specified price, with that right lasting until a particular date. These options are traded on several stock exchanges.

Suppose that you thought the price of Alcan (which sold for $49.10 per share on August 15, 2000) was going to go up. You might buy a call option giving you the right to buy 100 shares of Alcan any time in the next two months at a so-called *strike price* of $65. If the stock rose to $75 before October, you would exercise your call option. Your profit would be $10 per share ($75 – $65) less the price you paid to buy the option. However, if the

stock option The purchased right to buy or sell a stock.

call option The purchased right to buy a particular stock at a certain price until a specified date.

put option The purchased right to sell a particular stock at a certain price until a specified date.

stock price fell instead of rising, you would not exercise your call option because Alcan would be available on the open market for less than $65 per share. Your stock option would be "under water," that is, it would be worthless. You would lose whatever you paid for the option. In recent years, there has been much negative publicity about stock options that are *given* to executives to motivate them to work hard for the company.

BUYING AND SELLING SECURITIES

6 Explain the process by which securities are bought and sold.

The process of buying and selling stocks, bonds, and other financial instruments is complex. You need to gather information about possible investments and match them to your investment objectives. Then you must decide whether you want to use a broker to buy and sell stocks, or whether you want to do it yourself.

Using Financial Information Services

Have you ever looked at the financial section of your daily newspaper and found yourself wondering what all those tables and numbers mean? If you cannot read stock and bond quotations, you probably should not invest in these issues. Fortunately, this skill is easily mastered.

Stock Quotations

Figure 15.5 shows the type of information newspapers provide about daily market transactions of individual stocks. The corporation's name is shown along with the number of shares sold, the high and low prices of the stock for that trading day, the closing price of the stock, and the change from the closing price on the previous day.

Bond Quotations

Bond prices also change from day to day. These changes form the *coupon rate*, which provides information for firms about the cost of borrowing funds. Prices of domestic corporation bonds, Canadian government bonds,

- *Stock*
  Vale Inco (Name of Company)
- *Volume*
  18 640 (total number of shares traded on this date [in 100s]).
- *High and Low*
  During the trading day, the highest price was $58.82 and the lowest price was $57.01.
- *Close*
  At the close of trading on this date, the last price paid per share was $58.05.
- *Net Change*
  Difference between today's closing price and the previous day's closing price. Price increased by 84 cents per share.

Company	Volume	High	Low	Close	Change
Four Seasons	663	67.49	65.27	66.15	−1.13
Goldcorp	35 233	31.99	30.65	31.15	+0.83
GW Life	54	25.80	25.57	25.80	−0.22
Hudson Bay	32 376	15.06	15.00	15.04	−0.02
Vale Inco	**18 640**	**58.82**	**57.01**	**58.05**	**+0.84**
Ipsco	4341	106.40	104.09	105.75	−0.25
Jean Cou	6918	14.56	14.31	14.31	−0.06
Kinross	72 321	13.68	12.92	13.10	+0.27

Figure 15.5 How to read a daily stock quotation.

and foreign bonds are reported separately. Bond prices are expressed in terms of 100, even though most have a face value of $1000. Thus, a quote of 85 means that the bond's price is 85 percent of its face value, or $850.

A corporate bond selling at 155 1/4 would cost a buyer $1552.50 ($1000 face value multiplied by 1.5525), plus commission. The interest rate on bonds is also quoted as a percentage of par, or face, value. Thus "6 1/2s" pay 6.5 percent of par value per year. Typically, interest is paid semi-annually at half of the stated interest or coupon rate.

The market value (selling price) of a bond at any given time depends on three things: its stated interest rate, the "going rate" of interest in the market, and its redemption or maturity date. A bond with a higher stated interest rate than the going rate on similar quality bonds will probably sell at a premium above its face value—its selling price will be above its redemption price. A bond with a lower stated interest rate than the going rate on similar quality bonds will probably sell at a discount—its selling price will be below its redemption price. How much the premium or discount is depends largely on how far in the future the maturity date is. The maturity date is shown after the interest rate. Figure 15.6 shows the type of information daily newspapers give about bond transactions.

Bond Yield. Suppose you bought a $1000 par-value bond in 1993 for $650. Its stated interest rate is 6 percent, and its maturity or redemption date is 2013. You therefore receive $60 per year in interest. Based on your actual investment of $650, your yield is 9.2 percent. If you hold it to maturity, you get $1000 for a bond that originally cost you only $650. This extra $350 increases your true, or effective, yield.

Market Indexes

Although they do not indicate how specific securities are doing, **market indexes** provide a useful summary of trends in specific industries and the stock market as a whole. Such information can be crucial in choosing

market index
A measure of the market value of stocks; provides a summary of price trends in a specific industry or of the stock market as a whole.

- *Bond*
  Company name is British Columbia Telephone.
- *Coupon*
  The annual rate of interest at face value is 9.65 percent.
- *Maturity*
  The maturity date is April 8, 2022.
- *Price*
  On this date, $138.48 was the price of the last transaction.
- *Yield*
  The yield is computed by dividing the annual interest paid by the current market price.

Issuer	Coupon	Maturity	Price	Yield
		GOVERNMENT OF CANADA		
Canada	3.00	June 1, 07	99.85	4.08
Canada	6.00	June 1, 08	103.83	4.08
Canada	5.00	June 1, 14	103.71	4.45
Canada	8.00	June 1, 27	145.92	4.58
		PROVINCIALS		
BC	6.00	June 9, 08	103.61	4.20
Hy Que	6.50	Feb. 15, 11	108.55	4.50
Man	7.75	Dec. 22, 25	135.19	4.93
		CORPORATE		
BC Tel	**9.65**	**Apr 8, 22**	**138.49**	**6.48**
Loblaw	6.65	Nov. 8, 27	107.91	5.99
Royal Bank	4.18	June 1, 09	99.04	4.51
Suncor	6.10	Aug 7, 07	100.95	5.96

Figure 15.6 How to read a bond quotation.

bull market
A period of rising stock prices; a period in which investors act on a belief that stock prices will rise.

bear market
A period of falling stock prices; a period in which investors act on a belief that stock prices will fall.

Dow Jones Industrial Average (DJIA)
Market index based on the prices of 30 of the largest firms listed on NYSE.

S&P/TSX index
An average computed from 225 different large Canadian stocks from various industry groups.

Standard & Poor's Composite Index (S&P 500)
Market index based on the performance of 400 industrial firms, 40 utilities, 40 financial institutions, and 20 transportation companies.

NASDAQ Composite Index
Value-weighted market index that includes all NASDAQ-listed companies, both domestic and foreign.

market order
An order to a broker to buy or sell a certain security at the current market price.

limit order
An order to a broker to buy a certain security only if its price is less than or equal to a given limit.

stop order
An order to a broker to sell a certain security if its price falls to a certain level or below.

round lot
The purchase or sale of stock in units of 100 shares.

odd lot
The purchase or sale of stock in units of other than 100 shares.

appropriate investments. For example, market indexes reveal bull and bear market trends. **Bull markets** are periods of upward-moving stock prices. The years 1981–89, 1993–99, and 2004-06 were bull markets. Periods of falling stock prices are called **bear markets**. The years 1972–74, 1991–92, and 2000–02 were bear markets.

The Dow Jones Industrial Average. The most widely cited market index is the **Dow Jones Industrial Average (DJIA)**. The Dow is the sum of market prices for 30 of the largest industrial firms listed on the NYSE. By tradition, the Dow is an indicator of blue-chip (top quality) stock price movements. Because of the small number of firms it considers, however, it is a limited gauge of the overall stock market. The Dow increased sharply in the 1990s. It reached 11 000 in early in 2000, but dropped to less than 8000 in 2002. By mid-2007, it had climbed to 13 400.

The S&P/TSX Average. The **S&P/TSX index** is an average computed from 225 different large Canadian stocks from various industry groups.[27] The index (formerly called the TSE 300) has also been very volatile during the last few years. It moved sharply upwards during the bull market of the 1990s, and topped 11 000 in the summer of 2000. It then dropped to 6500 by the end of 2000. By mid-2007, it had risen to 14 100.

The S&P 500. **Standard & Poor's Composite Index (S&P 500)** consists of 500 stocks, including 400 industrial firms, 40 utilities, 40 financial institutions, and 20 transportation companies. The index average is weighted according to market capitalization of each stock, so the more highly valued companies exercise a greater influence on the index.

The NASDAQ Composite. Because it considers more stocks, some stock market observers regard the **NASDAQ Composite Index** as the most important of all market indexes. Unlike the Dow and the S&P 500, all NASDAQ-listed companies are included in the index. The NASDAQ market has been very volatile. In early 2000, it reached 5000, but by 2001 had dropped to just 1300. By 2007, it had increased to 2800.

Buying and Selling Stocks

Based on your own investigations and/or recommendations from your broker, you can place many types of orders. A **market order** requests the broker to buy or sell a certain security at the prevailing market price at the time. A **limit order** authorizes the purchase of a stock only if its price is less than or equal to a given limit. For example, a limit order to buy a stock at $80 per share means that the broker is to buy it if and only if the stock becomes available for a price of $80 or less. Similarly, a **stop order** instructs the broker to sell a stock if its price falls to a certain level. For example, a stop order of $85 on a particular stock means that the broker is to sell it if and only if its price falls to $85 or below.

You can also place orders of different sizes. A **round lot** order requests 100 shares or some multiple thereof. Fractions of a round lot are called **odd lots**. Trading odd lots is usually more expensive than trading round lots, because an intermediary called an odd-lot broker is often involved, which increases brokerage fees.

The business of buying and selling stocks is changing rapidly. Formerly, a person had to have a broker to buy and sell stocks. More and more individuals are now buying and selling stocks on the internet, and traditional brokers are worried that before long customers will avoid using their services. To make matters worse for brokers, it will soon be possible for Canadians to purchase shares of stock directly from the companies that issue them instead of having to go through a broker or the internet. The fees that customers will have to pay for these direct purchases will be even lower than the fees currently charged by discount brokers.[28]

Financing Securities Purchases

When you place a buy order of any kind, you must tell your broker how you will pay for the purchase. You might maintain a cash account with your broker. Then, as stocks are bought and sold, proceeds are added into the account and commissions and costs of purchases are withdrawn by the broker. You can also buy shares on credit.

Margin Trading

As with futures contracts, you can buy stocks on *margin*—putting down only a portion of the stock's price. You borrow the rest from your broker, who, in turn, borrows from the banks at a special rate and secures the loans with stock. Suppose you purchased $100 000 worth of stock in WestJet. Let's also say that you paid $50 000 of your own money and borrowed the other $50 000 from your broker at 10 percent interest. Valued at its market price, your stock serves as your collateral. If shares have risen in value to $115 000 after one year, you can sell them and pay your broker $55 000 ($50 000 principal plus $5000 interest). You will have $60 000 left over. Your original investment of $50 000 will have earned a 20 percent profit of $10 000. If you had paid the entire price out of your own pocket, you would have earned only a 15 percent return.

Although investors often recognize possible profits to be made in margin trading, they sometimes fail to consider that losses, too, can be amplified. Suppose, for example, that you decided on January 4, 2004, to buy 1000 shares of Canadian Petroleum for $53 per share. You put up $26 500 of your own money and borrow $26 500 from your broker. As the stock rises, you reason, the loan will enable you to profit from twice as many shares. Now let us say that shortly after you purchase your stock, its market price begins to fall. You decide to hold on until it recovers. By January 4, 2006, when the price has fallen to $23 per share, you give up hope and sell.

Now let us see how margin trading has amplified your losses. If you had invested your own $26 500 instead of borrowing it, you would recover $23 000 of your $53 000 investment (excluding commissions). Your loss, therefore, would be nearly 57 percent ($30 000 loss divided by $53 000 invested). By trading on margin, however, even though you still recover $23 000 of your $26 500 investment, you must repay the $26 500 that you

If you're a day trader, are volatile markets good or bad? When the market's volatile, there are often wider spreads between bid prices (what traders pay for a share of stock) and ask prices (what they charge for it). The difference isn't necessarily large, but if you can make a number of quick hits during the day, you can make a dime here and a dollar there. That strategy appeals to traders at large firms, but also to individual traders working on their own.

borrowed, plus $2650 in loan interest (at a 10 percent annual rate). In this case, your losses total $32 650 ($55 650 in outlays less $23 000 recovered). The percentage loss is 123 percent of your investment ($32 650 loss divided by $26 500 investment)—much greater than the 57-percent loss you would have suffered without margin trading.

The problems with margin trading became evident at online brokerages when stock markets began falling in 2000. Inexperienced *day traders* were borrowing at an alarming rate, and some were using the borrowed funds for risky and speculative day trading. They visited websites online to buy and sell a stock in the same day (so-called *intraday trades*), seeking quick, in-and-out, small gains on large volumes (many shares) of each stock. While some day traders were successful, most ended up financial losers.

Short Sales

short sale
Selling borrowed shares of stock in the expectation that their price will fall before they must be replaced, so that replacement shares can be bought for less than the original shares were sold for.

In addition to money, brokerages also lend buyers securities. A **short sale** begins when you borrow a security from your broker and sell it (one of the few times it is legal to sell what you do not own). At a given time in the future, you must restore an equal number of shares of that issue to the brokerage, along with a fee.

For example, suppose that in June you believe the price of Alcan stock will soon fall. You order your broker to sell short 100 shares at the market price of $38 per share. Your broker will make the sale and credit $3800 to your account. If Alcan's price falls to $32 per share in July, you can buy 100 shares for $3200 and give them to your broker, leaving you with a $600 profit (before commissions). The risk is that Alcan's price will not fall but will hold steady or rise, leaving you with a loss.

SECURITIES REGULATION

blue-sky laws
Laws regulating how corporations must back up securities.

prospectus
A detailed registration statement about a new stock filed with a provincial securities exchange; must include any data helpful to a potential buyer.

insider trading
The use of special knowledge about a firm to make a profit on the stock market.

In 1912, the Manitoba government was a Canadian pioneer in making laws applying mainly to the sale of new securities. Under these "**blue-sky laws**," corporations issuing securities must back them up with something more than the blue sky. Similar laws were passed in other provinces. Provincial laws also generally require that stockbrokers be licensed and securities be registered before they can be sold. In each province, issuers of proposed new securities must file a prospectus with the provincial securities exchange. A **prospectus** is a detailed registration statement that includes information about the firm, its operation, its management, the purpose of the proposed issue, and any other data helpful to a potential buyer of these securities. The prospectus must be made available to prospective investors.

The Ontario Securities Act, for example, contains disclosure provisions for new and existing issues, prevention of fraud, regulation of the Toronto Stock Exchange, and takeover bids. It also prohibits **insider trading**, which is the use of special knowledge about a firm to make a profit in the stock market. The Toronto Stock Exchange provides an example of self-regulation by the industry. The TSE has regulations concerning listing and delisting of securities, disclosure requirements, and issuing of prospectuses for new securities.

Unlike the United States with its Securities and Exchange Commission (SEC), Canada does not yet have comprehensive federal securities legislation or a federal regulatory body. In fact, Canada is the only country in the industrialized world that does not have a single regulator.[29] A report by a government-appointed committee that studied Canada's system of securities regulation concluded that it is in dire need of reform. It recommended a single regulator for Canada. The main complaints the committee noted were lack of meaningful enforcement of securities laws, and unnecessary costs and time delays that make Canada's capital markets uncompetitive internationally.[30]

Summary of Learning Objectives

1. Define *money* and identify the different forms it takes in Canada's money supply. Any item that is portable, divisible, durable, and stable satisfies the four basic characteristics of *money*. Money also serves three functions: it is a medium of exchange, a store of value, and a unit of account. The nation's money supply is often determined by two measures. *M-1* includes liquid (or spendable) forms of money: currency (bills and coins), demand deposits, and other "chequable" deposits (such as chequing accounts and ATM withdrawals). *M-2* includes M-1 plus items that cannot be directly spent but that can be easily converted to spendable forms: time deposits, money market funds, and savings deposits. *Credit* must also be considered as a factor in the money supply.
2. Describe the different kinds of *financial institutions* that make up the Canadian financial system and explain the services they offer. The financial intermediaries that form the "four financial pillars" in Canada are chartered banks, alternate banks, life insurance companies, and investment dealers. The chartered banks, which are at the heart of our financial system, are the most important source of short-term funds for business firms. The chartered banking system creates money in the form of expanding demand deposits. The four kinds of financial institutions offer services like financial advice and brokerage services, electronic funds transfer, pension and trust services, and lending of money.
3. Explain the functions of the *Bank of Canada* and describe the tools it uses to control the money supply. The Bank of Canada manages the Canadian economy, controls the money supply, and regulates certain aspects of chartered banking operations. If the Bank of Canada wants to increase the money supply, it can buy government securities or lower the bank rate. If it wants to decrease the money supply, it can sell government securities or increase the bank rate.
4. Discuss the value of *common stock* and *preferred stock* to stockholders and describe the secondary market for each type of security. *Common stock* affords investors the prospect of capital gains, dividend income, or both. Common stock values are expressed in three ways: as *par value* (the face value of a share when it is issued), *market value* (the current market price of a share), and *book value* (the value of stockholders' equity compared with that of other stocks). Market value is the most important value to investors. *Preferred* stock is less risky than common stock. Both common and preferred stock are traded on *stock exchanges* (institutions formed to conduct the trading of existing securities) and in *over-the-counter (OTC) markets* (dealer organizations formed to trade securities outside stock exchange settings). "Members" who hold seats on exchanges act as *brokers*—agents who execute buy-and-sell orders—for non-members. Exchanges include the New York Stock Exchange, the Toronto Stock Exchange, and regional and foreign exchanges. In the OTC market, licensed traders serve functions similar to those of exchange members.
5. Describe the investment opportunities offered by *bonds*, *mutual funds*, and *commodities*. Like stocks and bonds, *mutual funds*—companies that pool investments to purchase portfolios of financial instruments—offer investors different levels of risk and growth potential. *Load funds* require investors to pay commissions of 2 to 8 percent; *no-load funds* do not charge commissions when investors buy in or out. *Futures contracts*—agreements to buy specified amounts of commodities at given prices on preset dates—are traded in the *commodities market*. Commodities traders often buy on *margins*, percentages of total sales prices that must be put up to order futures contracts.
6. Explain the process by which securities are bought and sold. Investors generally use such financial information services as newspaper and online stock, bond, and OTC quotations to learn about possible investments. *Market indexes* such as the Toronto Stock Exchange index, the Dow Jones Industrial Average, the Standard & Poor's Composite Index, and the NASDAQ Composite provide useful summaries of trends, both in specific industries and in the market as a whole. Investors can then place different types of orders. *Market orders* are orders to buy or sell at current prevailing prices. Because investors do not know exactly what prices will be when market orders are executed, they may issue *limit* or *stop orders* that are to be executed only if prices rise to or fall below specified levels. *Round lots* are purchased in multiples of 100 shares. *Odd lots* are purchased in fractions of round lots. Securities can be bought on margin or as part of *short sales*—sales in which investors sell securities that are borrowed from brokers and returned at a later date.

QUESTIONS AND EXERCISES

Questions for Analysis

1. What kinds of changes in banking are shifting banks away from their historical role?
2. Do we really need all the different types of financial institutions we have in Canada? Could we make do with just chartered banks? Why or why not?
3. Should credit cards be counted in the money supply? Why or why not? Support your definition by using the definition of money.
4. Should banks be regulated, or should market forces be allowed to determine the money supply? Defend your answer.
5. Assume that the price of gold on the open market was \$400 per ounce on March 31, 2003. Assume also that futures contracts for June 2004 gold were selling for \$428 per ounce. This price reflected investors' judgments that gold prices would be higher the following December. Now suppose that you purchased a 100-ounce gold futures contract in October 2003 for \$42 800 (428 × 100). If in December 2003 the June gold futures sold for \$453, what could you sell your contract for? What would your profit be after the two months?
6. Suppose you decided to invest in common stocks as a personal investment. Which kind of broker—full-service or online discount—would you use for buying and selling stock? Why?
7. Choose a stock from the TSX and find a newspaper listing of a recent day's transactions for the stock. Explain what each element in the listing means.

Application Exercises

8. Interview the manager of a local chartered bank branch. Identify the ways in which the Bank of Canada helps the bank and the ways in which it limits the bank.
9. Interview the financial manager of a local business firm. What are the investment goals of the organization? What mix of securities does it use? What strengths and weaknesses do you see in its portfolio?
10. Contact a broker for information about setting up a personal account for trading securities. Prepare a report on the broker's requirements for placing buy/sell orders, credit terms, cash account requirements, services available to investors, and commissions/fees schedules.

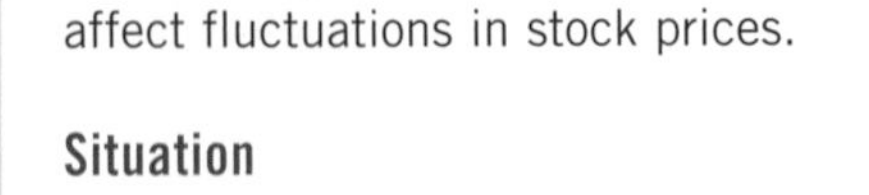

BUILDING YOUR BUSINESS SKILLS

Market Ups and Downs

Goal

To encourage students to understand the forces that affect fluctuations in stock prices.

Situation

Investing in stocks requires an understanding of the various factors that affect stock prices. These factors may be intrinsic to the company itself or part of the external environment.

- Internal factors relate to the company itself, such as an announcement of poor or favourable earnings, earnings that are more or less than expected, major layoffs, labour problems, management issues, and mergers.
- External factors relate to world or national events, such as a threatened war in the Persian Gulf, the SARS epidemic, weather conditions that affect sales, the Bank of Canada's adjustment of interest rates, and employment figures that were higher or lower than expected. By analyzing these factors, you will often learn a lot about why a stock did well or why it did poorly. Being aware of these influences will help you anticipate future stock movements.

Method

Step 1 Working alone, choose a common stock that has experienced considerable price fluctuations in the past few years. Here are several examples (but there are many others): Nortel Networks, IBM, Amazon.com, and Apple Computer. Find the symbol for the stock and the exchange on which it is traded.

Step 2 At your library, find the *Daily Stock Price Record*, a publication that provides a historical picture of daily stock closings. There are separate copies for the various stock exchanges. Find your stock, and study its trading pattern.

▶▶▶

Step 3 Find four or five days over a period of several months or even a year when there have been major price fluctuations in the stock. (A two- or three-point price change from one day to the next is considered major.) Then research what happened on that day that might have contributed to the fluctuation. The best place to begin is with *The Globe and Mail* or *The Wall Street Journal*.

Step 4 Write a short analysis that links changes in stock price to internal and external factors. As you analyze the data, be aware that it is sometimes difficult to know why a stock price fluctuates.

Step 5 Get together with three other students who studied different stocks. As a group, discuss your findings, looking for fluctuation patterns.

Follow-Up Questions

1. Do you see any similarities in the movement of the various stocks during the same period? For example, did the stocks move up or down at about the same time? If so, do you think the stocks were affected by the same factors? Explain your thinking.
2. Based on your analysis, did internal or external factors have the greater impact on stock price? Which factors had the longer-lasting effect? Which factors had the shorter effect?
3. Why do you think it is so hard to predict changes in stock price on a day-to-day basis?

EXERCISING YOUR ETHICS: TEAM EXERCISE

Serving Two Masters: Torn Between Company and Client

The Situation

Employees in financial services firms are sometimes confronted by conflicting allegiances between the company and its clients. In managing customers' stock portfolios, for example, the best timing for buy and sell decisions for clients' financial positions may not be the most profitable for the financial manager's firm. Investment managers, as a result, must choose a "right" course of action for reconciling possible conflicting interests.

The Dilemma

George Michaels is a customer portfolio manager employed by Premier Power Investments. His 35 clients—individual investors—have portfolios with market values ranging from $200 000 to $2 million in stocks, bonds, and mutual funds. Clients generally rely on George's recommendations to buy, sell, or hold each security based on his knowledge of their investment goals and risk tolerance, along with his experience in keeping up with market trends and holding down transactions costs. Premier Power Investments Company earns sales commissions ranging from 2 percent to 4 percent of market value for each buy and sell transaction.

On Monday morning, George's boss, Vicky Greene, informs George that due to Premier Power Investments Company's sagging revenues, it is to everyone's benefit to increase the number of transactions in customers' portfolios. She suggests that he find some different and attractive securities to replace existing securities for his customers. As George thinks about possible ways for accelerating his buy and sell recommendations, he has qualms about the motivation behind Vicky's comments. He is unsure what to do.

Team Activity

Assemble a group of four students and assign each group member to one of the following roles:

- George Michaels (employee)
- Vicky Greene (employer)
- Portfolio owner (customer)
- Owner (one of many outside shareholders of Premier Power Investments Company)

Action Steps

1. Before discussing the situation with your group, and from the perspective of your assigned role, do you think there are any ethical issues in this situation? If so, write them down.
2. Return to your group and reveal any ethical issues that were identified by each member. Be especially aware to see if the different roles resulted in different kinds of ethical issues. Why might role differences result in dissimilar priorities on ethical issues?
3. For the various ethical issues that were identified, decide as a group which one is the most important for Premier Power Investments to resolve. Which issue is second in importance?
4. From an ethical standpoint, what does your group finally recommend be done to resolve the most important ethical issue? To resolve the second most important ethical issue?

BUSINESS CASE 15

Scandal in the Mutual Fund Industry

During the past 20 years, Canadians have invested heavily in the stock market. Some of them do their own trading, and some use the services of a broker, but most of them buy shares in mutual funds. Fund managers pool the money of many individual investors and then decide which companies they will invest in and how much they will invest. Mutual funds are touted as a good deal for individual investors who do not have the time or expertise to intelligently invest in the stock market.

This sounds pretty good, but in the last five years or so, mutual funds have received some very negative publicity because their actions are not always in the best interests of the average investor. Concerns have been raised about mutual funds in three areas: management fees, market timing, and late trading.

Management fees. It is important to investors that mutual fund managers are efficient in their work so that management costs do not unduly reduce the returns that mutual funds earn. In 2004, the *Globe and Mail* reported the results of a study that assessed the performance of 615 mutual funds during the period 1999–2004. The study used a key measure of mutual fund performance: the "*Fee-to-Performance Value Indicator*" (which shows how much of a fund's returns are used for fees like managers' salaries and commissions). The study found that the typical mutual fund has a score of 25 on the fee-for-performance indicator, meaning that about 25 cents out of every dollar earned goes to cover management fees. But fee-to-performance scores varied a lot. The *best* funds in the study were Ferique Equity (where only 6.5 cents of every dollar earned was used for management fees), PH&N Dividend Income (7.4 cents), and Sprott Canadian Equity (7.4 cents). The *worst* funds were Investors Canadian Enterprise (where 88.9 cents of every dollar was used for management fees), Clarica Canadian Diversified (76.9 cents), and Ethical Growth (62.7 cents).

The study also found that billions of dollars have been invested by Canadians in mutual funds that are not giving them good value for their money. During the period 1999–2004, $32.7 billion was contributed to mutual funds like AGF American Growth Class and BMO International Equity Fund that actually lost money. These funds delivered no value at all to investors (and because they lost money, it is not possible to calculate a negative fee-to-performance score for these funds). But these same mutual funds collected millions of dollars in fees from investors. Canadians also invested $21 billion dollars in mutual funds where more than 50 percent of the gross revenue of the fund was used to pay management fees. These firms delivered questionable value to investors.

Ken Kivenko, a spokesman for the Small Investor Protection Association said that most individual investors don't even realize that they are paying fees to mutual funds. He found it surprising that some mutual funds can attract billions of dollars of investment from Canadians even though their fees are uncompetitive. Mutual funds that charge high fees counter these claims by noting that they provide better service to customers than do mutual funds that charge lower fees.

Market timing. This refers to the practice of rapid in-and-out trading in mutual fund shares in order to profit from near-term price changes. While it is not technically illegal, it violates a basic principle of fairness because mutual funds typically have a strategy of long-term investing and do not normally allow people to do in-and-out trading (unless they pay a penalty). If a select few traders are allowed to engage in market timing without paying the penalty, this obviously works to the detriment of small investors who are not given this deal.

In 2004, four large Canadian mutual funds were fined a total of $156 million for allowing certain traders to engage in market timing. These traders made a total of $301 million in profits by using market timing. Three brokerages that were owned by banks were also fined a total of $46.5 million. All of the money will be used to reimburse investors who were disadvantaged by market timing. Paul Moore, the vice-chairman of the Ontario Securities Commission, said that by allowing only certain people to make market timing trades, these companies reduced returns for their long-term investors and failed in their duty to protect their interests. He also said that the fines will remind mutual fund managers that they have a responsibility to be vigilant in monitoring the activities of the people who work in their firms.

Michael Watson, the OSC's enforcement director, said he was disturbed by the fact that the problem of market timing was brought to the OSC's attention by New York Attorney General Elliot Spitzer, who was prosecuting U.S. mutual funds that allowed the practice. Watson said there must have been many people in Canada who knew that market timing was going on, but no one said anything.

In the United States, charges were filed against several firms, including Putnam Investments, which is the fifth-largest mutual fund firm in the United States, with $272 billion in assets. Regulators allege that executives knew that two of the firm's managers were market timing their own funds for personal profit, told them to stop, but didn't fire them, and let them keep the profits they made from market timing. After this became known, CEO Lawrence Lasser and four managers were fired.

Late trading. Sounds incredible, doesn't it, that someone can bet on events from the past? It turns out that's what's been going on in the $7 trillion scandal-laden mutual funds industry. Some mutual fund managers have been making transactions after the market outcomes are known. It's what you might call a "sure thing"—a great way to erase market risk and take profits that are inaccessible to honest investors.

It's called "late trading"—trading in fund shares after the market closes, but at the close-of-trade price—and it's illegal. After the 4:00 p.m. (Eastern Time) cutoff, when the day's closing price is known, preferred customers get to trade—buy or sell—at the pre-4:00 p.m. price. It's like betting after the game is over. Late trading gives an unfair information advantage over other investors because when big news breaks after the 4:00 p.m. closing—news that will almost certainly affect the next day's securities markets—late traders are nearly assured of a next-day quick profit or avoidance of a loss.

In the United States, the Securities and Exchange Commission's (SEC) enforcement director, Stephen Cutler, told a Senate hearing that about 10 percent of fund groups may have engaged in late trading and as many as one-fourth of America's largest mutual funds helped favoured clients by allowing illegal late trading. Preferential trading arrangements for big-money clients can be draining off billions of dollars from ordinary investors in mutual funds.

The SEC, the New York Attorney General's Office, and the Wisconsin Department of Financial Institutions are all looking into alleged market-timing transactions by Richard Strong, the board chairman of Strong Mutual Funds, that may have benefited him, his family, and friends. Strong Mutual Funds has policies against market timing because it hurts long-term shareholders and increases the fund's costs of operations. Under those conditions, regulators say, it's fraudulent to allow favoured people to do market timing without disclosing it to shareholders. The company confirmed that Strong invested assets in a small number of short-term, next-day transactions taking advantage of market-moving news. Strong resigned as board chairman of the $42 billion fund and said he would reimburse investors for any losses they suffered because of his trading.

What should be done to reduce the problems of marketing timing and late trading? An indignant U.S. Congress proposed possible remedies and pledged that new, stiffer SEC regulations will eventually emerge. Meanwhile, the SEC and the National Association of Securities Dealers brought actions seeking injunctions, penalties, and financial relief for investors against several more illicit brokerages and mutual funds. But fixing the problem won't be easy because each proposal seems to create new potential problems, and there's no agreement on the best course of action. For example, proposals by the Investment Company Institute to outlaw all late trading could extend the time to process a trade—what now takes one day could take three or more days. That means mutual fund insiders would know about investment movements underway by big pension funds, and have more time to use that information for self-gain. The trick is to fix the old problems without causing new ones.

Questions for Discussion

1. Why do you suppose the Ontario Securities Commission was slow in detecting the industry's market-timing abuses?
2. What remedies do you believe would be appropriate for fund managers who are found guilty of market timing and late trading? Defend your answer.
3. Suppose you are the manager of one of the equity funds for a large mutual funds firm. What steps would you take to ensure compliance with OSC regulations by your employees?
4. As a Chartered Financial Analyst (CFA) working at a mutual funds firm, what would you do if you suspected other employees of doing market timing or late trading?
5. Think of an after-hours news event that resulted in a next-day decline in the stock market. Then think of an after-hours news event that resulted in a next-day increase in the stock market. Why do you think the market would fall for the one example and would increase for the other?

MYBUSINESSLAB PEARSON mybusinesslab

To improve your grade, visit the MyBusinessLab website at **www.pearsoned.ca/mybusinesslab**. This online homework and tutorial system allows you to test your understanding and generates a personalized study plan just for you. It provides you with study and practice tools directly related to this chapter's content. MyBusinessLab puts you in control of your own learning!

CHAPTER 16

Financial Decisions and Risk Management

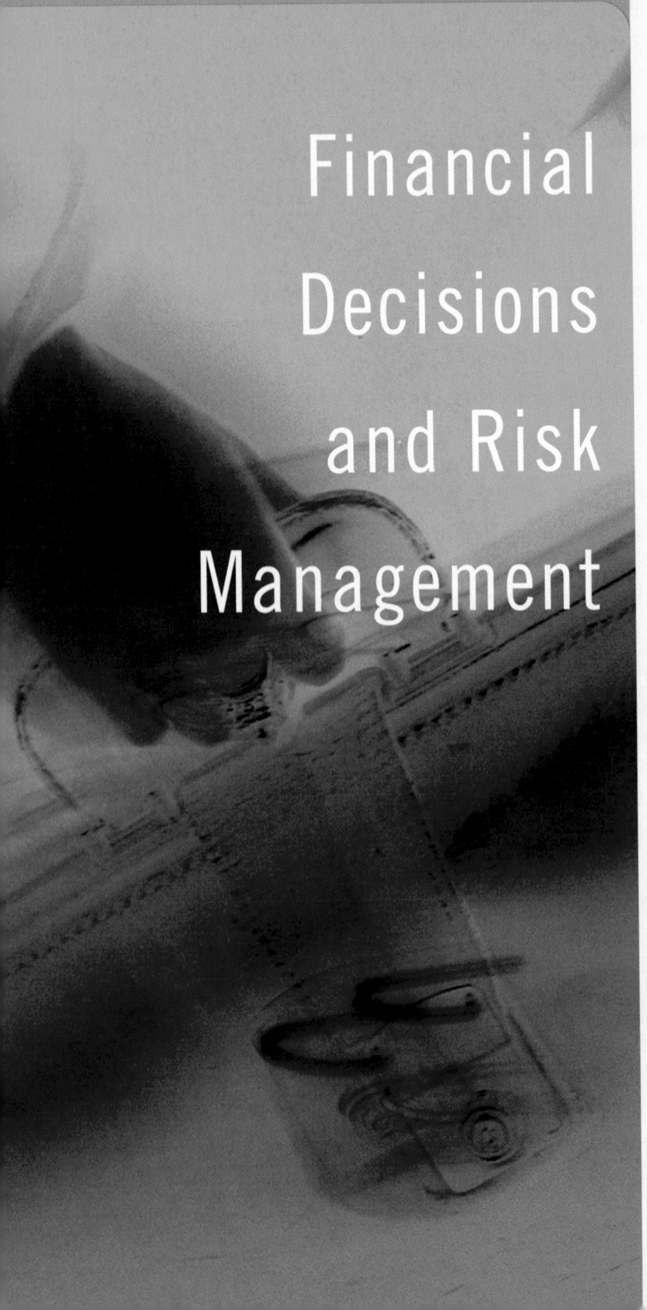

After reading this chapter, you should be able to:

1. Describe the responsibilities of a *financial manager*.
2. Distinguish between *short-term (operating)* and *long-term (capital)* expenditures.
3. Identify four sources of *short-term financing* for businesses.
4. Distinguish among the various sources of *long-term financing* and explain the risks involved in each.
5. Discuss some key issues in financial management for small businesses.
6. Explain how *risk* affects business operations and identify the five steps in the *risk-management process*.

The Increasing Importance of Risk Management

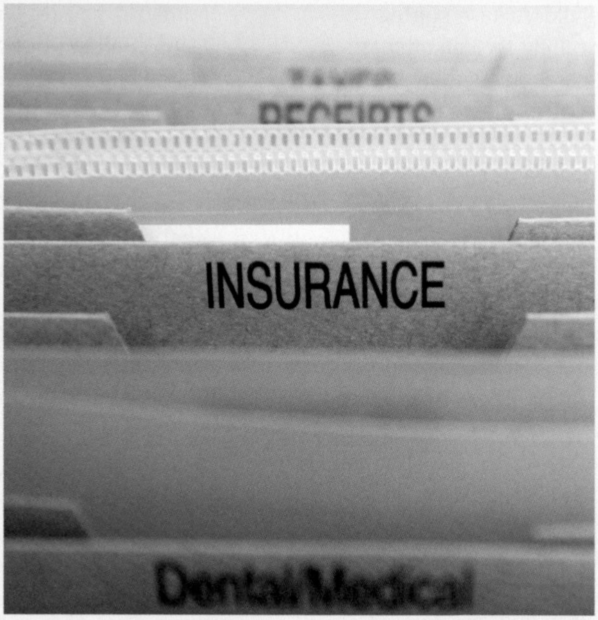

Canadian business firms face risks in many different areas. The company's computer network may be hacked into, interest rates may change, executive talent may be raided by another company, a natural disaster or terrorist attack may occur, consumers may sue the company, or all of the above may happen. How do business firms cope with these risks? There are several things that can be done including the creation of a top-level executive position to oversee risk management, buying insurance to shield the company from various kinds of risks, and instituting control systems that will reduce the risk that inappropriate employee behaviour will cause financial harm to the company.

Creating a top-level position to oversee risk management. Companies usually have a Chief Executive Officer (CEO), a Chief Operating Officer (COO), and a Chief Financial Officer (CFO), but not too many of them have a Chief Risk Officer (CRO). At least not yet. But the realization is growing that a business needs a high-level executive who is responsible for developing and implementing plans for dealing with risk, rather than just trying to respond to risk after something unexpected happens. Forrester Research predicts that by 2007, 75 percent of large organizations in North America will have a CRO.

Hydro One Inc. already has a CRO, partly because the deregulation of electricity means that it needs to manage the risk of price fluctuations in the new market-based pricing system. But it's not just pricing risk that Hydro One needs to deal with. John Fraser, Hydro One's CRO, has already dealt with a major risk situation that has little to do with pricing. When Hydro One offered an early retirement package to employees, 1400 people took the offer. This was far more than the company expected, so Fraser was charged with analyzing how the loss of so many people might affect the company's ability to achieve its objectives. After a department-by-department analysis, he concluded that by hiring 125 people and paying consultants to do some other critical work, Hydro One could reduce its risks to an acceptable level.

Buying insurance. There are many different types of business insurance that are available. Risk managers must decide what kind of insurance the company needs to carry and whether it can afford to carry such insurance. Consider what happened to Kitchener, Ontario–based Kentain Products, which manufactures chemical tank liners. Its products have been very successful in Canada, so owner Glen Lippert thought it was a natural extension of the business to begin exporting the products to the United States. He was in for a rude shock. When his insurance company found out what he was planning, they would no longer sell him liability insurance because they felt that selling to the United States was too risky. When Lippert checked with other insurance companies, he discovered that it would cost him $50 000 in annual premiums to get liability insurance. Since that figure exceeded the profit he expected to make in the United States, he abandoned his export plans.

It's not just companies that export that are having trouble with insurance premiums. One Waterloo, Ontario–based company that sells industrial air compressors had its premiums increased from $6500 to $40 000 in one year. A cabinet maker saw its premiums double from $10 000 to $20 000 in one year, and then to $60 000 two years later. Many small businesses can't get insurance at any price. This is a big problem because banks usually demand that a company have liability insurance before they will loan it money. A survey by the Federation of Independent Business found that most small businesses have faced increases in the 30 percent range during each of the last few years. In the survey, 83 percent of the respondents said that high insurance premiums were their single biggest cost.

The insurance industry gives a variety of reasons for the rapidly escalating insurance premiums—uncertainty in the stock market (where insurance companies have much of their money invested), low interest rates, terrorist activity, natural disasters, and liability lawsuits against companies. Put simply, insurance companies are not getting enough revenue from premium payments and their investments to pay all the claims that are arising. So they increase premiums and refuse to cover some high-risk activities.

Some people think that the insurance business is not very interesting, what with all the mathematical calculations and actuarial tables that are required. But insurance is not only practical and important; it can also be very interesting. Consider the following situations:

- Canadian companies routinely buy liability insurance for members of their board of directors to shield them from lawsuits that allege negligence or failure to carry out their duty to shareholders. Lately, lawyers for disgruntled shareholders have started suing boards of directors for failing to protect shareholders. Some big wins for shareholders meant that insurance companies had to pay out large sums of money. After this became a trend, insurance companies started sharply raising their rates.
- Producers of the Broadway show *Titanic* paid about U.S.$400 000 for insurance to cover things such as a member of the audience being hit by a flying deck chair, or a cast member being injured during the performance. Interestingly, Chubb Corp., the company that covered the real *Titanic* (the one that sank on April 15, 1912, claiming 1523 lives), also covered the Broadway show. That real *Titanic* disaster cost the insurance company $100 000, but the Broadway show was insured for U.S.$14 million.
- In the musical *Victor/Victoria*, an insurance policy was purchased on Julie Andrews. The policy premium—U.S.$157 985—insured the producers of the show for up to $2 million if Andrews missed some performances, and up to $8.5 million if she had to leave the show. Producers routinely buy this kind of insurance because if a star is unable to perform on a given night, many patrons who have bought tickets want their money back. As it happened, Andrews missed many performances because of various illnesses, and an unusually large number of patrons requested refunds. Total losses to the producers exceeded $1 million. But when the producers tried to collect their money, the insurance companies refused to pay, arguing that Andrews had given false answers to questions about her medical history.
- Rap artists such as Snoop Doggy Dogg can earn more than U.S.$50 000 per night on a multi-city concert tour. But national tours by rap artists have been virtually nonexistent for over a decade because stabbings and gunfire were becoming all too common at these shows and insurance was almost impossible to get.
- Diamond State Insurance Company, which issued an insurance policy to the band Limp Bizkit, claimed it had no liability for damages awarded following the death of a teenage fan at a Limp Bizkit rock concert in Australia in 2001. The insurance company argued that singer Fred Durst "incited" the crowd and that led to the teenager's death when she was trampled by the crowd.
- Reliance National Insurance is one of the largest underwriters of music events. It also insures many concerts by crooners and rappers. When musicians perform live, insurance costs are usually shared by the performer, the concert promoter, and the arena where the event is being held. Music companies also take out "key man" insurance on musicians.

Implementing effective control systems. There is always a risk that some employees will act in ways that are financially detrimental to the company. In recent years, several high-profile cases have demonstrated just how high the losses can be if effective risk control systems are not in place. For example, John Rusnak, a currency trader at Allfirst Financial, defrauded the company of $691 million by creating phoney currency trades. Stephen Humphries, a trader at Sussex Futures Ltd. in England engaged in so much fraudulent trading activity that he destroyed the company he worked for. He lost U.S.$1.1 million in just one 90-minute period. Sussex Futures ceased operations, and 70 people lost their jobs. Nicholas Leeson, who worked for Barings PLC, a British merchant bank, bought and sold futures contracts, particularly investments known as derivatives. Over a three-week period, Leeson managed to incur trading losses of nearly $1 billion. When losses spiralled out of control, Leeson fled, and Barings had to declare bankruptcy. Leeson was eventually sentenced to six-and-a-half years in prison.

In all of these cases, there was a failure to properly manage risk. That failure led to massive financial losses, corporate bankruptcies, and the loss of many jobs.

HOW WILL THIS BENEFIT YOU?

The opening case clearly shows the importance of managing risk with respect to the financial activities of business firms. The material in this chapter will benefit you in two ways: (1) You will be better able to use your knowledge about finance in your career as both an employee and as a manager, and (2) you will be a more informed consumer, with greater awareness of how businesses use financial instruments to support their activities.

In this chapter, we first describe the objectives and responsibilities of financial managers. We then identify the short-term and long-term expenditures that firms make, and the short- and long-term sources of funds that are available to support these expenditures. We conclude with a discussion of what is required to effectively manage risk in a business.

THE ROLE OF THE FINANCIAL MANAGER

Financial managers plan and control the acquisition and dispersal of the company's financial assets. The business activity known as **finance** (or corporate finance) typically involves four responsibilities:

- determining a firm's long-term investments
- obtaining funds to pay for those investments
- conducting the firm's everyday financial activities
- managing the risks that the firm takes

1 Describe the responsibilities of a *financial manager.*

financial managers
Those managers responsible for planning and overseeing the financial resources of a firm.

finance
The business function involving decisions about a firm's long-term investments and obtaining the funds to pay for those investments.

Objectives of the Financial Manager

A financial manager's overall objective is to increase a firm's value—and thus stockholders' wealth. Financial managers do many specific things to increase a firm's value: collect funds, pay debts, establish trade credit, obtain loans, control cash balances, and plan for future financial needs. Whereas accountants create data to reflect a firm's financial status, financial managers make decisions for improving that status. Financial managers, then, must ensure that a company's revenues exceed its costs—in other words, that it earns a profit. In sole proprietorships and partnerships, profits translate directly into increases in owners' wealth. In corporations, profits translate into an increase in the value of common stock.

Responsibilities of the Financial Manager

The various responsibilities of the financial manager in increasing a firm's wealth fall into three general categories: *cash flow management, financial control,* and *financial planning.*

Cash Flow Management

To increase a firm's value, financial managers must ensure that it always has enough funds on hand to purchase the materials and human resources that it needs to produce goods and services. Funds that are not needed immediately must be invested to earn more money for a firm. This activity—**cash flow management**—requires careful planning. If excess cash balances are allowed to sit idle instead of being invested, a firm loses the interest that it could have earned.

cash flow management
Managing the pattern in which cash flows into the firm in the form of revenues and out of the firm in the form of debt payments.

Financial Control

Because things never go exactly as planned, financial managers must be prepared to make adjustments for actual financial changes that occur each day. **Financial control** is the process of checking actual performance against plans to ensure that the desired financial outcome occurs. For example, planned revenues based on forecasts usually turn out to be higher or lower than actual revenues. Why? Simply because sales are unpredictable. Control involves monitoring revenue inflows and making appropriate financial adjustments. Higher-than-expected revenues, for instance, may be deposited in short-term interest-bearing accounts, or they may be used to pay off short-term debt. Otherwise earmarked resources can be saved or put to better use. In contrast, lower-than-expected revenues may necessitate short-term borrowing to meet current debt obligations.

financial control
The process of checking actual performance against plans to ensure that the desired financial status is achieved.

Budgets (as we saw in Chapter 11) are often the backbone of financial control. The budget provides the "measuring stick" against which performance is evaluated. The cash flows, debts, and assets not only of the whole

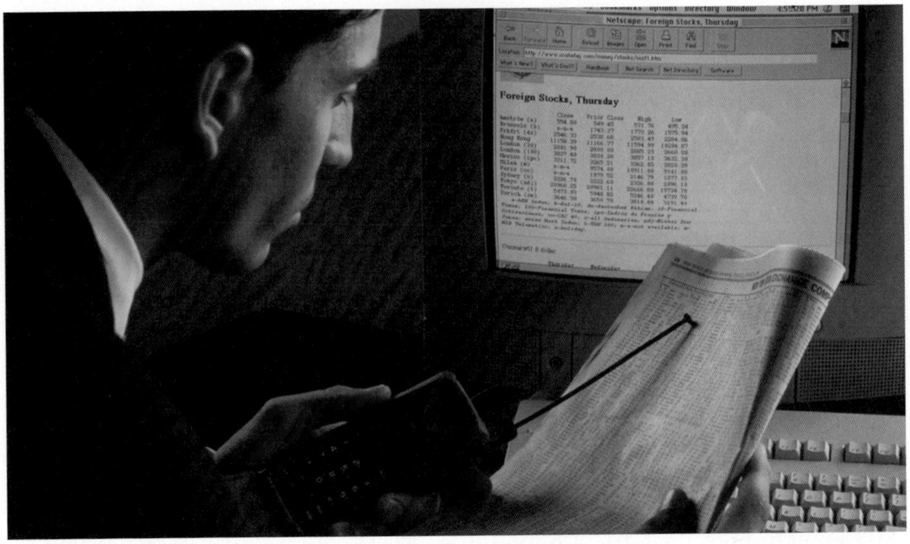

Financial managers have the responsibility of ensuring that the financial assets of a company are used effectively. This includes investments it may have in other companies in the form of shares of stock. Regular assessment of how these investments are performing is an important responsibility of financial managers.

company but of each department are compared at regular intervals against budgeted amounts. Discrepancies indicate the need for financial adjustments so that resources are used to the best advantage.

Financial Planning

financial plan
A description of how a business will reach some financial position it seeks for the future; includes projections for sources and uses of funds.

The cornerstone of effective financial management is the development of a **financial plan**, which describes a firm's strategies for reaching some future financial position. In constructing the plan, a financial manager must ask several questions:

- What funds are needed to meet immediate plans?
- When will it need more funds?
- Where can it get the funds to meet both its short- and long-term needs?

To answer these questions, a financial manager must develop a clear picture of why a firm needs funds. Managers must also assess the relative costs and benefits of potential funding sources. In the following sections, we examine the main reasons for which companies generate funds and describe the main sources of business funding, both for the short and long term.

WHY BUSINESSES NEED FUNDS

2 Distinguish between *short-term (operating)* and *long-term (capital)* expenditures.

Every company needs money to survive. Failure to make a contractually obligated payment can lead to bankruptcy and the dissolution of the firm. But the successful financial manager must distinguish between two different kinds of financial outlays: *short-term (operating)* expenditures and *long-term (capital)* expenditures.

Short-Term (Operating) Expenditures

A firm incurs short-term expenditures regularly in its everyday business activities. To handle these expenditures, financial managers must pay attention to *accounts payable, accounts receivable,* and *inventories*.

Accounts Payable

In Chapter 11, we defined *accounts payable* as unpaid bills owed to suppliers plus wages and taxes due within the upcoming year. For most companies, this is the largest single category of short-term debt. To plan for funding flows, financial managers want to know in advance the amounts of new accounts payable as well as when they must be repaid. For information about such obligations and needs—say, the quantity of supplies required by a certain department in an upcoming period—financial managers must rely on other managers. The Exercising Your Ethics box at the end of the chapter presents an interesting dilemma regarding accounts payable.

Accounts Receivable

As we also saw in Chapter 11, *accounts receivable* refers to funds due from customers who have bought on credit. A sound financial plan requires financial managers to project accurately both how much credit is advanced to buyers and when they will make payments on their accounts. For example, managers at Kraft Foods must know how many dollars' worth of cheddar cheese Safeway supermarkets will order each month; they must also know Safeway's payment schedule. Because accounts receivable represent an investment in products for which a firm has not yet received payment, they temporarily tie up its funds. Clearly, the seller wants to receive payment as quickly as possible.

Given that it is in the self-interest of buyers to delay payment as long as possible, how can a financial manager predict payment times? The answer lies in the development of a **credit policy**, the set of rules governing the extension of credit to customers. The credit policy sets standards as to which buyers are eligible for what type of credit. Financial managers extend credit to customers who have the ability to pay and honour their obligations to pay. They deny credit to firms with poor repayment histories.

credit policy
Rules governing a firm's extension of credit to customers.

The credit policy also sets payment terms. For example, credit terms of "2/10; net 30" mean that the selling company offers a 2 percent discount if the customer pays within 10 days. The customer has 30 days to pay the regular price. Thus, on a $1000 invoice, the buyer would have to pay only $980 on days 1 to 10 but all $1000 on days 11 to 30. The higher the discount, the more incentive buyers have to pay early. Sellers can thus adjust credit terms to influence when customers pay their bills. Often, however, credit terms can be adjusted only slightly without giving competitors an edge.

Inventories

Between the time a firm buys raw materials and the time it sells finished products, it ties up funds in **inventory**—materials and goods that it will sell within the year. Failure to manage inventory can have grave financial consequences. Too little inventory of any kind can cost a firm sales, while too much inventory means tied-up funds that cannot be used elsewhere. In extreme cases, a company may have to sell excess inventory at low prices simply to raise cash.

inventory
Materials and goods currently held by the company that will be sold within the year.

The basic supplies a firm buys to use in its production process are its **raw materials inventory**. Levi Strauss's raw materials inventory includes huge rolls of denim. **Work-in-process inventory** consists of goods partway through the production process. Cut-out but not-yet-sewn jeans are part of the work-in-process inventory at Levi's. Finally, **finished goods inventory** is the items that are ready for sale. Completed blue jeans ready for shipment to Levi dealers are finished goods inventory.

raw materials inventory
That portion of a firm's inventory consisting of basic supplies used to manufacture products for sale.

work-in-process inventory
That portion of a firm's inventory consisting of goods partway through the production process.

finished goods inventory
That portion of a firm's inventory consisting of completed goods ready for sale.

Long-Term (Capital) Expenditures

Companies need funds to cover long-term expenditures for fixed assets. As noted in Chapter 11, fixed assets are items that have a lasting use or value, such as land, buildings, and machinery. Long-term expenditures are usually more carefully planned than short-term outlays because they pose special problems. They differ from short-term outlays in the following ways, all of which influence the ways that long-term outlays are funded:

- unlike inventories and other short-term assets, they are not normally sold or converted to cash
- their acquisition requires a very large investment
- they represent a binding commitment of company funds that continues long into the future

SOURCES OF SHORT-TERM FUNDS

3 Identify four sources of *short-term financing* for businesses.

Firms can call on many sources for the funds they need to finance day-to-day operations and to implement short-term plans. These sources include *trade credit, secured and unsecured loans,* and *factoring of accounts receivable.*

Trade Credit

trade credit
The granting of credit by a selling firm to a buying firm.

open-book credit
Form of trade credit in which sellers ship merchandise on faith that payment will be forthcoming.

promissory note
Form of trade credit in which buyers sign promise-to-pay agreements before merchandise is shipped.

trade draft
Form of trade credit in which buyers must sign statements of payment terms attached to merchandise by sellers.

trade acceptance
Trade draft that has been signed by the buyer.

Accounts payable are not merely an expenditure. They are also a source of funds to the company, which has the use of both the product purchased and the price of the product until the time it pays its bill. **Trade credit**, the granting of credit by one firm to another, is effectively a short-term loan. Trade credit can take several forms.

- The most common form, **open-book credit**, is essentially a "gentlemen's agreement." Buyers receive merchandise along with invoices stating credit terms. Sellers ship products on faith that payment will be forthcoming.
- When sellers want more reassurance, they may insist that buyers sign legally binding **promissory notes** before merchandise is shipped. The agreement states when and how much money will be paid to the seller.
- The **trade draft** is attached to the merchandise shipment by the seller and states the promised date and amount of payment due. To take possession of the merchandise, the buyer must sign the draft. Once signed by the buyer, the document becomes a **trade acceptance**. Trade drafts and trade acceptances are useful forms of credit in international transactions.

Secured Short-Term Loans

secured loans
A short-term loan in which the borrower is required to put up collateral.

collateral
Any asset that a lender has the right to seize if a borrower does not repay a loan.

For most firms, bank loans are a vital source of short-term funding. Such loans almost always involve a promissory note in which the borrower promises to repay the loan plus interest. In **secured loans**, banks also require the borrower to put up **collateral**—to give the bank the right to seize certain assets if payments are not made as promised. Inventories, accounts receivable, and other assets may serve as collateral for a secured loan.

Secured loans allow borrowers to get funds when they might not qualify for unsecured credit. Moreover, they generally carry lower interest rates than unsecured loans. Collateral may be in the form of inventories or accounts receivable, and most businesses have other types of assets that can be pledged as well (for example, stocks and bonds the company owns). Most short-term business borrowing is secured by inventories and accounts receivable.

Inventory Loans

When a loan is made with inventory as a collateral asset, the lender lends the borrower some portion of the stated value of the inventory. Inventory is more attractive as collateral when it provides the lender with real security for the loan amount. For example, if the inventory can be readily converted into cash, it is relatively more valuable as collateral. Other inventory—say, boxes full of expensive, partially completed lenses for eyeglasses—is of little value on the open market. Meanwhile, a thousand crates of canned tomatoes might well be convertible into cash.

Accounts Receivable

When accounts receivable are used as collateral, the process is called **pledging accounts receivable**. In the event of non-payment, the lender may seize the receivables—that is, funds owed the borrower by its customers. If these assets are not enough to cover the loan, the borrower must make up the difference. This option is especially important to service companies such as accounting firms and law offices. Because they do not maintain inventories, accounts receivable are their main source of collateral. Typically, lenders who will accept accounts receivable as collateral are financial institutions with credit departments capable of evaluating the quality of the receivables.

pledging accounts receivable
Using accounts receivable as collateral for a loan.

Factoring Accounts Receivable. A firm can raise funds rapidly by *factoring* (that is, selling) its accounts receivable. The purchaser of the receivables (called a *factor*) might, for example, buy $40 000 worth of receivables for 60 percent of that sum ($24 000). The factor profits to the extent that the money it eventually collects exceeds the amount it paid. This profit depends on the quality of the receivables, the cost of collecting them, and interest rates.

Unsecured Short-Term Loans

With an **unsecured loan**, the borrower does not have to put up collateral. In many cases, however, the bank requires the borrower to maintain a *compensating balance:* the borrower must keep a portion of the loan amount on deposit with the bank in a non-interest-bearing account.

unsecured loan
A short-term loan in which the borrower is not required to put up collateral.

The terms of the loan—amount, duration, interest rate, and payment schedule—are negotiated between the bank and the borrower. To receive an

As CFO of *Nylon* magazine, which focuses on fashion and pop culture for women, Larry Rosenblum is responsible for collecting the money that advertisers owe the publication. The magazine depends on that money for its cash flow. To get the money, Rosenblum typically resorts to factors—lenders who buy the legal right to collect a company's outstanding invoices (in return for up to 3 percent of the amount due). Among Canadian and U.S. business firms, factoring accounts for more than $1 trillion in credit. The bill collecting business no longer has the unsavoury reputation that it once had.

unsecured loan, a firm must ordinarily have a good banking relationship with the lender. Once an agreement is made, a promissory note will be executed and the funds transferred to the borrower. Although some unsecured loans are one-time-only arrangements, many take the form of *lines of credit, revolving credit agreements,* or *commercial paper*.

Lines of Credit

line of credit
A standing agreement between a bank and a firm in which the bank specifies the maximum amount it will make available to the borrower for a short-term unsecured loan; the borrower can then draw on those funds, when available.

A standing agreement with a bank to lend a firm a maximum amount of funds on request is called a **line of credit**. With a line of credit, the firm knows the maximum amount it will be allowed to borrow if the bank has sufficient funds. The bank does not guarantee that the funds will be available when requested, however.

For example, suppose that TD Canada Trust gives Sunshine Tanning Inc. a $100 000 line of credit for the coming year. By signing promissory notes, Sunshine's borrowings can total up to $100 000 at any time. The bank may not always have sufficient funds when Sunshine needs them. But Sunshine benefits from the arrangement by knowing in advance that the bank regards the firm as creditworthy and will lend funds to it on short notice.

Revolving Credit Agreements

revolving credit agreement
A guaranteed line of credit for which the firm pays the bank interest on funds borrowed as well as a fee for extending the line of credit.

Revolving credit agreements are similar to bank credit cards for consumers. Under a **revolving credit agreement**, a lender agrees to make some amount of funds available on demand to a firm for continuing short-term loans. The lending institution guarantees that funds will be available when sought by the borrower. In return, the bank charges a *commitment fee*—a charge for holding open a line of credit for a customer even if the customer does not borrow any funds. The commitment fee is often expressed as a percentage of the loan amount, usually 0.5 to 1 percent of the committed amount.

For example, suppose that TD Canada Trust agrees to lend Sunshine Tanning up to $100 000 under a revolving credit agreement. If Sunshine borrows $80 000, it still has access to $20 000. If it pays off $50 000 of the debt, reducing its debt to $30 000, then $70 000 is available to it. Sunshine pays interest on the borrowed funds and also pays a fee on the unused funds in the line of credit.

Commercial Paper

commercial paper
A method of short-run fund-raising in which a firm sells unsecured notes for less than the face value and then repurchases them at the face value within 270 days; buyers' profits are the difference between the original price paid and the face value.

Some firms can raise short-term funds by issuing commercial paper. Since **commercial paper** is backed solely by the issuing firm's promise to pay, it is an option for only the largest and most creditworthy firms. Here's how it works: Corporations issue commercial paper with a face value. Companies that buy commercial paper pay less than that value. At the end of a specified period (usually 30 to 90 days but legally up to 270 days), the issuing company buys back the paper—*at the face value*. The difference between the price the buying company paid and the face value is the buyer's profit. For example, if Air Canada needs to borrow $10 million for 90 days, it might issue commercial paper with a face value of $10.2 million. Insurance companies with $10 million excess cash will buy the paper. After 90 days, Air Canada would pay $10.2 million to the insurance companies.

SOURCES OF LONG-TERM FUNDS

4 Distinguish among the various sources of *long-term financing* and explain the risks involved in each.

Firms need long-term funding to finance expenditures on fixed assets—the buildings and equipment necessary for conducting their business. They may seek long-term funds through *debt financing* (that is, from outside the firm) or through *equity financing* (by drawing on internal sources). We will discuss both options in this section, as well as a middle ground called *hybrid financing*. We will also analyze some of the options that enter into decisions about long-term financing, as well as the role of the *risk–return relationship* in attracting investors to a firm.

Debt Financing

Long-term borrowing from outside the company—**debt financing**—is a major component of most firms' long-term financial planning. The two primary sources of such funding are long-term loans and the sale of bonds.

debt financing
Raising money to meet long-term expenditures by borrowing from outside the company; usually takes the form of long-term loans or the sale of corporate bonds.

Long-Term Loans

Most corporations get their long-term loans from a chartered bank, usually one with which the firm has developed a long-standing relationship. But credit companies, insurance companies, and pension funds also grant long-term business loans.

Interest rates are negotiated between borrower and lender. Although some bank loans have fixed rates, others have floating rates tied to the prime rate that the bank charges its most creditworthy customers (see Chapter 15). A loan at 1 percent above prime, then, is payable at one percentage point higher than the prime rate. This rate may fluctuate, or float, because the prime rate itself goes up and down as market conditions change.

Long-term loans are attractive to borrowers for several reasons:

- because the number of parties involved is limited, loans can often be arranged very quickly
- the duration of the loan can easily be matched to the borrower's needs
- if the firm's needs change, loans usually contain clauses making it possible to change terms

Long-term loans also have some disadvantages. Large borrowers may have trouble finding lenders to supply enough funds. Long-term borrowers may also have restrictions placed on them as conditions of the loan. They may have to pledge long-term assets as collateral. And they may have to agree not to take on any more debt until the borrowed funds are repaid.

Corporate Bonds

Like commercial paper, a **corporate bond** is a contract—a promise by the issuing company or organization to pay the holder a certain amount of money on a specified date. Unlike commercial paper, however, bond issuers do not pay off quickly. In many cases, bonds may not be redeemed for 30 years from the time of issue. In addition, unlike commercial paper, most bonds pay the bondholder a stipulated sum of interest semi-annually or annually. If it fails to make a bond payment, the company is in default.

corporate bond
A promise by the issuing company to pay the holder a certain amount of money on a specified date, with stated interest payments in the interim; a form of long-term debt financing.

The terms of a bond, including the amount to be paid, the interest rate, and the **maturity date** (or payoff date), differ from company to company and from issue to issue. They are spelled out in the bond contract, or *bond indenture*. The indenture also identifies which of the firm's assets, if any, are pledged as collateral for the bonds.

maturity date
The date on or before which a company must pay off the principal of a particular bond issue.

Corporate bonds are the major source of long-term debt financing for most corporations. Bonds are attractive when companies need large amounts of funds for long periods of time. The issuing company gets access to large numbers of lenders through nationwide bond markets and stock exchanges. But bonds involve expensive administrative and selling costs. They also may require very high interest payments if the issuing company has a poor credit rating.

Equity Financing

equity financing
Raising money to meet long-term expenditures by issuing common stock or by retaining earnings.

Sometimes, looking inside the company for long-term funding is preferable to looking outside. In most cases, **equity financing** takes the form of issuing common stock or of retaining the firm's earnings. Both options involve putting the owners' capital to work.

Common Stock

By selling shares of stock, the company gets the funds it needs for buying land, buildings, and equipment. When stockholders purchase stock, they seek profits in the form of both dividends and capital appreciation. Overall, stockholders hope for an increase in the market value of their stock because the firm has profited and grown.

Suppose that Sunshine Tanning's founders invested $10 000 by buying the original 500 shares of common stock (at $20 per share) in 1997. If the company used these funds to buy equipment and succeeded financially, by 2006 it might need funds for expansion. A pattern of profitable operations and regularly paid dividends might allow Sunshine to raise $50 000 by selling 500 new shares of stock for $100 per share. This additional paid-in capital would increase the total stockholders' equity to $60 000, as shown in Table 16.1.

The use of equity financing via common stock can be expensive. Paying dividends is more expensive than paying bond interest because interest paid to bondholders is a business expense (and therefore a tax deduction for the firm), but stock dividends are not tax-deductible. If equity funding is so expensive, why don't firms rely instead on debt capital? Because long-term loans and bonds carry fixed interest rates and represent a fixed promise to pay, regardless of economic changes. If the firm defaults on its obligations, it may lose its assets and even go into bankruptcy. Because of the risk of default, debt financing appeals most strongly to companies in industries that have predictable profits and cash flow patterns. For example, demand for electric power is steady from year to year and predictable from month to month. So provincial electric utility companies, with their stable stream of income, can carry a substantial amount of debt.

Retained Earnings

Another approach to equity financing is to use retained earnings, which are profits not paid out in dividends. Using retained earnings means that the firm will not have to borrow money and pay interest on loans or bonds. A firm that has a history of eventually reaping much higher profits by successfully reinvesting retained earnings may be attractive to some investors. But the smaller dividends that can be paid to stockholders as a result of

Table 16.1 Stockholders' Equity for Sunshine Tanning

Common Stockholders' Equity, 1997	
Initial common stock (500 shares issued @ $20 per share, 1997)	$10 000
Total stockholders' equity	$10 000
Common Stockholders' Equity, 2006	
Initial common stock (500 shares issued @ $20 per share, 1997)	$10 000
Additional paid-in capital (500 shares issued @ $100 per share, 2006)	50 000
Total stockholders' equity	$60 000

If bond rating agencies like Moody's and Standard & Poor's downgrade a company's ratings to low enough levels, its bonds become junk bonds. That's what happened to The Gap after sales at virtually every store in the chain fell every single month for nearly two years. As a result, The Gap is finding it harder to raise money.

using retained earnings may decrease demand for—and thus the price of—the company's stock.

For example, if Sunshine Tanning had net earnings of $50 000 in 2006, it could pay a $50-per-share dividend on its 1000 shares of common stock. But if it plans to remodel at a cost of $30 000 and retains $30 000 of earnings to finance the project, only $20 000 is left to distribute for stock dividends ($20 per share).

Hybrid Financing: Preferred Stock

Preferred stock (see Chapter 4) is a hybrid because it has some of the features of corporate bonds and some of the features of common stock. As with bonds, payments on preferred stock are for fixed amounts, such as $6 per share per year. Unlike bonds, however, preferred stock never matures. It can be held indefinitely, like common stock. And dividends need not be paid if the company makes no profit. If dividends are paid, preferred stockholders receive them first in preference to dividends on common stock.

A major advantage of preferred stock to the issuing corporation is its flexibility. It secures funds for the firm without relinquishing control, since preferred stockholders have no voting rights. It does not require repayment of principal, or the payment of dividends in lean times.

Choosing Between Debt and Equity Financing

Financial planning involves striking a balance between debt and equity financing to meet the firm's long-term need for funds. Because the mix of debt and equity provides the firm's financial base, it is called the **capital structure** of the firm. Financial plans contain targets for the capital structure, such as 40 percent debt and 60 percent equity. But choosing a target is not easy. A wide range of debt-versus-equity mixes is possible.

capital structure Relative mix of a firm's debt and equity financing.

The most conservative strategy is to use all equity financing and no debt because a company has no formal obligations for financial payouts. But as we have noted, equity is a very expensive source of capital. The riskiest strategy would be to use all debt financing. While less expensive than equity funding, indebtedness increases the risk that a firm will be unable to meet its obligations and will go bankrupt. Somewhere between the two extremes, financial planners try to find a mix that will maximize stockholders' wealth.

ENTREPRENEURSHIP AND NEW VENTURES

The Personality of a Risk Taker

Thanks to the risks entailed in setting up and growing her own business, Lucy Marcus, founder of London-based Marcus Venture Consulting, has become an expert at assessing the risk involved in starting up a new business, investing in it, and managing it. In many ways, risk is the mainstay of Marcus's business. Her clients—mostly venture capital investors—want answers to such questions as "If I invest in XYZ Venture Capital Fund, how well will it be managed? How well does it treat entrepreneurial clients? What kind of financial return can I expect?" Her clients include individuals, companies, and pension funds—investors seeking a clear picture of the risks posed by potential investment opportunities. Her assessments help them determine the right balance between prospective gains and losses.

As one of a handful of senior female executives in the private equity industry, Marcus has to gain the trust of all sorts of clients by demonstrating dependable judgment about risk. It's a business with few women in leadership roles, but Marcus says it's just a matter of time until more women get into venture capital. "Private equity is all about managing risk," she says. "An investor will be drawn to what is familiar, where there is common ground, and familiarity—be it because two people are the same sex or from the same neighbourhood—is a way of eliminating some of that risk."

To encourage women in the equities industry, Marcus set up a network called HighTech Women—a 2500-member discussion group for women to meet and mentor one another. "HighTech Women was something I had to do," she explains. "I kept going to conferences and being one of four women in a roomful of 200 CEOs. I found that I'd meet the most interesting people in the ladies' room."

Marcus's success—she was selected as a World Economic Forum Global Leader for Tomorrow in 2002—stems from diverse career-building experiences, self-developed personal practices designed to sharpen creativity, and energetic drive. A native New Yorker, Marcus attended Wellesley College and did a summer internship with U.S. Senator Edward Kennedy. Before getting a master's degree in political philosophy from the University of Cambridge, she worked in public policy for the U.S. Treasury Department and Price-Waterhouse. She later held positions in various U.S. and European technology companies before opening Marcus Venture Consulting.

As an entrepreneur advising other entrepreneurs, Marcus's outlook is also influenced by a number of personal characteristics. For professional reasons, she won't tell anyone her age: "I'm too young for some people and too old for others." She regards herself as a maverick who's too outspoken for the average corporate environment, and she thinks people should be judged on what they achieve. She admires people who do different and interesting work, who buck trends, and who know what they're talking about. She prides herself on an ability to walk in other people's shoes and appreciate different points of view. She claims to be a quick judge of character and admits that she has to work hard at networking because she doesn't make friends with everybody. She wants to spend time with people in completely different industries. She avoids focussing solely on the business she's in, but that doesn't mean that she's not passionate about what she does. "I couldn't do something I wasn't passionate about," she says, "because I couldn't put the energy into it."

Figure 16.1 summarizes the factors management takes into account when deciding between debt and equity financing.

The Risk–Return Relationship

While developing plans for raising capital, financial managers must be aware of the different motivations of individual investors. Why, for example, do some individuals and firms invest in stocks while others invest only in bonds? Investor motivations, of course, determine who is willing to buy a given company's stocks or bonds. Everyone who invests money is expressing a personal preference for safety versus risk. Investors give money to firms and, in return, anticipate receiving future cash flows.

Some cash flows are more certain than others. Investors generally expect to receive higher payments for higher uncertainty. They do not generally

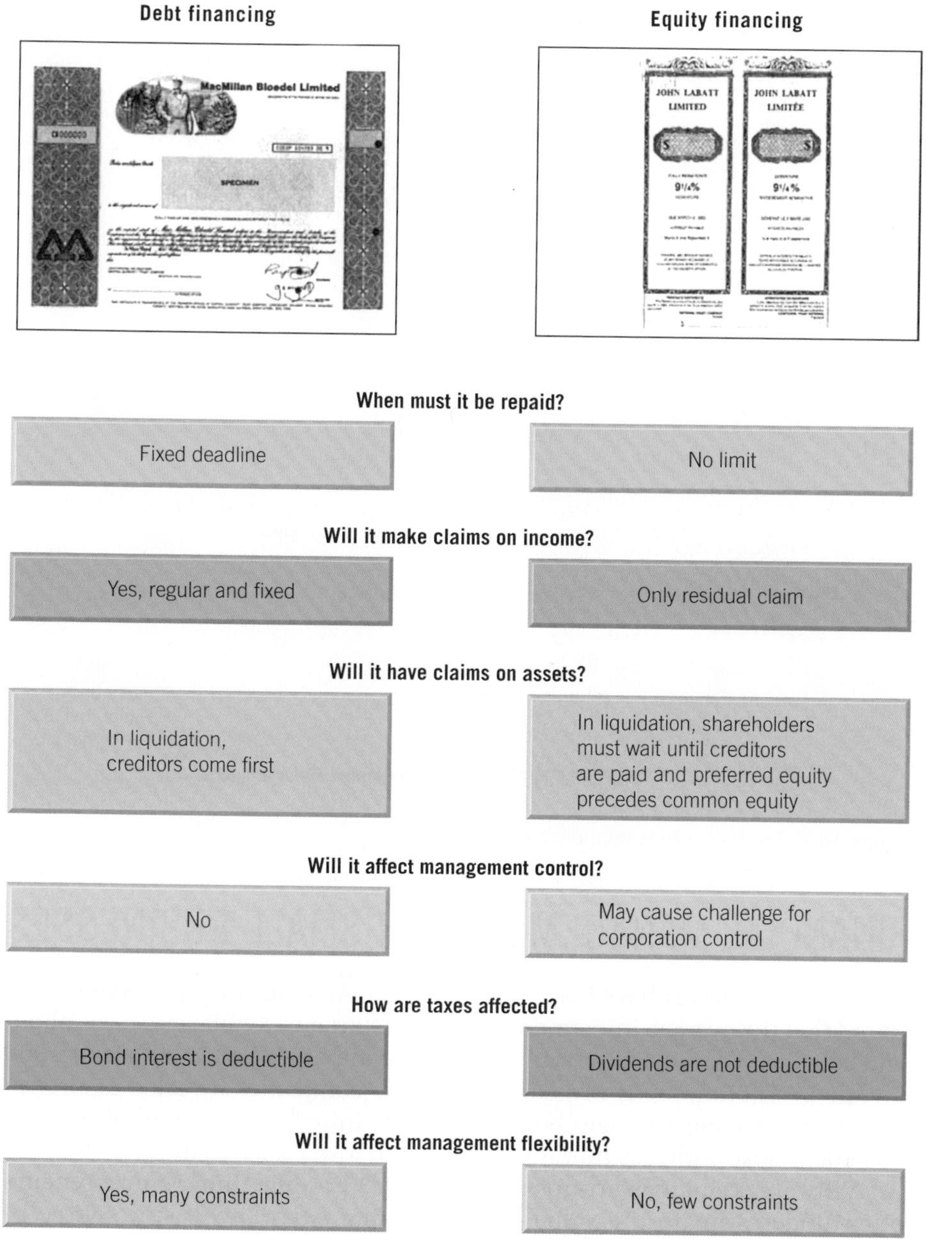
Debt financing
Equity financing
MacMillan Bloedel Limited
SPECIMEN
JOHN LABATT LIMITED
JOHN LABATT LIMITÉE
When must it be repaid?
Fixed deadline
No limit
Will it make claims on income?
Yes, regular and fixed
Only residual claim
Will it have claims on assets?
In liquidation, creditors come first
In liquidation, shareholders must wait until creditors are paid and preferred equity precedes common equity
Will it affect management control?
No
May cause challenge for corporation control
How are taxes affected?
Bond interest is deductible
Dividends are not deductible
Will it affect management flexibility?
Yes, many constraints
No, few constraints

Figure 16.1 Comparing debt and equity financing.

expect large returns for secure investments such as government-insured bonds. Each type of investment, then, has a **risk–return relationship**. Figure 16.2 shows the general risk–return relationship for various financial instruments. High-grade corporate bonds, for example, rate low in terms of risk on future returns but also low on size of expected returns. The reverse is true of junk bonds, those with a higher risk of default.

risk–return relationship Shows the amount of risk and the likely rate of return on various financial instruments.

Risk–return differences are recognized by financial planners, who try to gain access to the greatest funding at the lowest possible cost. By gauging investors' perceptions of their riskiness, a firm's managers can estimate how much it must pay to attract funds to their offerings. Over time, a company can reposition itself on the risk continuum by improving its record on dividends, interest payments, and debt repayment. The Entrepreneurship and New Ventures box describes the help that is available for those who want to determine the risk of investing in small businesses.

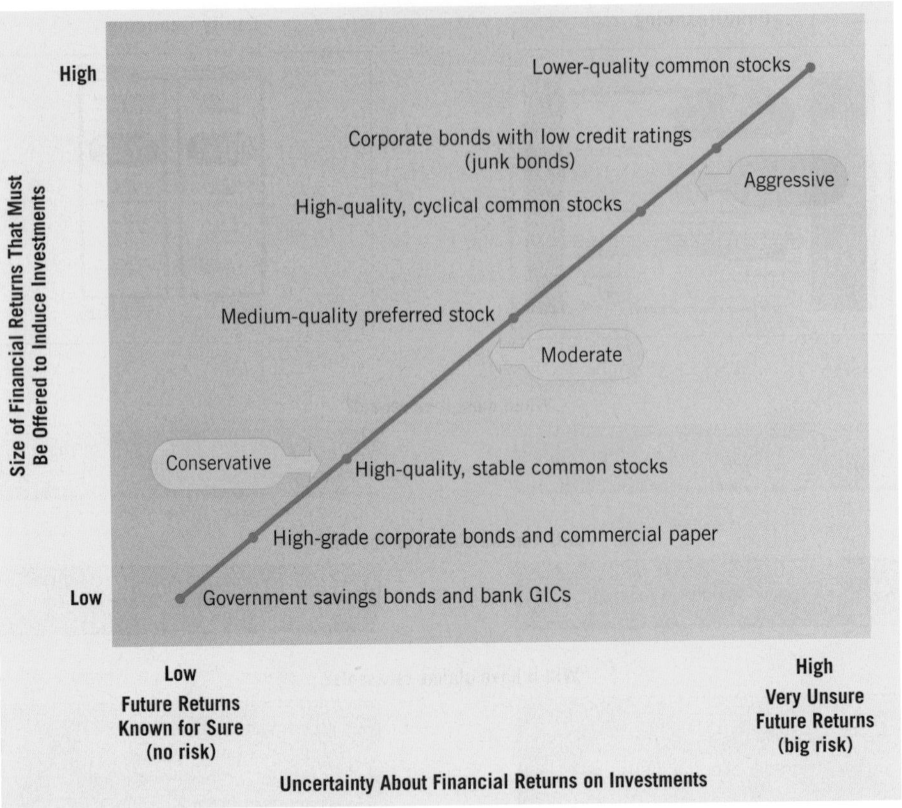

Figure 16.2 The risk–return relationship.

FINANCIAL MANAGEMENT FOR SMALL BUSINESSES

5 Discuss some key issues in financial management for small businesses.

Most new businesses have inadequate funding. An Ontario government study found that the average investment needed to start a new enterprise was about \$58 000, but that more than half of all new companies had less than \$15 000 invested.[1] Another study of nearly 3000 new companies revealed a survival rate of 84 percent for new businesses with initial investments of at least \$50 000. Those with less funding had a much lower survival rate.[2]

Why are so many start-ups underfunded? For one thing, entrepreneurs often underestimate the value of establishing *bank credit* as a source of funds and use *trade credit* ineffectively. In addition, they often fail to consider *venture capital* as a source of funding, and they are notorious for not *planning cash flow needs* properly.

Establishing Bank Credit and Trade Credit

Banks differ greatly in willingness to assume risk, ability to give professional advice, loyalty to customers, and maximum size of loans offered.[3] Some have liberal credit policies. Some offer financial analysis, cash flow planning, and suggestions based on experience with other local small businesses. Some provide loans to small businesses in bad times and work to keep them going. Others do not.

Credit-seekers must therefore be prepared to show they are worthy of the bank's help. A sound financial plan, a good credit history, and proven capability on the part of the entrepreneur can all convince bankers and other potential financiers that the business can succeed. Once it has obtained a line of credit, the small business can then attempt to gain more liberal credit policies from other businesses. Sometimes, suppliers will give customers longer credit periods, such as 45 or 60 days net rather than 30 days. Such liberal trade credit terms with suppliers allow the firm to increase its own short-term funds and avoid additional borrowing from banks.

The Business Plan as a Tool for Credit

Start-up firms without proven financial success usually must present a business plan (see Chapter 4) to demonstrate that the firm is a good credit risk.[4] Photographer David Cupp, for example, needed $50 000 in funding for his new firm, Photos Online Inc., which displays and sells photos over the internet. His business plan had to be rewritten many times until it became understandable, in financial terms, to potential lenders. The plan eventually reached 35 pages and contained information on the competition as well as cash flow projections. After four failed attempts, the fifth bank approved a $26 000 term loan and granted a $24 000 line of credit, to be used for computers, software, and living expenses to get the business started.[5]

Venture Capital

Many newer businesses—especially those undergoing rapid growth—cannot get the funds they need through borrowing alone. They may, therefore, turn to *venture capital*—outside equity funding provided in return for part ownership of the borrowing firm (see Chapter 4).

Planning for Cash Flow Requirements

Although all businesses should plan for their cash flows, it is especially important for small businesses to do so. Success or failure may hinge on anticipating times when cash will be short and when excess cash is expected.

Figure 16.3 shows possible cash inflows, cash outflows, and net cash position (inflows minus outflows), month by month, for Slippery Fish Bait Supply. In this highly seasonal business, bait stores buy heavily from Slippery during the spring and summer months. Revenues outpace expenses, leaving surplus funds that can be invested. During the fall and winter, expenses

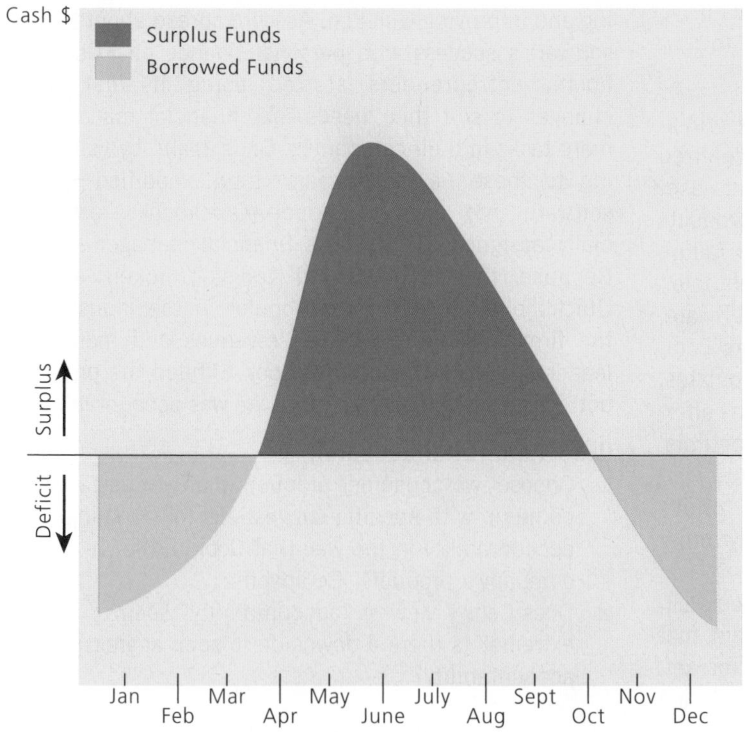

Figure 16.3 Cash flow for Slippery Fish Bait Supply Company.

exceed revenues. Slippery must borrow funds to keep going until sales revenues pick up again in the spring. Comparing predicted cash inflows from sales with outflows for expenses shows the firm's monthly cash flow position.

By anticipating shortfalls, a financial manager can seek funds in advance and minimize their cost. By anticipating excess cash, a manager can plan to put the funds to work in short-term, interest-earning investments. The Business Accountability box describes how one entrepreneur was successful by helping other individuals organize their financial matters.

BUSINESS ACCOUNTABILITY

A Quicken Course in Accountability

After deciding to hold himself accountable for designing new products, Scott Cook created some unique methods to ensure he'd meet those design obligations when he founded a company back in 1983. Cook is the former CEO of Intuit, the $1.7 billion company whose well-known software tools—Quicken and Quickbooks—have changed the way we manage our financial lives.

Cook initially envisioned three core principles for product design that eventually led to superb commercial success:

- First: It's the customer that's most important. Listen to the customer and design the product for customer value.
- Second: Be open-minded in identifying all competing ways the customer could perform the task, not just the obvious ways.
- Third: Simplify and improve the product so it provides the easiest way for the customer to complete the task to be performed.

From the beginning, Cook believed these principles would lead to superior, user-friendly preferred products that customers would buy and use. Accordingly, customer acceptance of the products would be the ultimate measure of success or failure of product designs for which Cook was accountable.

Although the firm was selling computer software, Cook didn't restrict his vision to just software competitors. As the second design principle stipulates, Intuit's products had to perform better than any alternative way of doing the task, including competitors' software, hand calculators, and pencil-and-paper methods. Otherwise, users wouldn't prefer Intuit's products for cheque writing and the many other financial tasks they had to perform.

While the initial version of Quicken worked well, Cook's insistence on pleasing customers meant that he wasn't satisfied when it first came on the market. Seeking user-based improvements, the first design principle was applied by assigning employees in computer stores to observe consumers when they bought Quicken off the shelf. Cook's imaginative "Follow Me Home" program surprised customers when they were asked if the employee could come home with them to watch their reaction to the software. Everything about the user's experience was noted, beginning with ease or difficulty in opening the package, reading instructions, installing the software on a computer, using it, and even turning away to write with pencil and paper. Cook insisted that anything preventing ease of use, no matter how small, was Intuit's fault, not the customer's. So watching for even the tiniest display of displeasure or frustration, the employee silently observed the user's facial expressions, body language, vocal reactions, pauses, and re-reading of instructions in each stage from opening the shrink-wrapped package to using the product.

Guided by what was learned from "Follow Me Home," the third principle was invoked for simplifying and improving Quicken. As word spread about the software's success with personal finance on PCs at home, entrepreneurs started using it—making changes to suit their needs—for financial management tasks in their companies. Once again, by listening to these new customers, Intuit modified the software into a new product—Quickbooks—especially designed for business financial management. Because these companion tools—Quicken and Quickbooks—are the most popular in the industry, the firm's $1.7 billion sales revenues and market leadership are evidence that Cook fulfilled the product-design obligations for which he was accountable.

QUESTIONS FOR DISCUSSION

1. Choose two consumer products that you use and come up with specific suggestions for pursuing accountability in the way that Cook did for his company's products. Be specific.
2. Does Cook's view of "accountability" seem extreme? Is there a downside to such aggressive accountability?

RISK MANAGEMENT

Because the outcome of management decisions cannot be known with certainty ahead of time, risk management is essential.[6] Firms should therefore devote considerable resources not only to recognizing potential risks, but also to positioning themselves to make the most advantageous decisions. A 2006 survey of risk management by Ernst & Young showed that 70 percent of Canadian business leaders felt that risk management is important to a company's long-term growth, but only 2 percent felt that their companies did a good job managing risk. The survey also showed that 78 percent of Canadian managers said that understanding risk in their organization was important, but only 11 percent of those felt they had such an understanding.[7]

6 Explain how *risk* affects business operations and identify the five steps in the *risk-management process.*

Coping with Risk

Businesses constantly face two basic types of **risk**—that is, uncertainty about future events. **Speculative risks**, such as financial investments, involve the possibility of gain or loss. **Pure risks** involve only the possibility of loss or no loss. Designing and distributing a new product, for example, is a speculative risk: The product may fail or it may succeed and earn high profits. The chance of a warehouse fire is a pure risk.

For a company to survive and prosper, it must manage both types of risk in a cost-effective manner. We can thus define the process of **risk management** as "conserving the firm's earning power and assets by reducing the threat of losses due to uncontrollable events."[8] The opening case for this chapter describes the importance of risk management. The risk-management process usually involves five steps.

risk Uncertainty about future events.

speculative risk An event that offers the chance for either a gain or a loss.

pure risk An event that offers no possibility of gain; it offers only the chance of a loss.

risk management Conserving a firm's (or an individual's) financial power or assets by minimizing the financial effect of accidental losses.

Step 1: Identify Risks and Potential Losses

Managers analyze a firm's risks to identify potential losses. For example, a firm with a fleet of delivery trucks can expect that one of them will eventually be involved in an accident. The accident may cause bodily injury to the driver or others, and may cause physical damage to the truck or other vehicles, or both.

Step 2: Measure the Frequency and Severity of Losses and Their Impact

To measure the frequency and severity of losses, managers must consider both past history and current activities. How often can the firm expect the loss to occur? What is the likely size of the loss in dollars? For example, our firm with the fleet of delivery trucks may have had two accidents per year in the past. If it adds more trucks to its fleet, it may reasonably expect the number of accidents to increase.

Step 3: Evaluate Alternatives and Choose the Techniques That Will Best Handle the Losses

Having identified and measured potential losses, managers are in a better position to decide how to handle them. They generally have four choices: *risk avoidance, control, retention,* or *transfer*.

Risk Avoidance. A firm opts for **risk avoidance** by declining to enter or by ceasing to participate in a risky activity. For example, the firm with the delivery trucks could avoid any risk of physical damage or bodily injury by closing down its delivery service. Similarly, a pharmaceutical maker may withdraw a new drug for fear of liability lawsuits.

risk avoidance Stopping participation in or refusing to participate in ventures that carry any risk.

Risk Control. When avoidance is not practical or desirable, firms can practise **risk control**—say, the use of loss-prevention techniques to minimize the frequency of losses. A delivery service, for instance, can prevent losses by training its drivers in defensive-driving techniques, mapping out safe routes, and conscientiously maintaining its trucks.

risk control
Techniques to prevent, minimize, or reduce losses or the consequences of losses.

Risk Retention. When losses cannot be avoided or controlled, firms must cope with the consequences. When such losses are manageable and predictable, they may decide to cover them out of company funds. The firm is thus said to "assume" or "retain" the financial consequences of the loss: hence the practice known as **risk retention**. For example, the firm with the fleet of trucks may find that each vehicle suffers vandalism totalling $300 per year. Depending on its coverage, the company may find it cheaper to pay for repairs out of pocket rather than to submit claims to its insurance company.

risk retention
The covering of a firm's unavoidable losses with its own funds.

Risk Transfer. When the potential for large risks cannot be avoided or controlled, managers often opt for **risk transfer**. They transfer the risk to another firm—namely, an insurance company. In transferring risk to an insurance company, a firm pays a sum called a *premium*. In return, the insurance company issues an insurance policy—a formal agreement to pay the policyholder a specified amount in the event of certain losses. In some cases, the insured party must also pay a *deductible*—an agreed-upon amount of the loss that the insured must absorb prior to reimbursement. Thus, the truck company may buy insurance to protect itself against theft, physical damage to trucks, and bodily injury to drivers and others involved in an accident.

risk transfer
The transfer of risk to another individual or firm, often by contract.

Every year in Canada, well over $1 billion is lost to insurance fraud. The insurance industry estimates that between $10 and $15 of every $100 dollars you pay in premiums goes to cover fraud losses. The Canadian Coalition Against Insurance Fraud (CCAIF) exists to curb this fraud. CCAIF members include mutual and private insurance companies, public automobile insurers, and representatives from health-care, law enforcement, and consumer advocacy groups. Part of the CCAIF's mandate is to ensure that consumers are aware of the connection between insurance fraud and higher insurance rates. Working with Crime Stoppers, the CCAIF offers a reward to tipsters who provide information leading to the discovery of fraud. Visit the CCAIF website at www.fraudcoalition.org.

When the National Highway Traffic Safety Administration in the United States informed General Motors that the suspension on its Saturn VUE had failed a new government rollover test, CEO Rick Wagoner decided to practise a little risk retention and recall 245 000 SUVs sold in Canada and the United States over the previous four years. GM then redesigned the vehicle's rear suspension, and dealers began making modifications at no cost to owners.

Step 4: Implement the Risk-Management Program

The means of implementing risk-management decisions depend on both the technique chosen and the activity being managed. For example, risk avoidance for certain activities can be implemented by purchasing those activities from outside providers, such as hiring delivery services instead of operating delivery vehicles. Risk control might be implemented by training employees and designing new work methods and equipment for on-the-job safety. For situations in which risk retention is preferred, reserve funds can be set aside out of revenues. When risk transfer is needed, implementation means selecting an insurance company and buying the right policies.

Step 5: Monitor Results

Because risk management is an ongoing activity, follow-up is always essential. New types of risks, for example, emerge with changes in customers, facilities, employees, and products. Insurance regulations change, and new types of insurance become available. Consequently, managers must continually monitor a company's risks, re-evaluate the methods used for handling them, and revise them as necessary.

Summary of Learning Objectives

1. Describe the responsibilities of a *financial manager.* A financial manager's overall objective is to increase a firm's value and stockholders' wealth. They must ensure that earnings exceed its costs—in other words, that the firm generates a profit. The responsibilities of the financial manager fall into two general categories: (1) *Cash flow management*: Financial managers must ensure that the company has enough funds on hand to purchase the resources that it needs to produce products. Funds not needed immediately must be invested to earn money; and (2) *Financial control:* The process of checking actual performance against plans to ensure that desired financial results occur.

2. Distinguish between *short-term (operating)* and *long-term (capital)* expenditures. *Short-term (operating)* expenditures are incurred in a firm's everyday business activities. To handle these expenditures, managers must pay attention to accounts payable, accounts receivable, and inventories. *Long-term (capital)* expenditures are required to purchase fixed assets.

3. Identify four sources of *short-term financing* for businesses. The four sources of short-term financing are *trade credit* (really a short-term loan from one firm to another), *secured short-term loans* (bank loans that usually involve promissory notes in which the borrower promises to repay the loan plus interest), *factoring accounts receivable* (selling the firm's accounts receivable), and *unsecured short-term loans* (the borrower does not have to put up collateral).

4. Distinguish among the various sources of *long-term financing* and explain the risks involved in each. Firms may seek long-term funds to pay for fixed assets through two channels: *debt financing* (*long-term loans* from chartered banks, or selling *corporate bonds*) or *equity financing* (issuing common stock or using retaining earnings). All-debt financing is the most speculative, while all-equity is the most conservative. A middle ground between debt financing and equity financing is the use of *preferred stock*, which is a "hybrid" because it has features of both corporate bonds and common stocks.

5. Discuss some key issues in financial management for small businesses. Obtaining credit begins with finding a bank that will support a small firm's financial needs. Once a *line of credit* is obtained, the small business can seek more liberal credit policies from other businesses. Obtaining long-term loans is more difficult for new businesses than for established companies, and start-ups pay higher interest rates than older firms. To demonstrate that it's a good credit risk, a start-up must usually present a *business plan*—a document explaining why the money is needed, the amount, how it will be used to improve the company, and when it will be paid back.

6. Explain how *risk* affects business operations and identify the five steps in the *risk-management process.* Businesses face two basic types of *risk*—that is, uncertainty about future events. (1) *Speculative risks*, such as financial investments, involve the possibility of gain or loss. (2) *Pure risks* (such as the chance of a warehouse

fire) involve only the possibility of loss or no loss. *Risk management* entails conserving earning power and assets by reducing the threat of losses due to uncontrollable events. The process has five steps: (1) Step 1: *Identify risks and potential losses:* Analyze risks to identify potential losses. (2) Step 2: *Measure the frequency and severity of losses and their impact:* To measure the frequency and severity of losses, consider past history and current activities. (3) Step 3: *Evaluate alternatives, and choose the techniques that will best handle the losses:* Decide how to handle risks from among four choices: *risk avoidance, risk control, risk retention, or risk transfer.* (4) Step 4: *Implement the risk-management program:* The means of implementing risk-management decisions depend on both the technique chosen and the activity being managed. (5) Step 5: *Monitor results:* Managers must monitor risks, re-evaluate methods for handling them, and revise them as necessary.

QUESTIONS AND EXERCISES

Questions for Analysis

1. In what ways do the two sources of debt financing differ from each other? How do they differ from the two sources of equity financing?
2. Describe the relationship between investment risk and return. In what ways might the risk–return relationship affect a company's financial planning?
3. What is the basic relationship between the amount of risk associated with a project and the likelihood of gains (or losses) on the project? Explain how several financial instruments (GICs, common stocks, preferred stocks, corporate bonds) illustrate this basic relationship.
4. How would you decide on the best mix of debt and equity for a company?
5. Why would a business "factor" its accounts receivable?
6. As a risk manager of a large firm, what risks do you think your firm faces? What risks would the manager of a small firm face? What accounts for the most important differences?
7. Look at the balance sheets of three different corporations. Determine the relative emphasis each business has placed on raising money through debt versus equity. Why might these differences exist?
8. What are the risks and benefits associated with the sources of short-term funds (trade credit, secured and unsecured loans, and factoring accounts receivable)? How do these risks and benefits compare with those associated with sources of long-term funds (debt and equity)?

Application Exercises

9. Interview the owner of a small local business. Identify the types of short-term and long-term funding that this firm typically uses. Why has the company made the financial management decisions that it has?
10. Interview the owner of a small local business. Ask this person to describe the risk-management process that he or she follows. What role, for example, is played by risk transfer? Why has the company made the risk-management decisions that it has?

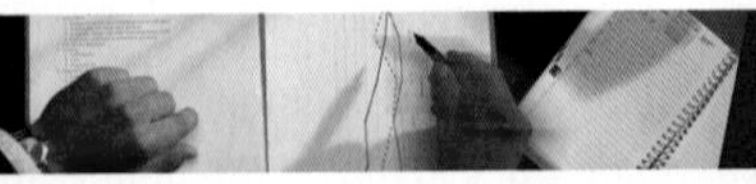

BUILDING YOUR BUSINESS SKILLS

Understanding Risk-Management Issues

Goal

To encourage students to gain a better understanding of the major financial and risk-management issues that face large companies.

Method

During the last few years, all of the following companies reported financial problems relating to risk management:

- Air Canada
- Bombardier
- EarthLink Inc.
- Levi Strauss & Co.
- Nortel Networks

▶▶▶

Step 1 Working alone, research one of the companies listed above to learn more about the financial risks that were reported in the news.
Step 2 Write a short explanation of the risks and financial-management issues that were faced by the firm you researched.
Step 3 Join in teams with students who researched other companies and compare your findings.

Follow-Up Questions

1. Were there common themes in the "big stories" in financial management?
2. What have the various companies done to minimize future risks and losses?

EXERCISING YOUR ETHICS: TEAM EXERCISE

Doing Your Duty when Payables Come Due

The Situation

Sarah Keats is the vice-president of finance at Multiverse, a large firm that manufactures consumer products. On December 15, 2007 (two weeks before the end of the fiscal year), she attends an Executive Committee meeting at which Jack Malvo, the CEO, expresses concern that the firm's year-end cash position will be less favourable than projected. The firm has exceeded analysts' performance expectations in each of his eight years at the helm and Malvo is determined that stockholders will never be disappointed as long as he is CEO. The purpose of the meeting is to find solutions to the cash problem and decide on a course of action.

The Dilemma

To open the meeting, Malvo announces, "We have just two weeks either to reduce expenses or to increase revenues. We need a $100 million swing to get us where market analysts predicted we'd be on cash flows for the year. Any suggestions?"

In the discussion that ensues, it is noted that Multiverse owes $150 million to about 80 different companies that supply component parts and other operating supplies to Multiverse. The money is due before year-end. Sarah Keats says, "Our cash outflows for the year will be lower if we delay paying suppliers, which will help the bottom line. And, it's like getting a free loan." The procurement director, Julie Levin expresses the following concern: "Our agreements with suppliers call for faithful payments at designated times, and many of the smaller firms depend on receiving that cash to meet their obligations. Also, we've worked hard for two years at improving relationships with all suppliers, and that effort could go down the drain if we don't meet our financial commitments as promised."

As the meeting draws to a close, Malvo announces, "Keep me posted on any unexpected developments, but if nothing helpful comes up in the next few days, let's go ahead and withhold supplier payments for three weeks."

Team Activity

Assemble a group of four students and assign each group member one of the following roles:

- Jack Malvo (CEO of Multiverse)
- Sarah Keats (vice-president of finance)
- Julie Levin (procurement director)
- A stockholder of Multiverse

Action Steps

1. Before discussing the situation with your group, and from the perspective of your assigned role, do you think there are any ethical issues here?
2. Before discussing the situation with your group, and from the perspective of your assigned role, what action do you think should be taken? Write down your recommended action.
3. Gather your group together and reveal, in turn, each member's comments and recommendations.
4. Appoint someone to record the main points of agreement and disagreement within the group. How do you explain the results? What accounts for any disagreements?
5. From an ethical standpoint, what does your group recommend?

BUSINESS CASE 16

Brascan Is Making Progress

When Bruce Flatt took over as CEO of Brascan Corp. in 2002, the company owned a diverse group of other companies, including Noranda Inc. (mining), Nexfor (paperboard), Brookfield Properties Corp. (real estate), Great Lakes Power Inc. (hydroelectric generation), Trilon Corp. (financial services), and two Brazilian cattle ranches. Flatt quickly announced that he was going to convert the company from a conglomerate (i.e., a company that owns a diverse group of other companies) into an asset management company that would focus on just three areas: real estate, power generation, and infrastructure.

Flatt's strategy contrasted sharply with that of his predecessor, Jack Cockwell, who is remembered as the last of a dying breed of conglomerate moguls who once ruled the Canadian business scene. Cockwell's strategy was to buy undervalued companies, even if they were very diverse. For example, in the early 1990s, he took $20 million of stock owned by Peter and Edward Bronfman and parlayed it into Canada's most powerful and controversial conglomerate—Edper Group. But when real estate prices dropped, Edper faced bankruptcy because it was unable to pay its debts. The company sold assets to stay alive and by the mid-1990s had sold nearly $5 billion in assets and had raised $6.6 billion in new financing. The company was renamed Brascan in 2000.

Flatt made his decision to move Brascan away from the conglomerate model because stock markets now like so-called "pure play" companies that are highly focused, and because investors had essentially attached a "holding company discount" to Brascan's stock price. That occurred in spite of the fact that Brascan had regularly been profitable. By the middle of 2005, Flatt had made some progress toward his goal. Brascan bought controlling interest in an office property in London's Canary Wharf, purchased B.C. coastal timberlands to boost its infrastructure assets, and purchased several hydroelectric generating plants in the United States and Brazil. Brascan now owns about $20 billion in assets, including 70 office towers and 120 power plants. The stock market liked what it saw, and the price of Brascan stock rose from $23 per share in September 2003 to $38 per share in July 2004.

The purchase of the B.C. timberlands included two lumber processing plants, five sawmills, and rights to harvest large tracts of crown land. Brascan will likely sell the sawmills and logging rights, perhaps for $300 million. Brascan executives point out that timberlands are a much more stable investment than lumber or paper companies, and will generate predictable cash returns. Trees also rise in value over time. Unlike mining, which is cyclical, tree harvesting is predictable. If prices decline, a company can simply let the trees keep growing until prices improve.

Other initiatives designed to change the look of Brascan have also been positive (after a few bumps in the road). At one point, it looked like China Minmetals Corp. would buy Noranda, but that deal fell through. Then, Noranda and Falconbridge Nickel merged, but that meant that Brascan was still involved in the resource industry. Finally, in 2005 Noranda was sold to Inco.

Financial analysts say Brascan is making progress, but think the company still has a way to go. Flatt thinks the market is finally recognizing Brascan's progress, but says that some people expect too much in a short period of time. He points out that just 10 years ago 80 percent of Brascan's assets were in resource-based industries, but the figure now is less than 10 percent.

Flatt says that assets must meet a threshold return or they won't be kept. He wants to achieve a 15 percent annual growth in sustainable cash flow and a 20 percent cash return on equity. These goals may be achievable in real estate, financial services, and power generation, but not in highly cyclical businesses like mining and paperboard.

In 2005, Brascan changed its name to Brookfield Asset Management to distance itself from its conglomerate past, and to suggest its new focus.

Questions for Discussion

1. Why might a profitable company like Brascan be out of favour with investment analysts? What can a company do to regain favour?
2. What are the advantages and disadvantages of debt and equity financing? How did these advantages and disadvantages manifest themselves at Brascan?
3. Discuss the risk–return relationship as it applies to Brascan.
4. How is Bruce Flatt's view of the organization different from that of former CEO Jack Cockwell?

MYBUSINESSLAB mybusinesslab

To improve your grade, visit the MyBusinessLab website at **www.pearsoned.ca/mybusinesslab**. This online homework and tutorial system allows you to test your understanding and generates a personalized study plan just for you. It provides you with study and practice tools directly related to this chapter's content. MyBusinessLab puts you in control of your own learning!

CRAFTING A BUSINESS PLAN

Part 5: Managing Financial Issues

Goal of the Exercise

In this final part of the business plan project, you'll consider how you'll finance your business as well as create an executive summary for your plan.

Exercise Background: Part 5 of the Business Plan

In a previous part of the business plan, you discussed the costs of doing business, as well as how much revenue that you expect to earn in one year. It's now time to think about how to finance the business. To get a "great idea" off the ground requires money. But how will you get these funds?

You'll then conclude this project by creating an *executive summary*. The purpose of the executive summary is to give the reader a quick snapshot into your proposed business. Although this exercise comes at the end of the project, once you're done writing it, you'll end up placing the executive summary at the *beginning* of your completed business plan.

YOUR ASSIGNMENT mybusinesslab

Step 1

Open the saved *Business Plan* file you have been working on.

Step 2

For the purposes of this assignment, you will answer the following questions, shown in "Part 5: Managing Financial Issues."

1. How much money will you need to get your business started?

   Hint: Refer back to Part 3 of the plan, where you analyzed the costs involved in running your business. Approximately how much will you need to get your business started?

2. How will you finance your business? For example, will you seek out a bank loan? Borrow from friends? Sell stocks or bonds initially or as your business grows?

   Hint: Refer to Chapter 15 for information on securities such as stocks and bonds. Refer also to Chapters 4 and 16 for more information on sources of short-term and long-term funds.

3. Now, create an executive summary for your business plan. The executive summary should be brief—no more than two pages long—and should cover the following points:

   - The name of your business
   - Where your business will be located
   - The mission of your business
   - The product or service you are selling
   - Who your ideal customers are
   - How your product or business will stand out in the crowd
   - Who the owners of the business are and what experience they have
   - An overview of the future prospects for your business and industry

   Hint: At this point, you've already answered all of these questions, so what you need to do here is put the ideas together into a "snapshot" format. The executive summary is really a sales pitch—it's the investor's first impression of your idea. Therefore, as with all parts of the plan, write in a clear and professional way.

Congratulations on completing the business plan project!

CBC VIDEO CASE V-1

The Cost of Counterfeiting

Wesley Weber is one of Canada's most famous counterfeiters. In just a few short years, he was able to print over $16 million in counterfeit $100 bills. He says that he was running a business (albeit an illegal one), and just like a regular manager, he hired employees, paid wages, worried about efficient operations, and tried to improve the quality of his product. Unfortunately, he was an example of the entrepreneurial instinct gone wrong.

Why did he do it? He says he got a real "rush" from counterfeiting, and, of course, it also allowed him to buy whatever he wanted—cars, boats, expensive televisions, trips, and so forth. Weber, who sees himself as a classic computer geek, says he had a strong urge to make money when he was quite young. When he got his first computer, he put a $10 bill in the scanner to see what would happen. His father was very upset.

Computer technology facilitated his illegal activities. All he needed was a computer, a printer, and some software. He began by making counterfeit $20 bills, but he was soon caught and spent three months in jail. After he got out of jail, he and some friends started making fake $100 bills. He chose that denomination because it was more efficient to make and required smaller amounts of supplies than making $20 bills. In order to get the equipment he needed, he passed himself off as a legitimate businessman. He was able to get a supply of the material needed to make the shiny square on the $100 bill by posing as an employee of Ford Motor Co. (he said he needed the material to make patches for car seats). To get the material needed to create the proper texture on the $100 bill he told an engraver he needed special metal stamps for replacement parts for a manufacturing operation. He always wore a suit and tie, and this apparently increased the legitimacy of his requests and helped him talk people into selling him what he wanted.

At first, Weber simply spent his fake cash. But then he increased the scale of his operations and began selling the $100 bills to distributors who paid $24 for each one. When Weber's fake bills started getting noticed, police alerted people to flaws in the bills. Weber responded by improving the bills and getting rid of their deficiencies. In the end, he was making very good fakes.

He was living the high life, but he became careless and greedy. The RCMP tracked him to a cottage where he was making the fake bills and put him under surveillance from a building next door. Weber says he was so engrossed in making money that he didn't see the obvious fact that the RCMP had a command headquarters next door. One July day, Weber met his "neighbours" as they burst into his cottage with guns drawn and placed him under arrest.

Weber was convicted of counterfeiting and sentenced to three years in prison. After serving his time, he was out on day parole. He became a regular at a local internet café, where he helped the owner detect fake bills. He also earned his living as a day trader. Shortly before completing his parole period, he went on an unauthorized trip and was arrested for parole violation. He will now have to pay the price (possibly 18 more months in jail).

Reflecting on his escapades, he now says that the counterfeit money brought him nothing but heartache. His girlfriend left him, his parents were devastated, and he has nothing from the proceeds of his crime (but he knows that people will think he has money buried all over the province). He thinks that perhaps $6 million of his counterfeit bills are still circulating in the Canadian economy.

Because of the activities of people like Wesley Weber, Canadian businesses are becoming more and more wary of accepting $100 or $50 bills. If a business accepts a counterfeit bill, it must eat the cost of the bill. Fears about counterfeiting are well-founded, since counterfeiting is becoming more and more common. One study found that counterfeiting is up 300 percent in the last few years. In some retail businesses (e.g., sports bars) it is relatively easy for crooks to pass bad bills because the pace of activity is so hectic. As well, patrons often leave money for their bill on the table, and by the time the staff check the bill for authenticity, the patrons are gone. Studies show that 6 out 10 retailers check the $100 bill, but only one in 10 checks lower denominations.

The Bank of Canada has responded to the counterfeiting problem by redesigning Canadian paper money to make it harder to copy. The new bills have more security features such as new holographic images, more raised printing, and images that show up only when a bill is held up to a light. The Bank of Canada has also spent $1 million on publicity about the new bills. But the bad guys are clever, and they are always improving their product.

Questions for Discussion

1. What is the meaning of the term "money supply?" What are the different measures of the money supply?
2. What is the impact of counterfeiting on the money supply?
3. How does counterfeiting harm individuals, business owners, and the Canadian economy?

Source: "Easy Money," *Venture*, September 22, 2002.

CBC VIDEO CASE V-2

Canadian Emeralds

At Regal Ridge in the Yukon, True North mining is developing an emerald mine, and millions of dollars of investment money is at stake. Publicity is very important to small mining companies, so True North has hired a TV crew to produce a promotional video showing the mine's prospects. The video shows real emeralds being dug out of the ground. But the big question is this: Are there enough emeralds to make a mine worthwhile? And what about the quality? Many of the surface emeralds have been damaged by frost, so the company is planning to dig deeper and sift through tonnes of rock in the hope of finding undamaged (and bigger) stones.

A lot of money is required to develop a mine, so True North's CEO—Andy Smith—needs to find new investors who are willing to put money into True North, and he needs to keep current investors happy. One big investor—Dundee Securities—is concerned about its $1 million investment. Its managers want to know when a commercial mine is likely to be built, and when retail sales of emeralds are likely to begin. Smith asks Dundee for patience. He points out that the emerald find is a unique story with potentially huge value for shareholders. After listening to Smith, Dundee Securities decides to stick with the company. But Smith knows that the underground results had better be good or investors like Dundee could cash out quickly.

Small investors are important too. Smith knows that True North needs visibility in Whitehorse, because many of True North's investors live there (and they own more than half the company's stock). As well, the emerald business means a lot to the people in Whitehorse, so Smith wants to keep investor confidence high. Don Murphy, a government geologist says that any new mining activity is welcome in the Yukon, but he is cautious when predicting what effect True North's hoped-for mine will have on the area.

A few weeks later, the underground emeralds are being sorted at True North's headquarters. Smith can't resist taking a peek at how things are going. The news is quite promising. Some of the emeralds that have been found may retail for as much as U.S.$3000. True North has also discovered a new kind of gem at Regal Ridge that is apparently found only in Canada. It is called a true blue beryl. The value of the new blue gem is unknown, but the media attention it receives is very valuable for True North. The day after the discovery is reported on The National, over 1 million shares of True North are traded, and the stock jumps to $1.24 per share.

On the eve of the shareholders meeting two weeks later, the first results are in. The deeper underground the company digs, the better the quality and size of the emeralds. But the sample is small, and the company doesn't know how much the total deposit may be worth. But at least this year the company can show investors real emeralds. At its meeting last year, they didn't have any emeralds, and investors were not happy.

Just before the shareholders meeting, Andy meets with the company geologist in a strategy session. They need to figure out what message they want to give to investors. He can't hype the company too much or he will run into trouble with securities regulators. But he also can't be too negative or vague, because investors want to see some action. At the meeting, Smith reports that the emerald sector looks comparable to the diamond sector (although it is less well developed at the moment). He emphasizes that the company has found bigger stones underground in recent digging, and he tells the shareholders that True North's emerald deposit could eventually be worth billions of dollars. The company's geologist is more cautious, and simply says that that the results look interesting from an economic point of view.

The geologist then shows shareholders some real emeralds taken from the Yukon property. Investors are happy with this hard evidence that something real is happening. Emerald fever is still alive, but until True North starts actually selling stones at the retail level, nothing is for sure. For now, shareholders seem willing to continue backing the company. But an operating mine is at least two years away, and many tasks remain to be completed: various permits are needed, more testing must be done at Regal Ridge, and there are environmental questions that must be answered.

Questions for Discussion

1. Explain the difference between par value, market value, and book value of a company's stock. Which of these values are investors of True North concerned about? Why?
2. What subjective factors influence the price of a company's stock? Which of these are relevant for this case? Explain.
3. Briefly describe the major sources of short- and long-term funds for businesses. Which of these sources would a firm like True North be most likely to use? Why?
4. What are the factors that a company must take into account when deciding between debt and equity financing? Explain which of these are relevant for True North, and the type of financing that the company would likely choose, given a consideration of these factors.

Source: "Canadian Emeralds," *Venture*, March 28, 2004.

CHAPTER 17

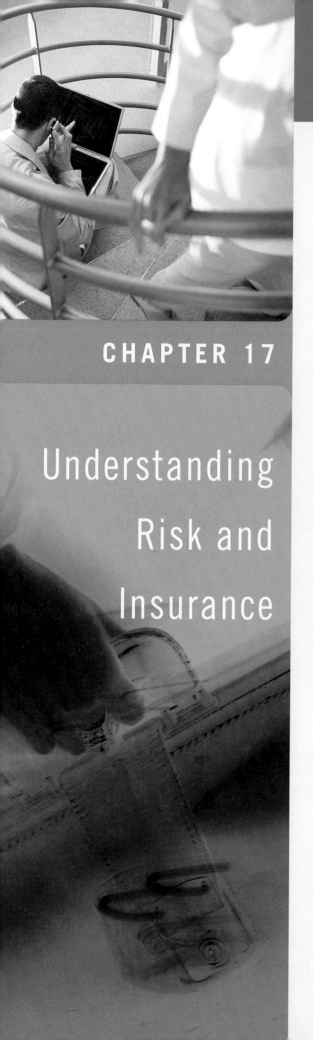

Understanding Risk and Insurance

Define risk, explain how to manage risk, and describe the role the insurance industry plays in our social, political and economic environment.

Learning Outcomes:

1. Explain how *risk* affects business operations and identify the five steps in the *risk-management process.*
2. Define terms relevant to a discussion of the Property & Casualty insurance market.
3. Discuss how a business transfers its risks by purchasing insurance.
4. Identify the types of business risks that cannot be transferred, and discuss what insurance is not intended to be used for.
5. Outline the function of insurance within the Canadian economy.
6. Describe the relationships between the major stakeholders within the insurance industry; consumer, intermediary, insurer, reinsurer, and government regulator.

RISK MANAGEMENT

1 Explain how *risk* affects business operations and identify the five steps in the *risk-management process*.

Risk is a factor in every manager's job, and because nearly every managerial action involves risk—that is, the possibility of either desirable outcomes or negative results—risk management is essential. (8) Not surprisingly, firms devote considerable resources to recognizing potential risks but also to positioning themselves to make the most advantageous decisions.

Coping with Risk

Businesses constantly face two basic types of risk—that is, uncertainty about future events. **Speculative risks**, such as financial investments, involve the possibility of gain or loss. **Pure risks** involve only the possibility of loss or no loss. Designing and distributing a new product, for example, is a speculative risk: the product may fail or it may succeed and earn high profits. The chance of a warehouse fire is a pure risk.

For the company to survive and prosper, it must manage both types of risk in a cost-effective manner. We can then define the process of risk management as "conserving the firm's earning power and assets by reducing the threat of losses due to uncontrollable events." (9) In every company, each manager must be alert for risks to the firm and their impact on profits. The risk management process usually involves five steps.

Step 1: Identify Risks and Potential Losses

Managers analyze a firm's risks to identify potential losses. For example, a furniture store with a fleet of delivery trucks can expect one of them will eventually be involved in an accident. The accident may cause bodily injury to the driver or others, and may cause physical damage to the truck or other vehicles.

Step 2: Measure the Frequency and Severity of Losses and Their Impact

To measure the frequency and severity of losses, managers must consider both past history and current activities. How often can a firm expect a loss to occur? What is the likely size of the loss in dollars? For example, our firm with the fleet of delivery trucks may have had two accidents per year in the past. If it adds trucks, however, it may reasonably expect the frequency of accidents to increase.

Step 3: Evaluate Alternatives and Choose the Techniques that Will Best Handle the Losses

Having identified and measured potential losses, managers are in a better position to decide how to handle them. With this third step, they generally have four choices: risk avoidance, control, retention or transfer.

Risk Avoidance. A firm opts for risk avoidance by declining to enter or by ceasing to participate in a risky activity. For example, the furniture store with the delivery trucks could avoid any risk of physical damage or bodily injury by closing down its delivery service and hiring an independent delivery service. Similarly, a pharmaceutical maker may withdraw a new drug for fear of liability suits.

Risk Control. When avoidance is not practical or desirable, firms can practice risk control—say the use of loss prevention techniques to minimize the frequency of losses. **Loss prevention** is the use of techniques to prevent a loss from occurring. A delivery service, for instance, can prevent losses by training its drivers in defensive-driving techniques, mapping out safe routes, and conscientiously maintaining its trucks. **Loss reduction** is the process of reducing the adverse affects of losses that do happen. For example, a company will install a sprinkler system to help contain a fire; an individual wears a seatbelt so that if an accident does occur the seatbelt will protect them against serious injury.

Risk Retention. When losses cannot be avoided or controlled, firms must cope with the consequences. When such losses are manageable and predictable, they may decide to cover them out of company funds. The firms is thus said to "assume" or "retain" the financial consequences of the loss; hence the practice known as risk retention. For example, a firm with the fleet of trucks may find that vehicles suffer vandalism totaling \$100 to \$500 per year. Depending on its coverage, the company may find it cheaper to pay for repairs out of pocket rather than submit claims to its insurance company. Another example would be when a company chooses not to purchase insurance against an earthquake loss because they understand that the probability of that type of loss occurring is so low.

Risk Transfer. When the potential for large risks cannot be avoided or controlled, managers often opt for risk transfer. They transfer the risk to another firm—namely an insurance company. In transferring the risk to an insurance company, the firm pays a sum called a premium. In return the insurance company issues an insurance policy—a formal agreement to pay the policyholder a specified amount in the event of certain losses. In some cases the insured party must also pay a deductible—an agreed upon amount of the loss that the insured must absorb prior to reimbursement. Thus, our furniture store may buy insurance to protect itself against theft or fire damage to its building, stock or equipment, physical damage to the delivery vehicles or injury to drivers and others involved in an accident. The Trends and Challenges box describes some interesting insurance situations.

Every year in Canada, well over \$1 billion is lost to insurance fraud. The Canadian Coalition Against Insurance Fraud (CCAIF) exists to curb this fraud. Coalition members include mutual and private insurance companies, public automobile insurers, and representatives from health-care, law enforcement, and consumer advocacy groups. Part of the CCAIF's mandate is to ensure that consumers are aware of the connection between insurance fraud and higher insurance rates. Visit the CCAIF website at www.fraudcoalition.org.

Step 4: Implement the Risk Management Program

The means of implementing the risk management decisions depend on both the technique chosen and the activity being managed. For example, risk avoidance for certain activities can be implemented by purchasing those activities from outside providers, such as hiring delivery services instead of operating delivery vehicles. Risk control might be implemented by training employees and designing new work methods and equipment for on-the-job safety. For situations in which risk retention is preferred, reserve funds can be set aside out of revenues. When risk transfer is needed, implementation means selecting an insurance company and buying the right policies.

Step 5: Monitor Results

Because risk management is an ongoing activity, follow-up is always essential. New types of risks, for example, emerge with changes in customers, facilities, employees and products. Insurance regulations change, and new types of insurance products become available. Consequently, managers must continually monitor a company's risks, re-evaluate the methods used for handling them and revise them as necessary.

INSURANCE AS RISK MANAGEMENT

2 Define terms relevant to a discussion of the Property & Casualty insurance market.

To deal with certain risks, both businesses and individuals chose to transfer that risk by purchasing the products offered by insurance companies. In exchange for a specified amount of money, known as the **premium**, the individual or business is protected from the effects of specific events that can cause them financial loss, many of which may be devastating.

Insurance is a simple concept that has spawned a very complex industry. Insurance is a risk sharing tool whereby the premiums contributed by a large group are used to pay the losses suffered by a small number of members within that group that suffer a loss. This is known as the risk sharing principle. The amount of premiums contributed by each member of the group is based on the probability that the individual or business will suffer a loss. This is known as the fairness principle. The higher the risk, or chance of loss, presented by the individual or business, the higher the premium they will contribute to the pool. Thus a business that uses dangerous chemicals in its manufacturing process is more likely to suffer a fire loss than a small retail outlet that sells ladies clothing. In accordance with the fairness principle then the manufacturing plant will pay more premium for their insurance than the retailer does.

More simply stated the concept of insurance is based on two underlying principles;

- The premiums of the many pay the losses of the few.
- The premiums are commensurate with the risk.

Purchasing insurance is purchasing peace of mind, or protection against the unknown. It is designed to protect the business or individual from a financial loss from which they could not recover. In order for the insurance policy to respond to a loss the event that caused the loss, or **peril**, must be a future event, and fortuitous or accidental and not at the direction of the insured.

Insurance companies are also concerned with identifying **hazards** which is a condition which may cause the peril to occur or to make the loss more severe. Hazards are classified into two categories; physical hazards and moral hazards. Physical hazards refer to the item being insured such as slippery floors, poorly maintained heating units or bare electrical wires. These hazards can usually be identified by an inspection of the properly and steps can be taken to reduce or remove these hazards. Moral hazards refer to the human element of the risk and stems from the attitudes and character of the insured such as a history of careless claims, dishonesty or financial problems.

The Insurance Act of Ontario defines **insurance** as "the undertaking by one person to indemnify another person against loss or liability for loss in respect of a certain risk or peril to which the object of insurance may be exposed or to pay a sum of money or other thing of value upon the happening of a certain event". Insurance is a contract of indemnity. To **indemnify** means to put back in the same financial position as just prior to the loss. A business or individual should not profit from the loss occurring but neither should they be in a worse position.

The **policy** issued by the insurance company is evidence of the contract, an agreement enforceable at law, and contains all of the terms and conditions of that agreement. The contract exists between the first party, or the insured, and the second party, or the insurer. A third party under an insurance contract is a person who makes a claim against the policy but is not a party to it.

Much of the confusion surrounding insurance is misconceptions about what the contract entitles the policyholder is entitled to in case of a loss, as well as the practicalities of measuring risk fairly.

It is as important to understand as well what insurance is not. Insurance is not an investment that is designed to "pay off" at some future date. When you purchase a policy of insurance it is designed to provide financial security should an insured event occur during the policy period. If a loss does not occur than the contract expires and no refund is owing. Remember that the premiums you pay go into a pot and even if you do not suffer a loss during that policy period others have and the money was available to pay their losses. The money collected is fully "used" by the end of each year. It should also be noted that insurance is not a maintenance contract designed to pay for small losses that the policyholder could easily absorb without threat to their financial security. Many policyholders see small losses as a way of getting back some of the money they contributed through their premium payments. Insurance is not designed to respond to minor losses. Withdrawing unnecessarily from the pool only means that more money is needed to replenish it and everyone's premiums will be increased accordingly.

INSURABLE RISKS

Both individuals and businesses face risks everyday. It is important to be able to recognize the exposures to loss in order to make informed and knowledgeable decisions about what to insure.

3 Discuss how a business transfers its risks by purchasing insurance.

Property Losses

Property can be divided into two general categories; **real property** such as land and buildings, and **personal property** which is anything that is personal, moveable or separate from the real property. Not only should you be concerned about the **direct loss** of this property, that is the loss of the economic value of the property caused by an insured peril, but also about the **indirect loss**, which is the loss of use of that property. When you have a fire in your building, not only do you suffer the economic loss caused by damage to your property, but you can no longer live or work there while it is being repaired. The financial burden of those additional expenses is also insurable.

Liability Losses

If you are **negligent** and cause injury to another person or damage their property you can be held legally liable to compensate them for their financial loss. You can insure against your legal liability by purchasing insurance, either individually for your personal actions or on a commercial policy for the actions of your business. This would include a slip and fall on your premises, injury caused by a malfunction of your product, or an automobile accident. This type of coverage also extends to **personal injury**, if you are held legally liable for defamation (libel or slander), invasion of privacy or false arrest or imprisonment.

Human Asset Loss

Many businesses would be devastated by the death or disability of a key person within the company, such as the loss of the head chef in a popular restaurant. Although you cannot replace the person, insurance provides necessary funds for the company to purchase the shares from a deceased partner or offset the costs involved in hiring and training a replacement. It is also important to protect your employees against injuries or accidents that could result in their inability to work. Many companies purchase life insurance, disability benefits or employee benefit plans to protect against these eventualities. These products are generally provided by life insurance companies are essentially outside the scope of this discussion.

Uninsurable Losses

Although there are many perils insured under a contract of insurance, businesses face many risks every day that cannot be transferred to an insurance company. Insurance is not designed to protect a business from being under-capitalized or failing to compete in their markets. It also does not protect against economic downturn, increased interest rates or obsolete products. Those are some of the many risks that the business must manage on their own.

THE INSURANCE PRODUCT

4 Identify the types of business risks that cannot be transferred, and discuss what insurance is not intended to be used for.

Property and Casualty Insurance, also referred to as General Insurance, is distinguished from life and health insurance as it concentrates mostly on insurance for property, automobile and liability risks. The insurance products covering these three primary exposures are numerous so we will focus on the types of insurance products available to an individual to insure the risks they face in everyday life, and on commercial insurance, which is essential when your own or operate a business.

Property Insurance

Property insurance is designed to protect against the direct loss of the assets being insured. An individual would purchase insurance on their home, their condominium or to protect their contents if they are tenants. Insurance is also available if you own a cottage or trailer. A business would purchase insurance to protect their building, stock and equipment. There are two important decisions to make when insuring your property. The first is to choose an amount of insurance that would allow for the property to be replaced or rebuilt should a loss occur. The second is to chose a policy that covers the perils, or events that could cause the loss, to which your home or business is exposed. For example, in 2005, theft accounted for 18% of all homeowners' claims. Other causes, including hail and wind, accounted for about 41% of all claims. Water damage to homes accounted for 31% of claims, followed by fires, which accounted for 10%. (FACTS 2006, IBC Publication). Although the loss of your property may be devastating it sometimes cannot compare to the indirect loss of your revenue while your business is closed. Although many expenses may be reduced or suspended when your business is closed down you often will have to continue to pay taxes, loans and wages to key employees. To protect against the financial hardship associated with loss of income insurance companies offer Business Interruption Insurance.

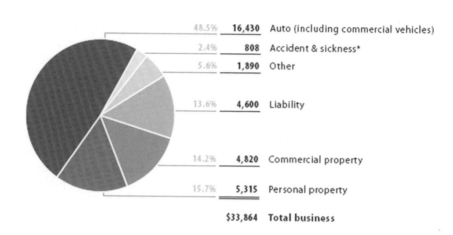

Net premiums written, by line of business, 2005 ($000,000)

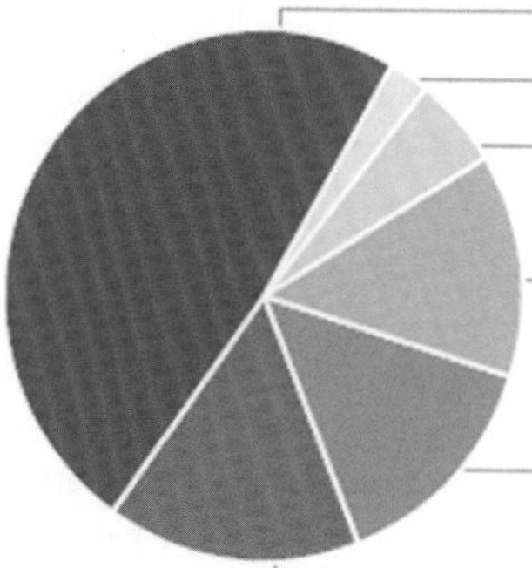

%	$000,000	Line of business
48.5%	16,430	Auto (including commercial vehicles)
2.4%	808	Accident & sickness*
5.6%	1,890	Other
13.6%	4,600	Liability
14.2%	4,820	Commercial property
15.7%	5,315	Personal property
	$33,864	**Total business**

Source: IBC, based upon data from MSA Researcher, OSFI and *Canadian Insurance*.

* A few general insurance companies sell a small amount of accident and sickness insurance; the majority of such insurance, however, is sold by life and health insurers.

Automobile Insurance

An automobile insurance policy protects the insured against liability arising from the ownership, use or operation of an owned or non-owned vehicle, from expenses incurred because death or an injury to their self or their passengers while operating the motor vehicle, and for physical damage to the vehicle itself. Automobile insurance is mandatory in Canada, although purchasing coverage for damage to the vehicle itself is optional.

Liability Insurance

You are legally liable for injuries or damage caused to others or their property by your negligence, and may be compelled by the courts to pay compensation. Liability insurance reimburses, or indemnifies the insured for the amount of the lawsuit up to the policy limit. Liability insurance is sold to individuals in connection with their home, condominium or tenants insurance and as a part of your automobile policy. Businesses purchase a Commercial General Liability policy to cover exposures from their premises, operations and products.

FUNCTIONS OF INSURANCE

As we have discussed the primary function of insurance is as a mechanism to spread risk; to share the losses of the few among the many. The insurance industry, however, also fulfills a number of other important functions within our economy and our society as a whole.

Outline the function of insurance within the Canadian economy. 5

Spread of Risk

Individuals and businesses spread their risk by purchasing insurance. It allows the individual to remove the burden of a large financial loss and share it with the rest of the community. The individual only has to pay a small known amount of money, the premium, in exchange for protection against an unknown loss.

Insurance companies further spread that risk in a number of ways in order to better monitor the fund of monies collected from those individuals and ensure their obligation to meet the policy agreements.

- Volume
  - Insurers write a large volume of risks and a number of different types of insurance. This allows them to balance significant losses in one line, say personal automobile insurance, against more manageable losses in another line, like commercial property insurance.
- Diversity of Type of Risk
  - Insurers write as many types of risk as possible in order to better achieve an underwriting profit. For example, there may be a number of fire losses in commercial property but fewer law suits affecting commercial liability. The average profit allows the insurer to remain in business.
- Diversity of Location
  - An insurance company will try to write policies at as many different locations as possible. One significant fire that damages a whole block of downtown Toronto businesses will probably affect a number of insurance companies with no one company losing too much. Catastrophic losses, such as Hurricane Katrina are also more manageable when a large number of companies are involved.

Security

Insurance is peace of mind. It allows individuals and businesses to plan for the future without having to set aside large reserves of cash in case a loss occurs. Although the probability of a loss occurring does not change with the purchase of insurance, the uncertainty connected to it is removed.

Aid to Credit

Credit is an integral part of today's economy. It allows individuals to purchase homes, cars and other necessities. A business needs credit to purchase stock, for capital expansion and for research and development. These are all an essential part of the growth and development of our economy. A financial institution would not be willing to extend credit unless their loan was secured by other assets. Insurance protects not only the individual's interest in the property but also the financial institutions investment.

Capital

The insurance industry manages vast sums of money. Premiums are paid in advance but losses often do not happen until well into the future or are spread out over the policy term. Insurance companies make use of the premiums collected by investing the money back into the economy until it is needed to pay claims. Insurance companies invest in government and corporate bonds and other secure investments within the stock market. The monies invested have a positive impact by helping governments finance capital work projects, and businesses to expand, which in turn create jobs and stimulate our economy. Because premiums collected are usually insufficient to pay the claims that occur insurance companies also use their investment income to pay claims and keep premiums lower than they might otherwise be.

Loss Prevention

Although the insurance industry is in the business of paying losses when they occur, the also focus on the reduction and prevention of losses to not only reduce the costs of insurance to the consumer, but to prevent the inconvenience and suffering that are part of any loss. The industry has long lobbied for safer products and practices, such as the use of fire brigades and sprinkler systems, encouraged safe driving practices and safety devices in vehicles, and crime prevention. The insurance industry was one of the foremost proponents for the graduated licensing program which has reduced the number of accidents among new drivers. "The crash rate for drivers age 16–19 declined 27 percent in 1995 compared to 1993, the year before the law was implemented." (http://www.nhtsa.dot.gov/people/injury/newdriver/SaveTeens/sect4.html).

Employment

The insurance industry requires a high level of service for its customers. Although the head offices of many of the large insurance providers are located in major Canadian cities, the workforce is spread across Canada, with brokers and agencies situated in the heart of many small towns. There are currently at least 215 private Property & Casualty insurers in Canada as well as government-owned automobile insurers in British Columbia, Manitoba, Saskatchewan and Quebec. (FACTS 2008, IBC Publication)

As of 2006, the industry employed over 107,500 people across Canada, the majority of which are in Ontario and Quebec. Of that total, 40.5% are employed by insurance companies, 52.8% are with brokerages, 5.4% are independent adjusters and appraisers, and 1.3% are employees of reinsurance companies throughout Canada. (FACTS 2008, IBC publication). There are very few industries that offer such a wide range of opportunities and variety of occupations.

This number does not take into account the number of people in health care, the legal profession, automotive repair and property restoration and construction companies that support the industry as well. Payment of claims enable these services to continue to thrive, and is further evidence of how essential the insurance industry is to our economy. Keep in mind as well that all individuals, whether employed directly by the industry or indirectly, are also consumers, thus further stimulating the economy.

INSURANCE STAKEHOLDERS

In order to better understand insurance it is important to understand the relationship between the major stakeholders in the insurance industry. Whether you are a consumer of the insurance product or an employee within the industry how the parties interact is important in developing a better understanding of the importance of insurance in our economy, and our society.

6 Describe the relationships between the major stakeholders within the insurance industry; consumer, intermediary, insurer, reinsurer, and government regulator.

Consumer

The consumer is the purchaser of the insurance products. It is their need for financial security that justifies the existence of the other parties. Regarded by many as a "necessary evil", insurance is often misunderstood and resented by consumers. Many will pay premiums for years without ever making a claim. Consumers mistrust the insurance industry because they do not see the value in their purchase. Consumer education has, and will continue to be an important focus for the industry in order to better inform consumers about the importance and value of their insurance purchase.

Intermediary

The intermediary is the middleman, or distribution system for the insurance industry. They are responsible for determining the consumer's exposure to loss and finding the product that will best protect them. Intermediaries work on behalf of the consumer while still representing the interests of the insurance companies they represent. There are three primary distribution systems in Canada; the broker, the agent and the direct writer. The **broker** is an independent businessperson that represents a number of insurance companies and can offer their clients alternatives to meet their insurance needs. Marsh Canada, and Aon Reed Steenhouse are examples of brokerages that operate throughout Canada. The **agent** represents one insurance company and recommends coverage from the products their company offers. State Farm is an example of an agency. **Direct Writers** are companies that sell their products directly to the consumer, such as Belair Direct and Meloche Monex.

Insurance Company

The company is the risk taker. They design the products and services, as well as administer the fund and pay the claims. Insurance companies employ underwriters to assess the risks submitted to determine if they fit are to be accepted or rejected, what terms and conditions to apply and what premium to charge. The underwriter is responsible as well for implementing the strategic plan of the company by investing in risks that will generate a profit.

Reinsurance Company

The reinsurer is the risk sharer. They help to further spread the risk by taking part of it from the primary insurer. Reinsurance helps to spread out the fluctuations of claims experience, such as in the case of catastrophic losses like the ice storm in Quebec and eastern Ontario in 1998.

Government Regulators

Insurance is regulated by the provincial governments in Canada. The regulators are the protectors of public interest. The regulate the solvency of insurance companies to ensure they are capable of meeting their obligations into the future, as well as guarantee both the availability of insurance products and their affordability to the purchasing public.

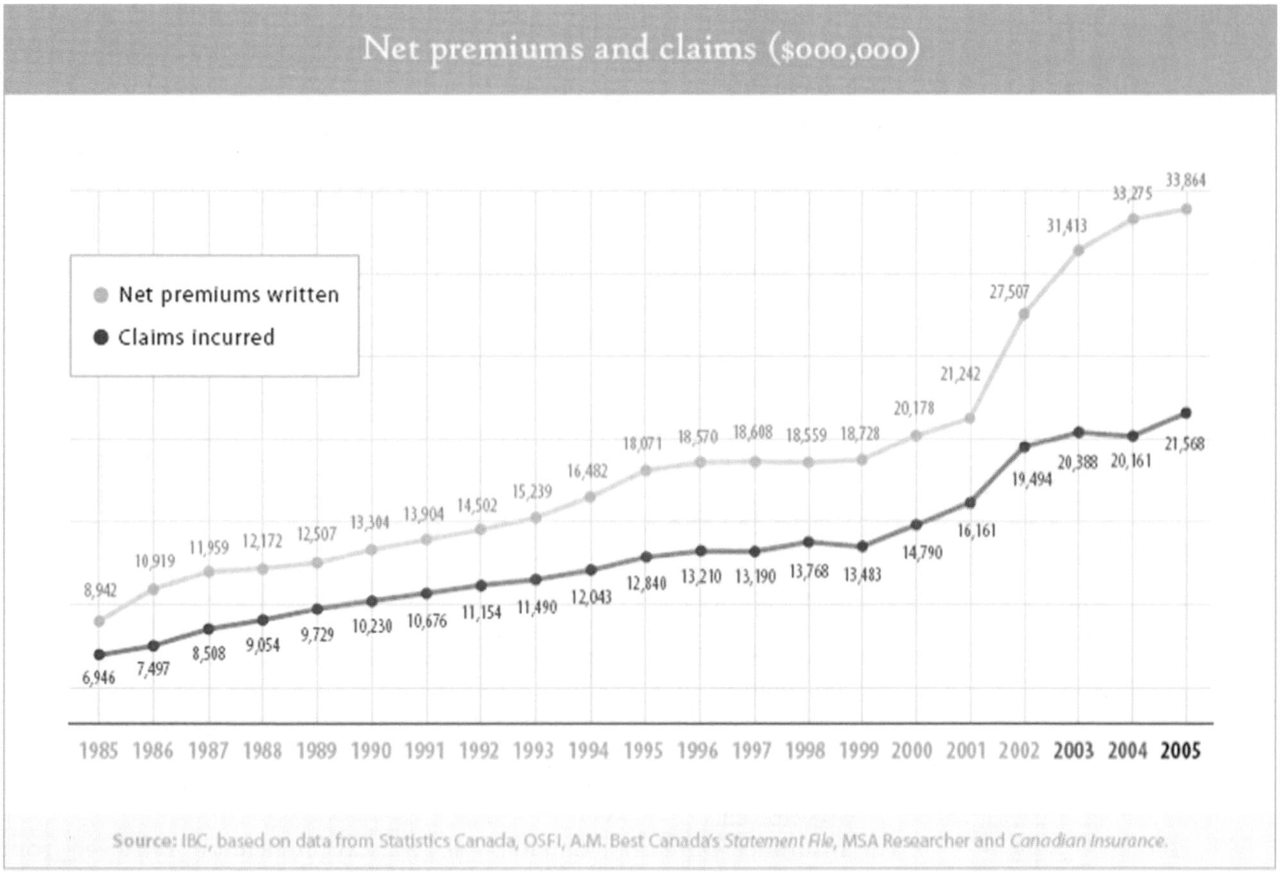

DEFINITIONS

Speculative Risks: involve the possibility of loss or gain, such as an investment

Pure Risks: involve only the possibility of loss or no loss, such as a fire

Loss Prevention: the use of loss control techniques to prevent a loss from occurring

Loss Reduction: the process of reducing the adverse effects of a loss that do happen

Risk: the chance of loss, or the object being insured against a loss

Premium: the amount of money paid by the insured in exchange for protection from loss under an insurance policy

Peril: the event or happening that could cause a loss

Insurance: The undertaking by one person to indemnify another person against loss or liability for loss in respect of a certain risk or peril to which the object of insurance may be exposed or to pay a sum of money or the thing of value upon the happening of a certain event.

Indemnify: to be put back in the same financial position you were in prior to loss, no more and no less

Policy: evidence of the contract

Real Property: Is the land and buildings

Personal Property: Is anything that is personal, moveable or separate from the real property

Direct Loss: Loss of the economic value of the item insured.

Indirect Loss: Damage which is not the direct consequence of the peril but flows from it.

Negligence: Doing something a prudent person would not do or not doing something a prudent person would do, resulting in loss by damage or injury

Personal Injury: Damage to the character or reputation of the third party in the community

Broker: Acting as an independent business person, a broker places insurance with numerous insurance companies.

Agent: A representative of an insurance company responsible for the sales and servicing of their clients.

Direct Writer: An employee of the insurance company.

REFERENCES

Insurance Institute of Canada, *C11 – Principles and Practices of Insurance*, 2002 edition

Insurance Institute of Canada, *C81 – General Insurance Essentials, Part 1*, 2004 edition

Insurance Institute of Canada, *C16 – The Business of Insurance*, 2002 edition

The Insurance Bureau of Canada, *FACTS 2006* publication, retrieved from www.ibc.ca.

The Insurance Bureau of Canada, *FACTS 2008* publication, retrieved from http://www.ibc.ca/en/Need_More_Info/documents/FactsBook2008.pdf, May 15, 2008

MANAGING YOUR PERSONAL FINANCES

Appendix A

For many people, the goal of financial success isn't *being* wealthy; it's the things that they can *do* with wealth. That's why chapter one in so many financial success stories deals with a hard reality: Like it or not, dealing with personal finances is a life-long job. As a rule, it involves a life-altering choice between two options:

- committing to the rational management of your personal finances—controlling them as a way of life and helping them grow
- letting the financial chips fall where they may and hoping for the best (which seldom happens)

Not surprisingly, option 1 results in greater personal satisfaction and financial stability. Ignoring your finances, on the other hand, invites frustration, disappointment, and, quite often, acute financial distress.

TAKING YOUR FINANCES PERSONALLY

In Chapter 16, we explored some basic financial-management activities, including the role of financial managers in cash flow management, financial planning and control, and debt and equity financing. We discussed the activities of financial managers—clarifying financial goals, determining short-term and long-term funding needs, and managing risk. Many of the principles of *organizational* finance pertain to *personal* finance as well. Recall, for example, the principle of reducing organizational financial risk by diversifying investments. When Enron collapsed, many employees lost their entire savings because their retirement portfolios consisted of just one security—Enron common stock—instead of a broader selection of investments.

In managing your own finances and pursuing your own personal financial goals, you must consider the activities that we'll revisit in the following sections: cash management, financial planning and control, investment alternatives, and risk management. We start by describing a key factor in success: the personal financial plan. Then we'll detail the steps in the planning process and relate them to some core concepts and crucial decisions in personal financial management.

BUILDING YOUR FINANCIAL PLAN

Financial planning is the process of looking at your current financial condition, identifying your goals, and anticipating your requirements for meeting those goals. Once you've determined the assets you need to meet your goals, you'll then identify the best sources and uses of those assets for eventually reaching your goals. But remember: Because your goals and financial position will change as you enter different life stages, your plan should always make room for revision. Figure A.1 summarizes a step-by-step approach to personal financial planning.

Knowing Your Net Worth

Begin by assessing your current financial position (Step 1). Your personal net worth is the value of all your assets minus all your liabilities or debts.

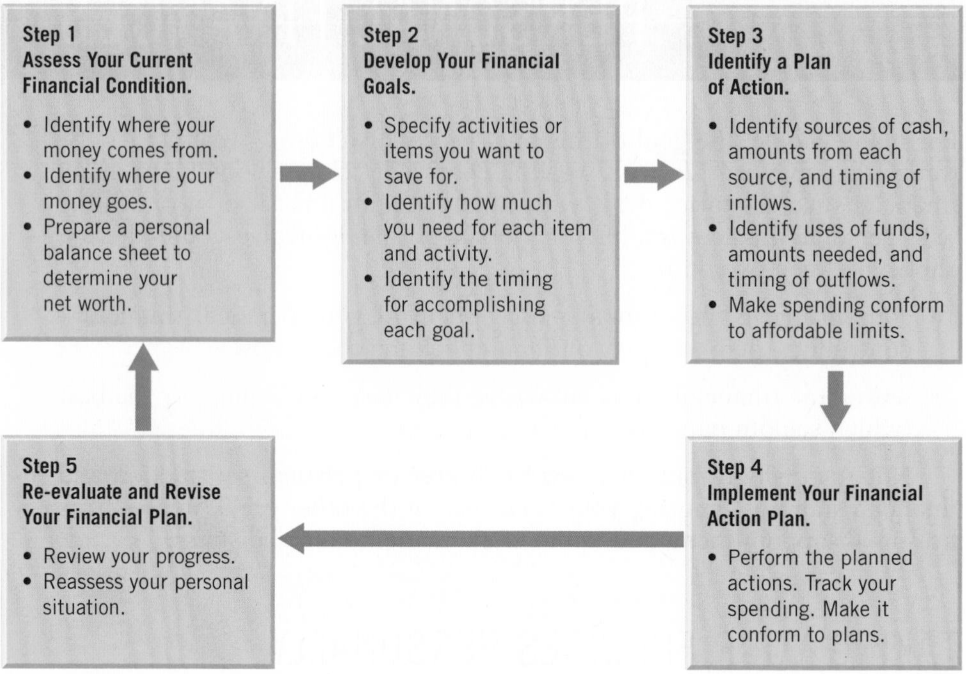
Step 1
Assess Your Current Financial Condition.
• Identify where your money comes from.
• Identify where your money goes.
• Prepare a personal balance sheet to determine your net worth.
Step 2
Develop Your Financial Goals.
• Specify activities or items you want to save for.
• Identify how much you need for each item and activity.
• Identify the timing for accomplishing each goal.
Step 3
Identify a Plan of Action.
• Identify sources of cash, amounts from each source, and timing of inflows.
• Identify uses of funds, amounts needed, and timing of outflows.
• Make spending conform to affordable limits.
Step 4
Implement Your Financial Action Plan.
• Perform the planned actions. Track your spending. Make it conform to plans.
Step 5
Re-evaluate and Revise Your Financial Plan.
• Review your progress.
• Reassess your personal situation.

Figure A.1

Bear in mind that personal net worth doesn't refer to the resources that you plan to manage in the future (as in a budget): It's a measure of *your wealth* at the present time. The worksheet in Figure A.2 provides some sample calculations for developing your own personal "balance sheet." Because assets and liabilities change over time, updating your balance sheet not only allows you to monitor changes but also provides more accurate information for realistic budgeting and planning.

Using Your Net Worth to Set and Evaluate Goals

Your personal balance sheet lets you review your *current* overall financial condition. Once you know where you presently stand, you can move on to Step 2 in financial planning: setting specific goals for the future by calculating *changes in net worth.* The worksheet in Figure A.3 allows for goal setting in three time frames: *immediate* (within one year), *intermediate* (within five years), and *long term* (over more than five years). This kind of planning should encourage you to set measurable goals and completion times when calculating your future financial needs. It also lets you set priorities for rationing your resources if, at some point, you don't have the wherewithal to pursue all of your goals.

Because subsequent planning steps—beginning with Step 3 (identifying a plan of action) and including implementation—will affect assets and liabilities, your balance sheet will change over time. That's why it needs periodic updating to reflect your current net worth, to monitor your progress, and to help you start a new planning cycle.

The Time Value of Money

The time value of money is perhaps the single most important concept in personal finance. It's especially relevant for setting financial goals and evaluating investments. The concept of *time value* recognizes the basic fact that, while it's invested, money grows by earning interest or yielding some other form of return. Thus, whenever you make everyday purchases, you're

Assets: What You Own		Example Numbers	Your Numbers
LIQUID ASSETS			
1. Cash	$	300	_______
2. Savings	+	3700	_______
3. Chequing	+	1200	_______
INVESTMENTS:			
4. RRSPs	+	12 400	_______
5. Securities	+	500	_______
6. Retirement Plan	+	—	_______
7. Real Estate (other than primary residence)	+	—	_______
HOUSEHOLD:			
8. Cars (market value)	+	18 000	_______
9. House (market value)	+	84 000	_______
10. Furniture	+	3400	_______
11. Personal Property	+	6600	_______
12. Other assets		—	_______
13. Total Assets (add lines 1–12)		**= $130 100**	_______
Liabilities (Debt): What You Owe			
CURRENT LIABILITIES:			
14. Credit card balance	$	1300	_______
15. Unpaid bills due	+	1800	_______
16. Alimony and child support	+	—	_______
LONG-TERM LIABILITIES:			
17. Home mortgage	+	72 500	_______
18. Home equity loan	+	—	_______
19. Car loan	+	4100	_______
20. Student loan	+	3600	_______
21. Other liabilities	+	2400	_______
22. Total Liabilities (add lines 14–21)		**= $85 700**	_______
Net Worth			
23. Total Assets (line 13)	$	130 100	_______
24. Less: Total Debt (line 22)	+	85 700	_______
25. Results: Net Worth		**= $44 400**	_______

Figure A.2

giving up interest that you could have earned with the same money if you'd invested it instead. From a financial standpoint, "idle" or uninvested money—money that could be put to work earning more money—is a wasted resource.

Why Money Grows

The value of time stems from the principle of compound growth—the compounding of interest paid over given time periods. With each additional time period, interest payments accumulate and earn even more interest, thus multiplying the earning capacity of the investment. Let's say, for example, that you invest $1 today at 10 percent annual interest. As you can see from Table A.1, you'll have $1.10 at the end of one year (your $1 original investment plus $0.10 in interest). If you reinvest your whole $1.10, you'll earn interest on both your first year's interest and your original investment. During year 2, therefore, your savings will grow to $1.21 (your $1.10 reinvestment plus $0.11 in interest). Obviously, each year's interest will be

Name the Goal	Financial requirement (amount) for this goal	Time frame for accomplishing goal	Importance (1 = highest, 5 = lowest)
Immediate Goals:			
Live in a better apartment	______	______	______
Obtain adequate life, disability, liability, property insurance	______	______	______
Establish an emergency cash fund	______	______	______
Pay off credit card debt	______	______	______
Other	______	______	______
Intermediate Goals:			
Save for wedding	______	______	______
Save to buy new car	______	______	______
Establish regular savings program (5% of gross income)	______	______	______
Save for college for self	______	______	______
Pay off major outstanding debt	______	______	______
Make a major purchase	______	______	______
Save for home remodeling	______	______	______
Save for down payment on a home	______	______	______
Other	______	______	______
Long-Term Goals:			
Pay off home mortgage	______	______	______
Save for college for children	______	______	______
Save for vacation home	______	______	______
Increase personal net worth to $__ in __ years.	______	______	______
Achieve retirement nest egg of $__ in __ years.	______	______	______
Accumulate funds for travel in retirement	______	______	______
Save for long-term care needs	______	______	______
Other	______	______	______

Figure A.3

Table A.1 Calculating Compound Growth

Year	Beginning Amount	+	Annual Interest Earned	=	Ending Amount
1	$1.000	+	$0.100 [0.10 × $1.000 = $0.100]	=	$1.100
2	1.100	+	0.110 [0.10 × $1.100 = $0.110]	=	1.210
3	1.210	+	0.121 [0.10 × $1.210 = $0.121]	=	1.331
4	1.331	+	0.133 [0.10 × $1.331 = $0.133]	=	1.464
5	1.464	+	0.146 [0.10 × $1.464 = $0.146]	=	1.610
6	1.610	+	0.161 [0.10 × $1.610 = $0.161]	=	1.771
7	1.771	+	0.177 [0.10 × $1.771 = $0.177]	=	1.948
8	1.948	+	0.195 [0.10 × $1.948 = $0.195]	=	2.143

greater than the previous year's. The interest accumulated over a single time period may seem rather modest, but when you add it up over many periods, the growth can be impressive. After about $7^1/_2$ years at 10 percent, your original $1 will have doubled. In other words, if you had invested $10 000, you'd have $20 000.

The Rule of 72

How long does it take to double an investment? A handy rule of thumb is called the "Rule of 72." You can find the number of years needed to double your money by dividing the annual interest rate (in percent) into 72. If, for example, you reinvest annually at 8 percent, you'll double your money in about 9 years:

$$\frac{72}{8} = 9$$

The Rule of 72 can also calculate how much interest you must get if you want to double your money in a given number of years. Simply divide 72 by the desired number of years. Thus, if you want to double your money in 10 years, you need to get 7.2 percent:

$$\frac{72}{10} = 7.2$$

Finally, the Rule of 72 highlights the downside as well as the upside of the compound-growth principle. The process means greater wealth for savers but increased indebtedness for borrowers. As we have seen, for example, an 8 percent rate doubles the principal every 9 years:

$$\frac{72}{8} = 9$$

Over a period of 36 years, the amount doubles four times:

$$\frac{36}{9} = 4$$

At 4 percent, by contrast, it doubles only twice over 36 years. Table A.2 charts the accumulation of the difference—$16 000 versus $4000—between investments (or loans) made at 8 percent versus 4 percent. The lesson for the personal-finance manager is clear: When investing (or saving), seek higher interest rates because money doubles more frequently; when borrowing, seek lower interest rates because indebtedness grows more slowly.

Table A.2 The Power of Doubling

Initial Investment (or Initial Unpaid Debt) = $1000

Number of Times Doubled	Value after Doubling
1	$2000
2	$4000
3	$8000
4	$16 000

Making Better Use of Your Time Value

Most people want to save for the future, either for things they need (down payments on a house, university or college tuition, retirement nest eggs) or for nonessentials (luxury items and recreation). Needless to say, the sooner you get started, the greater your financial power will be. You will have taken advantage of the time value of money for a longer period of time.

Consider the following illustration. Co-workers Ellen and Barbara are both planning to retire in 25 years. Let's assume that they are planning for a 10 percent annual return on investment (stock markets in North America have averaged about 10 percent over the past 75 years, with higher returns in some years and lower returns in others). Their savings strategies, however, are different. Whereas Barbara begins saving immediately, Ellen plans to start later but invest larger sums. Barbara will invest \$2000 annually for each of the next five years (years 1–5), for a total investment of \$10 000. She'll let interest accumulate through year 25. Ellen, meanwhile, wants to live a little larger by spending rather than saving for the next 10 years. Then, for years 11–20, she'll start saving \$2000 annually, for a total investment of \$20 000. She, too, will allow annual returns to accumulate until year 25, when both she and Barbara retire. Will Ellen have a larger retirement fund in year 25 because she's ultimately contributing twice as much as Barbara?

Not by a long shot. Barbara's retirement wealth will be much larger—\$90 358 versus Ellen's \$56 468—even though she invested only half as much (\$10 000 versus \$20 000). We explain the disparity by crunching all the

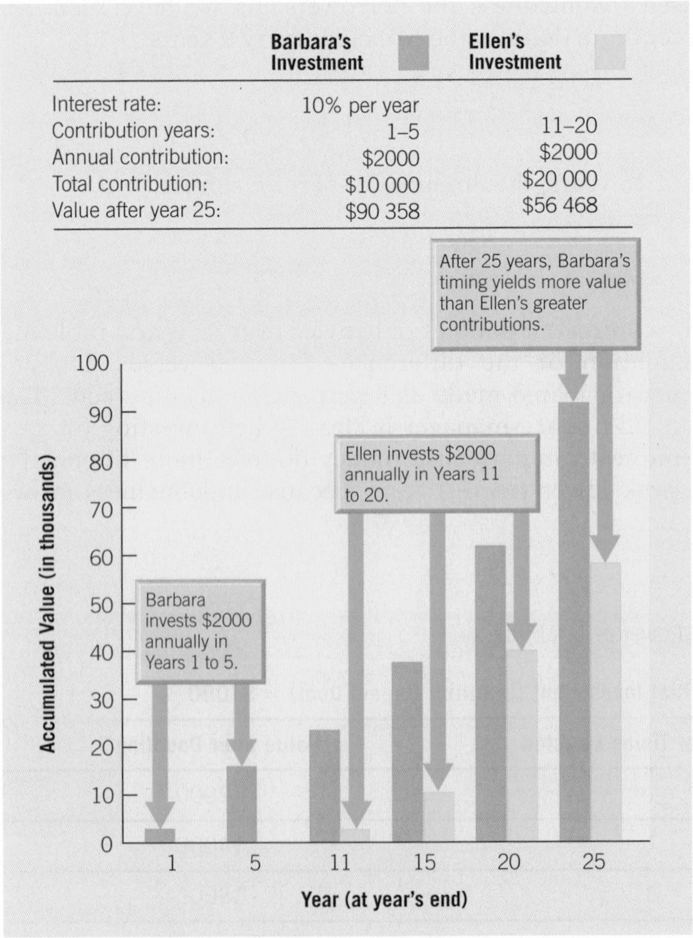

Figure A.4

numbers in Figure A.4. As you can see, Barbara's advantage lies in timing—namely, the length of her savings program. Her money is invested longer—over a period of 21 to 25 years—with interest compounding over that range of time. Ellen's earnings are compounded over a shorter period—6 to 15 years. Granted, Ellen may have had more fun in years 1 to 5, but Barbara's retirement prospects look brighter.

Time Value as a Financial-Planning Tool

How much must you set aside today to accumulate enough money for something you want tomorrow? By its very nature, financial planning takes into account not only future needs (retirement, vacations, a wedding, major purchases) but also sources of funds for meeting those needs. Timing, however, is important. The timing of financial transactions will determine whether your plan works or doesn't work the way you intend. Start by considering the time value of money at the outset of your planning cycle. In this respect, various time-based tables for financial calculations are quite useful.[1] Table A.3, for example, shows how much a $1 investment will grow over different lengths of time and at different interest rates. Let's see how we can use this tool for financial planning.

Having recently inherited $50 000, Jason wants to invest for his old age. Specifically, he wants to accumulate a $200 000 nest egg by the time he reaches 55 (30 years from now). He also wants to spend some of the money while he's young enough to enjoy it, but he doesn't know how much he'll have left to spend after he's determined the amount needed to meet his retirement goal.

To help Jason with his planning, we first need to focus on our 30-year investment; thus $n = 30$ in Table A.3. As you can see, the accumulated value of that investment depends on the annual interest rate. At 4 percent, for instance, the growth factor is 3.243. Over 30 years, therefore, $1 invested now will grow to $3.243. Our question, then, is this: If $1 invested now yields $3.243, how many dollars must we invest now to accumulate $200 000 in 30 years? The answer is fairly simple. If $1 provides $3.243 in 30 years, and if we want to accumulate $200 000, we divide $200 000 by $3.243 to determine Jason needs to invest $61 671 to reach his retirement goal.

Jason's worksheet, which is shown in Table A.4, reveals trial calculations made with three different interest rates—conservative, moderate, optimistic—available from alternative investments. As you can see, a 4 percent return on investment won't provide the desired $200 000. If he gets only 4 percent, Jason would have to invest $61 671; but, as we know, he has only $50 000. As a matter of fact, if he invested the entire $50 000 at 4 percent, he'd end up with just $162 150 ($50 000 × $3.243 = $162 150), which is well below his $200 000 goal.

Thus Jason has two choices: find a higher-paying investment or, if he's willing to settle for 4 percent, reduce the amount of his desired nest egg. To make his decision, Jason can use the trial data contained in Table A.4. Projecting an investment at 8 percent, he needs to allocate only about $20 000 to start his nest egg and still have more than $30 000 for other uses. If he considers the 8 percent investment too risky, he may opt for the safer 6 percent return; in that case, he'd still have $15 175 left ($50 000 – $34 825).

Table A.3 Timetable for Growing $1

n	1%	2%	3%	4%	5%	6%	7%	8%	9%	10%
1	1.010	1.020	1.030	1.040	1.050	1.060	1.070	1.080	1.090	1.100
2	1.020	1.040	1.061	1.082	1.102	1.124	1.145	1.166	1.188	1.210
3	1.030	1.061	1.093	1.125	1.158	1.191	1.225	1.260	1.295	1.331
4	1.041	1.082	1.126	1.170	1.216	1.262	1.311	1.360	1.412	1.464
5	1.051	1.104	1.159	1.217	1.276	1.338	1.403	1.469	1.539	1.611
6	1.062	1.126	1.194	1.265	1.340	1.419	1.501	1.587	1.677	1.772
7	1.072	1.149	1.230	1.316	1.407	1.504	1.606	1.714	1.828	1.949
8	1.083	1.172	1.267	1.369	1.477	1.594	1.718	1.851	1.993	2.144
9	1.094	1.195	1.305	1.423	1.551	1.689	1.838	1.999	2.172	2.358
10	1.105	1.219	1.344	1.480	1.629	1.791	1.967	2.159	2.367	2.594
11	1.116	1.243	1.384	1.539	1.710	1.898	2.105	2.332	2.580	2.853
12	1.127	1.268	1.426	1.601	1.796	2.012	2.252	2.518	2.813	3.138
13	1.138	1.294	1.469	1.665	1.886	2.133	2.410	2.720	3.066	3.452
14	1.149	1.319	1.513	1.732	1.980	2.261	2.579	2.937	3.342	3.797
15	1.161	1.346	1.558	1.801	2.079	2.397	2.759	3.172	3.642	4.177
16	1.173	1.373	1.605	1.873	2.183	2.540	2.952	3.426	3.970	4.595
17	1.184	1.400	1.653	1.948	2.292	2.693	3.159	3.700	4.328	5.054
18	1.196	1.428	1.702	2.026	2.407	2.854	3.380	3.996	4.717	5.560
19	1.208	1.457	1.753	2.107	2.527	3.026	3.616	4.316	5.142	6.116
20	1.220	1.486	1.806	2.191	2.653	3.207	3.870	4.661	5.604	6.727
21	1.232	1.516	1.860	2.279	2.786	3.399	4.140	5.034	6.109	7.400
22	1.245	1.546	1.916	2.370	2.925	3.603	4.430	5.436	6.658	8.140
23	1.257	1.577	1.974	2.465	3.071	3.820	4.740	5.871	7.258	8.954
24	1.270	1.608	2.033	2.563	3.225	4.049	5.072	6.341	7.911	9.850
25	1.282	1.641	2.094	2.666	3.386	4.292	5.427	6.848	8.623	10.834
30	1.348	1.811	2.427	3.243	4.322	5.743	7.612	10.062	13.267	17.449
40	1.489	2.208	3.262	4.801	7.040	10.285	14.974	21.724	31.408	45.258
50	1.645	2.691	4.384	7.106	11.467	18.419	29.456	46.900	74.354	117.386

continued

Table A.3 *continued*

n	11%	12%	13%	14%	15%	16%	17%	18%	19%	20%
1	1.110	1.120	1.130	1.140	1.150	1.160	1.170	1.180	1.190	1.200
2	1.232	1.254	1.277	1.300	1.322	1.346	1.369	1.392	1.416	1.440
3	1.368	1.405	1.443	1.482	1.521	1.561	1.602	1.643	1.685	1.728
4	1.518	1.574	1.630	1.689	1.749	1.811	1.874	1.939	2.005	2.074
5	1.685	1.762	1.842	1.925	2.011	2.100	2.192	2.288	2.386	2.488
6	1.870	1.974	2.082	2.195	2.313	2.436	2.565	2.700	2.840	2.988
7	2.076	2.211	2.353	2.502	2.660	2.826	3.001	3.185	3.379	3.583
8	2.305	2.476	2.658	2.853	3.059	3.278	3.511	3.759	4.021	4.300
9	2.558	2.773	3.004	3.252	3.518	3.803	4.108	4.435	4.785	5.160
10	2.839	3.106	3.395	3.707	4.046	4.411	4.807	5.234	5.695	6.192
11	3.152	3.479	3.836	4.226	4.652	5.117	5.624	6.176	6.777	7.430
12	3.498	3.896	4.334	4.818	5.350	5.936	6.580	7.288	8.064	8.916
13	3.883	4.363	4.898	5.492	6.153	6.886	7.699	8.599	9.596	10.699
14	4.310	4.887	5.535	6.261	7.076	7.987	9.007	10.147	11.420	12.839
15	4.785	5.474	6.254	7.138	8.137	9.265	10.539	11.974	13.589	15.407
16	5.311	6.130	7.067	8.137	9.358	10.748	12.330	14.129	16.171	18.488
17	5.895	6.866	7.986	9.276	10.761	12.468	14.426	16.672	19.244	22.186
18	6.543	7.690	9.024	10.575	12.375	14.462	15.879	19.673	22.900	26.623
19	7.263	8.613	10.197	12.055	14.232	16.776	19.748	23.214	27.251	31.948
20	8.062	9.646	11.523	13.743	16.366	19.461	23.105	27.393	32.429	38.337
21	8.949	10.804	13.021	15.667	18.821	22.574	27.033	32.323	38.591	46.005
22	9.933	12.100	14.713	17.861	21.644	26.186	31.629	38.141	45.923	55.205
23	11.026	13.552	16.626	20.361	24.891	30.376	37.005	45.007	54.648	66.247
24	12.239	15.178	18.788	23.212	28.625	35.236	43.296	53.108	65.031	79.496
25	13.585	17.000	21.230	26.461	32.918	40.874	50.656	62.667	77.387	95.395
30	22.892	29.960	39.115	50.949	66.210	85.849	111.061	143.367	184.672	237.373
40	64.999	93.049	132.776	188.876	267.856	378.715	533.846	750.353	1051.642	1469.740
50	184.559	288.996	450.711	700.197	1083.619	1670.669	2566.080	3927.189	5988.730	9100.191

n = Number of time periods
% = Various interest rates

Table A.4 Nest Egg Worksheet

	Investment Returns (annual rate)			Your numbers
	Conservative 4%	Moderate 6%	Optimistic 8%	%
Ending amount after 30 years:	$200 000	$200 000	$200 000	___
Growth factor (from table):	3.243	5.743	10.062	___
Amount* to invest now (end amount/ growth factor):	$61 671**	$34 825	$19 877	___
	($200 000/3.243)	($200 000/5.743)	($200 000/10.062)	

*Rounded to nearest whole dollar.
**This amount is greater than the available $50 000.

CONSERVING MONEY BY CONTROLLING IT

Several steps in the financial planning process call for conserving money by paying attention to where it goes—by keeping spending within affordable limits and understanding on what you're spending your money.[2] As too many people have found out the hard way, a major pitfall in any financial plan is the temptation to spend too much, especially when credit is so easy to get. Consumers often lose track of how much they spend, and, to make matters worse, some don't consider the costly finance charges associated with easy credit. Because many credit-card issuers target university and college students and recent graduates with tempting offers appealing to the desire for financial independence, we'll use the following section to explain the financial costs entailed by credit cards. Keep in mind, however, that the same lessons apply equally to home-equity loans, consumer finance agreements, and other sources of credit.

Credit Cards: Keys to Consumer Satisfaction or Fiscal Handcuffs?

Although some credit cards don't charge annual fees, all of them charge interest on unpaid (outstanding) balances. Because credit-card debt is one of the most expensive sources of funds, you need to understand the costs before you start charging instead of being surprised when you open the bill. For one thing, many card users don't realize how much interest they're paying or how long it will take them to pay off their bills.

Table A.5 reprints a page from California's "Minimum Payment Credit Card Calculation." Using the table as a guide, let's consider the following situation. Suppose you owe $5000 for credit-card purchases and your card company requires a minimum monthly payment of 5 percent of the unpaid balance. The interest rate is 18 percent APR (annual percentage rate) on the outstanding balance. (By the way, these aren't too high: Some rates are well above 20 percent.)

Thus, Table A.5 reflects an account with $5000 outstanding balance at the end of last month. This is the amount on which your interest of 18 percent APR is charged. Remember, too, that your card company requires a minimum monthly payment (minimum payment due—or MPD) of 5 percent (of the current balance). Let's assume that you pay only the monthly minimum and ask ourselves two questions:

1. How many months will it take to pay off the $5000?
2. How much interest will you have paid when you do pay it off?

In Table A.5, the column labelled "MPD 5%" reveals that at 18 percent APR it will take you 115 months to pay off $5000. That's approximately 91/2 years! And remember: This number assumes that your balance gradually diminishes to zero because you add no other purchases to the card. Your total payment of $7096.70 covers your $5000 debt plus interest charges. An immediate cash payoff, therefore, would avoid $2096.70 in interest payments.

Why does repayment take so long? In Table A.6, we run through some sample calculations for the first two months in your 115-month repayment process. As you can see, your minimum monthly payment decreases because your ending balance gets smaller with each monthly payment.

Table A.5 Paying Off Credit-Card Debt

Balance = $5000.00

	MPD 2%		MPD 3%		MPD 4%		MPD 5%		MPD 10%	
APR	**Months**	**Cost**	**Months**	**Cost**	**Months**	**Cost**	**Months**	**Cost**	**Months**	**Cost**
6%	211	$6576.80	144	$5965.56	111	$5696.30	92	$5544.58	50	$5260.74
7%	221	$6945.82	148	$6164.85	114	$5831.99	93	$5647.25	50	$5306.87
8%	233	$7360.22	153	$6378.23	116	$5974.39	95	$5753.83	51	$5353.84
9%	246	$7829.02	158	$6607.24	119	$6124.04	96	$5864.56	51	$5401.63
10%	262	$8363.77	163	$6853.67	122	$6281.51	98	$5979.70	52	$6450.30
11%	279	$8979.59	169	$7119.61	125	$6447.40	100	$6099.50	52	$5499.87
12%	299	$9696.61	175	$7407.50	128	$6622.45	102	$6224.26	53	$5550.32
13%	323	$10 542.23	182	$7720.16	131	$6807.42	104	$6354.29	53	$5601.75
14%	351	$11 554.78	189	$8060.94	134	$7003.17	106	$6489.94	53	$5654.11
15%	385	$12 789.56	197	$8433.88	138	$7210.72	108	$6631.59	54	$5707.49
16%	428	$14 329.44	206	$8843.78	142	$7431.13	110	$6779.63	54	$5761.88
17%	482	$16 304.46	216	$9296.40	146	$7665.64	112	$6934.49	55	$5817.33
18%	553	$18 931.11	226	$9798.89	150	$7915.67	115	$7096.70	55	$5873.86
19%	652	$22 598.52	238	$10 359.98	155	$8182.84	117	$7266.77	56	$5931.51
20%	799	$28 083.97	251	$10 990.60	160	$8468.95	120	$7445.32	56	$5990.30
21%	1040	$37 198.63	266	$11 704.63	165	$8776.09	123	$7632.92	57	$6050.28
22%	1518	$55 367.78	283	$12 519.87	171	$9106.71	126	$7830.38	58	$6111.48
23%	2930	$109 673.97	303	$13 459.58	177	$9463.60	129	$8038.42	58	$6173.93
24%	*	*	325	$14 554.76	184	$9850.03	132	$8257.96	59	$6237.69
25%	*	*	352	$15 847.75	191	$10 269.86	135	$8489.97	59	$6302.77

Table A.6 Calculating Minimum Monthly Payments

Month	Minimum Monthly Payment (5% of Previous Ending Balance)	=	Interest Owed on Previous Balance* ($^1/_{12}$ × 18%) Previous Balance)	+	Payment on Principal	Ending Balance Owed on Principal
January	—		—		—	$5000
February	$250 [0.05 × $5000]	=	$75 [1/12 × 0.18 × $5000]	+	$175	$4825 [5000 – 175]
March	$241.25 [0.05 × 4825]	=	$72.38 [1/12 × 0.18 × 4825]	+	$168.87	$4656.13 [4825 – 168.87]

*Monthly interest is calculated using $^1/_{12}$ of annual interest rate.

Your $250 payment in February includes $75 in interest owed on the $5000 balance in the previous month. At 18 percent APR, interest on $5000 would be $900 for a year (0.18 × $5000), but for one month (January), it's only 1/12 of that amount—$75. You're paying the rest of your February instalment of $175 ($250 – $75) on the principal amount, thereby reducing the month-end balance to $4825. If we carry out these calculations over 115 months, we find that, when your account is paid in full, you've made "payments on principal" of $5000 and interest payments of $2096.70.

Practise Paying Off Your Debt

Using the method illustrated in Table A.6, you should be able to answer the following questions about credit-card repayment (the answers appear at the end of this appendix):

1. According to the data in Table A.6, your minimum monthly payment for April would be which of the following? [select one] (a) $232.81; (b) $253.47; (c) $230.56; (d) $226.18.
2. According to the data in Table A.6, for April, the interest owed on your previous balance would be which of the following? [select one] (a) $70.43; (b) $71.94; (c) $69.84; (d) $68.32.
3. According to the data in Table A.6, for April, your ending balance owed on principal would be which of the following? [select one] (a) $4182.16; (b) $4493.16; (c) $4517.22; (d) $4334.97.

Save Your Money: Lower Interest Rates and Faster Payments

A closer look at Table A.5 confirms two principles for saving money that you can apply when borrowing from any source, not just credit cards: Look for lower interest rates and make faster repayments.

Seeking Lower Interest Rates

Because higher interest rates obviously mean more expensive money, you save money with lower interest rates (money that you can "stretch" by using it for other things). With a little research, you'll find that potential creditors charge different rates (ranging from below 10 percent to over 20 percent APR among credit-card issuers). How much can you save? Look again at Table A.5 and compare the cost of borrowing $5000 at 18 percent with the cost of borrowing it at 9 percent. If you assume the same 5 percent minimum monthly payment, how much interest does 9 percent save you over the life of the repayment? The answer is \$1232.14 (\$864.56 instead of \$2096.70). That's a nearly 59 percent savings.

Making Faster Payments

Because money has a time value, lenders charge borrowers according to the length of time for which they borrow it. In general, longer lending periods increase the cost, while shorter periods are cheaper. Accordingly, borrowers often speed up payments to cut interest costs. Using Table A.5, for example, compare the costs of the "5% MPD" (required monthly payment of 5 percent on the remaining balance) with the faster "10% MPD." The faster schedule cuts the repayment period from 115 to 55 months and, at 18 percent APR, reduces interest costs by \$1222.84 (7096.70 – 5873.86).

What if you combined both faster repayment and the lower interest rate (9 percent versus 18 percent)? You'd cut your total interest cost to just \$450.30—a savings of \$1695.07 over the amount you'd pay if you made slower repayments at the higher rate.

FINANCIAL COMMITMENTS OF HOME OWNERSHIP

Should you rent or buy the roof you need over your head? The answer to that question involves a variety of considerations, including life stage, family needs, career, financial situation, and preferred lifestyle. If you decide to buy, for example, you have to ask yourself how much house you can afford. To answer that question, you need to ask yourself a number of questions about your personal financial condition and your capacity for borrowing.

To Buy or Not to Buy: That Is the Question

Renting is attractive because you can move in without making an initial investment (or at least making a hefty down payment). That's why it's a popular choice among young adults, especially singles with limited budgets and people whose lifestyles aren't congenial to settling down in a fixed location. Flexibility, mobility, and freedom from obligations of maintenance and upkeep are important advantages. Financially speaking, however, rent payments are cash outflows that provide future financial benefits to owners instead of renters.

By the same token, first-time homebuyers cite the prospect of future financial gain as an attractive reason for buying. The financial inducements are in fact powerful, including home equity, increasing property values, and tax advantages. You can see if buying is a good idea for you by consulting a "rent-versus-buy calculator" on the Web, such as the one at www.ginniemae.gov/. By letting you try various interest rates, down payments, loan lengths, and rental costs, calculators specify the financial advantages of renting or buying under a wide range of financial circumstances.

Many younger adults with children report that they choose to buy because they want privacy, space, and the freedom to choose a neighbourhood. Finally, most home buyers say that they get satisfaction from a sense of ownership—from having their own property. Table A.7 summarizes the key considerations in deciding whether to rent or buy a place to live.

How Much House Can You Afford?

For most people, buying a home is the biggest investment they'll ever make. But even though ownership, as we've seen, bestows several benefits, many people make the regrettable mistake of buying a house that's too expensive

Table A.7 To Buy or Not to Buy

Renting	Buying
• No down payment to get started	• Must make payments for mortgage, property taxes, and insurance
• Flexibility to leave	• Equity builds up over time
• No obligation for upkeep or improvements	• More privacy
• No groundskeeping	• Value of property may increase
• Easy cash flow planning (a single monthly payment)	
• May provide access to recreation and social facilities	• Financial gains from selling house can be exempt from taxes
• Rental conditions may be changed by owner	• Greater control over use of property and improvements
• Timing for repairs controlled by owner	• The home can become a source of cash by refinancing with another mortgage loan or a home-equity loan

for their pocketbooks. Don't saddle yourself with house payments that you can't afford. In addition, new homebuyers quickly discover that the typical demands of ownership—especially the demand on their time and other resources for maintaining and improving a home—tend to cut into the money left over for recreation, eating out, taking vacations, and buying new cars. You can reduce the financial pressure by calculating in advance a realistic price range—one that not only lets you buy a house but also lets you live a reasonably pleasant life once you're in it.

Most people need a loan to buy a house or a condominium. A mortgage loan is a loan that's secured by the property—the home—being purchased. Because the size of a loan depends on the cost of the property, both borrowers and lenders want to know whether the buyer can afford the house they want. How can you determine how much you can afford? One time-tested (though somewhat conservative) rule of thumb cautions the buyer to keep the price below 2 1/2 times his or her annual income. Thus, if your income is \$48 000, look for a house priced below \$120 000.

Any such calculation, however, will give you just a rough estimate of what you can afford. There are other considerations. What you can afford also depends on how much money you have for a down payment and how much you can borrow. Lending institutions use two guidelines for estimating a buyer's borrowing capacity: (1) the borrower's ability to meet the recurring costs of buying and owning, and (2) other long-term debt that the buyer has already incurred.

PITI

What are those recurring costs? Every month, the homeowner must pay principal, interest, taxes, and insurance—*PITI,* for short. Because all four costs are greater for more expensive homes, the buyer's monthly obligation depends on how much house he or she has bought. The size of principal and interest payments depends on the mortgage amount, the length of the mortgage loan, and the interest rate. Obviously, if you borrow a fixed amount, the larger your monthly payment, the faster you'll pay off your loan. As Table A.8 shows, monthly payments on conventional loans are lower for longer-term loans and higher for larger interest rates.

In evaluating loan applications, lenders use PITI calculations to estimate the buyer's financial capacity—his or her ability to meet monthly pay-

Table A.8 Monthly Mortgage Payments on a $10 000 Loan

	Length of Loan					
Interest Rate (%)	**10 Years**	**15 Years**	**20 Years**	**25 Years**	**30 Years**	**40 Years**
5.0	$106.07	$79.08	$66.00	$58.46	$53.68	$48.22
5.5	108.53	81.71	68.79	61.41	56.79	51.58
6.0	111.02	84.39	71.64	64.43	59.96	50.22
6.5	113.55	87.11	74.56	67.52	63.21	58.55
7.0	116.11	89.88	77.53	70.68	66.53	62.14
7.5	118.71	92.71	80.56	73.90	69.93	65.81
8.0	121.33	95.57	83.65	77.19	73.38	69.53
8.5	123.99	98.48	86.79	80.53	76.90	73.31
9.0	126.68	101.43	89.98	83.92	80.47	77.14
9.5	129.40	104.43	93.22	87.37	84.09	81.01
10.0	132.16	107.47	96.51	90.88	87.76	84.91
10.5	134.94	110.54	99.84	94.42	91.48	88.86
11.0	137.76	113.66	103.22	98.02	95.24	92.83
11.5	140.60	116.82	106.65	101.65	99.03	96.83
12.0	143.48	120.02	110.11	105.33	102.86	100.85
12.5	146.38	123.26	113.62	109.04	106.73	104.89
13.0	149.32	126.53	117.16	112.79	110.62	108.95
13.5	152.27	129.83	120.74	116.56	114.54	113.03
14.0	155.27	133.17	124.35	120.38	118.49	117.11
14.5	158.29	136.55	128.00	124.22	122.46	121.21
15.0	161.33	139.96	131.68	128.08	126.44	125.32

ments. To determine how much someone is likely to lend you, calculate 28 percent of your gross monthly income (that is, before taxes and other deductions). If your PITI costs don't exceed that figure, you'll probably get the loan. With a monthly gross income of $4000, for example, your PITI costs shouldn't exceed $1120 (28 percent of $4000). Figure A.5 gives a sample calculation, and you should be able to make step-by-step computations by plugging your own numbers into the worksheet.

Other Long-Term Debt

In evaluating financial capacity, lenders also look at any outstanding debt that will take the borrower more than 10 months to pay off, such as car loans, child support and alimony payments, student loans, and credit-card bills. In general, they will accept long-term indebtedness (including PITI) that amounts to 36 percent of gross income. Remember: Because PITI itself

ASSUMPTIONS:

30-year mortgage
Closing costs (fees for property survey, credit report, title search, title insurance, attorney, interest advance, loan origination) = \$5000
Funds available for closing costs and down payment = \$25 000
Interest rate on mortgage = $6\frac{1}{2}\%$ per year
Estimated real estate taxes = \$200 per month
Estimated homeowner's insurance = \$20 per month

Example Numbers		Your Numbers
1. Monthly income, gross (before taxes or deductions).......	\$4000	______
2. Apply PITI ratio (0.28 x amount on line 1) to determine borrower's payment capacity: 0.28 x \$4000 = ...	\$1120	______
3. Determine mortgage payment (principal and interest) by subtracting taxes and insurance from PITI (line 2):............	– \$ 220	______
4. Result: Maximum mortgage payment (principal and interest)............	**\$ 900**	______
5. Using Table A.8, find the monthly mortgage payment on a \$10 000 loan at $6\frac{1}{2}\%$ interest for 30 years............	\$63.21	______
6. Since each \$10 000 loan requires a \$63.21 monthly payment, how many \$10 000 loans can the borrower afford with the \$900 payment capacity? The answer is determined as follows: \$900.00/\$63.21 = 14.2382 loans of \$10 000 each.		______
7. Result: Maximum allowable mortgage loan calculated as follows: 14.2382 loans (from line 6 above) x \$10 000 per loan] = ...	**\$142 382**	______
8. Result: Maximum house price borrower can afford using PITI (amount of house that can be bought with available funds):		
From loan..................	\$142 382	______
From down payment....	\$ 25 000	______
Less closing cost.......	–\$ 5 000	______
....	**\$162 382**	______

Figure A.5

can be up to 28 percent, you might be allowed as little as 8 percent in other long-term debt. With your \$4000 monthly gross income, your total debt should be less than \$1440 (which allows \$1120 for PITI and \$320 for other debt). If your total debt exceeds \$1440, you may have to settle for a smaller loan than the one you calculated with the PITI method. Figure A.6 gives an example of such an alternative calculation; again, you can plug your own numbers into the worksheet.

If you want to go into more detail about your own payment capabilities, search for websites that provide mortgage calculators for testing interest rates, lengths of loans, and other personal financial information.

ASSUMPTIONS:

30-year mortgage
Closing costs = $5000
Funds available for closing costs and down payment = $25 000
Interest rate on mortgage = $6\frac{1}{2}$% per year
Estimated real estate taxes = $200 per month
Estimated homeowner's insurance = $20 per month

Example Numbers		Your Numbers
1. Monthly income, gross (before taxes or deductions)............	$4000	________
2. Apply debt ratio (0.36 x amount on line 1) to determine borrower's payment capacity: 0.36 x $4000 = ...	$1440	________
3. Less current payments on non-mortgage debts that will last more than 10 months: car loan......................–$ 300; student loan...............–$ 100; credit card debt...........–$ 100	–$ 500	
4. Less taxes and insurance for house................................	–$ 220	________
5. Result: Maximum mortgage payment (principal and interest)...	**$ 720**	________
6. Using Table A.8, find the monthly mortgage payment payment on a $10 000 loan at $6\frac{1}{2}$% interest for 30 years..	$63.21	________
7. Since each $10 000 loan requires a $63.21 monthly payment, how many $10 000 loans can the borrower afford with the $720 payment capacity? The answer is determined as follows: $720.00/$63.21 = 11.3906 loans of $10 000 each		________
8. Result: Maximum allowable mortgage loan [calculated as follows: 11.3906 loans (from line 7 above) x $10 000 per loan]......................................	**$113 906**	________
9. Result: Maximum house price borrower can afford (amount of house that can be bought with available funds):		
From loan.................$113 906		________
From down payment...$ 25 000		________
Less closing costs.....–$ 5 000		________
....	**$133 906**	________

Figure A.6

PROTECTING YOUR NET WORTH

With careful attention, thoughtful saving and spending, and skilful financial planning (and a little luck), you can build up your net worth over time. In addition to steps for accumulating net worth, therefore, every financial plan should consider steps for preserving it. One approach involves the risk–return relationship that we discussed in Chapter 16. Do you prefer to protect your current assets, or are you willing to risk them in return for greater growth? At various life stages, and whenever you reach a designated level of wealth, you should adjust your asset portfolio to conform to your risk and return preferences—conservative, moderate, or aggressive. Another approach is life insurance.

Life Insurance

You can also think of life insurance as a tool for financial preservation. A life insurance policy is a promise to pay beneficiaries after the death of an insured party. In return, of course, insurance companies collect *premiums*—payments from the insurance purchaser—during his or her lifetime.

What Does Life Insurance Do?

From a personal-finance perspective, the purpose of life insurance is to replace income upon the death of the policyholder. Accordingly, the amount of insurance you need depends on how many other people rely on your income. Insurance, for example, is crucial for the married parent who is a family's sole source of income. On the other hand, a single person with no financial dependents needs little or no insurance and will probably prefer to put money into higher-paying investments.

How Much Should I Buy?

To estimate the amount you need, begin by adding up all of the annual expenses—rent, food, clothing, transportation, schooling, debts to be paid—that you pay for the dependents who would survive you. Then multiply the total by the number of years that you want the insurance to cover your dependents. Typically, this sum will amount to several times your current annual income. Thus many policyholders, especially during the life stages of highest need—are insured for 10 to 20 times their annual salaries.

Two Basic Types of Insurance

Term insurance pays a predetermined benefit when death occurs during the stipulated term—say, 10, 20, or 30 years—covered by the policy. If the insured outlives the term, the policy loses its value and simply ceases. When it is in force, however, the insured knows that it will provide funds to beneficiaries if he or she dies. Premiums for term life insurance are significantly lower than premiums for whole life insurance.

Unlike term life, *whole-life insurance*—also known as *cash-value insurance*—remains in force as long as premiums are paid. In addition to paying a death benefit, whole life accumulates cash value over time—a form of savings. Once the insured reaches a point at which he or she no longer needs the coverage, paid-in money can be withdrawn. Whole-life savings, however, earn less interest than most alternative forms of investment.

How Much Does It Cost?

The cost of insurance, of course, depends on how much you buy. But it also depends on your life expectancy and other risk factors that insurers determine statistically. Premiums are higher for people whose life expectancies are shorter, whether because of gender, age, weight, occupation, or pre-existing health conditions.

The lower cost of term insurance is an important consideration, not just for people on limited incomes, but also for those seeking higher returns from other types of investment. A healthy, 30-year-old, non-smoking female, for example, can expect to pay about $360 a year for a $300 000 term policy and about $600 to $700 a year for a $1 million term policy. Depending on the insurer and the conditions of coverage, whole life may cost the same person up to 10 times as much as term. To get the best match between your policy and your personal situation, therefore, you should evaluate the terms and conditions of a variety of policies. You can get convenient comparisons on websites such as IntelliQuote.com (www.intelliquote.com).

ANSWERS TO "PRACTISE PAYING OFF YOUR DEBT"

1. Item (a) is the correct answer, obtained as follows:

   Minimum monthly payment
   (5% of previous ending balance):
   April $232.81 = (0.05 × $4656.13)

2. Item (c) is the correct answer, obtained as follows:

   Interest owed on previous balance
   ($^1/_{12}$ × 0.18 previous balance):
   April $69.84 = ($^1/_{12}$ × 0.18 × $4656.13)

3. Item (b) is the correct answer, obtained as follows:

Payment on principal (monthly payment – monthly interest)	Ending balance owed on principal (previous balance – payment on principal)
April $162.97 = ($232.81 – $69.84)	$4493.16 = ($4656.13 – $162.97)

THE IMPACT OF INFORMATION TECHNOLOGY (IT)

No matter where we go, we can't escape the impact of **information technology (IT)**—the various devices for creating, storing, exchanging, and using information in diverse modes, including visual images, voice, multimedia, and business data. We see ads all the time for the latest cell phones, iPods, laptops, and software products, and most of us connect daily to the internet. Email has become a staple in business, and even such traditionally "low-tech" businesses as hair salons and garbage collection companies are becoming dependent on the internet, computers, and networks. As consumers, we interact with databases every time we withdraw money from an ATM, order food at McDonald's, or check on the status of a package at UPS or FedEx.

IT has had an immense effect on businesses—in fact, the growth of IT has changed the very structure of business organizations. Its adoption has altered the workforces in many companies, contributed to greater flexibility in dealing with customers, and changed the way that employees interact with each other. **Ecommerce** (short for *electronic commerce*)—the use of the internet and other electronic means for retailing and business-to-business transactions—has created new market relationships around the globe. In this section, we'll look at how businesses are using IT to bolster productivity, improve operations and processes, create new opportunities, and communicate and work in ways not possible before.

ecommerce
The use of the Internet and other electronic means for retailing and business-to-business transactions.

Creating Portable Offices: Providing Remote Access to Instant Information

The packing list for Barry Martin's upcoming fishing trip reflects his new outlook on where, when, and how he gets his work done. It reads, in part, as follows: (1) fly rod, (2) dry-pack food, (3) tent, and (4) BlackBerry. Five years ago, a much longer list would have included a cell phone, road and area maps, phone directory, appointments calendar, office files, and client project folders, all of which are replaced now by just one item—his BlackBerry—a wireless handheld messaging device that allows him to take the office with him wherever he goes.

For a project manager like Martin, the BlackBerry is more than just a cellphone. With its continuous connection, there's no dialing in, and his email is displayed the same moment it arrives on his PC back at the office. Even in the Canadian wilderness, Martin can place phone calls and read new email messages. Along with internet browsing, there's access to desktop tools—such as an organizer and an address book—for managing work and staying in touch with customers, suppliers, and employees from any location.

The mobile messaging capabilities of devices like the BlackBerry offer businesses powerful tools that save time and travel expenses. They also mean that employees no longer work only at the office or the factory, nor are all of a company's operations performed at one place. When using such devices, offsite employees have continuous access to information instead of being forced to be at a desk to access their files and the internet. Such benefits have attracted several million enthusiastic subscribers, making BlackBerry the leader in the handheld wireless industry.[1]

The BlackBerry wireless handheld messaging device allows employees to take the office with them.

Enabling Better Service by Coordinating Remote Deliveries

With access to the internet, company activities may be geographically scattered but remain coordinated through a networked system that provides better service for customers. Many businesses, for example, coordinate activities from one centralized location, but their deliveries flow from several remote locations, often at lower cost. When you order furniture from an internet storefront—for example, a chair, a sofa, a table, and two lamps—the chair may come from a warehouse in Toronto, the lamps from a manufacturer in China, and the sofa and table from a supplier in North Carolina. Beginning with the customer's order, activities are coordinated through the company's network, as if the whole order were being processed at one place. This avoids the expensive in-between step of first shipping all the items to a central location.

Creating Leaner, More Efficient Organizations

Networks and technology are also leading to leaner companies with fewer employees and simpler structures. Because networks enable firms to maintain information linkages between employees and customers, more work and customer satisfaction can be accomplished with fewer people. Bank customers can access 24-hour information systems and monitor their accounts without employee assistance. Instructions that once were given to assembly workers by supervisors are now delivered to workstations electronically. Truck drivers delivering freight used to return to the trucking terminal to receive instructions from supervisors on reloading for the next delivery, but now instructions arrive on electronic screens in the trucks so drivers know in advance what will be happening next.

Enabling Increased Collaboration

Collaboration among internal units and with outside firms is greater when firms use collaboration software and other IT communications devices (we discuss these later in this appendix). Companies are learning that complex problems can be solved better through IT-supported collaboration, either with formal teams or spontaneous interaction among people and departments. The design of new products, for example, was once largely an engineering responsibility. Now it is a shared activity using information from people in marketing, finance, production, engineering, and purchasing who, collectively, determine the best design. For example, when Boeing designed its new 777 aircraft, information came not just from engineers but also from passengers (who said they wanted electronic outlets to recharge personal electronic devices), cabin crews (who wanted more bathrooms and wider aisles), and air-traffic controllers (who wanted larger, safer airbrakes).

Enabling Global Exchange

The global reach of IT is enabling business collaboration on a scale that was unheard of just a few years ago. Consider Lockheed Martin's contract for designing the Joint Strike Fighter and supplying thousands of the planes in different versions for Canada, the United States, Britain, Italy, Denmark, and Norway. Lockheed can't do the job alone, so it is collaborating with Britain's BAE Systems and more than 70 U.S. and 18 international subcontractors at some 190 locations. An Australian manufacturer of aviation communications and a Turkish electronics supplier entered the project in 2005, joining seven other Australian and two other Turkish firms that were already involved. Over the project's 20-year life, more than 1500 firms will supply everything from radar systems to engines to bolts. Collaboration on this massive scale is essential for coordinating design, testing, and construction while avoiding delays, holding down costs, and maintaining quality.[2]

Improving Management Processes

IT has also changed the nature of the management process. At one time, upper-level managers didn't concern themselves with all of the detailed information filtering upward from the workplace because it was expensive to gather, slow in coming, and quickly became out of date. Rather, workplace management was delegated to middle and first-line managers. With databases, specialized software, and networks, however, instantaneous information is accessible and useful to all levels of management.

For example, consider *enterprise resource planning (ERP)*, a system for organizing and managing a firm's activities across product lines, departments, and geographic locations. The ERP stores real-time information on work status and upcoming transactions and notifies employees when action is required if certain schedules are to be met. It coordinates internal operations with activities of outside suppliers and notifies customers of upcoming deliveries and billings. Consequently, more managers use it routinely for planning and controlling operations. A manager at Hershey Foods, for example, uses ERP to check on the current status of any customer order for Hershey Kisses or Jolly Ranchers, to inspect productivity statistics for each workstation, and to analyze the delivery performance on any shipment. Managers can better coordinate company-wide performance because they can identify departments that are working well together and those that are lagging behind schedule and creating bottlenecks.

Providing Flexibility for Customization

IT has also created new manufacturing capabilities that enable businesses to offer customers greater variety and faster delivery cycles. Whether it's a personal computer from Dell, one of Nokia's cordless phones, or a Rawlings baseball glove, today's design-it-yourself world has become possible through fast, flexible manufacturing using IT networks. At Timbuk2's website, for example, you can "build your own" custom messenger bag at different price levels with choices of size, fabric, colour combinations, accessories, liner material, strap, and even left- or right-hand access.[3] The principle is called **mass-customization**: Although companies produce in large volumes, each unit features the unique options the customer prefers. As shown in Figure B.1, flexible production and speedy delivery depend on an integrated network of information to coordinate all the activities among customers, manufacturers, suppliers, and shippers.

mass-customization
Although companies produce in large volumes, each unit features the unique options the customer prefers.

Providing New Business Opportunities

Not only is IT improving existing businesses, it is creating entirely new businesses where none existed before. For big businesses, this means developing new products, offering new services, and reaching new clients. Only a few years ago, the multibillion-dollar behemoth known as Google was a fledgling search engine. Today, that company boasts not just a search engine but instant messaging, email, and auction features as well.

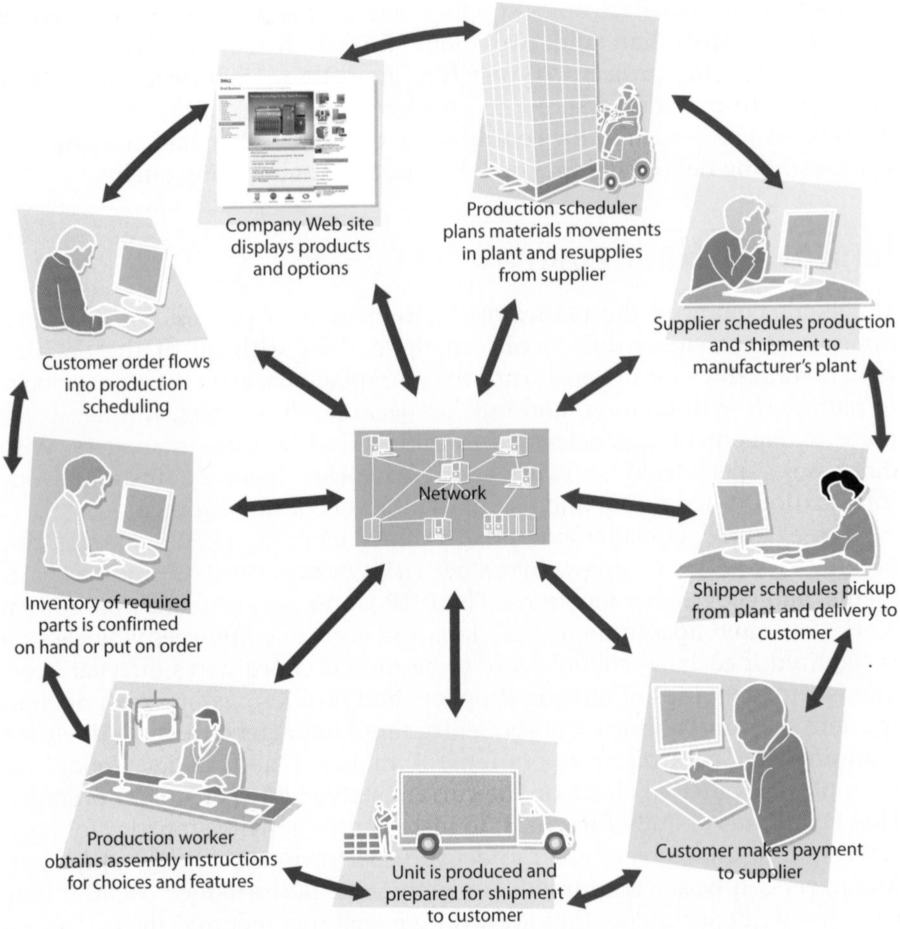

Figure B.1 Networking for mass-customization.

The IT landscape has also presented small business owners with new ebusiness opportunities. Consider Richard Smith, who began collecting stamps at age seven. Now, some 40 years later, he's turned his hobby into a profitable eBay business. Each day begins at the PC in his home office, scanning eBay's listings for items available and items wanted by sellers and buyers around the world. With more than 3000 sales transactions to date, Richard maintains a perfect customer rating and recently earned more than $4000 on a single eBay transaction.

Just how does Richard, like others, make eBay work for him? To assist start-up businesses, eBay's services network is a ready-made online business model, not just an auction market. Services range from credit financing to protection from fraud and misrepresentation, information security, international currency exchanges, and post-sales management. These activities enable users like Richard to complete sales transactions, deliver merchandise, and get new merchandise for future resale, all from the comfort of their own homes.

Meanwhile, eBay's PayPal system—an online financial institution—processes $20 billion in transactions annually. As a seller, Richard receives payments into his PayPal account from buyers using credit cards, debit cards, bank accounts, or from their PayPal accounts. When buying merchandise, he can pay in any of six currencies, including the Euro and Japanese Yen, with PayPal making the conversion between Canadian dollars and the seller's currency.

Improving the World and our Lives

Can advancements in IT really make the world a better place? Hospitals and medical equipment companies certainly think so. For example, when treating combat injuries, surgeons at Walter Reed National Military Medical Center in the United States now rely on high-tech graphics displays that are converted into three-dimensional physical models for presurgical planning. These 3-D mock-ups of shoulders, femurs, and facial bones give doctors the opportunity to see and feel the anatomy as it will be seen in the operating room, before they even use their scalpels.[4] Meanwhile, vitamin-sized cameras that patients swallow are providing doctors with computer images of the insides of the human body, helping them to make better diagnoses for such ailments as ulcers and cancer.[5]

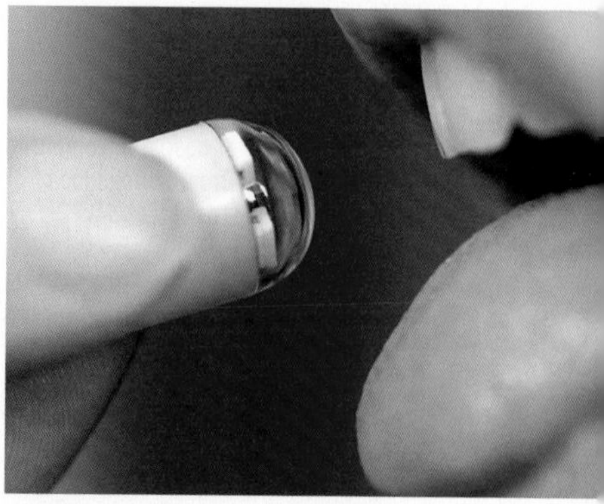

After this capsule is swallowed, the camera inside it can transmit 50 000 images during its eight-hour journey through the digestive tract.

IT BUILDING BLOCKS: BUSINESS RESOURCES

The material in the preceding section shows how dramatically IT is affecting the global business landscape. The *tools* that make it work are things like the internet, email and other communications technologies, networks, hardware devices, and software. In this section, we'll take a brief look at these IT resources that businesses can use.

The Internet and Other Communication Resources

The internet—and its companion system, the World Wide Web—are today among the world's most powerful communication technologies. More than two-thirds of Canadians use the **internet**, a system of more than 100 million interconnected computers in over 100 countries. The **World Wide Web** is a standardized code for accessing information and transmitting data over the internet. It provides the common language that allows information sharing on the internet. For thousands of businesses, the internet is replacing the telephone, fax machine, and standard mail as the primary communication tool.

The internet has spawned a number of other business communications technologies, including *intranets, extranets, electronic conferencing,* and *VSAT satellite* communications.

internet
A gigantic system of interconnected computers; more than 100 million computers in over 100 countries.

World Wide Web
A standardized code for accessing information and transmitting data over the Internet; the common language that allows information sharing on the Internet.

Intranets

Many companies maintain internal websites linked throughout the firm. These private networks, or **intranets**, are accessible only to employees. For example, Ford Motor Company's intranet connects 175 000 workstations in Asia, Europe, and North America to thousands of Ford websites containing private information on Ford's employee benefits, production management tools, and product design resources. Sharing information on engineering, distribution, and marketing has reduced the lead time for getting new models into production and has shortened customer delivery times.[6]

intranets
An organization's private network of internally linked websites accessible only to employees.

Extranets

Extranets allow outsiders limited access to a firm's internal information network. The most common application allows buyers to enter a system to see which products are available for sale and delivery, thus providing convenient product-availability information. Industrial suppliers are often linked into customers' information networks so that they can see planned production schedules and prepare supplies for customers' upcoming operations. The extranet at Chaparral Steel, for example, lets customers shop

extranets
A system that allows outsiders limited access to a firm's internal information network.

electronically through its storage yards and gives them electronic access to Chaparral's planned inventory of industrial steel products.

Electronic Conferencing

electronic conferencing
IT that allows groups of people to communicate simultaneously from various locations via email, phone, or video.

Electronic conferencing allows groups of people to communicate simultaneously from various locations via email, phone, or video. One form, called *dataconferencing*, allows people in remote locations to work simultaneously on one document. Working as a team, they can revise a marketing plan or draft a press release. *Videoconferencing* allows participants to see one another on video screens while the conference is in progress. For example, Lockheed Martin's Joint Strike Fighter project, discussed earlier, uses internet collaboration systems with both voice and video capabilities. Although separated by oceans, partners can communicate as if they were in the same room as they redesign components and alter production schedules. Electronic conferencing is attractive to many businesses because it eliminates travel and saves money. Recent improvements in video technology mean sharper pictures and better voice coordination than that found in the older videoconferencing systems.[7]

VSAT Satellite Communications

VSAT satellite communications
A network of geographically dispersed transmitter-receivers (transceivers) that send signals to and receive signals from a satellite, exchanging voice, video, and data transmissions.

Another internet technology businesses use to communicate is **VSAT satellite communications**. VSAT (short for *Very Small Aperture Terminal*) systems have a transmitter-receiver (*transceiver*) that sits outdoors with a direct line of sight to a satellite. The hub—a ground station computer at the company's headquarters—sends signals to and receives signals from the satellite, exchanging voice, video, and data transmissions. An advantage of VSAT is privacy. A company that operates its own VSAT system has total control over its communications without dependence on other companies. A firm might use VSAT to exchange sales and inventory information, advertising messages, and visual presentations between headquarters and store managers at remote sites.

Networks: System Architecture

computer network
A group of two or more computers linked together by some form of cabling or by wireless technology to share data or resources, such as a printer.

client-server network
A common business network in which clients make requests for information or resources and servers provide the services.

A **computer network** is a group of two or more computers linked together by some form of cabling (fibre-optic, coaxial, or twisted wire) or by wireless technology to share data or resources, such as a printer. The most common type of network used in businesses is a **client-server network**. In client-server networks, *clients* are usually the laptop or desktop computers through which users make requests for information or resources. *Servers* are the computers that provide the services shared by users. In big organizations, servers are usually assigned a specific task. For example, in a local university or college network, an *application server* stores the word-processing, spreadsheet, and other programs used by all computers connected to the network. A *print server* controls the printer, stores printing requests from client computers, and routes jobs as the printer becomes available. An *email server* handles all incoming and outgoing email. With a client-server system, users can share resources and internet connections—and avoid costly duplication.

Wide Area Networks (WANs)

wide area networks (WANs)
Computers that are linked over long distances through telephone lines, microwave signals, or satellite communications.

Computers that are linked over long distances—province-wide or even nationwide—through telephone lines, microwave signals, or satellite communications make up what are called **wide area networks (WANs)**. Firms can lease lines from communications vendors or maintain private WANs. Wal-Mart, for example, depends on a private satellite network that links 5000 retail stores to its Bentonville, Arkansas, headquarters.

Local Area Networks (LANs)

In **local area networks (LANs)**, computers are linked in a smaller area, such as all of a firm's computers within a single building. On cable TV's Home Shopping Network (HSN), for example, hundreds of operators at the HSN facility are united by a LAN for entering call-in orders. The arrangement requires only one computer system with one database and one software system.

local area networks (LANs) Computers that are linked in a small area, such as all of a firm's computers within a single building.

Wireless Networks

Wireless networks use airborne electronic signals to link network computers and devices. Like wired networks, wireless networks can reach across long distances or exist within a single building or small area. For example, the BlackBerry system shown in Figure B.2 consists of devices that send and receive transmissions on **wireless wide area networks (WWANS)** of more than 100 service providers in over 40 countries. The wireless format that the system relies on to control wireless messaging is supplied by Research in Motion (RIM), the Canadian company that makes the BlackBerry, and is installed on the user-company's computer. The *firewall* provides privacy protection (we discuss firewalls in more detail later).

wireless wide area networks A network that uses airborne electronic signals instead of wires to link computers and electronic devices over long distances.

Wi-Fi

Hotspots are specific locations such as coffee shops, hotels, and airport terminals that provide wireless internet connections for people on the go. Each hotspot, or **Wi-Fi** (short for *wi*reless *fi*delity) access point, is actually its own small network, called a **wireless local area network (Wireless LAN or WLAN)**.

The benefit of Wi-Fi is that you're not tethered to a wire for accessing the internet. Employees can wait for a delayed plane in the airport and still be connected to the internet through their wireless-enabled laptop. However, as with every technology, Wi-Fi has limitations, including a short range of distance. This means that your laptop's internet connection can be severed if you move further than about 300 feet from the hotspot. So, while a city may have hundreds of hotspots, your laptop must remain near one to stay connected. This distance limitation is expected to be improved soon by *WiMax* (*Worldwide Interoperability for Microwave Access*), the next step in wireless advancements, with its wireless range of 30 miles.

Wi-Fi Short for wireless fidelity; a wireless local area network.

wireless local area network (Wireless LAN or WLAN) A local area network with wireless access points for PC users.

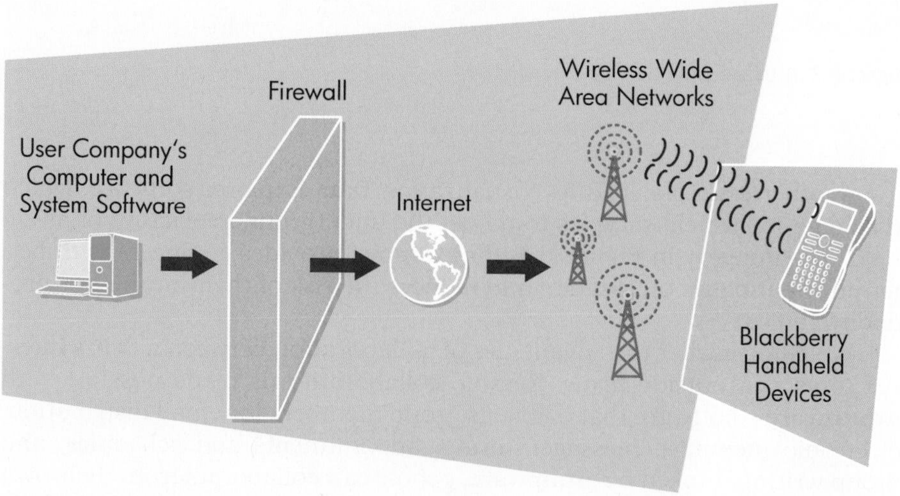

Figure B.2 BlackBerry wireless internet architecture.

Hardware and Software

hardware
The physical components of a computer network, such as keyboards, monitors, system units, and printers.

Any computer network or system needs **hardware**—the physical components, such as keyboards, monitors, system units, and printers. In addition to the laptops, desktop computers, and BlackBerrys mentioned earlier, *handheld computers* are also used in businesses. For example, Wal-Mart employees roam store aisles using handhelds to identify, count, and order items, track deliveries, and update backup stock at distribution centres to keep store shelves replenished with merchandise.

software
Programs that tell the computer's hardware what resources to use and how.

The other essential in any computer system is **software—**programs that tell the computer how to function. Software includes *system software,* such as Microsoft Windows, which tells the computer's hardware how to interact with the software. It also includes *application software,* which meets the needs of specific users. Examples of application software include word processing programs like Microsoft Word, spreadsheet programs like Lotus 1-2-3, graphics programs like Corel Draw, message centre software like WinFax Pro, integrated programs like Quicken, and database programs like Access.

computer graphics
Programs that convert numeric and character data into pictorial information like charts and graphs.

groupware
Software that connects group members for email distribution, electronic meetings, message storing, appointments and schedules, and group writing.

One illustrative example of a software program is **computer graphics**, which converts numeric and character data into pictorial information like charts and graphs. These allow managers to see relationships more easily and generate clearer and more persuasive reports and presentations. As Figure B.3 shows, both types of graphics can convey different kinds of information—in this case, the types of materials that should be ordered by a picture framing shop like Artists' Frame Service.

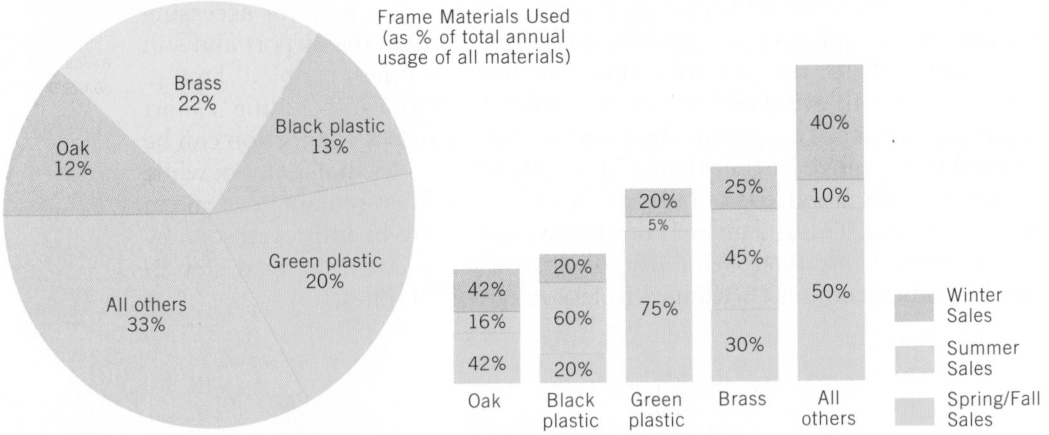

Figure B.3 Artists Frame Service.

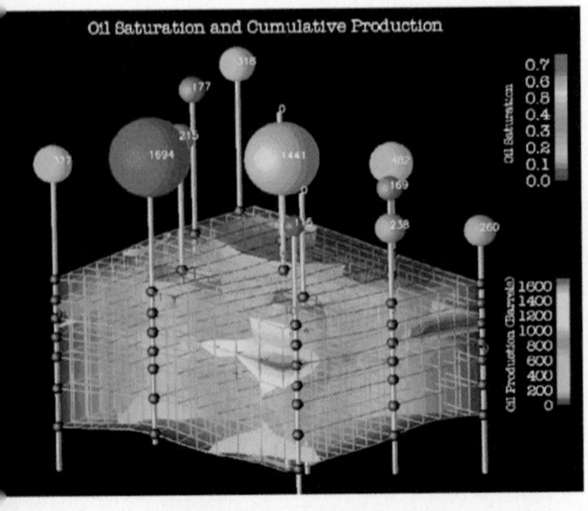

Figure B.4 3-D computer modelling software gives engineers a better idea of where oil might be located.

Another example is IBM's Visualization Data Explorer software, which uses data from field samples to model the underground structure of an oil field. The imagery in Figure B.4, for example, provides engineers with better information on oil location and reduces the risk of their hitting less productive holes.

We noted earlier the advantages of collaboration between a firm's internal units and outside firms. Remote collaboration is made possible with **groupware**—software that connects group members for email distribution, electronic meetings, message storing, appointments and schedules, and group writing. Linked by groupware, people can collaborate from their own desktop PCs, even if they're remotely located. Groupware systems include IBM Lotus Domino 6.5, Microsoft Exchange Server 2003, and Novell GroupWise 6.5.

HARNESSING THE COMPETITIVE POWER OF INFORMATION TECHNOLOGY

Business today relies on information management in ways that no one could foresee even a decade ago. Managers now treat IT as a basic organizational resource for conducting daily business. At major firms, every activity—designing services, ensuring product delivery and cash flow, evaluating personnel—is linked to *information systems*. An **information system (IS)** uses IT resources and enables managers to take **data**—raw facts and figures that, by themselves, may not have much meaning—and turn that data into **information**—the meaningful, useful interpretation of data. Information systems also enable managers to collect, process, and transmit that information for use in decision making.

information system (IS)
A system that uses IT resources to convert data into information and to collect, process, and transmit that information for use in decision making.

data
Raw facts and figures that, by themselves, may not have much meaning.

information
The meaningful, useful interpretation of data.

One of the most widely publicized examples of the strategic use of information systems is Wal-Mart. The IS drives down costs and increases efficiency because the same methods and systems are applied for all 5000-plus stores in Europe, Asia, and North America. Data on the billions of sales transactions—time, date, place—flows to company headquarters in Bentonville, Arkansas. Keeping track of nearly 700 million stock keeping units (SKUs) weekly, the information system enforces uniform reordering and delivery procedures—on packaging, timing, and quantities—for more than 30 000 suppliers. It also regulates the flow of the more than five billion cases through its distribution centres, and deliveries by nearly 8000 Wal-Mart truck drivers, to its stores.

The top priority for Wal-Mart's IS—improving in-stock reliability—requires integration of Wal-Mart's and suppliers' activities with store sales. That's why P&G, Johnson & Johnson, and other suppliers connect into Wal-Mart's information system to observe up-to-the-minute sales data on individual items, by store. They can use the system's computer-based tools—spreadsheets, sales forecasting, weather information—to forecast sales demand and plan delivery schedules. Coordinated planning avoids excessive inventories, speeds up deliveries, and holds down costs throughout the supply chain while keeping shelves stocked for retail customers.

Information systems managers operate the systems used for gathering, organizing, and distributing information. Incoming information arrives in various forms—reports, memos, databases, and emails—and managers use many of the IT resources we discussed earlier to sift through this information and apply it to their jobs. The question facing many businesses today, however, is how to use that information most effectively. In this section, we'll explore the process of *data mining* as well as the types of information systems that are available to businesses.

information systems managers
Managers who operate the systems used for gathering, organizing, and distributing information.

Data Warehousing and Data Mining

Almost everything you do leaves a trail of information about you—your preferences in movie rentals, television viewing, internet sites, and groceries; the destinations of your phone calls; your credit card charges; your financial status; and personal information about age, gender, marital status, and health. These are just a few of the items about each of us that are stored in scattered databases. The behaviour patterns of millions of users can be traced by analyzing this information. The collection, storage, and retrieval of such data in electronic files is called **data warehousing**. For managers, the data warehouse is a goldmine of information about their business.[8] The Wal-Mart data warehouse, for example, has a storage capacity

data warehousing
The collection, storage, and retrieval of data in electronic files.

of over 570 terabytes (a thousand billion bytes) of data. That's larger than all the web pages on the internet. Think about this: if each byte was a car, there would be nearly 88 000 cars for every person on earth.

data mining
The application of electronic technologies for searching, sifting, and reorganizing pools of data to uncover useful information.

After collecting information, managers use **data mining**—the application of electronic technologies for searching, sifting, and reorganizing pools of data to uncover useful information. By mining the data in the data warehouse, managers can better plan for new products, set prices, and identify trends and shopping patterns. For example, companies use data collected on the internet to gather information on user behaviour—who has bought which products and how many, over what websites individuals bought the products, how they paid, and so on. By analyzing what consumers actually do, businesses can determine what subsequent purchases they are likely to make and then send them tailor-made ads.

Types of Information Systems

The term *information system* is actually something of a misnomer. It suggests that there is one system when, in fact, the IS may be several information systems that share data while serving different areas of the organization. Since employees have many different responsibilities and decision-making needs, one IS can't handle such a range of requirements. Managers and their subordinates need access to the specialized information systems that satisfy their different information needs.

In addition to different types of users, each business *function*—marketing, human resources, accounting, production, finance—has its own information needs, as do groups working on major projects. Each user group and department, therefore, may need a special IS.

Information Systems for Knowledge Workers

knowledge information systems
Information system that supports knowledge workers by providing resources to create, store, use, and transmit new knowledge for useful applications.

As we discussed in Chapter 8, *knowledge workers* such as engineers and scientists are employees for whom information and knowledge are the raw materials of their work. For example, to develop new materials at a flooring company, knowledge workers may need information on the chemical properties of adhesives. Therefore, they use **knowledge information systems** that provide resources to create, store, use, and transmit new knowledge for useful applications. The purpose of such systems is to supply a flow of new knowledge that can be integrated into the company to strengthen it. It provides databases to organize and retrieve information, and computational power for data analysis. Word processing programs, spreadsheets, graphics capabilities, and desktop publishing are examples of knowledge information systems.

computer-aided design (CAD)
IS with software that helps knowledge workers design products by simulating them and displaying them in three-dimensional graphics.

Specialized support systems, such as computer-aided design and simulation modelling, have also increased the productivity of knowledge workers. **Computer-aided design (CAD)** helps knowledge workers design products by simulating them and displaying them in 3-D graphics. Products ranging from cellphones to auto parts are created with CAD because it creates faster designs at lower cost than manual modelling methods.

Information Systems for Managers

Each manager's information activities and IS needs vary according to his or her functional area (accounting or marketing and so forth) and management level. The following are some popular information systems used by managers for different purposes.

management information systems (MISs)
Computer system that supports managers by providing information—reports, schedules, plans, and budgets—that can be used for making decisions.

Management information systems. **Management information systems (MISs)** support managers by providing reports, schedules, plans, and budgets that can then be used for making decisions. For day-to-day activities, managers use information to oversee the details of departments or projects. For example, at a publishing company, managers rely on detailed information—current customer orders, staffing schedules, employee attendance, production schedules, equipment status, materials availability—for moment-to-moment decisions during the day. For mid-range action—looking weeks or months ahead—they rely on information to plan such activities as personnel training, materials movements, and cash flows. They also need to anticipate the status of the jobs and projects assigned to their departments. What stage is a job at now? When will it be finished? When will there be openings so other jobs can start? Many MISs—cash flow, sales, production scheduling, shipping—are indispensable for helping managers find answers to such questions.

For longer-range decisions on issues like business strategy, managers need information to analyze trends in the publishing industry and overall company performance in order to make long-range plans. They need both external and internal information, current and future, to compare current performance data to data from previous years and to analyze consumer trends and economic forecasts.

The 3-D computer model of this dinosaur is constructed from digital scans of fossilized tissue.

Decision support systems. Managers that face a particular kind of decision repeatedly can get assistance from **decision support systems (DSSs)**—interactive systems that create virtual business models and test them with different data to see how they respond. When faced with decisions on plant capacity, for example, managers can use a capacity DSS. The manager inputs data on anticipated sales, working capital, and customer-delivery requirements. The data flows into the DSS processor, which then simulates the plant's performance under the proposed data conditions. After experimenting with various data conditions, the DSS makes recommendations on the best levels of plant capacity for each future time period.

decision support systems (DSSs) Interactive system that creates virtual business models for a particular kind of decision and tests them with different data to see how they respond.

Artificial Intelligence (AI). AI refers to the development of computer systems to imitate human behaviour—in other words, systems that perform physical tasks, use thought processes, and learn. In developing AI systems, business specialists, modellers, and information-technology experts try to design computer-based systems capable of reasoning so that computers, instead of people, can perform certain activities. For example, a credit-evaluation system may decide which loan applicants are creditworthy and which are too risky, and it may then compose acceptance and rejection letters accordingly.

Some AI systems possess sensory capabilities, such as lasers that "see," "hear," and "feel." AND Corp. of Toronto has developed a software program—called Hnet—that can learn to recognize faces. This may seem like a simple thing, but millions of dollars had been spent on this problem without success until AND Corp. developed the software. The system can be used to improve airport security and to track terrorists.[9]

A special form of AI, the **expert system**, is designed to imitate the thought processes of human experts in a particular field.[10] Expert systems incorporate the rules that an expert applies to specific types of problems, such as the judgments a physician makes when diagnosing illnesses. In effect, expert systems supply everyday users with "instant expertise." For example, Campbell Soup developed an expert system to mimic complex decision processes and save the expert knowledge that was going to be lost when a long-time expert soup maker announced his intention to retire.[11]

expert system A form of AI designed to imitate the thought processes of human experts in a particular field.

IT RISKS AND THREATS

Unfortunately, IT has attracted abusers that are intent on doing mischief, with severity ranging from mere nuisance to outright destruction. In this section, we look at various IT threats, and in the next section we describe steps that businesses have taken to protect themselves.

Hackers

hackers
Cyber-criminal who gains unauthorized access to a computer or network, either to steal information, money, or property or to tamper with data.

Hackers are cyber-criminals who gain unauthorized access to a computer or network, either to steal information, money, or property or to tamper with data. For example, one 16-year-old British hacker recently got into the U.S. Air Force's top command-and-control facility 150 different times. From there, he got into the computers of several defence contractors and the South Korean Atomic Research Institute.

Wireless mooching is a growing industry for cyber-criminals. Once hackers get inside an unsecured wireless network, they use it to commit identity theft and to steal credit card numbers, among other activities. When police try to track down these criminals, they're long gone, leaving the network host exposed to criminal prosecution.

One common reason hackers break into a computer network is to launch *denial of service (DOS) attacks*. DOS attacks flood networks or websites with bogus requests for information and resources, thereby shutting down the networks or websites and making it impossible for legitimate users to access them. Such attacks cost companies millions in lost productive time and revenue.

Identity Theft

identity theft
Unauthorized stealing of personal information (such as social insurance number and address) to get loans, credit cards, or other monetary benefits by impersonating the victim.

Identity theft refers to the unauthorized stealing of personal information (such as social insurance number and addresses) to get loans, credit cards, or other monetary benefits by impersonating the victim. Clever crooks get information on unsuspecting victims by digging in trash, luring internet users to bogus websites, and stealing mail. Some America Online customers, for example, received an email notifying them of a billing problem with their AOL accounts. The email, displaying AOL logos and legitimate-looking links, requested personal information like credit card numbers, social security numbers, and banking accounts with passwords and PIN numbers. When the customers clicked on the AOL Billing Center link, they were transferred to a spoofed (falsified) AOL-looking web page, where they submitted the requested information—into the hands of the thief. The accounts were soon empty. The thieves in this case used *phishing* or *pharming*—emailing a deceptive, real-looking imitation of a popular website (e.g., AOL, PayPal, or your local bank) as bait, to masses of recipients, tricking them into giving up personal information.

Identity theft is rapidly becoming a major problem. Identity thieves are not often caught, but when they are, they may receive stiff penalties. One hacker was sentenced to nine years in prison for breaking into a computer system and stealing credit card account numbers of customers of a Lowe's home improvement store.[12]

Intellectual Property Theft

intellectual property
A product of the mind that has commercial value.

Information is so valuable that most companies enforce security precautions to protect it. Nearly every company faces the dilemma of protecting product plans, new inventions, and industrial processes. **Intellectual property** is a product of the mind—something produced by the intellect, with great expenditure of human effort—that has commercial value. Its ownership and right to its use may be protected by patent, copyright, trademark, and other means. Hackers often break into company networks to steal such intellectual property, but it's not just hackers who are doing the stealing. Because the chances of getting caught seem slim, home users continue, illegally, to download unpaid-for movies, music, and other resources from file-swapping networks. Recent estimates conservatively indicate industry losses in North America at more than $5 billion in music, $13 billion for software, and $4 billion in movies each year.[13]

Computer Viruses, Worms, and Trojan Horses

Another IT risk facing businesses is rogue programmers who disrupt IT operations by contaminating and destroying software, hardware, or data files. Viruses, worms, and Trojan horses are three kinds of malicious programs that, once installed, can shut down any computer system. A *computer virus* exists in a file that attaches itself to a program and migrates from computer to computer as a shared program or as an email attachment. It does not infect the system unless the user opens the contaminated file, and users typically are unaware they are spreading the virus by file-sharing. It can, for example, quickly copy itself over and over again, using up all available memory and effectively shutting down the computer.

Worms are a particular kind of virus that travel from computer to computer within networked computer systems, without your needing to open any software to spread the contaminated file. In a matter of days, the notorious Blaster Worm infected some 400 000 computer networks, destroying files and even allowing outsiders to take over computers remotely. The worm replicates itself rapidly, sending out thousands of copies to other computers in the network. Travelling through internet connections and email address books in the network's computers, it absorbs system memory and shuts down network servers, web servers, and individual computers.

Unlike viruses, a *Trojan horse* does not replicate itself. Instead, it most often comes into the computer, at your request, masquerading as a harmless, legitimate software product or data file. Once installed, the damage begins. For instance, it may simply redesign desktop icons or, more maliciously, delete files and destroy information.

Spyware

As if forced intrusion isn't bad enough, internet users unwittingly invite spies—masquerading as a friendly file available as a "giveaway" or shared among individual users on their PCs. This so-called **spyware** is downloaded by users that are lured by "free" software. Once installed, it crawls around to monitor the host's computer activities, gathering email addresses, credit card numbers, passwords, and other inside information that it transmits back to someone outside the host system. Spyware authors assemble incoming stolen information to create their own "intellectual property" that they then sell to other parties to use for marketing/advertising purposes or for identity theft.[14]

spyware
Program unknowingly downloaded by users that monitors their computer activities, gathering e-mail addresses, credit card numbers, and other information that it transmits to someone outside the host system.

Spam

Spam is junk email sent to a mailing list or a newsgroup (an online discussion group).[15] Spam is a greater nuisance than postal junk mail because the internet is open to the public, email costs are negligible, and massive mailing

spam
Junk email sent to a mailing list or a newsgroup.

lists are accessible through file-sharing or by theft. Spam operators send unwanted messages ranging from explicit pornography to hate mail to advertisements, and even destructive computer viruses. In addition to wasting users' time, it also consumes a network's bandwidth, thereby reducing the amount of data that can be transmitted in a fixed amount of time for useful purposes. Industry experts estimate spam's damage in lost time and productivity at more than $9 billion annually.[16]

IT PROTECTION MEASURES

Security measures against intrusion and viruses are a constant challenge. Businesses guard themselves against intrusion, identity theft, and viruses by using firewalls, special software, and encryption.

Firewalls

firewall
Security system with special software or hardware devices designed to keep computers safe from hackers.

Many systems guard against unauthorized access by requiring users to have protected passwords. This helps ensure that intruders are unable to access your computer or the data on it. However, many firms rely on additional safeguards, such as **firewalls**, which are security systems with special software or hardware devices designed to keep computers safe from hackers. Figure B.5 shows how a firewall works. The firewall is located where the two networks—the internet and the company's internal network—meet. It contains two components for filtering each incoming message:

- The company's *security policy*—Access rules that identify every type of message that the company doesn't want to pass through the firewall.
- A *router*—A table of available routes or paths, a "traffic switch" that determines which routes or paths on the network to send each message to after it is tested against the security policy.

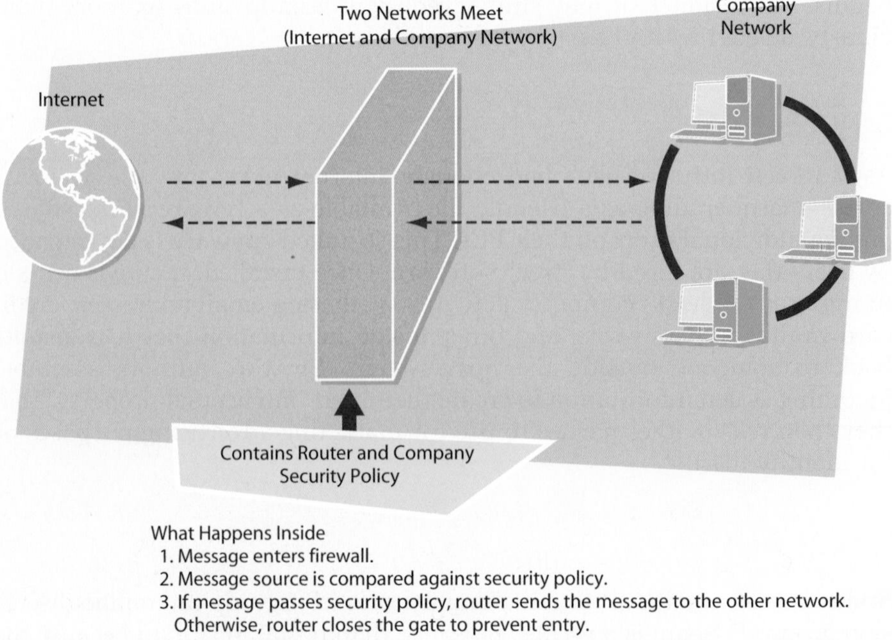

Figure B.5 How a firewall works.

Only those messages that meet the conditions of the user's security policy are routed through the firewall and permitted to flow between the two networks. Messages that fail the access test are blocked and cannot flow between the two networks. As we saw earlier, a firewall is used for protecting the BlackBerry wireless system from intrusion.

Preventing Identity Theft

Internet privacy experts say that a completely new identity verification system is needed to stop the rising tide of internet identity theft. One possibility is an "infocard," which would act like a credit card and would allow websites to verify a customer's identity without keeping personal information on the customer.[17] While foolproof prevention is impossible, steps can be taken to reduce the chance that you will be victimized. A visit to the Identity Theft Resource Center (*www.idtheftcenter.org*) is a valuable first step to get information on everything from scam alerts to victim issues—including assistance on lost and stolen wallets—to media resources, current laws, and prevention of identity theft in the workplace.

Preventing Viruses: Anti-Virus Software

Combating viruses, worms, and Trojan horses has become a major industry for systems designers and software developers. Installation of **anti-virus software** products protects systems by searching incoming email and data files for "signatures" of known viruses and virus-like characteristics. Contaminated files are discarded or placed in quarantine for safekeeping. Many viruses take advantage of weaknesses in operating systems in order to spread and propagate. Network administrators must make sure that the computers on their systems are using the most up-to-date operating system that includes the latest security protection.

anti-virus software
Product that protects systems by searching incoming emails and data files for "signatures" of known viruses and virus-like characteristics.

Encryption Software

Unprotected email can be intercepted, diverted to unintended computers, and opened, revealing contents to intruders. Protective software is available to guard against those intrusions, adding a layer of security by encoding emails so that only intended recipients can open them. The **encryption system** works by locking an email message to a unique code number (digital fingerprint) for each computer so only that computer can open and read the message.[18]

encryption system
Software that assigns an email message to a unique code number (digital fingerprint) for each computer so only that computer, not others, can open and read the message.

Avoiding Spam and Spyware

To help their employees avoid privacy invasion and to improve productivity, businesses often install anti-spyware and spam filtering software on their systems. Dozens of anti-spyware products provide protection—software such as Webroot's Spy Sweeper and the Microsoft AntiSpyware Beta—but they must be continually updated to keep pace with new spyware techniques.

While it cannot be prevented entirely, spam is abated by many internet service providers (ISPs) that ban the spamming of ISP subscribers. One ISP was recently awarded $1 billion in a lawsuit against 300 spammers that jammed the ISP system with an astounding 10 million emails a day. Anti-spam groups, too, promote the public's awareness of known spammers. The Spamhaus Project (www.spamhaus.org), for example, maintains a list—Register of Known Spam Operators (ROKSO)—of over 200 professional spammers that are responsible for over 80 percent of spam traffic in North America and Europe.

NOTES, SOURCES, AND CREDITS

Endnotes

Chapter 1

1. *Financial Post Business*, Special Edition, 2006, p. 64.

2. See Robert A. Collinge and Ronald M. Ayers, *Economics by Design: Principles and Issues*, 2nd ed. (Upper Saddle River, NJ: Prentice Hall, 2000), 41–42; Michael J. Mandel, "The New Economy," *Business Week* (January 31, 2000): 73–77.

3. Karl E. Case and Ray C. Fair, *Principles of Economics*, 6th ed. (Upper Saddle River, NJ: Prentice Hall, 2003), 224–225.

4. Richard I. Kirkland, Jr., "The Death of Socialism," *Fortune* (January 4, 1988): 64–72.

5. See Karl E. Case and Ray C. Fair, *Principles of Economics*, 5th ed. (Upper Saddle River, NJ: Prentice Hall, 1999), 69–74; Robert A. Collinge and Ronald M. Ayers, *Economics by Design: Principles and Issues*, 2nd ed. (Upper Saddle River, NJ: Prentice Hall, 2000), 51–52.

6. Geoffrey York, "Russian Miner Sees Privatization Payoff," *The Globe and Mail*, July 23, 2001, pp. B1, B4.

7. Andres Oppenheimer, "While Latin America Nationalizes, India Opens Up," *Orlando Sentinel*, January 22, 2007, p. A11.

8. Deborah Orr, "The Post Office with a Ticker," *Forbes* (November 29, 1999): 77–78; Matthew L. Wald, "Canada's Private Control Towers," *The New York Times*, October 23, 1999, p. C1. See also National Center for Policy Analysis, "Privatization," http://www.public-policy.org/~ncpa/pd/private/privat.html, March 8, 2000.

9. Andy Hoffman, "Labatt Convicted in Quebec Discount Beer Case," *The Globe and Mail*, November 24, 2005, p. B10.

10. Shirley Won and Jacquie McNish, "Antitrust Watchdog Loses Beer Battle," *The Globe and Mail*, March 29, 2007, pp. B1, B6.

11. John Gray, "Texas Fold 'Em," *Canadian Business* (October 9–22, 2006): 44–46.

12. Barrie McKenna, "Hyundai Gorged on Federal Funds," *The Globe and Mail*, March 25, 1994, p. B3.

13. Wendy Stueck, "Ginseng Growers at Root of Problem," *The Globe and Mail*, May 21, 2001, pp. B1, B3.

14. Claire Leow and Saijel Kishan, "It's Official: Money Grows on Trees," *The Globe and Mail*, August 29, 2006, p. B12.

15. Patrick Barta and Jane Spencer, "As Alternative Fuels Heat Up, Environmental Concerns Grow," *The Wall Street Journal*, December 5, 2006, pp. A1, A13.

16. Joel Millman, Metal is so Precious that Scrap Thieves Now Tap Beer Kegs," *The Wall Street Journal*, March 14, 2006, pp. A1, A15.

17. See Paul Heyne, Peter J. Boettke, and David L. Prychitko, *The Economic Way of Thinking*, 10th ed. (Upper Saddle River, NJ: Prentice Hall, 2003), 190, 358–59.

18. *Hoover's Handbook of World Business 2002* (Austin, TX: Hoover's Business Press, 2002), 74–75.

19. Karl E. Case and Ray C. Fair, *Principles of Economics*, 6th ed., updated (Upper Saddle River, NJ: Prentice Hall, 2003), 300–309.

20. John Partridge and Lawrence Surtees, "Rogers Faces Assault from Telcos," *The Globe and Mail*, March 28, 1994, pp. B1–B2.

21. "Royal Mail's Reign Comes to an End," *The Globe and Mail*, January 2, 2006, p. B7.

22. Eric Bellman, "As Economy Zooms, India's Postmen Struggle to Adapt," *The Wall Street Journal*, October 3, 2006, pp. A1, A12.

23. Madelaine Drohan, "Ottawa Targets Interprovincial Barriers," *The Globe and Mail*, May 14, 1991, p. B5.

Chapter 2

1. See Jay B. Barney and William G. Ouchi (eds.), *Organizational Economics* (San Francisco: Jossey-Bass, 1986), for a detailed analysis of linkages between economics and organizations.

2. Karl E. Case and Ray C. Fair, *Principles of Economics*, 6th ed., updated (Upper Saddle River, NJ: Prentice Hall, 2003), 432–433.

3. Karl E. Case and Ray C. Fair, *Principles of Economics*, 6th ed., updated (Upper Saddle River, NJ: Prentice Hall, 2003), 15.

4. Karl E. Case and Ray C. Fair, *Principles of Economics*, 6th ed., updated (Upper Saddle River, NJ: Prentice Hall, 2003), 15.

5. *Bank of Canada Banking and Financial Statistics*, Table H1 (April 2006): S94.

6. Barry Marquardson, "GDP Fails as a Measurement," *The Globe and Mail*, July 16, 1998, p. B2.

7. Richard Bloom, "Report Analyzes Income Gap with U.S.," *The Globe and Mail*, October 6, 2003, pp. B1, B4.

8. Olivier Blanchard, *Macroeconomics*, 3rd ed. (Upper Saddle River, NJ: Prentice Hall, 2003), 24–26.

9. Jay Heizer and Barry Render, *Operations Management*, 6th ed. (Upper Saddle River, NJ: Prentice Hall, 2001), 15–16.

10. *Bank of Canada Banking and Financial Statistics*, Table J1 (April 2006): S108.

11. Greg Hitt and Murray Hiebert, "U.S. Trade Deficit Ballooned to a Record in 2005," *The Wall Street Journal*, February 11–12, 2006, pp. A1, A10.

12. *Bank of Canada Banking and Financial Statistics*, Table G1 (May 2006): S-83.

13. Tavia Grant, "Lard in 1913, Plasma TV Now: CPI Tracks Changes," *The Globe and Mail*, April 21, 2005, pp. B1, B15.

14. Bruce Little, "There's Been a Huge Shift in How Consumers Spend," *The Globe and Mail*, July 5, 2004, p. B4. Figure 2.3 shows how inflation has varied over the last 20 years in Canada.

15. L.G. Franko, "Global Corporate Competition: Who's Winning, Who's Losing, and the R&D Factor as One Reason Why," *Strategic Management Journal* (September–October 1989): 449–474.

16. Statistics Canada, Industrial Research and Development, *2005 Intentions*, 10.

17. Statistics Canada, Industrial Research and Development, *2005 Intentions*, 10.

18. Statistics Canada, Industrial Research and Development, *2005 Intentions*, 17.

19. Statistics Canada, Industrial Research and Development, *2002 Intentions*, 19.

20. Statistics Canada, Industrial Research and Development, *2005 Intentions*, 10.

21. Thomas Wheelen and J. David Hunger, *Strategic Management and Business Policy* (Upper Saddle River, NJ: Pearson, 2004), 280.

22. Brian Laghi, "U.S. Backlash Seen Growing," *The Globe and Mail*, March 27, 2003, pp. B1, B10.

23. Sinclair Stewart, "CIBC's Solid Profit Overshadowed by Woes," *The Globe and Mail*, February 27, 2004, pp. B1, B6.

24. Richard Blackwell, "The Greening of the Corner Office," *The Globe and Mail*, March 26, 2007, pp. B1, B4.

25. Michael Porter. *Competitive Strategy: Techniques for Analyzing Industries and Competitors* (New York: The Free Press, 1980).

26. Judy Strauss and Raymond Frost, *E-Marketing* (Upper Saddle River, NJ: Prentice Hall, 2001), 245–246.

27. Tessa Wegert, "Advertisers Get Creative in Bid to Infect the Internet," *The Globe and Mail*, October 27, 2005, p. B13.

28. Lee J. Krajewski and Larry P. Ritzman, *Operations Management: Strategy and Analysis*, 6th ed. (Upper Saddle River, NJ: Prentice Hall, 2002), 3–4.

29. Lee J. Krajewski and Larry P. Ritzman, *Operations Management: Strategy and Analysis*, 6th ed. (Upper Saddle River, NJ: Prentice Hall, 2002), Chapter 3.

30. Romina Maurino, "Wave of Consolidation Isn't Over Yet," *Winnipeg Free Press*, December 26, 2006, p. B6.

31. Lawrence Surtees, "Takeover Concern Prompts BCE Poison Pill Plan," *The Globe and Mail*, February 25, 2000, p. B5.

32. Margot Gibb-Clark, "Share Plans Can Benefit More Than Employees," *The Globe and Mail*, February 14, 2000, p. B6.

Chapter 3

1. Constance L. Hays, "Aide Was Reportedly Ordered to Warn Stewart on Stock Sales," *New York Times*, August 6, 2002, pp. C1, C2.

2. Thomas Donaldson and Thomas W. Dunfee, "Toward a Unified Conception of Business Ethics: An Integrative Social Contracts Theory," *Academy of Management Review* 19, no. 2 (1994): 252–284.

3. "Drug Companies Face Assault on Prices," *Wall Street Journal*, May 11, 2000, pp. B1, B4.

4. John Saunders, "Bitter Air Carrier Dogfight Heads to Court," *The Globe and Mail*, July 8, 2004, p. B3.

5. Mike Esterl and David Crawford, "'Rocky Future' Ahead As Siemens Probe Widens," *The Globe and Mail*, April 27, 2007, p. B7; David Crawford and Mike Esterl, "At Siemens, Witnesses Cite Pattern of Bribery," *The Wall Street Journal*, January 31, 2007, pp. A1, A10.

6. Ann Zimmerman and Anita Raghavan, "Diamond Group Widens Probe of Bribe Charges, *The Wall Street Journal*, March 8, 2006, pp. B1–B2.

7. This section follows the logic of Gerald F. Cavanaugh, *American Business Values with International Perspectives*, 4th ed. (Upper Saddle River, NJ: Prentice Hall, 1998), Chapter 3.

8. Patricia Sellers, "Crunch Time for Coke," *Fortune* (July 19, 1999): 72–74.

9. Mark Schwartz, "Heat's on to Get an Effective Code," *The Globe and Mail*, November 27, 1997, p. B2.

10. Julie Schmidt, "Nike's Image Problem," *USA Today*, October 4, 1999, p. 1B, 2B.

11. Milton Friedman, *Capitalism and Freedom* (Chicago: University of Chicago Press, 1962), 133.

12. Alix M. Freedman, "As Unicef Battles Baby-Formula Makers, African Infants Sicken," *The Wall Street Journal*, December 5, 2000, pp. A1, A18.

13.. Jeremy Main, "Here Comes the Big New Cleanup," *Fortune* (November 21, 1988): 102–118.

14. Neil Reynolds, "The Dirty Truth of China's Energy," *The Globe and Mail*, March 28, 2007, p. B2.

15. R. Timothy Patterson, "Read the Sunspots," *National Post*, June 20, 2007, p. FP17.

16. Lawrence Solomon, "Open Mind Sees Climate Clearly," *National Post*, June 29, 2007, p. FP15.

17. Lauren Etter, "For Icy Greenland, Global Warming Has a Bright Side," *The Wall Street Journal*, July 18, 2006, pp. A1, A12.

18. David Ebner, "The Greening of the Oil Sands," *The Globe and Mail*, January 6, 2007, p. B4.

19. Bill Curry, "Ottawa Wants Kyoto Softened," *The Globe and Mail*, May 12, 2006, pp. A1, A7.

20. Richard Blackwell, "Canada Becoming a Wind Powerhouse," *The Globe and Mail*, March 9, 2007, p. B3.

21. Richard Blackwell, "In Ontario and Alberta, How Much Wind Power Is Too Much?" *The Globe and Mail*, October 30, 2006, pp. B1, B15.

22. Catherine Collins, "The Race for Zero," *Canadian Business* (March 1991): 52–56.

23. Allan Robinson and Allan Freeman, "Mining's Dam Problem," *The Globe and Mail*, May 16, 1998, pp. B1–B2.

24. Egle Procuta, "One Man's Garbage Is Another's Gold," *The Globe and Mail*, April 11, 2006, p. B7.

25. Geoffrey Scotton, "Cleanups Can Hurt, Companies Warned," *The Financial Post*, June 25, 1991, p. 4.

26. Marc Huber, "A Double-Edged Endorsement," *Canadian Business* (January 1990): 69–71.

27. Daniel Machalaba, "As Old Pallets Pile Up, Critics Hammer Them as New Eco-Menace," *The Wall Street Journal*, April 1, 1998, p. A1.

28. Patrick Barta, "Goro No Tropical Paradise for Inco," *The Globe and Mail*, July 12, 2006, p. B5.

29. John Saunders, "Polar Plastic Plot Flops," *The Globe and Mail*, June 10, 1994, p. B1.

30. John Wilke, "Cases, Fines, Soar in Fraud Probes of Drug Pricing," *The Wall Street Journal*, June 7, 2005, pp. A1, A10.

31. Jonathan Cheng, "False Ads: Chinese Consumers Awaken to a Western Problem," *The Wall Street Journal*, July 8, 2005, p. B9.

32. Shawn McCarthy, "Crackdown on New York's Canal Street," *The Globe and Mail*, August 30, 2004, pp. B1, B11.

33. Jeff Sanford, "Knock-off Nation," *Canadian Business* (November 8–21, 2004): 67–71.

34. Gordon Fairclough, "Tobacco Firms Trace Fakes to North Korea," *The Wall Street Journal*, January 27, 2006, pp. B1–B2.

35. Tim Barker, "Word-of-Mouth Advertising Grows in Influence, Concern," *Orlando Sentinel*, March 17, 2006, pp. A1, A19.

36. Michael McCarthy and Lorrie Grant, "Sears Drops Benetton After Controversial Death Row Ads," *USA Today*, February 18, 2000, p. 2B.

37. Shona McKay, "Willing and Able," *Report on Business Magazine* (October 1991): 58–63.

38. J. Southerst, "In Pursuit of Drugs," *Canadian Transportation* (November 1989): 58–65.

39. Jerald Greenberg and Robert A. Baron, *Behavior in Organizations: Understanding and Managing the Human Side of Work*, 7th ed. (Upper Saddle River, NJ: Prentice Hall, 2000), 374–375.

40. Rick Lyman, "A Tobacco Whistle-Blower's Life Is Transformed," *New York Times*, October 15, 1999, p. A24.

41. Brent Jang and Patrick Brethour, "This WestJet Staffer Blew the Whistle on his Employer's Corporate Spying. He's Still Waiting for Someone to Say Thanks," *The Globe and Mail*, October 18, 2006, pp. A1, A12.

42. "Scandalist," CBC *Venture* series, November 6, 2005.

43. Larry Neumeister, "Allegations of Insider Trading Hit 'Top Tier' Wall Street Firms," *The Globe and Mail*, March 2, 2007, p. B8.

44. Daniel Stoffman, "Good Behaviour and the Bottom Line," *Canadian Business* (May 1991): 28–32.

45. Tom Kierans, "Charity Begins at Work," *Report on Business Magazine* (June 1990): 23.

46. Theresa Ebden and Dawn Walton, "Walkerton Recipient of New-Style Corporate Giving," *The Globe and Mail*, June 3, 2000, pp. B1, B6.

47. "Private Sector Comes to Rescue in Asia," *The Globe and Mail*, December 30, 2004, p. B5.

48. Paul Waldie, "Firms Mull Response to Disaster," *The Globe and Mail*, December 31, 2004, pp. B1–B2.

49. Sandra Waddock and Neil Smith, "Corporate Responsibility Audits: Doing Well by Doing Good," *Sloan Management Review* (Winter 2000), 75–85.

50. Janet McFarland, "Are You Making Yourself Accountable?" *The Globe and Mail*, April 20, 2006, p. B12.

51. Alison Arnot, "The Triple Bottom Line," *CGA Magazine* (January–February 2004): 27–32.

Chapter 4

1. Statistics Canada, *Business Dynamics in Canada*, Catalogue no. 61–534-XIE (Ottawa: Minister of Industry, 2006).

2. P.D. Reynolds, S.M. Camp, W.D. Bygrave, E. Autio, and M. Hay, *Global Entrepreneurship Monitor: 2001 Executive Report* (Kansas City, MO: Kauffman Center for Entrepreneurial Leadership, 2001); P.D. Reynolds, M. Hay, W.D. Bygrave, S.M. Camp, and E. Autio, *Global Entrepreneurship Monitor: 2000 Executive Report* (Kansas City, MO: Kauffman Center for Entrepreneurial Leadership, 2000).

3. Industry Canada, *Key Small Business Statistics* (Ottawa: Public Works and Government Services Canada, 2006), 24.

4. Industry Canada, *Key Small Business Statistics* (Ottawa: Public Works and Government Services Canada, 2006), 3.

5. Monica Diochon, Teresa Menzies, and Yvon Gasse, "Exploring the relationship between start-up activities and new venture emergence: A longitudinal study of Canadian nascent entrepreneurs," *International Journal of Management and Enterprise Development* 2, no. 3/4, (2005): 408–426.

6. Industry Canada, *Key Small Business Statistics* (Ottawa: Public Works and Government Services Canada, 2006), 23.

7. Nancy M. Carter, William B. Gartner, and Paul D. Reynolds, "Firm Founding," in W.B. Gartner, K.G. Shaver, N.M. Carter, and P. D. Reynolds (eds), *Handbook of Entrepreneurial Dynamics: The Process of Business Creation* (Thousand Oaks, CA: Sage, 2004), 311–323.

8. William D. Bygrave and C.W. Hofer, "Theorizing about entrepreneurship," *Entrepreneurship Theory and Practice* 16, no. 2 (Winter 1991): 14; Donald Sexton and Nancy Bowman-Upton, *Entrepreneurship: Creativity and Growth* (New York, NY: MacMillan Publishing Company, 1991), 7.

9. John Cooper, "A Pint of Success," *CMA Management* (December 1999/ January 2000): 44–46.

10. http://www.heritage.org/research/features/index/countries.cfm.

11. Angela Dale, "Self-employment and entrepreneurship: notes on two problematic concepts," in Roger Burrows, ed. *Deciphering the Enterprise Culture* (London: Routledge, 1991), 45, 48; Holt 1992, 11.

12. Donald Sexton and Nancy Bowman-Upton, *Entrepreneurship: Creativity and Growth* (New York, NY: MacMillan Publishing Company, 1991), 11: Kao, 1991, 21.

13. Allan A. Gibb, "The enterprise culture and education: Understanding enterprise education and its links with small business, entrepreneurship and wider educational goals," *International Small Business Journal* 11, no. 3, (1993): 13–34; Donald Sexton and Nancy Bowman-Upton, *Entrepreneurship: Creativity and Growth* (New York, NY: MacMillan Publishing Company, 1991).

14. Terrence Belford, "Intrapreneurs combine big-biz clout with entrepreneurial style," *CanWest News* (March 23, 2005). Retrieved June 25, 2006, from CBCA Current Events database. (Document ID: 1009719591).

15. Statistics Canada, *Business Register, National Income and Expenditure Accounts 2005; Estimates of Population by Age and Sex for Canada, the Provinces and the Territories* (June 2005).

16. Industry Canada, *Key Small Business Statistics* (Ottawa: Public Works and Government Services Canada, 2006), 10.

17. Industry Canada, *Key Small Business Statistics* (Ottawa: Public Works and Government Services Canada, 2006), 10.

18. William B. Gartner, Kelly G. Shaver, Nancy M. Carter, and Paul D. Reynolds, *Handbook of Entrepreneurial Dynamics* (Thousand Oaks, CA: Sage Publications, Inc., 2004), ix.

19. Statistics Canada, *Business Dynamics in Canada 2003* (Ottawa: Minister Of Industry, March 2006), Catalogue no. 61–534-XIE, 6.

20. Richard Bloom, "Building a Future on Sweet Dreams," *The Globe and Mail*, October 21, 2004, p. B9.

21. Virginia Galt, "Female Entrepreneurs to be Honoured Tonight," *The Globe and Mail*, November 22, 2005, p. B9.

22. Roma Luciw, "Stay-At-Home Moms Stay the Business Course," *The Globe and Mail*, March 3, 2007, p. B10.

23. rbcroyalbank.com/sme/women/top_news.html.

24. Murray McNeill, "Patience Pays Off for Native Owner," *The Winnipeg Free Press*, November 6, 2002, p. B3.

25. Sarah Kennedy, "Self-Styled Pioneer Aims to Alter Face of Fashion," *The Globe and Mail*, July 1, 2002, p. B12.

26. Geoff Kirbyson, "Market-Research Firm Lands Major Contract," *The Winnipeg Free Press*, July 19, 2004, p. D7.

27. Donald F. Kuratko and Richard M. Hodgetts, *Entrepreneurship: Theory, Process, Practice*, 7th ed. (Mason, OH: Thomson South-Western, 2007), 118–125; John A. Hornday, "Research about Living Entrepreneurs," in *Encyclopedia of Entrepreneurship*, ed. Calvin Kent, Donald Sexton, and Karl Vesper (Englewood Cliffs, NJ: Prentice-Hall, 1982), 26–27; Jeffry A. Timmons and Stephen Spinelli, *New Venture Creation: Entrepreneurship for the 21st Century* (Boston, MA: McGraw-Hill Irwin, 2007), 9.

28. J.D. Kyle, R. Blais, R. Blatt, and A.J. Szonyi, "The Culture of the Entrepreneur: Fact or Fiction," *Journal of Small Business and Entrepreneurship* (1991): 3–14.

29. R.H. Brockhaus and Pam S. Horwitz, "The Psychology of the Entrepreneur," in *The Art and Science of Entrepreneurship*, D.L Sexton and Raymond W. Smilor, eds. (Cambridge, MA: Ballinger Pub. Co., 1986); William B. Gartner, "What Are We Talking About When We Talk About Entrepreneurship?" *Journal of Business Venturing* 5, no. 1 (1990): 15–29; Allan A. Gibb, "The Enterprise Culture and Education: Understanding Enterprise Education and Its Links with Small Business, Entrepreneurship and Wider Educational Goals," *International Small Business Journal* 11, no. 3, (1993): 13–34; J.C. Mitchell, "Case and Situation Analysis," *Sociological Review* 31, no. 2 (1983): 187–211.

30. Donald Sexton and Nancy Bowman-Upton, *Entrepreneurship: Creativity and Growth* (New York, NY: MacMillan Publishing Company, 1991); Karl H. Vesper, *New Venture Strategies* (Englewood Cliffs, NJ: Prentice Hall, 1990); W. D. Bygrave and C.W. Hofer, "Theorizing about Entrepreneurship," *Entrepreneurship Theory and Practice* 16, no. 2 (Winter 1991): 14.

31. Walter Good, *Building a Dream* (Toronto: McGraw-Hill Ryerson, 1998), 40.

32. Wayne A. Long and W. Ed McMullan. *Developing New Ventures* (San Diego: Harcourt Brace Jovanovich, 1990), 374–375.

33. "Sally Fox: Innovation in the Field," *www.vreseis.com/sally_fox_story.htm*, June 27, 2006.

34. Michael E. Porter, "Know Your Place," *Inc.* 13, no. 9 (September 1992): 90–93.

35. Howard H. Stevenson, H. Irving Grousbeck, Michael J. Roberts, and Amarnath Bhide, *New Business Ventures and the Entrepreneur* (Boston: Irwin McGraw-Hill, 1999), 19.

36. Howard H. Stevenson, H. Irving Grousbeck, Michael J. Roberts, and Amarnath Bhide, *New Business Ventures and the Entrepreneur* (Boston: Irwin McGraw-Hill, 1999), 21.

37. Marc J. Dollinger, *Entrepreneurship: Strategies and Resources* (Upper Saddle River, NJ: Prentice Hall, 1999), 94–101.

38. Thomas W. Zimmerer and Norman M. Scarborough, *Essentials of Entrepreneurship and Small Business Management*, 4th ed. (Upper Saddle River, NJ: Pearson Prentice Hall), 359.

39. Michael E. Porter, "Know your Place," *Inc.* 13, no. 9 (September 1992): 90–93.

40. Karen Mazurkewich, "Revenge of the Angel Investor," *National Post*, July 9, 2007, pp. FP1, FP3.

41. Karen Mazurkewich, "Revenge of the Investor Angel," *National Post*, July 9, 2007, pp. FP1, FP3.

42. Karl H. Vesper, *New Venture Mechanics* (Englewood Cliffs, NJ: Prentice Hall, 1993), 105.

43. Jeffry A. Timmons, *New Venture Creation* (Boston: Irwin McGraw-Hill, 1999), 277.

44. Lisa Stephens, "With Some Shape Shifting, This Company Has Legs," *The Globe and Mail*, October 5, 2005, p. B10.

45. Gordon Pitts, "An Empire Looks to the Future," *The Globe and Mail*, March 26, 2005, p. B4.

46. George Anders, Carol Hymowitz, Joann Lublin, and Don Clark, "All in the Family," *The Wall Street Journal*, August 1, 2005, pp. B1, B4.

47. Ronad J. Ebert, Ricky W. Griffin, and Frederick A. Starke, *Business Essentials*, 4th Canadian ed. (Toronto: Pearson Education Canada, 2006), 63.

48. Mary Agnes Welch, "When Name Is Everything," *The Winnipeg Free Press*, May 12, 2002, pp. B1–B2.

49. Richard Bloom, "IPO's Surge on Mood Swing," *The Globe and Mail*, February 8, 2005, p. B3.

50. Richard Bloom, "Cara Shareholders Vote to Take Company Private," *The Globe and Mail*, February 25, 2005, p. B7; Keith McArthur, "Magnotta Winery Plans to Go Private," *The Globe and Mail*, February 8, 2007, p. B6.

51. Sean Silcoff, "Bell Fee Bonanza Seen," *National Post*, June 28, 2007, p. FP1.

52. Terry Pedwell, "Income Trusts Face Tough Rules," *The Winnipeg Free Press*, November 1, 2006, p. B7.

53. "An Overview of Available Business Structures," INK "http://www.umanitoba.ca/afs/agric_economics/MRAC/structures.html#Cooperatives", July 2, 2006.

54. Monica Diochon, Teresa Menzies, and Yvon Gasse, "Nascent Entrepreneurs' Start-Up Efforts: Outcomes and Individual Influences on Sustainability," *Journal of Small Business and Entrepreneurship* (2005): 53–74.

55. Kevin Marron, "Want to Succeed? Read This," *The Globe and Mail*, October 19, 2005, pp. E1, E5. Several excellent articles on starting and operating a small business are found in Section E, "Report on Small Business" in *The Globe and Mail*, October 19, 2005.

56. See Norman M. Scarborough and Thomas W. Zimmerer, *Effective Small Business Management: An Entrepreneurial Approach*, 7th ed. (Upper Saddle River, NJ: Prentice Hall, 2003).

Chapter 5

1. Ricky Griffin and Michael W. Pustay, *International Business: A Managerial Perspective*, 5th ed. (Upper Saddle River, NJ: Prentice Hall, 2007).

2. Thomas Friedman, *The World Is Flat* (New York: Farrar, Straus, and Giroux, 2005).

3. Barrie McKenna, "China, India Crowd G7 in Driver's Seat," *The Globe and Mail*, July 19, 2006, p. B11; Andrew Batson, "China's Rise as Auto-Parts Power Reflects New Manufacturing Edge," *The Wall Street Journal*, August 1, 2006, pp. A1, A6.

4. Ricky W. Griffin and Michael W. Pustay, *International Business: A Managerial Perspective*, 2nd ed. (Reading, MA: Addison-Wesley, 1999), Chapter 3; Dominick Salvatore, *International Economics*, 6th ed. (Upper Saddle River, NJ: Prentice Hall, 1998), 27–33; Karl E. Case and Ray C. Fair, *Principles of Economics*, 5th ed. (Upper Saddle River, NJ: Prentice Hall, 1999), 813–817.

5. This section is based on Michael Porter, *The Competitive Advantage of Nations* (Boston: Harvard Business School Press, 1990), Chapters 3 and 4; Warren J. Keegan, *Global Marketing Management*, 6th ed. (Upper Saddle River, NJ: Prentice Hall, 1999), 312–321; John J. Wild, Kenneth L. Wild, and Jerry C.Y. Han, *International Business: An Integrated Approach* (Upper Saddle River, NJ: Prentice Hall, 2000), 175–178.

6. Heather Scoffield, "Canada's Slipping on the World Stage, WEF Study shows," *The Globe and Mail*, September 27, 2006, p. B7.

7. Madelaine Drohan, "Dependency on U.S. Leaves Canada 'Vulnerable': WTO," *The Globe and Mail*, November 20, 1996.

8. Table J2, *Bank of Canada Banking and Financial Statistics* (April 2006): S-110.

9. Karl E. Case and Ray C. Fair, *Principles of Economics*, 5th ed. (Upper Saddle River, NJ: Prentice Hall, 1999), 818–821.

10. Robyn Meredith, "Dollar Makes Canada a Land of the Spree," *The New York Times*, August 1, 1999, sec. 3, pp. 1, 11.

11. Deborah Ball and Cecilie Rohwedder, "Shopping as the Dollar Drops," *The Wall Street Journal*, December 1, 2006, pp. B1, B4.

12. "Exports, Eh?" *Canadian Business* (January 1997): 21.

13. "China Rising: Where We're At," *The Globe and Mail*, October 29, 2005, introduction to the "Report on Business" section.

14. Shirley Won, "Small Firms Beating a Path to the Middle Kingdom," *The Globe and Mail*, August 31, 2004, p. B7.

15. Ray August, *International Business Law: Text, Cases, and Readings*, 3rd ed. (Upper Saddle River, NJ: Prentice Hall, 2000), 192–197.

16. Paola Hjelt, "The Fortune Global 500," *Fortune* (July 22, 2003): 144–147.

17. Celeste Mackenzie, "Rumble in the Jungle," *Canadian Business* (February 28–March 13, 2005): 57–63.

18. Warren J. Keegan, *Global Marketing Management*, 6th ed. (Upper Saddle River, NJ: Prentice Hall, 1999), 290–292; Ricky W. Griffin and Michael W. Pustay, *International Business: A Managerial Perspective*, 2nd ed. (Reading, MA: Addison-Wesley, 1999), 427–431; John J. Wild, Kenneth L. Wild, and Jerry C.Y. Han, *International Business: An Integrated Approach* (Upper Saddle River, NJ: Prentice Hall, 2000), 454–456.

19. Ricky W. Griffin and Michael W. Pustay, *International Business: A Managerial Perspective*, 2nd ed. (Reading, MA: Addison-Wesley, 1999), 431–433; John J. Wild, Kenneth L. Wild, and Jerry C.Y. Han, *International Business: An Integrated Approach* (Upper Saddle River, NJ: Prentice Hall, 2000), 456–458.

20. Shirley Won, "Small Firms Beating a Path to the Middle Kingdom," *The Globe and Mail*, August 31, 2004, p. B7.

21. Shirley Won, "Small Firms Beating a Path to the Middle Kingdom," *The Globe and Mail*, August 31, 2004, p. B7.

22. John J. Wild, Kenneth L. Wild, and Jerry C.Y. Han, *International Business: An Integrated Approach* (Upper Saddle River, NJ: Prentice Hall, 2000), Chapter 7; Ricky W. Griffin and Michael W. Pustay, *International Business: A Managerial Perspective*, 2nd ed. (Reading, MA: Addison-Wesley, 1999), 436–439.

23. Eric Beauchesne, "Foreign Control of Economy Hits 30-Year High," *Winnipeg Free Press*, November 19, 2005, p. B7.

24. Eric Beauchesne, "Foreign Control of Economy Hits 30-Year High," *Winnipeg Free Press*, November 19, 2005, p. B7.

25. Roma Luciw, "Hollowed Out Fears? Relax, Foreigners Lead on Hiring," *The Globe and Mail*, July 14, 2006, pp. B1–B2.

26. Gordon Pitts, "Mixed Messages on Danger of Foreign Takeovers," *The Globe and Mail*, September 18, 2006, pp. B1, B3. For an extensive analysis of the effect of foreign takeovers of Canadian business firms, see Roger Martin and Gordon Nixon, "Whoa, Canada," *The Globe and Mail*, July 2, 2007, pp. B1–B3.

27. Steven Chase, "Canada Slaps Duties on Chinese-made Barbecues," *The Globe and Mail*, August 28, 2004, p. B2.

28. Peter Kennedy, "Softwood Decision Gets Mixed Reviews," *The Globe and Mail*, December 8, 2005, p. B6.

29. Jennifer Ditchburn, "Canada, U.S. Pen Deal to End Lumber Dispute," *The Winnipeg Free Press*, July 2, 2006, p. A6.

30. Paul Veira, "Emerson Warns Lumber Leaders of 'Consequences'," *Financial Post*, August 1, 2006, pp. FP1, FP5; also Steve Merti, "Lumber Exporters Taste Sting of Softwood Deal," *The Winnipeg Free Press*, September 22, 2006, p. B5.

31. Scott Kilman and Roger Thurow, "In Fight Against Farm Subsidies, Even Farmers are Joining Foes," *The Wall Street Journal*, March 14, 2006, pp. A1, A16.

32. Roger Thurow and Geoff Winestock, "How an Addiction to Sugar Subsidies Hurts Development," *The Wall Street Journal*, September 16, 2002, pp. A1, A10.

33. "WTO Strikes Down U.S. Cotton Subsidy Appeal," *The Globe and Mail*, March 4, 2005, p. B10.

34. Scott Kilman and Roger Thurow, "To Soothe Anger Over Subsidies, U.S. Cotton Tries Wooing Africa," *The Wall Street Journal*, August 5, 2005, pp. A1, A6.

35. Simon Tuck, "Farmers to WTO: If It Ain't Broke...," *The Globe and Mail*, August 9, 2004, p. B1–B2.

36. Anthony DePalma, "Chiquita Sues Europeans, Citing Banana Quota Losses," *New York Times*, January 26, 2001, p. C5; Brian Lavery, "Trade Feud on Bananas Not as Clear as It Looks," *New York Times*, February 7, 2001, p. W1; David E. Sanger, "Miffed at Europe, U.S. Raises Tariffs for Luxury Goods," *New York Times*, March 4, 1999, pp. A1, A5.

37. Wendy Stueck, "Mining Firms Hit Again By Chavez Threat," *The Globe and Mail*, September 23, 2005, p. B4; also Barrie McKenna, "A Nation of Big Riches, Bigger Risks," *The Globe and Mail*, September 24, 2005, p. B4.

38. Konrad Yakabuski, "Quebec Courts Margarine War," *The Globe and Mail*, October 14, 1997, pp. B1, B4.

39. Bertrand Marotte, "Ontario Calls for Dispute Panel in Quebec Margarine Battle," *The Globe and Mail*, March 26, 2002, p. B10.

40. Neville Nankivell, "Spilled Milk Over Provincial Trade," *The National Post*, April 24, 2000, p. C9.

41. Gerry Stobo, "Cross-Border Mobility," *CGA Magazine* (May–June 2005): 13–16.

42. Sinclair Stewart, "Uncle Sam Nabs Net Millionaires," *The Globe and Mail*, January 17, 2007, pp. B1, B8.

43. Dawn Walton, "Builders Most Likely to Bribe, Report Finds," *The Globe and Mail*, January 21, 2000, p. B5.

44. Nicholas Bray, "OECD Ministers Agree to Ban Bribery as Means for Companies to Win Business," *The Wall Street Journal*, May 27, 1997, p. A2.

45. www.transparency.org/policy_research/surveys_indices/cpi/2006

46. Geoffrey York, "Blowout in Bangladesh," *The Globe and Mail*, April 1, 2006, pp. B4–B5.

47. Barrie McKenna, "Aluminum Producers Whispering Dirty Word," *The Globe and Mail*, March 5, 1994, pp. B1, B5.

48. Jalil Hamid, "Coffee Rally Reignited," *The Globe and Mail*, May 22, 1997, p. B9.

49. Oliver Bertin, "Coffee Cartel Moves Fast on Price," *The Globe and Mail*, May 20, 2000, p. B3.

50. Steven Chase, "Canadian Bike Makers Fear Hit from Cheap Chinese Imports," *The Globe and Mail*, September 7, 2004, p. B4.

51. Michelle MacAfee, "Trade Protest Turns Violent," *The Winnipeg Free Press*, July 29, 2003, p. A9.

52. "European Union Expands Into 10 New Countries," *Reuters News Release*, April 30, 2004.

53. Bruce Little, "Free-Trade Pact Gets Mixed Reviews," *The Globe and Mail*, June 7, 2004, p. B3.

54. Andrew Purvis, "Super Exporter," *Time* (April 28, 1997): 36.

55. Geoffrey York, "Asian Trade Bloc Would Rival NAFTA, EU," *The Globe and Mail*, August 24, 2006, pp. B1, B8.

Chapter 6

1. *Hoover's Handbook of American Business 2006* (Austin, Texas: Hoover's Business Press, 2006).

2. Alex Taylor III, "How a Top Boss Manages His Day," *Fortune* (June 19, 1989): 95–100.

3. "On a Roll," *Canadian Business* (October 9–22, 2006): 51.

4. Roma Luciw, "No. 1 Employee Not Always Your No. 1 Manager," *The Globe and Mail*, February 17, 2007, p. B10.

5. "Our Annual Report on Executive Compensation," *The Globe and Mail*, June 4, 2007, p. B4.

6. Jerry Useem, "Boeing vs. Boeing," *Fortune* (October 2, 2000): 148–160; "Airbus Prepares to 'Bet the Company' as it Builds a Huge New Jet," *The Wall Street Journal*, November 3, 1999, pp. A1, A10.

7. Charles P. Wallace, "Adidas—Back in the Game," *Fortune* (August 18, 1997): 176–182.

8. Barry M. Staw and Jerry Ross, "Good Money After Bad," *Psychology Today* (February 1988): 30–33.

9. Gerry McNamara and Philip Bromiley, "Risk and Return in Organizational Decision Making," *Academy of Management Journal*, Vol. 42 (1999): 330–339.

10. Brian O'Reilly, '"What It Takes to Start a Startup," *Fortune* (June 7, 1999): 135–140.

11. Sinclair Stewart and Derek DeCloet, "It's Mr. Focus v. Mr. Diversification," *The Globe and Mail*, June 3, 2006, p. B4.

12. Michael Porter, *Competitive Strategy: Techniques for Analyzing Industries and Competitors* (New York: The Free Press, 1980).

13. Bertrand Marotte, "Gildan Takes T-Shirt Making to the Cutting-Edge of Casual Apparel," *The Globe and Mail*, July 3, 2004, p. B3.

14. "Cruise-Ship Delays Leave Guests High and Dry," *The Wall Street Journal*, October 24, 1997, pp. B1, B10; *Hoover's Handbook of American Business 2000* (Austin, TX: Hoover's Business Press, 2000), 1512–1513.

15. Richard Bloom, "How Parmalat Juggled the Struggle," *The Globe and Mail*, May 23, 2005, p. B3.

16. Ric Dolphin, "Magna Force," *Canadian Business* (May 1988).

17. Isadore Sharp, "Quality for All Seasons," *Canadian Business Review* (Spring 1990): 21–23.

18. Andrew Wahl, "Culture Shock," *Canadian Business* (October 10–23, 2005): 115–116.

19. Calvin Leung, "Culture Club," *Canadian Business* (October 9–22, 2006): 115, 116, 118, 120.

20. Doug Nairne, "Mounties Riding the Vision Thing," *The Winnipeg Free Press*, September 16, 1996, p. A5.

21. Meagen Fitzpatrick, "RCMP 'Horribly Broken,' Need Fix Quickly: Report," *The Winnipeg Free Press*, June 16, 2007, p. A9.

22. Sinclair Stewart and Andrew Willis, "Hunkin Is De-Risking the Place," *The Globe and Mail*, December 11, 2004, p. B4.

23. Gordon Pitts, "It Boiled Down to a Culture Clash," *The Globe and Mail*, June 11, 2005, p. B5.

Chapter 7

1. Robert L. Simison, "Ford Rolls Out New Model of Corporate Culture," *The Wall Street Journal*, January 13, 1999, pp. B1, B4.

2. Joann Muller, "Ford: Why It's Worse Than You Think," *Business Week* (June 25, 2001): 80–84.

3. John A. Wagner and John R. Hollenbeck, *Management of Organizational Behavior* (Englewood Cliffs, NJ: Prentice Hall, 1992), 563–565.

4. Jay Diamond and Gerald Pintel, *Retailing*, 6th ed. (Upper Saddle River, NJ: Prentice Hall, 1996), 83–84.

5. Industry Report: Restaurant Industry," *U.S. Business Reporter*, July 19, 2001, "http://www.activemedia-guide.com/print_restaurant.htm"; Michael Arndt, "There's Life in the Old Bird Yet," *Business Week*, May 14, 2001: 77–78.

6. Michael E. Raynor and Joseph L. Bower, "Lead from the Center," *Harvard Business Review* (May 2001): 93–102.

7. Bruce Horovitz, "Restoring the Golden-Arch Shine," *USA Today*, June 16, 1999: p. 3B.

8. Lee Hawkins, "Reversing 80 Years of History, GM is Reining in Global Fiefs," *The Wall Street Journal*, October 6, 2004, pp. A1, A14.

9. Donna Fenn, "The Buyers," *Inc.* (June 1996): 46–48.

10. Nelson Wyatt, "Bell Canada Plan Creates 3 Divisions," *The Winnipeg Free Press*, May 8, 2003, p. B7.

11. Robert Berner and Kevin Helliker, "Heinz's Worry: 4,000 Products, Only One Star," *The Wall Street Journal*, September 17, 1999, pp. B1, B4.

12. J. Galbraith, "Matrix Organization Designs: How to Combine Functional and Project Forms," *Business Horizons* (1971): 29–40; H.F. Kolodny, "Evolution to a Matrix Organization," *Academy of Management Review* 4 (1979): 543–553.

13. Interview with Tom Ward, operations manager for Genstar Shipyards.

14. Diane Brady, "Martha Inc.," *Business Week* (January 17, 2000): 62–66.

15. Gail Edmondson, "Danone Hits Its Stride," *Business Week* (February 1, 1999): 52–53.

16. Frank Rose, "Think Globally, Script Locally," *Fortune* (November 8, 1999): 156–160.

17. Thomas A. Stewart, "See Jack. See Jack Run," *Fortune* (September 27, 1999): 124–127.

18. James P. Sterba, "At the Met Opera, It's Not Over Till the Fat Man Folds," *The Wall Street Journal*, January 1998, pp. 1, 6.

19. Jerald Greenberg and Robert A. Baron, *Behavior in Organizations: Understanding and Managing the Human Side of Work*, 7th ed. (Upper Saddle River, NJ: Prentice Hall, 2000), 308–09.

20. Tyler Hamilton, "Welcome to the World Wide Grapevine," *The Globe and Mail*, May 6, 2000, pp. B1, B6.

Chapter 8

1. See Angelo S. DeNisi and Ricky W. Griffin, *Human Resource Management* (Boston: Houghton Mifflin, 2001) for a complete overview.

2. Patrick Brethour and Heather Scoffield, "Plenty of Work, not Enough Bodies," *The Globe and Mail*, August 21, 2006, p. B4.

3. Heather Scoffield, "Amid Jobs Boom, Hundreds of Thousands Left Behind," *The Globe and Mail*, August 21, 2006, p. B5.

4. Elizabeth Church, "Store Owners Struggle with Staffing," *The Globe and Mail*, November 25, 1996, p. B6.

5. Caroline Alphonso, "Job Fairs Draw a Crowd," *The Globe and Mail*, August 25, 2000, p. B7.

6. Elizabeth Church, "Nortel Recruits to a Different Beat," *The Globe and Mail*, August 23, 2000, p. M1.

7. Virginia Galt, "Extreme Blue is the Taj Mahal of Internships," *The Globe and Mail*, July 17, 2004, p. B9.

8. Wallace Immen, "Prospective Hires Put to the Test," *The Globe and Mail*, January 26, 2005, pp. C1, C2.

9. Wallace Immen, "Prospective Hires Put to the Test," *The Globe and Mail*, January 26, 2005, pp. C1, C2.

10. Katie Rook, "Curveball Job Questions: How Not To Strike Out," *The Globe and Mail*, September 3, 2005, p. B9.

11. Margot Gibb-Clark, "Ruling Narrows Options for Drug Testing," *The Globe and Mail*, July 28, 1998, p. B11.

12. Scott Feschuk, "Phi Beta Cuppa," *The Globe and Mail*, March 6, 1993, pp. B1, B4.

13. Mark Blanchard, "Pilots Enter Superjumbo Virtual Reality," *The Globe and Mail*, January 20, 2005, p. B8.

14. Paddy Kamen, "Circular Logic," *University Affairs* (November 2003): 24–25.

15. "The 2005 Rankings," *The Globe and Mail*, May 9, 2006, p. B8.

16. Joann Lublin and Scott Thrum, "Behind Soaring Executive Pay, Decades of Failed Restraints," *The Wall Street Journal*, October 12, 2006, pp. A1, A16.

17. Peter Verburg, "The Man of Steel's Fed Up," *Canadian Business* (June 26–July 10, 1998): 69.

18. David Roberts, "A Long Way from Cambodia," *The Globe and Mail*, July 5, 1994, p. B18.

19. "EI Premiums to Drop on Jan. 1," *The Winnipeg Free Press*, November 7, 2006, p. B7.

20. Dale Jackson, "Pumped Up and Ready to Pay Out," *The Globe and Mail*, October 21, 2006, p. B13.

21. Virginia Galt, "Companies, Unions, Expect Little Relief," *The Globe and Mail*, September 15, 2004, p. B4.

22. Virginia Galt, "Gift of Time Pays off for Savvy Employers," *The Globe and Mail*, December 28, 2004, p. B3.

23. Virginia Galt, "Gift of Time Pays off for Savvy Employers," *The Globe and Mail*, December 28, 2004, p. B3.

24. Elizabeth Church, "Workplace Daycare Takes Baby Steps Toward Acceptance, but Some Not Sold," *The Globe and Mail*, July 2, 2001, pp. B1, B3.

25. Kamal Dib, "Diversity Works," *Canadian Business* (March 29, 2004): 53–54.

26. Virginia Galt, "How to Hammer the Glass Ceiling," *The Globe and Mail*, April 5, 2007, pp. B1, B4.

27. Marie Drolet, "The Male-Female Wage Gap," Perspectives on Labour and Income, the Online Edition, December, 2001, www.statcan.ca/english/freepub/75-001-XIE/01201/hi-fs_200112_01_a.html.

28. Richard Blackwell and Brent Jang, "Top Court Sides with Airline Attendants," *The Globe and Mail*, January 27, 2006, pp. B1, B6.

29. Neco Cockburn, "Clerks to Get $150 Million in Back Pay," *The Winnipeg Free Press*, October 8, 2005, p. A3.

30. Keith McArthur, "Criticism of Women's Fitness for Top Jobs Causes International Stir," *The Globe and Mail*, October 21, 2005, pp. A1, A14.

31. Wallace Immen, "Post-65 Workers 'Productive and Engaged'," *The Globe and Mail*, March 18, 2005, p. C1.

32. Omar El Akkad, "A Woman's Work May Never Be Done," *The Globe and Mail*, March 28, 2006, pp. B1, B4.

33. Michael Moss, "For Older Employees, On-the-Job Injuries Are More Often Deadly," *The Wall Street Journal*, June 17, 1997, pp. A1, A10.

34. Max Boisot, *Knowledge Assets* (Oxford: Oxford University Press, 1998).

35. Thomas Stewart, "In Search of Elusive Tech Workers," *Fortune* (February 16, 1998): 171–172.

36. Aaron Bernstein, "When Is a Temp Not a Temp?" *Business Week* (December 7, 1998): 90–92.

37. David Lipsky and Clifford Donn, *Collective Bargaining in American Industry* (Lexington, MA: Lexington Books, 1981).

38. *Statistics Canada*, "Perspectives in Labour and Income," 15, 3 (Autumn 2003): 50.

39. *Statistics Canada*, "Perspectives in Labour and Income," 15, 3 (Autumn 2003): 50.

40. *Statistics Canada*, Perspectives in Labour and Income," 15, 3 (Autumn 2003): 51.

41. Greg Keenan, "CAW Rewriting Playbook to Keep Factories Running," *The Globe and Mail*, September 5, 2006, p. B3.

42. Virginia Galt, "Worn-Out Middle Managers May Get Protection," *The Globe and Mail*, January 3, 2005, pp. B1, B8.

43. Paul Waldie, "How Health Costs Hurt the Big Three," *The Globe and Mail*, March 22, 2005, pp. B1–B2; Virginia Galt, "Companies, Unions Expect Little Relief," *The Globe and Mail*, September 15, 2004, p. B4.

44. Brent Jang, "CN Strike Takes Mounting Toll as Rail Delays Hit Manufacturers," *The Globe and Mail*, February 19, 2007, pp. B1, B8; Brent Jang, "CN Rail Strike Ends With Fragile Truce," *The Globe and Mail*, February 26, 2007, pp. B1, B3.

45. William Watson, "Strike Champs," *National Post*, May 24, 2007, p. FP15.

46. Jack Mintz, "The Perils of the Picket Line," *Canadian Business* (February 27–March 12, 2006): 15.

47. Alison Auld, "NS. Nurses Defy Strike Law," *The Globe and Mail*, June 28, 2001, pp. B1, B2.

48. Murray McNeill, "Hotel Workers Sever Relationship With Union," *The Winnipeg Free Press*, July 22, 2005, p. B14.

49. Martin Cash, "Tractor Plant Workers Locked Out," *Winnipeg Free Press*, March 28, 2001, p. B3; also Paul McKie, "A Bitter End at Versatile," *The Winnipeg Free Press*, August 14, 2001, pp. A1–A2.

Chapter 9

1. Virginia Galt, "Keeping Key Workers a Tougher Task," *The Globe and Mail*, October 25, 2005, p. B6.

2. Daniel Goleman, *Emotional Intelligence: Why It Can Matter More than IQ* (New York: Bantam Books, 1995); also Kenneth Law, chi-Sum Wong, and Lynda Song, "The Construct and Criterion Validity of Emotional Intelligence and Its Potential Utility for Management Studies," *Journal of Applied Psychology* (2004): 483–496.

3. Daniel Goleman, "Leadership That Gets Results," *Harvard Business Review* (March–April 2000): 78–90.

4. "A Better Workplace," *Time* (April 17, 2000): 87.

5. Stephanie Armour, "More Dads Tap into Family Benefits at Work," *USA Today*, June 16, 2000, p. 1B.

6. Employee-Friendly Workplaces Raises Issues for Unions," *The Globe and Mail*, December 27, 2000, pp. B1, B4.

7. Frederick W. Taylor, *Principles of Scientific Management* (New York: Harper and Brothers, 1911).

8. See Daniel Wren, *The History of Management Thought*, 5th ed. (New York: John Wiley & Sons, 2004).

9. Douglas McGregor, *The Human Side of Enterprise* (New York: McGraw-Hill, 1960).

10. Abraham Maslow, "A Theory of Human Motivation," *Psychological Review* (July 1943): 370–396.

11. Frederick Herzberg, Bernard Mausner, and Barbara Bloch Snydeman, *The Motivation to Work* (New York: Wiley, 1959).

12. Victor Vroom, *Work and Motivation* (New York: Wiley, 1964); Craig Pinder, *Work Motivation* (Glenview, IL: Scott, Foresman, 1984).

13. J. Stacy Adams, "Toward an Understanding of Inequity," *Journal of Abnormal and Social Psychology* 75, no. 5 (1963): 422–436.

14. Andy Holloway, "How the Game Is Played," *Canadian Business* (April 2, 2001): 26–35.

15. Edwin Locke, "Toward a Theory of Task Performance and Incentives," *Organizational Behavior and Human Performance*, 3 (1968): 157–189.

16. Interviews with Sterling McLeod and Wayne Walker, senior vice-presidents of sales for Investors Group Financial Services.

17. Wilfred List, "On the Road to Profit," *The Globe and Mail*, July 10, 1991, pp. B1, B3.

18. Virginia Galt, "Change Is a Good Thing When Everyone Is Involved," *The Globe and Mail*, June 25, 2005, p. B11.

19. Patricia Kitchen, "Tap Your Employees," *Orlando Sentinel*, March 14, 2007, p. F1.

20. Brent Jang, "High-Flying WestJet Morale Gets Put to the Test," *The Globe and Mail*, November 25, 2005, p. B3.

21. Russ Forrester, "Empowerment: Rejuvenating a Potent Idea," *Academy of Management Executive* (2002): 67–78.

22. Gregory Moorhead and Ricky W. Griffin, *Organizational Behavior*, 6th ed. (Boston: Houghton Mifflin, 2001), Chapter 7.

23. Ricky Griffin, *Task Design* (Glenview, IL: Scott, Foresman, 1982).

24. Richard J. Hackman and Greg Oldham, *Work Redesign* (Reading, MA: Addison-Wesley, 1980).

25. Virginia Galt, "More Firms Offering Flex-Time Options," *The Globe and Mail*, August 11, 2003, p. B9.

26. Virginia Galt, "Flex-Time Helps to Attract, Keep Best Workers," *The Winnipeg Free Press*, August 12, 2003, p. D7.

27. Margot Gibb-Clark, "Banks' Short Work Week Improves Service," *The Globe and Mail*, September 23, 1991, p. B4.

28. Virginia Galt, "More Firms Offering Flex-Time Options," *The Globe and Mail*, August 11, 2003, p. B9.

29. "Telecommuting Causing Work Condition Worries," *The Globe and Mail*, January 7, 2000, p. B8.

30. Margot Gibb-Clark, "What Shaped the Workplace in 1998," *The Globe and Mail*, December 29, 1998, p. B6.

31. Margot Gibb-Clark, "Satellite Office a Hit with Staff," *The Globe and Mail*, November 18, 1991, p. B4.

32. "Slaves of the New Economy," *Canadian Business* (April 1996): 86–92.

33. Dawn Walton, "Survey Focuses on Job Sharing," *The Globe and Mail*, June 10, 1997, p. B4.

34. Gordon Pitts, "Taking a Stand: How One CEO Gained Respect," *The Globe and Mail*, January 31, 2006, p. B8.

35. John Kotter, "What Leaders Really Do," *Harvard Business Review* (December 2001): 85–94.

36. Ronald Heifetz and Marty Linsky, "A Survival Guide for Leaders," *Harvard Business Review* (June 2002): 65–74.

37. Frederick Reichheld, "Lead for Loyalty," *Harvard Business Review* (July–August 2001): 76–83.

38. Daniel Goleman, "What Makes a Leader?" *Harvard Business Review* (November–December 1998): 93–99.

39. David Dorsey, "Andy Pearson Finds Love," *Fast Company* (August 2001): 78–86.

40. David A. Waldman and Francis J. Yammarino, "CEO Charismatic Leadership: Levels-of-Management and Levels-of-Analysis Effects," *Academy of Management Review* (1999): Vol. 24, 266–285.

41. Jane Howell and Boas Shamir, "The Role of Followers in the Charismatic Leadership Process: Relationships and Their Consequences," *Academy of Management Review* (January 2005): 96–112.

42. J. Richard Hackman and Ruth Wageman, "A Theory of Team Coaching," *Academy of Management Review* (April 2005): 269–287.

43. "How Women Lead," *Newsweek* (October 24, 2005): 46–70.

44. Sinclair Stewart, "Passed by at TD, CEO hits stride in New York, *The Globe and Mail*, December 5, 2006, pp. B1, B21.

45. Zena Olijnyk, Mark Brown, Andy Holloway, Calvin Leung, Alex Mlynek, Erin Pooley, Jeff Sanford, Andrew Wahl, and Thomas Watson, "Canada's Global Leaders," *Canadian Business* (March 28–April 10, 2005): 37–43.

46. Madelaine Drohan, "What Makes a Canadian Manager?" *The Globe and Mail*, February 25, 1997, p. B18.

Chapter 10

1. *Our Time: GE Annual Report*: 2004. Fairfield, CT. (General Electric Co., 2005): 4–5.

2. Judy Strauss and Raymond Frost, *Marketing on the Internet* (Upper Saddle River, NJ: Prentice Hall, 1999), 266–271.

3. Mark Lander, "Slovakia No Longer a Laggard in Automaking," nytimes.com, April 13, 2004, www.nytimes.com/2004/04/13/business/worldbusiness.

4. Christina Passariello, "Louis Vuitton Tries Modern Methods On Factory Lines," *The Wall Street Journal*, October 9, 2006, pp. A1, A15.

5. Neal Boudette, "Chrysler Gains Edge by Giving New Flexibility to Its Factories," *The Wall Street Journal*, April 11, 2006, pp. A1, A15.

6. Greg Keenan, "Ford's New Maxim: Flex Manufacturing," *The Globe and Mail*, May 10, 2006, p. B3.

7. Gordon Pitts, "Industrial Evolution," *The Globe and Mail*, May 29, 2006, pp. B1, B4.

8. Don Marshall, "Time for Just in Time," *P&IM Review* (June 1991): 20–22; Gregg Stocker, "Quality Function Deployment: Listening to the Voice of the Customer," *APICS: The Performance Advantage* (September 1991): 44–48.

9. "The Disney Institute," http://www.disney.go.com/DisneyWorld/DisneyInstitute/ProfessionalPrograms/DisneyDifference/index.html, April 25, 2000.

10. Bruce Little, "Stock Answers," *The Globe and Mail*, June 6, 1995, p. B12.

11. Steven Chase, "Border Foils 'Just-in-Time' Delivery," *The Globe and Mail*, June 15, 2007, pp. B1, B5.

12. Harvey Enchin, "Canada Urged to Stop Living Off Fat of the Land," *The Globe and Mail*, October 25, 1991, pp. B1, B6.

13. Jon Hilsenrath, "Behind Surging Productivity: The Service Sector Delivers," *The Wall Street Journal*, November 7, 2003, pp. A1, A8.

14. Peter Kennedy, "Canfor Goes High Tech to Cut Costs," *The Globe and Mail*, July 29, 2000, p. 3.

15. Nathan VanderKlippe, "Pulp Producers Squeezed," *Financial Post*, June 23, 2007, p. 3.

16. Lee J. Krajewski and Larry P. Ritzman, *Operations Management: Strategy and Analysis*, 5th ed. (Reading, MA: Addison-Wesley, 1999), 229–230.

17. Bruce McDougall, "The Thinking Man's Assembly Line," *Canadian Business* (November 1991): 40.

18. Ted Wakefield, "No Pain, No Gain," *Canadian Business* (January 1993): 50–54.

19. Thomas Foster Jr., *Managing Quality: An Integrative Approach* (Upper Saddle River, NJ: Prentice Hall, 2001), 325–339.

20. Thomas Foster Jr., *Managing Quality: An Integrative Approach* (Upper Saddle River, NJ: Prentice Hall, 2001), 325–329.

21. James Evans and James Dean Jr., *Total Quality: Management, Organization, and Strategy*, 2nd ed. (Cincinnati, OH: South-Western, 2000), 230.

22. Margot Gibb-Clark, "Hospital Managers Gain Tool to Compare Notes," *The Globe and Mail*, September 9, 1996, p. B9.

23. Del Jones, "Baldrige Award Honors Record 7 Quality Winners," *USA Today*, November 26, 2003, p. 6B.

24. "Customer Service You Can Taste," *Canadian Business* (July 1991): 19–20.

25. Roberta S. Russell and Bernard W. Taylor III, *Operations Management*, 4th ed. (Upper Saddle River, NJ: Prentice Hall, 2003), 658–662; and Thomas Foster Jr., *Managing Quality: An Integrative Approach* (Upper Saddle River, NJ: Prentice Hall, 2001), 85–86.

26. Roberta S. Russell and Bernard W. Taylor III, *Operations Management*, 4th ed. (Upper Saddle River, NJ: Prentice Hall, 2003), 137–140.

27. Sunil Chopra and Peter Meindl, *Supply Chain Management: Strategy, Planning, and Operation*, 6th ed. (Upper Saddle River, NJ: Prentice Hall, 2001), 3–6; Lee J. Krajewski and Larry P. Ritzman, *Operations Management: Strategy and Analysis*, 5th ed. (Reading, MA: Addison-Wesley, 1999), Chapter 11; Roberta S. Russell and Bernard W. Taylor III, *Operations Management*, 4th ed. (Upper Saddle River, NJ: Prentice Hall, 2003), Chapter 7; and Thomas Foster Jr., *Managing Quality: An Integrative Approach* (Upper Saddle River, NJ: Prentice Hall, 2001), Chapter 9.

28. Sunil Chopra and Peter Meindl, *Supply Chain Management: Strategy, Planning, and Operation*, 6th ed. (Upper Saddle River, NJ: Prentice Hall, 2001), Chapter 20.

29. Christina Passariello, "Louis Vuitton Tries Modern Methods On Factory Lines," *The Wall Street Journal*, October 9, 2006, pp. A1, A15.

Chapter 11

1. Ronald Hilton, *Managerial Accounting*, 2nd ed. (New York: McGraw-Hill, 1994), 7.

2. Brian Christmas, "Buttoned Down and In Demand," *The Globe and Mail*, April 19, 2006, p. B13.

3. Brian Christmas, "Buttoned Down and in Demand," *The Globe and Mail*, April 19, 2006, p. B13.

4. Brian Christmas, "Buttoned Down and in Demand," *The Globe and Mail*, April 19, 2006, p. B13.

5. Elizabeth MacDonald, "Accounting Sleuths Ferret Hidden Assets," *The Wall Street Journal*, December 18, 1996, pp. B1–B2.

6. Rebecca Dube, "Changing the Rules," *The Globe and Mail*, October 21, 2006, pp. B17–B18.

7. Charles T. Horngren, Walter T. Harrison Jr., and Linda Smith Bamber, *Accounting*, 5th ed. (Upper Saddle River, NJ: Prentice Hall, 2002), 11–12, 39–41.

8. Charles T. Horngren, Walter T. Harrison Jr., and Linda Smith Bamber, *Accounting*, 5th ed. (Upper Saddle River, NJ: Prentice Hall, 2002), 17–20.

9. Charles T. Horngren, Walter T. Harrison, Jr., and Linda Smith Bamber, *Accounting*, 4th ed. (Upper Saddle River, NJ: Prentice Hall, 1999), 201–202.

Chapter 12

1. American Marketing Association, "Marketing Services Guide," www.ama.org/about/ama/ markdef.asp, August 23, 2001.

2. Philip Kotler, *Marketing Management*, 11th ed. (Upper Saddle River, NJ: Prentice Hall, 2003), 76–78.

3. *Harley-Davidson Inc.: 1995 Annual Report* (Milwaukee: Harley-Davidson, 1995), 33; Philip Kotler, *Marketing Management: Analysis, Planning, Implementation, and Control*, 9th ed. (Upper Saddle River, NJ: Prentice Hall, 1997), 12–13, 48–51.

4. Philip Kotler, *Marketing Management: Analysis, Planning, Implementation, and Control*, 7th ed. (Upper Saddle River, NJ: Prentice Hall, 1991).

5. Philip Kotler and Peggy Cunningham, *Marketing Management* (Toronto: Prentice-Hall, 2004), 18.

6. Chris Isadore, "Sweet Spot: Luxury SUV's are Hot," *CNN/Money*, January 7, 2004, cnnmoney.com.

7. Aparita Bhandari, "Ethnic Marketing—It's More Than Skin Deep," *The Globe and Mail*, September 7, 2005, p. B3.

8. Lauren Goldstein, "Dressing Up an Old Brand," *Fortune* (November 9, 1998): 154–156.

9. Jane Perlez, "Joy of Debts: Eastern Europe on Credit Fling," *The New York Times*, May 30, 1998, p. A3.

10. Philip Kotler, *Marketing Management*, 11th ed. (Upper Saddle River, NJ: Prentice Hall, 2003), 292–294.

11. Marina Strauss, "The Secret to Gaining Success in Quebec," *The Globe and Mail*, September 27, 2005, p. B4.

12. Lauren Goldstein, "Dressing Up an Old Brand," *Fortune* (November 9, 1998): 154–156.

13. Barrie McKenna, "Coke Plans Major Revamp to Put Fizz Back in its Shares," *The Globe and Mail*, November 12, 2004, pp. B1, B6.

14. John Morton, "How to Spot the Really Important Prospects," *Business Marketing* (January 1990): 62–67.

15. Marina Strauss, "First You Have to Get Their Attention," *The Globe and Mail*, July 12, 1991, p. B1.

16. Emily Nelson, "P&G Checks Out Real Life," *The Wall Street Journal*, May 17, 2001, pp. B1, B4.

17. Joseph Pereira, "Spying on the Sales Floor," *The Wall Street Journal*, December 21, 2004, pp. B1, B4.

18. Alvin C. Burns and Ronald F. Bush, *Marketing Research*, 3rd ed. (Upper Saddle River, NJ: Prentice Hall, 2000), Chapter 9.

19. Marina Strauss, "Mining Customer Feedback, Firms Go Undercover and Online," *The Globe and Mail*, May 13, 2004, pp. B1, B25.

20. Deborah Ball, Sarah Ellison, and Janet Adamy, "Probing Shoppers' Psyche," *The Wall Street Journal*, October 28, 2004, pp. B1, B8.

21. Peter Morton, "Marketing at Face Value," *National Post*, July 11, 2007, p. FP3.

22. Emily Nelson, "P&G Checks Out Real Life," *The Wall Street Journal*, May 17, 2001, pp. B1, B4.

23. Robyn Greenspan, "The Web as a Way of Life," www.cyberatlas.com, May 21, 2002.

24. Thomas Russell, Glenn Verrill, an W. Ronald Lane, *Kleppner's Advertisir Procedure*, 11th ed. (Englewood Cliff NJ: Prentice-Hall, 1990); James Enge Martin Warshaw, and Thomas Kinne *Promotional Strategy*, 6th ed. (Homewood, IL: Richard D. Irwin, 1

Chapter 13

1. Patricia Lush, "From Pipe Dream Profit," *The Globe and Mail*, Decemb 1994, p. B6.

2. Simon Tuck, "Bombardier To Ga on New Jet," *The Globe and Mail*, March 16, 2005, pp. A1–A2; Bertrand Marotte, "Bombardier Shelves C Series," *The Globe and Mail*, February 1, 2006, pp. B1, B6.

3. Richard Blackwell, "High-Definition TV a Bit Fuzzy, Poll Finds," *The Globe and Mail*, May 2, 2005, p. B4; Catherine McLean, "Cool Reception for High Definition," *The Globe and Mail*, December 21, 2006, p. B3.

4. James C. Anderson and James A. Narus, *Business Market Management: Understanding, Creating, and Delivering Value* (Upper Saddle River, NJ: Prentice Hall, 1999), 203–206.

5. Philip Kotler, *Marketing Management*, 11th ed. (Upper Saddle River, NJ: Prentice Hall, 2003), 328–339.

6. Keith McArthur, "What's 10 Years Old and Worth More than Coke?" *The Globe and Mail*, April 24, 2007, p. B5.

7. Other bases can also be used to rank brands. For example, in the 2007 Brand Finance Canada rankings, financial assets are an important consideration. The top three Canadian brands in their list were RBC, TD, and Manulife Financial.

8. Gordon Pitts, "New Irving Generation Broadens Horizons," *The Globe and Mail*, January 18, 2003, pp. B1, B4.

9. John Gray, "What's in a Brand?" *Canadian Business* (December 26, 2005–

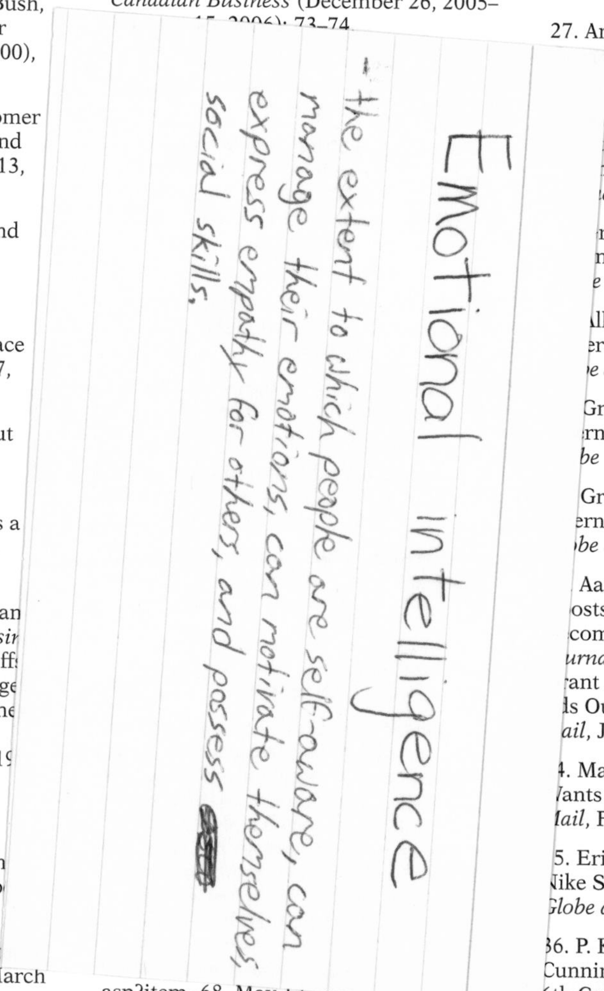
Emotional intelligence
- the extent to which people are self-aware, can
manage their emotions, can motivate themselves,
express empathy for others, and possess
social skills.

asp?item=68, May 17, 2001.

18. Eloise Coupey, *Marketing and the Internet* (Upper Saddle River, NJ: Prentice Hall, 2001), 174–179.

19. John Frook, "Cisco Scores with Its Latest Generation of Empowering Tools," *B to B* (August 20, 2001): 20.

20. David Square, "Mouse Pad Gets Oodles of Nibbles," *The Winnipeg Free Press*, July 26, 1997, p. B10.

21. Paul Waldie, "How RIM's Big Deal Was Done," *The Globe and Mail*, March 6, 2006, pp. B1, B14.

22. Deborah Ball, "The Perils of Packaging: Nestle Aims for Easier Openings," *The Wall Street Journal*, November 17, 2005, pp. B1, B5.

23. Keith McArthur, "Oh? Canada? Ads Beg to Differ," *The Globe and Mail*, July 1, 2004, pp. B1, B18.

24. Robert Berner, "The Rolls-Royce of Leather Jackets Is Hard to Come By," *The Wall Street Journal*, November 22, 1996, pp. A1, A10.

25. John Heinzl, "Buckley Wants U.S. to Swallow Its Bad Taste," *The Globe and Mail*, November 11, 1999, pp. B1, B12.

26. Grant Robertson, "Growth in Internet Ads Outpaces All Others," *The Globe and Mail*, June 23, 2006, p. B4.

27. Andrew Wahl, "Red All Over," *ian Business* (February 13–26, 53–54.

ron O. Patrick, "Technology s Outdoor Ads as Competition nes Fiercer," *The Wall Street al*, August 28, 2006, pp. A1, A10.

rant Robertson, "Growth in net Ads Outpaces All Others," *The e and Mail*, June 23, 2006, p. B4.

llan Kreda, "Advertisers Lured by er Bowl's Glitz, Huge Ratings," *The e and Mail*, December 30, 2004, p. B3.

Grant Robertson, "Growth in rnet Ads Outpaces All Others," *The be and Mail*, June 23, 2006, p. B4.

Grant Robertson, "Growth in ernet Ads Outpaces All Others," *The be and Mail*, June 23, 2006, p. B4.

Aaron O. Patrick, "Technology osts Outdoor Ads As Competition comes Fiercer," *The Wall Street urnal*, August 28, 2006, pp. A1, A10; ant Robertson, "Growth in Internet ls Outpaces All Others," *The Globe and ail*, June 23, 2006, p. B4.

4. Marina Strauss, "This Billboard ants to Pass You By," *The Globe and ail*, February 27, 1992, p. B4.

5. Erin White, "Word of Mouth Makes Nike Slip-On Sneakers Take Off," *The Globe and Mail*, June 7, 2001, pp. B1, B4.

36. P. Kotler, G. Armstrong, and P. Cunningham, *Principles of Marketing*, 6th Canadian ed. (Toronto: Pearson, 2005), 88.

37. Aaron O. Patrick, "Technology Boosts Outdoor Ads As Competition Becomes Fiercer," *The Wall Street Journal*, August 28, 2006, pp. A1, A10.

38. Keith McArthur, "Internet Advertising in Canada Surpasses the $1 Billion Mark," *The Globe and Mail*, April 30, 2007, p. B3.

39. Andrew Wahl, "Red All Over," *Canadian Business* (February 13–26, 2006): 53–54.

40. P. Kotler, G. Armstrong, and P. Cunningham, *Principles of Marketing*, 6th Canadian ed. (Toronto: Pearson, 2005), 89–91.

41. Simon Tuck, "Security Rated Top On-Line Fear," *The Globe and Mail*, July 5, 1999, p. B5.

42. James Hagerty and Dennis Berman, "New Battleground in Web Privacy War: Ads that Snoop," *The Wall Street Journal*, August 27, 2003, pp. A1, A8.

43. Stuart Elliott, "Real or Virtual? You Call It," *The New York Times*, October 1, 1999, pp. C1, C6.

44. Amol Sharma, "Companies Vie For Ad Dollars on Mobile Web," *The Wall Street Journal*, January 17, 2007, pp. A1, A17.

45. "Regulators Wary of Ads Rapping Rivals," *The Globe and Mail*, May 23, 1991, p. B4.

46. Ira Teinowitz and Cara B. Dipasquale, "Direct Marketers Take Issue with Proposed FTC Rules," *Advertising Age* (January 28, 2002): 3, 29; Larry Neilson, "Look Out for Telemarketing Speed Bumps," *National Underwriter* (September 17, 2001): 12–14.

47. John Heinzl, "Beer Firms Rethink Giveaways," *The Globe and Mail*, March 3, 2003, pp. B1, B5.

48. Joanna Slater, "Coke, Pepsi Fight Product-Contamination Charges in India," *The Wall Street Journal*, August 15, 2003, pp. B1, B4.

49. Warren J. Keegan, *Global Marketing Management*, 7th ed. (Upper Saddle River, NJ: Prentice Hall, 2002), Chapter 14.

50. Richard Bloom, "Cossette Scarfs McDonald's Global French Fry Contract," *The Globe and Mail*, December 5, 2003, p. B9.

Chapter 14

1. Stefan Fatsis, "The Barry Bonds Tax: Teams Raise Prices for Good Games," *The Wall Street Journal*, December 3, 2002, pp. D1, D8.

2. Leila Abboud and Jenny Clevstrom, "Swedes Try Toll Plan to Unsnarl Traffic," *The Globe and Mail*, August 29, 2006, p. B10; Lawrence Solomon, "Sweden Proves Congestion Tolls Work," *National Post*, August 4, 2007, p. FP13.

3. Lawrence Solomon, "Revolution on the Road: Pay-Per-Mile Insurance," *National Post*, October 14, 2006, p. FP15.

4. Stephen Kindel, "Tortoise Gains on Hare," *Financial World* (February 23, 1988): 18–20.

5. Judy Strauss and Raymond Frost, *E-Marketing*, 2nd ed. (Upper Saddle River, NJ: Prentice Hall, 2001), 166–167; Eloise Coupey, *Marketing and the Internet* (Upper Saddle River, NJ: Prentice Hall, 2001), 281–283.

6. Judy Strauss, Adel El-Ansary, and Raymond Frost. *E-Marketing*, 3rd ed. (Upper Saddle River, NJ: Prentice Hall, 2003), 320–323.

7. "Odd Prices Hurt Image of Prices," *Business Month* (July 1987): 23.

8. Paul Waldie, "Battle Over Real Estate Listings Spurs Probe," *The Globe and Mail*, March 26, 2007, pp. B1–B2.

9. Marina Strauss, "Taking 'e' Out of E-commerce: Meet the eBay Middleman," *The Globe and Mail*, October 6, 2004, pp. B1, B19.

10. Expedia.com, June 23, 2005, at www.expedia.com.

11. Ann Bednarz, "Acquisitions Tighten Supply-Chain Market," *Network World* (February 9, 2004): 21–22.

12. Marina Strauss, "E-tailing in Age of Refinement," *The Globe and Mail*, August 3, 2005, p. B6.

13. "Did You Know?" *Catalog News.com*, www.catalog-news.com, April 8, 2002; Judy Strauss and Raymond Frost, *E-Marketing*, 2nd ed. (Upper Saddle River, NJ: Prentice Hall, 2001), 140.

14. Zena Olijnyk, "Dot-Com wonder Boys, *Canadian Business* (April 14, 2003): 30–36.

15. Michelle MacAfee, "More Canadians Going Online for Shopping," *The Globe and Mail*, November 2, 2006, p. B9; Marina Strauss, "No Thanks, Just Browsing, Online Shoppers Say, *The Globe and Mail*, December 22, 2006, pp. B1, B4.

16. Gordon Jaremko, "River Highway in Canada's North Open for Business," *The Winnipeg Free Press*, July 25, 2006, p. B10.

Chapter 15

1. Andrew Higgins, "Lacking Money to Pay, Russian Firms Survive on Deft Barter System," *The Wall Street Journal*, August 27, 1998, pp. A1, A6.

2. *Bank of Canada Banking and Financial Statistics*, Table E1 (April 2006): S50.

3. John Partridge, "Phony $10, $20 Bills Rampant in '04," *The Globe and Mail*, March 15, 2005, p. B5.

4. "Counterfeit Coppers Fear Explosion of Funny Money," *The Winnipeg Free Press*, November 20, 2006, p. A9.

5. Omar El Akkad, "Canada's $5 Bill Offers New Security Features, "*The Globe and Mail*, April 5, 2006, p. B5.

6. *Bank of Canada Banking and Financial Statistics*, Table E1 (April 2006): S50.

7. Geoff Kirbyson, "Stop Taking Credit," *The Winnipeg Free Press*, October 22, 2006, pp. E1, E6.

8. *Bank of Canada Banking and Financial Statistics*, Table C1 (May 2006): S-1.

9. Tara Perkins and Tavia Grant, "You Can Make a Lot of Money in This Business," *The Globe and Mail*, April 23, 2007, p. B6.

10. Geoff Kirbyson, "Stop Taking Credit," *The Winnipeg Free Press*, October 22, 2006, pp. E1, E6.

11. "Statistics for Smart Cards," ePaynews.com (June 14, 2004), www.epaynews.com/statistics/scardstats.html.

12. Nancy Carr, "More Canadians Turning to Alternative Banks," *The Winnipeg Free Press*, July 21, 2003, p. B7.

13. Karen Horcher, "Reconstruction Zone," *CGA Magazine* (June 1997): 19.

14. Andrew Willis, "American VC Firms Trouncing Canadians At Home," *The Globe and Mail*, June 13, 2005, pp. B1, B3.

15. Andrew Willis, "CIBC Leads Underwriting Pack for Fourth Year," *The Globe and Mail*, January 26, 2005, p. B7.

16. Andrew Willis, "RBC Dominion King of the Debt Dealers," *The Globe and Mail*, January 26, 2005, p. B7.

17. Robert J. Carbaugh, *International Economics*, 5th ed. (Cincinnati: South-Western, 1995), Chapter 11.

18. Louise Lee and Lauren Young, "Is Schwab's Latest Come-On Enough?" *Business Week* (June 7, 2004): 44.

19. Lee and Young, "Is Schwab's Latest Come-on Enough?" 44; Theresa W. Carey, "Online Trading Revives," *Barron's* (February 28, 2005): T6.

20. Richard Blackwell, "TSE Sees Few Gains from Realignment," *The Globe and Mail*, May 23, 2000, p. 12.

21. Gordon J. Alexander, William F. Sharpe, and Jeffery V. Bailey, *Fundamentals of Investments*, 3rd ed. (Upper Saddle River, NJ: Prentice Hall, 2001), 36–39.

22. Geoffrey York and Sinclair Stewart, "China's Market Myths," *The Globe and Mail*, March 3, 2007, p. B4.

23. *NASDAQ*, www.nasdaq.com/ about/ timeline.stm, June 25, 2000.

24. Keith Damsell, "Ethical Investing Proving a Hard Sell in Canada," *The Globe and Mail*, August 12, 2004, p. B10.

25. Rob Carrick, "Tread Carefully in the World of Hedge Funds," *The Globe and Mail*, May 27, 2006, p. B8

26. Paul Waldie and Sinclair Stewart, "Hedge Funds in the Crosshairs," *The Globe and Mail*, May 30, 2005, p. B4; Sinclair Stewart and Paul Waldie, "The New Breed of 800-Pound Gorilla," *The Globe and Mail*, May 31, 2005, p. B7.

27. Richard Blackwell, "TSE 300 Shift Will Shrink Index," *The Globe and Mail*, January 31, 2002, B17.

28. Rob Carrick, "Direct Plans Cut Brokers Out," *The Globe and Mail*, August 21, 1999, p. B8.

29. Richard Mackie, "Ontario Pursues Single Regulator," *The Globe and Mail*, December 22, 2003, pp. B1, B4.

30. Karen Howlett, "Overhaul of Securities Industry Urged," *The Globe and Mail*, December 18, 2003, pp. B1, B20.

Chapter 16

1. *The State of Small Business, 1989 Annual Report on Small Business in Ontario* (Toronto: Ministry of Industry, Trade and Technology, 1990).

2. J.W. Duncan, *D&B Reports* (September–October 1991): 8.

3. E.F. Brigham, *Fundamentals of Financial Management*, 5th ed. (Chicago: Dryden, 1989).

4. Norman M. Scarborough and Thomas W. Zimmerer, *Effective Small Business Management: An Entrepreneurial Approach*, 6th ed. (Upper Saddle River, NJ: Prentice Hall, 2000), 298–300.

5. Susan Hodges, "One Big Step Toward a Loan," *Nation's Business* (August 1997): 34–36.

6. Richard S. Boulton, Barry D. Libert, and Steve M. Samek, "Managing Risk in an Uncertain World," *Upside* (June 2000): 268–278.

7. Thomas Watson, "Risky Business," *Canadian Business* (October 23–November 5, 2006): 153, 154, 156.

8. Thomas P. Fitch, *Dictionary of Banking Terms*, 2nd ed. (Hauppauge, NY: Barron's, 1993), 531.

Appendix A

1. See Chris Arthur J. Keown, *Personal Finance*, 3rd ed. (Upper Saddle River, NJ: Pearson Prentice Hall, 2004), 600–609.

2. Christopher Farrell, "No Need to Hit the Panic Button," *Business Week* (July 26, 2004): 76–84.

Appendix B

1. Mike Lazaridis, "Because Someone Had to Stand Up for All Those Frustrated Engineers," *Inc. Magazine* (April 2005): 98; "BlackBerry Subscribers Surge to over Three Million," May 9, 2005.

2. "Northrop Grumman Awards International Contracts for F-35 Joint Strike Fighter," *Northrop Grumman News Release* (September 29, 2005) at www.irconnect.com/noc/pages/news_printer.html?=86963&print=1; Faith Keenan and Spencer E. Ante, "The New Teamwork," *BusinessWeekOnline*, February 18, 2002.

3. Emily Walzer, "Have it Your Way," *SGB*, vol. 38, no. 1 (January 2005): 42.

4. 3D Systems, "3D Systems Helps Walter Reed Army Medical Center Rebuild Lives" (July 6, 2005), at www.3dsystems.com.

5. "Wireless Endoscopy—The Camera in a Pill" (August 17, 2005), at www.gihealth.com; "Expanding the Scope of GI," Given Imaging (July 6, 2005), at www.givenimaging.com.

6. "An Intranet's Life Cycle," *morebusiness.com* (November 6, 2005), at www.morebusiness.com/getting_started/website/d928247851.brc; "Calling all Workers," *CIO Magazine* (December 1, 2001), at www.cio.com/archive/120101/rule_ford.html.

7. William Bulkeley, "Better Virtual Meetings, "*The Wall Street Journal*, September 28, 2006, pp. B1, B5.

8. See James A. Senn, *Information Technology: Principles, Practices, Opportunities*, 3rd ed. (Upper Saddle River, NJ: Prentice Hall, 2004), 294–97.

9. Geoffrey Rowan, "Unique Software Thinks Like a Human," *The Globe and Mail*, December 31, 1996, pp. B1, B4.

10. Kenneth C. Laudon and Jane P. Laudon, *Essentials of Management Information Systems*, 3rd ed. (Upper Saddle River, NJ: Prentice-Hall, 1999), 383–388; E. Wainwright Martin, et al. *Managing Information Technology: What Managers Need to Know*, 3rd ed. (Upper Saddle River, NJ: Prentice-Hall, 1999), 225–227.

11. Emily Smith, "Turning an Expert's Skills into Computer Software," *Business Week* (October 7, 1985): 104–107.

12. U.S. Department of Justice, "Hacker Sentenced to Prison for Breaking into Lowe's Companies' Computers with Intent to Steal Credit Card Information," (Charlotte, NC: Department of Justice, Western District of North Carolina), December 15, 2004.

13. Hiawatha Bray, "Music Industry Aims to Send in Radio Cops," *Boston Globe* (November 15, 2004) at www.boston.com/business/technology/articles/2004/11/15/music_industry_aims_to_send_in_radio_cops?mode=PF; "Bush Creates Intellectual Property Czar," Patent Baristas (July 28, 2005) at www. patentbaristas.com/archives/000217.php; Howard Paul, "What You Cannot Protect, You Cannot Own," *Sai Global* (January 29, 2004), at www.sai-global.com/newsroom/tgs/2004-02/digital/digital.htm.

14. For information on spyware see www.webopedia.com/TERM/S/spyware.html.

15. www.webopedia.com.

16. "ISP Wins $1 Billion in Spam Suit," *CNET News.com* (December 19, 2004) at http://news.com.com/2102-1028_3-5497211.html?tag-st.util.print; Mike Wendland, "Innocents Suffer in War on Spam," *Detroit Free Press* (July 11, 2003), at www.freep.com/cgi-bin/forms/printerfriendly.pl.

17. Allison Jones, "Verification Revamp Urged Vs. Net Fraud," *The Winnipeg Free Press*, October 19, 2006, p. B10.

18. Jason Stein, "Madison, Wis., Company Offers Software that Protects Clients' Information," *The Wisconsin State Journal Distributed by Knight Ridder/Tribune Business News*, July 20, 2005, 1.

Source Notes

Chapter 1

Canadian Megaprojects Romina Maurino, "Wave of Consolidation Isn't Over Yet," *The Winnipeg Free Press*, December 26, 2006, p. B6; Wendy Stueck, "Vindication of Voisey's Bay," *The Globe and Mail*, September 3, 2005, p. B4; Dave Ebner, "CNQ Bets $25 Billion on Oil Sands," *The Globe and Mail*, November 3, 2005, pp. B1, B6; Patrick Brethour, "Alberta's Earth-Shaking Ambitions," *The Globe and Mail*, April 4, 2005, pp. B4–B5; Wendy Stueck, "Voisey's Bay at Last Getting Off the Ground," *The Globe and Mail*, June 17, 2004, pp. B1, B4; Wendy Stueck, "Nickel Prices Continue to Shine" *The Globe and Mail*, October 13, 2003; Wendy Stueck, "Inco Shares Fall on Voisey's Overrun," *The Globe and Mail*, March 21, 2003, p. B13; Allan Robinson, "Inco, Province Inch Toward Deal on Voisey's Bay," *The Globe and Mail*, October 12, 2001, p. B3; James Stevenson, "Inco Grilled Despite Impressive Rebound," *The Winnipeg Free Press*, April 20, 2000, p. B7; "Giant Newfoundland Nickel Project May Soon Proceed," *The Winnipeg Free Press*, November 23, 1999, p. B8; Allan Robinson, "Inco President Willing to Compromise on Voisey's Bay," *The Globe and Mail*, April 29, 1999, pp. B1, B4; Allan Robinson, "Inco to Halt Voisey's Bay Work," *The Globe and Mail*, July 28, 1998, pp. B1, B6; Allan Robinson, "Inco Chairman Defends Actions," *The Globe and Mail*, April 23, 1998, p. B3. **Business Accountability: Whatever Happened to Communism?** Mike Williams, "Private Enterprise in Cuba," *National Post*, May 28, 2007, p. FP3; Andres Oppenheimer, "Latin America Is Skeptical," *The Orlando Sentinel*, February 20, 2006, p. A19; Bradley Martin, "Hermit Kingdom Mixes Stalin, Profits," *The Globe and Mail*, December 29, 2005, pp. B1, B8; James Kynge, "Private Firms' Growth in China Striking: Report," *National Post*, May 11, 2000, p. C14; Howard French, "On the Street, Cubans Fondly Embrace Capitalism," *The New York Times*, February 3, 1994, p. A4. **Entrepreneurship and New Ventures: Putting Canadian Lentils on the International Map** Bruce Johnstone, "Al-Katib Wins Another Laurel," *The Leader-Post* (Regina), October 18, 2005, p. B6, material reprinted with the express permission of Regina Leader Post Group Inc., a CanWest Partnership; also supplemented with news article on the company's website: http://www.saskcan.com/news.html; also Business Development Bank of Canada website: http://www.bdc.ca/en/about/events_publications/young_entrepreneur_awards/award_ceremony_2005.htm; also http://www.bdc.ca/en/about/mediaroom/news_releases/2005/2005101811.htm. **Business Case 1: Supply and Demand: Some Practical Lessons** Claudia Carpenter and Millie Munshi,

"Palladium's Time To Shine," *National Post*, May 22, 2007, p. FP9; Neil Reynolds, "'Peak Oil' Doomsayers Fall Silent as Reserves Grow Ever Larger," *The Globe and Mail*, April 11, 2007, p. B2; Elizabeth Holmes, "Palladium, Platinum's Cheaper Sister, Makes a Bid for Love," *The Wall Street Journal*, February 13, 2007, pp. B1–B2; David Parkinson, "Platinum Supplies Limit Prospect of ETF," *The Globe and Mail*, November 22, 2006, p. B13; Patrick Brethour, "Peak Oil Theorists Don't Know Jack," *The Globe and Mail*, September 6, 2006, pp. B1, B6; Barrie McKenna, "Welcome to the Age of Scarcity," *The Globe and Mail*, May 21, 2005, p. B15; Harris Anwar, "Are Saudi Reserves Drying Up?" *The Globe and Mail*, May 21, 2005, p. B19; Peter Tertzakian, "Canada: Energy Superpower?" *The Globe and Mail*, May 28, 2005, p. B6; Michael Lynch, "Oil Discovery Forecasts Doomed," *The Globe and Mail*, May 28, 2005, p. B6; John Heinzl, "Now's a Good Time to cut Back on that Coffee Drinking Habit," *The Globe and Mail*, February 25, 2005, p. B10; "Price of Oil Spurts to $42.90 a Barrel," *USA Today*, July 29, 2004, p. 1B; "Higher and Higher—Again: Gasoline Prices Set Record," *USA Today*, May 25, 2004, p. 1B; Brad Foss, "Drivers Pay Price for Imported Gas," Associated Press Wire Story, May 22, 2004; Allan Sloan, "Why $2 Gas Isn't the Real Energy Problem," *Newsweek* (May 24, 2004): 40; Gregory L. White, "How Ford's Big Batch of Rare Metal Led to $1 Billion Write-Off," *The Wall Street Journal*, February 6, 2002, pp. A1, A6.

Chapter 2

Productivity and the Standard of Living Heather Scoffield, "Standard-of-Living Gap with U.S. Closing," *The Globe and Mail*, March 27, 2007, p. B3; Heather Scoffield, "Equality 'Myth' Seen Holding Canada Back," *The Globe and Mail*, January 18, 2007, p. B5; Virginia Galt, "Laid-Back Canadians? Not On Your Life," *The Globe and Mail*, December 23, 2006, p. B9; Virginia Galt, "Productivity Buckling Under the Strain of Stress, CEO's Say," *The Globe and Mail*, June 9, 2005, pp. B1, B15; John Partridge, "Several Causes Seen Possible for 'Unprecedented' Productivity Gap," *The Globe and Mail*, June 24, 2005, p. B6; "Canada Lags in Productivity, Investment: Study," *The Winnipeg Free Press*, October 19, 2005, p. B12; Gordon Pitts, "Ottawa's New, Improved Mantra: Productivity," The *Globe and Mail*, October 3, 2005, pp. B1, B6; Simon Tuck, "Canada's Standard of Living Takes Downturn," *The Globe and Mail*, March 3, 2005, pp. B1, B9; Jacquie McNish, "'Mediocre' Report Card says Canada not Making the Grade," *The Globe and Mail*, October 4, 2004, pp. B1, B10; Bruce Little, "Board Warns Productivity Must Rise," *The Globe and Mail*, October 5, 2004, p. B3; "Canada's Standard of Living," *National Post Business*, June, 2003, pp. 19–20; Pierre Fortin, "Differences in Annual Work Hours per Capita Between the United States and Canada," *International Productivity Monitor* (Spring 2003): 38–46; Frank Graves and Richard Jenkins, "Canadian Attitudes Towards Productivity: Balancing Standard of Living and Quality of Life," *The Review of Economic Performance and Social Progress* (2002): 243–258; Andrew Sharpe, "Why Are Americans More Productive Than Canadians?" *International Productivity Monitor* (Spring 2003): 19–37; Pierre Fortin, "Canadian Productivity: When Do We Catch Up?" *ISUMA* (Spring 2002). **Figure 2.3** 2005 data is from the *Bank of Canada Banking and Financial Statistics*, Table H8, May, 2006, S-102–103. **Figure 2.4** *Bank of Canada Banking and Financial Statistics*, Table H5, May, 2006, S-99. **Figure 2.5** Statistics Canada, Industrial Research and Development, 2005 *Intentions*, 13. **Business Accountability: Outsourcing: Good or Bad?** Barrie McKenna, "Offshoring May Not Be The Real Job Killer," *The Globe and Mail*, May 22, 2007, p. B8; John Partridge, "Agency Predicts Further Outsourcing," *The Globe and Mail*, April 26, 2005, p. B5; Norihiko Shirouzu, "Big Three's Outsourcing Plan: Makes Parts Suppliers Do It," *The Wall Street Journal*, June 10, 2004, pp. A1, A6; Lee J. Krajewski and Larry P. Ritzman, *Operations Management: Strategy and Analysis*, 6th ed. (Upper Saddle River, NJ: Prentice Hall, 2002), 102–106. **Business Case 2: Corporate Reputations: Mixed Evidence** Ronald Alsop, "How Boss's Deeds Buff A Firm's Reputation," *The Wall Street Journal*, January 31, 2007, pp. B1–B2; Gordon Pitts, "The RBC Dynasty Continues," *The Globe and Mail*, January 30, 2006.

Chapter 3

The Price of Bad Behaviour Mary Vallis, Barbara Shecter, and Theresa Tedesco, "Former Press Baron Faces 20 Years in Jail," *National Post*, July 14, 2007, pp. FW1, FW11; James Bagnall, "Enron Verdict Sends CEO's Strong Message," *The Winnipeg Free Press*, May 27, 2006, p. B10; Mark Maremont, "Tyco Ex-Officials Get Jail Terms, Big Fines," *The Wall Street Journal*, September 20, 2005, pp. C1, C4; Simon Houpt and Shawn McCarthy, "Ebbers' Storied Career Ends With Record-Fraud Conviction," *The Globe and Mail*, March 16, 2005, pp. B1, B7; Peter Brieger, "$2.4 Billion Gets CIBC out of Class Action," *The Winnipeg* Free Press, August 3, 2005, p. B7; Paul Waldie and Richard Blackwell, "Several Charges Against Drabinsky Dropped," *The Globe and Mail*, September 23, 2005, p. B5; Karen Howlett, "Livent's Auditors Charged With Misconduct," *The Globe and Mail*, April 6, 2004, pp. B1, B4; Barbara Shecter, "Black's $80 Million Fraud Charges," *The Winnipeg Free Press*, November 18, 2005, pp. A1, A4; Shawn McCarthy, "The Case Against Black," *The Globe and Mail*, November 18, 2005, pp. B1, B6; Jacquie McNish, "How the OSC Tipped the Scales on Rankin," *The Globe and Mail*, November 2, 2005, p. B13; Shirley Won, "Rankin Gets Six Months in Jail," *The Globe and Mail*, October 28, 2005, pp. B1, B16; Elena Cherney, "Radler Pleas May Trigger Showdown," *The Globe and Mail*, September 19, 2005, p. B4; Sinclair Stewart, "RBC Pays Enron to Resolve Lawsuit," *The Globe and Mail*, July 29, 2005, pp. B1–B2; Paul Waldie, "Black's Right-Hand Man Pleads Guilty to Fraud," *The Globe and Mail*, September 21, 2005, pp. A1, A7; Jacquie McNish and Shirley Won, "OSC Wins Trading Case Against Andrew Rankin," *The Globe and Mail*, July 16, 2005, pp. B1, B3; Gillian Livingston, "Scandal Hits Canada," *The Globe and Mail*, October 23, 2002, p. B3; David Wessel, "Why the Bad Guys of the Boardroom Emerged en Masse," *The Wall Street Journal*, June 20, 2002, pp. A1, A6; Barrie McKenna, "Andersen Hit with Charges," *The Globe and Mail*, March 15, 2002, pp. B1, B4. **Business Accountability: Crossing the Ethical Line?** Andrew Willis and Sinclair Stewart, "Two Years On, Genuity Hits Its Stride," *The Globe and Mail*, February 9, 2007, p. B; Andrew Willis, "CIBC Puts Ethics on the Line," *The Globe and Mail*, January 8, 2005, p. B2; Sinclair Stewart, "CIBC Sues 6 Former Employees, Alleges they Took confidential Data, Recruited Colleagues to Upstart Genuity," *The Globe and Mail*, January 6, 2005, pp. B1, B4; Andrew Willis, "CIBC Sues 6 Former Employees, Lawsuit Makes Both Parties Look Bad—But the Bank Gets the Worst of the Deal," *The Globe and Mail*, January 6, 2005, pp. B1, B13. **Figure 3.1** Guiding principles of Great-West Life Assurance Company, Winnipeg, Manitoba. Reproduced with permission. **Figure 3.2** David P. Baron, *Business and Its Environment*, 4th ed. (Upper Saddle River, NJ: Prentice Hall, 2003), 768. **Entrepreneurship and New Ventures: Mountain Equipment Co-Op** Ralph Shaw, "Peak Performance: Mountain Equipment Co-op Has a Better Way of Climbing," *Alternatives Journal*, Vol. 31, Issue 1 (Jan/Feb 2005): 19–20, reprinted with permission from *Alternatives Journal*, 31:1 (2005), www.alternativesjournal.ca and Ralph Shaw. **Figure 3.3** Based on Andrew C. Revkin, "Who Cares about a Few Degrees?" *The New York Times*, December 12, 1997, p. F1. **Business Case 3: High Seas Dumping** Bill McAllister, "Alaska Still Out Front on Environmental Monitoring," *The Juneau Empire*, May 29, 2004; Marilyn Adams, "Former Carnival Exec Says He Was Fired for Helping Federal Inquiry," *USA Today*, November 8–10, 2003; Adams, "Cruise-Ship Dumping Poisons Seas, Frustrates U.S. Enforcers," *USA Today*, November 8–10, 2003; Michael Connor,

"Norwegian Cruise Line Pleads Guilty in Pollution Case," Reuters, December 7, 2002; "What Is a Dead Zone?" *Oceana Interactive* (June 10, 2004), at www.oceana.org/index.cfm? sectionID 511&fuseaction59#25.

Chapter 4

Stepping Up Robeez Footwear Ltd. website:http://www.robeez.com/en-us/about/sandra.htm?PriceCat=1& Lang= EN-US; Rebecca Gardiner, "It Pays to Be Nice," *Profit* 24, no. 6 (December 2005): 23. Courtesy of Robeez Footwear Ltd. (www.robeez.com) and *Profit* Magazine. **Figures 4.1, 4.2, and 4.3** Adapted from Statistics Canada *Business Register*, June 2005. **Figures 4.4 and 4.5** Adapted from Statistics Canada, *Survey of Employment, Payrolls and Hours (SEPH)*, March 2005, and calculations by Industry Canada. Industry data are classified in accordance with the North American Industry Classification System (NAICS). **Entrepreneurship and New Ventures: A Web-Hosting Vision** Rick Spence, "The Fastest Five," *Profit* 24, no. 3, (June 2005): 49. Reprinted by permission of Rick Spence. Retrieved May 14, 2006, from ABI/INFORM Global database. (Document ID: 856224751); BDC website, http://www.bdc.ca/en/about/mediaroom/news_releases/2005/2005101808.htm, accessed June 12, 2006. **Table 4.2** *Financial Post Business*, Special Edition, 2006, p. 64. **Business Accountability: Getting on Boards** "Report on Business Corporate Governance Rankings," *The Globe and Mail*, October 17, 2005, p. B5; Louis Lavelle, "The Best and Worst Boards," *Business Week* (April 7, 2004); Stefani Eads, "Why Amazon's Board is Part of the Problem," *Business Week* (April 7, 2004); "Mixing It Up," *Corporate Board Member* (November/December, 2003); Jacquie McNish, "Onex Chief Ripped for Appointing Wife," *The Globe and Mail*, May 9, 2003, pp. B1, B7; Jennifer Reingold, "Dot.Com Boards are Flouting the Rules," *Business Week* (December 20, 2003); Janet McFarland, "How ROB Created the Rating System," *The Globe and Mail*, October 7, 2002, p. B6. **Business Case 4: Getting in on the Ground Floor** Marlene Cartash, "My Best Sale: Asked to Recall the Defining Moment of their Selling Careers, 10 Celebrated Entrepreneurs Cited Gutsy Moves that Still Fill Them with Pride," *Profit* 13, no. 4, (1995): 34–41; Bruce Erskine, "Gibson got in on ground floor," *The Halifax Herald Limited*, Wednesday, April 26, 2006. Retrieved July 3, 2006 from http://www.thechronicleherald.ca/external/bbi/index11.html. Republished with permission from The Halifax Herald Limited.

Chapter 5

Canadian Exporters: Opportunities and Problems Gordon Pitts, "Manulife's Army of Agents on the March for Middle Class," *The Globe and Mail*, October 23, 2004, p. B4; Rick Cash, "Dealing with the Dragon," *The Globe and Mail*, October 23, 2004, P. B3; Stephanie Nolen, "McCain Learns Tough Cultural Lesson on South Africa," *The Globe and Mail*, October 21, 2004, pp. B1, B19; Bertrand Marotte, "Coutu Takes on Fortress Retail, U.S.A.," *The Globe and Mail*, September 4, 2004, p. B5; Gordon Pitts, "Learn This Mantra: Customer is King in China," *The Globe and Mail*, July 12, 2004, pp. B1, B5; Gordon Pitts, "McCain Boss Picks up Pace of Global French Fry Assault," *The Globe and Mail*, June 14, 2004, pp. B1, B12; John Heinzl, "China Feasts on Canada's Resources," *The Globe and Mail*, May 22, 2004, p. B6; Oliver Bertin, "Firms Face Major Hurdles En Route to U.S. Markets," *The Globe and Mail*, April 29, 2004, p. B16; Shirley Won, "Small Furniture Firm Pegged for Success," *The Globe and Mail*, April 10, 2004, p. B5; "Exports, Eh?" *Canadian Business* (January 1997): 21; also Peggy Berkowitz, "You Say Potato, They Say McCain," *Canadian Business* (December 1991): 44–48. **Table 5.1** *Bank of Canada Banking and Financial Statistics*, Table J3, May, 2006, S111. **Entrepreneurship and New Ventures: Rolling in the Worldwide Dough** Ron Lieber, "Give Us This Day Our Global Bread," *Fast Company* (March 2001): 164–167. **Table 5.2** *Financial Post Business*, Special Edition, 2006, p. 121. Material reprinted with the express permission of National Post Company, a CanWest Partnership. **Business Accountability: How to Wake Up a Zombie** Clay Chandler, "Japan's Horror Show," *Fortune* (November 10, 2003): 114–118; "Quick Studies," *Business Week* (November 18, 2003): 48–49. **Business Case 5: International Challenges in the Clothing Industry** Bernard Marotte, "Gildan Dresses Up for Retail," *The Globe and Mail*, July 8, 2006, p. B4; Bernard Marotte, "Gildan Unravels North America Production, Shifts Jobs South," *The Globe and Mail*, September 28, 2006, pp. B1, B4; Martin Cash, "China Wins Apparel War?" *The Winnipeg Free Press*, July 30, 2005, pp. B8, B11; Gordon Pitts, "Peerless on a Mission: Stop China Now," *The Globe and Mail*, January 14, 2005, p. B8; Bertrand Marotte, "Gildan Takes T-Shirt Making to the Cutting-Edge of Casual Apparel," *The Globe and Mail*, July 3, 2004, p. B3; Gordon Pitts, "Who will be the Next Huntingdon?" *The Globe and Mail*, January 8, 2005, p. B7.

Chapter 6

Looking for Redemption? Shawn McCarthy, "Bronfman is Eager to Gain Redemption for his Music Gambit," *The Globe and Mail*, January 4, 2005, p. B4; Allen Swift, "Bronfman Jr. Wants His Toy Again," *The Winnipeg Free Press*, May 26, 2003, p. B7; Shawn McCarthy, "Bronfman Jumps Back Into Music with Winning Bid," *The Globe and Mail*, November 25, 2003; Brian Milner, "Broken Spirits," *Report on Business Magazine* (September 2002): 26–38; Allan Swift, "Polygram Bid Heats Up," *The Winnipeg Free Press*, November 5, 1998, p. B12; Brian Milner, "Seagram's Top Gun Shoots for the Stars," *The Globe and Mail*, June 6, 1998, pp. B1, B6; Brian Milner, "Seagram Snares Polygram," *The Globe and Mail*, May 22, 1998, pp. B1, B4; Brian Milner, "The Selling of Edgar Bronfman Jr.," *The Globe and Mail*, February 15, 1999, p. B15. **Figure 6.1** Ricky W. Griffin, *Management*, 8th ed. (Boston: Houghton Mifflin Company, 2005), 282. Used with Persmission. **Business Accountability: What Do Managers Actually Do?** Henry Mintzberg, *The Nature of Managerial Work* (New York: Harper and Row, 1973); Harvey Schachter, "Monday Morning Manager," *The Globe and Mail*, November 8, 2005, p. B2. **Entrepreneurship and New Ventures: Best in Show** Rick Spence, The Fastest Five," *Profit*, Vol. 24, Issue 23 (June 2005): 49–60; also "Pethealth Inc. Named one of Canada's Fastest-Growing Companies in 18th Annual PROFIT 100 Ranking of Canada's Fastest-Growing Companies," *CCNMatthews Newswire*, June 5, 2006. p. 1. Reprinted by permission of Rick Spence and Pethealth Inc. **Figure 6.5** Based on Thomas L. Wheelan and J. David Hunger, *Strategic Management and Business Policy*, 7th ed. (Upper Saddle River, NJ: Prtentice Hall, 2000), 13. **Business Case 6: Remaking BCE** Dene Moore, "Telecom Giant BCE Inc. Up For Grabs," *The Winnipeg Free Press*, April 18, 2007, p. B7; Andrew Willis, "A Bird in the Hand Versus Seven in the Sky," *The Globe and Mail*, December 23, 2006, p. B3; Derek DeCloet, "The CEO Craves Respect, but it Won't Come Until Fixes are Made," *The Globe and Mail*, October 12, 2006, pp. B1, B5; Catherine McLean, "Bell's Hope: George Cope," *The Globe and Mail*, September 16, 2006, p. B4; Andrew Willis, "The Conversion of Mr. Sabia," *The Globe and Mail*, October 12, 2006, pp. B1, B4; Catherine McLean, "Analysts Urge BCE to Focus on the Basics," *The Globe* and Mail, July 14, 2006, p. B10; Andrew Willis, Jacquie McNish, and Grant Robertson, "How the Deal Was Done: Embarking on Project Odyssey's Stormy Water," *The Globe and Mail*, December 3, 2005, p. B4; Gordon Pitts, "Bell Adopts a New Party Line," *The Globe and Mail*, May 14, 2005, p. B4; also Simon Avery, "Sabia Lays Out a New BCE: Lower Costs, More Wireless," *The Globe and Mail*, December 16, 2004, pp. B1, B7; Dave Ebner, "BCE Cutting Costs, Staff, Focusing on Bell Canada," *The Globe and Mail*, December 19, 2002, pp. B1, B4; Jacquie McNish and Paul Waldie, "BCE Reacquiring 20% Stake in Bell Canada," *The Globe and Mail*, June 29, 2002, pp. B1, B4; Karen Howlett and John Saunders, "Teleglobe to Abandon Huge Internet Investment, *The Globe and Mail*, May 16, 2002, pp. B1, B11; Ian Austen, "On the Hook," *Canadian*

Business (May 13, 2002): 35–39; Bertrand Marotte, "Sabia: BCE Committed to Emergis," *The Globe and Mail*, May 8, 2002, p. B5; Eric Reguly, "Decision Time for BCE Boss Is Now," *The Globe and Mail*, March 22, 2002, pp. B1–B2; Gordon Pitts, "Monty Ends 28 Years with a Clean Break," *The Globe and Mail*, April 25, 2002, p. B3.

Chapter 7

Frantic Films Is Getting More Organized Interviews with Jamie Brown, CEO of Frantic Films, as well as documents provided by Frantic Films. **Business Accountability: Product Versus Geographic Departmentalization: What's the Right Choice?** Joann Lublin, "Place vs. Product: It's Tough to Choose a Management Model," *The Wall Street Journal*, June 27, 2001, pp. A1, A4; Richard Blackwell, "New CIBC Boss Promises Shakeup," *The Globe and Mail*, April 2, 1999, pp. B1, B4; Rekha Bach, "Heinz's Johnson to Divest Operations, Scrap Management of Firm by Region," *The Wall Street Journal*, December, 1997, pp. B10-B12; Jana Parker-Pope and Joann Lublin, "P&G Will Make Jager CEO Ahead of Schedule," *The Wall Street Journal*, September, 1998, pp. B1, B8. **Entrepreneurship and New Ventures: The Techie Trio** BDC website:http://www.bdc.ca/en/about/mediaroom/news_releases/2005/2005101808.htm accessed June 12, 2006. **Business Case 7: Cooking Up a New Structure** "Our Brands," Sara Lee (July 3, 2002), at www.saralee.com; Deborah Cohen, "Sara Lee Opens Alternative to Victoria's Secret," *The Wall Street Journal*, January 3, 2003, p. B4; Julie Forster, "Sara Lee: Changing the Recipe—Again," *Business Week* (September 10, 2001): 87–89; "Sara Lee: Looking Shapely," *Business Week* (October 21, 2002): 52.

Chapter 8

Celebrating Workforce Diversity Virginia Galt, "P & G Leverages its Cultural Diversity," *The Globe and Mail*, April 7, 2005, pp. B1, B18; Jill Mahoney, "Visible Majority by 2017," *The Globe and Mail*, March 23, 2005, pp. A1, A7; Kamal Dib, "Diversity Works," *Canadian Business* (March 29, 2004): 53–54; Valerie Marchant, "The New Face of Work," *Canadian Business* (March 29, 2004): 38; Ann Zimmerman, "Defending Wal-Mart," *The Wall Street Journal*, October 4, 2004, pp. B1, B10; Virginia Galt, "Western Union Remakes 'Canadian' Image," *The Globe and Mail*, November 23, 2004, pp. B1, B24. **Business Accountability: Behaviour-Based Interviewing** Celene Adams, "Interview Style Probes Past to Predict Future," *The Globe and Mail*, April 29, 2002, p. B16. **Entrepreneurship and New Ventures: Benchmarking Labour Relations Through Sustainable Development** http://www.arcelor.com/index.php?lang=en&page=49&tb0=103.

Chapter 9

Keeping Employees Satisfied and Motivated Wallace Immen, "The Continuing Divide Over Stress Leave," *The Globe and Mail*, June 10, 2005, p. C1; Jeff Buckstein, "In Praise of Praise in the Workplace," *The Globe and Mail*, June 15, 2005, pp. C1, C5; Virginia Galt, "This Just In: Half Your Employees Ready to Jump Ship," *The Globe and Mail*, January 26, 2005, pp. B1, B9; David Sirota, Louis Mischkind, and Michael Meltzer, "Nothing Beats an Enthusiastic Employee," *The Globe and Mail*, July 29, 2005, p. C1; Virginia Galt, "Business's Next Challenge: Tackling Mental Health in the Workplace," *The Globe and Mail*, April 12, 2005, pp. B1, B20; Virginia Galt, "Canadian Take Dour View on Jobs, Bosses, Angels," *The Globe and Mail*, October 18, 2004, pp. B1, B7; Virginia Galt, "Worker Stress Costing Economy Billions, Panel Warns," *The Globe and Mail*, July 21, 2000, p. B9. **Business Accountability: Encouraging Employees to Share Ideas** "Neat as it Sounds," *The Wall Street Journal*, September 8, 1997, pp. A1, 13. **Table 9.1** Reprinted with permission of The Free Press, a division of Simon & Schuster Adult Publishing Group, from *A Force of Change: How Leadership Differs from Management* by John P. Kotter. Copyright© 1990 by John P. Kotter, Inc. All rights reserved. **Figure 9.5** Reprinted by permission of *Harvard Business Review*. Exhibit from "How to Choose Leadership Patterns" by Robert Tannenbaum & Warren Schmidt, May–June 1973. Copyright © 1973 by the Harvard Business School Publishing Corporation. All rights reserved. Reprinted by permission of the *Harvard Business Review*. **Figure 9.6** Copyright © 1990, by The Regents of the University of California. Reprinted from the *California Management Review*, Vol. 32, No. 2. By the permission of The Regents. **Entrepreneurship and New Ventures: An Apple a Day** Steven Berglas, "What You Can Learn from Steve Jobs," www.inc.com; "Apple's Bold Swim Downstream," *Business Week* (January 24, 2006): 32–35; "The Seed of Apple's Innovation," *Business Week* (October 12, 2005): 86–87; Alan Deutschman, *The Second Coming of Steve Jobs* (New York: Broadway Publishing, 2001); Brent Schlender, "How Big Can Apple Get?" *Fortune* (February 21, 2005): 122–128; "Steve Jobs' Magic Kingdom," *Business Week* (February 6, 2006): 62–69 (source of quote); **Business Case 9: Bringing the Bounty Back to P&G** A.G. Lafley, "Letter to Shareholders," Procter & Gamble, *2002 Annual Report*; "A Healthy Gamble," *Time* (September 16, 2002): 46–48; Katrina Booker, "The Un-CEO," *Fortune* (September 16, 2002): 88–96; Robert Berner, "Procter & Gamble's Renovator-in-Chief," *Business Week* (December 11, 2002): 98–100; Robert Berner, "The Best and Worst Managers: A.G. Lafley, Procter & Gamble," *Business Week* (January 13, 2003): 67.

Chapter 10

Meeting the Productivity Challenge Joe Castaldo, "On A Roll," *Canadian Business* (October 9–22, 2006): 51–56; Gordon Pitts, "Ottawa's New, Improved Mantra: Productivity," *The Globe and Mail*, October 3, 2005, pp. B1, B6; Greg Keenan, "GM Oshawa Cranks Out Productivity Award," *The Globe and Mail*, June 3, 2005, pp. B1, B8; Grant Robertson, "In the Boardroom at the General Motors Oshawa Plant is a Baseball Bat. Two Words are Carved on It: Beat Toyota," *The Globe and Mail*, September 15, 2005, p. B16; Gordon Pitts, "Manufacturers' Choice—Compete or Die," *The Globe and Mail*, October 5, 2005, p. B7; "Canada's Standard of Living," *National Post Business* (June 2003): 19–20; Jeffrey Bernstein, Richard Harris, and Andrew Sharpe, "The Widening Canada–US Manufacturing Productivity Gap," *International Productivity Monitor* (Fall 2002): 3–22; Pierre Fortin, "Differences in Annual Work Hours per Capita Between the United States and Canada," *International Productivity Monitor* (Spring 2003): 38–46; Frank Graves and Richard Jenkins, "Canadian Attitudes Towards Productivity: Balancing Standard of Living and Quality of Life," *The Review of Economic Performance and Social Progress* (2002): 243–258; Andrew Sharpe, "Why Are Americans More Productive Than Canadians?" *International Productivity Monitor* (Spring 2003): 19–37; Jason Myers, "Back to Basics: Canada's Productivity Challenge," *Canadian Manufacturers and Exporters* (April 2003): 14–18; Pierre Fortin, "Canadian Productivity: When Do We Catch Up?" *ISUMA* (Spring 2002). **Entrepreneurship and New Ventures: The Silencers** BDC website:http://www.bdc.ca/en/about/mediaroom/news_releases/2005/2005101812.htm. **Figure 12.1** Bart Van Ark and Robert McGuckin, "International Comparisons of Labor Productivity and Per Capita Income," *Monthly Labor Review* (July 1999): 33–41. **Business Accountability: Rating the Quality of Diamonds** Betsy Vereckey, "Diamond Sellers Scramble to Polish Their Image," *The Globe and Mail*, December 8, 2006, p. B10; Mark Brown, "Diamond in the Rough," *Canadian Business* (October 23–November 5, 2006): 71–73; Calvin Leung, "Diamonds in the Rough," *Canadian Business* (February 28–March 13, 2005): 65–67; Joel Baglole, "Political Correctness by the Carat," *The Wall Street Journal*, April 17, 2003, pp. B1, B3; Matthew Hart, "The Ice Storm," *Canadian Business* (November 2002): 52–62. **Figure 12.2** Adapted from D. Daryl Wickoff, "New Tools for Achieving Service Quality." *The Cornell Hotel and Restaurant Administrative Quarterly* (November 1984): 89. Cornell HRA Quarterly. Used by permission. All rights reserved. **Business Case 10: Supply Chain Management at Loblaws** Marina Strauss, "Battered Loblaw

Makes Deep Job Cuts," *The Globe and Mail*, January 23, 2007, pp. B1, B7; Marina Strauss, "New Team at Loblaw to Trim Stores, Wares," *The Globe and Mail*, November 17, 2006, pp. B1, B6; Zena Olijnyk, "All in the Family," *Canadian Business* (September 25–October 8, 2006): 75–76; Marina Strauss, "Loblaw's Supply Chain Reaction," *The Globe and Mail*, February 25, 2006, p. B4; "Canadian Retailer Loblaw's Earnings Hit Due to Delays and Challenges in Supply Chain Network Redesign Project," www.scdigest.com/assets, November 17, 2005; Blaise Robinson, "Bay Street Week Ahead—Food Fight in Canada Grocery Aisle," www.globeinvestor.com/servlet/ArticleNews/story/ROC, January 6, 2006; "Analysts Dismiss Loblaw's Woes," www.canada.com/national/nationalpost/financialpost/investing/story.html, April 28, 2006.

Chapter 11

Accounting for Pensions Richard Blackwell, "Pension Plans Staging Strong Recovery, Study Shows," *The Globe and Mail*, April 12, 2007, p. B3; Luis Millan, "Death Knell of the Nest Egg?" *CGA Magazine* (May–June, 2006): 13–19; "Addressing the Pension Dilemma in Canada" and "The State of Defined Benefit Pension Plans in Canada," www.cga-online.org/canada/ar; Elizabeth Church, "Pension Fund Shortfall Soars in First Half," *The Globe and Mail*, November 23, 2005, pp. B1, B7; Elizabeth Church, "Cost of Retiree Benefit Liabilities 'Sleeping Giant'," *The Globe and Mail*, August 23, 2004, p. B4; Elizabeth Church, "Accounting Overhaul Coming," *The Globe and Mail*, December 23, 2002, pp. B1, B6. **Business Accountability: Who's Accountable for Offshore Oversight?** Thomas J. Smedinghoff and Creighton R. Meland, Jr., "Financial Institution Outsourcing: Managing the Risks," *Outsourcing Journal* (May 2002), at www.outsourcing-journal.com; Lawrence M. Gill, "Questions Loom as Accountants Outsource Work Abroad," *Chicago Lawyer* (January 26, 2004); Jim Peterson, "Turf Battle Shows Signs of Truce," *International Herald Tribune*, November 8, 2003, p. 17; Beth Ellyn Rosenthal, "Deloitte Study Discovers 75 Percent of Global Financial Institutions Plan to Outsource Offshore," *BPO Outsourcing Journal* (June 2003), at www.bpo-outsourcing-journal.cm; "How to Evaluate an Outsourcing Provider and Watch the Bottom Line," *The CPA Journal* (June 2002): 19; Liz Loxton, "Offshoring—Offshore Accounting," *Accountancy* (February 2004): 48; Todd Furniss and Michel Janssen, "Offshore Outsourcing Part 1: The Brand of India," OutsourcingAsia.com, April 2003, at www.outsourcing-asia.com; Todd Furniss, "China: The Next Big Wave in Offshore Outsourcing"; "Cover Feature—Outsourcing the Finance Function—Out with the Count," *Accountancy* (September 1, 2001): 32. **Entrepreneurship and New Ventures: How Can You Account for a Good Beer?** "Brew Tour Update Form," *The Real Beer Page* (February 14, 2003), www.realbeer.com; "Black Oak Nut Brown Ale," Beer Advocate.com (February 14, 2003), www.beeradvocate.com; Stephen Beaumont, "Lament for a Brewpub—February 2003," *Stephen Beaumont's World of Beer* (February 14, 2003), www.worldofbeer.com; "Brewery Profile," *The Bar Towel* (February 14, 2003), www.bartowel.com/breweries/blackoak.phtml; John Cooper, "A Pint of Success," *CMA Management* (December 1999/January 2000): 44–46. **Business Case 11: Continuing Concerns in the Accounting Profession** Elizabeth Church, "Pension Funding Shortfall Increases Dramatically," *The Globe and Mail*, November 8, 2005, p. B5; Elizabeth Church, "Pension Fund Shortfall Soars in First Half," *The Globe and Mail*, November 23, 2005, pp. B1, B7; Elizabeth Church, "Cost of Retiree Benefit Liabilities 'Sleeping Giant'," *The Globe and Mail*, August 23, 2004, p. B4; Paul Waldie and Karen Howlett, "Reports Reveal Tight Grip of Ebbers on WorldCom," *The Globe and Mail*, June 11, 2003, pp. B1, B7; Barrie McKenna, Karen Howlett, and Paul Waldie, "Probes Cite Ebbers in 'Fraud,'" *The Globe and Mail*, June 10, 2003, pp. B1, B16; Elizabeth Church, "Accounting Overhaul Coming," *The Globe and Mail*, December 23, 2002, pp. B1, B6; Richard Blackwell," OSC Targets Tech Accounting," *The Globe and Mail*, September 26, 2000, pp. B1, B6.

Chapter 12

Marketers Pay Attention to the Older Folks Ethan Smith, "Tuning Into the Tween Set," *The Wall Street Journal*, December 21, 2006, pp. B1–B2; David Pringle, "In Mobile Phones, Older Users Say, More Is Less," *The Wall Street Journal*, August 15, 2005, pp. A1, A9; John Partridge, "Leisureworld Purchase Revs Up Retirement Debate," *The Globe and Mail*, March 24, 2005, p. B15; Kelly Greene, "Marketing Surprise: Older Consumers Buy Stuff, Too," *The Wall Street Journal*, April 6, 2004, pp. A1, A12; Andre Mayer, "Star's New Paper Woos Tween Readers," *The Globe and Mail*, March 12, 2003, p. B7; Gautam Naik, Leslie Chang, and Joanna Slater, "Leveraging the Age Gap," *The Wall Street Journal*, February 27, 2003, pp. B1, B4; Cris Prystay and Sarah Ellison, "Time for Marketers to Grow Up?" *The Wall Street Journal*, February 27, 2003, pp. B1, B4; Sebastian Moffett, "For Ailing Japan, Longevity Begins to Take Its Toll," *The Wall Street Journal*, February 11, 2003, pp. A1, A12; John Heinzl, "Crayon Maker Draws in an Older Kid," *The Globe and Mail*, March 5, 1998; Shawna Steinberg, "Have Allowance, Will Transform Economy," *Canadian Business* (March 13, 1998): 59–71; Lisa Bannon, "Little Big Spenders," *The Wall Street Journal*, October 13, 1998, pp. A1, A6; Sheryl Ubelacker, "Magazines Target Over-50 Crowd," *The Winnipeg Free Press*, April 9, 2000, p. B3; Allen St. John, "Baseball's Billion Dollar Question: Who's On Deck?" *American Demographics* (October 1998): 60–62, 65–69. **Business Accountability: When Smoke Gets in Your Eyes** Keith McArthur, "A Year Later: No Medium for the Message," *The Globe and Mail*, November 1, 2004, p. B3; Cheryl Healton and Kathleen Nelson, "Reversal of Misfortune: Viewing Tobacco as a Social Justice Issue," *American Journal of Public Health* (February 2004): 186t.; *Federal Trade Commission Cigarette Report for 2001* (June 15, 2003) at www.ftc.gov/os/2003/06/ cigreport.pdf. **Figure 12.2** From Kotler, *Principles of Marketing*, 6th Canadian ed., p. 358. Copyright 2005 Pearson Education Canada. Based on material by Mark E. Smith. **Figure 12.3** Adapted from Naresh K. Malhorta, *Marketing Research: An Applied Orientation*, 3rd ed. (Upper Saddle River, NJ: Prentice Hall, 1999), 10. **Entrepreneurship and New Ventures: When in Rome** http://www.canadianbusiness.com/entrepreneur/sales_marketing/article.jsp?content=20060210_125140_5560 (Accessed June 12, 2006); also Susanne Ruder, "PROFIT 100 Profile: When in Rome...," *PROFIT* (March 2006) © Suzanne Ruder, *PROFIT* Magazine, March 2006. **Business Case 12: Television Viewership: How Do You Measure It?** Brooks Barnes, "New TV Ratings Will Produce Ad-Price Fight," *The Wall Street Journal*, December 22, 2005, pp. B1, B3; Brooks Barnes, "Where Are the Ratings, Dude?" *The Wall Street Journal*, March 7, 2005, pp. B1, B6; Keith McArthur, "New TV Ratings Devices Know What You're Watching," *The Globe and Mail*, November 29, 2004, pp. B1, B12; Keith McArthur, "Advertisers Wary of Plan to Fuse TV Ratings Systems," *The Globe and Mail*, July 13, 2004, pp. B1, B20; Brooks Barnes, "For Nielsen, Fixing Old Ratings System Causes New Static," *The Wall Street Journal*, September 16, 2004, pp. A1, A8; Elizabeth Jensen, "Networks Blast Nielsen, Blame Faulty Ratings for Drop in Viewership," *The Wall Street Journal*, November 22, 1996, pp. A1, A8.

Chapter 13

The Fuel Cell: Still a Long, Rough Road Ahead Yuri Kageyama, "Toyota's Hybrid Sales Top 1 Million Vehicles," *The Winnipeg Free Press*, June 8, 2007, p. B16; Peter Kennedy, "Ballard's Celebrated Drive Hits a Bumpy Road," *The Globe and Mail*, July 17, 2004, p. B6; Peter Kennedy, "GM Aims to Finish First in Fuel Cell Race," *The Globe and Mail*, June 10, 2003, p. B5; Chris Nuttall-Smith, "Waiting for the Revolution," *Report on Business* (February, 2003): 44–54; Jeffrey Ball, "Hydrogen Fuel May Be Clean, But Getting It Here Looks Messy," *The Wall Street Journal*, March 7, 2003; Rebecca Blumenstein, "Auto Industry Reaches Surprising Consensus:

It Needs New Engines," *The Wall Street Journal*, January 5, 1998, pp. A1, A10. **Entrepreneurship and New Ventures: The Patriotic Entrepreneur** Cris Prystay, "Bio-Boost," *Far Eastern Economic Review* (February 6, 2003): 38; Charles Bickers, "Medicine Man Returns," *Far Eastern Economic Review* (August 23, 2001): 30–33. **Business Accountability: Who's Accountable for Results?** Joe Mandese, "The Age of Accountability," *TelevisionWeek* (February 16, 2004): 28; also Joe Mandese, "Shifting Ad Accountability to Media," *TelevisionWeek* (October 6, 2003): 15; also Erin White, "Media & Marketing—Advertising: Making Sure the Work Fits the Bill," *The Wall Street Journal*, February 3, 2004, p. B8. **Business Case 13: Advertising: Not What it Used to Be** Grant Robertson, "Radio Rivals Resort to Merger," *The Globe and Mail*, February 20, 2007, pp. B1, B6; Keith McArthur and Grant Robertson, "CRTC Ponders Impact of Product Placement," *The Globe and Mail*, November 21, 2005, pp. B1, B10; Grant Robertson and Richard Blackwell, "Eased Satellite Radio Rules Could 'Shock' System," *The Globe and Mail*, September 23, 2005, p. B7; Tessa Wegert, "On-Line Marketing Concept Gives Consumers a Say," *The Globe and Mail*, October 13, 2005, p. B13; Aaron Patrick, "Commercials by Cellphone," *The Wall Street Journal*, August 22, 2005, pp. B1, B3; Frazier Moore, "You Can't Fast-Forward Past These Commercials," *The Winnipeg Free Press*, July 25, 2005, p. D3; Simon Tuck, "CRTC Turns Radio on its Head with Landmark Satellite Ruling," *The Globe and Mail*, June 17, 2005, pp. B1, B6; Eric Reguly, "Blame the Act, Not the Regulator," *The Globe and Mail*, June 16, 2005, p. B2; Joe Flint and Brian Steinberg, "Procter & Gamble Tweaks Its Traditional TV Ad Strategy," *The Wall Street Journal*, June 13, 2005, p. B6; Peter Grant, "Interactive Ads Start to Click on Cable and Satellite TV," *The Wall Street Journal*, May 26, 2005, pp. B1, B6; Keith McArthur, "Branded Content Generates Buzz," *The Globe and Mail*, April 6, 2005, p. B4; Keith McArthur, "A Year Later: No Medium for the Message," *The Globe and Mail*, November 1, 2004, p. B3.

Chapter 14

The Importance of Price Joe Castaldo, "Smoke Signals," *Canadian Business* (November 20–December 3, 2006): 20–21; Andy Hoffman, "Cheap Suds Give Lakeport Rivals Brand Hangover," *The Globe and Mail*, March 14, 2006, p. B6; Derek DeCloet, "Trouble Brewing in Beer Industry," *The Globe and Mail*, May 7, 2005, p. B4; Jon Swartz, "Some eBay Sellers are Going, Going, Gone," *USA Today*, February 2, 2005, p. 3B; Keith McArthur, "In Hamilton, They Like Beer Cold... and Cheap," *The Globe and Mail*, July 10, 2004, p. B4; also Keith McArthur, "Why Molson is Crying In Its Beer," *The Globe and Mail*, July 10, 2004, p. B4; Greg Keenan, "Toyota Kills No-Haggle Sales Price Strategy," *The Globe and Mail*, June 17, 2004, pp. B1, B25; Ann Zimmerman, "Behind the Dollar-Store Boom: A Nation of Bargain Hunters," *The Wall Street Journal*, December 13, 2004, pp. A1, A10; Gordon Fairclough, "Four Biggest Cigarette Makers Can't Raise Prices As They Did," *The Wall Street Journal*, October 25, 2002, pp. A1, A8; Timothy Aeppel, "After Cost Cutting, Companies Turn Toward Price Increases," *The Wall Street Journal*, September 18, 2002, pp. A1, A12. **Business Accountability: Pricing in the Airline Industry: The Sky is No Longer the Limit** David Wessel and Susan Carey, "Airlines Captive to Costs and Competition," *The Wall Street Journal*, September 19, 2005, p. B8; Evan Perez and Nicole Harris, "Despite Early Signs of Victory, Discount Airlines Get Squeezed," *The Wall Street Journal*, January 17, 2005, pp. A1, A6; Melanie Trottman, "Equalizing Air Fares," *The Wall Street Journal*, August 17, 2004, pp. B1, B4; Julia Boorstin, "JetBlue's IPO Takes Off," *Fortune* (April 29, 2002): 96–100; Melanie Wells, "Lord of the Skies," *Forbes* (October 14, 2002): 130–138; Paul C. Judge, "How Will Your Company Adapt?" *Fast Company* (February 2003): 105–110. **Entrepreneurship and New Ventures: There Must Be a Better Way to Distribute Confusion, Demand, and Dysfunction** Chris McDougall, "Closing the Deal," *Inc.* (March 2004): 70–84. **Business Case 14: Changes in Distribution Channels: Downloading Music from the Internet** Julia Angwin, Sarah McBride, and Ethan Smith, "Record Labels Turn Piracy Into a Marketing Opportunity," *The Wall Street Journal*, October 18, 2006, pp. B1, B10; Shawn McCarthy, "U.S. Court Shuts Door on Internet File-Sharing," *The Globe and Mail*, June 28, 2005, p. B3; "File Sharing Firm Will Shut Down," *The Winnipeg Free Press*, November 8, 2005, p. A11; Nick Wingfield, "Online Music's Latest Tune," *The Wall Street Journal*, August 27, 2004, pp. B1, B2; Nick Wingfield, "New File-Swapping Software Limits Sharers to a Select Few," *The Wall Street Journal*, October 4, 2004, pp. B1, B4; Sarah McBride, "Stop the Music!," *The Wall Street Journal*, August 23, 2004, p. B1; also Vauhini Vara, "On Campus, iTunes Finds an Illicit Groove, *The Wall Street Journal*, August 23, 2004, pp. B1–B2; Nick Wingfield and Sarah McBride, "Green Light for Grokster," *The Wall Street Journal*, August 20, 2004, pp. B1, B3; Nick Wingfield, "The Day the Music Died," *The Wall Street Journal*, May 2, 2003, p. B8; "The End of File-Shares as We Know Them," *The Winnipeg Free Press*, July 4, 2003, p. A8; Ted Birdis, "Music Industry Escalates Net Fight," *The Winnipeg Free Press*, June 26, 2003, p. A12; Matthew Ingram, "Digital Music Industry Gets New Spin on Napster Judge's Decision," *The Globe and Mail*, February 26, 2002; Nick Wingfield, "Napster Boy, Interrupted," *The Wall Street Journal*, October 1, 2002, pp. B1, B3; Anna Matthews and Charles Goldsmith, "Music Industry Faces New Threats on Web," *The Wall Street Journal*, February 21, 2003, pp. B1, B4.

Chapter 15

Who Could Have Imagined This? Tim Campbell, "Hockey Plays Dollar Game," *The Winnipeg Free Press*, June 30, 2006, p. D8; Murray McNeill and Larry Kusch, "Manitoba's Manufacturing Sector Suffers While Buck Rises," *The Winnipeg Free Press*, May 2, 2006, pp. B1, B6; Eric Beauchesne, "Loonie Predicted to Hit Par Next Fall," *The Winnipeg Free Press*, May 2, 2006, pp. B1, B6; "20 Ways the Rising Loonie Is Changing Canada's Landscape," *The Globe and Mail*, July 5, 2003, pp. B1, B4; John Saunders, "Exporters Facing Some Loonie Math," *The Globe and Mail*, May 7, 2003, pp. B1, B4. **Entrepreneurship and New Ventures: Check It Out!** "Announcing CHEQ-IT Ltd. System Sales," Canada NewsWire, Oct 13, 2005, 1 (Copyright Canada Newswire), also CHEQ-IT Ltd. home page: http://www.cheqiteft.com/index.htm. Reprinted with permission of CHEQ-IT Ltd. **Business Accountability: Fixing the System on a National Scale** Nicolas Parent, Phoebe Munro, and Ron Parker, "An Evaluation of Fixed Announcement Dates," *Bank of Canada Review* (Autumn 2003): 3. **Table 15.1** "The Big Mac Index," http://economist.com, June 9, 2005. Copyright © The Economist Newspaper Ltd. All rights reserved. Reprinted with permission. **Table 15.2** *National Post,* June 2000 p. 168. **Business Case 15: Scandal in the Mutual Fund Industry** Karen Howlett and John Saunders, "Fund Firms Admit Role in Market Timing Trades," *The Globe and Mail*, December 17, 2004, pp. B1, B4; Janet McFarland and Rob Carrick, "The Fee Crunch: Not All Investors Get Value for Money," *The Globe and Mail*, June 24, 2004, p. B6; Christine Dugas, "Putnam Ousts CEO in Midst of Fund Probe," *USA Today*, November 3, 2003, at www.usatoday.com/money; "Senators Blast SEC over Mutual Fund Trading Scandal," *USA Today*, November 3, 2003, at www.usatoday.com/money; John Waggoner, Christine Dugas, and Thomas A. Fogarty, "Scandal Outrage Keeps Growing," *USA Today*, November 3, 2003, at www.usatoday.com/money; "NYC Pensions Pull Assets from Putnam," *CNNmoney*, November 4, 2003, at www.cnnmoney.com; "Chairman of Strong Mutual Resigns," *USA Today*, November 3, 2003, at www.usatoday.com/money.

Chapter 16

The Increasing Importance of Risk Management Oliver Bertin, "Sector Hit Hard by Sharp Increases in Premiums," *The Globe and Mail*, April 27, 2004, p. B14; Oliver Bertin, "Firms Face Major Hurdles En Route to U.S. Markets," *The Globe and Mail*, April 29, 2004, p. B16; Harris Anwar, "Chief Risk Officer: A Valuable addition to the C-Suite," *The Globe and Mail*, June 20, 2005, p. B13; "Singer 'Incited' Crowd," *The Winnipeg Free Press*, August 15, 2005, p. D2; Leslie Scism," If Disaster Strikes This 'Titanic,' Chubb Could Lose Millions," *The Wall Street Journal*, April 9, 1997, pp. A1, A4; Leslie Scism, "Maybe Julie Andrews Could Offer Insurers a Spoonful of Sugar," *The Wall Street Journal*, April 4, 1997, pp. A1, A4; Patrick Reilly, "Insurers Are Downbeat on Rap Concert Tours," *The Wall Street Journal*, March 26, 1997, pp. B1, B12. **Entrepreneurship and New Ventures: The Personality of a Risk Taker** Tom Stein, "Every Step You Take, LP's will be Watching You, *Venture Capital Journal*, January 1, 2003, at www.marcusventures.com/financialness.html; Yasmine Chinwala, "U.S. Survey Shows Gender Gap," *eFinancial News*, February 5, 2002, at marcusventures.com/financial news.html; Alison Maitland, "An Idea from the Ladies Room," FT.com/*Financial Times* (February 2, 2003), at www.marcusventures.com/FT.html. **Business Accountability: A Quicken Course in Accountability** Michael S. Hopkins, "Because He Learns, and Teaches," *Inc.* (April 2004): 119–20. **Business Case 16: Brascan Is Making Progress** Shirley Won, "What's in a Name? Plenty, If It's Brascan," *The Globe and Mail*, September 16, 2005, p. B3; Shirley Won, "Brascan's Plan Pleases Analysts, but Some Preach Wait-and-See," *The Globe and Mail*, March 18, 2005, p. B12; Andrew Willis, "Brascan Remakes Itself, This Time With Trees," *The Globe and Mail*, February 19, 2005, p. B7; Andrew Willis, "How Flatt is Reforging Brascan," *The Globe and Mail*, September 25, 2004, p. B6; John Partridge, "Brascan Looks to Power Plants for Added Juice in Bottom Line," *The Globe and Mail*, August 6, 2004, p. B9; Andrew Willis, "Investors Betting on Brascan Dismantling," *The Globe and Mail*, July 19, 2004, pp. B1, B10.

Appendix B

Figure B.2 Major modification of diagrams at the Blackberry website, modified from Research in Motion Limited, technical images, at www.blackberry.com/images/technical/bes_exchange_architecture.gif. **Figure B.4** Reprint courtesy of International Business Machines Corporation copyright 2006 © International Business Machines Corporation. Reprinted by permission of Paul Huang.

Photo Credits

Prologue Bettmann/CORBIS, page xxviii; Dave Olecko/Bloomberg News/Landov, page xxix (top); Courtesy of ANDI, page xxix (bottom); Maureen Jenkins, page xxx (top); Starbucks Coffee Company, page xxx (centre); © Paul A. Souders/CORBIS, page xxx (bottom); © Alamy, page xxxi (top); AP, page xxxi (bottom)

Part One © Ron Fehling/Masterfile, page 1

Chapter 1 Courtesy of Inco, page 3; AP, page 9; Ritz Sino/New York Times Pictures, page 22; Namas Bhojani, page 23

Chapter 2 © Steve Craft/Masterfile, page 29; © Louie Psihoyos/CORBIS, page 35; AP, page 41; © Fredrik Renander/Alamy, page 46

Chapter 3 CP (Jessica Kourkounis), page 57; CP (Kenneth Lambert), page 59; AFP/Getty Images, page 67; Donna Terek Photography, page 71; McDonald's Restaurant, page 76

Chapter 4 Courtesy of Robeez Footwear Ltd. www.robeez.com, page 85; S. Houston, page 87; Dick Hemingway, page 92; Dick Hemingway, page 102

Chapter 5 © Robert Holmes/CORBIS, page 119; Amit Barghava/CORBIS, page 122; Everett Collection, page 125; Uriel Sinai/Getty Images, page 133; Mark Gibson/Digital Vision/Getty Images, page 136; Namas Bhojani, page 140

Part Two © Rick Gomez/CORBIS, page 151

Chapter 6 CP (Laurent Rebours), page 153; Najlah Feanny/CORBIS, page 157; Frank Siteman/agefotostock/firstlight.ca, page 159 (top left); © PhotoAlto/Alamy, page 159 (top centre); ColorBlind Images/Getty Images, page 159 (top bottom); Corbis-NY, page 159 (bottom right); EPA/Sergei Chirikov/Landov LLC, page 162; Neema Frederic/CORBIS/Sygma, page 167; © Matthew Mcvay/CORBIS, page 172; Courtesy of Mainframe Entertainment Inc., page 173

Chapter 7 Courtesy of Frantic Films, page 181; Everett Collection, page 185; Dick Hemingway, page 186; Adamsmith/Taxi/Getty Images, page 193; AP, page 196; Bob Scott/Image Bank, page 200

Chapter 8 © ImageSource, page 207; Javier Larrea/agefotostock/firstlight.ca, page 211; © Creatas, page 213; CP (Kathy Willens), page 218; © Chris Sattlberger/CORBIS, page 224; Mark Richards, page 225; CP/Chicoutimi Le Quotidien (Jeannot Lévesque), page 226

Chapter 9 © Masterfile (Royalty-Free Div.) www.masterfile.com, page 241; Courtesy Western Electric, page 248; © Masterfile (Royalty-Free Div.) www.masterfile.com, page 252; Loren Santow/Stone/Getty Images, page 253; CP (Frank Gunn), page 257

Part Three © George Steinmetz/CORBIS, page 277

Chapter 10 © Masterfile (Royalty-Free Div.) www.masterfile.com, page 279; © Masterfile (Royalty-Free Div.) www.masterfile.com, page 282; PlusPix/Firstlight.ca, page 284 (top left); CP, page 284 (top centre, top right, bottom left); Photodisc/Getty Images, page 284 (bottom right); Toyota Motor Manufacturing Canada Inc., page 292; Ted Rice, page 297; Ray Ng, page 302

Chapter 11 © kolvenbach/Alamy, page 313; Photodisc/Getty Images, page 318; AP, page 319; Hulton Archive/Getty Images, page 328

Part Four Werner Dieterich/Photographer's Choice/Getty Images, page 337

Chapter 12 © Rick Gomez/CORBIS, page 339; Courtesy of Nutrisoya Foods Inc., page 341 (left); Courtesy of Curves International, Inc. and Publicis, USA Dallas, page 341 (centre); Text and advertisement © Queen's Printer for Ontario, 2006. Reproduced with permission. Photo: Philip Lee Harvey/Stone +/Getty Images, page 341 (right); Grand & Toy, page 345; © Rachel Epstein/Photo Edit, Inc., page 350; © Bryan F. Peterson/CORBIS, page 353; Feathercraft Products, Ltd., page 355

Chapter 13 Ballard Power Systems Inc. (www.ballard.com), page 363; Photodisc/Getty Images, page 368; Scouting Canada, page 375 (bottom left); CP (Didier Debusschere), page 375 (centre right); CP (Tom Hanson), page 375 (bottom right); Contact Press Images, Inc., page 377; Agence France-Presse AFP, page 381 (left); Getty Images, page 381 (right)

Chapter 14 © Najlah Feanny/Corbis, page 391; New York Times Pictures, page 394; Daniel Acker/Bloomberg News/Landov LLC, page 398; Jim West, page 400; QVC, Inc., page 407; Canadian National, page 409

Part Five Courtesy of TSX, page 419

Chapter 15 © Design Pics Inc./Alamy, page 421; coin image © 2008 Royal Canadian Mint—All Rights Reserved, photo: CP (Tom Hanson), page 423; Macduff Everton/CORBIS, page 425; Bob Carroll/Leucar, page 429 (top); Nikolai Ignatiev/Network Photographers, Ltd., page 429 (bottom); Jeremy Sutton-

Hibbert/Network Photographers Ltd., page 441; D. Loek/Toronto Star, page 442; Reproduced with the permission of the Minister of Finance, page 445; Bloomberg/Landov LLC, page 447; Dan Krauss/New York Times Pictures, page 451

Chapter 16 © Russell Underwood/CORBIS, page 459; © Stock Connection Blue/Alamy, page 462; Naomi Harris, page 465; Aileen Tat Photography, page 469; Joe Polimeni/GM/Bloomberg News/Landov LLC, page 476

Appendix B Courtesy of Blackberry Research in Motion Ltd., page B-1; © Reuters/CORBIS, page B-5; Reprint courtesy of International Business Machines Corporation. Reprinted by permission of Paul Huang, page B-8; © Roger Harris/Photo Researchers, page B-11

NAME AND ORGANIZATION INDEX

D

E

F

SUBJECT INDEX

Note: Key terms and the pages on which they are defined appear in boldface. *f* denotes a figure, and *t* denotes a table.

D

E

J

K

L

M

Q

R

T